Sapling Plus

Pre-class Tutorials

Introduce new topics in a more manageable, less intimidating way, to help students better retain what they've learned for class time.

Everything You Need in a Single Learning Path

SaplingPlus is the first system to support students and instructors at every step, from the first point of contact with new content to demonstrating mastery of concepts and skills. It is simply the best support for Principles of Economics.

Classroom Activities

Foster student curiosity and understanding through "clicker" questions (via iClicker Campus) and curated active learning activities.

Test Bank

Multiple-choice and short-answer questions to help instructors assess students' comprehension, interpretation, and ability to synthesize.

Developing Understanding

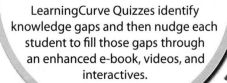

LearningCurve Quizzes identify knowledge gaps and then nudge each student to fill those gaps through an enhanced e-book, videos, and interactives.

Assessment

Homework Assignments—with an intuitive approach to graphing—offer multi-part questions and targeted feedback.

For more information on SaplingPlus, visit www.macmillanlearning.com.

Paul Krugman
Graduate Center of the City University of New York

Robin Wells

 **worth publishers**
Macmillan Learning
New York

To beginning students everywhere,
which we all were at one time.

Senior Vice President, Content Strategy: **Charles Linsmeier**
Program Director: **Shani Fisher**
Executive Program Manager: **Simon Glick**
Executive Development Editor: **Sharon Balbos**
Consultant: **Ryan Herzog**
Assessment Manager: **Kristyn Brown**
Assessment Editor: **Joshua Hill**
Marketing Manager: **Clay Bolton**
Associate Digital Marketing Specialist: **Chelsea Simens**
Director of Media Editorial and Assessment: **Noel Hohnstine**
Media Editor: **Stephany Harrington**
Assistant Editor: **Amanda Gaglione**
Director of Content Management Enhancement: **Tracey Kuehn**
Senior Managing Editor: **Lisa Kinne**
Senior Content Project Manager: **Edgar Doolan**
Director of Design, Content Management: **Diana Blume**
Design Services Manager: **Natasha Wolfe**
Cover Design: **John Callahan**
Photo Editor: **Cecilia Varas**
Senior Workflow Project Supervisor: **Susan Wein**
Production Supervisor: **Lawrence Guerra**
Media Project Manager: **Andrew Vaccaro**
Composition: **Lumina Datamatics, Inc.**
Printing and Binding: **LSC Communications**

Interior Design Icon Credits: Globe: Design Collection/Shutterstock; Head icons: Le_Mon/Shutterstock; Smartphone icon: Web icon/Shutterstock

See page xxv for cover credits information. Page xxv is an extension of this copyright page.

ISBN-13: 978-1-319-22131-7
ISBN-10: 1-319-22131-9

Library of Congress Control Number: 2019946847
© 2020, 2017, 2014, 2011 by Worth Publishers

Printed in the United States of America
1 2 3 4 5 6   23 22 21 20 19

Worth Publishers
One New York Plaza
Suite 4600
New York, NY 10004-1562
www.macmillanlearning.com

PAUL KRUGMAN, recipient of the 2008 Nobel Memorial Prize in Economic Sciences, is a faculty member of the Graduate Center of the City University of New York, associated with the Luxembourg Income Study, which tracks and analyzes income inequality around the world. Prior to that, he taught at Princeton University for 14 years. He received his BA from Yale and his PhD from MIT. Before Princeton, he taught at Yale, Stanford, and MIT. He also spent a year on the staff of the Council of Economic Advisers in 1982–1983. His research has included pathbreaking work on international trade, economic geography, and currency crises. In 1991, Krugman received the American Economic Association's John Bates Clark medal. In addition to his teaching and academic research, Krugman writes extensively for nontechnical audiences. He is a regular op-ed columnist for the *New York Times*. His best-selling trade books include *End This Depression Now!*, *The Return of Depression Economics and the Crisis of 2008*, a history of recent economic troubles and their implications for economic policy, and *The Conscience of a Liberal*, a study of the political economy of economic inequality and its relationship with political polarization from the Gilded Age to the present. His earlier books, *Peddling Prosperity* and *The Age of Diminished Expectations*, have become modern classics.

Ligaya Franklin

ROBIN WELLS was a Lecturer and Researcher in Economics at Princeton University. She received her BA from the University of Chicago and her PhD from the University of California at Berkeley; she then did postdoctoral work at MIT. She has taught at the University of Michigan, the University of Southampton (United Kingdom), Stanford, and MIT.

This is a book about economics as the study of what people do and how they interact, a study very much informed by real-world experience. These words, this spirit, have served as a guiding principle for us in every edition.

While we were driven to write this book by many small ideas about particular aspects of economics, we also had one big idea: an economics textbook should be built around narratives, many of them pulled from real life, and it should never lose sight of the fact that economics is, in the end, a set of stories about what people do.

Many of the stories economists tell take the form of models—for whatever else they are, economic models are stories about how the world works. But we believe that student understanding of and appreciation for models are greatly enhanced if they are presented, as much as possible, in the context of stories about the real world that both illustrate economic concepts and touch on the concerns we all face living in a world shaped by economic forces.

You'll find a rich array of stories in every chapter, in the chapter openers, Economics in Actions, Global Comparisons, and Business Cases. As always, we include many new stories and update others. We also integrate an international perspective throughout, more extensively than ever before. It starts with the Chapter 1 opening story on China's Pearl River Delta that sets the stage for new attention to China's ascendance in the global economy. An overview of the types of narrative-based features in the text is on page x.

We also include pedagogical features that reinforce learning. For example, most major sections end with three related elements devised with the student in mind: (1) the Economics in Action: a real-world application to help students achieve a fuller understanding of concepts they just read about; (2) a Quick Review of key ideas in list form; and (3) Check Your Understanding self-test questions with answers at the back of the book. Our thought-provoking end-of-chapter Discussion Questions and Problems are another strong feature. The Work It Out feature appears in all end-of-chapter problem sets, offering students online tutorials that guide them step-by-step through solving key problems. With the Fifth Edition, a new feature, Discovering Data exercises, offers students the opportunity to use interactive graphs to analyze interesting economic questions. An overview of the text's tools for learning is on page xi.

Students also benefit from the impressive set of online resources that are linked to specific chapter content. These include several exciting new digital features as well as adaptive quizzing, tutorials, interactive activities, graphing questions, and data-analysis questions. All have been devised with the goal of supporting instructor teaching and student learning in principles of economics courses.

We hope your experience with *Essentials of Economics* is a good one. Thank you for introducing it into your classroom.

Paul Krugman   Robin Wells

We are committed to the belief that students learn best from a complete textbook program built around narratives, steeped in real life and current events, with a strong emphasis on global matters and with proven technology that supports student success.

Narrative Approach

This is a textbook built around narratives and stories, many pulled from real life. In every chapter, stories are used to teach core concepts and motivate learning. We believe that the best way to introduce concepts and reinforce them is through memorable, real-world stories; students simply relate more easily to them.

Global Focus

This book is unrivaled in the attention paid to global matters. We have thoroughly integrated an international perspective into the text, in the numerous applications, cases, and stories and, of course, in the data-based Global Comparison feature.

Technology That Builds Success

Essentials of Economics is not just a textbook. It has evolved to become a complete program with interactive features designed and built to extend the goals of the text. This program encourages even stronger student engagement, mastery of the material, and success in the course.

> **interactive activity** Look for this Interactive Activity icon to find materials that are enhanced by our online tools.

What's New in the Fifth Edition?

Technology that offers the best value and price. Because students' needs are changing, our most powerful learning option is now our most affordable. SaplingPlus is a new digital solution that combines LearningCurve with an integrated e-book, robust homework, improved graphing, and fully digital end-of-chapter problems, including Work It Outs. And if print is important, a package with a loose-leaf copy of the text is only a few dollars more.

Discovering Data exercises help students interpret, analyze, share, and report on data. Students develop data literacy by completing these new interactive exercises: step-by-step problems that have students use up-to-the-minute FRED data.

Current events framed by the world's best communicators of economics. No other text stays as fresh as this one. The authors—who have explained economics to millions through trade books and

newspaper columns—offer a new online feature, News Analysis, that pairs journalistic takes on pressing issues with questions based on Bloom's taxonomy. This complements the text's unparalleled coverage of current topics: sustainability, the economic impact of technology, pressing policy debates, and much more.

A richer commitment to broadening students' understanding of the global economy. With unparalleled insight and clarity, the authors use their hallmark narrative approach to take students outside of the classroom and into our global world, starting in Chapter 1 with a new opening story on the economic transformation in China's Pearl River Delta. The global focus is carried throughout in chapter openers, Economics in Action, Business Cases, and Global Comparisons. There is now more on the ascendance of China's economy, along with real-world stories about the economies of Europe, Bangladesh, and Japan, among many others.

Engaging Students with a Narrative Approach

2 Economic Models: Trade-offs and Trade

FROM KITTY HAWK TO DREAMLINER

BOEING'S 787 DREAMLINER was the result of an aerodynamic revolution—a super-efficient airplane designed to cut airline operating costs and the first to use superlight composite materials.

To ensure that the Dreamliner was sufficiently lightweight and aerodynamic, it underwent over 15,000 hours of wind tunnel tests, resulting in subtle design changes that improved its performance.

making it more fuel efficient and less pollutant emitting than existing passenger jets. In fact, some budget airlines such as Norwegian Air (Europe's third-largest budget airline) have been offering transatlantic flights at half the price of their rivals, expecting that the super-fuel-efficient Dreamliner will shrink fuel costs enough to make their discount strategy profitable.

The first flight of the Dreamliner was a spectacular advance from the 1903 maiden voyage of the Wright Flyer, the first successful powered airplane, in Kitty Hawk, North Carolina. Yet the Boeing engineers—and all aeronautical engineers—owe an enormous debt to the Wright Flyer's inventors, Wilbur and Orville Wright.

What made the Wrights truly visionary was their invention of the wind tunnel, an apparatus that let them experiment with many different designs for wings and control surfaces. Doing experiments with a miniature airplane, inside a wind tunnel the size of a shipping crate, gave the Wright brothers the knowledge that would make heavier-than-air flight possible.

Neither a miniature airplane inside a packing crate nor a miniature model of the Dreamliner inside Boeing's state-of-the-art Transonic Wind Tunnel is the same thing as an actual aircraft in flight. But it is a very useful model of a flying plane—a simplified representation of the real thing that can be used to answer crucial questions, such as how much lift a given wing shape will generate at a given airspeed.

Needless to say, testing an airplane design in a wind tunnel is cheaper and safer than building a full-scale version and hoping it will fly. More generally, models play a crucial role in almost all scientific research—economics very much included.

In fact, you could say that economic theory consists mainly of a collection of models, a series of simplified representations of economic reality that allow us to understand a variety of economic issues.

In this chapter, we'll look at two economic models that are crucially important in their own right and illustrate why such models are so useful. We'll conclude with a look at how economists actually use models in their work. ■

The Wright brothers' model made modern airplanes, including the Dreamliner, possible.

WHAT YOU WILL LEARN
- What are economic **models** and why are they so important to economists?
- How do three simple models—the **production possibility frontier**, **comparative advantage**, and the **circular-flow diagram**—help us understand how modern economies work?
- Why is an understanding of the difference between **positive economics** and **normative economics** important for the real-world application of economic principles?
- Why do economists sometimes disagree?

ECONOMICS >> *in Action*
An Economic Breakthrough in Bangladesh

Western news media rarely mention Bangladesh: it's not a political hot spot, it doesn't have oil, and it's overshadowed by its immense neighbor, India. Yet it is home to more than 160 million people—and although it is still very poor, it is nonetheless one of the greatest economic success stories of the past generation.

As recently as the 1980s, real GDP per capita in Bangladesh—which achieved independence from Pakistan in 1971, after a brutal war—was barely higher than it had been in 1950, when the country was so poor that it literally lived on the edge of starvation. In the early 1990s, however, the nation began a process of political and economic reform, making the transition from military rule to democracy, freeing up markets, and achieving monetary and fiscal stability. And growth took off, most notably with the rise of Bangladesh as a major exporter of clothing to Western markets. Real GDP per capita grew at over 3% per year, from the late 1980s through 2010, doubling over the 20-year period from 1990 to 2010.

By 2015 real GDP per capita was almost 2½ times what it had been in 1990. Other measures also showed dramatic improvements in the quality of life: life expectancy rose by a dozen years, child mortality fell by 70%, school enrollment rose sharply, especially for girls.

Make no mistake, Bangladesh is still incredibly poor by American standards. Wages are very low, although rising, while working conditions are often terrible and dangerous—a point highlighted in 2013, when a factory complex collapsed, killing more than a thousand workers. But compared with its own past,

Although Bangladesh remains a very poor country, a high growth rate has improved living standards over the last 25 years.

GLOBAL COMPARISON   WHEAT YIELDS AROUND THE WORLD

Wheat yields differ substantially around the world. The disparity between France and the United States that you see in this graph is particularly striking, given that they are both wealthy countries with comparable agricultural technology. Yet the reason for that disparity is straightforward: differing government policies. In the United States, farmers receive payments from the government to supplement their incomes, but European farmers benefit from price floors. Since European farmers get higher prices for their output than American farmers, they employ more variable inputs and produce significantly higher yields.

Interestingly, in poor countries like Uganda and Ethiopia, foreign aid can lead to significantly depressed yields. Foreign aid from wealthy countries has often taken the form of surplus food, which depresses local market prices, severely hurting local agriculture that poor countries normally depend on. Charitable organizations like Oxfam have asked wealthy food-producing countries to modify their aid policies—principally, to give aid in cash rather than in

food products except in the case of acute food shortages—to avoid this problem.

Wheat yield (bushels per acre)

Data from: FAO STATS, 2016.

BUSINESS CASE   Parking Your Money at PayPal

Officially, PayPal, the electronic funds–transfer firm—which is also the owner of Venmo, a mobile-phone payment service that has become extremely popular—isn't considered a bank. Instead, regulators consider it a *money transmitter*, an entity that sends your money someplace rather than holding it and keeping it safe.

However, as users accumulate substantial sums in their PayPal accounts, that distinction has started to look questionable. Venmo users, in particular, often seem willing to let incoming payments sit in their accounts until the funds are spent. As a result, PayPal's accounts were estimated to total more than $13 billion in 2016. If those billions were considered bank deposits, PayPal would be considered among the 50 largest banks in the United States.

At first glance, leaving significant sums in PayPal accounts seems counterintuitive for two reasons. First,

these accounts aren't protected by federal deposit insurance. Second, they pay no interest. But upon closer examination, this behavior makes good economic sense. People will typically hold only a tiny fraction of their wealth in their PayPal account, thereby making the lack of federal deposit insurance an acceptable risk. And interest rates on bank accounts are so low at the time of this writing (around 0.06% in Spring 2019) that losing that interest is a reasonable price to pay to avoid the hassle of moving funds back and forth between a bank account and a PayPal or Venmo account.

The result is that many people are behaving like one user quoted by the *Wall Street Journal*, who now waits a while before transferring funds out of her Venmo account to her regular bank account: "I'm starting to intentionally keep my money in there a little bit longer."

But will PayPal/Venmo or something like it begin to make major inroads into traditional banking? Some analysts think so. Others suggest, however, that conventional banks will find ways to make mobile payments easier, and that rising interest rates will lure customers back to conventional bank deposits. Time will tell.

QUESTIONS FOR THOUGHT
1. PayPal accounts aren't counted as part of the money supply. Should they be? Why or why not?
2. In 2010, only around 25% of mobile phones in the United States were smartphones. In 2017, that number increased to more than 80%. How does this situation play into the PayPal story, and how does it fit into the broader pattern of monetary history?
3. How might future actions by the Federal Open Market Committee affect the future of PayPal and similar services?

- To engage students, every chapter begins with a compelling story. **What You Will Learn** questions help students focus on key chapter concepts.

- So students can immediately see economic concepts applied in the real world, **Economics in Action** applications appear throughout chapters.

- To provide students with an international perspective, the **Global Comparison** feature uses data and graphs to illustrate why countries reach different economic outcomes.

- So students can see key economic principles applied to real-life business situations, each major part concludes with **Business Cases.**

Engaging Students with Effective Tools for Learning

ECONOMICS >> in Action
How the Sharing Economy Reduces Fixed Cost

The *sharing economy* is a relatively new phenomenon in which technology allows unrelated parties (firms and individuals) to share assets like office space, homes, computing capacity, software, cars, small jets, machinery, financial capital, books, and even clothes. Uber and Airbnb are probably the most prominent examples of how the sharing economy works: their web platforms allow both drivers with cars and homeowners with rooms to spare to share their assets with others. But even the Cloud itself, the vast digital network into which you upload your photos and team-project term papers to share with others, is a feature of the sharing economy because it allows firms and individuals to rent computing capacity, storage, and software.

So what does the sharing have to do with fixed cost? A lot. If the use of an asset can be obtained only when needed, then it goes from incurring a fixed cost to incurring a variable cost. Take, for example, a company jet. Instead of incurring the fixed cost of owning and maintaining a company jet full time (one which might sit on the runway for a significant amount of time), a company can now purchase, through NetJets or similar firms, the services of a jet on an as-needed basis. In effect, by turning the fixed cost of ownership and operation into a variable cost, the sharing economy might allow smaller companies to operate in markets that would have previously been unprofitable for them. Likewise, sharing allows individuals to afford assets (a car, a home, a designer handbag) that were previously unaffordable because the assets can now be used to generate income.

And the sharing economy marketplace makes for a more efficient use of society's resources overall, as it improves the allocation of resources to those who can make the best use of them.

NetJets and other firms like it in the sharing economy help convert fixed costs to variable costs and allow for a more efficient use of resources.

>> Check Your Understanding 6-3
Solutions appear at back of book.

1. The accompanying table shows three possible combinations of fixed cost and average variable cost. Average variable cost is constant in this example (it does not vary with the quantity of output produced).

Choice	Fixed cost	Average variable cost
1	$8,000	$1.00
2	12,000	0.75
3	24,000	0.25

   a. For each of the three choices, calculate the average total cost of producing 12,000, 22,000, and 30,000 units. For each of these quantities, which choice results in the lowest average total cost?
   b. Suppose that the firm, which has historically produced 12,000 units, experiences a sharp, permanent increase in demand that leads it to produce 22,000 units. Explain how its average total cost will change in the short run and in the long run.
   c. Explain what the firm should do instead if it believes the change in demand is temporary.

2. In each of the following cases, explain what kind of scale effects you think the firm will experience and why.
   a. A telemarketing firm in which employees make sales calls using computers and telephones
   b. An interior design firm in which design projects are based on the expertise of the firm's owner
   c. A diamond-mining company

3. Draw a graph like Figure 6-12 and insert a short-run average total cost curve corresponding to a long-run output choice of 5 cases of salsa per day. Use the graph to show why Selena should change her fixed cost if she expects to produce only 4 cases per day for a long period of time.

>> Quick Review

- In the long run, firms choose fixed cost according to expected output. Higher fixed cost reduces average total cost when output is high. Lower fixed cost reduces average total cost when output is low.
- There are many possible short-run average total cost curves, each corresponding to a different level of fixed cost. The **long-run average total cost curve, LRATC,** shows average total cost over the long run, when the firm has chosen fixed cost to minimize average total cost for each level of output.
- A firm that has fully adjusted its fixed cost for its output level will operate at a point that lies on both its current short-run and long-run average total cost curves. A change in output moves the firm along its current short-run average total cost curve. Once it has readjusted its fixed cost, the firm will operate on a new short-run average total cost curve and on the long-run average total cost curve.
- Scale effects arise from the technology of production. **Increasing returns to scale** tend to make firms larger. **Network externalities** are one reason for increasing returns to scale. **Decreasing returns to scale** tend to limit their size. With **constant returns to scale,** scale has no effect.

- To reinforce learning, most sections within chapters conclude with three tools: an application of key concepts in the **Economics in Action;** a **Quick Review** of key concepts; and a comprehension check with **Check Your Understanding** questions. Solutions for these questions appear at the back of the book.

- **Pitfalls** teach students to identify and avoid common misconceptions about economic concepts.

- End-of-chapter **Solved Problems** guide students step by step through solving specific problems tied to real-world events.

- **Discovering Data** exercises offer students the opportunity to use interactive graphs to analyze interesting economic questions.

- **Work It Out** skill-building problems provide interactive step-by-step help with solving select problems from the textbook.

WORK IT OUT Interactive step-by-step help with solving this problem can be found online.

14. There is only one labor market in Profunctia. All workers have the same skills, and all firms hire workers with these skills. Use the accompanying diagram, which shows the supply and demand for labor, to answer the following questions. Illustrate each answer with a diagram.

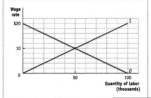

   a. What is the equilibrium wage rate in Profunctia? At this wage rate, what are the level of employment, the size of the labor force, and the unemployment rate?
   b. If the government of Profunctia sets a minimum wage equal to $12, what will be the level of employment, the size of the labor force, and the unemployment rate?
   c. If unions bargain with the firms in Profunctia and set a wage rate equal to $14, what will be the level of employment, the size of the labor force, and the unemployment rate?
   d. If the concern for retaining workers and encouraging high-quality work leads firms to set a wage rate equal to $16, what will be the level of employment, the size of the labor force, and the unemployment rate?

5. Access the Discovering Data exercise for Chapter 14 Problem 5 online to answer the following questions.
   a. What is the current federal minimum wage?
   b. In what year was the federal minimum wage last increased?
   c. What is the current value for the real minimum wage?
   d. In what year was the real minimum wage the highest? The lowest?
   e. In general, since 1970, how has the purchasing power of the minimum wage changed over time?

PITFALLS

DEMAND VERSUS QUANTITY DEMANDED

When economists say "an increase in demand," they mean a rightward shift of the demand curve, and when they say "a decrease in demand," they mean a leftward shift of the demand curve—that is, when they're being careful.

In ordinary speech most of us, professional economists included, use the word *demand* casually. For example, an economist might say "the demand for air travel has doubled over the past 15 years, partly because of falling airfares," when he or she really means that the *quantity demanded* has doubled.

This is OK in casual conversation. But when you're doing economic analysis, it's important to make the distinction between changes in the quantity demanded, which involve movements along a demand curve, and shifts of the demand curve (see Figure 3-3 for an illustration). Sometimes students end up writing something like this: "If demand increases, the price will go up, but that will lead to a fall in demand, which pushes the price down . . ." and then go around in circles.

By making a clear distinction between changes in *demand,* which mean shifts of the demand curve, and changes in *quantity demanded,* which means movement along the demand curve, you can avoid a lot of confusion.

SOLVED PROBLEM   Production Challenges for Tesla

Tesla Inc. produces electric cars in a former Toyota factory in Fremont, California. The Tesla Roadster, a sports car, was the company's first design, available for sale in 2008. Their latest design, the Tesla Model 3, hit the road in 2017. The Model 3 is an all-wheel-drive, mid-size luxury, four-door sedan. It uses no gasoline, has a range of 220 to 310 miles per charge, and has zero tailpipe emissions. It has the ability to be fully self-driving.

Pre-orders for the Model 3 exceeded 450,000 units, nearly triple those for the previous model, the 2013 Tesla Model X. Despite the strong demand, production of the Model 3 at the Fremont plant was slower than expected.

To meet demand for the Model 3, Tesla announced it will increase production at the plant to 6,000 cars per week, or about 300,000 cars per year. Currently, the plant is equipped to produce about 100,000 cars per year, which is the total number of cars sold by Tesla in 2017. Using the following table, find Tesla's average total cost of production across the various plants for each level of production. Explain why the production costs with the size A plant are higher than they would be if Tesla could build a new plant that was equipped to produce 300,000 vehicles.

	Total cost (billions of U.S. dollars)		
Plant size	100,000 cars sold	200,000 cars sold	300,000 cars sold
A	$1.75	$3.25	$5.5
B	2.0	3.0	5.0
C	2.5	4.0	4.5

STEP 1 Find Tesla's average total cost of production at the various plant sizes and production levels. *Review pages 181–183.*

	Average total cost		
Plant size	100,000 cars sold	200,000 cars sold	300,000 cars sold
A	$17,500	$16,250	$18,333
B	$20,000	$15,000	$16,667
C	$25,000	$20,000	$15,000

Average total cost is found by dividing total cost by the quantity of output. So, if Tesla has a total cost of $1,750,000,000 at an output of 100,000 cars we calculate $1,750,000,000/100,000 = $17,500. Average total cost for each plant size and production level from the previous table are given in the table at left.

STEP 2 Explain why the production cost with a size A plant is higher than it would be if Tesla could build a new plant that was best equipped to produce 300,000 vehicles. *Review pages 186–189.*

If Tesla were to build a new plant based on the production of 300,000 vehicles, it would build a size C plant. Tesla would be able to adjust its fixed cost to a new level that minimizes average total cost for its new output level. If Tesla could easily change its plant size, it would always build the plant size that minimizes its average total cost on its long-run average total cost curve. However, if the size of the plant is fixed at size A, then it will be on its short-run average total cost curve based on a size A plant.

Engaging Students with Technology

The technology for this new edition has been developed to spark student engagement and improve outcomes while offering instructors flexible, high-quality, research-based tools for teaching this course.

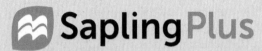 Sapling Plus

NEW! SaplingPlus combines powerful multimedia resources with an integrated e-book and the robust problem library of Sapling Learning, creating an extraordinary new learning resource for students. Online homework helps students get better grades with targeted instructional feedback tailored to the individual. And it saves instructors time preparing for and managing a course by providing personalized support from a PhD or Master's level colleague trained in Sapling's system.

NEW! Pre-Lecture Tutorials foster basic understanding of core economic concepts before students ever set foot in class. Developed by two pioneers in active-learning methods — Eric Chiang, Florida Atlantic University, and José Vazquez, University of Illinois at Urbana–Champaign — this resource is part of the SaplingPlus learning path. Students watch Pre-Lecture videos and complete Bridge Question assessments that prepare them to engage in class. Instructors receive data about student comprehension that can inform their lecture preparation.

<< LearningCurve Adaptive Quizzing

Embraced by students and instructors alike, this incredibly popular and effective adaptive quizzing engine offers individualized question sets and feedback tailored to each student based on correct and incorrect responses. Questions are hyperlinked to relevant e-book sections, encouraging students to read and use the resources at hand to enrich their understanding.

NEW! Graphing Questions >>

Powered by improved graphing, multi-step questions paired with helpful feedback guide students through the process of problem solving. Students are asked to demonstrate their understanding by simply clicking, dragging, and dropping a line to a predetermined location. The graphs have been designed so that students' entire focus is on moving the correct curve in the correct direction, virtually eliminating grading issues for instructors.

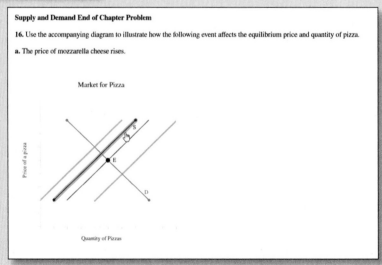

Work It Out >>

These skill-building activities pair sample end-of-chapter problems with targeted feedback and video explanations to help students solve problems step-by-step. This approach allows students to work independently, tests their comprehension of concepts, and prepares them for class and exams.

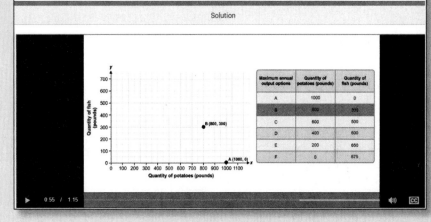

Trade-Offs and Trade Work It Out: Question 1 of 4

Atlantis is a small, isolated island in the South Atlantic. The inhabitants grow potatoes and catch fish. The accompanying table shows the maximum annual output combinations of potatoes and fish that can be produced. Obviously, given their limited resources and available technology, as they use more of their resources for potato production, there are fewer resources available for catching fish.

Using the data in the table, place the points in the accompanying graph to depict Atlantis's production possibilities frontier.

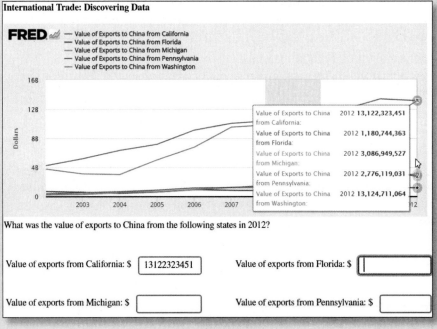

International Trade: Discovering Data

What was the value of exports to China from the following states in 2012?

Value of exports from California: $ | 13122323451 |

Value of exports from Florida: $ | |

Value of exports from Michigan: $ | |

Value of exports from Pennsylvania: $ | |

<< NEW! Discovering Data Exercises help students
interpret and analyze data by completing interactive, stepped-out exercises that use up-to-the-minute FRED data. These exercises help students develop data literacy and synthesizing skills, encourage economic analysis based on recent trends, and build an understanding of the broader economy.

"FRED®" graphs ©Federal Reserve Bank of St. Louis. 2016. All rights reserved. All "FRED®" graphs appear courtesy of Federal Reserve Bank of St. Louis. https://fred.stlouisfed.org/

Powerful Support for Instructors

FOR ASSESSMENT

Test Bank Containing multiple-choice and short-answer questions, this test bank helps instructors assess students' comprehension, interpretation, and ability to synthesize.

End-of-Chapter and Work It Out Questions The in-text end-of-chapter problems have been converted to a multiple-choice format accompanied by answer-specific feedback. **Work It Out** activities walk students through each step of solving an end-of-chapter problem using choice specific feedback and video explanations for each step.

Homework Assignments Each chapter concludes with homework of various question types, including graphing questions featuring our updated graphing player, providing instructors with a curated set of multiple-choice and graphing questions that are easily assigned for graded assessment.

Practice Quizzes Designed to be used as a study tool for students, Practice Quizzes allow for multiple attempts as students familiarize themselves with chapter content.

ADDITIONAL RESOURCES

A Gradebook This useful resource offers clear feedback to students and instructors on individual assignments and on performance in the course.

LMS Integration Included so that online homework is easily integrated into a school's learning management system and that an instructor's Gradebook and roster are always in sync.

Instructor's Resource Manual This manual offers instructors teaching materials and tips to enhance the classroom experience, along with chapter objectives, outlines, and other ideas.

Solutions Manual Prepared by the authors of the text, this manual offers detailed solutions to all of the text's end-of-chapter Discussion Questions and Problems and the Business Case questions.

Interactive Presentation Slides These brief, interactive, and visually interesting slides are designed to hold students' attention in class with graphics and animations demonstrating key concepts, real-world examples, and opportunities for active learning.

WHAT'S NEW IN THIS EDITION?

There are 44 new opening stories, Business Cases, and Economics in Action applications in this edition — ensuring that the Fifth Edition is truly current and relevant. Many other stories have been updated and refreshed.

9 New Opening Stories

A Day in the Megacity
Big City, Not So Bright Ideas
Regulators Give Bridgestone a Flat Tire
Greek Tragedies
China Hits the Big Time
A Tale of Two Numbers
Different Generations, Different Policies
Spending Our Way Out of a Recession
Not So Funny Money

11 New Business Cases

How Priceline Went from Barely Surviving to Thriving
Uber Gives Riders a Lesson in Supply and Demand
Ticket Prices and Music's Reigning Couple, Jay-Z and Beyoncé
Bricks-and-Mortar Retailers Go Toe to Toe with Mobile Shopping Apps
Xcel Energy Goes for a Win-Win
Can America's Entrepreneurial Spirit Survive Threats to the ACA?
Betting on Bad Numbers
TaskRabbit
Raising the Bar(code)
Toyota Makes Its Move
Parking Your Money at PayPal

24 New Economics in Action Applications

The Fundamental Law of Traffic Congestion
When Economists Agree
Where's the Guacamole?
Why Price Controls in Venezuela Proved Useless
China and the Global Commodities Glut of 2016
Finding the Optimal Team Size
How the Sharing Economy Reduces Fixed Cost
Farmers Know How
The Monopoly that Wasn't: China and the Market for Rare Earths
The (R)Evolution of the American High-Speed Internet Market
The Case Against Chocolate Producers Melts
The Demise of OPEC
Abbondanza!
American Infrastructure Gets a D+
Greece's Costly Surplus
Structural Unemployment in Spain
An Economic Breakthrough in Bangladesh
The Rise, Fall, and Return of the Productivity Paradox
What's the Matter with Italy?
A Tale of Two Stimuli
Trying to Balance Budgets in a Recession
From Bucks to Bitcoin
Up the Down Staircase
Strong Dollar Woes

Our deep appreciation and heartfelt thanks go out to **Ryan Herzog,** Gonzaga University, for his hard work and extensive contributions during every stage of this revision. Ryan's creativity and insights helped us make this Fifth Edition possible. And special thanks to Thomas Dunn, who did an outstanding job helping to insure the accuracy of page proof.

We must also thank the many wonderful and talented people at Worth Publishers for their work on this edition: Shani Fisher, Simon Glick, Sharon Balbos, Amanda Gaglione, Stephany Harrington, Noel Hohnstine, Joshua Hill, Andrew Zierman, Catherine Woods, Lisa Kinne, Tracey Kuehn, Susan Wein, Edgar Doolan, Jean Erler, and Cecilia Varas.

And many thanks to the following reviewers, whose input helped us shape this Fifth Edition.

Valbona Cela, *Tri-County Technical College*
Carmen Dybwad, *University of Regina*
Tom Flesher, *Suffolk County Community College*
Daniel Giedeman, *Grand Valley State University*
Rajeev K. Goel, *Illinois State University*
Miren Ivankovic, *Anderson University*
Sukanya Kemp, *University of Akron*
Haiyong Liu, *East Carolina University*
Michael E. Martell, *Bard College*
Diego Mendez-Carbajo, *Illinois Wesleyan University*
Geoffrey Schneider, *Bucknell University*
Ariuntungalag Taivan, *University of Minnesota, Duluth*
Michele T. Villinski, *DePauw University*

Thank you to all the instructors who reviewed past editions of this text.

Carlos Aguilar, *El Paso Community College*
Gbenga Ajilore, *University of Toledo*
Irma T. Alonso, *Florida International University*
Jack Amariglio, *Merrimack College*
Clive Belfield, *Queens College, CUNY*
Doris Bennett, *Jacksonville State University*
McKinley Blackburn, *University of South Carolina*
Amy Boswell, *Anne Arundel Community College*
Elizabeth Breitbach, *University of South Carolina*
Rob Catlett, *Emporia State University*
Semih Emre Cekin, *Texas Tech University*
Eric Chiang, *Florida Atlantic University*
Norman R. Cloutier, *University of Wisconsin–Parkside*
Michael Coon, *University of Wisconsin–Milwaukee*
Tom Creahan, *Morehead State University*
Abel Embaye, *University of Arkansas*
Jose Esteban, *Palomar College*
Randall Filer, *Hunter College, CUNY*
Todd Gabe, *University of Maine*
Satyajit Ghosh, *University of Scranton*
Chris Gingrich, *Eastern Mennonite University*
Seth Gitter, *Towson University*
Devra Golbe, *Hunter College*
Patricia Graham, *University of Northern Colorado*
George Greenlee, *St. Petersburg College, Clearwater*
Thomas Hardin, *Mater Dei Catholic High School*
Ryan Herzog, *Gonzaga University*
Terence Hunady, *Bowling Green State University*

Arthur Janssen, *Emporia State University*
Matthew Jaremski, *Colgate University*
Nicholas Karatjas, *Indiana University of Pennsylvania*
Susan Kask, *Warren Wilson College*
Hisaya Kitaoka, *Franklin College*
Katie Kontak, *Bowling Green State University*
Andrew F. Kozak, *St. Mary's College of Maryland*
Richard Langlois, *University of Connecticut*
Frances F. Lea, *Germanna Community College*
Noreen E. Lephardt, *Marquette University*
Stephen Lile, *Western Kentucky University*
Solina Lindahl, *California Polytechnic University, San Luis Obispo*
Mike Martell, *Franklin and Marshall College*
Parul Mathur, *Simpson College*
Dennis C. McCornac, *Anne Arundel Community College*
Chris N. McGrew, *Purdue University*
Mary Helen McSweeney-Feld, *Iona College*
Marshall Medoff, *California State University, Long Beach*
Diego Mendez-Carbajo, *Illinois Wesleyan University*
Garrett Milam, *University of Puget Sound*
Ellen Mutari, *Richard Stockton College of New Jersey*
Kevin O'Brien, *Bradley University*
Inge O'Connor, *Syracuse University*
John Perry, *Centre College*
Iordanis Petsas, *University of Scranton*
H. Mikael Sandberg, *University of Florida*
Elizabeth Sawyer-Kelly, *University of Wisconsin–Madison*
Amy Scott, *DeSales University*
Chace Stiehl, *Bellevue College*
Abdulhamid Sukar, *Cameron University*
Leonore Taga, *Rider University*
Patrick Taylor, *Millsaps College*
Robert Teitelbaum, *State University of New York, Empire State College*
Theo Thedford, *Shorter University*
Jose J. Vazquez-Cognet, *University of Illinois at Urbana-Champaign*
Matt Warning, *University of Puget Sound*
Thomas Watkins, *Eastern Kentucky University*

And lastly, to all of you who have introduced our books to your students and colleagues, and who continue to shape our experience as textbook authors, we thank you and encourage your feedback.

PART 3 The Production Decision

PART 8 Stabilization Policy

Chapter 17
Fiscal Policy / 473

Chapter 18
Money, Banking, and the Federal
Reserve System / 503

PART 9 The International Economy

Chapter 20
International Trade, Capital Flows, and Exchange Rates / 567

Cover Credits

Front Cover

Credits are listed left to right.

First Row: Fireman, Kris Timken/AGE Fotostock

Second Row: Commuter train, tovovan/Shutterstock; Fruit Stand, Richard A McMillin/Shutterstock

Third Row: Cows, Stockbyte/Photodisc; Business woman giving presentation, Tinpixels/Getty Images; Solarpanels, iurii/Shutterstock

Fourth Row: Gas Prices, Nickolay Stanev/Shutterstock; Depression Era Man holding sign, akg-images/The Image Works; Wall Street Sign, Thinkstock

Fifth Row: Woman looking in Microscope, Tetra Images/AGE Fotostock; Money Exchange Rates, Bankoo/Shutterstock; Shopping for a mobile phone, Juice Images/AGE Fotostock

Sixth Row: Busy Asian Street, Tom Bonaventure/Getty Images; Construction workers, mikeledray/Shutterstock; Cargoship, EvrenKalinbacak/Shutterstock

Seventh Row: Baby having heartbeat checked, Darren Brode/Shutterstock; Powerlines, Brand X Pictures; Smoking Coal Power Plant, iStockphoto/Thinkstock; Lightbulbs, fStop Images GmbH/Alamy

Eight Row: Workers examining boxes, Jupiterimages/Getty Images; Infrastructure repair, Nightman1965/Shutterstock; Currency, Lucia Pitter/Shutterstock

Back Cover

First Row: Filing Taxes, PTstock/Shutterstock

Second Row: Stack of Cargo Containers, rodho/Shutterstock; Printing Money, matthiashaas/Thinkstock; Coral reef and fish, John_Walker/Shutterstock

Third Row: Waiter, Steven Miric/Getty Images; Cupcakes, Tobias Titz/AGE Fotostock; Shopper Deciding, Noel Hendrickson/Getty Images; Graduates, Prasit Rodphan/Shutterstock

Fourth Row: Flags, yui/Shutterstock; Cars in lot, Matushchak Anton/Shutterstock; Robotic arm for packing, wellphoto/Shutterstock;

Fifth Row: Traffic, Artens/Shutterstock; Shopping in City street, Peathegee Inc/AGE Fotostock; Fracking Rig, CSP_LonnyGarris/AGE Fotostock; Concert, Wittybear/Shutterstock

Sixth Row: Stacks of Wood, Fedor Selivanov/Shutterstock; Soybean Farm, Fotokostic/Shutterstock

Seventh Row: Sushi, Ipatov/Shutterstock; Credit Cards, Olleg/Shutterstock; Diamonds, The Adventurer/Shutterstock

1 First Principles

A DAY IN THE MEGACITY

LONDON, NEW YORK, AND TOKYO have something in common: they are megacities—huge metropolitan complexes that contain tens of millions of people and are spread over immense tracts of land. While most people are familiar with these megacities, not everyone knows about the biggest of them all: the vast urban complex known as China's Pearl River Delta (the PRD). Roughly the same size as the state of Maryland the PRD is home to more than 55 million people.

Nearly forty years ago China was very poor with a backward economy. Now it produces sophisticated goods for the world, allowing it to deliver relatively comfortable incomes to many of its people.

What are all those people doing? A significant percentage of them are engaged in producing goods for world markets, especially, but by no means only, electronic components: just about every smartphone, tablet, and computer contains components produced in the PRD. But the megacity's residents are consumers as well as producers. While the wage of an average worker in the PRD is relatively low by U.S. standards, overall wages and income are high enough to support a vast retail sector, ranging from mom-and-pop local stores to shops selling expensive luxury goods.

But not so long ago, neither the PRD nor the economic dynamism it embodies was visible. As recently as 1980, 800 million people in China subsisted on less than $1.50 a day. The average Chinese citizen more or less had enough to eat and a roof over his or her head, but not much more than that. In fact, the standard of living wasn't much higher than it had been centuries earlier.

However, in the years since 1980, Chinese incomes have soared more than tenfold in real terms as the poverty rate (percentage of population subsisting on less than $1.90 a day) has fallen from 88% in 1981 to 0.7% in 2015. The rise of the PRD is one chapter of an incredible success story in which hundreds of millions of Chinese have been lifted out of abject poverty over the past few decades. Never in human history have so many seen so much progress.

Although this is a remarkable story, it is not entirely unprecedented. From 1840 to 1910, British workers also experienced a marked rise in their standard of living. And this success was repeated soon afterward in the United States, setting the stage for the high levels of prosperity we now enjoy. Commenting on how English workers were lifted out of poverty, the great economist Alfred Marshall made an observation that is equally relevant for Chinese workers today: "The hope that poverty and ignorance may gradually be extinguished, derives indeed much support from the steady progress of the working classes during the nineteenth century."

These unprecedented sets of events have touched our lives today in many ways. You are using smartphones and laptops that are manufactured in the PRD as you pursue a first-rate education in the United States, one of the richest countries in the world.

What can economics say about all this? Quite a lot, it turns out. What you will learn from this book is how these momentous changes, which lifted hundreds of millions of people out of poverty, are related to a simple, but very important, set of questions involving economics. Among these questions are:

- How does our economic system work? That is, how does it manage to deliver the goods?
- When and why does our economic system sometimes go astray, leading people into counterproductive behavior?
- Why are there ups and downs in the economy? That is, why does the economy sometimes have a bad year?
- Why is the long run mainly a story of ups rather than downs? That is, why has China, like Great Britain and the United States, become much richer over time?

Let's take a look at these questions and offer a brief preview of what you will learn in this book. ●

WHAT YOU WILL LEARN

- What are the fundamental terms that relate to economics and the economy and what do they mean?
- What four principles guide the choices made by individuals?
- What five principles govern how individual choices interact?
- What three principles illustrate economy-wide interactions?

An **economy** is a system for coordinating society's productive activities.

Economics is the social science that studies the production, distribution, and consumption of goods and services.

A **market economy** is an economy in which decisions about production and consumption are made by individual producers and consumers.

The Invisible Hand

The massive industrial and consumer complex that is today's Pearl River Delta is a quite new creation. As recently as 1980 much of the region was an economic backwater; the nucleus, Shenzhen, was then a small and very poor fishing village. How did this backwater turn into the electronics workshop of the world, making it a dynamic creator of wealth?

To achieve the level of prosperity we have in America, a level the average resident of the PRD can only now begin to aspire to, you need a well-functioning system for coordinating productive activities—the activities that create the goods and services people want and get them to the people who want them. That kind of system is what we mean when we talk about the **economy.** And **economics** is the social science that studies the production, distribution, and consumption of goods and services.

An economy succeeds to the extent that it, literally, delivers the goods. And as we've discussed, over the past 40 years the Chinese economy has achieved a spectacular increase in the amount of goods it delivers both to its own citizens and to the rest of the world.

So China's economy must be doing something right, and we might want to compliment the people in charge. But guess what? There isn't anyone in charge—not anymore.

In the 1970s, before the incredible rise of the PRD, China was a *command economy* in which decisions about what factories would produce and what goods would be delivered to households were made by government officials. But experience shows that command economies don't work very well. Producers in command economies like China before 1980 or the Soviet Union before 1991 routinely found themselves unable to produce because they did not have crucial raw materials, or if they succeeded in producing, they found nobody wanted their products. Consumers were often unable to find necessities like toilet paper or milk. From 1959 to 1961, in what is now known as "The Great Leap Backward," the Chinese government got its command economy terribly wrong, inflicting enormous hardship and causing millions of unnecessary deaths.

In 1978 the Chinese government finally admitted that its economic model wasn't working, and began a remarkable transformation into a **market economy,** one in which production and consumption are the result of decentralized decisions by many firms and individuals. The United States has a market economy. And in today's China there is no central authority telling people what to produce or where to ship it. Each individual producer makes what he or she thinks will be most profitable; each consumer buys what he or she chooses. It's important to realize, however, that the Chinese government intervenes in markets much more than the U.S. government does; in particular, while China's government rarely tells producers what to produce, it often tells banks how much to lend and to whom.

If you had never seen a market economy in action, you might imagine that it would be chaotic. After all, nobody is in charge. But market economies are able to coordinate even highly complex activities and reliably provide consumers with the goods and services they want. Indeed, people quite casually trust their lives to the market system: residents of any major city would starve in days if the unplanned yet somehow orderly actions of thousands of businesses did not deliver a steady supply of food. Surprisingly, the unplanned "chaos" of a market economy turns out to be far more orderly than the planning of a command economy. And that's why almost every country in the world—North Korea, Vietnam, Laos, and Cuba are the only exceptions—has become a market economy.

In 1776, in a famous passage in his book *The Wealth of Nations,* the pioneering Scottish economist Adam Smith wrote about how individuals, in pursuing their own interests, often end up serving the interests of society as a whole. Of a businessman whose pursuit of profit makes the nation wealthier, Smith wrote: "[H]e intends only his own gain, and he is in this, as in many other cases, led by an invisible hand to promote an end which was no part of his intention." Ever since, economists have used the term **invisible hand** to refer to the way a market economy manages to harness the power of self-interest for the good of society.

The study of how individuals make decisions and how these decisions interact is called **microeconomics.** One of the key themes in microeconomics is the validity of Adam Smith's insight: individuals pursuing their own interests often do promote the interests of society as a whole.

So the answer to our first question—"How does our economic system manage to deliver the goods?"—is that we rely on the virtues of a market economy and the power of the invisible hand.

But the invisible hand isn't always our friend. It's also important to understand when and why the individual pursuit of self-interest can lead to counterproductive behavior.

The **invisible hand** refers to the way in which the individual pursuit of self-interest can lead to good results for society as a whole.

Microeconomics is the branch of economics that studies how people make decisions and how these decisions interact.

When the individual pursuit of self-interest leads to bad results for society as a whole, there is **market failure.**

My Benefit, Your Cost

In most ways, life in the PRD is immensely better than it was in 1980. Two things have, however, gotten much worse: traffic congestion and air quality. At rush hour, the average speed on the PRD's roads is only around 12 miles an hour and the air is seriously unhealthy much of the year.

Why do these problems represent failures of the invisible hand? Consider the case of traffic congestion.

When traffic is congested, each driver is imposing a cost on all the other drivers on the road—he is literally getting in their way (and they are getting in his way). This cost can be substantial: one estimate found that someone driving a car into lower Manhattan on a weekday causes more than three hours of delays to other drivers, and around $160 in monetary losses. Yet when deciding whether or not to drive, commuters have no incentive to take the costs they impose on others into account.

Traffic congestion is a familiar example of a much broader problem: **market failure,** which happens when the individual pursuit of one's own interest, instead of promoting the interests of society as a whole, actually makes society worse off. Another important example of market failure is air pollution, which is all too visible, literally, in the PRD. Water pollution and the overexploitation of natural resources such as fish and forests reflect the same problem.

The environmental costs of self-interested behavior can sometimes be huge. And as the world becomes more crowded and the environmental footprint of human activity continues to grow, issues like climate change and ocean acidification will become increasingly important.

The good news, as you will learn if you study microeconomics, is that economic analysis can be used to diagnose cases of market failure. And often, economic analysis can also be used to devise solutions for the problem.

Good Times, Bad Times

China has become an enormous economic powerhouse in the last 40 years. (And, depending upon the data source used, China and the United States vie for top place among the world's economies.) One somewhat ironic consequence of China's

"Remember, an economic boom is usually followed by an economic kaboom."

rise is that people around the world get nervous at any signs of trouble in Chinese industry, because it's such a big source of demand for raw materials. And in 2016, there was a lot to be nervous about. Although official data said that the Chinese economy was still strong, many independent observers looked at indicators like electricity consumption and saw them as evidence that a sharp slowdown was in progress.

Such troubled periods are a regular feature of modern economies. The fact is that the economy does not always run smoothly: it experiences fluctuations, a series of ups and downs. By middle age, a typical American will have experienced three or four downs, known as **recessions.** The U.S. economy experienced serious recessions beginning in 1973, 1981, 1990, 2001, and 2007. During a severe recession, millions of workers may be laid off.

Like market failure, recessions are a fact of life; but also like market failure, they are a problem for which economic analysis offers some solutions. Recessions are one of the main concerns of the branch of economics known as **macroeconomics,** which is concerned with the overall ups and downs of the economy. If you study macroeconomics, you will learn how economists explain recessions and how government policies can be used to minimize the damage from economic fluctuations.

Despite the occasional recession, however, over the long run the stories of all major economies contain many more ups than downs. And that long-run ascent is the subject of our final question.

Onward and Upward

The overall standard of living of the average resident of the PRD, while immensely higher than it was in 1980, is still pretty low by American standards. But then, America wasn't always as rich as it is today. Indeed, at the beginning of the twentieth century, most Americans lived under conditions that we would now think of as extreme poverty. Only 10% of homes had flush toilets, only 8% had central heating, only 2% had electricity, and almost nobody had a car, let alone a washing machine or air conditioning. But over the course of the following century America achieved a remarkable rise in living standards that ultimately led to the great wealth that we see around us today.

Such comparisons are a stark reminder of how much lives around the world have been changed by **economic growth,** the increasing ability of the economy to produce goods and services. Why does the economy grow over time? And why does economic growth occur faster in some places and times than in others? These are key questions for economics, because economic growth is a good thing, as the residents of the PRD can attest, and most of us want more of it.

However, it is important for economic growth to take place without irreparable damage to the environment. What we need is *sustainable long-run economic growth*, which is economic growth over time that balances protection of the environment with improved living standards for current and future generations. Today, the goal of balancing the production of goods and services with the health of the environment is an increasingly pressing concern, and economic analysis has a key role to play, particularly in the analysis of market failure.

An Engine for Discovery

We hope we have convinced you that what the great economist Alfred Marshall called the "ordinary business of life," the economic actions and transactions that go on every day not just in the PRD but around the world, is really quite

A **recession** is a downturn in the economy.

Macroeconomics is the branch of economics that is concerned with overall ups and downs in the economy.

Economic growth is the growing ability of the economy to produce goods and services.

extraordinary, if you stop to think about it, and that it can lead us to ask some very interesting and important questions.

In this book, we will describe the answers economists have given to these questions. But this book, like economics as a whole, isn't a list of answers: it's an introduction to a discipline, a way to address questions like those we asked earlier. Or as Alfred Marshall put it: "Economics . . . is not a body of concrete truth, but an engine for the discovery of concrete truth."

So let's turn the key and start the ignition.

>> Check Your Understanding 1-1
Solutions appear at back of book.

1. Explain whether each of the following statements describes features of a market economy.
   a. The invisible hand harnesses the power of self-interest for the good of society.
   b. A central authority makes decisions about production and consumption.
   c. The pursuit of one's own self-interest sometimes results in market failure.
   d. Growth in a market economy is steady and without fluctuations.

>> Quick Review

• **Economics** is the study of the production, distribution, and consumption of goods and services and how the **economy** coordinates these activities. In a **market economy,** the **invisible hand** works through individuals pursuing their own self-interest.

• **Microeconomics** is the study of how individuals make decisions and how these decisions interact, which sometimes leads to **market failure. Macroeconomics** is concerned with economic fluctuations, such as **recessions,** that can temporarily slow **economic growth.**

Principles That Underlie Individual Choice: The Core of Economics

Every economic issue involves, at its most basic level, **individual choice**—decisions by an individual about what to do and what not to do. In fact, you might say that it isn't economics if it isn't about choice.

Take Walmart or Amazon. There are thousands of different products available, and it is extremely unlikely that you—or anyone else—could afford to buy everything you might want to have. And anyway, there's only so much space in your dorm room or apartment. So will you buy another bookcase or a mini-refrigerator? Given limitations on your budget and your living space, you must choose which products to buy and which to leave at the store.

The fact that those products are available for purchase in the first place involves choice—the store manager chose to put them there, and the manufacturers of the products chose to produce them. All economic activities involve individual choice.

Four economic principles underlie the economics of individual choice, as shown in Table 1-1. We'll now examine each of these principles.

Principle #1: Choices Are Necessary Because Resources Are Scarce

You can't always get what you want. Everyone would like to have a beautiful house in a great location, a new car or two, and a nice vacation in a fancy hotel. But even in a rich country like the United States, not many families can afford all that. So they must make choices—whether to go to Disney World this year or buy a better car, whether to make do with a small house or accept a longer commute to live where land is cheaper.

Limited income isn't the only thing that keeps people from having everything they want. Time is also in limited supply: there are only 24 hours in a day. Choosing to spend time on one activity means choosing not to spend time on a different activity—studying for an exam means forgoing a night spent watching a movie. Indeed, many people faced with the limited number of hours in the day are willing to trade money for time. For example, convenience stores normally charge higher

TABLE 1-1 The Principles of Individual Choice

1. People must make choices because resources are scarce.

2. The opportunity cost of an item—what you must give up to get it—is its true cost.

3. "How much" decisions require making trade-offs at the margin: comparing the costs and benefits of doing a little bit more of an activity versus doing a little bit less.

4. People usually respond to incentives, exploiting opportunities to make themselves better off.

Individual choice is the decision by an individual of what to do, which necessarily involves a decision of what not to do.

A **resource** is anything that can be used to produce something else.

Resources are **scarce**—not enough of the resources are available to satisfy all the various ways a society wants to use them.

The real cost of an item is its **opportunity cost:** what you must give up to get it.

Resources are scarce.

prices than a regular supermarket. But they fulfill a valuable role by catering to time-pressed customers who would rather pay more than travel farther to the supermarket. This leads to our first principle of individual choice:

People must make choices because resources are scarce.

A **resource** is anything that can be used to produce something else. Lists of the economy's resources usually begin with land, labor (the time of workers), physical capital (machinery, buildings, and other man-made productive assets), and human capital (the educational achievements and skills of workers).

A resource is **scarce** when there's not enough of the resource available to satisfy all the ways a society wants to use it. For example, there is a limited supply of natural resources that come from the physical environment, such as minerals, lumber, and petroleum. There is also a limited quantity of human resources, such as labor, skill, and intelligence. And in a growing world economy with a rapidly increasing human population, even clean air and water have become scarce resources.

Just as individuals must make choices, the scarcity of resources means that society as a whole must make choices. One way to do this in a market economy is to allow the choices to emerge as the result of many individual choices. For example, Americans as a group have only so many hours in a week: how many of those hours will they spend going to supermarkets to get lower prices, rather than saving time by shopping at convenience stores or online? The answer is the sum of individual decisions: each of the millions of individuals in the economy makes a choice about where to shop, and the overall choice is simply the sum of those individual decisions.

For various reasons, there are some decisions that a society decides are best not left to individual choice. And often, economic analysis can also be used to devise the best solutions in these cases. Take the case of cod fishing. By 1992, excessive fishing by individual fishermen had left the stocks of cod in the North Atlantic close to extinction. The Canadian government intervened to limit the amount harvested by fishermen; as a result, cod stocks were on their way to recovery as of 2016.

Principle #2: The True Cost of Something Is Its Opportunity Cost

It is the last term before you graduate, and your class schedule allows you to take only one elective. There are two, however, that you would really like to take: Intro to Web Design and History of Jazz.

Suppose you decide to take the History of Jazz course. What's the cost of that decision? It is the fact that you can't take the web design class, your next best alternative choice. Economists call that kind of cost—what you must give up to get an item you want—the **opportunity cost** of that item. This leads us to our second principle:

The opportunity cost of an item—what you must give up to get it—is its true cost.

So the opportunity cost of taking the History of Jazz class is the benefit you would have derived from the Intro to Web Design class.

The concept of opportunity cost is crucial to understanding individual choice because, in the end, all costs are opportunity costs. That's because every choice you make means forgoing some other alternative.

Sometimes critics claim that economists are concerned only with costs and benefits that can be measured in dollars and cents. But that is not true. Much economic analysis involves cases like our elective course example, where it costs no extra tuition to take one elective course—that is, there is no direct monetary cost. Nonetheless, the elective you choose has an opportunity cost—the other desirable

Ben Heys/Shutterstock

elective course that you must forgo because your limited time permits taking only one. More specifically, the opportunity cost of a choice is what you forgo by not choosing your next best alternative.

You might think that opportunity cost is an add-on—that is, something *additional* to the monetary cost of an item. Suppose that an elective class costs additional tuition of $750; now there is a monetary cost to taking History of Jazz. Is the opportunity cost of taking that course something separate from that monetary cost?

Well, consider two cases. First, suppose that taking Intro to Web Design also costs $750. In this case, you would have to spend that $750 no matter which class you take. So what you give up to take the History of Jazz class is still the web design class, period. But suppose there isn't any fee for the web design class. In that case, what you give up to take the jazz class is the benefit from the web design class *plus* the benefit you could have gained from spending the $750 on other things.

Either way, the real cost of taking your preferred class is what you must give up to get it. As you expand the set of decisions that underlie each choice—whether to take an elective or not, whether to finish this term or not, whether to drop out or not—you'll realize that all costs are ultimately opportunity costs.

Sometimes the money you have to pay for something is a good indication of its opportunity cost. But many times it is not.

One very important example of how poorly monetary cost can indicate opportunity cost is the cost of attending college. Tuition and housing are major monetary expenses for most students; but even if these things were free, attending college would still be an expensive proposition because most college students, if they were not in college, would have a job. That is, by going to college, students *forgo* the income they could have earned if they had worked instead. This means that the opportunity cost of attending college is what you pay for tuition and housing plus the forgone income you would have earned in a job.

It's easy to see that the opportunity cost of going to college is especially high for people who could be earning a lot during what would otherwise have been their college years. That is why star athletes like LeBron James and entrepreneurs like Mark Zuckerberg, founder of Facebook, often skip or drop out of college.

> You make a **trade-off** when you compare the costs with the benefits of doing something.

Mark Zuckerberg understood the concept of opportunity cost.

Principle #3: "How Much" Is a Decision at the Margin

Some important decisions involve an "either–or" choice—for example, you decide either to go to college or to begin working; you decide either to take economics or to take something else. But other important decisions involve "how much" choices—for example, if you are taking both economics and chemistry this semester, you must decide how much time to spend studying for each. When it comes to understanding "how much" decisions, economics has an important insight to offer: "how much" is a decision made at the margin.

Suppose you are taking both economics and chemistry. And suppose you are a pre-med student, now your grade in chemistry matters more to you than your grade in economics. Does that therefore imply that you should spend *all* your study time on chemistry and wing it on the economics exam? Probably not; even if you think your chemistry grade is more important, you should put some effort into studying economics.

Spending more time studying chemistry involves a benefit (a higher expected grade in that course) and a cost (you could have spent that time doing something else, such as studying to get a higher grade in economics). That is, your decision involves a **trade-off**—a comparison of costs and benefits.

How do you decide this kind of "how much" question? The typical answer is that you make the decision a bit at a time, by asking how you should spend the next hour. Say both exams are on the same day, and the night before you spend time reviewing your notes for both courses. At 6:00 P.M., you decide that it's a good idea

Decisions about whether to do a bit more or a bit less of an activity are **marginal decisions.**

The study of such decisions is known as **marginal analysis.**

An **incentive** is anything that offers rewards to people to change their behavior.

to spend at least an hour on each course. At 8:00 P.M., you decide you'd better spend another hour on each course. At 10:00 P.M., you are getting tired and figure you have one more hour to study before bed—chemistry or economics? If you are pre-med, it's likely to be chemistry; if you are a business major, it's likely to be economics.

Note how you've made the decision to allocate your time: at each point the question is whether or not to spend *one more hour* on either course. And in deciding whether to spend another hour studying for chemistry, you weigh the costs (an hour forgone of studying for economics or an hour forgone of sleeping) versus the benefits (a likely increase in your chemistry grade). As long as the benefit of studying chemistry for one more hour outweighs the cost, you should choose to study for that additional hour.

Decisions of this type—whether to do a bit more or a bit less of an activity, like what to do with your next hour, your next dollar, and so on—are **marginal decisions.** This brings us to our third principle:

> *"How much" decisions require making trade-offs at the margin: comparing the costs and benefits of doing a little bit more of an activity versus doing a little bit less.*

The study of such decisions is known as **marginal analysis.** Many of the questions that we face in real life involve marginal analysis: How many minutes should I exercise? How many workers should I hire? Marginal analysis plays a central role in economics because it is the key to our deciding "how much" of an activity to do.

Principle #4: People Usually Respond to Incentives, Exploiting Opportunities to Make Themselves Better Off

One day, while listening to the financial news, the authors heard a great tip about how to park cheaply in Manhattan. Garages in the Wall Street area charge as much as $30 per day. But according to this news report, some people had found a better way: instead of parking in a garage, they had their oil changed at the Manhattan Jiffy Lube for $19.95—where they will keep your car all day!

It's a great story, but unfortunately it turned out not to be true—in fact, there is no Jiffy Lube in Manhattan. But if there were, you can be sure there would be a lot of oil changes there. Why? Because when people are offered opportunities to make themselves better off, they normally take them—and if they could find a way to park their car all day for $19.95 rather than $30, they would.

In this example, economists say that people are responding to an **incentive**—an opportunity to make themselves better off, which brings us to our fourth principle:

> *People usually respond to incentives, exploiting opportunities to make themselves better off.*

When you try to predict how individuals will behave in an economic situation, it is a very good bet that they will respond to incentives—that is, exploit opportunities to make themselves better off. Furthermore, individuals will *continue* to exploit these opportunities until they have been fully exhausted. If there really were a Manhattan Jiffy Lube and an oil change really were a cheap way to park your car, we can safely predict that before long the waiting list for oil changes would be weeks, if not months.

In fact, the principle that people will exploit opportunities to make themselves better off is the basis of *all* predictions by economists about individual behavior.

If the earnings of those who get MBAs soar while the earnings of those who get law degrees decline, expect more students to go to business school and fewer to go to law school. If the price of gasoline rises and stays high for an extended period of time, expect people to buy smaller cars with higher gas mileage—making themselves better off by driving more fuel-efficient cars.

One last point: economists tend to be skeptical of any attempt to change behavior that *doesn't* change incentives. For example, a plan that calls on manufacturers to reduce pollution voluntarily probably won't be effective. In contrast, a plan that gives manufacturers a financial reward to reduce pollution is a lot more likely to succeed because it has changed their incentives.

So are we ready to do economics? Not yet—because most of the interesting things that happen in the economy are the result not merely of individual choices but of the way in which individual choices interact.

ECONOMICS >> *in Action* 🌐
Boy or Girl? It Depends on the Cost

One fact about China is indisputable: it has lots of people. As of 2018, the estimated Chinese population is over 1,415,000,000. That's right: over *one billion four hundred million* people. And trends in Chinese demographics have shifted the cost of having a child over time; in particular, the cost of having a boy or a girl.

In the 1970s, China was a very, very poor country with an already large and growing population. Concerned that it would be unable to adequately provide and care for such a large number of people, the Chinese government introduced the one-child policy in 1979. It restricted most couples to only one child and imposed penalties on those that defied the mandate. By 2016 the average number of children per Chinese woman had fallen to 1.6, from more than 5 in the 1970s.

But the one-child policy has had an unfortunate unintended consequence. Until recently China was an overwhelmingly rural country. In the countryside, because of the physical demands of farming, sons are strongly preferred over daughters. In addition, tradition dictated that it was sons, not daughters, who took care of elderly parents. The effect of the one-child policy was to greatly increase the perceived cost to a Chinese family of a female child. As a result, while some were given up for adoption abroad, many Chinese females simply "disappeared" during the first year of life, victims of neglect and mistreatment.

In fact, in 1990 Nobel-prize-winning Indian-born economist Amartya Sen calculated that there were 100 million "missing women" in Asia due to the perceived higher cost of female children, with estimates rising to 160 million.

Recent events, however, have shifted the relative costs of a boy versus a girl toward a greater balance. Because China is quickly urbanizing, boys are no longer prized to do manual labor. So the gender imbalance between Chinese boys and girls peaked in 1995 and has fallen toward the biologically natural ratio since then. And in 2015 the Chinese government officially ended the one-child policy.

Yet the consequences will endure for many more years. There are now estimated to be over 30 million *excess men* in China—the number of men in excess of the number of women who will reach adulthood by 2020. There have also been reports of Chinese villages full of lonely men. Not surprisingly, websites have popped up advising couples on how to have a girl rather than a boy.

ED JONES/Getty Images

In China, the cost of having a baby girl compared to a baby boy has fallen due to changes in the economy and in government policy.

>> **Quick Review**

• All economic activities involve **individual choice.**

• People must make choices because **resources** are **scarce.**

• The real cost of something is its **opportunity cost**—what you must give up to get it. All costs are opportunity costs. Monetary costs are sometimes a good indicator of opportunity costs, but not always.

• Many choices involve not *whether* to do something but *how much* of it to do. "How much" choices call for making a **trade-off** at the margin. The study of **marginal decisions** is known as **marginal analysis.**

• Because people usually exploit opportunities to make themselves better off, **incentives** can change people's behavior.

>> *Check Your Understanding* 1-2

Solutions appear at back of book.

1. Explain how each of the following illustrates one of the four principles of individual choice.
   a. You are on your third trip to a restaurant's all-you-can-eat dessert buffet and are feeling very full. Although it would cost you no additional money, you forgo a slice of coconut cream pie but have a slice of chocolate cake.
   b. Even if there were more resources in the world, there would still be scarcity.
   c. Different teaching assistants teach several Economics 101 tutorials. Those taught by the teaching assistants with the best reputations fill up quickly, with spaces left unfilled in the ones taught by assistants with poor reputations.

Interaction of choices—my choices affect your choices, and vice versa—is a feature of most economic situations. The results of this interaction are often quite different from what the individuals intend.

In a market economy, individuals engage in **trade:** they provide goods and services to others and receive goods and services in return.

There are **gains from trade:** people can get more of what they want through trade than they could if they tried to be self-sufficient. This increase in output is due to **specialization:** each person specializes in the task that he or she is good at performing.

d. To decide how many hours per week to exercise, you compare the health benefits of one more hour of exercise to the effect on your grades of one fewer hour spent studying.

2. You make $45,000 per year at your current job with Whiz Kids Consultants. You are considering a job offer from Brainiacs, Inc., that will pay you $50,000 per year. Which of the following are elements of the opportunity cost of accepting the new job at Brainiacs, Inc.?

a. The increased time spent commuting to your new job

b. The $45,000 salary from your old job

c. The more spacious office at your new job

Interaction: How Economies Work

An economy is a system for coordinating the productive activities of many people. In a market economy like we live in, coordination takes place without any coordinator: each individual makes his or her own choices.

Yet those choices are by no means independent of one another: each individual's opportunities, and hence choices, depend to a large extent on the choices made by other people. So to understand how a market economy behaves, we have to examine this **interaction** in which my choices affect your choices, and vice versa.

When studying economic interaction, we quickly learn that the end result of individual choices may be quite different from what any one individual intends. For example, over the past century farmers in the United States have eagerly adopted new farming techniques and crop strains that have reduced their costs and increased their yields. Clearly, it's in the interest of each farmer to keep up with the latest farming techniques.

But the end result of each farmer trying to increase his or her own income has actually been to drive many farmers out of business. Because American farmers have been so successful at producing larger yields, agricultural prices have steadily fallen. These falling prices have reduced the incomes of many farmers, and as a result, fewer people find it worthwhile to farm. That is, an individual farmer who plants a better variety of corn is better off; but when many farmers plant a better variety of corn, the result may be to make farmers as a group worse off.

The farmer who plants a new and improved corn variety doesn't just grow more corn. This farmer also affects *the market* for corn through the increased yields attained, with consequences that will be felt by other farmers, consumers, and beyond.

In addition to the four economic principles that underlie individual choice, there are five principles underlying the economics of interaction. These principles are summarized in Table 1-2.

TABLE 1-2 The Principles of the Interaction of Individual Choices

5. There are gains from trade.

6. Because people respond to incentives, markets move toward equilibrium.

7. Resources should be used as efficiently as possible to achieve society's goals.

8. Because people usually exploit gains from trade, markets usually lead to efficiency.

9. When markets don't achieve efficiency, government intervention can improve society's welfare.

Principle #5: There Are Gains from Trade

Why do the choices I make interact with the choices you make? A family could try to take care of all its own needs—growing its own food, sewing its own clothing, providing itself with entertainment, writing its own economics textbooks. But trying to live that way would be very hard.

The key to a much better standard of living for everyone is **trade,** in which people divide tasks among themselves and each person provides a good or service that other people want in return for different goods and services that she or he wants.

The reason we have an economy, and not many self-sufficient individuals, is that there are **gains from trade:** by dividing tasks and trading, two people (or 7 billion people) can each get more of what they want than they could get by being self-sufficient. This leads to our fifth principle:

There are gains from trade.

Gains from trade arise from this division of tasks, which economists call **specialization**—a situation in which different people each engage in a different task, specializing in those tasks that they are good at performing. The advantages of specialization, and the resulting gains from trade, were the starting point for Adam Smith's 1776 book *The Wealth of Nations*, which many regard as the beginning of economics as a discipline. Smith's book begins with a description of an eighteenth-century pin factory where, rather than each of the 10 workers making a pin from start to finish, each worker specialized in one of the many steps in pin-making:

"I hunt and she gathers—otherwise, we couldn't make ends meet."

> One man draws out the wire, another straights it, a third cuts it, a fourth points it, a fifth grinds it at the top for receiving the head; to make the head requires two or three distinct operations; to put it on, is a particular business, to whiten the pins is another; it is even a trade by itself to put them into the paper; and the important business of making a pin is, in this manner, divided into about eighteen distinct operations. . . . Those ten persons, therefore, could make among them upwards of forty-eight thousand pins in a day. But if they had all wrought separately and independently, and without any of them having been educated to this particular business, they certainly could not each of them have made twenty, perhaps not one pin a day. . . .

The same principle applies when we look at how people divide tasks among themselves and trade in an economy. *The economy, as a whole, can produce more when each person specializes in a task and trades with others.*

The benefits of specialization are the reason a person typically chooses only one career. It takes many years of study and experience to become a doctor or a commercial airline pilot. Many doctors might well have had the potential to become excellent pilots, and vice versa; but it is very unlikely that anyone who decided to pursue both careers would be as good a pilot or as good a doctor as someone who decided at the beginning to specialize in just one field. So it is to everyone's advantage that individuals specialize in their career choices.

Markets are what allow a doctor and a pilot to specialize in their own fields. Because markets for commercial flights and for doctors' services exist, a doctor is assured that she can find a flight and a pilot is assured that he can find a doctor. As long as individuals know that they can find the goods and services they want in the market, they are willing to forgo self-sufficiency and to specialize. But what assures people that markets will deliver what they want? The answer to that question leads us to our next principle.

Principle #6: Markets Move Toward Equilibrium

It's a busy afternoon at the supermarket; there are long lines at the checkout counters. Then one of the previously closed cash registers opens. What happens? The first thing, of course, is a rush to that register. After a couple of minutes, however, things will have settled down; shoppers will have rearranged themselves so that the line at the newly opened register is about the same length as the lines at all the other registers.

How do we know that? We know from Principle #4 that people will exploit opportunities to make themselves better off. This means that people will rush to the newly opened register to save time standing in line. And things will settle down when shoppers can no longer improve their position by switching lines—that is, when the opportunities to make themselves better off have all been exploited.

Witness equilibrium in action at the checkout line.

An economic situation is in **equilibrium** when no individual would be better off doing something different.

A story about supermarket checkout lines illustrates an important economic principle: a situation in which individuals cannot make themselves better off by doing something different—as is the case when all the checkout lines are the same length—is what economists call an **equilibrium.**

Recall the story about the mythical Jiffy Lube, where it was supposedly cheaper to leave your car for an oil change than to pay for parking. If the opportunity had really existed and people were still paying $30 to park in garages, the situation would *not* have been an equilibrium. And that should have been a giveaway that the story couldn't be true. In reality, people would have seized an opportunity to park cheaply, just as they seize opportunities to save time at the checkout line. And in so doing they would have eliminated the opportunity! Either it would have become very hard to get an appointment for an oil change or the price of a lube job would have increased to the point that it was no longer an attractive option (unless you really needed an oil change). This brings us to our sixth principle:

Because people respond to incentives, markets move toward equilibrium.

As we will see, markets usually reach equilibrium via changes in prices, which rise or fall until no opportunities for individuals to make themselves better off remain.

The concept of equilibrium is extremely helpful in understanding economic interactions because it provides a way to cut through the sometimes complex details of those interactions. To understand what happens when a new line is opened at a supermarket, you don't need to worry about exactly how shoppers rearrange themselves, who moves ahead of whom, which register just opened, and so on. What you need to know is that *any time there is a change, the situation will move to an equilibrium.*

The fact that markets move toward equilibrium is why we can depend on them to work in a predictable way. In fact, we can trust markets to supply us with the essentials of life. For example, residents of big cities can be sure that supermarket shelves will always be fully stocked. Why? Because if some merchants who distribute food *didn't* maintain shelves full of food, a big profit opportunity would be created for any merchant who did—and there would be a rush to supply food, just like the rush to a newly opened cash register.

So the market ensures that food will always be available for city dwellers. And, returning to our fifth principle, this allows city dwellers to be city dwellers—to specialize in doing city jobs rather than living on farms and growing their own food.

A market economy, as we have seen, allows people to achieve gains from trade. But how do we know how well such an economy is doing? The next principle gives us a standard to use in evaluating an economy's performance.

Principle #7: Resources Should Be Used Efficiently to Achieve Society's Goals

Suppose you are taking a course in which the classroom is too small for the number of students—many are forced to stand or sit on the floor—despite the fact that large, empty classrooms are available nearby. You would say, correctly, that this is no way to run a college. Economists would call this an *inefficient* use of resources. But if an inefficient use of resources is undesirable, just what does it mean to use resources *efficiently*?

You might imagine that the efficient use of resources has something to do with money, maybe that it is measured in dollars-and-cents terms. But in economics, as in life, money is only a means to other ends. The measure that economists really care about is not money but people's happiness or welfare. Economists say that *an economy's resources are used efficiently when they are used in a way that has fully exploited all opportunities to make everyone better off.* To put it another way, an economy is **efficient** if it takes all opportunities to make some people better off without making other people worse off.

In our classroom example, there clearly is a way to make everyone better off—moving the class to a larger room would make people in the class better off without hurting anyone else in the college—it would have been an efficient use of the college's resources. Assigning the course to the smaller classroom is an inefficient use of the college's resources.

When an economy is efficient, it is producing the maximum gains from trade possible given the resources available, because there is no way to rearrange how resources are used so that everyone can be made better off. When an economy is efficient, one person can be made better off by rearranging how resources are used *only* by making someone else worse off.

In our classroom example, if all larger classrooms were already occupied, the college would have been run in an efficient way: your class could be made better off by moving to a larger classroom only by making people in the larger classroom worse off by making them move to a smaller classroom. We now have our seventh principle:

> *Resources should be used as efficiently as possible to achieve society's goals.*

Should policy makers always strive to achieve economic efficiency? Well, not quite, because efficiency is only a means to achieving society's goals. Sometimes efficiency may conflict with a goal that society has deemed worthwhile to achieve. For example, in most societies, people also care about issues of fairness, or **equity.** And there is typically a trade-off between equity and efficiency: policies that promote equity often come at a cost of decreased efficiency in the economy, and vice versa.

To see this, consider the case of disabled-designated parking spaces in public parking lots. Many people have difficulty walking due to age or disability, so it seems only fair to assign closer parking spaces specifically for their use. You may have noticed, however, that a certain amount of inefficiency is involved. To insure that there is always a parking space available should a disabled person want one, there are typically more of these spaces available than there are disabled people who want to park in one. As a result, desirable parking spaces are unused. (And the temptation for nondisabled people to use them is so great that they must be dissuaded by fear of getting a ticket.)

So, short of hiring parking attendants to allocate spaces, there is a conflict between *equity,* making life "fairer" for disabled people, and *efficiency,* making sure that all opportunities to make people better off have been fully exploited by never letting available parking spaces go unused.

Exactly how far policy makers should go in promoting equity over efficiency is a difficult question that goes to the heart of the political process. As such, it is not a question that economists can answer. What is important for economists, however, is always to seek to use the economy's resources as efficiently as possible in the pursuit of society's goals, whatever those goals may be.

Principle #8: Markets Usually Lead to Efficiency

No branch of the U.S. government is entrusted with ensuring the general economic efficiency of our market economy—we don't have agents tasked with checking that brain surgeons aren't plowing fields or that Minnesota farmers aren't trying to grow oranges. The government doesn't need to enforce the efficient use of resources, because in most cases the invisible hand does the job.

The incentives built into a market economy ensure that resources are usually put to good use and that opportunities to make people better off are not wasted. If a college were known for its habit of crowding students into small classrooms

An economy is **efficient** if it takes all opportunities to make some people better off without making other people worse off.

Equity means that everyone gets his or her fair share. Since people can disagree about what's "fair," equity isn't as well defined a concept as efficiency.

Sometimes equity trumps efficiency.

while large classrooms went unused, it would soon find its enrollment dropping, putting the jobs of its administrators at risk. The "market" for college students would respond in a way that induced administrators to run the college efficiently.

A detailed explanation of why markets are usually very good at making sure that resources are used well will have to wait until we have studied how markets actually work. But the most basic reason is that in a market economy, in which individuals are free to choose what to consume and what to produce, people normally take opportunities for mutual gain—that is, gains from trade.

If there is a way in which some people can be made better off, people will usually be able to take advantage of that opportunity. And that is exactly what defines efficiency: all the opportunities to make some people better off without making other people worse off have been exploited, leading to our eighth principle:

> *Because people usually exploit gains from trade, markets usually lead to efficiency.*

However, there are exceptions to the principle that markets are generally efficient. In cases of *market failure,* the individual pursuit of self-interest found in markets makes society worse off—that is, the market outcome is inefficient. And, as we will see in examining the next principle, when markets fail, government intervention can help. But short of market failure, the general rule is that markets are a remarkably good way of organizing an economy.

Principle #9: When Markets Don't Achieve Efficiency, Government Intervention Can Improve Society's Welfare

Recall the nature of the market failure caused by traffic congestion—a commuter driving to work has no incentive to take into account the cost that his or her action inflicts on other drivers in the form of increased traffic.

There are several possible remedies to this situation. Examples include charging road tolls, subsidizing the cost of public transportation, and taxing sales of gasoline to individual drivers. All these remedies work by changing the incentives of would-be drivers, motivating them to drive less and use alternative transportation. But these remedies share another feature: each relies on government intervention in the market. This brings us to our ninth principle:

> *When markets don't achieve efficiency, government intervention can improve society's welfare.*

When markets go wrong, an appropriately designed government policy can sometimes move society closer to an efficient outcome by changing how society's resources are used.

An important part of your education in economics is learning to identify not just when markets work but also when they don't work, and to judge what government policies are appropriate in each situation.

ECONOMICS >> *in Action*
The Fundamental Law of Traffic Congestion

Driving through the middle of Boston used to be a nightmarish experience. The Central Artery—the stretch of Interstate 93 that goes through the heart of the city—was a continuous traffic jam from early morning into evening. What could be done? Boston's answer was the Big Dig, a huge project that involved putting 3½ miles of highway underground, adding a new tunnel to Logan Airport, and building a new bridge over the Charles River.

The Big Dig took much longer—15 years—and cost far more—over $20 billion—than anyone had predicted. Still, once it was completed in 2007, the effect was

In building more roads, planners failed to understand the equilibrium outcome: congestion was not reduced because more people chose to drive.

striking: traffic in central Boston flowed much faster than before. This was a big win for commuters, right?

Well, maybe not. A 2008 study by the *Boston Globe* found that while traffic congestion inside Boston was much reduced, traffic had gotten much worse on roads leading into Boston, so that typical commute times probably hadn't decreased much if at all. The explanation, the paper suggested, was that reduced congestion along the Central Artery induced more people to drive into the city, creating congestion in other places, and that this process continued until the overall driving time was back to its original level.

It's a plausible story, because similar results have been seen in many places. Researchers call it the "fundamental law of traffic congestion": if a city builds more roads, this induces more driving, and this increase in traffic continues until a new equilibrium is reached, with commuting times more or less back where they started. And it really does seem to be a law: a statistical analysis published in 2011 found that a 10% increase in the mileage of interstate highways within a metropolitan area leads to a 10.3% increase in the number of vehicle-miles driven, as more trucks take to the roads and commuters move farther out from the city center.

By the way, expanding public transit also has little effect on traffic congestion, for the same reason: any increase in traffic speed simply induces more driving, which pushes commute times back up.

The fundamental law of traffic congestion is a discouraging result for urban planners trying to make commuters' lives easier. It is, however, a good illustration of the importance of thinking about equilibrium.

>> Check Your Understanding 1-3
Solutions appear at back of book.

1. Explain how each of the following illustrates one of the five principles of interaction.
   a. Using Amazon, any student who wants to sell a used textbook for at least $30 is able to sell it to someone who is willing to pay $30.
   b. At a college tutoring co-op, students can arrange to provide tutoring in subjects they are good in (like economics) in return for receiving tutoring in subjects they are poor in (like philosophy).
   c. The local municipality imposes a law that requires bars and nightclubs near residential areas to keep their noise levels below a certain threshold.
   d. To provide better care for low-income patients, the local municipality has decided to close some underutilized neighborhood clinics and shift funds to the main hospital.
   e. On Amazon, books of a given title with approximately the same level of wear and tear sell for about the same price.
2. Which of the following describes an equilibrium situation? Which does not? Explain your answer.
   a. The restaurants across the street from the university dining hall serve better-tasting and cheaper meals than those served at the university dining hall. The vast majority of students continue to eat at the dining hall.
   b. You currently take the subway to work. Although taking the bus is cheaper, the ride takes longer. So you are willing to pay the higher subway fare to save time.

‖ Economy-Wide Interactions

The economy as a whole has its ups and downs. For example, in 2007 the U.S. economy entered a severe recession in which millions of people lost their jobs, while those who remained employed saw their wages stagnate. It took 7 years—until May 2014—for the number of Americans employed to return to its pre-recession level. And it took until late 2016 for wages to exceed their pre-recession levels.

To understand recessions and recoveries, we need to understand economy-wide interactions, and understanding the big picture of the economy requires three more economic principles, which are summarized in Table 1-3.

Principle #10: One Person's Spending Is Another Person's Income

Between 2005 and 2011, home construction in America plunged more than 60% as builders found it increasingly difficult to make sales. At first the damage was mainly limited to the construction industry. But over time the slump spread into just about every part of the economy, with consumer spending falling across the board.

But why should a fall in home construction mean empty stores in shopping malls? After all, malls are places where families, not builders, do their shopping.

The answer is that lower spending on construction led to lower incomes throughout the economy; people who had been employed either directly in construction, producing goods and services builders need (like roofing shingles), or in producing goods and services new homeowners need (like new furniture), either lost their jobs or were forced to take pay cuts. And as incomes fell, so did spending by consumers. This example illustrates our tenth principle:

> *One person's spending is another person's income.*

In a market economy, people make a living selling things—including their labor—to other people. If some group in the economy decides, for whatever reason, to spend more, the income of other groups will rise. If some group decides to spend less, the income of other groups will fall.

Because one person's spending is another person's income, a chain reaction of changes in spending behavior tends to have repercussions that spread through the economy. For example, a fall in consumer spending at shopping malls leads to reduced family incomes; families respond by reducing consumer spending; this leads to another round of income cuts; and so on. These repercussions play an important role in our understanding of recessions and recoveries.

Principle #11: Overall Spending Sometimes Gets Out of Line with the Economy's Productive Capacity

Macroeconomics emerged as a separate branch of economics in the 1930s, when a collapse of consumer and business spending, a crisis in the banking industry, and other factors led to a plunge in overall spending. This plunge in spending, in turn, led to a period of very high unemployment known as the Great Depression.

The lesson economists learned from the troubles of the 1930s is that overall spending—the amount of goods and services that consumers and businesses want to buy—sometimes doesn't match the amount of goods and services the economy is capable of producing. In the 1930s, spending fell far short of what was needed to keep American workers employed, and the result was a severe economic slump. In fact, shortfalls in spending are responsible for most, though not all, recessions.

It's also possible for overall spending to be too high. In that case, the economy experiences *inflation*, a rise in prices throughout the economy. This rise in prices occurs because when the amount that people want to buy outstrips the supply, producers can raise their prices and still find willing customers. Taking account of both shortfalls in spending and excesses in spending brings us to our eleventh principle:

> *Overall spending sometimes gets out of line with the economy's productive capacity.*

When this happens, what can be done about it? The answer to that questions leads to our last principle.

Principle #12: Government Policies Can Change Spending

The government does a lot of spending on everything—from military equipment to health care—and it can choose to do more or less. The government can also vary how much it collects from the public in taxes, which in turn affects how much income consumers and businesses have left to spend. And the government's control of the quantity of money in circulation gives it another powerful tool with which to affect total spending. Our twelfth and final principle is then:

Government policies can change spending.

Government spending, taxes, and control of money are the tools of *macroeconomic policy.* Modern governments deploy these macroeconomic policy tools in an effort to manage overall spending in the economy, trying to steer it between the perils of recession and inflation. These efforts aren't always successful—recessions still happen, and so do periods of inflation. But it's widely believed that aggressive efforts to sustain spending in 2008 and 2009 helped prevent the financial crisis of 2008 from turning into a full-blown depression.

>> Check Your Understanding 1-4

Solutions appear at back of book.

1. Explain how each of the following illustrates one of our principles of economy-wide interactions.
   a. The White House urged Congress to pass a package of temporary spending increases and tax cuts in early 2009, a time when employment was plunging and unemployment soaring.
   b. With oil prices plummeting, Canadian and U.S. oil companies have been forced to shut down their productive wells. In cities throughout North Dakota, Wyoming, Texas, and Alaska, restaurants and other consumer businesses are failing.
   c. In the mid-2000s, Spain, which was experiencing a big housing boom, also had the highest inflation rate in Europe.

>> Quick Review

- In a market economy, one person's spending is another person's income. As a result, changes in spending behavior have repercussions that spread through the economy.

- Overall spending sometimes gets out of line with the economy's capacity to produce goods and services. When spending is too low, the result is a recession. When spending is too high, it causes inflation.

- Modern governments use macroeconomic policy tools to affect the overall level of spending in an effort to steer the economy between recession and inflation.

SUMMARY

1. An **economy** is a system for coordinating society's productive activities, and **economics** is the social science that studies the production, distribution, and consumption of goods and services. The United States has a **market economy**—an economy in which decisions about production and consumption are made by individual producers and consumers pursuing their own self-interest. The **invisible hand** harnesses the power of self-interest for the good of society.

2. **Microeconomics** is the branch of economics that studies how people make decisions and how these decisions interact. **Market failure** occurs when the individual pursuit of self-interest leads to bad results for society as a whole.

3. **Macroeconomics** is the branch of economics that is concerned with overall ups and downs in the economy. Despite occasional **recessions,** the U.S. economy has achieved long-run **economic growth.**

4. All economic analysis is based on a set of basic principles that apply to three levels of economic

activity. First, we study how individuals make choices; second, we study how these choices interact; and third, we study how the economy functions overall.

5. Everyone has to make choices about what to do and what *not* to do. **Individual choice** is the basis of economics—if it doesn't involve choice, it isn't economics.

6. The reason choices must be made is that **resources**—anything that can be used to produce something else—are **scarce.** Individuals are limited in their choices by money and time; economies are limited by their supplies of human and natural resources.

7. Because you must choose among limited alternatives, the true cost of anything is what you must give up to get it—all costs are **opportunity costs.**

8. Many economic decisions involve questions not of "whether" but of "how much"—how much to spend on a particular good, how much to produce, and so on. Such decisions must be made by performing a **trade-off** *at the margin*—by comparing the costs and benefits of doing a bit more or a bit less. Decisions of this type are called

marginal decisions; the study of them, **marginal analysis,** plays a central role in economics.

9. The study of how people *should* make decisions is also a good way to understand actual behavior. Individuals usually respond to **incentives**—exploiting opportunities to make themselves better off.

10. The next level of economic analysis is the study of **interaction**—how my choices depend on your choices, and vice versa. When individuals interact, the end result may be different from what anyone intends.

11. Individuals interact because there are **gains from trade:** by engaging in the **trade** of goods and services with one another, the members of an economy can all be made better off. **Specialization**—each person specializes in the task he or she is good at—is the source of gains from trade.

12. Because individuals usually respond to incentives, markets normally move toward **equilibrium**—a situation in which no individual can make himself or herself better off by taking a different action.

13. An economy is **efficient** if all opportunities to make some people better off without making other people worse off are taken. Resources should be used as efficiently as possible to achieve society's goals. But efficiency is not the sole way to evaluate an economy: **equity,** or fairness, is also desirable, and there is often a trade-off between equity and efficiency.

14. Markets usually lead to efficiency, with some well-defined exceptions.

15. When markets fail and do not achieve efficiency, government intervention can improve society's welfare.

16. Because people in a market economy earn income by selling things, including their own labor, one person's spending is another person's income. As a result, changes in spending behavior can spread throughout the economy.

17. Overall spending in the economy can get out of line with the economy's productive capacity. Spending below the economy's productive capacity leads to a recession; spending in excess of the economy's productive capacity leads to inflation.

18. Governments have the ability to strongly affect overall spending, an ability they use in an effort to steer the economy between recession and inflation.

KEY TERMS

Economy, p. 2
Economics, p. 2
Market economy, p. 2
Invisible hand, p. 3
Microeconomics, p. 3
Market failure, p. 3
Recession, p. 4
Macroeconomics, p. 4

Economic growth, p. 4
Individual choice, p. 5
Resource, p. 6
Scarce, p. 6
Opportunity cost, p. 6
Trade-off, p. 7
Marginal decisions, p. 8
Marginal analysis, p. 8

Incentive, p. 8
Interaction, p. 10
Trade, p. 10
Gains from trade, p. 10
Specialization, p. 10
Equilibrium, p. 12
Efficient, p. 13
Equity, p. 13

PROBLEMS

Interactive Activity

1. In each of the following situations, identify which of the twelve principles is at work.

   a. You choose to purchase your textbooks online through Chegg rather than paying a higher price for the same books through your college bookstore.

   b. On your spring break trip, your budget is limited to $35 a day.

   c. Craigslist allows departing students to sell items such as used books, appliances, and furniture rather than give them away as they formerly did.

   d. After a hurricane did extensive damage to homes on the island of St. Crispin, homeowners wanted to purchase many more building materials and hire many more workers than were available on the island. As a result, prices for goods and services rose dramatically across the board.

   e. You buy a used textbook from your roommate. Your roommate uses the money to buy music from iTunes.

   f. You decide how many cups of coffee to have when studying the night before an exam by considering how much more work you can do by having another cup versus how much jittery it will make you feel.

   g. There is limited lab space available to do the project required in Chemistry 101. The lab supervisor assigns lab time to each student based on when that student is able to come.

   h. You realize that you can graduate a semester early by forgoing a semester of study abroad.

   i. At the student center, there is a bulletin board on which people advertise used items for sale, such as bicycles. Once you have adjusted for differences in quality, all the bikes sell for about the same price.

j. You are better at performing lab experiments, and your lab partner is better at writing lab reports. So the two of you agree that you will do all the experiments and she will write up all the reports.

k. State governments mandate that it is illegal to drive without passing a driving exam.

l. Your parents' after-tax income has increased because of a tax cut passed by Congress. They therefore increase your allowance, which you spend on a spring break vacation.

2. Describe some of the opportunity costs when you decide to do the following.

a. Attend college instead of taking a job

b. Watch a movie instead of studying for an exam

c. Ride the bus instead of driving your car

3. Liza needs to buy a textbook for the next economics class. The price at the college bookstore is $65. One website offers it for $55, and another site, for $57. All prices include sales tax. The accompanying table indicates the typical shipping and handling charges for the textbook ordered online.

Shipping method	Delivery time	Charge
Standard shipping	3–7 days	$3.99
Second-day air	2 business days	8.98
Next-day air	1 business day	13.98

a. What is the opportunity cost of buying online instead of at the bookstore? Note that if you buy the book online, you must wait to get it.

b. Show the relevant choices for this student. What determines which of these options the student will choose?

4. Use the concept of opportunity cost to explain the following.

a. More people choose to get graduate degrees when the job market is poor.

b. More people choose to do their own home repairs when the economy is slow and hourly wages are down.

c. There are more parks in suburban than in urban areas.

d. Convenience stores, which have higher prices than supermarkets, cater to busy people.

e. Fewer students enroll in classes that meet before 10:00 A.M.

5. For the following examples, state how you would use the principle of marginal analysis to make a decision.

a. Deciding how many days to wait before doing your laundry

b. Deciding how much time to spend researching before writing your term paper

c. Deciding how many bags of chips to eat

d. Deciding how many class lectures to skip

6. This morning you made the following individual choices: you bought a bagel and coffee at the local café, you drove to school in your car during rush hour, and you typed your course notes for your roommate because she was texting in class—in return for which she will do your laundry for a month. For each of these actions, describe how your individual choices interacted with the individual choices made by others. Were other people left better off or worse off by your choices in each case?

7. The Hatfield family lives on the east side of the Hatatoochie River, and the McCoy family lives on the west side. Each family's diet consists of fried chicken and corn-on-the-cob, and each is self-sufficient, raising their own chickens and growing their own corn. Explain the conditions under which each of the following would be true.

a. The two families are made better off when the Hatfields specialize in raising chickens, the McCoys specialize in growing corn, and the two families trade.

b. The two families are made better off when the McCoys specialize in raising chickens, the Hatfields specialize in growing corn, and the two families trade.

8. Which of the following situations describes an equilibrium? Which does not? If the situation does not describe an equilibrium, what would an equilibrium look like?

a. Many people regularly commute from the suburbs to downtown Pleasantville. Due to traffic congestion, the trip takes 30 minutes via highway but only 15 minutes via side streets.

b. At the intersection of Main and Broadway are two gas stations. One station charges $3.00 per gallon for regular gas and the other charges $2.85 per gallon. Customers can get service immediately at the first station but must wait in a long line at the second.

c. Every student enrolled in Economics 101 must also attend a weekly tutorial. This year there are two sections offered: section A and section B, which meet at the same time in adjoining classrooms and are taught by equally competent instructors. Section A is overcrowded, with people sitting on the floor and often unable to see what is written on the board at the front of the room. Section B has many empty seats.

9. For each of the following, explain whether you think the situation is efficient or not. If it is not efficient, why not? What actions would make it efficient?

a. Electricity is included in the rent at your dorm. Some residents in your dorm leave lights, computers, and appliances on when they are not in their rooms.

b. Although they cost the same amount to prepare, the cafeteria in your dorm consistently provides too many dishes that diners don't like, such as tofu casserole, and too few dishes that diners do like, such as roast turkey with dressing.

c. The enrollment for a particular course exceeds the spaces available. Some students who need to take this course to complete their major are unable to get a space even though others who are taking it as an elective do get a space.

10. Discuss the efficiency and equity implications of each of the following. How would you go about balancing the concerns of equity and efficiency in these areas?

a. The government pays the full tuition for every college student to study whatever subject he or she wishes.

b. When people lose their jobs, the government provides unemployment benefits until they find new ones.

11. Governments often adopt certain policies to promote desired behavior among their citizens. For each of the following policies, determine what the incentive is and what behavior the government wishes to promote. In each case, why do you think that the government might wish to change people's behavior, rather than allow their actions to be solely determined by individual choice?

a. A tax of $5 per pack is imposed on cigarettes.

b. The government pays parents $100 when their child is vaccinated for measles.

c. The government pays college students to tutor children from low-income families.

d. The government imposes a tax on the amount of air pollution that a company discharges.

12. In each of the following situations, explain how government intervention could improve society's welfare by changing people's incentives. In what sense is the market going wrong?

a. Pollution from auto emissions has reached unhealthy levels.

b. Everyone in Woodville would be better off if streetlights were installed in the town. But no individual resident is willing to pay for installation of a streetlight in front of his or her house because it is impossible to recoup the cost by charging other residents for the benefit they receive from it.

13. Tim Geithner, a former U.S. Treasury Secretary, has said, "The recession that began in late 2007 was extraordinarily severe. But the actions we took at its height to stimulate the economy helped arrest the free fall, preventing an even deeper collapse and putting the economy on the road to recovery." Which two of the three principles of economy-wide interaction are at work in this statement?

14. A sharp downturn in the U.S. housing market in August 2007 reduced the income of many who worked in the home construction industry. A *Wall Street Journal* news article reported that Walmart's wire-transfer business was likely to suffer because many construction workers are Hispanics who regularly send part of their wages back to relatives in their home countries via Walmart. With this information, use one of the principles of economy-wide interaction to trace a chain of links that explains how reduced spending for U.S. home purchases is likely to affect the performance of the Mexican economy.

15. In August 2017, Hurricane Harvey caused massive destruction to Texas, Louisiana, and many Caribbean Islands. Catastrophic flooding occurred, with hundreds of people requiring rescue, 68 killed, and estimated damage of $125 billion. Even those who weren't directly affected by the destruction were hurt because businesses failed or contracted and jobs dried up. Using one of the principles of economy-wide interaction, explain how government intervention can help in this situation.

16. During the Great Depression, food was left to rot in the fields or fields that had once been actively cultivated were left fallow. Use one of the principles of economy-wide interaction to explain why.

2 | Economic Models: Trade-offs and Trade

FROM KITTY HAWK TO DREAMLINER

BOEING'S 787 DREAMLINER was the result of an aerodynamic revolution—a super-efficient airplane designed to cut airline operating costs and the first to use superlight composite materials.

To ensure that the Dreamliner was sufficiently lightweight and aerodynamic, it underwent over 15,000 hours of wind tunnel tests, resulting in subtle design changes that improved its performance,

The Wright brothers' model made modern airplanes, including the Dreamliner, possible.

making it more fuel efficient and less pollutant emitting than existing passenger jets. In fact, some budget airlines such as Norwegian Air (Europe's third-largest budget airline) have been offering transatlantic flights at half the price of their rivals, expecting that the super-fuel-efficient Dreamliner will shrink fuel costs enough to make their discount strategy profitable.

The first flight of the Dreamliner was a spectacular advance from the 1903 maiden voyage of the Wright Flyer, the first successful powered airplane, in Kitty Hawk, North Carolina. Yet the Boeing engineers—and all aeronautical engineers—owe an enormous debt to the Wright Flyer's inventors, Wilbur and Orville Wright.

What made the Wrights truly visionary was their invention of the wind tunnel, an apparatus that let them experiment with many different designs for wings and control surfaces. Doing experiments with a miniature airplane, inside a wind tunnel the size of a shipping crate, gave the Wright brothers the knowledge that would make heavier-than-air flight possible.

Neither a miniature airplane inside a packing crate nor a miniature model of the Dreamliner inside Boeing's state-of-the-art Transonic Wind Tunnel is the same thing as an actual aircraft in flight. But it is a very useful *model* of a flying plane—a simplified representation of the real thing that can be used to answer crucial questions, such as how much lift a given wing shape will generate at a given airspeed.

Needless to say, testing an airplane design in a wind tunnel is cheaper and safer than building a full-scale version and hoping it will fly. More generally, models play a crucial role in almost all scientific research—economics very much included.

In fact, you could say that economic theory consists mainly of a collection of models, a series of simplified representations of economic reality that allow us to understand a variety of economic issues.

In this chapter, we'll look at two economic models that are crucially important in their own right and illustrate why such models are so useful. We'll conclude with a look at how economists actually use models in their work. ●

WHAT YOU WILL LEARN

- What are economic **models** and why are they so important to economists?
- How do three simple models—the **production possibility frontier**, **comparative advantage**, and the **circular-flow diagram**—help us understand how modern economies work?
- Why is an understanding of the difference between **positive economics** and **normative economics** important for the real-world application of economic principles?
- Why do economists sometimes disagree?

A **model** is a simplified representation of a real situation that is used to better understand real-life situations.

The **other things equal assumption** means that all other relevant factors remain unchanged.

‖ Models in Economics: Some Important Examples

A **model** is any simplified representation of reality that is used to better understand real-life situations. But how do we create a simplified representation of an economic situation?

One possibility—an economist's equivalent of a wind tunnel—is to find or create a real but simplified economy. Take, for example, an economist who wants to know how an increase in the government-mandated minimum wage would affect the U.S. economy. It would be impossible to do an experiment that involved raising the minimum wage across the country and seeing what happens. Instead, the economist will observe the effects of a smaller economy that is raising its minimum wage (like the city of Seattle did in 2015) and then extrapolate those results to the larger U.S. economy.

Another possibility is to simulate the workings of the economy on a computer. For example, when changes in tax law are proposed, government officials use *tax models*—large mathematical computer programs—to assess how the proposed changes would affect different types of people.

Models are important because their simplicity allows economists to focus on the effects of only one change at a time. That is, they allow us to hold everything else constant and study how one change affects the overall economic outcome. Thus an important assumption when building economic models is the **other things equal assumption,** which means that all other relevant factors remain unchanged.

But you can't always find or create a small-scale version of the whole economy, and a computer program is only as good as the data it uses. For many purposes, the most effective form of economic modeling is the construction of "thought experiments": simplified, hypothetical versions of real-life situations.

We use the example of how customers checking out at a supermarket rearrange themselves when a new cash register opens to illustrate the concept of equilibrium in Chapter 1. Although we didn't say it, this is an example of a simple model—an imaginary supermarket, in which many details are ignored. (What were customers buying? Never mind.) This simple model can be used to answer a "what if" question: for example, what if another cash register were to open?

As the checkout story shows, it is possible to describe and analyze a useful economic model in plain English. However, because much of economics involves changes in quantities—in the price of a product, the number of units produced, or the number of workers employed in its production—economists often find that using some mathematics helps clarify an issue. In particular, a numerical example, a simple equation, or—especially—a graph can be key to understanding an economic concept.

Whatever form it takes, a good economic model can be a tremendous aid to understanding. We'll now look at three simple but important economic models and what they tell us:

- The *production possibility frontier,* a model that helps economists think about the trade-offs every economy faces.

- *Comparative advantage,* a model that clarifies the principle of gains from trade between individuals and between countries.

- The *circular-flow diagram,* a schematic representation that helps us understand how flows of money, goods, and services are channeled through the economy.

In discussing these models, we make considerable use of graphs to represent mathematical relationships. If you are already familiar with how graphs are used, you can skip the appendix to this chapter, which provides a brief introduction to the use of graphs in economics. If not, this would be a good time to turn to it.

Trade-offs: The Production Possibility Frontier

The first principle of economics we introduced in Chapter 1 is that resources are scarce and, as a result, any economy faces trade-offs—whether it's an isolated group of a few dozen hunter-gatherers or the nearly 7.5 billion people making up the twenty-first-century global economy. No matter how lightweight the Boeing Dreamliner is, no matter how efficient Boeing's assembly line, producing Dreamliners means using resources that therefore can't be used to produce something else.

To think about the trade-offs that face any economy, economists often use the model known as the **production possibility frontier.** The idea behind this model is to improve our understanding of trade-offs by considering a simplified economy that produces only two goods. This simplification enables us to show the trade-off graphically.

Suppose, for a moment, that the United States was a one-company economy, with Boeing its sole employer and aircraft its only product. But there would still be a choice of what kinds of aircraft to produce—say, Dreamliners versus small commuter jets. Figure 2-1 shows a hypothetical production possibility frontier representing the trade-off this one-company economy would face. The frontier—the line in the diagram—shows the maximum quantity of small jets that Boeing can produce per year *given* the quantity of Dreamliners it produces per year, and vice versa. That is, it answers questions of the form, "What is the maximum quantity of small jets that Boeing can produce in a year if it also produces 9 (or 15, or 30) Dreamliners that year?"

There is a crucial distinction between points *inside* or *on* the production possibility frontier (the shaded area) and *outside* the frontier. If a production point lies inside or on the frontier—like point *C*, at which Boeing produces 20 small jets and 9 Dreamliners in a year—it is feasible. After all, the frontier tells us that if Boeing produces 20 small jets, it could also produce a maximum of 15 Dreamliners that year, so it could certainly make 9 Dreamliners.

However, a production point that lies outside the frontier—such as the hypothetical production point *D*, where Boeing produces 40 small jets and 30 Dreamliners—isn't feasible. Boeing can produce 40 small jets and no Dreamliners, *or* it can produce 30 Dreamliners and no small jets, but it can't do both.

In Figure 2-1 the production possibility frontier intersects the horizontal axis at 40 small jets. This means that if Boeing dedicated all its production capacity

The **production possibility frontier** illustrates the trade-offs facing an economy that produces only two goods. It shows the maximum quantity of one good that can be produced for any given quantity produced of the other.

FIGURE 2-1 The Production Possibility Frontier

The production possibility frontier illustrates the trade-offs Boeing faces in producing Dreamliners and small jets. It shows the maximum quantity of one good that can be produced given the quantity of the other good produced. Here, the maximum quantity of Dreamliners manufactured per year depends on the quantity of small jets manufactured that year, and vice versa. Boeing's feasible production is shown by the area *inside* or *on* the curve. Production at point *C* is feasible but not efficient. Points *A* and *B* are feasible and efficient in production, but point *D* is not feasible.

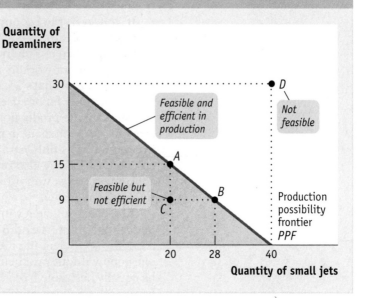

to making small jets, it could produce 40 small jets per year but could produce no Dreamliners. The production possibility frontier intersects the vertical axis at 30 Dreamliners. This means that if Boeing dedicated all its production capacity to making Dreamliners, it could produce 30 Dreamliners per year but no small jets.

The figure also shows less extreme trade-offs. For example, if Boeing's managers decide to make 20 small jets this year, they can produce at most 15 Dreamliners; this production choice is illustrated by point *A*. And if Boeing's managers decide to produce 28 small jets, they can make at most 9 Dreamliners, as shown by point *B*.

Thinking in terms of a production possibility frontier simplifies the complexities of reality. The real-world U.S. economy produces millions of different goods. Even Boeing can produce more than two different types of planes. Yet it's important to realize that even in its simplicity, this stripped-down model gives us important insights about the real world.

By simplifying reality, the production possibility frontier helps us understand some aspects of the real economy better than we could without the model: efficiency, opportunity cost, and economic growth.

Efficiency   First of all, the production possibility frontier is a good way to illustrate the general economic concept of *efficiency*. Recall from Chapter 1 that an economy is efficient if there are no missed opportunities—there is no way to make some people better off without making other people worse off.

One key element of efficiency is that there are no missed opportunities in production—there is no way to produce more of one good without producing less of other goods. As long as Boeing operates on its production possibility frontier, its production is efficient. At point *A*, 15 Dreamliners are the maximum quantity feasible given that Boeing has also committed to producing 20 small jets; at point *B*, 9 Dreamliners are the maximum number that can be made given the choice to produce 28 small jets; and so on.

But suppose for some reason that Boeing was operating at point *C*, making 20 small jets and 9 Dreamliners. In this case, it would not be operating efficiently and would therefore be *inefficient*: it could be producing more of both planes.

Although we have used an example of the production choices of a one-firm, two-good economy to illustrate efficiency and inefficiency, these concepts also carry over to the real economy, which contains many firms and produces many goods. If the economy as a whole could not produce more of any one good without producing less of something else—that is, if it is on its production possibility frontier—then we say that the economy is *efficient in production*.

If, however, the economy could produce more of some things without producing less of others—which typically means that it could produce more of everything—then it is inefficient in production. For example, an economy in which large numbers of workers are involuntarily unemployed is clearly inefficient in production. And that's a bad thing because these workers could be employed in the production of more useful goods and services.

Although the production possibility frontier helps clarify what it means for an economy to be efficient in production, it's important to understand that efficiency in production is only *part* of what's required for the economy as a whole to be efficient. Efficiency also requires that the economy allocate its resources so that consumers are as well off as possible. If an economy does this, we say that it is *efficient in allocation*.

To see why efficiency in allocation is as important as efficiency in production, notice that points *A* and *B* in Figure 2-1 both represent situations in which the economy is efficient in production, because in each case it can't produce more of one good without producing less of the other. But these two situations may not be equally desirable from society's point of view. Suppose that society prefers to have more small jets and fewer Dreamliners than at point *A*; say, it prefers to have

28 small jets and 9 Dreamliners, corresponding to point *B*. In this case, point *A* is inefficient in allocation from the point of view of the economy as a whole because it would rather have Boeing produce at point *B* instead of point *A*.

This example shows that efficiency for the economy as a whole requires *both* efficiency in production and efficiency in allocation: to be efficient, an economy must produce as much of each good as it can given the production of other goods, produce the mix of goods that people want to consume, and deliver those goods to the right people. An economy that gives small jets to international airlines and Dreamliners to commuter airlines serving small rural airports is inefficient, too.

In the real world, command economies, such as the former Soviet Union, are notorious for inefficiency in allocation. For example, consumers would often find stores well stocked with items few people wanted but lacking basics such as soap and toilet paper.

Opportunity Cost The production possibility frontier is also useful as a reminder of the fundamental point that the true cost of any good isn't the money it costs to buy, but what must be given up to get that good—the *opportunity cost*. If, for example, Boeing decides to change its production from point *A* to point *B*, it will produce 8 more small jets but 6 fewer Dreamliners. So the opportunity cost of 8 small jets is 6 Dreamliners—the 6 Dreamliners that must be forgone to produce 8 more small jets. This means that each small jet has an opportunity cost of $\frac{6}{8} = \frac{3}{4}$ of a Dreamliner.

Is the opportunity cost of an extra small jet in terms of Dreamliners always the same, no matter how many small jets and Dreamliners are currently produced? In the example illustrated by Figure 2-1, the answer is yes. If Boeing increases its production of small jets from 28 to 40, the number of Dreamliners it produces falls from 9 to zero. So Boeing's opportunity cost per additional small jet is $\frac{9}{12} = \frac{3}{4}$ of a Dreamliner, the same as it was when Boeing went from 20 small jets produced to 28 produced.

However, the fact that in this example the opportunity cost of a small jet in terms of a Dreamliner is always the same is a result of an assumption we've made, an assumption that's reflected in how Figure 2-1 is drawn. Specifically, whenever we assume that the opportunity cost of an additional unit of a good doesn't change regardless of the output mix, the production possibility frontier is a straight line.

Moreover, as you might have already guessed, the slope of a straight-line production possibility frontier is equal to the opportunity cost—specifically, the opportunity cost for the good measured on the horizontal axis in terms of the good measured on the vertical axis. In Figure 2-1, the production possibility frontier has a *constant slope* of $-\frac{3}{4}$, implying that Boeing faces a *constant opportunity cost* for 1 small jet equal to $\frac{3}{4}$ of a Dreamliner. (A review of how to calculate the slope of a straight line is found in this chapter's appendix.) This is the simplest case, but the production possibility frontier model can also be used to examine situations in which opportunity costs change as the mix of output changes.

Figure 2-2 illustrates a different assumption, a case in which Boeing faces *increasing opportunity cost*. Here, the more small jets it produces, the more costly it is to produce yet another small jet in terms of forgone production of a Dreamliner. And the same holds true in reverse: the more Dreamliners Boeing produces, the more costly it is to produce yet another Dreamliner in terms of forgone production of small jets. For example, to go from producing zero small jets to producing 20, Boeing has to forgo producing 5 Dreamliners. That is, the opportunity cost of those 20 small jets is 5 Dreamliners. But to increase its production of small jets to 40—that is, to produce an additional 20 small jets—it must forgo producing 25 more Dreamliners, a much higher opportunity cost. As you can see in Figure 2-2, when opportunity costs are increasing rather than constant, the production possibility frontier is a bowed-out curve rather than a straight line.

FIGURE 2-2 Increasing Opportunity Cost

The bowed-out shape of the production possibility frontier reflects increasing opportunity cost. In this example, to produce the first 20 small jets, Boeing must forgo producing 5 Dreamliners. But to produce an additional 20 small jets, Boeing must forgo manufacturing 25 more Dreamliners.

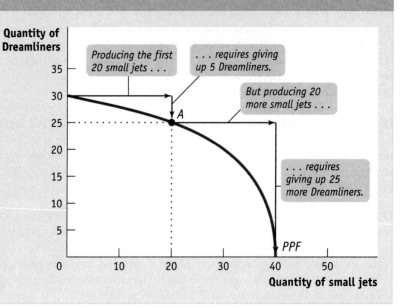

Although it's often useful to work with the simple assumption that the production possibility frontier is a straight line, economists believe that in reality opportunity costs are typically increasing. When only a small amount of a good is produced, the opportunity cost of producing that good is relatively low because the economy needs to use only those resources that are especially well suited for its production.

For example, if an economy grows only a small amount of corn, that corn can be grown in places where the soil and climate are perfect for corn-growing but less suitable for growing anything else, like wheat. So growing that corn involves giving up only a small amount of potential wheat output. Once the economy grows a lot of corn, however, land that is well suited for wheat but isn't so great for corn must be used to produce corn anyway. As a result, the additional corn production involves sacrificing considerably more wheat production. In other words, as more of a good is produced, its opportunity cost typically rises because well-suited inputs are used up and less adaptable inputs must be used instead.

Economic Growth Finally, the production possibility frontier helps us understand what it means to talk about *economic growth*. In Chapter 1, we defined the concept of economic growth as *the growing ability of the economy to produce goods and services*. As we saw, economic growth is one of the fundamental features of the real economy. But are we really justified in saying that the economy has grown over time? After all, although the U.S. economy produces more of many things than it did a century ago, it produces less of other things—for example, horse-drawn carriages. Production of many goods, in other words, is actually down. So how can we say for sure that the economy as a whole has grown?

The answer is illustrated in Figure 2-3, where we have drawn two hypothetical production possibility frontiers for the economy. In them we have assumed once again that everyone in the economy works for Boeing and, consequently, the economy produces only two goods, Dreamliners and small jets. Notice how the two curves are nested, with the one labeled "Original *PPF*" lying completely inside the one labeled "New *PPF*." Now we can see graphically what we mean by economic growth of the economy: economic growth means an *expansion of the economy's production possibilities;* that is, the economy *can* produce more of everything.

FIGURE 2-3 Economic Growth

Economic growth results in an *outward shift* of the production possibility frontier because production possibilities are expanded. The economy can now produce more of everything. For example, if production is initially at point *A* (25 Dreamliners and 20 small jets), economic growth means that the economy could move to point *E* (30 Dreamliners and 25 small jets).

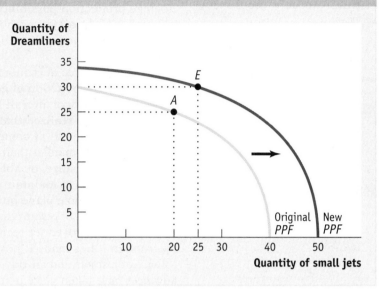

For example, if the economy initially produces at point *A* (25 Dreamliners and 20 small jets), economic growth means that the economy could move to point *E* (30 Dreamliners and 25 small jets). *E* lies outside the original frontier; so in the production possibility frontier model, growth is shown as an outward shift of the frontier.

What can lead the production possibility frontier to shift outward? There are basically two sources of economic growth. One is an increase in the economy's **factors of production,** the resources used to produce goods and services. Economists usually use the term *factor of production* to refer to a resource that is not used up in production. For example, in traditional airplane manufacture workers used riveting machines to connect metal sheets when constructing a plane's fuselage; the workers and the riveters are factors of production, but the rivets and the sheet metal are not. Once a fuselage is made, a worker and riveter can be used to make another fuselage, but the sheet metal and rivets used to make one fuselage cannot be used to make another.

Broadly speaking, the main factors of production are the resources land, labor, physical capital, and human capital. Land is a resource supplied by nature; labor is the economy's pool of workers; physical capital refers to created resources such as machines and buildings; and human capital refers to the educational achievements and skills of the labor force, which enhance its productivity. Of course, each of these is actually a broad category rather than a single factor: land in North Dakota is very different from land in Florida.

To see how adding to an economy's factors of production leads to economic growth, suppose that Boeing builds another construction hangar that allows it to increase the number of planes—small jets or Dreamliners or both—it can produce in a year. The new construction hangar is a factor of production, a resource Boeing can use to increase its yearly output. We can't say how many more planes of each type Boeing will produce; that's a management decision

Factors of production are resources used to produce goods and services.

The four factors of production: land, labor, physical capital, and human capital.

Technology is the technical means for producing goods and services.

that will depend on, among other things, customer demand. But we can say that Boeing's production possibility frontier has shifted outward because it can now produce more small jets without reducing the number of Dreamliners it makes, or it can make more Dreamliners without reducing the number of small jets produced.

The other source of economic growth is progress in **technology,** the technical means for the production of goods and services. Composite materials had been used in some parts of aircraft before the Boeing Dreamliner was developed. But Boeing engineers realized that there were large additional advantages to building a whole plane out of composites. The plane would be lighter, stronger, and have better aerodynamics than a plane built in the traditional way. It would therefore have longer range, be able to carry more people, and use less fuel, in addition to being able to maintain higher cabin pressure. So in a real sense Boeing's innovation—a whole plane built out of composites—was a way to do more with any given amount of resources, pushing out the production possibility frontier.

Because improved jet technology has pushed out the production possibility frontier, it has made it possible for the economy to produce more of everything, not just jets and air travel. Over the past 30 years, the biggest technological advances have taken place in information technology, not in construction or food services. Yet many Americans have chosen to buy bigger houses and eat out more than they used to because the economy's growth has made it possible to do so.

The production possibility frontier is a very simplified model of an economy. Yet it teaches us important lessons about real-life economies. It gives us our first clear sense of what constitutes economic efficiency, it illustrates the concept of opportunity cost, and it makes clear what economic growth is all about.

Comparative Advantage and Gains from Trade

Another of the twelve principles of economics described in Chapter 1 is the principle of *gains from trade*—the mutual gains that individuals can achieve by specializing in doing different things and trading with one another. Our second illustration of an economic model is a particularly useful model of gains from trade—trade based on *comparative advantage*.

One of the most important insights in all of economics is that there are gains from trade: it makes sense to produce the things you're especially good at producing and to buy from other people the things you aren't as good at producing. This would be true even if you could produce everything for yourself: even if a brilliant brain surgeon *could* repair her own dripping faucet, it's probably a better idea for her to call in a professional plumber.

How can we model the gains from trade? Let's stay with our aircraft example and once again imagine that the United States is a one-company economy where everyone works for Boeing, producing airplanes. Let's now assume, however, that the United States has the ability to trade with Brazil—another one-company economy where everyone works for the Brazilian aircraft company Embraer, which is, in the real world, a successful producer of small commuter jets. (If you fly from one major U.S. city to another, your plane is likely to be a Boeing, but if you fly into a small city, the odds are good that your plane will be an Embraer.)

In our example, the only two goods produced are large jets and small jets. Both countries could produce both kinds of jets. But as we'll see in a moment, they can gain by producing different things and trading with each other. For the purposes of this example, let's return to the simpler case of straight-line production possibility frontiers. America's production possibilities are represented by the production possibility frontier in panel (a) of Figure 2-4, which is similar to the production possibility frontier in Figure 2-1. According to this diagram, the United States can produce 40 small jets if it makes no large jets and can manufacture 30 large jets if it produces no small jets. Recall that this means that the slope of the U.S.

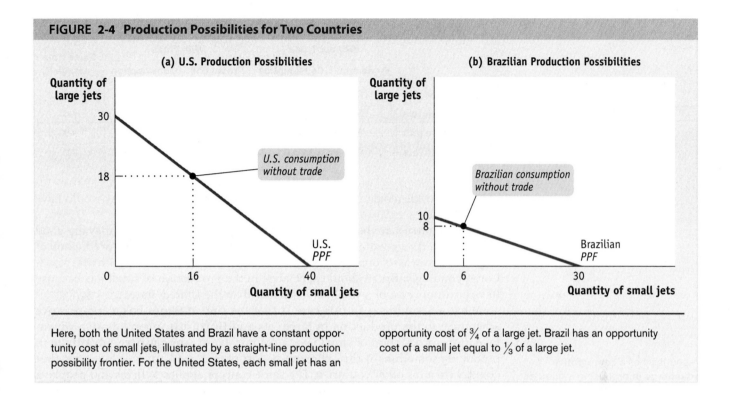

FIGURE 2-4 Production Possibilities for Two Countries

(a) U.S. Production Possibilities

Quantity of
large jets

30

18 · · · · · · · · · · · ·

*U.S. consumption
without trade*

U.S.
PPF

0   16   40
Quantity of small jets

(b) Brazilian Production Possibilities

Quantity of
large jets

*Brazilian consumption
without trade*

10
8 · · ·

Brazilian
PPF

0   6   30
Quantity of small jets

Here, both the United States and Brazil have a constant opportunity cost of small jets, illustrated by a straight-line production
possibility frontier. For the United States, each small jet has an

opportunity cost of ¾ of a large jet. Brazil has an opportunity
cost of a small jet equal to ⅓ of a large jet.

production possibility frontier is –¾: its opportunity cost of 1 small jet is ¾ of a
large jet.

Panel (b) of Figure 2-4 shows Brazil's production possibilities. Like the United
States, Brazil's production possibility frontier is a straight line, implying a constant
opportunity cost of a small jet in terms of large jets. Brazil's production possibility
frontier has a constant slope of – ⅓. Brazil can't produce as much of anything as the
United States can: at most it can produce 30 small jets or 10 large jets. But it is relatively better at manufacturing small jets than the United States; whereas the United
States sacrifices ¾ of a large jet per small jet produced, for Brazil the opportunity
cost of a small jet is only ⅓ of a large jet. Table 2-1 summarizes the two
countries' opportunity costs of small jets and large jets.

Now, the United States and Brazil could each choose to make their
own large and small jets, not trading any of them and consuming only
what each produced within its own country. (An airplane is "consumed"
when it is owned by a domestic resident.) Let's suppose that the two
countries start out this way and make the consumption choices shown in
Figure 2-4: in the absence of trade, the United States produces and consumes 16 small jets and 18 large jets per year, while Brazil produces and
consumes 6 small jets and 8 large jets per year.

But is this the best the two countries can do? No, it isn't. Given that the two
producers—and therefore the two countries—have different opportunity costs, the
United States and Brazil can strike a deal that makes both of them better off.

Table 2-2 shows how such a deal works: the United States specializes in the
production of large jets, manufacturing 30 per year, and sells 10 to Brazil. Meanwhile, Brazil specializes in the production of small jets, producing 30 per year,
and sells 20 to the United States. The result is shown in Figure 2-5. The United
States now consumes more of both small jets and large jets than before: instead
of 16 small jets and 18 large jets, it now consumes 20 small jets and 20 large jets.
Brazil also consumes more, going from 6 small jets and 8 large jets to 10 small jets
and 10 large jets. As Table 2-2 also shows, both the United States and Brazil reap

**TABLE 2-1 U.S. and Brazilian
Opportunity Costs of Small Jets and
Large Jets**

	U.S. Opportunity Cost		Brazilian Opportunity Cost
1 small jet	¾ large jet	>	⅓ large jet
1 large jet	4/3 small jets	<	3 small jets

TABLE 2-2 How the United States and Brazil Gain from Trade

		Without Trade		With Trade		Gains from Trade
		Production	Consumption	Production	Consumption	
United States	Large jets	18	18	30	20	+2
	Small jets	16	16	0	20	+4
Brazil	Large jets	8	8	0	10	+2
	Small jets	6	6	30	10	+4

gains from trade, consuming more of both types of planes than they would have without trade.

Both countries are better off when they each specialize in what they are good at and trade. It's a good idea for the United States to specialize in the production of large jets because its opportunity cost of a large jet is smaller than Brazil's: $\frac{4}{3} < 3$. Correspondingly, Brazil should specialize in the production of small jets because its opportunity cost of a small jet is smaller than the United States': $\frac{1}{3} < \frac{3}{4}$.

What we would say in this case is that the United States has a comparative advantage in the production of large jets and Brazil has a comparative advantage in the production of small jets. A country has a **comparative advantage** in producing something if the opportunity cost of that production is lower for that country than for other countries. The same concept applies to firms and people: a firm or an individual has a comparative advantage in producing something if its, his, or her opportunity cost of production is lower than for others.

One point of clarification before we proceed further. You may have wondered why the United States traded 10 large jets to Brazil in return for 20 small jets. Why not some other deal, like trading 10 large jets for 12 small jets? The answer to that question has two parts. First, there may indeed be other trades that the United States and Brazil might agree to. Second, there are some deals that we can safely rule out—one like 10 large jets for 10 small jets.

A country has a **comparative advantage** in producing a good or service if its opportunity cost of producing the good or service is lower than other countries' cost. Likewise, an individual has a comparative advantage in producing a good or service if his or her opportunity cost of producing the good or service is lower than it is for other people.

FIGURE 2-5 Comparative Advantage and Gains from Trade

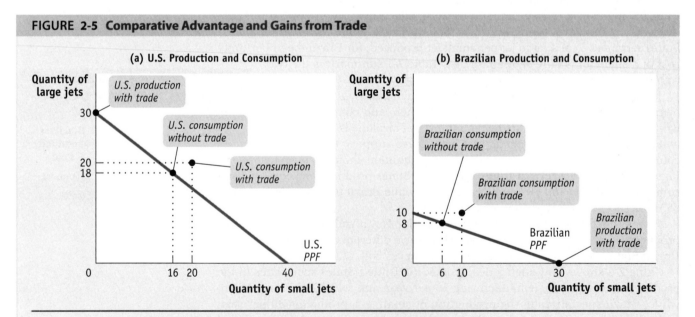

By specializing and trading, the United States and Brazil can produce and consume more of both large jets and small jets. The United States specializes in manufacturing large jets, its comparative advantage, and Brazil—which has an *absolute* disadvantage in both goods but a *comparative* advantage in small jets—specializes in manufacturing small jets. With trade, both countries can consume more of both goods than either could without trade.

To understand why, reexamine Table 2-1 and consider the United States first. Without trading with Brazil, the U.S. opportunity cost of a small jet is $\frac{3}{4}$ of a large jet. So it's clear that the United States will not accept any trade that requires it to give up more than $\frac{3}{4}$ of a large jet for a small jet. Trading 10 large jets in return for 12 small jets would require the United States to pay an opportunity cost of $\frac{10}{12} = \frac{5}{6}$ of a large jet for a small jet. Because $\frac{5}{6}$ is greater than $\frac{3}{4}$, this is a deal that the United States would reject. Similarly, Brazil won't accept a trade that gives it less than $\frac{1}{3}$ of a large jet for a small jet.

The point to remember is that the United States and Brazil will be willing to trade only if the "price" of the good each country obtains in the trade is less than its own opportunity cost of producing the good domestically. Moreover, this is a general statement that is true whenever two parties—countries, firms, or individuals—trade voluntarily.

While our story clearly simplifies reality, it teaches us some very important lessons that apply to the real economy, too.

First, the model provides a clear illustration of the gains from trade: through specialization and trade, both countries produce more and consume more than if they were self-sufficient.

Second, the model demonstrates a very important point that is often overlooked in real-world arguments: each country has a comparative advantage in producing something. This applies to firms and people as well: *everyone has a comparative advantage in something, and everyone has a comparative disadvantage in something.*

Crucially, in our example it doesn't matter if, as is probably the case in real life, U.S. workers are just as good as or even better than Brazilian workers at producing small jets. Suppose that the United States is actually better than Brazil at all kinds of aircraft production. In that case, we would say that the United States has an **absolute advantage** in both large-jet and small-jet production: in an hour, an American worker can produce more of either a large jet or a small jet than a Brazilian worker. You might be tempted to think that in that case the United States has nothing to gain from trading with the less productive Brazil.

But we've just seen that the United States can indeed benefit from trading with Brazil because *comparative, not absolute, advantage is the basis for mutual gain.* It doesn't matter whether it takes Brazil more resources than the United States to make a small jet; what matters for trade is that for Brazil the opportunity cost of a small jet is lower than the U.S. opportunity cost. So Brazil, despite its absolute disadvantage, even in small jets, has a comparative advantage in the manufacture of small jets. Meanwhile the United States, which can use its resources most productively by manufacturing large jets, has a comparative *dis*advantage in manufacturing small jets.

A country has an **absolute advantage** in producing a good or service if the country can produce more output per worker than other countries. Likewise, an individual has an absolute advantage in producing a good or service if he or she is better at producing it than other people. Having an absolute advantage is not the same thing as having a comparative advantage.

Comparative Advantage and International Trade, in Reality

Look at the label on a manufactured good sold in the United States, and there's a good chance you will find that it was produced in some other country—in China, or Japan, or even in Canada. On the other side, many U.S. industries sell a large fraction of their output overseas. This is particularly true of agriculture, high technology, and entertainment.

Should all this international exchange of goods and services be celebrated, or is it cause for concern? Politicians and the public often question the desirability of international trade, arguing that the nation should produce goods for itself rather than buying them from foreigners. Industries around the world demand protection from foreign competition: Japanese farmers want to keep out American rice,

PITFALLS

MISUNDERSTANDING COMPARATIVE ADVANTAGE

Students do it, pundits do it, and politicians do it all the time: they confuse *comparative advantage* with *absolute advantage*. For example, back in the 1980s, when the U.S. economy seemed to be lagging behind that of Japan, commentators could be heard warning that if we didn't improve our productivity, we would soon have no comparative advantage in anything.

What those commentators meant was that we would have no *absolute* advantage in anything—that there might come a time when the

Japanese were better at everything than we were. (It didn't turn out that way, but that's another story.) And they had the idea that in that case we would no longer be able to benefit from trade with Japan.

But just as Brazil, in our example, was able to benefit from trade with the United States (and vice versa) despite the fact that the United States was better at manufacturing both large and small jets, in real life nations can still gain from trade even if they are less productive in all industries than the countries they trade with.

American steelworkers want to keep out European steel. And these demands are often supported by public opinion.

Economists, however, have a very positive view of international trade. Why? Because they view it in terms of comparative advantage. As we learned from our example of U.S. large jets and Brazilian small jets, international trade benefits both countries. Each country can consume more than if it doesn't trade and remains self-sufficient. Moreover, these mutual gains don't depend on each country being better than other countries at producing one kind of good. Even if one country has, say, higher output per worker in both industries—that is, even if one country has an absolute advantage in both industries—there are still gains from trade. The following Global Comparison illustrates just this point.

🌐 GLOBAL COMPARISON | PAJAMA REPUBLICS

When a building that housed five clothing factories collapsed in Bangladesh in 2013, killing more than a thousand garment workers trapped inside, attention soon focused on the substandard working conditions in those factories, as well as the many violations of building codes and safety procedures—including those required by Bangladeshi law—that set the stage for the tragedy.

While this industrial disaster provoked a justified outcry, it also highlighted the remarkable rise of Bangladesh's clothing industry, which has become a major player in world markets—second only to China in total exports—and a desperately needed source of income and employment in a very poor country.

It's not that Bangladesh has especially high productivity in clothing manufacturing. In fact, estimates by the consulting firm McKinsey and Company suggest that it's about a quarter less productive than China. Rather, it has even lower productivity in other industries, giving it a comparative advantage in clothing manufacturing. This is typical in poor countries, which often rely heavily on clothing exports during the early phases of their economic development. An official from one such country once joked, "We are not a banana republic—we are a pajama republic."

The figure plots the per capita income of several such "pajama republics" (the total income of the country divided by the size of the population) against the share of total exports accounted for by clothing; per capita income is measured as a percentage of the U.S.

level to give you a sense of just how poor these countries are. As you can see, they are very poor indeed—and the poorer they are, the more they depend on clothing exports.

It's worth pointing out, by the way, that relying on clothing exports is not necessarily a bad thing, despite tragedies like the one in Bangladesh. Indeed, Bangladesh, although still desperately poor, is more than twice as rich as it was two decades ago, when it began its dramatic rise as a clothing exporter.

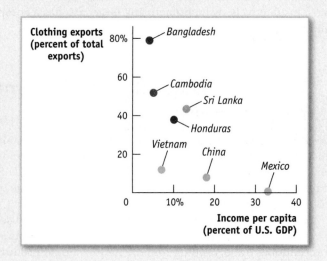

Data from: WTO.

Transactions: The Circular-Flow Diagram

The model economies that we've studied so far—each containing only one firm—are huge simplifications. We've also greatly simplified trade between the United States and Brazil, assuming that they engage only in the simplest of economic transactions, **barter,** in which one party directly trades a good or service for another good or service without using money. In a modern economy, simple barter is rare: usually people trade goods or services for money—pieces of colored paper with no inherent value—and then trade those pieces of colored paper for the goods or services they want. That is, they sell goods or services and buy other goods or services.

And they both sell and buy a lot of different things. The U.S. economy is a vastly complex entity, with more than a hundred million workers employed by millions of companies, producing millions of different goods and services. Yet you can learn some very important things about the economy by considering the simple graphic shown in Figure 2-6, the **circular-flow diagram.** This diagram represents the transactions that take place in an economy by two kinds of flows around a circle: flows of physical things such as goods, services, labor, or raw materials in one direction, and flows of money that pay for these physical things in the opposite direction. In this case the physical flows are shown in blue, the money flows in green.

The simplest circular-flow diagram illustrates an economy that contains only two kinds of inhabitants: **households** and **firms.** A household consists of either an individual or a group of people (usually, but not necessarily, a family) that share their income. A firm is an organization that produces goods and services for sale—and that employs members of households.

As you can see in Figure 2-6, there are two kinds of markets in this simple economy. On the left side, there are **markets for goods and services** in which households buy the goods and services they want from firms. This produces a flow of goods and services to households and a return flow of money to firms.

On the right side, there are **factor markets** in which firms buy the resources they need to produce goods and services. Recall from earlier that the main factors of production are land, labor, physical capital, and human capital.

Trade takes the form of **barter** when people directly exchange goods or services that they have for goods or services that they want.

The **circular-flow diagram** represents the transactions in an economy by flows around a circle.

A **household** is a person or a group of people that share their income.

A **firm** is an organization that produces goods and services for sale.

Firms sell goods and services that they produce to households in **markets for goods and services.**

Firms buy the resources they need to produce goods and services in **factor markets.**

FIGURE 2-6 The Circular-Flow Diagram

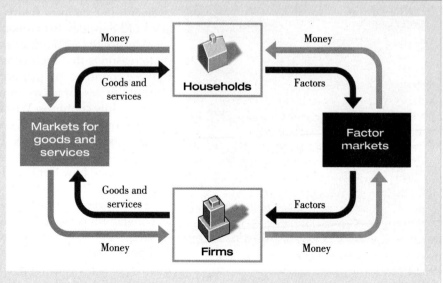

This diagram represents the flows of money and of goods and services in the economy. In the markets for goods and services, households purchase goods and services from firms, generating a flow of money to the firms and a flow of goods and services to the households. The money flows back to households as firms purchase factors of production from the households in factor markets.

An economy's **income distribution** is the way in which total income is divided among the owners of the various factors of production.

The factor market most of us know best is the labor market, in which workers sell their services. In addition, we can think of households as owning and selling the other factors of production to firms. For example, when a firm buys physical capital in the form of machines, the payment ultimately goes to the households that own the machine-making firm. In this case, the transactions occur in the *capital market,* the market in which capital is bought and sold. As we'll examine in detail later, factor markets ultimately determine an economy's **income distribution,** how the total income created in an economy is allocated between less skilled workers, highly skilled workers, and the owners of capital and land.

The circular-flow diagram ignores a number of real-world complications in the interests of simplicity. A few examples:

- In the real world, the distinction between firms and households isn't always that clear-cut. Consider a small, family-run business—a farm, a shop, a small hotel. Is this a firm or a household? A more complete picture would include a separate box for family businesses.

- Many of the sales that firms make are not to households but to other firms; for example, steel companies sell mainly to other companies such as auto manufacturers, not to households. A more complete picture would include these flows of goods, services, and money within the business sector.

- The figure doesn't show the government, which in the real world diverts quite a lot of money out of the circular flow in the form of taxes but also injects a lot of money back into the flow in the form of spending.

Figure 2-6, in other words, is by no means a complete picture either of all the types of inhabitants of the real economy or of all the flows of money and physical items that take place among these inhabitants.

Despite its simplicity, however, the circular-flow diagram is a very useful aid to thinking about the economy.

ECONOMICS >> *in Action*
Rich Nation, Poor Nation

Try taking off your clothes—at a suitable time and in a suitable place, of course— and taking a look at the labels inside that say where they were made. It's a very good bet that much, if not most, of your clothes were manufactured overseas, in a country that is much poorer than the United States— say, in El Salvador, Sri Lanka, or Bangladesh.

Why are these countries so much poorer than we are? The immediate reason is that their economies are much less *productive*—firms in these countries are just not able to produce as much from a given quantity of resources as comparable firms in the United States or other wealthy countries. Why countries differ so much in productivity is a deep question—indeed, one of the main questions that preoccupy economists. But in any case, the difference in productivity is a fact.

But if the economies of these countries are so much less productive than ours, how is it that they make so much of our clothing? Why don't we do it for ourselves?

The answer is "comparative advantage." Just about every industry in Bangladesh is much less productive than the corresponding industry in the United States. But the productivity difference between rich and poor countries varies across goods; it is very large in the production of sophisticated goods like aircraft but not that large in the production of simpler goods like clothing. So Bangladesh's position

Although less productive than American workers, Bangladeshi workers have a comparative advantage in clothing production.

Robert Nickelsberg/Getty Images

with regard to clothing production is like Embraer's position with respect to producing small jets: it's not as good at it as Boeing, but it's the thing Embraer does comparatively well.

Although Bangladesh is at an absolute disadvantage compared with the United States in almost everything, it has a comparative advantage in clothing production. This means that both the United States and Bangladesh are able to consume more because they specialize in producing different things, with Bangladesh supplying our clothes and the United States supplying Bangladesh with more sophisticated goods.

>> Check Your Understanding 2-1
Solutions appear at back of book.

1. True or false? Explain your answer.
   a. An increase in the amount of resources available to Boeing for use in producing Dreamliners and small jets does not change its production possibility frontier.
   b. A technological change that allows Boeing to build more small jets for any amount of Dreamliners built results in a change in its production possibility frontier.
   c. The production possibility frontier is useful because it illustrates how much of one good an economy must give up to get more of another good, regardless of whether resources are being used efficiently.

2. In Italy, an automobile can be produced by 8 workers in one day and a washing machine by 3 workers in one day. In the United States, an automobile can be produced by 6 workers in one day and a washing machine by 2 workers in one day.
   a. Which country has an absolute advantage in the production of automobiles? In washing machines?
   b. Which country has a comparative advantage in the production of washing machines? In automobiles?
   c. What pattern of specialization results in the greatest gains from trade between the two countries?

3. Using the numbers from Table 2-1, explain why the United States and Brazil are willing to engage in a trade of 10 large jets for 15 small jets.

4. Use the circular-flow diagram to explain how an increase in the amount of money spent by households results in an increase in the number of jobs in the economy. Describe in words what the circular-flow diagram predicts.

> ## >> Quick Review
> • Most economic **models** are "thought experiments" or simplified representations of reality that rely on the **other things equal assumption.**
>
> • The **production possibility frontier** model illustrates the concepts of efficiency, opportunity cost, and economic growth.
>
> • Every person and every country has a **comparative advantage** in something, giving rise to gains from trade. Comparative advantage is often confused with **absolute advantage.**
>
> • In the simplest economies people **barter** rather than transact with money. The **circular-flow diagram** illustrates transactions within the economy as flows of goods and services, **factors of production,** and money between **households** and **firms.** These transactions occur in **markets for goods and services** and **factor markets.** Ultimately, factor markets determine the economy's **income distribution.**

‖ Using Models

We have now seen how economics is mainly a matter of creating models that draw on a set of basic principles but add some more specific assumptions that allow the modeler to apply those principles to a particular situation. But what do economists actually *do* with their models?

Positive Versus Normative Economics

Imagine that you are an economic adviser to the governor of your state. What kinds of questions might the governor ask you to answer?

Well, here are three possible questions:

1. How much revenue will the tolls on the state turnpike yield next year?

2. How much would that revenue increase if the toll were raised from $1 to $1.50?

3. Should the toll be raised, bearing in mind that a toll increase will reduce traffic and air pollution near the road but will impose some financial hardship on frequent commuters?

Positive economics is the branch of economic analysis that describes the way the economy actually works.

Normative economics makes prescriptions about the way the economy should work.

A **forecast** is a simple prediction of the future.

There is a big difference between the first two questions and the third one. The first two are questions about facts. Your forecast of next year's toll collection will be proved right or wrong when the numbers actually come in. Your estimate of the impact of a change in the toll is a little harder to check—revenue depends on other factors besides the toll, and it may be hard to disentangle the causes of any change in revenue. Still, in principle there is only one right answer.

But the question of whether tolls should be raised may not have a "right" answer—two people who agree on the effects of a higher toll could still disagree about whether raising the toll is a good idea. For example, someone who lives near the turnpike but doesn't commute on it will care a lot about noise and air pollution but not so much about commuting costs. A regular commuter who doesn't live near the turnpike will have the opposite priorities.

This example highlights a key distinction between two roles of economic analysis. Analysis that tries to answer questions about the way the world works, which have definite right and wrong answers, is known as **positive economics.** In contrast, analysis that involves saying how the world *should* work is known as **normative economics.** To put it another way, positive economics is about description; normative economics is about prescription.

Positive economics occupies most of the time and effort of the economics profession. And models play a crucial role in almost all positive economics. As we mentioned earlier, the U.S. government uses a computer model to assess proposed changes in national tax policy, and many state governments have similar models to assess the effects of their own tax policy.

It's worth noting that there is a subtle but important difference between the first and second questions we imagined the governor asking. Question 1 asked for a simple prediction about next year's revenue—a **forecast.** Question 2 was a "what if" question, asking how revenue would change if the tax law were changed. Economists are often called upon to answer both types of questions, but models are especially useful for answering "what if" questions.

The answers to such questions often serve as a guide to policy, but they are still predictions, not prescriptions. That is, they tell you what will happen if a policy were changed; they don't tell you whether or not that result is good.

Suppose your economic model tells you that the governor's proposed increase in highway tolls will raise property values in communities near the road but will hurt people who must use the turnpike to get to work. Does that make this proposed toll increase a good idea or a bad one? It depends on whom you ask. As we've just seen, someone who is very concerned with the communities near the road will support the increase, but someone who is very concerned with the welfare of drivers will feel differently. That's a value judgment—it's not a question of economic analysis.

Still, economists often do engage in normative economics and give policy advice. How can they do this when there may be no "right" answer?

One answer is that economists are also citizens, and we all have our opinions. But economic analysis can often be used to show that some policies are clearly better than others, regardless of anyone's opinions.

Suppose that policies A and B achieve the same goal, but policy A makes everyone better off than policy B—or at least makes some people better off without making other people worse off. Then A is clearly more efficient than B. That's not a value judgment: we're talking about how best to achieve a goal, not about the goal itself.

For example, two different policies have been used to help low-income families obtain housing: rent control, which limits the rents landlords are allowed to charge, and rent subsidies, which provide families with additional money to pay rent. Almost all economists agree that subsidies are the more efficient policy. And so the great majority of economists, whatever their personal politics, favor subsidies over rent control.

When policies can be clearly ranked in this way, then economists generally agree. But it is no secret that economists sometimes disagree.

When and Why Economists Disagree

Economists have a reputation for arguing with each other. Where does this reputation come from, and is it justified?

One important answer is that media coverage tends to exaggerate the real differences in views among economists. If nearly all economists agree on an issue—for example, the proposition that rent controls lead to housing shortages—reporters and editors are likely to conclude that it's not a story worth covering, leaving the professional consensus unreported. But an issue on which prominent economists take opposing sides—for example, whether cutting taxes right now would help the economy—makes a news story worth reporting. So you hear much more about the areas of disagreement within economics than you do about the large areas of agreement.

It is also worth remembering that economics is, unavoidably, often tied up in politics. On a number of issues, powerful interest groups know what opinions they want to hear; they therefore have an incentive to find and promote economists who profess those opinions, giving these economists a prominence and visibility out of proportion to their support among their colleagues.

While the appearance of disagreement among economists exceeds the reality, it remains true that economists often *do* disagree about important things. For example, some well-respected economists argue vehemently that the U.S. government should replace the income tax with a *value-added tax* (a national sales tax, which is the main source of government revenue in many European countries). Other equally respected economists disagree. Why this difference of opinion?

One important source of differences lies in values: as in any diverse group of individuals, reasonable people can differ. In comparison to an income tax, a value-added tax typically falls more heavily on people of modest means. So an economist who values a society with more social and income equality for its own sake will tend to oppose a value-added tax. An economist with different values will be less likely to oppose it.

A second important source of differences arises from economic modeling. Because economists base their conclusions on models, which are simplified representations of reality, two economists can legitimately disagree about which simplifications are appropriate—and therefore arrive at different conclusions.

Suppose that the U.S. government were considering introducing a value-added tax. Economist A may rely on a model that focuses on the administrative costs of tax systems—that is, the costs of monitoring, processing papers, collecting the tax, and so on. This economist might then point to the well-known high costs of administering a value-added tax and argue against the change. But economist B may think that the right way to approach the question is to ignore the administrative costs and focus on how the proposed law would change savings behavior. This economist might point to studies suggesting that value-added taxes promote higher consumer saving, a desirable result.

Because the economists have used different models—that is, made different simplifying assumptions—they arrive at different conclusions. And so the two economists may find themselves on different sides of the issue.

ECONOMICS >> *in Action*

When Economists Agree

These three economists are on the panel (clockwise from top left): Amy Finkelstein of MIT, Hilary Hoynes of UC Berkeley, and Raj Chetty of Harvard.

"If all the economists in the world were laid end to end, they still couldn't reach a conclusion," goes an economist joke. But do economists really disagree that much? Not according to an ongoing survey. The Booth School of Business at the University of Chicago has assembled a panel of 51 economists, all with exemplary professional reputations, representing a mix of regions, schools, and political affiliations. They are regularly polled on questions of policy or political interest, often ones on which there are bitter divides among politicians or the general public.

Yet the survey shows much more agreement among economists than rumor would have it, even on supposedly controversial topics. For example, 85% of the panel agreed that trade with China makes most Americans better off and nearly the same percentage agreed that Americans who work in the production of competing goods, like clothing, are made worse off by trade with China. Roughly the same percentage (82%) disagreed with the proposition that rent control increases the supply of quality, affordable housing.

In the first case, the panel overwhelmingly agreed with a position widely considered liberal in American politics, while in the second case they agreed with one widely considered politically conservative.

Disagreements tended to involve untested economic policies. There was, for example, an almost even split over whether new Federal Reserve tactics aimed at boosting the economy would work. Ideology played a limited role in these disagreements: Economists known to be liberals did have slightly different positions, on average, from those known to be conservatives, but the differences weren't nearly as large as those among the general public.

So economists do disagree quite a lot on some issues, especially in macroeconomics. But there is a large area of common ground.

>> *Quick Review*

• **Positive economics**—the focus of most economic research—is the analysis of the way the world works, in which there are definite right and wrong answers. It often involves making **forecasts**. But in **normative economics,** which makes prescriptions about how things *ought to be*, inevitably involves value judgments.

• Economists do disagree—though not as much as legend has it—for two main reasons. One, they may disagree about which simplifications to make in a model. Two, economists may disagree—like everyone else—about values.

>> *Check Your Understanding* 2-2

Solutions appear at back of book.

1. Which of the following is a positive statement? Which is a normative statement?
   a. Society should take measures to prevent people from engaging in dangerous personal behavior.
   b. People who engage in dangerous personal behavior impose higher costs on society through higher medical costs.

2. True or false? Explain your answer.
   a. Policy choice A and policy choice B attempt to achieve the same social goal. Policy choice A, however, results in a much less efficient use of resources than policy choice B. Therefore, economists are more likely to agree on choosing policy choice B.
   b. When two economists disagree on the desirability of a policy, it's typically because one of them has made a mistake.

SOLVED PROBLEM   Heavy Metal and High Protein

If you look at one of the bottom rows of the periodic table of elements, you will find the lanthanides, also known as rare earths, fifteen metallic chemical elements, from lanthanum to lutetium. Unlike other more commonly known elements like hydrogen and gold, you have probably never heard of rare earths, even though you use them every day when you reach for a smartphone or a tablet, or watch TV. In fact, there are more than a dozen rare earth elements in an iPhone. These essential elements can also be found in hybrid cars, wind turbines, lasers, and satellites.

Despite their name, rare earth elements are not rare at all. They are embedded in the earth's crust. It just happens to be the case that China is the largest miner and exporter of rare earths, controlling nearly 95% of world production.

Meanwhile, the United States is the world's largest exporter of soybeans, a high-protein crop essential to the production of livestock feed but also used for human consumption in the form of products like soy milk, edamame, and tofu. Nearly 90% of all soybeans traded globally are grown in the United States.

Fortunately, the United States and China can trade with each other. But what if China refused to export rare earths, forcing the United States to find ways to extract these rare earths on its own? What if China stopped purchasing soybeans from other countries and reverted to self-production?

Now suppose that China and the United States can produce either soybeans or rare earths—a hypothetical example based on an actual trading pattern. Assume that the production possibilities for rare earths and soybeans are as follows:

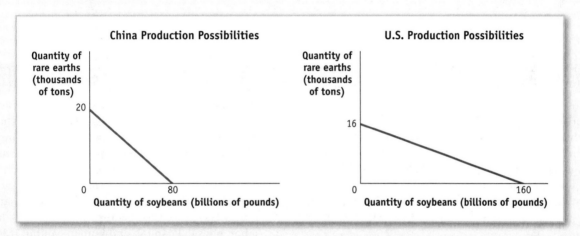

Calculate the opportunity cost of rare earths and soybeans for both countries. Does the United States have a comparative advantage in producing rare earths? Suppose China wishes to consume 64 billion pounds of soybeans and 12 thousand tons of rare earths. Show this point on a graph of the production possibilities. Is this possible without trade?

STEP | 1 Calculate the opportunity cost of rare earths and soybeans for both countries. *Review pages 28–31.*

The production possibility frontiers for both countries are straight lines, which implies a constant opportunity cost of soybeans in terms of rare earths. The slope of China's production possibility frontier is $-\frac{1}{4}$ (the slope is defined as the change in the y-variable—rare earths—divided by the change in the x-variable—soybeans—which in this case is $-\frac{20}{80} = -\frac{1}{4}$), and the slope of the production possibility frontier for the United States is $-\frac{1}{10}$. Thus, the opportunity cost for China of producing 1 thousand tons of rare earths is 4 billion pounds of soybeans, and the opportunity cost for the United States of producing 1 thousand tons of rare earths is 10 billion pounds of soybeans. Likewise, the opportunity cost for China of producing 1 billion pounds of soybeans is $\frac{1}{4}$ of a thousand tons of rare earths (250 tons), and the opportunity cost for the United States of producing 1 billion pounds of soybeans is $\frac{1}{10}$ of a thousand tons (100 tons) of rare earths.

STEP | 2 Does China have a comparative advantage at producing soybeans? *Review pages 28–31.*

A country has a comparative advantage in the production of a good if the opportunity cost of production is lower for that country than for another country. In this case, the

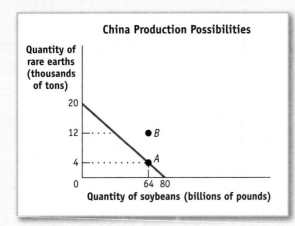

China Production Possibilities

Quantity of rare earths (thousands of tons)

Quantity of soybeans (billions of pounds)

opportunity cost of producing 1 billion pounds of soybeans is $\frac{1}{4}$ of a thousand tons of rare earths (250 tons) for China and $\frac{1}{10}$ of a thousand tons (100 tons) of rare earths for the United States. Since $\frac{1}{10}$ is less than $\frac{1}{4}$, the United States, not China, has a comparative advantage in the production of soybeans.

STEP | 3 Suppose China wishes to consume 64 billion pounds of soybeans and 12 thousand tons of rare earths. Show this point on a graph of the production possibilities. Is this possible without trade? *Review pages 28–31 and Figure 2-5.*

As shown on the graph, China's consumption of 64 billion pounds of soybeans and 12 thousand tons of rare earths, demonstrated at point B, is outside the production possibility frontier without trade. If China consumed 64 billion pounds of soybeans, without trade, it could consume only 4 thousand tons of rare earths, shown at point A. Thus, without trade, this level of consumption of both goods would be impossible.

SUMMARY

1. Almost all economics is based on **models,** "thought experiments" or simplified versions of reality, many of which use mathematical tools such as graphs. An important assumption in economic models is the **other things equal assumption,** which allows analysis of the effect of a change in one factor by holding all other relevant factors unchanged.

2. One important economic model is the **production possibility frontier.** It illustrates *opportunity cost* (showing how much less of one good can be produced if more of the other good is produced); *efficiency* (an economy is efficient in production if it produces on the production possibility frontier and efficient in allocation if it produces the mix of goods and services that people want to consume); and *economic growth* (an outward shift of the production possibility frontier). There are two basic sources of growth: an increase in **factors of production**—resources such as land, labor, capital, and human capital, inputs that are not used up in production—and improved **technology.**

3. Another important model is **comparative advantage,** which explains the source of gains from trade between individuals and countries. Everyone has a comparative advantage in something—some good or service in which that person has a lower opportunity cost than everyone else. But it is often confused with **absolute advantage,** an ability to produce a particular good or service better than anyone else. This confusion leads some to erroneously conclude that there are no gains from trade between people or countries.

4. In the simplest economies people **barter**—trade goods and services for one another—rather than trade them for money, as in a modern economy. The **circular-flow diagram** represents transactions within the economy as flows of goods, services, and money between **households** and **firms.** These transactions occur in **markets for goods and services** and **factor markets,** markets for factors of production—land, labor, physical capital, and human capital. It is useful in understanding how spending, production, employment, income, and growth are related in the economy. Ultimately, factor markets determine the economy's **income distribution,** how an economy's total income is allocated to the owners of the factors of production.

5. Economists use economic models for both **positive economics,** which describes how the economy works, and for **normative economics,** which prescribes how the economy *should* work. Positive economics often involves making **forecasts.** Economists can determine correct answers for positive questions but typically not for normative questions, which involve value judgments. The exceptions are when policies designed to achieve a certain objective can be clearly ranked in terms of efficiency.

6. There are two main reasons economists disagree. One, they may disagree about which simplifications to make in a model. Two, economists may disagree—like everyone else—about values.

KEY TERMS

Model, p. 22
Other things equal assumption, p. 22
Production possibility frontier, p. 23
Factors of production, p. 27
Technology, p. 28
Comparative advantage, p. 30

Absolute advantage, p. 31
Barter, p. 33
Circular-flow diagram, p. 33
Household, p. 33
Firm, p. 33
Markets for goods and services, p. 33

Factor markets, p. 33
Income distribution, p. 34
Positive economics, p. 36
Normative economics, p. 36
Forecast, p. 36

DISCUSSION QUESTIONS

1. Peter Pundit, an economics reporter, states that the European Union (EU) is increasing its productivity very rapidly in all industries. He claims that this productivity advance is so rapid that output from the EU in these industries will soon exceed that of the United States and, as a result, the United States will no longer benefit from trade with the EU.

    a. Do you think Peter Pundit is correct or not? If not, what do you think is the source of his mistake?

    b. If the EU and the United States continue to trade, what do you think will characterize the goods that the EU sells to the United States and the goods that the United States sells to the EU?

2. The inhabitants of the fictional economy of Atlantis use money in the form of cowry shells. Draw a circular-flow diagram showing households and firms. Firms produce potatoes and fish, and households buy potatoes and fish. Households also provide the land and labor to firms. Identify where in the flows of cowry shells or physical things (goods and services, or resources) each of the following impacts would occur. Describe how this impact spreads around the circle.

    a. A devastating hurricane floods many of the potato fields.

    b. A very productive fishing season yields a very large number of fish caught.

    c. The inhabitants of Atlantis discover Bruno Mars and spend several days a month at dancing festivals.

3. An economist might say that colleges and universities "produce" education, using faculty members and students as inputs. According to this line of reasoning, education is then "consumed" by households. Construct a circular-flow diagram to represent the sector of the economy devoted to college education: colleges and universities represent firms, and households both consume education and provide faculty and students to universities. What are the relevant markets in this diagram? What is being bought and sold in each direction? What would happen in the diagram if the government decided to subsidize 50% of all college students' tuition?

4. A representative of the American clothing industry recently made the following statement: "Workers in Asia often work in sweatshop conditions earning only pennies an hour. American workers are more productive and as a result earn higher wages. To preserve the dignity of the American workplace, the government should enact legislation banning imports of low-wage Asian clothing."

    a. Which parts of this quote are positive statements? Which parts are normative statements?

    b. Is the policy that is being advocated consistent with the preceding statements about the wages and productivities of American and Asian workers?

    c. Would such a policy make some Americans better off without making any other Americans worse off? That is, would this policy be efficient from the viewpoint of all Americans?

    d. Would low-wage Asian workers benefit from or be hurt by such a policy?

5. Evaluate the following statement: "It is easier to build an economic model that accurately reflects events that have already occurred than to build an economic model to forecast future events." Do you think this is true or not? Why? What does this imply about the difficulties of building good economic models?

6. Economists who work for the government are often called on to make policy recommendations. Why do you think it is important for the public to be able to differentiate normative statements from positive statements in these recommendations?

7. Assess the accuracy of the following statement: "If economists just had enough data, they could solve all policy questions in a way that maximizes the social good. There would be no need for divisive political debates, such as whether the government should provide free medical care for all." Frame your answer using the concepts of positive and normative economics.

PROBLEMS

1. Two important industries on the island of Bermuda are fishing and tourism. According to data from the Food and Agriculture Organization of the United Nations and the Bermuda Department of Statistics, in 2014 the 315 registered fishermen in Bermuda caught 497 metric tons of marine fish. And the 2,446 people employed by hotels produced 580,209 hotel stays (measured by the number of visitor arrivals). Suppose that this production point is efficient in production. Assume also that the opportunity cost of 1 additional metric ton of fish is 2,000 hotel stays and that this opportunity cost is constant (the opportunity cost does not change).

   a. If all 315 registered fishermen were to be employed by hotels (in addition to the 2,446 people already working in hotels), how many hotel stays could Bermuda produce?

   b. If all 2,446 hotel employees were to become fishermen (in addition to the 315 fishermen already working in the fishing industry), how many metric tons of fish could Bermuda produce?

   c. Draw a production possibility frontier for Bermuda, with fish on the horizontal axis and hotel stays on the vertical axis, and label Bermuda's actual production point for the year 2014.

2. According to data from the U.S. Department of Agriculture's National Agricultural Statistics Service, 124 million acres of land in the United States were used for wheat or corn farming in a recent year. Of those 124 million acres, farmers used 50 million acres to grow 2.158 billion bushels of wheat and 74 million acres to grow 11.807 billion bushels of corn. Suppose that U.S. wheat and corn farming is efficient in production. At that production point, the opportunity cost of producing 1 additional bushel of wheat is 1.7 fewer bushels of corn. However, because farmers have increasing opportunity costs, additional bushels of wheat have an opportunity cost greater than 1.7 bushels of corn. For each of the following production points, decide whether that production point is (i) feasible and efficient in production, (ii) feasible but not efficient in production, (iii) not feasible, or (iv) unclear as to whether or not it is feasible.

   a. Farmers use 40 million acres of land to produce 1.8 billion bushels of wheat, and they use 60 million acres of land to produce 9 billion bushels of corn. The remaining 24 million acres are left unused.

   b. From their original production point, farmers transfer 40 million acres of land from corn to wheat production. They now produce 3.158 billion bushels of wheat and 10.107 bushels of corn.

   c. Farmers reduce their production of wheat to 2 billion bushels and increase their production of corn to 12.044 billion bushels. Along the production possibility frontier, the opportunity cost of going from 11.807 billion bushels of corn to 12.044 billion bushels of corn is 0.666 bushel of wheat per bushel of corn.

3. In the ancient country of Roma, only two goods, spaghetti and meatballs, are produced. There are two tribes in Roma, the Tivoli and the Frivoli. By themselves, the Tivoli each month can produce either 30 pounds of spaghetti and no meatballs, or 50 pounds of meatballs and no spaghetti, or any combination in between. The Frivoli, by themselves, each month can produce 40 pounds of spaghetti and no meatballs, or 30 pounds of meatballs and no spaghetti, or any combination in between.

   a. Assume that all production possibility frontiers are straight lines. Draw one diagram showing the monthly production possibility frontier for the Tivoli and another showing the monthly production possibility frontier for the Frivoli. Show how you calculated them.

   b. Which tribe has the comparative advantage in spaghetti production? In meatball production?

   In A.D. 100 the Frivoli discover a new technique for making meatballs that doubles the quantity of meatballs they can produce each month.

   c. Draw the new monthly production possibility frontier for the Frivoli.

   d. After the innovation, which tribe now has an absolute advantage in producing meatballs? In producing spaghetti? Which has the comparative advantage in meatball production? In spaghetti production?

4. One July, the United States sold aircraft worth $1 billion to China and bought aircraft worth only $19,000 from China. During the same month, however, the United States bought $83 million worth of men's trousers, slacks, and jeans from China but sold only $8,000 worth of trousers, slacks, and jeans to China. Using what you have learned about how trade is determined by comparative advantage, answer the following questions.

   a. Which country has the comparative advantage in aircraft production? In production of trousers, slacks, and jeans?

   b. Can you determine which country has the absolute advantage in aircraft production? In production of trousers, slacks, and jeans?

5. You are in charge of allocating residents to your dormitory's baseball and basketball teams. You are down to the last four people, two of whom must be allocated to baseball and two to basketball. The accompanying table gives each person's batting average and free-throw average.

Name	Batting average	Free-throw average
Kelley	70%	60%
Jackie	50%	50%
Curt	10%	30%
Gerry	80%	70%

a. Explain how you would use the concept of comparative advantage to allocate the players. Begin by establishing each player's opportunity cost of free throws in terms of batting average.

b. Why is it likely that the other basketball players will be unhappy about this arrangement but the other baseball players will be satisfied? Nonetheless, why would an economist say that this is an efficient way to allocate players for your dormitory's sports teams?

6. Your dormitory roommate plays loud music most of the time; you, however, would prefer more peace and quiet. You suggest that she buy some headphones. She responds that although she would be happy to use headphones, she has many other things that she would prefer to spend her money on right now. You discuss this situation with a friend who is an economics major. The following exchange takes place:

He: How much would it cost to buy headphones?

You: $15.

He: How much do you value having some peace and quiet for the rest of the semester?

You: $30.

He: It is efficient for you to buy the headphones and give them to your roommate. You gain more than you lose; the benefit exceeds the cost. You should do that.

You: It just isn't fair that I have to pay for the headphones when I'm not the one making the noise.

a. Which parts of this conversation contain positive statements and which parts contain normative statements?

b. Construct an argument supporting your viewpoint that your roommate should be the one to change her behavior. Similarly, construct an argument from the viewpoint of your roommate that you should be the one to buy the headphones. If your dormitory has a policy that gives residents the unlimited right to play music, whose argument is likely to win? If your dormitory has a rule that a person must stop playing music whenever a roommate complains, whose argument is likely to win?

7. Are the following statements true or false? Explain your answers.

a. "When people must pay higher taxes on their wage earnings, it reduces their incentive to work" is a positive statement.

b. "We should lower taxes to encourage more work" is a positive statement.

c. Economics cannot always be used to completely decide what society ought to do.

d. "The system of public education in this country generates greater benefits to society than the cost of running the system" is a normative statement.

e. All disagreements among economists are generated by the media.

8. The mayor of Gotham City, worried about a potential epidemic of deadly influenza this winter, asks an economic adviser the following series of questions. Determine whether a question requires the economic adviser to make a positive assessment or a normative assessment.

a. How much vaccine will be in stock in the city by the end of November?

b. If we offer to pay 10% more per dose to the pharmaceutical companies providing the vaccines, will they provide additional doses?

c. If there is a shortage of vaccine in the city, whom should we vaccinate first—the elderly or the very young? (Assume that a person from one group has an equal likelihood of dying from influenza as a person from the other group.)

d. If the city charges $25 per shot, how many people will pay?

e. If the city charges $25 per shot, it will make a profit of $10 per shot, money that can go to pay for inoculating poor people. Should the city engage in such a scheme?

WORK IT OUT Interactive step-by-step help with solving this problem can be found online.

9. Atlantis is a small, isolated island in the South Atlantic. The inhabitants grow potatoes and catch fish. The accompanying table shows the maximum annual output combinations of potatoes and fish that can be produced. Obviously, given their limited resources and available technology, as they use more of their resources for potato production, there are fewer resources available for catching fish.

Maximum annual output options	Quantity of potatoes (pounds)	Quantity of fish (pounds)
A	1,000	0
B	800	300
C	600	500
D	400	600
E	200	650
F	0	675

a. Draw a production possibility frontier with potatoes on the horizontal axis and fish on the vertical axis illustrating these options, showing points A–F.

b. Can Atlantis produce 500 pounds of fish and 800 pounds of potatoes? Explain. Where would this point lie relative to the production possibility frontier?

c. What is the opportunity cost of increasing the annual output of potatoes from 600 to 800 pounds?

d. What is the opportunity cost of increasing the annual output of potatoes from 200 to 400 pounds?

e. Can you explain why the answers to parts c and d are not the same? What does this imply about the slope of the production possibility frontier?

Graphs in Economics

Getting the Picture

Whether you're reading about economics in the *Wall Street Journal* or in your economics textbook, you will see many graphs. Visual images can make it much easier to understand verbal descriptions, numerical information, or ideas. In economics, graphs are the type of visual image used to facilitate understanding. To fully understand the ideas and information being discussed, you need to be familiar with how to interpret and construct these visual aids. This appendix explains how to do this.

Graphs, Variables, and Economic Models

One reason to attend college is that a bachelor's degree provides access to higher-paying jobs. Additional degrees, such as MBAs or law degrees, increase earnings even more. If you were to read an article about the relationship between educational attainment and income, you would probably see a graph showing the income levels for workers with different amounts of education. And this graph would depict the idea that, in general, more education increases income.

This graph, like most of those in economics, would depict the relationship between two economic variables. A **variable** is a quantity that can take on more than one value, such as the number of years of education a person has, the price of a can of soda, or a household's income.

As you learned in this chapter, economic analysis relies heavily on *models,* simplified descriptions of real situations. Most economic models describe the relationship between two variables, simplified by holding constant other variables that may affect the relationship.

For example, an economic model might describe the relationship between the price of a can of soda and the number of cans of soda that consumers will buy, assuming that everything else affecting consumers' purchases of soda stays constant. This type of model can be described mathematically or verbally, but illustrating the relationship in a graph makes it easier to understand, as you'll see next.

How Graphs Work

Most graphs in economics are based on a grid built around two perpendicular lines that show the values of two variables, helping you visualize the relationship between them. So a first step in understanding the use of such graphs is to see how this system works.

Two-Variable Graphs

Figure 2A-1 shows a typical two-variable graph. It illustrates the data in the accompanying table on outside temperature and the number of sodas a typical vendor can expect to sell at a baseball stadium during one game. The first column shows the values of outside temperature (the first variable) and the second column shows the values of the number of sodas sold (the second variable). Five combinations or pairs of the two variables are shown, each denoted by *A* through *E* in the third column.

A quantity that can take on more than one value is called a **variable.**

FIGURE 2A-1 Plotting Points on a Two-Variable Graph

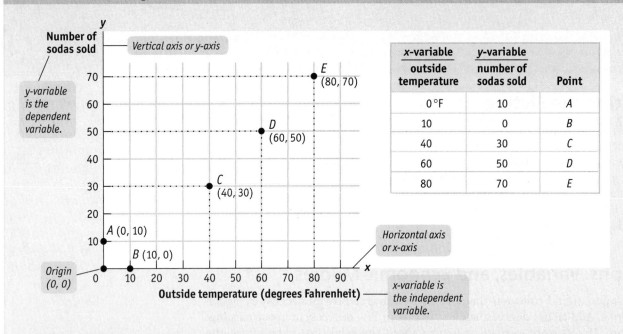

x-variable outside temperature	y-variable number of sodas sold	Point
0 °F	10	A
10	0	B
40	30	C
60	50	D
80	70	E

The data from the table are plotted where outside temperature (the independent variable) is measured along the horizontal axis and number of sodas sold (the dependent variable) is measured along the vertical axis. Each of the five combinations of temperature and sodas sold is represented by a point: *A, B, C, D,* and *E.* Each point in the graph is identified by a pair of values. For example, point *C* corresponds to the pair (40, 30)—an outside temperature of 40°F (the value of the *x*-variable) and 30 sodas sold (the value of the *y*-variable).

Now let's turn to graphing the data in this table. In any two-variable graph, one variable is called the *x*-variable and the other is called the *y*-variable. Here we have made outside temperature the *x*-variable and number of sodas sold the *y*-variable. The solid horizontal line in the graph is called the **horizontal axis** or ***x*-axis,** and values of the *x*-variable—outside temperature—are measured along it. Similarly, the solid vertical line in the graph is called the **vertical axis** or ***y*-axis,** and values of the *y*-variable—number of sodas sold—are measured along it.

At the **origin,** the point where the two axes meet, each variable is equal to zero. As you move rightward from the origin along the *x*-axis, values of the *x*-variable are positive and increasing. As you move up from the origin along the *y*-axis, values of the *y*-variable are positive and increasing.

You can plot each of the five points *A* through *E* on this graph by using a pair of numbers—the values that the *x*-variable and the *y*-variable take on for a given point. In Figure 2A-1, at point *C*, the *x*-variable takes on the value 40 and the *y*-variable takes on the value 30. You plot point *C* by drawing a line straight up from 40 on the *x*-axis and a horizontal line across from 30 on the *y*-axis. We write point *C* as (40, 30). We write the origin as (0, 0).

Looking at point *A* and point *B* in Figure 2A-1, you can see that when one of the variables for a point has a value of zero, it will lie on one of the axes. If the value of the *x*-variable is zero, the point will lie on the vertical axis, like point *A*. If the value of the *y*-variable is zero, the point will lie on the horizontal axis, like point *B*.

Most graphs that depict relationships between two economic variables represent a **causal relationship,** a relationship in which the value taken by one variable directly influences or determines the value taken by the other variable. In a causal relationship, the determining variable is called the **independent variable;** the variable it determines is called the **dependent variable.** In our example of

The line along which values of the *x*-variable are measured is called the **horizontal axis** or ***x*-axis.** The line along which values of the *y*-variable are measured is called the **vertical axis** or ***y*-axis.** The point where the axes of a two-variable graph meet is the **origin.**

A **causal relationship** exists between two variables when the value taken by one variable directly influences or determines the value taken by the other variable. In a causal relationship, the determining variable is called the **independent variable;** the variable it determines is called the **dependent variable.**

soda sales, the outside temperature is the independent variable. It directly influences the number of sodas that are sold, the dependent variable in this case.

By convention, we put the independent variable on the horizontal axis and the dependent variable on the vertical axis. Figure 2A-1 is constructed consistent with this convention; the independent variable (outside temperature) is on the horizontal axis and the dependent variable (number of sodas sold) is on the vertical axis.

An important exception to this convention is in graphs showing the economic relationship between the price of a product and quantity of the product: although price is generally the independent variable that determines quantity, it is always measured on the vertical axis.

> A **curve** is a line on a graph that depicts a relationship between two variables. It may be either a straight line or a curved line. If the curve is a straight line, the variables have a **linear relationship.** If the curve is not a straight line, the variables have a **nonlinear relationship.**

Curves on a Graph

Panel (a) of Figure 2A-2 contains some of the same information as Figure 2A-1, with a line drawn through the points *B, C, D,* and *E.* Such a line on a graph is called a **curve,** regardless of whether it is a straight line or a curved line. If the curve that shows the relationship between two variables is a straight line, or linear, the variables have a **linear relationship.** When the curve is not a straight line, or nonlinear, the variables have a **nonlinear relationship.**

A point on a curve indicates the value of the *y*-variable for a specific value of the *x*-variable. For example, point *D* indicates that at a temperature of 60°F, a vendor can expect to sell 50 sodas. The shape and orientation of a curve reveal the general

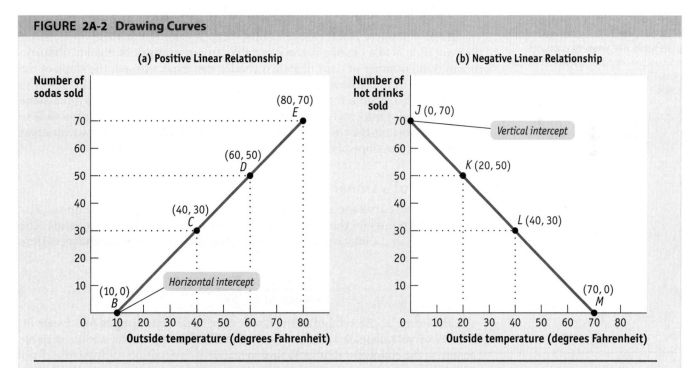

FIGURE 2A-2 Drawing Curves

(a) Positive Linear Relationship

(b) Negative Linear Relationship

The curve in panel (a) illustrates the relationship between the two variables, outside temperature and number of sodas sold. The two variables have a positive linear relationship: positive because the curve has an upward tilt, and linear because it is a straight line. It implies that an increase in the *x*-variable (outside temperature) leads to an increase in the *y*-variable (number of sodas sold). The curve in panel (b) is also a straight line, but it tilts downward. The two variables here, outside temperature and number of hot drinks sold, have a negative linear relationship: an increase in the *x*-variable (outside temperature) leads to a decrease in the *y*-variable (number of hot drinks sold). The curve in panel (a) has a horizontal intercept at point *B,* where it hits the horizontal axis. The curve in panel (b) has a vertical intercept at point *J,* where it hits the vertical axis, and a horizontal intercept at point *M,* where it hits the horizontal axis.

Two variables have a **positive relationship** when an increase in the value of one variable is associated with an increase in the value of the other variable. It is illustrated by a curve that slopes upward from left to right.

Two variables have a **negative relationship** when an increase in the value of one variable is associated with a decrease in the value of the other variable. It is illustrated by a curve that slopes downward from left to right.

The **horizontal intercept** of a curve is the point at which it hits the horizontal axis; it indicates the value of the *x*-variable when the value of the *y*-variable is zero.

The **vertical intercept** of a curve is the point at which it hits the vertical axis; it shows the value of the *y*-variable when the value of the *x*-variable is zero.

The **slope** of a line or curve is a measure of how steep it is. The slope of a line is measured by "rise over run"—the change in the *y*-variable between two points on the line divided by the change in the *x*-variable between those same two points.

nature of the relationship between the two variables. The upward tilt of the curve in panel (a) of Figure 2A-2 means that vendors can expect to sell more sodas at higher outside temperatures.

When variables are related this way—that is, when an increase in one variable is associated with an increase in the other variable—the variables are said to have a **positive relationship.** It is illustrated by a curve that slopes upward from left to right. Because this curve is also linear, the relationship between outside temperature and number of sodas sold illustrated by the curve in panel (a) of Figure 2A-2 is a positive linear relationship.

When an increase in one variable is associated with a decrease in the other variable, the two variables are said to have a **negative relationship.** It is illustrated by a curve that slopes downward from left to right, like the curve in panel (b) of Figure 2A-2. Because this curve is also linear, the relationship it depicts is a negative linear relationship. Two variables that might have such a relationship are the outside temperature and the number of hot drinks a vendor can expect to sell at a baseball stadium.

Return for a moment to the curve in panel (a) of Figure 2A-2 and you can see that it hits the horizontal axis at point *B*. This point, known as the **horizontal intercept,** shows the value of the *x*-variable when the value of the *y*-variable is zero. In panel (b) of Figure 2A-2, the curve hits the vertical axis at point *J*. This point, called the **vertical intercept,** indicates the value of the *y*-variable when the value of the *x*-variable is zero.

A Key Concept: The Slope of a Curve

The **slope** of a curve is a measure of how steep it is and indicates how sensitive the *y*-variable is to a change in the *x*-variable. In our example of outside temperature and the number of cans of soda a vendor can expect to sell, the slope of the curve would indicate how many more cans of soda the vendor could expect to sell with each 1 degree increase in temperature. Interpreted this way, the slope gives meaningful information. Even without numbers for *x* and *y*, it is possible to arrive at important conclusions about the relationship between the two variables by examining the slope of a curve at various points.

The Slope of a Linear Curve

Along a linear curve the slope, or steepness, is measured by dividing the *rise* between two points on the curve by the *run* between those same two points. The rise is the amount that *y* changes, and the run is the amount that *x* changes. Here is the formula:

$$\frac{\text{Change in } y}{\text{Change in } x} = \frac{\Delta y}{\Delta x} = \text{Slope}$$

In the formula, the symbol Δ (the Greek uppercase delta) stands for *change in*. When a variable increases, the change in that variable is positive; when a variable decreases, the change in that variable is negative.

The slope of a curve is positive when the rise (the change in the *y*-variable) has the same sign as the run (the change in the *x*-variable). That's because when two numbers have the same sign, the ratio of those two numbers is positive. The curve in panel (a) of Figure 2A-2 has a positive slope: along the curve, both the *y*-variable and the *x*-variable increase.

The slope of a curve is negative when the rise and the run have different signs. That's because when two numbers have different signs, the ratio of those two numbers is negative. The curve in panel (b) of Figure 2A-2 has a negative slope: along the curve, an increase in the *x*-variable is associated with a decrease in the *y*-variable.

FIGURE 2A-3   Calculating the Slope

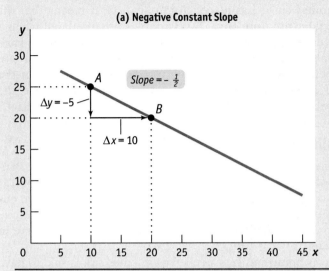

(a) Negative Constant Slope

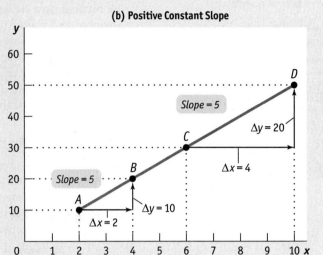

(b) Positive Constant Slope

Panels (a) and (b) show two linear curves. Between points A and B on the curve in panel (a), the change in y (the rise) is -5 and the change in x (the run) is 10. So the slope from A to B is $\frac{\Delta y}{\Delta x} = \frac{-5}{10} = -\frac{1}{2} = -0.5$, where the negative sign indicates that the curve is downward sloping. In panel (b), the curve has a slope from A to B of $\frac{\Delta y}{\Delta x} = \frac{10}{2} = 5$. The slope from C to D

is $\frac{\Delta y}{\Delta x} = \frac{20}{4} = 5$. The slope is positive, indicating that the curve is upward sloping. Furthermore, the slope between A and B is the same as the slope between C and D, making this a linear curve. The slope of a linear curve is constant: it is the same regardless of where it is measured along the curve.

Figure 2A-3 illustrates how to calculate the slope of a linear curve. Let's focus first on panel (a). From point A to point B the value of the y-variable changes from 25 to 20 and the value of the x-variable changes from 10 to 20. So the slope of the line between these two points is:

$$\frac{\text{Change in } y}{\text{Change in } x} = \frac{\Delta y}{\Delta x} = \frac{-5}{10} = -\frac{1}{2} = -0.5$$

Because a straight line is equally steep at all points, the slope of a straight line is the same at all points. In other words, a straight line has a constant slope. You can check this by calculating the slope of the linear curve between points A and B and between points C and D in panel (b) of Figure 2A-3.

Between A and B: $\dfrac{\Delta y}{\Delta x} = \dfrac{10}{2} = 5$

Between C and D: $\dfrac{\Delta y}{\Delta x} = \dfrac{20}{4} = 5$

Horizontal and Vertical Curves and Their Slopes

When a curve is horizontal, the value of the y-variable along that curve never changes—it is constant. Everywhere along the curve, the change in y is zero. Now, zero divided by any number is zero. So, regardless of the value of the change in x, the slope of a horizontal curve is always zero.

If a curve is vertical, the value of the x-variable along the curve never changes—it is constant. Everywhere along the curve, the change in x is zero. This means that the slope of a vertical curve is a ratio with zero in the denominator.

A **nonlinear curve** is one in which the slope is not the same between every pair of points.

The **absolute value** of a negative number is the value of the negative number without the minus sign.

A ratio with zero in the denominator approaches infinity—that is, an infinitely large number. So the slope of a vertical curve is equal to infinity.

A vertical or a horizontal curve has a special implication: it means that the *x*-variable and the *y*-variable are unrelated. Two variables are unrelated when a change in one variable (the independent variable) has no effect on the other variable (the dependent variable). Or to put it a slightly different way, two variables are unrelated when the dependent variable is constant regardless of the value of the independent variable. If, as is usual, the *y*-variable is the dependent variable, the curve is horizontal. If the dependent variable is the *x*-variable, the curve is vertical.

The Slope of a Nonlinear Curve

A **nonlinear curve** is one in which the slope changes as you move along it. Panels (a), (b), (c), and (d) of Figure 2A-4 show various nonlinear curves. Panels (a) and (b) show nonlinear curves whose slopes change as you move along them, but the slopes always remain positive. Although both curves tilt upward, the curve in panel (a) gets steeper as you move from left to right in contrast to the curve in panel (b), which gets flatter.

A curve that is upward sloping and gets steeper, as in panel (a), is said to have *positive increasing* slope. A curve that is upward sloping but gets flatter, as in panel (b), is said to have *positive decreasing* slope.

When we calculate the slope along these nonlinear curves, we obtain different values for the slope at different points. How the slope changes along the curve determines the curve's shape. For example, in panel (a) of Figure 2A-4, the slope of the curve is a positive number that steadily increases as you move from left to right, whereas in panel (b), the slope is a positive number that steadily decreases.

The slopes of the curves in panels (c) and (d) are negative numbers. Economists often prefer to express a negative number as its **absolute value,** which is the value of the negative number without the minus sign. In general, we denote the absolute value of a number by two parallel bars around the number; for example, the absolute value of –4 is written as $|-4| = 4$.

In panel (c), the absolute value of the slope steadily increases as you move from left to right. The curve therefore has *negative increasing* slope. And in panel (d), the absolute value of the slope of the curve steadily decreases along the curve. This curve therefore has *negative decreasing* slope.

Calculating the Slope Along a Nonlinear Curve

We've just seen that along a nonlinear curve, the value of the slope depends on where you are on that curve. So how do you calculate the slope of a nonlinear curve? We will focus on two methods: the *arc method* and the *point method*.

The Arc Method of Calculating the Slope An arc of a curve is some piece or segment of that curve. For example, panel (a) of Figure 2A-4 shows an arc consisting of the segment of the curve between points *A* and *B*. To calculate the slope along a nonlinear curve using the arc method, you draw a straight line between the two end-points of the arc. The slope of that straight line is a measure of the average slope of the curve between those two endpoints.

You can see from panel (a) of Figure 2A-4 that the straight line drawn between points *A* and *B* increases along the *x*-axis from 6 to 10 (so that $\Delta x = 4$) as it increases along the *y*-axis from 10 to 20 (so that $\Delta y = 10$). Therefore the slope of the straight line connecting points *A* and *B* is:

$$\frac{\Delta y}{\Delta x} = \frac{10}{4} = 2.5$$

This means that the average slope of the curve between points *A* and *B* is 2.5.

FIGURE 2A-4 Nonlinear Curves

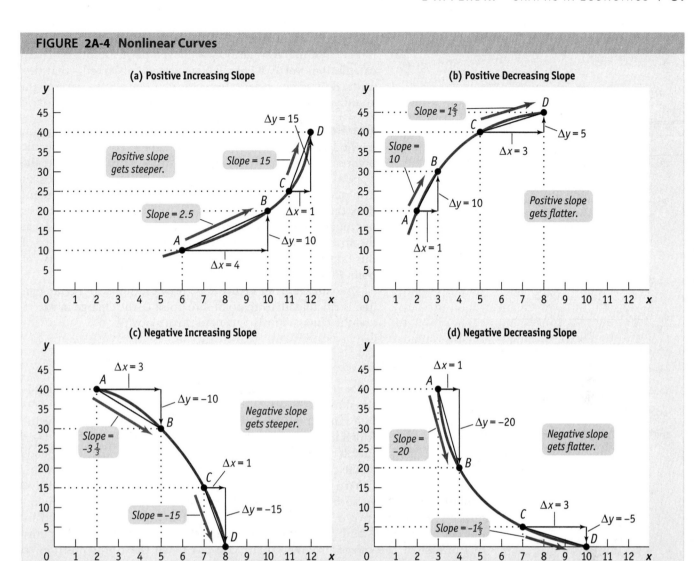

In panel (a) the slope of the curve from A to B is $\dfrac{\Delta y}{\Delta x} = \dfrac{10}{4} = 2.5$, and from C to D it is $\dfrac{\Delta y}{\Delta x} = \dfrac{15}{1} = 15$. The slope is positive and increasing; the curve gets steeper as you move to the right. In panel (b) the slope of the curve from A to B is $\dfrac{\Delta y}{\Delta x} = \dfrac{10}{1} = 10$, and from C to D it is $\dfrac{\Delta y}{\Delta x} = \dfrac{5}{3} = 1\dfrac{2}{3}$. The slope is positive and decreasing; the curve gets flatter as you move to the right. In panel (c) the slope from A to B is $\dfrac{\Delta y}{\Delta x} = \dfrac{-10}{3} = -3\dfrac{1}{3}$, and from C to D it is $\dfrac{\Delta y}{\Delta x} = \dfrac{-15}{1} = -15$. The slope is negative and

increasing; the curve gets steeper as you move to the right. And in panel (d) the slope from A to B is $\dfrac{\Delta y}{\Delta x} = \dfrac{-20}{1} = -20$, and from C to D it is $\dfrac{\Delta y}{\Delta x} = \dfrac{-5}{3} = -1\dfrac{2}{3}$. The slope is negative and decreasing; the curve gets flatter as you move to the right. The slope in each case has been calculated by using the arc method—that is, by drawing a straight line connecting two points along a curve. The average slope between those two points is equal to the slope of the straight line between those two points.

Now consider the arc on the same curve between points C and D. A straight line drawn through these two points increases along the x-axis from 11 to 12 ($\Delta x = 1$) as it increases along the y-axis from 25 to 40 ($\Delta y = 15$). So the average slope between points C and D is:

$$\frac{\Delta y}{\Delta x} = \frac{15}{1} = 15$$

FIGURE 2A-5 Calculating the Slope Using the Point Method

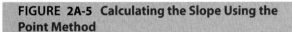
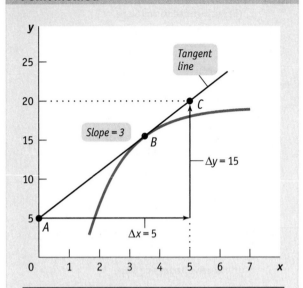

Here a tangent line has been drawn, a line that just touches the curve at point *B*. The slope of this line is equal to the slope of the curve at point *B*. The slope of the tangent line, measuring from *A* to *C*, is $\frac{\Delta y}{\Delta x} = \frac{15}{5} = 3$.

A **tangent line** is a straight line that just touches, or is tangent to, a nonlinear curve at a particular point. The slope of the tangent line is equal to the slope of the nonlinear curve at that point.

A nonlinear curve may have a **maximum** point, the highest point along the curve. At the maximum, the slope of the curve changes from positive to negative.

Therefore the average slope between points *C* and *D* is larger than the average slope between points *A* and *B*. These calculations verify what we have already observed—that this upward-tilted curve gets steeper as you move from left to right and therefore has positive increasing slope.

The Point Method of Calculating the Slope The point method calculates the slope of a nonlinear curve at a specific point on that curve. Figure 2A-5 illustrates how to calculate the slope at point *B* on the curve. First, we draw a straight line that just touches the curve at point *B*. Such a line is called a **tangent line:** the fact that it just touches the curve at point *B* and does not touch the curve at any other point on the curve means that the straight line is *tangent* to the curve at point *B*. The slope of this tangent line is equal to the slope of the nonlinear curve at point *B*.

You can see from Figure 2A-5 how the slope of the tangent line is calculated: from point *A* to point *C*, the change in *y* is 15 and the change in *x* is 5, generating a slope of:

$$\frac{\Delta y}{\Delta x} = \frac{15}{5} = 3$$

By the point method, the slope of the curve at point *B* is equal to 3.

A natural question to ask at this point is how to determine which method to use—the arc method or the point method—in calculating the slope of a nonlinear curve. The answer depends on the curve itself and the data used to construct it.

You use the arc method when you don't have enough information to be able to draw a smooth curve. For example, suppose that in panel (a) of Figure 2A-4 you have only the data represented by points *A*, *C*, and *D* and don't have the data represented by point *B* or any of the rest of the curve. Clearly, then, you can't use the point method to calculate the slope at point *B*; you would have to use the arc method to approximate the slope of the curve in this area by drawing a straight line between points *A* and *C*.

But if you have sufficient data to draw the smooth curve shown in panel (a) of Figure 2A-4, then you could use the point method to calculate the slope at point *B*—and at every other point along the curve as well.

Maximum and Minimum Points

The slope of a nonlinear curve can change from positive to negative or vice versa. When the slope of a curve changes from positive to negative, it creates what is called a *maximum* point of the curve. When the slope of a curve changes from negative to positive, it creates a *minimum* point.

Panel (a) of Figure 2A-6 illustrates a curve in which the slope changes from positive to negative as you move from left to right. When *x* is between 0 and 50, the slope of the curve is positive. At *x* equal to 50, the curve attains its highest point—the largest value of *y* along the curve. This point is called the **maximum** of the curve. When *x* exceeds 50, the slope becomes negative as the curve turns downward. Many important curves in economics, such as the curve that represents how the profit of a firm changes as it produces more output, are hill-shaped like this.

In contrast, the curve shown in panel (b) of Figure 2A-6 is U-shaped: it has a slope that changes from negative to positive. At *x* equal to 50, the curve reaches

FIGURE 2A-6 Maximum and Minimum Points

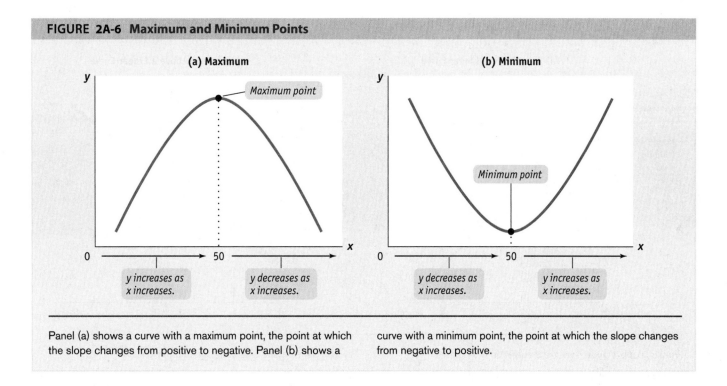

Panel (a) shows a curve with a maximum point, the point at which the slope changes from positive to negative. Panel (b) shows a curve with a minimum point, the point at which the slope changes from negative to positive.

its lowest point—the smallest value of *y* along the curve. This point is called the **minimum** of the curve. Various important curves in economics, such as the curve that represents how the per-unit costs of some firms change as output increases, are U-shaped like this.

Calculating the Area Below or Above a Curve

Sometimes it is useful to be able to measure the size of the area below or above a curve. For the sake of simplicity, we'll only calculate the area below or above a linear curve.

How large is the shaded area below the linear curve in panel (a) of Figure 2A-7? First note that this area has the shape of a right triangle. A right triangle is a triangle that has two sides that make a right angle with each other. We will refer to one of these sides as the *height* of the triangle and the other side as the *base* of the triangle. For our purposes, it doesn't matter which of these two sides we refer to as the base and which as the height.

Calculating the area of a right triangle is straightforward: multiply the height of the triangle by the base of the triangle, and divide the result by 2. The height of the triangle in panel (a) of Figure 2A-7 is $10 - 4 = 6$. And the base of the triangle is $3 - 0 = 3$. So the area of that triangle is

$$\frac{6 \times 3}{2} = 9$$

How about the shaded area above the linear curve in panel (b) of Figure 2A-7? We can use the same formula to calculate the area of this right triangle. The height of the triangle is $8 - 2 = 6$. And the base of the triangle is $4 - 0 = 4$. So the area of that triangle is

$$\frac{6 \times 4}{2} = 12$$

A nonlinear curve may have a **minimum** point, the lowest point along the curve. At the minimum, the slope of the curve changes from negative to positive.

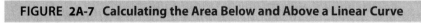

FIGURE 2A-7 Calculating the Area Below and Above a Linear Curve

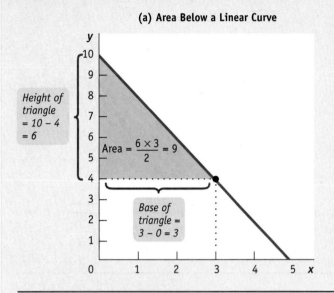

(a) Area Below a Linear Curve

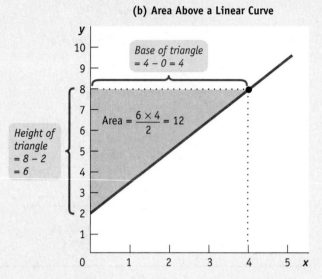

(b) Area Above a Linear Curve

The area above or below a linear curve forms a right triangle. The area of a right triangle is calculated by multiplying the height of the triangle by the base of the triangle, and dividing the result by 2. In panel (a) the area of the shaded triangle is $\frac{6 \times 3}{2} = 9$. In panel (b) the area of the shaded triangle is $\frac{6 \times 4}{2} = 12$.

Graphs That Depict Numerical Information

Graphs can also be used as a convenient way to summarize and display data without assuming some underlying causal relationship. Graphs that simply display numerical information are called *numerical graphs*. Here we will consider four types of numerical graphs: *time-series graphs, scatter diagrams, pie charts,* and *bar graphs*. These are widely used to display real, empirical data about different economic variables because they often help economists and policy makers identify patterns or trends in the economy. But as we will also see, you must be aware of both the usefulness and the limitations of numerical graphs to avoid misinterpreting them or drawing unwarranted conclusions from them.

Types of Numerical Graphs

You have probably seen graphs that show what has happened over time to economic variables such as the unemployment rate or stock prices. A **time-series graph** has successive dates on the horizontal axis and the values of a variable that occurred on those dates on the vertical axis.

For example, Figure 2A-8 shows real gross domestic product (GDP) per capita—a rough measure of a country's standard of living—in the United States from 1947 to 2016. A line connecting the points that correspond to real GDP per capita for each calendar quarter during those years gives a clear idea of the overall trend in the standard of living over these years.

Figure 2A-9 is an example of a different kind of numerical graph. It represents information from a sample of 186 countries on the standard of living, again measured by GDP per capita, and the amount of carbon emissions per capita, a measure of environmental pollution. Each point here indicates an average resident's standard of living and his or her annual carbon emissions for a given country.

A **time-series graph** has dates on the horizontal axis and values of a variable that occurred on those dates on the vertical axis.

The points lying in the upper right of the graph, which show combinations of a high standard of living and high carbon emissions, represent economically advanced countries such as the United States. (The country with the highest carbon emissions, at the top of the graph, is Qatar.) Points lying in the bottom left of the graph, which show combinations of a low standard of living and low carbon emissions, represent economically less advanced countries such as Afghanistan and Sierra Leone.

The pattern of points indicates that there is a positive relationship between living standard and carbon emissions per capita: on the whole, people create more pollution in countries with a higher standard of living.

This type of graph is called a **scatter diagram,** in which each point corresponds to an actual observation of the *x*-variable and the *y*-variable. In scatter diagrams, a curve is typically fitted to the scatter of points; that is, a curve is drawn that approximates as closely as possible the general relationship between the variables. As you can see, the fitted line in Figure 2A-9 is upward sloping, indicating the underlying positive relationship between the two variables. Scatter diagrams are often used to show how a general relationship can be inferred from a set of data.

A **pie chart** shows the share of a total amount that is accounted for by various components, usually expressed in percentages. For example, Figure 2A-10 is a pie chart that depicts the education levels of workers who in 2015 were paid the

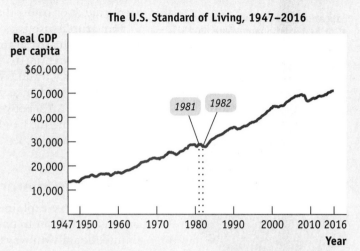

FIGURE 2A-8 Time-Series Graph

The U.S. Standard of Living, 1947–2016

Time-series graphs show successive dates on the *x*-axis and values for a variable on the *y*-axis. This time-series graph shows real gross domestic product per capita, a measure of a country's standard of living, in the United States from 1947 to early 2016.
Data from: The Federal Reserve Bank of St. Louis.

A **scatter diagram** shows points that correspond to actual observations of the *x*- and *y*-variables. A curve is usually fitted to the scatter of points.

A **pie chart** shows how some total is divided among its components, usually expressed in percentages.

FIGURE 2A-9 Scatter Diagram

In a scatter diagram, each point represents the corresponding values of the *x*- and *y*-variables for a given observation. Here, each point indicates the GDP per capita and the amount of carbon emissions per capita for a given country for a sample of 186 countries. The upward-sloping fitted line here is the best approximation of the general relationship between the two variables.
Data from: World Development Indicators.

Standard of Living and Carbon Emissions, 2011

Education Levels of Workers Paid at or Below Minimum Wage, 2015

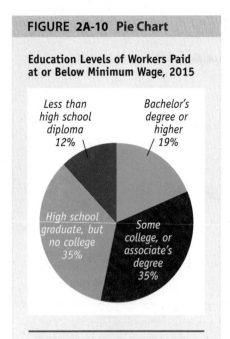

A pie chart shows the percentages of a total amount that can be attributed to various components. This pie chart shows the percentages of workers with given education levels who were paid at or below the federal minimum wage in 2015. (Numbers don't add to 100 due to rounding.)

Data from: Bureau of Labor Statistics.

federal minimum wage or less. As you can see, the majority of workers paid at or below the minimum wage had no college degree. Only 19% of workers who were paid at or below the minimum wage had a bachelor's degree or higher.

Bar graphs use bars of various heights or lengths to indicate values of a variable. In the bar graph in Figure 2A-11, the bars show the percent change in GDP per capita from 2014 to 2015 for the United States, China, and Indonesia. Exact values of the variable that is being measured may be written at the end of the bar, as in this figure. For instance, GDP per capita for China increased by 6.7% between 2014 and 2015. But even without the precise values, comparing the heights or lengths of the bars can give useful insight into the relative magnitudes of the different values of the variable.

Problems in Interpreting Numerical Graphs

Although we've explained that graphs are visual images that make ideas or information easier to understand, graphs can be constructed (intentionally or unintentionally) in ways that are misleading and can lead to inaccurate conclusions. This section raises some issues to be aware of when you are interpreting graphs.

Features of Construction Before drawing any conclusions about what a numerical graph implies, pay close attention to the scale, or size of increments, shown on the axes. Small increments tend to visually exaggerate changes in the variables, whereas large increments tend to visually diminish them. So the scale used in construction of a graph can influence your interpretation of the significance of the changes it illustrates—perhaps in an unwarranted way.

Take, for example, Figure 2A-12, which shows real GDP per capita in the United States from 1981 to 1982 using increments of $500. You can see that real GDP per capita fell from $28,957 to $27,859. A decrease, sure, but is it as enormous as the scale chosen for the vertical axis makes it seem?

If you go back and reexamine Figure 2A-8, which shows real GDP per capita in the United States from 1947 to 2016, you can see that this would be a misguided conclusion. Figure 2A-8 includes the same data shown in Figure 2A-12, but it is constructed with a scale having increments of $10,000 rather than $500. From it you can see that the fall in real GDP per capita from 1981 to 1982 was, in fact, relatively insignificant.

In fact, the story of real GDP per capita—a measure of the standard of living—in the United States is mostly a story of ups, not downs. This comparison shows that if you are not careful to factor in the choice of scale in interpreting a graph, you can arrive at very different, and possibly misguided, conclusions.

Related to the choice of scale is the use of *truncation* in constructing a graph. An axis is **truncated** when part of the range is omitted. This is indicated by two slashes (//) in the axis near the origin. You can see that the vertical axis of Figure 2A-12 has been truncated—some of the range of values from 0 to $27,000 have been omitted and a // appears in the axis. Truncation saves space in the presentation of a graph and allows smaller increments to be used in constructing it. As a result, changes in the variable depicted on a graph that has been

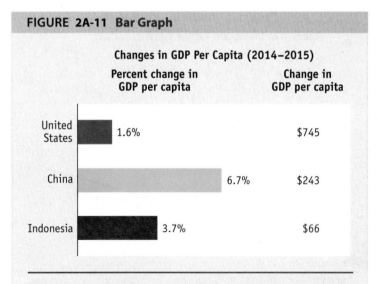

A bar graph measures a variable by using bars of various heights or lengths. This bar graph shows the percent change in GDP per capita (measured in 2005 dollars) for the United States, China, and Indonesia.

Data from: World Bank, World Development Indicators.

FIGURE 2A-12 Interpreting Graphs: The Effect of Scale

Some of the same data for the years 1981 and 1982 used in Figure 2A-8 are represented here, except that here they are shown using increments of $500 rather than increments of $10,000. As a result of this change in scale, changes in the standard of living look much larger in this figure compared to Figure 2A-8.

Data from: Bureau of Economic Analysis.

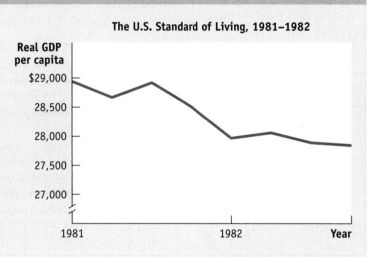

The U.S. Standard of Living, 1981–1982

truncated appear larger compared to a graph that has not been truncated and that uses larger increments.

You must also consider exactly what a graph is illustrating. For example, in Figure 2A-11, you should recognize that what is being shown are *percent* changes in GDP per capita, not *numerical* changes. The growth rate for China increased by the highest percentage, 6.7% in this example. If you were to confuse numerical changes with percent changes, you would erroneously conclude the country with the greatest change in GDP per capita was China.

In fact, a correct interpretation of Figure 2A-11 shows that the greatest dollar change in GDP per capita was for the United States: GDP per capita increased by $745 for the United States, which is greater than the increase in GDP per capita for China, which is $243 in this example. Although there was a higher percentage increase in GDP per capita for China, the dollar increase for China from 2014 to 2015 was smaller than the change for the United States, leading to a smaller change in GDP per capita for China than the United States. The same can be said for Indonesia, where GDP per capita grew by 3.7%, but that only resulted in a $66 increase in actual GDP per capita.

Omitted Variables From a scatter diagram that shows two variables moving either positively or negatively in relation to each other, it is easy to conclude that there is a causal relationship. But relationships between two variables are not always due to direct cause and effect. Quite possibly an observed relationship between two variables is due to the *unobserved* effect of a third variable on each of the other two variables.

An unobserved variable that, through its influence on other variables, creates the erroneous appearance of a direct causal relationship among those variables is called an **omitted variable.** For example, in New England, a greater amount of snowfall during a given week will typically cause people to buy more snow shovels. It will also cause people to buy more de-icer fluid. But if you omitted the influence of the snowfall and simply plotted the number of snow shovels sold versus the number of bottles of de-icer fluid sold, you would produce a scatter diagram that showed an upward tilt in the pattern of points, indicating a positive relationship between snow shovels sold and de-icer fluid sold.

To attribute a causal relationship between these two variables, however, is misguided; more snow shovels sold do not cause more de-icer fluid to be sold, or vice versa. They move together because they are both influenced by a third, determining, variable—the weekly snowfall, which is the omitted variable in this case.

A **bar graph** uses bars of varying heights or lengths to show the comparative sizes of different observations of a variable.

An axis is **truncated** when some of the values on the axis are omitted, usually to save space.

An **omitted variable** is an unobserved variable that, through its influence on other variables, creates the erroneous appearance of a direct causal relationship among those variables.

The error of **reverse causality** is committed when the true direction of causality between two variables is reversed.

So before assuming that a pattern in a scatter diagram implies a cause-and-effect relationship, it is important to consider whether the pattern is instead the result of an omitted variable. Or to put it succinctly: correlation is not causation.

Reverse Causality Even when you are confident that there is no omitted variable and that there is a causal relationship between two variables shown in a numerical graph, you must also be careful that you don't make the mistake of **reverse causality**—coming to an erroneous conclusion about which is the dependent and which is the independent variable by reversing the true direction of causality between the two variables.

For example, imagine a scatter diagram that depicts the grade point averages (GPAs) of 20 of your classmates on one axis and the number of hours that each classmate spends studying on the other. A line fitted between the points will probably have a positive slope, showing a positive relationship between GPA and hours of studying. We could reasonably infer that hours spent studying is the independent variable and that GPA is the dependent variable. But you could make the error of reverse causality: you could infer that a high GPA causes a student to study more, whereas a low GPA causes a student to study less.

As you've just seen, it is important to understand how graphs can mislead or be interpreted incorrectly. Policy decisions, business decisions, and political arguments are often based on interpretation of the types of numerical graphs we've just discussed. Problems of misleading features of construction, omitted variables, and reverse causality can lead to important and undesirable consequences.

PROBLEMS

interactive activity

1. Study the four accompanying diagrams. Consider the following statements and indicate which diagram matches each statement. Which variable would appear on the horizontal and which on the vertical axis? In each of these statements, is the slope positive, negative, zero, or infinity?

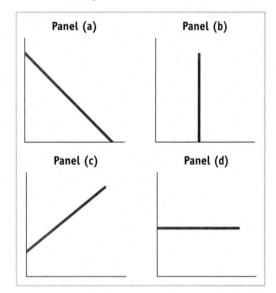

Panel (a)   Panel (b)

Panel (c)   Panel (d)

a. If the price of movies increases, fewer consumers go to see movies.

b. More experienced workers typically have higher incomes than less experienced workers.

c. Whatever the temperature outside, Americans consume the same number of hot dogs per day.

d. Consumers buy more frozen yogurt when the price of ice cream goes up.

e. Research finds no relationship between the number of diet books purchased and the number of pounds lost by the average dieter.

f. Regardless of its price, Americans buy the same quantity of salt.

2. During the Reagan administration, economist Arthur Laffer argued in favor of lowering income tax rates in order to increase tax revenues. Like most economists, he believed that at tax rates above a certain level, tax revenue would fall because high taxes would discourage some people from working and that people would refuse to work at all if they received no income after paying taxes. This relationship between tax rates and tax revenue is graphically summarized in what is widely known as the Laffer curve. Plot the Laffer curve relationship assuming that it has the shape of a nonlinear curve. The following questions will help you construct the graph.

a. Which is the independent variable? Which is the dependent variable? On which axis do you therefore measure the income tax rate? On which axis do you measure income tax revenue?

b. What would tax revenue be at a 0% income tax rate?

c. The maximum possible income tax rate is 100%. What would tax revenue be at a 100% income tax rate?

d. Estimates now show that the maximum point on the Laffer curve is (approximately) at a tax rate of 80%. For tax rates less than 80%, how would you describe the relationship between the tax rate and tax revenue, and how is this relationship reflected in the slope? For tax rates higher than 80%, how would you describe the relationship between the tax rate and tax revenue, and how is this relationship reflected in the slope?

3. In the accompanying figures, the numbers on the axes have been lost. All you know is that the units shown on the vertical axis are the same as the units on the horizontal axis.

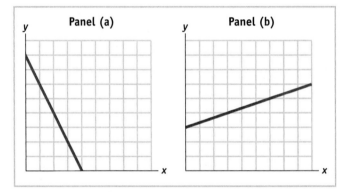

a. In panel (a), what is the slope of the line? Show that the slope is constant along the line.

b. In panel (b), what is the slope of the line? Show that the slope is constant along the line.

4. Answer each of the following questions by drawing a schematic diagram.

a. Taking measurements of the slope of a curve at three points farther and farther to the right along the horizontal axis, the slope of the curve changes from −0.3, to −0.8, to −2.5, measured by the point method. Draw a schematic diagram of this curve. How would you describe the relationship illustrated in your diagram?

b. Taking measurements of the slope of a curve at five points farther and farther to the right along the horizontal axis, the slope of the curve changes from 1.5, to 0.5, to 0, to −0.5, to −1.5, measured by the point method. Draw a schematic diagram of this curve. Does it have a maximum or a minimum?

5. For each of the accompanying diagrams, calculate the area of the shaded right triangle.

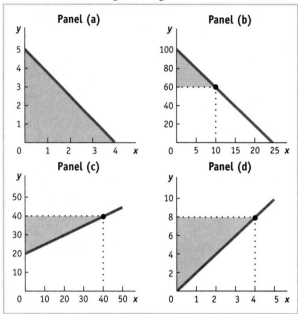

6. The base of a right triangle is 10, and its area is 20. What is the height of this right triangle?

7. The accompanying table shows the relationship between workers' hours of work per week and their hourly wage rate. Apart from the fact that they receive a different hourly wage rate and work different hours, these five workers are otherwise identical.

Name	Quantity of labor (hours per week)	Wage rate (per hour)
Athena	30	$15
Boris	35	30
Curt	37	45
Diego	36	60
Emily	32	75

a. Which variable is the independent variable? Which is the dependent variable?

b. Draw a scatter diagram illustrating this relationship. Draw a (nonlinear) curve that connects the points. Put the hourly wage rate on the vertical axis.

c. As the wage rate increases from $15 to $30, how does the number of hours worked respond according to the relationship depicted here? What is the average slope of the curve between Athena's and Boris's data points using the arc method?

d. As the wage rate increases from $60 to $75, how does the number of hours worked respond according to the relationship depicted here? What is the average slope of the curve between Diego's and Emily's data points using the arc method?

8. An insurance company has found that the severity of property damage in a fire is positively related to the number of firefighters arriving at the scene.

  a. Draw a diagram that depicts this finding with number of firefighters on the horizontal axis and amount of property damage on the vertical axis. What is the argument made by this diagram? Suppose you reverse what is measured on the two axes. What is the argument made then?

  b. Should the insurance company ask the city to send fewer firefighters to any fire to reduce its payouts to policy holders?

9. This table illustrates annual salaries and income tax owed by five individuals. Despite receiving different annual salaries and owing different amounts of income tax, these five individuals are otherwise identical.

Name	Annual salary	Annual income tax owed
Susan	$22,000	$3,304
Eduardo	63,000	14,317
John	3,000	454
Camila	94,000	23,927
Peter	37,000	7,020

  a. If you were to plot these points on a graph, what would be the average slope of the curve between the points for Eduardo's and Camila's salaries and taxes using the arc method? How would you interpret this value for the slope?

  b. What is the average slope of the curve between the points for John's and Susan's salaries and taxes using the arc method? How would you interpret that value for the slope?

  c. What happens to the slope as salary increases? What does this relationship imply about how the level of income taxes affects a person's incentive to earn a higher salary?

WORK IT OUT Interactive step-by-step help with solving this problem can be found online.

10. Studies have found a relationship between a country's yearly rate of economic growth and the yearly rate of increase in airborne pollutants. It is believed that a higher rate of economic growth allows a country's residents to have more cars and travel more, thereby releasing more airborne pollutants.

  a. Which variable is the independent variable? Which is the dependent variable?

  b. Suppose that in the country of Sudland, when the yearly rate of economic growth fell from 3.0% to 1.5%, the yearly rate of increase in airborne pollutants fell from 6% to 5%. What is the average slope of a nonlinear curve between these points using the arc method?

  c. Assume that when the yearly rate of economic growth rose from 3.5% to 4.5%, the yearly rate of increase in airborne pollutants rose from 5.5% to 7.5%. What is the average slope of a nonlinear curve between these two points using the arc method?

  d. How would you describe the relationship between the two variables here?

Investors who held onto their shares of Booking Holdings over the past several years were happy campers in spring 2018. That is when the share price of Booking Holdings, the parent company of Priceline.com, the online provider of travel-related bookings, hit an all-time high of over $2,000—a 30,000% plus increase over its lowest point of $6.60 per share in October 2002.

Even more remarkable is the fact that in 2002, the company was in such deep trouble that many doubted it would survive. From 1999 to 2002, the company lost 95% of its value, going from a valuation of $9 billion to a paltry $425 million. What went so right, then so terribly wrong, and then so incredibly right again?

When the company was formed in 1998, investors were immediately impressed by how it revolutionized the travel industry. Its success lay in its ability to spot exploitable opportunities for itself and its customers. The company understood that when a plane departs with empty seats or a hotel has empty beds, there is a cost—the revenue that would have been earned if the seat or bed were filled. Priceline.com's innovation was to bring airlines and hotels with unsold capacity together with travelers.

It worked this way: customers specify the price they are willing to pay for a given flight or hotel, and then, after booking, Priceline presents them with a list of airlines or hotels willing to accept that price. Typically, price declines as the trip date nears. Although some travelers like the security of booking their trips well in advance and are willing to pay extra for that assurance, others are quite happy to wait until the last minute and risk not getting their first choice of flight or hotel to benefit from a lower price.

Priceline, then, found a way to make everyone better off, including itself, since it charged a small fee for each booking it facilitated.

Yet, in 2002 the company was at risk of going under. After the terrorist attacks of September 11, 2001, many Americans simply stopped flying. As the economy went into a deep slump, airplanes sat empty on the tarmac and the airlines lost billions of dollars. Several major airlines spiraled toward bankruptcy, and Priceline.com was losing several million dollars a year.

In order to avert a meltdown of the airline industry, Congress passed a $15 billion aid package that was critical in stabilizing the industry.

That was the seed of the company's turnaround. Quick on its feet when it saw its market challenged by newcomers Expedia and Orbitz, it responded aggressively by moving more of its business toward hotel bookings and into Europe, where the online travel industry was still quite small. Its network was particularly valuable in the European hotel market, composed of many more small hotels, compared to the U.S. market, which is dominated by nationwide chains. The efforts paid off, and by 2003 Priceline.com was turning a profit. From 2005 to 2018, Priceline.com expanded by acquiring the travel websites Booking.com, Kayak.com, Agoda.com, Rentalcars.com, and OpenTable.com, transforming itself into Booking Holdings, with revenues of $12.7 billion in 2017, and a revenue growth rate averaging 15% for the past 3 years.

QUESTION FOR THOUGHT

1. Explain how each of the twelve principles of economics is illustrated in this case.

Boeing is back at the drawing board. In 2015, after releasing the Boeing 777X, an update to the widely popular 777, they announced plans to redevelop their production process. Boeing hoped to extend the extremely successful process known as *lean production* to incorporate robotics and standardize production further, leading to what Boeing calls *advanced manufacturing*.

Lean manufacturing, pioneered by Toyota Motors of Japan, is based on the practice of having parts arrive on the factory floor just as they are needed for production. This reduces the amount of parts Boeing holds in inventory as well as the amount of the factory floor needed for production. To help move from lean production to advanced manufacturing Boeing has turned to Toyota, hiring some of their top engineers.

Boeing first adopted lean manufacturing in 1999 in the manufacture of the 737, the most popular commercial airplane. By 2005, after constant refinement, it achieved a 50% reduction in the time it takes to produce a plane and a nearly 60% reduction in parts inventory. An important feature is a continuously moving assembly line, moving products from one assembly team to the next at a steady pace and eliminating the need for workers to wander across the factory floor from task to task or in search of tools and parts.

Toyota's lean production techniques have been the most widely adopted, revolutionizing manufacturing worldwide. In simple terms, lean production is focused on organization and communication. Workers and parts are organized so as to ensure a smooth and consistent workflow that minimizes wasted effort and materials. Lean production is also designed to be highly responsive to changes in the desired mix of output—for example, quickly producing more sedans and fewer minivans according to changes in customer demand. Coming full circle, advanced manufacturing was used in the production of the redeveloped 737, the 737 MAX, which started shipping to customers in 2017.

Toyota's methods were so successful that they transformed the global auto industry and severely threatened once-dominant American automakers. Until the 1980s, the "Big Three"—Chrysler, Ford, and General Motors—dominated the American auto industry, with virtually no foreign-made cars sold in the United States. In the 1980s, however, Toyotas became increasingly popular due to their high quality and relatively low price—so popular that the Big Three eventually prevailed upon the U.S. government to protect them by restricting the sale of Japanese autos in the United States. Over time, Toyota responded by building assembly plants in the United States, bringing along its lean production techniques, which then spread throughout American manufacturing.

QUESTIONS FOR THOUGHT

1. What is the opportunity cost associated with having a worker wander across the factory floor from task to task or in search of tools and parts?

2. Explain how lean manufacturing improves the economy's efficiency in allocation.

3. Before lean manufacturing innovations, Japan mostly sold consumer electronics to the United States. How did lean manufacturing innovations alter Japan's comparative advantage vis-à-vis the United States?

4. How do you think the shift in the location of Toyota's production from Japan to the United States has altered the pattern of comparative advantage in automaking between the two countries?

A NATURAL GAS BOOM

IN JUST FIVE YEARS, from 2010 to 2015, Karnes County went from producing a relatively small amount of oil and natural gas to becoming the largest producing county in Texas. What accounted for the swift change was hydraulic fracturing, or fracking.

In those few years, Karnes County also went through an extreme cycle of boom and bust as the price of oil plunged from $100 a barrel in 2014 to under $45 a barrel in 2015, while the price of natural gas (per thousand cubic feet) went from nearly $8 to under $2. What accounted for this reversal of fortune? Once again, it was fracking. *Fracking* is a method of extracting natural gas (and to a lesser extent, oil) from deposits trapped between layers of shale rock thousands of feet underground using powerful jets of chemical-laden water. For almost a century in the United States, vast deposits of natural gas within these shale formations lay untapped because drilling for them was too difficult.

Until recently, that is. A few decades ago, new drilling technologies were developed that made it possible to reach these deeply embedded deposits. But what finally pushed energy companies to invest in these new extraction technologies was the high price of natural gas over the last decade—a quadrupling from 2002 to 2006. Two principal factors explain the high prices: the demand for natural gas and the supply of natural gas.

First, the demand side. In 2002, the U.S. economy was mired in recession; with economic activity low and job losses high, people and businesses cut their energy consumption. For example, to save money, homeowners turned down their thermostats in winter and turned them up in the summer. But by 2006, the U.S. economy came roaring back, and natural gas consumption rose.

Second, the supply side. In 2005, Hurricane Katrina devastated the American Gulf Coast, site of most of the country's natural gas production at the time. So by 2006, the demand for natural gas surged while supply was severely curtailed. As a result, natural gas prices peaked at around $14 per thousand cubic feet, up from around $2 in 2002.

Fast-forward to 2013: natural gas prices once again fell to $2 per thousand cubic feet. But this time a slow economy was not the principal explanation—it was the impact of new technologies on oil and natural gas production. To illustrate, the United States produced 8.13 trillion cubic feet of natural gas from shale deposits in 2012, nearly doubling the total from 2010. That total increased to nearly 10 trillion cubic feet of natural gas in 2015, making the United States the world's largest producer of both oil and natural gas—overtaking both Russia and Saudi Arabia. Despite a brief surge in the winter of 2013–2014 due to high demand for heating fuel during a very cold winter, by late 2015 the price fell to under $2 as fracking technology advanced and more drilling expanded production.

The benefits of much lower natural gas prices have led to lower heating costs for consumers, and have cascaded through American industries. For example, electricity-generating power plants are switching from coal to natural gas, and mass-transit vehicles are switching from gasoline to natural gas. The effect has been so significant that many European manufacturers, paying four times more for gas than their U.S. rivals, have been forced to relocate plants to American soil to survive. In addition, the revived U.S. natural gas industry has directly created tens of thousands of new jobs.

Yet the benefits of natural gas have been accompanied by deep reservations and controversy over the environmental effects of fracking. While there are clear environmental benefits from the switch to natural gas (which burns cleaner than the other, heavily polluting fossil fuels, gasoline and coal), fracking has sparked another set of environmental worries. One is the potential for contamination of local groundwater by chemicals used in fracking. Another is that cheap natural gas may discourage the adoption of more expensive renewable energy sources like solar and wind power, furthering our dependence on fossil fuel.

The debate over fracking has been highly charged and is ongoing. We, the authors, do not espouse one side or the other, believing that science as well as economics should provide guidance about the best course to follow.

But let's return to the topic of supply and demand. How, exactly, does the high price of natural gas nearly a decade ago translate into today's switch to vehicles powered by natural gas? The short answer is that it's a matter of supply and demand. But what does that mean? Many people use "supply and demand" as a sort of catchphrase to mean "the laws of the marketplace at work."

To economists, however, the concept of supply and demand has a precise meaning: it is a *model of how a market behaves* that is extremely useful for understanding many—but not all—markets.

In this chapter, we lay out the pieces that make up the *supply and demand model,* put them together, and show how this model can be used. ●

Supply and Demand: A Model of a Competitive Market

Natural gas sellers and natural gas buyers constitute a market—a group of producers and consumers who exchange a good or service for payment. In this chapter, we'll focus on a particular type of market known as a *competitive market*. A **competitive market** is a market in which there are many buyers and sellers of the same good or service. More precisely, the key feature of a competitive market is that no individual's actions have a noticeable effect on the price at which the good or service is sold. It's important to understand, however, that this is not an accurate description of every market.

For example, it's not an accurate description of the market for cola beverages. That's because in this market, Coca-Cola and Pepsi account for such a large proportion of total sales that they are able to influence the price at which cola beverages are bought and sold. But it is an accurate description of the market for natural gas. The global marketplace for natural gas is so huge that even the biggest U.S. driller for natural gas—Exxon Mobil—accounts for such a small share of total global transactions that it is unable to influence the price at which natural gas is bought and sold.

It's a little hard to explain why competitive markets are different from other markets until we've seen how a competitive market works. So let's take a rain check—we'll return to that issue at the end of this chapter. For now, let's just say that it's easier to model competitive markets than other markets. Just as when taking an exam, it's always a good strategy to begin by answering the easier questions. We will now start by talking about the easier model: competitive markets.

When a market is competitive, its behavior is well described by the **supply and demand model.** And because many markets are competitive, the supply and demand model is a very useful one indeed.

There are five key elements in this model:

- The *demand curve*
- The *supply curve*
- The set of factors that cause the demand curve to shift and the set of factors that cause the supply curve to shift
- The *market equilibrium*, which includes the *equilibrium price* and *equilibrium quantity*
- The way the market equilibrium changes when the supply curve or demand curve shifts

To understand the supply and demand model, we will examine each of these elements.

The Demand Curve

How much natural gas will American consumers want to buy in a given year? You might at first think that we can answer this question by simply adding up the amounts each American household and business consumes in that year. But that's not enough to answer the question, because how much natural gas Americans want to buy depends upon the price of natural gas.

A **competitive market** is a market in which there are many buyers and sellers of the same good or service, none of whom can influence the price at which the good or service is sold.

The **supply and demand model** is a model of how a competitive market behaves.

When the price of natural gas falls, as it did from 2006 to 2015, consumers will generally respond to the lower price by using more natural gas—for example, by turning up their thermostats to keep their houses warmer in the winter or switching to vehicles powered by natural gas. In general, the amount of natural gas, or of any good or service that people want to buy, depends upon the price. The higher the price, the less of the good or service people want to purchase; alternatively, the lower the price, the more they want to purchase.

So, the answer to the question "How many units of natural gas do consumers want to buy?" depends on the price of a unit of natural gas. If you don't yet know what the price will be, you can start by making a table of how many units of natural gas people would want to buy at a number of different prices. Such a table is known as a *demand schedule*. This, in turn, can be used to draw a *demand curve*, which is one of the key elements of the supply and demand model.

The Demand Schedule and the Demand Curve

A **demand schedule** is a table showing how much of a good or service consumers will want to buy at different prices. At the right of Figure 3-1, we show a hypothetical demand schedule for natural gas. It's expressed in BTUs (British thermal units), a commonly used measure of quantity of natural gas. It's a hypothetical demand schedule—it doesn't use actual data on American demand for natural gas.

According to the table, if a BTU of natural gas costs $3, consumers will want to purchase 10 trillion BTUs of natural gas over the course of a year. If the price is $3.25 per BTU, they will want to buy only 8.9 trillion BTUs; if the price is only $2.75 per BTU, they will want to buy 11.5 trillion BTUs. The higher the price, the fewer BTUs of natural gas consumers will want to purchase. So, as the price rises, the **quantity demanded** of natural gas—the actual amount consumers are willing to buy at some specific price—falls.

A **demand schedule** shows how much of a good or service consumers will want to buy at different prices.

The **quantity demanded** is the actual amount of a good or service consumers are willing to buy at some specific price.

FIGURE 3-1 The Demand Schedule and the Demand Curve

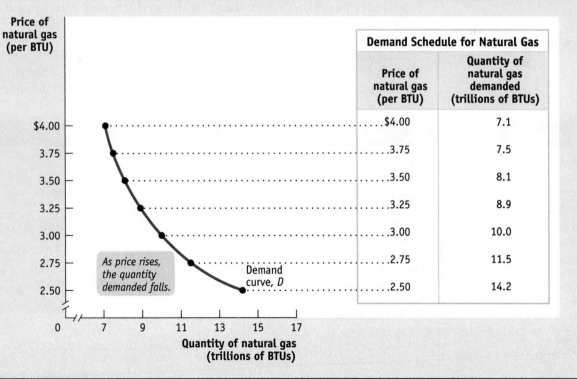

The demand schedule for natural gas yields the corresponding demand curve, which shows how much of a good or service consumers want to buy at any given price. The demand curve and the demand schedule reflect the law of demand: as price rises, the quantity demanded falls. Similarly, a fall in price raises the quantity demanded. As a result, the demand curve is downward sloping.

A **demand curve** is a graphical representation of the demand schedule. It shows the relationship between quantity demanded and price.

The **law of demand** says that a higher price for a good or service, other things equal, leads people to demand a smaller quantity of that good or service.

The graph in Figure 3-1 is a visual representation of the information in the table. (You might want to review the discussion of graphs in economics in the appendix to Chapter 2.) The vertical axis shows the price of a BTU of natural gas and the horizontal axis shows the quantity of natural gas in trillions of BTUs. Each point on the graph corresponds to one of the entries in the table. The curve that connects these points is a **demand curve.** A demand curve is a graphical representation of the demand schedule, another way of showing the relationship between the quantity demanded and price.

Note that the demand curve shown in Figure 3-1 slopes downward. This reflects the inverse relationship between price and the quantity demanded: a higher price reduces the quantity demanded, and a lower price increases the quantity demanded. We can see this from the demand curve in Figure 3-1. As price falls, we move down the demand curve and quantity demanded increases. And as price increases, we move up the demand curve and quantity demanded falls.

In the real world, demand curves almost always *do* slope downward. (The exceptions are so rare that for practical purposes we can ignore them.) Generally, the proposition that a higher price for a good, *other things equal,* leads people to demand a smaller quantity of that good is so reliable that economists are willing to call it a "law"—the **law of demand.**

Shifts of the Demand Curve

Although natural gas prices in 2006 were higher than they had been in 2002, U.S. consumption of natural gas was higher in 2006. How can we reconcile this fact with the law of demand, which says that a higher price reduces the quantity demanded, other things equal?

The answer lies in the crucial phrase *other things equal*. In this case, other things weren't equal: the U.S. economy had changed between 2002 and 2006 in ways that increased the amount of natural gas demanded at any given price. For one thing, the U.S. economy was much stronger in 2006 than in 2002. Figure 3-2 illustrates this phenomenon using the demand schedule and demand curve for natural gas. (As before, the numbers in Figure 3-2 are hypothetical.)

The table in Figure 3-2 shows two demand schedules. The first is the demand schedule for 2002, the same as shown in Figure 3-1. The second is the demand schedule for 2006. It differs from the 2002 schedule because of the stronger U.S. economy, leading to an increase in the quantity of natural gas demanded at any

---

GLOBAL COMPARISON **PAY MORE, PUMP LESS**

For a real-world illustration of the law of demand, consider how gasoline consumption varies according to the prices consumers pay at the pump. Because of high taxes, gasoline and diesel fuel are more than twice as expensive in most European countries and in many East Asian countries than in the United States. According to the law of demand, this should lead Europeans to buy less gasoline than Americans—and they do. As you can see from the figure, per person, Europeans consume less than half as much fuel as Americans, mainly because they drive smaller cars with better mileage.

Prices aren't the only factor affecting fuel consumption, but they're probably the main cause of the difference between European and American fuel consumption per person.

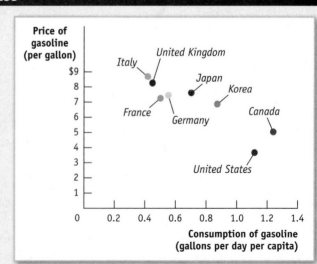

Data from: World Development Indicators and U.S. Energy Information Administration, 2013.

FIGURE 3-2 An Increase in Demand

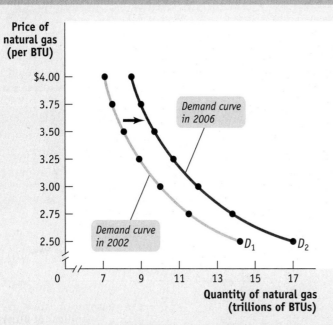

Demand Schedules for Natural Gas		
Price of natural gas (per BTU)	Quantity of natural gas demanded (trillions of BTUs)	
	in 2002	in 2006
$4.00	7.1	8.5
3.75	7.5	9.0
3.50	8.1	9.7
3.25	8.9	10.7
3.00	10.0	12.0
2.75	11.5	13.8
2.50	14.2	17.0

A strong economy is one factor that increases the demand for natural gas—a rise in the quantity demanded at any given price. This is represented by the two demand schedules—one showing the demand in 2002 when the economy was weak, the other showing the demand in 2006, when the economy was strong—and their corresponding demand curves. The increase in demand shifts the demand curve to the right.

given price. So, at each price the 2006 schedule shows a larger quantity demanded than the 2002 schedule. For example, the quantity of natural gas consumers wanted to buy at a price of $3 per BTU increased from 10 trillion to 12 trillion BTUs per year; the quantity demanded at $3.25 per BTU went from 8.9 trillion to 10.7 trillion, and so on.

What is clear from this example is that the changes that occurred between 2002 and 2006 generated a *new* demand schedule, one in which the quantity demanded was greater at any given price than in the original demand schedule. The two curves in Figure 3-2 show the same information graphically. As you can see, the demand schedule for 2006 corresponds to a new demand curve, D_2, that is to the right of the demand schedule for 2002, D_1. This **shift of the demand curve** shows the change in the quantity demanded at any given price, represented by the change in position of the original demand curve D_1 to its new location at D_2.

It's crucial to make the distinction between such shifts of the demand curve and **movements along the demand curve,** changes in the quantity demanded of a good arising from a change in that good's price. Figure 3-3 illustrates the difference.

The movement from point A to point B is a movement along the demand curve: the quantity demanded rises due to a fall in price as you move down D_1. Here, a fall in the price of natural gas from $3.50 to $3 per BTU generates a rise in the quantity demanded from 8.1 trillion to 10 trillion BTUs per year. But the quantity demanded can also rise when the price is unchanged if there is an *increase in demand*—a rightward shift of the demand curve. This is illustrated in Figure 3-3 by the shift of the demand curve from D_1 to D_2. Holding the price constant at $3.50 per BTU, the quantity demanded rises from 8.1 trillion BTUs at point A on D_1 to 9.7 trillion BTUs at point C on D_2.

A **shift of the demand curve** is a change in the quantity demanded at any given price, represented by the shift of the original demand curve to a new position, denoted by a new demand curve.

A **movement along the demand curve** is a change in the quantity demanded of a good arising from a change in the good's price.

FIGURE 3-3 Movement Along the Demand Curve versus Shift of the Demand Curve

The rise in quantity demanded when going from point *A* to point *B* reflects a movement along the demand curve: it is the result of a fall in the price of the good. The rise in quantity demanded when going from point *A* to point *C* reflects a shift of the demand curve: it is the result of a rise in the quantity demanded at any given price.

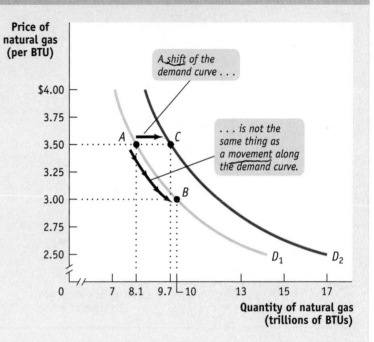

When economists say "the demand for *X* increased" or "the demand for *Y* decreased," they mean that the demand curve for *X* or *Y* shifted—not that the quantity demanded rose or fell because of a change in the price.

Understanding Shifts of the Demand Curve

Figure 3-4 illustrates the two basic ways in which demand curves can shift.

1. When economists talk about an *increase in demand*, they mean a *rightward* shift of the demand curve: at any given price, consumers demand a larger quantity of the good or service than before. This is shown by the rightward shift of the original demand curve D_1 to curve D_2.

2. When economists talk about a *decrease in demand*, they mean a *leftward* shift of the demand curve: at any given price, consumers demand a smaller quantity of the good or service than before. This is shown by the leftward shift of the original demand curve D_1 to curve D_3.

What caused the demand curve for natural gas to shift? As we mentioned earlier, the reason was the stronger U.S. economy in 2006 compared to 2002. If you think about it, you can come up with other factors that would be likely to shift the demand curve for natural gas. For example, suppose that the price of heating oil rises.

PITFALLS

DEMAND VERSUS QUANTITY DEMANDED

When economists say "an increase in demand," they mean a rightward shift of the demand curve, and when they say "a decrease in demand," they mean a leftward shift of the demand curve—that is, when they're being careful.

In ordinary speech most of us, professional economists included, use the word *demand* casually. For example, an economist might say "the demand for air travel has doubled over the past 15 years, partly because of falling airfares," when he or she really means that the *quantity demanded* has doubled.

This is OK in casual conversation. But when you're doing economic analysis, it's important to make the distinction between changes in the quantity demanded, which involve movements along a demand curve, and shifts of the demand curve (see Figure 3-3 for an illustration). Sometimes students end up writing something like this: "If demand increases, the price will go up, but that will lead to a fall in demand, which pushes the price down . . ." and then go around in circles.

By making a clear distinction between changes in *demand*, which mean shifts of the demand curve, and changes in *quantity demanded*, which means movement along the demand curve, you can avoid a lot of confusion.

FIGURE 3-4 Shifts of the Demand Curve

Any event that increases demand shifts the demand curve to the right, reflecting a rise in the quantity demanded at any given price. Any event that decreases demand shifts the demand curve to the left, reflecting a fall in the quantity demanded at any given price.

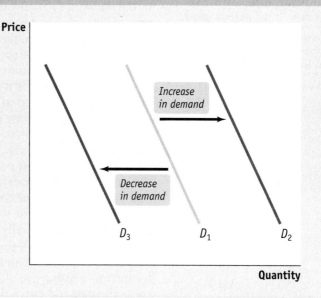

This will induce some consumers, who heat their homes and businesses in winter with heating oil, to switch to natural gas instead, increasing the demand for natural gas.

Economists believe that there are five principal factors that shift the demand curve for a good or service:

- Changes in the prices of related goods or services
- Changes in income
- Changes in tastes
- Changes in expectations
- Changes in the number of consumers

Although this is not an exhaustive list, it contains the five most important factors that can shift demand curves. When we say that the quantity of a good or service demanded falls as its price rises, *other things equal*, we are in fact stating that the factors that shift demand are remaining unchanged. Let's now explore how those factors shift the demand curve.

Changes in the Prices of Related Goods or Services Heating oil is what economists call a *substitute* for natural gas. A pair of goods are **substitutes** if a rise in the price of one good (heating oil) makes consumers more likely to buy the other good (natural gas). Substitutes are usually goods that in some way serve a similar function: coffee and tea, muffins and doughnuts, train rides and air flights. A rise in the price of the alternative good induces some consumers to purchase the original good *instead* of the substitute, shifting demand for the original good to the right.

But sometimes a rise in the price of one good makes consumers *less* willing to buy another good. Such pairs of goods are known as **complements.** Complements are usually goods that in some sense are consumed together: smartphones and apps, coffee and Egg McMuffins, and cars and gasoline. Because consumers like to consume a good and its complement together, a change in the price of one of the goods will affect the demand for its complement. In particular, when the price of one good rises, the demand for its complement decreases, shifting the demand curve for the complement to the left. So, for example, when the price of gasoline began to rise in 2009 from under $3 per gallon to close to $4 per gallon in 2011, the demand for gas-guzzling cars fell.

Two goods are **substitutes** if a rise in the price of one of the goods leads to an increase in the demand for the other good.

Two goods are **complements** if a rise in the price of one good leads to a decrease in the demand for the other good.

When a rise in income increases the demand for a good—the normal case—it is a **normal good.**

When a rise in income decreases the demand for a good, it is an **inferior good.**

Changes in Income Why did the stronger economy in 2006 lead to an increase in the demand for natural gas compared to the demand during the weak economy of 2002? It was because the economy was stronger and Americans had more income, making them more likely to purchase more of *most* goods and services at any given price. For example, with a higher income you are likely to keep your house warmer in the winter than if your income is low.

And, the demand for natural gas, a major source of fuel for electricity-generating power plants, is tied to the demand for other goods and services. For example, businesses must consume power to provide goods and services to households. So, when the economy is strong and household incomes are high, businesses will consume more electricity and, indirectly, more natural gas.

Why do we say that people are likely to purchase more of "most goods," not "all goods"? Most goods are **normal goods**—the demand for them increases when consumer income rises. However, the demand for some products falls when income rises. Goods for which demand decreases when income rises are known as **inferior goods.** Usually an inferior good is considered less desirable than more expensive alternatives—such as a bus ride versus a taxi ride. When they can afford to, people stop buying an inferior good and switch their consumption to the preferred, more expensive alternative. So, when a good is inferior, a rise in income shifts the demand curve to the left. And, not surprisingly, a fall in income shifts the demand curve to the right.

One example of the distinction between normal and inferior goods that has drawn attention in the business press is the difference between so-called casual-dining restaurants such as Chipotle's or Olive Garden and fast-food chains such as Burger King or McDonald's. When their incomes rise, Americans tend to eat out more at casual-dining restaurants. However, some of that increased dining out comes at the expense of fast-food venues—to some extent, people visit McDonald's less often once they can afford to move upscale. So casual dining is a normal good, whereas fast-food consumption appears to be an inferior good.

Changes in Tastes Why do people want what they want? Fortunately, we don't need to answer that question—we just need to acknowledge that people have certain preferences, or tastes, that determine what they choose to consume and that these tastes can change. Economists usually lump together changes in demand due to trends, beliefs, cultural shifts, and so on under the heading of changes in tastes or preferences.

For example, once upon a time men wore hats. Up until around World War II, a respectable man wasn't fully dressed unless he wore a dignified hat along with his suit. But after the war, returning troops adopted a more informal style, perhaps due to the rigors of the war. And President Eisenhower, who had been supreme commander of Allied Forces before becoming president, often went hatless. After World War II, it was clear that the demand curve for hats had shifted leftward, reflecting a decrease in the demand for hats.

Economists have relatively little to say about the forces that influence consumers' tastes. (Although marketers and advertisers have plenty to say about them!) However, a change in tastes does have a predictable impact on demand. When tastes change in favor of a good, more people want to buy it at any given price, so the demand curve shifts to the right. When tastes change against a good, fewer people want to buy it at any given price, so the demand curve shifts to the left.

Changes in Expectations When consumers have some choice about when to make a purchase, current demand for a good is often affected by expectations about its future price. For example, savvy shoppers often wait for seasonal sales— say, buying next year's holiday decorations during the post-holiday markdowns. In this case, expectations of a future drop in price lead to a decrease in demand today. Alternatively, expectations of a future rise in price are likely to cause an increase in demand today.

In addition, the fall in gas prices in recent years to around $2 per BTU has spurred more consumers to switch to natural gas from other fuel types than when natural gas fell to $2 per BTU in 2002. But why are consumers more willing to switch now? Because in 2002, consumers didn't expect the fall in the price of natural gas to last—and they were right.

In 2002, natural gas prices fell because of the weak economy. That situation changed in 2006 when the economy came roaring back and the price of natural gas rose dramatically. In contrast, consumers have come to expect that the more recent fall in the price of natural gas will not be temporary because it is based on a permanent change: the ability to tap much larger deposits of natural gas.

Expected changes in future income can also lead to changes in demand: if you expect your income to rise in the future, you will typically borrow today and increase your demand for certain goods; if you expect your income to fall in the future, you are likely to save today and reduce your demand for some goods.

Changes in the Number of Consumers Another factor that can cause a change in demand is a change in the number of consumers of a good or service. For example, population growth in the United States eventually leads to higher demand for natural gas as more homes and businesses need to be heated in the winter and cooled in the summer.

Let's introduce a new concept: the **individual demand curve,** which shows the relationship between quantity demanded and price for an individual consumer. For example, suppose that the Gonzalez family is a consumer of natural gas for heating and cooling their home. Panel (a) of Figure 3-5 shows how many BTUs of natural gas they will buy per year at any given price. The Gonzalez family's individual demand curve is $D_{Gonzalez}$.

The *market demand curve* shows how the combined quantity demanded by all consumers depends on the market price of the good. (Most of the time when

> An **individual demand curve** illustrates the relationship between quantity demanded and price for an individual consumer.

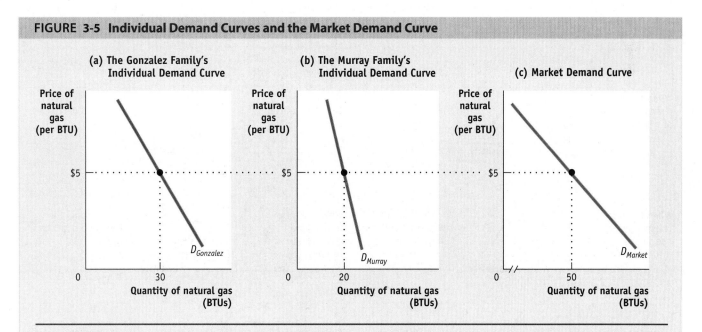

FIGURE 3-5 Individual Demand Curves and the Market Demand Curve

The Gonzalez family and the Murray family are the only two consumers of natural gas in the market. Panel (a) shows the Gonzalez family's individual demand curve: the number of BTUs they will buy per year at any given price. Panel (b) shows the Murray family's individual demand curve. Given that the Gonzalez family and the Murray family are the only two consumers, the *market demand curve*, which shows the quantity of BTUs demanded by all consumers at any given price, is shown in the panel (c). The market demand curve is the *horizontal sum* of the individual demand curves of all consumers. In this case, at any given price, the quantity demanded by the market is the sum of the quantities demanded by the Gonzalez family and the Murray family.

TABLE 3-1 Factors That Shift Demand

When this happens...	...demand increases	But when this happens...	...demand decreases
When the price of a substitute rises...	Price / Quantity / D_1 D_2 / ...demand for the original good increases.	When the price of a substitute falls...	Price / Quantity / D_2 D_1 / ...demand for the original good decreases.
When the price of a complement falls...	Price / Quantity / D_1 D_2 / ...demand for the original good increases.	When the price of a complement rises...	Price / Quantity / D_2 D_1 / ...demand for the original good decreases.
When income rises...	Price / Quantity / D_1 D_2 / ...demand for a normal good increases.	When income falls...	Price / Quantity / D_2 D_1 / ...demand for a normal good decreases.
When income falls...	Price / Quantity / D_1 D_2 / ...demand for an inferior good increases.	When income rises...	Price / Quantity / D_2 D_1 / ...demand for an inferior good decreases.
When tastes change in favor of a good...	Price / Quantity / D_1 D_2 / ...demand for the good increases.	When tastes change against a good...	Price / Quantity / D_2 D_1 / ...demand for the good decreases.
When the price is expected to rise in the future...	Price / Quantity / D_1 D_2 / ...demand for the good increases today.	When the price is expected to fall in the future...	Price / Quantity / D_2 D_1 / ...demand for the good decreases today.
When the number of consumers rises...	Price / Quantity / D_1 D_2 / ...market demand for the good increases.	When the number of consumers falls...	Price / Quantity / D_2 D_1 / ...market demand for the good decreases.

economists refer to the demand curve they mean the market demand curve.) The market demand curve is the *horizontal sum* of the individual demand curves of all consumers in that market.

To see what we mean by the term *horizontal sum*, assume for a moment that there are only two consumers of natural gas, the Gonzalez family and the Murray family. The Murray family consumes natural gas to fuel their natural gas–powered car. The Murray family's individual demand curve, D_{Murray}, is shown in panel (b). Panel (c) shows the market demand curve. At any given price, the quantity demanded by the market is the sum of the quantities demanded by the Gonzalez family and the Murray family. For example, at a price of $5 per BTU, the Gonzalez family demands 30 BTUs of natural gas per year and the Murray family demands 20 BTUs per year. So the quantity demanded by the market is 50 BTUs per year, as seen on the market demand curve, D_{Market}.

Clearly, the quantity demanded by the market at any given price is larger with the Murray family present than it would be if the Gonzalez family were the only consumer. The quantity demanded at any given price would be even larger if we added a third consumer, then a fourth, and so on. So an increase in the number of consumers leads to an increase in demand.

For a review of the factors that shift demand, see Table 3-1.

ECONOMICS >> *in Action*
Beating the Traffic

All big cities have traffic, and many local authorities try to discourage driving in the crowded city center. If we think of an auto trip to the city center as a good that people consume, we can use the economics of demand to analyze anti-traffic policies.

One common strategy is to reduce the demand for auto trips by lowering the prices of substitutes. Many metropolitan areas subsidize bus and rail service, hoping to lure commuters out of their cars. An alternative is to raise the price of complements: several major U.S. cities impose high taxes on commercial parking garages and impose short time limits on parking meters, both to raise revenue and to discourage people from driving into the city.

A few major cities—including Singapore, London, Oslo, Stockholm, and Milan—have been willing to adopt a direct and politically controversial approach: reducing congestion by raising the price of driving. Under *congestion pricing,* a charge is imposed on cars entering the city center during business hours. Drivers buy passes, which are then debited electronically as they drive by monitoring stations. Compliance is monitored with cameras that photograph license plates.

In 2012, Moscow adopted a modest charge for parking in certain areas in an attempt to reduce its traffic jams, considered the worst of all major cities. After the approximately $1.60 charge was applied, city officials estimated that Moscow traffic decreased by 4%.

The standard cost of driving into London is currently £11.50 (about $15). Drivers who don't pay and are caught pay a fine of £130 (about $170) for each transgression.

Not surprisingly, studies have shown that after the implementation of congestion pricing, traffic does decrease. In the 1990s, London had some of the worst traffic in Europe. The introduction of its congestion charge in 2003 immediately reduced traffic in the city center by about 15%. And there has been increased use of substitutes, such as public transportation, bicycles, and ride-sharing. From 2001 to 2011, bike trips in London increased by 79%, and bus usage was up by 30%.

And less congestion led not just to fewer accidents, but to a lower *rate* of accidents as fewer cars jostled for space. One study found that from 2000 to 2010 the

Cities can reduce traffic congestion by raising the price of driving.

>> Quick Review

• The **supply and demand model** is a model of a **competitive market**—one in which there are many buyers and sellers of the same good or service.

• The **demand schedule** shows how the **quantity demanded** changes as the price changes. A **demand curve** illustrates this relationship.

• The **law of demand** asserts that a higher price reduces the quantity demanded. Thus, demand curves normally slope downward.

• An increase in demand leads to a rightward **shift of the demand curve:** the quantity demanded rises for any given price. A decrease in demand leads to a leftward shift: the quantity demanded falls for any given price. A change in price results in a change in the quantity demanded and a **movement along the demand curve.**

• The five main factors that can shift the demand curve are changes in (1) the price of a related good, such as a **substitute** or a **complement,** (2) income, (3) tastes, (4) expectations, and (5) the number of consumers.

• The market demand curve is the horizontal sum of the **individual demand curves** of all consumers in the market.

number of accidents per mile driven in London fell by 40%. Stockholm experienced effects similar to those in London: traffic fell by 22% in 2013 compared to pre-congestion charge levels, transit times fell by one-third to one-half, and air quality measurably improved.

>> Check Your Understanding 3-1
Solutions appear at back of book.

1. Explain whether each of the following events represents (i) a *shift of* the demand curve or (ii) a *movement along* the demand curve.
   a. A store owner finds that customers are willing to pay more for umbrellas on rainy days.
   b. When Circus Cruise Lines offered reduced prices for summer cruises in the Caribbean, their number of bookings increased sharply.
   c. People buy more long-stem roses the week of Valentine's Day, even though the prices are higher than at other times during the year.
   d. A sharp rise in the price of gasoline leads many commuters to join carpools to reduce their gasoline purchases.

‖ The Supply Curve

Some deposits of natural gas are easier to tap than others. Before the widespread use of fracking, drillers would limit their natural gas wells to deposits that lay in easily reached pools beneath the earth. How much natural gas they would tap from existing wells, and how extensively they searched for new deposits and drilled new wells, depended on the price they expected to get for the natural gas. The higher the price, the more they would tap existing wells as well as drill and tap new wells.

So just as the quantity of natural gas that consumers want to buy depends upon the price they have to pay, the quantity that producers of natural gas, or of any good or service, are willing to produce and sell—the **quantity supplied**—depends upon the price they are offered.

The Supply Schedule and the Supply Curve

The table in Figure 3-6 shows how the quantity of natural gas made available varies with the price—that is, it shows a hypothetical **supply schedule** for natural gas.

A supply schedule works the same way as the demand schedule shown in Figure 3-1: in this case, the table shows the number of BTUs of natural gas that producers are willing to sell at different prices. At a price of $2.50 per BTU, producers are willing to sell only 8 trillion BTUs of natural gas per year. At $2.75 per BTU, they're willing to sell 9.1 trillion BTUs. At $3, they're willing to sell 10 trillion BTUs, and so on.

In the same way that a demand schedule can be represented graphically by a demand curve, a supply schedule can be represented by a **supply curve,** as shown in Figure 3-6. Each point on the curve represents an entry from the table.

Suppose that the price of natural gas rises from $3 to $3.25; we can see that the quantity of natural gas that producers are willing to sell rises from 10 trillion to 10.7 trillion BTUs. This is the normal situation for a supply curve, that a higher price leads to a higher quantity supplied. So just as demand curves normally slope downward, supply curves normally slope upward: the higher the price being offered, the more of any good or service producers will be willing to sell.

The **quantity supplied** is the actual amount of a good or service people are willing to sell at some specific price.

A **supply schedule** shows how much of a good or service would be supplied at different prices.

A **supply curve** shows the relationship between quantity supplied and price.

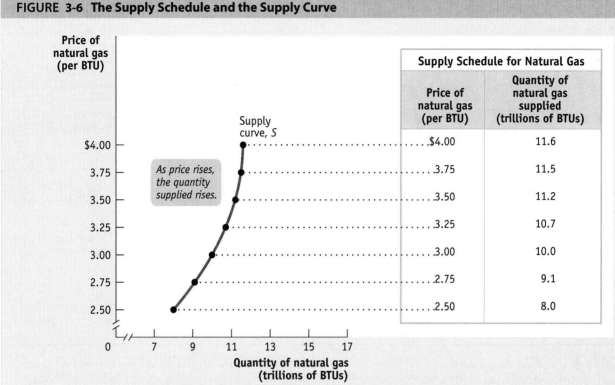

FIGURE 3-6 The Supply Schedule and the Supply Curve

The supply schedule for natural gas is plotted to yield the corresponding supply curve, which shows how much of a good producers are willing to sell at any given price. The supply curve and the supply schedule reflect the fact that supply curves are usually upward sloping: the quantity supplied rises when the price rises.

Shifts of the Supply Curve

Innovations in the technology of drilling natural gas deposits have led to a huge increase in U.S. production of natural gas—a 40% increase in daily production from 2005 through 2014. Figure 3-7 illustrates these events in terms of the supply schedule and the supply curve for natural gas. The table in Figure 3-7 shows two supply schedules. The schedule before improved natural gas–drilling technology was adopted is the same one as in Figure 3-6. The second schedule shows the supply of natural gas *after* the improved technology was adopted.

Just as a change in demand schedules leads to a shift of the demand curve, a change in supply schedules leads to a **shift of the supply curve**—a change in the quantity supplied at any given price. This is shown in Figure 3-7 by the shift of the supply curve before the adoption of new natural gas–drilling technology, S_1, to its new position after the adoption of new natural gas–drilling technology, S_2. Notice that S_2 lies to the right of S_1, a reflection of the fact that quantity supplied rises at any given price.

As in the analysis of demand, it's crucial to draw a distinction between such shifts of the supply curve and **movements along the supply curve**—changes in the quantity supplied arising from a change in price. We can see this difference in Figure 3-8. The movement from point A to point B is a movement along the supply curve: the quantity supplied rises along S_1 due to a rise in price. Here, a rise in price from $3 to $3.50 leads to a rise in the quantity supplied from 10 trillion to 11.2 trillion BTUs of natural gas. But the quantity supplied can also rise when the

A **shift of the supply curve** is a change in the quantity supplied of a good or service at any given price. It is represented by the change of the original supply curve to a new position, denoted by a new supply curve.

A **movement along the supply curve** is a change in the quantity supplied of a good arising from a change in the good's price.

FIGURE 3-7 An Increase in Supply

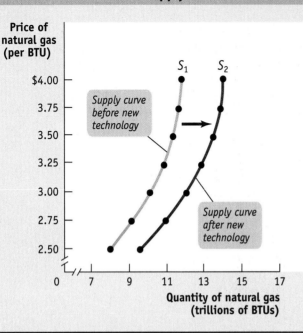

Supply Schedules for Natural Gas		
Price of natural gas (per BTU)	Quantity of natural gas supplied (trillions of BTUs)	
	Before new technology	After new technology
$4.00	11.6	13.9
3.75	11.5	13.8
3.50	11.2	13.4
3.25	10.7	12.8
3.00	10.0	12.0
2.75	9.1	10.9
2.50	8.0	9.6

The adoption of an improved natural gas–drilling technology generated an increase in supply–a rise in the quantity supplied at any given price. This event is represented by the two supply schedules–one showing supply before the new technology was adopted, the other showing supply after the new technology was adopted–and their corresponding supply curves. The increase in supply shifts the supply curve to the right.

price is unchanged if there is an increase in supply—a rightward shift of the supply curve. This is shown by the rightward shift of the supply curve from S_1 to S_2. Holding the price constant at $3, the quantity supplied rises from 10 trillion BTUs at point A on S_1 to 12 billion BTUs at point C on S_2.

FIGURE 3-8 Movement Along the Supply Curve versus Shift of the Supply Curve

The increase in quantity supplied when going from point A to point B reflects a movement along the supply curve: it is the result of a rise in the price of a good. The increase in quantity supplied when going from point A to point C reflects a shift of the supply curve: it is the result of an increase in the quantity supplied at any given price.

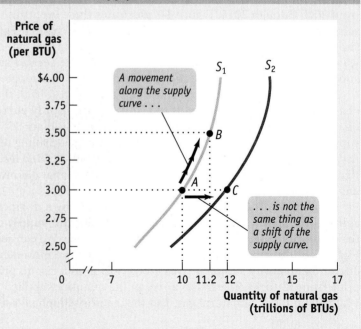

Understanding Shifts of the Supply Curve

Figure 3-9 illustrates the two basic ways in which supply curves can shift. When economists talk about an "increase in supply," they mean a *rightward* shift of the supply curve: at any given price, producers supply a larger quantity of the good than before. This is shown in Figure 3-9 by the rightward shift of the original supply curve S_1 to S_2. And when economists talk about a "decrease in supply," they mean a *leftward* shift of the supply curve: at any given price, producers supply a smaller quantity of the good than before. This is represented by the leftward shift of S_1 to S_3.

Economists believe that shifts of the supply curve for a good or service are mainly the result of five factors (though, as with demand, there are other possible causes):

- Changes in input prices
- Changes in the prices of related goods or services
- Changes in technology
- Changes in expectations
- Changes in the number of producers

Changes in Input Prices To produce output, you need inputs. For example, to make vanilla ice cream, you need vanilla beans, cream, sugar, and so on. An **input** is any good or service that is used to produce another good or service. Inputs, like outputs, have prices. And an increase in the price of an input makes the production of the final good more costly for those who produce and sell it. So producers are less willing to supply the final good at any given price, and the supply curve shifts to the left. That is, supply decreases. For example, fuel is a major cost for airlines. When oil prices surged in 2007–2008, airlines began cutting back on their flight schedules and some went out of business.

Similarly, a fall in the price of an input makes the production of the final good less costly for sellers. They are more willing to supply the good at any given price, and the supply curve shifts to the right. That is, supply increases.

Changes in the Prices of Related Goods or Services A single producer often produces a mix of goods rather than a single product. For example, an oil

> An **input** is a good or service that is used to produce another good or service.

FIGURE 3-9 Shifts of the Supply Curve

Any event that increases supply shifts the supply curve to the right, reflecting a rise in the quantity supplied at any given price. Any event that decreases supply shifts the supply curve to the left, reflecting a fall in the quantity supplied at any given price.

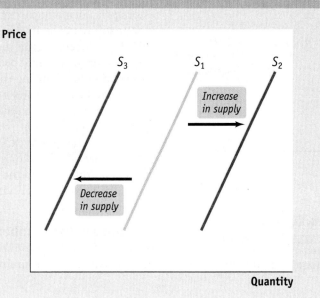

refinery produces gasoline from crude oil, but it also produces heating oil and other products from the same raw material. When a producer sells several products, the quantity of any one good it is willing to supply at any given price depends on the prices of its other co-produced goods.

This effect can run in either direction. An oil refiner will supply less gasoline at any given price when the price of heating oil rises, shifting the supply curve for gasoline to the left. But it will supply more gasoline at any given price when the price of heating oil falls, shifting the supply curve for gasoline to the right. This means that gasoline and other co-produced oil products are *substitutes in production* for refiners.

In contrast, due to the nature of the production process, other goods can be *complements in production*. Producers of natural gas often find that natural gas wells also produce oil as a by-product of extraction. The higher the price at which a driller can sell its oil, the more willing it will be to drill natural gas wells and the more natural gas it will supply at any given price. Higher oil prices then lead to more natural gas supplied at any given price because oil and natural gas can be tapped simultaneously. As a result, oil is a complement in the production of natural gas. The reverse is also true: natural gas is a complement in the production of oil.

Changes in Technology As the opening story illustrates, changes in technology affect the supply curve. Technology improvements enable producers to spend less on inputs (in this case, drilling equipment, labor, land purchases, and so on), yet still produce the same amount of output. When a better technology becomes available reducing the cost of production, supply increases and the supply curve shifts to the right.

Improved technology enabled natural gas producers to more than double output in less than two years. Technology is also the main reason that natural gas has remained relatively cheap, even as demand has grown.

Changes in Expectations Just as changes in expectations can shift the demand curve, they can also shift the supply curve. When suppliers have some choice about when they put their good up for sale, changes in the expected future price of the good can lead a supplier to supply less or more of the good today.

Consider the fact that gasoline and other oil products are often stored for significant periods of time at oil refineries before being sold to consumers. In fact, storage is normally part of producers' business strategy. Knowing that the demand for gasoline peaks in the summer, oil refiners normally store some of their gasoline produced during the spring for summer sale. Similarly, knowing that the demand for heating oil peaks in the winter, they normally store some of their heating oil produced during the fall for winter sale.

In each case, there's a decision to be made between selling the product now versus storing it for later sale. The choice a producer makes depends on a comparison of the current price and the expected future price. This example illustrates how changes in expectations can alter supply: an increase in the anticipated future price of a good or service reduces supply today, a leftward shift of the supply curve. But a fall in the anticipated future price increases supply today, a rightward shift of the supply curve.

An **individual supply curve** illustrates the relationship between quantity supplied and price for an individual producer.

Changes in the Number of Producers Just as changes in the number of consumers affect the demand curve, changes in the number of producers affect the supply curve. Let's examine the **individual supply curve,** by looking at panel (a)

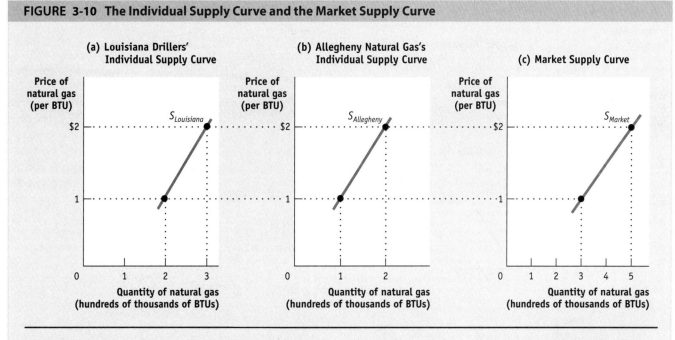

FIGURE 3-10 The Individual Supply Curve and the Market Supply Curve

Panel (a) shows the individual supply curve for Louisiana Drillers $S_{Louisiana}$, the quantity it will sell at any given price. Panel (b) shows the individual supply curve for Allegheny Natural Gas, $S_{Allegheny}$. The market supply curve, which shows the quantity of natural gas supplied by all producers at any given price is shown in panel (c). The market supply curve is the horizontal sum of the individual supply curves of all producers.

in Figure 3-10. The individual supply curve shows the relationship between quantity supplied and price for an individual producer. For example, suppose that Louisiana Drillers is a natural gas producer and that panel (a) of Figure 3-10 shows the quantity of BTUs it will supply per year at any given price. Then $S_{Louisiana}$ is its individual supply curve.

The *market supply curve* shows how the combined total quantity supplied by all individual producers in the market depends on the market price of that good. Just as the market demand curve is the horizontal sum of the individual demand curves of all consumers, the market supply curve is the horizontal sum of the individual supply curves of all producers. Assume for a moment that there are only two natural gas producers, Louisiana Drillers and Allegheny Natural Gas. Allegheny's individual supply curve is shown in panel (b). Panel (c) shows the market supply curve. At any given price, the quantity supplied to the market is the sum of the quantities supplied by Louisiana Drillers and Allegheny Natural Gas. For example, at a price of $1 per BTU, Louisiana Drillers supplies 200,000 BTUs and Allegheny Natural Gas supplies 100,000 BTUs per year, making the quantity supplied to the market 300,000 BTUs.

Clearly, the quantity supplied to the market at any given price is larger when Allegheny Natural Gas is also a producer than it would be if Louisiana Drillers were the only supplier. The quantity supplied at a given price would be even larger if we added a third producer, then a fourth, and so on. So an increase in the number of producers leads to an increase in supply and a rightward shift of the supply curve.

For a review of the factors that shift supply, see Table 3-2.

TABLE 3-2 Factors That Shift Supply

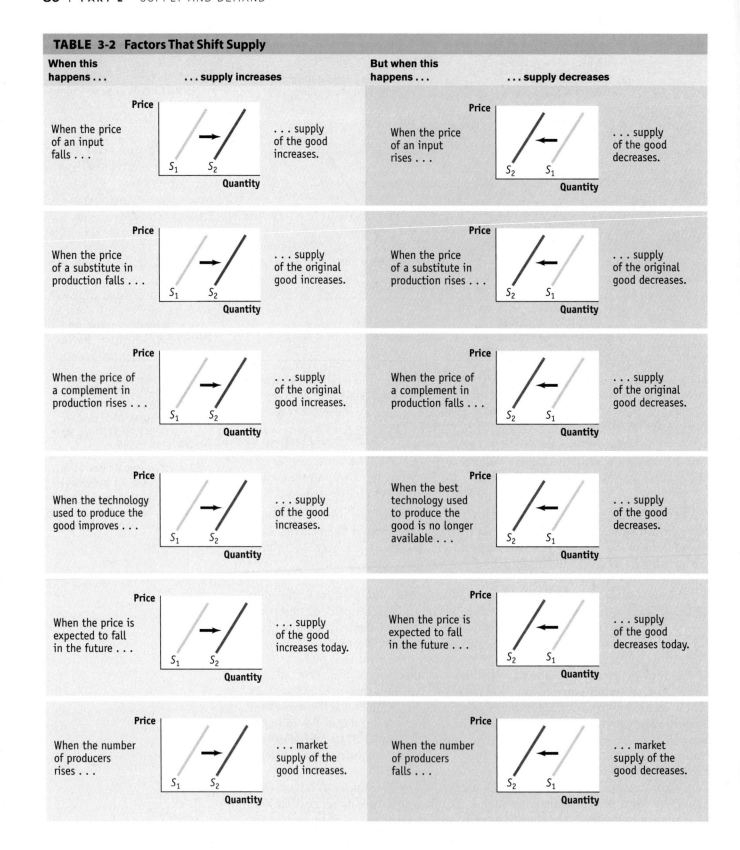

When this happens . . .	. . . supply increases	But when this happens . . .	. . . supply decreases
When the price of an input falls . . .	. . . supply of the good increases.	When the price of an input rises . . .	. . . supply of the good decreases.
When the price of a substitute in production falls . . .	. . . supply of the original good increases.	When the price of a substitute in production rises . . .	. . . supply of the original good decreases.
When the price of a complement in production rises . . .	. . . supply of the original good increases.	When the price of a complement in production falls . . .	. . . supply of the original good decreases.
When the technology used to produce the good improves . . .	. . . supply of the good increases.	When the best technology used to produce the good is no longer available . . .	. . . supply of the good decreases.
When the price is expected to fall in the future . . .	. . . supply of the good increases today.	When the price is expected to fall in the future . . .	. . . supply of the good decreases today.
When the number of producers rises . . .	. . . market supply of the good increases.	When the number of producers falls . . .	. . . market supply of the good decreases.

1. Explain whether each of the following events represents (i) a *shift of* the supply curve or (ii) a *movement along* the supply curve.
   a. More homeowners put their houses up for sale during a real estate boom that causes house prices to rise.
   b. Many strawberry farmers open temporary roadside stands during harvest season, even though prices are usually low at that time.
   c. Immediately after the school year begins, fast-food chains must raise wages, which represent the price of labor, to attract workers.
   d. Many construction workers temporarily move to areas that have suffered hurricane damage, lured by higher wages.
   e. Since new technologies have made it possible to build larger cruise ships (which are cheaper to run per passenger), Caribbean cruise lines offer more cabins, at lower prices, than before.

Supply, Demand, and Equilibrium

We have now covered the first three key elements in the supply and demand model: the demand curve, the supply curve, and the set of factors that shift each curve. The next step is to put these elements together to show how they can be used to predict the actual price at which the good is bought and sold, as well as the actual quantity transacted.

What determines the price at which a good or service is bought and sold? What determines the quantity transacted of the good or service? In Chapter 1 we learned the general principle that *markets move toward equilibrium*, a situation in which no individual would be better off taking a different action. In the case of a competitive market, we can be more specific: a competitive market is in equilibrium when the price has moved to a level at which the quantity of a good demanded equals the quantity of that good supplied. At that price, no individual seller could make herself better off by offering to sell either more or less of the good and no individual buyer could make himself better off by offering to buy more or less of the good. In other words, at the market equilibrium, price has moved to a level that exactly matches the quantity demanded by consumers to the quantity supplied by sellers.

The price that matches the quantity supplied and the quantity demanded is the **equilibrium price;** the quantity bought and sold at that price is the **equilibrium quantity.** The equilibrium price is also known as the **market-clearing price:** it is the price that "clears the market" by ensuring that every buyer willing to pay that price finds a seller willing to sell at that price, and vice versa. So how do we find the equilibrium price and quantity?

Finding the Equilibrium Price and Quantity

The easiest way to determine the equilibrium price and quantity in a market is by putting the supply curve and the demand curve on the same diagram. Since the supply curve shows the quantity supplied at any given price and the demand curve shows the quantity demanded at any given price, the price at which the two curves cross is the equilibrium price: the price at which quantity supplied equals quantity demanded.

Figure 3-11 combines the demand curve from Figure 3-1 and the supply curve from Figure 3-6. They *intersect* at point E, which is the equilibrium of this market; $3 is the equilibrium price and 10 trillion BTUs is the equilibrium quantity.

A competitive market is in equilibrium when price has moved to a level at which the quantity of a good or service demanded equals the quantity of that good or service supplied. The price at which this takes place is the **equilibrium price,** also referred to as the **market-clearing price.** The quantity of the good or service bought and sold at that price is the **equilibrium quantity.**

FIGURE 3-11 Market Equilibrium

Market equilibrium occurs at point *E*, where the supply curve and the demand curve intersect. In equilibrium, the quantity demanded is equal to the quantity supplied. In this market, the equilibrium price is $3 per BTU and the equilibrium quantity is 10 trillion BTUs per year.

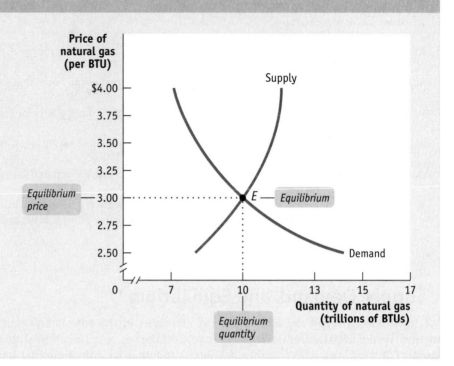

Let's confirm that point *E* fits our definition of equilibrium. At a price of $3 per BTU, natural gas producers are willing to sell 10 trillion BTUs a year and natural gas consumers want to buy 10 trillion BTUs a year. So at the price of $3 per BTU, the quantity of natural gas supplied equals the quantity demanded. Notice that at any other price the market would not clear: every willing buyer would not be able to find a willing seller, or vice versa. More specifically, if the price were more than $3, the quantity supplied would exceed the quantity demanded; if the price were less than $3, the quantity demanded would exceed the quantity supplied.

The model of supply and demand, then, predicts that given the demand and supply curves shown in Figure 3-11, 10 trillion BTUs would change hands at a price of $3 per BTU. But how can we be sure that the market will arrive at the equilibrium price? We begin by answering three simple questions:

1. Why do all sales and purchases in a market take place at the same price?
2. Why does the market price fall if it is above the equilibrium price?
3. Why does the market price rise if it is below the equilibrium price?

1. Why Do All Sales and Purchases in a Market Take Place at the Same Price?
There are some markets in which the same good can sell for many different prices, depending on who is selling or who is buying. For example, have you ever bought a souvenir in a tourist trap and then seen the same item on sale somewhere else for a lower price? Because tourists don't know which shops offer the best deals and don't have time for comparison shopping, sellers in tourist areas can charge different prices for the same good.

But in any market in which both buyers and sellers have been around for some time, sales and purchases tend to converge at a generally uniform price, so we can safely talk about *the* market price. It's easy to see why. Suppose a seller offered a potential buyer a price noticeably above what the buyer knew other people to be paying. The buyer would clearly be better off shopping elsewhere—unless the seller were prepared to offer a better deal.

Conversely, a seller would not be willing to sell for significantly less than the amount he knew most buyers were paying; he would be better off waiting to get a more reasonable customer. Thus, in any well-established, ongoing market, all sellers receive and all buyers pay approximately the same price. This is what we call the *market price.*

2. Why Does the Market Price Fall if It Is Above the Equilibrium Price?

Suppose the supply and demand curves are as shown in Figure 3-11 but the market price is above the equilibrium level of $3—say, $3.50. This situation is illustrated in Figure 3-12. Why can't the price stay there?

As the figure shows, at a price of $3.50 there would be more BTUs of natural gas available than consumers wanted to buy: 11.2 trillion BTUs versus 8.1 trillion BTUs. The difference of 3.1 trillion BTUs is the **surplus**—also known as the *excess supply*—of natural gas at $3.50.

This surplus means that some natural gas producers are frustrated: at the current price, they cannot find consumers who want to buy their natural gas. The surplus offers an incentive for those frustrated would-be sellers to offer a lower price to poach business from other producers and entice more consumers to buy. The result of this price cutting will be to push the prevailing price down until it reaches the equilibrium price. So the price of a good will fall whenever there is a surplus—that is, whenever the market price is above its equilibrium level.

3. Why Does the Market Price Rise if It Is Below the Equilibrium Price?

Now suppose the price is below its equilibrium level—say, at $2.75 per BTU, as shown in Figure 3-13. In this case, the quantity demanded, 11.5 trillion BTUs, exceeds the quantity supplied, 9.1 trillion BTUs, implying that there are

There is a **surplus** of a good or service when the quantity supplied exceeds the quantity demanded. Surpluses occur when the price is above its equilibrium level.

FIGURE 3-12 Price Above Its Equilibrium Level Creates a Surplus

The market price of $3.50 is above the equilibrium price of $3. This creates a surplus: at a price of $3.50, producers would like to sell 11.2 trillion BTUs but consumers want to buy only 8.1 trillion BTUs, so there is a surplus of 3.1 trillion BTUs. This surplus will push the price down until it reaches the equilibrium price of $3.

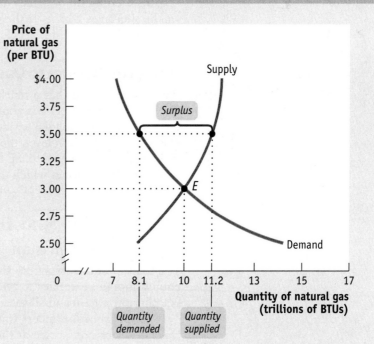

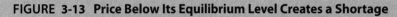

FIGURE 3-13 Price Below Its Equilibrium Level Creates a Shortage

The market price of $2.75 is below the equilibrium price of $3. This creates a shortage: consumers want to buy 11.5 trillion BTUs, but only 9.1 trillion BTUs are for sale, so there is a shortage of 2.4 trillion BTUs. This shortage will push the price up until it reaches the equilibrium price of $3.

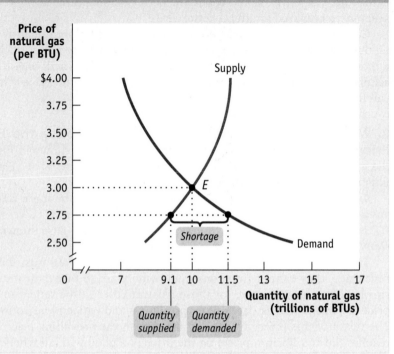

There is a **shortage** of a good or service when the quantity demanded exceeds the quantity supplied. Shortages occur when the price is below its equilibrium level.

would-be buyers who cannot find natural gas: there is a **shortage,** also known as an *excess demand,* of 2.4 trillion BTUs.

When there is a shortage, there are frustrated would-be buyers—people who want to purchase natural gas but cannot find willing sellers at the current price. In this situation, either buyers will offer more than the prevailing price or sellers will realize that they can charge higher prices. Either way, the result is to drive up the prevailing price.

This bidding up of prices happens whenever there are shortages—and there will be shortages whenever the price is below its equilibrium level. So the market price will always rise if it is below the equilibrium level.

Using Equilibrium to Describe Markets

We have now seen that a market tends to have a single price, the equilibrium price. If the market price is above the equilibrium level, the ensuing surplus leads buyers and sellers to take actions that lower the price. And if the market price is below the equilibrium level, the ensuing shortage leads buyers and sellers to take actions that raise the price. So the market price always *moves toward* the equilibrium price, the price at which there is neither surplus nor shortage.

ECONOMICS >> *in Action*
The Price of Admission

The market equilibrium, so the theory goes, is pretty egalitarian because the equilibrium price applies to everyone. That is, all buyers pay the same price—the equilibrium price—and all sellers receive that same price. But is this realistic?

The market for concert tickets is an example that seems to contradict the theory—there's one price at the box office, and there's another price (typically much higher) for the same event online where people who already have tickets resell them, such as StubHub.com eBay owns StubHub. For example, compare the box office price for a Demi Lovato concert in Nashville, Tennessee, in March 2018 to the StubHub price for seats in the same location: $95.45 versus $169.98.

Puzzling as this may seem, there is no contradiction once we take opportunity costs and tastes into account. For major events, buying tickets from the box office can mean waiting in very long lines. Ticket buyers who use online resellers have decided that the opportunity cost of their time is too high to spend waiting in line. And tickets for major events being sold at face value by online box offices often sell out within minutes. In this case, some people who want to go to the concert badly but have missed out on the opportunity to buy cheaper tickets from the online box office are willing to pay the higher online reseller price.

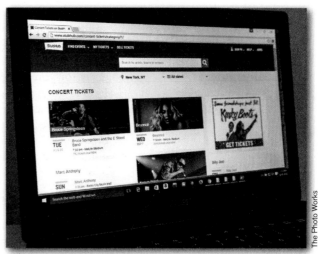

The competitive market model determines the price you pay for concert tickets.

Not only that, by comparing prices across sellers for seats close to one another, you can see that markets really do move to equilibrium. For example, for a seat in Section 107, Row 3, StubHub's price is $169.99 while ScoreBig's price for a nearby seat is $168. As the competitive market model predicts, units of the same good will end up selling for approximately the same price.

In fact, e-commerce is making markets move to equilibrium more quickly by doing the price comparisons for you. The website SeatGeek compares ticket prices across more than 100 ticket resellers, allowing customers to instantly choose the best deal. Tickets that are priced lower than those of competitors will be up, while higher-priced tickets will languish unsold.

And tickets on StubHub can sell for less than the face value for events with little appeal, while they can skyrocket for events in high demand. For example, in 2016 some fans paid over $20,000 to watch the Chicago Cubs win their first World Series Championship in 108 years. Even StubHub's chief executive says the site is "the embodiment of supply-and-demand economics."

So the theory of competitive markets isn't just speculation. If you want to experience it for yourself, try buying tickets to a concert (or the World Series).

>> Check Your Understanding 3-3

Solutions appear at back of book.

1. In the following three situations, the market is initially in equilibrium. Explain the changes in either supply or demand that result from each event. After each event described below, does a surplus or shortage exist at the original equilibrium price? What will happen to the equilibrium price as a result?
   a. 2015 was a very good year for California wine-grape growers, who produced a bumper crop.
   b. After a hurricane, Florida hoteliers often find that many people cancel their upcoming vacations, leaving them with empty hotel rooms.
   c. After a heavy snowfall, many people want to buy second-hand snowblowers at the local tool shop.

>> Quick Review

• Price in a competitive market moves to the **equilibrium price,** or **market-clearing price,** where the quantity supplied is equal to the quantity demanded. This quantity is the **equilibrium quantity.**

• All sales and purchases in a market take place at the same price. If the price is above its equilibrium level, there is a **surplus** that drives the price down to the equilibrium level. If the price is below its equilibrium level, there is a **shortage** that drives the price up to the equilibrium level.

Changes in Supply and Demand

The huge fall in the price of natural gas from $14 to $2 per BTU from 2006 to 2013 may have come as a surprise to consumers, but to suppliers it was no surprise at all. Suppliers knew that advances in drilling technology had opened up vast reserves of natural gas that had been too costly to tap in the past. And, predictably, an increase in supply reduces the equilibrium price.

The adoption of improved drilling technology is an example of an event that shifted the supply curve for a good without having an effect on the demand curve. There are many such events. There are also events that shift the demand curve without shifting the supply curve. For example, a medical report that chocolate is good for you increases the demand for chocolate but does not affect the supply. Events often shift either the supply curve or the demand curve, but not both; it is therefore useful to ask what happens in each case.

We have seen that when a curve shifts, the equilibrium price and quantity change. We will now concentrate on exactly how the shift of a curve alters the equilibrium price and quantity.

What Happens When the Demand Curve Shifts

Heating oil and natural gas are substitutes: if the price of heating oil rises, the demand for natural gas will increase, and if the price of heating oil falls, the demand for natural gas will decrease. But how does the price of heating oil affect the *market equilibrium* for natural gas?

Figure 3-14 shows the effect of a rise in the price of heating oil on the market for natural gas. The rise in the price of heating oil increases the demand for natural gas. Point E_1 shows the equilibrium corresponding to the original demand curve, with P_1 the equilibrium price and Q_1 the equilibrium quantity bought and sold.

An increase in demand is indicated by a *rightward* shift of the demand curve from D_1 to D_2. At the original market price P_1, this market is no longer in equilibrium: a shortage occurs because the quantity demanded exceeds the quantity supplied. So the price of natural gas rises and generates an increase in the quantity supplied, an upward *movement along the supply curve*. A new equilibrium is established at point E_2, with a higher equilibrium price, P_2, and higher equilibrium quantity, Q_2. This sequence of events reflects a general principle: *When demand for a good or service increases, the equilibrium price and the equilibrium quantity of the good or service both rise.*

What would happen in the reverse case, a fall in the price of heating oil? A fall in the price of heating oil reduces the demand for natural gas, shifting the

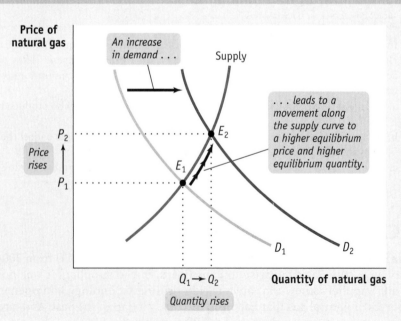

FIGURE 3-14 Equilibrium and Shifts of the Demand Curve

The original equilibrium in the market for natural gas is at E_1, at the intersection of the supply curve and the original demand curve, D_1. A rise in the price of heating oil, a substitute, shifts the demand curve rightward to D_2. A shortage exists at the original price, P_1, causing both the price and quantity supplied to rise, a movement along the supply curve. A new equilibrium is reached at E_2, with a higher equilibrium price, P_2, and a higher equilibrium quantity, Q_2. When demand for a good or service increases, the equilibrium price and the equilibrium quantity of the good or service both rise.

demand curve to the *left*. At the original price, a surplus occurs as quantity supplied exceeds quantity demanded. The price falls and leads to a decrease in the quantity supplied, resulting in a lower equilibrium price and a lower equilibrium quantity. This illustrates another general principle: *When demand for a good or service decreases, the equilibrium price and the equilibrium quantity of the good or service both fall.*

To summarize how a market responds to a change in demand: *An increase in demand leads to a rise in both the equilibrium price and the equilibrium quantity. A decrease in demand leads to a fall in both the equilibrium price and the equilibrium quantity.*

What Happens When the Supply Curve Shifts

For most goods and services, it is a bit easier to predict changes in supply than changes in demand. Physical factors that affect supply, like weather or the availability of inputs, are easier to get a handle on than the fickle tastes that affect demand. Still, with supply as with demand, what we can best predict are the *effects* of shifts of the supply curve.

As we mentioned in the opening story, improved drilling technology significantly increased the supply of natural gas from 2006 onward. Figure 3-15 shows how this shift affected the market equilibrium. The original equilibrium is at E_1, the point of intersection of the original supply curve, S_1, with an equilibrium price P_1 and equilibrium quantity Q_1. As a result of the improved technology, supply increases and S_1 shifts *rightward* to S_2. At the original price P_1, a surplus of natural gas now exists and the market is no longer in equilibrium. The surplus causes a fall in price and an increase in the quantity demanded, a *downward movement along the demand curve*. The new equilibrium is at E_2, with an equilibrium price P_2 and an equilibrium quantity Q_2. In the new equilibrium E_2, the price is lower and the equilibrium quantity is higher than before. This can be stated as a general principle: *When supply of a good or service increases, the equilibrium price of the good or service falls and the equilibrium quantity of the good or service rises.*

What happens to the market when supply falls? A fall in supply leads to a *leftward* shift of the supply curve. At the original price a shortage now exists. As a result, the equilibrium price rises and the quantity demanded falls. This describes

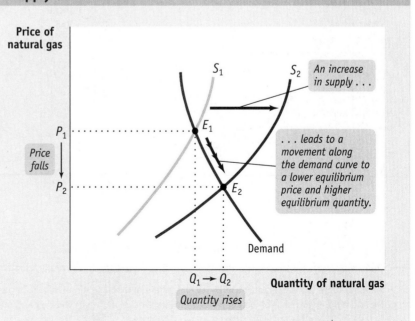

FIGURE 3-15 Equilibrium and Shifts of the Supply Curve

The original equilibrium in the market is at E_1. Improved technology causes an increase in the supply of natural gas and shifts the supply curve rightward from S_1 to S_2. A new equilibrium is established at E_2, with a lower equilibrium price, P_2, and a higher equilibrium quantity, Q_2.

Price of natural gas

S_1

S_2 An increase in supply . . .

E_1

P_1

Price falls

. . . leads to a movement along the demand curve to a lower equilibrium price and higher equilibrium quantity.

P_2

E_2

Demand

$Q_1 \rightarrow Q_2$ **Quantity of natural gas**

Quantity rises

PITFALLS

WHICH CURVE IS IT?

When the price of a good or service changes, in general, we can say that this reflects a change in either supply or demand. But which one is it? A helpful clue is the direction of change in the quantity. If the quantity sold changes in the *same* direction as the price—for example, if both the price and the quantity rise—it is likely that the demand curve has shifted. If the price and the quantity move in *opposite* directions, the likely cause is a shift of the supply curve.

what happened to the market for natural gas after Hurricane Katrina damaged natural gas production in the Gulf of Mexico in 2005. We can formulate a general principle: *When supply of a good or service decreases, the equilibrium price of the good or service rises and the equilibrium quantity of the good or service falls.*

To summarize how a market responds to a change in supply: *An increase in supply leads to a fall in the equilibrium price and a rise in the equilibrium quantity. A decrease in supply leads to a rise in the equilibrium price and a fall in the equilibrium quantity.*

Simultaneous Shifts of Supply and Demand Curves

Finally, it sometimes happens that events shift *both* the demand and supply curves at the same time. This is not unusual; in real life, supply curves and demand curves for many goods and services shift quite often because the economic environment continually changes.

Figure 3-16 illustrates two examples of simultaneous shifts. In both panels there is an increase in supply—that is, a rightward shift of the supply curve from S_1 to S_2—representing, for example, adoption of an improved drilling technology. Notice that the rightward shift in panel (a) is smaller than the one in panel (b): we can suppose that panel (a) represents a small, incremental change in technology while panel (b) represents a big advance in technology.

Both panels show a decrease in demand—that is, a leftward shift from D_1 to D_2. Also notice that the leftward shift in panel (a) is relatively larger than the one in panel (b): we can suppose that panel (a) reflects the effect on demand of a deep recession in the overall economy, while panel (b) reflects the effect of a mild winter.

In both cases the equilibrium price falls from P_1 to P_2 as the equilibrium moves from E_1 to E_2. But what happens to the equilibrium quantity, the quantity of natural gas bought and sold? In panel (a) the decrease in demand is large relative to the increase in supply, and the equilibrium quantity falls as a result. In panel (b) the increase in supply is large relative to the decrease in demand, and the equilibrium

FIGURE 3-16 Simultaneous Shifts of the Demand and Supply Curves

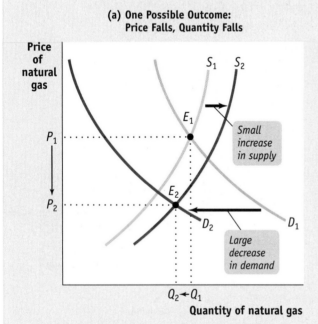

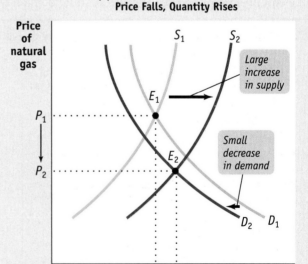

In panel (a) there is a simultaneous leftward shift of the demand curve and a rightward shift of the supply curve. Here the decrease in demand is relatively larger than the increase in supply, so the equilibrium quantity falls as the equilibrium price

also falls. In panel (b) there is also a simultaneous leftward shift of the demand curve and rightward shift of the supply curve. Here the increase in supply is large relative to the decrease in demand, so the equilibrium quantity rises as the equilibrium price falls.

quantity rises as a result. That is, when demand decreases and supply increases, the actual quantity bought and sold can go either way, depending on *how much* the demand and supply curves have shifted.

In general, when supply and demand shift in opposite directions, we can't predict what the ultimate effect will be on the quantity bought and sold. What we can say is that a curve that shifts a disproportionately greater distance than the other curve will have a disproportionately greater effect on the quantity bought and sold. That said, we can make the following prediction about the outcome when the supply and demand curves shift in opposite directions:

- When demand decreases and supply increases, the equilibrium price falls but the change in the equilibrium quantity is ambiguous.
- When demand increases and supply decreases, the equilibrium price rises but the change in the equilibrium quantity is ambiguous.

But suppose that the demand and supply curves shift in the same direction. This is what has happened in the United States, as the economy made a gradual recovery from the recession of 2008, resulting in an increase in both demand and supply. Can we safely make any predictions about the changes in price and quantity? In this situation, the change in quantity bought and sold can be predicted, but the change in price is ambiguous. The two possible outcomes when the supply and demand curves shift in the same direction are as follows:

- When both demand and supply increase, the equilibrium quantity rises but the change in equilibrium price is ambiguous.
- When both demand and supply decrease, the equilibrium quantity falls but the change in equilibrium price is ambiguous.

ECONOMICS >> *in Action*
Where's the Guacamole?

In 2015, a case of avocados could be purchased in California for $30 to $40. But by August 2017, the price had nearly tripled to approximately $120 per case. And for consumers, average supermarket prices also shot up—doubling in many parts of the country. As one market trader commented at the time, "The avocado market is crazy right now."

Actually, the market for avocados wasn't crazy at all—it was just responding to the forces of supply and demand. First, you can thank Americans' fast-growing appetite for all things avocado: guacamole, avocado toast, avocado smoothies, and the like. The average American eats 7 pounds of guacamole per year, compared to 1.1 pounds per year in 1989, according to the Agriculture Marketing Resource Center. Adding to the increase in American demand is burgeoning demand in Europe and China.

Increased demand and decreased supply can take a bite out of your budget.

Second, there's supply. Five years of high heat and drought in California, where about 10% of avocados consumed in the United States are grown, sharply reduced the state's supply. The 2016 California avocado harvest was only half of what it had been the year before. Mexico and Peru, which account for much of the remaining 90%, have had their own supply problems. Peru experienced poor growing weather as well. And Mexico, which supplies 82% of U.S. consumption, had been hit by a *growers' strike.*

Observing the rising prices of avocados in the United States due to the California drought, Mexican avocado growers became dissatisfied with the prices they received. So they essentially went on strike, holding back their crop to get a higher price. In a typical week, about 40 million pounds of Mexican avocados are imported into the United States. But in the midst of the strike, that amount fell by nearly 68%, to only 13 million pounds per week. One produce buyer said, "[Mexican growers are] holding out for more money because the California season is running dry, and there's no other sources."

So an increase in demand coupled with a sharp fall in supply leads to sharply rising prices. It's economic logic, after all. Until demand falls, or supply rises, or both, the price of satisfying America's avocado cravings will remain high.

>> Check Your Understanding 3-4

Solutions appear at back of book.

1. For each of the following, determine (i) the market in question; (ii) whether a shift in demand or supply occurred, the direction of the shift, and what induced the shift; and (iii) the effect of the shift on the equilibrium price and the equilibrium quantity.
   a. As U.S. gasoline prices fall, more people buy large cars.
   b. As technological innovation has lowered the cost of recycling used paper, fresh paper made from recycled stock is used more frequently.
   c. When a local cable company offers cheaper on-demand films, local movie theaters have more unfilled seats.

2. When a new, faster computer chip is introduced, demand for computers using the older, slower chips decreases. Simultaneously, computer makers increase their production of computers containing the old chips to clear out their stocks of old chips.
   a. Draw two diagrams of the market for computers containing the old chips: one in which the equilibrium quantity falls in response to these events, and one in which the equilibrium quantity rises.
   b. What happens to the equilibrium price in each diagram?

Competitive Markets—and Others

Earlier in this chapter we defined a competitive market and explained that the supply and demand framework is a model of competitive markets. But why does it matter whether or not a market is competitive? Now that we've seen how the supply and demand model works, we can offer some explanation.

To understand why competitive markets are different from other markets, compare the problems facing two individuals: a wheat farmer who must decide whether to grow more wheat and the president of a giant aluminum company—say, Alcoa—who must decide whether to produce more aluminum.

For the wheat farmer, the question is simply whether the extra wheat can be sold at a price high enough to justify the extra production cost. The farmer need not worry about whether producing more wheat will affect the price of the wheat he or she was already planning to grow. That's because the wheat market is competitive. There are thousands of wheat farmers, and one farmer's decision will not impact the market price.

But for the Alcoa executive, the aluminum market is *not* competitive. There are only a few big producers, including Alcoa, and each of them is well aware that its actions *do* have a noticeable impact on the market price. This adds a whole new level of complexity to the decisions producers have to make. Alcoa can't decide whether or not to produce more aluminum just by asking whether the additional product will sell for more than it costs to make. The company also has to ask whether producing more aluminum will drive down the market price and reduce its *profit*, its net gain from producing and selling its output.

When a market is competitive, individuals can base decisions on less complicated analyses than those used in a noncompetitive market. This in turn means that it's easier for economists to build a model of a competitive market than of a noncompetitive market.

This doesn't mean that economic analysis has nothing to say about noncompetitive markets. On the contrary, economists can offer some very important insights into how other kinds of markets work. But those insights require other models.

SOLVED PROBLEM   Sugar, Sugar

"U.S. Sugar Soars Above World Prices." So read a headline in the *Wall Street Journal*. Although the price for sugar on the international market was $0.15 per pound at the time, American buyers were paying 50% more, nearly $0.25 per pound. The impact was felt by candy companies like PEZ Candy, which purchases 75,000 pounds of sugar each week. Why was there a disparity in price?

To protect sugar farmers, the U.S. government limits the quantity of sugar that domestic buyers, like PEZ Candy, can purchase from international suppliers. These restrictions leave U.S. buyers with virtually no other choice; they have to purchase the higher-priced sugar from domestic suppliers.

The table is a hypothetical supply and demand schedule for the U.S. sugar market.

Price of sugar (per pound)	Quantity of sugar (millions of tons)	
	Quantity demanded	Quantity supplied
$0.45	1.6	2.8
0.35	1.8	2.4
0.25	2.0	2.0
0.15	2.2	1.6
0.05	2.4	1.2

Use a supply and demand graph to find the equilibrium quantity and price for sugar in the United States. Show how a shortage would occur if U.S. sugar farmers were forced to set prices equal to the world price of $0.15 per pound.

STEP | 1 Draw and label supply and demand curves. Find the equilibrium quantity demanded. *Review pages 64–66, 74–75, and 81–84.*

The equilibrium quantity demanded is at point *E*, the point at which quantity supplied equals quantity demanded. As shown both in the supply and demand schedule and in the figure, this occurs at an equilibrium quantity of 2.0 billion pounds and an equilibrium price of $0.25.

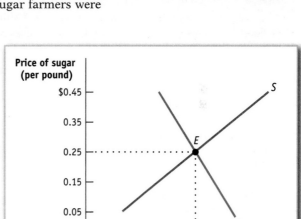

STEP | 2 Calculate the shortage of sugar that would occur at a price of $0.15. *Review pages 81–84.*

As shown in the accompanying graph, a price of $0.15 corresponds to point *A* on the supply curve. The quantity supplied at a price of $0.15 can be found by starting at point *A*, following the dotted line down to the horizontal axis, and observing that the quantity supplied by U.S. sugar farmers is 1.6 billion pounds. Similarly, a price of $0.15 corresponds to point *B* on the demand curve. The quantity demanded at a price of $0.15 can be found by starting at point *B*, following the dotted line down to the horizontal axis, and observing that the quantity demanded is 2.2 billion pounds. The difference between the quantity demanded and the quantity supplied is 2.2 – 1.6 = 0.6 billion pounds. This difference can also be found from the supply and demand schedule. As shown in the schedule, at a price of $0.15, the quantity supplied (1.6 billion pounds) is less than the quantity demanded (2.2 billion pounds) by 0.6 billion pounds.

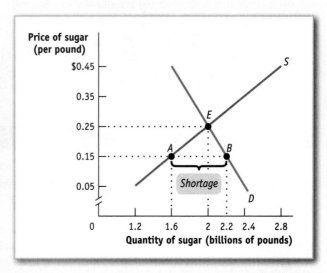

SUMMARY

1. The **supply and demand model** illustrates how a **competitive market,** one with many buyers and sellers, none of whom can influence the market price, works.

2. The **demand schedule** shows the **quantity demanded** at each price and is represented graphically by a **demand curve.** The **law of demand** says that demand curves slope downward; that is, a higher price for a good or service leads people to demand a smaller quantity, other things equal.

3. A **movement along the demand curve** occurs when a price change leads to a change in the quantity demanded. When economists talk of increasing or decreasing demand, they mean **shifts of the demand curve**—a change in the quantity demanded at any given price. An increase in demand causes a rightward shift of the demand curve. A decrease in demand causes a leftward shift.

4. There are five main factors that shift the demand curve:
   - A change in the prices of related goods or services, such as **substitutes** or **complements**
   - A change in income: when income rises, the demand for **normal goods** increases and the demand for **inferior goods** decreases
   - A change in tastes
   - A change in expectations
   - A change in the number of consumers

5. The market demand curve for a good or service is the horizontal sum of the **individual demand curves** of all consumers in the market.

6. The **supply schedule** shows the **quantity supplied** at each price and is represented graphically by a **supply curve.** Supply curves usually slope upward.

7. A **movement along the supply curve** occurs when a price change leads to a change in the quantity supplied. When economists talk of increasing or decreasing supply, they mean **shifts of the supply curve**—a change in

the quantity supplied at any given price. An increase in supply causes a rightward shift of the supply curve. A decrease in supply causes a leftward shift.

8. There are five main factors that shift the supply curve:
   - A change in **input** prices
   - A change in the prices of related goods and services
   - A change in technology
   - A change in expectations
   - A change in the number of producers

9. The market supply curve for a good or service is the horizontal sum of the **individual supply curves** of all producers in the market.

10. The supply and demand model is based on the principle that the price in a market moves to its **equilibrium price,** or **market-clearing price,** the price at which the quantity demanded is equal to the quantity supplied. This quantity is the **equilibrium quantity.** When the price is above its market-clearing level, there is a **surplus** that pushes the price down. When the price is below its market-clearing level, there is a **shortage** that pushes the price up.

11. An increase in demand increases both the equilibrium price and the equilibrium quantity; a decrease in demand has the opposite effect. An increase in supply reduces the equilibrium price and increases the equilibrium quantity; a decrease in supply has the opposite effect.

12. Shifts of the demand curve and the supply curve can happen simultaneously. When they shift in opposite directions, the change in equilibrium price is predictable but the change in equilibrium quantity is not. When they shift in the same direction, the change in equilibrium quantity is predictable but the change in equilibrium price is not. In general, the curve that shifts the greater distance has a greater effect on the changes in equilibrium price and quantity.

KEY TERMS

DISCUSSION QUESTIONS

1. Aaron Hank is a star hitter for the Bay City baseball team. He is close to breaking the major league record for home runs hit during one season, and it is widely anticipated that in the next game he will break that record. As a result, tickets for the team's next game have been a hot commodity. But today it is announced that, due to a knee injury, he will not in fact play in the team's next game. Assume that season ticket-holders are able to resell their tickets if they wish. Use supply and demand diagrams to explain your answers to parts a and b.

a. Show the case in which this announcement results in a lower equilibrium price and a lower equilibrium quantity than before the announcement.

b. Show the case in which this announcement results in a lower equilibrium price and a higher equilibrium quantity than before the announcement.

c. What accounts for whether case a or case b occurs?

d. Suppose that a scalper had secretly learned before the announcement that Aaron Hank would not play in the next game. What actions do you think he would take?

2. In each of the following, what is the mistake that underlies the statement? Explain the mistake in terms of supply and demand and the factors that influence them.

a. Consumers are illogical because they are buying more Starbucks beverages in 2016 despite the fact that Starbucks has raised prices from 10 to 30 cents per drink.

b. Consumers are illogical because they buy less at Cost-U-Less Warehouse Superstore when their incomes go up.

c. Consumers are illogical for buying an iPhone X when an iPhone 8 costs less.

3. In 2016 the price of oil fell to a 12-year low. For drivers, the cost of driving fell significantly as gasoline prices plunged. For the airline industry, the cost of operation also fell significantly because jet fuel is a major expense.

a. Draw a supply and demand diagram that illustrates the effect of a fall in the price of jet fuel on the supply of air travel.

b. Draw a supply and demand diagram that illustrates the effect of a fall in the price of oil on the demand for air travel. (*Hint:* Think about this in terms of the substitutes for air travel, like driving.)

c. Put the diagrams from parts a and b together. What happens to the equilibrium price and quantity of air travel?

Despite the fall in the cost of driving, many more Americans chose to fly to their destinations during 2014 to 2016, as incomes rose and people splurged on vacations that had been postponed during the Great Recession.

d. Using your results from part c, modify your diagram to illustrate an outcome in which the equilibrium price of air travel rises as people take more vacations by air.

PROBLEMS

interactive activity

1. A study conducted by Yahoo! revealed that chocolate is the most popular flavor of ice cream in America. For each of the following, indicate the possible effects on demand, supply, or both, as well as equilibrium price and quantity of chocolate ice cream.

a. A severe drought in the Midwest causes dairy farmers to reduce the number of milk-producing cattle in their herds by a third. These dairy farmers supply cream that is used to manufacture chocolate ice cream.

b. A new report by the American Medical Association reveals that chocolate does, in fact, have significant health benefits.

c. The discovery of cheaper synthetic vanilla flavoring lowers the price of vanilla ice cream.

d. New technology for mixing and freezing ice cream lowers manufacturers' costs of producing chocolate ice cream.

2. In a supply and demand diagram, draw the shift of the demand curve for hamburgers in your hometown due to the following events. In each case, show the effect on equilibrium price and quantity.

a. The price of tacos increases.

b. All hamburger sellers raise the price of their french fries.

c. Income falls in town. Assume that hamburgers are a normal good for most people.

d. Income falls in town. Assume that hamburgers are an inferior good for most people.

e. Hot dog stands cut the price of hot dogs.

3. The market for many goods changes in predictable ways according to the time of year, in response to events such as holidays, vacation times, seasonal changes in production, and so on. Using supply and demand, explain the change in price in each of the following cases. Note that supply and demand may shift simultaneously.

a. Lobster prices usually fall during the summer peak lobster harvest season, despite the fact that people like to eat lobster during the summer more than at any other time of year.

b. The price of a Christmas tree is lower after Christmas than before but fewer trees are sold.

c. The price of a round-trip ticket to Paris on Air France falls by more than $200 after the end of school vacation in September. This happens despite the fact that generally worsening weather increases the cost of operating flights to Paris, and Air France therefore reduces the number of flights to Paris at any given price.

4. Show in a diagram the effect on the demand curve, the supply curve, the equilibrium price, and the equilibrium quantity of each of the following events.

a. The market for newspapers in your town

Case 1: The salaries of journalists go up.

Case 2: There is a big news event in your town, which is reported in the newspapers.

b. The market for Seattle Seahawks cotton T-shirts

Case 1: The Seahawks win the Super Bowl.

Case 2: The price of cotton increases.

c. The market for bagels

Case 1: People realize how fattening bagels are.

Case 2: People have less time to make themselves a cooked breakfast.

d. The market for the Krugman and Wells economics textbook

Case 1: Your professor makes it required reading for all of his or her students.

Case 2: Printing costs for textbooks are lowered by the use of synthetic paper.

5. Let's assume that each person in the United States consumes an average of 37 gallons of soft drinks (nondiet) at an average price of $2 per gallon and that the U.S. population is 294 million. At a price of $1.50 per gallon, each individual consumer would demand 50 gallons of soft drinks. From this information about the individual demand schedule, calculate the market demand schedule for soft drinks for the prices of $1.50 and $2 per gallon.

6. Suppose that the supply schedule of Maine lobsters is as follows:

Price of lobster (per pound)	Quantity of lobster supplied (pounds)
$25	800
20	700
15	600
10	500
5	400

Suppose that Maine lobsters can be sold only in the United States. The U.S. demand schedule for Maine lobsters is as follows:

Price of lobster (per pound)	Quantity of lobster demanded (pounds)
$25	200
20	400
15	600
10	800
5	1,000

a. Draw the demand curve and the supply curve for Maine lobsters. What are the equilibrium price and quantity of lobsters?

Now suppose that Maine lobsters can be sold in France. The French demand schedule for Maine lobsters is as follows:

Price of lobster (per pound)	Quantity of lobster demanded (pounds)
$25	100
20	300
15	500
10	700
5	900

b. What is the demand schedule for Maine lobsters now that French consumers can also buy them? Draw a supply and demand diagram that illustrates the new equilibrium price and quantity of lobsters. What will happen to the price at which fishermen can sell lobster? What will happen to the price paid by U.S. consumers? What will happen to the quantity consumed by U.S. consumers?

7. Find the flaws in reasoning in the following statements, paying particular attention to the distinction between shifts of and movements along the supply and demand curves. Draw a diagram to illustrate what actually happens in each situation.

a. "A technological innovation that lowers the cost of producing a good might seem at first to result in a reduction in the price of the good to consumers. But a fall in price will increase demand for the good, and higher demand will send the price up again. It is not certain, therefore, that an innovation will really reduce price in the end."

b. "A study shows that eating a clove of garlic a day can help prevent heart disease, causing many consumers to demand more garlic. This increase in demand results in a rise in the price of garlic. Consumers, seeing that the price of garlic has gone up, reduce their demand for garlic. This causes the demand for garlic to decrease and the price of garlic to fall. Therefore, the ultimate effect of the study on the price of garlic is uncertain."

8. The following table shows a demand schedule for a normal good.

Price	Quantity demanded
$23	70
21	90
19	110
17	130

a. Do you think that the increase in quantity demanded (say, from 90 to 110 in the table) when price decreases (from $21 to $19) is due to a rise in consumers' income? Explain clearly (and briefly) why or why not.

b. Now suppose that the good is an inferior good. Would the demand schedule still be valid for an inferior good?

c. Lastly, assume you do not know whether the good is normal or inferior. Devise an experiment that would allow you to determine which one it was. Explain.

9. In recent years, the number of car producers in China has increased rapidly. In fact, China now has more car brands than the United States. In addition, car sales have climbed every year and automakers have increased their output at even faster rates, causing fierce competition and a decline in prices. At the same time, Chinese consumers' incomes have risen. Assume that cars are a normal good. Draw a diagram of the supply and demand curves for cars in China to explain what has happened in the Chinese car market.

10. Fans of music often bemoan the high price of concert tickets. One rock superstar has argued that it isn't worth hundreds, even thousands, of dollars to hear him and his band play. Let's assume this star sold out arenas around the country at an average ticket price of $75.

a. How would you evaluate the argument that ticket prices are too high?

b. Suppose that due to this star's protests, ticket prices were lowered to $50. In what sense is this price too low? Draw a diagram using supply and demand curves to support your argument.

c. Suppose the superstar really wanted to bring down ticket prices. Since he and his band control the supply of their services, what do you recommend they do? Explain by using a supply and demand diagram.

d. Suppose the band's next album was a total dud. Do you think they would still have to worry about ticket prices being too high? Why or why not? Draw a supply and demand diagram to support your argument.

e. Suppose the group announced their next tour was going to be their last. What effect would this likely have on the demand for and price of tickets? Illustrate with a supply and demand diagram.

11. After several years of decline, the market for handmade acoustic guitars is making a comeback. These guitars are usually made in small workshops employing relatively few highly skilled luthiers. Assess the impact on the equilibrium price and quantity of handmade acoustic guitars as a result of each of the following events. In your answers indicate which curve(s) shift(s) and in which direction.

a. Environmentalists succeed in having the use of Brazilian rosewood banned in the United States, forcing luthiers to seek out alternative, more costly woods.

b. A foreign producer reengineers the guitar-making process and floods the market with identical guitars.

c. Music featuring handmade acoustic guitars makes a comeback as audiences tire of heavy metal and alternative rock music.

d. The country goes into a deep recession and the income of the average American falls sharply.

12. *Demand twisters:* Sketch and explain the demand relationship in each of the following statements.

a. I would never buy a Taylor Swift album! You couldn't even give me one for nothing.

b. I generally buy a bit more coffee as the price falls. But once the price falls to $2 per pound, I'll buy out the entire stock of the supermarket.

c. I spend more on orange juice even as the price rises. (Does this mean that I must be violating the law of demand?)

d. Due to a tuition rise, most students at a college find themselves with less disposable income. Almost all of them eat more frequently at the school cafeteria and less often at restaurants, even though prices at the cafeteria have risen, too. (This one requires that you draw both the demand and the supply curves for school cafeteria meals.)

13. Will Shakespeare is a struggling playwright in sixteenth-century London. As the price he receives for writing a play increases, he is willing to write more plays. For the following situations, use a diagram to illustrate how each event affects the equilibrium price and quantity in the market for Shakespeare's plays.

a. The playwright Christopher Marlowe, Shakespeare's chief rival, is killed in a bar brawl.

b. The Bubonic plague, a deadly infectious disease, breaks out in London.

c. To celebrate the defeat of the Spanish Armada, Queen Elizabeth declares several weeks of festivities, which involves commissioning new plays.

14. Three years ago, the small town of Middling experienced a sudden doubling of the birth rate. Today, the birth rate has returned to normal. Use a diagram to illustrate the effect of these events on the following.

a. The market for an hour of babysitting services in Middling this year.

b. The market for an hour of babysitting services 14 years into the future, after the birth rate has returned to normal, by which time children born today are old enough to work as babysitters

c. The market for an hour of babysitting services 30 years into the future, when children born today are likely to be having children of their own

15. Use a diagram to illustrate how each of the following events affects the equilibrium price and quantity of pizza.

a. The price of mozzarella cheese rises.

b. The health hazards of hamburgers are widely publicized.

c. The price of tomato sauce falls.

d. The incomes of consumers rise, and pizza is an inferior good.

e. Consumers expect the price of pizza to fall next week.

16. Although he was a prolific artist, Pablo Picasso painted only 1,000 canvases during his "Blue Period." Picasso is now dead, and all of his Blue Period works are currently on display in museums and private galleries throughout Europe and the United States.

a. Draw a supply curve for Picasso Blue Period works. Why is this supply curve different from ones you have seen?

b. Given the supply curve from part a, the price of a Picasso Blue Period work will be entirely dependent on what factor(s)? Draw a diagram showing how the equilibrium price of such a work is determined.

c. Suppose rich art collectors decide that it is essential to acquire Picasso Blue Period art for their collections. Show the impact of this on the market for these paintings.

17. Draw the appropriate curve in each of the following cases. Is it like or unlike the curves you have seen so far? Explain.

a. The demand for cardiac bypass surgery, given that the government pays the full cost for any patient

b. The demand for elective cosmetic plastic surgery, given that the patient pays the full cost

c. The supply of reproductions of Rembrandt paintings

WORK IT OUT Interactive step-by-step help with solving this problem can be found online.

18. The accompanying table gives the annual U.S. demand and supply schedules for pickup trucks.

Price of truck	Quantity of trucks demanded (millions)	Quantity of trucks supplied (millions)
$20,000	20	14
25,000	18	15
30,000	16	16
35,000	14	17
40,000	12	18

a. Plot the demand and supply curves using these schedules. Indicate the equilibrium price and quantity on your diagram.

b. Suppose the tires used on pickup trucks are found to be defective. What would you expect to happen in the market for pickup trucks? Show this on your diagram.

c. Suppose that the U.S. Department of Transportation imposes costly regulations on manufacturers that cause them to reduce supply by one-third at any given price. Calculate and plot the new supply schedule and indicate the new equilibrium price and quantity on your diagram.

THE MARKET STRIKES BACK!

IN 2015, A REAL ESTATE DEVELOPER purchased a New York City apartment building and wanted to evict three elderly tenants who had lived in their apartment for decades.

But inducing the tenants to leave was no easy matter because their apartment was one of 27,000 units covered by New York's *rent control* law. The law prevents landlords from raising rents or evicting tenants in rent-controlled apartments except when specifically given permission by a city agency. In fact, under the law it would have been virtually impossible to evict these tenants against their will.

So, how was the situation resolved? After intense negotiations, the three tenants finally agreed to move after receiving a payment of $25 million from the developer. Yes, *$25 million.*

Why was the developer willing to pay so much? Because in New York City's highly lucrative housing market, with its shortage of places to live, the developer stood to make a lot more money by constructing a larger building with apartments that are not rent-controlled and that will rent for very high prices. Some developers argue that the difficulty they have dislodging rent-controlled tenants in New York limits their ability to build more housing, leading to a shortage of all apartments, whether affordable or expensive.

Rent control is a type of *market intervention,* a policy imposed by government to prevail over the market forces of supply and demand—in this case, over the market forces of the supply and demand for New York City rental apartments.

Although rent control laws were introduced during World War II in many major American cities to protect the interests of tenants, the problems they create have led most cities to discard them. New York City and San Francisco are notable exceptions, although rent control covers only a small and diminishing proportion of rental apartments in both cities.

In Chapter 3 we learned the principle that a market moves to equilibrium—that the market price rises or falls to the level at which the quantity of a good that people are willing to supply is equal to the quantity that other people demand. However, when governments intervene in markets, they try to defy that principle.

When a government tries to dictate either a market price or a market quantity that's different from the equilibrium price or quantity, the market strikes back in predictable ways. The shortage of apartments is one example of what happens when the logic of the market is defied: a market intervention like rent control keeps the price of apartment rentals below market equilibrium level, creating a shortage and other serious problems. And, as we'll see, those problems inevitably create winners and losers.

Our ability to predict what will happen when governments try to defy supply and demand shows the power and usefulness of supply and demand analysis.

We will also examine another form of market intervention used in New York and other cities—a licensing system for taxis that reduces the number of taxis offering rides below the market equilibrium level. Originally intended to protect the interests of both drivers and customers, like rent control, it led to a shortage of taxis. In recent years, however, the rise of companies like Uber and Lyft has upended market interventions in the taxi industry and moved it closer to market equilibrium.

We begin this chapter by looking at *consumer surplus,* the benefit from being able to purchase a good or a service. We will then look at a corresponding measure, *producer surplus,* which shows the benefit sellers receive from being able to sell a good. We move on to examine what happens when governments try to control prices in a competitive market, keeping the price in a market either below its equilibrium level—a price ceiling such as rent control—or above it—a price floor such as the minimum wage paid to workers in many countries. We then turn to schemes such as taxi medallions that attempt to dictate the quantity of a good bought and sold.

Although there are specific winners and losers from market intervention, we will learn how and why society as a whole loses—a result that has led economists to be generally skeptical of market interventions except in certain well-defined situations. ●

WHAT YOU WILL LEARN

- What is **consumer surplus?**
- What is **producer surplus?**
- What is **total surplus** and why is it used to illustrate the gains from trade in a market?
- What is a market intervention and why are **price controls** and **quantity controls** the two main forms it takes?
- Why do price and quantity controls create **deadweight losses?**
- Who benefits and who loses from market interventions?

Consumer Surplus and the Demand Curve

The market in used textbooks is a big business in terms of dollars and cents—several billion dollars each year. More importantly for us, it is a convenient starting point for developing the concepts of consumer and producer surplus. We'll use the concepts of consumer and producer surplus to understand exactly how buyers and sellers benefit from a competitive market and how big those benefits are. In addition, these concepts play important roles in analyzing what happens when competitive markets don't work well or there is interference in the market.

So let's begin by looking at the market for used textbooks, starting with the buyers. The key point, as we'll see in a minute, is that the demand curve is derived from their tastes or preferences—and that those same preferences also determine how much they gain from the opportunity to buy used books.

Willingness to Pay and the Demand Curve

A used book is not as good as a new book—it will be battered and coffee-stained, may include someone else's highlighting, and may not be completely up to date. How much this bothers you depends on your preferences. Some potential buyers would prefer to buy the used book even if it is only slightly cheaper than a new one; others would buy the used book only if it is considerably cheaper.

Let's define a potential buyer's **willingness to pay** as the maximum price at which he or she would buy a good, in this case a used textbook. An individual won't buy the good if it costs more than this amount but is eager to do so if it costs less. If the price is just equal to an individual's willingness to pay, he or she is indifferent between buying and not buying. For the sake of simplicity, we'll assume that the individual buys the good in this case.

Table 4-1 shows five potential buyers of a used book that costs $100 new, listed in order of their willingness to pay. At one extreme is Aleisha, who will buy a second-hand book even if the price is as high as $59. Brad is less willing to have a used book and will buy one only if the price is $45 or less. Claudia is willing to pay only $35 and Darren, only $25. And Edwina, who really doesn't like the idea of a used book, will buy one only if it costs no more than $10.

How many of these five students will actually buy a used book? It depends on the price. If the price of a used book is $55, only Aleisha buys one; if the price is $40, Aleisha and Brad both buy used books, and so on. So the information in the table can be used to construct the *demand schedule* for used textbooks.

TABLE 4-1   Consumer Surplus if the Price of a Used Textbook = $30

Potential buyer	Willingness to pay	Price paid	Individual consumer surplus = Willingness to pay − Price paid
Aleisha	$59	$30	$29
Brad	45	30	15
Claudia	35	30	5
Darren	25	–	–
Edwina	10	–	–
All buyers			**Total consumer surplus = $49**

Willingness to Pay and Consumer Surplus

Suppose that the campus bookstore makes used textbooks available at a price of $30. In that case, Aleisha, Brad, and Claudia will buy books. Do they gain from their purchases, and if so, how much?

The answer, also shown in Table 4-1, is that each student who purchases a book does achieve a net gain but that the amount of the gain differs among students.

Aleisha would have been willing to pay $59, so her net gain is $59 − $30 = $29. Brad would have been willing to pay $45, so his net gain is $45 − $30 = $15. Claudia

A consumer's **willingness to pay** for a good is the maximum price at which he or she would buy that good.

would have been willing to pay $35, so her net gain is $35 – $30 = $5. Darren and Edwina, however, won't be willing to buy a used book at a price of $30, so they neither gain nor lose.

The net gain that a buyer achieves from the purchase of a good is called that buyer's **individual consumer surplus.** What we learn from this example is that whenever a buyer pays a price less than his or her willingness to pay, the buyer achieves some individual consumer surplus.

The sum of the individual consumer surpluses achieved by all the buyers of a good is known as the **total consumer surplus** achieved in the market. In Table 4-1, the total consumer surplus is the sum of the individual consumer surpluses achieved by Aleisha, Brad, and Claudia: $29 + $15 + $5 = $49.

Economists often use the term **consumer surplus** to refer to both individual and total consumer surplus. We will follow this practice; it will always be clear in context whether we are referring to the consumer surplus achieved by an individual or by all buyers. Total consumer surplus can be represented graphically. As we saw in Chapter 3, we can use the demand schedule to derive the market demand curve shown in Figure 4-1. Because we are considering only a small number of consumers, this curve doesn't look like the smooth demand curves of Chapter 3, where markets contained hundreds or thousands of consumers.

This demand curve is stepped, with alternating horizontal and vertical segments. Each horizontal segment—each step—corresponds to one potential buyer's willingness to pay. Each step in that demand curve is one book wide and represents one consumer. For example, the height of Aleisha's step is $59, her willingness to pay. This step forms the top of a rectangle, with $30—the price she actually pays for a book—forming the bottom.

The area of Aleisha's rectangle, ($59 – $30) × 1 = $29, is her consumer surplus from purchasing one book at $30. So the individual consumer surplus Aleisha gains is the *area of the dark blue rectangle* shown in Figure 4-1.

Individual consumer surplus is the net gain to an individual buyer from the purchase of a good. It is equal to the difference between the buyer's willingness to pay and the price paid.

Total consumer surplus is the sum of the individual consumer surpluses of all the buyers of a good in a market.

The term **consumer surplus** is often used to refer both to individual and to total consumer surplus.

FIGURE 4-1 Consumer Surplus in the Used-Textbook Market

At a price of $30, Aleisha, Brad, and Claudia each buy a book but Darren and Edwina do not. Aleisha, Brad, and Claudia receive individual consumer surpluses equal to the difference between their willingness to pay and the price, illustrated by the areas of the shaded rectangles. Both Darren and Edwina have a willingness to pay less than $30, so they are unwilling to buy a book in this market; they receive zero consumer surplus. The total consumer surplus is given by the entire shaded area—the sum of the individual consumer surpluses of Aleisha, Brad, and Claudia—equal to $29 + $15 + $5 = $49.

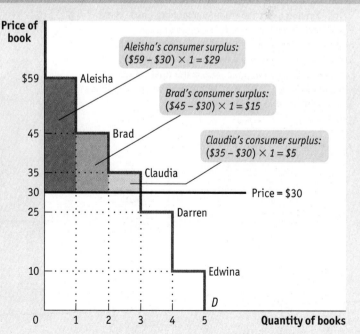

In addition to Aleisha, Brad and Claudia will also each buy a book when the price is $30. Like Aleisha, they benefit from their purchases, though not as much, because they each have a lower willingness to pay. Figure 4-1 also shows the consumer surplus gained by Brad and Claudia; again, this can be measured by the areas of the appropriate rectangles. Darren and Edwina, because they do not buy books at a price of $30, receive no consumer surplus.

The total consumer surplus achieved in this market is just the sum of the individual consumer surpluses received by Aleisha, Brad, and Claudia. So total consumer surplus is equal to the combined area of the three rectangles—the entire shaded area in Figure 4-1. Another way to say this is that total consumer surplus is equal to the area below the demand curve but above the price.

Figure 4-1 illustrates the following general principle: *The total consumer surplus generated by purchases of a good at a given price is equal to the area below the demand curve but above that price.* The same principle applies regardless of the number of consumers.

When we consider large markets, this graphical representation of consumer surplus becomes extremely helpful. Consider, for example, the sales of iPads to millions of potential buyers. Each potential buyer has a maximum price that he or she is willing to pay. With so many potential buyers, the demand curve will be smooth, like the one shown in Figure 4-2.

Suppose that at a price of $500, a total of 1 million iPads are purchased. How much do consumers gain from being able to buy those 1 million iPads? We could answer that question by calculating the individual consumer surplus of each buyer and then adding these numbers up to arrive at a total. But it is much easier just to look at Figure 4-2 and use the fact that total consumer surplus is equal to the shaded area. As in our original example, consumer surplus is equal to the area below the demand curve but above the price. (To refresh your memory on how to calculate the area of a right triangle, see the appendix to Chapter 2.)

FIGURE 4-2 Consumer Surplus

The demand curve for iPads is smooth because there are many potential buyers. At a price of $500, 1 million iPads are demanded. The consumer surplus at this price is equal to the shaded area: the area below the demand curve but above the price. This is the total net gain to consumers generated from buying and consuming iPads when the price is $500.

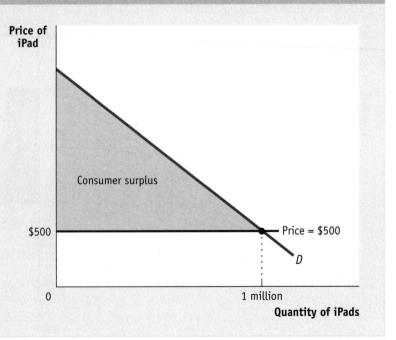

Producer Surplus and the Supply Curve

Just as some buyers of a good would have been willing to pay more for their purchase than the price they actually pay, some sellers of a good would have been willing to sell it for less than the price they actually receive. So, just as there are consumers who receive consumer surplus from buying in a market, there are producers who receive producer surplus from selling in a market.

Cost and Producer Surplus

Consider a group of students who are potential sellers of used textbooks. Because they have different preferences, the various potential sellers differ in the price at which they are willing to sell their books. Table 4-2 shows the prices at which several different students would be willing to sell. Andrew is willing to sell the book as long as he can get at least $5; Betty won't sell unless she can get at least $15; Carlos, unless he can get $25; Donna, unless she can get $35; Engelbert, unless he can get $45.

The lowest price at which a potential seller is willing to sell has a special name in economics: it is called the seller's **cost.** So Andrew's cost is $5, Betty's is $15, and so on.

Using the term *cost*, which people normally associate with the monetary cost of producing a good, may sound a little strange when applied to sellers of used textbooks. The students don't have to manufacture the books, so it doesn't cost the student who sells a used textbook anything to make that book available for sale, does it?

TABLE 4-2 Producer Surplus When the Price of a Used Textbook = $30			
Potential seller	Cost	Price received	Individual producer surplus = Price received − Cost
Andrew	$ 5	$30	$25
Betty	15	30	15
Carlos	25	30	5
Donna	35	–	–
Engelbert	45	–	–
All sellers			**Total producer surplus = $45**

Yes, it does. A student who sells a book won't have it later, as part of his or her personal collection. So there is an *opportunity* cost to selling a textbook, even if the owner has completed the course for which it was required. And remember that one of the basic principles of economics is that the true measure of the cost of doing something is always its opportunity cost. That is, the real cost of something is what you must give up to get it.

So it is good economics to talk of the minimum price at which someone will sell a good as the "cost" of selling that good, even if he or she doesn't spend any money to make the good available for sale. Of course, in most real-world markets the sellers are also those who produce the good and therefore *do* spend money to make it available for sale. In this case, the cost of making the good available for sale includes monetary costs, but it may also include other opportunity costs.

Getting back to the example, suppose that Andrew sells his book for $30. Clearly he has gained from the transaction: he would have been willing to sell for only $5, so he has gained $25. This net gain, the difference between the price he actually gets and his cost—the minimum price at which he would have been willing to sell—is known as his **individual producer surplus.**

As in the case of consumer surplus, we can add the individual producer surpluses of sellers to calculate the **total producer surplus,** the total net gain to all sellers in the market. Economists use the term **producer surplus** to refer to either individual or total producer surplus. Table 4-2 shows the net gain to each of the students who would sell a used book at a price of $30: $25 for Andrew, $15 for Betty, and $5 for Carlos. The total producer surplus is $25 + $15 + $5 = $45.

As with consumer surplus, the producer surplus gained by those who sell books can be represented graphically. Just as we derived the demand curve from the

A seller's **cost** is the lowest price at which he or she is willing to sell a good.

Individual producer surplus is the net gain to an individual seller from selling a good. It is equal to the difference between the price received and the seller's cost.

Total producer surplus is the sum of the individual producer surpluses of all the sellers of a good in a market.

Economists use the term **producer surplus** to refer both to individual and to total producer surplus.

willingness to pay of different consumers, we first derive the supply curve from the cost of different producers. The step-shaped curve in Figure 4-3 shows the supply curve implied by the cost shown in Table 4-2. Each step in that supply curve is one book wide and represents one seller. The height of Andrew's step is $5, his cost. This forms the bottom of a rectangle, with $30, the price he actually receives for his book, forming the top. The area of this rectangle, ($30 – $5) × 1 = $25, is his producer surplus. So the producer surplus Andrew gains from selling his book is the *area of the red rectangle* shown in the figure.

Let's assume that the campus bookstore is willing to buy all the used copies of this book that students are willing to sell at a price of $30. Then, in addition to Andrew, Betty and Carlos will also sell their books. They will also benefit from their sales, though not as much as Andrew, because they have higher costs. Andrew, as we have seen, gains $25. Betty gains a smaller amount: since her cost is $15, she gains only $15. Carlos gains even less, only $5.

Again, as with consumer surplus, we have a general rule for determining the total producer surplus from sales of a good: *The total producer surplus from sales of a good at a given price is the area above the supply curve but below that price.*

This rule applies both to examples like the one shown in Figure 4-3, where there are a small number of producers and a step-shaped supply curve, and to more realistic examples, where there are many producers and the supply curve is smooth.

Consider, for example, the supply of wheat. Figure 4-4 shows how producer surplus depends on the price per bushel. Suppose that, as shown in the figure, the price is $5 per bushel and farmers supply 1 million bushels. What is the benefit to the farmers from selling their wheat at a price of $5? Their producer surplus is equal to the shaded area in the figure—the area above the supply curve but below the price of $5 per bushel.

‖ The Gains from Trade

Let's return to the market in used textbooks but now consider a much bigger market—say, one at a large state university. There are many potential buyers and sellers, so the market is competitive. Let's line up incoming students who are

---

FIGURE 4-3 Producer Surplus in the Used-Textbook Market

At a price of $30, Andrew, Betty, and Carlos each sell a book but Donna and Engelbert do not. Andrew, Betty, and Carlos get individual producer surpluses equal to the difference between the price and their cost, illustrated here by the shaded rectangles. Donna and Engelbert each have a cost that is greater than the price of $30, so they are unwilling to sell a book and so receive zero producer surplus. The total producer surplus is given by the entire shaded area, the sum of the individual producer surpluses of Andrew, Betty, and Carlos, equal to $25 + $15 + $5 = $45.

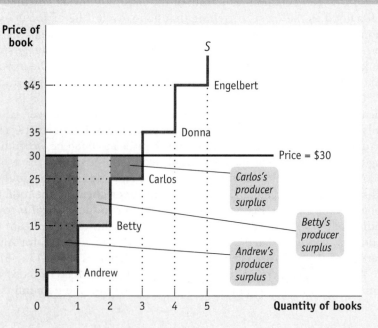

FIGURE 4-4 Producer Surplus

Here is the supply curve for wheat. At a price of $5 per bushel, farmers supply 1 million bushels. The producer surplus at this price is equal to the shaded area: the area above the supply curve but below the price. This is the total gain to producers–farmers in this case–from supplying their product when the price is $5.

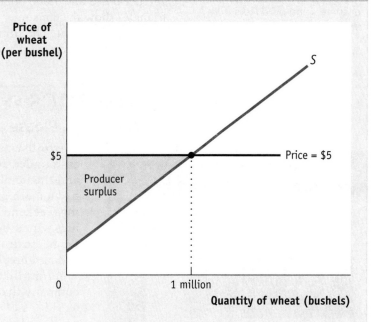

potential buyers of a book in order of their willingness to pay, so that the entering student with the highest willingness to pay is potential buyer number 1, the student with the next-highest willingness to pay is number 2, and so on. Then we can use their willingness to pay to derive a demand curve like the one in Figure 4-5.

Similarly, we can line up outgoing students, who are potential sellers of the book, in order of their cost—starting with the student with the lowest cost, then the student with the next lowest cost, and so on—to derive a supply curve like the one shown in the same figure.

FIGURE 4-5 Total Surplus

In the market for used textbooks, the equilibrium price is $30 and the equilibrium quantity is 1,000 books. Consumer surplus is given by the blue area, the area below the demand curve but above the price. Producer surplus is given by the red area, the area above the supply curve but below the price. The sum of the blue and the red areas is total surplus, the total benefit to society from the production and consumption of the good.

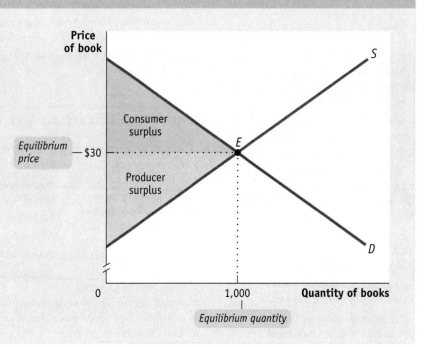

The **total surplus** generated in a market is the total net gain to consumers and producers from trading in the market. It is the sum of the producer and the consumer surplus.

As we have drawn the curves, the market reaches equilibrium at a price of $30 per book, and 1,000 books are bought and sold at that price. The two shaded triangles show the consumer surplus (blue) and the producer surplus (red) generated by this market. The sum of consumer and producer surplus is known as the **total surplus** generated in a market.

ECONOMICS >> *in Action*
Take the Keys, Please

Owners use marketplaces like Airbnb to turn unused resources into cash.

M4OS Photos/Alamy Stock Photo

"Airbnb was really born from a math problem," said its co-founder, Joe Gebbia. "We quit our jobs to be entrepreneurs, and the landlord raised our rent beyond our means. And so we had a math problem to solve. It just so happened that that coming weekend, a design conference came to San Francisco that just wiped out the hotels in the city. We connected the dots. We had extra space in our apartment. So thus was born the air bed-and-breakfast."

From that bout of desperation-induced ingenuity sprang a company that is now the largest single source of lodging in the world. As of 2014, 20 million people searching for a bed have availed themselves of Airbnb's marketplace, half of them in 2014 alone. The website now lists four million dwellings worldwide. Airbnb is the most famous and successful purveyor in what is called "the sharing economy": companies that provide a marketplace in which people can share the use of goods. And there is a dizzying array of others: Turo and Getaround let you rent cars from their owners; Boatbound facilitates boat rentals, Desktime offers office space for rent, and JustPark offers parking spaces.

What's motivating all this sharing? Well, it isn't an outbreak of altruism—it's plain dollars and cents. If there are unused resources sitting around, why not make money by renting them to someone else? As Judith Chevalier, a Yale School of Management economist, says, "These companies let you wring a little bit of value out of . . . goods that are just sitting there." And generating a bit more surplus from your possessions leads to a more efficient use of those resources. As a result, says Arun Sundararajan, a professor at the NYU Stern School of Business, "That makes it possible for people to rethink the way they consume."

>> *Quick Review*

• The demand curve for a good is determined by each potential consumer's **willingness to pay.**

• **Individual consumer surplus** is the net gain an individual consumer gets from buying a good.

• The **total consumer surplus** in a given market is equal to the area below the market demand curve but above the price.

• Economists use the term **consumer surplus** to refer to both individual and total consumer surplus.

• The supply curve for a good is determined by each seller's **cost.**

• The difference between the price and cost is the seller's **individual producer surplus.**

>> *Check Your Understanding* 4-1

Solutions appear at back of book.

1. Two consumers, Casey and Josey, want cheese-stuffed jalapeño peppers for lunch. Two producers, Cara and Jamie, can provide them. The accompanying table shows the consumers' willingness to pay and the producers' costs. Note that consumers and producers in this market are not willing to consume or produce more than four peppers at any price.

Quantity of peppers	Casey's willingness to pay	Josey's willingness to pay	Cara's cost	Jamie's cost
1st pepper	$0.90	$0.80	$0.10	$0.30
2nd pepper	0.70	0.60	0.10	0.50
3rd pepper	0.50	0.40	0.40	0.70
4th pepper	0.30	0.30	0.60	0.90

   a. Use the table to construct a demand schedule and a supply schedule for prices of $0.00, $0.10, and so on, up to $0.90.

  b. Find the equilibrium price and quantity in the market for cheese-stuffed jalapeño peppers.

  c. Find consumer, producer, and total surplus in equilibrium in this market.

2. Show how each of the following three actions reduces total surplus:

  a. Having Josey consume one fewer pepper and Casey one more pepper than in the market equilibrium.

  b. Having Cara produce one fewer pepper and Jamie one more pepper than in the market equilibrium.

  c. Having Josey consume one fewer pepper and Cara produce one fewer pepper than in the market equilibrium.

- The **total producer surplus** is equal to the area above the market supply curve but below the price.

- Economists use the term **producer surplus** to refer to either total or individual producer surplus.

- **Total surplus** measures the gains from trade in a market.

Why Governments Control Prices

As we know from Chapter 3, a market moves to equilibrium—the market price moves to the level at which the quantity supplied equals the quantity demanded. But this equilibrium price does not necessarily please either buyers or sellers.

After all, buyers would always like to pay less if they could, and sometimes they can make a strong moral or political case that they should pay lower prices. For example, what if the equilibrium between supply and demand for apartments in a major city leads to rental rates that an average working person can't afford? In that case, a government might well be under pressure to impose limits on the rents landlords can charge.

Sellers, however, would always like to get more money for what they sell, and sometimes they can make a strong moral or political case that they should receive higher prices. For example, consider the labor market: the price for an hour of a worker's time is the wage rate. What if the equilibrium between supply and demand for less skilled workers leads to wage rates that yield an income below the poverty level? In that case, a government might well be pressured to require employers to pay a rate no lower than some specified minimum wage.

In other words, there is often a strong political demand for governments to intervene in markets. And powerful interests can make a compelling case that a market intervention favoring them is "fair." When a government intervenes to regulate prices, we say that it imposes **price controls.** These controls typically take the form either of an upper limit, a **price ceiling,** or a lower limit, a **price floor.**

Unfortunately, it's not that easy to tell a market what to do. As we will now see, when a government tries to legislate prices—whether it legislates them down by imposing a price ceiling or up by imposing a price floor—there are certain predictable and unpleasant side effects.

Price Ceilings

Aside from rent control, there are not many price ceilings in the United States today. But at times they have been widespread. Price ceilings are typically imposed during crises—wars, harvest failures, natural disasters—because these events often lead to sudden price increases that hurt many people but produce big gains for a lucky few.

The U.S. government imposed ceilings on many prices during World War II: the war sharply increased demand for raw materials, such as aluminum and steel, and price controls prevented those with access to these raw materials from earning huge profits. Price controls on oil were imposed in 1973, when an embargo by Arab oil-exporting countries seemed likely to generate huge profits for U.S. oil companies. Price controls were instituted again in 2012 by New York and New Jersey authorities in the aftermath of Hurricane Sandy, as gas shortages led to rampant price-gouging.

Price controls are legal restrictions on how high or low a market price may go. They can take two forms: a **price ceiling,** a maximum price sellers are allowed to charge for a good or service, or a **price floor,** a minimum price buyers are required to pay for a good or service.

Rent control in New York is, as we mention in the opening story, a legacy of World War II: it was imposed because wartime production led to an economic boom that increased demand for apartments at a time when the labor and raw materials that might have been used to build them were being used to win the war instead. Although most price controls were removed soon after the war ended, New York's rent limits were retained and gradually extended to buildings not previously covered, leading to some very strange situations.

You can rent a one-bedroom apartment in Manhattan on fairly short notice—if you are able and willing to pay several thousand dollars a month and live in a less desirable area. Yet some people pay only a small fraction of this for comparable apartments, and others pay hardly more for bigger apartments in better locations.

Aside from producing great deals for some renters, however, what are the broader consequences of New York's rent-control system? To answer this question, we turn to the model we developed in Chapter 3: the supply and demand model.

Modeling a Price Ceiling

To see what can go wrong when a government imposes a price ceiling on an efficient market, consider Figure 4-6, which shows a simplified model of the market for apartments in New York. For the sake of simplicity, we imagine that all apartments are exactly the same and would rent for the same price in an unregulated market.

The table in Figure 4-6 shows the demand and supply schedules; the demand and supply curves are shown on the left. We show the quantity of apartments on the horizontal axis and the monthly rent per apartment on the vertical axis. You can see that in an unregulated market the equilibrium would be at point *E*: 2 million apartments would be rented for $1,000 each per month.

Now suppose that the government imposes a price ceiling, limiting rents to a price below the equilibrium price—say, no more than $800.

Figure 4-6 The Market for Apartments in the Absence of Price Controls

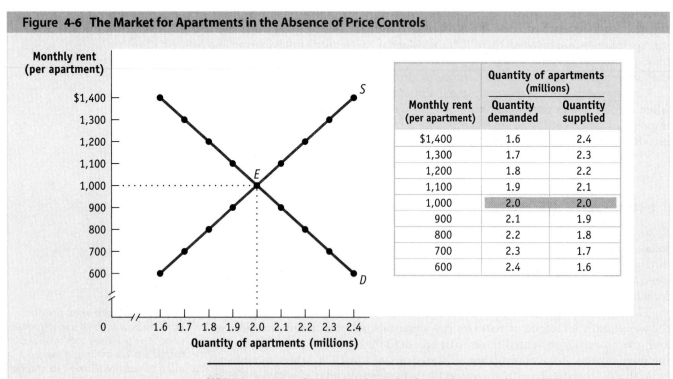

Monthly rent (per apartment)	Quantity of apartments (millions)	
	Quantity demanded	Quantity supplied
$1,400	1.6	2.4
1,300	1.7	2.3
1,200	1.8	2.2
1,100	1.9	2.1
1,000	2.0	2.0
900	2.1	1.9
800	2.2	1.8
700	2.3	1.7
600	2.4	1.6

Without government intervention, the market for apartments reaches equilibrium at point *E* with a market rent of $1,000 per month and 2 million apartments rented.

Figure 4-7 shows the effect of the price ceiling, represented by the line at $800. At the enforced rental rate of $800, landlords have less incentive to offer apartments, so they won't be willing to supply as many as they would at the equilibrium rate of $1,000. They will choose point *A* on the supply curve, offering only 1.8 million apartments for rent, 200,000 fewer than in the unregulated market.

At the same time, more people will want to rent apartments at a price of $800 than at the equilibrium price of $1,000; as shown at point *B* on the demand curve, at a monthly rent of $800 the quantity of apartments demanded rises to 2.2 million, 200,000 more than in the unregulated market and 400,000 more than are actually available at the price of $800. So there is now a persistent shortage of rental housing: at that price, 400,000 more people want to rent than are able to find apartments.

Do price ceilings always cause shortages? No. If a price ceiling is set above the equilibrium price, it won't have any effect. Suppose that the equilibrium rental rate on apartments is $1,000 per month and the city government sets a ceiling of $1,200. Who cares? In this case, the price ceiling won't be *binding*—it won't actually constrain market behavior—and it will have no effect.

How a Price Ceiling Causes Inefficiency

The housing shortage shown in Figure 4-7 is not merely annoying: like any shortage induced by price controls, it can be seriously harmful because it leads to inefficiency. In other words, there are gains from trade that go unrealized.

Rent control, like all price ceilings, creates inefficiency in at least four distinct ways.

1. It reduces the quantity of apartments rented below the efficient level.
2. It typically leads to inefficient allocation of apartments among would-be renters.
3. It leads to wasted time and effort as people search for apartments.
4. It leads landlords to maintain apartments in inefficiently low quality or condition.

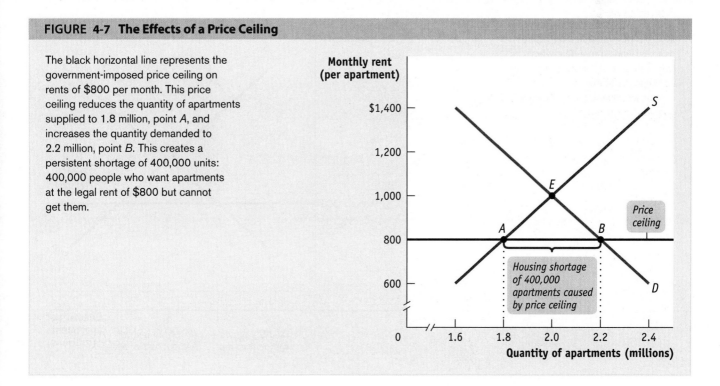

FIGURE 4-7 The Effects of a Price Ceiling

The black horizontal line represents the government-imposed price ceiling on rents of $800 per month. This price ceiling reduces the quantity of apartments supplied to 1.8 million, point *A*, and increases the quantity demanded to 2.2 million, point *B*. This creates a persistent shortage of 400,000 units: 400,000 people who want apartments at the legal rent of $800 but cannot get them.

Deadweight loss is the loss in total surplus that occurs whenever an action or a policy reduces the quantity transacted below the efficient market equilibrium quantity.

In addition to inefficiency, price ceilings give rise to illegal behavior as people try to circumvent them.

We'll now look at each of these inefficiencies caused by price ceilings.

Inefficiently Low Quantity Because rent controls reduce the number of apartments supplied, they reduce the number of apartments rented, too.

Figure 4-8 shows the implications for total surplus. Recall that total surplus is the sum of the area above the supply curve and below the demand curve. If the only effect of rent control was to reduce the number of apartments available, it would cause a loss of surplus equal to the area of the shaded triangle in the figure.

The area represented by that triangle has a special name in economics, **deadweight loss:** the lost surplus associated with the transactions that no longer occur due to the market intervention. In this example, the deadweight loss is the lost surplus associated with the apartment rentals that no longer occur due to the price ceiling, a loss that is experienced by both disappointed renters and frustrated landlords. Economists often call triangles like the one in Figure 4-8 a *deadweight-loss triangle.*

Deadweight loss is a key concept in economics, one that we will encounter whenever an action or a policy leads to a reduction in the quantity transacted below the efficient market equilibrium quantity. It is important to realize that deadweight loss is a *loss to society*—it is a reduction in total surplus, a loss in surplus that accrues to no one as a gain. It is not the same as a loss in surplus to one person that then accrues as a gain to someone else, what an economist would call a *transfer* of surplus from one person to another. For an example, in the next section we will explore how a price ceiling can create deadweight loss as well as a transfer of surplus between renters and landlords. Deadweight loss is not the only type of inefficiency that arises from a price ceiling. The types of inefficiency created by rent control go beyond reducing the quantity of apartments available. These additional inefficiencies—inefficient allocation to consumers,

---

FIGURE 4-8 A Price Ceiling Causes Inefficiently Low Quantity

A price ceiling reduces the quantity supplied below the market equilibrium quantity, leading to a deadweight loss. The area of the shaded triangle corresponds to the amount of total surplus lost due to the inefficiently low quantity transacted.

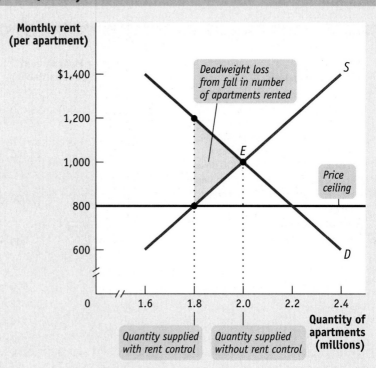

wasted resources, and inefficiently low quality—lead to a loss of surplus over and above the deadweight loss.

Inefficient Allocation to Consumers Rent control doesn't just lead to too few apartments being available. It can also lead to misallocation of the apartments that are available: people who badly need a place to live may not be able to find an apartment, but some apartments may be occupied by people with much less urgent needs.

In the case shown in Figure 4-7, 2.2 million people would like to rent an apartment at $800 per month, but only 1.8 million apartments are available. Of those 2.2 million who are seeking an apartment, some want one badly and are willing to pay a high price to get it. Others have a less urgent need and are only willing to pay a low price, perhaps because they have alternative housing. An efficient allocation of apartments would reflect these differences: people who really want an apartment will get one and people who aren't all that anxious to find an apartment won't. In an inefficient distribution of apartments, the opposite will happen: some people who are not especially anxious to find an apartment will get one and others who are very anxious to find an apartment won't.

Because people usually get apartments through luck or personal connections, under rent control, it generally results in an **inefficient allocation to consumers** of the few apartments available.

To see the inefficiency involved, consider the plight of the Lees, a family with young children who have no alternative housing and would be willing to pay up to $1,500 for an apartment—but are unable to find one. Also consider George, a retiree who lives most of the year in Florida but still has a lease on the New York apartment he moved into 40 years ago. George pays $800 per month for this apartment, but if the rent were even slightly more—say, $850—he would give it up and stay with his children when he visits New York.

This allocation of apartments—George has one and the Lees do not—is a missed opportunity: there is a way to make the Lees and George both better off at no additional cost. The Lees would be happy to pay George, say, $1,200 a month to sublease his apartment, which he would happily accept since the apartment is worth no more than $849 a month to him. George would prefer the money he gets from the Lees to keeping his apartment; the Lees would prefer to have the apartment rather than the money. So both would be made better off by this transaction—and nobody else would be made worse off.

Generally, if people who really want apartments could sublease them from people who are less eager to live there, both those who gain apartments and those who trade their occupancy for money would be better off. However, subletting is illegal under rent control because it would occur at prices above the price ceiling.

The fact that subletting is illegal doesn't mean it never happens. In fact, chasing down illegal subletting is a major business for New York private investigators who are hired to prove that the legal tenants in rent-controlled apartments actually live somewhere else and have sublet their apartments at two or three times the controlled rent.

Although landlords and legal agencies actively discourage the practice of illegal subletting, the problem of inefficient allocation of apartments remains.

Wasted Resources Another reason a price ceiling causes inefficiency is that it leads to **wasted resources:** people expend money, effort, and time to cope with the shortages caused by the price ceiling. Back in 1979, U.S. price controls on gasoline led to shortages that forced millions of Americans to wait in lines at gas stations for hours each week. The opportunity cost of the time spent in gas lines—the wages not earned, the leisure time not enjoyed—constituted wasted resources from the point of view of consumers and of the economy as a whole.

Price ceilings often lead to inefficiency in the form of **inefficient allocation to consumers:** some people who want the good badly and are willing to pay a high price don't get it, and some who care relatively little about the good and are only willing to pay a low price do get it.

Price ceilings typically lead to inefficiency in the form of **wasted resources:** people expend money, effort, and time to cope with the shortages caused by the price ceiling.

Price ceilings often lead to inefficiency in that the goods being offered are of **inefficiently low quality:** sellers offer low-quality goods at a low price even though buyers would prefer a higher quality at a higher price.

A **black market** is a market in which goods or services are bought and sold illegally—either because it is illegal to sell them at all or because the prices charged are legally prohibited by a price ceiling.

Because of rent control, the Lees will spend all their spare time for several months searching for an apartment, time they would rather have spent working or in family activities. That is, there is an opportunity cost to the Lees' prolonged search for an apartment—the leisure or income they had to forgo.

If the market for apartments worked freely, the Lees would quickly find an apartment at the equilibrium rent of $1,000, leaving them time to earn more or to enjoy themselves—an outcome that would make them better off without making anyone else worse off. Again, rent control creates missed opportunities.

Inefficiently Low Quality Yet another way a price ceiling creates inefficiency is by causing goods to be of inefficiently low quality. **Inefficiently low quality** means that sellers offer low-quality goods at a low price even though buyers would rather have higher quality and would be willing to pay a higher price for it.

Again, consider rent control. Landlords have no incentive to provide better conditions because they cannot raise rents to cover their repair costs but are able to find tenants easily. In many cases, tenants would be willing to pay much more for improved conditions than it would cost for the landlord to provide them—for example, upgrading an outdated electrical system that cannot safely run air conditioners or computers. But any additional payment for such improvements would be legally considered a rent increase, which is prohibited.

Indeed, rent-controlled apartments are notoriously badly maintained, rarely painted, subject to frequent electrical and plumbing problems, sometimes even hazardous to inhabit. As one manager of a Manhattan building described: "At unregulated apartments we'd do most things that the tenants requested. But on the rent-regulated units, we did absolutely only what the law required. . . . We had a perverse incentive to make those tenants unhappy." This whole situation is a missed opportunity—some tenants would be happy to pay for better conditions, and landlords would be happy to provide them for payment. But such an exchange would occur only if the market were allowed to operate freely.

Black Markets In addition to these four inefficiencies there is a final aspect of price ceilings: the incentive they provide for illegal activities, specifically the emergence of **black markets.** We have already described one kind of black market activity—illegal subletting by tenants. But it does not stop there. Clearly, there is a temptation for a landlord to say to a potential tenant, "Look, you can have the place if you slip me an extra few hundred in cash each month"—and for the tenant to agree if he or she is one of those people who would be willing to pay much more than the maximum legal rent.

What's wrong with black markets? In general, it's a bad thing if people break any law, because it encourages disrespect for the law in general. Worse yet, in this case illegal activity worsens the position of those who are honest. If the Lees are scrupulous about upholding the rent-control law but other people—who may need an apartment less than the Lees—are willing to bribe landlords, the Lees may never find an apartment.

Winners, Losers, and Rent Control

We've just seen how price controls can lead to inefficiencies. These inefficiencies, in turn, create winners and losers as some people benefit from policies like rent control while others are made worse off.

Using consumer and producer surplus, we can graphically evaluate the winners and the losers from rent control. Panel (a) of Figure 4-9 shows the consumer surplus and producer surplus in the equilibrium of the unregulated market for apartments before rent control. Recall that the *consumer surplus,* represented by the area below the demand curve and above the price, is the total net gain to consumers in the market equilibrium. Likewise, *producer surplus,* represented by the area above the supply curve and below the price, is the total net gain to producers in the market equilibrium.

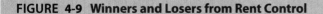

FIGURE 4-9 Winners and Losers from Rent Control

(a) Before Rent Control

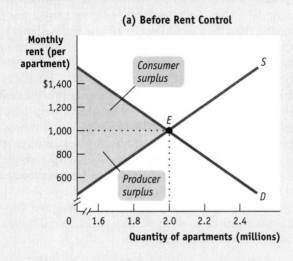

(b) After Rent Control

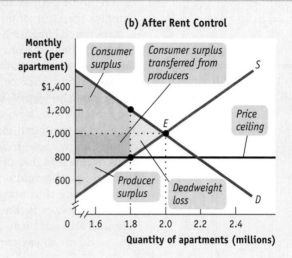

In the market for apartments, total surplus is maximized before rent control, as shown in panel (a). After rent controls are introduced, total surplus is reduced by the deadweight loss equal to the yellow triangle, shown in panel (b), but consumers are often better off, as indicated by the purple rectangle showing the amount of producer surplus transferred to consumers after rent control.

Panel (b) of this figure shows the consumer and producer surplus in the market after the price ceiling of $800 has been imposed. As you can see, for consumers who can still obtain apartments under rent control, consumer surplus has increased. These renters are clearly winners: they obtain an apartment at $800, paying $200 less than the unregulated market price. These people receive a direct transfer of surplus from landlords in the form of lower rent.

But not all renters win: there are fewer apartments to rent now than if the market had remained unregulated, making it hard, if not impossible, for some to find a place to call home.

Without direct calculation of the surpluses gained and lost, it is generally unclear whether renters as a whole are made better or worse off by rent control. What we can say is that the greater the deadweight loss—the larger the reduction in the quantity of apartments rented—the more likely it is that renters as a whole lose.

However, we can say unambiguously that landlords are worse off: producer surplus has clearly decreased. Landlords who continue to rent out their apartments get $200 a month less in rent, and others withdraw their apartments from the market altogether. The deadweight-loss triangle, shaded yellow in panel (b), represents the value lost to both renters and landlords from rentals that essentially vanish thanks to rent control.

So Why Are There Price Ceilings?

We have seen three common results of price ceilings:

- A persistent shortage of the good
- Inefficiency arising from this persistent shortage in the form of inefficiently low quantity (deadweight loss), inefficient allocation of the good to consumers, resources wasted in searching for the good, and the inefficiently low quality of the good offered for sale
- The emergence of illegal, black market activity

Given these unpleasant consequences of price ceilings, why do governments still sometimes impose them? Why does rent control, in particular, persist in New York?

One answer is that although price ceilings may have adverse effects, they do benefit some people. In practice, New York's rent-control rules—which are more complex than our simple model—hurt most residents but give a small minority of renters much cheaper housing than they would get in an unregulated market. And those who benefit from the controls are typically better organized and more vocal than those who are harmed by them.

Also, when price ceilings have been in effect for a long time, buyers may not have a realistic idea of what would happen without them. In our previous example, the rental rate in an unregulated market (Figure 4-6) would be only 25% higher than in the regulated market (Figure 4-7): $1,000 instead of $800. But how would renters know that? Indeed, they might have heard about black market transactions at much higher prices—the Lees or some other family paying George $1,200 or more—and would not realize that these black market prices are much higher than the price that would prevail in a fully unregulated market.

A last answer is that government officials often do not understand supply and demand analysis! It is a great mistake to suppose that economic policies in the real world are always sensible or well informed.

ECONOMICS >> *in Action*
Why Price Controls in Venezuela Proved Useless

Venezuela's food shortages show how price controls disproportionately hurt the people they were designed to benefit.

By all accounts, Venezuela, as one of the world's top producers of oil, is a rich country. But despite its wealth, by 2016, price controls had so distorted its economy that the country was struggling to feed its citizens. Basic items like toilet paper, rice, coffee, corn, flour, milk, and meat were chronically lacking.

Venezuelans lined up for hours to purchase price-controlled goods at state-run stores, but they often came away empty handed. "Empty shelves and no one to explain why a rich country has no food. It's unacceptable," said Jesús López, a 90-year old farmer.

The origins of the shortages can be traced to policies espoused by Venezuela's former president, Hugo Chávez. First elected in 1998 on a platform that promised to favor the poor and working classes over the country's economic elite, Chávez implemented price controls on basic foodstuffs. Prices were set so low that farmers reduced production, so that by 2006 shortages were severe. As a result, Venezuela went from being self-sufficient in food in 1998 to importing more than 70% of its food by 2016.

At the same time, generous government programs for the poor and working class created higher demand. The reduced supply of goods due to price controls combined with higher demand led to sharply rising prices for black market goods that, in turn, generated even greater demand for goods sold at the controlled prices. Smuggling became rampant, since a bottle of milk sold across the border in Colombia for seven or eight times the controlled price in Venezuela. Not surprisingly, fresh milk was rarely seen in Venezuelan markets.

The irony of the situation is that the policies put in place to help the poor and working classes have disproportionately hurt them. By 2016, a basket of basic foodstuffs on the black market cost six times the Venezuelan minimum monthly salary and people were spending up to 12 hours at a time in line. As one shopper in a low-income area said, "It fills me with rage to have to spend the one free day I have wasting my time for a bag of rice. I end up paying more at the resellers [the black market]. In the end, all these price controls proved useless."

By late 2016, the lack of basic necessities—food and medicine—coupled with soaring crime, led to a mass exodus from Venezuela to neighboring countries that continues. As one woman said, "I'm leaving with nothing. But I have to do this. Otherwise, we will just die hungry here."

>> Check Your Understanding 4-2

Solutions appear at back of book.

1. On game days, homeowners near Middletown University's stadium used to rent parking spaces in their driveways to fans at a going rate of $11. A new town ordinance now sets a maximum parking fee of $7. Use the accompanying supply and demand diagram to explain how each of the following corresponds to a price-ceiling concept.

   a. Some homeowners now think it's not worth the hassle to rent out spaces.

   b. Some fans who used to carpool to the game now drive alone.

   c. Some fans can't find parking and leave without seeing the game.

   Explain how each of the following adverse effects arises from the price ceiling.

   d. Some fans now arrive several hours early to find parking.

   e. Friends of homeowners near the stadium regularly attend games, even if they aren't big fans. But some serious fans have given up because of the parking situation.

   f. Some homeowners rent spaces for more than $7 but pretend that the buyers are nonpaying friends or family.

2. True or false? Explain your answer. A price ceiling below the equilibrium price of an otherwise efficient market does the following:

   a. Increases quantity supplied

   b. Makes some people who want to consume the good worse off

   c. Makes all producers worse off

3. Which of the following create deadweight loss? Which do not and are simply a transfer of surplus from one person to another? Explain your answer.

   a. You have been evicted from your rent-controlled apartment after the landlord discovered your pet boa constrictor. The apartment is quickly rented to someone else at the same price. You and the new renter do not necessarily have the same willingness to pay for the apartment.

   b. In a contest, you won a ticket to a jazz concert. But you can't go to the concert because of an exam, and the terms of the contest do not allow you to sell the ticket or give it to someone else. Would your answer to this question change if you could not sell the ticket but could give it to someone else?

   c. Your school's dean of students, who is a proponent of a low-fat diet, decrees that ice cream can no longer be served on campus.

   d. Your ice-cream cone falls on the ground and your dog eats it. (Take the liberty of counting your dog as a member of society, and assume that, if he could, your dog would be willing to pay the same amount for the ice-cream cone as you.)

Price Floors

Sometimes governments intervene to push market prices up instead of down. *Price floors* have been widely legislated for agricultural products, such as wheat and milk, as a way to support the incomes of farmers. Historically, there were also price floors—legally mandated minimum prices—on such services as trucking and air travel, although these were phased out by the U.S. government in the 1970s.

If you have ever worked in a fast-food restaurant, you are likely to have encountered a price floor: governments in the United States and many other countries

The **minimum wage** is a legal floor on the wage rate, which is the market price of labor.

maintain a lower limit on the hourly wage rate of a worker's labor; that is, a floor on the price of labor called the **minimum wage.**

Just like price ceilings, price floors are intended to help some people but generate predictable and undesirable side effects. Figure 4-10 shows hypothetical supply and demand curves for butter. Left to itself, the market would move to equilibrium at point *E*, with 10 million pounds of butter bought and sold at a price of $1 per pound.

Now suppose that the government, to help dairy farmers, imposes a price floor on butter of $1.20 per pound. Its effects are shown in Figure 4-11, where the line at $1.20 represents the price floor. At a price of $1.20 per pound, producers would want to supply 12 million pounds (point *B* on the supply curve) but consumers would want to buy only 9 million pounds (point *A* on the demand curve). So the price floor leads to a persistent surplus of 3 million pounds of butter.

Does a price floor always lead to an unwanted surplus? No. Just as in the case of a price ceiling, the floor may not be binding—that is, it may be irrelevant. If the equilibrium price of butter is $1 per pound but the floor is set at only $0.80, the floor has no effect.

But suppose that a price floor is binding: what happens to the unwanted surplus? The answer depends on government policy. In the case of agricultural price floors, governments buy up unwanted surplus. As a result, the U.S. government has at times found itself warehousing thousands of tons of butter, cheese, and other farm products. (The European Commission, which administers price floors for a number of European countries, once found itself the owner of a so-called butter mountain, equal in weight to the entire population of Austria.) The government then has to find a way to dispose of these unwanted goods.

Some countries pay exporters to sell products at a loss overseas; this is standard procedure for the European Union. The United States gives surplus food away to

---

FIGURE 4-10   The Market for Butter in the Absence of Government Controls

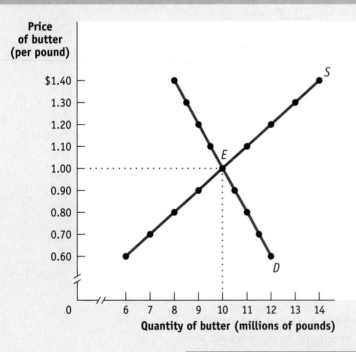

Price of butter (per pound)	Quantity of butter (millions of pounds)	
	Quantity demanded	Quantity supplied
$1.40	8.0	14.0
1.30	8.5	13.0
1.20	9.0	12.0
1.10	9.5	11.0
1.00	10.0	10.0
0.90	10.5	9.0
0.80	11.0	8.0
0.70	11.5	7.0
0.60	12.0	6.0

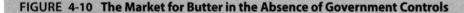

Without government intervention, the market for butter reaches equilibrium at a price of $1 per pound with 10 million pounds of butter bought and sold.

FIGURE 4-11 The Effects of a Price Floor

The black horizontal line represents the government-imposed price floor of $1.20 per pound of butter. The quantity of butter demanded falls to 9 million pounds, and the quantity supplied rises to 12 million pounds, generating a persistent surplus of 3 million pounds of butter.

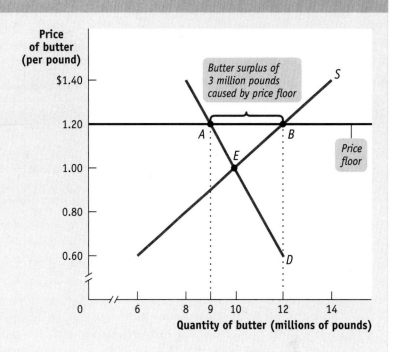

citizens in need as well as to schools, which use the products in school lunches. In some cases, governments have actually destroyed the surplus production.

When the government is not prepared to purchase the unwanted surplus, a price floor means that would-be sellers cannot find buyers. This is what happens when there is a price floor on the wage rate paid for an hour of labor, the minimum wage: when the minimum wage is above the equilibrium wage rate, some people who are willing to work—that is, sell labor—cannot find buyers—that is, employers—willing to give them jobs.

How a Price Floor Causes Inefficiency

The persistent surplus that results from a price floor creates missed opportunities—inefficiencies—that resemble those created by the shortage that results from a price ceiling. Like a price ceiling, a price floor creates inefficiency in at least four ways:

1. It creates deadweight loss by reducing the quantity transacted to below the efficient level.
2. It leads to an inefficient allocation of sales among sellers.
3. It leads to a waste of resources.
4. It leads to sellers providing an inefficiently high-quality level.

In addition to inefficiency, like a price ceiling, a price floor leads to illegal behavior as people break the law to sell below the legal price.

Inefficiently Low Quantity Because a price floor raises the price of a good to consumers, it reduces the quantity of that good demanded; because sellers can't sell more units of a good than buyers are willing to buy, a price floor reduces the quantity of a good bought and sold below the market equilibrium quantity and leads to a deadweight loss. Notice that this is the *same* effect as a price ceiling. You might be tempted to think that a price floor and a price ceiling have opposite effects, but both have the effect of reducing the quantity of a good bought and sold (see the upcoming Pitfalls).

FIGURE 4-12 A Price Floor Causes Inefficiently Low Quantity

A price floor reduces the quantity demanded below the market equilibrium quantity and leads to a deadweight loss.

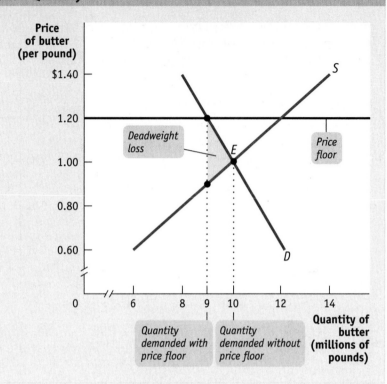

Price floors can lead to **inefficient allocation of sales among sellers:** sellers who are willing to sell at the lowest price are unable to make sales while sales go to sellers who are only willing to sell at a higher price.

Since the equilibrium of an efficient market maximizes the sum of consumer and producer surplus, a price floor that reduces the quantity below the equilibrium quantity reduces total surplus. Figure 4-12 shows the implications for total surplus of a price floor on the price of butter. Total surplus is the sum of the area above the supply curve and below the demand curve.

By reducing the quantity of butter sold, a price floor causes a deadweight loss equal to the area of the shaded triangle in the figure. As in the case of a price ceiling, however, deadweight loss is only one of the forms of inefficiency that the price control creates.

Inefficient Allocation of Sales Among Sellers Like a price ceiling, a price floor can lead to *inefficient allocation*—in this case, an **inefficient allocation of sales among sellers:** sellers who are willing to sell at the lowest price are unable to make sales, while sales go to sellers who are only willing to sell at a higher price.

One example of the inefficient allocation of selling opportunities caused by a price floor was the labor market situation in many European countries from the 1980s onward. A high minimum wage led to a two-tier labor system, composed of the fortunate who had good jobs in the formal labor market, and the rest who were locked out without any prospect of ever finding a good job.

PITFALLS

CEILINGS, FLOORS, AND QUANTITIES

A price ceiling pushes the price of a good *down*. A price floor pushes the price of a good *up*. So it's easy to assume that the effects of a price floor are the opposite of the effects of a price ceiling. In particular, if a price ceiling reduces the quantity of a good bought and sold, doesn't a price floor increase the quantity?

No, it doesn't. In fact, both floors and ceilings reduce the quantity bought and sold. Why? When the quantity of a good supplied

isn't equal to the quantity demanded, the actual quantity sold is determined by the "short side" of the market—whichever quantity is less. If sellers don't want to sell as much as buyers want to buy, it's the sellers who determine the actual quantity sold, because buyers can't force unwilling sellers to sell. If buyers don't want to buy as much as sellers want to sell, it's the buyers who determine the actual quantity sold, because sellers can't force unwilling buyers to buy.

Either unemployed or underemployed in dead-end jobs in the black market for labor, the unlucky ones were disproportionately young, from the ages of 18 to early 30s. Although eager for good jobs in the formal sector and willing to accept less than the minimum wage—that is, willing to sell their labor for a lower price—it was illegal for employers to pay them less than the minimum wage.

The inefficiency of unemployment and underemployment was compounded as a generation of young people was unable to get adequate job training, develop careers, and save for their future. These young people were also more likely to engage in crime. And many of these countries saw their best and brightest young people emigrate, leading to a permanent reduction in the future performance of their economies. The social losses grew to such an extent that in recent years European countries have undertaken labor market reforms that have significantly reduced the problem.

Wasted Resources Also like a price ceiling, a price floor generates inefficiency by *wasting resources*. The most graphic examples involve government purchases of the unwanted surpluses of agricultural products caused by price floors. The surplus production is sometimes destroyed, which is pure waste; in other cases, the stored produce goes, as officials euphemistically put it, "out of condition" and must be thrown away.

Price floors also lead to wasted time and effort. Consider the minimum wage. Would-be workers who spend many hours searching for jobs, or waiting in line in the hope of getting jobs, play the same role in the case of price floors as hapless families searching for apartments in the case of price ceilings.

Inefficiently High Quality Again like price ceilings, price floors lead to inefficiency in the quality of goods produced.

We saw that when there is a price ceiling, suppliers produce products that are of inefficiently low quality: buyers prefer higher-quality products and are willing to pay for them, but sellers refuse to improve the quality of their products because the price ceiling prevents their being compensated for doing so. This same logic applies to price floors, but in reverse: suppliers offer goods of **inefficiently high quality.**

How can this be? Isn't high quality a good thing? Yes, but only if it is worth the cost. Suppose that suppliers spend a lot to make goods of very high quality but that this quality isn't worth much to consumers, who would rather receive the money spent on that quality in the form of a lower price. This represents a missed opportunity: suppliers and buyers could make a mutually beneficial deal in which buyers got goods of lower quality for a much lower price.

A good example of the inefficiency of excessive quality comes from the days when transatlantic airfares were set artificially high by international treaty. Forbidden to compete for customers by offering lower ticket prices, airlines instead offered expensive services, like lavish in-flight meals that went largely uneaten—an especially wasteful practice, considering that what passengers really wanted was less food and lower airfares.

Since the deregulation of U.S. airlines in the 1970s, American passengers have experienced a large decrease in ticket prices accompanied by a decrease in the quality of in-flight service—smaller seats, lower-quality food, and so on. Everyone complains about the service—but thanks to lower fares, the number of people flying on U.S. carriers has grown from 130 billion passenger miles, when deregulation began, to over 1 trillion miles in 2018.

Illegal Activity In addition to the four inefficiencies we analyzed, like price ceilings, price floors provide incentives for illegal activity. For example, in countries where the minimum wage is far above the equilibrium wage rate, workers

Price floors often lead to inefficiency in that goods of **inefficiently high quality** are offered: sellers offer high-quality goods at a high price, even though buyers would prefer a lower quality at a lower price.

desperate for jobs sometimes agree to work off the books for employers who conceal their employment from the government—or bribe the government inspectors. This practice, known in Europe as *black labor*, is especially common in Southern European countries such as Italy and Spain.

So Why Are There Price Floors?

To sum up, a price floor creates various negative side effects:

- A persistent surplus of the good
- Inefficiency arising from the persistent surplus in the form of inefficiently low quantity (deadweight loss), inefficient allocation of sales among sellers, wasted resources, and an inefficiently high level of quality offered by suppliers
- The temptation to engage in illegal activity, particularly bribery and corruption of government officials

So why do governments impose price floors when they have so many negative side effects? The reasons are similar to those for imposing price ceilings. Government officials often disregard warnings about the consequences of price floors either because they believe that the relevant market is poorly described by the supply and demand model or, more often, because they do not understand the model. Above all, just as price ceilings are often imposed because they benefit some influential buyers of a good, price floors are often imposed because they benefit some influential sellers.

"We have an opening for a part-time upaid intern, which could lead to a full-time unpaid internship."

Aaron Bacall/www.Cartoonstock.com

ECONOMICS >> *in Action*
The Rise and Fall of the Unpaid Intern

The best-known example of a price floor is the minimum wage. Most economists believe, however, that the minimum wage has relatively little effect on the overall job market in the United States, mainly because the floor is set so low. In 1964, the U.S. minimum wage was 53% of the average wage of blue-collar production workers; by 2015, it had fallen to about 35%. However, there is one sector of the U.S. job market where it appears that the minimum wage can indeed be binding: the market for interns.

Starting in 2011, a spate of lawsuits brought by former unpaid interns claiming they were cheated out of wages brought the matter to public attention. A common thread in these complaints was that interns were assigned grunt work with no educational value, such as tracking lost cell phones. In other cases, unpaid interns complained that they were given the work of full-salaried employees. And by 2015, many of those lawsuits proved successful: Condé Nast Publications settled for $5.8 million, Sirius Satellite XM Radio settled for $1.3 million, and Viacom Media settled for $7.2 million. In 2017, even the Olsen twins had to cough up $140,000 in payments to unpaid interns for their fashion company, Dualstar Entertainment.

As a result, unless their programs can clearly demonstrate an educational component such as course credit, companies have to pay their interns minimum wage or shut down their programs altogether.

Some observers worry that the end of the unpaid internship means that programs that once offered valuable training will be lost. But as one lawyer commented, "The law says that when you work, you have to get paid [at least the minimum wage]."

>> *Check Your Understanding* 4-3

Solutions appear at back of book.

1. The state legislature mandates a price floor for gasoline of P_F per gallon. Assess the following statements and illustrate your answer using this figure.
   a. Proponents of the law claim it will increase the income of gas station owners. Opponents claim it will hurt gas station owners because they will lose customers.
   b. Proponents claim consumers will be better off because gas stations will provide better service. Opponents claim consumers will be generally worse off because they prefer to buy gas at cheaper prices.
   c. Proponents claim that they are helping gas station owners without hurting anyone else. Opponents claim that consumers are hurt and will end up doing things like buying gas in a nearby state or on the black market.

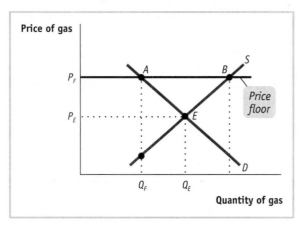

- The most familiar price floor is the **minimum wage.** Price floors are also commonly imposed on agricultural goods.

- A price floor above the equilibrium price benefits successful sellers but causes predictable adverse effects such as a persistent surplus, which leads to four kinds of inefficiencies: deadweight loss from inefficiently low quantity, **inefficient allocation of sales among sellers,** wasted resources, and **inefficiently high quality.**

- Price floors encourage illegal activity, such as workers who work off the books, often leading to official corruption.

‖ Controlling Quantities

In the 1930s, New York City instituted a system of licensing for taxicabs: only taxis with a "medallion" were allowed to pick up passengers hailing them from the street. Because this system was intended to assure quality, medallion owners were supposed to maintain certain standards, including safety and cleanliness. A total of 11,787 medallions were issued, with taxi owners paying $10 for each medallion.

In 1995, there were still only 11,787 licensed taxicabs in New York, even though the city had meanwhile become the financial capital of the world, a place where hundreds of thousands of people in a hurry tried to hail a cab every day. By 2015, the number of licensed cabs had risen to only 13,635. And up until a few years ago, this restriction on the number of New York City taxi medallions made them a very valuable item: if you want to operate a taxi in the city, you must lease a medallion from someone or buy one.

Yet restrictions on the number of taxis induced people to try to circumvent them, eventually leading to the emergence of mobile-app-based car services like Uber and Lyft. Their cars aren't hailed from the street like taxis—in fact, their drivers are forbidden from picking up riders from the street. Instead, riders quickly arrange trips on their smartphones, directing available drivers to their location. Of course, the ubiquity of smartphones also contributed to the emergence of these car services.

Since 2013, Uber and Lyft have had a significant effect on the market for car rides in New York City and most other major cities. But let's postpone the discussion of those effects until we learn more about how the market worked when only licensed taxicabs could operate.

A taxi medallion is a form of **quantity control,** or **quota,** by which the government regulates the quantity of a good that can be bought and sold rather than the price at which it is transacted. It is another way that government intervenes in markets along with price ceilings and price floors. The total amount of the good that can be transacted under the quantity control is called the **quota limit.** Typically, the government limits quantity in a market by issuing **licenses;** only people with a license can legally supply the good.

A taxi medallion is just such a license. The government of New York City limited the number of taxi rides that can be sold by limiting the number of taxis to only those

A **quantity control,** or **quota,** is an upper limit on the quantity of some good that can be bought or sold. The total amount of the good that can be legally transacted is the **quota limit.**

A **license** gives its owner the right to supply a good.

who hold medallions. More generally, quantity controls, or quotas, set an upper limit on the quantity of a good that can be transacted. For example, quotas have been used frequently to limit the size of the catch of endangered fish stocks. In this case, quotas are implemented for good economic reasons: to protect endangered fish stocks.

But some quotas are implemented for bad economic reasons, typically for the purpose of enriching the quota holder. For example, quantity controls introduced to address a temporary problem such as assuring that only safe and clean taxis are allowed to operate, become difficult to remove later, once the problem disappears, because quota holders benefit from them and exert political pressure.

The Anatomy of Quantity Controls

To understand why a New York taxi medallion is worth so much money, we consider a simplified version of the market for taxi rides, shown in Figure 4-13. Just as we assumed in the analysis of rent control that all apartments are the same, we now suppose that all taxi rides are the same—ignoring the real-world complication that some taxi rides are longer, and so more expensive, than others.

The table in the figure shows supply and demand schedules. The equilibrium—indicated by point *E* in the figure and by the shaded entries in the table—is a fare of $5 per ride, with 10 million rides taken per year. (You'll see in a minute why we present the equilibrium this way.)

The New York medallion system limits the number of taxis, but each taxi driver can offer as many rides as he or she can manage. To simplify our analysis, however, we will assume that a medallion system limits the number of taxi rides that can legally be given to 8 million per year.

Until now, we have derived the demand curve by answering questions of the form: "How many taxi rides will passengers want to take if the price is $5 per ride?" But it is possible to reverse the question and ask instead: "At what price will consumers want to buy 10 million rides per year?" The price at which consumers want to buy a given quantity—in this case, 10 million rides at $5 per ride—is the **demand price** of that quantity. You can see from the demand schedule in

The **demand price** of a given quantity is the price at which consumers will demand that quantity.

FIGURE 4-13 The Market for Taxi Rides in the Absence of Government Controls

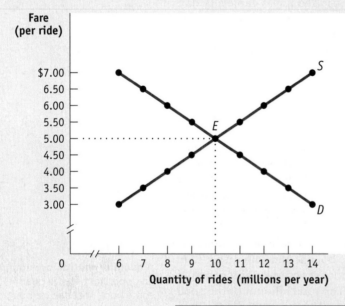

Fare (per ride)	Quantity of rides (millions per year)	
	Quantity demanded	Quantity supplied
$7.00	6	14
6.50	7	13
6.00	8	12
5.50	9	11
5.00	10	10
4.50	11	9
4.00	12	8
3.50	13	7
3.00	14	6

Without government intervention, the market reaches equilibrium with 10 million rides taken per year at a fare of $5 per ride.

Figure 4-13 that the demand price of 6 million rides is $7 per ride, the demand price of 7 million rides is $6.50 per ride, and so on.

Similarly, the supply curve represents the answer to questions of the form: "How many taxi rides would taxi drivers supply at a price of $5 each?" But we can also reverse this question to ask: "At what price will suppliers be willing to supply 10 million rides per year?" The price at which suppliers will supply a given quantity—in this case, 10 million rides at $5 per ride—is the **supply price** of that quantity. We can see from the supply schedule in Figure 4-13 that the supply price of 6 million rides is $3 per ride, the supply price of 7 million rides is $3.50 per ride, and so on.

Now we are ready to analyze a quota. We have assumed that the city government limits the quantity of taxi rides to 8 million per year. Medallions, each of which carries the right to provide a certain number of taxi rides per year, are made available to selected people in such a way that a total of 8 million rides will be provided. Medallion-holders may then either drive their own taxis or rent their medallions to others for a fee.

Figure 4-14 shows the resulting market for taxi rides, with the black vertical line at 8 million rides per year representing the quota limit. Because the quantity of rides is limited to 8 million, consumers must be at point *A* on the demand curve, corresponding to the shaded entry in the demand schedule: the demand price of 8 million rides is $6 per ride. Meanwhile, taxi drivers must be at point *B* on the supply curve, corresponding to the shaded entry in the supply schedule: the supply price of 8 million rides is $4 per ride.

But how can the price received by taxi drivers be $4 when the price paid by taxi riders is $6? The answer is that in addition to the market in taxi rides, there is

> The **supply price** of a given quantity is the price at which producers will supply that quantity.

FIGURE 4-14 Effect of a Quota on the Market for Taxi Rides

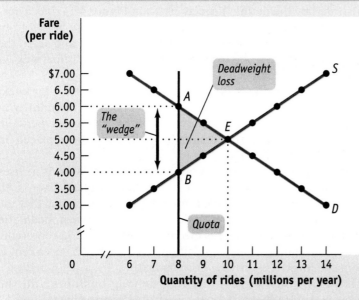

Fare (per ride)	Quantity of rides (millions per year)	
	Quantity demanded	Quantity supplied
$7.00	6	14
6.50	7	13
6.00	8	12
5.50	9	11
5.00	10	10
4.50	11	9
4.00	12	8
3.50	13	7
3.00	14	6

The table shows the demand price and the supply price corresponding to each quantity: the price at which that quantity would be demanded and supplied, respectively. The city government imposes a quota of 8 million rides by selling licenses for only 8 million rides, represented by the black vertical line. The price paid by consumers rises to $6 per ride, the demand price of 8 million rides, shown by point *A*.

The supply price of 8 million rides is only $4 per ride, shown by point *B*. The difference between these two prices is the quota rent per ride, the earnings that accrue to the owner of a license. The quota rent drives a wedge between the demand price and the supply price. And since the quota discourages mutually beneficial transactions, it creates a deadweight loss equal to the shaded triangle.

also a market in medallions. Medallion-holders may not always want to drive their taxis: they may be ill or on vacation. Those who do not want to drive their own taxis will sell the right to use the medallion to someone else.

So we need to consider two sets of transactions here, and so two prices: (1) the transactions in taxi rides and the price at which these will occur, and (2) the transactions in medallions and the price at which these will occur. It turns out that since we are looking at two markets, the $4 and $6 prices will both be right.

To see how this all works, consider two imaginary New York taxi drivers, Ali and Jean. Ali has a medallion but he can't use it because he's recovering from a severely sprained wrist, so he's looking to rent his medallion out to someone else. Jean doesn't have a medallion but would like to rent one. Furthermore, at any point in time there are many other people like Jean who would like to rent a medallion. Suppose Ali agrees to rent his medallion to Jean. To make things simple, assume that any driver can give only one ride per day and that Ali is renting his medallion to Jean for one day. What rental price will they agree on?

To answer this question, we need to look at the transactions from the viewpoints of both drivers. Once she has the medallion, Jean knows she can make $6 per day—the demand price of a ride under the quota. And she is willing to rent the medallion only if she makes at least $4 per day—the supply price of a ride under the quota. So Ali cannot demand a rent of more than $2—the difference between $6 and $4. And if Jean offered Ali less than $2—say, $1.50—there would be other eager drivers willing to offer him more, up to $2. So, to get the medallion, Jean must offer Ali at least $2. Since the rent can be no more than $2 and no less than $2, it must be exactly $2.

It is no coincidence that $2 is exactly the difference between $6, the demand price of 8 million rides, and $4, the supply price of 8 million rides. In every case in which the supply of a good is legally restricted, there is a **wedge** between the demand price of the quantity transacted and the supply price of the quantity transacted.

This wedge, illustrated by the double-headed arrow in Figure 4-14, has a special name: the **quota rent.** It is the earnings that accrue to the license-holder from ownership of a valuable commodity, the license. In the case of Ali and Jean, the quota rent of $2 goes to Ali because he owns the license, and the remaining $4 from the total fare of $6 goes to Jean.

So Figure 4-14 also illustrates the quota rent in the market for New York taxi rides. The quota limits the quantity of rides to 8 million per year, a quantity at which the demand price of $6 exceeds the supply price of $4. The wedge between these two prices, $2, is the quota rent that results from the restrictions placed on the quantity of taxi rides in this market.

But wait a second. What if Ali doesn't rent out his medallion? What if he uses it himself? Doesn't this mean that he gets a price of $6? No, not really. Even if Ali doesn't rent out his medallion, he could have rented it out, which means that the medallion has an *opportunity cost* of $2: if Ali decides to use his own medallion and drive his own taxi rather than renting his medallion to Jean, the $2 represents his opportunity cost of not renting out his medallion. That is, the $2 quota rent is now the rental income he forgoes by driving his own taxi.

In effect, Ali is in two businesses—the taxi-driving business and the medallion-renting business. He makes $4 per ride from driving his taxi and $2 per ride from renting out his medallion. It doesn't make any difference that in this particular case he has rented his medallion to himself!

So regardless of whether the medallion owner uses the medallion himself or herself, or rents it to others, it is a valuable asset. And this is represented in the going price for a New York City taxi medallion: in 2013, medallions regularly sold for over $1 million. At that time, an owner of a medallion who leased it to a driver could expect to earn about $2,500 per month, or a 3% return—an attractive rate of return compared to other investments.

A quantity control, or quota, drives a **wedge** between the demand price and the supply price of a good; that is, the price paid by buyers ends up being higher than that received by sellers.

The difference between the demand and supply price at the quota limit is the **quota rent,** the earnings that accrue to the license-holder from ownership of the right to sell the good. It is equal to the market price of the license when the licenses are traded.

Notice, by the way, that quotas—like price ceilings and price floors—don't always have a real effect. If the quota were set at 12 million rides—that is, above the equilibrium quantity in an unregulated market—it would have no effect because it would not be binding.

The Costs of Quantity Controls

Like price controls, quantity controls can have some predictable and undesirable side effects. The first is the by-now-familiar problem of inefficiency due to missed opportunities: quantity controls create deadweight loss by preventing mutually beneficial transactions from occurring, transactions that would benefit both buyers and sellers.

Looking back at Figure 4-14, you can see that starting at the quota limit of 8 million rides, New Yorkers would be willing to pay at least $5.50 per ride when 9 million rides are offered, 1 million more than the quota, and that taxi drivers would be willing to provide those rides as long as they got at least $4.50 per ride. These are rides that would have taken place if there were no quota limit.

The same is true for the next 1 million rides: New Yorkers would be willing to pay at least $5 per ride when the quantity of rides is increased from 9 to 10 million, and taxi drivers would be willing to provide those rides as long as they got at least $5 per ride. Again, these rides would have occurred without the quota limit.

Only when the market has reached the unregulated market equilibrium quantity of 10 million rides are there no "missed-opportunity rides." The quota limit of 8 million rides has caused 2 million "missed-opportunity rides."

Generally, *as long as the demand price of a given quantity exceeds the supply price, there is a deadweight loss.* A buyer would be willing to buy the good at a price that the seller would be willing to accept, but such a transaction does not occur because it is forbidden by the quota. The deadweight loss arising from the 2 million in missed-opportunity rides is represented by the shaded triangle in Figure 4-14.

And because there are transactions that people would like to make but are not allowed to, quantity controls generate an incentive to circumvent them. In the days before Uber and Lyft, a substantial number of unlicensed taxis simply defied the law and picked up passengers without a medallion. These unregulated, unlicensed taxis contributed to a disproportionately large share of accidents.

However, Uber and Lyft cars legally circumvent the restriction that a car without a medallion can't be hailed from the street. By 2018, Uber had over 65,000 cars in New York City, significantly more than the 13,587 licensed taxicabs.

Clearly, the quantity restriction on New York City taxicabs has been substantially undermined. In effect, the quota line in Figure 4-14 has shifted rightward, closer to the equilibrium quantity, with the entry of Uber and Lyft.

In the past few years, as quota rents to owners of a taxi medallion have fallen, the prices of taxi medallions have fallen significantly as well. In sum, quantity controls typically create the following undesirable side effects:

- Deadweight loss because some mutually beneficial transactions don't occur
- Incentives for illegal activities

ECONOMICS >> *in Action*
Crabbing, Quotas, and Saving Lives in Alaska

Alaskan king and snow crab are considered delicacies worldwide. And crab fishing is one of the most important industries in the Alaskan economy. So, many were justifiably concerned when, in 1983, the annual crab catch fell by 90% due to overfishing. In response, marine biologists set a *total allowable catch quota system,*

Jean-Erick PASQUIER/Getty Images

The quota-share system protects Alaska's crab population and saves the lives of crabbers.

which limited the amount of crab that could be harvested annually to allow the crab population to return to a healthy, sustainable level.

Notice, by the way, that the Alaskan crab quota is an example of a quota that was justified by broader economic and environmental considerations—unlike the New York taxicab quota, which has long since lost any economic rationale. Another important difference is that, unlike New York taxicab medallions, owners of Alaskan crab boats did not have the ability to buy or sell individual quotas. So although depleted crab stocks eventually recovered with the total catch quota system in place, there was another, unintended and deadly consequence.

The Alaskan crabbing season is fairly short, running roughly from October to January, and it can be further shortened by bad weather. By the 1990s, Alaskan crab fishermen were engaging in "fishing derbies." To stay within the quota limit when the crabbing season began, boat crews rushed to fish for crab in dangerous, icy, rough water, straining to harvest in a few days a haul that could be worth several hundred thousand dollars. As a result, boats often became overloaded and capsized, making Alaskan crab fishing one of the most dangerous jobs, with an average of 7.3 deaths a year, about 80 times the fatality rate for an average worker. And after the brief harvest, the market for crab was flooded with supply, lowering the prices fishermen received.

In 2006 fishery regulators instituted another quota system called *quota share*—aimed at protecting Alaska's crabbers and crabs. Under individual quota share, each boat received a quota to fill during the three-month season. Moreover, the individual quotas could be sold or leased. These changes transformed the industry as owners of bigger boats bought the individual quotas of smaller boats, shrinking the number of crabbing boats dramatically. Bigger boats are much less likely to capsize, improving crew safety.

In addition, by extending the fishing season, the quota-share system boosted the crab population and crab prices. With more time to fish, fishermen could make sure that juvenile and female crabs were returned to the sea rather than harvested. And with a longer fishing season, the catch comes to market more gradually, eliminating the downward plunge in prices when supply hits the market. Predictably, an Alaskan crab fisherman earns more money under the quota-share system than under the total catch quota system.

>> Quick Review

• **Quantity controls,** or **quotas,** are government-imposed limits on how much of a good may be bought or sold. The quantity allowed for sale is the **quota limit.** The government then issues a **license**—the right to sell a given quantity of a good under the quota.

• When the quota limit is smaller than the equilibrium quantity in an unregulated market, the **demand price** is higher than the **supply price**—there is a **wedge** between them at the quota limit.

• This wedge is the **quota rent,** the earnings that accrue to the license-holder from ownership of the right to sell the good—whether by actually supplying the good or by renting the license to someone else. The market price of a license equals the quota rent.

• Like price controls, quantity controls create deadweight loss and encourage illegal activity.

>> Check Your Understanding 4-4

Solutions appear at back of book.

1. Suppose that the supply and demand for taxi rides is given by Figure 4-13 but the quota is set at 6 million rides instead of 8 million. Find the following and indicate them on Figure 4-13.
   a. The price of a ride
   b. The quota rent
   c. The deadweight loss
   d. Suppose the quota limit on taxi rides is increased to 9 million. What happens to the quota rent? To the deadweight loss?

2. Assume that the quota limit is 8 million rides. Suppose demand decreases due to a decline in tourism. What is the smallest parallel leftward shift in demand that would result in the quota no longer having an effect on the market? Illustrate your answer using Figure 4-13.

SOLVED PROBLEM   The World's Second-Most Expensive City

Up until recently, London was one of the most expensive places in the world to rent an apartment. If you've visited London, you might have noticed an area around the city known as the "Green Belt," where urban growth is discouraged in favor of nature and openness. Zoning laws make it nearly impossible to build new residential housing on land designated as the Green Belt. Consider the following hypothetical market for apartments in London in the absence of zoning controls.

Monthly rent (per apartment)	Quantity of apartments (millions)	
	Quantity demanded	Quantity supplied
£1,400	1.6	2.4
1,300	1.7	2.3
1,200	1.8	2.2
1,100	1.9	2.1
1,000	2.0	2.0
900	2.1	1.9
800	2.2	1.8
700	2.3	1.7
600	2.4	1.6

This figure should look familiar to you—it is Figure 4-6, but the currency is the British pound rather than the U.S. dollar. At the time of this writing, the British pound was worth about 1.3 dollars.

Now, let's go back to the reality of zoning controls in the Green Belt. Use a diagram to show the effect of a quota of 1.7 million apartments. What is the quota rent, and who gets it?

STEP | 1 Use a diagram to show the effect of a quota of 1.7 million apartments. *Review pages 119–123.*

In this figure, the black vertical line represents the quota limit of 1.7 million apartments. Because the quantity of apartments is limited, consumers must be at point *A* on the demand curve. The demand price of 1.7 million apartments is £1,300 each. The supply price, corresponding to point *B* on the diagram, of 1.7 million apartments is only £700 each, creating a "wedge" of £1,300 – £700 = £600.

STEP | 2 What is the quota rent in this case, and who gets it? *Review pages 119–123.*

In the case of taxis, the quota rent is the earnings that accrue to the license-holder from ownership of the right to sell the good. In the case of apartments inside the Green Belt in London, the quota rent is the "wedge" of £600 created by the difference in the demand price and the supply price. The wedge goes to current owners of property or flats in London. Current owners benefit from the strict application of zoning laws.

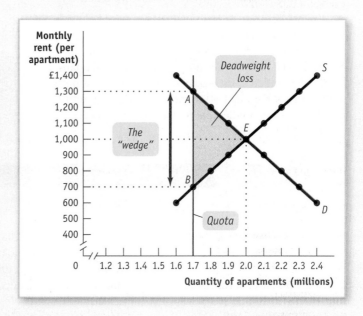

SUMMARY

1. The **willingness to pay** of each individual consumer determines the demand curve. When price is less than or equal to the willingness to pay, the potential consumer purchases the good. The difference between willingness to pay and price is the net gain to the consumer, the **individual consumer surplus. Total consumer surplus** in a market, the sum of all individual consumer surpluses in a market, is equal to the area below the market demand curve but above the price. The term **consumer surplus** is often used to refer to both individual and total consumer surplus.

2. The **cost** of each potential producer, the lowest price at which he or she is willing to supply a unit of a particular good, determines the supply curve. If the price of a good is above a producer's cost, a sale generates a net gain to the producer, known as the **individual producer surplus. Total producer surplus** in a market, the sum of the individual producer surpluses in a market, is equal to the area above the market supply curve but below the price. The term **producer surplus** is often used to refer to both individual and total producer surplus.

3. **Total surplus,** the total gain to society from the production and consumption of a good, is the sum of consumer and producer surplus.

4. Even when a market is efficient, governments often intervene to pursue greater fairness or to please a powerful interest group. Interventions can take the form of **price controls** or quantity controls, both of which generate predictable and undesirable side effects consisting of various forms of inefficiency and illegal activity.

5. A **price ceiling,** a maximum market price below the equilibrium price, benefits successful buyers but creates persistent shortages. Because the price is maintained below the equilibrium price, the quantity demanded is increased and the quantity supplied is decreased compared to the equilibrium quantity. This leads to predictable problems: inefficiencies

in the form of **deadweight loss** from inefficiently low quantity, **inefficient allocation to consumers, wasted resources,** and **inefficiently low quality.** It also encourages illegal activity as people turn to **black markets** to get the good. Because of these problems, price ceilings have generally lost favor as an economic policy tool. But some governments continue to impose them either because they don't understand the effects or because the price ceilings benefit some influential group.

6. A **price floor,** a minimum market price above the equilibrium price, benefits successful sellers but creates persistent surplus. Because the price is maintained above the equilibrium price, the quantity demanded is decreased and the quantity supplied is increased compared to the equilibrium quantity. This leads to predictable problems: inefficiencies in the form of deadweight loss from inefficiently low quantity, **inefficient allocation of sales among sellers,** wasted resources, and **inefficiently high quality.** It also encourages illegal activity and black markets. The most well-known kind of price floor is the **minimum wage,** but price floors are also commonly applied to agricultural products.

7. **Quantity controls,** or **quotas,** limit the quantity of a good that can be bought or sold. The quantity allowed for sale is the **quota limit.** The government issues **licenses** to individuals, giving them the right to sell a given quantity of the good. The owner of a license earns a **quota rent,** earnings that accrue from ownership of the right to sell the good. It is equal to the difference between the **demand price** at the quota limit, what consumers are willing to pay for that quantity, and the **supply price** at the quota limit, what suppliers are willing to accept for that quantity. Economists say that a quota drives a **wedge** between the demand price and the supply price; this wedge is equal to the quota rent. Quantity controls lead to deadweight loss in addition to encouraging illegal activity.

KEY TERMS

Willingness to pay, p. 98
Individual consumer surplus, p. 99
Total consumer surplus, p. 99
Consumer surplus, p. 99
Cost, p. 101
Individual producer surplus, p. 101
Total producer surplus, p. 101
Producer surplus, p. 101
Total surplus, p. 104
Price controls, p. 105

Price ceiling, p. 105
Price floor, p. 105
Deadweight loss, p. 108
Inefficient allocation to consumers, p. 109
Wasted resources, p. 109
Inefficiently low quality, p. 110
Black market, p. 110
Minimum wage, p. 114
Inefficient allocation of sales among sellers, p. 116

Inefficiently high quality, p. 117
Quantity control, p. 119
Quota, p. 119
Quota limit, p. 119
License, p. 119
Demand price, p. 120
Supply price, p. 121
Wedge, p. 122
Quota rent, p. 122

PROBLEMS

interactive activity

1. Determine the amount of consumer surplus generated in each of the following situations.

   a. Leon goes to the clothing store to buy a new T-shirt, for which he is willing to pay up to $10. He picks out one he likes with a price tag of exactly $10. When he is paying for it, he learns that the T-shirt has been discounted by 50%.

   b. Alberto goes to the music store hoping to find a used copy of Nirvana's *Nevermind* for up to $30. The store has one copy of the record selling for $30, which he purchases.

   c. After soccer practice, Stacey is willing to pay $2 for a bottle of mineral water. The 7-Eleven sells mineral water for $2.25 per bottle, so she declines to purchase it.

2. Determine the amount of producer surplus generated in each of the following situations.

   a. Gordon lists his old Lionel electric trains on eBay. He sets a minimum acceptable price, known as his reserve price, of $75. After five days of bidding, the final high bid is exactly $75. He accepts the bid.

   b. So-Hee advertises her car for sale in the used-car section of the student newspaper for $2,000, but she is willing to sell the car for any price higher than $1,500. The best offer she gets is $1,200, which she declines.

   c. Sanjay likes his job so much that he would be willing to do it for free. However, his annual salary is $80,000.

3. You are the manager of Fun World, a small amusement park. The accompanying diagram shows the demand curve of a typical customer at Fun World.

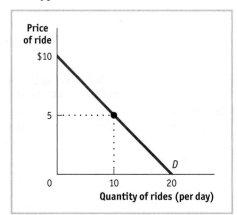

   a. Suppose that the price of each ride is $5. At that price, how much consumer surplus does an individual consumer get? (Recall that the area of a right triangle is ½ × the height of the triangle × the base of the triangle.)

   b. Suppose that Fun World considers charging an admission fee, even though it maintains the price of each ride at $5. What is the maximum admission fee

   it could charge? (Assume that all potential customers have enough money to pay the fee.)

   c. Suppose that Fun World lowered the price of each ride to zero. How much consumer surplus does an individual consumer get? What is the maximum admission fee Fun World could charge?

4. The accompanying diagram illustrates a taxi driver's individual supply curve (assume that each taxi ride is the same distance).

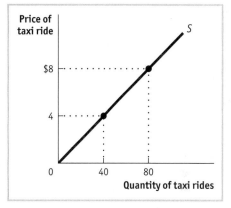

   a. Suppose the city sets the price of taxi rides at $4 per ride, and at $4 the taxi driver is able to sell as many taxi rides as he desires. What is this taxi driver's producer surplus? (Recall that the area of a right triangle is ½ × the height of the triangle × the base of the triangle.)

   b. Suppose that the city keeps the price of a taxi ride set at $4, but it decides to charge taxi drivers a "licensing fee." What is the maximum licensing fee the city could extract from this taxi driver?

   c. Suppose that the city allowed the price of taxi rides to increase to $8 per ride. Again assume that, at this price, the taxi driver sells as many rides as he is willing to offer. How much producer surplus does an individual taxi driver now get? What is the maximum licensing fee the city could charge this taxi driver?

5. To ingratiate himself with voters, the mayor of Gotham City decides to lower the price of taxi rides. Assume, for simplicity, that all taxi rides are the same distance and therefore cost the same. The accompanying table shows the demand and supply schedules for taxi rides.

Fare (per ride)	Quantity of rides (millions per year)	
	Quantity demanded	Quantity supplied
$7.00	10	12
6.50	11	11
6.00	12	10
5.50	13	9
5.00	14	8
4.50	15	7

a. Assume that there are no restrictions on the number of taxi rides that can be supplied (there is no medallion system). Find the equilibrium price and quantity.

b. Suppose that the mayor sets a price ceiling at $5.50. How large is the shortage of rides? Illustrate with a diagram. Who loses and who benefits from this policy?

c. Suppose that the stock market crashes and, as a result, people in Gotham City are poorer. This reduces the quantity of taxi rides demanded by 6 million rides per year at any given price. What effect will the mayor's new policy have now? Illustrate with a diagram.

d. Suppose that the stock market rises and the demand for taxi rides returns to normal (that is, returns to the demand schedule given in the table). The mayor now decides to ingratiate himself with taxi drivers. He announces a policy in which operating licenses are given to existing taxi drivers; the number of licenses is restricted such that only 10 million rides per year can be given. Illustrate the effect of this policy on the market, and indicate the resulting price and quantity transacted. What is the quota rent per ride?

6. In the late eighteenth century, the price of bread in New York City was controlled, set at a predetermined price above the market price.

a. Draw a diagram showing the effect of the policy. Did the policy act as a price ceiling or a price floor?

b. What kinds of inefficiencies were likely to have arisen when the controlled price of bread was above the market price? Explain in detail.

One year during this period, a poor wheat harvest caused a leftward shift in the supply of bread and therefore an increase in its market price. New York bakers found that the controlled price of bread in New York was below the market price.

c. Draw a diagram showing the effect of the price control on the market for bread during this one-year period. Did the policy act as a price ceiling or a price floor?

d. What kinds of inefficiencies do you think occurred during this period? Explain in detail.

7. European governments tend to make greater use of price controls than does the U.S. government. For example, the French government sets minimum starting yearly wages for new hires who have completed *le bac*, certification roughly equivalent to a high school diploma. The demand schedule for new hires with *le bac* and the supply schedule for similarly credentialed new job seekers are given in the accompanying table. The price here—given in euros, the currency used in France—is the same as the yearly wage.

Wage (per year)	Quantity demanded (new job offers per year)	Quantity supplied (new job seekers per year)
€45,000	200,000	325,000
40,000	220,000	320,000
35,000	250,000	310,000
30,000	290,000	290,000
25,000	370,000	200,000

a. In the absence of government interference, what are the equilibrium wage and number of graduates hired per year? Illustrate with a diagram. Will there be anyone seeking a job at the equilibrium wage who is unable to find one—that is, will there be anyone who is involuntarily unemployed?

b. Suppose the French government sets a minimum yearly wage of €35,000. Is there any involuntary unemployment at this wage? If so, how much? Illustrate with a diagram. What if the minimum wage is set at €40,000? Also illustrate with a diagram.

c. Given your answer to part b and the information in the table, what do you think is the relationship between the level of involuntary unemployment and the level of the minimum wage? Who benefits from such a policy? Who loses? What is the missed opportunity here?

8. The waters off the North Atlantic coast were once teeming with fish. But because of overfishing by the commercial fishing industry, the stocks of fish became seriously depleted. In 1991, the National Marine Fisheries Service of the U.S. government implemented a quota to allow fish stocks to recover. In 2016 the quota limited the amount of swordfish caught per year by all U.S.-licensed fishing boats to 7 million pounds. As soon as the U.S. fishing fleet had met the quota limit, the swordfish catch was closed down for the rest of the year. The accompanying table gives the hypothetical demand and supply schedules for swordfish caught in the United States per year.

Price of swordfish (per pound)	Quantity of swordfish (millions of pounds per year)	
	Quantity demanded	Quantity supplied
$20	6	15
18	7	13
16	8	11
14	9	9
12	10	7

a. Use a diagram to show the effect of the quota on the market for swordfish in 1991. In your diagram, illustrate the deadweight loss from inefficiently low quantity.

b. How do you think fishermen will change how they fish in response to this policy?

9. In Maine, you must have a license to harvest lobster commercially; these licenses are issued yearly. The state of Maine is concerned about the dwindling supplies of lobsters found off its coast. The state fishery department has decided to place a yearly quota of 80,000 pounds of lobsters harvested in all Maine waters. It has also decided to give licenses this year only to those fishermen who had licenses last year. The accompanying diagram shows the demand and supply curves for Maine lobsters.

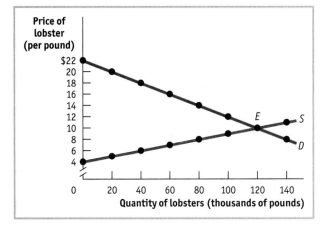

Price of lobster (per pound) / Quantity of lobsters (thousands of pounds)

a. In the absence of government restrictions, what are the equilibrium price and quantity?

b. What is the *demand price* at which consumers wish to purchase 80,000 pounds of lobsters?

c. What is the *supply price* at which suppliers are willing to supply 80,000 pounds of lobsters?

d. What is the *quota rent* per pound of lobster when 80,000 pounds are sold? Illustrate the quota rent and the deadweight loss on the diagram.

e. Explain a transaction that benefits both buyer and seller but is prevented by the quota restriction.

10. The Venezuelan government has imposed a price ceiling on the retail price of roasted coffee beans. The accompanying diagram shows the market for coffee beans. In the absence of price controls, the equilibrium is at point *E*, with an equilibrium price of P_E and an equilibrium quantity bought and sold of Q_E.

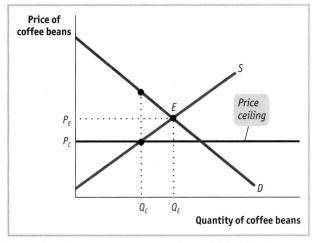

Price of coffee beans / Quantity of coffee beans

a. Show the consumer and producer surplus before the introduction of the price ceiling.

After the introduction of the price ceiling, the price falls to P_C and the quantity bought and sold falls to Q_C.

b. Show the consumer surplus after the introduction of the price ceiling (assuming that the consumers with the highest willingness to pay get to buy the available coffee beans; that is, assuming that there is no inefficient allocation to consumers).

c. Show the producer surplus after the introduction of the price ceiling (assuming that the producers with the lowest cost get to sell their coffee beans; that is, assuming that there is no inefficient allocation of sales among producers).

d. Using the diagram, show how much of what was producer surplus before the introduction of the price ceiling has been transferred to consumers as a result of the price ceiling.

e. Using the diagram, show how much of what was total surplus before the introduction of the price ceiling has been lost. That is, how great is the deadweight loss?

11. In 2014, the U.S. House of Representatives approved a new farm bill establishing the Margin Protection Program (MPP) for dairy producers. The MPP supports dairy farmers when the margin between feed costs and milk prices falls below $0.08 per pound. Current feed costs are $0.10 per pound, which means the program creates a price floor for milk at $0.18 per pound. At that price, in 2015, the quantity of milk supplied was 240 billion pounds, and the quantity demanded was 140 billion pounds. To support the price of milk at the price floor, the U.S. Department of Agriculture (USDA) has to buy up 100 billion pounds of surplus milk. The supply and demand curves in the following diagram illustrate the market for milk.

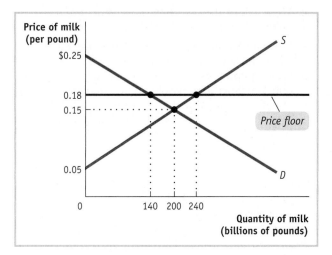

Price of milk (per pound) / Quantity of milk (billions of pounds)

a. In the absence of a price floor, how much consumer surplus is created? How much producer surplus? What is the total surplus (producer surplus plus consumer surplus)?

b. With the price floor at $0.18 per pound of milk, consumers buy 140 billion pounds of milk. How much consumer surplus is created now?

c. With the price floor at $0.18 per pound of milk, producers sell 240 billion pounds of milk (some to consumers and some to the USDA). How much producer surplus is created now?

d. How much money does the USDA spend to buy surplus milk?

e. Taxes must be collected to pay for the purchases of surplus milk by the USDA. As a result, total surplus is reduced by the amount the USDA spent buying surplus milk. Using your answers from parts b, c, and d, what is the total surplus when there is a price floor? How does this total surplus compare to the total surplus without a price floor from part a?

12. The accompanying table shows hypothetical demand and supply schedules for milk per year. The U.S. government decides that the incomes of dairy farmers should be maintained at a level that allows the traditional family dairy farm to survive. So it implements a price floor of $1 per pint by buying surplus milk until the market price is $1 per pint.

Price of milk (per pint)	Quantity of milk (millions of pints per year)	
	Quantity demanded	Quantity supplied
$1.20	550	850
1.10	600	800
1.00	650	750
0.90	700	700
0.80	750	650

a. In a diagram, show the deadweight loss from the inefficiently low quantity bought and sold.

b. How much surplus milk will be produced as a result of this policy?

c. What will be the cost to the government of this policy?

d. Since milk is an important source of protein and calcium, the government decides to provide the surplus milk it purchases to elementary schools at a price of only $0.60 per pint. Assume that schools will buy any amount of milk available at this low price. But parents now reduce their purchases of milk at any price by 50 million pints per year because they know their children are getting milk at school. How much will the dairy program now cost the government?

e. Explain how inefficiencies in the form of inefficient allocation to sellers and wasted resources arise from this policy.

13. For the last 80 years the U.S. government has used price supports to provide income assistance to American farmers. To implement these price supports, at times the government has used price floors, which it maintains by buying up the surplus farm products. At other times, it has used target prices, a policy by which the government gives the farmer an amount equal to the difference between the market price and the target price for each unit sold. Consider the market for corn depicted in the accompanying diagram.

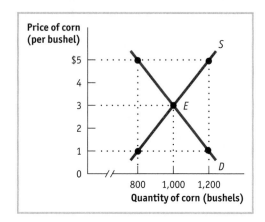

a. If the government sets a price floor of $5 per bushel, how many bushels of corn are produced? How many are purchased by consumers? By the government? How much does the program cost the government? How much revenue do corn farmers receive?

b. Suppose the government sets a target price of $5 per bushel for any quantity supplied up to 1,000 bushels. How many bushels of corn are purchased by consumers and at what price? By the government? How much does the program cost the government? How much revenue do corn farmers receive?

c. Which of these programs (in parts a and b) costs corn consumers more? Which program costs the government more? Explain.

d. Is one of these policies less inefficient than the other? Explain.

14. In many European countries high minimum wages have led to high levels of unemployment and underemployment, and to a two-tier labor system. In the formal labor market, workers have good jobs that pay at least the minimum wage. In the informal, or black market for labor, workers have poor jobs and receive less than the minimum wage.

a. Draw a demand and supply diagram showing the effect of the imposition of a minimum wage on the overall market for labor, with wage on the vertical axis and hours of labor on the horizontal axis. Your supply curve should represent the hours of labor offered by workers according to the wage, and the demand curve should represent the hours of labor demanded by employers according to the wage. On your diagram show the deadweight loss from the imposition of a minimum wage. What type of shortage is created? Illustrate on your diagram the size of the shortage.

b. Assume that the imposition of the high minimum wage causes a contraction in the economy so that employers in the formal sector cut their production and their demand for workers. Illustrate the effect of this on the overall market for labor. What happens to the size of the deadweight loss? The shortage? Illustrate with a diagram.

c. Assume that the workers who cannot get a job paying at least the minimum wage move into the informal labor market where there is no minimum wage. What happens to the size of the informal market for labor as a result of the economic contraction? What happens to the equilibrium wage in the informal labor market? Illustrate with a supply and demand diagram for the informal market.

15. The accompanying diagram shows data from the U.S. Bureau of Labor Statistics on the average price of an airline ticket in the United States from 1975 until 1985, adjusted to eliminate the effect of *inflation* (the general increase in the prices of all goods over time). In 1978, the United States Airline Deregulation Act removed the price floor on airline fares, and it also allowed the airlines greater flexibility to offer new routes.

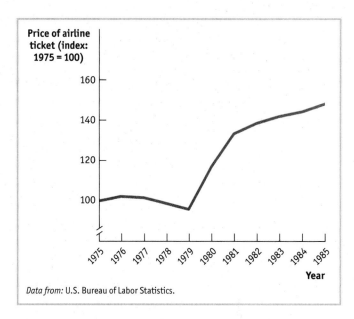

Data from: U.S. Bureau of Labor Statistics.

a. Looking at the data on airline ticket prices in the diagram, do you think the price floor that existed before 1978 was binding or nonbinding? That is, do you think it was set above or below the equilibrium price? Draw a supply and demand diagram, showing where the price floor that existed before 1978 was in relation to the equilibrium price.

b. Most economists agree that the average airline ticket price per mile traveled actually *fell* as a result of the Airline Deregulation Act. How might you reconcile that view with what you see in the diagram?

WORK IT OUT Interactive step-by-step help with solving this problem can be found online.

16. Suppose it is decided that rent control in New York City will be abolished and that market rents will now prevail. Assume that all rental units are identical, and, for this reason, are offered at the same rent. To address the plight of residents who may be unable to pay the market rent, an income supplement will be paid to all low-income households equal to the difference between the old controlled rent and the new market rent.

a. Use a diagram to show the effect on the rental market of the elimination of rent control. What will happen to the quality and quantity of rental housing supplied?

b. Use a second diagram to show the additional effect of the income-supplement policy on the market. What effect does it have on the market rent and quantity of rental housing supplied in comparison to your answers to part a?

c. Are tenants better or worse off as a result of these policies? Are landlords better or worse off? Is society as a whole better or worse off?

d. Why do you think cities have been more likely to resort to rent control rather than implement a policy of income supplements to help low-income families pay for housing?

TAKEN FOR A RIDE

IF YOU ARE EXPERIENCING a true emergency, you aren't likely to quibble about the price of an ambulance ride to the nearest emergency room. But what if it isn't an emergency? Take the case of Kira Milas, who doesn't even know who called an ambulance after she swam into the side of a swimming pool, breaking three teeth. Shaken, she accepted the ambulance ride to a local hospital, 15 minutes away. A week later, she received the bill: $1,772.42. Stunned, she said: "We only drove nine miles and it was a non-life-threatening injury. I needed absolutely no emergency treatment."

Kira's experience is by no means exceptional. Although ambulances are often requested by a bystander or by 911 dispatchers, it is the patient who receives the bill. Undoubtedly, in a true medical emergency, a patient feels fortunate when an ambulance pulls up. But in nonemergency cases, like Kira's, many patients feel obliged to get into the ambulance once it arrives. And just like Kira, they are uninformed about the cost of the ride to the hospital. And while many people have health insurance that will cover some or all of the cost of the ambulance service, the patient is ultimately responsible for paying the rest.

Each year an estimated 40 million ambulance trips, at a cost of $14 billion, are provided by nonprofit entities, such as local fire departments, and by for-profit companies in the United States. Sensing profit-making opportunities, in recent years for-profit companies have significantly expanded their operations, often taking over from nonprofit operators. And big investors are betting that ambulance services will generate significant profits: two private ambulance providers were recently bought by investors, one for $3 billion and another for $438 million. A similar dynamic has occurred in the air ambulance market, where high profits have led to explosive growth and patients have been handed bills for tens of thousands of dollars for trips that would have been shorter and more safely taken by land.

Charges for an ambulance ride vary wildly across the country, from several hundred dollars to tens of thousands of dollars. The price may depend on many things other than the patient's medical needs, from the level of skill of the ambulance team to the distance traveled, or in some cases whether a friend or relative rides along (which can add hundreds of dollars to the cost).

What accounts for the extreme variation in the cost of ambulance services? How are these services able to charge thousands of dollars, regardless of whether an ambulance is actually needed? Or to charge for an ambulance equipped with heart resuscitation capabilities when the patient only has a broken leg? The answer to these questions is *price unresponsiveness*: in the heat of the moment,

many consumers—particularly those with true emergencies—are *unresponsive* to the price of an ambulance. Ambulance operators judge correctly that a significant number of patients won't ask "How much is this ride to the emergency room going to cost?" before getting onboard. In other words, a large increase in the price of an ambulance ride leaves the quantity demanded by a significant number of consumers relatively unchanged.

Let's consider a very different scenario. Suppose that the maker of a particular brand of breakfast cereal decided to charge 10 times the original price. It would be extremely difficult, if not impossible, to find consumers willing to pay the much higher price. In other words, consumers of breakfast cereal are much more responsive to price than the consumers of ambulance rides.

But how do we define *responsiveness*? Economists measure responsiveness of consumers to price with a particular number, called the *price elasticity of demand*. In this chapter we will show how the price elasticity of demand is calculated and why it is the best measure of how the quantity demanded responds to changes in price. We will then see that the price elasticity of demand is only one of a family of related concepts, including the *income elasticity of demand, cross-price elasticity of demand,* and *price elasticity of supply*.

We will finish our discussion of elasticities by looking at how the price elasticity of supply and demand influence the costs and benefits of taxation. ●

WHAT YOU WILL LEARN

- Why is **elasticity** used to measure the response to changes in prices or income?
- What are the different elasticity measures and what do they mean?
- What factors influence the size of these various elasticities?
- Why is it vitally important to determine the size of the relevant elasticity before setting prices or government fees?
- How do taxes affect supply and demand?
- How does the elasticity of supply and demand affect the costs and benefits of taxation?

The **price elasticity of demand** is the ratio of the percent change in the quantity demanded to the percent change in the price as we move along the demand curve.

Defining and Measuring Elasticity

For investors to know whether they can earn significant profits in the ambulance business, they need to know the *price elasticity of demand* for ambulance rides. With this information, investors can accurately predict whether or not a significant rise in the price of an ambulance ride results in an increase in revenue.

Calculating the Price Elasticity of Demand

Figure 5-1 shows a hypothetical demand curve for an ambulance ride. At a price of $200 per ride, consumers would demand 10 million rides per year (point *A*); at a price of $210 per ride, consumers would demand 9.9 million rides per year (point *B*).

Figure 5-1, then, tells us the change in the quantity demanded for a particular change in the price. But how can we turn this into a measure of price responsiveness? The answer is to calculate the *price elasticity of demand*.

The **price elasticity of demand** is the ratio of the *percent change in quantity demanded* to the *percent change in price* as we move along the demand curve. As we'll see later in this chapter, the reason economists use percent changes is to obtain a measure that doesn't depend on the units in which a good is measured (say, a 1-mile ambulance trip versus a 10-mile ambulance trip). But before we get to that, let's look at how elasticity is calculated.

To calculate the price elasticity of demand, we first calculate the *percent change in the quantity demanded* and the corresponding *percent change in the price* as we move along the demand curve. These are defined as follows:

$$\text{(5-1)} \quad \% \text{ change in quantity demanded} = \frac{\text{Change in quantity demanded}}{\text{Initial quantity demanded}} \times 100$$

And

$$\text{(5-2)} \quad \% \text{ change in price} = \frac{\text{Change in price}}{\text{Initial price}} \times 100$$

In Figure 5-1, we see that when the price rises from $200 to $210, the quantity demanded falls from 10 million to 9.9 million rides, yielding a change in the

FIGURE 5-1 The Demand for Ambulance Rides

At a price of $200 per ambulance ride, the quantity of ambulance rides demanded is 10 million per year (point *A*). When price rises to $210 per ambulance ride, the quantity demanded falls to 9.9 million ambulance rides per year (point *B*).

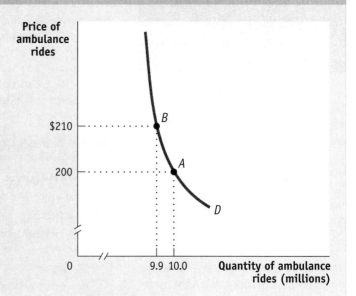

quantity demanded of 0.1 million rides. So the percent change in the quantity demanded is

$$\% \text{ change in quantity demanded} = \frac{-0.1 \text{ million rides}}{10 \text{ million rides}} \times 100 = -1\%$$

The initial price is $200 and the change in the price is $10, so the percent change in price is

$$\% \text{ change in price} = \frac{\$10}{\$200} \times 100 = 5\%$$

To calculate the price elasticity of demand, we find the ratio of the percent change in the quantity demanded to the percent change in the price:

(5-3) $\text{Price elasticity of demand} = \dfrac{\% \text{ change in quantity demanded}}{\% \text{ change in price}}$

In Figure 5-1, the price elasticity of demand is therefore

$$\text{Price elasticity of demand} = \frac{1\%}{5\%} = 0.2$$

Notice that the minus sign that appeared in the calculation of the percent change in the quantity demanded has been dropped when we calculate this last equation, the price elasticity of demand. Why have we done this? The *law of demand* says that demand curves are downward sloping, so price and quantity demanded always move in opposite directions. In other words, a positive percent change in price (a rise in price) leads to a negative percent change in the quantity demanded; a negative percent change in price (a fall in price) leads to a positive percent change in the quantity demanded. This means that the price elasticity of demand is, in strictly mathematical terms, a negative number.

However, it is inconvenient to repeatedly write a minus sign. So when economists talk about the price elasticity of demand, they usually drop the minus sign and report the *absolute value* of the price elasticity of demand. In this case, for example, economists would usually say "the price elasticity of demand is 0.2," taking it for granted that you understand they mean *minus* 0.2. We follow this convention here.

The larger the price elasticity of demand, the more responsive the quantity demanded is to the price. When the price elasticity of demand is large—when consumers change their quantity demanded by a large percentage compared to the percent change in the price—economists say that demand is highly elastic.

As we'll see shortly, a price elasticity of 0.2 indicates a small response of quantity demanded to price. That is, the quantity demanded will fall by a relatively small amount when price rises. This is what economists call *inelastic* demand. And inelastic demand is exactly what enables an ambulance operator to increase the total amount earned by raising the price of an ambulance ride.

An Alternative Way to Calculate Elasticities: The Midpoint Method

Price elasticity of demand compares the *percent change in quantity demanded* with the *percent change in price*. When we look at some other elasticities, which we will do shortly, we'll learn why it is important to focus on percent changes. But at this point we need to discuss a technical issue that arises when you calculate percent changes in variables.

The best way to understand the issue is with a real example. Suppose you were trying to estimate the price elasticity of demand for gasoline by comparing gasoline prices and consumption in different countries. Because of high taxes, gasoline usually costs about three times as much per gallon in Europe as it does in the

The **midpoint method** is a technique for calculating the percent change. In this approach, we calculate changes in a variable compared with the average, or midpoint, of the starting and final values.

United States. So what is the percent difference between American and European gas prices?

Well, it depends on which way you measure it. Because the price of gasoline in Europe is approximately three times higher than in the United States, it is 200% higher. Because the price of gasoline in the United States is one-third as high as in Europe, it is 66.7% lower.

This is a nuisance: we'd like to have a percent measure of the difference in prices that doesn't depend on which way you measure it. To avoid computing different elasticities for rising and falling prices we use the *midpoint method*.

The **midpoint method** replaces the usual definition of the percent change in a variable, X, with a slightly different definition:

(5-4) $\% \text{ change in } X = \dfrac{\text{Change in } X}{\text{Average value of } X} \times 100$

where the average value of X is defined as

$$\text{Average value of } X = \dfrac{\text{Starting value of } X + \text{Final value of } X}{2}$$

When calculating the price elasticity of demand using the midpoint method, both the percent change in the price and the percent change in the quantity demanded are found using this method. To see how this method works, suppose you have the following data for some good:

Situation	Price	Quantity demanded
A	$0.90	1,100
B	1.10	900

To calculate the percent change in quantity going from situation A to situation B, we compare the change in the quantity demanded—a fall of 200 units—with the *average* of the quantity demanded in the two situations. So we calculate

$$\% \text{ change in quantity demanded} = \dfrac{-200}{(1,100 + 900)/2} \times 100 = \dfrac{-200}{1,000} \times 100 = -20\%$$

In the same way, we calculate

$$\% \text{ change in price} = \dfrac{\$0.20}{(\$0.90 + \$1.10)/2} \times 100 = \dfrac{\$0.20}{\$1.00} \times 100 = 20\%$$

So in this case we would calculate the price elasticity of demand to be

$$\text{Price elasticity of demand} = \dfrac{\% \text{ change in quantity demanded}}{\% \text{ change in price}} = \dfrac{20\%}{20\%} = 1$$

again dropping the minus sign.

The important point is that we would get the same result, a price elasticity of demand of 1, whether we go up the demand curve from situation A to situation B or down the demand curve from situation B to situation A.

To arrive at a more general formula for price elasticity of demand, suppose that we have data for two points on a demand curve. At point 1 the quantity demanded and price are (Q_1, P_1); at point 2 they are (Q_2, P_2). Then the formula for calculating the price elasticity of demand is:

(5-5) $\text{Price elasticity of demand} = \dfrac{\dfrac{Q_2 - Q_1}{(Q_1 + Q_2)/2}}{\dfrac{P_2 - P_1}{(P_1 + P_2)/2}}$

As before, when finding a price elasticity of demand calculated by the midpoint method, we drop the minus sign and use the absolute value.

ECONOMICS >> *in Action*

Estimating Elasticities

You might think it's easy to estimate price elasticities of demand from real-world data: just compare percent changes in prices with percent changes in quantities demanded. Unfortunately, it's rarely that simple because changes in price aren't the only thing affecting changes in the quantity demanded: other factors—such as changes in income, changes in tastes, and changes in the prices of other goods—shift the demand curve, thereby changing the quantity demanded at any given price.

To estimate price elasticities of demand, economists must use careful statistical analysis to separate the influence of the change in price, holding other things equal.

Economists have estimated price elasticities of demand for a number of goods and services. Table 5-1 summarizes some of these and shows a wide range of price elasticities. There are some goods, like gasoline, for which demand hardly responds at all to changes in the price. There are other goods, such as airline travel for leisure, or Coke and Pepsi, for which the quantity demanded is very sensitive to the price.

Notice that Table 5-1 is divided into two parts: inelastic and elastic demand. We'll explain the significance of that division in the next section.

TABLE 5-1 Some Estimated Price Elasticities of Demand	
Good	**Price elasticity of demand**
Inelastic demand	
Gasoline (short-run)	0.09
Gasoline (long-run)	0.24
College (in-state tuition)	0.60–0.75
Airline travel (business)	0.80
Soda	0.80
Elastic demand	
Housing	1.2
College (out-of-state tuition)	1.2
Airline travel (leisure)	1.5
Coke/Pepsi	3.3

>> Check Your Understanding 5-1

Solutions appear at back of book.

1. The price of strawberries falls from $1.50 to $1.00 per carton and the quantity demanded goes from 100,000 to 200,000 cartons. Use the midpoint method to find the price elasticity of demand.

2. At the present level of consumption, 4,000 movie tickets, and at the current price, $5 per ticket, the price elasticity of demand for movie tickets is 1. Using the midpoint method, calculate the percentage by which the owners of movie theaters must reduce price to sell 5,000 tickets.

3. The price elasticity of demand for ice-cream sandwiches is 1.2 at the current price of $0.50 per sandwich and the current consumption level of 100,000 sandwiches. Calculate the change in the quantity demanded when price rises by $0.05. Use Equations 5-1 and 5-2 to calculate percent changes and Equation 5-3 to relate price elasticity of demand to the percent changes.

>> Quick Review

• The **price elasticity of demand** is equal to the percent change in the quantity demanded divided by the percent change in the price as you move along the demand curve, and dropping any minus sign.

• In practice, percent changes are best measured using the **midpoint method,** in which the percent changes are calculated using the average of starting and final values.

‖ Interpreting the Price Elasticity of Demand

In a true emergency, a patient is unlikely to question the price of the ambulance ride to the hospital. But even in a nonemergency, like Kira's broken teeth, patients are often unlikely to respond to an increase in the price of an ambulance by reducing their quantity demanded, because they are unaware of the cost. As a result, investors in private ambulance companies see profit-making opportunities in delivering ambulance services, because the price elasticity of demand is small. But what does that mean? How low does a price elasticity have to be for us to classify it as low? How high does it have to be for us to consider it high? And what determines whether the price elasticity of demand is high or low anyway?

To answer these questions, we need to look more deeply at the price elasticity of demand.

Demand is **perfectly inelastic** when the quantity demanded does not respond at all to changes in the price. When demand is perfectly inelastic, the demand curve is a vertical line.

Demand is **perfectly elastic** when any price increase will cause the quantity demanded to drop to zero. When demand is perfectly elastic, the demand curve is a horizontal line.

How Elastic Is Elastic?

As a first step toward classifying price elasticities of demand, let's look at the extreme cases.

First, consider the demand for a good when people pay no attention to the price—say, snake anti-venom. Suppose that consumers will buy 1,000 doses of anti-venom per year regardless of the price. In this case, the demand curve for anti-venom would look like the curve shown in panel (a) of Figure 5-2: it would be a vertical line at 1,000 doses of anti-venom. Since the percent change in the quantity demanded is zero for *any* change in the price, the price elasticity of demand in this case is zero. The case of a zero price elasticity of demand is known as **perfectly inelastic demand.**

The opposite extreme occurs when even a tiny rise in the price will cause the quantity demanded to drop to zero or even a tiny fall in the price will cause the quantity demanded to get extremely large.

Panel (b) of Figure 5-2 shows the case of pink tennis balls; we suppose that tennis players really don't care what color their balls are and that other colors, such as neon green and vivid yellow, are available at $5 per dozen balls. In this case, consumers will buy no pink balls if they cost more than $5 per dozen but will buy only pink balls if they cost less than $5. The demand curve will therefore be a horizontal line at a price of $5 per dozen balls. As you move back and forth along this line, there is a change in the quantity demanded but no change in the price. Roughly speaking, when you divide a number by zero, you get infinity, denoted by the symbol ∞. So, a horizontal demand curve implies an infinite price elasticity of demand. When the price elasticity of demand is infinite, economists say that demand is **perfectly elastic.**

The price elasticity of demand for the vast majority of goods is somewhere between these two extreme cases. Economists use one main criterion for classifying these intermediate cases: they ask whether the price elasticity of demand

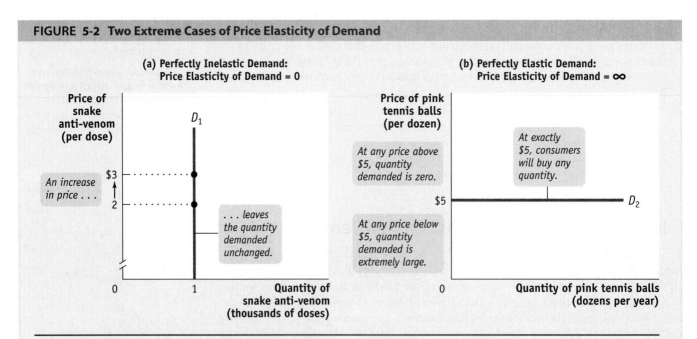

FIGURE 5-2 Two Extreme Cases of Price Elasticity of Demand

(a) Perfectly Inelastic Demand: Price Elasticity of Demand = 0

Price of snake anti-venom (per dose)

D_1

An increase in price . . .

$3

2

. . . leaves the quantity demanded unchanged.

0   1   Quantity of snake anti-venom (thousands of doses)

(b) Perfectly Elastic Demand: Price Elasticity of Demand = ∞

Price of pink tennis balls (per dozen)

At any price above $5, quantity demanded is zero.

At exactly $5, consumers will buy any quantity.

$5 D_2

At any price below $5, quantity demanded is extremely large.

0   Quantity of pink tennis balls (dozens per year)

Panel (a) shows a perfectly inelastic demand curve, which is a vertical line. The quantity of snake anti-venom demanded is always 1,000 doses, regardless of price. As a result, the price elasticity of demand is zero—the quantity demanded is unaffected by the price. Panel (b) shows a perfectly elastic demand curve, which is a horizontal line. At a price of $5, consumers will buy any quantity of pink tennis balls, but they will buy none at a price above $5. If the price falls below $5, they will buy an extremely large number of pink tennis balls and none of any other color.

is greater than or less than 1. When the price elasticity of demand is greater than 1, economists say that demand is **elastic.** When the price elasticity of demand is less than 1, they say that demand is **inelastic.** The borderline case is **unit-elastic demand,** where the price elasticity of demand is—surprise—exactly 1.

To see why a price elasticity of demand equal to 1 is a useful dividing line, let's consider a hypothetical example: a toll bridge operated by the state highway department. Other things equal, the number of drivers who use the bridge depends on the toll, the price the highway department charges for crossing the bridge: the higher the toll, the fewer the drivers who use the bridge.

Figure 5-3 shows three hypothetical demand curves—one in which demand is unit-elastic, one in which it is inelastic, and one in which it is elastic. In each case, point *A* shows the quantity demanded if the toll is $0.90 and point *B* shows the quantity demanded if the toll is $1.10. An increase in the toll from $0.90 to $1.10 is an increase of 20% if we use the midpoint method to calculate percent changes.

Panel (a) shows what happens when the toll is raised from $0.90 to $1.10 and the demand curve is unit-elastic. Here the 20% price rise leads to a fall in the quantity of cars using the bridge each day from 1,100 to 900, which is a

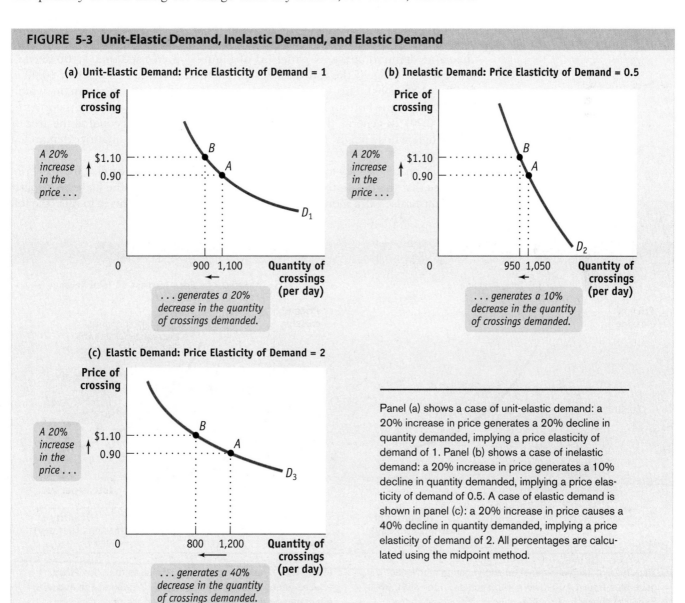

FIGURE 5-3 Unit-Elastic Demand, Inelastic Demand, and Elastic Demand

Panel (a) shows a case of unit-elastic demand: a 20% increase in price generates a 20% decline in quantity demanded, implying a price elasticity of demand of 1. Panel (b) shows a case of inelastic demand: a 20% increase in price generates a 10% decline in quantity demanded, implying a price elasticity of demand of 0.5. A case of elastic demand is shown in panel (c): a 20% increase in price causes a 40% decline in quantity demanded, implying a price elasticity of demand of 2. All percentages are calculated using the midpoint method.

The **total revenue** is the total value of sales of a good or service. It is equal to the price multiplied by the quantity sold.

20% decline (again using the midpoint method). So the price elasticity of demand is 20%/20% = 1.

Panel (b) shows a case of inelastic demand when the toll is raised from $0.90 to $1.10. The same 20% price rise reduces the quantity demanded from 1,050 to 950. That's only a 10% decline, so in this case the price elasticity of demand is 10%/20% = 0.5.

Panel (c) shows a case of elastic demand when the toll is raised from $0.90 to $1.10. The 20% price increase causes the quantity demanded to fall from 1,200 to 800—a 40% decline, so the price elasticity of demand is 40%/20% = 2.

Why does it matter whether demand is unit-elastic, inelastic, or elastic? Because this classification predicts how changes in the price of a good will affect the *total revenue* earned by producers from the sale of that good. In many real-life situations, it is crucial to know how price changes affect total revenue. **Total revenue** is defined as the total value of sales of a good or service, equal to the price multiplied by the quantity sold.

(5-6) Total revenue = Price × Quantity sold

Total revenue has a useful graphical representation that can help us understand why knowing the price elasticity of demand is crucial when we ask whether a price rise will increase or reduce total revenue. Panel (a) of Figure 5-4 shows the same demand curve as panel (a) of Figure 5-3. We see that 1,100 drivers will use the bridge if the toll is $0.90. So the total revenue at a price of $0.90 is $0.90 × 1,100 = $990. This value is equal to the area of the green rectangle, which is drawn with the bottom left corner at the point (0, 0) and the top right corner at (1,100, 0.90). In general, the total revenue at any given price is equal to the area of a rectangle whose height is the price and whose width is the quantity demanded at that price.

To get an idea of why total revenue is important, consider the following scenario. Suppose that the toll on the bridge is currently $0.90 but that the highway department must raise extra money for road repairs. One way to do this is to raise the toll

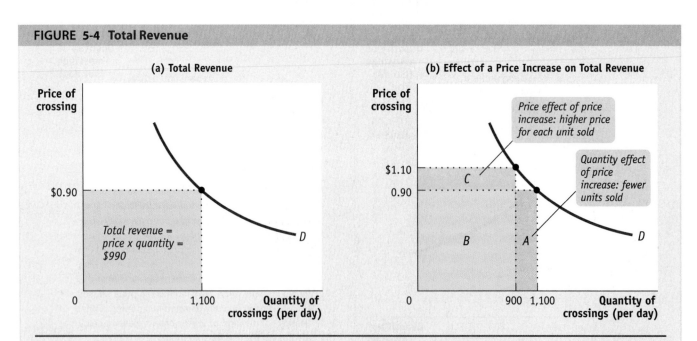

FIGURE 5-4 Total Revenue

(a) Total Revenue

Price of crossing

$0.90

Total revenue = price x quantity = $990

D

0   1,100   **Quantity of crossings (per day)**

(b) Effect of a Price Increase on Total Revenue

Price of crossing

Price effect of price increase: higher price for each unit sold

$1.10

C

0.90

Quantity effect of price increase: fewer units sold

B   *A*

D

0   900 1,100   **Quantity of crossings (per day)**

The green rectangle in panel (a) shows the total revenue generated from 1,100 drivers who each pay a toll of $0.90. Panel (b) shows how total revenue is affected when the price increases from $0.90 to $1.10. Due to the quantity effect, total revenue falls by area *A*. Due to the price effect, total revenue increases by the area *C*. In general, the overall effect can go either way, depending on the price elasticity of demand.

on the bridge. But this plan might backfire, since a higher toll will reduce the number of drivers who use the bridge. And if traffic on the bridge dropped a lot, a higher toll would actually reduce total revenue instead of increasing it. So it's important for the highway department to know how drivers will respond to a toll increase.

We can see graphically how the toll increase affects total bridge revenue by examining panel (b) of Figure 5-4. At a toll of $0.90, total revenue is given by the sum of the areas *A* and *B*. After the toll is raised to $1.10, total revenue is given by the sum of areas *B* and *C*. So when the toll is raised, revenue represented by area *A* is lost but revenue represented by area *C* is gained.

These two areas have important interpretations. Area *C* represents the revenue gain that comes from the additional $0.20 paid by drivers who continue to use the bridge. That is, the 900 drivers who continue to use the bridge contribute an additional $0.20 × 900 = $180 per day to total revenue, represented by area *C*. But 200 drivers who would have used the bridge at a price of $0.90 no longer do so, generating a loss to total revenue of $0.90 × 200 = $180 per day, represented by area *A*. (In this particular example, because demand is unit-elastic—the same as in panel (a) of Figure 5-3—the rise in the toll has no effect on total revenue; areas *A* and *C* are the same size.)

Except in the rare case of a good with perfectly elastic or perfectly inelastic demand, when a seller raises the price of a good, two countervailing effects are present:

The highway department uses the price elasticity of demand to calculate the change in revenue from higher tolls.

- *A price effect:* After a price increase, each unit sold sells at a higher price, which tends to raise revenue.

- *A quantity effect:* After a price increase, fewer units are sold, which tends to lower revenue.

But then, you may ask, what is the ultimate net effect on total revenue: does it go up or down? The answer is that, in general, the effect on total revenue can go either way—a price rise may either increase total revenue or lower it. If the price effect, which tends to raise total revenue, is the stronger of the two effects, then total revenue goes up. If the quantity effect, which tends to reduce total revenue, is the stronger effect, then total revenue goes down. And if the strengths of the two effects are exactly equal—as in our toll bridge example, where a $180 gain offsets a $180 loss—total revenue is unchanged by the price increase.

The price elasticity of demand tells us what happens to total revenue when price changes: its size determines which effect—the price effect or the quantity effect—is stronger. Specifically:

- If demand for a good is *unit-elastic* (the price elasticity of demand is 1), an increase in price does not change total revenue. In this case, the quantity effect and the price effect exactly offset each other.

- If demand for a good is *inelastic* (the price elasticity of demand is less than 1), a higher price increases total revenue. In this case, the quantity effect is weaker than the price effect.

- If demand for a good is *elastic* (the price elasticity of demand is greater than 1), an increase in price reduces total revenue. In this case, the quantity effect is stronger than the price effect.

Table 5-2 shows how the effect of a price increase on total revenue depends on the price elasticity of demand, using the same data as in Figure 5-3. An increase in the price from $0.90 to $1.10 leaves total revenue unchanged at $990 when demand is unit-elastic. When

TABLE 5-2 Price Elasticity of Demand and Total Revenue

	Price of toll = $0.90	Price of toll = $1.10
Unit-elastic demand (price elasticity of demand = 1)		
Quantity demanded	1,100	900
Total revenue	$990	$990
Inelastic demand (price elasticity of demand = 0.5)		
Quantity demanded	1,050	950
Total revenue	$945	$1,045
Elastic demand (price elasticity of demand = 2)		
Quantity demanded	1,200	800
Total revenue	$1,080	$880

demand is inelastic, the quantity effect is dominated by the price effect; the same price increase leads to an increase in total revenue from $945 to $1,045. And when demand is elastic, the quantity effect dominates the price effect; the price increase leads to a decline in total revenue from $1,080 to $880.

The price elasticity of demand also predicts the effect of a *fall* in price on total revenue. When the price falls, the same two countervailing effects are present, but they work in the opposite directions as compared to the case of a price rise. There is the price effect of a lower price per unit sold, which tends to lower revenue. This is countered by the quantity effect of more units sold, which tends to raise revenue. Which effect dominates depends on the price elasticity. Here is a quick summary:

- When demand is *unit-elastic,* the two effects exactly balance; so a fall in price has no effect on total revenue.

- When demand is *inelastic,* the quantity effect is dominated by the price effect; so a fall in price reduces total revenue.

- When demand is *elastic,* the quantity effect dominates the price effect; so a fall in price increases total revenue.

Price Elasticity Along the Demand Curve

Suppose an economist says that "the price elasticity of demand for coffee is 0.25." What he or she means is that *at the current price* the elasticity is 0.25. In the previous discussion of the toll bridge, what we were really describing was the elasticity *at the toll price* of $0.90. Why this qualification? Because for the vast majority of demand curves, the price elasticity of demand at one point along the curve is different from the price elasticity of demand at other points along the same curve.

To see this, consider the table in Figure 5-5, which shows a hypothetical demand schedule. It also shows in the last column the total revenue generated at each price and quantity combination in the demand schedule. The upper panel of the graph in Figure 5-5 shows the corresponding demand curve. The lower panel illustrates the same data on total revenue: the height of the bar at each quantity demanded—which corresponds to a particular price—measures the total revenue generated at that price.

In Figure 5-5, you can see that when the price is low, raising the price increases total revenue: starting at a price of $1, raising the price to $2 increases total revenue from $9 to $16. This means that when the price is low, demand is inelastic. Moreover, you can see that demand is inelastic on the entire section of the demand curve from a price of $0 to a price of $5.

When the price is high, however, raising it further reduces total revenue: starting at a price of $8, raising the price to $9 reduces total revenue, from $16 to $9. This means that when the price is high, demand is elastic. Furthermore, you can see that demand is elastic over the section of the demand curve from a price of $5 to $10.

For the vast majority of goods, the price elasticity of demand changes along the demand curve. So whenever you measure a good's elasticity, you are really measuring it at a particular point or section of the good's demand curve.

What Factors Determine the Price Elasticity of Demand?

Investors in private ambulance companies believe that the price elasticity of demand for an ambulance ride is low for two important reasons. First, in many if not most cases, an ambulance ride is a medical necessity. Second, in an emergency there really is no substitute for the standard of care that an ambulance provides. And even among ambulances there are typically no substitutes because in any given geographical area there is usually only one ambulance provider. The exceptions are very densely populated areas, but even in those locations an ambulance

FIGURE 5-5 The Price Elasticity of Demand Changes Along the Demand Curve

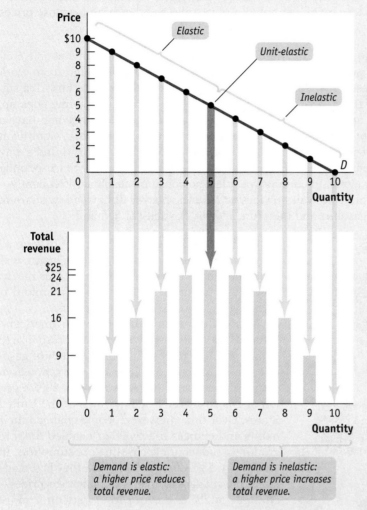

Demand Schedule and Total Revenue for a Linear Demand Curve		
Price	Quantity demanded	Total revenue
$0	10	$0
1	9	9
2	8	16
3	7	21
4	6	24
5	5	25
6	4	24
7	3	21
8	2	16
9	1	9
10	0	0

The upper panel of the graph shows a demand curve corresponding to the demand schedule in the table. The lower panel shows how total revenue changes along that demand curve: at each price and quantity combination, the height of the bar represents the total revenue generated. You can see that at a low price, raising the price increases total revenue. So demand is inelastic at low prices. At a high price, however, a rise in price reduces total revenue. So demand is elastic at high prices.

dispatcher is unlikely to give you a choice of ambulance providers with an accompanying price list.

In general there are four main factors that determine elasticity: whether a good is a necessity or luxury, the availability of close substitutes, the share of income a consumer spends on the good, and how much time has elapsed since a change in price. We'll briefly examine each of these factors.

Whether the Good Is a Necessity or a Luxury As our opening story illustrates, the price elasticity of demand tends to be low if a good is something you must have, like a life-saving ambulance ride to the hospital. The price elasticity of demand tends to be high if the good is a luxury—something you can easily live without. For example, most people would consider a 110-inch ultra-high-definition TV a luxury—nice to have, but something they can live without. Therefore, the price elasticity of demand for it will be much higher than for a life-saving ambulance ride to the hospital.

The Availability of Close Substitutes As we just noted, the price elasticity of demand tends to be low if there are no close substitutes or if they are very difficult to obtain. In contrast, the price elasticity of demand tends to be high if there are other readily available goods that consumers regard as similar and would be willing to consume instead. For example, most consumers believe that there are fairly close substitutes to their favorite brand of breakfast cereal. As a result, if the maker of a particular brand of breakfast cereal raised the price significantly, that maker is likely to lose much—if not all—of its sales to other brands whose prices have not risen.

Share of Income Spent on the Good Consider a good that some people consume frequently, such as gasoline—say, for a long commute to and from work every day. For these consumers, spending on gasoline will typically absorb a significant share of their income. As a result, when the price of gasoline goes up, these consumers are likely to be very responsive to the price change and have a higher elasticity of demand. Why? Because when the good absorbs a significant share of these consumers' income, it is worth their time and effort to find a way to reduce their demand when the price goes up—such as switching to car-pooling instead of driving alone. In contrast, people who consume gasoline infrequently—for example, people who walk to work or take the bus—will have a low share of income spent on gasoline and therefore a lower elasticity of demand.

Time Elapsed Since Price Change In general, the price elasticity of demand tends to increase as consumers have more time to adjust. This means that the long-run price elasticity of demand is often higher than the short-run elasticity.

A good illustration is the changes in Americans' behavior over the past two decades in response to higher gasoline prices. In 1998, a gallon of gasoline was only about $1. Over the years, however, gasoline prices steadily rose, so that by 2008 a gallon of gas cost over $4.00 in much of the United States. Over time, however, people changed their habits and choices in ways that enabled them to gradually reduce their gasoline consumption. In one survey, 53% of responders said they had made major life changes to cope with higher gas prices—changes such as driving less, getting a more fuel-efficient car, and using other modes of transportation like buses or bicycles. Some even moved to a more convenient location to save gas. These changes are reflected in the data on American gasoline consumption: the trend line of consumption fluctuated until about 2003, then took a nosedive. So by 2013, Americans were purchasing less than 350 million gallons of gas daily, less than the nearly 380 million gallons purchased daily in 2007, and far less than 450 million gallons a day, the amount Americans would have purchased if they had followed previous trends of ever-increasing gasoline consumption. This confirms that the long-run price elasticity of demand for gasoline is indeed much larger than the short-run elasticity.

Gas prices dropped dramatically from 2014 to early 2017, with the average price down to around $2.25. Not surprisingly, gasoline consumption started to rise again. And if the fall in prices persists, it is very likely that gas consumption will rise dramatically as consumers switch back to their gas-guzzlers.

ECONOMICS >> *in Action*
Responding to Your Tuition Bill

If it seems like the cost of college keeps going up—it's because it has. It is estimated that over the past 10 years the average annual increase in tuition has exceeded the inflation rate by approximately 5% to 6% every year. An important question for educators and policy makers is whether the rise in tuition deters people from going to college. And if so, by how much?

Several studies have shown that tuition increases lead to consistently negative effects on enrollment numbers, with estimates of the price elasticity of demand ranging from 0.67 to 0.76 for four-year institutions. So a 3% rise in tuition at a four-year institution leads to a fall in enrollment of approximately 2% (3 × 0.67) to 2.3% (3 × 0.76). Two-year institutions were found to have a significantly higher response: a 3% increase in tuition leads to a 2.7% fall in enrollment, implying a price elasticity of demand of 0.9. One other study found that for financial aid students, the price elasticity of demand rises to 1.18, implying that a 3% rise in tuition leads to a 3.54% fall in enrollment. While grant and loan disbursements lead to increases in enrollment, their effects are modest: with a price elasticity of demand of 0.33, a 3% increase in grant monies leads to a 1% increase in enrollment, and with an elasticity of 0.12, a 3% increase in loan monies leads to a 0.36% increase in enrollment.

These results indicate that an increase in tuition accompanied by an equal increase in financial aid leads to lower enrollment. That is, students care not just about *net tuition*, defined as the full price of tuition minus financial aid, but they also care about the composition of how their tuition bill is paid, preferring a lower full-price tuition to one with higher tuition and more financial aid.

So the increase in tuition *is* a barrier to college, and it is more of a barrier for students at two-year institutions than four-year institutions. This makes sense in light of evidence suggesting that students at two-year schools are more likely to be paying their own way, so they are spending a higher share of income on tuition compared to students at four-year institutions (who are more likely to be counting on their parents' income).

Students at two-year schools are also more responsive to changes in the unemployment rate. Higher unemployment leads to higher enrollments, indicating that these students are making a trade-off by going to school instead of working, and they consider school a substitute for their time. Both of these factors—the high share of income spent on tuition and viewing school as a substitute for their time—will lead students at two-year colleges to be more responsive to changes in tuition than students at four-year colleges.

An increase in tuition is also more of a barrier for financial aid students than for students paying full tuition. Financial aid students may be more responsive to the full cost of tuition due to fear of losing their grant money or concerns about the cost of paying back their student loans.

Students at two-year schools are more responsive to the price of tuition than students at four-year schools.

>> Check Your Understanding 5-2

Solutions appear at back of book.

1. For each case, choose the condition that characterizes demand: elastic demand, inelastic demand, or unit-elastic demand.
   a. Total revenue decreases when price increases.
   b. The additional revenue generated by an increase in quantity sold is exactly offset by revenue lost from the fall in price received per unit.
   c. Total revenue falls when output increases.
   d. Producers in a particular industry find they can increase their total revenues by coordinating a reduction in industry output.
2. What is the elasticity of demand for the following goods? Explain. What is the shape of the demand curve?
   a. Demand for a blood transfusion by an accident victim
   b. Demand by students for green erasers

>> Quick Review

• Demand is **perfectly inelastic** if it is completely unresponsive to price. It is **perfectly elastic** if it is infinitely responsive to price.

• Demand is **elastic** if the price elasticity of demand is greater than 1. It is **inelastic** if the price elasticity of demand is less than 1. It is **unit-elastic** if the price elasticity of demand is exactly 1.

• When demand is elastic, the quantity effect of a price increase dominates the price effect and **total revenue** falls. When demand is inelastic, the quantity effect is dominated by the price effect and total revenue rises.

• Because the price elasticity of demand can change along the demand curve, economists refer to a particular point on the demand curve when speaking of the price elasticity of demand.

• Ready availability of close substitutes makes demand for a good more elastic, as does a longer length of time elapsed since the price change. Demand for a necessity is less elastic, and demand for a luxury good is more elastic. Demand tends to be inelastic for goods that absorb a small share of a consumer's income and elastic for goods that absorb a large share of income.

‖ Other Demand Elasticities

The quantity of a good demanded depends not only on the price of that good but also on other variables. In particular, demand curves shift because of changes in the prices of related goods and changes in consumers' incomes. It is often important to have a measure of these other effects, and the best measures are—you guessed it—elasticities. Specifically, we can best measure how the demand for a good is affected by prices of other goods by using a measure called the *cross-price elasticity of demand*, and we can best measure how demand is affected by changes in income by using the *income elasticity of demand*.

The Cross-Price Elasticity of Demand

In Chapter 3 you learned that the demand for a good is often affected by the prices of other, related goods—goods that are substitutes or complements. There you saw that a change in the price of a related good shifts the demand curve of the original good, reflecting a change in the quantity demanded at any given price. The strength of such a "cross" effect on demand can be measured by the **cross-price elasticity of demand,** defined as the ratio of the percent change in the quantity demanded of one good to the percent change in the price of the other. Like the price elasticity of demand, the cross-price elasticity is calculated using the midpoint method.

(5-7) Cross-price elasticity of demand between goods A and B

$$= \frac{\% \text{ change in quantity of A demanded}}{\% \text{ change in price of B}}$$

When two goods are substitutes, like hot dogs and hamburgers, the cross-price elasticity of demand is positive: a rise in the price of hot dogs increases the demand for hamburgers—that is, it causes a rightward shift of the demand curve for hamburgers. If the goods are close substitutes, the cross-price elasticity will be positive and large; if they are not close substitutes, the cross-price elasticity will be positive and small. So when the cross-price elasticity of demand is positive, its size is a measure of how closely substitutable the two goods are.

When two goods are complements, like hot dogs and hot dog buns, the cross-price elasticity is negative: a rise in the price of hot dogs decreases the demand for hot dog buns—that is, it causes a leftward shift of the demand curve for hot dog buns. As with substitutes, the size of the cross-price elasticity of demand between two complements tells us how strongly complementary they are: if the cross-price elasticity is only slightly below zero, they are weak complements; if it is very negative, they are strong complements.

Note that in the case of the cross-price elasticity of demand, the sign (plus or minus) is very important: it tells us whether the two goods are complements or substitutes. So we cannot drop the minus sign as we did for the price elasticity of demand.

Our discussion of the cross-price elasticity of demand is a useful place to return to a point we made earlier: elasticity is a *unit-free* measure—that is, it doesn't depend on the units in which goods are measured.

To see the potential problem, suppose someone told you that "if the price of hot dog buns rises by $0.30, Americans will buy 10 million fewer hot dogs this year." If you've ever bought hot dog buns, you'll immediately wonder: is that a $0.30 increase in the price *per bun*, or is it a $0.30 increase in the price *per package*? Buns are usually sold in packages of eight. It makes a big difference what units we are talking about! However, if someone says that the cross-price elasticity of demand between buns and hot dogs is –0.3, it doesn't matter whether buns are

The **cross-price elasticity of demand** between two goods measures the effect of the change in one good's price on the quantity demanded of the other good. It is equal to the percent change in the quantity demanded of one good divided by the percent change in the other good's price.

sold individually or by the package. So elasticity is defined as a ratio of percent changes, as a way of making sure that confusion over units doesn't arise.

The Income Elasticity of Demand

The **income elasticity of demand** is a measure of how much the demand for a good is affected by changes in consumers' incomes. It allows us to determine whether a good is a normal or inferior good as well as to measure how intensely the demand for the good responds to changes in income.

(5-8) Income elasticity of demand $= \dfrac{\%\text{ change in quantity demanded}}{\%\text{ change in income}}$

Just as the cross-price elasticity of demand between two goods can be either positive or negative, depending on whether the goods are substitutes or complements, the income elasticity of demand for a good can also be either positive or negative. Recall from Chapter 3 that goods can be either *normal goods*, for which demand increases when income rises, or *inferior goods*, for which demand decreases when income rises. These definitions relate directly to the sign of the income elasticity of demand:

- When the income elasticity of demand is positive, the good is a normal good. In this case, the quantity demanded at any given price increases as income increases. Correspondingly, the quantity demanded at any given price decreases as income falls.

- When the income elasticity of demand is negative, the good is an inferior good. In this case, the quantity demanded at any given price decreases as income increases. Likewise, the quantity demanded at any given price increases as income falls.

> The **income elasticity of demand** is the percent change in the quantity of a good demanded when a consumer's income changes, divided by the percent change in the consumer's income.
>
> Demand for a good is **income-elastic** if the income elasticity of demand for that good is greater than 1.

GLOBAL COMPARISON   FOOD'S BITE IN WORLD BUDGETS

If the income elasticity of demand for food is less than 1, we would expect to find that people in poor countries spend a larger share of their income on food than people in rich countries. And that's exactly what the data show. In this graph, we compare per capita income—a country's total income, divided by the population—with the share of income that is spent on food. (To make the graph a manageable size, per capita income is measured as a percentage of U.S. per capita income.)

In very poor countries like Pakistan, people spend a large percent of their income on food. In middle-income countries, like Israel and Mexico, the share of spending that goes to food is much lower. And it's even lower in rich countries like the United States.

Data from: USDA and World Bank, World Development Indicators.

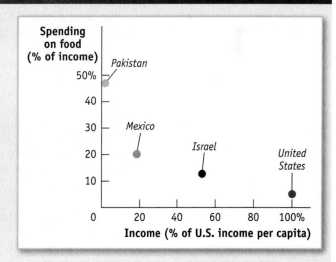

Economists often use estimates of the income elasticity of demand to predict which industries will grow most rapidly as the incomes of consumers grow over time. In doing this, they often find it useful to make a further distinction among normal goods, identifying which are *income-elastic* and which are *income-inelastic*.

The demand for a good is **income-elastic** if the income elasticity of demand for that good is greater than 1. When income rises, the demand for income-elastic goods rises *faster* than income. Luxury goods such as second homes and

>> **Quick Review**

• Goods are substitutes when the **cross-price elasticity of demand** is positive. Goods are complements when the cross-price elasticity of demand is negative.

• Inferior goods have a negative **income elasticity of demand.** Most goods are normal goods, which have a positive income elasticity of demand.

• Normal goods may be either **income-elastic,** with an income elasticity of demand greater than 1, or **income-inelastic,** with an income elasticity of demand that is positive but less than 1.

international travel tend to be income-elastic. The demand for a good is **income-inelastic** if the income elasticity of demand for that good is positive but less than 1. When income rises, the demand for income-inelastic goods rises, but more slowly than income. Necessities such as food and clothing tend to be income-inelastic.

>> **Check Your Understanding 5-3**
Solutions appear at back of book.

1. After Chelsea's income increased from $12,000 to $18,000 a year, her purchases of album downloads increased from 10 to 40 downloads a year. Calculate Chelsea's income elasticity of demand for albums using the midpoint method.

2. Expensive restaurant meals are income-elastic goods for most people, including Sanjay. Suppose his income falls by 10% this year. What can you predict about the change in Sanjay's consumption of expensive restaurant meals?

3. As the price of margarine rises by 20%, a manufacturer of baked goods increases its quantity of butter demanded by 5%. Calculate the cross-price elasticity of demand between butter and margarine. Are butter and margarine substitutes or complements for this manufacturer?

‖ The Price Elasticity of Supply

A fundamental characteristic of any market for ambulance services, no matter where it is located, is limited supply. For example, it would have been much harder to charge Kira Milas $1,772.42 for a 15-minute ride to the hospital if there had been many ambulance providers cruising nearby and offering a lower price. But there are good economic reasons why there are not: who among those experiencing a true health emergency would trust their health and safety to a low-price ambulance? And who would want to be a supplier, paying the expense of providing quality ambulance services, without being able to charge high prices to recoup costs? Not surprisingly, then, in most locations there is only one ambulance provider available.

In sum, a critical element in the ability of ambulance providers to charge high prices is limited supply: a low responsiveness in the quantity of output supplied to the higher prices charged for an ambulance ride. To measure the response of ambulance providers to price changes, we need a measure parallel to the price elasticity of demand—the *price elasticity of supply*, as we'll see next.

Measuring the Price Elasticity of Supply

The **price elasticity of supply** is defined the same way as the price elasticity of demand, although since it is always positive there is no minus sign to be eliminated:

(5-9) $\text{Price elasticity of supply} = \dfrac{\%\ \text{change in quantity supplied}}{\%\ \text{change in price}}$

The demand for a good is **income-inelastic** if the income elasticity of demand for that good is positive but less than 1.

The **price elasticity of supply** is a measure of the responsiveness of the quantity of a good supplied to the price of that good. It is the ratio of the percent change in the quantity supplied to the percent change in the price as we move along the supply curve.

The only difference is that now we consider movements along the supply curve rather than movements along the demand curve.

Suppose that the price of tomatoes rises by 10%. If the quantity of tomatoes supplied also increases by 10% in response, the price elasticity of supply of tomatoes is 1 (10%/10%) and supply is unit-elastic. If the quantity supplied increases by 5%, the price elasticity of supply is 0.5 and supply is inelastic; if the quantity increases by 20%, the price elasticity of supply is 2 and supply is elastic.

As in the case of demand, the extreme values of the price elasticity of supply have a simple graphical representation. Panel (a) of Figure 5-6 shows the supply of cell phone frequencies, the portion of the radio spectrum that is suitable for

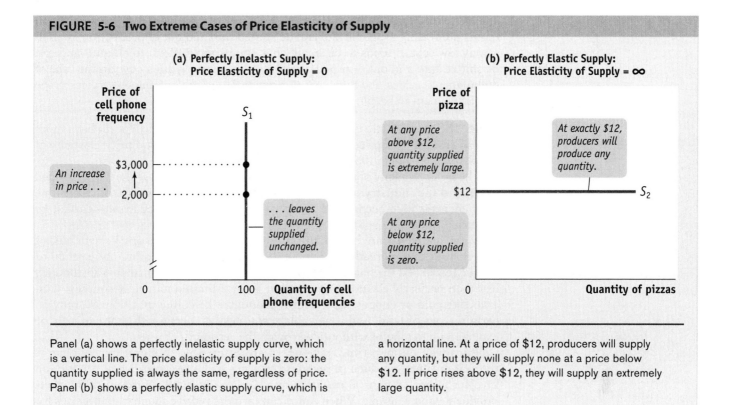

FIGURE 5-6 Two Extreme Cases of Price Elasticity of Supply

(a) Perfectly Inelastic Supply:
Price Elasticity of Supply = 0

Price of cell phone frequency

S_1

An increase in price . . .

$3,000

2,000

. . . leaves the quantity supplied unchanged.

0   100   Quantity of cell phone frequencies

(b) Perfectly Elastic Supply:
Price Elasticity of Supply = ∞

Price of pizza

At any price above $12, quantity supplied is extremely large.

At exactly $12, producers will produce any quantity.

$12 S_2

At any price below $12, quantity supplied is zero.

0   Quantity of pizzas

Panel (a) shows a perfectly inelastic supply curve, which is a vertical line. The price elasticity of supply is zero: the quantity supplied is always the same, regardless of price. Panel (b) shows a perfectly elastic supply curve, which is a horizontal line. At a price of $12, producers will supply any quantity, but they will supply none at a price below $12. If price rises above $12, they will supply an extremely large quantity.

sending and receiving cell phone signals. Governments own the right to sell the use of this part of the radio spectrum to cell phone operators inside their borders. But governments can't increase or decrease the number of cell phone frequencies that they have to offer—for technical reasons, the quantity of frequencies suitable for cell phone operation is a fixed quantity.

So the supply curve for cell phone frequencies is a vertical line, which we have assumed is set at the quantity of 100 frequencies. As you move up and down that curve, the change in the quantity supplied by the government is zero, whatever the change in price. So panel (a) illustrates a case in which the price elasticity of supply is zero. This is a case of **perfectly inelastic supply.**

Panel (b) shows the supply curve for pizza. We suppose that it costs $12 to produce a pizza, including all opportunity costs. At any price below $12, it would be unprofitable to produce pizza and all the pizza parlors in America would go out of business. Alternatively, there are many producers who could operate pizza parlors if they were profitable. The ingredients—flour, tomatoes, cheese—are plentiful. And if necessary, more tomatoes could be grown, more milk could be produced to make mozzarella, and so on. So any price above $12 would elicit an extremely large quantity of pizzas supplied. The implied supply curve is therefore a horizontal line at $12.

Since even a tiny increase in the price would lead to a huge increase in the quantity supplied, the price elasticity of supply would be more or less infinite. This is a case of **perfectly elastic supply.**

As our cell phone frequencies and pizza examples suggest, real-world instances of both perfectly inelastic and perfectly elastic supply are easy to find—much easier than their counterparts in demand.

What Factors Determine the Price Elasticity of Supply?

Our examples tell us the main determinant of the price elasticity of supply: the availability of inputs. In addition, as with the price elasticity of demand, time may also play a role in the price elasticity of supply. Here we briefly summarize the two factors.

There is **perfectly inelastic supply** when the price elasticity of supply is zero, so that changes in the price of the good have no effect on the quantity supplied. A perfectly inelastic supply curve is a vertical line.

There is **perfectly elastic supply** when even a tiny increase or reduction in the price will lead to very large changes in the quantity supplied, so that the price elasticity of supply is infinite. A perfectly elastic supply curve is a horizontal line.

The Availability of Inputs The price elasticity of supply tends to be large when inputs are readily available and can be shifted into and out of production at a relatively low cost. It tends to be small when inputs are difficult to obtain—and can be shifted into and out of production only at a relatively high cost. In the case of ambulance services, the high cost of providing quality ambulance services is the crucial element in keeping the elasticity of supply very low.

Time The price elasticity of supply tends to grow larger as producers have more time to respond to a price change. This means that the long-run price elasticity of supply is often higher than the short-run elasticity.

The price elasticity of the supply of pizza is very high because the inputs needed to expand the industry are readily available. The price elasticity of cell phone frequencies is zero because an essential input—the radio spectrum—cannot be increased at all.

Many industries are like pizza production and have large price elasticities of supply: they can be readily expanded because they don't require any special or unique resources. In contrast, the price elasticity of supply is usually substantially less than perfectly elastic for goods that involve limited natural resources: minerals like gold or copper, agricultural products like coffee that flourish only on certain types of land, and renewable resources like ocean fish that can only be exploited up to a point without destroying the resource.

But given enough time, producers are often able to significantly change the amount they produce in response to a price change, even when production involves a limited natural resource or a very costly input. Agricultural markets provide a good example. When American farmers receive much higher prices for a given commodity, like wheat (because of a drought in a big wheat-producing country like Australia), in the next planting season they are likely to switch their acreage planted from other crops to wheat.

For this reason, economists often make a distinction between the short-run elasticity of supply, usually referring to a few weeks or months, and the long-run elasticity of supply, usually referring to several years. In most industries, the long-run elasticity of supply is larger than the short-run elasticity.

ECONOMICS >> *in Action*
China and the Global Commodities Glut of 2016

Over the past decade, the rapidly growing Chinese economy has been a voracious consumer of commodities—metals, foodstuffs, and fuel—as its economy rapidly expanded to become a global manufacturing powerhouse. As China's demand for commodities to support its transformation soared, the countries providing those commodities also saw their incomes soar.

However, in 2016, it all came to a screeching halt as the Chinese economy faltered. Global commodity producers saw the demand for their goods fall dramatically, just as many of them were investing in costly projects to increase supplies. For example, Chile, the world's major copper producer, had undertaken a massive expansion of its copper mines, digging up 1.7 billion tons of material as copper prices plummeted around the world. India was building railroad lines to connect its underused coal mines to the export market just as a worldwide glut of coal opened up. And Australia was planning to increase its natural gas production by 150% just as natural gas companies around the world went bankrupt due to shrinking fuel demand and plunging prices.

Because these countries had invested many billions of dollars into increasing their supply capacity over several years, they could not simply shut down production. So it continued, making the existing glut of commodities even worse.

What the commodity producers appear to have forgotten is the logic of the price elasticity of supply: combine persistently high prices with the easy availability of inputs to increase supply capacity (in this case, the chief input was financial capital), and the predictable result is a big increase in the supply of commodities (a rightward shift of the supply curve).

Also predictable is that once the growth in demand for the commodities slowed down, a steep fall in prices would result. As Michael Levi, a commodities expert at the Council of Foreign Relations said, "Producers ended up being their own worst enemies. No one ever worried they would produce too much, but that is exactly what has happened and gotten them into this mess."

>> Check Your Understanding 5-4
Solutions appear at back of book.

1. Using the midpoint method, calculate the price elasticity of supply for web-design services when the price per hour rises from $100 to $150 and the number of hours transacted increases from 300,000 to 500,000. Is supply elastic, inelastic, or unit-elastic?

2. Are each the following statements true or false? Explain.
   a. If the demand for milk rose, then, in the long run, milk drinkers would be better off if supply were elastic rather than inelastic.
   b. Long-run price elasticities of supply are generally larger than short-run price elasticities of supply. As a result, short-run supply curves are generally flatter than long-run supply curves.
   c. When supply is perfectly elastic, changes in demand have no effect on price.

>> Quick Review

• The **price elasticity of supply** is the percent change in the quantity supplied divided by the percent change in the price.

• Under **perfectly inelastic supply,** the quantity supplied is completely unresponsive to price and the supply curve is a vertical line. Under **perfectly elastic supply,** the supply curve is horizontal at some specific price. If the price falls below that level, the quantity supplied is zero. If the price rises above that level, the quantity supplied is extremely large.

• The price elasticity of supply depends on the availability of inputs, the ease of shifting inputs into and out of alternative uses, and the period of time that has elapsed since the price change.

An Elasticity Menagerie

We've just run through quite a few different elasticities. Keeping them all straight can be a challenge. So in Table 5-3 (page 152) we provide a summary of all the elasticities we have discussed and their implications.

The Benefits and Costs of Taxation

When a government is considering whether to impose a tax or how to design a tax system, it has to weigh the benefits of a tax against its costs. We don't usually think of a tax as something that provides benefits, but governments need money to provide things people want, such as national defense and health care for those unable to afford it. The benefit of a tax is the revenue it raises for the government to pay for these services. Unfortunately, this benefit comes at a cost—a cost that is normally greater than the amount consumers and producers pay. Let's look first at what determines how much money a tax raises, then at the costs a tax imposes, both of which are dependent upon the elasticity of supply and demand. To understand the economics of taxes, it's helpful to look at a simple type of tax known as an **excise tax**—a tax charged on each unit of a good or service that is sold.

An **excise tax** is a tax on sales of a good or service.

"What taxes would you like to see imposed on other people?"

The Revenue from an Excise Tax

Suppose that the supply and demand for hotel rooms in the city of Potterville are as shown in Figure 5-7. For simplicity, assume that all hotel rooms offer the same features. In the absence of taxes, the equilibrium price of a room is $80.00 per night and the equilibrium quantity of hotel rooms rented is 10,000 per night.

Now suppose that Potterville's city council imposes an excise tax of $40 per night on hotel rooms—that is, every time a room is rented for the night, the owner

TABLE 5-3 An Elasticity Menagerie

Price elasticity of demand $= \dfrac{\text{\% change in quantity demanded}}{\text{\% change in price}}$ (dropping the minus sign)	
0	**Perfectly inelastic:** price has no effect on quantity demanded (vertical demand curve).
Between 0 and 1	**Inelastic:** a rise in price increases total revenue.
Exactly 1	**Unit-elastic:** changes in price have no effect on total revenue.
Greater than 1, less than ∞	**Elastic:** a rise in price reduces total revenue.
∞	**Perfectly elastic:** any rise in price causes quantity demanded to fall to 0. Any fall in price leads to an infinite quantity demanded (horizontal demand curve).
Cross-price elasticity of demand $= \dfrac{\text{\% change in quantity demanded of } \textit{one good}}{\text{\% change in price of } \textit{another good}}$	
Negative	**Complements:** quantity demanded of one good falls when the price of another rises.
Positive	**Substitutes:** quantity demanded of one good rises when the price of another rises.
Income elasticity of demand $= \dfrac{\text{\% change in quantity demanded}}{\text{\% change in income}}$	
Negative	**Inferior good:** quantity demanded falls when income rises.
Positive, less than 1	**Normal good, income-inelastic:** quantity demanded rises when income rises, but not as rapidly as income.
Greater than 1	**Normal good, income-elastic:** quantity demanded rises when income rises, and more rapidly than income.
Price elasticity of supply $= \dfrac{\text{\% change in quantity supplied}}{\text{\% change in price}}$	
0	**Perfectly inelastic:** price has no effect on quantity supplied (vertical supply curve).
Greater than 0, less than ∞	Ordinary upward-sloping supply curve.
∞	**Perfectly elastic:** any fall in price causes quantity supplied to fall to 0. Any rise in price elicits an infinite quantity supplied (horizontal supply curve).

of the hotel must pay the city $40. For example, if a customer pays $80, $40 is collected as a tax, leaving the hotel owner with only $40.

How much revenue does the government collect from an excise tax? In our hotel tax example, the revenue is equal to the area of the shaded rectangle in Figure 5-7.

To see why this area represents the revenue collected by a $40 tax on hotel rooms, notice that the height of the rectangle is $40, equal to the tax per room. It is also, as we've seen, the size of the wedge that the tax drives between the supply price (the price received by producers) and the demand price (the price paid by consumers). Meanwhile, the width of the rectangle is 5,000 rooms, equal to the

FIGURE 5-7   The Revenue from an Excise Tax

The revenue from a $40 excise tax on hotel rooms is $200,000, equal to the tax rate, $40—the size of the wedge that the tax drives between the supply price and the demand price—multiplied by the number of rooms rented, 5,000. This is equal to the area of the shaded rectangle.

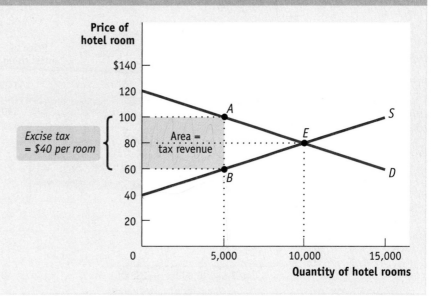

equilibrium quantity of rooms given the $40 tax. With that information, we can make the following calculations.

The tax revenue collected is:

$$\text{Tax revenue} = \$40 \text{ per room} \times 5{,}000 \text{ rooms} = \$200{,}000$$

The area of the shaded rectangle is:

$$\text{Area} = \text{Height} \times \text{Width} = \$40 \text{ per room} \times 5{,}000 \text{ rooms} = \$200{,}000$$

or

$$\text{Tax revenue} = \text{Area of shaded rectangle}$$

This is a general principle: *The revenue collected by an excise tax is equal to the area of the rectangle whose height is the tax wedge between the supply and demand curves and whose width is the quantity transacted under the tax.*

Tax Rates and Revenue

In Figure 5-7, $40 per room is the *tax rate* on hotel rooms. A **tax rate** is the amount of tax levied per unit of the taxed item. Sometimes tax rates are defined in terms of dollar amounts per unit of a good or service; for example, $2.46 per pack of cigarettes sold. In other cases, they are defined as a percentage of the price; for example, the payroll tax is 15.3% of a worker's earnings up to $128,400 in 2018.

There's obviously a relationship between tax rates and revenue. That relationship is not, however, one-for-one. In general, doubling the excise tax rate on a good or service won't double the amount of revenue collected, because the tax increase will reduce the quantity of the good or service transacted. And the relationship between the level of the tax and the amount of revenue collected may not even be positive: in some cases raising the tax rate actually *reduces* the amount of revenue the government collects.

We can illustrate these points using our hotel room example. Figure 5-7 showed the revenue the government collects from a $40 tax on hotel rooms. Figure 5-8 shows the revenue the government would collect from two alternative tax rates—a lower tax of only $20 per room and a higher tax of $60 per room.

A **tax rate** is the amount of tax people are required to pay per unit of whatever is being taxed.

FIGURE 5-8 Tax Rates and Revenue

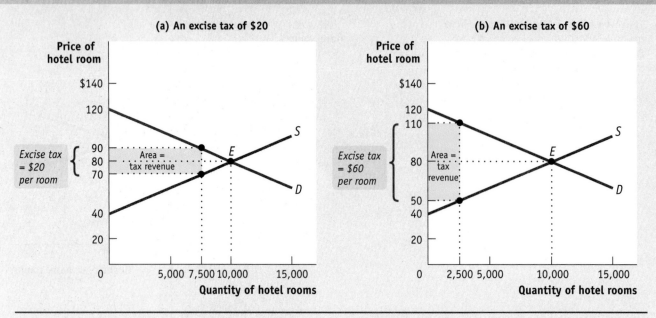

In general, doubling the excise tax rate on a good or service won't double the amount of revenue collected, because the tax increase will reduce the quantity of the good or service bought and sold. And the relationship between the level of the tax and the amount of revenue collected may not even be positive. Panel (a) shows the revenue raised by a tax of $20 per room, only half the tax rate in Figure 5-7. The tax revenue raised, equal to the area of the shaded rectangle, is $150,000. That is 75% of $200,000, the revenue raised by a $40 tax rate. Panel (b) shows that the revenue raised by a $60 tax is also $150,000. So raising the tax rate from $40 to $60 actually reduces tax revenue.

Panel (a) of Figure 5-8 shows the case of a $20 tax, equal to half the tax rate illustrated in Figure 5-7. At this lower tax rate, 7,500 rooms are rented, generating tax revenue of:

$$\text{Tax revenue} = \$20 \text{ per room} \times 7,500 \text{ rooms} = \$150,000$$

Recall that the tax revenue collected from a $40 tax rate is $200,000. So the revenue collected from a $20 tax rate, $150,000, is only 75% of the amount collected when the tax rate is twice as high ($150,000/$200,000 × 100 = 75%). To put it another way, a 100% increase in the tax rate from $20 to $40 per room leads to only a one-third, or 33.3%, increase in revenue, from $150,000 to $200,000 (($200,000 − $150,000)/$150,000 × 100 = 33.3%).

Panel (b) depicts what happens if the tax rate is raised from $40 to $60 per room, leading to a fall in the number of rooms rented from 5,000 to 2,500. The revenue collected at a $60 per room tax rate is:

$$\text{Tax revenue} = \$60 \text{ per room} \times 2,500 \text{ rooms} = \$150,000$$

This is also *less* than the revenue collected by a $40 per room tax. So raising the tax rate from $40 to $60 actually reduces revenue. More precisely, in this case raising the tax rate by 50% (($60 − $40)/$40) × 100 = 50% lowers the tax revenue by 25% (($150,000 − $200,000)/$200,000) × 100 = −25%). Why did this happen? Because the fall in tax revenue caused by the reduction in the number of rooms rented more than offset the increase in the tax revenue caused by the rise in the tax rate. In other words, setting a tax rate so high that it deters a significant number of transactions will likely lead to a fall in tax revenue.

One way to think about the revenue effect of increasing an excise tax is that the tax increase affects tax revenue in two ways. On one side, the tax increase means that the government raises more revenue for each unit of the good sold, which other things equal would lead to a rise in tax revenue. On the other side, the tax increase reduces the quantity of sales, which other things equal would lead to a fall in tax revenue. The end result depends both on the price elasticities of supply and demand and on the initial level of the tax.

If the price elasticities of both supply and demand are low, the tax increase won't reduce the quantity of the good sold very much, so tax revenue will definitely rise. If the price elasticities are high, the result is less certain; if they are high enough, the tax reduces the quantity sold so much that tax revenue falls. Also, if the initial tax rate is low, the government doesn't lose much revenue from the decline in the quantity of the good sold, so the tax increase will definitely increase tax revenue. If the initial tax rate is high, the result is again less certain. Tax revenue is likely to fall or rise very little from a tax increase only in cases where the price elasticities are high and there is already a high tax rate.

The possibility that a higher tax rate can reduce tax revenue, and the corresponding possibility that cutting taxes can increase tax revenue, is a basic principle of taxation that policy makers take into account when setting tax rates. That is, when considering a tax created for the purpose of raising revenue (in contrast to taxes created to discourage undesirable behavior, known as *sin taxes*), a well-informed policy maker won't impose a tax rate so high that cutting the tax would increase revenue.

In the real world, however, policy makers aren't always well informed, but they usually aren't complete fools either. That's why it's very hard to find real-world examples in which raising a tax reduced revenue or cutting a tax increased revenue.

The Costs of Taxation

What is the cost of a tax? You might be inclined to answer that it is the money taxpayers pay to the government. In other words, you might believe that the cost of a tax is the tax revenue collected. But suppose the government uses the tax revenue to provide services that taxpayers want. Or suppose that the government simply hands the tax revenue back to taxpayers. Would we say in those cases that the tax didn't actually cost anything?

No—because a tax, like a quota, prevents mutually beneficial transactions from occurring. Consider Figure 5-7 once more. Here, with a $40 tax on hotel rooms, guests pay $100 per room but hotel owners receive only $60 per room. Because of the wedge created by the tax, we know that some transactions don't occur that would have occurred without the tax.

For example, we know from the supply and demand curves that after the $40 tax is imposed there are some potential guests who would be willing to pay up to $90 per night and some hotel owners who would be willing to supply rooms if they received at least $70 per night. If these two sets of people were allowed to trade with each other without the tax, they would engage in mutually beneficial transactions—hotel rooms would be rented.

But such deals would be illegal, because the $40 tax would not be paid. In our example, 5,000 potential hotel room rentals that would have occurred in the absence of the tax, to the mutual benefit of guests and hotel owners, do not take place because of the tax. Specifically, 5,000 (the number of lost rentals) is equal to 10,000 (the equilibrium quantity at an untaxed rate of $80) minus 5,000 (the rooms that are rented with the tax).

So an excise tax imposes costs over and above the tax revenue collected in the form of inefficiency, which occurs because the tax discourages mutually beneficial transactions. As we learned in Chapter 4, the cost to society of this kind of inefficiency—the value of forgone mutually beneficial transactions—is called the deadweight loss. While all real-world taxes impose some deadweight loss, a badly designed tax imposes a larger deadweight loss than a well-designed one.

To measure the deadweight loss from a tax, we turn to the concepts of producer and consumer surplus. Figure 5-9 shows the effects of an excise tax on consumer and producer surplus. In the absence of the tax, the equilibrium is at E and the equilibrium price and quantity are P_E and Q_E, respectively. An excise tax drives a wedge equal to the amount of the tax between the price received by producers and the price paid by consumers, reducing the quantity sold. In this case, where the tax is T dollars per unit, the quantity sold falls to Q_T. The price paid by consumers rises to P_C, the demand price of the reduced quantity, Q_T, and the price received by producers falls to P_P, the supply price of that quantity. The difference between these prices, $P_C - P_P$, is equal to the excise tax, T.

The rise in the price paid by consumers causes a loss equal to the sum of the areas of a rectangle and a triangle: the dark blue rectangle labeled A and the area of the light blue triangle labeled B in Figure 5-9.

Meanwhile, the fall in the price received by producers leads to a fall in producer surplus. This, too, is equal to the sum of the areas of a rectangle and a triangle. The loss in producer surplus is the sum of the areas of the red rectangle labeled C and the pink triangle labeled F in Figure 5-9.

Of course, although consumers and producers are hurt by the tax, the government gains revenue. The revenue the government collects is equal to the tax per unit sold, T, multiplied by the quantity sold, Q_T. This revenue is equal to the area of a rectangle Q_T wide and T high. And we already have that rectangle in the figure: it is the sum of rectangles A and C. So the government gains part of what consumers and producers lose from an excise tax.

But a portion of the loss to producers and consumers from the tax is not offset by a gain to the government—specifically, the two triangles B and F. The deadweight loss caused by the tax is equal to the combined area of these two triangles. It represents the total surplus lost to society because of the tax—that is, the amount of surplus that would have been generated by transactions that now do not take place because of the tax.

Figure 5-10 is a version of Figure 5-9 that leaves out rectangles A (the surplus shifted from consumers to the government) and C (the surplus shifted from

---

FIGURE 5-9 A Tax Reduces Consumer and Producer Surplus

Before the tax, the equilibrium price and quantity are P_E and Q_E, respectively. After an excise tax of T per unit is imposed, the price to consumers rises to P_C and consumer surplus falls by the sum of the dark blue rectangle, labeled A, and the light blue triangle, labeled B. The tax also causes the price to producers to fall to P_P; producer surplus falls by the sum of the red rectangle, labeled C, and the pink triangle, labeled F. The government receives revenue from the tax equal to $Q_T \times T$, which is given by the sum of the areas A and C. Areas B and F represent the losses to consumer and producer surplus that are not collected by the government as revenue. They are the deadweight loss to society of the tax.

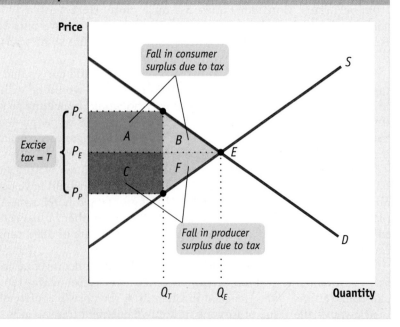

FIGURE 5-10   The Deadweight Loss of a Tax

A tax leads to a deadweight loss because it creates inefficiency: some mutually beneficial transactions never take place because of the tax—namely, the transactions $Q_E - Q_T$. The yellow area here represents the value of the deadweight loss: it is the total surplus that would have been gained from the $Q_E - Q_T$ transactions. If the tax had not discouraged transactions—had the number of transactions remained at Q_E because of either perfectly inelastic supply or perfectly inelastic demand—no deadweight loss would have been incurred.

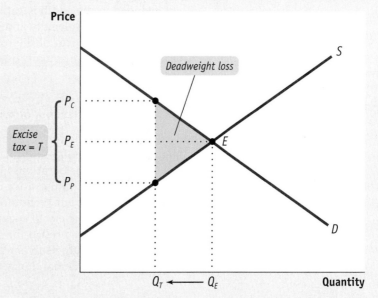

producers to the government) and shows only the deadweight loss, here drawn as a triangle shaded yellow. The base of that triangle is equal to the tax wedge, T; the height of the triangle is equal to the reduction in the quantity transacted due to the tax, $Q_E - Q_T$. Clearly, the larger the tax wedge and the larger the reduction in the quantity transacted, the greater the inefficiency from the tax.

But also note an important, contrasting point: if the excise tax somehow *didn't* reduce the quantity bought and sold in this market—if Q_T remained equal to Q_E after the tax was levied—the yellow triangle would disappear and the deadweight loss from the tax would be zero. This observation is simply the flip-side of the principle found earlier in the chapter: a tax causes inefficiency because it discourages mutually beneficial transactions between buyers and sellers. So if a tax does not discourage transactions, which would be true if either supply or demand were perfectly inelastic, it causes no deadweight loss. In this case, the tax simply shifts surplus straight from consumers and producers to the government.

Using a triangle to measure deadweight loss is a technique used in many economic applications. For example, triangles are used to measure the deadweight loss produced by types of taxes other than excise taxes. They are also used to measure the deadweight loss produced by monopoly, another kind of market distortion. And deadweight-loss triangles are often used to evaluate the benefits and costs of public policies besides taxation—such as whether to impose stricter safety standards on a product.

In considering the total amount of inefficiency caused by a tax, we must also take into account something not shown in Figure 5-10: the resources actually used by the government to collect the tax, and by taxpayers to pay it, over and above the amount of the tax. These lost resources are called the **administrative costs** of the tax. The most familiar administrative cost of the U.S. tax system is the time individuals spend filling out their income tax forms or the money they pay for tax return preparation services like those provided by H&R Block and companies like it. (The latter is considered an inefficiency from the point of view of society

The **administrative costs** of a tax are the resources used for its collection, for the method of payment, and for any attempts to evade the tax.

Society ultimately pays the administrative costs of taxes.

because resources spent on return preparation could be used for other, non-tax-related purposes.)

Included in the administrative costs that taxpayers incur are resources used to evade the tax, both legally and illegally. The costs of operating the Internal Revenue Service, the arm of the federal government tasked with collecting the federal income tax, are actually quite small in comparison to the administrative costs paid by taxpayers.

So we get:

$$\text{Total inefficiency of tax} = \text{Deadweight loss} + \text{Administrative costs}$$

The general rule for economic policy is that, other things equal, a tax system should be designed to minimize the total inefficiency it imposes on society. In practice, other considerations also apply, but this principle nonetheless gives valuable guidance. Administrative costs are usually well known, more or less determined by the current technology of collecting taxes (for example, filing paper returns versus filing electronically).

But how can we predict the size of the deadweight loss associated with a given tax? Not surprisingly, as in our analysis of the incidence of a tax, the price elasticities of supply and demand play crucial roles in making such a prediction.

Elasticities and the Deadweight Loss of a Tax

We know that the deadweight loss from an excise tax arises because it prevents some mutually beneficial transactions from occurring. In particular, the producer and consumer surplus that is forgone because of these missing transactions is equal to the size of the deadweight loss itself. This means that the larger the number of transactions that are prevented by the tax, the larger the deadweight loss.

This fact gives us an important clue in understanding the relationship between elasticity and the size of the deadweight loss from a tax. Recall that when demand or supply is elastic, the quantity demanded or the quantity supplied is relatively responsive to changes in the price. So a tax imposed on a good for which either demand or supply, or both, is elastic will cause a relatively large decrease in the quantity transacted and a relatively large deadweight loss. In addition, the greater the elasticity of either demand or supply, the greater the deadweight loss from a tax.

And when we say that demand or supply is inelastic, we mean that the quantity demanded or the quantity supplied is relatively unresponsive to changes in the price. As a result, a tax imposed when demand or supply, or both, is inelastic will cause a relatively small decrease in the quantity transacted and a relatively small deadweight loss.

The four panels of Figure 5-11 illustrate the positive relationship between a good's price elasticity of either demand or supply and the deadweight loss from taxing that good. Each panel represents the same amount of tax imposed but on a different good; the size of the deadweight loss is given by the area of the shaded triangle. In panel (a), the deadweight-loss triangle is large because demand for this good is relatively elastic—a large number of transactions fail to occur because of the tax. In panel (b), the same supply curve is drawn as in panel (a), but demand for this good is relatively inelastic; as a result, the triangle is small because only a small number of transactions are forgone. Likewise, panels (c) and (d) contain the same demand curve but different supply curves. In panel (c), an elastic supply curve gives rise to a large deadweight-loss triangle, but in panel (d) an inelastic supply curve gives rise to a small deadweight-loss triangle.

The implication of this result is clear: if you want to minimize the efficiency costs of taxation, you should choose to tax only those goods for which demand or supply, or both, is relatively inelastic. For such goods, a tax has little effect on behavior because behavior is relatively unresponsive to changes in the price. In the extreme case in which demand is perfectly inelastic (a vertical demand curve), the quantity demanded is unchanged by the imposition of the tax. As a result, the tax imposes no

FIGURE 5-11 Deadweight Loss and Elasticities

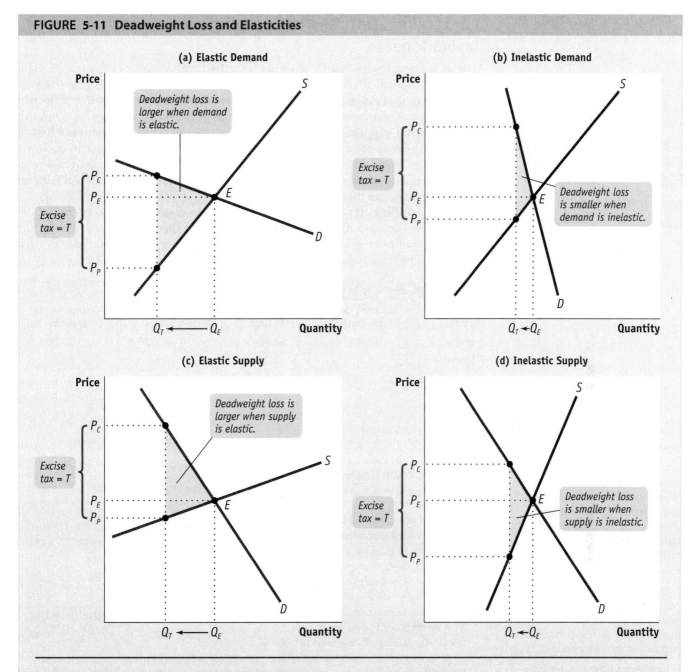

Demand is elastic in panel (a) and inelastic in panel (b), but the supply curves are the same. Supply is elastic in panel (c) and inelastic in panel (d), but the demand curves are the same. The yellow-shaded deadweight losses are larger in panels (a) and (c) than in panels (b) and (d) because the greater the price elasticity of demand or supply, the greater the tax-induced fall in the quantity transacted. In contrast, the lower the price elasticity of demand or supply, the smaller the tax-induced fall in the quantity transacted and the smaller the deadweight loss.

deadweight loss. Similarly, if supply is perfectly inelastic (a vertical supply curve), the quantity supplied is unchanged by the tax and there is also no deadweight loss.

So if the goal in choosing whom to tax is to minimize deadweight loss, then taxes should be imposed on goods and services that have the most inelastic response—that is, goods and services for which consumers or producers will change their behavior the least in response to the tax. And this lesson carries a flip-side: using a tax to purposely decrease the amount of a harmful activity, such as underage drinking, will have the most impact when that activity is elastically demanded or supplied.

ECONOMICS >> *in Action*

Taxing Tobacco

One of the most important excise taxes in the United States is the tax on cigarettes. The federal government imposes a tax of $1.01 a pack; state governments impose taxes that range from $0.17 cents per pack in Missouri to $4.35 per pack in New York; and many cities impose further taxes. In general, tax rates on cigarettes have increased over time, because more governments have seen them not just as a source of revenue but as a way to discourage smoking. But the rise in cigarette taxes has not been gradual. Usually, once a state government decides to raise cigarette taxes, it raises them a lot—which provides economists with useful data on what happens when there is a big tax increase.

Table 5-4 shows the results of big increases in cigarette taxes. In each case, sales fell, just as our analysis predicts. Although it's theoretically possible for tax revenue to fall after such a large tax increase, in reality tax revenue rose in each case. That's because cigarettes have a low price elasticity of demand.

TABLE 5-4 Results of Increases in Cigarette Taxes

State	Increase in tax (per pack)	New state tax (per pack)	Change in quantity transacted	Change in tax revenue
Illinois	$1.00	$1.98	−31.2%	39.0%
Minnesota	1.60	2.83	−24.0	56.0
New Mexico	0.75	1.66	−7.8	67.5
Florida	1.00	1.33	−27.8	193.2
Washington	1.00	3.03	−20.5	17.0

Data from: Orzechowski & Walker, *Tax Burden on Tobacco*. U.S. Alcohol and Tobacco Tax and Trade Bureau.

>> *Quick Review*

• An **excise tax** generates tax revenue equal to the **tax rate** times the number of units of the good or service transacted but reduces consumer and producer surplus. It creates inefficiency by distorting incentives and creating missed opportunities.

• The government tax revenue collected is less than the loss in total surplus because the tax creates inefficiency by discouraging some mutually beneficial transactions.

• The difference between the tax revenue from an excise tax and the reduction in total surplus is the deadweight loss from the tax. The total amount of inefficiency resulting from a tax is equal to the dead-weight loss plus the **administrative costs** of the tax.

• The larger the number of transactions prevented by a tax, the larger the deadweight loss. As a result, taxes on goods with a greater price elasticity of supply or demand, or both, generate higher deadweight losses. There is no deadweight loss when the number of transactions is unchanged by the tax. (That is, when supply or demand is perfectly inelastic.)

>> *Check Your Understanding* 5-5

Solutions appear at back of book.

1. The accompanying table shows five consumers' willingness to pay for one can of diet soda each, as well as five producers' costs of selling one can of diet soda each. Each consumer buys at most one can of soda; each producer sells at most one can of soda. The government asks your advice about the effects of an excise tax of

Consumer	Willingness to pay	Producer	Cost
Ana	$0.70	Zhang	$0.10
Bernice	0.60	Yves	0.20
Chizuko	0.50	Xavier	0.30
Dagmar	0.40	Walter	0.40
Ella	0.30	Vern	0.50

$0.40 per can of diet soda. Assume that there are no administrative costs from the tax.

   a. Without the excise tax, what is the equilibrium price and the equilibrium quantity of soda transacted?
   b. The excise tax raises the price paid by consumers post-tax to $0.60 and lowers the price received by producers post-tax to $0.20. With the excise tax, what is the quantity of soda transacted?
   c. Without the excise tax, how much individual consumer surplus does each of the consumers gain? How much with the tax? How much total consumer surplus is lost as a result of the tax?
   d. Without the excise tax, how much individual producer surplus does each of the producers gain? How much with the tax? How much total producer surplus is lost as a result of the tax?
   e. How much government revenue does the excise tax create?
   f. What is the deadweight loss from the imposition of this excise tax?

2. In each of the following cases, focus on the price elasticity of demand and use a diagram to illustrate the likely size—small or large—of the deadweight loss resulting from a tax. Explain your reasoning.
   a. Gasoline
   b. Milk chocolate bars

SOLVED PROBLEM   Drive We Must

Late in 2013, U.S. gasoline prices started to drop from over $4.00 a gallon to under $2.50 by 2015. You've learned that when prices fall, quantity demanded rises. But, in the case of gasoline, it can take time for consumers to change their behavior. So despite the lower gas prices, in the short run, consumers didn't immediately run out to buy gas-guzzling sport-utility vehicles (SUVs) or change their driving behavior by taking long road trips. But with lower gas prices holding steady, consumer behavior did change in the long run. In 2015, the *New York Times* reported that consumers were buying fewer electric and hybrid cars while SUV sales were reaching record highs.

Because consumers are slow to change their behavior in response to a change in gas prices, economists have to make different elasticity estimates of demand. Specifically, economists estimate the short-run elasticity for gasoline to be about 0.10, and the long-run elasticity of demand for gasoline to be about 0.30.

As we've seen, gasoline prices decreased from about $4.00 per gallon in 2013 to about $2.50 per gallon where they remained into 2016. Using the long- and short-run elasticities just noted, what is the predicted change in consumption of gasoline in the short and long runs? Draw and label a demand curve that reflects the long-run elasticity, assuming that at $4.00 per gallon, motorists in the United States consume 10 million barrels per day of gasoline.

STEP | 1 Find the percent change in the consumption of gasoline in the short run.
  Review pages 134–136.

It is the following:

$$\% \text{ change in price} = \text{Change in price/Initial price} \times 100$$

Looking at Equation 5-3, we see that

  Price elasticity of demand = % change in quantity demanded/% change in price

This equation can be rearranged as follows:

% change in quantity demanded = Price elasticity of demand × % change in price

Using Equation 5-2, we can first find the percent change in price. Since price went from $4.00 per gallon to $2.50 per gallon, we divide the change in price, which is $4.00 − $2.50 = $1.50, by the initial price, which is $4.00. The percent change in price is therefore $1.50/$4.00 × 100 = 37.5%. By rearranging Equation 5-3 as above, we find that the percent change in quantity demanded is the short-run price elasticity of demand (0.10) multiplied by the percent change in price (37.5%), so 0.10 × 37.5% = 3.75%.

STEP | 2 Find the percent change in the consumption of gasoline in the long run.

Use the same method as above to find the long-run percent change, but substitute 0.30 (the long-run elasticity) for 0.10 (the short-run elasticity).

As we found above, the percent change in price was 37.5%. We know that by rearranging Equation 5-3, we find that the percent change in quantity demanded is the long-run price elasticity of demand (0.30) multiplied by the percent change in price (37.5%), so 0.30 × 37.5% = 11.25%.

STEP | 3 Draw and label a demand curve that reflects the long-run elasticity, assuming that at $4.00 per gallon, motorists in the United States consume 10 million barrels per day of gasoline.

Use the next two steps to devise this curve.

STEP | 4 Find the relevant numerical quantities for the horizontal axis by finding the amount demanded at $2.50 per gallon. *Again, review pages 134–136.*

$$\% \text{ change in quantity demanded} =$$
$$\text{Change in quantity demanded/Initial quantity demanded} \times 100$$

Rearranging, we find that the

$$\text{Change in quantity demanded} =$$
$$\% \text{ change in quantity demanded} \times \text{Initial quantity demanded/100}$$

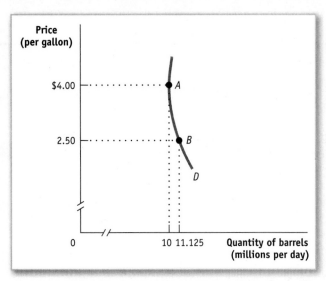

From the question, we know that a price of $4.00 corresponds to a quantity of 10 million barrels per day. If the price were to fall to $2.50 and the elasticity is 0.30, we know from Step 2 that the percent change in consumption is 11.25%. Using the above rearranged equation, the change in quantity demanded = (11.25 × 10 million barrels)/100 = 1.125 million barrels. Hence, the new quantity at a price of $2.50 equals the initial quantity plus the change in quantity demanded: 10 million barrels + 1.125 million barrels = 11.125 million barrels.

STEP | 5 Draw and label the demand curve. *Review pages 138–140.*

Carefully examine panel (b) of Figure 5-3 and consider how the figure would change if the elasticity were 0.30 rather than 0.50 as in the figure.

An elasticity of demand of 0.30 is slightly more inelastic than an elasticity of demand of 0.50, so we would draw the curve to be slightly more vertical than that of the figure. That is, we would rotate the curve slightly to the right. As shown in the figure, point A now corresponds to a price of $4.00 and a quantity of 10 million barrels per day, and point B now corresponds to a price of $2.50 and a quantity of 11.125 million barrels, as calculated in Step 4.

SUMMARY

1. Many economic questions depend on the size of consumer or producer responses to changes in prices or other variables. *Elasticity* is a general measure of responsiveness that can be used to answer such questions.

2. The **price elasticity of demand**—the percent change in the quantity demanded divided by the percent change in the price (dropping the minus sign)—is a measure of the responsiveness of the quantity demanded to changes in the price. In practical calculations, it is usually best to use the **midpoint method,** which calculates percent changes in prices and quantities based on the average of starting and final values.

3. The responsiveness of the quantity demanded to price can range from **perfectly inelastic demand,** where the quantity demanded is unaffected by the price, to **perfectly elastic demand,** where there is a unique price at which consumers will buy as much or as little as they are offered. When demand is perfectly inelastic, the demand curve is a vertical line; when it is perfectly elastic, the demand curve is a horizontal line.

4. The price elasticity of demand is classified according to whether it is more or less than 1. If it is greater than 1, demand is **elastic;** if it is less than 1, demand is **inelastic;** if it is exactly 1, demand is **unit-elastic.** This classification determines how **total revenue,** the total value of sales, changes when the price changes.

If demand is elastic, total revenue falls when the price increases and rises when the price decreases. If demand is inelastic, total revenue rises when the price increases and falls when the price decreases. If demand is unit-elastic, total revenue is unchanged by a change in price.

5. The price elasticity of demand depends on whether there are close substitutes for the good in question (it is higher), whether the good is a necessity (it is lower) or a luxury (it is higher), the share of income spent on the good (it is higher), and the length of time that has elapsed since the price change (it is higher).

6. The **cross-price elasticity of demand** measures the effect of a change in one good's price on the quantity demanded of another good. The cross-price elasticity of demand can be positive, in which case the goods are substitutes, or negative, in which case they are complements.

7. The **income elasticity of demand** is the percent change in the quantity of a good demanded when a consumer's income changes divided by the percent change in income. The income elasticity of demand indicates how intensely the demand for a good responds to changes in income. It can be negative; in that case the good is an inferior good. Goods with positive income elasticities of demand are normal goods. If the income elasticity is greater than 1, a good is **income-elastic;** if it is positive and less than 1, the good is **income-inelastic.**

8. The **price elasticity of supply** is the percent change in the quantity of a good supplied divided by the percent change in the price. If the quantity supplied does not change at all, we have an instance of **perfectly inelastic supply;** the supply curve is a vertical line. If the quantity supplied is zero below some price but infinite above that price, we have an instance of **perfectly elastic supply;** the supply curve is a horizontal line.

9. The price elasticity of supply depends on the availability of resources to expand production and on time. It is higher when inputs are available at relatively low cost and the longer the time elapsed since the price change.

10. The tax revenue generated by a tax depends on the **tax rate** and on the number of taxed units transacted. Excise taxes cause inefficiency in the form of deadweight loss because they discourage some mutually beneficial transactions. Taxes also impose **administrative costs:** resources used to collect the tax, to pay it (over and above the amount of the tax), and to evade it.

11. An **excise tax** generates revenue for the government but lowers total surplus. The loss in total surplus exceeds the tax revenue, resulting in a deadweight loss to society. This deadweight loss is represented by a triangle, the area of which equals the value of the transactions discouraged by the tax. The greater the elasticity of demand or supply, or both, the larger the deadweight loss from a tax. If either demand or supply is perfectly inelastic, there is no deadweight loss from a tax.

KEY TERMS

Price elasticity of demand, p. 134
Midpoint method, p. 136
Perfectly inelastic demand, p. 138
Perfectly elastic demand, p. 138
Elastic demand, p. 139
Inelastic demand, p. 139

Unit-elastic demand, p. 139
Total revenue, p. 140
Cross-price elasticity of demand, p. 146
Income elasticity of demand, p. 147
Income-elastic demand, p. 147
Income-inelastic demand, p. 148

Price elasticity of supply, p. 148
Perfectly inelastic supply, p. 149
Perfectly elastic supply, p. 149
Excise tax, p. 151
Tax rate, p. 153
Administrative costs, p. 157

DISCUSSION QUESTIONS

1. There is a debate about whether sterile hypodermic needles should be passed out free of charge in cities with high drug use. Proponents argue that doing so will reduce the incidence of diseases, such as HIV/AIDS, that are often spread by needle sharing among drug users. Opponents believe that doing so will encourage more drug use by reducing the risks of this behavior. As an economist asked to assess the policy, you must know the following: (i) how responsive the spread of diseases like HIV/AIDS is to the price of sterile needles and (ii) how responsive drug use is to the price of sterile needles. Assuming that you know these two things, use the concepts of price elasticity of demand for sterile needles and the cross-price elasticity between drugs and sterile needles to answer the following questions.

   a. In what circumstances do you believe this is a beneficial policy?

   b. In what circumstances do you believe this is a bad policy?

2. Worldwide, the average coffee grower has increased the amount of acreage under cultivation over the past few years. The result has been that the average coffee plantation produces significantly more coffee than it did 10 to 20 years ago. Unfortunately for the growers, however, this has also been a period in which their total revenues have plunged. In terms of an elasticity, what must be true for these events to have occurred? Illustrate these events with a diagram, indicating the quantity effect and the price effect that gave rise to these events.

3. In 1990, the United States began to levy a tax on sales of luxury cars. For simplicity, assume that the tax was an excise tax of $6,000 per car. The accompanying figure shows hypothetical demand and supply curves for luxury cars.

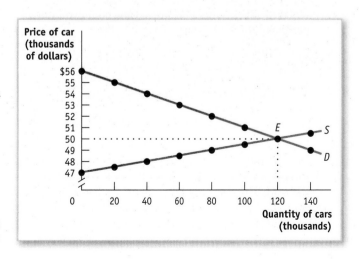

a. Under the tax, what is the price paid by consumers? What is the price received by producers? What is the government tax revenue from the excise tax?

Over time, the tax on luxury automobiles was slowly phased out (and completely eliminated in 2002). Suppose that the excise tax falls from $6,000 per car to $4,500 per car.

b. After the reduction in the excise tax from $6,000 to $4,500 per car, what is the price paid by consumers? What is the price received by producers? What is tax revenue now?

c. Compare the tax revenue created by the taxes in parts a and b. What accounts for the change in tax revenue from the reduction in the excise tax?

PROBLEMS

interactive activity

1. Do you think the price elasticity of demand for Ford sport-utility vehicles (SUVs) will increase, decrease, or remain the same when each of the following events occurs? Explain your answer.

a. Other car manufacturers, such as General Motors, decide to make and sell SUVs.

b. SUVs produced in foreign countries are banned from the American market.

c. Due to ad campaigns, Americans believe that SUVs are much safer than ordinary passenger cars.

d. The time period over which you measure the elasticity lengthens. During that longer time, new models such as four-wheel-drive cargo vans appear.

2. In the United States, 2015 was a bad year for growing wheat. And as wheat supply decreased, the price of wheat rose dramatically, leading to a lower quantity demanded (a movement along the demand curve). The accompanying table describes what happened to prices and the quantity of wheat demanded.

	2014	2015
Quantity demanded (bushels)	2.2 billion	2.0 billion
Average price (per bushel)	$3.42	$4.26

a. Using the midpoint method, calculate the price elasticity of demand for wheat.

b. What is the total revenue for U.S. wheat farmers in 2014 and 2015?

c. Did the bad harvest increase or decrease the total revenue of U.S. wheat farmers? How could you have predicted this from your answer to part a?

3. The accompanying table gives part of the supply schedule for personal computers in the United States.

Price of computer	Quantity of computers supplied
$1,100	12,000
900	8,000

a. Calculate the price elasticity of supply when the price increases from $900 to $1,100 using the midpoint method. Is it elastic, inelastic or unit-elastic?

b. Suppose firms produce 1,000 more computers at any given price due to improved technology. As price increases from $900 to $1,100, is the price elasticity of supply now greater than, less than, or the same as it was in part a?

c. Suppose a longer time period under consideration means that the quantity supplied at any given price is 20% higher than the figures given in the table. As price increases from $900 to $1,100, is the price elasticity of supply now greater than, less than, or the same as it was in part a?

4. The accompanying table lists the cross-price elasticities of demand for several goods, where the percent quantity change is measured for the first good of the pair, and the percent price change is measured for the second good.

Good	Cross-price elasticities of demand
Air-conditioning units and kilowatts of electricity	−0.34
Coke and Pepsi	+0.63
High-fuel-consuming sport-utility vehicles (SUVs) and gasoline	−0.28
McDonald's burgers and Burger King burgers	+0.82
Butter and margarine	+1.54

a. Explain the sign of each of the cross-price elasticities. What does it imply about the relationship between the two goods in question?

b. Compare the absolute values of the cross-price elasticities and explain their magnitudes. For example, why is the cross-price elasticity of McDonald's burgers and Burger King burgers less than the cross-price elasticity of butter and margarine?

c. Use the information in the table to calculate how a 5% increase in the price of Pepsi affects the quantity of Coke demanded.

d. Use the information in the table to calculate how a 10% decrease in the price of gasoline affects the quantity of SUVs demanded.

5. What can you conclude about the price elasticity of demand in each of the following statements?

   a. "The pizza delivery business in this town is very competitive. I'd lose half my customers if I raised the price by as little as 10%."

   b. "I owned both of the two Jerry Garcia autographed lithographs in existence. I sold one on eBay for a high price. But when I sold the second one, the price dropped by 80%."

   c. "My economics professor has chosen to use the Krugman/Wells textbook for this class. I have no choice but to buy this book."

   d. "I always spend a total of exactly $10 per week on coffee."

6. The accompanying table shows the price and yearly quantity of souvenir T-shirts demanded in the town of Crystal Lake according to the average income of the tourists visiting.

Price of T-shirt	Quantity of T-shirts demanded when average tourist income is $20,000	Quantity of T-shirts demanded when average tourist income is $30,000
$4	3,000	5,000
5	2,400	4,200
6	1,600	3,000
7	800	1,800

   a. Using the midpoint method, calculate the price elasticity of demand when the price of a T-shirt rises from $5 to $6 and the average tourist income is $20,000. Also calculate it when the average tourist income is $30,000.

   b. Using the midpoint method, calculate the income elasticity of demand when the price of a T-shirt is $4 and the average tourist income increases from $20,000 to $30,000. Also calculate it when the price is $7.

7. A recent study determined the following elasticities for Volkswagen Jettas:

   Price elasticity of demand = 2

   Income elasticity of demand = 1.5

   The supply of Jettas is elastic. Based on this information, are the following statements true or false? Explain your reasoning.

   a. A 10% increase in the price of a Jetta will reduce the quantity demanded by 20%.

   b. An increase in consumer income will increase the price and quantity of Jettas sold.

8. In each of the following cases, do you think the price elasticity of supply is (i) perfectly elastic; (ii) perfectly inelastic; (iii) elastic, but not perfectly elastic; or (iv) inelastic, but not perfectly inelastic? Explain using a diagram.

   a. An increase in demand this summer for luxury cruises leads to a huge jump in the sales price of a cabin on the *Queen Mary 2*.

   b. The price of a kilowatt of electricity is the same during periods of high electricity demand as during periods of low electricity demand.

   c. Fewer people want to fly during February than during any other month. The airlines cancel about 10% of their flights as ticket prices fall about 20% during this month.

   d. Owners of vacation homes in Maine rent them out during the summer. Due to the soft economy this year, a 30% decline in the price of a vacation rental leads more than half of homeowners to occupy their vacation homes themselves during the summer.

9. Use an elasticity concept to explain each of the following observations.

   a. During economic booms, the number of new personal care businesses, such as gyms and tanning salons, is proportionately greater than the number of other new businesses, such as grocery stores.

   b. Cement is the primary building material in Mexico. After new technology makes cement cheaper to produce, the supply curve for the Mexican cement industry becomes relatively flatter.

   c. Some goods that were once considered luxuries, like a telephone, are now considered virtual necessities. As a result, the demand curve for telephone services has become steeper over time.

   d. Consumers in a less developed country like Guatemala spend proportionately more of their income on equipment for producing things at home, like sewing machines, than consumers in a more developed country like Canada.

10. According to data from the U.S. Department of Energy, sales of the fuel-efficient Toyota Prius hybrid fell from 194,108 vehicles sold in 2014 to 180,603 in 2015. Over the same period, according to data from the U.S. Energy Information Administration, the average price of regular gasoline fell from $3.36 to $2.43 per gallon. Using the midpoint method, calculate the cross-price elasticity of demand between Toyota Prii (the official plural of "Prius" is "Prii") and regular gasoline. According to your estimate of the cross-price elasticity, are the two goods complements or substitutes? Does your answer make sense?

11. A 2015 article published by the *American Journal of Preventive Medicine* studied the effects of an increase in alcohol prices on the incidence of new cases of sexually transmitted diseases. In particular, the researchers studied the effects that a Maryland policy increasing alcohol taxes had on the decline in gonorrhea cases. The report concluded that an increase in the alcohol tax rate by 3% resulted in 1,600 fewer cases of gonorrhea. Assume that prior to the tax increase, the number of gonorrhea cases was 7,450. Use the midpoint method to determine the percent decrease in gonorrhea cases, and then

calculate the cross-price elasticity of demand between alcohol and the incidence of gonorrhea. According to your estimate of this cross-price elasticity of demand, are alcohol and gonorrhea complements or substitutes?

12. The United States imposes an excise tax on the sale of domestic airline tickets. Let's assume that in 2015 the total excise tax was $6.10 per airline ticket (consisting of the $3.60 flight segment tax plus the $2.50 September 11 fee). According to data from the Bureau of Transportation Statistics, in 2015, 643 million passengers traveled on domestic airline trips at an average price of $380 per trip. The accompanying table shows the supply and demand schedules for airline trips. The quantity demanded at the average price of $380 is actual data; the rest is hypothetical.

Price of trip	Quantity of trips demanded (millions)	Quantity of trips supplied (millions)
$380.02	642	699
380.00	643	698
378.00	693	693
373.90	793	643
373.82	913	642

a. What is the government tax revenue in 2015 from the excise tax?

b. On January 1, 2016, the total excise tax increased to $6.20 per ticket. What is the quantity of tickets transacted now? What is the average ticket price now? What is the 2016 government tax revenue?

c. Does this increase in the excise tax increase or decrease government tax revenue?

13. All states impose excise taxes on gasoline. According to data from the Federal Highway Administration, the state of California imposes an excise tax of $0.40 per gallon of gasoline. In 2015, gasoline sales in California totaled 14.6 billion gallons. What was California's tax revenue from the gasoline excise tax? If California doubled the excise tax, would tax revenue double? Why or why not?

WORK IT OUT Interactive step-by-step help with solving these problems can be found online.

---

14. The U.S. government wants to help the American auto industry compete against foreign automakers that sell trucks in the United States. It can do this by imposing an excise tax on each foreign truck sold in the United States. The hypothetical pre-tax demand and supply schedules for imported trucks are given in this table.

Price of imported truck	Quantity of imported trucks (thousands)	
	Quantity demanded	Quantity supplied
$32,000	100	400
31,000	200	350
30,000	300	300
29,000	400	250
28,000	500	200
27,000	600	150

a. In the absence of government interference, what is the equilibrium price of an imported truck? The equilibrium quantity? Illustrate with a diagram.

b. Assume that the government imposes an excise tax of $3,000 per imported truck. Illustrate the effect of this excise tax in your diagram from part a. How many imported trucks are now purchased and at what price? How much does the foreign automaker receive per truck?

c. Calculate the government revenue raised by the excise tax in part b. Illustrate it on your diagram.

d. How does the excise tax on imported trucks benefit American automakers? Whom does it hurt? How does inefficiency arise from this government policy?

15. Nile.com, the online bookseller, wants to increase its total revenue. One strategy is to offer a 10% discount on every book it sells. Nile.com knows that its customers can be divided into two distinct groups according to their likely responses to the discount. The accompanying table shows how the two groups respond to the discount.

	Group A (sales per week)	Group B (sales per week)
Volume of sales before the 10% discount	1.55 million	1.50 million
Volume of sales after the 10% discount	1.65 million	1.70 million

a. Using the midpoint method, calculate the price elasticities of demand for group A and group B.

b. Explain how the discount will affect total revenue from each group.

c. Suppose Nile.com knows which group each customer belongs to when he or she logs on and can choose whether or not to offer the 10% discount. If Nile.com wants to increase its total revenue, should discounts be offered to group A or to group B, to neither group, or to both groups?

Created in 2009 by two young entrepreneurs, Garrett Camp and Travis Kalanick, Uber was designed to alleviate a common frustration: how to find a taxi when there aren't any available. In a densely populated city like New York, finding a taxi is relatively easy on most days—stand on a corner, stick out your arm, and before long a taxi will stop to pick you up. And you know exactly what taxi fare rates will be before you step into the car, because they are set by city regulators.

But at other times, it is not so easy to find a taxi, and you can wait a very long time for one—for example, on rainy days or during rush hour. As you wait, you will probably notice empty taxis passing you by—drivers who have quit working for the day and are headed home. Moreover, there are times when it is simply impossible to hail a taxi—such as during a snowstorm or on New Year's Eve.

Uber was created to address this problem. Using an app, Uber connects people who want a ride to drivers with cars. It also registers drivers, sets fares, and automatically collects payment from a registered rider's credit card. Uber then keeps 25% of the fare, with the rest going to the driver. As of 2018, Uber was operating in 85 countries and in more than 903 cities, and booked $12 billion in rides.

In New York City, Uber fares are roughly comparable to regular taxi fares *during normal driving hours*. The qualification *during normal driving hours* is important because at other times Uber's rates fluctuate. When there are more people looking for a ride than cars available, Uber uses what it calls *surge pricing:* setting the rate higher until everyone who wants a car at the going price can get one. For example, during a snowstorm or on New Year's Eve, Uber rides cost around 9 to 10 times the standard price. Enraged, some Uber customers have accused it of price gouging.

But according to Kalanick, Uber's surge pricing is simply a method of keeping customers happy because the surge price is calculated to leave as few people as possible without a ride. As he explains, "We do not own cars nor do we employ drivers. Higher prices are required to get cars on the road and keep them on the road during the busiest times." However, with more drivers joining Uber's fleet, drivers are finding that it takes longer hours to make sufficient income. So in cities where passengers have limited access to taxi services, Uber drivers have banded together to take "synchronized breaks" during peak hours, such as Saturday nights. These breaks cause prices to surge, which prompts the drivers to jump into their cars. Clearly these Uber drivers know how supply and demand works.

QUESTIONS FOR THOUGHT

1. What accounts for the fact that before Uber's arrival, there were typically enough taxis available for everyone who wanted one on good weather days, but not enough available on bad weather days?

2. How does Uber's surge pricing solve the problem? Assess Kalanick's claim that the price is set to leave as few people as possible without a ride.

3. Use a supply and demand diagram to illustrate how Uber drivers can cause prices to surge by taking coordinated breaks. Why is this strategy unlikely to work in New York, a large city with an established fleet of taxis?

The reigning couple of music, Jay-Z and Beyoncé, had a very profitable year in 2014. Until then, these long-standing individual artists had never headlined a tour together. When they combined their creative forces for their "On the Run" tour, the demand for Jay-Z and Beyoncé tickets went through the roof. When the tour wrapped up in August 2014, its 19 shows had grossed over $100 million in ticket sales with 90% of the seats sold.

One music industry expert noted that no one should be surprised by this. "With nearly 200 million records sold between them and 36 total Grammys, Jay-Z and Beyoncé are a creative force to be reckoned with. When their talents are combined, the sky is the limit—at least as far as ticket prices are concerned." And the market agreed, with tickets selling on the websites of ticket resellers such as StubHub and TicketsNow for an average price of $342.67.

Yet, despite the high demand for their tickets, Jay-Z and Beyoncé received significantly less than $342.67 for an average ticket. Why? Omar Al-Joulani, the producer of the tour explained that tickets were priced to be *inclusive* with tickets starting at $40 and running no higher than $275. "Our strategy was to price tickets so that wherever you were on that ticket chain you had an opportunity to attend the show."

So if you were able to obtain a ticket directly, either by lining up at the venue box office, or getting a ticket online from a direct seller such as Ticketmaster, you could have made a pretty penny by reselling your ticket at the market price. Perhaps this was Jay-Z and Beyoncé's way of sharing the wealth as well as their music.

QUESTIONS FOR THOUGHT

1. Use the concepts of consumer surplus and producer surplus to analyze the exchange between Jay-Z and Beyoncé and their fans in the absence of ticket resellers. (That is, assume that everyone buys a ticket directly and goes to the concert.) Draw a diagram to illustrate.

2. Referring to the diagram drawn in response to question 1, explain the effect of resellers on the allocation of consumer surplus and producer surplus among Jay-Z and Beyoncé and their fans.

The airline industry made $36 billion in profits in 2015, up from nearly $12 billion in 2013. But in 2008, during the recession, the industry was teetering on the edge of disaster. According to the International Air Transport Association, the industry lost $11 billion that year.

However, by 2009, despite the fact that the economy was still extremely weak and airline traffic was still well below normal, profitability began to rebound. And by 2010, despite continued economic weakness, the airline industry had definitely recovered, achieving an $8.9 billion profit that year.

How did the airline industry achieve such a dramatic turnaround? Simple: fly less and charge more. In 2011, fares were 8% higher than they had been the previous year and 17% higher compared to 2009. Flights were more crowded than they had been in decades, with fewer than one in five seats empty on domestic flights. And that trend continues today.

In addition to cutting back on the number of flights—particularly money-losing ones—airlines began to vary ticket prices based on time of departure and when the ticket was purchased. For example, the cheapest days to fly are Tuesday or Wednesday, with Friday and Saturday the most expensive days to travel. The first flight of the morning (the one that requires you to get up at 4 A.M.) is cheaper than later flights. And the cheapest time to buy a ticket is Tuesday at 3 P.M. Eastern Standard Time, with tickets purchased over the weekend carrying the highest prices.

It doesn't stop there. As every beleaguered traveler knows, airlines have tacked on a wide variety of new fees and increased old ones—fees for food, blankets, baggage, even the right to board first or choose your seat in advance. Airlines have also become more inventive at imposing fees that are hard for travelers to track in advance—such as imposing a holiday surcharge while claiming that fares have not increased for the holiday.

In 2007, airlines earned $2.45 billion from fees, a relatively small amount. But by 2016 that number had exploded to nearly $70 billion, an increase of almost 2,500% from 2007. The increase in revenue continued despite fuel being at its lowest level in six years. Yet many airlines continued to charge passengers a fuel surcharge, which federal airline regulators allowed airlines to impose in times of very high fuel costs.

But industry analysts question whether airlines can maintain such high levels of profitability. In the past, as travel demand picked up, airlines increased capacity—added seats—too quickly, leading to falling airfares. "The wild card is always capacity discipline," says an airline industry researcher. "All it takes is one carrier to begin to add capacity aggressively, and then we follow and we undo all the good work that's been done."

QUESTIONS FOR THOUGHT

1. How would you describe the price elasticity of demand for airline flights given the information in this case? Explain.

2. Using the concept of elasticity, explain why airlines would create such great variations in the price of a ticket depending on when it is purchased and the day and time the flight departs. Assume that some people are willing to spend time shopping for deals as well as fly at inconvenient times, but others are not.

3. Using the concept of elasticity, explain why airlines have imposed fees on things such as checked bags. Why might they try to hide or disguise fees?

4. Use an elasticity concept to explain under what conditions the airline industry will be able to maintain its high profitability in the future. Explain.

THE FARMER'S MARGIN

"O BEAUTIFUL FOR SPACIOUS SKIES, for amber waves of grain." So begins the song "America the Beautiful." And those amber waves of grain are for real: though farmers are now only a small minority of America's population, our agricultural industry is immensely productive and feeds much of the world.

If you look at agricultural statistics, however, something may seem rather surprising: when it comes to yield per acre, U.S. farmers are often nowhere near the top. Farmers in Western European countries grow much more: about three times as much wheat per acre as their

U.S. counterparts. Are the Europeans better at growing wheat than we are?

No: European farmers are very skillful, but no more so than Americans. They produce more wheat per acre because they employ more inputs—more fertilizer and, especially, more labor—per acre. Of course, this means that European farmers have higher costs than their American counterparts. But because of government policies, European farmers receive a much higher price for their wheat than American farmers. This gives them an incentive to use more inputs and to expend more effort at the margin to increase the crop yield per acre.

Notice our use of the phrase "at the margin." Like most decisions that involve a comparison of benefits and costs, decisions about inputs and production involve a comparison of marginal quantities—the marginal cost versus the marginal benefit of producing a bit more from each acre.

In this chapter and the next we will show how marginal analysis can be used to understand these output decisions—decisions that lie behind the supply curve. The first step in this analysis is to show how the relationship between a firm's inputs and its output—its *production function*—determines its *cost curves,* the relationship between cost and quantity of output produced. That is what we will examine in this chapter. In Chapter 7, we will use our understanding of the firm's cost curves to derive the individual and the market supply curves. ●

WHAT YOU WILL LEARN

- What is the firm's **production function?**
- Why is production often subject to **diminishing returns to inputs?**
- What types of costs does a firm face and how does the firm generate its marginal and **average cost** curves?
- Why does a firm's costs differ in the **short run** and in the **long run?**
- What is **increasing returns to scale** and what advantage does it give?

A **production function** is the relationship between the quantity of inputs a firm uses and the quantity of output it produces.

A **fixed input** is an input whose quantity is fixed for a period of time and cannot be varied.

A **variable input** is an input whose quantity the firm can vary at any time.

The **long run** is the time period in which all inputs can be varied.

The **short run** is the time period in which at least one input is fixed.

The **total product curve** shows how the quantity of output depends on the quantity of the variable input, for a given quantity of the fixed input.

The Production Function

A *firm* is an organization that produces goods or services for sale. To do this, it must transform inputs into output. The quantity of output a firm produces depends on the quantity of inputs; this relationship is known as the firm's **production function.** As we'll see, a firm's production function underlies its *cost curves.* As a first step, let's look at the characteristics of a hypothetical production function.

Inputs and Output

To understand the concept of a production function, let's consider a farm that we assume, for the sake of simplicity, produces only one output, wheat, and uses only two inputs, land and labor. This particular farm is owned by a couple named George and Martha. They hire workers to do the actual physical labor on the farm. Moreover, we will assume that all potential workers are of the same quality—they are all equally knowledgeable and capable of performing farmwork.

George and Martha's farm sits on 10 acres of land. No more acres are available to them, and they are currently unable to either increase or decrease the size of their farm by selling, buying, or leasing acreage. Land here is what economists call a **fixed input**—an input whose quantity is fixed for a period of time and cannot be varied. George and Martha are, however, free to decide how many workers to hire. The labor provided by these workers is called a **variable input**—an input whose quantity the firm can vary at any time.

In reality, whether or not the quantity of an input is really fixed depends on the time horizon. In the **long run,** that is, given that a long enough period of time has elapsed—firms can adjust the quantity of any input. For example, in the long run, George and Martha can vary the amount of land they farm by buying or selling land. So there are no fixed inputs in the long run.

In contrast, the **short run** is defined as the time period during which at least one input is fixed. Later in this chapter, we'll look more carefully at the distinction between the short run and the long run. But for now, we will restrict our attention to the short run and assume that at least one input is fixed.

George and Martha know that the quantity of wheat they produce depends on the number of workers they hire. Using modern farming techniques, one worker can cultivate the 10-acre farm, albeit not very intensively. When an additional worker is added, the land is divided equally among all the workers: each worker has 5 acres to cultivate when 2 workers are employed, each cultivates $3\frac{1}{3}$ acres when 3 are employed, and so on. So as additional workers are employed, the 10 acres of land are cultivated more intensively and more bushels of wheat are produced.

The relationship between the quantity of labor and the quantity of output, for a given amount of the fixed input, constitutes the farm's production function. The production function for George and Martha's farm, where land is the fixed input and labor is a variable input, is shown in the first two columns of the table in Figure 6-1; the diagram there shows the same information graphically. The curve in Figure 6-1 shows how the quantity of output depends on the quantity of the variable input, for a given quantity of the fixed input. It is called the farm's **total product curve.**

The physical quantity of output, bushels of wheat, is measured on the vertical axis; the quantity of the variable input, labor (that is, the number of workers employed), is measured on the horizontal axis. The total product curve here slopes upward, reflecting the fact that more bushels of wheat are produced as more workers are employed.

Although the total product curve in Figure 6-1 slopes upward along its entire length, the slope isn't constant: as you move up the curve to the right, it flattens

FIGURE 6-1   Production Function and Total Product Curve for George and Martha's Farm

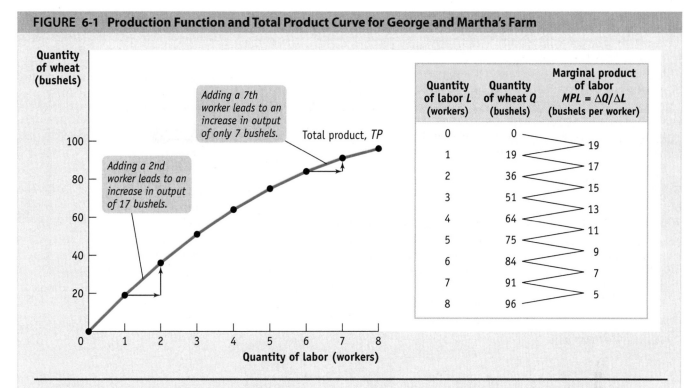

Quantity of labor *L* (workers)	Quantity of wheat *Q* (bushels)	Marginal product of labor $MPL = \Delta Q/\Delta L$ (bushels per worker)
0	0	
		19
1	19	
		17
2	36	
		15
3	51	
		13
4	64	
		11
5	75	
		9
6	84	
		7
7	91	
		5
8	96	

The table shows the production function, the relationship between the quantity of the variable input (labor, measured in number of workers) and the quantity of output (wheat, measured in bushels) for a given quantity of the fixed input. It also calculates the marginal product of labor on George and Martha's farm. The total product curve shows the production function graphically. It slopes upward because more wheat is produced as more workers are employed. It also becomes flatter because the marginal product of labor declines as more and more workers are employed.

out. To understand why the slope changes, look at the third column of the table in Figure 6-1, which shows the *change in the quantity of output* that is generated by adding one more worker. This is called the *marginal product* of labor, or *MPL:* the additional quantity of output from using one more unit of labor (where one unit of labor is equal to one worker). In general, the **marginal product** of an input is the additional quantity of output that is produced by using one more unit of that input.

In this example, we have data on changes in output at intervals of 1 worker. Sometimes data aren't available in increments of 1 unit—for example, you might have information only on the quantity of output when there are 40 workers and when there are 50 workers. In this case, we use the following equation to calculate the marginal product of labor:

$$\textbf{(6-1)}\quad \begin{matrix}\text{Marginal} \\ \text{product} \\ \text{of labor}\end{matrix} = \begin{matrix}\text{Change in quantity of} \\ \text{output produced by one} \\ \text{additional unit of labor}\end{matrix} = \frac{\text{Change in quantity of output}}{\text{Change in quantity of labor}}$$

or

$$MPL = \frac{\Delta Q}{\Delta L}$$

In this equation, Δ, the Greek uppercase delta, represents the change in a variable.

Now we can explain the significance of the slope of the total product curve: it is equal to the marginal product of labor. The slope of a line is equal to "rise" over "run" (explained in the Chapter 2 graph appendix). This implies that the slope of the total product curve is the change in the quantity of output (the "rise," ΔQ)

The **marginal product** of an input is the additional quantity of output that is produced by using one more unit of that input.

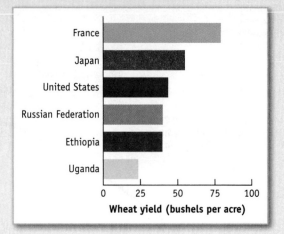

GLOBAL COMPARISON   **WHEAT YIELDS AROUND THE WORLD**

Wheat yields differ substantially around the world. The disparity between France and the United States that you see in this graph is particularly striking, given that they are both wealthy countries with comparable agricultural technology. Yet the reason for that disparity is straightforward: differing government policies. In the United States, farmers receive payments from the government to supplement their incomes, but European farmers benefit from price floors. Since European farmers get higher prices for their output than American farmers, they employ more variable inputs and produce significantly higher yields.

Interestingly, in poor countries like Uganda and Ethiopia, foreign aid can lead to significantly depressed yields. Foreign aid from wealthy countries has often taken the form of surplus food, which depresses local market prices, severely hurting the local agriculture that poor countries normally depend on. Charitable organizations like Oxfam have asked wealthy food-producing countries to modify their aid policies—principally, to give aid in cash rather than in food products except in the case of acute food shortages—to avoid this problem.

Data from: FAO STATS, 2016.

divided by the change in the quantity of labor (the "run," ΔL). And this, as we can see from Equation 6-1, is simply the marginal product of labor. So in Figure 6-1, the fact that the marginal product of the first worker is 19 also means that the slope of the total product curve in going from 0 to 1 worker is 19. Similarly, the slope of the total product curve in going from 1 to 2 workers is the same as the marginal product of the second worker, 17, and so on.

In this example, the marginal product of labor steadily declines as more workers are hired—that is, each successive worker adds less to output than the previous worker. So as employment increases, the total product curve gets flatter.

Figure 6-2 shows how the marginal product of labor depends on the number of workers employed on the farm. The marginal product of labor, *MPL*, is measured on the vertical axis in units of physical output—bushels of wheat—produced per additional worker, and the number of workers employed is measured on the horizontal axis. You can see from the table in Figure 6-1 that if 5 workers are employed instead of 4, output rises from 64 to 75 bushels; in this case the marginal product of labor is 11 bushels—the same number found in Figure 6-2. To indicate that 11 bushels is the marginal product when employment rises from 4 to 5, we place the point corresponding to that information halfway between 4 and 5 workers.

In this example the marginal product of labor falls as the number of workers increases. That is, there are *diminishing returns to labor* on George and Martha's farm. In general, there are **diminishing returns to an input** when an increase in the quantity of that input, holding the quantity of all other inputs fixed, reduces that input's marginal product. Due to diminishing returns to labor, the *MPL* curve is negatively sloped.

There are **diminishing returns to an input** when an increase in the quantity of that input, holding the levels of all other inputs fixed, leads to a decline in the marginal product of that input.

To grasp why diminishing returns can occur, think about what happens as George and Martha add more and more workers without increasing the number of acres of land. As the number of workers increases, the land is farmed more intensively and the number of bushels produced increases. But each additional worker is working with a smaller share of the 10 acres—the fixed input—than the previous worker. As a result, the additional worker cannot produce as much output as the previous worker. So it's not surprising that the marginal product of the additional worker falls.

FIGURE 6-2   Marginal Product of Labor Curve for George and Martha's Farm

The marginal product of labor curve plots each worker's marginal product, the increase in the quantity of output generated by each additional worker. The change in the quantity of output is measured on the vertical axis and the number of workers employed on the horizontal axis. On George and Martha's 10-acre farm, the first worker employed generates an increase in output of 19 bushels, the second worker generates an increase of 17 bushels, and so on. The curve slopes downward due to diminishing returns to labor.

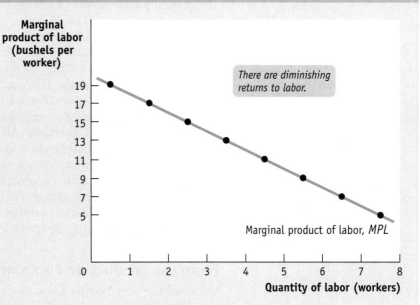

The crucial point to emphasize about diminishing returns is that, like many propositions in economics, it is an "other things equal" proposition: each successive unit of an input will raise production by less than the last *if the quantity of all other inputs is held fixed.*

What would happen if the levels of other inputs were allowed to change? You can see the answer illustrated in Figure 6-3. Panel (a) shows two total product

FIGURE 6-3   Total Product, Marginal Product, and the Fixed Input

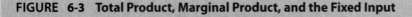

(a) Total Product Curves

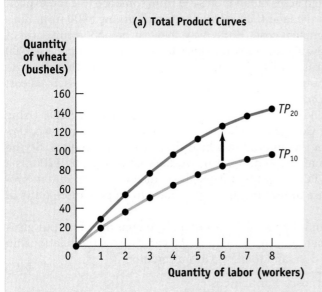

(b) Marginal Product Curves

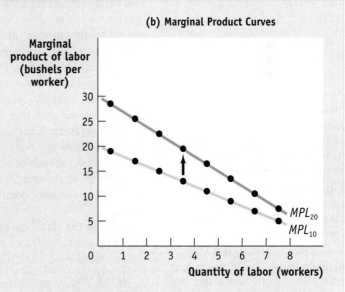

This figure shows how the quantity of output and the marginal product of labor depend on the level of the fixed input. Panel (a) shows two total product curves for George and Martha's farm, TP_{10} when their farm is 10 acres and TP_{20} when it is 20 acres. With more land, each worker can produce more wheat. So an increase in the fixed input shifts the total product curve up from

TP_{10} to TP_{20}. This implies that the marginal product of each worker is higher when the farm is 20 acres than when it is 10 acres. Panel (b) shows the marginal product of labor curves. The increase in acreage also shifts the marginal product of labor curve up from MPL_{10} to MPL_{20}. Note that both marginal product of labor curves still slope downward due to diminishing returns to labor.

curves, TP_{10} and TP_{20}. TP_{10} is the farm's total product curve when its total area is 10 acres (the same curve as in Figure 6-1). TP_{20} is the total product curve when the farm has increased to 20 acres. Except when 0 workers are employed, TP_{20} lies everywhere above TP_{10} because with more acres available, any given number of workers produces more output. Panel (b) shows the corresponding marginal product of labor curves. MPL_{10} is the marginal product of labor curve given 10 acres to cultivate (the same curve as in Figure 6-2), and MPL_{20} is the marginal product of labor curve given 20 acres.

Both curves slope downward because, in each case, the amount of land is fixed, albeit at different levels. But MPL_{20} lies everywhere above MPL_{10}, reflecting the fact that the marginal product of the same worker is higher when he or she has more of the fixed input to work with.

Figure 6-3 demonstrates a general result: the position of the total product curve of a given input depends on the quantities of other inputs. If you change the quantity of the other inputs, both the total product curve and the marginal product curve of the remaining input will shift.

From the Production Function to Cost Curves

Once George and Martha know their production function, they know the relationship between inputs of labor and land and output of wheat. But if they want to maximize their profits, they need to translate this knowledge into information about the relationship between the quantity of output and cost. Let's see how they can do this.

To translate information about a firm's production function into information about its costs, we need to know how much the firm must pay for its inputs. We will assume that George and Martha face either an *explicit cost* or an *implicit cost* of $400 for the use of the land. An **explicit cost** is a cost that involves actually laying out money. An **implicit cost** does not require an outlay of money; it is measured by the value, in dollar terms, of benefits that are forgone. It is irrelevant whether George and Martha must rent the ten acres of land for $400 from someone else (an explicit cost), or whether they own the land themselves and forgo earning $400 from renting it to someone else (an implicit cost). Either way, they pay an opportunity cost of $400 by using the land to grow wheat. Moreover, since the land is a fixed input, the $400 George and Martha pay for it is a **fixed cost,** denoted by *FC*—a cost that does not depend on the quantity of output produced (in the short run). In business, fixed cost is often referred to as *overhead cost*.

We also assume that George and Martha must pay each worker $200. Using their production function, George and Martha know that the number of workers they must hire depends on the amount of wheat they intend to produce. So the cost of labor, which is equal to the number of workers multiplied by $200, is a **variable cost,** denoted by *VC*—a cost that depends on the quantity of output produced. It is variable because to produce more they have to employ more units of input.

Adding the fixed cost and the variable cost of a given quantity of output gives the **total cost,** or *TC*, of that quantity of output. We can express the relationship among fixed cost, variable cost, and total cost as an equation:

(6-2) Total cost = Fixed cost + Variable cost

or

$$TC = FC + VC$$

The table in Figure 6-4 shows how total cost is calculated for George and Martha's farm. The second column shows the number of workers employed, *L*.

An **explicit cost** is a cost that requires an outlay of money.

An **implicit cost** does not require an outlay of money. It is measured by the value, in dollar terms, of benefits that are forgone.

A **fixed cost** is a cost that does not depend on the quantity of output produced. It is the cost of the fixed input.

A **variable cost** is a cost that depends on the quantity of output produced. It is the cost of the variable input.

The **total cost** of producing a given quantity of output is the sum of the fixed cost and the variable cost of producing that quantity of output.

FIGURE 6-4 Total Cost Curve for George and Martha's Farm

The table shows the variable cost, fixed cost, and total cost for various output quantities on George and Martha's 10-acre farm. The total cost curve shows how total cost (measured on the vertical axis) depends on the quantity of output (measured on the horizontal axis). The labeled points on the curve correspond to the rows of the table. The total cost curve slopes upward because the number of workers employed, and hence total cost, increases as the quantity of output increases. The curve gets steeper as output increases due to diminishing returns to labor.

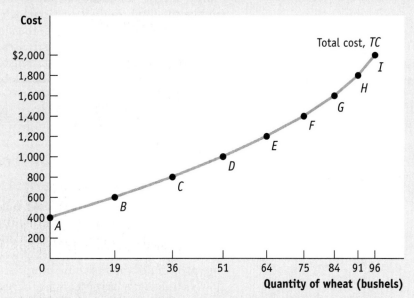

Point on graph	Quantity of labor L (workers)	Quantity of wheat Q (bushels)	Variable cost VC	Fixed cost FC	Total cost TC = FC + VC
A	0	0	$0	$400	$400
B	1	19	200	400	600
C	2	36	400	400	800
D	3	51	600	400	1,000
E	4	64	800	400	1,200
F	5	75	1,000	400	1,400
G	6	84	1,200	400	1,600
H	7	91	1,400	400	1,800
I	8	96	1,600	400	2,000

The third column shows the corresponding level of output, *Q*, taken from the table in Figure 6-1. The fourth column shows the variable cost, *VC*, equal to the number of workers multiplied by $200, the cost per worker. The fifth column shows the fixed cost, *FC*, which is $400 regardless of how many workers are employed. The sixth column shows the total cost of output, *TC*, which is the variable cost plus the fixed cost.

The first column labels each row of the table with a letter, from *A* to *I*. These labels will be helpful in understanding our next step: drawing the **total cost curve,** a curve that shows how total cost depends on the quantity of output.

George and Martha's total cost curve is shown in the diagram in Figure 6-4, where the horizontal axis measures the quantity of output in bushels of wheat and the vertical axis measures total cost in dollars. Each point on the curve corresponds to one row of the table in Figure 6-4. For example, point *A* shows the situation when 0 workers are employed: output is 0, and total cost is equal to fixed cost, $400. Similarly, point *B* shows the situation when 1 worker is employed: output is 19 bushels, and total cost is $600, equal to the sum of $400 in fixed cost and $200 in variable cost.

The **total cost curve** shows how total cost depends on the quantity of output.

Like the total product curve, the total cost curve slopes upward: due to the variable cost, the more output produced, the higher the farm's total cost. But unlike the total product curve, which gets flatter as employment rises, the total cost curve gets *steeper*. That is, the slope of the total cost curve is greater as the amount of output produced increases. As we will soon see, the steepening of the total cost curve is also due to diminishing returns to the variable input. Before we can understand this, we must first look at the relationships among several useful measures of cost.

ECONOMICS >> *in Action*
Finding the Optimal Team Size

In both offices and learning environments, team projects are a favorite way of organizing work. According to one study, the most efficient team size is between 4 and 5 people (4.6 team members, to be exact). Yet researchers have found that project designers routinely create teams that are too large to be efficient. What are project designers failing to understand?

It's true that a larger team has access to more resources, specifically more labor and more human capital. But keep in mind that how large a team should be is a decision at the margin. And studies have shown that adding another person to a team of 5 generally *reduces* the marginal product of existing members. This result is due to a phenomenon called *social loafing*: as the size of the team increases, it's easier to hide individual lack of effort, and the connection between individual effort and reward weakens. So team members loaf. As a result, the marginal product of the 6th member is equal to his personal contribution *minus* the loss due to social loafing that his presence inflicts on other team members.

A larger team must spend more time coordinating its activities, which reduces the marginal product of each team member. With the addition of each member, team losses get larger. So at some point, team losses from social loafing and coordination costs outweigh the individual contribution made by the 6th team member. This result is well documented among teams of software programmers: at some point, adding another team member reduces the output of the entire team.

This situation is illustrated in Figure 6-5. The top part of the figure shows how the value of the team project varies with the number of team members. Each additional member accomplishes less than the previous one, and beyond a certain point an additional member is actually counterproductive. The bottom part of the figure shows the marginal product of each successive team member, which falls as more team members are employed and eventually becomes negative. In other words, the 6th team member has a negative marginal product.

It appears that project designers are creating teams that are too large by mistakenly focusing on the individual contribution of an additional team member, rather than on the marginal product generated by the *entire* team when another person is added. So, instead of having one large project performed by a team of 10 people, it would be more efficient and productive to split the large project into two smaller projects performed by teams of 5 people. By thinking at the margin, we can understand why, in teamwork, 5 + 5 doesn't equal 10: two teams of 5 people will produce more than one team of 10 people.

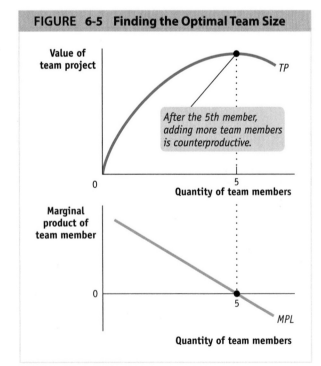

FIGURE 6-5 Finding the Optimal Team Size

After the 5th member, adding more team members is counterproductive.

1. Bernie's ice-making company produces ice cubes using a 10-ton machine and electricity. The quantity of output, measured in terms of pounds of ice, is given in the accompanying table.
   a. What is the fixed input? What is the variable input?
   b. Construct a table showing the marginal product of the variable input. Does it show diminishing returns?
   c. Suppose a 50% increase in the size of the fixed input increases output by 100% for any given amount of the variable input. What is the fixed input now? Construct a table showing the quantity of output and marginal product in this case.

Quantity of electricity (kilowatts)	Quantity of ice (pounds)
0	0
1	1,000
2	1,800
3	2,400
4	2,800

Two Key Concepts: Marginal Cost and Average Cost

Now that we've learned how to derive a firm's total cost curve from its production function, let's take a deeper look at total cost by deriving two extremely useful measures: *marginal cost* and *average cost*. As we'll see, these two measures of the cost of production have a somewhat surprising relationship to each other. Moreover, they will prove to be vitally important later when we use them to analyze the firm's output decision and the market supply curve.

Marginal Cost

Marginal cost is the change in total cost generated by producing one more unit of output. We've already seen that the marginal product of an input is easiest to calculate if data on output are available in increments of one unit of that input. Similarly, marginal cost is easiest to calculate if data on total cost are available in increments of one unit of output. When the data come in less convenient increments, it's still possible to calculate marginal cost. But for the sake of simplicity, let's work with an example in which the data come in convenient one-unit increments.

Selena's Gourmet Salsas produces bottled salsa, and Table 6-1 shows how its costs per day depend on the number of cases of salsa it produces per day. The firm has a fixed cost of $108 per day, shown in the second column, which represents the daily cost of its food-preparation equipment. The third column shows the variable cost, and the fourth column shows the total cost. Panel (a) of Figure 6-6 plots the total cost curve. Like the total cost curve for George and Martha's farm in Figure 6-4, this curve slopes upward, getting steeper as you move up it to the right.

The significance of the slope of the total cost curve is shown by the fifth column of Table 6-1, which calculates *marginal cost:* the additional cost of each additional unit. The general formula for marginal cost is:

(6-3) Marginal cost = $\dfrac{\text{Change in total cost generated by one additional unit of output}}{}$ = $\dfrac{\text{Change in total cost}}{\text{Change in quantity of output}}$

or

$$MC = \frac{\Delta TC}{\Delta Q}$$

The **marginal cost** of producing a good or service is the additional cost incurred by producing one more unit of that good or service.

TABLE 6-1 Costs at Selena's Gourmet Salsas

Quantity of salsa Q (cases)	Fixed cost FC	Variable cost VC	Total cost TC = FC + VC	Marginal cost of case MC = TC/ΔQ
0	$108	$0	$108	
				$12
1	108	12	120	
				36
2	108	48	156	
				60
3	108	108	216	
				84
4	108	192	300	
				108
5	108	300	408	
				132
6	108	432	540	
				156
7	108	588	696	
				180
8	108	768	876	
				204
9	108	972	1,080	
				228
10	108	1,200	1,308	

As in the case of marginal product, marginal cost is equal to "rise" (the increase in total cost) divided by "run" (the increase in the quantity of output). So just as marginal product is equal to the slope of the total product curve, marginal cost is equal to the slope of the total cost curve.

Now we can understand why the total cost curve gets steeper as we move up it to the right: as you can see in Table 6-1, marginal cost at Selena's Gourmet Salsas rises as output increases. Panel (b) of Figure 6-6 shows the marginal cost curve corresponding to the data in Table 6-1. Notice that, as in Figure 6-2, we plot the marginal cost for increasing output from 0 to 1 case of salsa halfway between 0 and 1, the marginal cost for increasing output from 1 to 2 cases of salsa halfway between 1 and 2, and so on.

Why does the marginal cost curve slope upward? Because there are diminishing returns to inputs in this example. As output increases, the marginal product of the variable input declines. This implies that more and more of the variable input must be used to produce each additional unit of output as the amount of output already produced rises. And since each unit of the variable input must be paid for, the additional cost per additional unit of output also rises.

In addition, recall that the flattening of the total product curve is also due to diminishing returns: the marginal product of an input falls as more of that input is used if the quantities of other inputs are fixed. The flattening of the total product curve as output increases and the steepening of the total cost curve as output increases are just flip-sides of the same phenomenon. That is, as output increases, the marginal cost of output also increases because the marginal product of the variable input decreases.

We will return to marginal cost in Chapter 7, when we consider the firm's profit-maximizing output decision. Our next step is to introduce another measure of cost: *average cost*.

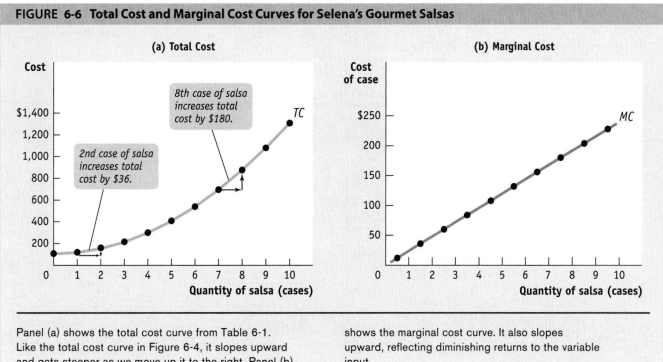

FIGURE 6-6 Total Cost and Marginal Cost Curves for Selena's Gourmet Salsas

(a) Total Cost

(b) Marginal Cost

Panel (a) shows the total cost curve from Table 6-1. Like the total cost curve in Figure 6-4, it slopes upward and gets steeper as we move up it to the right. Panel (b) shows the marginal cost curve. It also slopes upward, reflecting diminishing returns to the variable input.

Average Total Cost

In addition to total cost and marginal cost, it's useful to calculate another measure, **average total cost,** often simply called **average cost.** The average total cost is total cost divided by the quantity of output produced; that is, it is equal to total cost per unit of output. If we let *ATC* denote average total cost, the equation looks like this:

> **Average total cost,** often referred to simply as **average cost,** is total cost divided by quantity of output produced.

(6-4) $ATC = \dfrac{\text{Total cost}}{\text{Quantity of output}} = \dfrac{TC}{Q}$

Average total cost is important because it tells the producer how much the *average* or *typical* unit of output costs to produce. Marginal cost, meanwhile, tells the producer how much *one more* unit of output costs to produce. Although they may look very similar, these two measures of cost typically differ.

Table 6-2 uses data from Selena's Gourmet Salsas to calculate average total cost. For example, the total cost of producing 4 cases of salsa is $300, consisting of $108 in fixed cost and $192 in variable cost (from Table 6-1). So the average total cost of producing 4 cases of salsa is $300/4 = $75. You can see from Table 6-2 that as quantity of output increases, average total cost first falls, then rises.

Figure 6-7 plots that data to yield the *average total cost curve,* which shows how average total cost depends on output. As before, cost in dollars is measured on the vertical axis and quantity of output is measured on the horizontal axis. The average total cost curve has a distinctive U shape that corresponds to how average total cost first falls and then rises

TABLE 6-2 Average Costs for Selena's Gourmet Salsas

Quantity of salsa Q (cases)	Total cost TC	Average total cost of case ATC = TC / Q	Average fixed cost of case AFC = FC / Q	Average variable cost of case AVC = VC / Q
1	$120	$120.00	$108.00	$12.00
2	156	78.00	54.00	24.00
3	216	72.00	36.00	36.00
4	300	75.00	27.00	48.00
5	408	81.60	21.60	60.00
6	540	90.00	18.00	72.00
7	696	99.43	15.43	84.00
8	876	109.50	13.50	96.00
9	1,080	120.00	12.00	108.00
10	1,308	130.80	10.80	120.00

FIGURE 6-7 Average Total Cost Curve for Selena's Gourmet Salsas

The average total cost curve at Selena's Gourmet Salsas is U-shaped. At low levels of output, average total cost falls because the *spreading effect* of falling average fixed cost dominates the *diminishing returns effect* of rising average variable cost. At higher levels of output, the opposite is true and average total cost rises. At point *M*, corresponding to an output of three cases of salsa per day, average total cost is at its minimum level, the minimum average total cost.

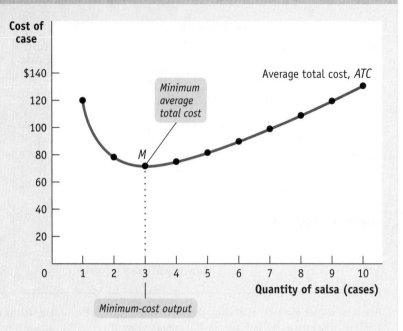

as output increases. Economists believe that such **U-shaped average total cost curves** are the norm for producers in many industries.

To help our understanding of why the average total cost curve is U-shaped, Table 6-2 breaks average total cost into its two underlying components, *average fixed cost* and *average variable cost*. **Average fixed cost,** or *AFC,* is fixed cost divided by the quantity of output, also known as the fixed cost per unit of output. For example, if Selena's Gourmet Salsas produces 4 cases of salsa, average fixed cost is $108/4 = $27 per case. **Average variable cost,** or *AVC,* is variable cost divided by the quantity of output, also known as variable cost per unit of output. At an output of 4 cases, average variable cost is $192/4 = $48 per case.

Writing these in the form of equations:

$$\textbf{(6-5) } AFC = \frac{\text{Fixed cost}}{\text{Quantity of output}} = \frac{FC}{Q}$$

$$AVC = \frac{\text{Variable cost}}{\text{Quantity of output}} = \frac{VC}{Q}$$

Average total cost is the sum of average fixed cost and average variable cost. It has a U shape because these components move in opposite directions as output rises.

Average fixed cost falls as more output is produced because the numerator (the fixed cost) is a fixed number but the denominator (the quantity of output) increases as more is produced. Another way to think about this relationship is that, as more output is produced, the fixed cost is spread over more units of output; the end result is that the fixed cost *per unit of output*—the average fixed cost—falls. You can see this effect in the fourth column of Table 6-2: average fixed cost drops continuously as output increases.

Average variable cost, however, rises as output increases. As we've seen, this reflects diminishing returns to the variable input: each additional unit of output incurs more variable cost to produce than the previous unit. So variable cost rises at a faster rate than the quantity of output increases.

So increasing output has two opposing effects on average total cost:

1. *The spreading effect.* The larger the output, the greater the quantity of output over which fixed cost is spread, leading to lower average fixed cost.

A **U-shaped average total cost curve** falls at low levels of output, then rises at higher levels.

Average fixed cost is the fixed cost per unit of output.

Average variable cost is the variable cost per unit of output.

2. *The diminishing returns effect.* The larger the output, the greater the amount of variable input required to produce additional units, leading to higher average variable cost.

At low levels of output, the spreading effect is very powerful because even small increases in output cause large reductions in average fixed cost. So at low levels of output, the spreading effect dominates the diminishing returns effect and causes the average total cost curve to slope downward. But when output is large, average fixed cost is already quite small, so increasing output further has only a very small spreading effect.

Diminishing returns, however, usually grow increasingly important as output rises. As a result, when output is large, the diminishing returns effect dominates the spreading effect, causing the average total cost curve to slope upward. At the bottom of the U-shaped average total cost curve, point *M* in Figure 6-7, the two effects exactly balance each other. At this point average total cost is at its minimum level, the minimum average total cost.

Figure 6-8 brings together in a single picture four members of the family of cost curves that we have derived from the total cost curve for Selena's Gourmet Salsas: the marginal cost curve (*MC*), the average total cost curve (*ATC*), the average variable cost curve (*AVC*), and the average fixed cost curve (*AFC*). All are based on the information in Tables 6-1 and 6-2. As before, cost is measured on the vertical axis and the quantity of output is measured on the horizontal axis.

Let's take a moment to note some features of the various cost curves.

- Marginal cost slopes upward—the result of diminishing returns that make an additional unit of output more costly to produce than the one before.

- Average variable cost also slopes upward—again, due to diminishing returns— but is flatter than the marginal cost curve. This is because the higher cost of an additional unit of output is averaged across all units, not just the additional units, in the average variable cost measure.

- Average fixed cost slopes downward because of the spreading effect.

- The marginal cost curve intersects the average total cost curve from below, crossing it at its lowest point, point *M* in Figure 6-8. This last feature is our next subject of study.

FIGURE 6-8 Marginal Cost and Average Cost Curves for Selena's Gourmet Salsas

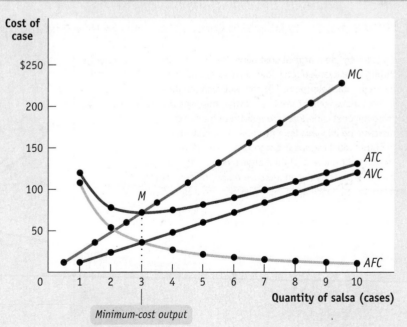

Here we have the family of cost curves for Selena's Gourmet Salsas: the marginal cost curve (*MC*), the average total cost curve (*ATC*), the average variable cost curve (*AVC*), and the average fixed cost curve (*AFC*). Note that the average total cost curve is U-shaped and the marginal cost curve crosses the average total cost curve at the bottom of the U, point *M*, corresponding to the minimum average total cost from Table 6-2 and Figure 6-7.

The **minimum-cost output** is the quantity of output at which average total cost is lowest—the bottom of the U-shaped average total cost curve.

Minimum Average Total Cost

For a U-shaped average total cost curve, average total cost is at its minimum level at the bottom of the U. Economists call the quantity of output that corresponds to the minimum average total cost the **minimum-cost output.** In the case of Selena's Gourmet Salsas, the minimum-cost output is three cases of salsa per day.

In Figure 6-8, the bottom of the U is at the level of output at which the marginal cost curve crosses the average total cost curve from below. Is this an accident? No—it reflects three general principles that are always true about a firm's marginal cost and average total cost curves:

1. At the minimum-cost output, average total cost *is equal to* marginal cost.
2. At output less than the minimum-cost output, marginal cost *is less than* average total cost and average total cost is falling.
3. At output greater than the minimum-cost output, marginal cost *is greater than* average total cost and average total cost is rising.

To understand these principles, think about how your grade in one course—say, a 3.0 in sociology—affects your overall grade point average. If your GPA before receiving that grade was more than 3.0, the new grade lowers your average.

Similarly, if marginal cost—the cost of producing one more unit—is less than average total cost, producing that extra unit lowers average total cost. This is shown in Figure 6-9 by the movement from A_1 to A_2. In this case, the marginal cost of producing an additional unit of output is low, as indicated by the point MC_L on the marginal cost curve. When the cost of producing the next unit of output is less than average total cost, increasing production reduces average total cost. So any quantity of output at which marginal cost is less than average total cost must be on the downward-sloping segment of the U.

But if your grade in sociology is more than the average of your previous grades, this new grade raises your GPA. Similarly, if marginal cost is greater than average total cost, producing that extra unit raises average total cost. This is illustrated by the movement from B_1 to B_2 in Figure 6-9, where the marginal cost, MC_H, is higher than average total cost. So any quantity of output at which marginal cost is greater than average total cost must be on the upward-sloping segment of the U.

FIGURE 6-9 The Relationship Between the Average Total Cost and the Marginal Cost Curves

To see why the marginal cost curve (*MC*) must cut through the average total cost curve at the minimum average total cost (point *M*), corresponding to the minimum-cost output, we look at what happens if marginal cost is different from average total cost. If marginal cost is *less* than average total cost, an increase in output must reduce average total cost, as in the movement from A_1 to A_2. If marginal cost is *greater* than average total cost, an increase in output must increase average total cost, as in the movement from B_1 to B_2.

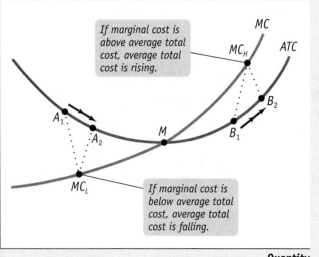

Finally, if a new grade is exactly equal to your previous GPA, the additional grade neither raises nor lowers that average—it stays the same. This corresponds to point *M* in Figure 6-9: when marginal cost equals average total cost, we must be at the bottom of the U, because only at that point is average total cost neither falling nor rising.

Does the Marginal Cost Curve Always Slope Upward?

Up to this point, we have emphasized the importance of diminishing returns, which led to a marginal product curve that always slopes downward and a marginal cost curve that always slopes upward. In practice, however, economists believe that marginal cost curves often slope *downward* as a firm increases its production from zero up to some low level, sloping upward only at higher levels of production: they look like the curve *MC* in Figure 6-10.

This initial downward slope occurs because a firm often finds that, when it starts with only a very small number of workers, employing more workers and expanding output allows its workers to specialize in various tasks. This, in turn, lowers the firm's marginal cost as it expands output. For example, one individual producing salsa would have to perform all the tasks involved: selecting and preparing the ingredients, mixing the salsa, bottling and labeling it, packing it into cases, and so on. As more workers are employed, they can divide the tasks, with each worker specializing in one or a few aspects of salsa-making.

This specialization leads to *increasing returns* to the hiring of additional workers and results in a marginal cost curve that initially slopes downward. But once there are enough workers to have completely exhausted the benefits of further specialization, diminishing returns to labor set in and the marginal cost curve changes direction and slopes upward. So, typical marginal cost curves actually have the "swoosh" shape shown by *MC* in Figure 6-10. For the same reason, average variable cost curves typically look like *AVC* in Figure 6-10: they are U-shaped rather than strictly upward sloping.

However, as Figure 6-10 also shows, the key features we saw from the example of Selena's Gourmet Salsas remain true: the average total cost curve is U-shaped, and the marginal cost curve passes through the point of minimum average total cost.

FIGURE 6-10 More Realistic Cost Curves

A realistic marginal cost curve has a "swoosh" shape. Starting from a very low output level, marginal cost often falls as the firm increases output. That's because hiring additional workers allows greater specialization of their tasks and leads to increasing returns. Once specialization is achieved, however, diminishing returns to additional workers set in and marginal cost rises. The corresponding average variable cost curve is now U-shaped, like the average total cost curve.

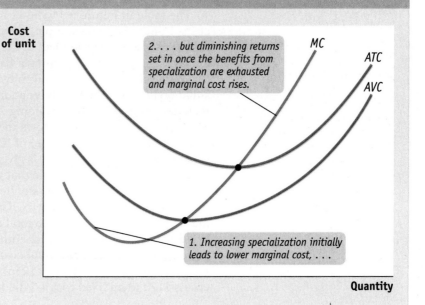

2. . . . but diminishing returns set in once the benefits from specialization are exhausted and marginal cost rises.

1. Increasing specialization initially leads to lower marginal cost, . . .

>> Quick Review

• **Marginal cost**—the change in total cost resulting from a change in output—is equal to the slope of the total cost curve. Diminishing returns cause the marginal cost curve to slope upward.

• **Average total cost** (or **average cost**) is equal to the sum of **average fixed cost** and **average variable cost**. When the **U-shaped average total cost curve** slopes downward, the spreading effect dominates: fixed cost is spread over more units of output. When it slopes upward, the diminishing returns effect dominates: an additional unit of output requires more variable inputs.

• Marginal cost is equal to average total cost at the **minimum-cost output**. At higher output levels, marginal cost is greater than average total cost and average total cost is rising. At lower output levels, marginal cost is lower than average total cost and average total cost is falling.

• At low levels of output there are often increasing returns to the variable input due to the benefits of specialization, making the marginal cost curve "swoosh"-shaped: initially sloping downward before sloping upward.

>> Check Your Understanding 6-2
Solutions appear at back of book.

1. Alicia's Apple Pies is a roadside business. Alicia must pay $9.00 in rent each day. In addition, it costs her $1.00 to produce the first pie of the day, and each subsequent pie costs 50% more to produce than the one before. For example, the second pie costs $1.00 \times 1.5 = $1.50 to produce, and so on.

   a. Calculate Alicia's marginal cost, variable cost, average total cost, average variable cost, and average fixed cost as her daily pie output rises from 0 to 6. (*Hint:* The variable cost of two pies is just the marginal cost of the first pie, plus the marginal cost of the second, and so on.)

   b. Indicate the range of pies for which the spreading effect dominates and the range for which the diminishing returns effect dominates.

   c. What is Alicia's minimum-cost output? Explain why making one more pie lowers Alicia's average total cost when output is lower than the minimum-cost output. Similarly, explain why making one more pie raises Alicia's average total cost when output is greater than the minimum-cost output.

Short-Run versus Long-Run Costs

Up to this point, we have treated fixed cost as completely outside the control of a firm because we have focused on the short run. But as we noted earlier, all inputs are variable in the long run: this means that in the long run fixed cost may also be varied. *In the long run, in other words, a firm's fixed cost becomes a variable it can choose.* For example, given time, Selena's Gourmet Salsas can acquire additional food-preparation equipment or dispose of some of its existing equipment.

In this section, we will examine how a firm's costs behave in the short run and in the long run. We will also see that the firm will choose its fixed cost in the long run based on the level of output it expects to produce.

Let's begin by supposing that Selena's Gourmet Salsas is considering whether to acquire additional food-preparation equipment. Acquiring additional machinery will affect its total cost in two ways. First, the firm will have to either rent or buy the additional equipment; either way, that will mean higher fixed cost in the short run. Second, if the workers have more equipment, they will be more productive: fewer workers will be needed to produce any given output, so variable cost for any given output level will be reduced.

The table in Figure 6-11 shows how acquiring an additional machine affects costs. In our original example, we assumed that Selena's Gourmet Salsas had a fixed cost of $108. The left half of the table shows variable cost as well as total cost and average total cost assuming a fixed cost of $108. The average total cost curve for this level of fixed cost is given by ATC_1 in Figure 6-11. Let's compare that to a situation in which the firm buys additional food-preparation equipment, doubling its fixed cost to $216 but reducing its variable cost at any given level of output. The right half of the table shows the firm's variable cost, total cost, and average total cost with this higher level of fixed cost. The average total cost curve corresponding to $216 in fixed cost is given by ATC_2.

From the figure you can see that when output is small, 4 cases of salsa per day or fewer, average total cost is smaller when Selena forgoes the additional equipment and maintains the lower fixed cost of $108: ATC_1 lies below ATC_2. For example, at 3 cases per day, average total cost is $72 without the additional machinery and $90 with the additional machinery. But as output increases beyond 4 cases per day, the firm's average total cost is lower if it acquires the additional equipment, raising its fixed cost to $216. So, at 9 cases of salsa per day, average total cost is $120 when fixed cost is $108 but only $78 when fixed cost is $216.

FIGURE 6-11 Choosing the Level of Fixed Cost for Selena's Gourmet Salsas

For any given level of output, there is a trade-off: a choice between lower fixed cost and higher variable cost, or higher fixed cost and lower variable cost. ATC_1 is the average total cost curve corresponding to a fixed cost of $108; it leads to lower fixed cost and higher variable cost. ATC_2 is the average total cost curve corresponding to a higher fixed cost of $216 but lower variable cost. At low output levels, at 4 or fewer cases of salsa per day, ATC_1 lies below ATC_2: average total cost is lower with only $108 in fixed cost. But as output goes up, average total cost is lower with the higher amount of fixed cost, $216: at more than 4 cases of salsa per day, ATC_2 lies below ATC_1.

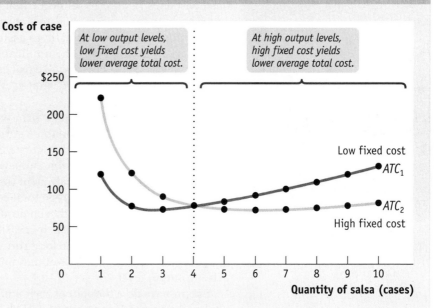

	Low fixed cost (FC = $108)			High fixed cost (FC = $216)		
Quantity of salsa (cases)	High variable cost	Total cost	Average total cost of case ATC_1	Low variable cost	Total cost	Average total cost of case ATC_2
1	$12	$120	$120.00	$6	$222	$222.00
2	48	156	78.00	24	240	120.00
3	108	216	72.00	54	270	90.00
4	192	300	75.00	96	312	78.00
5	300	408	81.60	150	366	73.20
6	432	540	90.00	216	432	72.00
7	588	696	99.43	294	510	72.86
8	768	876	109.50	384	600	75.00
9	972	1,080	120.00	486	702	78.00
10	1,200	1,308	130.80	600	816	81.60

Why does average total cost change like this when fixed cost increases? When output is low, the increase in fixed cost from the additional equipment outweighs the reduction in variable cost from higher worker productivity—that is, there are too few units of output over which to spread the additional fixed cost. So if Selena plans to produce 4 or fewer cases per day, she would be better off choosing the lower level of fixed cost, $108, to achieve a lower average total cost of production. When planned output is high, however, she should acquire the additional machinery.

In general, for each output level there is some choice of fixed cost that minimizes the firm's average total cost for that output level. So, when the firm has a desired output level that it expects to maintain over time, it should choose the level of fixed cost optimal for that level—that is, the level of fixed cost that minimizes its average total cost.

Now that we are studying a situation in which fixed cost can change, we need to take time into account when discussing average total cost. All the average total cost curves we have considered until now are defined for a given level of fixed cost—that is, they are defined for the short run, the period of time over which fixed cost doesn't vary. To reinforce that distinction, for the rest of this chapter we will refer to these average total cost curves as *short-run average total cost curves*.

For most firms, it is realistic to assume that there are many possible choices of fixed cost, not just two. The implication: for such a firm, many possible short-run average total cost curves will exist, each corresponding to a different choice of fixed cost and so giving rise to what is called a firm's "family" of short-run average total cost curves.

At any given point in time, a firm will find itself on one of its short-run cost curves, the one corresponding to its current level of fixed cost; a change in output will cause it to move along that curve. If the firm expects that change in output level to be long-standing, then it is likely that the firm's current level of fixed cost is no longer optimal. Given sufficient time, it will want to adjust its fixed cost to a new level that minimizes average total cost for its new output level.

For example, if Selena had been producing 2 cases of salsa per day with a fixed cost of $108 but found herself increasing her output to 8 cases per day for the foreseeable future, then in the long run she should purchase more equipment and increase her fixed cost to a level that minimizes average total cost at the 8-cases-per-day output level.

Suppose we do a thought experiment and calculate the lowest possible average total cost that can be achieved for each output level if the firm were to choose its fixed cost for each output level. Economists have given this thought experiment a name: the *long-run average total cost curve*. Specifically, the **long-run average total cost curve,** or *LRATC*, is the relationship between output and average total cost when fixed cost has been chosen to minimize average total cost *for each level of output*. If there are many possible choices of fixed cost, the long-run average total cost curve will have the familiar, smooth U shape, as shown by *LRATC* in Figure 6-12.

We can now draw the distinction between the short run and the long run more fully. In the long run, when a producer has had time to choose the fixed cost appropriate for its desired level of output, that producer will be at some point on the long-run average total cost curve. But if the output level is altered, the firm will no longer be on its long-run average total cost curve and will instead be moving along

To understand how firms operate over time, be sure to distinguish between short-run and long-run average costs.

The **long-run average total cost curve** shows the relationship between output and average total cost when fixed cost has been chosen to minimize average total cost for each level of output.

KalSyer/iStock/Getty Images

FIGURE 6-12 Short-Run and Long-Run Average Total Cost Curves

Short-run and long-run average total cost curves differ because a firm can choose its fixed cost in the long run. If Selena has chosen the level of fixed cost that minimizes short-run average total cost at an output of 6 cases, and actually produces 6 cases, then she will be at point *C* on *LRATC* and *ATC₆*. But if she produces only 3 cases, she will move to point *B*. If she expects to produce only 3 cases for a long time, in the long run she will reduce her fixed cost and move to point *A* on *ATC₃*. Likewise, if she produces 9 cases (putting her at point *Y*) and expects to continue this for a long time, she will increase her fixed cost in the long run and move to point *X* on *ATC₉*.

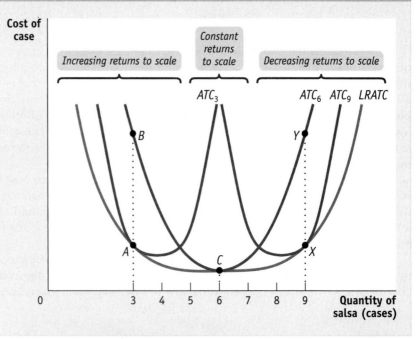

its current short-run average total cost curve. It will not be on its long-run average total cost curve again until it readjusts its fixed cost for its new output level.

Figure 6-12 illustrates this point. The curve ATC_3 shows short-run average total cost if Selena has chosen the level of fixed cost that minimizes average total cost at an output of 3 cases of salsa per day. This is confirmed by the fact that at 3 cases per day, ATC_3 touches *LRATC*. Similarly, ATC_6 shows short-run average total cost if Selena has chosen the level of fixed cost that minimizes average total cost if her output is 6 cases per day. It touches *LRATC* at 6 cases per day. And ATC_9 shows short-run average total cost if Selena has chosen the level of fixed cost that minimizes average total cost if her output is 9 cases per day. It touches *LRATC* at 9 cases per day.

Suppose that Selena initially chose to be on ATC_6. If she actually produces 6 cases of salsa per day, her firm will be at point *C* on both its short-run and long-run average total cost curves. Suppose, however, that Selena ends up producing only 3 cases of salsa per day. In the short run, her average total cost is indicated by point *B* on ATC_6; it is no longer on *LRATC*. If Selena had known that she would be producing only 3 cases per day, she would have been better off choosing a lower level of fixed cost, the one corresponding to ATC_3, thereby achieving a lower average total cost. She could do this, for example, by selling her production plant and purchasing a smaller one. Then her firm would have found itself at point *A* on the long-run average total cost curve, which lies below point *B*.

Suppose, conversely, that Selena ends up producing 9 cases per day even though she initially chose to be on ATC_6. In the short run her average total cost is indicated by point *Y* on ATC_6. But she would be better off purchasing more equipment and incurring a higher fixed cost to reduce her variable cost and move to ATC_9. This would allow her to reach point *X* on the long-run average total cost curve, which lies below *Y*.

The distinction between short-run and long-run average total costs is extremely important in making sense of how real firms operate over time. A company that has to increase output suddenly to meet a surge in demand will typically find that in the short run its average total cost rises sharply because it is hard to get extra production out of existing facilities. But given time to build new factories or add machinery, short-run average total cost falls.

Returns to Scale

What determines the shape of the long-run average total cost curve? The answer is that *scale*, the size of a firm's operations, is often an important determinant of its long-run average total cost of production. Firms that experience scale effects in production find that their long-run average total cost changes substantially depending on the quantity of output they produce. There are **increasing returns to scale** (also known as *economies of scale*) when long-run average total cost declines as output increases.

As you can see in Figure 6-12, Selena's Gourmet Salsas experiences increasing returns to scale over output levels ranging from 0 up to 5 cases of salsa per day—the output levels over which the long-run average total cost curve is declining. In contrast, there are **decreasing returns to scale** (also known as *dis-economies of scale*) when long-run average total cost increases as output increases. For Selena's Gourmet Salsas, decreasing returns to scale occur at output levels greater than 7 cases, the output levels over which its long-run average total cost curve is rising.

There is also a third possible relationship between long-run average total cost and scale: firms experience **constant returns to scale** when long-run average total cost is constant as output increases. In this case, the firm's long-run average total cost curve is horizontal over the output levels for which there are constant returns to scale. As you see in Figure 6-12, Selena's Gourmet Salsas has constant returns to scale when it produces anywhere from 5 to 7 cases of salsa per day.

There are **increasing returns to scale** when long-run average total cost declines as output increases.

There are **decreasing returns to scale** when long-run average total cost increases as output increases.

There are **constant returns to scale** when long-run average total cost is constant as output increases.

A **network externality** exists when the value of a good or service to an individual is greater when many other people use the good or service as well.

What explains these scale effects in production? The answer ultimately lies in the firm's technology of production. Increasing returns often arise from the increased *specialization* that larger output levels allow—a larger scale of operation means that individual workers can limit themselves to more specialized tasks, becoming more skilled and efficient at doing them.

Another source of increasing returns is the very large initial setup cost; in some industries—such as auto manufacturing, electricity generating, or petroleum refining—incurring a high fixed cost in the form of plant and equipment is necessary to produce any output.

A third source of increasing returns, found in certain high-tech industries such as software development, is that the value of a good or service to an individual increases when a large number of others own or use the same good or service, known as **network externalities.** The classic example is computer operating systems. Worldwide, most personal computers run on Microsoft Windows. Although many believe that Apple has a superior operating system, the wider use of Windows in the early days of personal computers attracted more software development and technical support, giving it lasting dominance. As we'll see in Chapter 8, where we study monopoly, increasing returns have very important implications for how firms and industries interact and behave.

Decreasing returns—the opposite scenario—typically arise in large firms due to problems of coordination and communication: as the firm grows in size, it becomes ever more difficult, and so more costly, to communicate and to organize its activities. Although increasing returns induce firms to get larger, decreasing returns tend to limit their size. And when there are constant returns to scale, scale has no effect on a firm's long-run average total cost: it is the same regardless of whether the firm produces 1 unit or 100,000 units.

Summing Up Costs: The Short and Long of It

If a firm is to make the best decisions about how much to produce, it has to understand how its costs relate to the quantity of output it chooses to produce. Table 6-3 provides a quick summary of the concepts and measures of cost you have learned about.

TABLE 6-3   Concepts and Measures of Cost

	Measurement	Definition	Mathematical term
Short run	Fixed cost	Cost that does not depend on the quantity of output produced	FC
	Average fixed cost	Fixed cost per unit of output	$AFC = FC/Q$
Short run and long run	Variable cost	Cost that depends on the quantity of output produced	VC
	Average variable cost	Variable cost per unit of output	$AVC = VC/Q$
	Total cost	The sum of fixed cost (short run) and variable cost	$TC = FC$ (short run) $+ VC$
	Average total cost (average cost)	Total cost per unit of output	$ATC = TC/Q$
	Marginal cost	The change in total cost generated by producing one more unit of output	$MC = TC/Q$
Long run	Long-run average total cost	Average total cost when fixed cost has been chosen to minimize average total cost for each level of output	$LRATC$

ECONOMICS >> *in Action*
How the Sharing Economy Reduces Fixed Cost

The *sharing economy* is a relatively new phenomenon in which technology allows unrelated parties (firms and individuals) to share assets like office space, homes, computing capacity, software, cars, small jets, machinery, financial capital, books, and even clothes. Uber and Airbnb are probably the most prominent examples of how the sharing economy works: their web platforms allow both drivers with cars and homeowners with rooms to spare to share their assets with others. But even the Cloud itself, the vast digital network into which you upload your photos and team-project term papers to share with others, is a feature of the sharing economy because it allows firms and individuals to rent computing capacity, storage, and software.

NetJets and other firms like it in the sharing economy help convert fixed costs to variable costs and allow for a more efficient use of resources.

So what does the sharing have to do with fixed cost? A lot. If the use of an asset can be obtained only when needed, then it goes from incurring a fixed cost to incurring a variable cost. Take, for example, a company jet. Instead of incurring the fixed cost of owning and maintaining a company jet full time (one which might sit on the runway for a significant amount of time), a company can now purchase, through NetJets or similar firms, the services of a jet on an as-needed basis. In effect, by turning the fixed cost of ownership and operation into a variable cost, the sharing economy might allow smaller companies to operate in markets that would have previously been unprofitable for them. Likewise, sharing allows individuals to afford assets (a car, a home, a designer handbag) that were previously unaffordable because the assets can now be used to generate income.

And the sharing economy marketplace makes for a more efficient use of society's resources overall, as it improves the allocation of resources to those who can make the best use of them.

>> Check Your Understanding 6-3
Solutions appear at back of book.

1. The accompanying table shows three possible combinations of fixed cost and average variable cost. Average variable cost is constant in this example (it does not vary with the quantity of output produced).

Choice	Fixed cost	Average variable cost
1	$8,000	$1.00
2	12,000	0.75
3	24,000	0.25

   a. For each of the three choices, calculate the average total cost of producing 12,000, 22,000, and 30,000 units. For each of these quantities, which choice results in the lowest average total cost?
   b. Suppose that the firm, which has historically produced 12,000 units, experiences a sharp, permanent increase in demand that leads it to produce 22,000 units. Explain how its average total cost will change in the short run and in the long run.
   c. Explain what the firm should do instead if it believes the change in demand is temporary.

2. In each of the following cases, explain what kind of scale effects you think the firm will experience and why.
   a. A telemarketing firm in which employees make sales calls using computers and telephones
   b. An interior design firm in which design projects are based on the expertise of the firm's owner
   c. A diamond-mining company

3. Draw a graph like Figure 6-12 and insert a short-run average total cost curve corresponding to a long-run output choice of 5 cases of salsa per day. Use the graph to show why Selena should change her fixed cost if she expects to produce only 4 cases per day for a long period of time.

>> Quick Review

• In the long run, firms choose fixed cost according to expected output. Higher fixed cost reduces average total cost when output is high. Lower fixed cost reduces average total cost when output is low.

• There are many possible short-run average total cost curves, each corresponding to a different level of fixed cost. The **long-run average total cost curve, LRATC,** shows average total cost over the long run, when the firm has chosen fixed cost to minimize average total cost for each level of output.

• A firm that has fully adjusted its fixed cost for its output level will operate at a point that lies on both its current short-run and long-run average total cost curves. A change in output moves the firm along its current short-run average total cost curve. Once it has readjusted its fixed cost, the firm will operate on a new short-run average total cost curve and on the long-run average total cost curve.

• Scale effects arise from the technology of production. **Increasing returns to scale** tend to make firms larger. **Network externalities** are one reason for increasing returns to scale. **Decreasing returns to scale** tend to limit their size. With **constant returns to scale,** scale has no effect.

SOLVED PROBLEM | Production Challenges for Tesla

Tesla Inc. produces electric cars in a former Toyota factory in Fremont, California. The Tesla Roadster, a sports car, was the company's first design, available for sale in 2008. Their latest design, the Tesla Model 3, hit the road in 2017. The Model 3 is an all-wheel-drive, mid-size luxury, four-door sedan. It uses no gasoline, has a range of 220 to 310 miles per charge, and has zero tailpipe emissions. It has the ability to be fully self-driving.

Pre-orders for the Model 3 exceeded 450,000 units, nearly triple those for the previous model, the 2013 Tesla Model X. Despite the strong demand, production of the Model 3 at the Fremont plant was slower than expected.

To meet demand for the Model 3, Tesla announced it will increase production at the plant to 6,000 cars per week, or about 300,000 cars per year. Currently, the plant is equipped to produce about 100,000 cars per year, which is the total number of cars sold by Tesla in 2017. Using the following table, find Tesla's average total cost of production across the various plants for each level of production. Explain why the production costs with the size A plant are higher than they would be if Tesla could build a new plant that was equipped to produce 300,000 vehicles.

	Total cost (billions of U.S. dollars)		
Plant size	100,000 cars sold	200,000 cars sold	300,000 cars sold
A	$1.75	$3.25	$5.5
B	2.0	3.0	5.0
C	2.5	4.0	4.5

STEP | 1 Find Tesla's average total cost of production at the various plant sizes and production levels. *Review pages 181–183.*

	Average total cost		
Plant size	100,000 cars sold	200,000 cars sold	300,000 cars sold
A	$17,500	$16,250	$18,333
B	$20,000	$15,000	$16,667
C	$25,000	$20,000	$15,000

Average total cost is found by dividing total cost by the quantity of output. So, if Tesla has a total cost of $1,750,000,000 at an output of 100,000 cars we calculate $1,750,000,000/100,000 = $17,500. Average total cost for each plant size and production level from the previous table are given in the table at left.

STEP | 2 Explain why the production cost with a size A plant is higher than it would be if Tesla could build a new plant that was best equipped to produce 300,000 vehicles. *Review pages 186–189.*

If Tesla were to build a new plant based on the production of 300,000 vehicles, it would build a size C plant. Tesla would be able to adjust its fixed cost to a new level that minimizes average total cost for its new output level. If Tesla could easily change its plant size, it would always build the plant size that minimizes its average total cost on its long-run average total cost curve. However, if the size of the plant is fixed at size A, then it will be on its short-run average total cost curve based on a size A plant.

SUMMARY

1. The relationship between inputs and output is a producer's **production function.** In the **short run,** the quantity of a **fixed input** cannot be varied but the quantity of a **variable input** can. In the **long run,** the quantities of all inputs can be varied. For a given amount of the fixed input, the **total product curve** shows how the quantity of output changes as the quantity of the variable input changes. We may also calculate the **marginal product** of an input, the increase in output from using one more unit of that input.

2. There are **diminishing returns to an input** when its marginal product declines as more of the input is used, holding the quantity of all other inputs fixed.

3. **Total cost,** represented by the **total cost curve,** is equal to the sum of **fixed cost,** which does not depend on output, and **variable cost,** which does depend on output. Total cost takes into account **explicit costs,** which involve an actual outlay of cash, as well as **implicit costs,** which do not require an outlay of cash. Due to diminishing returns, **marginal cost,** the

increase in total cost generated by producing one more unit of output, normally increases as output increases.

4. **Average total cost** (also known as **average cost**), total cost divided by quantity of output, is the cost of the average unit of output, and marginal cost is the cost of one more unit produced. Economists believe that **U-shaped average total cost curves** are typical, because average total cost consists of two parts: **average fixed cost,** which falls when output increases (the spreading effect), and **average variable cost,** which rises with output (the diminishing returns effect).

5. When average total cost is U-shaped, the bottom of the U is the level of output at which average total cost is minimized, the point of **minimum-cost output.** This is also the point at which the marginal cost curve crosses the average total cost curve from below. Due to gains from specialization, the marginal cost curve may slope downward initially before sloping upward, giving it a "swoosh" shape.

6. In the long run, a producer can change its fixed input and its level of fixed cost. By accepting higher fixed cost, a firm can lower its variable cost for any given output level, and vice versa. The **long-run average total cost curve** shows the relationship between output and average total cost when fixed cost has been chosen to minimize average total cost at each level of output. A firm moves along its short-run average total cost curve as it changes the quantity of output, and it returns to a point on both its short-run and long-run average total cost curves once it has adjusted fixed cost to its new output level.

7. As output increases, there are **increasing returns to scale** if long-run average total cost declines; **decreasing returns to scale** if it increases; and **constant returns to scale** if it remains constant. **Network externalities** are a source of increasing returns to scale. Scale effects depend on the technology of production.

KEY TERMS

Production function, p. 172
Fixed input, p. 172
Variable input, p. 172
Long run, p. 172
Short run, p. 172
Total product curve, p. 172
Marginal product, p. 173
Diminishing returns to an input, p. 174
Explicit cost, p. 176

Implicit cost, p. 176
Fixed cost, p. 176
Variable cost, p. 176
Total cost, p. 176
Total cost curve, p. 177
Marginal cost, p. 179
Average total cost, p. 181
Average cost, p. 181
U-shaped average total cost curve, p. 182

Average fixed cost, p. 182
Average variable cost, p. 182
Minimum-cost output, p. 184
Long-run average total cost curve, p. 188
Increasing returns to scale, p. 189
Decreasing returns to scale, p. 189
Constant returns to scale, p. 189
Network externality, p. 190

DISCUSSION QUESTIONS

1. Magnificent Blooms is a florist specializing in floral arrangements for weddings, graduations, and other events. Magnificent Blooms has a fixed cost associated with space and equipment of $100 per day. Each worker is paid $50 per day. The daily production function for Magnificent Blooms is shown in the accompanying table.

Quantity of labor (workers)	Quantity of floral arrangements
0	0
1	5
2	9
3	12
4	14
5	15

a. Calculate the marginal product of each worker. What principle explains why the marginal product per worker declines as the number of workers employed increases?

b. Calculate the marginal cost of each level of output. What principle explains why the marginal cost per floral arrangement increases as the number of arrangements increases?

2. In your economics class, each homework problem set is graded on the basis of a maximum score of 100. You have completed 9 out of 10 of the problem sets for the term, and your current average grade is 88. What range of grades for your 10th problem set will raise your overall average? What range will lower your overall average? Explain your answer.

PROBLEMS

1. Changes in the prices of key commodities have a significant impact on a company's bottom line. For virtually all companies, the price of energy is a substantial portion of their costs. In addition, many industries—such as those that produce beef, chicken, high-fructose corn syrup, and ethanol—are highly dependent on the price of corn. In particular, corn has seen a significant increase in price.

  a. Explain how the cost of energy can be both a fixed cost and a variable cost for a company.

  b. Suppose energy is a fixed cost and energy prices rise. What happens to the company's average total cost curve? What happens to its marginal cost curve? Illustrate your answer with a diagram.

  c. Explain why the cost of corn is a variable cost but not a fixed cost for an ethanol producer.

  d. When the cost of corn goes up, what happens to the average total cost curve of an ethanol producer? What happens to its marginal cost curve? Illustrate your answer with a diagram.

2. Marty's Frozen Yogurt is a small shop that sells cups of frozen yogurt in a university town. Marty owns three frozen-yogurt machines. His other inputs are refrigerators, frozen-yogurt mix, cups, sprinkle toppings, and, of course, workers. He estimates that his daily production function when he varies the number of workers employed (and at the same time, of course, yogurt mix, cups, and so on) is as shown in the accompanying table.

Quantity of labor (workers)	Quantity of frozen yogurt (cups)
0	0
1	110
2	200
3	270
4	300
5	320
6	330

  a. What are the fixed inputs and variable inputs in the production of cups of frozen yogurt?

  b. Draw the total product curve. Put the quantity of labor on the horizontal axis and the quantity of frozen yogurt on the vertical axis.

  c. What is the marginal product of the first worker? The second worker? The third worker? Why does marginal product decline as the number of workers increases?

3. The production function for Marty's Frozen Yogurt is given in Problem 2. Marty pays each of his workers $80 per day. The cost of his other variable inputs is $0.50 per cup of yogurt. His fixed cost is $100 per day.

  a. What is Marty's variable cost and total cost when he produces 110 cups of yogurt? 200 cups? Calculate variable and total cost for every level of output given in Problem 2.

  b. Draw Marty's variable cost curve. On the same diagram, draw his total cost curve.

  c. What is the marginal cost per cup for the first 110 cups of yogurt? For the next 90 cups? Calculate the marginal cost for all remaining levels of output.

4. The production function for Marty's Frozen Yogurt is given in Problem 2. The costs are given in Problem 3.

  a. For each of the given levels of output, calculate the average fixed cost (*AFC*), average variable cost (*AVC*), and average total cost (*ATC*) per cup of frozen yogurt.

  b. On one diagram, draw the *AFC*, *AVC*, and *ATC* curves.

  c. What principle explains why the *AFC* declines as output increases? What principle explains why the *AVC* increases as output increases? Explain your answers.

  d. How many cups of frozen yogurt are produced when average total cost is minimized?

5. Labor costs represent a large percentage of total costs for many firms. According to data from the Bureau of Labor Statistics, U.S. labor costs went up 2.0% in 2015, compared to 2014.

  a. When labor costs increase, what happens to average total cost and marginal cost? Consider a case in which labor costs are only variable costs and a case in which they are both variable and fixed costs.

An increase in labor productivity means each worker can produce more output. Recent data on productivity show that labor productivity in the U.S. nonfarm business sector grew by 1.7% between 1970 and 1999, by 2.6% between 2000 and 2009, and by 1.1% between 2010 and 2015.

  b. When productivity growth is positive, what happens to the total product curve and the marginal product of labor curve? Illustrate your answer with a diagram.

  c. When productivity growth is positive, what happens to the marginal cost curve and the average total cost curve? Illustrate your answer with a diagram.

  d. If labor costs are rising over time on average, why would a company want to adopt equipment and methods that increase labor productivity?

6. You have the information shown in the accompanying table about a firm's costs. Complete the missing data.

Quantity of output	TC	MC	ATC	AVC
0	$20		–	–
		$20		
1	?		?	?
		10		
2	?		?	?
		16		
3	?		?	?
		20		
4	?		?	?
		24		
5	?		?	?

7. Evaluate each of the following statements. If a statement is true, explain why; if it is false, identify the mistake and try to correct it.

   a. A decreasing marginal product tells us that marginal cost must be rising.

   b. An increase in fixed cost increases the minimum-cost output.

   c. An increase in fixed cost increases marginal cost.

   d. When marginal cost is above average total cost, average total cost must be falling.

8. Mark and Jeff operate a small company that produces souvenir footballs. Their fixed cost is $2,000 per month. They can hire workers for $1,000 per worker per month. Their monthly production function for footballs is as given in the accompanying table.

Quantity of labor (workers)	Quantity of footballs
0	0
1	300
2	800
3	1,200
4	1,400
5	1,500

   a. For each quantity of labor, calculate average variable cost (*AVC*), average fixed cost (*AFC*), average total cost (*ATC*), and marginal cost (*MC*).

   b. On one diagram, draw the *AVC, ATC,* and *MC* curves.

   c. At what level of output is Mark and Jeff's average total cost minimized?

9. You produce widgets. Currently you produce four widgets at a total cost of $40.

   a. What is your average total cost?

   b. Suppose you could produce one more (the fifth) widget at a marginal cost of $5. If you do produce that fifth widget, what will your average total cost be?

Has your average total cost increased or decreased? Why?

   c. Suppose instead that you could produce one more (the fifth) widget at a marginal cost of $20. If you do produce that fifth widget, what will your average total cost be? Has your average total cost increased or decreased? Why?

10. Don owns a small concrete-mixing company. His fixed cost is the cost of the concrete-batching machinery and his mixer trucks. His variable cost is the cost of the sand, gravel, and other inputs for producing concrete; the gas and maintenance for the machinery and trucks; and his workers. He is trying to decide how many mixer trucks to purchase. He has estimated the costs shown in the accompanying table based on estimates of the number of orders his company will receive per week.

Quantity of trucks	FC	VC		
		20 orders	40 orders	60 orders
2	$6,000	$2,000	$5,000	$12,000
3	7,000	1,800	3,800	10,800
4	8,000	1,200	3,600	8,400

   a. For each level of fixed cost, calculate Don's total cost for producing 20, 40, and 60 orders per week.

   b. If Don is producing 20 orders per week, how many trucks should he purchase and what will his average total cost be? Answer the same questions for 40 and 60 orders per week.

11. Consider Don's concrete-mixing business described in Problem 10. Assume that Don purchased 3 trucks, expecting to produce 40 orders per week.

   a. Suppose that, in the short run, business declines to 20 orders per week. What is Don's average total cost per order in the short run? What will his average total cost per order in the short run be if his business booms to 60 orders per week?

   b. What is Don's long-run average total cost for 20 orders per week? Explain why his short-run average total cost of producing 20 orders per week when the number of trucks is fixed at 3 is greater than his long-run average total cost of producing 20 orders per week.

   c. Draw Don's long-run average total cost curve. Draw his short-run average total cost curve if he owns 3 trucks.

12. True or false? Explain your reasoning.

   a. The short-run average total cost can never be less than the long-run average total cost.

   b. The short-run average variable cost can never be less than the long-run average total cost.

   c. In the long run, choosing a higher level of fixed cost shifts the long-run average total cost curve upward.

13. Wolfsburg Wagon (WW) is a small automaker. The accompanying table shows WW's long-run average total cost.

Quantity of cars	LRATC of car
1	$30,000
2	20,000
3	15,000
4	12,000
5	12,000
6	12,000
7	14,000
8	18,000

a. For which levels of output does WW experience increasing returns to scale?

b. For which levels of output does WW experience decreasing returns to scale?

c. For which levels of output does WW experience constant returns to scale?

WORK IT OUT Interactive step-by-step help with solving this problem can be found online.

14. The accompanying table shows a car manufacturer's total cost of producing cars.

Quantity of cars	TC
0	$500,000
1	540,000
2	560,000
3	570,000
4	590,000
5	620,000
6	660,000
7	720,000
8	800,000
9	920,000
10	1,100,000

a. What is this manufacturer's fixed cost?

b. For each level of output, calculate the variable cost (VC). For each level of output except zero output, calculate the average variable cost (AVC), average total cost (ATC), and average fixed cost (AFC). What is the minimum-cost output?

c. For each level of output, calculate this manufacturer's marginal cost (MC).

d. On one diagram, draw the manufacturer's AVC, ATC, and MC curves.

7

Perfect Competition and the Supply Curve

DECK THE HALLS

ONE SURE SIGN it's the holiday season is the sudden appearance of Christmas tree sellers, setting up shop in vacant lots, parking lots, and garden centers all across the country. Until the 1950s, virtually all Christmas trees were obtained by individuals going to local forests to cut down their own. However, by the 1950s increased demand from population growth and diminished supply from the loss of forests created a market opportunity. Seeing an ability to profit by growing and selling Christmas trees, farmers responded to the demand.

Richard Levine/Corbis via Getty Images

Whether it's Christmas trees or smartphones, how a good is produced determines its cost of production.

So rather than venturing into the forest to cut your own tree, you now have a wide range of tree sizes and varieties to choose from—and they are available close to home. In 2017, nearly 27 million farmed trees were sold in the United States for a total of $2 billion.

Note that the supply of Christmas trees is relatively price inelastic for two reasons: it takes time to acquire land for planting, and it takes time for the trees to grow. However, these limits apply only in the short run. Over time, farms that are already in operation can increase their capacity and new tree farmers can enter the business. And, over time, the trees will mature and be ready to harvest. So the increase in the quantity supplied in response to an increase in price will be much larger in the long run than in the short run.

Where does the supply curve come from? Why is there a difference between the short-run and the long-run supply curve? In this chapter we will use our understanding of costs, developed in Chapter 6, as the basis for an analysis of the supply curve. As we'll see, this will require that we understand the behavior both of individual firms and of an entire industry, composed of these many individual firms.

Our analysis in this chapter assumes that the industry in question is characterized by *perfect competition*. We begin by explaining the concept of perfect competition, providing a brief introduction to the conditions that give rise to a perfectly competitive industry. We then show how a producer under perfect competition decides how much to produce. Finally, we use the cost curves of individual producers to derive the *industry supply curve* under perfect competition.

By analyzing the way a competitive industry evolves over time, we will come to understand the distinction between the short-run and long-run effects of changes in demand on a competitive industry—such as, for example, the effect of America's preference for readily available trees for the holidays on the Christmas tree farming industry. We will conclude with a deeper discussion of the conditions necessary for an industry to be perfectly competitive. ●

WHAT YOU WILL LEARN

- What is perfect competition and why do economists consider it an important benchmark?
- What factors make a firm or an industry perfectly competitive?
- How does a **perfectly competitive industry** determine the profit-maximizing output level?
- What determines if a firm is profitable or unprofitable?
- Why does it make sense for a firm to behave differently in the short run versus the long run?
- How does the **short-run industry supply curve** differ from the **long-run industry supply curve**?

A **price-taking producer** is a producer whose actions have no effect on the market price of the good or service it sells.

A **price-taking consumer** is a consumer whose actions have no effect on the market price of the good or service he or she buys.

A **perfectly competitive market** is a market in which all market participants are price-takers.

A **perfectly competitive industry** is an industry in which producers are price-takers.

‖ Perfect Competition

Suppose that Yves and Zoe are neighboring farmers, both of whom grow Christmas trees. Both sell their output to the same set of Christmas tree consumers, so, in a real sense, Yves and Zoe compete with each other.

Does this mean that Yves should try to stop Zoe from growing Christmas trees or that Yves and Zoe should form an agreement to grow less? Almost certainly not: there are thousands of Christmas tree farmers, and Yves and Zoe are competing with all those other growers as well as with each other. Because so many farmers sell Christmas trees, if any one of them produced more or less, there would be no measurable effect on market prices.

When people talk about business competition, the image they often have in mind is a situation in which two or three rival firms are intensely struggling for advantage. But economists know that when an industry consists of only a few main competitors, it's actually a sign that competition is fairly limited. As the example of Christmas trees suggests, when there is enough competition, it doesn't even make sense to identify your rivals: there are so many competitors that you cannot single out any one of them as a rival.

We can put it another way: Yves and Zoe are **price-taking producers.** A producer is a price-taker when its actions cannot affect the market price of the good or service it sells. As a result, a price-taking producer considers the market price as given. When there is enough competition—when competition is what economists call "perfect"—then every producer is a price-taker.

And there is a similar definition for consumers: a **price-taking consumer** is a consumer who cannot influence the market price of the good or service by his or her actions. That is, the market price is unaffected by how much or how little of the good the consumer buys.

Defining Perfect Competition

In a **perfectly competitive market,** all market participants, both consumers and producers, are price-takers. That is, neither consumption decisions by individual consumers nor production decisions by individual producers affect the market price of the good.

The supply and demand model, which we introduced in Chapter 3 and have used repeatedly since then, is a model of a perfectly competitive market. It depends fundamentally on the assumption that no individual buyer or seller of a good, such as coffee beans or Christmas trees, believes that it is possible to affect the price at which he or she can buy or sell the good.

As a general rule, consumers are indeed price-takers. Instances in which consumers are able to affect the prices they pay are rare. It is, however, quite common for producers to have a significant ability to affect their selling price, a phenomenon we'll address in the next chapter. So the model of perfect competition is appropriate for some but not all markets. An industry in which producers are price-takers is called a **perfectly competitive industry.** Clearly, some industries aren't perfectly competitive; in later chapters we'll learn how to analyze industries that don't fit the perfectly competitive model.

Under what circumstances will all producers be price-takers? In the next section we will find that there are two necessary conditions for a perfectly competitive industry and that a third condition is often present as well.

Two Necessary Conditions for Perfect Competition

The markets for major grains, like wheat and corn, are perfectly competitive: individual wheat and corn farmers, as well as individual buyers of wheat and corn, take market prices as given. In contrast, the markets for some of the food items made from these grains—in particular, breakfast cereals—are by no means perfectly competitive. There is intense competition among cereal brands, but not *perfect* competition. To understand the difference between the market for wheat and the market for shredded wheat cereal is to understand the importance of the two necessary conditions for perfect competition. For an industry to be perfectly competitive:

1. The industry must contain many producers, none of whom have a large market share. A producer's **market share** is the fraction of the total industry output accounted for by that producer's output. The distribution of market share constitutes a major difference between the grain industry and the breakfast cereal industry.

In the market for wheat, there are thousands of producers—wheat farmers—none of whom account for more than a tiny fraction of total wheat sales. In contrast, the breakfast cereal industry is dominated by four producers: Kellogg's, General Mills, Post Foods, and the Quaker Oats Company. Kellogg's and General Mills alone account for 65% of all cereal sales in the United States. Kellogg's executives know that if they try to sell more cornflakes, they are likely to drive down the market price of cornflakes. That is, they know that their actions influence market prices, simply because they are such a large part of the market that changes in their production will significantly affect the overall quantity supplied. It makes sense to assume that producers are price-takers only when an industry does *not* contain any large producers like Kellogg's.

2. Every firm in the industry must produce a standardized product. A product that consumers regard as the same good, even when it comes from different producers, is known as a **standardized product** or a **commodity.** Wheat is an example of a standardized product because consumers regard the output of one wheat producer as a perfect substitute for that of another producer. Consequently, one farmer cannot increase the price for his or her wheat without losing all sales to other wheat farmers.

But what is true for wheat is clearly not true for shredded wheat breakfast cereal, which is not a standardized product: consumers don't consider Cap'n Crunch to be a good substitute for Wheaties. As a result, the maker of Wheaties has some ability to increase its price without fear that it will lose all its customers to the maker of Cap'n Crunch.

Another Feature of Perfect Competition: Free Entry and Exit

Most perfectly competitive industries are also characterized by one more feature: it is easy for new firms to enter the industry or for firms that are currently in the industry to leave. That is, no obstacles in the form of government regulations or limited access to key resources prevent new producers from entering the market. And no additional costs are associated with shutting down a company and leaving the industry.

Economists refer to the arrival of new firms into an industry as *entry;* they refer to the departure of firms from an industry as *exit.* When there are no obstacles to entry into or exit from an industry, we say that the industry has **free entry and exit.**

Free entry and exit is not strictly necessary for perfect competition. In Chapter 4 we described the case of Alaskan crab fishing, where regulations place a quota on the amount of Alaskan crab that can be caught during a season, so entry is limited to established boat owners that have been given quotas. Despite this, there are enough boats operating that the crab fishermen are price-takers. But free entry and exit is a key factor in most competitive industries. It ensures that the number of firms in an industry can adjust to changing market conditions. And, in particular, it ensures that firms in an industry cannot act to keep other firms out.

A producer's **market share** is the fraction of the total industry output accounted for by that producer's output.

A good is a **standardized product,** also known as a **commodity,** when consumers regard the products of different producers as the same good.

An industry has **free entry and exit** when new producers can easily enter into an industry and existing producers can easily leave that industry.

To sum up, then, perfect competition depends on two necessary conditions.

1. The industry must contain many producers, each with a small market share.

2. The industry must produce a standardized product.

In addition, perfectly competitive industries are typically characterized by free entry and exit.

How does an industry that meets these three criteria behave? As a first step toward answering that question, let's look at how an individual producer in a perfectly competitive industry maximizes profit.

ECONOMICS >> *in Action*
Pay for Delay

Sometimes it is possible to watch an industry become perfectly competitive. This is the case in the pharmaceutical industry, when the patent on a popular drug expires and a *generic* rival drug enters the market.

Patents allow drug makers to have a legal monopoly on new medications for 20 years.

A company that develops a new drug is given a *patent*, which gives it a *legal monopoly*—the exclusive right to sell the drug—for 20 years. Legally, no one else can sell the drug without the patent-holder's permission.

When the patent expires, the market is open for other companies to produce and sell *generics*, alternative versions of the drug, and the price drops dramatically. On average, a generic drug costs about 15% of the price of the equivalent patent-protected drug, which will lose up to 90% of its market share. In the case of Lipitor, Pfizer's blockbuster drug for cholesterol, the generic version was only 8% of the price of Lipitor.

However, that sequence of events is what is *supposed* to happen. Makers of the original patent-protected drugs have employed a variety of strategies to block or forestall the entry of generic competitors. One very successful tactic is *pay for delay*, an agreement in which the patent-holder pays the generic drug maker to delay the entry of the generic drug in return for compensation. As a result, the patent-holder continues to charge high prices, the generic drug maker gets a lucrative payment, and the consumer suffers.

Pay-for-delay agreements have cost consumers an estimated $3.5 billion dollars annually from 2005 to 2013. But in 2014 the number of such deals dropped dramatically after a ruling by the U.S. Supreme Court gave federal regulators the authority to prosecute the deals as anti-competitive. With that authority the Federal Trade Commission scored a $1.2 billion settlement from drug maker Teva over allegations it engaged in pay for delay over their sleep-disorder drug Provigil. According to industry observers, increased competition is saving consumers many billions of dollars a year.

>> Quick Review

• Neither the actions of a **price-taking producer** nor those of a **price-taking consumer** can influence the market price of a good.

• In a **perfectly competitive market** all producers and consumers are price-takers. Consumers are almost always price-takers, but this is often not true of producers. An industry in which producers are price-takers is a **perfectly competitive industry**.

• A perfectly competitive industry contains many producers, each of which produces a **standardized product** (also known as a **commodity**) but none of which has a large **market share.**

• Most perfectly competitive industries are also characterized by **free entry and exit.**

>> Check Your Understanding 7-1

Solutions appear at back of book.

1. In each of the following situations, do you think the industry described will be perfectly competitive or not? Explain your answer.

a. There are two producers of aluminum in the world, a good sold in many places.

b. The price of natural gas is determined by global supply and demand. A small share of that global supply is produced by a handful of companies located in the North Sea.

c. Dozens of designers sell high-fashion clothes. Each designer has a distinctive style and a loyal clientele.

d. There are many baseball teams in the United States, one or two in each major city and each selling tickets to its hometown events.

Production and Profits

Consider Noelle, who runs a Christmas tree farm. Suppose that the market price of Christmas trees is $18 per tree and that Noelle is a price-taker—she can sell as many as she likes at that price. Then we can use the data in Table 7-1 to find her profit-maximizing level of output by direct calculation.

The first column shows the quantity of output in number of trees, and the second column shows Noelle's total revenue from her output: the market value of trees she produced. Total revenue, *TR*, is equal to the market price multiplied by the quantity of output:

(7-1) $TR = P \times Q$

In this example, total revenue is equal to $18 per tree times the quantity of output in trees.

The third column of Table 7-1 shows Noelle's total cost. The fourth column shows her profit, equal to total revenue minus total cost:

(7-2) $Profit = TR - TC$

As indicated by the numbers in the table, profit is maximized at an output of 50 trees, where profit is equal to $180. But we can gain more insight into the profit-maximizing choice of output by viewing it as a problem of marginal analysis, a task we'll do next.

Using Marginal Analysis to Choose the Profit-Maximizing Quantity of Output

Recall the definition of *marginal cost* from Chapter 6: the additional cost incurred by producing one more unit of that good or service. Similarly, the **marginal benefit** of a good or service is the additional benefit gained from producing one more unit of a good or service. We are now ready to use the **principle of marginal analysis,** which says that the optimal amount of an activity is the level at which marginal benefit is equal to marginal cost.

To apply this principle, consider the effect on a producer's profit of increasing output by one unit. The marginal benefit of that unit is the additional revenue generated by selling it; this measure has a name—it is called the **marginal revenue** of that unit of output. The general formula for marginal revenue is:

(7-3) $\text{Marginal revenue} = \dfrac{\text{Change in total revenue generated by one additional unit of output}}{} = \dfrac{\text{Change in total revenue}}{\text{Change in quantity of output}}$

or

$$MR = \frac{\Delta TR}{\Delta Q}$$

So Noelle maximizes her profit by producing trees up to the point at which the marginal revenue is equal to marginal cost. We can summarize this as the producer's **optimal output rule:** profit is maximized by producing the quantity at which the marginal revenue of the last unit produced is equal to its marginal cost. That is, $MR = MC$ at the optimal quantity of output.

We can learn how to apply the optimal output rule with the help of Table 7-2, which provides various short-run cost measures for Noelle's farm. The second column contains the farm's variable cost, and the third column shows its total cost of output based on the assumption that the farm incurs a fixed cost of $140. The fourth column shows marginal cost. Notice that, in this example, the marginal cost initially falls but then rises as output increases. This gives the marginal cost curve the "swoosh" shape described in Chapter 6. It will soon become clear that this shape has important implications for short-run production decisions.

TABLE 7-1 Profit for Noelle's Farm When Market Price Is $18

Quantity of trees Q	Total revenue TR	Total cost TC	Profit TR – TC
0	$0	$140	–$140
10	180	300	–120
20	360	360	0
30	540	440	100
40	720	560	160
50	900	720	180
60	1,080	920	160
70	1,260	1,160	100

The **marginal benefit** of a good or service is the additional benefit derived from producing one more unit of that good or service.

The **principle of marginal analysis** says that the optimal amount of an activity is the quantity at which marginal benefit equals marginal cost.

Marginal revenue is the change in total revenue generated by an additional unit of output.

According to the **optimal output rule,** profit is maximized by producing the quantity of output at which the marginal revenue of the last unit produced is equal to its marginal cost.

TABLE 7-2 Short-Run Costs for Noelle's Farm

Quantity of trees Q	Variable cost VC	Total cost TC	Marginal cost of tree $MC = \Delta TC/\Delta Q$	Marginal revenue of tree MR	Net gain of tree = MR − MC
0	$0	$140			
			$16	$18	$2
10	160	300			
			6	18	12
20	220	360			
			8	18	10
30	300	440			
			12	18	6
40	420	560			
			16	18	2
50	580	720			
			20	18	−2
60	780	920			
			24	18	−6
70	1,020	1,160			

The fifth column contains the farm's marginal revenue, which has an important feature: Noelle's marginal revenue equal to price is constant at $18 for every output level. The sixth and final column shows the calculation of the net gain per tree, which is equal to marginal revenue minus marginal cost—or, equivalently in this case, market price minus marginal cost. As you can see, it is positive for the 1st through 50th trees; producing each of these trees raises Noelle's profit. For the 51st through 70th trees, however, net gain is negative: producing them would decrease, not increase, profit. So to maximize profits, Noelle will produce up to the point at which the marginal revenue of the last unit produced is greater than or equal to the marginal cost of the last unit produced. Any more reduces her profit. Hence, 50 trees is Noelle's profit-maximizing output.

Because Noelle receives $18 for every tree produced, we know that her farm is a price-taking firm. A price-taking firm cannot influence the market price by its actions. It always takes the market price as given because it cannot lower the market price by selling more or raise the market price by selling less. So, for a price-taking firm, the additional revenue generated by producing one more unit is always the market price. Be sure to keep this fact in mind in future chapters, where we will learn that marginal revenue is not equal to the market price if the industry is not perfectly competitive. As a result, firms are not price-takers when an industry is not perfectly competitive. For the remainder of this chapter, we will assume that the industry in question is like Christmas tree farming, perfectly competitive.

Figure 7-1 shows that Noelle's profit-maximizing quantity of output is, indeed, 50 trees. The figure shows the marginal cost curve, MC, drawn from the data in the fourth column of Table 7-2. As in Chapter 6, we plot the marginal cost of

FIGURE 7-1 The Price-Taking Firm's Profit-Maximizing Quantity of Output

At the profit-maximizing quantity of output, the market price is equal to marginal cost. It is located at the point where the marginal cost curve crosses the marginal revenue curve, which is a horizontal line at the market price. Here, the profit-maximizing point is at an output of 50 trees, the output quantity at point E.

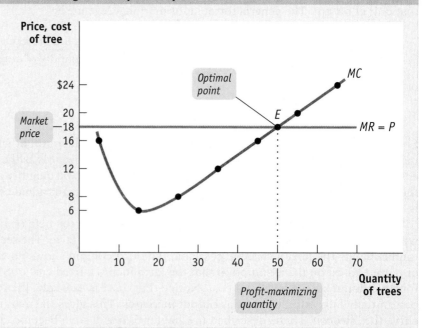

increasing output from 10 to 20 trees halfway between 10 and 20, and so on. The *MC* curve is smooth, allowing us to see how *MC* changes as one more tree is produced. The horizontal line at $18 is Noelle's **marginal revenue curve.**

Note that whenever a firm is a price-taker, its marginal revenue curve is a horizontal line at the market price: it can sell as much as it likes at the market price. Regardless of whether it sells more or less, the market price is unaffected. In effect, the individual firm faces a horizontal, perfectly elastic demand curve for its output. The marginal cost curve crosses the marginal revenue curve at point *E* where *MC* = *MR*. Sure enough, the quantity of output at *E* is 50 trees.

This example illustrates another general rule derived from marginal analysis—the **price-taking firm's optimal output rule,** which says that a price-taking firm's profit is maximized by producing the quantity of output up to the point at which the market price is equal to the marginal cost of the last unit produced. That is, *P* = *MC* at the price-taking firm's optimal quantity of output. In fact, the price-taking firm's optimal output rule is just an application of the optimal output rule to the particular case of a price-taking firm. Why? Because *in the case of a price-taking firm, marginal revenue is equal to the market price.*

Does this mean that the price-taking firm's production decision can be entirely summed up as "produce up to the point where the marginal cost of production is equal to the price"? No, not quite. Before applying the profit-maximizing principle of marginal analysis to determine how much to produce, a potential producer must as a first step answer an "either–or" question: should it produce at all? If the answer to that question is yes, it then proceeds to the second step—a "how much" decision: maximizing profit by choosing the quantity of output at which marginal cost is equal to price.

To understand why the first step in the production decision involves an "either–or" question, we need to ask how we determine whether it is profitable or unprofitable to produce at all. That is, we need to determine whether the firm should produce or shut down.

When Is Production Profitable?

A firm's decision whether or not to stay in a given business depends on its **economic profit**—the firm's revenue minus the opportunity cost of resources used in the business. To put it a slightly different way: in the calculation of economic profit, a firm's total cost incorporates the *implicit cost*—the benefits forgone in the next best use of the firm's resources—as well as the *explicit cost* in the form of actual cash outlays.

In contrast, **accounting profit** is profit calculated using only the explicit costs incurred by the firm. This means that economic profit incorporates the opportunity cost of resources owned by the firm and used in the production of output, while accounting profit does not.

A firm may make positive accounting profit while making zero or even negative economic profit. It's important to understand clearly that a firm's decision to produce or not, to stay in business or to close down permanently, should be based on economic profit, not accounting profit.

We will assume, as we always do, that the cost numbers given in Tables 7-1 and 7-2 include all costs, implicit as well as explicit, and that the profit numbers in Table 7-1 are therefore economic profit. So what determines whether Noelle's farm earns a profit or generates a loss? The answer is that, *given the farm's cost curves, whether or not it is profitable depends on the market price of trees—specifically, whether the market price is more or less than the farm's minimum average total cost.*

In Table 7-3 we calculate short-run average variable cost and short-run average total cost for Noelle's farm. These are short-run values because we take fixed cost as given. (We'll turn to the effects of changing fixed cost shortly.)

The **marginal revenue curve** shows how marginal revenue varies as output varies.

According to the **price-taking firm's optimal output rule,** a price-taking firm's profit is maximized by producing the quantity of output at which the market price is equal to the marginal cost of the last unit produced.

Economic profit is the firm's revenue minus the opportunity cost of resources used in business.

Accounting profit is profit calculated using only the explicit costs incurred by the firm.

TABLE 7-3 Short-Run Average Costs for Noelle's Farm

Quantity of trees Q	Variable cost VC	Total cost TC	Short-run average variable cost of tree AVC = VC/Q	Short-run average total cost of tree ATC = TC/Q
10	$160.00	$300.00	$16.00	$30.00
20	220.00	360.00	11.00	18.00
30	300.00	440.00	10.00	14.67
40	420.00	560.00	10.50	14.00
50	580.00	720.00	11.60	14.40
60	780.00	920.00	13.00	15.33
70	1,020.00	1,160.00	14.57	16.57

The short-run average total cost curve, *ATC*, is shown in Figure 7-2, along with the marginal cost curve, *MC*, from Figure 7-1. As you can see, average total cost is minimized at point *C*, corresponding to an output of 40 trees—the *minimum-cost output*—and an average total cost of $14 per tree.

To see how these curves can be used to decide whether production is profitable or unprofitable, recall that profit is equal to total revenue minus total cost, *TR − TC*. This means:

- If the firm produces a quantity at which $TR > TC$, the firm is profitable.
- If the firm produces a quantity at which $TR = TC$, the firm breaks even.
- If the firm produces a quantity at which $TR < TC$, the firm incurs a loss.

We can also express this idea in terms of revenue and cost per unit of output. If we divide profit by the number of units of output, *Q*, we obtain the following expression for profit per unit of output:

(7-4) $\text{Profit}/Q = TR/Q - TC/Q$

TR/Q is average revenue, which is the market price. *TC/Q* is average total cost. So a firm is profitable if the market price for its product is more than the average total cost of the quantity the firm produces; a firm loses money if the market price is less than average total cost of the quantity the firm produces. This means:

- If the firm produces a quantity at which $P > ATC$, the firm is profitable.
- If the firm produces a quantity at which $P = ATC$, the firm breaks even.
- If the firm produces a quantity at which $P < ATC$, the firm incurs a loss.

FIGURE 7-2 Costs and Production in the Short Run

This figure shows the marginal cost curve, *MC*, and the short-run average total cost curve, *ATC*. When the market price is $14, output will be 40 trees (the minimum-cost output), represented by point *C*. The price of $14, equal to the firm's minimum average total cost, is the firm's *break-even price*.

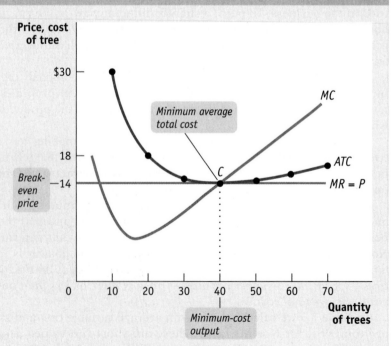

Figure 7-3 illustrates this result, showing how the market price determines whether a firm is profitable. It also shows how profits are depicted graphically. Each panel shows the marginal cost curve, *MC*, and the short-run average total cost curve, *ATC*. Average total cost is minimized at point *C*. Panel (a) shows the case we have already analyzed, in which the market price of trees is $18 per tree. Panel (b) shows the case in which the market price of trees is lower, $10 per tree.

In panel (a), we see that at a price of $18 per tree the profit-maximizing quantity of output is 50 trees, indicated by point *E*, where the marginal cost curve, *MC*, intersects the marginal revenue curve—which for a price-taking firm is a

---

FIGURE 7-3 Profitability and the Market Price

In panel (a) the market price is $18. The farm is profitable because price exceeds minimum average total cost, the break-even price, $14. The farm's optimal output choice is indicated by point *E*, corresponding to an output of 50 trees. The average total cost of producing 50 trees is indicated by point *Z* on the *ATC* curve, corresponding to an amount of $14.40. The vertical distance between *E* and *Z* corresponds to the farm's per-unit profit, $18.00 − $14.40 = $3.60. Total profit is given by the area of the shaded rectangle, 50 × $3.60 = $180.00. In panel (b) the market price is $10; the farm is unprofitable because the price falls below the minimum average total cost, $14. The farm's optimal output choice when producing is indicated by point *A*, corresponding to an output of 30 trees. The farm's per-unit loss, $14.67 − $10.00 = $4.67, is represented by the vertical distance between *A* and *Y*. The farm's total loss is represented by the shaded rectangle, 30 × $4.67 = $140.00 (adjusted for rounding error).

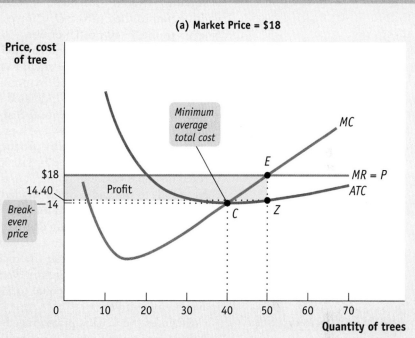

(a) Market Price = $18

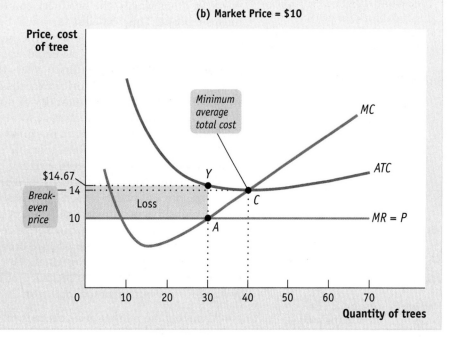

(b) Market Price = $10

horizontal line at the market price. At that quantity of output, average total cost is $14.40 per tree, indicated by point Z. Since the price per tree exceeds average total cost per tree, Noelle's farm is profitable.

Noelle's total profit when the market price is $18 is represented by the area of the shaded rectangle in panel (a). To see why, notice that total profit can be expressed in terms of profit per unit:

(7-5) $\text{Profit} = TR - TC = (TR/Q - TC/Q) \times Q$

or, equivalently,

$$\text{Profit} = (P - ATC) \times Q$$

since P is equal to TR/Q and ATC is equal to TC/Q. The height of the shaded rectangle in panel (a) corresponds to the vertical distance between points E and Z. It is equal to $P - ATC = \$18.00 - \$14.40 = \$3.60$ per tree. The shaded rectangle has a width equal to the output: $Q = 50$ trees. So the area of that rectangle is equal to Noelle's profit: $3.60 profit per tree $\times$ 50 trees = $180.

What about the situation illustrated in panel (b)? Here the market price of trees is $10 per tree. Setting price equal to marginal cost leads to a profit-maximizing output of 30 trees, indicated by point A. At this output, Noelle has an average total cost of $14.67 per tree, indicated by point Y. At the profit-maximizing output quantity—30 trees—average total cost exceeds the market price. This means that Noelle's farm generates a loss, not a profit.

How much does she lose by producing when the market price is $10? On each tree she loses $ATC - P = \$14.67 - \$10.00 = \$4.67$, an amount corresponding to the vertical distance between points A and Y. And she would produce 30 trees, which corresponds to the width of the shaded rectangle. So the total value of the losses is $4.67 \times 30 = \$140.00$ (adjusted for rounding error), an amount that corresponds to the area of the shaded rectangle in panel (b).

But how does a producer know, in general, whether or not its business will be profitable? It turns out that the crucial test lies in a comparison of the market price to the producer's *minimum average total cost*. On Noelle's farm, minimum average total cost, which is equal to $14, occurs at an output quantity of 40 trees, indicated by point C.

Whenever the market price exceeds minimum average total cost, the producer can find some output level for which the average total cost is less than the market price. In other words, the producer can find a level of output at which the firm makes a profit. Thus, Noelle's farm will be profitable whenever the market price exceeds $14. And she will achieve the highest possible profit by producing the quantity at which marginal cost equals the market price.

Conversely, if the market price is less than minimum average total cost, there is no output level at which price exceeds average total cost. As a result, the firm will be unprofitable at any quantity of output. As we saw, at a price of $10—an amount less than minimum average total cost—Noelle did indeed lose money. By producing the quantity at which marginal cost equals the market price, Noelle did the best she could, but the best that she could do was a loss of $140. Any other quantity would have increased the size of her loss.

The minimum average total cost of a price-taking firm is called its **break-even price,** the price at which it earns zero profit. (Recall that's *economic profit.*) A firm will earn positive profit when the market price is above the break-even price, and it will suffer losses when the market price is below the break-even price. Noelle's break-even price of $14 is the price at point C in Figures 7-2 and 7-3.

So the rule for determining whether a producer of a good is profitable depends on a comparison of the market price of the good to the producer's break-even price—its minimum average total cost:

The **break-even price** of a price-taking firm is the market price at which it earns zero profit.

• Whenever the market price exceeds minimum average total cost, the producer is profitable.

- Whenever the market price equals minimum average total cost, the producer breaks even.
- Whenever the market price is less than minimum average total cost, the producer is unprofitable.

The Short-Run Production Decision

You might be tempted to say that if a firm is unprofitable because the market price is below its minimum average total cost, it shouldn't produce any output. In the short run, however, this conclusion isn't correct.

In the short run, sometimes the firm should produce even if price falls below minimum average total cost. The reason is that total cost includes *fixed cost*—cost that does not depend on the amount of output produced and can only be altered in the long run.

In the short run, fixed cost must still be paid, regardless of whether or not a firm produces. For example, if Noelle rents a refrigerated truck for the year, she has to pay the rent on the truck regardless of whether she produces any trees. *Since it cannot be changed in the short run, her fixed cost is irrelevant to her decision about whether to produce or shut down in the short run.*

Although fixed cost should play no role in the decision about whether to produce in the short run, other costs—variable costs—do matter. An example of variable costs is the wages of workers who must be hired to help with planting and harvesting. Since variable costs can be saved by *not* producing, they should play a role in determining whether or not to produce in the short run.

Let's turn to Figure 7-4: it shows both the short-run average total cost curve, *ATC*, and the short-run average variable cost curve, *AVC*, drawn from the information in Table 7-3. Recall that the difference between the two curves—the vertical distance between them—represents average fixed cost, the fixed cost per unit of output, FC/Q.

Because the marginal cost curve has a "swoosh" shape—falling at first before rising—the short-run average variable cost curve is U-shaped: the initial fall in marginal cost causes average variable cost to fall as well, before rising marginal cost eventually pulls it up again. The short-run average variable cost curve reaches its minimum value of $10 at point *A*, at an output of 30 trees.

We are now prepared to fully analyze the optimal production decision in the short run. We need to consider two cases: (1) when the market price is below minimum average *variable* cost and (2) when the market price is greater than or equal to minimum average *variable* cost.

1. **When the Market Price Is Below Minimum Average Variable Cost:** in this case, the price the firm receives per unit is not covering its variable cost per unit. A firm in this situation should cease production immediately because there is no level of output at which the firm's total revenue covers its variable costs—the costs it can avoid by not operating. In this case the firm maximizes its profits by not producing at all—by, in effect, minimizing its losses. It will still incur a fixed cost in the short run, but it will no longer incur any variable cost. This means that the minimum average variable cost is equal to the **shut-down price,** the price at which the firm ceases production in the short run. In the example of Noelle's tree farm, she will cease production in the short run by laying off workers and halting all planting and harvesting of trees.

2. **When Price Is Greater Than Minimum Average Variable Cost:** In this case, the firm maximizes profit—or minimizes loss—by choosing the output quantity at which its marginal cost is equal to the market price. A firm in this situation should produce in the short run. For example, if the market price of each tree is $18, Noelle should produce at point *E* in Figure 7-4, corresponding to an output of 50 trees. Note that point *C* in Figure 7-4 corresponds to the farm's

A firm will cease production in the short run if the market price falls below the **shut-down price,** which is equal to minimum average variable cost.

break-even price of $14 per tree. Since *E* lies above *C*, Noelle's farm will be profitable; she will generate a per-tree profit of $18.00 – $14.40 = $3.60 when the market price is $18.

But what if the market price lies between the shut-down price and the break-even price—that is, between minimum average *variable* cost and minimum average *total* cost? In the case of Noelle's farm, this corresponds to prices anywhere between $10 and $14—say, a market price of $12. At $12, Noelle's farm is not profitable; since the market price is below minimum average total cost, the farm is losing the difference between price and average total cost per unit produced.

Yet even if it isn't covering its total cost per unit, it is covering its variable cost per unit and some—but not all—of the fixed cost per unit. If a firm in this situation shuts down, it would incur no variable cost but would still incur the *full* fixed cost. As a result, shutting down generates an even greater loss than continuing to operate.

This means that whenever price lies between minimum average total cost and minimum average variable cost, the firm is better off producing some output in the short run. The reason is that by producing, it can cover its variable cost per unit and at least some of its fixed cost, even though it is incurring a loss. In this case, the firm maximizes profit—that is, minimizes loss—by choosing the quantity of output at which its marginal cost is equal to the market price. So if Noelle faces a market price of $12 per tree, her profit-maximizing output is given by point *B* in Figure 7-4, corresponding to an output of 35 trees.

It's worth noting that the decision to produce when the firm is covering its variable costs but not all of its fixed cost is similar to the decision to ignore *sunk costs*. A **sunk cost** is a cost that has already been incurred and cannot be recouped; and because it cannot be changed, it should have no effect on any current decision.

In the short-run production decision, fixed cost is, in effect, like a sunk cost—it has been spent, and it can't be recovered in the short run. This comparison also illustrates why variable cost does indeed matter in the short run: it can be avoided by not producing.

And what happens if market price is exactly equal to the shut-down price, which occurs at the minimum average variable cost? In this instance, the firm is indifferent between producing 30 units or 0 units. As we'll see shortly, this is an important point when looking at the behavior of an industry as a whole. For the sake of clarity, we'll assume that the firm, although indifferent, does indeed produce output when price is equal to the shut-down price.

Putting everything together, we can now draw the **short-run individual supply curve** of Noelle's farm, the red line in Figure 7-4; it shows how the profit-maximizing quantity of output in the short run depends on the price. As you can see, the curve is in two segments. The upward-sloping red segment starting at point *A* shows the short-run profit-maximizing output when market price is equal to or above the shut-down price of $10 per tree.

As long as the market price is equal to or above the shut-down price, Noelle produces the quantity of output at which marginal cost is equal to the market price. That is, at market prices equal to or above the shut-down price, the firm's short-run supply curve corresponds to its marginal cost curve. But at any market price below minimum average variable cost—in this case, $10 per tree—the firm shuts down and output drops to zero in the short run. This corresponds to the vertical segment of the curve that lies on top of the vertical axis.

Do firms really shut down temporarily without going out of business? Yes. In fact, in some businesses temporary shut-downs are routine. The most common examples are industries in which demand is highly seasonal, like outdoor amusement parks in climates with cold winters. Such parks would have to offer very low prices to entice customers during the colder months—prices so low that the owners would not cover their variable costs (principally wages and electricity). The wiser choice economically is to shut down until warm weather brings enough customers who are willing to pay a higher price.

A **sunk cost** is a cost that has already been incurred and is nonrecoverable.

The **short-run individual supply curve** shows how an individual producer's profit-maximizing output quantity depends on the market price, taking fixed cost as given.

FIGURE 7-4 The Short-Run Individual Supply Curve

When the market price equals or exceeds Noelle's *shut-down price* of $10, the minimum average variable cost indicated by point *A*, she will produce the output quantity at which marginal cost is equal to price. So, at any price equal to or above the minimum average *variable* cost, the short-run individual supply curve is the firm's marginal cost curve; this corresponds to the upward-sloping segment of the individual supply curve. When market price falls below minimum average variable cost, the firm ceases operation in the short run. This corresponds to the vertical segment of the individual supply curve along the vertical axis.

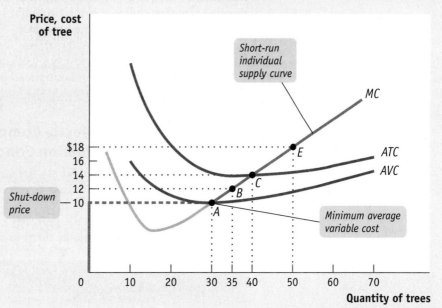

Long-Run Production: Changing Fixed Cost, Entry and Exit

Although fixed cost cannot be altered in the short run, in the long run firms can acquire or get rid of machines, buildings, and so on. In the long run the level of fixed cost is a matter of choice. A firm will choose the level of fixed cost that minimizes the average total cost for its desired output quantity. Now we will focus on an even bigger question facing a firm when choosing its fixed cost: whether to incur *any* fixed cost at all by remaining in its current business.

In the long run, a producer can always eliminate fixed cost by selling off its plant and equipment. If it does this, it can no longer produce: it has exited the industry. In contrast, a potential producer that takes on some fixed cost by acquiring machines and other resources is in a position to produce: it can enter the industry.

This means that in perfectly competitive industries, the number of producers is fixed in the short run. In contrast, because fixed cost can be changed in the long run, the number of producers can change as firms enter or exit the industry.

Consider Noelle's farm once again. To simplify our analysis, we will sidestep the problem of choosing among several possible levels of fixed cost. Instead, we will assume from now on that Noelle has only one possible choice of fixed cost if she operates, the amount of $140. Alternatively, she can choose a fixed cost of zero if she exits the industry. It is changes in fixed cost that cause short-run average total cost curves to differ from long-run average total cost curves. With this assumption then, Noelle's short-run average total cost curve and long-run average total cost curve are one and the same.

Suppose that the market price of trees is consistently less than $14 over an extended period of time. In that case, Noelle never fully covers her fixed cost: her business runs at a persistent loss. In the long run, then, she can do better by closing her business and leaving the industry. In other words, *in the long run* firms will exit an industry if the market price is consistently less than their break-even price—their minimum average total cost.

Conversely, suppose that the price of Christmas trees is consistently above the break-even price, $14, for an extended period of time. Because her farm is profitable, Noelle will remain in the industry and continue producing.

But things won't stop there. The perfectly competitive Christmas tree industry meets the criterion of *free entry:* there are many potential tree producers because

Buying or selling equipment allows a firm to change its fixed cost.

the necessary inputs are easy to obtain. And the cost curves of those potential producers are likely to be similar to Noelle's, since the technology used by other producers is likely to be very similar to what Noelle uses. If the price is high enough to generate profits for existing producers, it will also attract some of these potential producers into the industry. *In the long run,* then, a price in excess of $14 should lead to entry: new producers will come into the Christmas tree industry.

As we will see next, exit and entry lead to an important distinction between the *short-run industry supply curve* and the *long-run industry supply curve.*

Summing Up: The Perfectly Competitive Firm's Profitability and Production Conditions

In this chapter, we've studied where the supply curve for a perfectly competitive, price-taking firm comes from. Every perfectly competitive firm makes its production decisions by maximizing profit, and these decisions determine the supply curve. Table 7-4 summarizes the perfectly competitive firm's profitability and production conditions. It also relates them to entry into and exit from the industry.

TABLE 7-4 Summary of the Perfectly Competitive Firm's Profitability and Production Conditions

Profitability condition (minimum *ATC* = break-even price)	Result
$P >$ minimum *ATC*	Firm profitable. Entry into industry in the long run.
$P =$ minimum *ATC*	Firm breaks even. No entry into or exit from industry in the long run.
$P <$ minimum *ATC*	Firm unprofitable. Exit from industry in the long run.

Profitability condition (minimum *AVC* = shut-down price)	Result
$P >$ minimum *AVC*	Firm produces in the short run. If $P <$ minimum *ATC*, firm covers variable cost and some but not all of fixed cost. If $P >$ minimum *ATC*, firm covers all variable cost and fixed cost.
$P =$ minimum *AVC*	Firm indifferent between producing in the short run or not. Just covers variable cost.
$P <$ minimum *AVC*	Firm shuts down in the short run. Does not cover variable cost.

Farmers show their economic acumen by moving up and down their supply curves as crop prices change.

ECONOMICS >> *in Action*
Farmers Know How

If there is one profession that requires a firm understanding of profit maximization, it's farming. Farmers must respond to constantly fluctuating prices for their output, as well as constantly changing input prices. Furthermore, the farming industry satisfies the condition of a competitive market because it is composed of thousands of individual price-taking farmers.

For a good illustration of farmers' economic acumen we can look at the recent history of American crop and farmland prices for the years 2003 to 2013. During this decade, prices for corn and soybeans rose steadily, reaching an all-time high in 2012 and 2013 as corn and soybean prices increased by 300% and 250%, respectively.

This long-term rise was mainly due to two demand-based factors. First, corn prices benefited from a congressional mandate to increase the use of corn-based ethanol, a biofuel that is blended into gasoline, as a means of reducing American dependency on imported oil. Second, crop prices were pushed upward by rapidly rising exports to China and other developing countries.

Being smart profit-maximizers, farmers responded by farming their land more intensively—using more fertilizer, for example—and by increasing their acreage. By 2013, fertilizer prices had doubled compared to 2005. And over the decade from 2003 to 2013, the average price of farmland tripled, with some farmland selling for 10 times its 2003 price.

Doing this made complete economic sense, as each farmer moved up his or her individual supply curve. And because the individual supply curve is the marginal cost curve, each farmer's costs also went up as more inputs were employed to produce more output.

By 2016, however, crop prices fell by more than 50% from their 2012 high as the oil boom from fracking pushed down the price of ethanol and a strong U.S. dollar reduced foreign buyers' demand for American crops. On the supply side, bumper harvests in 2014 sharply depressed crop prices.

Thinking like economists, farmers responded by moving back down their supply curve, withdrawing from production the most expensive land to cultivate and reducing their demand for additional acreage. As a result, the average price of Iowa farmland fell by 12% from 2012 to 2015, and, unsurprisingly, the price of fertilizer fell significantly as well.

>> Check Your Understanding 7-2
Solutions appear at back of book.

1. Draw a short-run diagram showing a U-shaped average total cost curve, a U-shaped average variable cost curve, and a "swoosh"-shaped marginal cost curve. On it, indicate the range of output and the range of price for which the following actions are optimal.
   a. The firm shuts down immediately.
   b. The firm operates in the short run despite sustaining a loss.
   c. The firm operates while making a profit.

2. Maine has a very active lobster industry, which harvests lobsters during the summer months. The rest of the year lobsters can be obtained from other parts of the world, but at a much higher price. Maine is also full of "lobster shacks," roadside restaurants serving lobster dishes that are open only during the summer. Explain why it is optimal for lobster shacks to operate only in the summer.

The Industry Supply Curve Under Perfect Competition

Why will an increase in the demand for Christmas trees lead to a large price increase at first but a much smaller increase in the long run? The answer lies in the behavior of the **industry supply curve**—the relationship between the price and the total output of an industry as a whole. The industry supply curve is what we referred to in earlier chapters as *the* supply curve or the market supply curve. But here we take some extra care to distinguish between the *individual supply curve* of a single firm and the supply curve of the industry as a whole.

As you might guess from the previous section, the industry supply curve must be analyzed in somewhat different ways for the short run and the long run. Let's start with the short run.

The Short-Run Industry Supply Curve

Recall that in the short run the number of producers in an industry is fixed—there is no entry or exit. And you may also remember from Chapter 3 that the market supply curve is the horizontal sum of the individual supply curves of all

The **industry supply curve** shows the relationship between the price of a good and the total output of the industry as a whole.

The **short-run industry supply curve** shows how the quantity supplied by an industry depends on the market price given a fixed number of producers.

There is a **short-run market equilibrium** when the quantity supplied equals the quantity demanded, taking the number of producers as given.

producers—you find it by summing the total output across all suppliers at every given price. We will do that exercise here under the assumption that all the producers are alike—an assumption that makes the derivation particularly simple. So let's assume there are 100 Christmas tree farms, each with the same costs as Noelle's farm.

Each of these 100 farms will have an individual short-run supply curve like the one in Figure 7-4. At a price below $10, no farms will produce. At a price of $10 or more, each farm will produce the quantity of output at which its marginal cost is equal to the market price. As you can see from Figure 7-4, this will lead each farm to produce 40 trees if the price is $14 per tree, 50 trees if the price is $18, and so on. So, if there are 100 tree farms and the price of Christmas trees is $18 per tree, the industry as a whole will produce 5,000 trees, corresponding to 100 farms × 50 trees per farm, and so on. The result is the **short-run industry supply curve,** shown as S in Figure 7-5. This curve shows the quantity that producers will supply at each price, *taking the number of producers as given.*

The demand curve D in Figure 7-5 crosses the short-run industry supply curve at E_{MKT}, corresponding to a price of $18 and a quantity of 5,000 trees. Point E_{MKT} is a **short-run market equilibrium:** the quantity supplied equals the quantity demanded, taking the number of producers as given. But the long run may look quite different, because in the long run farms may enter or exit the industry.

Long-Run Market Equilibrium

Suppose that in addition to the 100 farms currently in the Christmas tree business, there are many other potential producers. Suppose also that each of these potential producers would have the same cost curves as existing producers like Noelle if it entered the industry.

When will additional producers enter the industry? Whenever existing producers are making a profit—that is, whenever the market price is above the break-even price of $14 per tree, the minimum average total cost of production. For example, at a price of $18 per tree, new firms will enter the industry.

What will happen as additional producers enter the industry? Clearly, the quantity supplied at any given price will increase. The short-run industry supply curve will shift to the right. This will, in turn, alter the market equilibrium and result in a lower market price. Existing firms will respond to the lower market

FIGURE 7-5 The Short-Run Market Equilibrium

The short-run industry supply curve, S, is the industry supply curve taking the number of producers—here, 100—as given. It is generated by adding together the individual supply curves of the 100 producers. Below the shut-down price of $10, no producer wants to produce in the short run. Above $10, the short-run industry supply curve slopes upward, as each producer increases output as price increases. It intersects the demand curve, D, at point E_{MKT}, the point of short-run market equilibrium, corresponding to a market price of $18 and a quantity of 5,000 trees.

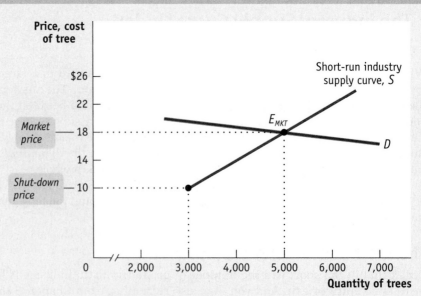

price by reducing their output, but the total industry output will increase because of the larger number of firms in the industry.

Figure 7-6 illustrates the effects of this chain of events on an existing firm and on the market; panel (a) shows how the market responds to entry, and panel (b) shows how an individual existing firm responds to entry. (Note that these two graphs have been rescaled in comparison to Figures 7-4 and 7-5 to better illustrate how profit changes in response to price.) In panel (a), S_1 is the initial short-run industry supply curve, based on the existence of 100 producers. The initial short-run market equilibrium is at E_{MKT}, with an equilibrium market price of $18 and a quantity of 5,000 trees. At this price existing producers are profitable, which is reflected in panel (b): an existing firm makes a total profit represented by the green-shaded rectangle labeled A when market price is $18.

These profits will induce new producers to enter the industry, shifting the short-run industry supply curve to the right. For example, the short-run industry supply curve when the number of producers has increased to 167 is S_2. Corresponding to this supply curve is a new short-run market equilibrium labeled D_{MKT}, with a market price of $16 and a quantity of 7,500 trees. At $16, each firm produces 45 trees, so that industry output is $167 \times 45 = 7{,}500$ trees (rounded).

From panel (b) you can see the effect of the entry of 67 new producers on an existing firm: the fall in price causes it to reduce its output, and its profit falls to the area represented by the striped rectangle labeled B.

Although diminished, the profit of existing firms at D_{MKT} means that entry will continue and the number of firms will continue to rise. If the number of

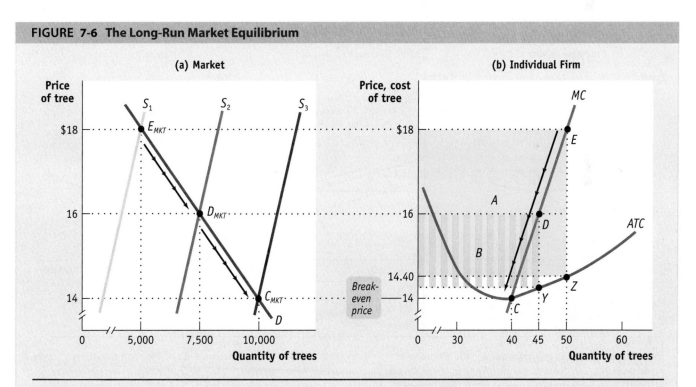

FIGURE 7-6 The Long-Run Market Equilibrium

Point E_{MKT} of panel (a) shows the initial short-run market equilibrium. Each of the 100 existing producers makes an economic profit, illustrated in panel (b) by the green rectangle labeled A, the profit of an existing firm. Profits induce entry by additional producers, shifting the short-run industry supply curve outward from S_1 to S_2 in panel (a), resulting in a new short-run equilibrium at point D_{MKT}, at a lower market price of $16 and higher industry output. Existing firms reduce output and profit falls to the area given by the striped rectangled labeled B in panel (b). Entry continues to shift out the short-run industry supply curve, as price falls and industry output increases yet again. Entry of new firms ceases at point C_{MKT} on supply curve S_3 in panel (a). Here market price is equal to the break-even price; existing producers make zero economic profits, and there is no incentive for entry or exit. So C_{MKT} is also a long-run market equilibrium.

A market is in **long-run market equilibrium** when the quantity supplied equals the quantity demanded, given that sufficient time has elapsed for entry into and exit from the industry to occur.

producers rises to 250, the short-run industry supply curve shifts out again to S_3, and the market equilibrium is at C_{MKT}, with a quantity supplied and demanded of 10,000 trees and a market price of $14 per tree.

Like E_{MKT} and D_{MKT}, C_{MKT} is a short-run equilibrium. But it is also something more. Because the price of $14 is each firm's break-even price, an existing producer makes zero economic profit—neither a profit nor a loss, earning only the opportunity cost of the resources used in production—when producing its profit-maximizing output of 40 trees.

At the break-even price there is no incentive either for potential producers to enter or for existing producers to exit the industry. So C_{MKT} corresponds to a **long-run market equilibrium**—a situation in which the quantity supplied equals the quantity demanded given that sufficient time has elapsed for producers to either enter or exit the industry. *In a long-run market equilibrium, all existing and potential producers have fully adjusted to their optimal long-run choices. As a result, all entry and exit ceases, and each firm makes zero economic profit.*

The Long-Run Industry Supply Curve

To explore further the significance of the difference between short-run and long-run equilibrium, consider the effect of an increase in demand on an industry with free entry that is initially in long-run equilibrium. Panel (b) in Figure 7-7 shows

FIGURE 7-7 The Effect of an Increase in Demand in the Short Run and the Long Run

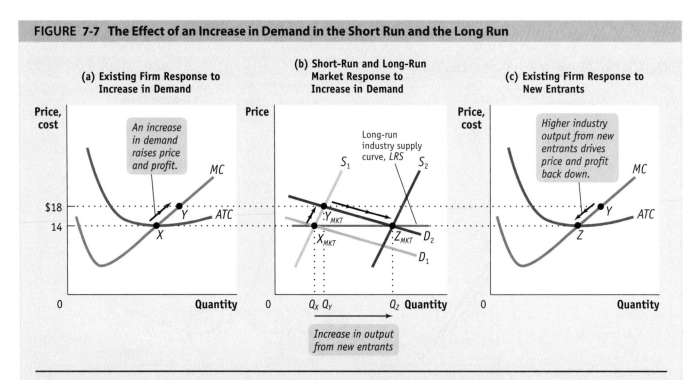

Panel (b) shows how an industry adjusts in the short and long run to an increase in demand; panels (a) and (c) show the corresponding adjustments by an existing firm. Initially the market is at point X_{MKT} in panel (b), a short-run and long-run equilibrium at a price of $14 and industry output of Q_X. An existing firm makes zero economic profit, operating at point X in panel (a) at minimum average total cost. Demand increases as D_1 shifts rightward to D_2 in panel (b), raising the market price to $18. Existing firms increase their output, and industry output moves along the short-run industry supply curve S_1 to a short-run equilibrium at Y_{MKT}. Correspondingly, the existing firm in panel (a) moves from point X to point Y. But at a price of $18 existing firms are profitable. As shown in panel (b),

in the long run new entrants arrive and the short-run industry supply curve shifts rightward, from S_1 to S_2. There is a new equilibrium at point Z_{MKT}, at a lower price of $14 and higher industry output of Q_Z. An existing firm responds by moving from Y to Z in panel (c), returning to its initial output level and zero economic profit. Production by new entrants accounts for the total increase in industry output, $Q_Z - Q_X$. Like X_{MKT}, Z_{MKT} is also a short-run and long-run equilibrium: with existing firms earning zero economic profit, there is no incentive for any firms to enter or exit the industry. The horizontal line passing through X_{MKT} and Z_{MKT}, *LRS*, is the long-run industry supply curve: at the break-even price of $14, producers will produce any amount that consumers demand in the long run.

the market adjustment; panels (a) and (c) show how an existing individual firm behaves during the process.

In panel (b) of Figure 7-7, D_1 is the initial demand curve and S_1 is the initial short-run industry supply curve. Their intersection at point X_{MKT} is both a short-run and a long-run market equilibrium because the equilibrium price of \$14 leads to zero economic profit—and therefore neither entry nor exit. It corresponds to point X in panel (a), where an individual existing firm is operating at the minimum of its average total cost curve.

Now suppose that the demand curve shifts out to D_2. As shown in panel (b), in the short run, industry output moves along the short-run industry supply curve S_1 to the new short-run market equilibrium at Y_{MKT}, the intersection of S_1 and D_2. The market price rises to \$18 per tree, and industry output increases from Q_X to Q_Y. This corresponds to an existing firm's movement from X to Y in panel (a) as the firm increases its output in response to the rise in the market price.

But we know that Y_{MKT} is not a long-run equilibrium, because \$18 is higher than minimum average total cost, and thus existing producers are making economic profits. This will lead additional firms to enter the industry.

Over time entry will cause the short-run industry supply curve to shift to the right. In the long run, the short-run industry supply curve will have shifted out to S_2, and the equilibrium will be at Z_{MKT}—with the price falling back to \$14 per tree and industry output increasing yet again, from Q_Y to Q_Z. Like X_{MKT} before the increase in demand, Z_{MKT} is both a short-run and a long-run market equilibrium.

The effect of entry on an existing firm is illustrated in panel (c), in the movement from Y to Z along the firm's individual supply curve. The firm reduces its output in response to the fall in the market price, ultimately arriving back at its original output quantity, corresponding to the minimum of its average total cost curve. In fact, every firm that is now in the industry—the initial set of firms and the new entrants—will operate at the minimum of its average total cost curve, at point Z. This means that the entire increase in industry output, from Q_X to Q_Z, comes from production by new entrants.

The line *LRS* that passes through X_{MKT} and Z_{MKT} in panel (b) is the **long-run industry supply curve.** It shows how the quantity supplied by an industry responds to the price, given that producers have had time to enter or exit the industry.

In this particular case, the long-run industry supply curve is horizontal at \$14. In other words, in this industry supply is *perfectly elastic* in the long run: given time to enter or exit, producers will supply any quantity that consumers demand at a price of \$14. Perfectly elastic long-run supply is actually a good assumption for many industries. In this case we speak of there being *constant costs across the industry:* each firm, regardless of whether it is an incumbent or a new entrant, faces the same cost structure (that is, they each have the same cost curves). Industries that satisfy this condition are those in which there is a perfectly elastic supply of inputs—industries like agriculture or bakeries.

In other industries, however, even the long-run industry supply curve slopes upward. The usual reason for this is that producers must use some input that is in limited supply (that is, inelastically supplied). As the industry expands, the price of that input is driven up. Consequently, later entrants in the industry find that they have a higher cost structure than early entrants. An example is beachfront resort hotels, which must compete for a limited quantity of prime beachfront property. Industries that behave like this are said to have *increasing costs across the industry.*

It is possible for the long-run industry supply curve to slope downward. This can occur when an industry faces increasing returns to scale, in which average costs fall as output rises. Notice that we said that the *industry* faces increasing returns. However, when increasing returns apply at the level of the individual firm, the industry usually ends up dominated by a small number of firms (an *oligopoly*) or a single firm (a *monopoly*).

The **long-run industry supply curve** shows how the quantity supplied responds to the price once producers have had time to enter or exit the industry.

In some cases, the advantages of large scale for an entire industry accrue to all firms in that industry. For example, the costs of new technologies such as solar panels tend to fall as the industry grows because that growth leads to improved knowledge, a larger pool of workers with the right skills, and so on.

Regardless of whether the long-run industry supply curve is horizontal or upward sloping or even downward sloping, the long-run price elasticity of supply is *higher* than the short-run price elasticity whenever there is free entry and exit. As shown in Figure 7-8, the long-run industry supply curve is always flatter than the short-run industry supply curve. The reason is entry and exit: a high price caused by an increase in demand attracts entry by new producers, resulting in a rise in industry output and an eventual fall in price; a low price caused by a decrease in demand induces existing firms to exit, leading to a fall in industry output and an eventual increase in price.

The distinction between the short-run industry supply curve and the long-run industry supply curve is very important in practice. We often see a sequence of events like that shown in Figure 7-7: an increase in demand initially leads to a large price increase, but prices return to their initial level once new firms have entered the industry. Or we see the sequence in reverse: a fall in demand reduces prices in the short run, but they return to their initial level as producers exit the industry.

The Cost of Production and Efficiency in Long-Run Equilibrium

Our analysis leads us to three conclusions about the cost of production and efficiency in the long-run equilibrium of a perfectly competitive industry. These results will be important in our discussion in Chapter 8 of how monopoly gives rise to inefficiency.

1. **In a perfectly competitive industry in equilibrium, the value of marginal cost is the same for all firms.** That's because all firms produce the quantity of output at which marginal cost equals the market price, and as price-takers they all face the same market price.

2. **In a perfectly competitive industry with free entry and exit, each firm will have zero economic profit in long-run equilibrium.** Each firm produces the quantity of output that minimizes its average total cost—corresponding to

---

FIGURE 7-8 Comparing the Short-Run and Long-Run Industry Supply Curves

The long-run industry supply curve may slope upward, but it is always flatter—more elastic—than the short-run industry supply curve. This is because of entry and exit: a higher price attracts new entrants in the long run, resulting in a rise in industry output and a fall in price; a lower price induces existing producers to exit in the long run, generating a fall in industry output and an eventual rise in price.

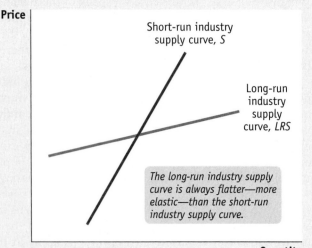

The long-run industry supply curve is always flatter—more elastic—than the short-run industry supply curve.

point *Z* in panel (c) of Figure 7-7. So the total cost of production of the industry's output is minimized in a perfectly competitive industry.

The exception is an industry with increasing costs across the industry. Given a sufficiently high market price, early entrants make positive economic profits, but the last entrants do not as the market price falls. Costs are minimized for later entrants, as the industry reaches long-run equilibrium, but not necessarily for the early ones.

3. **The long-run market equilibrium of a perfectly competitive industry is efficient: no mutually beneficial transactions go unexploited.** To understand this, recall a fundamental requirement for efficiency: all consumers who have a willingness to pay greater than or equal to sellers' costs actually get the good. In addition, when a market is efficient (except under certain, well-defined conditions), the market price matches all consumers with a willingness to pay greater than or equal to the market price to all sellers who have a cost of producing the good less than or equal to the market price.

So, in the long-run equilibrium of a perfectly competitive industry, production is efficient: costs are minimized and no resources are wasted. In addition, the allocation of goods to consumers is efficient: every consumer willing to pay the cost of producing a unit of the good gets it. Indeed, no mutually beneficial transaction is left unexploited. Moreover, this condition tends to persist over time as the environment changes: the force of competition makes producers responsive to changes in consumers' desires and to changes in technology.

ECONOMICS >> *in Action*
Thirsty? From Global Wine Glut to Shortage

In 2016, if you were a wine producer and still in business, you probably considered yourself very fortunate. Why? Because you had survived some very tough years in the wine industry caused by a global wine glut.

From 2004 to 2010, the wine industry was battered by an oversupply of wine arising from a long-term increase in wine grape acreage planted around the world, a series of large global harvests, and a sharp fall in demand in the wake of the global recession of 2008. When wine prices plunged, many wine producers were compelled to call it quits. The glut was so severe that European governments began paying farmers to grow fewer grapes. By 2012 French wine production had fallen 17% while Spanish production had fallen by 11%.

However, circumstances changed dramatically by 2016; the glut turned into a shortage and wine producers were happily struggling to keep up with demand. What caused the glut and then the sharp reversal into shortage? The answer is supply and demand forces leading to entry and exit in the wine industry. In the 2000s, growing global demand led to more entry into the wine industry as the industry moved up the short-run industry supply curve. Oversupply, along with the 2008 recession, led to a fall in demand and then to plunging prices and the exit of some wine producers, a move down the short-run industry supply curve.

But with the recovery in global demand and the reduced supply of wine, prices rose again. In France, 2016 grape prices were at a 10-year high. No doubt, higher prices will eventually draw more producers back into the industry. So hold onto your wine glasses—the present shortage could turn into a glut once again.

History shows that a wine shortage is likely to lead to a wine glut as more producers enter the industry.

>> *Quick Review*

>> *Quick Review*

• The **industry supply curve** corresponds to the supply curve of earlier chapters. In the short run, the time period over which the number of producers is fixed, the **short-run market equilibrium** is given by the intersection of the **short-run industry supply curve** and the demand curve. In the long run, the time period over which producers can enter or exit the industry, the **long-run market equilibrium** is given by the intersection of the **long-run industry supply curve** and the demand curve. In the long-run market equilibrium, no producer has an incentive to enter or exit the industry.

• The long-run industry supply curve is often horizontal, although it may slope upward when a necessary input is in limited supply. It is always more elastic than the short-run industry supply curve.

• In the long-run market equilibrium of a perfectly competitive industry, each firm produces at the same marginal cost, which is equal to the market price, and the total cost of production of the industry's output is minimized. It is also efficient.

>> *Check Your Understanding 7-3*
Solutions appear at back of book.

1. Which of the following events will induce firms to enter an industry? Which will induce firms to exit? When will entry or exit cease? Explain your answer.
   a. A technological advance lowers the fixed cost of production of every firm in the industry.
   b. The wages paid to workers in the industry go up for an extended period of time.
   c. A permanent change in consumer tastes increases demand for the good.
   d. The price of a key input rises due to a long-term shortage of that input.

2. Assume that the egg industry is perfectly competitive and is in long-run equilibrium with a perfectly elastic long-run industry supply curve. Health concerns about cholesterol then lead to a decrease in demand. Construct a figure similar to Figure 7-7, showing the short-run behavior of the industry and how long-run equilibrium is reestablished.

SOLVED PROBLEM   Is There a Catch?

Seattle's Pike Place Fish Market is well known for its freshly caught salmon, halibut, and Alaskan King Crab and for its entertaining staff, who hurl a fish into the air on its way to wrapping and checkout.

Consider the following hypothetical daily costs for one of the market's suppliers, a fisherman who runs a boat that fishes primarily for Chinook salmon. Each day begins with the decision of whether to take out the boat, given the price he expects to receive at the fish market. Whether he goes out or not, he incurs fixed costs such as dockage, licensing, and the mortgage on the boat. In addition to fixed costs, he incurs a variable cost for each fish brought back to port. So, he must also decide how much to catch.

Using the following table, calculate average variable cost, average total cost, and marginal cost to find the break-even price per fish. If the market price falls to $14.00 per fish, in the short run, how many fish will the fisherman bring to market?

Quantity of fish Q	Variable cost VC	Total cost TC
30	$280	$680
40	320	720
50	440	840
60	600	1,000
70	840	1,240
80	1,160	1,560
90	1,560	1,960
100	2,040	2,440

STEP | 1 Find the average variable cost, average total cost, and marginal cost of a box of fish. *Review pages 179–183 in Chapter 6, and Equations 6-3, 6-4, and 6-5.*

The average variable cost is equal to the variable cost divided by the quantity (VC/Q), the average total cost is equal to the total cost divided by the quantity (TC/Q), and the marginal cost is the change in the total cost divided by the change in the quantity ($\Delta TC/\Delta Q$). These costs are calculated for each row in the following table.

Quantity of fish Q	Variable cost VC	Total cost TC	Marginal cost MC = ΔTC/ΔQ	Average variable cost AVC = VC/Q	Average total cost ATC = TQ/Q
30	$280	$680		$9.33	$22.67
			$4.00		
40	320	720		8.00	18.00
			12.00		
50	440	840		8.80	16.80
			16.00		
60	600	1,000		10.00	16.67
			24.00		
70	840	1,240		12.00	17.71
			32.00		
80	1,160	1,560		14.50	19.50
			40.00		
90	1,560	1,960		17.33	21.78
			48.00		
100	2,040	2,440		20.40	24.40

STEP | 2 Find the break-even price per fish. *Review pages 203–207 and Figure 7-2.*

To find the break-even price, we need to find the minimum average total cost of production. In the table, the minimum average total cost occurs at 60 fish. Thus, the break-even price is $16.67 per fish.

STEP | 3 If the market price falls to $14.00 per fish, in the short run how many fish will be brought to market? *Review pages 201–203 and the Pitfalls on page 203.*

In the case of the price-taking firm, the marginal revenue is equal to the market price. So, to find the optimal quantity, we need to find the point where $P = MC$. If there is not a point on the table at which $P = MC$, then the fisherman will want to produce the largest quantity for which P exceeds MC. Going from 40 to 50 fish, the MC is $12.00, but going from 50 to 60 fish, the MC is $16.00. Hence, the largest quantity for which P exceeds MC is 50 fish. Although price is less than average total cost, he will still fish because the price is greater than his average variable cost.

SUMMARY

1. In a **perfectly competitive market** all producers are **price-taking producers** and all consumers are **price-taking consumers**—no one's actions can influence the market price. Consumers are normally price-takers, but producers often are not. In a **perfectly competitive industry,** all producers are price-takers.

2. There are two necessary conditions for a perfectly competitive industry: there are many producers, none of whom have a large **market share,** and the industry produces a **standardized product** or **commodity**—goods that consumers regard as equivalent. A third condition is often satisfied as well: **free entry and exit** into and from the industry.

3. The **marginal benefit** of a good or service is the additional benefit derived from producing one more unit of that good or service. The **principle of marginal analysis** says that the optimal amount of an activity is the level at which marginal benefit equals marginal cost.

4. A producer chooses output according to the **optimal output rule:** produce the quantity at which **marginal revenue** equals marginal cost. For a price-taking firm, marginal revenue is equal to price and its **marginal revenue curve** is a horizontal line at the market price. It chooses output according to the **price-taking firm's optimal output rule:** produce the quantity at which price equals marginal cost. However, a firm that produces the optimal quantity may not be profitable.

5. Companies should base decisions on **economic profit,** which takes into account explicit costs that involve an actual outlay of cash as well as implicit costs that do not require an outlay of cash, but are measured by the value, in dollar terms, of benefits that are forgone. The **accounting profit** is often considerably larger than the economic profit because it includes only explicit costs and depreciation, not implicit costs.

6. Whether a producer is profitable depends on a comparison of the market price of the good to the producer's **break-even price**—its minimum average total cost. If market price exceeds the break-even price, the firm is profitable; if it is less, the firm is unprofitable; if it is equal, the firm breaks even. When profitable, the firm's per-unit profit is $P - ATC;$ when unprofitable, its per-unit loss is $ATC - P$.

7. Like **sunk cost,** fixed cost is irrelevant to the firm's optimal short-run production decision, which depends on its **shut-down price**—its minimum average variable cost—and the market price. When the market price is equal to or exceeds the shut-down price, the firm produces the output quantity where marginal cost equals the market price. When the market price falls below the shut-down price, the firm should cease production. When price lies between minimum average total cost (break-even price) and minimum average variable cost (shut-down price), the firm produces in the short run to minimize loss. This defines the firm's **short-run individual supply curve.**

8. Fixed cost matters over time. If the market price is below minimum average total cost for an extended period of time, firms will exit the industry in the long run. If above, existing firms are profitable and new firms will enter the industry in the long run.

9. The **industry supply curve** under perfect competition depends on the time period. The **short-run industry supply curve** is the industry supply curve, given that the number of firms is fixed. The **short-run market equilibrium** is given by the intersection of the short-run industry supply curve and the demand curve.

10. The **long-run industry supply curve** is the industry supply curve given sufficient time for entry into and exit from the industry. In the **long-run market equilibrium**—given by the intersection of the long-run industry supply curve and the demand curve—no producer has an incentive to enter or exit. The long-run industry supply curve is often horizontal. It may slope upward if there is limited supply of an input, resulting in increasing costs across the industry. It may even slope downward, the case of decreasing costs across the industry. But it is always more elastic than the short-run industry supply curve.

11. In the long-run market equilibrium of a competitive industry, profit maximization leads each firm to produce at the same marginal cost, which is equal to market price. Free entry and exit means that each firm earns zero economic profit—producing the output corresponding to its minimum average total cost. So the total cost of production of an industry's output is minimized. The outcome is efficient because every consumer with a willingness to pay greater than or equal to marginal cost gets the good.

KEY TERMS

Price-taking producer, p. 198
Price-taking consumer, p. 198
Perfectly competitive market, p. 198
Perfectly competitive industry, p. 198
Market share, p. 199
Standardized product, p. 199
Commodity, p. 199
Free entry and exit, p. 199

Marginal benefit, p. 201
Principle of marginal analysis, p. 201
Marginal revenue, p. 201
Optimal output rule, p. 201
Marginal revenue curve, p. 203
Price-taking firm's optimal output rule, p. 203
Economic profit, p. 203
Accounting profit, p. 203

Break-even price, p. 206
Shut-down price, p. 207
Sunk cost, p. 208
Short-run individual supply curve, p. 208
Industry supply curve, p. 211
Short-run industry supply curve, p. 212
Short-run market equilibrium, p. 212
Long-run market equilibrium, p. 214
Long-run industry supply curve, p. 215

DISCUSSION QUESTIONS

1. The accompanying table, taken from a survey of California dry cleaners, presents prices for washing and ironing a shirt.

Dry cleaner	City	Price
A-1 Cleaners	Santa Barbara	$1.50
Regal Cleaners	Santa Barbara	1.95
St. Paul Cleaners	Santa Barbara	1.95
Zip Kleen Dry Cleaners	Santa Barbara	1.95
Effie the Tailor	Santa Barbara	2.00
Magnolia Too	Goleta	2.00
Master Cleaners	Santa Barbara	2.00
Santa Barbara Cleaners	Goleta	2.00
Sunny Cleaners	Santa Barbara	2.00
Casitas Cleaners	Carpinteria	2.10
Rockwell Cleaners	Carpinteria	2.10
Norvelle Bass Cleaners	Santa Barbara	2.15
Ablitt's Fine Cleaners	Santa Barbara	2.25
California Cleaners	Goleta	2.25
Justo the Tailor	Santa Barbara	2.25
Pressed 4 Time	Goleta	2.50
King's Cleaners	Goleta	2.50

a. What is the average price per shirt washed and ironed in Goleta? In Santa Barbara?

b. Draw typical marginal cost and average total cost curves for California Cleaners in Goleta, assuming it is a perfectly competitive firm but is making a profit on each shirt in the short run. Mark the short-run equilibrium point and shade the area that corresponds to the profit made by the dry cleaner.

c. Assume $2.25 is the short-run equilibrium price in Goleta. Draw a typical short-run demand and supply curve for the market. Label the equilibrium point.

d. Observing profits in the Goleta area, another dry cleaning service, Diamond Cleaners, enters the market. It charges $1.95 per shirt. What is the new average price of washing and ironing a shirt in Goleta? Illustrate the effect of entry on the average Goleta price by a shift of the short-run supply curve, the demand curve, or both.

e. Assume that California Cleaners now charges the new average price and just breaks even (that is, makes zero economic profit) at this price. Show the likely effect of the entry on your diagram in part b.

f. If the dry cleaning industry is perfectly competitive, what does the average difference in price between Goleta and Santa Barbara imply about costs in the two areas?

PROBLEMS

interactive activity

1. For each of the following, is the business a price-taking producer? Explain your answers.

   a. A cappuccino café in a university town where there are dozens of very similar cappuccino cafés

   b. The makers of Pepsi

   c. One of many zucchini sellers at a local farmers' market

2. For each of the following, is the industry perfectly competitive? Referring to market share, standardization of the product, and/or free entry and exit, explain your answers.

   a. Aspirin

   b. Alicia Keys concerts

   c. SUVs

3. Bob produces Blu-ray movies for sale, which requires a building and a machine that copies the original movie onto a Blu-ray. Bob rents a building for $30,000 per month and rents a machine for $20,000 a month. Those are his fixed costs. His variable cost per month is given in the accompanying table.

Quantity of Blu-rays	VC
0	$0
1,000	5,000
2,000	8,000
3,000	9,000
4,000	14,000
5,000	20,000
6,000	33,000
7,000	49,000
8,000	72,000
9,000	99,000
10,000	150,000

a. Calculate Bob's average variable cost, average total cost, and marginal cost for each quantity of output.

b. There is free entry into the industry, and anyone who enters will face the same costs as Bob. Suppose that currently the price of a Blu-ray is $25. What will Bob's profit be? Is this a long-run equilibrium? If not, what will the price of Blu-ray movies be in the long run?

4. Consider Bob's Blu-ray company described in Problem 3. Assume that Blu-ray production is a perfectly competitive industry. For each of the following questions, explain your answers.

a. What is Bob's break-even price? What is his shut-down price?

b. Suppose the price of a Blu-ray is $2. What should Bob do in the short run?

c. Suppose the price of a Blu-ray is $7. What is the profit-maximizing quantity of Blu-rays that Bob should produce? What will his total profit be? Will he produce or shut down in the short run? Will he stay in the industry or exit in the long run?

d. Suppose instead that the price of Blu-rays is $20. Now what is the profit-maximizing quantity of Blu-rays that Bob should produce? What will his total profit be now? Will he produce or shut down in the short run? Will he stay in the industry or exit in the long run?

5. Consider again Bob's Blu-ray company described in Problem 3.

a. Draw Bob's marginal cost curve.

b. Over what range of prices will Bob produce no Blu-rays in the short run?

c. Draw Bob's individual supply curve. In your graph, plot the price range from $0 to $60 in increments of $10.

6. a. A profit-maximizing business incurs an economic loss of $10,000 per year. Its fixed cost is $15,000 per year. Should it produce or shut down in the short run? Should it stay in the industry or exit in the long run?

b. Suppose instead that this business has a fixed cost of $6,000 per year. Should it produce or shut down in the short run? Should it stay in the industry or exit in the long run?

7. The first sushi restaurant opens in town. Initially people are very cautious about eating tiny portions of raw fish, as this is a town where large portions of grilled meat have always been popular. Soon, however, an influential health report warns consumers against grilled meat and suggests that they increase their consumption of fish, especially raw fish. The sushi restaurant becomes very popular and its profit increases.

a. What will happen to the short-run profit of the sushi restaurant? What will happen to the number of sushi restaurants in town in the long run? Will the first sushi restaurant be able to sustain its short-run profit over the long run? Explain your answers.

b. Local steakhouses suffer from the popularity of sushi and start incurring losses. What will happen to the number of steakhouses in town in the long run? Explain your answer.

8. A perfectly competitive firm has the following short-run total cost:

Quantity	TC
0	$5
1	10
2	13
3	18
4	25
5	34
6	45

Market demand for the firm's product is given by the following market demand schedule:

Price	Quantity demanded
$12	300
10	500
8	800
6	1,200
4	1,800

a. Calculate this firm's marginal cost and, for all output levels except zero, the firm's average variable cost and average total cost.

b. There are 100 firms in this industry that all have costs identical to those of this firm. Draw the short-run industry supply curve. In the same diagram, draw the market demand curve.

c. What is the market price, and how much profit will each firm make?

9. A new vaccine against a deadly disease has just been discovered. Presently, 55 people die from the disease each year. The new vaccine will save lives, but it is not completely safe. Some recipients of the shots will die from adverse reactions. The projected effects of the inoculation are given in the accompanying table:

Percent of population inoculated	Total deaths due to disease	Total deaths due to inoculation	Marginal benefit of inoculation	Marginal cost of inoculation	"Profit" of inoculation
0	55	0	–	–	–
10	45	0	–	–	–
20	36	1	–	–	–
30	28	3	–	–	–
40	21	6	–	–	–
50	15	10	–	–	–
60	10	15	–	–	–
70	6	20	–	–	–
80	3	25	–	–	–
90	1	30	–	–	–
100	0	35	–	–	–

a. What are the interpretations of "marginal benefit" and "marginal cost" here? Calculate marginal benefit and marginal cost per each 10% increase in the rate of inoculation. Write your answers in the table.

b. What proportion of the population should optimally be inoculated?

c. What is the interpretation of "profit" here? Calculate the profit for all levels of inoculation.

10. Evaluate each of the following statements. If a statement is true, explain why; if it is false, identify the mistake and try to correct it.

a. A profit-maximizing firm in a perfectly competitive industry should select the output level at which the difference between the market price and marginal cost is greatest.

b. An increase in fixed cost lowers the profit-maximizing quantity of output produced in the short run.

11. The production of agricultural products like wheat is one of the few examples of a perfectly competitive industry. In this question, we analyze results from a study released by the U.S. Department of Agriculture about wheat production in the United States in 2016.

a. The average variable cost per acre planted with wheat was $115 per acre. Assuming a yield of 44 bushels per acre, calculate the average variable cost per bushel of wheat.

b. The average price of wheat received by a farmer in 2016 was $4.89 per bushel. Do you think the average farm would have exited the industry in the short run? Explain.

c. With a yield of 44 bushels of wheat per acre, the average total cost per farm was $7.71 per bushel. The harvested acreage for wheat in the United States decreased from 48.8 million acres in 2013 to 43.9 million acres in 2016. Using the information on prices and costs here and in parts a and b, explain why this might have happened.

d. Using the above information, what do you think will happen to wheat production and prices after 2016?

WORK IT OUT Interactive step-by-step help with solving this problem can be found online.

12. Kate's Katering provides catered meals, and the catered meals industry is perfectly competitive. Kate's machinery costs $100 per day and is the only fixed input. Her variable cost consists of the wages paid to the cooks and the cost of the food ingredients. The variable cost per day associated with each level of output is given in the accompanying table.

Quantity of meals	VC
0	0
10	200
20	300
30	480
40	700
50	1,000

a. Calculate the total cost, the average variable cost, the average total cost, and the marginal cost for each quantity of output.

b. What is the break-even price and quantity? What is the shut-down price and quantity?

c. Suppose that the price at which Kate can sell catered meals is $21 per meal. In the short run, will Kate earn a profit? In the short run, should she produce or shut down?

d. Suppose that the price at which Kate can sell catered meals is $17 per meal. In the short run, will Kate earn a profit? In the short run, should she produce or shut down?

e. Suppose that the price at which Kate can sell catered meals is $13 per meal. In the short run, will Kate earn a profit? In the short run, should she produce or shut down?

If you like instant taste-bud gratification and live in one of the growing list of cities that enjoy Amazon's same-day one-hour restaurant delivery, life has become so much more gratifying. And if you live in one of the many locations where Amazon offers same-day delivery of merchandise, you may wait longer than an hour, but your goods will arrive at your doorstep that day.

We can thank Amazon's army of Kiva robots for the speedy deliveries. These robots spend their days hauling very tall shelves of merchandise, weighing up to 700 pounds, to human "pickers" who assemble orders, and to human "stockers" who sort incoming inventory.

By 2018 Amazon had more than 100,000 robots working in its 75 fulfillment centers, to help with distribution of the 5 billion items it carries. Before the arrival of bots, human employees did this tedious work, often walking 10 to 15 miles daily, carrying heavy loads. Without humans walking miles to the merchandise, warehouse operations have become much more efficient. In addition, because robots don't need aisles between shelves like people do, there's more room for merchandise storage in Amazon's fulfillment centers.

Over the past 20 years, Amazon has invested an enormous amount of money perfecting its warehouse management and order fulfillment operations to satisfy customers' desire to receive their items quickly. The company's spokesperson, Phil Hardin, explains the widespread use of robots this way: "It's an investment that has implications for a lot of elements of our cost structure. It has been a great innovation for us, . . . and we think it makes our warehouses more productive."

Analysts estimate that by using robots, Amazon has saved 48% of its costs of fulfilling an order.

And Amazon's competitors have definitely noticed. More companies, particularly other big-name retailers like Staples and Walmart, are using robotic systems for fast order fulfillment to compete with Amazon's speedy delivery times. However, with Amazon's huge advantage, it remains to be seen whether these other retailers can catch up.

QUESTIONS FOR THOUGHT

1. Describe the shift in Amazon's cost structure based on the concepts from this chapter. Is Amazon on a short-run or long-run cost curve? What are the relevant returns to scale in Amazon's operations?

2. What are the pros and cons of Amazon's strategy?

3. What advantage does a robotic system give Amazon over its rivals? How likely is it that they will catch up with Amazon? What market factors does it depend upon?

Brick-and-mortar retailers like Target, Best Buy, and Walmart have an exasperating problem that is threatening their very survival: shoppers who visit their stores, but not to buy the merchandise. Instead, these shoppers are *showrooming*—visiting a brick-and-mortar store to inspect the merchandise and then whipping out their smartphones to find the item at a cheaper price and then buying it online.

The explosive growth of mobile shopping apps has given customers a dizzying range of methods to pay less for their purchases. For example, Google Shopping and BuyVia allow shoppers to compare prices and make online purchases; ShopSavvy and ShopAdvisor send them discount alerts; and Coupons.com lets them search for coupon and promotion codes to apply to their purchases.

In 2017, U.S. sales on mobile devices grew to over $156 billion from $115 billion in 2016, and they are expected to nearly triple by 2021. The consulting firm Accenture found that 73% of customers with mobile devices prefer to shop with their phones rather than talk to a salesperson. Not surprisingly, by 2021, mobile phones will be responsible for nearly 54% of all retail e-commerce sales.

But brick-and-mortar retailers are fighting back. To combat showrooming, Target stocks products that manufacturers have slightly modified at Target's request, making it hard for showroomers to find an online comparison. Like other retailers, Target has been building its online presence, as well as sending coupons and discount alerts to customers' phones. Walmart offers free in-store delivery for online purchases so customers can avoid shipping charges. And Staples will give you a discount on a new printer if you bring in an old one.

However, traditional retailers know their survival rests on pricing. So Best Buy, Walmart, and Target will now match the prices of rival retailers. Walmart has even created a mobile app that allows shoppers to scan a Walmart receipt and compare the prices paid to competitors' advertised deals and get the difference back on a Walmart gift card.

It's clearly a race for survival. As one analyst said, "Only a couple of retailers can play the lowest-price game. This is going to accelerate the demise of retailers who do not have either competitive pricing or standout store experience."

QUESTIONS FOR THOUGHT

1. From the evidence in the case, what can you infer about whether or not the retail market for electronics satisfied the conditions for perfect competition before the advent of comparison price shopping via mobile app? What was the most important impediment to competition?

2. What effect is the introduction of shopping apps having on competition in the retail market for electronics? On the profitability of brick-and-mortar retailers like Best Buy? What, on average, will be the effect on the consumer surplus of purchasers of these items?

3. Why are some retailers responding by having manufacturers make slightly modified or exclusive versions of products for them? Is this trend likely to increase or diminish?

8 | Monopoly

EVERYBODY MUST GET STONES

SEVERAL YEARS AGO DE BEERS, the world's main supplier of diamonds, ran an ad urging husbands to buy their wives diamond jewelry. "She married you for richer, for poorer," read the ad. "Let her know how it's going."

Crass? Yes. Effective? No question. For generations diamonds have been a symbol of luxury, valued not only for their appearance but also for their rarity. But geologists will tell you that diamonds aren't all that rare. In fact, according to the *Dow Jones–Irwin Guide to Fine Gems and Jewelry,* diamonds are "more common than any other gem-quality colored stone. They only seem rarer . . ."

Why do diamonds seem rarer than other gems? Part of the answer is a brilliant marketing campaign. But mainly diamonds seem rare

because De Beers *makes* them rare: historically, the company controlled most of the world's diamond mines and limited the quantity of diamonds supplied to the market.

Up to now we have concentrated exclusively on perfectly competitive markets—markets in which the producers are perfect competitors. But De Beers isn't like the producers we've studied so far: it is a *monopolist,* the sole (or almost sole) producer of a good. Monopolists behave differently from producers in perfectly competitive industries: whereas perfect competitors take the price at which they can sell their output as given, monopolists know that their actions affect market prices and take that into account when deciding how much to produce.

Before we begin our analysis, let's step back and look at *monopoly* and perfect competition as parts of a broader system for classifying markets.

Perfect competition and monopoly are particular types of *market structure.* They are specific categories in a system economists use to classify markets and industries according to two main dimensions.

This chapter begins with a brief overview of types of market structure. It will help us here and in subsequent chapters to understand on a deeper level why markets differ and why producers in those markets behave quite differently. ●

"Got stones?"

WHAT YOU WILL LEARN

- What is the significance of **monopoly,** a type of industry in which only one producer, a **monopolist,** operates?

- How does being a monopolist affect a firm's price and output decisions?

- Why does the presence of monopoly typically reduce social welfare?

- What tools do policy makers use to address the problem of monopoly?

- What is **price discrimination** and why is it so prevalent in certain industries?

Types of Market Structure

In the real world, there is a mind-boggling array of different markets. We observe widely different behavior patterns by producers across markets. In some markets, firms are extremely competitive; in others, they seem somehow to coordinate their actions to avoid competing with one another; and, as we have just described in the opening story, some markets are monopolies in which there is no competition at all.

To develop principles and make predictions about markets and how producers will behave in them, economists have developed four primary models of market structure: *monopoly, oligopoly, perfect competition,* and *monopolistic competition.* This system of market structures is based on two dimensions:

1. The number of firms in the market (one, few, or many)

2. Whether the goods offered are identical or *differentiated*

Differentiated goods are goods that are different but considered somewhat substitutable by consumers (think Coke versus Pepsi).

Figure 8-1 provides a simple visual summary of the four types of market structure classified according to the two dimensions. In *monopoly,* a single producer sells a single, undifferentiated product. In *oligopoly,* a few producers—more than one but not a large number—sell products that may be either identical or differentiated. In *perfect competition,* as we know, many firms each sell an identical product. And finally, in *monopolistic competition,* many firms each sell a differentiated product (think of producers of economics textbooks).

You might wonder what determines the number of firms in a market: whether there is one (monopoly), a few (oligopoly), or many (perfect competition and monopolistic competition). We won't answer that question here because it will be covered in detail later in this chapter and in Chapter 9.

We will just briefly note that in the long run it depends on whether there are conditions that make it difficult for new firms to enter the market, such as control of necessary resources or inputs, increasing returns to scale in production, technological superiority, a network externality, or government regulations. When these conditions are present, industries tend to be monopolies or oligopolies; when they are not present, industries tend to be perfectly competitive or monopolistically competitive.

FIGURE 8-1 Types of Market Structure

The behavior of any given firm and the market it occupies are analyzed using one of four models of market structure—monopoly, oligopoly, perfect competition, or monopolistic competition. This system for categorizing market structure is based on two dimensions: (1) whether products are differentiated or identical, and (2) the number of producers in the industry—one, a few, or many.

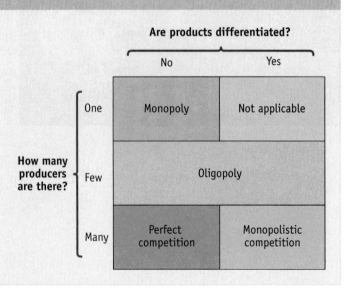

You might also wonder why some markets have differentiated products but others have identical ones. The answer is that it depends on the nature of the good and consumers' preferences. Some goods—soft drinks, economics textbooks, breakfast cereals—can readily be made into different varieties in the eyes and tastes of consumers. Other goods—Christmas trees or pencils, for example—are much less easy to differentiate.

Although this chapter is devoted to monopoly, important aspects of monopoly carry over to oligopoly and monopolistic competition. In the next section, we will define monopoly and review the conditions that make it possible. These same conditions, in less extreme form, also give rise to oligopoly. We then show how a monopolist can increase profit by limiting the quantity supplied to a market—behavior that also occurs in oligopoly and monopolistic competition.

As we'll see, this kind of behavior is good for the producer but bad for consumers; it also causes inefficiency. An important topic of study will be the ways in which public policy tries to limit the damage. Finally, we turn to one of the surprising effects of monopoly—one that is very often present in oligopoly and monopolistic competition as well: the fact that different consumers often pay different prices for the same good.

‖ The Meaning of Monopoly

The De Beers monopoly of South Africa was created in the 1880s by Cecil Rhodes, a British businessman. By 1880 mines in South Africa already dominated the world's supply of diamonds. There were, however, many mining companies, all competing with each other. During the 1880s Rhodes bought the great majority of those mines and consolidated them into a single company, De Beers. By 1889 De Beers controlled almost all of the world's diamond production.

De Beers, in other words, became a **monopolist.** A producer is a monopolist if it is the sole supplier of a good that has no close substitutes. When a firm is a monopolist, the industry is a **monopoly.**

Monopoly: Our First Departure from Perfect Competition

As we saw in Chapter 7, the supply and demand model of a market is not universally valid. Instead, it's a model of perfect competition, which is only one of several different types of market structure. A market will be perfectly competitive only if there are many producers, all of whom produce the same good. Monopoly is the most extreme departure from perfect competition.

In practice, true monopolies are hard to find in the modern American economy, partly because of legal obstacles. A contemporary entrepreneur who tried to consolidate all the firms in an industry the way that Rhodes did would soon land in court, accused of breaking *antitrust* laws, which are intended to prevent monopolies from emerging. Oligopoly, a market structure in which there is a small number of large producers, is much more common. In fact, most of the goods you buy, from cars to airline tickets, are supplied by oligopolies.

Monopolies do, however, play an important role in some sectors of the economy, such as pharmaceuticals. Furthermore, our analysis of monopoly will provide a foundation for our later analysis of other departures from perfect competition, such as oligopoly and monopolistic competition.

What Monopolists Do

Why did Rhodes want to consolidate South African diamond producers into a single company? What difference did it make to the world diamond market?

A **monopolist** is a firm that is the only producer of a good that has no close substitutes. An industry controlled by a monopolist is known as a **monopoly.**

Market power is the ability of a firm to raise prices.

Figure 8-2 offers a preliminary view of the effects of monopoly. It shows an industry in which the supply curve under perfect competition intersects the demand curve at C, leading to the price P_C and the output Q_C.

Suppose that this industry is consolidated into a monopoly. The monopolist *moves up the demand curve* by reducing quantity supplied to a point like M, at which the quantity produced, Q_M, is lower, and the price, P_M, is higher than under perfect competition.

The ability of a monopolist to raise its price above the competitive level by reducing output is known as **market power.** And market power is what monopoly is all about. A wheat farmer who is 1 of 100,000 wheat farmers has no market power: he or she must sell wheat at the going market price. Your local water utility company, though, does have market power: it can raise prices and still keep many (though not all) of its customers, because they have nowhere else to go. In short, it's a monopolist.

The reason a monopolist reduces output and raises price compared to the perfectly competitive industry levels is to increase profit. Cecil Rhodes consolidated the diamond producers into De Beers because he realized that the whole would be worth more than the sum of its parts—the monopoly would generate more profit than the sum of the profits of the individual competitive firms. Under perfect competition, economic profits normally vanish in the long run as competitors enter the market. Under monopoly the profits don't go away—a monopolist is able to continue earning economic profits in the long run.

In fact, monopolists are not the only types of firms that possess market power. In the next chapter we will study *oligopolists*, firms that can have market power as well. Under certain conditions, oligopolists can earn positive economic profits in the long run by restricting output like monopolists do.

But why don't profits get competed away? What allows monopolists to be monopolists?

FIGURE 8-2 What a Monopolist Does

Under perfect competition, the price and quantity are determined by supply and demand. Here, the competitive equilibrium is at C, where the price is P_C and the quantity is Q_C. A monopolist reduces the quantity supplied to Q_M and moves up the demand curve from C to M, raising the price to P_M.

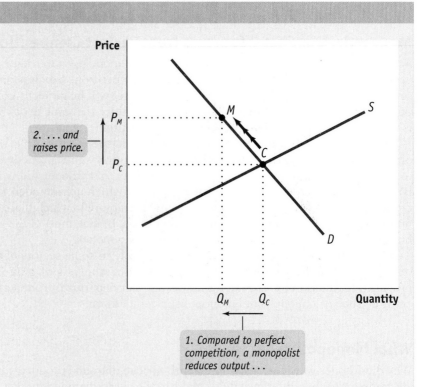

2. ...and raises price.

1. Compared to perfect competition, a monopolist reduces output . . .

Why Do Monopolies Exist?

A monopolist making profits will not go unnoticed by others. (Recall that we mean economic profit, revenue over and above the opportunity costs of the firm's resources.) But won't other firms crash the party, grab a piece of the action, and drive down prices and profits in the long run?

For a profitable monopoly to persist, something must keep others from going into the same business; that "something" is known as a **barrier to entry.** There are five principal types of barriers to entry: control of a scarce resource or input, increasing returns to scale, technological superiority, a network externality, and a government-created barrier to entry.

1. Control of a Scarce Resource or Input

A monopolist that controls a resource or input crucial to an industry can prevent other firms from entering its market. Cecil Rhodes created the De Beers monopoly by establishing control over the mines that produced the great bulk of the world's diamonds.

2. Increasing Returns to Scale

Many Americans have natural gas piped into their homes for cooking and heating. Invariably, the local gas company is a monopolist. But why don't rival companies compete to provide gas?

In the early nineteenth century, when the natural gas industry was just starting up, companies did compete for local customers. But this competition didn't last long; soon local gas suppliers became a monopoly in almost every town because of the large fixed costs of providing a town with gas lines. The cost of laying gas lines didn't depend on how much gas a company sold, so a firm with a larger volume of sales had a cost advantage: because it was able to spread the fixed costs over a larger volume, it had lower average total costs than smaller firms.

Local gas supply is an industry in which average total cost falls as output increases. As we learned in Chapter 6, this phenomenon is called *increasing returns to scale:* which leads to economies of scale. Economies of scale will encourage firms to grow larger. In an industry characterized by economies of scale, larger companies are more profitable and drive out smaller ones. For the same reason, established companies have a cost advantage over any potential entrant—a potent barrier to entry. So increasing returns to scale—economies of scale—can both give rise to and sustain monopoly.

A monopoly created and sustained by increasing returns to scale is called a **natural monopoly.** The defining characteristic of a natural monopoly is that it possesses increasing returns to scale over the range of output that is relevant for the industry. This is illustrated in Figure 8-3, showing the firm's average total cost curve and the market demand curve, *D*. Here we can see that the natural monopolist's *ATC* curve declines over the output levels at which price is greater than or equal to average total cost.

So the natural monopolist has increasing returns to scale over the entire range of output for which any firm would want to remain in the industry—the range of output at which the firm would at least break even in the long run. The source of this condition is large fixed costs: when large fixed costs are required to operate, a given quantity of output is produced at lower average total cost by one large firm than by two or more smaller firms.

The most visible natural monopolies in the modern economy are local utilities—water, gas, power generation, and fiber optic cable. As we'll see later, natural monopolies pose a special challenge to public policy.

3. Technological Superiority

A firm that maintains a consistent technological advantage over potential competitors can establish itself as a monopolist. For example, from the 1970s through the 1990s, the semiconductor chip manufacturer Intel was able to maintain a consistent advantage over potential competitors in both the design and production of microprocessors, the chips that run

To earn economic profits, a monopolist must be protected by a **barrier to entry**—something that prevents other firms from entering the industry.

A **natural monopoly** exists when increasing returns to scale provide a large cost advantage to a single firm that produces all of an industry's output.

FIGURE 8-3 **Increasing Returns to Scale Lead to Natural Monopoly**

A natural monopoly can arise when fixed costs required to operate are very high. When this occurs, the firm's *ATC* curve declines over the range of output at which price is greater than or equal to average total cost. This gives the firm increasing returns to scale over the entire range of output at which the firm would at least break even in the long run. As a result, a given quantity of output is produced more cheaply by one large firm than by two or more smaller firms.

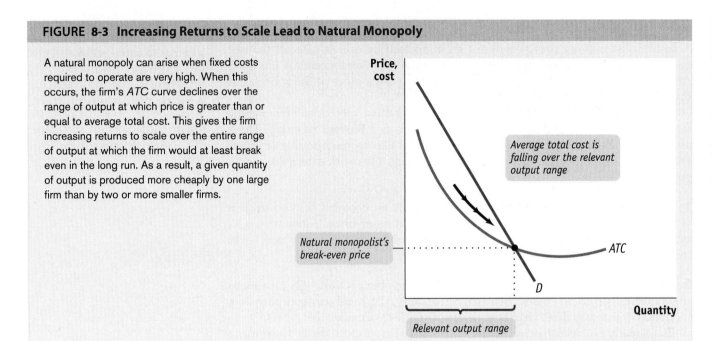

---

computers. But technological superiority is typically not a barrier to entry over the longer term: over time competitors will invest in upgrading their technology to match that of the technology leader.

In the last few years Intel found its technological superiority eroded by a competitor, Advanced Micro Devices (also known as AMD), which was able to produce chips approximately as fast and as powerful as Intel chips.

4. Network Externalities If you were the only person in the world with an internet connection, what would that connection be worth to you? The answer, of course, is nothing. Your internet connection is valuable only because other people are also connected. And, in general, the more people who are connected, the more valuable your connection is. This phenomenon, whereby the value of a good or service to an individual is greater when many others use the same good or service, is called a **network externality**—its value derives from enabling its users to participate in a network of other users.

The earliest form of network externalities arose in transportation, when the value of a road or airport increased as the number of people who had access to it rose. But network externalities are especially prevalent in the technology and communications sectors of the economy.

The classic case is computer operating systems. Worldwide, most personal computers run on Microsoft Windows. Although many believe that Apple has a superior operating system, the wider use of Windows in the early days of personal computers attracted more software development and technical support, giving it a lasting dominance. More recent examples of firms that came to dominate their industries through network externalities are eBay, iTunes, Facebook, Instagram, WhatsApp, PayPal, and Snapchat.

When a network externality exists, the firm with the largest network of customers using its product has an advantage in attracting new customers, one that may allow it to become a monopolist. At a minimum, the dominant firm can charge a higher price and so earn higher profits than competitors. Moreover, a network externality gives an advantage to the firm with the deepest pockets. Companies with the most money on hand can sell the most goods at a loss with the expectation that doing so will give them the largest customer base.

A **network externality** exists when the value of a good or service to an individual is greater when many other people use the good or service as well.

5. Government-Created Barriers The pharmaceutical company Merck introduced Propecia, a drug effective against baldness, in 1998. Although Propecia was very profitable and other drug companies had the know-how to produce it, no other firms challenged Merck's monopoly. That's because the U.S. government had given Merck the sole legal right to produce the drug in the United States. Propecia is an example of a monopoly protected by government-created barriers.

The most important legally created monopolies today arise from *patents* and *copyrights*. A **patent** gives an inventor the sole right to make, use, or sell that invention for a period that in most countries lasts between 14 and 20 years. Patents are given to the creators of new products, such as drugs or mechanical devices. Similarly, a **copyright** gives the creator of a literary or artistic work the sole right to profit from that work, usually for a period equal to the creator's lifetime plus 70 years.

The justification for patents and copyrights is a matter of incentives. If inventors were not protected by patents, they would gain little reward from their efforts: as soon as a valuable invention was made public, others would copy it and sell products based on it. And if inventors could not expect to profit from their inventions, then there would be no incentive to incur the costs of invention in the first place. Likewise for the creators of literary or artistic works. The law thus allows a monopoly to exist temporarily by granting property rights that encourage invention and creation.

Patents and copyrights are temporary because the law strikes a compromise. The higher price for the good that holds while the legal protection is in effect compensates inventors for the cost of invention; conversely, the lower price that results once the legal protection lapses benefits consumers.

Because the lifetime of the temporary monopoly cannot be tailored to specific cases, this system is imperfect and leads to some missed opportunities. In some cases there can even be significant welfare issues. For example, the violation of American drug patents by pharmaceutical companies in poor countries has been a major source of controversy, pitting the needs of poor patients who cannot afford to pay retail drug prices against the interests of the drug manufacturers who have incurred high research costs to discover these drugs.

To solve this problem, some American drug companies and poor countries have negotiated deals in which the patents are honored, but the American companies sell their drugs at deeply discounted prices. (This is an example of *price discrimination*, which we'll learn about shortly.)

A **patent** gives an inventor a temporary monopoly in the use or sale of an invention.

A **copyright** gives the creator of a literary or artistic work sole rights to profit from that work.

ECONOMICS >> *in Action*
The Monopoly That Wasn't: China and the Market for Rare Earths

A quiver of panic shot through the U.S. high-technology and military sectors in 2010. Rare earths, a group of 17 elements that are a critical input in the manufacture of high-tech products like smartphones and military jet components, had suddenly become much harder to obtain.

China controlled 85% to 97% of the global supply of rare earths and, until 2009, made them relatively abundant and cheap on world markets. However, in 2010 China adopted an *export quota*—a limit on the amount of rare earths that could be exported, severely restricting supply on the world market and leading to sharply higher prices. For example, the rare earth dysprosium went from $166 per kilo in 2010 to nearly $1,000 per kilo in 2011, a nearly sixfold increase.

But the panic proved to be temporary. China's dominance in rare earths was due to its low cost of production, and not to a monopoly position. In fact, only about a third of the world's rare earth reserves are found in China. Rare earths mines in Australia and the United States, which had been mothballed during the period of low prices, were reopened in response to the sharply higher prices. In addition, other sources emerged, such as recovering rare earths from discarded computer equipment.

The episode revealed to government and business leaders outside of China how vulnerable they were to disruptions in the supply of Chinese rare earths. As a result, they committed to keeping the alternative sources operating, even if prices should fall. And China's leaders learned that without control over the global sources of rare earths, what looked like a monopoly position, in fact, wasn't.

>> Check Your Understanding 8-1

Solutions appear at back of book.

1. Currently, Texas Tea Oil Co. is the only local supplier of home heating oil in Frigid, Alaska. This winter, residents were shocked that the price of a gallon of heating oil had doubled and believed that they were the victims of market power. Explain which of the following pieces of evidence support or contradict that conclusion.
   a. There is a national shortage of heating oil, and Texas Tea could procure only a limited amount.
   b. Last year, Texas Tea and several other competing local oil-supply firms merged into a single firm.
   c. The cost to Texas Tea of purchasing heating oil from refineries has gone up significantly.
   d. Recently, some nonlocal firms have begun to offer heating oil to Texas Tea's regular customers at a price much lower than Texas Tea's.
   e. Texas Tea has acquired an exclusive government license to draw oil from the only heating oil pipeline in the state.
2. Suppose the government is considering extending the length of a patent from 20 years to 30 years. How would this change each of the following?
   a. The incentive to invent new products
   b. The length of time during which consumers have to pay higher prices
3. Explain the nature of the network externality in each of the following cases.
   a. A new type of credit card, called Passport
   b. A new type of car engine, which runs on solar cells
   c. A website for trading locally provided goods and services

How a Monopolist Maximizes Profit

Once Cecil Rhodes consolidated the competing diamond producers of South Africa into a single company, the industry's behavior changed: the quantity supplied fell and the market price rose. We will now learn how a monopolist increases its profit by reducing output. And we will see the crucial role that market demand plays in leading a monopolist to behave differently from a perfectly competitive industry. (Remember that profit here is economic profit, not accounting profit.)

The Monopolist's Demand Curve and Marginal Revenue

Recall the firm's optimal output rule: a profit-maximizing firm produces the quantity of output at which the marginal cost of producing the last unit of output equals marginal revenue—the change in total revenue generated by that last unit of output. That is, $MR = MC$ at the profit-maximizing quantity of output.

Although the optimal output rule holds for all firms, we will see shortly that its application leads to different profit-maximizing output levels for a monopolist as compared to a firm in a perfectly competitive industry—that is, a price-taking firm. The source of that difference lies in comparing the demand curve faced by a monopolist to the demand curve faced by an individual perfectly competitive firm.

FIGURE 8-4   Comparing the Demand Curves of a Perfectly Competitive Producer and a Monopolist

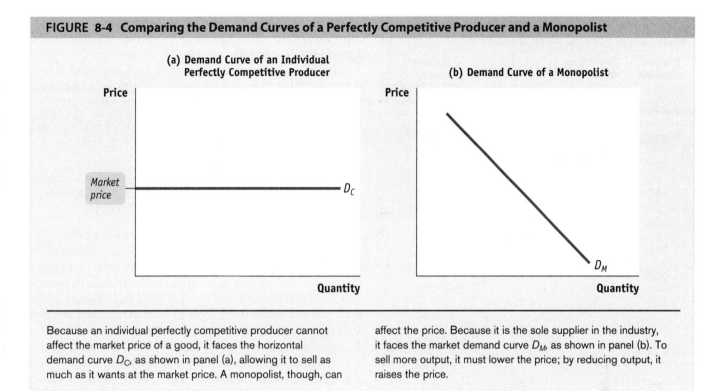

(a) Demand Curve of an Individual Perfectly Competitive Producer

(b) Demand Curve of a Monopolist

Because an individual perfectly competitive producer cannot affect the market price of a good, it faces the horizontal demand curve D_C, as shown in panel (a), allowing it to sell as much as it wants at the market price. A monopolist, though, can affect the price. Because it is the sole supplier in the industry, it faces the market demand curve D_M, as shown in panel (b). To sell more output, it must lower the price; by reducing output, it raises the price.

Comparing Demand Curves Recall that each of the firms in a perfectly competitive industry faces a *perfectly elastic* demand curve that is horizontal at the market price, like D_C in panel (a) of Figure 8-4. A perfectly competitive firm can sell as much as it likes at the market price, yet will lose all of its sales if it attempts to charge more.

Therefore the marginal revenue of a perfectly competitive producer is simply the market price. As a result, the price-taking firm's optimal output rule is to produce the output level at which the marginal cost of the last unit produced is equal to the market price.

In contrast, because a monopolist is the sole supplier of its good, its demand curve is simply the market demand curve. And like virtually all market demand curves, it slopes downward, like D_M in panel (b) of Figure 8-4. As a result, a monopolist must cut its price to sell more. *This downward slope creates a difference—a "wedge"—between the price of the good and the marginal revenue received by the monopolist for that good.*

Comparing Marginal Revenue and Price The first two columns of Table 8-1 show a hypothetical demand schedule for De Beers diamonds. For the sake of simplicity, we will assume that all diamonds are exactly alike. And to make the arithmetic easy, we suppose that the number of diamonds sold is far smaller than is actually the case. For instance, at a price of $500 per diamond, we assume that only 10 diamonds are sold. The demand curve implied by this schedule is shown in panel (a) of Figure 8-5.

The third column of Table 8-1 shows De Beers's total revenue from selling each quantity of diamonds—the price per diamond multiplied by the number of diamonds sold. The last column calculates marginal revenue, the change in total revenue from producing and selling another diamond.

The marginal revenue a monopolist receives from selling one more unit is less than the price at which that unit is sold. This is clear after the first diamond in Table 8-1. For example, if De Beers sells 10 diamonds, the price at which the

TABLE 8-1 Demand, Total Revenue, and Marginal Revenue for the De Beers Monopoly

Price of diamond P	Quantity of diamonds Q	Total revenue TR = P × Q	Marginal revenue MR = ΔTR/ΔQ
$1,000	0	$0	
			$950
950	1	950	
			850
900	2	1,800	
			750
850	3	2,550	
			650
800	4	3,200	
			550
750	5	3,750	
			450
700	6	4,200	
			350
650	7	4,550	
			250
600	8	4,800	
			150
550	9	4,950	
			50
500	10	5,000	
			−50
450	11	4,950	
			−150
400	12	4,800	
			−250
350	13	4,550	
			−350
300	14	4,200	
			−450
250	15	3,750	
			−550
200	16	3,200	
			−650
150	17	2,550	
			−750
100	18	1,800	
			−850
50	19	950	
			−950
0	20	0	

10th diamond is sold is $500. But the marginal revenue—the change in total revenue in going from 9 to 10 diamonds—is only $50.

The marginal revenue from that 10th diamond is less than the price because an increase in production by a monopolist has two opposing effects on revenue:

1. *A quantity effect.* One more unit is sold, increasing total revenue by the price at which the unit is sold (in this case +$500).

2. *A price effect.* To sell the last unit, the monopolist must cut the market price on *all* units sold. This decreases total revenue (in this case, by 9 × −$50 = −$450).

The quantity effect and the price effect when the monopolist goes from selling 9 diamonds to 10 diamonds are illustrated by the two shaded areas in panel (a) of Figure 8-5. Increasing diamond sales from 9 to 10 means moving down the demand curve from A to B, reducing the price per diamond from $550 to $500. The green-shaded area represents the quantity effect: De Beers sells the 10th diamond at a price of $500. This is offset, however, by the price effect, represented by the yellow-shaded area. To sell that 10th diamond, De Beers must reduce the price on all its diamonds from $550 to $500. So it loses 9 × $50 = $450 in revenue. As point C indicates, the total effect on revenue of selling one more diamond—the marginal revenue—derived from an increase in diamond sales from 9 to 10 is only $50.

Point C lies on the monopolist's marginal revenue curve, labeled MR in panel (a) of Figure 8-5 and taken from the last column of Table 8-1. The crucial point about the monopolist's marginal revenue curve is that it is always *below* the demand curve. That's because of the price effect: a monopolist's marginal revenue from selling an additional unit is always less than the price the monopolist receives for the previous unit. It is the price effect that creates the wedge between the monopolist's marginal revenue curve and the demand curve: to sell an additional diamond, De Beers must cut the market price on all units sold. In fact, this wedge exists for any firm that possesses market power, such as an oligopolist as well as a monopolist. Having market power means that the firm faces a downward-sloping demand curve. As a result, there will always be a price effect from an increase in its output. So for a firm with market power, the marginal revenue curve always lies below its demand curve.

Take a moment to compare the monopolist's marginal revenue curve with the marginal revenue curve for a perfectly competitive firm, one without market power. For such a firm there is no price effect from an increase in output: its marginal revenue curve is simply its horizontal demand curve. For a perfectly competitive firm, then, market price and marginal revenue are always equal.

To emphasize how the quantity and price effects offset each other for a firm with market power, De Beers's total revenue curve is shown in panel (b) of Figure 8-5. Notice that it is hill-shaped: as output rises from 0 to 10 diamonds, total revenue increases. This reflects the fact that at *low levels of output, the quantity effect is stronger than the price effect:* as the monopolist sells more, it has to

FIGURE 8-5   A Monopolist's Demand, Total Revenue, and Marginal Revenue Curves

Panel (a) shows the monopolist's demand and marginal revenue curves for diamonds from Table 8-1. The marginal revenue curve lies below the demand curve. To see why, consider point A on the demand curve, where 9 diamonds are sold at $550 each, generating total revenue of $4,950. To sell a 10th diamond, the price on all 10 diamonds must be cut to $500, as shown by point B. As a result, total revenue increases by the green area (the quantity effect: +$500) but decreases by the yellow area (the price effect: –$450). So the marginal revenue from the 10th diamond is $50 (the difference between the green and yellow areas), which is much lower than its price, $500. Panel (b) shows the monopolist's total revenue curve for diamonds. As output goes from 0 to 10 diamonds, total revenue increases. It reaches its maximum at 10 diamonds—the level at which marginal revenue is equal to 0—and declines thereafter. The quantity effect dominates the price effect when total revenue is rising; the price effect dominates the quantity effect when total revenue is falling.

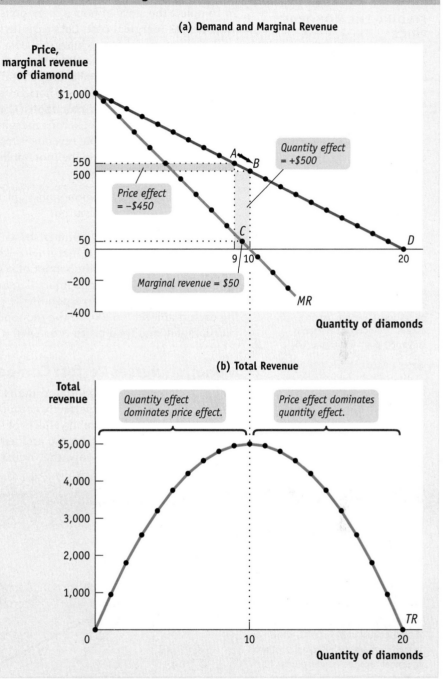

lower the price on only very few units, so the price effect is small. As output rises beyond 10 diamonds, total revenue actually falls. This reflects the fact that *at high levels of output, the price effect is stronger than the quantity effect:* as the monopolist sells more, it now has to lower the price on many units of output, making the price effect very large.

Correspondingly, the marginal revenue curve lies below 0 at output levels above 10 diamonds. For example, an increase in diamond production from 11 to 12 yields only $400 for the 12th diamond, simultaneously reducing the revenue from diamonds 1 through 11 by $550. As a result, the marginal revenue of the 12th diamond is –$150.

PITFALLS

FINDING THE MONOPOLY PRICE

In order to find the *profit-maximizing quantity of output* for a monopolist, look for the point where the marginal revenue curve crosses the marginal cost curve. Point *A* in Figure 8-6 is an example.

However, it's important not to make the mistake of imagining that point *A* also shows the *price* at which the monopolist sells its output. It doesn't. Instead, it shows the *marginal revenue* received by the monopolist, which is less than the price.

To find the monopoly price, you have to go up vertically from point *A* to the demand curve. There you find the price at which consumers demand the profit-maximizing quantity. So the profit-maximizing price–quantity combination is always a point on the demand curve, like point *B* in Figure 8-6.

The Monopolist's Profit-Maximizing Output and Price

To complete the story of how a monopolist maximizes profit, we now bring in the monopolist's marginal cost. Let's assume that there is no fixed cost of production; we'll also assume that the marginal cost of producing an additional diamond is constant at $200, no matter how many diamonds De Beers produces. Then marginal cost will always equal average total cost, and the marginal cost curve (and the average total cost curve) is a horizontal line at $200, as shown in Figure 8-6.

To maximize profit, the monopolist compares marginal cost with marginal revenue. If marginal revenue exceeds marginal cost, De Beers increases its profit by producing more; if marginal revenue is less than marginal cost, De Beers increases profit by producing less. So the monopolist maximizes its profit by using the optimal output rule:

(8-1) $MR = MC$ at the monopolist's profit-maximizing quantity of output

The monopolist's optimal point is shown in Figure 8-6. At point *A*, the marginal cost curve, *MC*, crosses the marginal revenue curve, *MR*. The corresponding output level, 8 diamonds, is the monopolist's profit-maximizing quantity of output, Q_M. The price at which consumers demand 8 diamonds is $600, so the monopolist's price, P_M, is $600—corresponding to point *B*. The average total cost of producing each diamond is $200, so the monopolist earns a profit of $600 − $200 = $400 per diamond, and total profit is $8 \times $400 = $3,200$, as indicated by the shaded area.

Monopoly versus Perfect Competition

When Cecil Rhodes consolidated many independent diamond producers into De Beers, he converted a perfectly competitive industry into a monopoly. We can now use our analysis to see the effects of such a consolidation.

Let's look again at Figure 8-6 and ask how this same market would work if, instead of being a monopoly, the industry were perfectly competitive. We will

---

FIGURE 8-6 The Monopolist's Profit-Maximizing Output and Price

This figure shows demand, marginal revenue, and marginal cost curves. Marginal cost per diamond is constant at $200, so the marginal cost curve is horizontal at $200. According to the optimal output rule, the profit-maximizing quantity of output for the monopolist is at $MR = MC$, shown by point *A*, where the marginal cost and marginal revenue curves cross at an output of 8 diamonds. The price De Beers can charge per diamond is found by going to the point on the demand curve directly above point *A*, which is point *B* here—a price of $600 per diamond. It makes a profit of $400 × 8 = $3,200. A perfectly competitive industry produces the output level at which $P = MC$, given by point *C*, where the demand curve and marginal cost curves cross. So, a competitive industry produces 16 diamonds, sells at a price of $200, and makes zero profit.

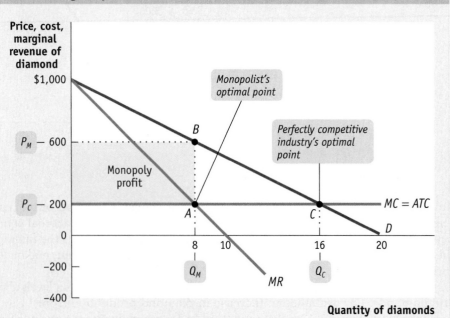

continue to assume that there is no fixed cost and that marginal cost is constant, so average total cost and marginal cost are equal.

If the diamond industry consists of many perfectly competitive firms, each of those producers takes the market price as given. For each firm, marginal revenue is equal to the market price. So, each firm within the industry uses the price-taking firm's optimal output rule:

(8-2) $P = MC$ at the perfectly competitive firm's profit-maximizing quantity of output

In Figure 8-6, this corresponds to producing at point C, where the price per diamond, P_C, is $200, equal to the marginal cost of production. So the profit maximizing output of an industry under perfect competition, Q_C, is 16 diamonds.

But does the perfectly competitive industry earn any profits at point C? No: the price of $200 is equal to the average total cost per diamond. So there are no economic profits for this industry when it produces at the perfectly competitive output level.

We've already seen that once the industry is consolidated into a monopoly, the result is very different. The monopolist's calculation of marginal revenue takes the price effect into account, so that marginal revenue is less than the price. That is,

(8-3) $P > MR = MC$ at the monopolist's profit-maximizing quantity of output

We've also seen that the monopolist produces less than the competitive industry—8 diamonds rather than 16. The price under monopoly is $600, compared with only $200 under perfect competition. The monopolist earns a positive profit, but the competitive firm does not.

So, just as we suggested earlier, compared with a competitive firm, a monopolist does the following:

- Produces a smaller quantity: $Q_M < Q_C$
- Charges a higher price: $P_M > P_C$
- Earns a profit

Monopoly: The General Picture

Figure 8-6 involved specific numbers and assumed that marginal cost was constant, that there was no fixed cost, and, therefore, that the average total cost curve was a horizontal line. Figure 8-7 shows a more general picture of monopoly in action: D is the market demand curve; MR, the marginal revenue curve; MC, the marginal cost curve; and ATC, the average total cost curve. Here we return to the usual assumption that the marginal cost curve has a "swoosh" shape and the average total cost curve is U-shaped.

Applying the optimal output rule, we see that the profit-maximizing level of output is the output at which marginal revenue equals marginal cost, indicated by point A. The profit-maximizing quantity of output is Q_M, and the price charged by the monopolist is P_M. At the profit-maximizing level of output, the monopolist's average total cost is ATC_M, shown by point C.

Profit is equal to the difference between total revenue and total cost. So we have:

(8-4) Profit $= TR - TC$
$$= (P_M \times Q_M) - (ATC_M \times Q_M)$$
$$= (P_M - ATC_M) \times Q_M$$

Profit is equal to the area of the shaded rectangle in Figure 8-7, with a height of $P_M - ATC_M$ and a width of Q_M.

From Chapter 7 we know that a perfectly competitive industry can have profits in the *short run but not in the long run*. In the short run, price can exceed

FIGURE 8-7 The Monopolist's Profit

In this case, the marginal cost curve has a "swoosh" shape and the average total cost curve is U-shaped. The monopolist maximizes profit by producing the level of output at which $MR = MC$, given by point A, generating quantity Q_M. It finds its monopoly price, P_M, from the point on the demand curve directly above point A, point B here. The average total cost of Q_M is shown by point C. Profit is given by the area of the shaded rectangle.

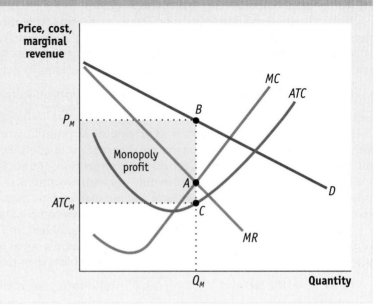

average total cost, allowing a perfectly competitive firm to make a profit. But we also know that this cannot persist.

In the long run, any profit in a perfectly competitive industry will be competed away as new firms enter the market. In contrast, barriers to entry allow a monopolist to make profits in *both the short run and the long run.*

ECONOMICS >> *in Action*
Shocked by the High Price of Electricity

Historically, electric utilities in the United States were recognized as natural monopolies. A utility serviced a defined geographical area and owned both the plants that generated electricity and the transmission lines that delivered it to retail customers. The rates that customers were charged were regulated by the government, set at a level to cover the utility's cost of operation plus a modest return on capital to its shareholders.

Beginning in the late 1990s, however, there was a move toward deregulation, based on the belief that competition would deliver lower retail electricity prices. Competition occurs at two junctures in the channel from power generation to retail customers: (1) distributors compete to sell electricity to retail customers, and (2) power generators compete to supply power to distributors.

That was the theory, at least. By 2018, only 16 states had instituted some form of electricity deregulation, while 7 had started but then suspended deregulation, leaving 27 states to continue with a regulated monopoly electricity provider. Why did so few states actually follow through on electricity deregulation?

One major obstacle is the lack of choice in power generators, the bulk of which still entail large up-front fixed costs. In many markets there is only one power generator. Although consumers appear to have a choice in their electricity distributor,

Although some electric utilities were deregulated in the 1990s, the current trend is to reregulate them.

the choice is illusory, as everyone must get their electricity from the same source in the end. And in cases in which there is actually choice in power generators, there is frequently no choice in transmission, which is controlled by monopoly power line companies.

In fact, deregulation can make consumers worse off when there is only one power generator because of the potential for the power generator to engage in market manipulation—intentionally reducing the amount of power supplied to distributors in order to drive up prices. The most shocking case occurred during the California energy crisis of 2000–2001 that brought blackouts and billions of dollars in electricity surcharges to homes and businesses. On audiotapes later acquired by regulators, executives could be heard discussing plans to shut down power plants during times of peak energy demand, joking about how they were "stealing" more than $1 million a day from California.

Another problem is that without prices set by regulators, producers aren't guaranteed a profitable rate of return on new power plants, subjecting them to far more risk. Many new power generators took on high debt levels to build their plants, then went bankrupt when demand did not rise to the level that would support their debt. As a result, new power generator builders are demanding much higher prices before they invest. And in states with deregulation, capacity has failed to keep up with growing demand. For example, Texas, a deregulated state, has experienced massive blackouts due to insufficient capacity, and in New Jersey and Maryland, regulators have intervened to compel producers to build more power plants.

Lastly, consumers in deregulated states have been subject to big spikes in their electricity bills, often paying much more than consumers in regulated states. So, angry customers and exasperated regulators have prompted many states to shift into reverse, with Illinois, Montana, and Virginia moving to regulate their industries. California and Montana have gone so far as to mandate that their electricity distributors reacquire power plants that were sold off during deregulation. In addition, regulators have been on the prowl, fining utilities in Texas, New York, and Illinois for market manipulation.

>> Check Your Understanding 8-2

Solutions appear at back of book.

1. Use the accompanying total revenue schedule of Emerald, Inc., a monopoly producer of 10-carat emeralds, to calculate the answers to parts a–d. Then answer part e.
   a. The demand schedule
   b. The marginal revenue schedule
   c. The quantity effect component of marginal revenue per output level
   d. The price effect component of marginal revenue per output level
   e. What additional information is needed to determine Emerald, Inc.'s profit-maximizing output?

2. Use Figure 8-6 to show what happens to the following when the marginal cost of diamond production rises from $200 to $400.
   • Marginal cost curve
   • Profit-maximizing price and quantity
   • Profit of the monopolist
   • Perfectly competitive industry profits

Quantity of emeralds demanded	Total revenue
1	$100
2	186
3	252
4	280
5	250

>> Quick Review

• The crucial difference between a firm with market power, such as a monopolist, and a firm in a perfectly competitive industry is that perfectly competitive firms are price-takers that face horizontal demand curves, but a firm with market power faces a downward-sloping demand curve.

• Due to the price effect of an increase in output, the marginal revenue curve of a firm with market power always lies below its demand curve. So a profit-maximizing monopolist chooses the output level at which marginal cost is equal to marginal revenue—*not* to price.

• As a result, the monopolist produces less and sells its output at a higher price than a perfectly competitive industry would. It earns profits in the short run and the long run.

‖ Monopoly and Public Policy

It's good to be a monopolist, but it's not so good to be a monopolist's customer. A monopolist, by reducing output and raising prices, benefits at the expense of consumers. But buyers and sellers always have conflicting interests: buyers want lower prices while sellers want higher prices. Is the conflict under monopoly any different than it is under perfect competition?

The answer is yes, because monopoly is a source of inefficiency: the losses to consumers from monopoly behavior are larger than the gains to the monopolist. Because monopoly leads to net losses to society's welfare, governments often try either to prevent the emergence of monopolies or to limit their effects. In this section, we will see why monopoly leads to inefficiency and examine the policies governments adopt in an attempt to prevent this inefficiency.

Welfare Effects of Monopoly

By restricting output below the level at which marginal cost is equal to the market price, a monopolist increases its profit but hurts consumers. When comparing the monopolist's gain in profit to the loss in consumer surplus, we learn that the loss in consumer surplus is larger than the monopolist's gain. As a result, monopoly causes a net loss for society.

To see why, let's return to the case in which the marginal cost curve is horizontal, as shown in the two panels of Figure 8-8. Here the marginal cost curve is MC, the demand curve is D, and, in panel (b), the marginal revenue curve is MR.

Panel (a) shows what happens if this industry is perfectly competitive. Equilibrium output is Q_C; the price of the good, P_C, is equal to marginal cost, and marginal cost is also equal to average total cost because there is no fixed cost, and marginal cost is constant. Each firm is earning exactly its average total cost per unit of output, so there is no profit and no producer surplus in this equilibrium.

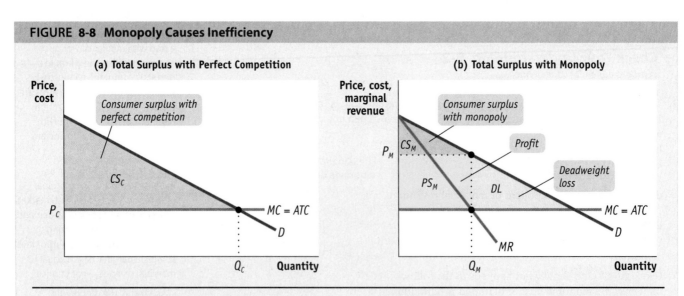

FIGURE 8-8 Monopoly Causes Inefficiency

Panel (a) depicts a perfectly competitive industry: output is Q_C, and market price, P_C, is equal to MC. Since price is exactly equal to each producer's average total cost of production per unit, there is no profit and no producer surplus. So total surplus is equal to consumer surplus, the entire shaded area. Panel (b) depicts the industry under monopoly: the monopolist decreases output to Q_M and charges P_M. Consumer surplus (blue area) has shrunk: a portion of it has been captured as profit (green area), and a portion of it has been lost to deadweight loss (yellow area), the value of mutually beneficial transactions that do not occur because of monopoly behavior. As a result, total surplus falls.

The consumer surplus generated by the market is equal to the area of the blue-shaded triangle CS_C shown in panel (a). Since there is no producer surplus when the industry is perfectly competitive, CS_C also represents the total surplus.

Panel (b) shows the results for the same market, but this time assuming that the industry is a monopoly. The monopolist produces the level of output Q_M, at which marginal cost is equal to marginal revenue, and it charges the price P_M. The industry now earns profit—which is also the producer surplus—equal to the area of the green rectangle, PS_M. Note that this profit is surplus captured from consumers as consumer surplus shrinks to the area of the blue triangle, CS_M.

By comparing panels (a) and (b), we see that in addition to the redistribution of surplus from consumers to the monopolist, another important change has occurred: the sum of profit and consumer surplus—total surplus—is *smaller* under monopoly than under perfect competition. That is, the sum of CS_M and PS_M in panel (b) is less than the area CS_C in panel (a). The total surplus shrinks by the yellow triangle DL as the market goes from perfect competition to monopoly. So, monopoly produces a net loss for society equal to the area DL.

This net loss arises because some mutually beneficial transactions do not occur. There are people for whom an additional unit of the good is worth more than the marginal cost of producing it but who don't consume it because they are not willing to pay P_M. The wedge between price and marginal cost created by monopoly operates much like the wedge created by a tax, which we learned about earlier. In other words, monopoly acts much like a tax on consumers and produces the same kind of inefficiency: a higher price on consumers and a lower quantity supplied.

Preventing Monopoly

Policy toward monopoly depends crucially on whether or not the industry in question is a natural monopoly, one in which increasing returns to scale ensure that a bigger producer has lower average total cost. If the industry is not a natural monopoly, the best policy is to prevent monopoly from arising or break it up if it already exists. Let's focus on that case first, then turn to the more difficult problem of dealing with natural monopoly.

The De Beers monopoly on diamonds didn't have to happen. Diamond production is not a natural monopoly: the industry's costs would be no higher if it consisted of a number of independent, competing producers (as is the case, for example, in gold production).

So if the South African government had been worried about how a monopoly would have affected consumers, it could have blocked Cecil Rhodes in his drive to dominate the industry or broken up his monopoly after the fact. Today, governments often try to prevent monopolies from forming and break up existing ones.

De Beers is a unique case. For complicated historical reasons, it was allowed to remain a monopoly. But over the last century, most similar monopolies have been broken up. The most celebrated example in the United States is Standard Oil, founded by John D. Rockefeller in 1870. By 1878 Standard Oil controlled almost all U.S. oil refining; but in 1911 a court order broke the company into a number of smaller units, including the companies that later became Exxon and Mobil (and merged in 1999 to become ExxonMobil).

The government policies used to prevent or eliminate monopolies are known as *antitrust policies*, which we will discuss in the next chapter.

Dealing with Natural Monopoly

Recall from earlier that natural monopoly arises from increasing returns to scale: The lowest average cost is achieved when there is only one producer in the industry. As a result, policies to encourage rivals to enter the market will lead to higher

In **public ownership** of a monopoly, the good is supplied by the government or by a firm owned by the government.

Price regulation limits the price that a monopolist is allowed to charge.

average total cost across the industry. For example, a town government that tried to prevent a single company from dominating local gas supply—which, as we've discussed, is almost surely a natural monopoly—would raise the cost of providing gas to its residents.

Yet even in the case of a natural monopoly, a profit-maximizing monopolist acts in a way that causes inefficiency—it charges consumers a price that is higher than marginal cost and, by doing so, prevents some potentially beneficial transactions. Also, it can seem unfair that a firm that has managed to establish a monopoly position earns a large profit at the expense of consumers.

What government policies should be adopted to deal with this? There are two common answers.

1. Public Ownership In many countries, the preferred answer to the problem of natural monopoly has been **public ownership.** Instead of allowing a private monopolist to control an industry, the government establishes a public agency to provide the good and protect consumers' interests. Some examples of public ownership in the United States include passenger rail service provided by the public company Amtrak, and regular mail delivery provided by the U.S. Postal Service. Some cities, including Los Angeles, have publicly owned electric power companies.

The advantage of public ownership, in principle, is that a publicly owned natural monopoly can set prices based on the criterion of efficiency rather than profit maximization. In a perfectly competitive industry, profit-maximizing behavior is efficient, because producers produce the quantity at which price is equal to marginal cost; that is why there is no economic argument for public ownership of, say, Christmas tree farms.

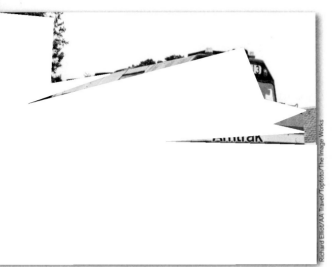

Amtrak, a public company, has provided train service, at a loss, to destinations that attract few passengers.

Richard Elliot/AA Travel/Topfoto/The Image Works

Experience suggests, however, that public ownership as a solution to the problem of natural monopoly often works badly in practice. One reason is that publicly owned firms are often less eager than private companies to keep costs down or offer high-quality products. Another is that publicly owned companies all too often end up serving political interests—providing contracts or jobs to people with the right connections. For example, Amtrak has notoriously provided train service at a loss to destinations that attract few passengers—but that are located in the districts of influential members of Congress.

2. Regulation In the United States, the more common policy toward natural monopoly has been to leave the industry in private hands but subject it to regulation. In particular, most local utilities like electricity, natural gas, and so on are covered by **price regulation** that limits the prices they can charge.

As we've learned, imposing a *price ceiling* on a competitive industry is a recipe for shortages, black markets, and other nasty side effects. Doesn't imposing a limit on the price that, say, a local gas company can charge have the same effects?

Not necessarily: a price ceiling on a monopolist need not create a shortage—in the absence of a price ceiling, a monopolist would charge a price that is higher than its marginal cost of production. So even if forced to charge a lower price—as long as that price is above M_C and the monopolist at least breaks even on total output—the monopolist still has an incentive to produce the quantity demanded at that price.

The upcoming Economics in Action describes the case of broadband internet, a natural monopoly that has been alternately regulated and deregulated as politicians change their minds about the appropriate policy.

Monopsony Is it possible for the buyer and not the seller to have market power? Put another way, is it possible to have a market in which there is only one buyer but many sellers, so that the buyer can use its power to capture surplus from the sellers? The answer is yes, and that market is called a **monopsony.**

Like a monopolist, a **monopsonist** will distort the competitive market outcome in order to capture more of the surplus, except that the monopsonist will do this through quantity purchased and price paid for goods rather than through quantity sold and price charged for goods.

Monopsony, although it does exist, is rarer than monopoly. The classic example is a single employer in a small town—say, the local factory—that is purchasing labor services from workers. Recall that a monopolist, realizing that it can affect the price at which its goods are sold, reduces output in order to get a higher price and increase its profits. A monopsonist does much the same thing, but with a twist. Realizing that it can affect the wage it pays its employees by moving down the labor supply curve, it reduces the number of employees hired in order to pay a lower wage and increase its profits.

Just as a monopolist creates a deadweight loss by producing too little of the output, a monopsonist creates a deadweight loss by hiring too few workers (and thereby producing too little output as well).

Monopsony seems to occur most frequently in markets in which workers have a specialized skill, and there is only one employer who hires based on that skill. For example, physicians have often complained that in some parts of the country where most patients are insured by one or two insurance companies, the companies act as monopsonists in setting the reimbursement rates they pay for medical procedures.

And in 2014, when the two largest cable providers, Time Warner Cable and Comcast, announced their intention to merge, questions of monopoly *and* monopsony arose: monopoly, because the combined company would cover 30 million subscribers, an overwhelming proportion of Americans with cable access; and monopsony because the combined company would be virtually the only purchaser of programming by companies that produce shows for broadcast. So it was no surprise that the FCC signaled to the two companies its strong opposition to the deal. As a result, in 2015 the two companies announced that the deal was off.

So although monopsony may be rare, it can be an important phenomenon.

What to Do About Monopoly? As our discussion has made clear, managing monopoly (and monopsony) can be tricky because trade-offs are often present. For example, in the case of drug monopolies, how can the prices consumers pay for existing drugs be reduced if the profits from those sales fund research and development of new drugs?

In the case of a regulated natural monopoly like power generation, how can power producers invest in cost-saving technology and new production capacity if they receive regulated returns and are therefore insulated from market forces? And on the flip side, when the electricity industry is deregulated, how can regulators assure that consumers are not gouged through market manipulation?

Economists and policy makers have struggled with these questions for decades because the best answer is often found through trial and error—as we've seen through the various attempts at electricity deregulation.

And there is always the danger of what is called *regulatory capture:* because vast sums of money are at stake, regulators can be unduly influenced by the companies they are supposed to oversee.

A **monopsony** exists when there is only one buyer of a good. A **monopsonist** is a firm that is the sole buyer in a market.

Perhaps, in dealing with monopolies, the best answer is for economists and policy makers to remain vigilant and admit that sometimes midcourse policy corrections are needed.

ECONOMICS >> *in Action*
The (R)Evolution of the American High-Speed Internet Market

If you are a resident of Seoul, South Korea, it takes about 7 seconds to download a high-definition movie and you'll pay less than $25 a month for the connection. But if you are a resident of an average U.S. city, that same download will take 1.4 minutes (for those with the fastest internet connections), and you will pay around $300 a month.

Compared to countries like South Korea and the Netherlands, internet access in the United States is slow and expensive. Figure 8-9 compares the average download speed and price per megabit across select countries. According to a 2015 study by the leading cloud service provider, Akami Technologies, the United States ranks 20th in terms of average download speeds.

Our example of American broadband service illustrates why it can be so hard to balance the short-run and long-term interests of consumers in the case of a natural monopoly. Cable service, the way most Americans have gotten their broadband service, is a natural monopoly because running cable to individual homes incurs large fixed costs. So in the early days, cable companies were regulated as monopolists, and prices were set by local governments.

But when Congress deregulated broadband service 20 years ago, the industry consolidated as two big companies, Time Warner and Comcast, and purchased smaller, local companies. So it's not surprising that consumers faced yearly price hikes. From 2010 to 2015, the average price of cable service increased by about 8% a year, more than four times the rate of inflation.

In addition, Americans have paid higher prices for their internet service because of differences in regulation compared to countries with a *common carrier rule*, which required cable companies to rent out some of their network capacity to other companies who then competed to provide internet service to consumers. Lacking this sort of regulation, the vast majority of Americans had only one cable provider and so faced monopoly pricing. A 2015 comparison of cable service in several U.S. cities found that even when several providers operated in a given city, they avoided competing with one another by carving up the area into subareas where only one company would operate.

Yet the market is changing rapidly. The big profits generated by American cable companies have attracted investment in infrastructure. Broadband companies have invested $1.4 trillion in their networks, deploying the latest in 4G, fiber optic, and satellite technology in certain areas. In densely populated cities such as New York, where the cost of laying fiber to homes is relatively low, entrants such as Verizon Fios have appeared, competition has heated up, and prices have plateaued. Moreover, many Americans are cancelling their cable service, instead choosing to access the internet on their smartphones. In rural areas, satellite offers an alternative to cable.

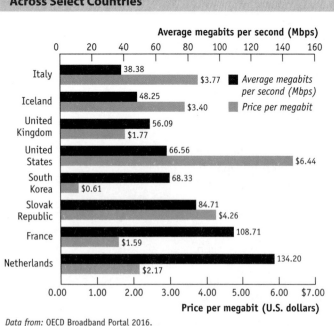

FIGURE 8-9 Comparing Broadband Speed and Price Across Select Countries

Data from: OECD Broadband Portal 2016.

>> Check Your Understanding 8-3

Solutions appear at back of book.

1. What policy should the government adopt in the following cases? Explain.
   a. Internet service in Anytown, Ohio, is provided by cable. Customers feel they are being overcharged, but the cable company claims it must charge prices that allow it to recover the costs of laying cable.
   b. The only two airlines that currently fly to Alaska need government approval to merge. Other airlines wish to fly to Alaska but need government-allocated landing slots to do so.
2. True or false? Explain your answer.
   a. Society's welfare is lower under monopoly because some consumer surplus is transformed into profit for the monopolist.
   b. A monopolist causes inefficiency because there are consumers who are willing to pay a price greater than or equal to marginal cost but less than the monopoly price.
3. Suppose a monopolist mistakenly believes that its marginal revenue is always equal to the market price. Assuming constant marginal cost and no fixed cost, draw a diagram comparing the level of profit, consumer surplus, total surplus, and deadweight loss for this misguided monopolist compared to a smart monopolist.

Price Discrimination

Up to this point, we have considered only the case of a **single-price monopolist,** one that charges all consumers the same price. As the term suggests, not all monopolists do this. In fact, many if not most monopolists find that they can increase their profits by charging different customers different prices for the same good: they engage in **price discrimination.**

The most striking example of price discrimination involves airline tickets. Although there are a number of airlines, most air routes in the United States are serviced by only one or two carriers, which, as a result, have market power and can set prices. So any regular airline passenger quickly becomes aware that the question "How much will it cost me to fly there?" rarely has a simple answer.

If you are willing to buy a nonrefundable ticket a month in advance and happen to purchase the ticket on Tuesday or Wednesday evening, the round trip may cost only $150—or less if you are a senior citizen or a student. But if you have to go on a business trip tomorrow, which happens to be Tuesday, and come back on Wednesday, the same round trip might cost $550. Yet the business traveler and the visiting grandparent receive the same product—the same cramped seat, the same awful food (if indeed any food is served).

You might argue that airlines are not usually monopolists—that in most flight markets the airline industry is an oligopoly. In fact, price discrimination takes place under oligopoly and monopolistic competition as well as monopoly. But it doesn't happen under perfect competition. And once we've seen why monopolists sometimes price-discriminate, we'll be in a good position to understand why it happens in oligopoly and monopolistic competition, too.

The Logic of Price Discrimination

To get a preliminary view of why price discrimination might be more profitable than charging all consumers the same price, imagine that Air Sunshine offers the only nonstop flights between Bismarck, North Dakota, and Fort Lauderdale, Florida. Assume that there are no capacity problems—the airline can fly as many planes as the number of passengers warrants. Also assume that there is no fixed cost. The marginal cost to the airline of providing a seat is $125, however many passengers it carries.

A **single-price monopolist** offers its product to all consumers at the same price.

Sellers engage in **price discrimination** when they charge different prices to different consumers for the same good.

FIGURE 8-10 Two Types of Airline Customers

Air Sunshine has two types of customers, business travelers willing to pay at most $550 per ticket and students willing to pay at most $150 per ticket. There are 2,000 of each kind of customer. Air Sunshine has a constant marginal cost of $125 per seat. If Air Sunshine could charge these two types of customers different prices, it would maximize its profit by charging business travelers $550 and students $150 per ticket. It would capture all of the consumer surplus as profit.

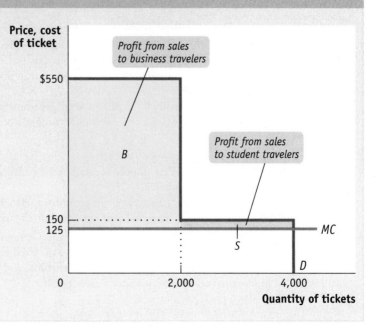

Further assume that the airline knows there are two kinds of potential passengers: 2,000 business travelers who want to travel between these destinations each week, and 2,000 students who want to do the same.

Will potential passengers take the flight? It depends on the price. The business travelers, it turns out, really need to fly; they will take the plane as long as the price is no more than $550. Since they are flying purely for business, we assume that cutting the price below $550 will not lead to any increase in business travel. The students, however, have less money and more time; if the price goes above $150, they will take the bus. The implied demand curve is shown in Figure 8-10.

So what should the airline do? If it has to charge everyone the same price, its options are limited. It could charge $550; that way it would get as much as possible out of the business travelers but lose the student market. Or it could charge only $150; that way it would get both types of travelers but would make significantly less money from sales to business travelers.

We can quickly calculate the profits from each of these alternatives. If the airline charged $550, it would sell 2,000 tickets to the business travelers, earning total revenue of 2,000 × $550 = $1.1 million and incurring costs of 2,000 × $125 = $250,000; in this case, its profit would be $850,000, illustrated by the shaded area *B* in Figure 8-10.

If the airline charged only $150, it would sell 4,000 tickets, receiving revenue of 4,000 × $150 = $600,000 and incurring costs of 4,000 × $125 = $500,000; in this case, its profit would be $100,000. If the airline must charge everyone the same price, charging the higher price and forgoing sales to students is clearly more profitable.

What the airline would really like to do, however, is charge the business travelers the full $550 but offer $150 tickets to the students. That's a lot less than the price paid by business travelers, but it's still above marginal cost; so if the airline could sell those extra 2,000 tickets to students, it would make an additional $50,000 in profit. That is, it would make a profit equal to the areas *B* plus *S* in Figure 8-10.

It would be more realistic to suppose that there is some "give" in each group's demand: at a price below $550, there would be some increase in business travel;

and at a price above $150, some students would still purchase tickets. But this, it turns out, does not do away with the argument for price discrimination.

The important point is that the two groups of consumers differ in their *sensitivity to price*—that a high price has a larger effect in discouraging purchases by students than purchases by business travelers. As long as different groups of customers respond differently to the price, a monopolist will find that it can capture more consumer surplus and increase its profit by charging them different prices.

Price Discrimination and Elasticity A more realistic description of the demand that airlines face would not specify particular prices at which different types of travelers would choose to fly. Instead, it would distinguish between the groups on the basis of their sensitivity to the price—their price elasticity of demand.

Suppose that a company sells its product to two easily identifiable groups of people—business travelers and students. It just so happens that business travelers are very insensitive to the price: there is a certain amount of the product they just have to have whatever the price, but they cannot be persuaded to buy much more than that no matter how cheap it is. Students, though, are more flexible: offer a good enough price and they will buy quite a lot, but raise the price too high and they will switch to something else. What should the company do?

The answer is the one already suggested by our simplified example: the company should charge business travelers, with their low price elasticity of demand, a higher price than it charges students, with their high price elasticity of demand.

Perfect Price Discrimination

Let's return to the example of business travelers and students traveling between Bismarck and Fort Lauderdale, illustrated in Figure 8-10, and ask what would happen if the airline could distinguish between the two groups of customers to charge each a different price.

Clearly, the airline would charge each group its willingness to pay—that is, the maximum that each group is willing to pay. For business travelers, the willingness to pay is $550; for students, it is $150. As we have assumed, the marginal cost is $125 and does not depend on output, making the marginal cost curve a horizontal line. As we noted earlier, we can easily determine the airline's profit: it is the sum of the areas of the rectangle *B* and the rectangle *S*.

In this case, the consumers do not get any consumer surplus! The entire surplus is captured by the monopolist in the form of profit. When a monopolist is able to capture the entire surplus in this way, we say that it achieves **perfect price discrimination.**

In general, the greater the number of different prices a monopolist is able to charge, the closer it can get to perfect price discrimination. Figure 8-11 shows a monopolist facing a downward-sloping demand curve, a monopolist who we assume is able to charge different prices to different groups of consumers, with the consumers who are willing to pay the most being charged the most.

In panel (a) the monopolist charges two different prices; in panel (b) the monopolist charges three different prices. Two things are apparent here:

1. The greater the number of prices the monopolist charges, the lower the lowest price—that is, some consumers will pay prices that approach marginal cost.

2. The greater the number of prices the monopolist charges, the more money it extracts from consumers.

With a very large number of different prices, the picture would look like panel (c), a case of perfect price discrimination. Here, consumers least willing to buy the good pay marginal cost, and the entire consumer surplus is extracted as profit.

Both our airline example and the example in Figure 8-11 can be used to make another point: a monopolist that can engage in perfect price discrimination

On many airline routes, the fare you pay depends on the type of traveler you are.

Perfect price discrimination takes place when a monopolist charges each consumer his or her willingness to pay—the maximum that the consumer is willing to pay.

FIGURE 8-11 Price Discrimination

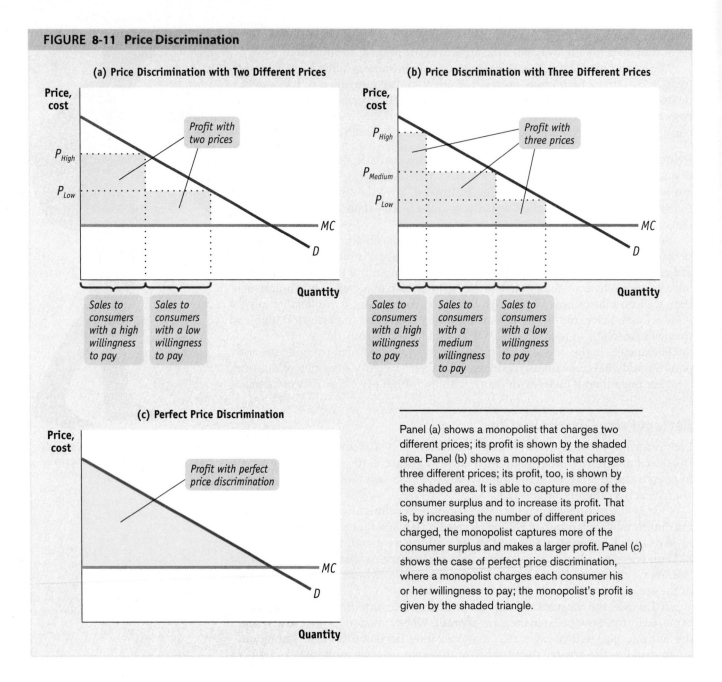

(a) Price Discrimination with Two Different Prices

Profit with two prices

Sales to consumers with a high willingness to pay

Sales to consumers with a low willingness to pay

(b) Price Discrimination with Three Different Prices

Profit with three prices

Sales to consumers with a high willingness to pay

Sales to consumers with a medium willingness to pay

Sales to consumers with a low willingness to pay

(c) Perfect Price Discrimination

Profit with perfect price discrimination

Panel (a) shows a monopolist that charges two different prices; its profit is shown by the shaded area. Panel (b) shows a monopolist that charges three different prices; its profit, too, is shown by the shaded area. It is able to capture more of the consumer surplus and to increase its profit. That is, by increasing the number of different prices charged, the monopolist captures more of the consumer surplus and makes a larger profit. Panel (c) shows the case of perfect price discrimination, where a monopolist charges each consumer his or her willingness to pay; the monopolist's profit is given by the shaded triangle.

doesn't cause any inefficiency! The reason is that the source of inefficiency is eliminated: all potential consumers who are willing to purchase the good at a price equal to or above marginal cost are able to do so. The perfectly price discriminating monopolist manages to scoop up all consumers by offering some of them lower prices than it charges others.

Perfect price discrimination is almost never possible in practice. At a fundamental level, the inability to achieve perfect price discrimination is a problem of prices as economic signals, a phenomenon we noted earlier.

When prices work as economic signals, they convey the information needed to ensure that all mutually beneficial transactions will indeed occur: the market price signals the seller's cost, and a consumer signals willingness to pay by purchasing the good whenever that willingness to pay is at least as high as the market price.

The problem in reality, however, is that prices are often not perfect signals: a consumer's true willingness to pay can be disguised, as by a business traveler who claims to be a student when buying a ticket to obtain a lower fare. When such disguises work, a monopolist cannot achieve perfect price discrimination.

However, monopolists do try to move in the direction of perfect price discrimination through a variety of pricing strategies. Common techniques for price discrimination include the following:

- *Advance purchase restrictions.* Prices are lower for those who purchase well in advance (or in some cases for those who purchase at the last minute). This separates those who are likely to shop for better prices from those who won't.

- *Volume discounts.* Often the price is lower if you buy a large quantity. For a consumer who plans to consume a lot of a good, the cost of the last unit—the marginal cost to the consumer—is considerably less than the average price. This separates those who plan to buy a lot and so are likely to be more sensitive to price from those who don't.

- *Two-part tariffs.* With a two-part tariff, a customer pays a flat fee upfront and then a per-unit fee on each item purchased. So in a discount club like Sam's Club (which is not a monopolist but a monopolistic competitor), you pay an annual fee in addition to the cost of the items you purchase. So, the cost of the first item you buy is in effect much higher than that of subsequent items, making the two-part tariff behave like a volume discount.

Our discussion also helps explain why government policies on monopoly typically focus on preventing deadweight losses, not preventing price discrimination—unless it causes serious issues of equity. Compared to a single-price monopolist, price discrimination—even when it is not perfect—can increase the efficiency of the market.

If sales to consumers formerly priced out of the market but who are now able to purchase the good at a lower price generate enough surplus to offset the loss in surplus to those now facing a higher price and no longer buying the good, then total surplus increases when price discrimination is introduced.

An example of this might be a drug that is disproportionately prescribed to senior citizens, who are often on fixed incomes and so are very sensitive to price. A policy that allows a drug company to charge senior citizens a low price and everyone else a high price may indeed increase total surplus compared to a situation in which everyone is charged the same price. But price discrimination that creates serious concerns about equity is likely to be prohibited—for example, an ambulance service that charges patients based on the severity of their emergency.

ECONOMICS >> *in Action*
Sales, Factory Outlets, and Ghost Cities

Have you ever wondered why department stores occasionally hold sales, offering their merchandise for considerably less than the usual prices? Or why, driving along America's highways, you sometimes encounter clusters of factory outlet stores a few hours away from the nearest city?

These familiar features of the economic landscape are actually rather peculiar if you think about them: why should sheets and towels be suddenly cheaper for a week each winter, or raincoats be offered for less in Freeport, Maine, than in Boston? In each case the answer is that the sellers—who are often oligopolists or monopolistic competitors—are engaged in a subtle form of price discrimination.

Why hold regular sales of sheets and towels? Stores are aware that some consumers buy these goods only when they discover that they need them; they are not likely to put a lot of effort into searching for the best price and so have a relatively low price elasticity of demand. So the store wants to charge high prices for customers who come in on an ordinary day.

Periodic sales allow stores to price-discriminate between their high-elasticity and low-elasticity customers.

But shoppers who plan ahead, looking for the lowest price, will wait until there is a sale. By scheduling such sales only now and then, the store is in effect able to price-discriminate between high-elasticity and low-elasticity customers.

An outlet store serves the same purpose: by offering merchandise for low prices, but only at a considerable distance away, a seller is able to establish a separate market for those customers who are willing to make the effort to search out lower prices—and who therefore have a relatively high price elasticity of demand.

Finally, let's return to airline tickets to mention one of the truly odd features of their prices. Often a flight from one major destination to another—say, from Chicago to Los Angeles—is cheaper than a much shorter flight to a smaller city—say, from Chicago to Salt Lake City. Again, the reason is a difference in the price elasticity of demand: customers have a choice of many airlines between Chicago and Los Angeles, so the demand for any one flight is quite elastic; customers have very little choice in flights to a small city, so the demand is much less elastic.

But often there is a flight between two major destinations that makes a stop along the way—say, a flight from Chicago to Los Angeles with a stop in Salt Lake City. In these cases, it is sometimes cheaper to fly to the more distant city than to the city that is a stop along the way. For example, it may be cheaper to purchase a ticket to Los Angeles and get off in Salt Lake City than to purchase a ticket to Salt Lake City! It sounds ridiculous but makes perfect sense given the logic of monopoly pricing.

So why don't passengers simply buy a ticket from Chicago to Los Angeles, but get off at Salt Lake City? Well, some do—but the airlines, understandably, make it difficult for customers to find out about such "ghost cities." In addition, the airline will not allow you to check baggage only part of the way if you have a ticket for the final destination. And airlines refuse to honor tickets for return flights when a passenger has not completed all the legs of the outbound flight. All these restrictions are meant to enforce the separation of markets necessary to allow price discrimination.

>> Quick Review

- Not every monopolist is a **single-price monopolist.** Many monopolists, as well as oligopolists and monopolistic competitors, engage in **price discrimination.**

- Price discrimination is profitable when consumers differ in their sensitivity to the price. A monopolist charges higher prices to low-elasticity consumers and lower prices to high-elasticity ones.

- A monopolist able to charge each consumer his or her willingness to pay for the good achieves **perfect price discrimination** and does not cause inefficiency because all mutually beneficial transactions are exploited.

>> Check Your Understanding 8-4

Solutions appear at back of book.

1. True or false? Explain your answer.
   a. A single-price monopolist sells to some customers that a price-discriminating monopolist refuses to.
   b. A price-discriminating monopolist creates more inefficiency than a single-price monopolist because it captures more of the consumer surplus.
   c. Under price discrimination, a customer with highly elastic demand will pay a lower price than a customer with inelastic demand.

2. Which of these are cases of price discrimination and which are not? In the cases of price discrimination, identify the consumers with high and those with low price elasticity of demand.
   a. Damaged merchandise is marked down.
   b. Restaurants have senior citizen discounts.
   c. Food manufacturers place discount coupons for their merchandise in newspapers.
   d. Airline tickets cost more during the summer peak flying season.

SOLVED PROBLEM | Painkiller Pricing

When suffering from sore muscles, a headache, or a fever, many of us turn to the painkiller ibuprofen for relief. Until 1986, a British pharmaceutical company, Boots Laboratories, held the patent for ibuprofen, which it sold under the brand name Advil. Boots, then, had a monopoly on producing and selling the drug. At the time, a 100-tablet bottle of ibuprofen cost about $5, which is equivalent to $10 in today's dollars. But, when the patent expired in 1986, generic drug manufacturers entered the market and the price of that 100-tablet bottle dropped below $2.

The accompanying table shows a hypothetical demand schedule for ibuprofen.

Assuming that the marginal cost of producing a 100-tablet bottle of ibuprofen is $2, calculate total revenue, marginal revenue, and the profit-maximizing price and quantity for a bottle of Advil before generic drug producers enter the market. Then, assuming a perfectly competitive industry, explain what happens to equilibrium price and quantity when generic drug producers enter the market.

Price	Quantity of 100-tablet bottle (millions)
$20	0
18	1
16	2
14	3
12	4
10	5
8	6
6	7
4	8
2	9

STEP | 1 Construct a marginal revenue schedule to find Advil's optimal price and quantity for producing bottles of ibuprofen. *Review pages 234–237.*

Total revenue is found by multiplying price and quantity ($TR = P \times Q$). The marginal revenue is the change in total revenue divided by the change in quantity ($MR = \Delta TR/\Delta Q$). In the upcoming table, the total revenue for producing 1 million 100-tablet bottles is $18 million or simply 1 million times $18. The total revenue for 2 million bottles is $32 million or 2 million times $16. The marginal revenue from producing an extra million bottles, 2 million bottles, is $(32 - 18)/(2 - 1)$ or $14, the change in total revenue from producing an extra 1 million bottles, $14 million, divided by the change in quantity or 1 million bottles.

Price	Quantity of 100-tablet bottle (millions)	Total revenue (millions of dollars) $TR = P \times Q$	Marginal revenue per 100-tablet bottles (dollars) $MR = \Delta TR/\Delta Q$
$20	0	$0	
			$18
18	1	18	
			14
16	2	32	
			10
14	3	42	
			6
12	4	48	
			2
10	5	50	
			−2
8	6	48	
			−6
6	7	42	
			−10
4	8	32	
			−14
2	9	18	

STEP | 2 Determine the optimal price and quantity of bottles of ibuprofen to produce.
Review pages 238–239.

A monopolist maximizes profit by producing the quantity at which marginal revenue equals marginal cost. In this case, Advil has a marginal cost of $2 per bottle. The purple shading in the table shows that marginal revenue is $2 at a quantity of 5 million bottles. You can also verify that profit is highest, $40 million, when price is set at $10 per bottle and Advil manufactures 5 million bottles.

STEP | 3 Determine what happens to equilibrium price and quantity when generic drug manufacturers are allowed to enter the industry and produce ibuprofen.
Review pages 242–243.

When the patent for ibuprofen expired, many firms began producing the drug, making the industry almost perfectly competitive—causing price to equal marginal cost. Looking at the area shaded green in the table, you can see that marginal cost, $2, is equal to price at a quantity of 9 million bottles.

SUMMARY

1. There are four main types of market structure based on the number of firms in the industry and product differentiation: perfect competition, monopoly, oligopoly, and monopolistic competition.

2. A **monopolist** is a producer who is the sole supplier of a good without close substitutes. An industry controlled by a monopolist is a **monopoly.**

3. The key difference between a monopoly and a perfectly competitive industry is that a single perfectly competitive firm faces a horizontal demand curve but a monopolist faces a downward-sloping demand curve. This gives the monopolist **market power,** the ability to raise the market price by reducing output compared to a perfectly competitive firm.

4. To persist, a monopoly must be protected by a **barrier to entry.** This can take the form of control of a natural resource or input, increasing returns to scale that give rise to **natural monopoly,** technological superiority, a **network externality,** or government rules that prevent entry by other firms, such as **patents** or **copyrights.**

5. The marginal revenue of a monopolist is composed of a quantity effect (the price received from the additional unit) and a price effect (the reduction in the price at which all units are sold). Because of the price effect, a monopolist's marginal revenue is always less than the market price, and the marginal revenue curve lies below the demand curve.

6. At the monopolist's profit-maximizing output level, marginal cost equals marginal revenue, which is less than market price. At the perfectly competitive firm's profit-maximizing output level, marginal cost equals the market price. So in comparison to perfectly competitive industries, monopolies produce less, charge higher prices, and earn profits in both the short run and the long run.

7. A monopoly creates deadweight losses by charging a price above marginal cost: the loss in consumer surplus exceeds the monopolist's profit. Thus monopolies are a source of market failure and should be prevented or broken up, except in the case of natural monopolies. **Monopsony,** an industry in which there is only one buyer of a good, is more rare than cases of monopoly. The **monopsonist** can affect the price of the good it buys: it captures surplus from sellers by reducing how much it purchases and thereby lowers the price. It creates deadweight loss by reducing the level of the good transacted to inefficiently low levels.

8. Natural monopolies can still cause deadweight losses. To limit these losses, governments sometimes impose **public ownership** and at other times impose **price regulation.** A price ceiling on a monopolist, as opposed to a perfectly competitive industry, need not cause shortages and can increase total surplus.

9. Not all monopolists are **single-price monopolists.** Monopolists, as well as oligopolists and monopolistic competitors, often engage in **price discrimination** to make higher profits, using various techniques to differentiate consumers based on their sensitivity to price, charging those with less elastic demand higher prices. A monopolist that achieves **perfect price discrimination** charges each consumer a price equal to his or her willingness to pay and captures the total surplus in the market. Although perfect price discrimination creates no inefficiency, it is practically impossible to implement.

KEY TERMS

DISCUSSION QUESTIONS

1. Skyscraper City has a subway system, for which a one-way fare is $1.50. There is pressure on the mayor to reduce the fare by one-third, to $1.00. The mayor is dismayed, thinking that this will mean Skyscraper City is losing one-third of its revenue from sales of subway tickets. The mayor's economic adviser reminds her that she is focusing only on the price effect and ignoring the quantity effect. Explain why the mayor's estimate of a one-third loss of revenue is likely to be an overestimate. Illustrate with a diagram.

2. This diagram illustrates your local electric company's natural monopoly. It shows the demand curve for kilowatt-hours (kWh) of electricity, the company's marginal revenue (*MR*) curve, its marginal cost (*MC*) curve, and its average total cost (*ATC*) curve. The government wants to regulate the monopolist by imposing a price ceiling.

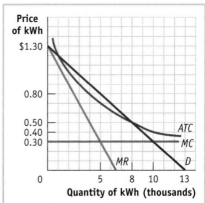

   a. If the government does not regulate this monopolist, which price will it charge? Illustrate the inefficiency this creates by shading the deadweight loss from monopoly.

   b. If the government imposes a price ceiling equal to the marginal cost, $0.30, will the monopolist make profits or lose money? Shade the area of profit (or loss) for the monopolist. If the government does impose this price ceiling, do you think the firm will continue to produce in the long run?

   c. If the government imposes a price ceiling of $0.50, will the monopolist make a profit, lose money, or break even?

3. A monopolist knows that in order to expand the quantity of output it produces from 8 to 9 units, it must

lower the price of its output from $2 to $1. Calculate the quantity effect and the price effect. Use these results to calculate the monopolist's marginal revenue of producing the 9th unit. The marginal cost of producing the 9th unit is positive. Is it a good idea for the monopolist to produce the 9th unit?

4. Explain the following situations.

   a. In Europe, when a service contract is purchased, many cell phone service providers give away for free what would otherwise be very expensive cell phones. Why might a company want to do that?

   b. In England, the country's antitrust authority prohibited the cell phone service provider Vodafone from offering a plan that gave customers free calls to other Vodafone customers. Why might Vodafone have wanted to offer these calls for free? Why might a government want to step in and ban this practice? Why might it not be a good idea for a government to interfere in this way?

5. For people with life-threatening allergies, carrying a device that can automatically inject epinephrine (called an *autoinjector*) is a necessity. In the summer of 2016, Mylan, the maker of the widely used autoinjector EpiPen, found itself with a virtual monopoly. A year earlier its primary competitor, Auvi-Q, was recalled amid fears that it would malfunction and deliver the wrong dose. In addition, the FDA denied the drug producer, Teva, from releasing a generic autoinjector. Prior to these events, a two-pack EpiPen sold for approximately $100. But, during that summer, Mylan raised the price to over $600 per pack, leading to extensive news coverage, popular online petitions, and outrage on the part of consumers. Mylan countered that many consumers received their EpiPens through their medical insurance, hence they were protected from the price increase. For those who didn't have insurance coverage and had to pay the full price, Mylan offered a $300 savings card.

   a. Draw a graph that shows consumer and producer surplus in a competitive market for epinephrine autoinjectors. Assume firms have a constant marginal cost of $100 per pack.

   b. Next, using that graph, show how much consumer surplus, producer surplus, and deadweight loss change after the Auvi-Q recall and the denied entry of Teva by the FDA.

c. How is the savings card offered to those without insurance an example of price discrimination? (*Hint:* Patients who are covered by medical insurance are like consumers who have high incomes and can therefore afford to pay full price.) Draw a graph showing how consumer and producer surplus will change under the savings card program.

PROBLEMS

interactive activity

1. Each of the following firms possesses market power. Explain its source.

   a. Merck, the producer of the patented cholesterol-lowering drug Zetia

   b. Waterworks, a provider of piped water

   c. Chiquita, a supplier of bananas and owner of most banana plantations

   d. The Walt Disney Company, the creators of Mickey Mouse

2. Bob, Bill, Ben, and Brad Baxter have just made a documentary movie about their basketball team. They are thinking about making the movie available for download on the internet, and they can act as a single-price monopolist if they choose to. Each time the movie is downloaded, their internet service provider charges them a fee of $4. The Baxter brothers are arguing about which price to charge customers per download. The accompanying table shows the demand schedule for their film.

Price of download	Quantity of downloads demanded
$10	0
8	1
6	3
4	6
2	10
0	15

   a. Calculate the total revenue and the marginal revenue per download.

   b. Bob is proud of the film and wants as many people as possible to download it. Which price would he choose? How many downloads would be sold?

   c. Bill wants as much total revenue as possible. Which price would he choose? How many downloads would be sold?

   d. Ben wants to maximize profit. Which price would he choose? How many downloads would be sold?

   e. Brad wants to charge the efficient price. Which price would he choose? How many downloads would be sold?

3. Mateo's room overlooks a major league baseball stadium. He decides to rent a telescope for $50.00 a week and charge his friends to use it to peep at the games for 30 seconds. He can act as a single-price monopolist for renting out "peeps." For each person who takes a 30-second peep, it costs Mateo $0.20 to clean the eyepiece. The accompanying table shows the information Mateo has gathered about the weekly demand for the service.

Price of peep	Quantity of peeps demanded
$1.20	0
1.00	100
0.90	150
0.80	200
0.70	250
0.60	300
0.50	350
0.40	400
0.30	450
0.20	500
0.10	550

   a. For each price in the table, calculate the total revenue from selling peeps and the marginal revenue per peep.

   b. At what quantity will Mateo's profit be maximized? What price will he charge? What will his total profit be?

   c. Mateo's landlady complains about all the visitors and tells him to stop selling peeps. But, if he pays her $0.20 for every peep he sells, she won't complain. What effect does the $0.20-per-peep bribe have on Mateo's marginal cost per peep? What is the new profit-maximizing quantity of peeps? What effect does the $0.20-per-peep bribe have on Mateo's total profit?

4. Suppose that De Beers is a single-price monopolist in the diamond market. De Beers has five potential customers: Raquel, Jackie, Joan, Mia, and Sophia. Each of these customers will buy at most one diamond—and only if the price is just equal to, or lower than, her willingness to pay. Raquel's willingness to pay is $400; Jackie's, $300; Joan's, $200; Mia's, $100; and Sophia's, $0. De Beers's marginal cost per diamond is $100. The result is a demand schedule for diamonds as follows:

Price of diamond	Quantity of diamonds demanded
$500	0
400	1
300	2
200	3
100	4
0	5

a. Calculate De Beers's total revenue and its marginal revenue. From your calculation, draw the demand curve and the marginal revenue curve.

b. Explain why De Beers faces a downward-sloping demand curve and why the marginal revenue from an additional diamond sale is less than the price of the diamond.

c. Suppose De Beers currently charges $200 for its diamonds. If it lowers the price to $100, how large is the price effect? How large is the quantity effect?

d. Add the marginal cost curve to your diagram from part a and determine which quantity maximizes De Beers's profit and which price De Beers will charge.

5. Use the demand schedule for diamonds given in Problem 4. The marginal cost of producing diamonds is constant at $100. There is no fixed cost.

a. If De Beers charges the monopoly price, how large is the individual consumer surplus that each buyer experiences? Calculate total consumer surplus by summing the individual consumer surpluses. How large is producer surplus?

Suppose that upstart Russian and Asian producers enter the market and it becomes perfectly competitive.

b. What is the perfectly competitive price? What quantity will be sold in this perfectly competitive market?

c. At the competitive price and quantity, how large is the consumer surplus that each buyer experiences? How large is total consumer surplus? How large is producer surplus?

d. Compare your answer to part c to your answer to part a. How large is the deadweight loss associated with monopoly in this case?

6. Use the demand schedule for diamonds given in Problem 4. De Beers is a monopolist, but it can now price-discriminate perfectly among all five of its potential customers. De Beers's marginal cost is constant at $100. There is no fixed cost.

a. If De Beers can price-discriminate perfectly, to which customers will it sell diamonds and at what prices?

b. How large is each individual consumer surplus? How large is total consumer surplus? Calculate producer surplus by summing the producer surplus generated by each sale.

7. Download Records decides to release an album by the group Mary and the Little Lamb. It produces the album with no fixed cost, but the total cost of creating a digital album and paying Mary her royalty is $6 per album. Download Records can act as a single-price monopolist. Its marketing division finds that the demand schedule for the album is as shown in the accompanying table.

Price of album	Quantity of albums demanded
$22	0
20	1,000
18	2,000
16	3,000
14	4,000
12	5,000
10	6,000
8	7,000

a. Calculate the total revenue and the marginal revenue per album.

b. The marginal cost of producing each album is constant at $6. To maximize profit, what level of output should Download Records choose, and which price should it charge for each album?

c. Mary renegotiates her contract and will be paid a higher royalty per album. So the marginal cost rises to be constant at $14. To maximize profit, what level of output should Download Records now choose, and which price should it charge for each album?

8. The Collegetown movie theater serves 900 students and 100 professors in town. Each student's willingness to pay for a movie ticket is $5. Each professor's willingness to pay is $10. Each will buy only one ticket. The movie theater's marginal cost per ticket is constant at $3, and there is no fixed cost.

a. Suppose the movie theater cannot price-discriminate and charges both students and professors the same price per ticket. If the movie theater charges $5, who will buy tickets and what will the movie theater's profit be? How large is consumer surplus?

b. If the movie theater charges $10, who will buy movie tickets and what will the movie theater's profit be? How large is consumer surplus?

c. Assume the movie theater can price-discriminate between students and professors by requiring students to show their student ID. If the movie theater charges students $5 and professors $10, how much profit will the movie theater make? How large is consumer surplus?

9. In the United States, the Federal Trade Commission (FTC) is charged with promoting competition and challenging mergers that would likely lead to higher prices. Several years ago, Staples and Office Depot, two of the largest office supply superstores, announced their agreement to merge.

a. Some critics of the merger argued that, in many parts of the country, a merger between the two companies would create a monopoly in the office supply superstore market. Based on the FTC's argument and its mission to challenge mergers that would likely lead to higher prices, do you think it allowed the merger?

b. Staples and Office Depot argued that, while in some parts of the country they might create a monopoly in the office supply superstore market, the FTC should consider the larger market for all office supplies, which includes many smaller stores that sell office supplies (such as grocery stores and other retailers). In that market, Staples and Office Depot would face competition from many other, smaller stores. If the market for all office supplies is the relevant market that the FTC should consider, would it make the FTC more or less likely to allow the merger?

10. Prior to the late 1990s, the same company that generated your electricity also distributed it to you over high-voltage lines. Since then, 16 states and the District of Columbia have begun separating the generation from the distribution of electricity, allowing competition between electricity generators and between electricity distributors.

a. Assume that the market for electricity distribution was and remains a natural monopoly. Use a graph to illustrate the market for electricity distribution if the government sets price equal to average total cost.

b. Assume that deregulation of electricity generation creates a perfectly competitive market. Also assume that electricity generation does not exhibit the characteristics of a natural monopoly. Use a graph to illustrate the cost curves in the long-run equilibrium for an individual firm in this industry.

11. In 2014, Time Warner and Comcast announced their intention to merge. This prompted questions

of monopoly because the combined company would supply cable access to an overwhelming majority of Americans. It also raised questions of monopsony since the combined company would be virtually the only purchaser of programming for broadcast shows. Although the merger was ultimately disallowed, assume that it had occurred. In each of the following, determine whether it is evidence of monopoly, monopsony, or neither.

a. The monthly cable fee for consumers increases significantly more than the increase in the cost of producing and delivering programs over cable.

b. Companies that advertise on cable TV find that they must pay higher rates for advertising.

c. Companies that produce broadcast shows find they must produce more shows for the same amount they were paid before.

d. Consumers find that there are more shows available for the same monthly cable fee.

12. Walmart is the world's largest retailer. As a consequence, it has sufficient bargaining power to push its suppliers to lower their prices so it can honor its slogan of "Save Money. Live Better" for its customers.

a. Is Walmart acting like a monopolist or monopsonist when purchasing goods from suppliers? Explain.

b. How does Walmart affect the consumer surplus of its customers? The producer surplus of its suppliers?

c. Over time, what is likely to happen to the quality of products produced by Walmart suppliers?

WORK IT OUT **Interactive step-by-step help with solving this problem can be found online.**

13. Consider an industry with the demand curve (*D*) and marginal cost curve (*MC*) shown in the accompanying diagram. There is no fixed cost. If the industry is a single-price monopoly, the monopolist's marginal revenue curve would be *MR*. Answer the following questions by naming the appropriate points or areas.

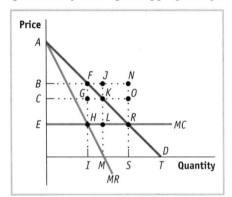

a. If the industry is perfectly competitive, what will be the total quantity produced? At what price?

b. Which area reflects consumer surplus under perfect competition?

c. If the industry is a single-price monopoly, what quantity will the monopolist produce? Which price will it charge?

d. Which area reflects the single-price monopolist's profit?

e. Which area reflects consumer surplus under single-price monopoly?

f. Which area reflects the deadweight loss to society from single-price monopoly?

g. If the monopolist can price-discriminate perfectly, what quantity will the perfectly price-discriminating monopolist produce?

9 Oligopoly and Monopolistic Competition

REGULATORS GIVE BRIDGESTONE A FLAT TIRE

WITH SALES OF OVER $27 BILLION in 2015, Bridgestone is the largest tire company by sales in the United States. But in 2014 it suffered a particularly humiliating turn of events, courtesy of U.S. regulators. That year Bridgestone admitted that for several years it had participated in meetings with competitors Hitachi Automotive and Mitsubishi Electric. At those meetings, the companies set prices and split up the market for rubber automotive parts, behavior called *price-fixing*. In all, 26 companies pled guilty to price-fixing for rubber automotive parts, 32 people were indicted, and a total of more than $2 billion in fines were assessed by the U.S. government.

What Bridgestone and their co-conspirators were doing was illegal. According to the indictment issued by the Justice Department, their actions were undertaken to "suppress and eliminate competition." The effect of these actions was to raise the price of auto parts to auto manufacturers throughout the country—from General Motors to Toyota to Chrysler. In this chapter we will come to understand how regulators made the determination of price-fixing, and how Bridgestone's actions hurt consumers.

The case brought against Bridgestone and its co-conspirators illustrates the issues posed by *oligopoly*—an industry that is neither perfectly competitive nor purely monopolistic. Oligopoly is a type of market structure in which there are only a few producers. In the real world, oligopoly occurs much more frequently than monopoly. And it is arguably more typical of modern economies than perfect competition.

The problems posed by oligopoly keep regulators at the U.S. Justice Department very busy investigating dozens of cases of allegedly anti-competitive behavior. Recent cases have involved fees charged by the American Express credit card company, e-book price-fixing on the part of Apple and book publishers, rigged financial transactions by several major international banks, and price-fixing in deep sea transport.

When there are only a few producers in an industry, as is the case with oligopoly, the issue of *strategic behavior* arises: how one firm behaves affects the behavior of other firms. Because firms can affect each other's behavior, they are tempted to coordinate their actions, or *collude*, in order to stifle competition and raise profits, as Bridgestone and its co-conspirators did. As a result of this behavior, regulators often intervene in oligopolistic industries to protect consumers.

In this chapter, we'll begin by examining what oligopoly is and why it is so important. Then we'll turn to the behavior of oligopolistic industries. Finally, we'll look at the meaning of monopolistic competition and how monopolistically competitive firms compete through product differentiation. •

The law catches up with a colluding oligopolist.

WHAT YOU WILL LEARN

- What is **oligopoly** and why does it occur?
- Why do **oligopolists** benefit from **collusion** and how are consumers hurt by it?
- Why is **antitrust policy,** which is aimed at preventing collusion among oligopolists, a critical function of government?
- How do the insights gained from **game theory** help us to understand the strategic behavior of oligopolists?
- What is **monopolistic competition** and why do monopolistically competitive firms differentiate their products?

An **oligopoly** is an industry with only a small number of producers. A producer in such an industry is known as an **oligopolist.**

When no one firm has a monopoly, but producers nonetheless realize that they can affect market prices, an industry is characterized by **imperfect competition.**

The Meaning of Oligopoly

During the period of price-fixing by Bridgestone and its co-conspirators, no one company controlled the world market for rubber auto parts. Instead, there were only a few major producers. An industry with only a few sellers is known as an **oligopoly;** a firm in such an industry is known as an **oligopolist.** Of course, oligopolists compete with one another for sales. But neither Bridgestone nor Mitsubishi was like a firm in a perfectly competitive industry, which takes the price at which it can sell its product as given. Each of these firms knew that its decision about how much to produce would affect the market price. That is, like monopolists, each of the firms had some *market power.* So the competition in this industry wasn't "perfect."

Economists refer to a situation in which firms compete but also possess market power—which enables them to affect market prices—as **imperfect competition.** As we saw in Chapter 8, there are actually two important forms of imperfect competition: oligopoly and *monopolistic competition.* Of these, oligopoly is probably the more important in practice.

Although rubber automotive parts is a multibillion-dollar business, it is not exactly a product familiar to most consumers. However, many familiar goods and services are supplied by only a few competing sellers, which means the industries in question are oligopolies. For example, Google has a market share of 63% in the American search engine market, while Bing and Yahoo! have a combined share of 34%. In the U.S. smartphone market, Apple and Samsung have market shares of 47% and 22%, respectively. In the American toothpaste market, Colgate-Palmolive accounts for 48% of the market, while Crest and Sensodyne account for 29% and 22%, respectively. Verizon, AT&T, and T-Mobile collectively account for about 85% of the American wireless telephone subscriptions, and most domestic airline routes are covered by only two to three carriers. The list could go on for several more pages.

It's important to realize that an oligopoly isn't necessarily made up of large firms. What matters isn't size per se; the question is how many competitors there are. When a small town has only two grocery stores, grocery service in that town is just as much an oligopoly as air shuttle service between New York and Washington.

Why are oligopolies so prevalent? Essentially, oligopoly is the result of the same factors that sometimes produce monopoly, but in weaker form. Probably the most important source of oligopoly is the existence of *increasing returns to scale,* which give bigger producers a cost advantage over smaller ones. When these effects are very strong, they lead to monopoly. When they are only moderately strong, they lead to an industry with a small number of firms.

For example, larger grocery stores typically have lower costs than smaller ones. But the advantages of large scale taper off once grocery stores are reasonably large, which is why two or three stores often survive in small towns.

If oligopoly is so common, why has most of this book focused on competition in industries where the number of sellers is very large? And why did we study monopoly, which is relatively uncommon, first? The answer has two parts.

First, much of what we learn from the study of perfectly competitive markets—about costs, entry and exit, and efficiency—remains valid despite the fact that many industries are not perfectly competitive. Second, the analysis of oligopoly turns out to present some puzzles for which there are no easy solutions. It is almost always a good idea—in exams and in life in general—first to deal with the questions you can easily answer, then to puzzle over the harder ones. We have followed the same strategy, developing the relatively clear-cut theories of perfect competition and monopoly first, and only then turning to the puzzles presented by oligopoly.

Understanding Oligopoly

Oligopolists can behave fundamentally differently than firms in other types of market structure because they operate in a state of **interdependence**. This means that the pricing and production decisions of one firm significantly affect the profits of its rivals. To begin to understand how oligopolies think and behave, we will start with an example.

A Duopoly Example We'll now examine the simplest version of oligopoly, an industry in which there are only two producing firms—a **duopoly**—and each is known as a **duopolist.**

Going back to our opening story, imagine that there are only two producers of auto tires, Bridgestone and Hitachi. To make things simpler, suppose that once a company has incurred the fixed cost needed to produce tires, the marginal cost of producing another tire is zero. So, the companies are concerned only with the revenue they receive from sales, and not with their costs.

Table 9-1 shows a hypothetical demand schedule for tires and the total revenue of the industry at each price–quantity combination.

If this were a perfectly competitive industry, each firm would have an incentive to produce more as long as the market price was above marginal cost. Since the marginal cost is assumed to be zero, this would mean that at equilibrium tires would be provided free. Firms would produce until price equals zero, yielding a total output of 120 million tires and zero revenue for both firms.

Yet, surely the firms would not be that stupid. With only two firms in the industry, each would realize that by producing more, it drives down the market price. So, each firm would, like a monopolist, realize that profits would be higher if it and its rival limited their production.

So how much will the two firms produce?

One possibility is that the two companies will engage in **collusion**—they will cooperate to raise their joint profits. The strongest form of collusion is a **cartel,** an arrangement between producers that determines how much each is allowed to produce. The world's most famous cartel is the Organization of the Petroleum Exporting Countries (OPEC), described in an Economics in Action later in the chapter.

As its name indicates, OPEC is actually an agreement among governments rather than firms. There's a reason this cartel is an agreement among governments: cartels among firms are illegal in the United States and many other jurisdictions. But let's ignore the law for a moment (which is, of course, what Bridgestone did in real life—to its detriment).

Let's illustrate with an example of a cartel formed by only two firms, Bridgestone and Hitachi. We'll assume that this cartel decided to act as if it were a monopolist, maximizing total industry profits. It's obvious from Table 9-1 that in order to maximize the combined profits of the two firms, the cartel should set total industry output at 60 million tires, which would sell at a price of $6 per tire, leading to revenue of $360 million, the maximum possible.

Then the only question would be how much of that 60 million tires each firm gets to produce. A fair solution might be for each firm to produce 30 million tires with revenues for each firm of $180 million.

But even if the two firms agreed on such a deal, they might have a problem: each of the firms would have an incentive to break its word and produce more than the agreed-upon quantity.

Collusion and Competition Suppose that the presidents of Bridgestone and Hitachi were to agree that each would

When a firm's decision significantly affects the profits of other firms in the industry, the firms are in a situation of **interdependence**.

An oligopoly consisting of only two firms is a **duopoly**. Each firm is known as a **duopolist**.

Sellers engage in **collusion** when they cooperate to raise their joint profits. A **cartel** is an agreement among several producers to obey output restrictions in order to increase their joint profits.

TABLE 9-1 Demand Schedule for Tires

Price of tire	Quantity of tires demanded (millions)	Total revenue (millions)
$12	0	$0
11	10	110
10	20	200
9	30	270
8	40	320
7	50	350
6	60	360
5	70	350
4	80	320
3	90	270
2	100	200
1	110	110
0	120	0

produce 30 million tires over the next year. Both would understand that this plan maximizes their combined profits. And both would have an incentive to cheat.

To see why, consider what would happen if Hitachi honored its agreement, producing only 30 million tires, but Bridgestone ignored its promise and produced 40 million tires. This increase in total output would drive the price down from $6 to $5 per tire, the price at which 70 million tires are demanded. The industry's total revenue would fall from $360 million ($6 × 60 million tires) to $350 million ($5 × 70 million tires). However, Bridgestone's revenue would *rise*, from $180 million ($6 × 30 million tires) to $200 million ($5 × 40 million tires). Since we are assuming a marginal cost of zero, this would mean a $20 million increase in Bridgestone's profits.

But Hitachi's president might make exactly the same calculation. And if both firms were to produce 40 million tires, the price would drop to $4 per tire. So each firm's profits would fall, from $180 million to $160 million.

Why do individual firms have an incentive to produce more than the quantity that maximizes their joint profits? Because neither firm has as strong an incentive to limit its output, as a true monopolist would.

Let's go back for a minute to the theory of monopoly. We know that a profit-maximizing monopolist sets marginal cost (which in this case is zero) equal to marginal revenue. But what is marginal revenue? Recall that, under monopoly, producing an additional unit of a good has two effects:

1. A positive *quantity* effect: one more unit is sold, increasing total revenue by the price at which that unit is sold.

2. A negative *price* effect: in order to sell one more unit, the monopolist must cut the market price on *all* units sold.

The negative price effect is the reason marginal revenue for a monopolist is less than the market price. In the case of oligopoly, when considering the effect of increasing production, a firm is concerned only with the price effect on its *own* units of output, not those of its fellow oligopolists. Both Bridgestone and Hitachi suffer a negative price effect if Bridgestone decides to produce extra tires and so drives down the price. But Bridgestone cares only about the negative price effect on the units it produces, not about the loss to Hitachi.

This tells us that an individual firm in an oligopolistic industry faces a smaller price effect from an additional unit of output than does a monopolist; therefore, the marginal revenue that such a firm calculates is higher. So it will seem to be profitable for any one company in an oligopoly to increase production, even if that increase reduces the profits of the industry as a whole. But if everyone thinks that way, the result is that everyone earns a lower profit!

Until now, we have been able to analyze producer behavior by asking what a producer should do to maximize profits. But even if Bridgestone and Hitachi are both trying to maximize profits, what does this predict about their behavior? Will they engage in collusion, reaching and holding to an agreement that maximizes their combined profits? Or will they engage in **noncooperative behavior,** with each firm acting in its own self-interest, even though this has the effect of driving down everyone's profits? Both strategies sound like profit maximization. Which will actually describe their behavior?

Now you see why oligopoly, with only a small number of players, makes collusion a real possibility. If there were dozens or hundreds of firms, it would be safe to assume they would behave noncooperatively. Yet even when there are only a handful of firms in an industry, collusion isn't inevitable. For reasons we explain in the next section, oligopolists are often unable to collude.

Since collusion is ultimately more profitable than noncooperative behavior, firms do have an incentive to collude if they can. One way to do so is to formalize it—sign an agreement (maybe even make a legal contract) or establish some financial incentives for the companies to set their prices high. But in the United

When firms ignore the effects of their actions on each other's profits, they engage in **noncooperative behavior.**

States and many other nations, you can't do that—at least not legally. Companies cannot make a legal contract to keep prices high: not only is the contract unenforceable, but writing it is a one-way ticket to jail. Neither can they sign an informal agreement, which lacks the force of law but perhaps rests on threats of retaliation—that's illegal, too.

In fact, executives from rival companies rarely meet without lawyers present, who make sure that the conversation does not stray into inappropriate territory. Even hinting at how nice it would be if prices were higher can bring you an unwelcome interview with the Justice Department or the Federal Trade Commission.

For example, in 2003 the Justice Department launched a price-fixing case against Monsanto and other large producers of genetically modified seed. The Justice Department was alerted by a series of meetings held between Monsanto and Pioneer Hi-Bred International, two companies that accounted for 60% of the U.S. market in corn and soybean seed. The two companies, parties to a licensing agreement involving genetically modified seed, claimed that no illegal discussions of price-fixing occurred in those meetings. But the fact that the two firms discussed prices as part of the licensing agreement was enough to trigger action by the Justice Department.

Sometimes, as we've seen, oligopolistic firms just ignore the rules. But more often they find ways to achieve collusion without a formal agreement, as we'll soon see.

Oligopoly in Practice

How do oligopolies usually work in practice? The answer depends both on the legal framework that limits what firms can do and on the underlying ability of firms in a given industry to cooperate without formal agreements.

The Legal Framework To understand oligopoly pricing in practice, we must be familiar with the legal constraints under which oligopolistic firms operate. In the United States, oligopoly first became an issue during the second half of the nineteenth century, when the growth of railroads—themselves an oligopolistic industry—created a national market for many goods.

Large firms producing oil, steel, and many other products soon emerged. The industrialists quickly realized that profits would be higher if they could limit price competition. So, many industries formed cartels—that is, they signed formal agreements to limit production and raise prices. Until 1890, when the first federal legislation against such cartels was passed, this was perfectly legal.

However, although these cartels were legal, they weren't legally *enforceable*—members of a cartel couldn't ask the courts to force a firm that was violating its agreement to reduce its production. And firms often did violate their agreements, for the reason already suggested by our duopoly example: there is always a temptation for each firm in a cartel to produce more than it is supposed to.

In 1881, clever lawyers at John D. Rockefeller's Standard Oil Company came up with a solution—the so-called *trust*. In a trust, shareholders of all the major companies in an industry placed their shares in the hands of a board of trustees who controlled the companies. This, in effect, merged the companies into a single firm that could then engage in monopoly pricing. In this way, the Standard Oil Trust established what was essentially a monopoly of the oil industry, and it was soon followed by trusts in sugar, whiskey, lead, cottonseed oil, and linseed oil.

Eventually there was a public backlash, driven partly by concern about the economic effects of the trust movement, partly by fear that the owners of the trusts were simply becoming too powerful. The result was the Sherman Antitrust Act of 1890, which was intended both to prevent the creation of more monopolies and to break up existing ones. At first this law went largely unenforced, but over the decades that followed, the federal government became increasingly committed to making

"Frankly, I'm dubious about amalgamated smelting and refining pleading innocent to their anti-trust violation due to insanity."

it difficult for oligopolistic industries either to become monopolies or to behave like them. Such efforts are known to this day as **antitrust policy.**

Among advanced countries, the United States is unique in its long tradition of antitrust policy. Until recently, other advanced countries did not have policies against price-fixing, and some had even supported the creation of cartels, believing that it would help their own firms against foreign rivals. But the situation has changed radically over the past 30 years, as the European Union (EU)—a supranational body tasked with enforcing antitrust policy for its member countries—has moved toward U.S. practices. Today, EU and U.S. regulators often target the same firms because price-fixing has "gone global" as international trade has expanded.

During the early 1990s, the United States instituted an amnesty program in which a price-fixer receives a much-reduced penalty if it informs on its co-conspirators. In addition, Congress increased the maximum fines levied upon conviction. These two new policies clearly made informing on your cartel partners a dominant strategy, and it has paid off because executives from Belgium, Great Britain, Canada, France, Germany, Italy, Mexico, the Netherlands, South Korea, and Switzerland, as well as from the United States, have been convicted of cartel crimes in U.S. courts. As one lawyer commented, "you get a race to the courthouse" as each conspirator seeks to be the first to come clean.

Life has gotten much tougher over the past few years if you want to operate a cartel.

Tacit Collusion and Price Wars If a real industry were as simple as our tire example, it probably wouldn't be necessary for the company presidents to meet or do anything that could land them in jail. Both firms would realize that it was in their mutual interest to restrict output to 30 million tires each and that any short-term gains to either firm from producing more would be much less than the later losses as the other firm retaliated. So even without any explicit agreement, the firms would probably achieve the tacit collusion needed to maximize their combined profits.

Firms are said to be engaged in **tacit collusion** when, as in our example, they restrict output in a way that raises the profits of another firm, and expect the favor to be returned, even without an enforceable agreement—although they act "as if" they had such an agreement and are in legal jeopardy if they even discuss price.

Real industries are nowhere near that simple. Nonetheless, in most oligopolistic industries, most of the time, the sellers do appear to succeed in keeping prices above their noncooperative level. Tacit collusion, in other words, is the normal state of oligopoly.

Although tacit collusion is common, it rarely allows an industry to push prices all the way up to their monopoly level; collusion is usually far from perfect. In particular, there are four factors that make it hard for an industry to coordinate on high prices.

1. Less Concentration: In a less concentrated industry, the typical firm will have a smaller market share than in a more concentrated industry. This tilts firms toward noncooperative behavior because when a smaller firm cheats and increases its output, it gains for itself all of the profit from the higher output. And if its rivals retaliate by increasing their output, the firm's losses are limited because of its relatively modest market share. A less concentrated industry is often an indication that there are low barriers to entry.

2. Complex Products and Pricing Schemes: In our tire example the two firms produce only one product. In reality, however, oligopolists often sell thousands or even tens of thousands of different products. Under these circumstances, keeping track of what other firms are producing and the prices they are charging is

Antitrust policy consists of efforts undertaken by the government to prevent oligopolistic industries from becoming or behaving like monopolies.

When firms limit production and raise prices in a way that raises one another's profits, even though they have not made any formal agreement, they are engaged in **tacit collusion.**

difficult. This makes it hard to determine whether a firm is cheating on the tacit agreement.

3. Differences in Interests: In the tire example, a tacit agreement for the firms to split the market equally is a natural outcome, probably acceptable to both firms. In real industries, however, firms often differ both in their perceptions about what is fair and in their real interests.

For example, suppose that Hitachi was a long-established tire producer and Bridgestone a more recent entrant to the industry. Hitachi might feel that it deserved to continue producing more than Bridgestone, but Bridgestone might feel that it was entitled to 50% of the business. Alternatively, suppose that Bridgestone's marginal costs were lower than Hitachi's. Even if they could agree on market shares, they would then disagree about the profit-maximizing level of output.

4. Bargaining Power of Buyers: Often oligopolists sell not to individual consumers but to large buyers—other industrial enterprises, nationwide chains of stores, and so on. These large buyers are in a position to bargain for lower prices from the oligopolists: they can ask for a discount from an oligopolist and warn that they will go to a competitor if they don't get it. An important reason that large retailers like Walmart are able to offer lower prices to customers than small retailers is precisely their ability to use their size to extract lower prices from their suppliers.

These difficulties in enforcing tacit collusion have sometimes led companies to defy the law and create illegal cartels, as we've seen in the case of the tire industry. In the following Economics in Action, we'll look at the chocolate industry.

Because tacit collusion is often hard to achieve, most oligopolies charge prices that are well below what the same industry would charge if it were controlled by a monopolist—or what they would charge if they were able to collude outright. In addition, sometimes collusion breaks down and there is a **price war.** A price war sometimes involves simply a collapse of prices to their noncooperative level. Sometimes prices even go *below* that level, as sellers try to put each other out of business or at least punish what they regard as cheating.

> A **price war** occurs when tacit collusion breaks down and prices collapse.

ECONOMICS >> *in Action*
The Case Against Chocolate Producers Melts

In the Bridgestone case, company executives admitted to price-fixing, giving investigators indisputable evidence of collusion that was used to prosecute the company. However, without solid evidence, the prosecution of price-fixing can be a tricky business. The differing outcomes of price-fixing allegations in the American and Canadian chocolate industry make that point abundantly clear.

In late 2015, an eight-year-long probe into collusion by the major Canadian chocolate makers finally ended. It started when Cadbury Canada disclosed that it had colluded with Hershey Canada, Nestlé Canada, and Mars Canada. In the ensuing court case, 13 Cadbury Canada executives revealed their contacts with the other companies, including one episode in which a Nestlé Canada executive handed over details about a forthcoming price hike to Cadbury Canada. According to court documents, top executives of Hershey Canada, Nestlé Canada, and Mars Canada secretly met to set prices. After protracted litigation, all four producers settled the case and paid fines totaling more than $23 million that were then distributed among consumers.

South of the border, several of the largest American grocery chains and snack retailers were convinced that they, too, had been victims of collusion by

Are chocolate makers engaging in price-fixing?

chocolate makers. In 2010, one of these stores, SuperValu, filed a lawsuit against the American divisions of the four chocolate makers. In contrast to Canada, where the big four controlled a little less than 50% of the market, in the U.S. market they controlled over 75%. SuperValu claimed that the American companies had been fixing prices since 2002, regularly increasing prices by mid-single-digit to double-digit amounts within a few days of one another.

Indeed, over that period the price of chocolate candy in the United States had soared, climbing by 17% from 2008 to 2010, far in excess of the rate of inflation. American chocolate makers, however, defended their actions, contending that they were simply passing on the higher costs of cocoa beans, dairy products, and sugar. And as antitrust experts pointed out, without solid evidence such as conversations or written agreements between companies, price-fixing can be very difficult to prove because it is not illegal for producers to raise prices at the same time.

In 2014, an American judge threw out the collusion case against the American chocolate producers, stating that closely timed price increases were not sufficient proof of collusion and that there was no evidence that American producers knew of the collusion between the Canadian counterparts. Federal Judge Christopher Conner concluded that the companies engaged in "rational, competitive behavior" when they increased prices to counter anticipated cost increases. In 2015, Canadian regulators finally closed their books on the case, deciding against bringing further criminal charges against the four companies.

>> Quick Review

- **Oligopoly** is a common market structure, one in which there are only a few firms, called **oligopolists,** in the industry. It arises from the same forces that lead to monopoly, except in a weaker form. Oligopolies operate in a state of **interdependence.**

- Some of the key issues in oligopoly can be understood by looking at the simplest case, a **duopoly**—an industry containing only two firms, called **duopolists.**

- By acting as if they were a single monopolist, oligopolists can maximize their combined profits. So there is an incentive to form a **cartel.**

- However, each firm has an incentive to cheat—to produce more than it is supposed to under the cartel agreement. So there are two principal outcomes: successful **collusion** or behaving **noncooperatively** by cheating.

- Oligopolies operate under legal restrictions in the form of **antitrust policy.** But many succeed in achieving **tacit collusion,** which occurs when firms, without any formal agreement, limit production and raise prices in a way that raises one another's profits.

- Tacit collusion is limited by a number of factors, including large numbers of firms, complex products and pricing, differences in interests among firms, and bargaining power of buyers. When collusion breaks down, there is a **price war.**

>> Check Your Understanding 9-1
Solutions appear at back of book.

1. Explain why each of the following industries is an oligopoly, not a perfectly competitive industry.
   a. The world oil industry, where a few countries near the Persian Gulf control much of the world's oil reserves
   b. The microprocessor industry, where two firms, Intel and its bitter rival AMD, dominate the technology
   c. The wide-body passenger jet industry, composed of the American firm Boeing and the European firm Airbus, where production is characterized by an extremely large fixed cost

2. Which of the following factors increase the likelihood that an oligopolist will collude with other firms in the industry? Which increase the likelihood that an oligopolist will act noncooperatively and raise output? Explain your answers.
   a. The firm's initial market share is small. (*Hint:* Think about the price effect.)
   b. The firm has a cost advantage over its rivals.

3. Which of the following factors are likely to support the conclusion that there is tacit collusion in this industry? Which are not? Explain.
   a. There has been considerable variation in the market shares of the firms in the industry over time.
   b. Firms in the industry build into their products unnecessary features that make it hard for consumers to switch from one company's products to another company's products.
   c. Firms meet yearly to discuss their annual sales forecasts.
   d. Firms tend to adjust their prices upward at the same time.

‖ Games Oligopolists Play

In our duopoly example and in real life, each oligopolistic firm realizes both that its profit depends on what its competitor does and that its competitor's profit depends on what it does. The two firms are in a state of interdependence, where each firm's decision significantly affects the profit of the other firm (or firms, in the case of more than two).

In effect, the two firms are playing a game in which the profit of each player depends not only on its own actions but on those of the other player (or players). To understand more fully how oligopolists behave, economists, along with mathematicians, developed the area of study of such games, known as **game theory.** It has many applications—not just to economics but also to military strategy, politics, and other social sciences.

Let's see how game theory helps us understand oligopoly.

The Prisoners' Dilemma

Game theory deals with any situation in which the reward to any one player—the **payoff**—depends not only on his or her own actions but also on those of other players in the game. In the case of oligopolistic firms, the payoff is simply the firm's profit.

When there are only two players, as in a duopoly, the interdependence between the players can be represented with a **payoff matrix** like that shown in Figure 9-1. Each row corresponds to an action by one player (in this case, Bridgestone); each column corresponds to an action by the other (in this case, Hitachi). For simplicity, let's assume that Bridgestone can pick only one of two alternatives: produce 30 million tires or produce 40 million tires. Hitachi has the same pair of choices.

The matrix contains four boxes, each divided by a diagonal line. Each box shows the payoff to the two firms that results from a pair of choices: the number below the diagonal shows Bridgestone's profits; the number above the diagonal shows Hitachi's profits.

These payoffs show what we concluded from our earlier analysis: the combined profit of the two firms is maximized if they each produce 30 million tires. Either firm can, however, increase its own profit by producing 40 million tires while the other produces only 30 million tires. But if both produce the larger quantity, both will have lower profits than if they had both held their output down.

The study of behavior in situations of interdependence is known as **game theory.**

The reward received by a player in a game, such as the profit earned by an oligopolist, is that player's **payoff.**

A **payoff matrix** shows how the payoff to each of the participants in a two-player game depends on the actions of both. Such a matrix helps us analyze situations of interdependence.

FIGURE 9-1 A Payoff Matrix

Two firms, Bridgestone and Hitachi, must decide how many tires to produce. The profits of the two firms are *interdependent:* each firm's profit depends not only on its own decision but also on the other's decision. Each row represents an action by Bridgestone; each column an action by Hitachi. Both firms will be better off if they both choose the lower output, but it is in each firm's individual interest to choose the higher output.

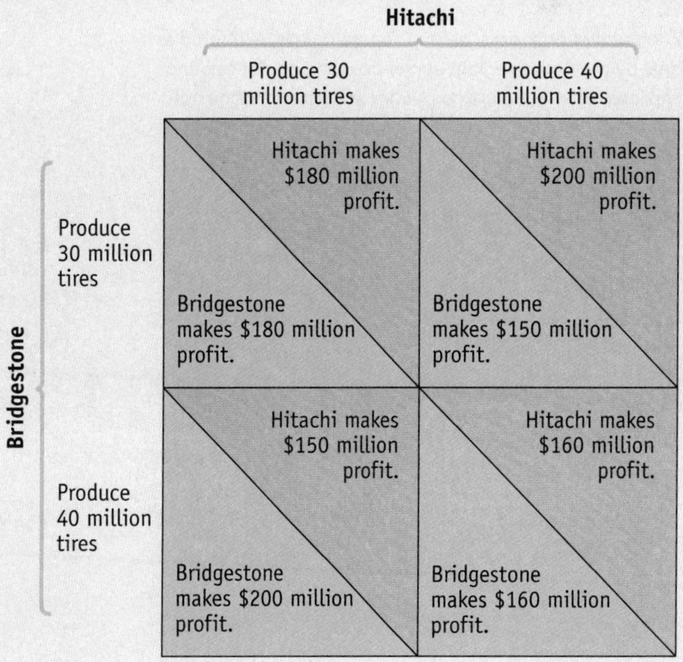

Prisoners' dilemma is a game based on two premises: (1) each player has an incentive to choose an action that benefits itself at the other player's expense; (2) when both players act in this way, both are worse off than if they had acted cooperatively.

The particular situation shown here is a version of a famous—and seemingly paradoxical—case of interdependence that appears in many contexts. Known as the **prisoners' dilemma**, it is a type of game in which the payoff matrix implies the following:

- Each player has an incentive, regardless of what the other player does, to cheat—to take an action that benefits it at the other's expense.

- When both players cheat, both are worse off than they would have been if neither had cheated.

The original illustration of the prisoners' dilemma occurred in a fictional story about two accomplices in crime—let's call them Thelma and Louise—who have been caught by the police. The police have enough evidence to put them behind bars for 5 years. They also know that the pair have committed a more serious crime, one that carries a 20-year prison sentence; unfortunately, they don't have enough evidence to convict the women on that charge. To do so, they would need each of the prisoners to implicate the other in the second crime.

So the police put the miscreants in separate cells and say the following to each: "Here's the deal: if neither of you confesses, you know that we'll send you to jail for 5 years. If you confess and implicate your partner, and she doesn't do the same, we'll reduce your sentence from 5 years to 2. But if your partner confesses and you don't, you'll get the maximum 20 years. And if both of you confess, we'll give you both 15 years."

Figure 9-2 shows the payoffs that face the prisoners, depending on the decision of each to remain silent or to confess. (Usually the payoff matrix reflects the players' payoffs, and higher payoffs are better than lower payoffs. This case is an exception: a higher number of years in prison is bad, not good!) Let's assume that the prisoners have no way to communicate and that they have not sworn an oath not to harm each other or anything of that sort. So each acts in her own self-interest. What will they do?

FIGURE 9-2 The Prisoners' Dilemma

Each of two prisoners, held in separate cells, is offered a deal by the police—a light sentence if she confesses and implicates her accomplice but her accomplice does not do the same, a heavy sentence if she does not confess but her accomplice does, and so on. It is in the joint interest of both prisoners not to confess; it is in each one's individual interest to confess.

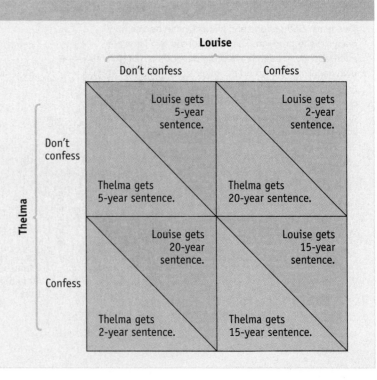

The answer is clear: both will confess. Look at it first from Thelma's point of view: she is better off confessing, regardless of what Louise does. If Louise doesn't confess, Thelma's confession reduces her own sentence from 5 years to 2. If Louise *does* confess, Thelma's confession reduces her sentence from 20 to 15 years. Either way, it's clearly in Thelma's interest to confess. And because she faces the same incentives, it's clearly in Louise's interest to confess, too. To confess in this situation is a type of action that economists call a *dominant strategy*. An action is a **dominant strategy** when it is the player's best action regardless of the action taken by the other player.

It's important to note that not all games have a dominant strategy—it depends on the structure of payoffs in the game. But in the case of Thelma and Louise, it is clearly in the interest of the police to structure the payoffs so that confessing is a dominant strategy for each person. So, as long as the two prisoners have no way to make an enforceable agreement that neither will confess (something they can't do if they can't communicate, and the police certainly won't allow them to do so because the police want to compel each one to confess), Thelma and Louise will each act in a way that hurts the other.

So if each prisoner acts rationally in her own interest, both will confess. Yet if neither of them had confessed, both would have received a much lighter sentence! In a prisoners' dilemma, each player has a clear incentive to act in a way that hurts the other player—but when both make that choice, it leaves both of them worse off.

When Thelma and Louise both confess, they reach an *equilibrium* of the game. We have used the concept of equilibrium many times; it is an outcome in which no individual or firm has any incentive to change his or her action.

In game theory, this kind of equilibrium, in which each player takes the action that is best for her given the actions taken by other players, and vice versa, is known as a **Nash equilibrium,** after the mathematician and Nobel laureate John Nash. (Nash's life was chronicled in the best-selling biography *A Beautiful Mind*, which was made into a movie.) Because the players in a Nash equilibrium do not take into account the effect of their actions on others, this is also known as a **noncooperative equilibrium.**

Now look back at Figure 9-1: Bridgestone and Hitachi are in the same situation as Thelma and Louise. Each firm is better off producing the higher output, regardless of what the other firm does. Yet if both produce 40 million tires, both are worse off than if they had followed their agreement and produced only 30 million tires. In both cases, then, the pursuit of individual self-interest—the effort to maximize profits or to minimize jail time—has the perverse effect of hurting both players.

Prisoners' dilemmas appear in many situations. Clearly, the players in any prisoners' dilemma would be better off if they had some way of enforcing cooperative behavior—if Thelma and Louise had both sworn to a code of silence or if Bridgestone and Hitachi had signed an enforceable agreement not to produce more than 30 million tires. In the United States, however, an agreement setting the output levels of two oligopolists isn't just unenforceable, it's illegal. So it seems that a noncooperative equilibrium is the only possible outcome. Or is it?

Overcoming the Prisoners' Dilemma: Repeated Interaction and Tacit Collusion

Thelma and Louise in their cells are playing what is known as a *one-shot* game—that is, they play the game with each other only once. They get to choose once and for all whether to confess or hang tough, and that's it. However, most of the games that oligopolists play aren't one-shot; instead, they expect to play the game repeatedly with the same rivals.

An action is a **dominant strategy** when it is a player's best action regardless of the action taken by the other player.

A **Nash equilibrium,** also known as a **noncooperative equilibrium,** results when each player in a game chooses the action that maximizes his or her payoff given the actions of other players, while ignoring the effects of his or her action on the payoffs received by those other players.

PITFALLS

PLAYING FAIR IN THE PRISONERS' DILEMMA

One common reaction to the prisoners' dilemma is to assert that it isn't really rational for either prisoner to confess. Thelma wouldn't confess because she'd be afraid Louise would beat her up, or Thelma would feel guilty because Louise wouldn't do that to her.

But this kind of answer is, well, cheating—it amounts to changing the payoffs in the payoff matrix. To understand the dilemma, you have to play fair and imagine prisoners who care *only* about the length of their sentences.

Luckily, when it comes to oligopoly, it's a lot easier to believe that the firms care only about their profits. There is no indication that anyone at Bridgestone felt either fear of or affection for Hitachi, or vice versa; it was strictly about business.

A firm engages in **strategic behavior** when it attempts to influence the future behavior of other firms.

A strategy of **tit for tat** involves playing cooperatively at first, then doing whatever the other player did in the previous period.

An oligopolist usually expects to be in business for many years, and it knows that its decision today about whether to cheat is likely to affect the way other firms treat it in the future. So a smart oligopolist doesn't decide what to do based solely on the effect on profit in the short run. Instead, it engages in **strategic behavior,** taking account of the effects of the action it chooses today on the future actions of other players in the game. And under some conditions oligopolists that behave strategically manage to behave as if they had a formal agreement to collude.

Suppose that Bridgestone and Hitachi expect to be in the tire business for many years and therefore expect to play the game of cheat versus collude shown in Figure 9-1 many times. Would they really betray each other time and again?

Probably not. Suppose that Bridgestone considers two strategies. In one strategy it always cheats, producing 40 million tires each year, regardless of what Hitachi does. In the other strategy, it starts with good behavior, producing only 30 million tires in the first year, and watches to see what its rival does. If Hitachi also keeps its production down, Bridgestone will stay cooperative, producing 30 million tires again for the next year. But if Hitachi produces 40 million tires, Bridgestone will take the gloves off and also produce 40 million tires the next year. This latter strategy—start by behaving cooperatively, but thereafter do whatever the other player did in the previous period—is generally known as **tit for tat.**

Tit for tat is a form of strategic behavior, which we have just defined as behavior intended to influence the future actions of other players. Tit for tat offers a reward to the other player for cooperative behavior—if you behave cooperatively, so will I. It also provides a punishment for cheating—if you cheat, don't expect me to be nice in the future.

The payoff to Bridgestone of each of these strategies would depend on which strategy Hitachi chooses. Consider the four possibilities, shown in Figure 9-3:

1. If Bridgestone plays tit for tat and so does Hitachi, both firms will make a profit of $180 million each year.

2. If Bridgestone plays always cheat but Hitachi plays tit for tat, Bridgestone makes a profit of $200 million the first year but only $160 million per year thereafter.

FIGURE 9-3 How Repeated Interaction Can Support Collusion

A strategy of tit for tat involves playing cooperatively at first, then following the other player's move. This rewards good behavior and punishes bad behavior. If the other player cheats, playing tit for tat will lead to only a short-term loss in comparison to playing always cheat. But if the other player plays tit for tat, also playing tit for tat leads to a long-term gain. So a firm that expects other firms to play tit for tat may well choose to do the same, leading to successful tacit collusion.

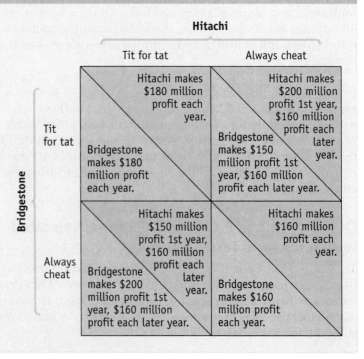

3. If Bridgestone plays tit for tat but Hitachi plays always cheat, Bridgestone makes a profit of only $150 million in the first year but $160 million per year thereafter.

4. If Bridgestone plays always cheat and Hitachi does the same, both firms will make a profit of $160 million each year.

Which strategy is better? In the first year, Bridgestone does better playing always cheat, whatever its rival's strategy: it assures itself that it will get either $200 million or $160 million (which of the two payoffs it actually receives depends on whether Hitachi plays tit for tat or always cheat). This is better than what it would get in the first year if it played tit for tat: either $180 million or $150 million. But by the second year, a strategy of always cheat gains Bridgestone only $160 million per year for the second and all subsequent years, regardless of Hitachi's actions.

Over time, the total amount gained by Bridgestone by playing always cheat is less than the amount it would gain by playing tit for tat: for the second and all subsequent years, it would never get any less than $160 million and would get as much as $180 million if Hitachi played tit for tat as well. Which strategy, always cheat or tit for tat, is more profitable depends on two things: how many years Bridgestone expects to play the game and what strategy its rival follows.

If Bridgestone expects the tire business to end in the near future, it is in effect playing a one-shot game. So it might as well cheat and grab what it can. Even if Bridgestone expects to remain in the tire business for many years (therefore to find itself repeatedly playing this game with Hitachi) and, for some reason, expects Hitachi always to cheat, it should also always cheat. That is, Bridgestone should follow the old rule "Do unto others before they do unto you."

But if Bridgestone expects to be in the business for a long time and thinks Hitachi is likely to play tit for tat, it will make more profits over the long run by playing tit for tat, too. It could have made some extra short-term profits by cheating at the beginning, but this would provoke Hitachi into cheating, too, and would, in the end, mean lower profits.

The lesson of this story is that when oligopolists expect to compete with one another over an extended period of time, each individual firm will often conclude that it is in its own best interest to be helpful to the other firms in the industry. So it will restrict its output in a way that raises the profits of the other firms, expecting them to return the favor, and without a formal agreement. In other words, the firms engage in tacit collusion.

ECONOMICS >> *in Action*
The Demise of OPEC

"Lots of people said OPEC was dead. OPEC itself just confirmed it," declared energy consultant Jamie Webster in late 2015. The death of OPEC, the most successful multinational cartel in history, was an event of epic proportions that was felt around the globe. The Organization of the Petroleum Exporting Countries (OPEC)—composed of the 17 countries of Algeria, Angola, Austria, Cameroon, Ecuador, Equatorial Guinea, Gabon, Iran, Iraq, Kuwait, Libya, Nigeria, Republic of Congo, Saudi Arabia, Syria, the United Arab Emirates, and Venezuela—is a cartel that controls 42% of the world oil exports, 80% of its proven oil reserves, and 47% of natural gas reserves. Unlike corporations that are legally prohibited from forming cartels, national governments can do whatever they like in setting prices.

For many years OPEC was the largest, most successful, and most economically important cartel in the world. Its members met regularly to set prices and production quotas for oil. Figure 9-4 shows the price of oil (in constant dollars) since 1947. OPEC first demonstrated its muscle in 1973: during the Yom Kippur War in the Middle East, OPEC producers limited their output—and they liked the resulting price increase so much that they decided to continue the practice. Following a second wave of turmoil due to the Iran–Iraq War in 1979, output quotas fell further and prices shot even higher.

FIGURE 9-4 Crude Oil Prices, 1947–2016 (in Constant 2016 Dollars)

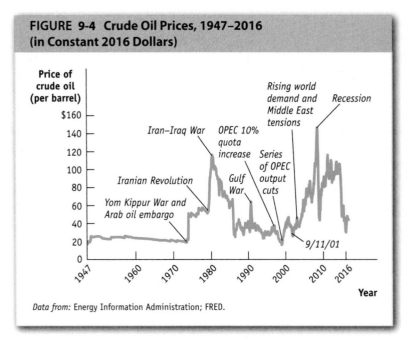

Data from: Energy Information Administration; FRED.

Higher oil prices spurred more exploration and production, so by the mid-1980s a growing glut of oil on world markets as well as cheating by cash-strapped OPEC members led to a price collapse. But in the late 1990s OPEC emerged successful once again, as Saudi Arabia, the largest producer by far, began acting as the "swing producer": allowing other members to produce as much as they wanted, then adjusting its own output to meet the overall production limit. By 2008, the price of oil had soared to $145 per barrel.

Yet, by the end of 2015, OPEC as a successful cartel was effectively dead, and in early 2016 the price had fallen to under $30 a barrel as a result of the rise of two non-OPEC oil superpowers: Russia and the United States. After a huge fall in production in the late 1990s, Russia thereafter ramped up its output. In addition, new fracking technology employed in the United States opened up large reserves of oil. Because neither Russia nor the United States agreed to production limits, OPEC's ability to determine the global price of oil declined dramatically. In 2016, with every oil-producing country operating at maximum capacity, Bhushan Bahree, an energy consultant, observed "OPEC and non-OPEC are irrelevant classifications."

>> Quick Review

- Economists use **game theory** to study firms' behavior when there is interdependence between their **payoffs.** The game can be represented with a **payoff matrix.** Depending on the payoffs, a player may or may not have a **dominant strategy.**

- When each firm has an incentive to cheat, but both are worse off if both cheat, the situation is known as a **prisoners' dilemma.**

- Players who don't take their interdependence into account arrive at a **Nash,** or **noncooperative, equilibrium.** But if a game is played repeatedly, players may engage in **strategic behavior,** sacrificing short-run profit to influence future behavior.

- In repeated prisoners' dilemma games, **tit for tat** is often a good strategy, leading to successful tacit collusion.

>> Check Your Understanding 9-2

Solutions appear at back of book.

1. Find the Nash (noncooperative) equilibrium actions for the following payoff matrix. Which actions maximize the total payoff of Nikita and Margaret? Why is it unlikely that they will choose those actions without some communication?

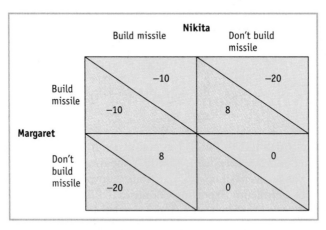

2. Which of the following factors make it more likely that oligopolists will play noncooperatively? Which make it more likely that they will engage in tacit collusion? Explain.

a. Each oligopolist expects several new firms to enter the market in the future.

b. It is very difficult for a firm to detect whether another firm has raised output.

c. The firms have coexisted while maintaining high prices for a long time.

‖ The Meaning of Monopolistic Competition

Leo owns the Wonderful Wok stand in the food court of a big shopping mall. He offers the only Chinese food there, but there are also more than a dozen alternatives, from Bodacious Burgers to Pizza Paradise. When deciding what to charge for a meal, Leo knows that he must take those alternatives into account: even people who normally prefer stir-fry won't order a $15 lunch from Leo when they can get a burger, fries, and drink for $4.

But Leo also knows that he won't lose all his business even if his lunches cost a bit more than the alternatives. Chinese food isn't the same thing as burgers or pizza. Some people will really be in the mood for Chinese that day, and they will buy from Leo even if they could dine more cheaply on burgers. Of course, the reverse is also true: even if Chinese is a bit cheaper, some people will choose burgers instead. In other words, Leo does have some market power: he has *some* ability to set his own price.

So how would you describe Leo's situation? He definitely isn't a price-taker, so he isn't in a situation of perfect competition. But you wouldn't exactly call him a monopolist, either. Although he's the only seller of Chinese food in that food court, he does face competition from other food vendors.

Yet it would also be wrong to call him an oligopolist. Oligopoly, remember, involves competition among a small number of interdependent firms in an industry protected by some—albeit limited—barriers to entry and whose profits are highly interdependent. Because their profits are highly interdependent, oligopolists have an incentive to collude, tacitly or explicitly. But in Leo's case there are *lots* of vendors in the shopping mall, too many to make tacit collusion feasible.

Economists describe Leo's situation as one of **monopolistic competition.** Monopolistic competition is particularly common in service industries like restaurants and gas stations, but it also exists in some manufacturing industries. It involves three necessary conditions: large numbers of competing producers, free entry into and exit from the industry in the long run, and differentiated products.

In a monopolistically competitive industry, each producer has some ability to set the price of her differentiated product. But exactly how high she can set it is limited by the competition she faces from other existing and potential producers that produce close, but not identical, products.

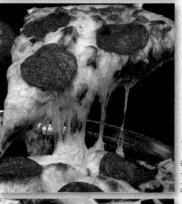

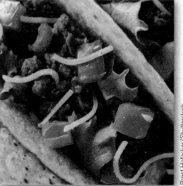

Competing for your taste buds.

Large Numbers

In a monopolistically competitive industry, there are many firms. Such an industry does not look either like a monopoly, where the firm faces no competition, or like an oligopoly, where each firm has only a few rivals. Instead, each seller has many competitors. For example, there are many vendors in a big food court, many gas stations along a major highway, and many hotels at a popular beach resort.

Free Entry and Exit in the Long Run

In monopolistically competitive industries, new producers, with their own distinct products, can enter the industry freely in the long run. For example, other food vendors would open outlets in the food court if they thought it would be profitable to do so. In addition, firms will exit the industry if they find they are not covering their costs in the long run.

Differentiated Products

In a monopolistically competitive industry, each firm has a product that consumers view as somewhat distinct from the products of competing firms. At the same time, though, consumers see these competing products as close substitutes. If Leo's food court contained 15 vendors selling exactly the same kind and quality of food, there would be perfect competition: any seller who tried to charge a higher price would have no customers. But suppose that Wonderful Wok is the only Chinese food vendor, Bodacious Burgers is the only hamburger stand, and so on.

Monopolistic competition is a market structure in which there are many competing producers in an industry, each producer sells a differentiated product, and there is free entry into and exit from the industry in the long run.

Product differentiation is an attempt by a firm to convince buyers that its product is different from the products of other firms in the industry.

The result of this differentiation is that each seller has some ability to set his own price: each producer has some—albeit limited—market power.

Product differentiation is the attempt by a firm to create the perception that its product is different. It is the only way monopolistically competitive firms can acquire some market power. How do firms in the same industry—such as fast-food vendors, gas stations, or chocolate makers—differentiate their products? Sometimes the difference is mainly in the minds of consumers rather than in the products. In general, however, firms differentiate their products by—surprise!—actually making them different.

The key to product differentiation is that consumers have different preferences and are willing to pay somewhat more to satisfy those preferences. Each producer can carve out a market niche by producing something that caters to the particular preferences of some group of consumers better than the products of other firms.

We'll now look at three forms of product differentiation: by style or type, by location, and by quality. Then we'll consider two important features of industries with differentiated products.

Differentiation by Style or Type   The other sellers in Leo's food court offer different types of fast food: hamburgers, pizza, Chinese food, Mexican food, and so on. Each consumer arrives at the food court with some preference for one or another of these offerings. This preference may depend on the consumer's mood, her diet, or what she has already eaten that day. These preferences will not make consumers indifferent to price: if Wonderful Wok were to charge $15 for an egg roll, everybody would go to Bodacious Burgers or Pizza Paradise instead. But some people will choose a more expensive meal if that type of food is closer to their preference. So the products of the different vendors are substitutes, but they aren't *perfect* substitutes—they are *imperfect substitutes*.

Vendors in a food court aren't the only sellers that differentiate their offerings by type. Clothing stores concentrate on women's or men's clothes, on business or casual clothes, on trendy or classic styles, and so on. Auto manufacturers offer sedans, minivans, sport-utility vehicles, and sports cars, each type aimed at drivers with different needs and tastes.

Books offer yet another example of differentiation by type and style. Mysteries are differentiated from romances; among mysteries, we can differentiate among hard-boiled detective stories, whodunits, and police procedurals. And no two writers of fantasy and science fiction are exactly alike: J. K. Rowling and George R. R. Martin each have their devoted fans.

In fact, product differentiation is characteristic of most consumer goods. As long as people differ in their tastes, producers find it possible and profitable to produce a wide variety of goods.

Differentiation by Location   Gas stations along a road offer differentiated products. True, the gas may be exactly the same. But the location of the stations is different, and location matters to consumers: it's more convenient to stop for gas near your home, near your workplace, or near wherever you are when the gas gauge shows you are low on fuel.

In fact, many monopolistically competitive industries supply goods differentiated by location. This is especially true in service industries, from dry cleaners to hairdressers, where customers often choose the seller who is closest rather than cheapest.

Differentiation by Quality   Do you have a craving for chocolate? How much are you willing to spend on it? You see, there's chocolate and then there's chocolate: although ordinary chocolate may not be very expensive, gourmet chocolate can cost several dollars per bite.

With chocolate, as with many goods, there is a range of possible qualities. You can get a usable bicycle for less than $100 or you can get a much fancier bicycle

For industries that differentiate by location, proximity is everything.

for 10 times as much. It all depends on how much the additional quality matters to you and how much you will miss the other things you could have purchased with that money.

Because consumers vary in what they are willing to pay for higher quality, producers can differentiate their products by quality—some offering lower-quality, inexpensive products and others offering higher-quality products at a higher price.

Features of Monopolistically Competitive Industries Product differentiation, then, can take several forms. Whatever form it takes, however, there are two important features of industries with differentiated products:

1. *There is competition among sellers*: even though sellers of differentiated products are not offering identical goods, they are to some extent competing for a limited market. If more businesses enter the market, each will find that it sells less quantity at any given price. For example, if a new gas station opens along a particular road, each of the existing gas stations will sell a bit less.

2. *There is value in variety*: consumers benefit from the proliferation of differentiated products. A food court with eight vendors makes consumers happier than one with only six vendors, even if the prices are the same, because some customers will get a meal that is closer to what they had in mind. A road on which there is a gas station every two miles is more convenient for motorists than a road where gas stations are five miles apart.

When a product is available in many different qualities, fewer people are forced to pay for more quality than they need or to settle for lower quality than they want. There are, in other words, benefits to consumers from a greater diversity of available products.

Monopolistic competition differs from the three market structures we have examined so far. It's not the same as perfect competition: firms have some power to set prices. It's not pure monopoly: firms face some competition. And it's not the same as oligopoly: because there are many firms and free entry, the potential for collusion so important in oligopoly doesn't exist.

ECONOMICS >> *in Action*
Abbondanza!

Has the experience of choosing a jar of pasta sauce from among the dozens of varieties on grocery store shelves ever left you feeling overwhelmed? If so, you have one person to thank and to blame: Howard Moskowitz. Twenty-five years ago, making your selection was much simpler: there was no Newman's Socka-rooni, no Barilla's Spicy Marinara with Roasted Garlic, no Mario Batali's Arrabbiata. In fact, there were only two brands available, Prego and Ragù. And they offered only one variety each—plain spaghetti sauce.

In the late 1980s, Prego was in a slump compared to its rival, Ragù. While searching for a way to turn their business around, the company concluded that Prego and Ragù pasta sauces were relatively indistinguishable. But rather than engage in a price war with its rival, Prego hired market researcher Howard Moskowitz, who realized that the answer to Prego's dilemma was to find out what appealed to consumers' taste buds and then use this to distinguish Prego from Ragù. Moskowitz proceeded to create 45 varieties of pasta sauces, varied on every conceivable measure: sweetness, spiciness, tartness, saltiness, thickness, and so on. He then taste-tested them around the country. What stood out was consumers' preference for extra chunky sauce—an unavailable option at the time, when both Prego and Ragù offered highly blended watery sauces.

A dizzying variety of pasta sauces is available—thanks to monopolistic competition.

In 1989 Prego launched its Extra Chunky variety, and it was extraordinarily successful. It's a measure of Moskowitz's success that today it is hard to appreciate the radicalness of his approach. Twenty years ago, the food industry believed it should strive to create a "platonic dish"—some ideal version that would completely satisfy consumers' tastes. Prego and Ragù offered thin pasta sauces because their ideal reflected how sauce was made in Italy. But Prego came to understand the importance of setting itself apart while avoiding head-to-head price competition with Ragù, which would ultimately be self-defeating. Along came Moskowitz, who freed the food industry to indulge American consumers' desire for variety and distinctive flavors.

>> **Quick Review**

• In **monopolistic competition** there are many competing producers, each with a differentiated product, and free entry and exit in the long run.

• **Product differentiation** takes three main forms: by style or type, by location, or by quality. The products of competing sellers are considered imperfect substitutes.

• Producers compete for the same market, so entry by more producers reduces the quantity each existing producer sells at any given price. In addition, consumers gain from the increased variety of products.

>> **Check Your Understanding 9-3**

Solutions appear at back of book.

1. Each of these goods and services is a differentiated product. Which are differentiated as a result of monopolistic competition and which are not? Explain your answers.
   a. Ladders
   b. Soft drinks
   c. Department stores
   d. Steel

2. You must determine which of two types of market structure better describes an industry, but you are allowed to ask only one question about the industry. What question should you ask to determine if an industry is:
   a. perfectly competitive or monopolistically competitive?
   b. a monopoly or monopolistically competitive?

SOLVED PROBLEM   The Ups (and Downs) of Oil Prices

The world's best known cartel is OPEC, the Organization of the Petroleum Exporting Countries, discussed in the preceding Economics in Action. The 17 national governments that comprise OPEC export nearly $1 trillion of petroleum products every year. As the largest producer, Saudi Arabia produces one-third of the annual output and it is the key decision maker. The result is a situation similar to the prisoners' dilemma faced by Thelma and Louise, but this time, the players are Saudi Arabia and the rest of OPEC.

Our players, Saudi Arabia and other OPEC members, must collectively decide whether to maintain or increase oil production levels:

• If both parties choose to maintain oil production levels, the price of oil and, subsequently, the total value of oil exports from each country will stay the same.

• If one of the parties decides to increase oil production the price of oil will decrease.

• If either party independently increases production, the value of oil exports will increase, but if both parties increase production the value of total exports will decrease.

The accompanying payoff matrix displays the actions that both Saudi Arabia and the rest of OPEC could take, as well as the outcomes for each (expressed as the annual total value of oil exports). Find the dominant strategies for Saudi Arabia and the rest of OPEC, the Nash (or noncooperative) equilibrium, and the outcome that results under tacit collusion.

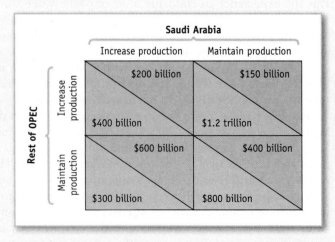

STEP | 1 **Determine the dominant strategy for Saudi Arabia and then for the rest of OPEC.** *Review pages 267–269.*

In this particular case, the dominant strategy for both Saudi Arabia and the rest of OPEC is to always increase production. Saudi Arabia is always better off increasing production independent of the actions taken by the rest of OPEC. Referring to the accompanying payoff matrix, you can see that if the other OPEC members choose to maintain production, Saudi Arabia can increase production and increase total exports to $600 billion, which is more than the $400 billion they would receive by maintaining production levels. If the rest of OPEC chooses to increase production, Saudi Arabia can offset some of their losses by increasing production as well, allowing them to earn $200 billion, instead of $150 billion. Because the rest of OPEC faces the same incentives as Saudi Arabia, it is in their best interest to increase production as well.

STEP | 2 **Find the noncooperative or Nash equilibrium. Then determine if Saudi Arabia and the rest of OPEC will choose to increase or decrease production.** *Review pages 267–269.*

The noncooperative, or Nash, equilibrium will occur when both parties increase production and Saudi Arabia exports $200 billion of oil and the rest of OPEC exports $400 billion. In this case both parties are following their dominant strategy. Despite leaving both parties worse off, neither party has an incentive to change their action, hence the prisoners' dilemma.

STEP | 3 **Explain what the outcome would be if Saudi Arabia and the rest of OPEC engaged in a repeated game and followed a tit-for-tat strategy.** *Review pages 269–271.*

In reality, both Saudi Arabia and the rest of OPEC play a repeated game. They are in a situation where they must choose their production levels for many years to come. If Saudi Arabia leads by maintaining production levels, the rest of OPEC, using a tit-for-tat strategy, will also choose to maintain production levels. In this case, both parties are engaging in tacit collusion, which results in a more desirable outcome. Using this strategy, Saudi Arabia will export $400 billion in oil and the rest of OPEC will export $800 billion. The repeated game continues until one party tries to cheat by taking advantage of the other and increasing production.

SUMMARY

1. Many industries are an **oligopoly:** where there are only a few sellers. In particular, a **duopoly** has only two sellers. Firms that operate in an oligopoly are called **oligopolists.** Oligopolies exist for more or less the same reasons that monopolies exist, but in weaker form. They are characterized **by imperfect competition:** firms compete but possess some market power.

2. Oligopolists operate in a state of **interdependence** in which the actions by one firm have a significant effect on the profits of its rivals. The firms in an oligopoly could maximize their combined profits by acting as a **cartel,** setting output levels for each firm as if they were a single monopolist; to the extent that firms manage to do this, they engage in **collusion.** But each individual firm has an incentive to produce more than it would in such an arrangement—to engage in **noncooperative behavior.**

3. In order to limit the ability of oligopolists to collude and act like monopolists, most governments pursue an **antitrust policy** designed to make collusion more difficult. In practice, however, tacit collusion is widespread.

4. A variety of factors make tacit collusion difficult: large numbers of firms, complex products and pricing, differences in interests, and bargaining power of buyers. When tacit collusion breaks down, there is a **price war.**

5. The situation of interdependence, in which each firm's profit depends noticeably on what other firms do, is the subject of **game theory.** In the case of a game with two players, the **payoff** of each player depends both on its own actions and on the actions of the other; this interdependence can be represented as a **payoff matrix.** Depending on the structure of payoffs in the payoff matrix, a player may have a **dominant strategy**—an action that is always the best regardless of the other player's actions.

6. **Duopolists** face a particular type of game known as a **prisoners' dilemma;** if each acts independently in its own interest, the resulting **Nash equilibrium** or **noncooperative equilibrium** will be bad for both. However, firms that expect to play a game repeatedly tend to engage in **strategic behavior,** trying to influence each other's future actions. A particular strategy that seems to work well in maintaining **tacit collusion** is **tit for tat.**

7. **Monopolistic competition** is a market structure in which there are many competing producers, each producing a differentiated product, and there is free entry and exit in the long run. **Product differentiation** takes three main forms: by style or type, by location, or by quality. Products of competing sellers are considered imperfect substitutes, and each firm has its own downward-sloping demand curve and marginal revenue curve.

KEY TERMS

PROBLEMS

interactive activity

1. The accompanying table shows the demand schedule for vitamin D. Suppose that the marginal cost of producing vitamin D is zero.

Price of vitamin D (per ton)	Quantity of vitamin D demanded (tons)
$8	0
7	10
6	20
5	30
4	40
3	50
2	60
1	70

a. Assume that BASF is the only producer of vitamin D and acts as a monopolist. It currently produces 40 tons of vitamin D at $4 per ton. If BASF were to produce 10 more tons, what would be the price effect for BASF? What would be the quantity effect? Would BASF have an incentive to produce those 10 additional tons?

b. Now assume that Roche enters the market by also producing vitamin D and the market is now a duopoly. BASF and Roche agree to produce 40 tons of vitamin D in total, 20 tons each. BASF cannot be punished for deviating from the agreement with Roche. If BASF, on its own, were to deviate from that agreement and produce 10 more tons, what would be the price effect for BASF? What would be the quantity effect for BASF? Would BASF have an incentive to produce those 10 additional tons?

2. The market for olive oil in New York City is controlled by two families, the Sopranos and the Contraltos. Both families will ruthlessly eliminate any other family that attempts to enter the New York City olive oil market. The marginal cost of producing olive oil is constant and equal to $40 per gallon. There is no fixed cost. The accompanying table gives the market demand schedule for olive oil.

Price of olive oil (per gallon)	Quantity of olive oil demanded (gallons)
$100	1,000
90	1,500
80	2,000
70	2,500
60	3,000
50	3,500
40	4,000
30	4,500
20	5,000
10	5,500

a. Suppose the Sopranos and the Contraltos form a cartel. For each of the quantities given in the table, calculate the total revenue for their cartel and the marginal revenue for each additional gallon. How many gallons of olive oil would the cartel sell in total and at what price? The two families share the market equally (each produces half of the total output of the cartel). How much profit does each family make?

b. Uncle Junior, the head of the Soprano family, breaks the agreement and sells 500 more gallons of olive oil than under the cartel agreement. Assuming the Contraltos maintain the agreement, how does this affect the price for olive oil and the profit earned by each family?

c. Anthony Contralto, the head of the Contralto family, decides to punish Uncle Junior by increasing sales by 500 gallons as well. How much profit does each family earn now?

3. In France, the market for bottled water is controlled by two large firms, Perrier and Evian. Each firm has a fixed cost of €1 million and a constant marginal cost of €2 per liter of bottled water (€1 = 1 euro). The following table gives the market demand schedule for bottled water in France.

Price of bottled water (per liter)	Quantity of bottled water demanded (millions of liters)
€10	0
9	1
8	2
7	3
6	4
5	5
4	6
3	7
2	8
1	9

a. Suppose the two firms form a cartel and act as a monopolist. Calculate marginal revenue for the cartel. What will the monopoly price and output be? Assuming the firms divide the output evenly, how much will each produce and what will each firm's profit be?

b. Now suppose Perrier decides to increase production by 1 million liters. Evian doesn't change its production. What will the new market price and output be? What is Perrier's profit? What is Evian's profit?

c. What if Perrier increases production by 3 million liters? Evian doesn't change its production. What would Perrier's output and profit be relative to those in part b?

d. What do your results tell you about the likelihood of cheating on such agreements?

4. Over the last 40 years the Organization of the Petroleum Exporting Countries (OPEC) has had varied success in forming and maintaining its cartel agreements. Explain how the following factors may contribute to the difficulty of forming and/or maintaining its price and output agreements.

a. New oil fields are discovered and increased drilling is undertaken in the Gulf of Mexico and the North Sea by nonmembers of OPEC.

b. Crude oil is a product that is differentiated by sulfur content: it costs less to refine low-sulfur crude oil into gasoline. Different OPEC countries possess oil reserves of different sulfur content.

c. Cars powered by hydrogen are developed.

5. Suppose you are an economist working for the Antitrust Division of the Justice Department. In each of the following cases you are given the task of determining whether the behavior warrants an antitrust investigation for possible illegal acts, or is just an example of undesirable, but not illegal, tacit collusion. Explain your reasoning.

a. Two companies dominate the industry for industrial lasers. Several people sit on the boards of directors of both companies.

b. The two oil companies that produce most of the petroleum for the western half of the United States have decided to forgo building their own pipelines and to share a common pipeline, the only means of transporting petroleum products to that market.

c. The two major companies that dominate the market for herbal supplements have each created a subsidiary that sells the same product as the parent company, but in larger quantities and with a generic name.

d. The two largest credit card companies, Passport and OmniCard, require all retailers who accept their cards to agree to limit their use of rival credit cards.

6. To preserve the North Atlantic fish stocks, it is decided that only two fishing fleets, one from the United States and the other from the European Union, can fish in those waters. Suppose that this fisheries agreement breaks down, and now the fleets behave noncooperatively. Assume that the United States and the European Union each can send out either one or two fleets. The more fleets in the area, the more fish they catch in total but the lower the catch of each fleet. The accompanying matrix shows the profit (in dollars) per week earned by each side.

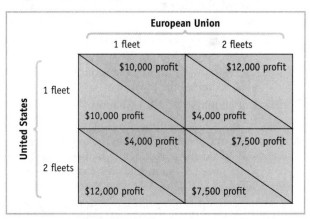

a. What is the noncooperative Nash equilibrium? Will each side choose to send out one or two fleets?

b. Suppose that the fish stocks are being depleted. Each region considers the future and comes to a tit-for-tat agreement whereby each side will send only one fleet out as long as the other does the same. If either of them breaks the agreement and sends out a second fleet, the other will also send out two and will continue to do so until its competitor sends out only one fleet. If both play this tit-for-tat strategy, how much profit will each make every week?

7. Untied and Air "R" Us are the only two airlines operating flights between Collegeville and Bigtown. That is, they operate in a duopoly. Each airline can charge either a high price or a low price for a ticket. The accompanying matrix shows their payoffs, in profits per seat (in dollars), for any choice that the two airlines can make.

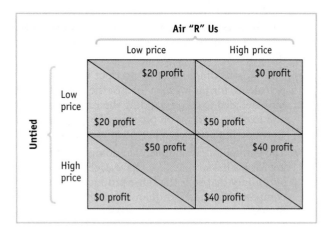

a. Suppose the two airlines play a one-shot game—that is, they interact only once and never again. What will be the Nash (noncooperative) equilibrium in this one-shot game?

b. Now suppose the two airlines play this game twice. And suppose each airline can play one of two strategies: it can play either always charge the low price or tit for tat—that is, it starts off charging the high price in the first period, and then in the second period it does whatever the other airline did in the previous period. Write down the payoffs to Untied from the following four possibilities:

   i. Untied plays always charge the low price when Air "R" Us also plays always charge the low price.

   ii. Untied plays always charge the low price when Air "R" Us plays tit for tat.

   iii. Untied plays tit for tat when Air "R" Us plays always charge the low price.

   iv. Untied plays tit for tat when Air "R" Us also plays tit for tat.

8. Suppose that Coke and Pepsi are the only two producers of cola drinks, making them duopolists. Both companies have zero marginal cost and a fixed cost of $100,000.

a. Assume first that consumers regard Coke and Pepsi as perfect substitutes. Currently both are sold for $0.20 per can, and at that price each company sells 4 million cans per day.

   i. How large is Pepsi's profit?

   ii. If Pepsi were to raise its price to $0.30 per can, and Coke did not respond, keeping its price at $0.20 per can, what would happen to Pepsi's profit?

b. Now suppose that each company advertises to differentiate its product from the other company's product. As a result of advertising, Pepsi realizes that if it raises or lowers its price, it will sell less or more of its product, as shown by the demand schedule in the accompanying table.

Price of Pepsi (per can)	Quantity of Pepsi demanded (millions of cans)
$0.10	5
0.20	4
0.30	3
0.40	2
0.50	1

If Pepsi now were to raise its price to $0.30 per can, what would happen to its profit?

c. Comparing your answer to part a (i) and to part b, what is the maximum amount Pepsi would be willing to spend on advertising?

9. Schick and Gillette spend huge sums of money each year to advertise their razors in an attempt to steal customers from each other. Suppose that each year Schick and Gillette have to decide whether or not they want to spend money on advertising. If neither firm advertises, each will earn a profit of $2 million. If they both advertise, each will earn a profit of $1.5 million. If one firm advertises and the other does not, the firm that advertises will earn a profit of $2.8 million and the other firm will earn $1 million.

a. Use a payoff matrix to depict this problem.

b. Suppose Schick and Gillette can write an enforceable contract about what they will do. What is the cooperative solution to this game?

c. What is the Nash equilibrium without an enforceable contract? Explain why this is the likely outcome.

10. Use the three conditions for monopolistic competition discussed in the chapter to decide which of the following firms are likely to be operating as monopolistic competitors. If they are not monopolistically competitive firms, are they monopolists, oligopolists, or perfectly competitive firms?

a. A local band that plays for weddings, parties, and so on

b. Minute Maid, a producer of individual-serving juice boxes

c. Your local dry cleaner

d. A farmer who produces soybeans

11. You are thinking of setting up a coffee shop. The market structure for coffee shops is monopolistic competition. There are three Starbucks shops and two other coffee shops very much like Starbucks in your town already. In order for you to have some degree of market power, you may want to differentiate your coffee shop. Thinking about the three different ways in which products can be differentiated, explain how you would decide whether you should copy Starbucks or whether you should sell coffee in a completely different way.

WORK IT OUT Interactive step-by-step help with solving this problem can be found online.

12. Let's revisit the fisheries agreement introduced in Problem 6, which stated that to preserve the North Atlantic fish stocks, only two fishing fleets, one from the United States (U.S.) and the other from the European Union (EU), can fish in those waters. The accompanying table shows the market demand schedule per week for fish from these waters. The only costs are fixed costs, so fishing fleets maximize profit by maximizing revenue.

Price of fish (per pound)	Quantity of fish demanded (pounds)
$17	1,800
16	2,000
15	2,100
14	2,200
12	2,300

a. If both fishing fleets collude, what is the revenue-maximizing output for the North Atlantic fishery? What price will a pound of fish sell for?

b. If both fishing fleets collude and share the output equally, what is the revenue to the EU fleet? To the U.S. fleet?

c. Suppose the EU fleet cheats by expanding its own catch by 100 pounds per week. The U.S. fleet doesn't change its catch. What is the revenue to the U.S. fleet? To the EU fleet?

d. In retaliation for the cheating by the EU fleet, the U.S. fleet also expands its catch by 100 pounds per week. What is the revenue to the U.S. fleet? To the EU fleet?

David Ryder/Getty Images

In May 2014, all-out war broke out between Amazon, the third-largest U.S. book retailer, and Hachette, the fourth-largest book publisher. Suddenly Amazon took weeks to deliver Hachette publications (paper and e-books), including best-sellers from authors like Stephen Colbert, Dan Brown, and J. D. Salinger, meanwhile offering shoppers suggestions for non-Hachette books as alternatives. In addition, pre-order options for forthcoming Hachette books—including one by J. K. Rowling of Harry Potter fame—disappeared from Amazon's website along with many other Hachette books. These same books were readily available, often at lower prices, at rival book retailers such as Barnes and Noble.

All publishers pay retailers a share of sales prices. In this case, hostilities were set off by Amazon's demand that Hachette raise that share from 30% to 50%. This was a familiar story: Amazon demanded ever-larger percentages during yearly contract negotiations. Since it won't carry a publisher's books without an agreement, a protracted disagreement and the resulting loss of sales are disastrous for publishers. This time, however, Hachette refused to give in and went public with Amazon's demands.

Amazon claimed that the publisher could pay more out of its profit margin—around 75% on e-books, 60% on paperbacks, and 40% on hardcovers. Indeed, Amazon openly admitted that its long-term objective was to displace publishers altogether, and deal directly with authors itself. And it received support from some authors who had been rejected by traditional publishers but succeeded by selling directly to readers via Amazon. But publishers countered that Amazon's calculations ignored the costs of editing, marketing, advertising, and at times supporting struggling writers until they became successful. Amazon, they claimed, would eventually destroy the book industry.

Over the course of the conflict, Amazon faced some very angry authors. Douglas Preston, a best-selling Hachette author of thrillers, saw his sales drop by at least 60%. Speaking of the comfortable lifestyle that his writing supported, Preston observed that if Amazon decided not to sell his books at all, "All this goes away." In the end, the conflict became a public relations disaster for Amazon as writers and even some readers turned against them. So, Amazon eventually capitulated and agreed to allow Hachette to set the price of its e-books. However, given Amazon's size and influence, authors remain wary about the future.

In fact, a few years later, Amazon became the largest U.S. book retailer. This is largely due to Amazon's costly investments in its website and its vast warehouse and speedy delivery system, despite sometimes charging higher prices than rival websites. These upgrades have been funded by Amazon investors, who waited patiently for 20 years, incurring billions of dollars in losses. But 2015 was a turning point for Amazon. That year, the company made a small profit, and each year since, it has experienced increased profitability. In 2018, Amazon made over $10 billion. The wait for its investors finally paid off. Over the same time period, Amazon's share price increased by nearly 500%.

QUESTIONS FOR THOUGHT

1. What is the source of surplus in this industry? Who generates it? How is it divided among the various agents (authors, publishers, and retailers)?

2. What are the various sources of market power here? What is at risk for the various parties?

Ian Waldie/Getty Images

The United Kingdom is home to two long-haul airline carriers (carriers that fly between continents): British Airways and its rival, Virgin Atlantic. Although British Airways is the dominant company, with a market share generally between 50% and 100% on routes between London and various American cities, Virgin has been a tenacious competitor.

The rivalry between the two has ranged from relatively peaceable to openly hostile over the years. In the 1990s, British Airways lost a court case alleging it had engaged in "dirty tricks" to drive Virgin out of business. In April 2010, however, British Airways may well have wondered if the tables had been turned.

It all began in mid-July 2004, when oil prices were rising. British prosecutors alleged that the two airlines had plotted to levy fuel surcharges on passengers. For the next two years, according to the prosecutors, the rivals had established a cartel through which they coordinated increases in surcharges. British Airways first introduced a £5 ($8.25) surcharge on long-haul flights when a barrel of oil traded at about $38. It increased the surcharge six times, so that by 2006, when oil was trading at about $69 a barrel, the surcharge was £70 ($115). At the same time, Virgin Atlantic also levied a £70 fee. These surcharges increased within days of each other.

Eventually, three Virgin executives decided to blow the whistle in exchange for immunity from prosecution. British Airways immediately suspended its executives under suspicion and paid fines of nearly $500 million to U.S. and U.K. authorities. And in 2010 four British Airways executives were prosecuted by British authorities for their alleged role in the conspiracy.

The lawyers for the executives argued that although the two airlines had swapped information, this was not proof of a criminal conspiracy. In fact, they argued, Virgin was so fearful of American regulators that it had admitted to criminal behavior before confirming that it had indeed committed an offense.

One of the defense lawyers, Clare Montgomery, argued that because U.S. laws against anti-competitive behavior are much tougher than those in the United Kingdom, companies may be compelled to blow the whistle to avoid investigation. "It's a race," she said. "If you don't get to them and confess first, you can't get immunity. The only way to protect yourself is to go to the authorities, even if you haven't [done anything]." The result was that the Virgin executives were given immunity in both the United States and the United Kingdom, but the British Airways executives were subject to prosecution (and possible multiyear jail terms) in both countries.

In late 2011 the case came to a shocking end for Virgin Atlantic and U.K. authorities. Citing e-mails that Virgin was forced to turn over by the court, the judge found insufficient evidence that there was ever a conspiracy between the two airlines. The court was incensed enough to threaten to rescind the immunity granted to the three Virgin executives.

QUESTIONS FOR THOUGHT

1. Explain why Virgin Atlantic and British Airways might collude in response to increased oil prices. Was the market conducive to collusion or not?

2. How would you determine whether illegal behavior actually occurred? What might explain these events other than illegal behavior?

3. Explain the dilemma facing the two airlines as well as their individual executives.

THE GREAT STINK

BY THE MIDDLE OF THE NINETEENTH century, London had become the world's largest city, with close to 2.5 million inhabitants. Unfortunately, all those people produced a

HIP/The Image Works

lot of waste—and there was no place for it to go except into the Thames, the river flowing through the city. Nobody with a working nose could ignore the results. And the river didn't just smell bad—it carried dangerous waterborne diseases like cholera and typhoid. London neighborhoods close to the Thames had death rates from cholera more than six times greater than the neighborhoods farthest away. And the great majority of Londoners drew their drinking water from the Thames.

The hot summer of 1858 brought what came to be known as the Great Stink, which was so bad that one health journal reported "men struck down with the stench." Even the privileged and powerful suffered: Parliament met in a building next to the river and after unsuccessful efforts to stop the smell by covering the windows with chemical-soaked curtains, Parliament finally approved a plan for an immense system of sewers and pumping stations to direct sewage away from the city. The system, opened in 1865, brought dramatic improvement in the city's quality of life.

By dumping waste into the Thames, individuals imposed costs on all of the residents of London. When individuals impose costs on or provide benefits to others, but don't have an economic incentive to take those costs or benefits into account, economists say that externalities are generated.

In this chapter we'll examine the economics of *externalities*, seeing how they can get in the way of economic efficiency and lead to market failure, why they provide a reason for government intervention in markets, and how economic analysis can be used to guide government policy.

The story of the Great Stink also illustrates an important reason for government intervention in the economy. London's new sewage system was a clear example of a *public good*—a good that benefits many people, whether or not they have paid for it, and whose benefits to any one individual do not depend on how many others also benefit. As we will see, public goods differ in important ways from the *private goods* we have studied so far—and these differences mean that public goods cannot be efficiently supplied by the market. ●

WHAT YOU WILL LEARN

- What are **externalities** and why do they lead to inefficiency and government intervention in the market?
- How do **negative externalities, positive externalities,** and *network externalities* differ?
- What is the **Coase theorem** and how does it explain that private individuals can sometimes remedy externalities?
- Why are some government policies created to deal with externalities efficient and others are not?
- What is a **public good** and how is it different from a private good?

An **external cost** is an uncompensated cost that an individual or firm imposes on others.

An **external benefit** is a benefit that an individual or firm confers on others without receiving compensation.

External costs and benefits are known as **externalities.** External costs are **negative externalities,** and external benefits are **positive externalities.**

The **marginal social cost of pollution** is the additional cost imposed on society as a whole by an additional unit of pollution.

Externalities

The environmental costs of pollution are the best known and most important example of an **external cost**—an uncompensated cost that an individual or firm imposes on others. In a modern economy there are many examples of an external cost that an individual or firm imposes on others. A very familiar one is the external cost of traffic congestion: an individual who chooses to drive during rush hour increases congestion and has no incentive to take into account the inconvenience inflicted on other drivers. Another familiar example is the cost created by those who text while driving, increasing the risk of deadly accidents.

We'll see later in this chapter that there are also important examples of **external benefits,** benefits that individuals or firms confer on others without receiving compensation. For example, when you get a flu shot, you are less likely to pass on the flu virus to your roommates. Yet you alone incur the monetary cost of the vaccination and the painful jab.

External costs and benefits are jointly known as **externalities.** Externalities occur when individuals or firms make private decisions that either impose a cost on society, a **negative externality,** or a benefit to society, a **positive externality.** In both cases the market fails to produce the optimal quantity for society. Let's take a closer look at why by focusing on the case of pollution.

The Economics of a Negative Externality: Pollution

Pollution is a bad thing. Yet most pollution is a side effect of activities that provide us with good things: our air is polluted by power plants generating the electricity that lights our cities, and our rivers are damaged by fertilizer runoff from farms that grow our food. And groundwater contamination may occur from hydraulic fracturing, or fracking, which also produces cleaner-burning fuel. Recall from Chapter 3 that *fracking* is a method of extracting natural gas or oil from deposits trapped between layers of shale rock thousands of feet underground, using powerful jets of liquid.

So, should we accept a certain amount of pollution as the cost of a good life? Actually, we do. Even highly committed environmentalists don't think that we can or should completely eliminate pollution—even an environmentally conscious society would accept *some* pollution as the cost of producing useful goods and services. What environmentalists argue is that unless there is a strong and effective environmental policy, our society will generate *too much* pollution—too much of a bad thing. And the great majority of economists agree.

To see why, we need a framework that lets us think about how much pollution a society *should* have. We'll then be able to see why a market economy, left to itself, will produce more pollution than it should. We'll start by adopting the simplest framework to study the problem—assuming that the amount of pollution emitted by a polluter is directly observable and controllable.

The Costs and Benefits of Pollution

How much pollution should society allow? To answer this "how much" question, recall the *principle of marginal analysis* from Chapter 7. This principle always involves comparing the marginal benefit from an additional unit of something with the marginal cost of that additional unit. The same is true of pollution.

The **marginal social cost of pollution** is the additional cost imposed on society as a whole by an additional unit of pollution.

For example, sulfur dioxide from coal-fired power plants mixes with rainwater to form acid rain, which damages fisheries, crops, and forests, while groundwater contamination, which may be a side effect of fracking, damages health. Typically, the marginal social cost of pollution is increasing—each additional unit of pollution emitted causes a greater level of damage than the unit before. That's because nature can often safely handle low levels of pollution but is increasingly harmed as pollution reaches higher levels.

The **marginal social benefit of pollution** is the benefit to society from an additional unit of pollution. This may seem like a confusing concept—how can there be any benefit to society from pollution? The answer lies in the understanding that pollution can be reduced—but at a cost. For example, air pollution from coal-fired power plants can be reduced by using more-expensive coal and expensive scrubbing technology; contamination of drinking water due to fracking can be limited with more-expensive drilling techniques; wastewater contamination of rivers and oceans can be reduced by building water treatment facilities.

All these methods of reducing pollution have an opportunity cost. That is, avoiding pollution requires using scarce resources that could have been employed to produce other goods and services. So the marginal social benefit of pollution is the goods and services that could be had by society if it tolerated another unit of pollution.

Comparisons between the pollution levels tolerated in rich and poor countries illustrate the importance of the level of the marginal social benefit of pollution in deciding how much pollution a society wishes to tolerate. Because poor countries have a higher opportunity cost of resources spent on reducing pollution than richer countries, they tolerate higher levels of pollution. For example, the World Health Organization has estimated that 3.8 million people in poor countries die prematurely from breathing polluted indoor air caused by burning dirty fuels like wood, dung, and coal to heat and cook—a situation that residents of rich countries can afford to avoid.

Using hypothetical numbers, Figure 10-1 shows how we can determine the **socially optimal quantity of pollution**—the quantity of pollution that society would choose if all the social costs and benefits were fully accounted for. The upward-sloping marginal social cost curve, *MSC*, shows how the marginal cost to society of an additional unit of pollution varies with the quantity of pollution. It is typically upward sloping because the harm inflicted by a unit of pollution typically increases since more pollution has already been emitted. In contrast, the marginal social benefit curve, *MSB*, is downward sloping. At high levels of pollution, the cost of achieving a reduction in pollution is fairly small. However, as pollution levels drop, it becomes progressively more costly to engineer a further fall in pollution as more expensive techniques must be used, so the *MSB* is higher at lower levels of pollution.

As we can see from Figure 10-1, the socially optimal quantity of pollution in this example isn't zero. It's Q_{OPT}, the quantity corresponding to point *O*, where *MSB* crosses *MSC*. At Q_{OPT}, the marginal social benefit from an additional unit of pollution and its marginal social cost are equalized at $200.

But will a market economy, left to itself, arrive at the socially optimal quantity of pollution? No, it won't. Let's see why.

Why a Market Economy Produces Too Much Pollution

While pollution yields both benefits and costs to society, in a market economy without government intervention, too much pollution will be produced. In that case it is polluters alone—owners of power plants or gas-drilling companies, for example—who decide how much pollution occurs. And they have no incentive to take into account the cost that pollution imposes on others. Instead, the company's incentives are determined by the private monetary costs and benefits of generating power, such as the price of coal, the price earned for a kilowatt of energy, and so on.

Figure 10-2 shows the result of this asymmetry between who reaps the benefits and who pays the costs. *In a market economy without government intervention,*

The **marginal social benefit of pollution** is the additional gain to society as a whole from an additional unit of pollution.

The **socially optimal quantity of pollution** is the quantity of pollution that society would choose if all the costs and benefits of pollution were fully accounted for.

FIGURE 10-1 The Socially Optimal Quantity of Pollution

Pollution yields both costs and benefits. Here the curve *MSC* shows how the marginal cost to society as a whole from emitting one more unit of pollution emissions depends on the quantity of emissions. The *MSC* curve is upward sloping, so the marginal social cost increases as pollution increases. The curve *MSB* shows how the marginal benefit to society as a whole of emitting an additional unit of pollution emissions depends on the quantity of pollution emissions. The *MSB* curve is downward sloping, so the marginal social benefit falls as pollution increases. The socially optimal quantity of pollution is Q_{OPT}; at that quantity, the marginal social benefit of pollution is equal to the marginal social cost, corresponding to $200.

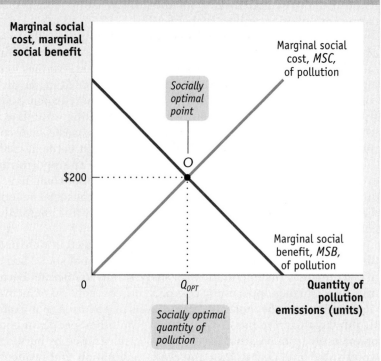

since polluters are the only ones making the decisions, only the private benefits of pollution are taken into account when choosing how much pollution to produce, not the costs to society. So instead of producing the socially optimal quantity, Q_{OPT}, the market economy will generate the amount Q_{MKT}. At Q_{MKT}, the marginal social benefit of an additional unit of pollution is zero, while the marginal social cost of an additional unit is much higher—$400.

FIGURE 10-2 Why a Market Economy Produces Too Much Pollution

In the absence of government intervention, the quantity of pollution will be Q_{MKT}, the level at which the marginal social benefit of pollution is zero. This is an inefficiently high quantity of pollution: the marginal social cost, $400, greatly exceeds the marginal social benefit, $0. An optimal Pigouvian tax* of $200, the value of the marginal social cost of pollution when it equals the marginal social benefit of pollution, can move the market to the socially optimal quantity of pollution, Q_{OPT}.

*Pigouvian taxes will be covered in the next section on pollution policy.

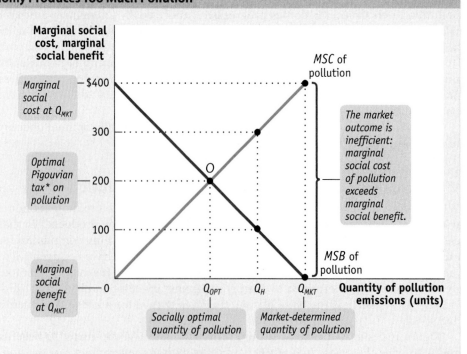

Why? Well, take a moment to consider what the polluter would do if he found himself emitting Q_{OPT} of pollution. Remember that the *MSB* curve represents the resources made available by tolerating one more unit of pollution. The polluter would notice that if he increases his emission of pollution by moving down the *MSB* curve from Q_{OPT} to Q_H, he would gain \$200 − \$100 = \$100. That gain of \$100 comes from using less-expensive but higher-emission production techniques. Remember, he suffers none of the costs of doing this—only others do. However, it won't stop there. At Q_H, he notices that if he increases his emissions from Q_H to Q_{MKT}, he would gain another \$100 as he moves down the *MSB* curve yet again. This would be achieved by using even cheaper and higher-emission production techniques. He will stop at Q_{MKT} because at this emission level the marginal social benefit of a unit of pollution is zero. That is, at Q_{MKT} he gains nothing by using yet cheaper and dirtier production techniques and emitting more pollution.

The market outcome, Q_{MKT}, is inefficient. Recall that an outcome is inefficient if someone could be made better off without someone else being made worse off. At an inefficient outcome, a mutually beneficial trade is being missed. At Q_{MKT}, the benefit accruing to the polluter of the last unit of pollution is very low—virtually zero. But the cost imposed on society of that last unit of pollution is quite high—\$400. So by reducing the quantity of pollution at Q_{MKT} by one unit, the total social cost of pollution falls by \$400 but the total social benefit falls by virtually zero.

So total surplus rises by approximately \$400 if the quantity of pollution at Q_{MKT} is reduced by one unit. At Q_{MKT}, society would be willing to pay the polluter up to \$400 not to emit the last unit of pollution, and the polluter would be willing to accept their offer, since that last unit gains him virtually nothing. But because there is no means in this market economy for this transaction to take place, an inefficient outcome occurs.

Private Solutions to Externalities

As we've just seen, externalities in a market economy cause inefficiency: there is a mutually beneficial trade that is being missed. So can the private sector solve the problem of externalities without government intervention? Will individuals be able to make that deal on their own?

In an influential 1960 article, the economist and Nobel laureate Ronald Coase pointed out that in an ideal world the private sector could indeed solve the problem of inefficiency caused by externalities. According to the **Coase theorem,** even in the presence of externalities an economy can always reach an efficient solution provided that the costs of making a deal are sufficiently low. The costs of making a deal are known as **transaction costs.**

For an illustration of how the Coase theorem might work, consider the case of groundwater contamination caused by drilling. There are two ways a private transaction can address this problem. First, landowners whose groundwater is at risk of contamination can pay drillers to use more-expensive, less-polluting technology. Second, the drilling companies can pay landowners the value of damage to their groundwater sources—say, by buying their properties outright so that the landowners move. If drillers legally have the right to pollute, then the first outcome is more likely. If drillers don't legally have the right to pollute, then the second is more likely.

What Coase argued is that, either way, if transaction costs are sufficiently low, then drillers and landowners can make a mutually beneficial deal. Regardless of how the transaction is structured, the social cost of the pollution is taken into account in decision making. When individuals take externalities into account when making decisions, economists say that they **internalize the externality.** In that case the outcome is efficient without government intervention.

According to the **Coase theorem,** even in the presence of externalities an economy can always reach an efficient solution as long as **transaction costs**—the costs to individuals of making a deal—are sufficiently low.

When individuals take external costs or benefits into account, they **internalize the externality.**

So why don't private parties always internalize externalities? The problem is transaction costs in one form or another that prevent an efficient outcome. Here is a sample:

- *The high cost of communication.* Suppose a power plant emits pollution that covers a wide area. The cost of communicating with the many people affected will be very high.

- *The high cost of making legally binding and timely agreements.* What if some landowners band together and pay a driller to reduce groundwater pollution? It can be very expensive to make an effective agreement, requiring lawyers, groundwater tests, engineers, and others. And there is no guarantee that the negotiations will go smoothly or quickly: some landowners may refuse to pay even if their groundwater is protected, while the drillers may hold out for a better deal.

To be sure, there are examples in the real world in which private parties internalize the externalities. Take the case of private communities that set rules for appearances—no cars on blocks in the driveway!—and behavior—no loud parties at midnight! These rules internalize the externality that one homeowner's lack of upkeep or rowdy behavior has on the market value of a neighbor's house. But for major externalities like widespread pollution, it is necessary to look for government solutions because transaction costs are just too high to achieve an efficient private outcome.

In some cases, people do find ways to reduce transaction costs, allowing them to internalize externalities. For example, a house with a junk-filled yard and peeling paint imposes a negative externality on the neighboring houses, diminishing their value in the eyes of potential home buyers. So, many people live in private communities that set rules for home maintenance and behavior, making bargaining between neighbors unnecessary. But in many other cases, transaction costs are too high to make it possible to deal with externalities through private action. For example, tens of millions of people are adversely affected by acid rain. It would be prohibitively expensive to try to make a deal among all those people and all those power companies.

When transaction costs prevent the private sector from dealing with externalities, it is time to look for government solutions. We turn to public policy in the next section.

ECONOMICS >> *in Action*
How Much Does Your Electricity Really Cost?

Three leading economists, Nicholas Z. Muller, Robert Mendelsohn, and William Nordhaus, published a 2011 paper estimating the external cost of pollution by various U.S. industries. The costs took a variety of forms, from harmful effects on health to reduced agricultural yields. In the case of the electricity-generation sector, the authors included costs from carbon dioxide emissions—one of the many *greenhouse gases* that cause *climate change*.

The authors used a conservative, relatively low estimate because valuing these costs is a contentious issue—in part because they will fall on future generations. For each industry they calculated the total external cost of pollution, or TEC. Remarkably, in a number of cases this cost actually exceeded the industry's value added (VA), that is, the market value of its output. This doesn't mean that these industries should be shut down, but it's a clear indication that markets weren't taking the costs of pollution into account.

What is the social cost of carbon?

Among other things, the paper compared the external costs associated with coal-fired and natural gas–fired power plants. The accompanying table shows the TEC to VA ratios and the TEC to kilowatt-hour ratios for the coal and natural gas industries. As you can see, both modes of electricity generation impose large external costs, exceeding their value added. But, the TEC per kilowatt-hour generated with natural gas is much lower than that of one generated with coal, because burning natural gas releases both less carbon dioxide and fewer other pollutants.

	TEC/ VA	TEC/ Kilowatt-hour
Coal	$2.83	$0.039
Natural gas	1.30	0.005

A conservative estimate is that the external cost of a kilowatt hour is one-third of the retail price of electricity when generated by coal, and one-twentieth when generated by natural gas.

In 2014, the Environmental Protection Agency (EPA) issued rules limiting carbon emissions from newly constructed power plants. The rules won't hinder the construction of gas-fired plants, which meet the EPA standard, but will block coal-fired plants unless they can use carbon-capture technology to divert carbon emissions and store them underground.

In addition, the falling price of natural gas due to fracking has induced power companies to substitute natural gas for coal in generating power. So in 2016, for the first time in history, more American energy was generated by using natural gas than by using coal.

>> Check Your Understanding 10-1

Solutions appear at back of book.

1. Wastewater runoff from large poultry farms adversely affects their neighbors. Explain the following:
   a. The nature of the external cost imposed
   b. The outcome in the absence of government intervention or a private deal
   c. The socially optimal outcome

2. According to Yasmin, any student who borrows a book from the university library and fails to return it on time imposes a negative externality on other students. She claims that rather than charging a modest fine for late returns, the library should charge a huge fine so that borrowers will never return a book late. Is Yasmin's economic reasoning correct?

‖ Government Policy and Pollution

By the 1960s, vast tracts of ghostly, withered trees in the northeastern United States and southeastern Canada revealed an ominous truth: these great forests were dying. Moreover, the lakes and streams within them were dying too, as the stock of fish and other aquatic life plummeted.

The culprit was acid rain, a phenomenon that occurs when rain mixes with airborne sulfur dioxide pollutants from coal-burning power plants. The result is highly acidic rain that poisons trees and aquatic life. Before 1970, there were no regulations governing the amount of sulfur dioxide that a U.S. power plant could emit.

In 1970, Congress adopted the Clean Air Act, which set rules forcing power plants to reduce their emissions. And it worked—the acidity of rainfall declined significantly. Economists, however, argued that a more flexible system of rules that exploits the effectiveness of markets could reduce pollution at a lower cost. In 1990 this theory was put into effect with a modified version of the Clean Air Act. And guess what? The economists were right!

In this section we'll look at the three types of policies governments typically use to deal with pollution: environmental standards, emissions taxes, and tradable emissions permits.

We will also see how economic analysis has been used to improve those policies. We will also look at the issue of climate change and how government policy can be used to address it.

Environmental Standards

Among the most serious negative externalities we face today are those associated with actions that damage the environment—air pollution, water pollution, habitat destruction, and so on. Protection of the environment has become a major role of government in all advanced nations. In the United States, the Environmental Protection Agency is the principal enforcer of environmental policies at the national level, supported by the actions of state and local governments.

"They have very strict anti-pollution laws in this state."

How does a country protect its environment? At present the main policy tools are **environmental standards,** rules that protect the environment by specifying actions by producers and consumers. A familiar example is the law that requires almost all vehicles to have catalytic converters, which reduce the emission of chemicals that can cause smog and lead to health problems. Other rules require communities to treat their sewage or factories to avoid or limit certain kinds of pollution. And as we just saw in the Economics in Action, environmental standards were put in place in 2014, compelling new coal- and gas-fired power plants to adopt cleaner-burning technologies.

Environmental standards came into widespread use in the 1960s and 1970s, and they have had considerable success in reducing pollution. For example, since the United States passed the Clean Air Act in 1970, overall emission of pollutants into the air has fallen by more than a third, even though the population has grown by a third and the size of the economy has more than doubled.

Emissions Taxes

Another policy tool to address pollution is to charge polluters an **emissions tax.** Emissions taxes depend on the amount of pollution a firm emits. As we learned in Chapter 5, a tax imposed on an activity will reduce the level of that activity.

Recall that without government intervention, polluters have an incentive to increase pollution beyond the socially optimal quantity of pollution. In fact, they will produce up to the point at which the marginal social benefit equals zero.

If the marginal social benefit and marginal social cost of an additional unit of pollution are equal at $200 (as shown in Figure 10-2), a tax on polluters of $200 per unit of pollution will induce polluters to reduce their emissions to the socially optimal quantity.

This illustrates a general result: an emissions tax equal to the marginal social cost at the socially optimal quantity of pollution induces polluters to internalize the externality—to take into account the true cost to society of their actions.

An emissions tax is also a more efficient (or cost-minimizing) way to reduce pollution than environmental standards because the tax ensures that the marginal benefit of pollution is equal for all sources of pollution. Environmental standards, by contrast, treat all polluters the same, despite the fact that polluters will face different costs for reducing their pollution.

The term *emissions tax* may convey the misleading impression that taxes are a solution to only one kind of negative externality, pollution. In fact, taxes can be used to discourage any activity that generates negative externalities, such as driving (which inflicts environmental damage greater than the cost of producing gasoline) or smoking (which inflicts health costs on society far greater than the cost of making a cigarette).

Environmental standards are rules that protect the environment by specifying actions by producers and consumers.

An **emissions tax** is a tax that depends on the amount of pollution a firm produces.

In general, taxes designed to reduce the costs imposed on society from a negative externality are known as **Pigouvian taxes,** after the economist A. C. Pigou, who emphasized their usefulness in his classic 1920 book, *The Economics of Welfare*. In our example, the optimal Pigouvian tax is $200, which sets the marginal social cost of pollution equal to the social optimal quantity. As you can see from Figure 10-2, this corresponds to the marginal social cost of pollution at the optimal output quantity, Q_{OPT}.

The main shortcoming of emissions taxes is that in practice, government officials usually aren't sure how high the tax should be set. If they set it too low, pollution reduction would be insufficient. If they set it too high, emissions will be reduced by more than is efficient. This uncertainty around the optimal level of the emissions tax can't be eliminated, but the nature of the risks can be changed by using an alternative policy: issuing tradable emissions permits.

> Taxes designed to reduce negative externalities are known as **Pigouvian taxes.**

 GLOBAL COMPARISON   **ECONOMIC GROWTH AND GREENHOUSE GASES IN SIX COUNTRIES**

At first glance, a comparison of the per capita greenhouse gas emissions of various countries, shown in panel (a) of this graph, suggests that Australia, the United States, and Canada are the worst offenders. The average American is responsible for 16.1 tonnes of greenhouse gas emissions (measured in carbon dioxide, CO_2, equivalents)—the pollution that causes climate change—compared to only 3.9 tonnes for the average Uzbek, 6.7 tonnes for the average Chinese, and 1.8 tonnes for the average Indian. (A tonne, also called a metric ton, equals 1.10 ton.)

Such a conclusion, however, ignores an important factor in determining the level of a country's greenhouse gas emissions: its gross domestic product, or GDP—the total value of a country's domestic output. Output typically cannot be produced without more energy, and more energy usage typically results in more pollution. In fact, some have argued that criticizing a country's level of greenhouse gases without taking account of its level of economic development is misguided. It would be equivalent to faulting a country for being at a more advanced stage of economic development.

A more meaningful way to compare pollution across countries is to measure emissions per $1 million of a country's GDP, as shown in panel (b). On this basis, the United States, Canada, and Australia

are now "green" countries, but Uzbekistan, China, and India are not. What explains the reversal once GDP is accounted for? The answer is scarce resources.

Countries that are poor, such as Uzbekistan and India (and, historically, China), have viewed resources spent on pollution reduction as better spent on other things. They have argued that they are too poor to afford the same environmental priorities as wealthy advanced countries. To impose a wealthy country's environmental standards on them would, they claimed, jeopardize their economic growth.

However, the scientific evidence pointing to *greenhouse gases* as the cause of *climate change* and the falling price of non-polluting energy sources has changed attitudes in poorer countries. Realizing that their citizens are likely to suffer disproportionately more from climate change, poor countries joined forces with rich countries to sign the *Paris Agreement* in 2015, an agreement initially between 196 countries to reduce their emissions of greenhouse gases to keep the global temperature below 2 degrees Celsius, the temperature at which the effects of climate change are considered to be catastrophic and irreversible. At the time of writing, the United States has announced its intent to withdraw from the agreement, the only country in the world to reject the agreement.

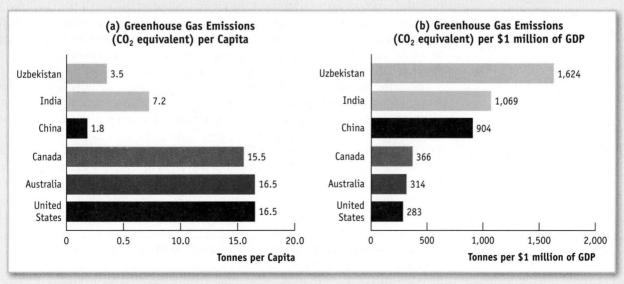

(a) Greenhouse Gas Emissions (CO_2 equivalent) per Capita

	Tonnes per Capita
Uzbekistan	3.5
India	7.2
China	1.8
Canada	15.5
Australia	16.5
United States	16.5

(b) Greenhouse Gas Emissions (CO_2 equivalent) per $1 million of GDP

	Tonnes per $1 million of GDP
Uzbekistan	1,624
India	1,069
China	904
Canada	366
Australia	314
United States	283

Data from: Global Carbon Atlas; IMF—World Economic Outlook.

Tradable Emissions Permits

Tradable emissions permits are licenses to emit limited quantities of pollutants
that can be bought and sold by polluters. Firms that pollute typically have different costs of reducing pollution—for example, it will be more costly for plants
using older technology to reduce pollution than plants using newer technology.
Regulators begin the system by issuing polluters with permits to pollute based on
some formula—say, for example, equal to 50% of a given firm's historical level of
emissions. Firms then have the right to trade permits among themselves.

Under this system, a market in permits to pollute will emerge. Polluters who
place a higher value on the right to pollute—those with older technology—will
purchase permits from polluters who place a lower value on the right to pollute—
those with newer technology. As a result, a polluter with a higher value for a unit
of emissions will pollute more than a polluter with a lower value.

In the end, those with the lowest cost of reducing pollution will reduce their
pollution the most, while those with the highest cost of reducing pollution will
reduce their pollution the least. The total effect is to allocate pollution reduction
efficiently—that is, in the least costly way.

Just like emissions taxes, tradable emissions permits provide polluters with an
incentive to take the marginal social cost of pollution into account. To see why,
suppose that the market price of a permit to emit one unit of pollution is $200.
Every polluter now has an incentive to limit its emissions to the point where its
marginal benefit of one unit of pollution is $200. Why?

If the marginal benefit of one more unit of pollution is greater than $200 then
it is cheaper to pollute more than to pollute less. In that case the polluter will buy
a permit and emit another unit. And if the marginal benefit of one more unit of
pollution is less than $200, then it is cheaper to reduce pollution than to pollute
more. In that scenario the polluter will reduce pollution rather than buy the $200
permit.

From this example we can see how an emissions permit leads to the same outcome as an emissions tax when they are the same amount: a polluter who pays
$200 for the right to emit one unit faces the same incentives as a polluter who
faces an emissions tax of $200 per unit. And it's equally true for polluters who
have received more permits from regulators than they plan to use: by not emitting
one unit of pollution, a polluter frees up a permit that it can sell for $200. In other
words, the opportunity cost of a unit of pollution to this firm is $200, regardless of
whether it is used.

Recall that when using emissions taxes to arrive at the optimal level of pollution, the problem arises of finding the right amount of the tax: if the tax is too low,
too much pollution is emitted; if the tax is too high, too little pollution is emitted
(in other words, too many resources are spent reducing pollution). A similar problem with tradable emissions permits is getting the quantity of permits right, which
is much like the flip-side of getting the level of the tax right.

Because it is difficult to determine the optimal quantity of pollution, regulators can find themselves either issuing too many permits, so that there is insufficient pollution reduction, or issuing too few, so that there is too much pollution
reduction.

In the case of sulfur dioxide pollution, the U.S. government first relied on environmental standards, but then turned to a system of tradable emissions permits.
Currently the largest emissions permit trading system is the European Union system for controlling emissions of carbon dioxide.

Comparing Environmental Policies with an Example

Figure 10-3 shows a hypothetical industry consisting of only two plants, plant A
and plant B. We'll assume that plant A uses newer technology, giving it a lower
cost of pollution reduction, while plant B uses older technology and has a higher

FIGURE 10-3 Comparing Environmental Policies

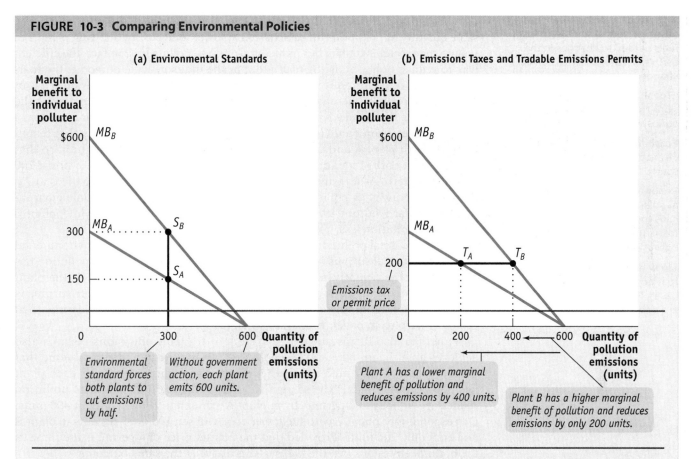

(a) Environmental Standards

Marginal benefit to individual polluter

MB_B

$600

300 MB_A.......... S_B

150 · · · · · · · · · · S_A

0   300   600   **Quantity of pollution emissions (units)**

Environmental standard forces both plants to cut emissions by half.

Without government action, each plant emits 600 units.

(b) Emissions Taxes and Tradable Emissions Permits

Marginal benefit to individual polluter

$600 MB_B

MB_A

200 T_A T_B
/
Emissions tax or permit price

0   200   400 ◄──── 600   **Quantity of pollution emissions (units)**

Plant A has a lower marginal benefit of pollution and reduces emissions by 400 units.

Plant B has a higher marginal benefit of pollution and reduces emissions by only 200 units.

In both panels, MB_A shows the marginal benefit of pollution to plant A and MB_B shows the marginal benefit of pollution to plant B. In the absence of government intervention, each plant would emit 600 units. However, the cost of reducing emissions is lower for plant A, as shown by the fact that MB_A lies below MB_B. Panel (a) shows the result of an environmental standard that requires both plants to cut emissions in half; this

is inefficient, because it leaves the marginal benefit of pollution higher for plant B than for plant A. Panel (b) shows that an emissions tax as well as a system of tradable permits achieves the same quantity of overall pollution efficiently. Faced with either an emissions tax of $200 per unit, or a market price of a permit of $200 per unit, each plant reduces pollution to the point where its marginal benefit is $200.

---

cost of pollution reduction. Reflecting this difference, plant A's marginal benefit of pollution curve, MB_A, lies below plant B's marginal benefit of pollution curve, MB_B. Because it is more costly for plant B to reduce its pollution at any output quantity, an additional unit of pollution is worth more to plant B than to plant A.

In the absence of government action, we know that polluters will pollute until the marginal social benefit of a unit of pollution is equal to zero. As a result, without government intervention each plant will pollute until its own marginal benefit of pollution is equal to zero. This corresponds to an emissions quantity of 600 units for each plant—the quantities of pollution at which MB_A and MB_B are equal to zero. So, although plant A and plant B have different costs of pollution reduction, they will each choose to emit the same amount of pollution.

Now suppose that regulators decide that the overall pollution from this industry should be cut in half, from 1,200 units to 600 units. Panel (a) of Figure 10-3 shows this might be achieved with an environmental standard that requires each plant to cut its emissions in half, from 600 to 300 units. The standard has the desired effect of reducing overall emissions from 1,200 to 600 units but accomplishes it inefficiently.

As you can see from panel (a), the environmental standard leads plant A to produce at point S_A, where its marginal benefit of pollution is $150, but plant B produces at point S_B, where its marginal benefit of pollution is twice as high, $300.

An accumulation of greenhouse gases caused by the use of fossil fuels has led to changes in the earth's climate, known as **climate change.**

Greenhouse gases are gas emissions that trap heat in Earth's atmosphere.

Fossil fuels such as coal and oil are fuels derived from fossil sources.

Renewable energy sources such as solar and wind power are inexhaustible sources of energy (unlike fossil fuel sources, which are exhaustible).

Clean energy sources are those that do not emit greenhouse gases. Renewable energy sources are also clean energy sources.

This difference in marginal benefits between the two plants tells us that the same quantity of pollution can be achieved at lower total cost by allowing plant B to pollute more than 300 units but inducing plant A to pollute less. In fact, the efficient way to reduce pollution is to ensure that at the industry-wide outcome, the marginal benefit of pollution is the same for all plants. When each plant values a unit of pollution equally, there is no way to rearrange pollution reduction among the various plants that achieves the optimal quantity of pollution at a lower total cost.

We can see from panel (b) how an emissions tax achieves exactly that result. Suppose both plant A and plant B pay an emissions tax of $200 per unit, so that the marginal cost of an additional unit of emissions to each plant is now $200 rather than zero. As a result, plant A produces at T_A and plant B produces at T_B. So plant A reduces its pollution more than it would under an inflexible environmental standard, cutting its emissions from 600 to 200 units; meanwhile, plant B reduces its pollution less, going from 600 to 400 units.

In the end, total pollution—600 units—is the same as under the environmental standard, but total surplus is higher. That's because the reduction in pollution has been achieved efficiently, allocating most of the reduction to plant A, the plant that can reduce emissions at a lower cost. (Remember that producer surplus is the area below the supply curve and above the price line. So, there is more total producer surplus in panel (b) than in panel (a).)

Panel (b) also illustrates why a system of tradable emissions permits also achieves an efficient allocation of pollution among the two plants. Assume that in the market for permits, the market price of a permit is $200 and each plant has 300 permits to start the system. Plant B, with the higher cost of pollution reduction, will buy 100 permits from plant A, enough to allow it to emit 400 units. Correspondingly, plant A, with the lower cost, will sell 100 of its permits to plant B and emit only 200 units. Provided that the market price of a permit is the same as the optimal emissions tax, the two systems arrive at the same outcome.

The Economics of Climate Change

One serious problem that the world will face in upcoming years is **climate change.** Science has conclusively shown that the emissions of *greenhouse gases* are changing the earth's climate. **Greenhouse gases** trap heat in Earth's atmosphere, leading to extreme weather patterns—drought, flooding, temperature fluctuations, destructive storm activity, and rising sea levels. Climate change inflicts huge costs and suffering, as crops fail, homes are washed away, tropical diseases spread, animal species are lost, and areas become uninhabitable. A recent estimate put the cost of unmitigated climate change at 20% of world gross domestic product by 2100.

The rise in Earth's temperature began in the first half of the nineteenth century and has accelerated since the 1980s. The source of the vast majority of greenhouse gases is human activity—specifically, the burning of **fossil fuels** such as coal, oil, and natural gas, which are derived from fossil sources and are used to generate electricity or power vehicles. While fossil fuels are in limited supply, **renewable energy sources** are inexhaustible. Examples are solar and wind-generated power. Unlike fossil fuels, renewables are **clean energy sources** because they do not emit greenhouse gases.

World energy consumption is overwhelmingly dependent upon fossil fuels, which account for 81.4% of total consumption, while renewables account for only 2.6%. Why? It's dollars and cents (or rupees, as the case may be). Historically, fossil fuels have been a cheaper source of energy than renewables.

However, it is now widely recognized that the direct cost of fossil fuel consumption greatly underestimates the social cost. In a study commissioned by the World Bank, economists Joseph Stiglitz and Nicholas Stern estimate that the true environmental cost of carbon emissions ranges from $50 to $100 per ton as of 2017, and climb to as high as $400 by 2050. To address climate change, humans will need to move from a heavy reliance on fossil fuels to using clean energy sources. But, because so much of the productive capacity of modern economies is dependent upon fossil fuel use, the transition will require economic changes and large-scale investment in clean energy capacity.

Examples of government policies that could be used to effect the transition include tax credits and subsidies to promote the shift; mandates to cut emissions; industrial and business commitments to clean energy use; greater efficiency standards for buildings, homes, and vehicles; and smart metering for home energy use.

ECONOMICS >> *in Action*
Cap and Trade

The tradable emissions permit systems for both acid rain in the United States and greenhouse gases in the European Union are examples of *cap and trade systems:* The government sets a *cap* (a maximum amount of pollutant that can be emitted), issues tradable emissions permits, and enforces a yearly rule that a polluter must hold a number of permits equal to the amount of pollutant emitted. The goal is to set the cap low enough to generate environmental benefits, while giving polluters flexibility in meeting environmental standards and motivating them to adopt new technologies that will lower the cost of reducing pollution.

In 1995 the United States began a cap and trade system for the sulfur dioxide emissions that cause acid rain by issuing permits to power plants based on their historical consumption of coal. Thanks to the system, sulfur dioxide emissions have fallen by 75% from 1994 to 2015. Economists who have analyzed the sulfur dioxide cap and trade system point to another reason for its success: it would have been a lot more expensive—80% more to be exact—to reduce emissions by this much using a non-market-based regulatory policy.

In 2005 the first cap and trade system for trading greenhouse gases—called *carbon trading*—was launched in the European Union. More than a decade later, carbon trading has grown rapidly around the world and now covers 8% of all man-made greenhouse gas emissions. In the past few years, several new greenhouse gas markets have been launched covering California, South Korea, Quebec, and three major industrial centers in China. In 2018, approximately $164 billion in permits were traded globally.

Yet cap and trade systems are not silver bullets for the world's pollution problems. Although they are appropriate for pollution that's geographically dispersed, like sulfur dioxide and greenhouse gases, they don't work for pollution that's localized, like groundwater contamination. And there must be vigilant monitoring of compliance for the system to work. Finally, the level at which the cap is set has become a difficult political issue for governments trying to run an effective cap and trade system.

The political problems stem from the fact that a lower cap imposes higher costs on companies, because they must either achieve great pollution reductions or because they must purchase permits that command a higher market price. So, companies lobby governments to set higher caps. As of 2018 only five countries (Finland, France, Sweden, Norway, and Switzerland) had caps that met or exceeded $44 per metric ton, the carbon price that the International Emissions Trading Association estimates is required to avert catastrophic climate change. In fact, most carbon trading prices are well below $15. As one energy economist stated, "It is politically difficult to get carbon prices to levels that have an effect." And the same applies for taxes on carbon, as higher taxes can be a hard sell to consumers and producers.

So, although carbon trading and carbon taxes are the efficient ways to reduce greenhouse emissions, their susceptibility to political pressure has policy makers turning to regulations instead. A case in point is the adoption in 2014 by the EPA of rules limiting the emissions from newly built coal-fired and natural gas–fired plants. And in 2012, the Obama administration adopted a mandate that doubles the fuel efficiency of cars by 2025.

>> Quick Review

• Governments often limit pollution with **environmental standards.** Generally, such standards are an inefficient way to reduce pollution because they are inflexible.

• Environmental goals can be achieved efficiently in two ways: **emissions taxes** and **tradable emissions permits.** These methods are efficient because they are flexible, allocating more pollution reduction to those who can do it more cheaply. They also motivate polluters to adopt new pollution-reducing technology. An emissions tax is a form of **Pigouvian tax.** The optimal Pigouvian tax is equal to the marginal social cost of pollution at the socially optimal quantity of pollution.

• Unlike fossil fuels, **renewable energy sources,** such as solar and wind power, are inexhaustible. Policies such as taxes, tax credits, subsidies, mandates, consumer use of smart metering, and industrial commitments, are needed.

New Jerseyans understand that preserving local farmland makes them better off.

>> Check Your Understanding 10-2

Solutions appear at back of book.

1. Some opponents of tradable emissions permits object to them on the grounds that polluters that sell their permits benefit monetarily from their contribution to polluting the environment. Assess this argument.

2. Explain the following:
   a. Why an emissions tax smaller than or greater than the marginal social cost at Q_{OPT} leads to a smaller total surplus compared to the total surplus generated if the emissions tax had been set optimally
   b. Why a system of tradable emissions permits that sets the total quantity of allowable pollution higher or lower than Q_{OPT} leads to a smaller total surplus compared to the total surplus generated if the number of permits had been set optimally
   c. How a carbon tax, which is a tax on carbon emissions, would encourage consumers to use more renewable energy sources

The Economics of Positive Externalities

New Jersey is the most densely populated state in the country, lying along the northeastern corridor, an area of almost continuous development stretching from Washington, D.C., to Boston. Yet a drive through New Jersey reveals a surprising feature: acre upon acre of farmland, growing everything from corn to pumpkins to the famous Jersey tomatoes. This is no accident: starting in 1961, New Jerseyans have voted in a series of measures that subsidize farmers to permanently preserve their farmland rather than sell it to developers. By 2016, the Green Acres Program, administered by the state, had preserved over 680,000 acres of open space.

Why have New Jersey citizens voted to raise their own taxes to subsidize the preservation of farmland? Because they believe that preserved farmland in an already heavily developed state provides benefits, such as natural beauty, access to fresh food, and the conservation of wild bird populations. In addition, preservation alleviates the negative externalities that come with more development, such as pressure on roads, water supplies, and municipal services—and, inevitably, more pollution.

In this section we'll explore the topic of positive externalities. They are, in many ways, the mirror images of negative externalities. Left to its own, the market will produce too little of a good (in this case, preserved New Jersey farmland) that generates benefits on others. But society as a whole is better off when policies are adopted that increase the supply of such a good.

Preserved Farmland: A Positive Externality

Preserved farmland yields both benefits and costs to society. In the absence of government intervention, the farmer who wants to sell his land incurs all the costs of preservation—namely, the forgone profit to be made from selling the farmland to a developer. But the benefits of preserved farmland accrue not to the farmer but to neighboring residents, who have no right to influence how the farmland is disposed of.

Figure 10-4 illustrates society's problem. The marginal social cost of preserved farmland, shown by the *MSC* curve, is the additional cost imposed on society by an additional acre of such farmland. This represents the forgone profits that would have accrued to farmers if they had sold their land to developers. The line is upward sloping because when very few acres are preserved and there is plenty of land available for development, the profit that could be made from selling an acre to a developer is small. But as the number of preserved acres increases and few are left for development, the amount a developer is willing to pay for them, and therefore the forgone profit, increases as well.

FIGURE 10-4 Why a Market Economy Preserves Too Little Farmland

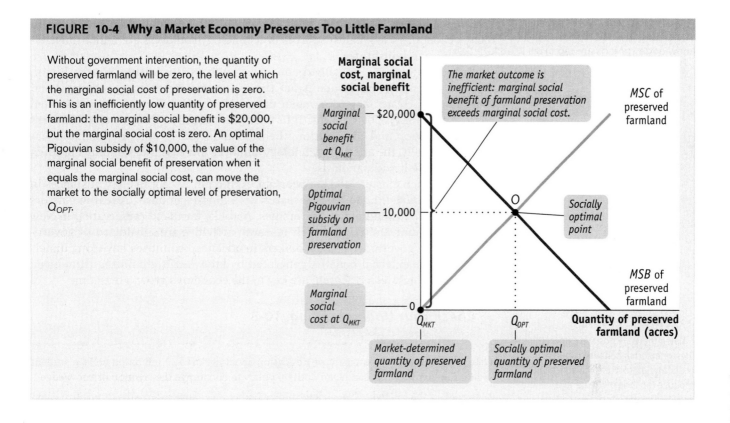

Without government intervention, the quantity of preserved farmland will be zero, the level at which the marginal social cost of preservation is zero. This is an inefficiently low quantity of preserved farmland: the marginal social benefit is $20,000, but the marginal social cost is zero. An optimal Pigouvian subsidy of $10,000, the value of the marginal social benefit of preservation when it equals the marginal social cost, can move the market to the socially optimal level of preservation, Q_{OPT}.

The *MSB* curve represents the marginal social benefit of preserved farmland. It is the additional benefit that accrues to society—in this case, the farmer's neighbors—when an additional acre of farmland is preserved. The curve is downward sloping because as more farmland is preserved, the benefit to society of preserving another acre falls.

As Figure 10-4 shows, the socially optimal point, *O*, occurs when the marginal social cost and the marginal social benefit are equalized—here, at a price of $10,000 per acre. At the socially optimal point, Q_{OPT} acres of farmland are preserved.

The market alone will not provide Q_{OPT} acres of preserved farmland. Instead, in the market outcome no acres will be preserved; the level of preserved farmland, Q_{MKT}, is equal to zero. That's because farmers will set the marginal social cost of preservation—their forgone profits—at zero and sell all their acres to developers. Because farmers bear the entire cost of preservation but gain none of the benefits, an inefficiently low quantity of acres will be preserved in the market outcome.

This is clearly inefficient because at zero acres preserved, the marginal social benefit of preserving an acre of farmland is $20,000. So how can the economy be induced to produce Q_{OPT} acres of preserved farmland, the socially optimal level? The answer is a **Pigouvian subsidy:** a payment designed to encourage activities that generate positive externalities. The optimal Pigouvian subsidy, as shown in Figure 10-4, is equal to the marginal social benefit of preserved farmland at the socially optimal level, Q_{OPT}—that is, $10,000 per acre.

So New Jersey voters are indeed implementing the right policy to raise their social welfare—taxing themselves in order to provide subsidies for farmland preservation.

Positive Externalities in Today's Economy

In the overall U.S. economy, the single most important source of positive externalities is the creation of knowledge. In high-tech industries such as programming, app design, robotics, green technology, and bioengineering, innovations by one firm are quickly emulated and improved upon by rival firms. Such spreading of

A **Pigouvian subsidy** is a payment designed to encourage activities that yield external benefits.

A **technology spillover** is a positive externality that results when knowledge spreads among individuals and firms.

knowledge across individuals and firms is known as a **technology spillover.** In today's economy, the greatest sources of technology spillovers are major universities and research institutes.

In technologically advanced countries such as the United States, Japan, England, Germany, France, and Israel, there is an ongoing exchange of people and ideas among private industries, major universities, and research institutes located in close proximity. The dynamic interplay that occurs in these *research clusters* spurs innovation and competition, theoretical advances, and practical applications. Ultimately, the areas of technology spillover increase the economy's productivity and raise living standards.

But research clusters don't appear out of thin air. Except in a few instances in which firms have funded basic research on a long-term basis, research clusters have grown up around major universities. And like farmland preservation in New Jersey, major universities and their research activities are subsidized by government. In fact, government policy makers in advanced countries have long understood that the external benefits generated by knowledge, stemming from basic education to high-tech research, are key to the economy's growth over time.

>> Quick Review

• When there are positive externalities, or external benefits, a market economy, left to itself, will typically produce too little of the good or activity. The socially optimal quantity of the good or activity can be achieved by an optimal **Pigouvian subsidy.**

• The most important example of a positive externality in the economy is the creation of knowledge through **technology spillover.**

>> Check Your Understanding 10-3

Solutions appear at back of book.

1. In 2016, the U.S. Department of Education spent almost $29 billion on college student aid. Explain why this can be an optimal policy to encourage the creation of knowledge.

2. In each of the following cases, determine whether a negative externality or positive externality is imposed and what an appropriate policy response would be.
   a. Trees planted in urban areas improve air quality and lower summer temperatures.
   b. Water-saving toilets reduce the need to pump water from rivers and aquifers. The cost of a gallon of water to homeowners is virtually zero.
   c. Bottled drinks are packaged in plastic that does not decompose when discarded. As a result, they take up vast amounts of landfill space or must be burned, releasing pollutants.

‖ Public Goods

The opening story describes the Great Stink of 1858, a negative externality created by individuals dumping waste into the Thames River.

What London needed, said reformers at the time, was a sewage system that would carry waste away from the river. Yet no private individual was willing to build such a system, and influential people were opposed to the idea that the government should take responsibility for the problem.

Eventually, Parliament approved a plan for an immense system of sewers and pumping stations, with the result that cholera and typhoid epidemics, which had been regular occurrences, completely disappeared. The Thames was turned from the filthiest to the cleanest metropolitan river in the world, and the sewage system's principal engineer, Sir Joseph Bazalgette, was lauded as having "saved more lives than any single Victorian public official." It was estimated at the time that Bazalgette's sewer system added 20 years to the life span of the average Londoner.

So, what's the difference between installing a new bathroom in a house and building a municipal sewage system? What's the difference between growing wheat and fishing in the open ocean?

These aren't trick questions. In each case there is a basic difference in the characteristics of the goods involved. Bathroom fixtures and wheat have the characteristics necessary to allow markets to work efficiently. Public sewage systems and fish in the sea do not.

Let's look at these crucial characteristics and why they matter.

Characteristics of Goods

Goods like bathroom fixtures or wheat have two characteristics that, as we'll soon see, are essential if a good is to be efficiently provided by a market economy.

- They are **excludable:** suppliers of the good can prevent people who don't pay from consuming it.
- They are **rival in consumption:** the same unit of the good cannot be consumed by more than one person at the same time.

When a good is both excludable and rival in consumption, it is called a **private good.** Wheat is an example of a private good. It is *excludable:* the farmer can sell a bushel to one consumer without having to provide wheat to everyone in the county. And it is *rival in consumption:* if I eat bread baked with a farmer's wheat, that wheat cannot be consumed by someone else.

But not all goods possess these two characteristics. Some goods are **nonexcludable**—the supplier cannot prevent consumption of the good by people who do not pay for it. Fire protection is one example: a fire department that puts out fires before they spread protects the whole city, not just people who have made contributions to the Firemen's Benevolent Association. An improved environment is another: the city of London couldn't have ended the Great Stink for some residents while leaving the River Thames foul for others.

Nor are all goods rival in consumption. Goods are **nonrival in consumption** if more than one person can consume the same unit of the good at the same time. TV shows are nonrival in consumption: your decision to watch a show does not prevent other people from watching the same show.

Because goods can be either excludable or nonexcludable, rival or nonrival in consumption, there are four types of goods, illustrated by the matrix in Figure 10-5:

- *Private goods,* which are excludable and rival in consumption, like wheat
- *Public goods,* which are nonexcludable and nonrival in consumption, like a public sewer system
- *Common resources,* which are nonexcludable but rival in consumption, like clean water in a river
- *Artificially scarce goods,* which are excludable but nonrival in consumption, like on-demand movies on Amazon Prime Video

A good is **excludable** if the supplier of that good can prevent people who do not pay from consuming it.

A good is **rival in consumption** if the same unit of the good cannot be consumed by more than one person at the same time.

A good that is both excludable and rival in consumption is a **private good.**

When a good is **nonexcludable,** the supplier cannot prevent consumption by people who do not pay for it.

A good is **nonrival in consumption** if more than one person can consume the same unit of the good at the same time.

FIGURE 10-5 Four Types of Goods

	Rival in consumption	Nonrival in consumption
Excludable	**Private goods** • Wheat • Bathroom fixtures	**Artificially scarce goods** • On-demand movies • Computer software
Non-excludable	**Common resources** • Clean water • Biodiversity	**Public goods** • Public sanitation • National defense

There are four types of goods. The type of a good depends on (1) whether or not it is excludable–whether a producer can prevent someone from consuming it; and (2) whether or not it is rival in consumption–whether it is impossible for the same unit of a good to be consumed by more than one person at the same time.

There are, of course, many other characteristics that distinguish between types of goods—necessities versus luxuries, normal versus inferior, and so on. Why focus on whether goods are excludable and rival in consumption?

Why Markets Can Supply Only Private Goods Efficiently

As we learned, markets are typically the best means for a society to deliver goods and services to its members; that is, markets are efficient except in the case of the well-defined problems of market power, externalities, or other instances of market failure. But there is yet another condition that must be met, one rooted in the nature of the good itself: markets cannot supply goods and services efficiently unless they are private goods—excludable and rival in consumption.

Goods that are nonexcludable suffer from the **free-rider problem:** many individuals are unwilling to pay for their own consumption and instead will take a "free ride" on anyone who does pay.

To see why excludability is crucial, suppose that a farmer had only two choices: either produce no wheat or provide a bushel of wheat to every resident of the county who wants it, whether or not that resident pays for it. It seems unlikely that anyone would grow wheat under those conditions.

Yet the operator of a municipal sewage system faces pretty much the same problem as our hypothetical farmer. A sewage system makes the whole city cleaner and healthier—but that benefit accrues to all the city's residents, whether or not they pay the system operator. That's why no private entrepreneur came forward with a plan to end London's Great Stink.

The general point is that if a good is nonexcludable, self-interested consumers won't be willing to pay for it—they will take a "free ride" on anyone who *does* pay. So there is a **free-rider problem.** Examples of the free-rider problem are familiar from daily life. One you may have encountered is when students are required to do a group project. There is often a tendency for some group members to shirk, relying on others in the group to get the work done. The shirkers *free-ride* on someone else's effort.

Because of the free-rider problem, the forces of self-interest alone do not lead to an efficient level of production for a nonexcludable good. Even though consumers would benefit from increased production of the good, no one individual is willing to pay for more, and so no producer is willing to supply it. The result is that nonexcludable goods suffer from *inefficiently low production*. That is, they are undersupplied in a market economy. In fact, in the face of the free-rider problem, self-interest may not ensure that any amount of the good—let alone the efficient quantity—is produced.

Goods that are excludable and nonrival in consumption, like on-demand movies, suffer from a different kind of inefficiency. As long as a good is excludable, it is possible to earn a profit by making it available only to those who pay. Therefore producers are willing to supply an excludable good. But the marginal cost of letting an additional viewer watch an on-demand movie is zero because it is nonrival in consumption. So the efficient price to the consumer is also zero—or, to put it another way, individuals should watch movies up to the point at which their marginal benefit is zero.

But if Amazon actually charges viewers $4 for on-demand movies, viewers will consume the good only up to the point at which their marginal benefit is $4. When consumers must pay a price greater than zero for a good that is nonrival in consumption, the price they pay is higher than the marginal cost of allowing them to consume that good, which is zero. So, in a market economy, goods that are nonrival in consumption suffer from *inefficiently low consumption*—they are underconsumed.

Now we can see why private goods are the only goods that can be efficiently produced and consumed in a competitive market. (That is, a private good will be efficiently produced and consumed in a market free of market power, externalities, or other instances of market failure.) Because private goods are excludable, producers can charge for them and so have an incentive to produce them. And because they are also rival in consumption, it is efficient for consumers to pay a positive price—a price equal to the marginal cost of production. If one or both of these characteristics are lacking, a market economy will not lead to efficient production and consumption of the good.

Fortunately for the market system, most goods are private goods. Food, clothing, shelter, and most other desirable things in life are excludable and rival in consumption, so markets can provide us with most things. Yet there are crucial goods that don't meet these criteria—and in most cases, that means that the government must step in.

PITFALLS

MARGINAL COST OF WHAT EXACTLY?

In the case of a good that is nonrival in consumption, it's easy to confuse the marginal cost of *producing* a unit of the good with the marginal cost of *allowing* a unit of the good *to be consumed*.

For example, Amazon Prime Video incurs a marginal cost in making an on-demand movie available to its subscribers that is equal to the cost of the resources it uses to produce and broadcast that movie. However, *once that movie is being broadcast,* no marginal cost is incurred by letting an additional family watch it. In other words, no costly resources are used up when one more family consumes a movie that has already been produced and is being broadcast.

This complication does not arise, however, when a good is rival in consumption. In that case, the resources used to produce a unit of the good are used up by a person's consumption of it—they are no longer available to satisfy someone else's consumption. So when a good is rival in consumption, the marginal cost to society of allowing an individual to consume a unit is equal to the resource cost of producing that unit—that is, equal to the marginal cost of producing it.

Providing Public Goods

A **public good** is the exact opposite of a private good: it is a good that is both nonexcludable and nonrival in consumption. A public sewer system is an example of a public good: you can't keep a river clean without making it clean for everyone who lives near its banks, and my protection from great stinks does not come at my neighbor's expense.

A **public good** is both nonexcludable and nonrival in consumption.

Here are some other examples of public goods:

- *Disease prevention.* When doctors act to stamp out an epidemic before it can spread, they protect people around the world.
- *National defense.* A strong military protects all citizens.
- *Scientific research.* More knowledge benefits everyone.

Because these goods are nonexcludable, they suffer from the free-rider problem, so no private firm would be willing to produce them. And because they are nonrival in consumption, it would be inefficient to charge people for consuming them. As a result, society must find nonmarket methods for providing these goods.

Public goods are provided through a variety of means. The government doesn't always get involved—in many cases a nongovernmental solution has been found for the free-rider problem. But these solutions are usually imperfect in some way.

Some public goods are supplied through voluntary contributions. For example, private donations support a considerable amount of scientific research. But they are insufficient to finance huge, socially important projects like basic medical research.

Some public goods are supplied by self-interested individuals or firms because those producing the goods are able to make money in an indirect way. The classic example is broadcast television, which in the United States is supported entirely by advertising. The downside of such indirect funding is that it skews the nature and quantity of the public goods that are supplied, as well as imposing additional costs on consumers. TV stations show the programs that yield the most advertising revenue (that is, programs best suited for selling prescription drugs, weight-loss remedies, and the like to the segment of the population that buys them), which are not necessarily the programs people most want to see. And viewers must also endure many commercials.

Some potentially public goods are deliberately made excludable and therefore subject to charge, like on-demand movies. However, as noted earlier, when suppliers charge a price greater than zero for a nonrival good, consumers will consume an inefficiently low quantity of that good.

In small communities, a high level of social encouragement or pressure can be brought to bear on people to contribute money or time to provide the efficient level of a public good. Volunteer fire departments, which depend both on the volunteered services of the firefighters themselves and on contributions from local residents, are a good example. But as communities grow larger and more anonymous, social pressure is increasingly difficult to apply, compelling larger towns and cities to tax residents to provide salaried firefighters for fire protection services.

As this last example suggests, when these other solutions fail, it is up to the government to provide public goods. Indeed, the most important public goods—national defense, the legal system, disease control, fire protection in large cities, and so on—are provided by government and paid for by taxes. Economic theory tells us that the provision of public goods is one of the crucial roles of government.

How Much of a Public Good Should Be Provided?

In some cases, provision of a public good is an "either–or" decision: London would either have a sewage system—or not. But in most cases, governments must decide not only whether to provide a public good but also *how much* of that public good to provide. For example, street cleaning is a public good—but how often should the streets be cleaned? Once a month? Twice a month? Every other day?

Imagine a city in which there are only two residents, Ted and Alice. Assume that the public good in question is street cleaning and that Ted and Alice truthfully tell the government how much they value a unit of the public good, where a unit is equal to one street cleaning per month. Specifically, each of them tells the government *his or her willingness to pay for another unit of the public good supplied*—an amount that corresponds to that *individual's marginal benefit* of another unit of the public good.

Using this information plus information on the cost of providing the good, the government can use marginal analysis to find the efficient level of providing the public good: the level at which the *marginal social benefit* of the public good is equal to the marginal cost of producing it. Earlier we explained that the marginal social benefit of a good is the benefit that accrues to society as a whole from the consumption of one additional unit of the good.

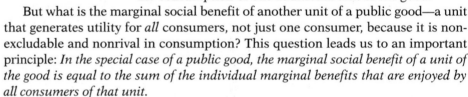

We all benefit when someone does the cleaning up.

But what is the marginal social benefit of another unit of a public good—a unit that generates utility for *all* consumers, not just one consumer, because it is nonexcludable and nonrival in consumption? This question leads us to an important principle: *In the special case of a public good, the marginal social benefit of a unit of the good is equal to the sum of the individual marginal benefits that are enjoyed by all consumers of that unit.*

Or to consider it from a slightly different angle, if a consumer could be compelled to pay for a unit before consuming it (the good is made excludable), then the marginal social benefit of a unit is equal to the *sum* of each consumer's willingness to pay for that unit. Using this principle, the marginal social benefit of an additional street cleaning per month is equal to Ted's individual marginal benefit from that additional cleaning *plus* Alice's individual marginal benefit.

Why? Because a public good is nonrival in consumption—Ted's benefit from a cleaner street does not diminish Alice's benefit from that same clean street, and vice versa. Because people can all simultaneously consume the same unit of a public good, the marginal social benefit of an additional unit of that good is the *sum* of the individual marginal benefits of all who enjoy the public good. And the efficient quantity of a public good is the quantity at which the marginal social benefit is equal to the marginal cost of providing it.

Figure 10-6 illustrates the efficient provision of a public good, showing three marginal benefit curves. Panel (a) shows Ted's individual marginal benefit curve from street cleaning, MB_T: he would be willing to pay $25 for the city to clean its streets once a month, an additional $18 to have it done a second time, and so on. Panel (b) shows Alice's individual marginal benefit curve from street cleaning, MB_A. Panel (c) shows the marginal social benefit curve from street cleaning, MSB: it is the vertical sum of Ted's and Alice's individual marginal benefit curves, MB_T and MB_A.

To maximize society's welfare, the government should clean the street up to the level at which the marginal social benefit of an additional cleaning is no longer greater than the marginal cost. Suppose that the marginal cost of street cleaning is $6 per cleaning. Then the city should clean its streets 5 times per month, because the marginal social benefit of going from 4 to 5 cleanings is $8, but going from 5 to 6 cleanings would yield a marginal social benefit of only $2.

FIGURE 10-6 A Public Good

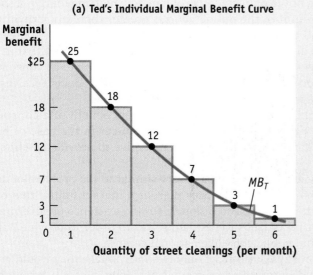

(a) Ted's Individual Marginal Benefit Curve

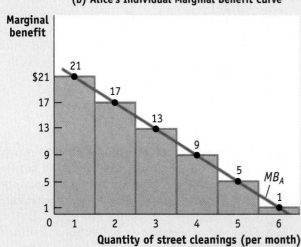

(b) Alice's Individual Marginal Benefit Curve

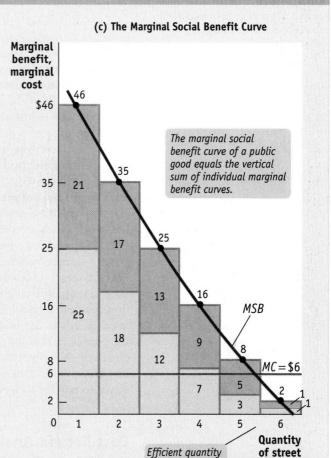

(c) The Marginal Social Benefit Curve

The marginal social benefit curve of a public good equals the vertical sum of individual marginal benefit curves.

Efficient quantity of the public good

Panel (a) shows Ted's individual marginal benefit curve of street cleanings per month, MB_T, and panel (b) shows Alice's individual marginal benefit curve, MB_A. Panel (c) shows the marginal social benefit of the public good, equal to the sum of the individual marginal benefits to all consumers (in this case, Ted and Alice). The marginal social benefit curve, MSB, is the vertical sum of the individual marginal benefit curves MB_T and MB_A. At a constant marginal cost of $6, there should be 5 street cleanings per month, because the marginal social benefit of going from 4 to 5 cleanings is $8 ($3 for Ted plus $5 for Alice), but the marginal social benefit of going from 5 to 6 cleanings is only $2.

Figure 10-6 can help reinforce our understanding of why we cannot rely on individual self-interest to yield provision of an efficient quantity of public goods. Suppose that the city did one fewer street cleaning than the efficient quantity and that either Ted or Alice was asked to pay for the last cleaning. Neither one would be willing to pay for it! Ted would personally gain only the equivalent of $3 in utility from adding one more street cleaning—so he wouldn't be willing to pay the $6 marginal cost of another cleaning. Alice would personally gain the equivalent of $5 in utility—so she wouldn't be willing to pay either.

The point is that the marginal social benefit of one more unit of a public good is always greater than the individual marginal benefit to any one

Cost-benefit analysis is the estimation and comparison of the social costs and social benefits of providing a public good.

individual. That is why no individual is willing to pay for the efficient quantity of the good.

Does this description of the public-good problem, in which the marginal social benefit of an additional unit of the public good is greater than any individual's marginal benefit, sound a bit familiar? It should: we encountered a somewhat similar situation in our discussion of *positive externalities*. Remember that in the case of a positive externality, the marginal social benefit accruing to all consumers of another unit of the good is greater than the price that the producer receives for that unit; as a result, the market produces too little of the good.

In the case of a public good, the individual marginal benefit of a consumer plays the same role as the price received by the producer in the case of positive externalities: both cases create insufficient incentive to provide an efficient amount of the good.

The problem of providing public goods is very similar to the problem of dealing with positive externalities; in both cases there is a market failure that calls for government intervention. One basic rationale for the existence of government is that it provides a way for citizens to tax themselves in order to provide public goods—particularly a vital public good like national defense.

Of course, if society really consisted of only two individuals, they would probably manage to strike a deal to provide the good. But imagine a city with a million residents, each of whose individual marginal benefit from provision of the good is only a tiny fraction of the marginal social benefit. It would be impossible for people to reach a voluntary agreement to pay for the efficient level of street cleaning—the potential for free-riding makes it too difficult to make and enforce an agreement among so many people. But they could and would vote to tax themselves to pay for a citywide sanitation department.

Cost-Benefit Analysis

How do governments decide in practice how much of a public good to provide? Sometimes policy makers just guess—or do whatever they think will get them reelected. However, responsible governments try to estimate and compare both the social benefits and the social costs of providing a public good, a process known as **cost-benefit analysis.**

It's straightforward to estimate the cost of supplying a public good. Estimating the benefit is harder. In fact, it is a very difficult problem.

Now you might wonder why governments can't figure out the marginal social benefit of a public good just by asking people their willingness to pay for it (their individual marginal benefit). But it turns out that it's hard to get an honest answer.

This is not a problem with private goods: we can determine how much an individual is willing to pay for one more unit of a private good by looking at his or her actual choices. But because people don't actually pay for public goods, the question of willingness to pay is always hypothetical.

Worse yet, it's a question that people have an incentive not to answer truthfully. People naturally want more rather than less. Because they cannot be made to pay for whatever quantity of the public good they use, people are apt to overstate their true feelings when asked how much they desire a public good. For example, if street cleaning were scheduled according to the stated wishes of homeowners alone, the streets would be cleaned every day—an inefficient level of provision.

So, governments must be aware that they cannot simply rely on the public's statements when deciding how much of a public good to provide—if they do, they are likely to provide too much. In contrast, relying on the public to indicate how much of the public good they want through voting has problems as well—and is likely to lead to too little of the public good being provided.

ECONOMICS >> *in Action*
American Infrastructure Gets a D+

New Jersey is the third-richest state in the country, with much of its income deriving from its close economic links to New York City's financial industry. Every day, several hundred thousand New Jerseyans take a train or a bus into New York City on the second busiest commuter route in the country. Public transportation is the lifeblood of New Jersey's economy, with nearly a million people—10% of the state's population—taking a bus or a train on an average day.

Yet, despite the critical importance of the public transportation system to New Jersey's economy, it has been chronically underfunded in recent years. In 2015 the state contribution to the system's operating budget was only 10% of what it had been in 2009, forcing it to run a $45 million deficit that year. Capital investment has plunged by 20% as ridership has increased by 20%. Predictably, buses are persistently late, overcrowded, and prone to break down. As one commuter said, "It's gotten me in trouble with work quite a bit. They think I'm making it up." And in September 2016 a packed New Jersey Transit commuter train slammed into a train station at full speed, injuring 114 people and killing 1. Tragically, New Jersey Transit Authority had delayed installation of an automatic braking system in its trains the previous year.

New Jersey's infrastructure woes are not unique; in fact, they are the norm across the country. A 2016 study showed that state and local spending on infrastructure—schools, water treatment plants, roads, highways, and bridges—is at a 30-year low. Every 4 years the American Society of Civil Engineers (ASCE) assesses the state of American infrastructure and issues a report card. In 2013, the United States received a D+ "based on a significant backlog of overdue maintenance across our infrastructure system [and] a pressing need for modernization" arising from decades of underfunding. According to ASCE, an estimated $3.6 trillion in spending is needed by 2020 in order to bring American infrastructure up to a grade B (good). Based on current funding gaps, it is estimated that $3.95 trillion in gross domestic product will be lost by 2025, translating into an annual loss to each household of $3,900.

Figure 10-7 shows the projected funding, the funding gap, and the 2013 grade for types of infrastructure. As you can see, the funding gaps for much of our basic infrastructure are extensive, with surface transportation, schools, and waterways suffering most from funding shortages. Across the board, grades for each of these infrastructure types are consistently bad. They make it clear that infrastructure improvements are needed.

Why has infrastructure in the United States been allowed to deteriorate so badly? It has been a casualty of both the political conflict in Congress and in-state legislatures, as well as short-sightedness that undervalues infrastructure as a long-term asset.

For years, political gridlock prevented federal and state governments from borrowing money or raising taxes to adequately fund infrastructure. As a result, the country has run down its existing stock to perilous levels. Congress has recently begun allocating larger sums, as the costs of deteriorating roads, schools, water quality, and more have grown too great to ignore. It's a start, but it will take many years of higher funding for the country to dig out of its infrastructure pothole.

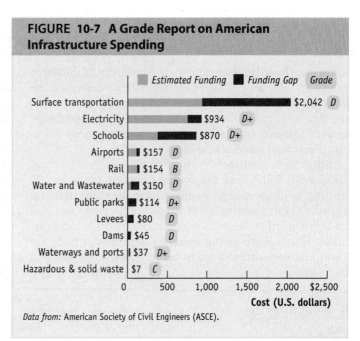

FIGURE 10-7 A Grade Report on American Infrastructure Spending

Data from: American Society of Civil Engineers (ASCE).

>> Check Your Understanding 10-4

Solutions appear at back of book.

1. Classify each of the following goods according to whether they are excludable and whether they are rival in consumption. What kind of good is each?
   a. Use of a public space such as a park
   b. A cheese burrito
   c. Information from a website that is password-protected
   d. Publicly announced information on the path of an incoming hurricane

2. The town of Centreville, population 16, has two types of residents, Homebodies and Revelers. Using the accompanying table, the town must decide how much to spend on its New Year's Eve party. No individual resident expects to directly bear the cost of the party.

   a. Suppose there are 10 Homebodies and 6 Revelers. Determine the marginal social benefit schedule of money spent on the party. What is the efficient level of spending?

   b. Suppose there are 6 Homebodies and 10 Revelers. How do your answers to part a change? Explain.

   c. Suppose that the individual marginal benefit schedules are known but no one knows the true proportion of Homebodies versus Revelers.

Money spent on party	Individual marginal benefit of additional $1 spent on party	
	Homebody	Reveler
$0		
	$0.05	$0.13
1		
	0.04	0.11
2		
	0.03	0.09
3		
	0.02	0.07
4		

Individuals are asked their preferences. What is the likely outcome if each person assumes that others will pay for any additional amount of the public good? Why is it likely to result in an inefficiently high level of spending? Explain.

SOLVED PROBLEM   The Not So Sweet Smell of Success

Americans have become passionate consumers of the Asian hot sauce, Sriracha. This red sauce with a rooster on the label can be found on condiment counters across the country. Fast-food chains like Pizza Hut and Subway have even created Sriracha-infused menu items such as honey Sriracha pizza crust and Sriracha chicken melt.

Sriracha is produced by Huy Fong Foods in Irwindale, California. Each year the company processes over 100 million pounds of chili peppers to make their delectable sauce. But roasting all of those chili peppers has had an unintended consequence: pollution. In 2013, local residents began complaining about a pungent odor from the plant that they believed led to heartburn, nosebleeds, and coughing.

The hypothetical table shows the estimated marginal social benefit (*MSB*) and marginal social cost (*MSC*) of pollution that arises from odor emissions. How can the pollution that results from Sriracha production have a marginal social benefit?

As we've seen, avoiding pollution requires using scarce resources that could have been used to produce other goods and services. The more pollution companies are allowed to emit, the lower the extra costs imposed on them. The social benefit from the pollution is the money the company saves by not having to invest in new equipment to reduce the odors that have resulted from Sriracha production. Generally, the costs of reducing pollution decrease with the amount of pollution that is allowed, so the marginal social benefit decreases as pollution increases.

Marginal Social Cost and Benefit of Odor

Quantity of odor emissions (thousands of odor units)	Marginal social benefit ($ per odor unit)	Marginal social cost ($ per odor unit)
0	$80	$0
1	72	8
2	64	16
3	56	24
4	48	32
5	40	40
6	32	48
7	24	56
8	16	64
9	8	72
10	0	80

Graph the marginal social cost and marginal social benefit of odor. What is the market-determined quantity of odor? What is the social gain from reducing the market-determined quantity of odor by one odor unit?

STEP | 1 Draw and label marginal social benefit and marginal social cost curves. Find the optimal level of odor units. *Review pages 286–287 and Figure 10-1.*

The optimal social quantity of pollution is at the point where the marginal social benefit of polluting equals the marginal social cost of polluting. As shown in the accompanying figure, this occurs at point *O*, the intersection of the marginal social cost curve and the marginal social benefit curve. At point *O*, the optimal quantity of odor emissions is 5 thousand odor units and the marginal social benefit of odor emissions, which equals the marginal social cost of odor emissions, is $40 per odor unit.

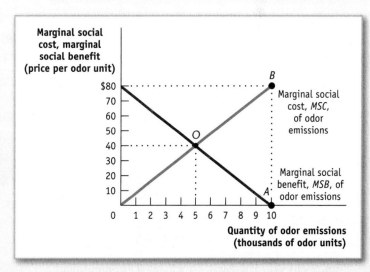

STEP | 2 Find the market-determined quantity of pollution. *Review pages 287–289.*

The market-determined quantity of pollution will be at the point where the marginal benefits to polluters are zero. As there are no marginal social benefits to pollution beyond the cost savings realized by the polluters themselves, the market-determined quantity will be at the point where the marginal social benefit of pollution is zero. This occurs at an odor emissions level of 10 thousand odor units, as shown at point A on the figure.

STEP | 3 Find the social gain from reducing the quantity of pollution by one odor unit from the market-determined level. *Review pages 287–289.*

Moving up from point A to point B in the figure, we can see that the marginal social cost of polluting at the market-determined level of 10 thousand odor units is high at $80 per unit. The marginal social benefit at point A is zero. As the marginal cost per odor unit of polluting at a level of 10 thousand odor units is $80 per unit and the marginal social benefit per unit of polluting at that level is zero, reducing the quantity of pollution by one odor unit leads to a net gain in total surplus of approximately $80 − 0 = $80.

SUMMARY

1. The costs to society of pollution are an example of an **external cost;** in some cases, however, economic activities yield **external benefits.** External costs and benefits are jointly known as **externalities.** Pollution is an example of a **negative externality,** an action that inflicts an uncompensated cost on others. In contrast, a **positive externality,** such as a flu shot, confers an uncompensated benefit on others.

2. When pollution can be directly observed and controlled, government policies should be geared directly to producing the **socially optimal quantity of pollution,** the quantity at which the **marginal social cost of pollution** is equal to the **marginal social benefit of pollution.** In the absence of government intervention, a market produces too much pollution because polluters take only their benefit from polluting into account, not the costs imposed on others.

3. According to the **Coase theorem,** individuals can find a way to **internalize the externality,** making government intervention unnecessary, as long as **transaction costs**—the costs of making a deal—are sufficiently low. However, in many cases transaction costs are too high to permit such deals.

4. Governments often deal with pollution by imposing **environmental standards,** a method, economists argue, that is usually an inefficient way to reduce pollution. Two efficient (cost-minimizing) methods for reducing pollution are **emissions taxes,** a form of **Pigouvian tax,** and **tradable emissions permits.** The optimal Pigouvian tax on pollution is equal to its marginal social cost at the socially optimal quantity of pollution. These methods also provide incentives for the creation and adoption of production technologies that cause less pollution.

5. A history of heavy reliance on **fossil fuels** that emit **greenhouse gases** has led to problems created by **climate change.** The Paris Agreement is a commitment signed by 196 countries to reduce greenhouse gases.

Unlike fossil fuels, **renewable energy sources** are inexhaustible.

6. When a good or activity yields external benefits, or positive externalities, such as **technology spillovers,** then an optimal **Pigouvian subsidy** to producers moves the market to the socially optimal quantity of production.

7. Free markets can deliver efficient levels of production and consumption for **private goods,** which are both excludable and rival in consumption. When goods are nonexcludable or nonrival in consumption, or both, free markets cannot achieve efficient outcomes.

8. Goods may be classified according to whether or not they are **excludable** and whether or not they are **rival in consumption.**

9. When goods are **nonexcludable,** there is a **free-rider problem:** some consumers will not pay for the good, consuming what others have paid for and leading to inefficiently low production. When goods are **nonrival in consumption,** they should be free, and any positive price leads to inefficiently low consumption.

10. A **public good** is nonexcludable and nonrival in consumption. In most cases a public good must be supplied by the government. The marginal social benefit of a public good is equal to the sum of the individual marginal benefits to each consumer. The efficient quantity of a public good is the quantity at which marginal social benefit equals the marginal cost of providing the good. Like a positive externality, marginal social benefit is greater than any one individual's marginal benefit, so no individual is willing to provide the efficient quantity.

11. One rationale for the presence of government is that it allows citizens to tax themselves in order to provide public goods. Governments use **cost-benefit analysis** to determine the efficient provision of a public good. Such analysis is difficult, however, because individuals have an incentive to overstate the good's value to them.

KEY TERMS

External cost, p. 286
External benefit, p. 286
Externalities, p. 286
Negative externalities, p. 286
Positive externalities, p. 286
Marginal social cost of pollution, p. 286
Marginal social benefit of pollution, p. 287
Socially optimal quantity of pollution, p. 287
Coase theorem, p. 289

Transaction costs, p. 289
Internalize the externality, p. 289
Environmental standards, p. 292
Emissions tax, p. 292
Pigouvian taxes, p. 293
Tradable emissions permits, p. 294
Climate change, p. 296
Greenhouse gases, p. 296
Fossil fuels, p. 296
Renewable energy sources, p. 296
Clean energy sources, p. 296

Pigouvian subsidy, p. 299
Technology spillover, p. 300
Excludable, p. 301
Rival in consumption, p. 301
Private good, p. 301
Nonexcludable, p. 301
Nonrival in consumption, p. 301
Free-rider problem, p. 302
Public good, p. 303
Cost-benefit analysis, p. 306

DISCUSSION QUESTIONS

1. In developing a vaccine for the SARS virus, a pharmaceutical company incurs a very high fixed cost. The marginal cost of delivering the vaccine to patients, however, is negligible (consider it to be equal to zero). The pharmaceutical company holds the exclusive patent to the vaccine. You are a regulator who must decide what price the pharmaceutical company is allowed to charge.

   a. Draw a diagram that shows the price for the vaccine that would arise if the company is unregulated, and label it P_M. What is the efficient price for the vaccine? Show the deadweight loss that arises from the price P_M.

   b. On another diagram, show the lowest price that the regulator can enforce that would still induce the pharmaceutical company to develop the vaccine. Label it P^*. Show the deadweight loss that arises from this price. How does it compare to the dead-weight loss that arises from the price P_M?

   c. Suppose you have accurate information about the pharmaceutical company's fixed cost. How could you use price regulation of the pharmaceutical company, combined with a subsidy to the company, to have the efficient quantity of the vaccine provided at the lowest cost to the government?

PROBLEMS

interactive activity

1. What type of externality (positive or negative) is present in each of the following examples? Is the marginal social benefit of the activity greater than or equal to the marginal benefit to the individual? Is the marginal social cost of the activity greater than or equal to the marginal cost to the individual? Without intervention, will there be too little or too much (relative to what would be socially optimal) of this activity?

   a. Mr. Chau plants lots of colorful flowers in his front yard.

   b. Your next-door neighbor likes to build bonfires in his backyard, and sparks often drift onto your house.

   c. Maija, who lives next to an apple orchard, decides to keep bees to produce honey.

   d. Justine buys a large SUV that consumes a lot of gasoline.

2. Many dairy farmers in California are adopting a new technology that allows them to produce their own electricity from methane gas captured from animal waste. (One cow can produce up to 2 kilowatts a day.) This practice reduces the amount of methane gas released into the atmosphere. In addition to reducing their own utility bills, the farmers are allowed to sell any electricity they produce at favorable rates.

   a. Explain how the ability to earn money from capturing and transforming methane gas behaves like a Pigouvian tax on methane gas pollution and can lead dairy farmers to emit the efficient amount of methane gas pollution.

   b. Suppose some dairy farmers have lower costs of transforming methane into electricity than others. Explain how this system of capturing and selling methane gas leads to an efficient allocation of emissions reduction among farmers.

3. According to a report from the U.S. Census Bureau, "the average [lifetime] earnings of a full-time, year-round worker with a high school education are about $1.2 million compared with $2.1 million for a college graduate." This indicates that there is a considerable benefit to a graduate from investing in his or her own education. Tuition at most state universities covers only about two-thirds to three-quarters of the cost, so the state applies a Pigouvian subsidy to college education.

   If a Pigouvian subsidy is appropriate, is the externality created by a college education a positive or a negative externality? What does this imply about the differences between the costs and benefits that accrue privately to students compared to social costs and benefits? What are some reasons for the differences?

4. The city of Falls Church, Virginia, subsidizes the planting of trees in homeowners' front yards when the yards are within 15 feet of the street.

   a. Using concepts in the chapter, explain why a municipality would subsidize planting trees on private property, but near the street.

   b. Draw a diagram similar to Figure 10-4 that shows the marginal social benefit, the marginal social cost, and the optimal Pigouvian subsidy on planting trees.

5. Fishing for sablefish has been so intensive that sablefish were threatened with extinction. After several years of banning such fishing, the government is now proposing to introduce tradable vouchers, each of which entitles its holder to a catch of a certain size. Explain how uncontrolled fishing generates a negative externality and how the voucher scheme may overcome the inefficiency created by this externality.

6. The two dry-cleaning companies in Collegetown, College Cleaners and Big Green Cleaners, are a major source of air pollution. Together they currently produce 350 units of air pollution, which the town wants to reduce to 200 units. The accompanying table shows the current pollution level produced by each company and each company's marginal cost of reducing its pollution. The marginal cost is constant.

Companies	Initial pollution level (units)	Marginal cost of reducing pollution (per unit)
College Cleaners	230	$5
Big Green Cleaners	120	2

a. Suppose that Collegetown passes an environmental standards law that limits each company to 100 units of pollution. What would be the total cost to the two companies of each reducing its pollution emissions to 100 units?

Suppose instead that Collegetown issues 100 pollution vouchers to each company, each entitling the company to one unit of pollution, and that these vouchers can be traded.

b. How much is each pollution voucher worth to College Cleaners? To Big Green Cleaners? (That is, how much would each company, at most, be willing to pay for one more voucher?)

c. Who will sell vouchers and who will buy them? How many vouchers will be traded?

d. What is the total cost to the two companies of the pollution controls under this voucher system?

7. The government is involved in providing many goods and services. For each of the goods or services listed, determine whether it is rival or nonrival in consumption and whether it is excludable or nonexcludable. What type of good is it? Without government involvement, would the quantity provided be efficient, inefficiently low, or inefficiently high?

a. Street signs

b. Amtrak rail service

c. Regulations limiting pollution

d. A congested interstate highway without tolls

e. A lighthouse on the coast

8. An economist gives the following advice to a museum director: "You should introduce 'peak pricing.' At times when the museum has few visitors, you should admit visitors for free. And at times when the museum has many visitors, you should charge a higher admission fee."

a. When the museum is quiet, is it rival or nonrival in consumption? Is it excludable or nonexcludable? What type of good is the museum at those times? What would be the efficient price to charge visitors during that time, and why?

b. When the museum is busy, is it rival or nonrival in consumption? Is it excludable or nonexcludable? What type of good is the museum at those times? What would be the efficient price to charge visitors during that time, and why?

9. In many planned communities, various aspects of community living are subject to regulation by a homeowners' association. These rules can regulate house architecture; require snow removal from sidewalks; exclude outdoor equipment, such as backyard swimming pools; require appropriate conduct in shared spaces such as the community clubhouse; and so on. Suppose there has been some conflict in one such community because some homeowners feel that some of the regulations mentioned above are overly intrusive. You have been called in to mediate. Using what you have learned about public goods and common resources, how would you decide what types of regulations are warranted and what types are not?

10. The accompanying table shows Tanisha's and Ari's individual marginal benefit of different amounts of street cleanings per month. Suppose that the marginal cost of street cleanings is constant at $9 each.

Quantity of street cleanings per month	Tanisha's individual marginal benefit	Ari's individual marginal benefit
0		
	$10	$8
1		
	6	4
2		
	2	1
3		

a. If Tanisha had to pay for street cleaning on her own, how many street cleanings would there be?

b. Calculate the marginal social benefit of street cleaning. What is the optimal number of street cleanings?

c. Consider the optimal number of street cleanings. The last street cleaning of the optimal number of street cleanings costs $9. Is Tanisha willing to pay for that last cleaning on her own? Is Ari willing to pay for that last cleaning on his own?

WORK IT OUT   Interactive step-by-step help with solving these problems can be found online.

11. The loud music coming from the sorority next to your dorm is a negative externality that can be directly quantified. The accompanying table shows the marginal social benefit and the marginal social cost per decibel (dB, a measure of volume) of music.

Volume of music (dB)	Marginal social benefit of dB	Marginal social cost of dB
90		
	$36	$0
91		
	30	2
92		
	24	4
93		
	18	6
94		
	12	8
95		
	6	10
96		
	0	12
97		

a. Draw the marginal social benefit curve and the marginal social cost curve. Use your diagram to determine the socially optimal volume of music.

b. Only the members of the sorority benefit from the music, and they bear none of the cost. Which volume of music will they choose?

c. The college imposes a Pigouvian tax of $3 per decibel of music played. From your diagram, determine the volume of music the sorority will now choose.

12. A residential community has 100 residents who are concerned about security. The accompanying table gives the total cost of hiring a 24-hour security service as well as each individual resident's total benefit.

Quantity of security guards	Total cost	Total individual benefit to each resident
0	$0	$0
1	150	10
2	300	16
3	450	18
4	600	19

a. Explain why the security service is a public good for the residents of the community.

b. Calculate the marginal cost, the individual marginal benefit for each resident, and the marginal social benefit.

c. If an individual resident were to decide about hiring and paying for security guards on his or her own, how many guards would that resident hire?

d. If the residents act together, how many security guards will they hire?

11 Poverty, Inequality, and the Welfare State

THE COMING OF OBAMACARE

ON JANUARY 1, 2014, Lou Vincent finally got health insurance.

Vincent, a resident of Ohio, had Type 2 diabetes, and as a result no insurance company was willing to offer him a policy, leaving him uninsured for 10 years. "We got 30 denial letters," his wife told a reporter. So what changed at the beginning of 2014? A major new government program, the Patient Protection and Affordable Care Act—often referred to as the Affordable Care Act, the ACA, or Obamacare—went into effect.

Implementation of the Affordable Care Act (ACA) was a major expansion of the U.S. welfare state.

Tens of millions of Americans receive health insurance directly from the government, mainly from Medicare (which covers those 65 and older) and Medicaid (which covers the poor and near-poor, and which was expanded under the ACA). The Affordable Care Act works differently, because it mainly operates through private insurance companies, although they are subject to extensive government regulation that tries to ensure that everyone, including people like Vincent, has access to health insurance.

In addition to regulating insurers, the ACA provides financial aid to help individuals gain coverage. The law expanded Medicaid, which directly insures low-income individuals; however, this expansion only took place in states that agreed to it, and as of 2019 there were 14 states that had not accepted the expansion. It also provided subsidies to help higher-income individuals purchase private policies.

The ACA has undergone some modifications since it was implemented. In particular, in what many believe was an effort to undermine the law, the Republican-sponsored Tax Cuts and Jobs Act of 2017 removed the tax penalty for individuals whose health insurance didn't meet certain minimum standards. Typically referred to as the *individual mandate*, this tax penalty was a central tenet of the ACA, put in place to keep the program viable. Overall, the ACA was a substantial expansion of the government's role in the economy. Specifically, it marked the biggest expansion since the 1960s of the *welfare state,* the collection of government programs designed to limit economic insecurity and reduce economic inequality.

There is intense political dispute about the appropriate size and role of the welfare state. Indeed, you can argue that this dispute is what politics is mainly about, with liberals seeking to expand the welfare state's reach and conservatives seeking to scale it back. So, opinions about the ACA, not surprisingly, are deeply divided. It's part of a larger debate in contemporary America, in which politicians often disagree about how much help financially troubled families should receive to pay for health care, housing, food, and other necessities.

Yet there is a broad political consensus that troubled families should receive some help. And they do. Even conservatives generally accept a fairly extensive welfare state as a fact of life. Governments of all wealthy nations play a large role in everything from health care, to retirement, to aid to the poor and jobless.

We start this chapter by discussing the rationale for welfare state programs. Then we look at the two main programs operating in the United States: *income support programs,* of which Social Security is by far the largest, and *health care programs,* dominated by Medicare and Medicaid, but with the Affordable Care Act playing a growing role. •

WHAT YOU WILL LEARN

- What is the **welfare state** and how does it benefit society?
- What are the causes and consequences of poverty?
- How has income inequality in America changed over time?
- How do **social insurance programs** like Social Security affect poverty and income inequality?
- What are the special concerns of **private health insurance** and how has government addressed them?
- What are the political debates over the size of the welfare state?

The **welfare state** is the collection of government programs designed to alleviate economic hardship.

A **government transfer** is a government payment to an individual or a family.

A **poverty program** is a government program designed to aid the poor.

A **social insurance program** is a government program designed to provide protection against unpredictable financial distress.

‖ Poverty, Inequality, and Public Policy

The term **welfare state** has come to refer to the collection of government programs that are designed to alleviate economic hardship. A large share of the government spending of all wealthy countries consists of **government transfers**—payments by the government to individuals and families—that provide financial aid to the poor, assistance to unemployed workers, guaranteed income for the elderly, and assistance in paying medical bills for those with large health care expenses.

The Logic of the Welfare State

There are three major economic rationales for the creation of the welfare state. Let's look at each.

1. Alleviating Income Inequality Suppose that the Taylor family, which has an income of only $15,000 a year, receives a government check that allows them to afford things that will significantly improve their quality of life, such as a better place to live or a more nutritious diet. Also suppose that the Fisher family, which has an income of $300,000 a year, faces an extra tax of $1,500. This probably wouldn't make much difference to their quality of life: at worst, they might have to give up a few minor luxuries.

This hypothetical exchange illustrates the first major rationale for the welfare state: *alleviating income inequality.* Because a marginal dollar is worth more to a poor person than to a rich one, modest transfers from the rich to the poor will do the rich little harm but benefit the poor a lot. So, according to this argument, a government that plays Robin Hood, taking modest amounts from the rich to give to the poor, does more good than harm. As long as the amounts are relatively modest, the inefficiencies created by the transfers will be outweighed by the benefits to society. Programs that are designed to aid the poor are known as **poverty programs.**

2. Alleviating Economic Insecurity The second major rationale for the welfare state is *alleviating economic insecurity.* When bad things happen, such as a flood, or an illness, they almost always happen to a limited number of people. For example, during the devastating floods that hit Texas in 2017, millions of Texans were rendered homeless. But the floods also left many Texans and the rest of the United States unscathed. Or, imagine 10 families, each of which can expect an income next year of $50,000 if nothing goes wrong. But suppose the odds are that something *will* go wrong for one of the families, although nobody knows which one. For example, suppose each of the families has a 1 in 10 chance of experiencing a sharp drop in income because one family member is laid off, or gets sick and incurs large medical bills. And assume that this event will produce severe hardship for the family—a family member will have to drop out of school or the family will lose its home.

Now suppose there's a government program that provides aid to families in distress, paying for that aid by taxing families that are having a good year. Arguably, this program will make all the families better off, because even families that don't currently receive aid from the program might need it at some point in the future. Each family will therefore feel safer knowing that the government stands ready to help when disaster strikes. Programs designed to provide protection against unpredictable financial distress are known as **social insurance programs.**

These two rationales for the welfare state, alleviating income inequality and alleviating economic insecurity, are closely related to a major principle of tax fairness, the *ability-to-pay principle,* according to which those with greater ability to pay a tax should pay more. The principle is usually interpreted to mean that people with low incomes, for whom an additional dollar makes a big difference to economic well-being, should pay a smaller fraction of their income in taxes than people with higher incomes, for whom an additional dollar makes much less difference. The same principle suggests that those with very low incomes should actually get money back from the tax system.

3. Reducing Poverty and Providing Access to Health Care The third and final major rationale for the welfare state involves the *social benefits of poverty reduction and access to health care*, especially when applied to children of poor households. Researchers have documented that such children, on average, suffer lifelong disadvantages.

Even after adjusting for ability, children from economically disadvantaged backgrounds are more likely to be underemployed or unemployed, engage in crime, and suffer chronic health problems—all of which impose significant social costs. So, according to the evidence, programs that help to alleviate poverty and provide access to health care generate external benefits to society.

More broadly, some political philosophers argue that principles of social justice demand that society take care of the poor and unlucky. Others disagree, arguing that welfare state programs go beyond the proper role of government. To an important extent, the difference between those two philosophical positions defines what we mean in politics by *liberalism* and *conservatism*.

But it's important to realize that things aren't quite that cut and dried. Even conservatives who believe in limited government typically support some welfare state programs. And even economists who support the goals of the welfare state are concerned about the effects of large-scale aid to the poor and the unlucky on their incentives to work and save. Like taxes, welfare state programs can create substantial deadweight losses, so their true economic costs can be considerably larger than the direct monetary cost.

We'll turn to the costs and benefits of the welfare state later in this chapter. First, however, let's examine the problems the welfare state is supposed to address.

The Problem of Poverty

Since the depths of the Great Depression, most U.S. presidents have promised to attempt to reduce poverty. In 1964 President Lyndon Johnson went so far as to declare a "war on poverty," creating a number of new programs to aid the poor. Antipoverty programs account for a significant part of the U.S. welfare state, although social insurance programs are an even larger part.

What, exactly, do we mean by poverty? Any definition is somewhat arbitrary. Since 1965, however, the U.S. government has maintained an official definition of the **poverty threshold,** a minimum annual income that is considered adequate to purchase the necessities of life. Families whose incomes fall below the poverty threshold are considered poor.

The official poverty threshold depends on the size and composition of a family and is adjusted every year to reflect changes in the cost of living. In 2018 the poverty threshold for an adult living alone was $12,140; for a household consisting of two adults and two children, it was $25,100.

Trends in Poverty

Although the U.S. economy has grown far more prosperous over the past several decades, the official U.S. **poverty rate,** which is the percentage of the U.S. population living below the poverty threshold, has not declined.

The orange line in Figure 11-1 shows the poverty rate from 1967 to 2017. As you can see, since 1967 it has fluctuated up and down, with no clear trend over the long run. In 2017, the poverty rate was approximately the same as it had been during the 1960s, even though America as a whole was far richer.

The **poverty threshold** is the annual income below which a family is officially considered poor.

The **poverty rate** is the percentage of the population living below the poverty threshold.

FIGURE 11-1 Trends in the U.S. Poverty Rate, 1967–2017

The official poverty rate has shown no clear trend since the late 1960s. However, an alternative measure, known as the supplemental poverty measure, or SPM, which most experts consider to be more accurate, has declined modestly.

Data from: U.S. Census Bureau; Fox, Liana, et al., NBER Report No. w19789.

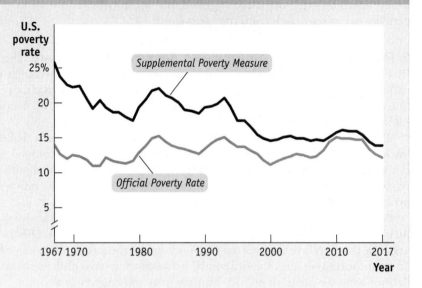

To provide some context for this perplexing result, economists have constructed the *Supplemental Poverty Measure,* which includes income from government aid such as food stamps. Some experts consider this measure to be more accurate than the poverty rate.

The burgundy line in Figure 11-1 shows how this measure has changed over time. While it shows more progress than the standard measure, the change is still surprisingly little considering that total real income in the United States has risen by more than 250%.

Who Are the Poor? There's a widely held image of poverty in America: an African-American or Hispanic family with no husband present and the female head of the household unemployed at least part of the time. This picture isn't completely off-base: poverty is disproportionately high among African-Americans and Hispanics as well as among female-headed households. But a majority of the poor don't fit the stereotype.

In 2017, 39.7 million Americans were in poverty—12.3% of the population, or slightly more than one in seven persons. Of those in poverty, the single largest group is non-Hispanic whites, making up 43% of the total. Hispanics follow, representing 27% of those in poverty; then African-Americans at 23%, and Asians at 5%. However, African-Americans, Hispanics, and Asians are more likely to be poor than non-Hispanic whites. And one-third of all people in poverty are children—about one in six children in the United States live in poverty.

There is also a correlation between family makeup and poverty. Female-headed families with no spouse present had a very high poverty rate: 25.6%. Married couples were much less likely to be poor, with a poverty rate of only 4.9%; still, about 39% of those in poverty were in married families with both spouses present.

What really stands out in the data, however, is the association between poverty and inadequate employment. Adults who work full time are very unlikely to be poor: only 2% of full-time workers were poor in 2017. Many industries, particularly in the retail and service sectors, now rely primarily on part-time workers who typically lack benefits such as health plans, paid vacation days, and retirement benefits. These jobs also usually pay a lower hourly wage than comparable full-time work. As a result, many of the poor are members of what analysts call the *working poor:* workers whose incomes fall at or below the poverty threshold.

What Causes Poverty? Poverty is often blamed on lack of education, and educational attainment clearly has a strong positive effect on income level—those with more education earn, on average, higher incomes than those with less education. For example, in 1979 the median weekly wage of men with a college degree was 29% higher than that of men with only a high school diploma; by 2017, the "college premium" had increased to 86%.

Lack of proficiency in English is also a barrier to higher income. For example, Mexican-born male workers in the United States—two-thirds of whom have not graduated from high school and many of whom have poor English skills—earn less than half of what native-born men earn.

And it's important not to overlook the role of racial and gender discrimination; although less pervasive today than 60 years ago, discrimination still erects formidable barriers to advancement for many Americans. Non-Whites earn less and are less likely to be employed than Whites with comparable levels of education. Studies find that African-American males suffer persistent discrimination by employers in favor of Whites, African-American women, and Hispanic immigrants. Women earn lower incomes than men with similar qualifications.

The United States has a high poverty rate compared to other rich countries.

In addition, one important source of poverty that should not be overlooked is bad luck. Many families find themselves impoverished when a wage-earner loses a job, a family business fails, or a family member falls seriously ill.

Consequences of Poverty The consequences of poverty are often severe and long-lasting, particularly for children. In 2017, 17.5% of children in the United States lived in poverty. Poverty is often associated with lack of access to health care, which can lead to health problems that erode the ability to attend school and work later in life. Affordable housing is also frequently a problem, leading poor families to move often, disrupting school and work schedules.

Recent medical studies have shown that children raised in severe poverty tend to suffer from lifelong learning disabilities. As a result, American children growing up in or near poverty tend to be at a disadvantage throughout their lives. Even talented children who come from poor families are unlikely to finish college.

A long-term survey conducted by the U.S. Department of Education tracked students, starting in eighth grade, according to ability and parental income and employment. Among students who scored in the top 25% on aptitude tests but who came from economically disadvantaged backgrounds, only 29% finished college. Equally talented students from families with higher incomes had a 74% chance of finishing. The results show that because children from less-advantaged backgrounds are much less likely to complete the education they need to overcome poverty, to an important degree, poverty is self-perpetuating.

Other studies have shown that the environment in which a poor child grows up also makes a difference. Poor children who grow up in highly segregated, inner city neighborhoods are much less likely to be employed as adults than those who are equally poor but grow up in areas that are economically diverse and less segregated. When families move to better neighborhoods, children are more likely to stay in school and graduate. These benefits increase with each year of childhood spent in the improved environment.

Economic Inequality

The United States is a rich country. The average household income in 2017 was $86,220. How is it possible, then, that so many Americans still live in poverty? The answer is that income is unequally distributed, with many households earning much less than the average and others earning much more.

TABLE 11-1 U.S. Income Distribution in 2017

Income group	Income range	Average income	Percent of total income
Bottom quintile	Less than $24,638	$13,258	3.1%
Second quintile	$24,638 to $47,110	35,401	8.2
Third quintile	$47,111 to $77,552	61,564	14.3
Fourth quintile	$77,553 to $126,855	99,030	23.0
Top quintile	More than $126,855	221,846	51.5
Top 5%	More than $237,034	385,289	22.3
Mean income = $81,331		**Median income = $61,372**	

Data from: U.S. Census Bureau.

Table 11-1 shows the distribution of pre-tax income—income before federal income taxes are paid—among U.S. families in 2017, as estimated by the Census Bureau. Households are grouped into *quintiles,* each containing 20%, or one-fifth, of the population. The first, or bottom, quintile contains households whose income put them below the 20th percentile in income, the second quintile contains households whose income put them between the 20th and 40th percentiles, and so on.

For each group, Table 11-1 shows three numbers. The second column shows the income ranges that define the group. For example, in 2017, the bottom quintile consisted of households with annual incomes of less than $24,638, the next quintile of households had incomes between $24,638 and $47,110, and so on. The third column shows the average income in each group, ranging from $13,258 for the bottom fifth to $385,289 for the top 5%. The fourth column shows the percentage of total U.S. income received by each group.

Mean Versus Median Household Income At the bottom of Table 11-1 are two useful numbers for thinking about the incomes of American households. **Mean household income,** also called average household income, is the total income of all U.S. households divided by the number of households. **Median household income** is the income of a household in the exact middle of the income distribution—the level of income at which half of all households have lower income and half have higher income. It's very important to realize that these two numbers do not measure the same thing.

Economists often illustrate the difference by asking people first to imagine a room containing several dozen more or less ordinary wage-earners, then to think about what happens to the mean and median incomes of the people in the room if a Silicon Valley tech billionaire walks into the room. The mean income soars, because the billionaire's income pulls up the average, but the median income hardly rises at all.

This example explains why economists regard median income as a better guide to the economic status of typical American families than mean income: mean income is strongly affected by the incomes of a relatively small number of very-high-income Americans, who are not representative of the population as a whole; median income is not.

What we learn from Table 11-1 is that income in the United States is quite unequally distributed. The average income of the poorest fifth of families is less than a quarter of the average income of families in the middle, and the richest fifth have an average income more than three times that of families in the middle. The incomes of the richest fifth of the population are, on average, about 17 times as high as those of the poorest fifth. In fact, the distribution of income in America has become more unequal since 1980, rising to a level that has made it a significant political issue. The upcoming Economics in Action discusses long-term trends in U.S. income inequality, which declined in the 1930s and 1940s, was stable for more than 30 years after World War II, but began rising again in the late 1970s.

A caveat about the data in Table 11-1. To some extent, it overstates the true degree of inequality in America. There are two reasons for this.

First, household incomes vary from year to year. In any given year, many households at the bottom of the income distribution are having a particularly bad year, just as many at the top are having a particularly good year. Over time, their incomes will stabilize, thereby reducing the level of measured inequality.

Mean household income is the average income across all households.

Median household income is the income of the household lying at the exact middle of the income distribution.

Second, household incomes vary over the lifetime. Young people and retired people, on average, have lower income than those in their prime working years. So data that mixes people of different ages will show more income inequality than data that makes comparisons among people of similar ages.

Despite those qualifications, however, there is a considerable amount of genuine income inequality in the United States.

The Gini Coefficient A good way to gain some perspective on the level of income inequality in the United States is to compare it to levels of inequality in other countries. To do that economists use the **Gini coefficient,** a measure of income inequality based on the type of data found in Table 11-1. Mathematically, a country's Gini coefficient can range from 0, indicating a perfectly equal distribution of income, to 1, indicating the most unequal distribution of income possible—one in which all the income goes to a single household.

Countries with a high degree of income inequality have a Gini coefficient close to 0.5. Aside from a few countries in Africa, the highest levels of income inequality are found in Latin America, especially Colombia. Countries with a very equal income distribution have Gini coefficients around 0.25. The most equal distributions of income are in Europe, especially in Scandinavia.

According to recent data, the United States has a Gini coefficient of 0.41. So, compared to other wealthy countries, the United States has unusually high inequality, though it isn't as unequal as in a country in Latin America. In 2016, the top 1% income bracket in the United States ($390,000 and up) garnered 20% of national income, compared to 6% in Denmark and 14% in Canada.

How serious an issue is income inequality? In a direct sense, high income inequality means that some people don't share in a nation's overall prosperity. Rising inequality explains how it's possible that the U.S. poverty rate has failed to fall for the past 50 years even though the country as a whole has become considerably richer.

And inequality not only persists for long periods of time for individuals, it extends across generations. The children of poor parents are much more likely to be poor than the children of affluent parents, and vice versa—a correlation that is even stronger in the United States than in other rich countries. Those born into low-income families may fail to receive adequate nutrition and health care, limiting their productivity as adults; they may also lack access to education and job opportunities, limiting their ability to make contributions to economic growth. In some cases, high inequality also contributes to social and political instability, which further damages economic performance.

Economic Insecurity

As stated earlier, although the rationale for the welfare state rests in part on the social benefits of reducing poverty and inequality, it also rests in part on the benefits of reducing economic insecurity, which afflicts even relatively well-off families.

One form economic insecurity takes is the risk of a sudden loss of income, which usually happens when a family member loses a job and either spends an extended period without work or is forced to take a new job that pays considerably less. In the aftermath of the Great Recession, one in six American families saw their income cut in half from the previous year. One study finds that almost half of individual workers will see their incomes fluctuate by 25%, with many falling below the poverty threshold.

Even if a family doesn't face a loss in income, it can face a surge in expenses. Until implementation of the Affordable Care Act in 2014, the most common reason for such a surge was a medical problem that required expensive treatment, such as heart disease or cancer. Estimates show that 60% of personal bankruptcies in the United States in 2009 were due to medical expenses.

The **Gini coefficient** is a number that summarizes a country's level of income inequality based on how unequally income is distributed across quintiles.

GLOBAL COMPARISON INCOME, REDISTRIBUTION, AND INEQUALITY IN RICH COUNTRIES

If you were to spend some time traveling around the United States and then do the same in Denmark, you're likely to come away with the impression that compared to America, Denmark has substantially less income inequality than America—the rich aren't as rich and the poor aren't as poor. And the numbers confirm this impression: the Gini coefficient for Denmark, and indeed for most of Western Europe, is substantially lower than in the United States. But why?

The answer, to an important extent, is the role of government, which, in the United States, plays a significant role in redistributing income away from those with the highest incomes to those who earn the least. But European nations have substantially bigger welfare states than we do, and do a lot more income redistribution.

The accompanying figure shows two measures of the Gini coefficient for a number of rich countries. (The figure focuses on households in which everyone is under 60, because differences in retirement ages skew results among older families.) A country with a perfectly equal income distribution—one in which every household had the same income—would have a Gini coefficient of zero. At the other extreme, a country in which all of the income goes to one household would have a Gini coefficient of 1. For each country, the purple bars show the actual Gini, a measure of the observed inequality in income before taxes and transfers are made. The orange bars show what each country's Gini would be after taxes and transfers are made. It turns out that the inequality of market incomes in Denmark is somewhat lower than that in the United States, but much of the difference in observed inequality is the result of Denmark's bigger welfare state.

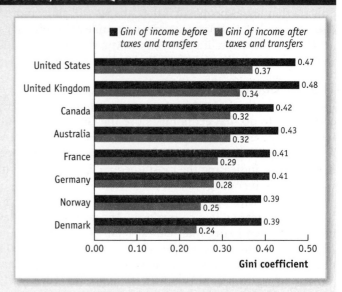

There are some caveats to this conclusion. On one side, the data probably don't do a very good job of tracking very high incomes, which are probably a bigger factor in the United States than elsewhere. On the other side, European welfare states may indirectly increase measured income inequality through their effects on incentives. Still, the data strongly suggest that differences in inequality among rich countries reflect different policies as well as differences in the underlying economic situation.

Data from: Janet C. Gornick and Branko Milanovic, "Income Inequality in the United States in Cross-National Perspective: Redistribution Revisited," Luxembourg Income Study Center, May 4, 2015.

ECONOMICS >> *in Action*
Long-Term Trends in Income Inequality in the United States

Does inequality tend to rise, fall, or stay the same over time? The answer is yes—all three. Over the course of the past century, the United States has gone through periods characterized by all three trends: an era of falling inequality during the 1930s and 1940s, an era of stable inequality for about 35 years after World War II, and an era of rising inequality over the past 40 years.

Detailed U.S. data on income by quintiles, as shown in Table 11-1, are available starting in 1947. Panel (a) of Figure 11-2 shows the annual rate of growth of income, adjusted for inflation, for each quintile over two periods: from 1947 to 1980, and from 1980 to 2017. There's a clear difference between the two periods. In the first period, income within each group grew at about the same rate—that is, there wasn't much change in the inequality of income, just growing incomes across the board.

After 1980, however, incomes grew much more quickly at the top than in the middle, and more quickly in the middle than at the bottom. So inequality has increased substantially since 1980. Overall, inflation-adjusted income for families in the top quintile rose 67% between 1980 and 2017, while actually falling slightly for families in the bottom quintile.

Although detailed data on income distribution aren't available before 1947, economists have used other information, such as income tax data, to estimate the share of income going to the top 10% of the population all the way back to 1917. Panel (b) of Figure 11-2 shows this measure from 1917 to 2017. These data, like the more detailed data available since 1947, show that American inequality was more or less stable between 1947 and the late 1970s but has risen substantially since.

The longer-term data also show, however, that the relatively equal distribution of 1947 was something new. In the late nineteenth century, often referred to as the Gilded Age, American income was very unequally distributed. This high level of inequality persisted into the 1930s. But inequality declined sharply between the late 1930s and the end of World War II. In a famous paper, Claudia Goldin and Robert Margo, two economic historians, dubbed this narrowing of income inequality *the Great Compression.*

The Great Compression roughly coincided with World War II, a period during which the U.S. government imposed special controls on wages and prices. Evidence indicates that these controls were applied in ways that reduced inequality—for example, it was much easier for employers to get approval to increase the wages of their lowest-paid employees than to increase executive salaries. What remains puzzling is that the equality imposed by wartime controls lasted for decades after those controls were lifted in 1946.

As we've already seen, inequality has increased substantially since the 1970s. In fact, pre-tax income appears to be as unequally distributed in America today as it was in the 1920s, prompting many commentators to describe the current state of the nation as a new Gilded Age—albeit one in which the effects of inequality are moderated by taxes and the existence of the welfare state.

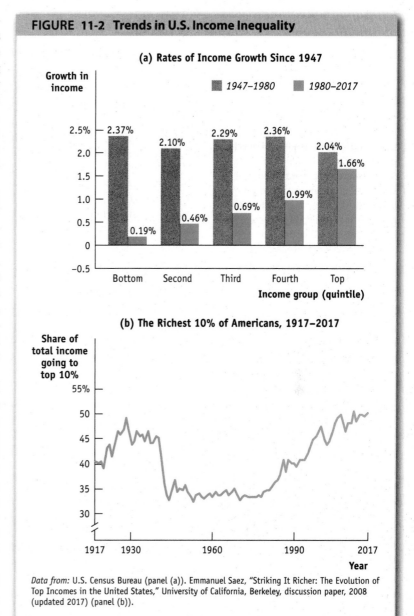

FIGURE 11-2 Trends in U.S. Income Inequality

Data from: U.S. Census Bureau (panel (a)). Emmanuel Saez, "Striking It Richer: The Evolution of Top Incomes in the United States," University of California, Berkeley, discussion paper, 2008 (updated 2017) (panel (b)).

There is intense debate among economists about the causes of this widening inequality. The most popular explanation is rapid technological change, which has increased the demand for highly skilled or talented workers more rapidly than the demand for other workers, leading to a rise in the wage gap between the highly skilled and other workers. Growing international trade may also have contributed by allowing the United States to import labor-intensive products from low-wage countries rather than making them domestically, reducing the demand for less-skilled American workers and depressing their wages. Rising immigration may be yet another source. On average, immigrants have lower education levels than native-born workers and increase the supply of low-skilled labor while depressing low-skilled wages.

However, these explanations fail to account for one key feature: much of the rise in inequality doesn't reflect a rising gap between highly educated workers and those with less education, but rather growing differences among highly educated

>> Quick Review

• **Welfare state** programs, which include **government transfers,** absorb a large share of government spending in wealthy countries.

• The ability-to-pay principle explains one rationale for the welfare state: alleviating income inequality. **Poverty programs** do this by aiding the poor. **Social insurance programs** address a second rationale: alleviating economic insecurity. The external benefits to society of poverty reduction and access to health care, especially for children, is a third rationale for the welfare state.

• The official U.S. **poverty threshold** is adjusted yearly to reflect changes in the cost of living but not in the average standard of living. But even though average income has risen significantly, the U.S. **poverty rate** is no lower than it was 40 years ago.

• The causes of poverty can include lack of education, the legacy of racial and gender discrimination, and bad luck. The consequences of poverty are dire for children.

• **Median household income** is a better indicator of typical household income than **mean household income.** A comparison of **Gini coefficients** across countries shows that the United States has less income inequality than poor countries but more than all other rich countries.

• The United States has seen both declining and increasing income inequality. Since 1980, income inequality has increased substantially, largely due to increased inequality among highly educated workers.

workers themselves. For example, schoolteachers and top business executives have similarly high levels of education, but executive paychecks have risen dramatically and teachers' salaries have not. For some reason, a few superstars—a group that includes literal superstars in the entertainment world but also such groups as Wall Street traders and top corporate executives—now earn much higher incomes than was the case a generation ago. It's still unclear what caused the change.

>> Check Your Understanding 11-1

Solutions appear at back of book.

1. Indicate whether each of the following programs is a poverty program or a social insurance program.
   a. A pension guarantee program, which provides pensions for retirees if they have lost their employment-based pension due to their employer's bankruptcy
   b. The federal program known as CHIP, which provides health care for children in families that are above the poverty threshold but still have relatively low income
   c. The Section 8 housing program, which provides housing subsidies for low-income households
   d. The federal flood program, which provides financial help to communities hit by major floods

2. Recall that the poverty threshold is not adjusted to reflect changes in the standard of living. As a result, is the poverty threshold a relative or an absolute measure of poverty? That is, does it define poverty according to how poor someone is relative to others or according to some fixed measure that doesn't change over time? Explain.

3. The accompanying table gives the distribution of income for a very small economy.
   a. What is the mean income? What is the median income? Which measure is more representative of the income of the average person in the economy? Why?
   b. What income range defines the first quintile? The third quintile?

	Income
Sephora	$39,000
Kelly	17,500
Raul	900,000
Vijay	15,000
Oskar	28,000

4. Which of the following statements more accurately reflects the principal source of rising inequality in the United States today?
   a. The salary of the manager of the local branch of Sunrise Bank has risen relative to the salary of the neighborhood gas station attendant.
   b. The salary of the CEO of Sunrise Bank has risen relative to the salary of the local branch bank manager, although the two have similar education levels.

The U.S. Welfare State

In 2017 the U.S. welfare state consisted of three huge programs (Social Security, Medicare, and Medicaid); several other fairly big programs, including the Affordable Care Act, Temporary Assistance for Needy Families, food stamps, and the Earned Income Tax Credit; and a number of smaller programs. Table 11-2 shows one useful way to categorize the programs existing in 2017, along with spending on each listed program.

First, the table distinguishes between programs that are **means-tested** and those that are not. In means-tested programs, benefits are available only to families or individuals whose income or wealth falls below some minimum. Basically, means-tested programs are poverty programs designed to help only those with low incomes. By contrast, non-means-tested programs provide their benefits to everyone, although, as we'll see, they tend in practice to reduce income inequality.

Second, the table distinguishes between programs that provide monetary transfers that beneficiaries can spend as they choose and those that provide **in-kind benefits,** which are given in the form of goods or services rather than

A **means-tested** program is a program available only to individuals or families whose incomes fall below a certain level.

An **in-kind benefit** is a benefit given in the form of goods or services.

money. As the numbers suggest, in-kind benefits are dominated by Medicare and Medicaid, which pay for health care. We'll discuss health care in the next section of this chapter. For now, let's examine the other major programs.

Means-Tested Programs

When people use the term *welfare,* they're often referring to monetary aid to poor families. The main source of such monetary aid in the United States is Temporary Assistance for Needy Families, or TANF. This program does not aid everyone who is poor; it is available only to poor families with children and only for a limited period of time.

TABLE 11-2 Major U.S. Welfare State Programs, 2017

	Monetary transfers	In-kind
Means-tested	Temporary Assistance for Needy Families (TANF): $21 billion	Food stamps: $72 billion
	Supplemental Security Income: $52 billion	Medicaid: $379 billion
	Earned Income Tax Credit (EITC): $61 billion	Affordable Care Act (ACA): $110 billion
Not means-tested	Social Security: $946 billion	Medicare: $701 billion
	Unemployment insurance: $29 billion	

Data from: U.S. Treasury.

TANF was introduced in the 1990s to replace a highly controversial program known as Aid to Families with Dependent Children, or AFDC. The older program was widely accused of creating perverse incentives for the poor, including encouraging family breakup. Partly as a result of the change in programs, the benefits of modern "welfare" are considerably less generous than those available a generation ago, once the data are adjusted for inflation. Also, TANF contains time limits, so welfare recipients—even single parents—must eventually seek work. As you can see from Table 11-2, TANF is a relatively small part of the modern U.S. welfare state.

Other means-tested programs, though more expensive, are less controversial. The Supplemental Security Income program aids disabled Americans who are unable to work and have no other source of income. The food stamp program, or SNAP—officially the Supplemental Nutrition Assistance Program, since it now provides debit cards rather than stamps—helps low-income families and individuals, who can use those debit cards to buy food staples but not other items.

Finally, economists use the term **negative income tax** for a program that supplements the earnings of low-income working families. The United States has a program known as the Earned Income Tax Credit (EITC), which provides additional income to millions of workers. It has become more generous as traditional welfare has become less generous. Only workers who earn income are eligible for the EITC. Over a certain range of incomes, the more a worker earns, the higher the amount of EITC received. That is, the EITC acts as a negative income tax for low-wage workers. In 2017, married couples with two children earning less than $14,050 per year received EITC payments equal to $5,616, approximately 40% of their earnings. (Payments were slightly lower for single-parent families or workers without children.) The EITC is phased out at higher incomes. As of 2017, the payment ceased at an income of $50,597 for married couples with two children.

One of every seven Americans receives food stamps, officially known as SNAP.

Social Security and Unemployment Insurance

Social Security, the largest program in the U.S. welfare state, is a non-means-tested program that guarantees retirement income to qualifying older Americans. It also provides benefits to workers who become disabled, and "survivor benefits" to family members of workers who die.

Social Security is supported by a dedicated tax on wages: the Social Security portion of the payroll tax pays for Social Security benefits. The benefits workers

A **negative income tax** is a program that supplements the income of low-income working families.

President Franklin D. Roosevelt signed the Social Security Act in 1935, creating the modern welfare state.

receive on retirement depend on their taxable earnings during their working years: the more you earn up to the maximum amount subject to Social Security taxes ($127,200 in 2017), the more you receive in retirement. Benefits are not, however, strictly proportional to earnings. Instead, they're determined by a formula that gives high earners more than low earners, but with a sliding scale that makes the program relatively more generous for low earners.

Because most seniors don't receive pensions from their former employers and most don't own enough assets to provide them with a living, Social Security benefits are an enormously important source of income for them. Fully 64% of Americans 65 and older rely on Social Security for more than half their income, and 20% have no income at all except for Social Security.

Unemployment insurance, although normally a much smaller amount of government transfers than Social Security, is another key social insurance program. It provides workers who lose their jobs with about 35% of their previous salary until they find a new job or until 26 weeks have passed. Like Social Security, unemployment insurance is not means-tested.

The Effects of the Welfare State on Poverty and Inequality

Because the people who receive government transfers tend to be different from those who are taxed to pay for those transfers, the U.S. welfare state has the effect of redistributing income from some people to others. Government statisticians have put considerable effort into calculating the effects of this redistribution, which makes a big difference to poverty rates and a somewhat smaller difference to overall inequality.

An important note: such reports calculate only the *direct* effect of taxes and transfers, without taking into account changes in behavior that the taxes and transfers might cause. For example, they don't try to estimate how many older Americans who are now retired would still be working if they weren't receiving Social Security checks. As a result, the estimates are only a partial indicator of the true effects of the welfare state. Nonetheless, the results are striking.

Table 11-3 shows how a number of government programs affected the poverty rate, as measured by the Supplemental Poverty Measure, for the population as a whole and for different age groups in 2012 (the most current data available). For each program it shows the amount, in percentage points, by which that group's poverty rate was reduced by the program. For example, it says that without Social Security, the poverty rate among older Americans would have been almost 40 percentage points higher than it was.

TABLE 11-3 Effects of Government Programs on Reducing the Rate of Poverty, 2012

	All people	Children	Nonelderly adults	65 years and older
Social Security	8.56%	1.97%	4.08%	39.86%
Refundable Tax Credits	3.02	6.66	2.25	0.20
SNAP (food stamps)	1.62	3.01	1.27	0.76
Unemployment insurance	0.79	0.82	0.88	0.31
Supplemental Security Income	1.07	0.84	1.12	1.21
Housing subsidies	0.91	1.39	0.66	1.12
School lunch	0.38	0.91	0.25	0.03
Temporary Assistance for Needy Families	0.21	0.46	0.14	0.05
WIC (Women, Infants, and Children)	0.13	0.29	0.09	0.00

Data from: Council of Economic Advisers.

Table 11-4 shows a Congressional Budget Office estimate of the effect of taxes and transfers on the share of aggregate income going to each quintile of the income distribution in 2013 (the latest available data). The effect of government programs was to increase the share of income going to the poorest 80% of the population, especially the share going to the poorest 20%, while reducing the share of income going to the richest 20%.

TABLE 11-4 Effects of Taxes and Transfers on Income Distribution, 2013

Quintiles	Share of aggregate income without taxes and transfers	Share of aggregate income with taxes and transfers
Bottom quintile	2.2%	9.3%
Second quintile	7.2	10.7
Third quintile	12.8	14.1
Fourth quintile	20.8	19.9
81st–99th percentiles	41.5	35.2
Top 1%	17.2	12.3

Data from: Congressional Budget Office.

ECONOMICS >> *in Action*
Welfare State Programs and Poverty Rates in the Great Recession, 2007–2010

In 2007 the U.S. economy entered a deep downturn, the worst since the 1930s. Recovery officially began in 2009, but it was slow and disappointing. It took over six years for both average and median family income, adjusted for inflation, to return to pre-recession levels.

Given this poor economic performance, you might have expected to see a sharp rise in poverty, and the official poverty rate did in fact move up, as you can see in Figure 11-1. But while the Great Recession and its aftermath certainly hurt many American families, the country never seemed as desperate as it did during the Great Depression, or even during the last big slump, in 1981–1982. And sure enough, the Supplemental Poverty Measure, which most experts consider a better measure of economic hardship, rose only slightly. Why?

The main answer, it turns out, was antipoverty programs, which automatically expanded during the slump and were further reinforced by legislation that temporarily expanded food stamps and other forms of aid. Figure 11-3 shows an estimate of how much the poverty rate would have risen between 2007 and 2010 in the absence of welfare state programs, compared with how much it actually rose. Without transfers and benefits the poverty rate would have risen by 4.50%; but with transfers and benefits it rose only 0.50%. The U.S. welfare state didn't prevent the slump or stop people from losing their jobs or homes. But it did strikingly limit the rise in poverty.

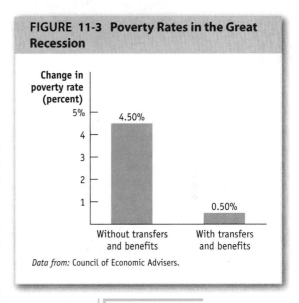

FIGURE 11-3 Poverty Rates in the Great Recession

Data from: Council of Economic Advisers.

>> Check Your Understanding 11-2

Solutions appear at back of book.

1. Explain how the negative income tax avoids the disincentive to work that characterizes poverty programs that simply give benefits based on low income.

2. According to Table 11-3, what effect does the U.S. welfare state have on the overall poverty rate? On the poverty rate for those aged 65 and over?

The Economics of Health Care

A large part of the welfare state, in both the United States and other wealthy countries, is devoted to paying for health care. In most wealthy countries, the government pays between 70% and 80% of all medical costs. The private sector plays a larger role in the U.S. health care system. Yet even in America, as of 2016 the

>> Quick Review

• **Means-tested** programs are designed to reduce poverty, but non-means-tested programs do so as well. Programs are classified according to whether they provide monetary or **in-kind benefits.**

• "Welfare," or TANF, is far less generous today than a generation ago due to concerns about its effect on incentives to work and family breakup. The **negative income tax** addresses these concerns: it supplements the incomes of only low-income working families.

• Social Security, the largest program in the U.S. welfare state, is a non-means-tested program that provides retirement income for the elderly. Unemployment insurance is also a key social insurance program that is not means-tested.

• Overall, the American welfare state is redistributive. It increases the share of income going to the poorest 80% while reducing the share going to the richest 20%.

FIGURE 11-4 Who Paid for U.S. Health Care in 2016?

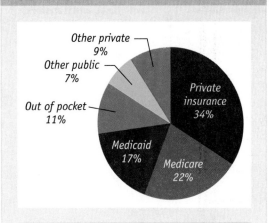

In the United States in 2016, insurance paid for 89% of health care consumption costs: the sum of 34% (private insurance), 22% (Medicare), 17% (Medicaid), 9% (other private), and 7% (other public). The percentage paid for by private insurance, 34%, was a uniquely high number among advanced countries. Even so, substantially more U.S. health care was paid for by Medicare, Medicaid, and other government programs than by other means.

Data from: Department of Health and Human Services Centers for Medicare and Medicaid Services.

government pays almost half of all health care costs; furthermore, it indirectly subsidizes private health insurance through the federal tax code.

Figure 11-4 shows who paid for U.S. health care in 2016. Only 11% of health care consumption spending (all spending on health care except investment in health care buildings and facilities) was expenses "out of pocket"—that is, paid directly by individuals. Most health care spending, 89%, was paid for by some kind of insurance. Of this 89%, considerably less than half was private insurance; the rest was some kind of government insurance, mainly Medicare and Medicaid. To understand why, we need to examine the special economics of health insurance.

The Need for Health Insurance

In 2016, U.S. personal health care expenses were $10,372 per person—18.1% of gross domestic product. This did not, however, mean that the typical American spent nearly $10,000 on medical treatment. In fact, in any given year half the population incurs only minor medical expenses. But a small percentage of the population faces huge medical bills, with 10% of the population typically accounting for almost two-thirds of medical costs.

Is it possible to predict who will have high medical costs? To a limited extent, yes: there are broad patterns to illness. For example, the elderly are more likely to need expensive surgery or drugs than the young. But the fact is that anyone can suddenly find himself or herself needing very expensive medical treatment, costing many thousands of dollars in a very short time—far beyond what most families can easily afford. Yet nobody wants to be unable to afford such treatment if it becomes necessary. As a result, most people would like to have *health insurance* to help cover the costs of medical care.

The U.S. health care system offers a mix of *private insurance*, mainly from employers, and *public insurance*, provided through the government. We'll look at each of these next.

Private Health Insurance Under **private health insurance**, each member of a large pool of individuals agrees to pay a fixed amount annually (called a *premium*) into a common fund that is managed by a private company, which then pays most of the medical expenses of the pool's members. Although members must pay fees even in years in which they don't have large medical expenses, they benefit from the reduction in risk: if they do turn out to have high medical costs, the pool will take care of those expenses. The problem with private health insurance is that it is subject to market failure. Let's examine why.

People typically don't want to purchase health insurance until they are already sick, to avoid paying premiums when they are healthy. As a result, the average person who purchases a private health insurance policy is sicker and has higher medical expenses than the average person who does not. Premiums have to be raised to account for the higher medical costs, which in turn will lead more of the relatively healthy insured people to stop buying insurance and leave the pool.

Without some type of intervention, this dynamic continues for more rounds until only extremely sick people are left in the pool and the private insurance company collapses, unable to charge high enough premiums to cover its medical cost outlays. Economists call this phenomenon the *private health insurance market death spiral*.

Private health insurers have adopted several methods to counteract the death spiral: refusing insurance to anyone who had any sign of a preexisting condition;

Under **private health insurance,** each member of a large pool of individuals pays a fixed amount annually to a private company that agrees to pay most of the medical expenses of the pool's members.

dropping those who did develop an illness while insured; and refusing to cover some procedures such as childbirth. As a result, private health insurance markets leave a significant number of people uninsured—particularly those with preexisting conditions, who need insurance the most.

Because private insurance markets perform so poorly, Americans typically get health insurance through employment-based health insurance and the government—whether government health insurance or government intervention in the market through the Affordable Care Act.

Employment-Based Health Insurance Private insurance can avoid the death spiral by selling insurance indirectly, to peoples' employers rather than to individuals. The advantage of *employment-based health insurance* is that employees are likely to contain a representative mix of healthy and less healthy people, rather than a group of people who want insurance because they expect to incur high medical bills. This is especially true if the employer is a large company with thousands of workers. Employers require their employees to participate in the company health insurance plan because allowing employees to opt out (which healthier ones will be tempted to do) raises the cost of providing insurance for everyone else.

There's another reason employment-based insurance is widespread in the United States: it gets special, favorable tax treatment. Workers pay taxes on their paychecks, but workers who receive health insurance from their employers don't pay taxes on the value of the benefit. So, employment-based health insurance is, in effect, subsidized by the U.S. tax system.

However, many working Americans don't receive employment-based health insurance from their employers (especially part-time workers). In addition, those who aren't covered include most older Americans, because relatively few employers offer workers insurance that continues after retirement, and the unemployed.

Government Health Insurance Table 11-5 shows the breakdown of health insurance coverage across the U.S. population in 2017. A majority of Americans, 181 million people, received health insurance through their employers. The majority of those who didn't have private insurance were covered by two government programs, Medicare and Medicaid. (The numbers don't add up because some people have more than one form of coverage. For example, many recipients of Medicare also have supplemental coverage either through Medicaid or private policies.)

Medicare, financed by payroll taxes, is available to all Americans 65 and older, regardless of their income and wealth. You can get an idea of how much difference Medicare makes to the finances of elderly Americans by comparing the median income per person of Americans 65 and older—$38,565—with average annual Medicare payments per recipient, which were more than $10,000 in 2016.

Unlike Medicare, Medicaid is a means-tested program, paid for with federal and state government revenues. There's no simple way to summarize the criteria for eligibility because it is partly paid for by state governments and each state sets its own rules. Of the nearly 62.5 million Americans covered by Medicaid in 2017, 32 million were children under 18 and many of the rest were parents of children under 18. Most of the cost of Medicaid, however, is accounted for by a small number of older Americans, especially those needing long-term care.

"For me, crime pays for what Medicare doesn't cover."

Frank Cotham The New Yorker Collection/The Cartoon Bank

TABLE 11-5 Number of Americans Covered by Health Insurance, 2017 (millions)	
Covered by private health insurance	**217.1**
Employment-based	181.0
Direct purchase	51.8
Covered by government	**122.0**
Medicaid	62.5
Medicare	55.6
Military health care	15.5
Not covered	**28.0**

Data from: U.S. Census Bureau.

More than 15.5 million Americans receive health insurance as a consequence of military service. Unlike Medicare and Medicaid, which pay medical bills but don't deliver health care directly, the Veterans Health Administration, which has more than 9 million clients, runs hospitals and clinics around the country.

The Affordable Care Act

When Congress passed the Affordable Care Act in 2010, the U.S. health care system was in trouble on two fronts.

First was the rapid growth in the ranks of the uninsured. The percentage of working-age Americans without health insurance grew from 1997 to 2010, peaking with almost a quarter of working-age Americans without insurance. One study found that most of the uninsured were low-wage workers, for whom health insurance benefits were unavailable at work, and private insurance was unaffordable because of its high cost.

Second, health care spending was rising rapidly, leading to sharply higher insurance premiums. In fact, health care spending has tripled as a share of U.S. income since 1965. The source of this higher spending is medical progress: as medical science advances, more illnesses are treatable, but at greater cost.

When implemented in 2014, the ACA was the largest expansion of the American welfare state since the creation of Medicare and Medicaid in 1965. It had three major objectives: covering the uninsured, reducing inefficiency, and cost control.

Covering the Uninsured To cover the uninsured, the ACA in many ways replicated the model of employer-based insurance, but extended it to all Americans. First, as in employee-based insurance, everyone had to participate. So, the ACA adopted what is known as the *individual mandate*, the requirement that all individuals be insured. Second, like the tax subsidies in employee-based insurance, government subsidies were provided to lower-income families to make purchasing insurance affordable. And third, as in employee-based insurance, insurers had to offer the same policies to everyone, at the same premiums, regardless of medical history, a rule called "community rating."

It's important to understand that this system was devised to work like a three-legged stool: all three components play important roles in making it work. Without community rating, those with preexisting conditions will be denied coverage. Without the individual mandate, healthy people may not buy insurance. And without subsidies, lower-income households wouldn't be able to afford to buy insurance. For these reasons, the Tax Cuts and Jobs Act of 2017, by eliminating the individual mandate and financing for subsidies, represented a real threat to the foundations of the program.

Reducing Inefficiency The United States spends far more on health care than other wealthy countries, but without clear evidence of better health outcomes. Economists believe one of the reasons is serious inefficiencies arising from the country's reliance on private health insurance markets compared to other countries, which rely much more on government-provided health care or health care insurance. Before the ACA, private insurers had high operating costs due to the amounts they spent on marketing and weeding out high-cost applicants, leading to high operating costs. But because the ACA eliminated insurers' ability to spend resources on weeding out applicants, it has the potential to increase efficiency.

Cost Control The ACA contained a number of measures, many of them involving Medicare, intended to help control health care costs. Health care providers were encouraged to band together to form "accountable care organizations," coordinating care in ways that save money; organizations that did so would receive a share of the savings. Hospitals were encouraged to provide effective care by rules that reduced payments to hospitals whose patients tend to be readmitted at high rates. Special taxes on "Cadillac" health insurance—extremely generous plans—aimed to discourage excessive treatment. And the ACA eliminated copayments for preventive care, in the hope that patients would be encouraged to take care of medical issues before they required expensive treatment.

As it turns out, the rate at which health costs were rising slowed sharply around 2010, just as the ACA was passed. It's unclear how much of this cost slowdown was caused by the law's provisions.

Results So Far The most important provisions of the ACA took effect at the start of 2014; by 2015 it was possible to get an initial view of its results.

The first effect can be seen in Figure 11-5, which shows the uninsured percentage of the working-age population. This percentage began dropping after 2010, partly because of a recovering economy, but also because some provisions of the ACA went into effect, notably a rule allowing Americans under the age of 26 to remain on their parents' policies. And after 2013, with the law in full effect, the number of uninsured fell sharply. By 2016 the percent of working-age adults without health insurance had been cut almost in half.

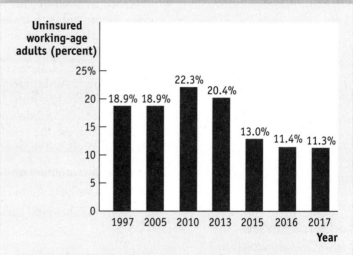

FIGURE 11-5 Uninsured Working-Age Americans, 1997–2017

Before the ACA was implemented, the share of uninsured working-age adults was rising dramatically. Since the ACA's implementation, the share has fallen sharply.
Data from: Kaiser Family Foundation, U.S. Census Bureau.

Yet a sizable number of people remain uninsured. The law does not cover undocumented immigrants, and roughly half the states have chosen not to accept a federally funded expansion of Medicaid, leaving several million people in a *gap* where they receive neither Medicaid nor subsidies to buy private insurance. So progress toward covering the uninsured has been substantial but incomplete.

Furthermore, as we've noted, in 2017 Republicans in Congress succeeded in repealing one important provision in the ACA, the individual mandate, although the rest of the law remained intact. This change was expected to raise premiums, because fewer healthy people would sign up. Many beneficiaries would be insulated from this premium increase thanks to the law's subsidies, but the move was nonetheless widely expected to shrink the number of insured Americans, perhaps by millions.

ECONOMICS >> *in Action*
What Medicaid Does

Do social insurance programs actually help their beneficiaries? The answer isn't always as obvious as you might think. Take the example of Medicaid, which provides health insurance to low-income Americans. Some of those skeptical about the program's effectiveness have argued that in the absence of Medicaid, the poor would still find ways to get essential health care, and that there is no clear evidence that receiving Medicaid actually leads to better health.

Testing such assertions is tricky. You can't just compare people who are on Medicaid with people who aren't, since the program's beneficiaries differ in many ways from

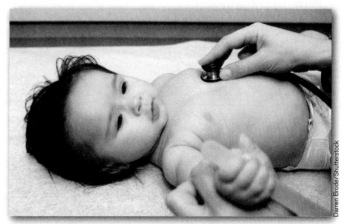

Medicaid has been shown to make a big difference in the well-being of recipients.

those who aren't on the program. And we don't normally get to do controlled experiments in which otherwise comparable groups receive different government benefits.

Once in a while, however, events provide the equivalent of a controlled experiment—and that's what happened with Medicaid. In 2008, the state of Oregon—which had sharply curtailed its Medicaid program because it lacked sufficient funds—found itself with enough money to put some but not all deserving recipients back on the program. To allocate the limited number of slots, the state used a lottery. And there you had it: in effect, a controlled experiment, in which researchers could compare a random sample of people receiving Medicaid with similar people who didn't win the lottery.

So what were the results? It turned out that Medicaid made a big difference. Those on Medicaid received

- 60% more mammograms
- 35% more outpatient care
- 30% more hospital care
- 20% more cholesterol checks

Medicaid recipients were also

- 70% more likely to have a consistent source of care
- 55% more likely to see the same doctor over time
- 45% more likely to have had a Pap test within the last year (for women)
- 40% less likely to need to borrow money or skip payment on other bills because of medical expenses
- 25% percent more likely to report themselves in "good" or "excellent" health
- 15% more likely to use prescription drugs
- 15% more likely to have had a blood test for high blood sugar or diabetes
- 10% percent less likely to screen positive for depression

In short, Medicaid led to major improvements in access to medical care and in the well-being of those receiving it. So although there is a valid debate over the size of a state's Medicaid program because it costs taxpayers a significant amount of money, the Oregon results show that one criticism of Medicaid—the claim that it doesn't work at all—isn't valid.

>> **Quick Review**
- Health insurance satisfies an important need because expensive medical treatment is unaffordable for most families. **Private health insurance** has an inherent problem: those who buy insurance are disproportionately sicker than the average person, which drives up costs and premiums, leading more healthy people to forgo insurance, further driving up costs and premiums and ultimately leading private insurance companies to fail. Screening by insurance companies reduces the problem, and employment-based health insurance, the way most Americans are covered, avoids it altogether.

- The majority of Americans not covered by private insurance are covered by Medicare, which is a non-means-tested **single-payer system** for those 65 and over, and Medicaid, which is means-tested.

- Health care costs everywhere are increasing rapidly due to medical progress. The ACA was designed to address the large and growing share of American uninsured and to reduce the rate of growth of health care spending.

A **single-payer system** is a health care system in which the government is the principal payer of medical bills funded through taxes.

>> Check Your Understanding 11-3

Solutions appear at back of book.

1. If you are enrolled in a four-year degree program, it is likely that you are required to enroll in a health insurance program run by your school unless you can show proof of existing insurance coverage.
   a. Explain how you and your parents benefit from this health insurance program even though, given your age, it is unlikely that you will need expensive medical treatment.
   b. Explain how your school's health insurance program avoids the problem of the adverse selection death spiral faced by private insurance.

The Debate over the Welfare State

The goals of the welfare state seem laudable: to help the poor, protect against severe economic hardship, and ensure access to essential health care. But good intentions don't always make for good policy. There is an intense debate about how large the welfare state should be, partly reflecting differences in philosophy but also reflecting concern about the possibly counterproductive effects on incentives of welfare state programs. Disputes about the size of the welfare state are one of the defining issues of modern American politics.

Arguments Against the Welfare State

There are two different arguments against the welfare state. One is based on philosophical concerns about the proper role of government. Some political theorists believe that redistributing income is not a legitimate role of government. Rather, they believe that government's role should be limited to maintaining the rule of law, providing public goods, and managing externalities.

The more conventional argument against the welfare state involves the trade-off between efficiency and equity. As we've learned, the *ability-to-pay-principle*—the argument that an extra dollar of income matters more to a less well-off individual than to a more well-off individual—implies that the government can help the poor at relatively little cost to the well-off. But this redistribution of income from well-off to poor requires that the well-off be taxed more heavily, paying a higher percentage of their income in taxes than those with lower incomes. This is the principle behind progressive taxation.

As a result, the goals of the welfare state must be balanced against the efficiency costs of higher tax rates on the well-off that can reduce their incentive to work hard or make risky investments. A progressive tax system, then, tends to make society as a whole somewhat poorer, and could hurt even those the system was intended to help. A larger welfare state requires higher tax revenue and higher tax rates than a smaller welfare state, which restricts itself to mainly providing public goods such as national defense. So in making policy that affects the size of the welfare state, government must make a trade-off between efficiency versus equity.

One way to reduce the cost of the welfare state is to means-test benefits: make them available only to those who need them. But means-testing creates a different kind of trade-off between equity and efficiency. Consider the following example: Suppose there is some means-tested benefit, worth $2,000 per year, that is available only to families with incomes of less than $20,000 per year. Now suppose that a family currently has an income of $19,500 but that one family member is deciding whether to take a new job that will raise the family's income to $20,500. Well, taking that job will actually make the family worse off because it will gain $1,000 in earnings but lose the $2,000 in government benefits. This effect is known as a *benefits notch*.

Unless means-testing is carefully designed, poor families can face a large fall in their effective income when their income rises to the level at which they are no longer eligible for benefits, reducing their incentive to work. One study found that a family of two adults and two children that raised its income from $20,000 a year—just above the poverty threshold in 2005—to $35,000 would find almost all its increase in after-tax income offset by loss of benefits such as food stamps, the Earned Income Tax Credit, and Medicaid.

The Politics of the Welfare State

Today, U.S. politicians also fall on a "right-left" divide, and they mainly disagree about the appropriate size of the welfare state. The debate over the ACA was an example, with the vote on the bill breaking down entirely according to party lines—Democrats (on the left) in favor of the ACA and Republicans (on the right) opposed.

You might think that it's a huge oversimplification to say political debate is really about just one thing—how big to make the welfare state. But political scientists have found that once you carefully rank members of Congress from right to left on past legislation, a congressperson's position in that ranking is a very good predictor of his or her votes on future legislation.

The same studies also show that American politics has become more polarized. Forty years ago, there was a substantial overlap between the parties: some Democrats were to the right of some Republicans, or, if you prefer, some Republicans were to the left of some Democrats. Today, however, the rightmost Democrats appear to be to the left of the leftmost Republicans.

Can economic analysis help resolve this political conflict? Only up to a point. Some of the political controversy involves differences in opinion about the trade-offs we have just discussed: if you believe that the disincentive effects of more generous benefits and higher taxes are very large, you will look less favorably on welfare state programs than if you believe they're fairly small.

Economic analysis, by improving our knowledge of the facts, can help resolve some of these differences. Yet some of the disagreements over the welfare state are the result of a misunderstanding of economics—for example, how health insurance markets work. And some of the conflict is based on a misunderstanding of how economic policy is made. For example, it is important to realize that a promise to maintain social programs cannot be met if, at the same time, cuts will be made to the tax revenue those programs depend upon.

To an important extent, however, differences of opinion on the size of the welfare state reflect differences in values and philosophy. And those are differences economics can't resolve.

>> Quick Review

• Intense debate on the size of the welfare state centers on philosophy and on equity-versus-efficiency concerns. The high marginal tax rates needed to finance an extensive welfare state can reduce the incentive to work. Holding down the cost of the welfare state by means-testing can also cause inefficiency by creating high effective marginal tax rates for benefit recipients.

• Politics is often depicted as an opposition between left and right; in the modern United States, that division mainly arises from three sources: differences in views on the size of the equity-versus-efficiency trade-off, a misunderstanding of economics, and philosophical differences.

>> Check Your Understanding 11-4

Solutions appear at back of book.

1. Explain how each of the following policies creates a disincentive to work or undertake a risky investment.
   a. A high sales tax on consumer items
   b. The complete loss of a housing subsidy when yearly income rises above $25,000
2. Over the past 40 years, has the polarization in Congress increased, decreased, or stayed the same?

SUMMARY

1. The **welfare state** absorbs a large share of government spending in all wealthy countries. **Government transfers** are the payments made by the government to individuals and families. **Poverty programs** alleviate income inequality by helping the poor; **social insurance programs** alleviate economic insecurity. Welfare state programs also deliver external benefits to society through poverty reduction and improved access to health care, particularly for children.

2. Despite the fact that the **poverty threshold** is adjusted according to the cost of living but not according to the standard of living, and that the average American income has risen substantially over the last 30 years, the **poverty rate,** the percentage of the population with an income below the poverty threshold, is no lower than it was 30 years ago. There are various causes of poverty: lack of education, the legacy of discrimination, and bad luck. The consequences of poverty are particularly harmful for children, resulting in more chronic disease, lower lifetime earnings, and higher rates of criminality.

3. **Median household income,** the income of a family at the center of the income distribution, is a better indicator of the income of the typical household than **mean household income** because it is not distorted by the inclusion of a small number of very wealthy households. The **Gini coefficient,** a number that summarizes a country's level of income inequality based on how unequally income is distributed across quintiles, is used to compare income inequality across countries.

4. Both **means-tested** and non-means-tested programs reduce poverty. The major **in-kind benefits** programs are Medicare and Medicaid, which pay for medical care. Due to concerns about the effects on incentives to work and on family cohesion, aid to poor families has become significantly less generous even as the **negative income tax** has become more generous. Social Security, the largest U.S. welfare state program, has significantly reduced poverty among the elderly. Unemployment insurance is also a key social insurance program.

5. Health insurance satisfies an important need because most families cannot afford expensive medical treatment. **Private health insurance,** unless it is employment-based or carefully screens applicants, has the potential to fall into an adverse selection

death spiral. Most Americans are covered by employment-based private health insurance; the majority of the remaining are covered by Medicare (a **single-payer system** for those 65 and over in which the government pays for most medical bills from tax revenue) or Medicaid (for those with low incomes).

6. Compared to other countries, the United States relies more heavily on private health insurance and has substantially higher health care costs per person without clearly providing better care. Health care costs are rising, largely due to advances in technology. The rising number of uninsured and the financial distress caused by lack of insurance prompted the passage of the Affordable Care Act, or ACA. Its objective is to reduce the number of those uninsured and to also reduce the rate of growth of health care costs.

7. Debates over the size of the welfare state are based on philosophical and equity-versus-efficiency considerations. The equity-versus-efficiency debate arises from the fact that an extensive welfare state requires high taxes on the well-off, which can diminish society's wealth by reducing their incentive to work and make risky investments. Means-testing of benefits can reduce the cost of the welfare state but must be carefully designed to avoid reducing the incentive to work by the poor.

8. Politicians on the left tend to favor a bigger welfare state and those on the right to oppose it. American politics has become more polarized in recent decades. Differences arise from views on the size of the equity-versus-efficiency trade-off, misunderstandings about how markets work, and philosophical differences.

KEY TERMS

Welfare state, p. 316
Government transfer, p. 316
Poverty program, p. 316
Social insurance program, p. 316
Poverty threshold, p. 317

Poverty rate, p. 317
Mean household income, p. 320
Median household income, p. 320
Gini coefficient, p. 321
Means-tested, p. 324

In-kind benefit, p. 324
Negative income tax, p. 325
Private health insurance, p. 328
Single-payer system, p. 332

PROBLEMS

interactive activity

1. The accompanying table contains data on the U.S. economy for the years 1983 and 2015. The second column shows the poverty threshold. The third column shows the consumer price index (CPI), a measure of the overall level of prices. And the fourth column shows U.S. gross domestic product (GDP) per capita, a measure of the standard of living.

Year	Poverty threshold	CPI (1982–1984 = 100)	GDP per capita
1983	$5,180	99.6	$15,525
2015	12,331	237.8	56,066

Data from: U.S. Census Bureau; Bureau of Labor Statistics; Bureau of Economic Analysis.

a. By what factor has the poverty threshold increased from 1983 to 2015? That is, has it doubled, tripled, and so on?

b. By what factor has the CPI (a measure of the overall price level) increased from 1983 to 2015? That is, has it doubled, tripled, and so on?

c. By what factor has GDP per capita (a measure of the standard of living) increased from 1983 to 2015? That is, has it doubled, tripled, and so on?

d. What do your results tell you about how people officially classified as "poor" have done economically relative to other U.S. citizens?

2. In the city of Metropolis, there are 100 residents, each of whom lives until age 75. Residents of Metropolis have the following incomes over their lifetime: Through age 14, they earn nothing. From age 15 until age 29, they earn 200 metros (the currency of Metropolis) per year. From age 30 to age 49, they earn 400 metros. From age 50 to age 64, they earn 300 metros. Finally, at age 65 they retire and are paid a pension of 100 metros per year until they die at age 75. Each year, everyone consumes whatever their income is that year (that is, there is no saving and no borrowing). Currently, 20 residents are 10 years old, 20 residents are 20 years old, 20 residents are 40 years old, 20 residents are 60 years old, and 20 residents are 70 years old.

a. Study the income distribution among all residents of Metropolis. Split the population into quintiles according to their income. How much income does a resident in the lowest quintile have? In the second, third, fourth, and top quintiles? What share of total income of all residents goes to the residents in each quintile? Construct a table showing the share of total income that goes to each quintile. Does this income distribution show inequality?

b. Now look only at the 20 residents of Metropolis who are currently 40 years old, and study the income distribution among only those residents. Split those 20 residents into quintiles according to their income. How much income does a resident in the lowest quintile have? In the second, third, fourth, and top quintiles? What share of total income of all 40-year-olds goes to the residents in each quintile? Does this income distribution show inequality?

c. What is the relevance of these examples for assessing data on the distribution of income in any country?

3. The accompanying table presents data from the U.S. Census Bureau on median and mean income of male workers for the years 1972 and 2015. The income figures are adjusted to eliminate the effect of inflation.

Year	Median income	Mean income
	(in 2015 dollars)	
1972	$37,760	$43,766
2015	37,138	54,757

Data from: U.S. Census Bureau.

a. By what percentage has median income changed over this period? By what percentage has mean income changed over this period?

b. Between 1972 and 2015, has the income distribution become less or more unequal? Explain.

4. There are 100 households in the economy of Equalor. Initially, 99 of them have an income of $10,000 each, and one household has an income of $1,010,000.

a. What is the median income in this economy? What is the mean income?

Through its poverty programs, the government of Equalor now redistributes income: it takes $990,000 away from the richest household and distributes it equally among the remaining 99 households.

b. What is the median income in this economy now? What is the mean income? Has the median income changed? Has the mean income changed? Which indicator (mean or median household income) is a better indicator of the typical Equalorian household's income? Explain.

5. The country of Marxland has the following income tax and social insurance system. Each citizen's income is taxed at an average tax rate of 100%. A social insurance system then provides transfers to each citizen such that each citizen's after-tax income is exactly equal. That is, each citizen gets (through a government transfer payment) an equal share of the income tax revenue. What is the incentive for one individual citizen to work and earn income? What will the total tax revenue in Marxland be? What will be the after-tax income (including the transfer payment) for each citizen? Do you think such a tax system that creates perfect equality will work?

6. The tax system in Taxilvania includes a negative income tax. For all incomes below $10,000, individuals pay an income tax of –40% (that is, they receive a payment of 40% of their income). For any income above the $10,000 threshold, the tax rate on that additional income is 10%.

a. For each scenario in the table, calculate the amount of income tax to be paid and after-tax income.

b. Can you find a situation in this tax system in which earning more pre-tax income actually results in less after-tax income? Explain.

Scenarios	
1	Lowani earns income of $8,000
2	Midram earns income of $40,000
3	Hi-Wan earns income of $100,000

7. In the city of Notchingham, each worker is paid a wage rate of $10 per hour. Notchingham administers its own unemployment benefit, which is structured as follows: If you are unemployed (that is, if you do not work at all), you get unemployment benefits (a transfer from the government) of $50 per day. As soon as you work for only one hour, the unemployment benefit is completely withdrawn. That is, there is a notch in the benefit system.

a. How much income does an unemployed person have per day? How much daily income does an individual who works four hours per day have? How many hours do you need to work to earn just the same as if you were unemployed?

b. Will anyone ever accept a part-time job that requires working four hours per day, rather than being unemployed?

c. Suppose that Notchingham now changes the way in which the unemployment benefit is withdrawn. For each additional dollar an individual earns, $0.50 of the unemployment benefit is withdrawn. How much daily income does an individual who works four hours per day now have? Is there an incentive now to work four hours per day rather than being unemployed?

8. The accompanying table shows data on the total number of people in the United States and the number of all people who were uninsured, for selected years from 2003 to 2015. It also shows data on the total number of poor children in the United States—those under 18 and below the poverty threshold—and the number of poor children who were uninsured.

Year	Total people	Uninsured people	Total poor children	Uninsured poor children
	(millions)			
2003	288.3	43.4	12.9	8.3
2005	293.8	44.8	12.9	8.0
2007	299.1	45.7	13.3	8.1
2009	304.3	50.7	15.5	7.5
2011	308.8	48.6	16.1	7.0
2013	313.1	41.8	15.8	5.4
2015	318.4	29.0	14.5	4.5

Data from: U.S. Census Bureau.

For each year, calculate the percentage of all people who were uninsured and the percentage of poor children who were uninsured. How have these percentages changed over time? What is a possible explanation for the change in the percentage of uninsured poor children?

9. The American National Election Studies conducts periodic research on the opinions of U.S. voters. The accompanying table shows the percentage of people, in selected years from 1952 to 2012, who agreed with the statement "There are important differences in what the Republicans and Democrats stand for." What do these data say about the degree of partisanship in U.S. politics over time?

Year	Agree with statement
1952	50%
1972	46
1992	60
2004	76
2008	78
2012	81

Data from: American National Election Studies.

10. For this Discovering Data exercise, go to FRED (fred.stlouisfed.org) to create a line graph that compares poverty rates for different counties across the United States. In the search bar enter "Estimated Percent of People of All Ages in Poverty for United States" and select the subsequent series. Follow the steps below to add the series for additional counties. Then answer the questions that follow.

   I. Select "Edit Graph" and under "Add Line" enter "Estimated Percent of People in Poverty for Wayne County, MI," which includes Detroit, Michigan.

   II. Repeat step I to add the following counties:
      i. King County, WA (for Seattle, Washington)
      ii. Miami-Dade County, FL (for Miami, Florida)
      iii. San Francisco County/City, CA (for San Francisco, California)
      iv. Cuyahoga County, OH (for Cleveland, Ohio)

   III. In the graph frame change the start date to 1997-01-01 and the end date to 2014-01-01.
      a. Which counties have the lowest poverty rates? Highest? How do poverty rates compare to the national average?
      b. How has the difference in poverty rates changed from 2004 (prior to the Great Recession) to 2012 (after the Great Recession)?
      c. Create a second line graph including "Estimated Percent of People of All Ages in Poverty for United States" and a second line with your home county. How does the poverty rate in your home county compare with that of the national average?

11. In a private insurance market, there are two different kinds of people: some who are more likely to require expensive medical treatment and some who are less likely to require medical treatment and who, if they do require treatment, require less expensive treatment. One health insurance policy is offered, tailored to the average person's health care needs: the premium is equal to the average person's medical expenses (plus the insurer's expenses and normal profit).

   a. Explain why such an insurance policy is unlikely to be feasible.

   In an effort to avoid the adverse selection death spiral, a private health insurer offers two health insurance policies: one that is intended for those who are more likely to require expensive treatment (and therefore the insurer charges a higher premium) and one that is intended for those who are less likely to require treatment (and therefore the insurer charges a lower premium).

   b. Could this system overcome the problem created by adverse selection?

   c. How does the British National Health Service avoid these problems?

The federal Energy Information Administration estimates that nearly 95% of all new power capacity installed in the United States in 2017 came from *renewables*. These are natural resources that are not depleted upon use, making them inexhaustible. Solar and wind power are two examples. But in 2017, long-standing federal subsidies for renewable energy were at risk as Congress debated whether to cut them.

Historically, renewables have been more expensive than fossil fuel, and subsidies have been critical in bringing cost down to consumers. However, fossil fuel industry backers claim that the cost of renewables have fallen so low that the subsidies to renewables unfairly undercut them.

Will the threat to end subsidies stall the meteoric rise of renewable energy, and lead the economy to return to fossil fuel sources?

Benjamin Fowke, the CEO of Xcel Energy, thinks not and is undeterred. Trained in finance and accounting, it's safe to say that he is no starry-eyed dreamer. Xcel Energy has announced that across its eight-state system, 60% of its energy will be generated by renewables, and its carbon emissions will be reduced by 80% by 2030.

Fowke is positioning Xcel Energy to take advantage of the "learning curve" associated with the cost of renewable energy. *Learning curve* is the term used to describe the dramatic fall in costs that is often achieved after a new technology is introduced—adoption of the new technology spreads because scientists, innovators, and manufacturers get better at exploiting it. A "virtuous cycle" is generated as costs fall and adoption of the new technology increases, spurring further investment and additional reductions in costs.

An example is solar energy: the price to consumers of a watt of solar energy has dropped by nearly 88% since 1998. The learning curve has been steepest in the last decade, with solar prices dropping by 70%. In the case of wind energy, prices have dropped 90% since 1980.

According to Fowke, it is now cheaper to build new wind turbines than to operate its lowest-cost existing coal plants. For example, in 2017 Xcel purchased wind energy at a cost of $15 to $20 per megawatt-hour, compared to $25 to $35 for natural-gas-generated power, the main energy source competing with renewables.

Unsurprisingly, competition with conventional fossil fuel producers encourages the solar and wind industries, along with producers of other renewables, to keep improving their product and prices to stay ahead of the competition.

QUESTIONS FOR THOUGHT

1. Explain how subsidies affect the future adoption of a new technology that is subject to steep learning curve effects. Relate this to the role of government intervention when externalities are present.

2. Is Fowke right or wrong to persist in the adoption of renewables when federal subsidies are under threat? Analyze the investment decision that a CEO like Fowke must make when deciding whether and when to invest more capacity in renewables instead of in fossil fuel sources.

3. How does this case illustrate the way in which business and government can work together in a market economy?

In 2016, Stinson Dean faced a critical decision. A savvy trader employed by a firm that traded lumber as a commodity, Dean could see that the lumber market was ripe for a dramatic upswing as the home construction industry recovered from the housing bust. Yet to personally profit from that upswing, he would have to quit his job and open his own firm.

But becoming an entrepreneur carried significant risk. By going out on his own, he would have to sacrifice the employer-provided health insurance that covered him, his wife, and their three young children. In making his decision, Dean declared: "One of the things I wasn't willing to risk was the health of my family." In fact, the tendency of workers to stay in a job that they would rather leave for fear of losing their health care benefits is so pervasive that economists have a term for it: *job lock*.

In the end, Dean made the jump because he was able to purchase affordable health insurance for himself and his family through the ACA. And the move paid off as the surge in home construction boosted Dean's business far beyond his expectations. In fact, business was so good that, by 2017, Dean wanted to expand and hire three or four new people. However, by that time Congressional threats to repeal the ACA generated a stumbling block not only to his expansion plans, but to his future as an entrepreneur in the long run.

"What that's doing for me is preventing me to convince folks who are in a similar situation to where I was—a nice corporate job, making good money, with great benefits, with kids—convincing them to leave that to come to work for me with no benefits," he says. As a result, in 2017, Dean was having trouble convincing others to take a chance and come work for him. Moreover, he wondered whether he would eventually be forced to close his firm and resume his corporate job in order to assure health insurance for his family.

QUESTIONS FOR THOUGHT

1. A recent study of employees with chronic health conditions who have employer-provided health care coverage found that these workers were 40% less likely to leave their jobs than similar employees without chronic health conditions. A RAND Corporation study found that making health insurance more accessible to individuals could increase self-employment and entrepreneurship in the United States by a third. What pattern would you expect to see in the size and number of newly created companies after the implementation of the ACA compared to before?

2. Historically, small businesses and entrepreneurs have been more innovative than larger companies. What does this imply for the rate of innovation in the United States before implementation of the ACA? After? And what would you expect now that the ACA has come under threat?

GREEK TRAGEDIES

IN THE SUMMER OF 2015, 28-year-old Christina Tsimpida was ready to give up on her native country. The Athens lawyer's office where she worked had shut, laying off all its employees; and, despite being highly qualified, she had no leads on where to find another job. She was not alone: in 2015, very few young Greeks were able to get jobs of any kind. The Greek *unemployment rate*— the percentage of Greeks seeking work who had been unable to find it—averaged 25% in 2015, and the unemployment rate among young workers exceeded 45%.

Yet it wasn't always like that. In the mid-2000s, Greek unemployment was only a third as high as it was in 2015, and someone with Tsimpida's education would have been virtually assured of a job. But then Greece plunged into a severe economic downturn, a *recession,* which led to a collapse in employment. Many businesses went bust and a great number of people suffered economic hardship. And Greece wasn't alone. Much of the world, including the United States, plunged into a deep recession after 2007, which came to be known as the *Great Recession.* By 2015 the United States had mostly recovered, but much of Europe had not.

Yet, as bad as things were during the Great Recession, the global economy had seen much worse. Beginning in 1929, a severe global economic slump known as the *Great Depression* hit and lasted over a decade, until the start of World War II in 1940. The Great Recession was less severe than the Great Depression for many reasons. But one significant factor was that economists had learned something about what to do from the earlier catastrophe. As the Great Depression began in 1929, political leaders and their economic advisers had no idea what policies might help or hinder recovery.

Microeconomics, which is concerned with the consumption and production decisions of individual consumers and producers and with the allocation of scarce resources among industries, was already a well-developed branch of economics. But *macroeconomics,* which focuses on the behavior of the economy as a whole, was still in its infancy. In contrast, by 2007 macroeconomics had advanced enough that economists knew what needed to be done when the Great Recession hit.

In normal economic times, when there is no recession or depression, workers who lose their jobs are able to find employment somewhere else. However, the Great Depression was no normal time: in the United States the unemployment rate hit 25% and the value of the economy's output (GDP) fell by 26%. Economists realized that they needed to understand the nature of the catastrophe that had overtaken the United States and much of the rest of the world in order to extricate themselves, as well as to learn how to avoid such economic disasters in the future. To this day, the effort to understand economic slumps and find ways to prevent them is at the core of macroeconomics. Over time, however, macroeconomics has broadened its reach to encompass a number of other subjects, such as long-run economic growth, inflation, and international macroeconomics.

This chapter offers an overview of macroeconomics. We start with a general description of the difference between macroeconomics and microeconomics, then briefly describe some of the field's major concerns. ●

WHAT YOU WILL LEARN

- What is the difference between macroeconomics and microeconomics?

- What are **business cycles** and why do policy makers try to diminish their severity?

- How does **long-run economic growth** determine a country's standard of living?

- What are **inflation** and **deflation,** and why is **price stability** preferred?

- Why does international macroeconomics matter, and how do economies interact through **trade deficits** and **trade surpluses**?

The Nature of Macroeconomics

Macroeconomics differs from microeconomics by focusing on the behavior of the economy as a whole.

Macroeconomic Questions

Table 12-1 lists some typical economic questions from the perspectives of microeconomists in the left column, and macroeconomists in the right column. By comparing the questions, you can begin to get a sense of the difference between microeconomics and macroeconomics.

As these questions illustrate, microeconomics focuses on how decisions are made by individuals and firms and the consequences of those decisions. For example, we use microeconomics to determine how much it would cost a university or college to offer a new course, including the instructor's salary, the cost of class materials, and so on. The school can then decide whether to offer the course by weighing the costs and benefits.

TABLE 12-1 Microeconomic versus Macroeconomic Questions

Microeconomic Questions	Macroeconomic Questions
Should I go to business school or take a job right now?	How many people are employed in the economy as a whole this year?
What determines the salary Google offers to Cherie Camajo, a new MBA?	What determines the overall salary levels paid to workers in a given year?
What determines the cost to a university or college of offering a new course?	What determines the overall level of prices in the economy as a whole?
What government policies should be adopted to make it easier for low-income students to attend college?	What government policies should be adopted to promote employment and growth in the economy as a whole?
What determines whether Citibank opens a new office in Shanghai?	What determines the overall trade in goods, services, and financial assets between the United States and the rest of the world?

Macroeconomics, in contrast, examines the *overall* behavior of the economy—how the actions of all the individuals and firms in the economy interact to produce a particular economy-wide level of economic performance. For example, macroeconomics is concerned with the general level of prices in the economy and how high or how low that level is relative to the general level of prices last year, rather than with the price of one particular good or service.

You might imagine that macroeconomic questions can be answered simply by adding up microeconomic answers. For example, the model of supply and demand introduced in Chapter 3 tells us how the equilibrium price of an individual good or service is determined in a competitive market. So you might think, then, that applying supply and demand analysis to every good and service in the economy, then summing the results, is the way to understand the overall level of prices in the economy as a whole.

But that is incorrect: although basic concepts such as supply and demand are essential to macroeconomics, answering macroeconomic questions requires an additional set of tools and an expanded frame of reference.

Macroeconomics: The Whole Is Greater Than the Sum of Its Parts

If you drive on a highway, you probably know what a rubber-necking traffic jam is and why it is so annoying. Someone pulls over to the side of the road, perhaps to fix a flat tire, and, pretty soon, a long traffic jam occurs as drivers slow down to take a look.

What makes it so annoying is that the length of the traffic jam is greatly out of proportion to the minor event that precipitated it. Because some drivers hit their brakes in order to rubber-neck, the drivers behind them must also hit their brakes, those behind them must do the same, and so on. The accumulation of all the individual hitting of brakes eventually leads to a long, wasteful traffic jam as each driver slows down a little bit more than the driver ahead. In other words, each person's response leads to an amplified response by the next person.

Just as individual actions on the road can unintentionally lead to a traffic jam, individual actions in the economy can produce an unintended macroeconomic effect.

Understanding rubber-necking gives us some insight into one very important way in which macroeconomics differs from microeconomics: many thousands or millions of individual actions compound upon one another to produce an outcome that isn't simply the sum of those individual actions.

Consider, for example, what macroeconomists call the *paradox of thrift:* when households and businesses are worried about the possibility of economic hard times, they prepare by cutting their spending. This reduction in spending depresses the economy as consumers spend less and businesses react by laying off workers. As a result, families and businesses may end up worse off than if they hadn't tried to act responsibly by cutting their spending.

This is a paradox because seemingly virtuous behavior—preparing for hard times by saving more—ends up harming everyone. The flip-side to this story is that when families and businesses are feeling optimistic about the future, they spend more today. This stimulates the economy, leading businesses to hire more workers, which further expands the economy. Seemingly profligate behavior leads to good times for all.

A key insight of macroeconomics, then, is that the combined effect of individual decisions can have results that are very different from what any one individual intended, results that are sometimes perverse. The behavior of the macroeconomy is, indeed, greater than the sum of individual actions and market outcomes.

Macroeconomics: Theory and Policy

To a much greater extent than microeconomists, macroeconomists are concerned with questions about *policy,* about what the government can do to make macroeconomic performance better. This policy focus was strongly shaped by history, in particular by the Great Depression of the 1930s.

Before the 1930s, economists tended to regard the economy as **self-regulating:** they believed that problems such as unemployment would be corrected through the working of the invisible hand and that government attempts to improve the economy's performance would be ineffective at best—and would probably make things worse.

The Great Depression changed all that. The sheer scale of the catastrophe, which left a quarter of the U.S. workforce without jobs and threatened the political stability of many countries, created a demand for action. It also led to a major effort on the part of economists to understand economic slumps and find ways to prevent them.

In 1936 the British economist John Maynard Keynes (pronounced "canes") published *The General Theory of Employment, Interest, and Money*, a book that transformed macroeconomics. According to **Keynesian economics,** a depressed economy is the result of inadequate spending. In addition, Keynes argued that government intervention can help a depressed economy through *monetary policy* and *fiscal policy*. **Monetary policy** uses changes in the quantity of money to alter interest rates, which in turn affect the level of overall spending. **Fiscal policy** uses changes in taxes and government spending to affect overall spending.

In general, Keynes established the idea that managing the economy is a government responsibility. Keynesian ideas continue to have a strong influence on both economic theory and public policy: in 2008 and 2009, Congress, the White House, and the Federal Reserve (a quasi-governmental agency that manages U.S. monetary policy) took steps to fend off an economic slump that were clearly Keynesian in spirit, as described in the following Economics in Action.

> In a **self-regulating economy,** problems such as unemployment are resolved without government intervention, through the working of the invisible hand.
>
> According to **Keynesian economics,** economic slumps are caused by inadequate spending, and they can be mitigated by government intervention.
>
> **Monetary policy** uses changes in the quantity of money to alter interest rates and affect overall spending.
>
> **Fiscal policy** uses changes in government spending and taxes to affect overall spending.

ECONOMICS >> *in Action*
Fending Off Depression

In 2008 the world economy experienced a severe financial crisis reminiscent of the early days of the Great Depression. Major banks teetered on the edge of collapse and world trade slumped. In reviewing the 2009 data, the economic historians Barry

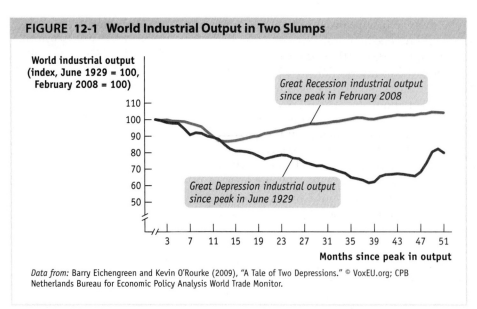

FIGURE 12-1 World Industrial Output in Two Slumps

Data from: Barry Eichengreen and Kevin O'Rourke (2009), "A Tale of Two Depressions." © VoxEU.org; CPB Netherlands Bureau for Economic Policy Analysis World Trade Monitor.

Eichengreen and Kevin O'Rourke pointed out that "globally we are tracking or doing even worse than the Great Depression."

But the worst did not, in the end, come to pass. Figure 12-1 shows one of Eichengreen and O'Rourke's measures of economic activity, world industrial production, during the Great Depression (the bottom line) and during the Great Recession (the top line). During the first year the two crises were indeed comparable. But fortunately, 11 months into the Great Recession, world production leveled off and turned around. In contrast, three years into the Great Depression world production continued to fall. Why the difference?

At least part of the answer is that policy makers responded very differently. During the Great Depression, it was widely argued that the slump should be allowed to run its course. Any attempt to mitigate the ongoing catastrophe, declared Joseph Schumpeter—the Austrian-born Harvard economist now famed for his work on innovation—would "leave the work of depressions undone." In the early 1930s, some countries' monetary authorities actually raised interest rates in the face of the slump, while governments cut spending and raised taxes—actions that deepened the recession.

In the aftermath of the 2008 crisis, by contrast, interest rates were slashed, and a number of countries, the United States included, used temporary increases in spending and reductions in taxes in an attempt to sustain spending. Governments also moved to shore up their banks with loans, aid, and guarantees.

Many of these measures were controversial, to say the least. But most economists believe that by responding actively to the Great Recession—and doing so using the knowledge gained from the study of macroeconomics—governments helped avoid a global economic catastrophe.

>> Check Your Understanding 12-1

Solutions appear at back of book.

1. Which of the following questions involve microeconomics, and which involve macroeconomics? In each case, explain your answer.
   a. Why did consumers switch to smaller cars in 2008?
   b. Why did overall consumer spending slow down in 2008?
   c. Why did the standard of living rise more rapidly in the first generation after World War II than in the second?
   d. Why have starting salaries for students with economics degrees risen sharply of late?
   e. What determines the choice between rail and road transportation?
   f. Why did laptops get much cheaper between 2000 and 2017?
   g. Why did inflation fall in the 2010s?

2. In 2008, problems in the financial sector led to a drying up of credit around the country: home-buyers were unable to get mortgages, students were unable to get student loans, car-buyers were unable to get car loans, and so on.
   a. Explain how the drying up of credit can lead to compounding effects throughout the economy and result in an economic slump.
   b. If you believe the economy is self-regulating, what would you advocate that policy makers do?
   c. If you believe in Keynesian economics, what would you advocate that policy makers do?

|| The Business Cycle

The Great Depression was by far the worst economic crisis in U.S. history. Although the economy managed to avoid catastrophe in the decades that followed, it has experienced many ups and downs.

It's true that the ups have consistently been bigger than the downs: a chart of any of the major numbers used to track the U.S. economy shows a strong upward trend over time. For example, panel (a) of Figure 12-2 shows total U.S. private-sector employment (the total number of jobs offered by private businesses) measured along the left vertical axis, with the data from 1985 to 2017 given by the purple line. The graph also shows the index of industrial production (a measure of the total output of U.S. factories) measured along the right vertical axis, with the data from 1985 to 2017 given by the red line. Both private-sector employment and industrial production were much higher at the end of this period than at the beginning, and in most years both measures rose.

But they didn't rise steadily. As you can see from the figure, there were three periods—in the early 1990s, in the early 2000s, and again beginning in late 2007—when both employment and industrial output stumbled. Panel (b) emphasizes these stumbles by showing the *rate of change* of employment and industrial production over the previous year. For example, the percent change in employment for October 2009 was –0.6 because employment in October 2009 was 0.6% lower than it had been in October 2008. The three big downturns stand out clearly.

What's more, a detailed look at the data makes it clear that in each period the stumble wasn't confined to only a few industries: in each downturn, just about every sector of the U.S. economy cut back on production and on the number of people employed.

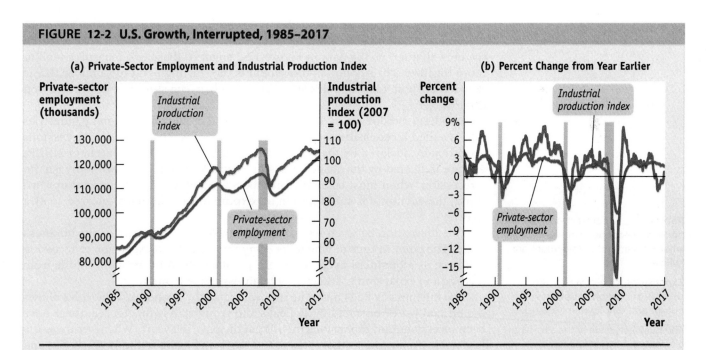

FIGURE 12-2 U.S. Growth, Interrupted, 1985–2017

(a) Private-Sector Employment and Industrial Production Index

(b) Percent Change from Year Earlier

Panel (a) shows two important economic numbers, the industrial production index and total private-sector employment. Both numbers grew substantially from 1985 to 2017, but they didn't grow steadily. Instead, both suffered from three downturns associated with recessions, which are indicated by the shaded areas in the figure. Panel (b) emphasizes those downturns by showing the annual rate of change of industrial production and employment, that is, the percentage increase over the past year. The simultaneous downturns in both numbers during the three recessions are clear.

Data from: Federal Reserve Bank of St. Louis.

FIGURE 12-3 The Business Cycle

This is a stylized picture of the business cycle. The vertical axis measures either employment or total output in the economy. Periods when these two variables turn down are *recessions*; periods when they turn up are *expansions*. The point at which the economy turns down is a *business-cycle peak*; the point at which it turns up again is a *business-cycle trough*.

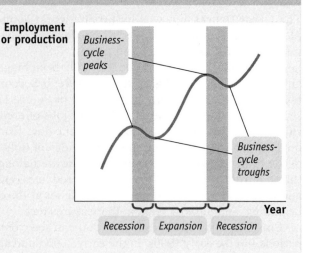

The economy's forward march, in other words, isn't smooth. And the uneven pace of the economy's progress, its ups and downs, is one of the main preoccupations of macroeconomics.

Charting the Business Cycle

Figure 12-3 shows a stylized representation of the way the economy evolves over time. The vertical axis shows either employment or an indicator of how much the economy is producing, such as industrial production or *real gross domestic product (real GDP)*, a measure of the economy's overall output that we'll learn about in the next chapter. As the data in Figure 12-2 suggest, these two measures tend to move together. Their common movement is the starting point for a major theme of macroeconomics: the economy's alternation between short-run downturns and upturns.

A widespread downturn, in which output and employment in many industries fall, is called a **recession** (sometimes referred to as a *contraction*). Recessions are officially declared by the National Bureau of Economic Research, or NBER, and are indicated by the shaded areas in Figure 12-3. When the economy isn't in a recession, when most economic numbers are following their normal upward trend, the economy is said to be in an **expansion** (sometimes referred to as a *recovery*).

Recessions, or contractions, are periods of economic downturn when output and employment are falling.

Expansions, or recoveries, are periods of economic upturn when output and employment are rising.

The **business cycle** is the short-run alternation between recessions and expansions.

The point at which the economy turns from expansion to recession is a **business-cycle peak.**

The point at which the economy turns from recession to expansion is a **business-cycle trough.**

The alternation between recessions and expansions is known as the **business cycle.** The point in time at which the economy shifts from expansion to recession is known as a **business-cycle peak;** the point at which the economy shifts from recession to expansion is known as a **business-cycle trough.**

The business cycle is an enduring feature of the economy. Table 12-2 shows the official list of business-cycle peaks and troughs. As you can see, there have been recessions and expansions for at least the past 160 years. Whenever there is a prolonged expansion, as there was in the 1960s and again in the 1990s, books and articles come out proclaiming the end of the business cycle. Such proclamations have always been proved wrong: the cycle always comes back.

The Pain of Recession

Not many people complain about the business cycle when the economy is expanding. Recessions, however, create a great deal of pain.

The most important effect of a recession is its effect on the ability of workers to find and hold jobs. The most widely used indicator of conditions in the labor market is the *unemployment rate*. We'll explain how that rate is calculated in Chapter 14, but for now it's enough to say that a high unemployment rate tells us that jobs are scarce and a low unemployment rate tells us that jobs are easy to find.

Figure 12-4 shows the unemployment rate from 1988 to early 2019. As you can see, the U.S. unemployment rate surged during and after each recession but eventually fell during periods of expansion. The rising unemployment rate in 2008 was a sign that a new recession might be under way, which was later confirmed by the NBER to have begun in December 2007.

Because recessions cause many people to lose their jobs and make it hard to find new ones, they reduce the standard of living of households across the country. Recessions are usually associated with a rise in the number of people living below the poverty line, an increase in the number of people who lose their homes because they can't afford the mortgage payments, and a fall in the percentage of Americans with health insurance coverage.

But workers are not the only group that suffers during a recession. Recessions are also bad for firms: profits fall during recessions, and many small businesses fail.

All in all, then, recessions are bad for almost everyone. Can anything be done to reduce their frequency and severity?

Taming the Business Cycle

Modern macroeconomics largely came into being as a response to the worst recession in history—the 43-month downturn that began in 1929 and continued into 1933, ushering in the Great Depression. The havoc wreaked by the 1929–1933 recession spurred economists to search both for understanding and for solutions: they wanted to know how such things could happen and how to prevent them.

As explained earlier, the work of John Maynard Keynes suggested that monetary and fiscal policies could be used to mitigate the effects

TABLE 12-2 The History of the Business Cycle

Business-Cycle Peak	Business-Cycle Trough
no prior data available	December 1854
June 1857	December 1858
October 1860	June 1861
April 1865	December 1867
June 1869	December 1870
October 1873	March 1879
March 1882	May 1885
March 1887	April 1888
July 1890	May 1891
January 1893	June 1894
December 1895	June 1897
June 1899	December 1900
September 1902	August 1904
May 1907	June 1908
January 1910	January 1912
January 1913	December 1914
August 1918	March 1919
January 1920	July 1921
May 1923	July 1924
October 1926	November 1927
August 1929	March 1933
May 1937	June 1938
February 1945	October 1945
November 1948	October 1949
July 1953	May 1954
August 1957	April 1958
April 1960	February 1961
December 1969	November 1970
November 1973	March 1975
January 1980	July 1980
July 1981	November 1982
July 1990	March 1991
March 2001	November 2001
December 2007	June 2009

Data from: National Bureau of Economic Research.

FIGURE 12-4 The U.S. Unemployment Rate, 1987–2019

The unemployment rate, a measure of joblessness, rises sharply during recessions and usually falls during expansions.

Data from: Bureau of Labor Statistics.

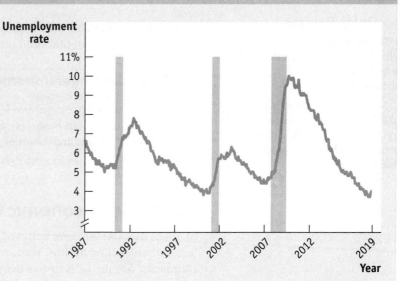

"I can't move in with my parents. They moved in with my grandparents."

of recessions, and to this day governments turn to Keynesian policies when recession strikes. Later work, notably that of another great macroeconomist, Milton Friedman, led to a consensus that it's important to rein in booms as well as to fight slumps. So modern policy makers try to "smooth out" the business cycle. They haven't been completely successful, as a look back at Figure 12-2 makes clear. It's widely believed, however, that policy guided by macroeconomic analysis has helped make the economy more stable.

Although the business cycle has historically played a crucial role in fostering development of the field, macroeconomists are also concerned with other issues, such as long-run growth, inflation, deflation, and international imbalances, which we examine next.

ECONOMICS >> *in Action*
Comparing Recessions

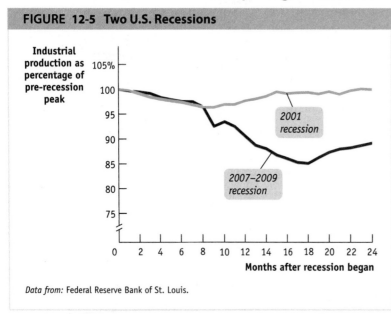

FIGURE 12-5 Two U.S. Recessions

Industrial production as percentage of pre-recession peak

Data from: Federal Reserve Bank of St. Louis.

The alternation of recessions and expansions seems to be an enduring feature of economic life. However, not all business cycles are created equal. In particular, some recessions have been much worse than others.

Let's compare the two most recent U.S. recessions: the 2001 recession and the Great Recession of 2007–2009. These recessions differed in duration: the first lasted only eight months, the second more than twice as long. Even more important, however, they differed greatly in depth.

In Figure 12-5 we compare the depth of the recessions by looking at what happened to industrial production over the months after the recession began. In each case, production is measured as a percentage of its level at the recession's start. Thus the line for the 2007–2009 recession shows that industrial production eventually fell to about 85% of its initial level.

Clearly, the 2007–2009 recession hit the economy vastly harder than the 2001 recession. Indeed, by comparison to many recessions, the 2001 slump was very mild.

Of course, this was no consolation to the millions of American workers who lost their jobs, even in that mild recession.

>> *Check Your Understanding* 12-2
Solutions appear at back of book.

1. Why do we talk about business cycles for the economy as a whole, rather than just talking about the ups and downs of particular industries?

2. Describe who gets hurt in a recession, and how.

Long-Run Economic Growth

In 1960, most Americans believed, rightly, that they were better off than the citizens of any other nation, past or present. Yet they were quite poor by today's standards. Figure 12-6 shows the percentage of American homes equipped with selected appliances in 1960 and 2011. In 1960 only a minority of households had a washing machine, very few had air conditioning, and of course nobody had smartphones or computers. And, if we turn the clock back to, say, 1900, we find that life for many Americans was startlingly primitive by today's standards.

Why are the vast majority of Americans today able to afford conveniences that many Americans lacked in 1960? The answer is **long-run economic growth,** the sustained rise in the quantity of goods and services the economy produces. Figure 12-7 shows estimates of *real GDP per capita*, a measure of total output per person, for two countries—the United States and the United Kingdom—for selected years going back to the Middle Ages. Both countries have experienced an enormous long-run rise in production per person, dwarfing the ups and downs of the business cycle.

Two points are, however, worth noting:

1. Long-run economic growth is a modern invention: the United Kingdom wasn't any richer in 1650 than it was two centuries earlier, and overall world incomes didn't start rising until around 1890.

2. Countries don't necessarily grow at the same rate. The United Kingdom was once substantially richer than the United States, but was overtaken by a rapidly growing America after 1875.

Long-run economic growth is fundamental to many of the most pressing economic questions today. Responses to key policy questions, such as the country's ability to bear the future costs of government programs such as Social Security and Medicare, depend in part on how fast the U.S. economy grows over the next few decades.

More broadly, the public's sense that the country is making progress depends crucially on success in achieving long-run growth. When growth slows, as it did in the 1970s, it can help generate a national mood of pessimism. In particular, *long-run growth per capita*—a sustained upward trend in output per person—is the key to higher wages and a rising standard of living. A major concern of macroeconomics—and the theme of Chapter 15—is trying to understand the forces behind long-run growth.

Long-run growth is an even more urgent concern in poorer, less developed countries. In these countries, which would like to achieve a higher standard of living, the question of how to accelerate long-run growth is the central concern of economic policy.

As we'll see, macroeconomists don't use the same models to think about long-run growth that they use to think about the business cycle. It's important to keep both sets of models in mind, because what is good in the long run can be bad in the short run, and vice versa. For example, we've already mentioned the paradox of thrift: an attempt by households to increase their savings can cause a recession. But a higher level of savings plays a crucial role in encouraging long-run economic growth.

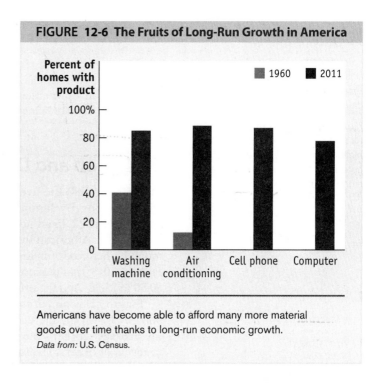

FIGURE 12-6 The Fruits of Long-Run Growth in America

Americans have become able to afford many more material goods over time thanks to long-run economic growth.

Data from: U.S. Census.

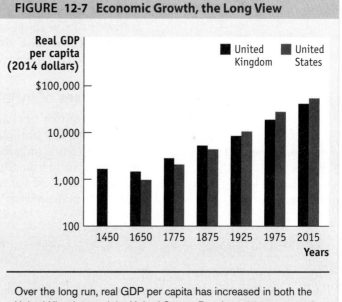

FIGURE 12-7 Economic Growth, the Long View

Over the long run, real GDP per capita has increased in both the United Kingdom and the United States. For about 300 years, real GDP per capita was greater in the United Kingdom. But early in the twentieth century, the United States surpassed the United Kingdom, becoming the richer country.

Data from: Maddison Data Project, Revision 2018.

Long-run economic growth is the sustained upward trend in the economy's output over time.

>> Check Your Understanding 12-3
Solutions appear at back of book.

1. Many poor countries have high rates of population growth. What does this imply about the long-run growth rates of overall output that they must achieve in order to generate a higher standard of living per person?

Inflation and Deflation

In January 1980 the average production worker in the United States was paid $6.61 an hour. By January 2018, the average hourly earnings for such a worker had risen to $22.45 an hour. Three cheers for economic progress!

But wait. American workers were paid much more in 2018, but they also faced a much higher cost of living. In January 1980, a dozen eggs cost only about $0.88; by January 2018, that was up to $1.77. The price of a loaf of white bread went from about $0.50 to $1.28. And the price of a gallon of gasoline rose from just $1.13 to $2.54.

Figure 12-8 compares the percentage increase in hourly earnings between 1980 and 2018 with the increases in the prices of some standard items. As you can see, the average worker's paycheck went farther in terms of some goods, but less far in terms of others. Overall, the 220% rise in the cost of living from 1980 to 2018 wiped out almost all of the wage gains of the typical American worker during that period. In other words, once inflation is taken into account, the living standard of the typical American worker barely rose from 1980 to the present.

The point is that between 1980 and 2018 the economy experienced substantial **inflation:** a rise in the overall level of prices. Understanding the causes of inflation and its opposite, **deflation**—a fall in the overall level of prices—is another main concern of macroeconomics.

The Causes of Inflation and Deflation

You might think that changes in the overall level of prices are just a matter of supply and demand. For example, higher gasoline prices reflect the higher price of crude oil, and higher crude oil prices reflect such factors as the exhaustion of major oil fields, growing demand from China and other emerging economies as more people grow rich enough to buy cars, and so on. But we can't just add up what happens in each of these markets to find out what happens to the overall level of prices.

A rising overall level of prices is **inflation.**

A falling overall level of prices is **deflation.**

FIGURE 12-8 Rising Prices

Between 1980 and 2018, American workers' hourly earnings rose by 240%. But the prices of just about all the goods bought by workers also rose, some by more, some by less. Overall, the rising cost of living offset most of the rise in the average U.S. worker's wage.

Data from: Bureau of Labor Statistics.

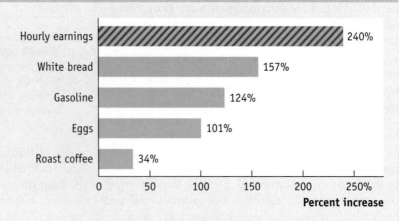

Supply and demand can only explain why a particular good or service becomes more expensive *relative to other goods and services*. It can't explain why, for example, the price of chicken has risen over time in spite of the fact that chicken production has become more efficient and that chicken has become substantially cheaper compared to other goods.

What causes the overall level of prices to rise or fall? As we'll learn in Chapter 14, in the short run, movements in inflation are closely related to the business cycle. When the economy is depressed and jobs are hard to find, inflation tends to fall; when the economy is booming, inflation tends to rise. For example, prices of most goods and services fell sharply during the terrible recession of 1929–1933.

In the long run, by contrast, the overall level of prices is mainly determined by changes in the money supply, the total quantity of assets that can be readily used to make purchases.

> The economy has **price stability** when the overall level of prices changes slowly or not at all.

The Pain of Inflation and Deflation

Both inflation and deflation can pose problems for the economy. Let's look at two examples:

First, inflation discourages people from holding onto cash, because cash loses value over time if the overall price level is rising. That is, the amount of goods and services you can buy with a given amount of cash falls. In extreme cases, people stop holding cash altogether and turn to barter.

Second, deflation can cause the reverse problem. If the price level is falling, cash gains value over time. In other words, the amount of goods and services you can buy with a given amount of cash increases. So, holding on to cash becomes more attractive than investing in new factories and other productive assets. This can deepen a recession.

We'll describe other costs of inflation and deflation in Chapters 13 and 14. For now, let's just note that, in general, economists regard **price stability**—in which the overall level of prices is changing, if at all, only slowly—as a desirable goal. Price stability is a goal that seemed far out of reach for much of the American economy during the post–World War II period. However, from the 1990s to the present, it has been achieved to the satisfaction of most macroeconomists.

ECONOMICS >> *in Action*
A Fast (Food) Measure of Inflation

The original McDonald's opened in 1948. It offered fast service—it was, indeed, the original fast-food restaurant. And it was also very inexpensive: hamburgers cost $0.15, $0.25 with fries. By 2018, a hamburger at a typical McDonald's cost more than six times as much, about $1.00. Has McDonald's lost touch with its fast-food roots? Have burgers become luxury cuisine?

No—in fact, compared with other consumer goods, a burger is a better bargain today than it was in 1948. Burger prices were about 6.5 times as high in 2018 as they were in 1948. But the consumer price index, the most widely used measure of the cost of living, was about 10 times as high in 2018 as it was in 1948.

Even though a burger costs six times more than it did when McDonald's first opened, it's still a good bargain compared to other consumer goods.

>> Quick Review

- A dollar today doesn't buy what it did in 1980, because the prices of most goods have risen. This rise in the overall price level has wiped out most if not all of the wage increases received by the typical American worker over the past 40 years.

- One area of macroeconomic study is in the overall level of prices. Because either **inflation** or **deflation** can cause problems for the economy, economists typically advocate maintaining **price stability.**

An **open economy** is an economy that trades goods and services with other countries.

A country runs a **trade deficit** when the value of goods and services bought from foreigners is more than the value of goods and services it sells to them. It runs a **trade surplus** when the value of goods and services bought from foreigners is less than the value of the goods and services it sells to them.

>> Check Your Understanding 12-4
Solutions appear at back of book.

1. Which of these sound like inflation, which sound like deflation, and which are ambiguous?
   a. Gasoline prices are up 10%, food prices are down 20%, and the prices of most services are up 1–2%.
   b. Gas prices have doubled, food prices are up 50%, and most services seem to be up 5% or 10%.
   c. Gas prices haven't changed, food prices are way down, and services have gotten cheaper, too.

International Imbalances

The United States is an **open economy:** an economy that trades goods and services with other countries. There have been times when that trade was more or less balanced—when the United States sold about as much to the rest of the world as it bought. But this isn't one of those times.

In 2018, the United States ran a big **trade deficit**—that is, the value of the goods and services U.S. residents bought from the rest of the world was a lot larger than the value of the goods and services American producers sold to foreign residents. Meanwhile, some other countries were in the opposite position, selling much more to foreigners than they bought.

Figure 12-9 shows the exports and imports of goods for three important economies in 2017. As you can see, the United States imported much more than it exported, but Germany and China did the reverse: they each ran a **trade surplus.** A country runs a trade surplus when the value of the goods and services it buys from the rest of the world is smaller than the value of the goods and services it sells abroad.

Was America's trade deficit a sign that something was wrong with our economy—that we weren't able to make things that people in other countries wanted to buy? No, not really. Trade deficits and their opposite, trade surpluses, are macroeconomic phenomena. They're the result of situations in which the whole is very different from the sum of its parts. You might think that countries with highly productive workers or widely desired products and services to sell run trade surpluses and countries with unproductive workers or poor-quality products and services run deficits. But the reality is that there's no simple relationship between the success of an economy and whether it runs trade surpluses or deficits.

FIGURE 12-9 Unbalanced Trade

In 2017, the goods and services the United States bought from the other countries were worth considerably more than the goods and services we sold abroad. Germany and China were in the reverse position. Trade deficits and trade surpluses reflect macroeconomic forces, especially differences in savings and investment spending.

Data from: Organization of Economics Co-operation Development.

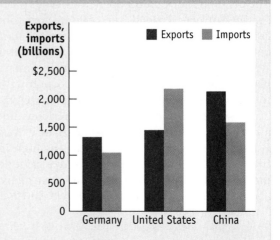

In Chapter 2 we learned that international trade is the result of comparative advantage: countries export goods they're relatively good at producing and import goods they're not as good at producing. That's why the United States exports wheat and imports coffee. What the concept of comparative advantage doesn't explain, however, is why the value of a country's imports is sometimes much larger than the value of its exports, or vice versa.

So, what does determine whether a country runs a trade surplus or a trade deficit? In Chapter 20 we'll learn the surprising answer: the determinants of the overall balance between exports and imports lie in decisions about savings and investment spending—spending on goods like machinery and factories that are in turn used to produce goods and services for consumers. Countries with high investment spending relative to savings run trade deficits; countries with low investment spending relative to savings run trade surpluses.

ECONOMICS >> *in Action*
Greece's Costly Surplus

In 1999 Greece took a momentous step: it gave up its national currency, the drachma, in order to adopt the euro, a shared currency intended to promote closer economic and political union among the nations of Europe. How did this affect Greece's international trade?

Figure 12-10 shows Greece's current account balance—a broad definition of its trade balance—from 1999 to 2017. A negative current account balance, as shown here, means the country is running a trade deficit. As you can see, after Greece switched to the euro it began running large trade deficits, which at their peak equaled almost 16% of the total value of goods and services Greece produced. After 2008, however, the trade deficit began shrinking rapidly, and by 2013 Greece was running a small surplus.

Did this mean that Greece's economy was doing badly in the mid-2000s, and better thereafter? Just the opposite. When Greece adopted the euro, foreign investors became highly optimistic about its prospects, and money poured into the country, fueling rapid economic expansion. Unfortunately, this optimism eventually evaporated, and the inflows of foreign capital dried up. One consequence was that Greece could no longer run large trade deficits, and by 2013 it was forced into running a surplus. Another consequence was a severe recession, leading to very high unemployment—including the unemployment of Christina Tsimpida, the jobless graduate described at the start of this chapter.

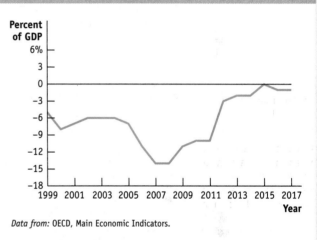

FIGURE 12-10 Greece's Current Account Balance, 1999–2017

Data from: OECD, Main Economic Indicators.

>> *Check Your Understanding* 12-5
Solutions appear at back of book.

1. Which of the following reflect comparative advantage, and which reflect macroeconomic forces?
   a. Thanks to the development of huge oil sands in the province of Alberta, Canada has become an exporter of oil and an importer of manufactured goods.
   b. Like many consumer goods, the Apple iPad is assembled in China, although many of the components are made in other countries.
   c. Since 2002, Germany has been running huge trade surpluses, exporting much more than it imports.
   d. The United States, which had roughly balanced trade in the early 1990s, began running large trade deficits later in the decade, as the technology boom took off.

>> *Quick Review*

• Comparative advantage can explain why an **open economy** exports some goods and services and imports others, but it can't explain why a country imports more than it exports, or vice versa.

• **Trade deficits** and **trade surpluses** are macroeconomic phenomena, determined by decisions about investment spending and savings.

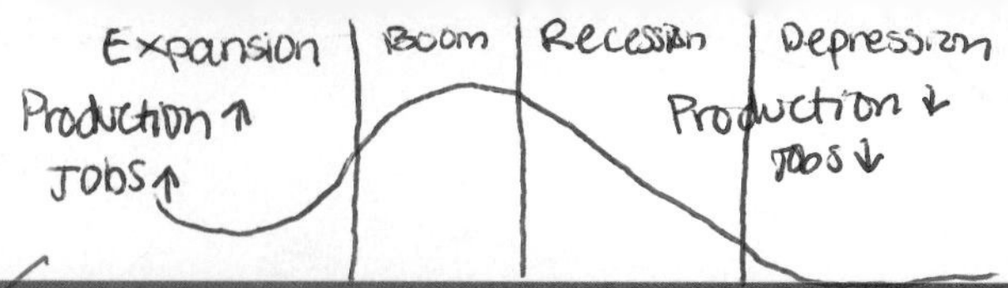

Handwritten annotations at top of page:

Expansion | Boom | Recession | Depression
Production ↑ | | | Production ↓
Jobs ↑ | | | Jobs ↓

SUMMARY

1. Macroeconomics is the study of the behavior of the economy as a whole, which can be different from the sum of its parts. Macroeconomics differs from microeconomics in the type of questions it tries to answer. Macroeconomics also has a strong policy focus: **Keynesian economics,** which emerged during the Great Depression, advocates the use of **monetary policy** and **fiscal policy** to fight economic slumps. Prior to the Great Depression, the economy was thought to be **self-regulating.**

2. One key concern of macroeconomics is the **business cycle,** the short-run alternation between **recessions,** periods of falling employment and output, and **expansions,** periods of rising employment and output. The point at which expansion turns to recession is a **business-cycle peak.** The point at which recession turns to expansion is a **business-cycle trough.**

3. Another key area of macroeconomic study is **long-run economic growth,** the sustained upward trend in the economy's output over time. Long-run economic growth is the force behind long-term increases in living standards and is important for financing some economic programs. It is especially important for poorer countries.

4. When the prices of most goods and services are rising, so that the overall level of prices is going up, the economy experiences **inflation.** When the overall level of prices is going down, the economy is experiencing **deflation.** In the short run, inflation and deflation are closely related to the business cycle. In the long run, prices tend to reflect changes in the overall quantity of money. Because both inflation and deflation can cause problems, economists and policy makers generally aim for **price stability.**

5. Although comparative advantage explains why **open economies** export some things and import others, macroeconomic analysis is needed to explain why countries run **trade surpluses** or **trade deficits.** The determinants of the overall balance between exports and imports lie in decisions about savings and investment spending.

KEY TERMS

Self-regulating economy, p. 343
Keynesian economics, p. 343
Monetary policy, p. 343
Fiscal policy, p. 343
Recession, p. 346
Expansion, p. 346

Business cycle, p. 346
Business-cycle peak, p. 346
Business-cycle trough, p. 346
Long-run economic growth, p. 349
Inflation, p. 350
Deflation, p. 350

Price stability, p. 351
Open economy, p. 352
Trade deficit, p. 352
Trade surplus, p. 352

DISCUSSION QUESTIONS

interactive activity

1. The U.S. Department of Labor reports statistics on employment and earnings that are used as key indicators by many economists to gauge the health of the economy. Figure 12-4 plots historical data on the unemployment rate each month. Noticeably, the numbers were high during the recessions in the early 1990s, in 2001, and in the aftermath of the Great Recession.

   a. Locate the latest data on the national unemployment rate. (*Hint:* Go to the Bureau of Labor Statistics at www.bls.gov; in the search bar enter "Employment Situation Summary" and select the subsequent page.)

   b. Compare the current numbers with those during the early 1990s, 2001, and during 2008–2017, as well as with the periods of relatively high economic growth just before the recessions. Are the current numbers indicative of a recessionary trend?

2. In the 1990s there were some dramatic economic events that came to be known as the *Asian financial crisis.* A decade later similar events came to be known as the *global financial crisis.* The accompanying figure shows the growth rate of real GDP in the United States and Japan from 1995 to 2014. Using the graph, explain why the two sets of events are referred to this way.

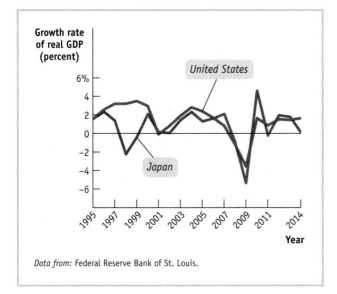

Data from: Federal Reserve Bank of St. Louis.

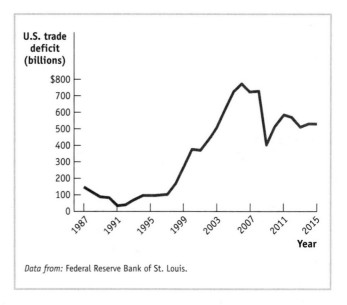

Data from: Federal Reserve Bank of St. Louis.

3. The accompanying figure illustrates the trade deficit of the United States since 1987. The United States has been consistently and, on the whole, increasingly importing more goods than it has been exporting. One of the countries it runs a trade deficit with is China. Which of the following statements are valid possible explanations of this fact? Explain.

a. Many products, such as televisions, that were formerly manufactured in the United States are now manufactured in China.

b. The wages of the average Chinese worker are far lower than the wages of the average American worker.

c. Investment spending in the United States is high relative to its level of savings.

PROBLEMS

interactive activity

1. Which of the following questions are relevant for the study of macroeconomics and which for microeconomics?

a. How will Ms. Martin's tips change when a large manufacturing plant near the restaurant where she works closes?

b. What will happen to spending by consumers when the economy enters a downturn?

c. How will the price of oranges change when a late frost damages Florida's orange groves?

d. How will wages at a manufacturing plant change when its workforce is unionized?

e. What will happen to U.S. exports as the dollar becomes less expensive in terms of other currencies?

f. What is the relationship between a nation's unemployment rate and its inflation rate?

2. When one person saves more, that person's wealth is increased, meaning that he or she can consume more in the future. But when everyone saves more, everyone's income falls, meaning that everyone must consume less today. Explain this seeming contradiction.

3. Before the Great Depression, the conventional wisdom among economists and policy makers was that the economy is largely self-regulating.

a. Is this view consistent or inconsistent with Keynesian economics? Explain.

b. What effect did the Great Depression have on conventional wisdom?

c. Contrast the response of policy makers during the 2007–2009 recession to the actions of policy makers during the Great Depression. What would have been the likely outcome of the 2007–2009 recession if policy makers had responded in the same fashion as policy makers during the Great Depression?

4. Access the Discovering Data exercise for Chapter 12 online to answer the following questions.

a. What is the percentage decline in industrial production for Greece from 2007 to 2009? What is it from 2007 to 2014?

b. What country has the largest decline in industrial production from 2007 to 2009? Rank the countries, in order, from the largest decline in industrial production to the smallest.

c. Find the decline in industrial production from 2007 to 2009 for each of the countries.

d. What country experienced the fastest recovery from the financial crisis? The slowest recovery?

e. How long did it take Germany to fully recover from the financial crisis? How long did it take the United States?

5. a. What three measures of the economy tend to move together during the business cycle? Which way do they move during an upturn? During a downturn?

b. Who in the economy is hurt during a recession? How?

c. How did Milton Friedman alter the consensus that had developed in the aftermath of the Great Depression on how the economy should be managed? What is the current goal of policy makers in managing the economy?

6. Why do we consider a business-cycle expansion different from long-run economic growth? Why do we care about the size of the long-run growth rate of real GDP relative to the size of the growth rate of the population?

7. In 1798, Thomas Malthus's *Essay on the Principle of Population* was published. In it, he wrote: "Population, when unchecked, increases in a geometrical ratio. Subsistence increases only in an arithmetical ratio. . . . This implies a strong and constantly operating check on population from the difficulty of subsistence." Malthus was saying that the growth of the population is limited by the amount of food available to eat; people will live at the subsistence level forever. Why didn't Malthus's description apply to the world after 1800?

8. Each year, *The Economist* publishes data on the price of the Big Mac in different countries and exchange rates. The accompanying table shows some data from 2007 and 2016. Use this information to answer the following questions.

Country	2007 Price of Big Mac (in local currency)	2007 Price of Big Mac (in U.S. dollars)	2016 Price of Big Mac (in local currency)	2016 Price of Big Mac (in U.S. dollars)
Argentina	peso8.25	$2.65	peso33.0	$2.39
Canada	C$3.63	$3.08	C$5.84	$4.14
Euro area	€2.94	$3.82	€3.72	$4.00
Japan	¥280	$2.31	¥370	$3.12
United States	$3.22	$3.22	$4.93	$4.93

a. Where was it cheapest to buy a Big Mac in U.S. dollars in 2007?

b. Where was it cheapest to buy a Big Mac in U.S. dollars in 2016?

c. Using the increase in the local currency price of the Big Mac in each country to measure the percent change in the overall price level from 2007 to 2016, which nation experienced the most inflation? Did any of the nations experience deflation?

9. College tuition has risen significantly in the last few decades. For the sake of this problem, let's assume that over the last 20 years the cost of college, including total tuition, room, and board paid by full-time undergraduate students went from $2,871 to $16,789 at public institutions, a 485% price increase, and from $6,330 to $33,716 at private institutions, a 433% increase. Over the same time, average personal income after taxes rose from $9,785 to $39,409 per year, an increase of 302%. Have these tuition increases made it more difficult for the average student to afford college tuition?

13 | GDP and the CPI: Tracking the Macroeconomy

CHINA HITS THE BIG TIME

WE OPENED THIS BOOK with a portrait of the Pearl River Delta, the huge urban complex in southeastern China that, taken as a whole, is now the world's biggest city. The world's biggest city also has a very big economy, larger than that of many nations. And China as a whole, by some measures, now has the world's largest economy. Other measures show that the U.S. economy is still larger.

China has become an economic superpower, surpassing Japan.

But what does it mean to have the largest economy in the world? If you compare China with the United States, you find that they do quite different things. China, for example, produces much of the world's clothing, while the U.S. clothing industry has largely disappeared. On the other hand, America produces around half of the world's passenger jets, while China is just getting into the aircraft industry. So you might think that trying to compare the sizes of the two economies would be a matter of comparing apples and oranges—well, pajamas and Boeings, but you get the idea.

In fact, however, economists routinely do compare the sizes of economies across both space and time—for example, they compare the size of the U.S. economy with that of China, and they also compare the size of the U.S. economy today with its size in the past. They do this using a measure known as *gross domestic product,* or GDP, the total value of goods and services produced in a country, and a closely related measure, *real GDP,* which corrects GDP for annual price changes. When number-crunchers say that one country's economy has overtaken the other's, they mean that China's real GDP has surpassed that of the United States (or that the United States' real GDP has surpassed that of China).

GDP and real GDP are two of the most important measures used to track the macroeconomy—that is, to quantify movements in the overall level of output and prices. Measures like GDP and *price indexes* play an important role in formulating economic policy, since policy makers need to know what's going on, and anecdotes are no substitute for hard data. Measures are also important for business decisions—to such an extent that corporations and other players seek independent estimates when they don't trust official numbers.

In this chapter, we explain how macroeconomists measure key aspects of the economy. We first explore ways to measure the economy's total output and total income. We then turn to the problem of how to measure the level of prices and the change in prices in the economy. ●

WHAT YOU WILL LEARN

- How do economists use aggregate measures to track the performance of the economy?
- What is **gross domestic product,** or **GDP,** and how is it calculated?
- What is the difference between **real GDP** and **nominal GDP,** and why is real GDP the appropriate measure of real economic activity?
- What is a **price index,** and how is it used to calculate the **inflation rate?**

The **national income and product accounts,** or **national accounts,** keep track of the flows of money between different sectors of the economy.

Final goods and services are goods and services sold to the final, or end, user.

Intermediate goods and services are goods and services—bought from one firm by another firm— that are inputs for production of final goods and services.

Gross domestic product, or GDP, is the total value of all final goods and services produced in the economy during a given year.

The National Accounts

Almost all countries calculate a set of numbers known as the *national income and product accounts*. In fact, the accuracy of a country's accounts is a remarkably reliable indicator of its state of economic development—in general, the more reliable the accounts, the more economically advanced the country. When international economic agencies seek to help a less developed country, typically the first order of business is to send a team of experts to audit and improve the country's accounts.

In the United States, these numbers are calculated by the Bureau of Economic Analysis, a division of the U.S. government's Department of Commerce. The **national income and product accounts,** often referred to simply as the **national accounts,** keep track of the spending of consumers, the sales of producers, business investment spending, government purchases, and a variety of other flows of money between different sectors of the economy. Let's see how they work.

Economists use the national accounts to measure the overall market value of the goods and services the economy produces. That measure has a name: it's a country's gross domestic product. But before we can formally define gross domestic product, or GDP, we have to examine an important distinction between classes of goods and services: the difference between *final goods and services* versus *intermediate goods and services*.

Gross Domestic Product

A consumer's purchase of a new car from a dealer is one example of a sale of **final goods and services:** goods and services sold to the final, or end, user. But an automobile manufacturer's purchase of steel from a steel foundry or glass from a glassmaker is an example of purchasing **intermediate goods and services:** goods and services that are inputs for production of final goods and services. In the case of intermediate goods and services, the purchaser—another firm—is *not* the final user.

Gross domestic product, or GDP, is the total value of all *final goods and services* produced in an economy during a given period, usually a year. In 2017 the GDP of the United States was $19,485 billion, or about $59,472 per person. If you are an economist trying to construct a country's national accounts, *one way to calculate GDP is to calculate it directly: survey firms and add up the total value of their production of final goods and services.* We'll soon explain why intermediate goods, and some other types of goods as well, are not included in the calculation of GDP.

But adding up the total value of final goods and services produced is only one of three ways of calculating GDP. A second way is based on total spending on final goods and services. This second method adds aggregate spending on domestically produced final goods and services in the economy. The third way of calculating GDP is based on total income earned in the economy. Firms and the factors of production that they employ are owned by households. So firms must ultimately pay out what they earn to households. And so, a third way of calculating GDP is to sum the total factor income earned by households from firms in the economy.

Calculating GDP

We've just explained the three methods for calculating GDP:

1. Add up total value of all final goods and services produced.
2. Add up spending on all domestically produced goods and services in the economy.
3. Add up the total factor income earned by households from firms in the economy.

FIGURE 13-1 Calculating GDP

In this simplified hypothetical economy consisting of three firms, GDP can be calculated in three different ways: (1) measuring GDP as the value of production of final goods and services by summing each firm's value added; (2) measuring GDP as aggregate spending on domestically produced final goods and services; and (3) measuring GDP as factor income earned by households from firms in the economy.

2. Aggregate spending on domestically produced final goods and services = $21,500

	American Ore, Inc.	American Steel, Inc.	American Motors, Inc.	Total factor income
Value of sales	$4,200 (ore)	$9,000 (steel)	$21,500 (car)	
Intermediate goods	0	4,200 (iron ore)	9,000 (steel)	
Wages	2,000	3,700	10,000	$15,700
Interest payments	1,000	600	1,000	2,600
Rent	200	300	500	1,000
Profit	1,000	200	1,000	2,200
Total expenditure by firm	4,200	9,000	21,500	
Value added per firm = Value of sales − Cost of intermediate goods	4,200	4,800	12,500	

3. Total payments to factors = $21,500

1. Value of production of final goods and services, sum of value added = $21,500

Government statisticians use all three methods. To illustrate how these three methods work, we will consider a simplified hypothetical economy, shown in Figure 13-1. This economy consists of three firms—American Motors, Inc., which produces one car per year; American Steel, Inc., which produces the steel that goes into the car; and American Ore, Inc., which mines the iron ore that goes into the steel. So GDP is $21,500, the value of the one car per year the economy produces. Let's look at how the three different methods of calculating GDP yield the same result.

Measuring GDP as the Value of Production of Final Goods and Services

The first method for calculating GDP is to add up the value of all the final goods and services produced in the economy—a calculation that excludes the value of intermediate goods and services. Why are intermediate goods and services excluded? After all, don't they represent a very large and valuable portion of the economy?

To understand why only final goods and services are included in GDP, look at the simplified economy described in Figure 13-1. Should we measure the GDP of this economy by adding up the total sales of the iron ore producer, the steel producer, and the auto producer? If we did, we would in effect be counting the value of the steel twice—once when it is sold by the steel plant to the auto plant, and again when the steel auto body is sold to a consumer as a finished car. And we would be counting the value of the iron ore *three* times—once when it is mined and sold to the steel company, a second time when it is made into steel and sold to the auto producer, and a third time when the steel is made into a car and sold to the consumer.

So counting the full value of each producer's sales would cause us to count the same items several times and artificially inflate the calculation of GDP. For example, in Figure 13-1, the total value of all sales, intermediate and final, is $34,700: $21,500 from the sale of the car, plus $9,000 from the sale of the steel, plus $4,200 from the sale of the iron ore. Yet we know that GDP is only $21,500. The way we

Steel is an intermediate good because it is sold to other product manufacturers, such as automakers, and rarely to final buyers, such as consumers.

The **value added** of a producer is the value of its sales minus the value of its purchases of intermediate goods and services.

Aggregate spending, the sum of consumer spending, investment spending, government purchases of goods and services, and exports minus imports, is the total spending on domestically produced final goods and services in the economy.

avoid double-counting is to count only each producer's **value added** in the calculation of GDP: the difference between the value of its sales and the value of the intermediate goods and services it purchases from other businesses.

That is, we subtract the cost of inputs—the intermediate goods—at each stage of the production process. In this case, the value added of the auto producer is the dollar value of the cars it manufactures *minus* the cost of the steel it buys, or $12,500. The value added of the steel producer is the dollar value of the steel it produces *minus* the cost of the ore it buys, or $4,800. Only the ore producer, which we have assumed doesn't buy any inputs, has value added equal to its total sales, $4,200. The sum of the three producers' value added is $21,500, equal to GDP.

Measuring GDP as Spending on Domestically Produced Final Goods and Services Another way to calculate GDP is by adding up *aggregate spending* on domestically produced final goods and services. The total flow of funds received by firms from sales in the goods and services market comprises total or **aggregate spending** on domestically produced final goods and services. It is the sum of consumer spending, investment spending, government purchases of goods and services, and exports minus imports. Like the method that estimates GDP as the value of domestic production of final goods and services, this measurement of the flow of funds into firms can be carried out in a way that avoids double-counting.

In terms of our steel and auto example, we don't want to count both consumer spending on a car (represented in Figure 13-1 by $21,500, the sales price of the car) and the auto producer's spending on steel (represented in Figure 13-1 by $9,000, the price of a car's worth of steel). If we counted both, we would be counting the steel embodied in the car twice.

We solve this problem by counting only the value of sales to *final buyers,* such as consumers, firms that purchase investment goods, the government, or foreign buyers. In other words, to avoid double-counting of spending, we omit sales of inputs from one business to another when estimating GDP using spending data. You can see from Figure 13-1 that aggregate spending on final goods and services—the finished car—is $21,500.

Mathematically we can represent GDP as the sum of the five components of aggregate spending:

(13-1) $GDP = C + I + G + X - IM$

Consumer spending is denoted by the symbol C: sales of investment goods to other businesses, or investment spending, is denoted by I; government purchases of goods and services is denoted by G; and sales to foreigners—that is, exports—is denoted by X.

One component of sales by firms is consumer spending, but in reality, not all of this final spending goes toward domestically produced goods and services. We must take account of spending on imports, which is denoted by IM in Equation 13-1. Income spent on imports is income not spent on domestic goods and services—it is income that has "leaked" across national borders. To accurately value domestic production using spending data, we must subtract out spending on imports to arrive at spending on domestically produced goods and services.

We'll see Equation 13-1 again in later chapters.

Measuring GDP as Factor Income Earned from Firms in the Economy
A final way to calculate GDP is to add up all the income earned by factors of production from firms in the economy—the wages earned by labor; the interest paid to those who lend their savings to firms and the government; the rent earned by those who lease their land or structures to firms; and dividends, the profits paid to the shareholders, the owners of the firms' physical capital. This is a valid measure because the money firms earn by selling goods and services must go somewhere;

whatever isn't paid as wages, interest, or rent is profit. Ultimately, profits are paid out to shareholders as dividends.

Figure 13-1 shows how this calculation works for our simplified economy. The numbers shaded in the column at far right in the figure show the total wages, interest, and rent paid by all these firms as well as their total profit. Summing up all of these items yields total factor income of $21,500—again, equal to GDP.

We won't emphasize factor income as much as the other two methods of calculating GDP. It's important to keep in mind, however, that all the money spent on domestically produced goods and services generates factor income to households.

What GDP Tells Us

We've now seen the various ways that gross domestic product is calculated. But what does the measurement of GDP tell us?

The most important use of GDP is as a measure of the size of the economy. For example, suppose you want to compare the economies of different nations. A natural approach is to compare their GDPs. In 2017, as we've seen, U.S. GDP was $19,485 billion, China's GDP was $12,237 billion, and the combined GDP of the 28 countries that make up the European Union was $17,281 billion.

But wait—didn't we open this chapter by stating that by some measures, China has the world's largest economy, while other measures show that the U.S. economy is still larger? Well, it turns out that one must be careful when using GDP numbers in comparing countries, and especially when making comparisons over time. That's because part of the increase in the value of GDP over time represents increases in the *prices* of goods and services rather than an increase in output. For example, U.S. GDP was $8,608 billion in 1997 and had more than doubled to $19,485 billion by 2017. But the U.S. economy didn't actually double in size over that period. To measure actual changes in aggregate output, we need a modified version of GDP that is adjusted for price changes, which is known as *real GDP*.

A similar issue arises when comparing the United States and China, because many goods and services sold inside China are much cheaper than they are in the United States, and estimates that take this into account find that China's real GDP is bigger than the unadjusted number suggests. We'll see next how real GDP is calculated.

>> Check Your Understanding 13-1

Solutions appear at back of book.

1. Explain why the three methods of calculating GDP produce the same estimate of GDP.

2. Consider the first row of Figure 13-1. Suppose you mistakenly believed that total value added was $30,500, the sum of the sales price of a car and a car's worth of steel. What items would you be counting twice?

‖ Real GDP: A Measure of Aggregate Output

The U.S. economy had a pretty good year in 2017: the nation gained 2.2 million jobs, while the unemployment rate fell from 4.7 to 4.1%. It was certainly a better year than 1982, when a severe recession reduced employment by 2 million and sent unemployment soaring. Strange to say, however, gross domestic product rose slightly faster in 1982 (4.2%) than it did in 2017 (4.1%). How is that possible? The answer is that back in 1982 GDP was rising for a bad reason—inflation, which raised the prices of the goods and services America produced—not because the economy was actually growing. Inflation was much lower in 2017 so the rise in GDP really did correspond to economic progress.

Aggregate output is the economy's total quantity of output of final goods and services.

Real GDP is the total value of all final goods and services produced in the economy during a given year, calculated using the prices of a selected base year.

Nominal GDP is the value of all final goods and services produced in the economy during a given year, calculated using the prices current in the year in which the output is produced.

In order to accurately measure the economy's growth, we need a measure of **aggregate output:** the total quantity of final goods and services the economy produces. The measure that is used for this purpose is known as *real GDP.* By tracking real GDP over time, we avoid the problem of changes in prices distorting the value of changes in production of goods and services over time. Let's look first at how real GDP is calculated, then at what it means.

Calculating Real GDP

To understand how real GDP is calculated, imagine an economy in which only two goods, apples and oranges, are produced and in which both goods are sold only to final consumers. The outputs and prices of the two fruits for two consecutive years are shown in Table 13-1.

The first thing we can say about these data is that the value of sales increased from year 1 to year 2. In the first year, the total value of sales was (2,000 billion × $0.25) + (1,000 billion × $0.50) = $1,000 billion; in the second it was (2,200 billion × $0.30) + (1,200 billion × $0.70) = $1,500 billion, which is 50% larger.

But it is also clear from the table that this increase in the dollar value of GDP overstates the real growth in the economy. Although the quantities of both apples and oranges increased, the prices of both apples and oranges also rose. So, part of the 50% increase in the dollar value of GDP from year 1 to year 2 simply reflects higher prices, not higher production of output.

TABLE 13-1 Calculating GDP and Real GPD in a Simple Economy		
	Year 1	Year 2
Quantity of apples (billions)	2,000	2,200
Price of apple	$0.25	$0.30
Quantity of oranges (billions)	1,000	1,200
Price of orange	$0.50	$0.70
GDP (billions of dollars)	$1,000	$1,500
Real GDP (billions of year 1 dollars)	$1,000	$1,150

To estimate the true increase in aggregate output produced, we have to ask: how much would GDP have gone up if prices had *not* changed? To answer this question, we need to find the value of output in year 2 expressed in year 1 prices. In year 1 the price of apples was $0.25 each and the price of oranges $0.50 each. So year 2 output *at year 1 prices* is (2,200 billion × $0.25) + (1,200 billion × $0.50) = $1,150 billion. And output in year 1 at year 1 prices was $1,000 billion. So in this example GDP measured in year 1 prices rose 15%—from $1,000 billion to $1,150 billion.

Now we can define **real GDP:** it is the total value of final goods and services produced in the economy during a year, calculated as if prices had stayed constant at the level of some given base year. A real GDP number always comes with information about what the base year is.

A GDP number that has not been adjusted for changes in prices is calculated using the prices in the year in which the output is produced. Economists call this measure **nominal GDP,** GDP at current prices. If we had used nominal GDP to measure the true change in output from year 1 to year 2 in our apples and oranges example, we would have overstated the true growth in output: we would have claimed it to be 50%, when in fact it was only 15%. By comparing output in the two years using a common set of prices—the year 1 prices in this example—we are able to focus solely on changes in the quantity of output by eliminating the influence of changes in prices.

Table 13-2 shows a real-life version of our apples and oranges example. The second column shows nominal GDP in 2007, 2012, and 2017. The third column shows real GDP for each year in 2012 dollars. For 2012 the two numbers are the same. But real GDP in 2007 expressed in 2012 dollars was higher than nominal GDP in 2007, reflecting the fact that prices were in general higher in 2012 than in 2007. Real GDP in 2017 expressed in 2012 dollars, however, was less than nominal GDP in 2017 because prices in 2012 were lower than in 2017.

TABLE 13-2 Nominal versus Real GDP in 2007, 2012, and 2017		
	Nominal GDP (billions of current dollars)	Real GDP (billions of 2012 dollars)
2007	$14,452	$15,626
2012	16,197	16,197
2017	19,485	18,051

You might have noticed that there is an alternative way to calculate real GDP using the data in Table 13-1. Why not measure it using the prices of year 2 rather than year 1 as the base-year prices? This procedure seems equally valid. According to that calculation, real GDP in year 1 at year 2 prices is (2,000 billion × $0.30) + (1,000 billion × $0.70) = $1,300 billion; real GDP in year 2 at year 2 prices is $1,500 billion, the same as nominal GDP in year 2. So, using year 2 prices as the base year, the growth rate of real GDP is equal to ($1,500 billion – $1,300 billion)/ $1,300 billion = 0.154, or 15.4%. This is slightly higher than the figure we got from the previous calculation, in which year 1 prices were the base-year prices. In that calculation, we found that real GDP increased by 15%. Neither answer, 15.4% versus 15%, is more "correct" than the other.

In reality, the government economists who put together the U.S. national accounts have adopted a method known as *chain-linking* to measure the change in real GDP; it uses the average between the GDP growth rate calculated using an early base year and the GDP growth rate calculated using a late base year. As a result, U.S. statistics on real GDP are always expressed in **chained dollars.**

What Real GDP Doesn't Measure

GDP, nominal or real, is a measure of a country's aggregate output. Other things equal, a country with a larger population will have higher GDP simply because there are more people working. So if we want to compare GDP across countries but want to eliminate the effect of differences in population size, we use the measure **GDP per capita**—GDP divided by the size of the population, equivalent to the average GDP per person.

Real GDP per capita can be a useful measure in some circumstances, such as in a comparison of labor productivity between countries. However, despite the fact that it is a rough measure of the average real output per person, real GDP per capita has well-known limitations as a measure of a country's living standards. Every once in a while economists are accused of believing that growth in real GDP per capita is the only thing that matters—that is, thinking that increasing real GDP per capita is a goal in itself. In fact, economists rarely make that mistake; the idea that economists care only about real GDP per capita is a sort of urban legend.

Let's take a moment to be clear about why a country's real GDP per capita is not a sufficient measure of human welfare in that country and why growth in real GDP per capita is not an appropriate policy goal in itself.

One way to think about this is to say that an increase in real GDP means an expansion in the economy's production possibility frontier. Because the economy has increased its productive capacity, society can achieve more things. But whether society actually makes good use of that increased potential to improve living standards is another matter. To put it in a slightly different way, your income may be higher this year than last year, but whether you use that higher income to improve your quality of life is your choice.

Real GDP per capita, then, is a measure of an economy's average aggregate output per person—and so of what it *can* do. It is not a sufficient goal in itself because it doesn't address how a country uses that output to affect living standards. A country with a high GDP can afford for its citizens to be healthy, to be well educated, and in general, to have a good quality of life. But there is not a one-to-one match between GDP and the quality of life.

Chained dollars is the method of calculating changes in real GDP using the average between the growth rate calculated using an early base year and the growth rate calculated using a late base year.

GDP per capita is GDP divided by the size of the population; it is equivalent to the average GDP per person.

ECONOMICS >> *in Action*
Miracle in Venezuela?

The South American nation of Venezuela has had a distinction that may surprise you: in recent years, it has had one of the world's fastest-growing nominal GDPs.

Between 2013 and 2017, in fact, Venezuelan nominal GDP grew at an estimated 9,000%—compared with growth of only 15% in the United States.

So, was Venezuela experiencing an economic miracle? On the contrary, its economy was a mess, partly because the price of oil—the country's main export—plunged and partly because of erratic government policies that disrupted production and led to widespread shortages of basic consumer goods. In fact, from 2013 to 2017 *real* GDP fell by an estimated 32%. And those shortages led to a surge in prices (especially on the black market, but even official prices rose rapidly). Furthermore, the government, lost much of its revenue thanks to the fall in oil exports, and paid some of its bills simply by printing money, which accelerated inflation.

In other words, Venezuela serves as an extreme illustration of the importance of distinguishing between nominal and real GDP: it produced fewer and fewer goods and services, but nominal GDP soared because the prices of the goods and services it did produce rose at triple-digit rates.

>> Quick Review

• To determine the actual growth in **aggregate output,** we calculate **real GDP** using prices from some given base year. In contrast, **nominal GDP** is the value of aggregate output calculated with current prices. U.S. statistics on real GDP are always expressed in **chained dollars.**

• Real **GDP per capita** is a measure of the average aggregate output per person. But it is not a sufficient measure of human welfare, nor is it an appropriate goal in itself, because it does not reflect important aspects of living standards within an economy.

>> Check Your Understanding 13-2
Solutions appear at back of book.

1. Assume there are only two goods in the economy, french fries and onion rings. In 2015, 1,000,000 servings of french fries were sold at $0.40 each and 800,000 servings of onion rings at $0.60 each. From 2015 to 2016 the price of french fries rose by 25% and the servings sold fell by 10%; the price of onion rings fell by 15% and the servings sold rose by 5%.
   a. Calculate nominal GDP in 2015 and 2016. Calculate real GDP in 2016 using 2015 prices.
   b. Why would an assessment of growth using nominal GDP be misguided?

2. From 2010 to 2015, the price of electronic equipment fell dramatically and the price of housing rose dramatically. What are the implications of this in deciding whether to use 2010 or 2015 as the base year in calculating 2013 real GDP?

⊪ Price Indexes and the Aggregate Price Level

In late 2016, drivers had something to celebrate: gasoline prices had tumbled to an average of $2.25 per gallon, down 38% from their peak, two and a half years earlier. But while driving was getting cheaper, having someplace to live when you arrived was getting more expensive: by the end of 2016, average rents were 10% higher than they had been when gas was its most expensive. So was the cost of living going up or down?

Clearly, there was a need for a single number summarizing what was happening to consumer prices. Just as macroeconomists find it useful to have a single number representing the overall level of output, they also find it useful to have a single number representing the overall level of prices: the **aggregate price level.** Yet a huge variety of goods and services are produced and consumed in the economy. How can we summarize the prices of all these goods and services with a single number? The answer lies in the concept of a *price index*—a concept best introduced with an example.

Market Baskets and Price Indexes

The **aggregate price level** is a measure of the overall level of prices in the economy.

Suppose that a frost in Florida destroys most of the citrus harvest. As a result, the price of an orange rises from $0.20 to $0.40, the price of a grapefruit rises from $0.60 to $1.00, and the price of a lemon rises from $0.25 to $0.45. How much has the price of citrus fruit increased?

One way to answer that question is to state three numbers—the changes in prices for oranges, grapefruit, and lemons. But this is a very cumbersome method. Rather than having to recite three numbers in an effort to track changes in the prices of citrus fruit, we would prefer to have some kind of overall measure of the *average* price change.

To measure average price changes for consumer goods and services, economists track changes in the cost of a typical consumer's *consumption bundle*—the typical basket of goods and services purchased before the price changes. A hypothetical consumption bundle, used to measure changes in the overall price level, is known as a **market basket.** Suppose that before the frost a typical consumer bought 200 oranges, 50 grapefruit, and 100 lemons over the course of a year, our market basket for this example.

Table 13-3 shows the pre-frost and post-frost cost of this market basket. Before the frost, it cost $95; after the frost, the same bundle of goods cost $175. Since $175/$95 = 1.842, the post-frost basket costs 1.842 times the cost of the pre-frost basket, a cost increase of 84.2%. In this example, the average price of citrus fruit has increased 84.2% since the base year as a result of the frost, where the base year is the initial year used in the measurement of the price change.

Economists use the same method to measure changes in the overall price level over time. For example, to measure the change in the overall price level from 2010 (the base year) to 2016, they compare the cost of purchasing the market basket in 2010 to the cost in 2016. They use a simplification to avoid tracking the market basket in the intervening years (2011 to 2015). So they *normalize* the measure of the aggregate price level, meaning that they set the cost of the market basket equal to 100 in the chosen base year. Working with a market basket and a base year, and after normalizing, we arrive at a **price index,** a normalized measure of the overall price level. It is always cited along with the year for which the aggregate price level is being measured and the base year. A price index can be calculated using the following formula:

(13-2) Price index in a given year $= \dfrac{\text{Cost of market basket in a given year}}{\text{Cost of market basket in base year}} \times 100$

In our example, the citrus fruit market basket cost $95 in the base year, the year before the frost. So by Equation 13-2 we define the price index for citrus fruit as (cost of market basket in a given year/$95) × 100, yielding an index of 100 for the period before the frost and 184.2 after the frost. You should note that the price index for the base year always results in a price index equal to 100. This is because the price index in the base year is equal to: (cost of market basket in base year/cost of market basket in base year) × 100 = 100.

Thus, the price index makes it clear that the average price of citrus has risen 84.2% as a consequence of the frost. Because of its simplicity and intuitive appeal, the method we've just described is used to calculate a variety of price indexes to track average price changes among a variety of different groups of goods and services. For example, the *consumer price index,* which we'll discuss shortly, is the most widely used measure of the aggregate price level, the overall price level of final consumer goods and services across the economy.

A **market basket** is a hypothetical set of consumer purchases of goods and services.

A **price index** measures the cost of purchasing a given market basket in a given year, in which that cost is normalized so that it is equal to 100 in the selected base year.

TABLE 13-3 Calculating the Cost of a Market Basket

	Pre-frost	Post-frost
Price of orange	$0.20	$0.40
Price of grapefruit	0.60	1.00
Price of lemon	0.25	0.45
Cost of market basket (200 oranges, 50 grapefruit, 100 lemons)	(200 × $0.20) + (50 × $0.60) + (100 × $0.25) = $95.00	(200 × $0.40) + (50 × $1.00) + (100 × $0.45) = $175.00

The **inflation rate** is the percent change per year in a price index—typically the consumer price index.

The **consumer price index,** or **CPI,** measures the cost of the market basket of a typical urban American family.

The **producer price index,** or **PPI,** measures changes in the prices of goods purchased by producers.

Price indexes are also the basis for measuring inflation. The **inflation rate** is the annual percent change in an official price index. The inflation rate from year 1 to year 2 is calculated using the following formula, where we assume that year 1 and year 2 are consecutive years.

$$(13\text{-}3) \quad \text{Inflation rate} = \frac{\text{Price index in year 2} - \text{Price index in year 1}}{\text{Price index in year 1}} \times 100$$

Typically, a news report that cites "the inflation rate" is referring to the annual percent change in the consumer price index.

The Consumer Price Index

The most widely used measure of prices in the United States is the **consumer price index** (often referred to simply as the **CPI**), which is intended to show how the cost of all purchases by a typical urban family has changed over time. It is calculated by surveying market prices for a market basket that is constructed to represent the consumption of a typical family of four living in a typical American city. The base period for the index is currently 1982–1984; that is, the index is calculated so that the average of consumer prices in 1982–1984 is 100.

The market basket used to calculate the CPI is far more complex than the three-fruit market basket we just described. In fact, to calculate the CPI, the Bureau of Labor Statistics sends its employees out to survey supermarkets, gas stations, hardware stores, and so on—some 23,000 retail outlets in 75 cities. Every month it tabulates about 80,000 prices, on everything from romaine lettuce to a medical check-up.

Figure 13-2 shows the weight of major categories in the consumer price index as of 2017. For example, motor fuel, mainly gasoline, accounted for 3% of the CPI. On the other hand, housing accounted for 42% of the CPI. So that 38% plunge in gasoline prices would have reduced the CPI by roughly 1% (0.38×3%), while the much smaller percentage rise in housing costs of 10% actually had a bigger, positive effect on the overall price index of 4.2% (0.1×42%).

Figure 13-3 shows how the CPI has changed since measurement began in 1913. Since 1940, the CPI has risen steadily, although its annual percent increases in recent years have been much smaller than those of the 1970s and early 1980s. (A logarithmic scale is used so that equal percent changes in the CPI have the same slope.)

The United States is not the only country that calculates a consumer price index. In fact, nearly every country has one. As you might expect, the market baskets that make up these indexes differ quite a lot from country to country. In poor countries, where people must spend a high proportion of their income just to feed themselves, food makes up a large share of the price index. Among high-income countries, differences in consumption patterns lead to differences in the price indexes: the Japanese price index puts a larger weight on raw fish and a smaller weight on beef than ours does, and the French price index puts a larger weight on wine.

FIGURE 13-2 The Makeup of the Consumer Price Index in 2017

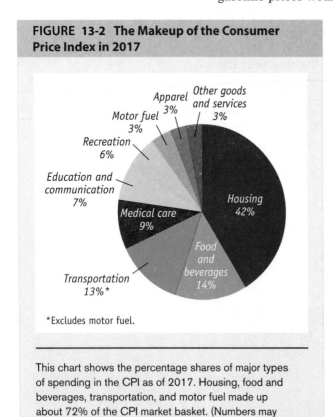

This chart shows the percentage shares of major types of spending in the CPI as of 2017. Housing, food and beverages, transportation, and motor fuel made up about 72% of the CPI market basket. (Numbers may not add to 100% due to rounding.)

Data from: Bureau of Labor Statistics.

Other Price Measures

There are two other price measures that are also widely used to track economy-wide price changes. One is the **producer price index** (or **PPI,** which used to be known as the *wholesale price index*). As its name suggests, the producer price index measures the cost of a typical basket of goods and services—containing raw commodities such as steel, electricity,

FIGURE 13-3 The CPI, 1913–2018

Since 1940, the CPI has risen steadily. But the annual percentage increases in recent years have been much smaller than those of the 1970s and early 1980s. (The vertical axis is measured on a logarithmic scale so that equal percent changes in the CPI have the same slope.)

Data from: Bureau of Labor Statistics.

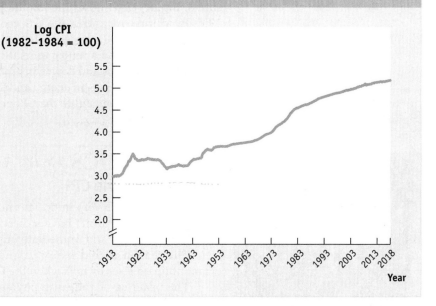

coal, and so on—purchased by producers. Because commodity producers are relatively quick to change prices when they perceive a change in overall demand for their goods, the PPI often responds to inflationary or deflationary pressures more quickly than the CPI. As a result, a change in the PPI is often regarded as an early warning signal of changes in the inflation rate.

The other widely used price measure is the *GDP deflator;* it isn't exactly a price index, although it serves the same purpose. Recall in our discussion of Table 13-2 we distinguished between *nominal GDP* (GDP in current prices) and *real GDP* (GDP calculated using the prices of a base year). The **GDP deflator** for a given year is equal to 100 times the ratio of nominal GDP for that year to real GDP for that year. Since real GDP is currently expressed in 2012 dollars, the GDP deflator for 2012 is equal to 100. If nominal GDP doubles but real GDP does not change, the GDP deflator indicates that the aggregate price level doubled.

Perhaps the most important point about the different inflation rates generated by these three measures of prices is that they usually move closely together (although

The **GDP deflator** for a given year is 100 times the ratio of nominal GDP to real GDP in that year.

FIGURE 13-4 The CPI, the PPI, and the GDP Deflator

As the figure shows, the three different measures of inflation, the PPI (orange), the CPI (green), and the GDP deflator (purple), usually move closely together. Each reveals a drastic acceleration of inflation during the 1970s and a return to relative price stability in the 1990s. With the exception of a brief period of deflation in 2009, prices have remained stable from 2000 to 2017.

Data from: Bureau of Labor Statistics; Bureau of Economic Analysis.

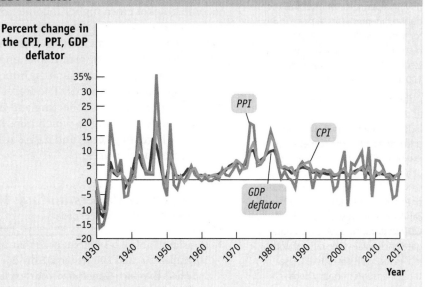

the producer price index tends to fluctuate more than either of the other two measures). Figure 13-4 shows the annual percent changes in the three indexes since 1930. By all three measures, the U.S. economy experienced deflation during the early years of the Great Depression, inflation during World War II, accelerating inflation during the 1970s, and a return to relative price stability in the 1990s. Notice, by the way, the dramatic ups and downs in producer prices from 2000 to 2017 on the graph; this reflects large swings in energy and food prices, which play a much bigger role in the PPI than they do in either the CPI or the GDP deflator.

ECONOMICS >> *in Action*

Indexing to the CPI

Although GDP is a very important number for shaping economic policy, official statistics on GDP don't have a direct effect on people's lives. The CPI, by contrast, has a direct and immediate impact on millions of Americans.

The reason is that many payments are tied, or *indexed*, to the CPI—the amount paid rises or falls when the CPI rises or falls.

The practice of indexing payments to consumer prices goes back to the dawn of the United States as a nation. In 1780 the Massachusetts State Legislature recognized that the pay of its soldiers fighting the British needed to be increased because of the inflation that occurred during the Revolutionary War. The legislature adopted a formula that made a soldier's pay proportional to the cost of a market basket that consisted of 5 bushels of corn, $68\frac{4}{7}$ pounds of beef, 10 pounds of sheep's wool, and 16 pounds of shoe leather.

Today, 64 million people receive payments from Social Security, a national retirement program that accounts for almost a quarter of current total federal spending—more than the defense budget. The amount of an individual's Social Security payment is determined by a formula that reflects each person's previous payments into the system and other factors. In addition, all Social Security payments are adjusted each year to offset any increase in consumer prices over the previous year. The CPI is used to calculate the official estimate of the inflation rate to adjust these payments yearly. So every percentage point added to the official estimate of the rate of inflation adds 1% to the checks received by tens of millions of individuals.

Other government payments, such as disability benefits, are also indexed to the CPI. In addition, income tax brackets, the bands of income levels that determine a taxpayer's income tax rate, are indexed to the CPI. (Individuals in a higher income bracket pay a higher income tax rate in a progressive tax system like ours.) Indexing also extends to the private sector, where some private contracts, including some wage settlements, contain cost-of-living allowances (called COLAs) that adjust payments in proportion to changes in the CPI.

Because the CPI plays such an important and direct role in people's lives, it's a politically sensitive number. The Bureau of Labor Statistics, which calculates the CPI, takes great care in collecting and interpreting price and consumption data. It uses a complex method in which households are surveyed to determine what they buy and where they shop, and a carefully selected sample of stores are surveyed to get representative prices.

A small change in the CPI has large consequences for those dependent on Social Security payments.

>> *Quick Review*

• Changes in the **aggregate price level** are measured by the cost of buying a particular **market basket** during different years. A **price index** for a given year is the cost of the market basket in that year normalized so that the price index equals 100 in a selected base year.

• The **inflation rate** is calculated as the percent change in a price index. The most commonly used price index is the **consumer price index,** or **CPI,** which tracks the cost of a basket of consumer goods and services. The **producer price index,** or **PPI,** does the same for goods and services used as inputs by firms. The **GDP deflator** measures the aggregate price level as the ratio of nominal to real GDP times 100. These three measures normally behave quite similarly.

>> *Check Your Understanding* 13-3

Solutions appear at back of book.

1. Consider Table 13-3 but suppose that the market basket is composed of 100 oranges, 50 grapefruit, and 200 lemons. How does this change the pre-frost and post-frost price indexes? Explain. Generalize your explanation to how the construction of the market basket affects the price index.

2. For each of the following events, how would an economist using a 10-year-old market basket create a bias in measuring the change in the cost of living today?
   a. A typical family owns more cars than it would have a decade ago. Over that time, the average price of a car has increased more than the average prices of other goods.
   b. Virtually no households had broadband internet access 20 years ago. Now many households have it, and the price has regularly fallen each year.
3. The consumer price index in the United States (base period 1982–1984) was 237.846 in 2015 and 242.821 in 2016. Calculate the inflation rate from 2015 to 2016.

SOLVED PROBLEM   A Change in Fortune?

Earlier we compared real versus nominal GDP in Venezuela. The following table shows the underlying data on nominal GDP (in billions of Venezuelan bolívares or VEB), real GDP (in billions of 1997 bolívares), and population (in millions) for the years 2005, 2007, 2009, 2011, 2013, 2015, and 2017. For each two-year period calculate the real growth rate in GDP per capita.

Year	Real GDP (billions of bolívares)	Nominal GDP (billions of 1997 bolívares)	Population (millions)
2005	VEB46.52	VEB304.09	26.78
2007	55.59	494.59	27.69
2009	56.65	707.26	28.59
2011	58.14	1357.49	29.46
2013	62.23	2245.84	30.32
2015	56.09	6025.33	31.16
2017	42.59	260,000.00	31.98

STEP | 1 Calculate real GDP per capita (in bolívares) for each year in the table.
Read pages 363–364.

Real GDP per capita is GDP divided by the size of the population.

Real GDP per capita for each of the years is listed in the accompanying table. Real GDP is expressed in billions of bolívares and population is expressed in millions. To get both variables in the same units we must multiply real GDP by 1,000 to express it in millions. For 2005, real GDP per capita is calculated by multiplying VEB46.52 by 1,000, and then dividing by 26.78: (VEB46.52 × 1,000)/26.78 = VEB1,737.12.

Year	Real GDP (billions of bolívares)	Population (millions)	Real GDP per capita (1997 bolívares)
2005	VEB46.52	26.78	VEB1,737.12
2007	55.59	27.69	2,007.58
2009	56.65	28.59	1,981.46
2011	58.14	29.46	1,973.52
2013	62.23	30.32	2,052.44
2015	56.09	31.16	1,800.06
2017	42.59	31.98	1,331.77

STEP | 2 Calculate the percent change in real GDP per capita for the periods 2005–2007, 2007–2009, 2009–2011, 2011–2013, and 2013–2015. *Read pages 363–364.*

The percent change in real GDP per capita between year 1 and year 2 is calculated using the following formula:

$$\% \text{ change in real GDP per capita} = \frac{\text{Real GDP per capita in year 2} - \text{Real GDP per capita in year 1}}{\text{Real GDP per capita in year 1}} \times 100$$

Note the similarity between this equation and Equation 13-2 in the chapter. Both equations measure the rate of change.

The percent change in real GDP per capita for each of the periods is presented in the second column of the table.

The percent change in real GDP per capita for 2005–2007 is calculated by subtracting real GDP per capita in 2005 from real GDP per capita in 2007, dividing by real GDP per capita in 2005, and then multiplying this expression by 100:

$$\frac{(\text{VEB2,000.58} - \text{VEB1,737.12})}{\text{VEB1,737.12}} \times 100 = 15.57\%$$

Year	% Change in real GDP per capita
2005–2007	15.57%
2007–2009	1.30%
2009–2011	−0.40%
2011–2013	4.00%
2013–2015	−12.3%
2015–2017	−26.02%

[handwritten note: thanksgiving Dinner price]

SUMMARY

1. Economists keep track of the flows of money between sectors with the **national income and product accounts,** or **national accounts.**

2. **Gross domestic product,** or **GDP,** measures the value of all **final goods and services** produced in the economy. It does not include the value of **intermediate** *[handwritten: (part of product)]* **goods and services.** It can be calculated in three ways: add up the **value added** by all producers; add up all spending on domestically produced final goods and services, leading to the equation $GDP = C + I + G + X - IM,$ also known as **aggregate spending;** or add up all the income paid by domestic firms to factors of production. These three methods are equivalent because in the economy as a whole, total income paid by domestic firms to factors of production must equal total spending on domestically produced final goods and services.

3. **Real GDP** is the value of the final goods and services produced calculated using the prices of a selected base year. Except in the base year, real GDP is not the same as **nominal GDP,** the value of **aggregate output** calculated *[handwritten margin note: measure price level]* using current prices. Analysis of the growth rate of aggregate output must use real GDP because doing so eliminates any change in the value of aggregate output due solely to price changes. Real **GDP per capita** is a measure of average aggregate output per person but is not in itself an appropriate policy goal. U.S. statistics on real GDP are always expressed in **chained dollars.**

4. To measure the **aggregate price level,** economists calculate the cost of purchasing a **market basket.** A **price index** is the ratio of the current cost of that market basket to the cost in a selected base year, multiplied by 100.

5. The **inflation rate** is the yearly percent change in a price index, typically based on the **consumer price index,** or **CPI,** the most common measure of the aggregate price level. A similar index for goods and services purchased by firms is the **producer price index,** or **PPI.** Finally, economists also use the **GDP deflator,** which measures the price level by calculating the ratio of nominal GDP to real GDP times 100.

[handwritten note: costs of goods and services]

KEY TERMS

National income and product accounts (national accounts), p. 358
Final goods and services, p. 358
Intermediate goods and services, p. 358
Gross domestic product (GDP), p. 358
Value added, p. 360
Aggregate spending, p. 360

Aggregate output, p. 362
Real GDP, p. 362
Nominal GDP, p. 362
Chained dollars, p. 363
GDP per capita, p. 363
Aggregate price level, p. 364

Market basket, p. 365
Price index, p. 365
Inflation rate, p. 366
Consumer price index (CPI), p. 366
Producer price index (PPI), p. 366
GDP deflator, p. 367

DISCUSSION QUESTIONS

1. Go to the Bureau of Labor Statistics home page at www.bls.gov. Place the cursor over the "Economic Releases" tab and then click on "Major Economic Indicators" in the drop-down menu that appears. Once on the "Major Economic Indicators" page, click on "Consumer Price Index." On that page, under "Table of Contents," click on "Table 1: Consumer Price Index for All Urban Consumers." Using the "unadjusted" figures, determine what the CPI was for the previous month. How did it change from the previous month? How does the CPI compare to the same month one year ago?

2. The cost of a college education in the United States is rising at a rate faster than inflation. The following table shows the average cost of a college education in the United States during the academic year that began in 2014 and the academic year that began in 2015 for public and private colleges. Assume the costs listed in the table are the only costs experienced by the various college students in a single year.

   a. Calculate the cost of living for an average college student in each category for 2014 and 2015.

   b. Calculate an inflation rate for each type of college student between 2014 and 2015.

	Cost of college education during academic year beginning 2014 (averages in 2014 dollars)			
	Tuition and fees	**Room and board**	**Books and supplies**	**Other expenses**
Two-year public college: commuter	$3,161	$7,810	$1,378	$3,809
Four-year public college: in-state, on-campus	8,199	9,495	1,250	3,203
Four-year public college: out-of-state, on-campus	22,203	9,495	1,250	3,203
Four-year private college: on-campus	30,177	10,506	1,251	2,488
	Cost of college education during academic year beginning 2015 (averages in 2015 dollars)			
	Tuition and fees	**Room and board**	**Books and supplies**	**Other expenses**
Two-year public college: commuter	$3,270	$7,918	$1,422	$3,761
Four-year public college: in-state, on-campus	8,445	9,760	1,275	3,272
Four-year public college: out-of-state, on-campus	23,107	9,760	1,275	3,272
Four-year private college: on-campus	31,177	10,827	1,248	2,511

PROBLEMS

interactive activity

1. The small economy of Pizzania produces three goods (bread, cheese, and pizza), each produced by a separate company. The bread and cheese companies produce all the inputs they need to make bread and cheese, respectively. The pizza company uses the bread and cheese from the other companies to make its pizzas. All three companies employ labor to help produce their goods, and the difference between the value of goods sold and the sum of labor and input costs is the firm's profit. The accompanying table summarizes the activities of the three companies when all the bread and cheese produced are sold to the pizza company as inputs in the production of pizzas.

	Bread company	Cheese company	Pizza company
Cost of inputs	$0	$0	$50 (bread) 35 (cheese)
Wages	15	20	75
Value of output	50	35	200

a. Calculate GDP as the value added in production.

b. Calculate GDP as spending on final goods and services.

c. Calculate GDP as factor income.

2. In the economy of Pizzania (from Problem 1), the bread and cheese produced are sold both to the pizza company for inputs in the production of pizzas and to consumers as final goods. The accompanying table summarizes the activities of the three companies.

	Bread company	Cheese company	Pizza company
Cost of inputs	$0	$0	$50 (bread) 35 (cheese)
Wages	25	30	75
Value of output	100	60	200

a. Calculate GDP as the value added in production.

b. Calculate GDP as spending on final goods and services.

c. Calculate GDP as factor income.

3. Which of the following transactions will be included in GDP for the United States?

a. Coca-Cola builds a new bottling plant in the United States.

b. Delta sells one of its existing airplanes to Korean Air.

c. Ms. Moneybags buys an existing share of Disney stock.

d. A California winery produces a bottle of Chardonnay and sells it to a customer in Montreal, Canada.

e. An American buys a bottle of French perfume in Paris.

f. A book publisher produces too many copies of a new book; the books don't sell this year, so the publisher adds the surplus books to inventories.

4. Access the Discovering Data exercise for Chapter 13 online to answer the following questions.

a. What was GDP for the United States last year?

b. Calculate the absolute change in U.S. GDP between last year and the year before.

c. Which component of GDP was the largest last year? Which was the smallest? What is the most recent year in which net exports were positive?

d. What happened to the size of government spending during the 1940s? What factors likely caused the shift?

e. How has each of the four components, as a percent of GDP, changed since the 1940s?

5. The accompanying table shows data on nominal GDP (in billions of dollars), real GDP (in billions of 2009 dollars), and population (in thousands) of the United States in 1965, 1975, 1985, 1995, 2005, and 2015. The U.S. price level rose consistently over the period 1965–2015.

Year	Nominal GDP (billions of dollars)	Real GDP (billions of 2009 dollars)	Population (thousands)
1965	$743.7	$3,976.7	194,250
1975	1,688.9	5,385.4	215,891
1985	4,346.7	7,593.8	238,416
1995	7,664.1	10,174.8	266,458
2005	13,093.7	14,234.2	296,115
2015	17,947.0	16,348.9	321,601

a. Why is real GDP greater than nominal GDP for all years until 2005 and lower for 2015?

b. Calculate the percent change in real GDP from 1965 to 1975, 1975 to 1985, 1985 to 1995, 1995 to 2005, and 2005 to 2015. Which period had the highest growth rate?

c. Calculate real GDP per capita for each of the years in the table.

d. Calculate the percent change in real GDP per capita from 1965 to 1975, 1975 to 1985, 1985 to 1995, 1995 to 2005, and 2005 to 2015. Which period had the highest growth rate?

e. How do the percent change in real GDP and the percent change in real GDP per capita compare? Which is larger? Do we expect them to have this relationship?

6. Eastland College is concerned about the rising price of textbooks that students must purchase. To better identify the increase in the price of textbooks, the dean asks you, the Economics Department's star student, to create an index of textbook prices. The average student purchases three English, two math, and four economics textbooks per year. The prices of these books are given in the accompanying table.

	2014	2015	2016
English textbook	$100	$110	$114
Math textbook	140	144	148
Economics textbook	160	180	200

a. What is the percent change in the price of an English textbook from 2014 to 2016?

b. What is the percent change in the price of a math textbook from 2014 to 2016?

c. What is the percent change in the price of an economics textbook from 2014 to 2016?

d. Using 2015 as a base year, create a price index for these books for all years.

e. What is the percent change in the price index from 2014 to 2016?

7. The consumer price index, or CPI, measures the cost of living for a typical urban household by multiplying the price for each category of expenditure (housing, food, and so on) times a measure of the importance of that expenditure in the average consumer's market basket and summing over all categories. However, using data from the consumer price index, we can see that changes in the cost of living for different types of consumers can vary a great deal. Let's compare the cost of living for a hypothetical retired person and a hypothetical college student. Let's assume that the market basket of a retired person is allocated in the following way: 10% on housing, 15% on food, 5% on transportation, 60% on medical care, 0% on education, and 10% on recreation. The college student's market basket is allocated as follows: 5% on housing, 15% on food, 20% on transportation, 0% on medical care, 40% on education, and 20% on recreation. The accompanying table shows the May 2016 CPI for each of the relevant categories.

	CPI May 2016
Housing	242.8
Food	248.0
Transportation	194.6
Medical care	460.5
Education	246.9
Recreation	117.2

Calculate the overall CPI for the retired person and for the college student by multiplying the CPI for each of the categories by the relative importance of that category to the individual and then summing each of the categories. The CPI for all items in May 2016 was 239.4. How do your calculations for the CPI for the retired person and the college student compare to the overall CPI?

8. The accompanying table provides the annual real GDP (in billions of 2009 dollars) and nominal GDP (in billions of dollars) for the United States.

a. Calculate the GDP deflator for each year.

b. Use the GDP deflator to calculate the inflation rate for all years except 2009.

	2009	2010	2011	2012	2013	2014	2015
Real GDP (billions of 2009 dollars)	$14,418.7	$14,783.8	$15,020.6	$15,354.6	$15,583.3	$15,961.7	$16,348.9
Nominal GDP (billions of dollars)	14,418.7	14,964.4	15,517.9	16,155.3	16,663.2	17,348.1	17,947.0

9. The accompanying table contains two price indexes for the years 2013, 2014, and 2015: the GDP deflator and the CPI. For each price index, calculate the inflation rate from 2013 to 2014 and from 2014 to 2015.

Year	GDP deflator	CPI
2013	106.929	232.964
2014	108.686	236.715
2015	109.775	236.995

WORK IT OUT Interactive step-by-step help with solving this problem can be found online.

10. The economy of Britannica produces three goods: computers, pens, and pizza. The accompanying table shows the prices and output of the three goods for the years 2014, 2015, and 2016.

a. What is the percent change in production of each of the goods from 2014 to 2015 and from 2015 to 2016?

b. What is the percent change in prices of each of the goods from 2014 to 2015 and from 2015 to 2016?

c. Calculate nominal GDP in Britannica for each of the three years. What is the percent change in nominal GDP from 2014 to 2015 and from 2015 to 2016?

d. Calculate real GDP in Britannica using 2014 prices for each of the three years. What is the percent change in real GDP from 2014 to 2015 and from 2015 to 2016?

	Computers		Pens		Pizzas	
Year	Price	Quantity	Price	Quantity	Price	Quantity
2014	$900	10	$10	100	$15	2
2015	1,000	10.5	12	105	16	2
2016	1,050	12	14	110	17	3

A TALE OF TWO NUMBERS

THERE ARE MANY official committees with impressive-sounding names but little impact on world events. The Federal Open Market Committee (FOMC), most certainly, is not one of them. The FOMC is part of the Federal Reserve system, a semi-autonomous federal agency that is responsible for making and implementing U.S. monetary policy.

The FOMC may have a drab-sounding name, but the decisions it makes eight times a year are critical, not just for the U.S. economy, but for the global economy as well. The committee, a 12-member panel under the directorship of the chair of the Federal Reserve, meets every six weeks to decide key aspects of monetary policy. When it announces its decisions, global financial markets move, sometimes dramatically.

In 2015, after seven long years of anemic growth precipitated by the 2008 financial crisis, the FOMC finally decided that the U.S. economy was on a self-sustaining upward trend. The evidence they had for that mainly came down to two numbers: the unemployment rate and the inflation rate. Unemployment had surged during the Great Recession, peaking at 10% in October 2009. By late 2015, the rate was down to a historically low 5%. In addition, the FOMC believed that inflation was moving to a range typically associated with a growing economy. These two pieces of evidence convinced the FOMC that the economy had finally recovered from the damage caused by the Great Recession.

As the FOMC knows, high unemployment and high inflation are the two great evils of macroeconomics: high unemployment incurs human and economic waste because willing workers can't find jobs. High inflation undermines the monetary system through rapidly rising prices. So the two principal goals of macroeconomic policy are low unemployment and price stability, usually defined as a low but positive rate of inflation. Sometimes these twin goals can be in conflict: at those times, macroeconomic policy makers must make a trade-off based on judgment and guesswork. At other times, such as during the extraordinary events of 2008, they aren't in conflict, and the making of macroeconomic policy is more straightforward.

In this chapter, we'll explore the dynamics of unemployment and inflation in the economy. We'll learn how they are measured and why accurate measurement is a critical function of government. From there we will go on to understand why low unemployment and price stability are the main goals of macroeconomic policy. Yet, as we just noted, sometimes those goals are in conflict; at other times they are not. It is the ability to cope with the dramatic shifts in the U.S. macroeconomy that makes the FOMC one of the most important committees in the world. ●

WHAT YOU WILL LEARN

- How is **unemployment** measured and how is the **unemployment rate** calculated?

- What is the significance of the unemployment rate for the economy?

- What is the relationship between the unemployment rate and economic growth?

- What factors determine the **natural rate of unemployment**?

- What are the economic costs of inflation?

- How do inflation and deflation create winners and losers?

- Why do policy makers try to maintain a stable rate of inflation?

Employment is the number of people currently employed in the economy, either full time or part time.

Unemployment is the number of people who are actively looking for work but aren't currently employed.

The **labor force** is equal to the sum of employment and unemployment.

The **labor force participation rate** is the percentage of the population aged 16 or older that is in the labor force.

‖ The Unemployment Rate

Figure 14-1 shows the U.S. unemployment rate from 1948 to 2019; as you can see, unemployment soared during the Great Recession of 2007–2009 and fell only gradually in the years that followed. What did the elevated unemployment rate mean, and why was it such a big factor in people's lives? To understand why policy makers pay so much attention to employment and unemployment, we need to understand how they both are defined and measured.

Defining and Measuring Unemployment

It's easy to define employment: you're employed if and only if you have a job. **Employment** is the total number of people currently employed, either full time or part time.

Unemployment, however, is a more subtle concept. Just because a person isn't working doesn't mean that we consider that person unemployed. For example, as of January 2019, there were more than 44 million retired workers in the United States receiving Social Security checks. Most of them were probably happy that they were no longer working, so we don't consider someone who has settled into a comfortable, well-earned retirement to be unemployed. There were also 8.5 million disabled U.S. workers receiving benefits because they were unable to work. Again, although they weren't working, we don't consider them to be unemployed.

The U.S. Census Bureau, the federal agency tasked with collecting data on unemployment, considers the unemployed only to be those who are "jobless, looking for jobs, and available for work." Retired people don't count because they aren't looking for jobs; the disabled don't count because they aren't available for work. More specifically, an individual is considered unemployed if he or she doesn't currently have a job and has been actively seeking a job during the past four weeks. So **unemployment** is defined as the total number of people who are actively looking for work but aren't currently employed.

A country's **labor force** is the sum of employment and unemployment—that is, of people who are currently working and people who are currently looking for work, respectively. The **labor force participation rate,** defined as the percentage of the working-age population that is in the labor force, is calculated as follows:

$$\textbf{(14-1)} \quad \text{Labor force participation rate} = \frac{\text{Labor force}}{\text{Population age 16 and older}} \times 100$$

FIGURE 14-1 The U.S. Unemployment Rate, 1948–2019

The unemployment rate has fluctuated widely over time. It always rises during recessions, which are shown by the shaded bars. It usually, but not always, falls during periods of economic expansion.

Data from: Bureau of Labor Statistics; National Bureau of Economic Research.

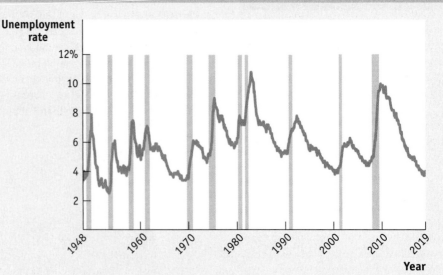

The **unemployment rate,** defined as the percentage of the total number of people in the labor force who are unemployed, is calculated as follows:

(14-2) $\text{Unemployment rate} = \dfrac{\text{Number of unemployed workers}}{\text{Labor force}} \times 100$

To estimate the numbers that go into calculating the unemployment rate, the U.S. Census Bureau carries out a monthly survey called the Current Population Survey, which involves interviewing a random sample of approximately 60,000 American households. People are asked whether they are currently employed. If they are not employed, they are asked whether they have been looking for a job during the past four weeks. The results are then scaled up, using estimates of the total population, to estimate the total number of employed and unemployed Americans.

The Significance of the Unemployment Rate

In general, the unemployment rate is a good indicator of how easy or difficult it is to find a job given the current state of the economy. When the unemployment rate is low, nearly everyone who wants a job can find one. In 2000, when the unemployment rate averaged just 4%, jobs were so abundant that employers spoke of a "mirror test" for getting a job: if you were breathing (therefore your breath would fog a mirror), you could find work. By contrast, in 2010, with the unemployment rate above 9% all year, it was very hard to find work. In fact, there were almost five times as many Americans seeking work as there were job openings.

Although the unemployment rate is a good indicator of current labor market conditions, it's not a literal measure of the percentage of people who want a job but can't find one. That's because in some ways the unemployment rate exaggerates the difficulty people have in finding jobs. But in other ways, the opposite is true—a low unemployment rate can conceal deep frustration over the lack of job opportunities.

How the Unemployment Rate Can Overstate the True Level of Unemployment
If you are searching for work, it's normal to take at least a few weeks to find a suitable job. Yet a worker who is quite confident of finding a job, but who has not yet accepted a position, is counted as unemployed. As a consequence, the unemployment rate never falls to zero, even in boom times when jobs are plentiful. Even in the buoyant labor market of 2000, when it was easy to find work, the unemployment rate was still 4%. Later in this chapter, we'll discuss in greater depth the reasons that measured unemployment persists even when jobs are abundant.

How the Unemployment Rate Can Understate the True Level of Unemployment
Frequently, people who would like to work but aren't working still don't get counted as unemployed. In particular, an individual who has given up looking for a job for the time being because there are no jobs available—say, a laid-off steelworker in a deeply depressed steel town—isn't counted as unemployed because he or she has not been searching for a job during the previous four weeks. Individuals who want to work but have told government researchers that they aren't currently searching because they see little prospect of finding a job given the state of the job market are called **discouraged workers.** Because it does not count discouraged workers, the measured unemployment rate may understate the percentage of people who want to work but are unable to find jobs.

Discouraged workers are part of a larger group—**marginally attached workers.** These are people who say they would like to have a job and have looked for work in the recent past but are not currently looking for work. They are also not included when calculating the unemployment rate. Finally, another category of workers who are frustrated in their ability to find work but aren't counted as unemployed are the **underemployed:** workers who would like to find full-time jobs but are currently working part time "for economic reasons"—that is, they can't find a full-time job. Again, they aren't counted in the unemployment rate.

The **unemployment rate** is the percentage of the total number of people in the labor force who are unemployed.

Discouraged workers are non-working people who are capable of working but have given up looking for a job given the state of the job market.

Marginally attached workers would like to be employed and have looked for a job in the recent past but are not currently looking for work.

Underemployment is the number of people who work part time because they cannot find full-time jobs.

FIGURE 14-2 Alternative Measures of Unemployment, 1994–2019

The unemployment number usually quoted in the news media counts individuals as unemployed only if they have been looking for work during the past four weeks. Broader measures also count discouraged workers, marginally attached workers, and the underemployed. These broader measures show a higher unemployment rate, but they move closely in parallel with the standard rate.

Data from: Bureau of Labor Statistics.

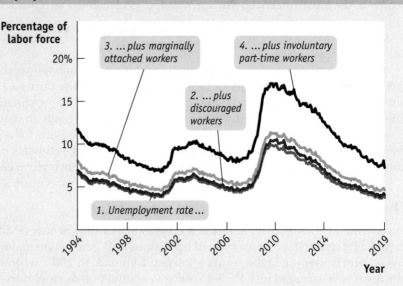

The Bureau of Labor Statistics is the federal agency that calculates the official unemployment rate. It also calculates broader "measures of labor underutilization" that include the three categories of frustrated workers. Figure 14-2 shows what happens to the measured unemployment rate once discouraged workers, other marginally attached workers, and the underemployed are counted. The broadest measure of unemployment and underemployment, known as *U-6,* is the sum of these three measures plus the unemployed. It is substantially higher than the rate usually quoted by the news media. But U-6 and the unemployment rate move very much in parallel, so changes in the unemployment rate remain a good guide to what's happening in the overall labor market, including frustrated workers.

Finally, it's important to realize that the unemployment rate varies greatly among demographic groups. Other things equal, jobs are generally easier to find for more experienced workers and for workers during their prime working years, that is, from ages 25 to 54. For younger workers, as well as workers nearing retirement age, jobs are typically harder to find, other things equal.

Figure 14-3 shows unemployment rates for different groups in 2007, when the overall unemployment rate was low by historical standards; in 2010, when the rate

FIGURE 14-3 Unemployment Rates of Different Groups in 2007, 2010, and 2019

Unemployment rates vary greatly among different demographic groups. For example, although the overall unemployment rate in February 2019 was 3.8%, the unemployment rate among African-American teenagers was 26.8%. As a result, even during periods of low overall unemployment, unemployment remains a serious problem for some groups.

Data from: Bureau of Labor Statistics.

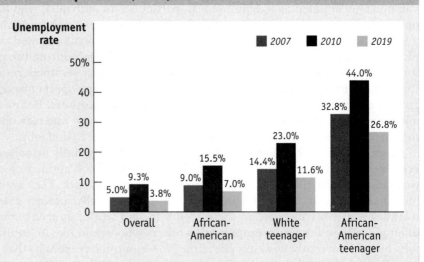

was high in the aftermath of the Great Recession; and in February 2019, when it had come down to pre-crisis levels. As you can see, the unemployment rate for African-American workers is consistently much higher than the national average; the unemployment rate for White teenagers (ages 16–19) is normally even higher; and the unemployment rate for African-American teenagers is higher still. (Bear in mind that a teenager isn't considered unemployed, even if he or she isn't working, unless that teenager is looking for work but can't find it.) So even at times when the overall unemployment rate is relatively low, jobs are hard to find for some groups.

So you should interpret the unemployment rate as an indicator of overall labor market conditions, not as an exact measure of the percentage of people unable to find jobs. The unemployment rate is, however, a very good indicator: its ups and downs closely reflect economic changes that have a significant impact on people's lives. Let's turn now to the causes of these fluctuations.

Growth and Unemployment

Compared to Figure 14-1, Figure 14-4 shows the U.S. unemployment rate over a somewhat shorter period, from 1979 through 2019. The shaded bars represent periods of recession. As you can see, during every recession, without exception, the unemployment rate rose. The severe recession of 2007–2009, like the earlier one of 1981–1982, led to a huge rise in unemployment.

Correspondingly, during periods of economic expansion the unemployment rate usually falls. The long economic expansion of the 1990s and the recovery from the Great Recession eventually brought the unemployment rate under 4%. However, it's important to recognize that *economic expansions aren't always periods of falling unemployment.* Look at the periods immediately following the recessions of 1990–1991 and 2001 in Figure 14-4. In each case the unemployment rate continued to rise for more than a year after the recession was officially over. The explanation in both cases is that although the economy was growing, it was not growing fast enough to reduce the unemployment rate.

Figure 14-5 is a scatter diagram showing U.S. data for the period from 1949 to 2016. The horizontal axis measures the annual rate of growth in real GDP—the percent by which each year's real GDP changed compared to the previous year's real GDP. (Notice that there were ten years in which growth was negative—that

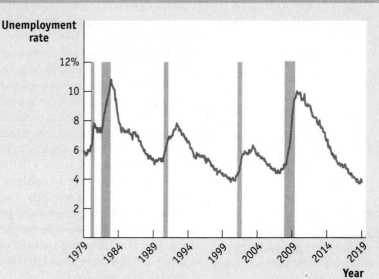

FIGURE 14-4 Unemployment and Recessions, 1979–2019

This figure shows a close-up of the unemployment rate for the past four decades, with the shaded bars indicating recessions. It's clear that unemployment always rises during recessions and *usually* falls during expansions. But in both the early 1990s and the early 2000s, unemployment continued to rise for some time after the recession was officially declared over.

Data from: Bureau of Labor Statistics; National Bureau of Economic Research.

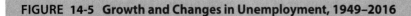

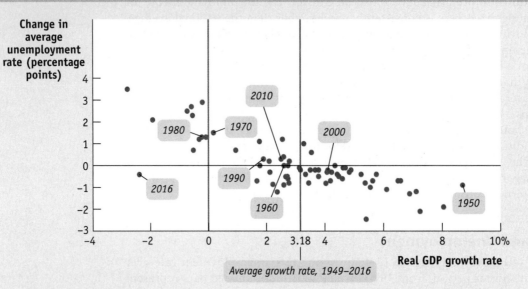

FIGURE 14-5 Growth and Changes in Unemployment, 1949–2016

Each dot shows the growth rate of the economy and the change in the unemployment rate for a specific year between 1949 and 2016. For example, in 2000 the economy grew 4.1% and the unemployment rate fell 0.2 percentage points, from 4.2% to 4.0%.

In general, the unemployment rate fell when growth was above its average rate of 3.18% a year and rose when growth was below average. Unemployment always rose when real GDP fell.

Data from: Bureau of Labor Statistics; Bureau of Economic Analysis.

is, real GDP shrank.) The vertical axis measures the *change* in the average unemployment rate over the previous year in percentage points—last year's unemployment rate minus this year's unemployment rate. Each dot represents the observed growth rate of real GDP and change in the unemployment rate for a given year. For example, in 2000 the average unemployment rate fell to 4.0% from 4.2% in 1999; this is shown as a value of –0.2 along the vertical axis for the year 2000. Over the same period, real GDP grew by 4.1%; this is the value shown along the horizontal axis for the year 2000.

The downward trend of the scatter diagram in Figure 14-5 shows that there is a generally strong negative relationship between growth in the economy and the rate of unemployment. Years of high growth in real GDP were also years in which the unemployment rate fell, and years of low or negative growth in real GDP were years in which the unemployment rate rose.

The green vertical line in Figure 14-5 at the value of 3.18% indicates the average growth rate of real GDP over the period from 1949 to 2016. Points lying to the right of the vertical line are years of above-average growth. In these years, the value on the vertical axis is usually negative, meaning that the unemployment rate fell. That is, years of above-average growth were usually years in which the unemployment rate was falling. Conversely, points lying to the left of the green vertical line were years of below-average growth. In these years, the value on the vertical axis is usually positive, meaning that the unemployment rate rose. That is, years of below-average growth were usually years in which the unemployment rate was rising.

A period in which real GDP is growing at a below-average rate and unemployment is rising is called a **jobless recovery** or a *growth recession*. Since 1990, there have been three recessions, each of which was followed by a period of jobless recovery. But true recessions, periods when real GDP falls, are especially painful for workers. As illustrated by the points to the left of the purple vertical line in Figure 14-5 (representing years in which the real GDP growth rate is negative), falling real GDP is always associated with a rising rate of unemployment, causing a great deal of hardship for families.

A **jobless recovery** is a period in which the real GDP growth rate is positive but the unemployment rate is still rising.

ECONOMICS >> *in Action*
Failure to Launch

In March 2010, when the U.S. job situation was near its worst, the *Harvard Law Record* published a brief note titled "Unemployed law student will work for $160K plus benefits." In a self-mocking tone, the author admitted to having graduated from Harvard Law School the previous year but not landing a job offer. "What mark on our résumé is so bad that it outweighs the crimson H?" the note asked.

The answer, of course, is that it wasn't about the résumé—it was about the economy. Times of high unemployment are especially hard on new graduates, who often find it hard to get any kind of full-time job.

How bad was it around the time that note was written? Figure 14-6 shows the unemployment rate by gender, for college graduates aged 20 to 24, from 2000 to 2018. The negative impact of the Great Recession was much worse than that of the previous slump shown, the recession of 2001. The downturn slammed the construction and manufacturing sectors especially hard, sending the unemployment rate for men into the double digits. The public and service sectors, where women are disproportionately employed, fared somewhat better. But women still saw their unemployment rate rise to over 8%. The effects of the Great Recession were prolonged, and the unemployment rate didn't return to pre-crisis level until 2016, nine years after the recession began.

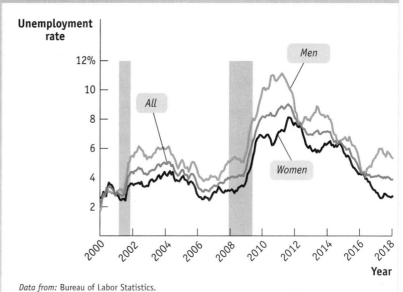

FIGURE 14-6 **Unemployment Rate for College Graduates Ages 20–24, 2000–2018**

Data from: Bureau of Labor Statistics.

>> *Check Your Understanding* 14-1
Solutions appear at back of book.

1. Suppose employment websites develop new software that enables job-seekers to find suitable jobs more quickly and employers to better screen potential employees. What effect will this have on the unemployment rate over time? Also suppose that these websites encourage job-seekers who had given up their searches to begin looking again. What effect will this have on the unemployment rate?

2. In which of these cases is a worker counted as unemployed? Explain.
   a. Rosa, an older worker who has been laid off and who gave up looking for work months ago
   b. Anthony, a schoolteacher who is not working during his three-month summer break
   c. Kanako, an investment banker who has been laid off and is currently searching for another position
   d. Sergio, a classically trained musician who can only find work playing for local parties
   e. Natasha, a graduate student who went back to school because jobs were scarce

3. Which of these are consistent with the observed relationship between growth in real GDP and changes in the unemployment rate as shown in Figure 14-5? Which are not?
   a. A rise in the unemployment rate accompanies a fall in real GDP.
   b. An exceptionally strong business recovery is associated with a greater percentage of the labor force being employed.
   c. Negative real GDP growth is associated with a fall in the unemployment rate.

>> *Quick Review*

• The **labor force,** equal to **employment** plus **unemployment,** does not include discouraged workers. Nor do labor statistics contain data on **underemployment.** The **labor force participation rate** is the percentage of the population age 16 and over in the labor force.

• The **unemployment rate** is an indicator of the state of the labor market, not an exact measure of the percentage of workers who can't find jobs. It can overstate the true level of unemployment because workers often spend time searching for a job even when jobs are plentiful. But it can also understate the true level of unemployment because it excludes **discouraged workers, marginally attached workers,** and **underemployed** workers.

• There is a strong negative relationship between growth in real GDP and changes in the unemployment rate. When growth is above average, the unemployment rate generally falls. When growth is below average, the unemployment rate generally rises—a period called a **jobless recovery** that typically follows a deep recession.

The Natural Rate of Unemployment

Fast economic growth tends to reduce the unemployment rate. So how low can the unemployment rate go? You might be tempted to say zero, but that isn't feasible. Over the past half-century, the national unemployment rate has never dropped below 2.9%.

How can there be so much unemployment even when many businesses are having a hard time finding workers? To answer this question, we need to examine the nature of labor markets and why they normally lead to substantial measured unemployment even when jobs are plentiful. Our starting point is the observation that even in the best of times, jobs are constantly being created and destroyed.

Job Creation and Job Destruction

Even during good times, most Americans know someone who has lost his or her job. In December 2018 the U.S. unemployment rate was only 3.9%, relatively low by historical standards. Yet in that month there were 5.5 million *job separations*—terminations of employment that occur because a worker is either fired or quits voluntarily.

There are many reasons for such job loss. One is structural change in the economy: industries rise and fall as new technologies emerge and consumers' tastes change, while some industries expand and create jobs while others contract and eliminate jobs. For example, employment in coal mining has declined to a small fraction of its one-time high due to both automation and a switch to other sources of energy. However, structural change also brings the creation of new jobs: employment in solar power surged after 2010 as a combination of rapidly improving technology and tax incentives led to a rapid growth in the use of solar panels.

Poor management performance or bad luck at individual companies also leads to job loss for employees. For example, in early 2018, JCPenney announced the closure of 140 stores and offered early retirement to 6,000 workers. That same year, Toys 'R' Us closed 735 stores, leading to 31,000 layoffs. Meanwhile, online retailers like Amazon continued to expand.

Continual job creation and destruction are features of modern economies, making a naturally occurring amount of unemployment inevitable. Within this naturally occurring amount, there are two types of unemployment—*frictional* and *structural*.

"At this point, I'm just happy to still have a job"

Frictional Unemployment

When a worker loses a job involuntarily due to job destruction, he or she often doesn't take the first new job offered. For example, suppose a skilled programmer, laid off because her software company's product line was unsuccessful, sees an online job posting for a receptionist. She might apply and get the job—but that would be foolish. Instead, she should take the time to look for a job that takes advantage of her skills and pays accordingly. In addition, individual workers are constantly leaving jobs voluntarily, typically for personal reasons—family moves, dissatisfaction, and better job prospects elsewhere.

Economists say that workers who spend time looking for employment are engaged in **job search.** If all workers and all jobs were alike, job search wouldn't be necessary; if information about jobs and workers was perfect, job search would be very quick. In practice, however, it's normal for a worker who loses a job, or a young worker seeking a first job, to spend at least a few weeks searching.

Frictional unemployment is unemployment due to the time workers spend in job search. A certain amount of frictional unemployment is inevitable due to the constant process of economic change. As we just mentioned, during the low-unemployment month of December 2018 there were nonetheless more than

Workers who spend time looking for employment are engaged in **job search.**

Frictional unemployment is unemployment due to the time workers spend in job search.

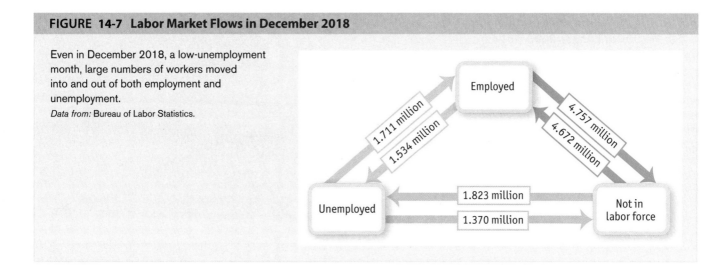

FIGURE 14-7 Labor Market Flows in December 2018

Even in December 2018, a low-unemployment month, large numbers of workers moved into and out of both employment and unemployment.
Data from: Bureau of Labor Statistics.

5.5 million job separations in which workers left or lost their jobs. Total employment grew because these separations were more than offset by almost 5.7 million hires. Inevitably, some of the workers who left or lost their jobs spent at least some time unemployed, as did some of the workers newly entering the labor force.

Figure 14-7 shows the average monthly flows of workers among three states: employed, unemployed, and not in the labor force during December 2018. What the figure suggests is how much churning is constantly taking place in the labor market. An inevitable consequence of that churning is a significant number of workers who haven't yet found their next job—that is, frictional unemployment.

A limited amount of frictional unemployment is relatively harmless and may even be a good thing. The economy is more productive if workers take the time to find jobs that are well matched to their skills, and workers who are unemployed for a brief period while searching for the right job don't experience great hardship. In fact, when there is a low unemployment rate, periods of unemployment tend to be quite short, suggesting that much of the unemployment is frictional.

Figure 14-8 shows the composition of unemployment in December 2018. Approximately 33% of the unemployed had been unemployed for less than 5 weeks, and only 35% had been unemployed for 15 or more weeks. Only about one in five unemployed workers were considered to be *long-term unemployed*—those unemployed for 27 or more weeks.

In periods of higher unemployment, however, workers tend to be jobless for longer periods of time, suggesting that a smaller share of unemployment is frictional. Figure 14-9 shows the fraction of the unemployed who had been out of work for six months or more from 2007 to 2018. It jumped to 45% after the Great Recession, but came gradually down as the economy recovered.

FIGURE 14-8 Distribution of the Unemployed by Duration of Unemployment, December 2018

When the unemployment rate is low, most unemployed workers are unemployed for only a short period. In December 2018, 33% of the unemployed had been unemployed for less than 5 weeks and 65% for less than 15 weeks. The short duration of unemployment for most workers suggests that much of the unemployment was frictional.
Data from: Bureau of Labor Statistics.

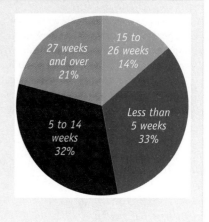

Structural Unemployment

Frictional unemployment exists even when the number of people seeking jobs is equal to the number of jobs being offered—that is, the existence of frictional unemployment doesn't mean that there is a surplus of labor. Sometimes, however,

FIGURE 14-9 Percentage of Unemployed U.S. Workers Who Had Been Unemployed for Six Months or Longer, 2007–2018

Before the Great Recession, relatively few U.S. workers had been unemployed for long periods. However, the percentage of long-term unemployed shot up after 2007, and came down only gradually.

Data from: Bureau of Labor Statistics.

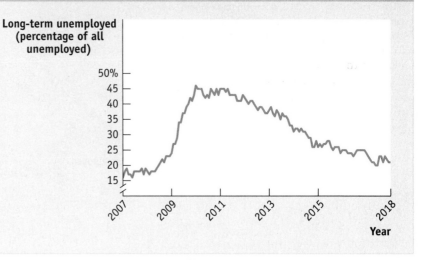

there is a *persistent surplus* of job-seekers in a particular labor market, even when the economy is at the peak of the business cycle. There may be more workers with a particular skill than there are jobs available using that skill, or there may be more workers in a particular geographic region than there are jobs available in that region. **Structural unemployment** is unemployment that results when there are more people seeking jobs in a particular labor market than there are jobs available at the current wage rate. The supply and demand model tells us that the price of a good, service, or factor of production tends to move toward an equilibrium level that matches the quantity supplied with the quantity demanded. This is equally true, in general, of labor markets.

Figure 14-10 shows a typical market for labor. The downward-sloping labor demand curve indicates that when the price of labor—the wage rate—increases, employers demand less labor. The upward-sloping labor supply curve indicates that when the price of labor increases, more workers are willing to supply labor at

In **structural unemployment,** more people are seeking jobs in a particular labor market than there are jobs available at the current wage rate, even when the economy is at the peak of the business cycle.

FIGURE 14-10 The Effect of a Minimum Wage on a Labor Market

When the government sets a minimum wage, W_F, that exceeds the market equilibrium wage rate in that market, W_E, the number of workers who would like to work at that minimum wage, Q_S, is greater than the number of workers demanded at that wage rate, Q_D. This surplus of labor is structural unemployment.

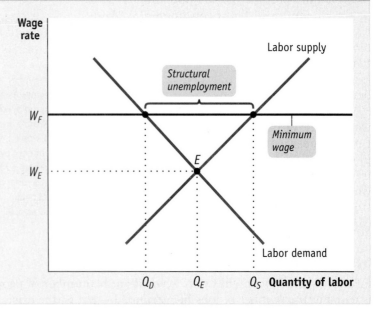

the prevailing wage rate. These two forces coincide to lead to an equilibrium wage rate for any given type of labor in a particular location. That equilibrium wage rate is shown as W_E.

Even at the equilibrium wage rate W_E, there will still be some frictional unemployment. That's because there will always be some workers engaged in job search even when the number of jobs available is equal to the number of workers seeking jobs. But there wouldn't be any structural unemployment in this labor market. *Structural unemployment occurs when the wage rate is, for some reason, persistently above W_E.* Several factors can lead to a wage rate in excess of W_E, the most important being minimum wages, unions, *efficiency wages,* the side effects of government policies, and mismatches between employees and employers.

Minimum Wages A *minimum wage* is a government-mandated floor on the price of labor. In the United States, the national minimum wage in early 2019 was $7.25 an hour. A number of state and local governments also determine the minimum wage within their jurisdictions, typically for the purpose of setting it higher than the federal level. For example, the city of Seattle has set a minimum wage at $15 an hour. For many American workers, the minimum wage is irrelevant; the market equilibrium wage for these workers is well above the national price floor. But for many less-skilled workers, the minimum wage is binding—it affects the wages that people are actually paid and can lead to structural unemployment in particular markets for labor. Other wealthy countries have higher minimum wages; for example, in 2019 the French minimum wage was 10.03 euros an hour, or around $11.33. In these countries, there are more workers for whom the minimum wage is binding.

California's minimum wage will be raised incrementally to $15 by 2022.

Figure 14-10 shows the effect of a binding minimum wage. In this market, the minimum wage is W_F, which is above the equilibrium wage rate, W_E. This leads to a persistent surplus in the labor market: the quantity of labor supplied, Q_S, is larger than the quantity demanded, Q_D. In other words, more people want to work than can find jobs at the minimum wage, leading to structural unemployment.

Given that minimum wages—that is, binding minimum wages—generally lead to structural unemployment, you might wonder why governments impose them. The rationale is to help ensure that people who work can earn enough income to afford at least a minimally comfortable lifestyle. However, this may come at a cost, because it may eliminate the opportunity to work for those who would have willingly worked for lower wages. As illustrated in Figure 14-10, not only are there more sellers of labor than there are buyers, but there are also fewer people working at a minimum wage (Q_D) than there would have been with no minimum wage at all (Q_E). The result is higher unemployment and, consequently, lower GDP. In addition, minimum wages, when they are binding, appear to disproportionately hurt younger workers with fewer skills to offer, and make it less costly for employers to engage in discrimination in hiring, since there are more willing workers than there are jobs.

Although economists broadly agree that a high minimum wage has the employment-reducing effects shown in Figure 14-10, there is widespread, although not universal, agreement that this isn't a good description of how the U.S. minimum wage actually works. The minimum wage in the United States is quite low compared with that in other wealthy countries, and as already noted, it isn't binding for the vast majority of workers.

In addition, researchers have produced evidence suggesting that minimum wage increases don't seem to be associated with employment declines and may actually lead to higher employment when, as was the case in the United States at one time, the minimum wage is low compared to average wages. They argue that firms employing a large percentage of workers in a particular market can keep wages low by restricting their hiring. Under these conditions, a moderate rise in the minimum wage will not lead to a loss of jobs. Most economists, however, agree that a sufficiently high minimum wage *does* lead to structural unemployment.

Labor Unions The actions of *labor unions* can have effects similar to those of minimum wages, leading to structural unemployment. By bargaining collectively for all of a firm's workers, unions can often win higher wages from employers than workers would have obtained by bargaining individually. This process, known as *collective bargaining*, is intended to tip the scales of bargaining power more toward workers and away from employers. Labor unions exercise bargaining power by threatening firms with a *labor strike*, a collective refusal to work. The threat of a strike can have serious consequences for firms. In such cases, workers acting collectively can exercise more power than they could if acting individually.

Employers have acted to counter the bargaining power of unions by threatening and enforcing *lockouts*—periods in which union workers are locked out and rendered unemployed—while they hire replacement workers.

When workers have increased bargaining power, they tend to demand and receive higher wages. Unions also bargain over benefits, such as health care and pensions, which we can think of as additional wages. Indeed, economists who study the effects of unions on wages find that unionized workers earn higher wages and more generous benefits than non-union workers with similar skills. The result of these increased wages can be the same as the result of a minimum wage: labor unions push the wage that workers receive above the equilibrium wage. Like a binding minimum wage, this leads to structural unemployment. In the United States, however, due to a low level of unionization, the amount of unemployment generated by union demands is likely to be very small. And in countries such as Germany and Japan, unions and management collaborate on devising more efficient work practices that support higher equilibrium wages.

Efficiency Wages Actions by firms can contribute to structural unemployment. Firms may choose to pay **efficiency wages**—wages that employers set above the equilibrium wage rate as an incentive for their workers to perform better.

Employers may feel the need for such incentives for several reasons. For example, employers often have difficulty directly observing how hard an employee works. They can, however, elicit more work effort by paying above-market wages: employees receiving these higher wages are more likely to work harder to ensure that they aren't fired, which would cause them to lose their higher wages.

For example, in 2018, Costco announced an increase in their minimum wage from $13 to $14 per hour, with the average hourly worker making over $22 per hour. Both the minimum and average wages paid by Costco far exceed the wages at Walmart and Sam's Club, Costco's largest competitors in the retail sector. By comparison, Walmart has a minimum wage of $11 per hour and an average wage of $14 per hour. In the end, Costco's employees are reported to be more satisfied with their jobs, more productive, and less likely to search for better opportunities elsewhere. When many firms pay efficiency wages, the result is a pool of workers who want jobs but can't find them. With Costco paying efficiency wages, a lot of workers are willing to work at Costco but not Walmart. So the use of efficiency wages by firms may lead to structural unemployment.

Side Effects of Government Policies In addition, government policies designed to help workers who lose their jobs can lead to structural unemployment as an unintended side effect. Most economically advanced countries provide benefits to laid-off workers as a way to tide them over until they find a new job. In the United States, these benefits typically replace only about 45% of a worker's income and expire after 26 weeks. (Benefits were extended in some cases to 99 weeks during the period of high unemployment in 2009–2011.) In other countries,

Efficiency wages are wages that employers set above the equilibrium wage rate as an incentive for better employee performance.

particularly in Europe, benefits are more generous and last longer. The drawback to this generosity is that it reduces a worker's incentive to quickly find a new job. During the 1980s, it was often argued that unemployment benefits in some European countries were one of the causes of *Eurosclerosis*, persistently high unemployment that afflicted a number of European economies.

Mismatches Between Employees and Employers It takes time for workers and firms to adjust to shifts in the economy. The result can be a mismatch between what employees have to offer and what employers are looking for. A skills mismatch is one form; for example, in the aftermath of the housing bust of 2009, there were more construction workers looking for jobs than were available. Another form is geographic, as in Michigan, which has had a long-standing surplus of workers after its auto industry declined. Until the mismatch is resolved through a big enough fall in wages of the surplus workers to induce retraining or relocation, there will be structural unemployment.

The Natural Rate of Unemployment

Because some frictional unemployment is inevitable and because many economies also suffer from structural unemployment, a certain amount of unemployment is normal, or "natural." Actual unemployment fluctuates around this normal level. The **natural rate of unemployment** is the normal unemployment rate around which the actual unemployment rate fluctuates. It is the rate of unemployment that arises from the effects of frictional plus structural unemployment.

Cyclical unemployment is the deviation of the actual rate of unemployment from the natural rate; that is, it is the difference between the actual and natural rates of unemployment. As the name suggests, cyclical unemployment is the share of unemployment that arises from the downturns of the business cycle.

We can summarize the relationships between the various types of unemployment as follows:

(14-3) Natural unemployment =
Frictional unemployment + Structural unemployment

(14-4) Actual unemployment =
Natural unemployment + Cyclical unemployment

Perhaps because of its name, people often imagine that the natural rate of unemployment is a constant that doesn't change over time and can't be affected by government policy. Neither proposition is true. Let's take a moment to stress two facts: The natural rate of unemployment changes over time, and it can be affected by government policies.

Changes in the Natural Rate of Unemployment

Private-sector economists and government agencies need estimates of the natural rate of unemployment both to make forecasts and to conduct policy analyses. Almost all these estimates show that the U.S. natural rate rises and falls over time. For example, the Congressional Budget Office, the independent agency that conducts budget and economic analyses for Congress, believes that the U.S. natural rate of unemployment was 5.3% in 1950, rose to 6.2% by the end of the 1970s, but fell to 4.6% by 2018. European countries have experienced even larger swings in their natural rates of unemployment.

What causes the natural rate of unemployment to change? The most important factors are changes in labor force characteristics, changes in labor market institutions, and changes in government policies. Let's look briefly at each factor.

Changes in Labor Force Characteristics Unemployment rates tend to be lower for experienced than for inexperienced workers. Because experienced workers tend to stay in a given job longer than do inexperienced ones, they have lower frictional

The **natural rate of unemployment** is the unemployment rate that arises from the effects of frictional plus structural unemployment.

Cyclical unemployment is the deviation of the actual rate of unemployment from the natural rate due to downturns in the business cycle.

unemployment. Also, because older workers are more likely than young workers to be family breadwinners, they have a stronger incentive to find and keep jobs. For example, in December 2018, American teenagers had an unemployment rate of 12.5% while workers age 25 to 34 had an unemployment rate of only 3.9%.

One reason the natural rate of unemployment rose during the 1970s was a large rise in the number of new workers—children of the post–World War II baby boom, as well as a rising percentage of women, entered the labor force. As Figure 14-11 shows, both the percentage of the labor force less than 25 years old and the percentage of women in the labor force grew rapidly in the 1970s. By the end of the 1990s, however, the share of women in the labor force had leveled off, and the percentage of workers under 25 had fallen sharply. As a result, the labor force as a whole is more experienced today than it was in the 1970s, one likely reason that the natural rate of unemployment is lower today than in the 1970s.

Changes in Labor Market Institutions As we pointed out earlier, unions that negotiate wages above the equilibrium level can be a source of structural unemployment. Some economists believe that the high natural rate of unemployment in Europe is caused, in part, by strong labor unions. In the United States, a sharp fall in union membership after 1980 may have been one reason the natural rate of unemployment fell between the 1970s and the 1990s.

Other institutional changes may also be at work. For example, some labor economists believe that temporary employment agencies have reduced frictional unemployment by helping match workers to jobs. Likewise, the proliferation of gig economy companies like Uber and TaskRabbit have reduced frictional and structural unemployment by making it easier for workers to earn money quickly and accept wages below a minimum wage.

Technological change, coupled with labor market institutions, can also affect the natural rate of unemployment. Technological change tends to increase the demand for skilled workers who are familiar with the relevant technology and reduce the demand for unskilled workers. Economic theory predicts that wages should increase for skilled workers and decrease for unskilled workers as technology advances. But if wages for unskilled workers cannot go down—say, due to a binding minimum wage—increased structural unemployment, and therefore a higher natural rate of unemployment, will result during periods of faster technological change.

Changes in Government Policies A high minimum wage can cause structural unemployment. Generous unemployment benefits can increase both structural

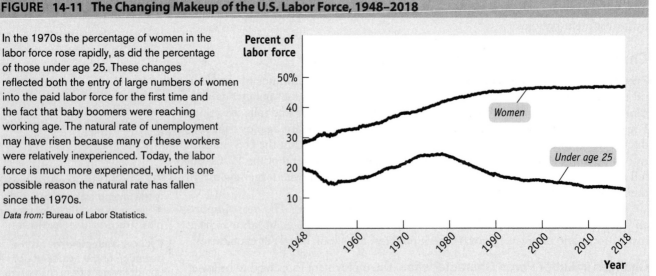

FIGURE 14-11 The Changing Makeup of the U.S. Labor Force, 1948–2018

In the 1970s the percentage of women in the labor force rose rapidly, as did the percentage of those under age 25. These changes reflected both the entry of large numbers of women into the paid labor force for the first time and the fact that baby boomers were reaching working age. The natural rate of unemployment may have risen because many of these workers were relatively inexperienced. Today, the labor force is much more experienced, which is one possible reason the natural rate has fallen since the 1970s.

Data from: Bureau of Labor Statistics.

and frictional unemployment as workers feel less financial pressure to accept a job immediately. So government policies intended to help workers can have the undesirable side effect of raising the natural rate of unemployment.

Some government policies, however, may reduce the natural rate. Two examples are job training and employment subsidies. *Job-training programs* are supposed to provide unemployed workers with skills that widen the range of jobs they can perform. *Employment subsidies* are payments either to workers or to employers that provide a financial incentive to accept or offer jobs.

ECONOMICS >> *in Action*
Structural Unemployment in Spain

Spain went through some dramatic ups and downs after 2000 when huge inflows of money from Germany and other northern European countries fed a giant housing boom. Then, after 2008, the boom went bust, causing both GDP and employment to slump, and unemployment to soar to more than 26%. Even before the crash, Spain's experience was somewhat unusual: during the height of the boom, unemployment was high by U.S. standards, bottoming out at about 8%. This suggests that Spain's natural rate of unemployment is very high, and several independent estimates do in fact put it in the range of 16% to 17%.

Why is Spain's natural rate so high? Researchers at the International Monetary Fund, the European Central Bank, and other institutions emphasize the role of laws that make it very hard to fire full-time workers, which in turn often allows these "insiders," many of whom are unionized, to demand relatively high wages even in the face of high unemployment among other workers. If these researchers are right, Spain is experiencing something like the possible effect of labor unions in causing structural unemployment.

Spain's seemingly high structural unemployment isn't unique: a number of other European countries seem to have similar issues, although none to such an extreme degree. For example, both Ireland and Portugal have a natural rate of unemployment over 10%. The important point to remember is that labor market institutions can differ greatly even among advanced economies, and that the result can be big differences in economic performance.

>> Check Your Understanding 14-2
Solutions appear at back of book.

1. Explain the following statements.
   a. Frictional unemployment is higher when the pace of technological advance quickens.
   b. Structural unemployment is higher when the pace of technological advance quickens.
   c. Frictional unemployment accounts for a larger share of total unemployment when the unemployment rate is low.
2. Why does collective bargaining have the same general effect on unemployment as a minimum wage? Illustrate your answer with a diagram.
3. Suppose that at the peak of the business cycle the United States dramatically increases benefits for unemployed workers. Explain what will happen to the natural rate of unemployment.

>> Quick Review

• Because of job creation and job destruction, as well as voluntary job separations, some level of unemployment is natural.

• **Frictional unemployment** occurs because unemployed workers engage in **job searches,** making some amount of unemployment inevitable.

• A variety of factors—minimum wages, unions, **efficiency wages,** the side effects of government policies such as unemployment benefits, and mismatches between employees and employers—lead to **structural unemployment** by raising wages above their market equilibrium level.

• Frictional plus structural unemployment equals natural unemployment, yielding a **natural rate of unemployment.** In contrast, **cyclical unemployment** changes with the business cycle. Actual unemployment is equal to the sum of natural unemployment and cyclical unemployment.

• The natural rate of unemployment can shift over time, due to changes in labor force characteristics, changes in institutions, and changes in government policies. Government policies designed to help workers are believed to be one reason for high natural rates of unemployment in Europe.

‖ Inflation and Deflation

As we mentioned in the opening story, macroeconomic policy makers are usually focused on two big evils, unemployment and inflation. It's easy to see why high unemployment is a problem. But why is inflation something to worry about? Why do policy makers even now get anxious about inflation going too high? The answer is that inflation can impose costs on the economy—but not in the way most people think.

The Level of Prices Doesn't Matter . . .

The most common complaint about *inflation*, which is an increase in the price level, is that it makes everyone poorer—after all, a given amount of money buys less. But inflation does not make everyone poorer. To see why, it's helpful to imagine what would happen if the United States did something other countries have done from time to time—replacing the dollar with a new currency.

An example of this kind of currency conversion happened in 2002, when France, like a number of other European countries, replaced its national currency, the franc, with the new pan-European currency, the euro. People turned in their franc coins and notes, and received euro coins and notes in exchange, at a rate of precisely 6.55957 francs per euro. At the same time, all contracts were restated in euros at the same rate of exchange. For example, if a French citizen had a home mortgage debt of 500,000 francs, this became a debt of 500,000/6.55957 = 76,224.51 euros. If a worker's contract specified that he or she should be paid 100 francs per hour, it became a contract specifying a wage of 100/6.55957 = 15.2449 euros per hour, and so on.

You could imagine doing the same thing in the case of the dollar, replacing the dollar with a "new dollar" at a rate of exchange of, say, 7 to 1. If you owed $140,000 on your home, that would become a debt of 20,000 new dollars. If you had a wage rate of $14 an hour, it would become 2 new dollars an hour, and so on. This would bring the overall U.S. price level back to about what it was in 1962, when John F. Kennedy was president.

So would everyone be richer as a result because prices would be only one-seventh as high? Of course not. Prices would be lower, but so would wages and incomes in general. If you cut a worker's wage to one-seventh of its previous value, but also cut all prices to one-seventh of their previous level, the worker's **real wage**—the wage rate divided by the price level—hasn't changed. In fact, bringing the overall price level back to what it was during the Kennedy administration would have no effect on overall purchasing power because doing so would reduce income exactly as much as it reduced prices.

Conversely, the rise in prices that has actually taken place since the early 1960s hasn't made America poorer because it has also raised incomes by the same amount: **real incomes**—incomes divided by the price level—haven't been affected by the rise in overall prices.

The moral of this story is that the *level* of prices doesn't matter: the United States would be no richer than it is now if the overall level of prices was still as low as it was in 1962; conversely, the rise in prices over the past half century hasn't made us any poorer.

. . . But the Rate of Change of Prices Does

The conclusion that the level of prices doesn't matter might seem to imply that the inflation rate doesn't matter either. But that's not true.

To see why, it's crucial to distinguish between the *level of prices* and the *inflation rate:* the percent increase in the overall level of prices per year. Recall that the inflation rate is defined as follows:

$$\text{Inflation rate} = \frac{\text{Price index in year 2} - \text{Price index in year 1}}{\text{Price index in year 1}} \times 100$$

Figure 14-12 highlights the difference between the price level and the inflation rate in the United States over the last half-century, with the price level measured along the left vertical axis and the inflation rate measured along the right vertical axis. In the 2000s, the overall level of prices in America was much higher than it had been in 1960—but that, as we've learned, didn't matter. The inflation rate in the 2000s, however, was much lower than in the 1970s—and that almost certainly made the economy richer than it would have been if high inflation had continued.

The **real wage** is the wage rate divided by the price level.

Real income is income divided by the price level.

FIGURE 14-12   The Price Level Versus the Inflation Rate, 1960–2019

With the exception of 2009, over the past half-century the price level has continuously increased. But the *inflation rate*—the rate at which prices are rising—has had both ups and downs. And in 2009, the inflation rate briefly turned negative, a phenomenon called *deflation*.

Data from: Bureau of Labor Statistics.

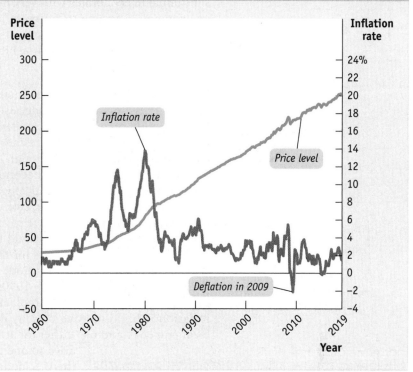

Economists believe that high rates of inflation impose significant economic costs. The most important of these costs are *shoe-leather costs, menu costs,* and *unit-of-account costs.* We'll discuss each in turn.

Shoe-Leather Costs People hold money—cash in their wallets and bank deposits—for convenience in making transactions. A high inflation rate, however, discourages people from holding money because the purchasing power of the cash in your wallet and the funds in your bank account steadily erode as the overall level of prices rises. This leads people to move funds into assets they believe will hold value and to reduce the amount of money they hold, often at considerable economic cost. For example, when Venezuelan inflation hit 800% in 2016, people began holding cigarettes and electronic currency (like Bitcoin) instead of Venezuelan currency.

During the most famous of all inflations, the German *hyperinflation* of 1921–1923, merchants employed runners to take their cash to the bank many times a day to convert it into something that would hold its value, such as a stable foreign currency. Hyperinflation occurs when prices rise by 50% or more per month, making an annual inflation rate of around 13,000%. In such cases, to avoid having the purchasing power of their money eroded, people use up valuable resources, such as the labor of the German runners, that can be used productively elsewhere. During the German hyperinflation, so many banking transactions were taking place that the number of employees at German banks nearly quadrupled—from around 100,000 in 1913 to 375,000 in 1923.

More recently, Brazil experienced hyperinflation during the early 1990s; during that episode, the Brazilian banking sector grew so large that it accounted for 15% of GDP, more than twice the size of the financial sector in the United States measured as a share of GDP. The large increase in the Brazilian banking sector needed to cope with the consequences of inflation, which represented a loss of real resources to its society.

Increased costs of transactions caused by inflation are known as **shoe-leather costs,** an allusion to the wear and tear caused by the extra running around that

Shoe-leather costs are the increased costs of transactions caused by inflation.

takes place when people are trying to avoid holding money. Shoe-leather costs are substantial in economies with very high inflation, as anyone who has lived in such an economy—say, one suffering inflation of 100% or more per year—can attest. Most estimates suggest, however, that the shoe-leather costs of inflation at the rates seen in the United States—which in peacetime has never had inflation above 15%—are quite small.

Menu Costs In a modern economy, most of the things we buy have a listed price. There's a price listed under each item on a supermarket shelf, a price listed for goods sold on any online retailer's website, such as Amazon or Zappos, and a price listed for each dish on a restaurant's menu. Changing a listed price has a real cost, called a **menu cost.** Although the potential burden imposed by menu costs have diminished in advanced economies as more sales have shifted online and prices can be changed electronically, they still exist. For example, to change prices in a supermarket or a clothing store requires sending clerks to change the listed price with each item. In the face of inflation, of course, firms are forced to change prices more often than they would if the aggregate price level was more or less stable. This means higher costs for the economy as a whole.

In times of very high inflation, menu costs can be substantial. During the Brazilian inflation of the early 1990s, for instance, supermarket workers reportedly spent half of their time replacing old price stickers with new ones. When inflation is high, merchants may decide to stop listing prices in terms of the local currency and use either an artificial unit—in effect, measuring prices relative to one another—or a more stable currency, such as the U.S. dollar. This is exactly what the Israeli real estate market began doing in the mid-1980s: prices were quoted in U.S. dollars, even though payment was made in Israeli shekels. And this is also what happened in Zimbabwe when, in May 2008, official estimates of the inflation rate reached 1,694,000%. By 2009, the government had suspended the Zimbabwean dollar, allowing Zimbabweans to buy and sell goods using foreign currencies.

When one hundred trillion dollar bills are in circulation as they were in Zimbabwe, menu costs are substantial.

Menu costs are also present in low-inflation economies, but they are not severe. In low-inflation economies, businesses might update their prices only sporadically—not daily or even more frequently, as is the case in high-inflation or hyperinflation economies.

Unit-of-Account Costs In the Middle Ages, contracts were often specified "in kind": a tenant might, for example, be obliged to provide his landlord with a certain number of cattle each year (the phrase *in kind* actually comes from an ancient word for *cattle*). This may have made sense at the time, but it would be an awkward way to conduct modern business. Instead, we state contracts in monetary terms: a renter owes a certain number of dollars per month, a company that issues a bond promises to pay the bondholder the dollar value of the bond when it comes due, and so on. We also tend to make our economic calculations in dollars: a family planning its budget, or a small business owner trying to figure out how well the business is doing, makes estimates of the amount of money coming in and going out.

This role of the dollar as a basis for contracts and calculation is called the *unit-of-account* role of money. It's an important aspect of the modern economy. Yet it's a role that can be degraded by inflation, which causes the purchasing power of a dollar to change over time—a dollar next year is worth less than a dollar this year. The effect, many economists argue, is to reduce the quality of economic decisions: the economy as a whole makes less efficient use of its resources because of the uncertainty caused by changes in the unit of account, the dollar.

The **menu cost** is the real cost of changing a listed price.

The **unit-of-account costs** of inflation are the costs arising from the way inflation makes money a less reliable unit of measurement.

Unit-of-account costs may be particularly important in the tax system because inflation can distort the measures of income on which taxes are collected. Here's an example: assume that the inflation rate is 10%, so the overall level of prices rises 10% each year. Suppose that a business buys an asset, such as a piece of land, for $100,000, then resells it a year later for $110,000. In a fundamental sense, the business didn't make a profit on the deal: in real terms, it got no more for the land than it paid for it. But U.S. tax law would say that the business made a capital gain of $10,000, and it would have to pay taxes on that phantom gain.

During the 1970s, when the United States had relatively high inflation, the distorting effects of inflation on the tax system were a serious problem. Some businesses were discouraged from productive investment spending because they found themselves paying taxes on phantom gains. Meanwhile, some unproductive investments became attractive because they led to phantom losses that reduced tax bills. When inflation fell in the 1980s—and tax rates were reduced—these problems became much less important.

Winners and Losers from Inflation As we've just learned, a high inflation rate imposes overall costs on the economy. In addition, inflation can produce winners and losers within the economy. The main reason inflation sometimes helps some people while hurting others is that economic transactions often involve contracts that extend over a period of time, such as loans, and these contracts are normally specified in nominal—that is, in dollar—terms.

In the case of a loan, the borrower receives a certain amount of funds at the beginning, and the loan contract specifies the *interest rate* on the loan and when it must be paid off. The **interest rate** is the return a lender receives for allowing borrowers the use of their savings for one year, calculated as a percentage of the amount borrowed.

What a dollar is worth in real terms—that is, in terms of purchasing power—depends greatly on the rate of inflation over the intervening years of the loan. Economists summarize the effect of inflation on borrowers and lenders by distinguishing between the *nominal* interest rate and the *real* interest rate. The **nominal interest rate** is the interest rate in dollar terms—for example, the interest rate on a student loan. The **real interest rate** is the nominal interest rate minus the rate of inflation. For example, if a loan carries an interest rate of 8%, but there is 5% inflation, the real interest rate is 8% − 5% = 3%.

When a borrower and a lender enter into a loan contract, the contract is normally written in dollar terms—that is, the interest rate it specifies is a nominal interest rate. (And in later chapters, when we say the interest rate we will mean the nominal interest rate unless noted otherwise.) But each party to a loan contract has an expectation about the future rate of inflation and therefore an expectation about the real interest rate on the loan. If the actual inflation rate is *higher* than expected, borrowers gain at the expense of lenders: borrowers will repay their loans with funds that have a lower real value than had been expected. Conversely, if the inflation rate is *lower* than expected, lenders will gain at the expense of borrowers: borrowers must repay their loans with funds that have a higher real value than had been expected.

In modern America, home mortgages are the most important source of gains and losses from inflation. While some mortgage interest rates are linked to the inflation rate, the vast majority are not, creating big winners and losers when inflation rates have changed unexpectedly. Americans who took out mortgages in the early 1970s quickly found the real cost of their payments reduced by higher-than-expected inflation. In contrast, those who took out mortgages in the early 1990s lost. The inflation rate fell to lower-than-expected levels in the following years and raised the cost of their payments.

The **unit-of-account costs** of inflation are the costs arising from the way inflation makes money a less reliable unit of measurement.

The **interest rate** on a loan is the price, calculated as a percentage of the amount borrowed, that lenders charge borrowers for the use of their savings for one year.

The **nominal interest rate** is the interest rate expressed in dollar terms.

The **real interest rate** is the nominal interest rate minus the rate of inflation.

Disinflation is the process of bringing the inflation rate down.

Because gains for some and losses for others result from inflation that is either higher or lower than expected, yet another problem arises: uncertainty about the future inflation rate discourages people from entering into any form of long-term contract. This is an additional cost of high inflation, because high rates of inflation are usually unpredictable. In countries with high and uncertain inflation, long-term loans are rare, which makes it difficult in many cases to make long-term investments.

One last point: unexpected *deflation*—a surprise fall in the price level—creates winners and losers, too. Between 1929 and 1933, as the U.S. economy plunged into the Great Depression, the consumer price index fell by 35%. This meant that debtors, including many farmers and homeowners, saw a sharp rise in the real value of their debts, which led to widespread bankruptcies and helped create a banking crisis, as lenders found their customers unable to pay back their loans. And as you can see in Figure 14-12, deflation occurred again in 2009, when the inflation rate fell to –2% at the trough of a deep recession. Like the Great Depression (but to a much lesser extent), the unexpected deflation of 2009 imposed heavy costs on debtors.

Inflation Is Easy; Disinflation Is Hard

There is not much evidence that a rise in the inflation rate from 2% to 5% would do a great deal of harm to the economy. Still, policy makers generally move forcefully to bring inflation back down when it creeps above 2% or 3%. Why? Because experience shows that bringing the inflation rate down—a process called **disinflation**—is very difficult and costly once a higher rate of inflation has become well established in the economy.

Figure 14-13 shows what happened during two major episodes of disinflation in the United States, in the mid-1970s and in the early 1980s. The horizontal axis shows the unemployment rate. The vertical axis shows *core inflation* over the previous year, a measure that excludes volatile food and energy prices and is widely considered a better measure of underlying inflation than overall consumer prices. Each marker represents the inflation rate and the unemployment rate for one month. In each episode, unemployment and inflation followed a sort of clockwise

---

FIGURE 14-13 The Cost of Disinflation

There were two major periods of disinflation in modern U.S. history: in the mid-1970s and the early 1980s. This figure shows the track of the unemployment rate and the core inflation rate, which excludes food and energy, during these two episodes. In each case bringing inflation down required a temporary but very large increase in the unemployment rate, demonstrating the high cost of disinflation.

Data from: Bureau of Labor Statistics.

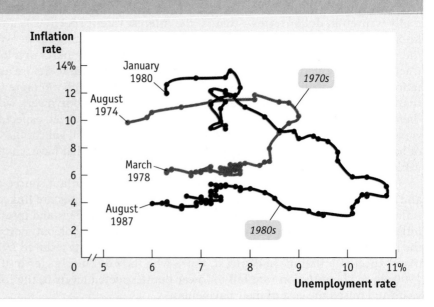

spiral, with high inflation gradually falling in the face of an extended period of very high unemployment.

According to many economists, these periods of high unemployment that temporarily depressed the economy were necessary to reduce inflation that had become deeply embedded in the economy. The best way to avoid having to put the economy through a wringer to reduce inflation, however, is to avoid having a serious inflation problem in the first place. So, as a form of preventive medicine for the economy, policy makers respond forcefully to signs that inflation may be accelerating.

>> Check Your Understanding 14-3
Solutions appear at back of book.

1. The widespread use of technology has revolutionized the banking industry, making it much easier for customers to access and manage their assets. Does this mean that the shoe-leather costs of inflation are higher or lower than they used to be?

2. Most people in the United States have grown accustomed to a modest inflation rate of around 2% to 3%. Who would gain and who would lose if inflation unexpectedly came to a complete stop over the next 15 or 20 years?

>> Quick Review

• The **real wage** and **real income** are unaffected by the level of prices.

• Inflation, like unemployment, is a major concern of policy makers—so much so that in the past they have accepted high unemployment as the price of reducing inflation.

• While the overall level of prices is irrelevant, high rates of inflation impose real costs on the economy: **shoe-leather costs, menu costs,** and **unit-of-account costs.**

• The **interest rate** is the return a lender receives for use of his or her funds for a year. The **real interest rate** is equal to the **nominal interest rate** minus the inflation rate. As a result, unexpectedly high inflation helps borrowers and hurts lenders. With high and uncertain inflation, people will often avoid long-term investments.

• **Disinflation** is very costly, so policy makers try to avoid getting into situations of high inflation in the first place.

SOLVED PROBLEM   The Current Population Survey

Every month, the U.S. Census Bureau surveys about 60,000 American households to gather information about the U.S. labor force for the Bureau of Labor Statistics. The survey, known as the Current Population Survey (CPS), provides information about employment, unemployment, earnings, work hours, and more. Once these data are collected, researchers at the Bureau of Labor Statistics publish a number of tables describing their findings. Please complete the following table and analyze the trend in the unemployment rate, the employment–population rate, and the labor force participation rate from December 2017 through December 2018. Then determine whether the unemployment rate in December 2018 is high or low by historical standards.

	Dec. 2017 (thousands)	Oct. 2018 (thousands)	Nov. 2018 (thousands)	Dec. 2018 (thousands)
Civilian noninstitutional population	256,109	258,514	258,708	258,888
Civilian labor force	160,636	162,694	162,821	163,240
Labor force participation rate	?	?	?	?
Employed	154,065	156,582	156,803	156,945
Employment–population ratio	?	?	?	?
Unemployed	6,572	6,112	6,018	6,294
Unemployment rate	?	?	?	?
Not in labor force	95,473	95,820	95,887	95,648

STEP | 1 Complete the table *Read pages 376–377 and use Equations 14-1 and 14-2.*

Equations 14-1 and 14-2 demonstrate how to calculate the labor force participation rate and the unemployment rate. The employment–population ratio is calculated as follows:

$$\text{Employment–Population Ratio} = \frac{\text{Employed}}{\text{Civilian noninstitutional population}} \times 100$$

This is the completed table.

	Dec. 2017 (thousands)	Oct. 2018 (thousands)	Nov. 2018 (thousands)	Dec. 2018 (thousands)
Civilian noninstitutional population	256,109	258,514	258,708	258,888
Civilian labor force	160,636	162,694	162,821	163,240
Labor force participation rate	62.7	62.9	62.9	63.1
Employed	154,065	156,582	156,803	156,945
Employment–population ratio	60.2	60.6	60.6	60.6
Unemployed	6,572	6,112	6,018	6,294
Unemployment rate	4.1	3.8	3.7	3.9
Not in labor force	95,473	95,820	95,887	95,648

As shown in Equation 14-1 in the chapter, the participation rate is calculated by dividing the civilian labor force by the civilian noninstitutional population and then multiplying by 100. The December 2018 labor force participation rate is therefore $\left(\dfrac{163,240}{258,888}\right) \times 100 = 63.1\%$. As shown in Equation 14-2 in the chapter, the unemployment rate is calculated by dividing the unemployed by the civilian labor force and then multiplying by 100. The December 2018 unemployment rate is therefore $\left(\dfrac{6,294}{163,240}\right) \times 100 = 3.9\%$. The employment–population ratio is calculated by dividing the employed by the civilian noninstitutional population and then multiplying by 100. The December 2018 employment–population ratio is therefore $\left(\dfrac{156,945}{258,888}\right) \times 100 = 60.6\%$.

STEP | 2 Analyze the trend in the unemployment rate, the employment-population rate, and the participation rate from December 2017 through December 2018. Is the unemployment rate in December 2018 high or low by historical standards? *Read pages 376–377 and study Figure 14-1.*

Both the unemployment rate and the labor force participation rate have steadily decreased over this period. The employment–population ratio first increased but has remained stable over the last three months, as well. By historical standards, as indicated in Figure 14-1, an unemployment rate of 3.9% is relatively low, previously reaching 3.9% in 2000.

SUMMARY

1. The two principal objectives of macroeconomic policy are price stability (a low, but positive, level of inflation) and low unemployment.

2. **Employment** is the number of people employed; **unemployment** is the number of people unemployed and actively looking for work. Their sum is equal to the **labor force;** the **labor force participation rate** is the percentage of the population age 16 or older that is in the labor force.

3. The **unemployment rate,** the percentage of the labor force that is unemployed and actively looking for work, can both overstate and understate the true level of unemployment. It can overstate because it counts as unemployed those who are continuing to search for a job despite having been offered one. It can understate because it ignores frustrated workers, such as **discouraged workers, marginally attached workers,** and the **underemployed.** In addition, the unemployment rate varies greatly among different groups in the population; it is typically higher for younger workers and for workers near retirement age than for workers in their prime working years.

4. The unemployment rate is affected by the business cycle. The unemployment rate generally falls when the growth rate of real GDP is above average and generally increases when the growth rate of real GDP is below average. A **jobless recovery,** a period in which real GDP is growing but unemployment rises, often follows recessions.

5. Job creation and destruction, as well as voluntary job separations, lead to **job search** and **frictional unemployment.** In addition, a variety of factors such as minimum wages, labor unions, **efficiency wages,** government policies designed to help laid-off workers, and a mismatch between employees and employers

result in a situation in which there is a surplus of labor at the market wage rate, creating **structural unemployment.** As a result, the **natural rate of unemployment,** the sum of frictional and structural unemployment, is well above zero, even when jobs are plentiful.

6. The actual unemployment rate is equal to the natural rate of unemployment, the share of unemployment that is independent of the business cycle, plus **cyclical unemployment,** the share of unemployment that depends on fluctuations in the business cycle.

7. The natural rate of unemployment changes over time, largely in response to changes in labor force characteristics, labor market institutions, and government policies.

8. Inflation does not, as many assume, make everyone poorer by raising the level of prices. That's because wages and incomes are adjusted to take into account a rising price level, leaving **real wages** and **real income** unaffected. However, a high inflation rate imposes overall costs on the economy: **shoe-leather costs, menu costs,** and **unit-of-account costs.**

9. Inflation can produce winners and losers within the economy, because long-term contracts are generally written in dollar terms. The **interest rate** specified in a loan is typically a **nominal interest rate,** which differs from the **real interest rate** due to inflation. A higher-than-expected inflation rate is good for borrowers and bad for lenders. A lower-than-expected inflation rate is good for lenders and bad for borrowers.

10. Many believe policies that depress the economy and produce high unemployment are necessary to reduce embedded inflation. Because **disinflation** is very costly, policy makers try to prevent inflation from becoming excessive in the first place.

KEY TERMS

Employment, p. 376
Unemployment, p. 376
Labor force, p. 376
Labor force participation rate, p. 376
Unemployment rate, p. 377
Discouraged workers, p. 377
Marginally attached workers, p. 377
Underemployment, p. 377

Jobless recovery, p. 380
Job search, p. 382
Frictional unemployment, p. 382
Structural unemployment, p. 384
Efficiency wages, p. 386
Natural rate of unemployment, p. 387
Cyclical unemployment, p. 387
Real wage, p. 390

Real income, p. 390
Shoe-leather costs, p. 391
Menu costs, p. 392
Unit-of-account costs, p. 393
Interest rate, p. 393
Nominal interest rate, p. 393
Real interest rate, p. 393
Disinflation, p. 394

DISCUSSION QUESTION

1. Each month, usually on the first Friday of the month, the Bureau of Labor Statistics releases the Employment Situation Summary for the previous month. Go to www.bls.gov and find the latest report. On the Bureau of Labor Statistics home page, at the top of the page, select the "Economic Releases" tab, find "Latest Releases," and select "Employment Situation." You will find the Employment Situation Summary listed at the top. How does the current unemployment rate compare to the rate one month earlier? How does the current unemployment rate compare to the rate one year earlier?

PROBLEMS

interactive activity

1. In general, how do changes in the unemployment rate vary with changes in real GDP? After several quarters of a severe recession, explain why we might observe a decrease in the official unemployment rate. Explain why we could see an increase in the official unemployment rate after several quarters of a strong expansion.

2. In each of the following situations, what type of unemployment is Melanie facing?

   a. After completing a complex programming project, Melanie is laid off. Her prospects for a new job requiring similar skills are good, and she has signed up with a programmer placement service. She has passed up offers for low-paying jobs.

   b. When Melanie and her co-workers refused to accept pay cuts, her employer outsourced their programming tasks to workers in another country. This phenomenon is occurring throughout the programming industry.

   c. Due to the current slump, Melanie has been laid off from her programming job. Her employer promises to rehire her when business picks up.

3. Part of the information released in the Employment Situation Summary concerns how long individuals have been unemployed. Go to www.bls.gov to find the latest report. Use the same technique as in Problem 1 to find the Employment Situation Summary. Near the end of the Employment Situation, click on Table A-12, titled "Unemployed persons by duration of unemployment." Use the seasonally adjusted numbers to answer the following questions.

   a. How many workers were unemployed less than 5 weeks? What percentage of all unemployed workers do these workers represent? How do these numbers compare to the previous month's data?

   b. How many workers were unemployed for 27 or more weeks? What percentage of all unemployed workers do these workers represent? How do these numbers compare to the previous month's data?

   c. How long has the average worker been unemployed (average duration, in weeks)? How does this compare to the average for the previous month's data?

   d. Comparing the latest month for which there are data with the previous month, has the problem of long-term unemployment improved or deteriorated?

4. A country's labor force is the sum of the number of employed and unemployed workers. The accompanying table provides data on the size of the labor force and the number of unemployed workers for different regions of the United States.

Region	Labor force (thousands)		Unemployed (thousands)	
	July 2015	July 2016	July 2015	July 2016
Northeast	28,397	28,565	1,459	1,377
South	57,297	58,022	2,978	2,720
Midwest	34,489	34,996	1,627	1,585
West	36,949	37,543	2,099	1,985

Data from: Bureau of Labor Statistics.

   a. Calculate the number of workers employed in each of the regions in July 2015 and July 2016. Use your answers to calculate the change in the total number of workers employed between July 2015 and July 2016.

   b. For each region, calculate the growth in the labor force from July 2015 to July 2016.

   c. Compute unemployment rates in the different regions of the country in July 2015 and July 2016.

   d. What can you infer about the fall in unemployment rates over this period? Was it caused by a net gain in the number of jobs or by a large fall in the number of people seeking jobs?

5. Access the Discovering Data exercise for Chapter 14 Problem 5 online to answer the following questions.

   a. What is the current federal minimum wage?

   b. In what year was the federal minimum wage last increased?

   c. What is the current value for the real minimum wage?

   d. In what year was the real minimum wage the highest? The lowest?

   e. In general, since 1970, how has the purchasing power of the minimum wage changed over time?

6. In which of the following cases is it more likely for efficiency wages to exist? Why?

   a. Jane and her boss work as a team selling ice cream.

b. Jane sells ice cream without any direct supervision by her boss.

c. Jane speaks Korean and sells ice cream in a neighborhood in which Korean is the primary language. It is difficult to find another worker who speaks Korean.

7. How will the following changes affect the natural rate of unemployment?

a. The government reduces the time during which an unemployed worker can receive unemployment benefits.

b. More teenagers focus on their studies and do not look for jobs until after college.

c. Greater access to the internet leads both potential employers and potential employees to use the internet to list and find jobs.

d. Union membership declines.

8. With its tradition of a job for life for most citizens, Japan once had a much lower unemployment rate than that of the United States; from 1960 to 1995, the unemployment rate in Japan exceeded 3% only once. However, since the crash of its stock market in 1989 and slow economic growth in the 1990s, the job-for-life system has broken down and unemployment rose to more than 5% in 2003.

a. Explain the likely effect of the breakdown of the job-for-life system in Japan on the Japanese natural rate of unemployment.

b. As the accompanying diagram shows, the rate of growth of real GDP has picked up in Japan after 2001 and before the global economic crisis of 2007–2009. Explain the likely effect of this increase in real GDP growth on the unemployment rate. Is the likely cause of the change in the unemployment rate during this period a change in the natural rate of unemployment or a change in the cyclical unemployment rate?

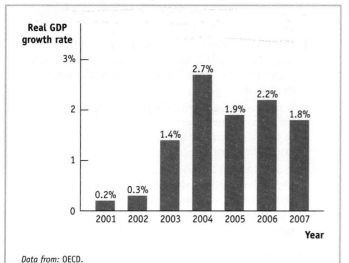

Data from: OECD.

9. In the following examples, is inflation creating winners and losers at no net cost to the economy, or is inflation imposing a net cost on the economy? If a net cost is being imposed, which type of cost is involved?

a. When inflation is expected to be high, workers get paid more frequently and make more trips to the bank.

b. Lanwei is reimbursed by her company for her work-related travel expenses. Sometimes, however, the company takes a long time to reimburse her. So when inflation is high, she is less willing to travel for her job.

c. Hector has a mortgage with a fixed nominal interest rate of 6% that he took out five years ago. Over the years, the inflation rate has crept up unexpectedly to its present level of 7%.

d. In response to unexpectedly high inflation, the manager of Cozy Cottages of Cape Cod must reprint and resend expensive color brochures correcting the price of rentals this season.

10. The accompanying diagram shows the interest rate on one-year loans and inflation from 2001–2016 in the economy of Albernia. When would one-year loans have been especially attractive and why?

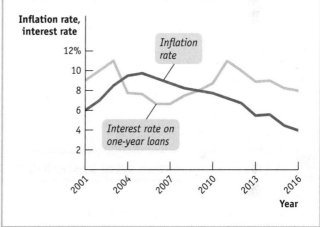

11. The accompanying table provides the inflation rate in the year 2005 and the average inflation rate over the period 2006–2015 for seven different countries.

Country	Inflation rate in 2005	Average inflation rate in 2006–2015
Brazil	6.87%	5.70%
China	1.82	2.89
France	1.90	1.47
Indonesia	10.46	6.82
Japan	−0.27	0.32
Turkey	8.18	8.30
United States	3.37	1.96

Data from: IMF.

a. Given the expected relationship between average inflation and menu costs, rank the countries in descending order of menu costs using average inflation over the period 2006–2015.

b. Rank the countries in order of inflation rates that most favored borrowers with ten-year loans that were taken out in 2005. Assume that the loans were agreed upon with the expectation that the inflation rate for 2006 to 2015 would be the same as the inflation rate in 2005.

c. Did borrowers who took out ten-year loans in Japan gain or lose overall versus lenders? Explain.

12. Access the Discovering Data exercise for Chapter 14 Problem 12 online to answer the following questions.

a. What is the current level of employment for individuals without a high school diploma?

b. How much has employment changed for high school graduates from 2007 through 2016?

c. Since 2007, which education group has experienced the largest increase in employment?

d. Since the end of the Great Recession in 2009, how has employment changed for the different education levels? Calculate the net gain (or loss) of jobs for each category to answer.

e. What percent of the employed had a bachelor's degree in January 1992? What percent has a bachelor's degree today?

f. Calculate the change in the share of employment by education level since 1992.

13. The accompanying diagram shows the inflation rate in the United Kingdom from 1980 to 2016.

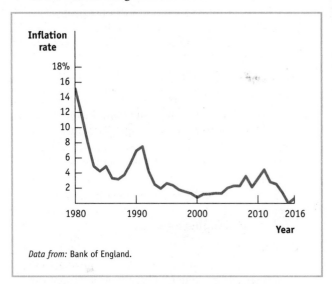

Data from: Bank of England.

a. Between 1980 and 1985, policy makers in the United Kingdom worked to lower the inflation rate. What would you predict happened to unemployment between 1980 and 1985?

b. Policy makers in the United Kingdom react forcefully when the inflation rate rises above a target rate of 2%. Why would it be harmful if inflation rose from 0.7% (the level in 2016) to, say, a level of 5%?

WORK IT OUT Interactive step-by-step help with solving this problem can be found online.

14. There is only one labor market in Profunctia. All workers have the same skills, and all firms hire workers with these skills. Use the accompanying diagram, which shows the supply of and demand for labor, to answer the following questions. Illustrate each answer with a diagram.

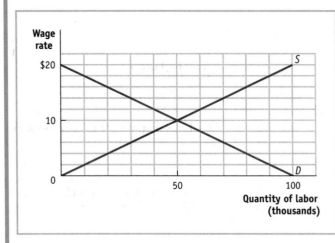

a. What is the equilibrium wage rate in Profunctia? At this wage rate, what are the level of employment, the size of the labor force, and the unemployment rate?

b. If the government of Profunctia sets a minimum wage equal to $12, what will be the level of employment, the size of the labor force, and the unemployment rate?

c. If unions bargain with the firms in Profunctia and set a wage rate equal to $14, what will be the level of employment, the size of the labor force, and the unemployment rate?

d. If the concern for retaining workers and encouraging high-quality work leads firms to set a wage rate equal to $16, what will be the level of employment, the size of the labor force, and the unemployment rate?

Chicago History Museum/Getty Images

Before there was the internet, there was mail order, and for rural and small-town America that meant, above all, the Montgomery Ward catalog. Starting in 1872, that catalog made it possible for families far from the big city to buy goods their local store wasn't likely to stock—everything from bicycles to pianos. In 1893 Sears, Roebuck and Co. introduced a competing catalog, and in the 1920s both companies opened physical stores around the country. The two firms struggled for dominance right up to World War II. After that, however, Montgomery Ward fell far behind. By 2001, it had closed all of its stores.

Why did Montgomery Ward falter? One key factor was that its management misjudged postwar prospects. The 1930s were a difficult time for retailers in general because of the catastrophic economic impact of the Great Depression. Figure 14-14 shows an index of department store sales, which plunged after 1930 and hadn't fully recovered by 1940. Montgomery Ward coped with this tough environment by cutting back: closing some stores, cutting costs, and accumulating a lot of cash. This strategy served the company well, restoring profitability and putting it in a very strong financial position.

Unfortunately for the company, it made the mistake of returning to this strategy after World War II—and the postwar environment was nothing like the environment of the 1930s. Overall department store sales surged: by 1960 they were more than four times their 1940 level. Sears and other retailers expanded to meet this surge in demand, especially in the rapidly growing suburbs. But Montgomery Ward, expecting the 1930s to return, just sat on its cash; it didn't open any new stores until 1959. By failing to expand with the market, Montgomery Ward suffered what turned out to be an irretrievable loss of market share, reputation, and name recognition.

Nothing in business is forever. Eventually Sears too entered a long, slow decline. First it was overtaken by newer retailers like Walmart, whose big box stores didn't sell large appliances but generally sold other goods more cheaply than Sears, in part by using information technology to hold costs down. More recently, the rise of online shopping has hurt traditional retailers of all kinds. But Montgomery Ward's self-inflicted defeat in the years after World War II nonetheless shows how important it is for businesses to understand what is happening in the broader economic environment— that is, to take macroeconomics into account.

FIGURE 14-14 Department Store Sales Index, 1919–1940

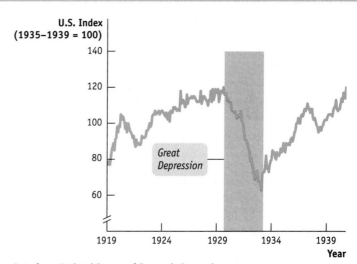

Data from: National Bureau of Economic Research.

QUESTIONS FOR THOUGHT

1. Why was it profitable for Montgomery Ward to close some of its stores during the Great Depression?

2. Use Figure 14-14 to compare the nature of the Great Depression to the Great Recession. What about the Great Depression made Montgomery Ward's decision not to expand in the 1940s appear rational? Would the same decision be rational now, in the aftermath of the Great Recession? Explain.

In early 2016 the *Wall Street Journal* reported that a number of big financial players, including the legendary speculator George Soros, had taken an interest in the future performance of the Chinese economy. Although China had achieved spectacular economic growth over the past 25 years, much of the *smart money* (cash invested or wagered by those considered to be experts) in the global financial system thought that boom times in China were over and that an economic crisis was looming. They believed that a weak Chinese economy would be especially devastating because Chinese companies had borrowed heavily during the boom times. Some even warned of political instability as tens of millions of Chinese citizens found their new-found prosperity slipping away.

That same year, global financial speculators placed their money in assets that would do well if the Chinese economy took a plunge.

What was the basis of this pessimism? And why did it merit betting hundreds of millions of dollars on it? Although official Chinese statistics did indicate some slowing of growth, they also showed a relatively robust growth rate of 6.9% in 2015 and forecast similar growth for 2016. Yet, this is what the smart money in global markets knew: nobody believed China's official numbers.

In fact, many in China knew this as well. In an unguarded moment, a rising Chinese official named Li Keqiang (shown in the accompanying photo) told the U.S. ambassador that China's official GDP figures were "man-made." That is, he effectively admitted they were concocted by Chinese officials to fit the optimistic story about the state of the economy that the government was communicating to its citizens. Li Keqiang also explained that in trying to understand the state of the Chinese economy he used three indicators that were easy to track and that weren't part of the Chinese national account: railway shipments, electricity consumption, and loans disbursed by banks. The revelation of this conversation made a splash around the world because it confirmed what many observers believed. Mr. Li knew what he was talking about. He soon went on to become China's Prime Minister, and if he didn't believe his own government's numbers, why should anyone else?

For businesses with interests in China, it is standard operating procedure to turn to independent estimates of Chinese GDP growth produced by a variety of researchers at places like Citibank, the British consulting firm Lombard Street Research, and the Conference Board, a research-oriented business association. Many of these estimates make use of some variation of the "Li Keqiang index"; that is, they rely on the data Li Keqiang uses, as well as other indicators like data on trade with neighboring countries like South Korea that have a reputation for clean statistics. For example, a fall in Chinese imports of components used in the production of goods from South Korea—which is also a fall in South Korea's exports to China—is a good indication of a slump in Chinese manufacturing.

So how much did these independent estimates differ from the official statistics? They generally suggested a much sharper slowdown than was indicated by the numbers coming from the Chinese government. Was this discrepancy enough to justify big bets against China? At the time of writing, it's too early to know.

QUESTIONS FOR THOUGHT

1. Why would an economic downturn cause problems for Chinese companies that borrowed heavily?

2. How do the three statistics that Li Keqiang cited fit into the three different ways to calculate GDP?

3. What business problems might China's untrustworthy numbers create?

We Do Chores.
You Live Life.

From major cleaning to minor repairs,
we make home work.

"Moving is the worst. Yard work is the worst. Building IKEA furniture is the worst." So began a 2015 report on TaskRabbit, a company founded in 2008 (under the name RunMyErrand), that helps people hire others to do their chores. As of 2019 there were about 140,000 of these freelancers, whom the company calls Taskers, and TaskRabbit operated in 53 U.S. cities, Great Britain, and Canada.

Why would becoming a Tasker seem appealing to some workers? The great majority of Taskers are part-time workers, who want flexibility in their employment; the company's pitch to potential Taskers contains the slogan "Start Tasking. Earn money your way." and features testimonials from workers who combined employment with parenting, careers in the arts, and so on.

Working part-time for a variety of clients isn't a new phenomenon. On urban street corners across America, workers still line up early each morning in the hope of getting day jobs in industries like construction, where the need for workers fluctuates, sometimes unpredictably. For more skilled workers, there are numerous online resources, as well as temporary staffing agencies like Allegis Group, that provide workers on a subcontracting basis, from a few days to months at a time. And some people still find temporary jobs by calling numbers listed in classified ads, or even going door to door.

But TaskRabbit—founded the year after Apple introduced its first iPhone—tries to use the ubiquity of smartphones to simplify the process. Originally it was set up as a kind of auction market, in which potential employers and workers placed bids, but since 2014 it has relied on a streamlined system that is very similar to the way car services like Uber or Lyft match riders with willing drivers. TaskRabbit's app let those seeking help make their needs known simply by tapping on one of a few common chores; potential workers can then offer to do jobs that match the locations and skills they have put in their profiles, again simply by tapping on jobs that appear on their smartphones. (They have already specified their hourly rate.) The process takes a lot less time and effort than standing on street corners, pounding the pavement, performing online job searches, or even calling the numbers from old-style classified ads.

How big a deal are enterprises like TaskRabbit? Some observers suggest that we're seeing the rise of a *gig economy,* in which large numbers of people freelance, moving from job to job rather than being formal employees of a large firm. There's probably some hype in these pronouncements, but real change does seem to be happening. In fact, one recent study concludes that the number of people with alternative work arrangements such as freelancing grew 50% from 2005 to 2015, accounting for *all* net U.S. job growth over that period. It's hard to estimate the number of workers in the gig economy. As of 2018, varying surveys find the share of independent workers in the U.S. economy to be between 10% and 36% of the workforce.

QUESTIONS FOR THOUGHT

1. How is the matching of job-seekers and employers through services like TaskRabbit likely to affect frictional unemployment?

2. What is the likely effect of such services on the number of people considered to be in the labor force?

3. Some analysts suggest that most freelancers have other jobs, and only do gig economy work on the side. How does that statement help explain the lack of clear evidence for a growing gig economy?

15 | Long-Run Economic Growth

AIRPOCALYPSE NOW

ON JANUARY 2, 2017, a video shot in Beijing went viral. It was a time-lapse recording showing a "wall of smog" overrunning China's capital, with blue skies quickly giving way to an almost complete lack of visibility. Unfortunately, the event wasn't all that exceptional. Severe pollution alerts have become common in Beijing and other major Chinese cities.

Rapid, uncontrolled economic growth has resulted in much higher living standards in China but at the cost of very high levels of pollution.

The *New York Times* has referred to the oppressive smog as an "airpocalypse." The severe air pollution that has become commonplace in China's cities makes the smog that used to afflict Los Angeles and other U.S. cities seem mild by comparison. The smog in U.S. cities is mostly gone now thanks to pollution regulations.

It goes without saying that the situation in China is a bad thing. But it is also a byproduct of a very good thing: China's extraordinary economic growth in the past few decades, which has raised literally hundreds of millions of people out of abject poverty. These newly enriched masses want what everyone wants if they can afford it:

better food, better housing, and consumer goods—including, in many cases, cars. As recently as 2007 there were fewer than 60 million motor vehicles in China, around 1 for every 20 people. By 2016 that number had tripled. Unfortunately, the growth in China's car population has run ahead of its pollution controls. And the result, combined with the emissions of the country's burgeoning industry, is epochal smog.

Despite its troubling environmental problems, China has made enormous economic strides over the past few decades. Indeed, its recent history is probably the world's most impressive example to date of *long-run economic growth*—a sustained increase in output per capita. Yet despite its impressive performance, in terms of per capita income, China is still playing catch-up with economically advanced countries like the United States and Japan. China is still a relatively poor country because these other nations began the process of long-run economic growth many decades ago. In the case of the United States and European countries, long-run economic growth began more than a century ago.

Many economists have argued that long-run economic growth—why it happens and how to achieve it—is the single most important issue in macroeconomics because of its direct effect on living standards.

In this chapter, we present some facts about long-run growth, look at the factors that economists believe determine the pace at which long-run growth takes place, and examine how government policies can help or hinder growth. We will also address questions about the environmental sustainability of long-run growth. ●

WHAT YOU WILL LEARN

- Why is long-run economic growth measured as the increase in real GDP per capita, and how has real GDP per capita changed over time in different countries?
- Why is **productivity** the key to long-run economic growth, and how is it driven by **physical capital, human capital,** and **technological progress**?
- Why do long-run growth rates differ so much among countries?
- How does growth vary among several important regions of the world and why does the **convergence hypothesis** apply to economically advanced countries?
- How do scarcity of natural resources and environmental degradation pose a challenge to **sustainable long-run economic growth**?

Comparing Economies Across Time and Space

Before we analyze the sources of long-run economic growth, it's useful to have a sense of just how much the U.S. economy has grown over time and how large the gaps are between wealthy countries like the United States and countries that have yet to achieve comparable growth. So let's take a look at the numbers.

Real GDP per Capita

The key statistic used to track economic growth is *real GDP per capita*—real GDP divided by the population size. We focus on GDP because, as we learned in Chapter 13, GDP measures the total value of an economy's production of final goods and services as well as the income earned in that economy in a given year. We use *real* GDP because we want to separate changes in the quantity of goods and services from the effects of a rising price level. We focus on real GDP *per capita* because we want to isolate the effect of changes in the population. For example, other things equal, an increase in the population lowers the standard of living for the average person—there are now more people to share a given amount of real GDP. An increase in real GDP that only matches an increase in population leaves the average standard of living unchanged.

Although we also learned that growth in real GDP per capita should not be a policy goal in and of itself, it does serve as a very useful summary measure of a country's economic progress over time. Figure 15-1 shows real GDP per capita for the United States, India, and China, measured in 2011 dollars, from 1900 to 2016. The vertical axis is drawn on a logarithmic scale so that equal percent changes in real GDP per capita across countries are the same size in the graph.

To give a sense of how much the U.S. economy grew during the last century, Table 15-1 shows real GDP per capita at selected years, expressed two ways: as a percentage of the 1900 level and as a percentage of the 2016 level. In 1920, the U.S. economy already produced 136% as much per person as it did in 1900. In 2016, it produced 848% as much per person as it did in 1900, more than an eightfold

FIGURE 15-1 Economic Growth in the United States, India, and China over the Past Century

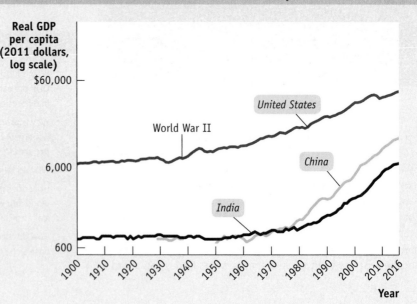

Real GDP per capita from 1900 to 2016, measured in 2011 dollars, is shown for the United States, India, and China. Equal percent changes in real GDP per capita are drawn the same size. As the steeper slopes of the lines representing China and India show, since 1980 India and China had a much higher growth rate than the United States. The standard of living achieved in the United States in 1900 was attained by China in 2000 and by India in 2016 (approximately for both). Note that the break in China data from 1940 to 1950 is due to war.

Data from: Maddison Project Database, version 2018. Bolt, Jutta, Robert Inklaar, Herman de Jong and Jan Luiten van Zanden (2018), "Rebasing 'Maddison': New income comparisons and the shape of long-run economic development," Maddison Project Working paper 10.

increase. Alternatively, in 1900 the U.S. economy produced only 12% as much per person as it did in 2016.

The income of the typical family normally grows more or less in proportion to per capita income. For example, a 1% increase in real GDP per capita corresponds, roughly, to a 1% increase in the income of the median or typical family—a family at the center of the income distribution. In 2016, the median American household had an income of about $57,500. Since Table 15-1 tells us that real GDP per capita in 1900 was only 12% of its 2016 level, a typical family in 1900 probably had a purchasing power only 12% as large as the purchasing power of a typical family in 2016. That's around $6,250 in today's dollars, representing a standard of living that we would now consider severe poverty. Today's typical American family, if transported back to the United States of 1900, would feel quite a lot of deprivation.

Many people in the world have a standard of living equal to or lower than that of the average American at the beginning of the last century. That's the message about China and India in Figure 15-1: despite dramatic economic growth in China over the last three decades and the more recent acceleration of economic growth in India, China has only recently exceeded the standard of living that the United States enjoyed in the early twentieth century, while India has matched it only recently. And much of the world today is poorer than China or India.

You can get a sense of how poor much of the world remains by looking at Figure 15-2, a map of the world in which countries are classified according to their 2015 levels of GDP per capita, in U.S. dollars. As you can see, large parts of the world have very low incomes. Generally speaking, the countries of Europe and North America, as well as a few in the Pacific, have high incomes. Many Asian countries, including China and India, have experienced rapid economic growth, moving them into the middle income categories. Africa, however, is dominated by countries with GDP less than $5,000 per capita. In fact, about 25% of the world's

TABLE 15-1 U.S. Real GDP per Capita

Year	Percentage of 1900 real GDP per capita	Percentage of 2016 real GDP per capita
1900	100%	12%
1920	136	16
1940	181	21
1980	474	56
2000	734	87
2016	848	100

Data from: Maddison Project Database, version 2018. Bolt, Jutta, Robert Inklaar, Herman de Jong, and Jan Luiten van Zanden (2018), "Rebasing 'Maddison': New income comparisons and the shape of long-run economic development," Maddison Project Working paper 10.

FIGURE 15-2 Incomes Around the World, 2015

Although the countries of Europe and North America—along with a few in the Pacific—have high incomes, much of the world is still very poor. Today, about a quarter of the world's population lives in countries with a lower standard of living than the United States had a century ago.

Data from: World Development Indicators, World Bank.

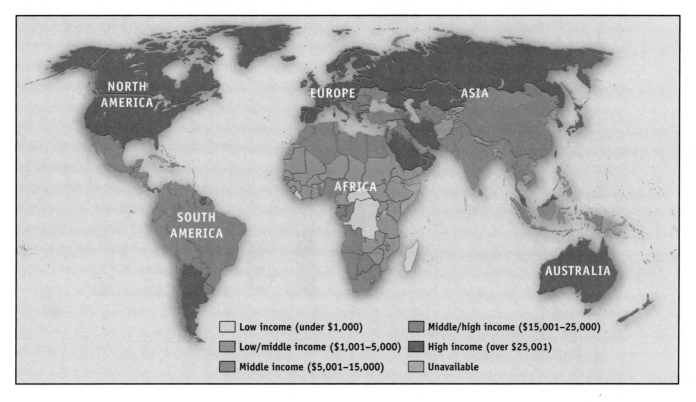

Low income (under $1,000)

Low/middle income ($1,001–5,000)

Middle income ($5,001–15,000)

Middle/high income ($15,001–25,000)

High income (over $25,001)

Unavailable

According to the **Rule of 70,** the time it takes a variable that grows gradually over time to double is approximately 70 divided by that variable's annual growth rate.

people live in countries with a lower standard of living than the United States had a century ago.

Growth Rates

How did the United States manage to produce over eight times as much real GDP per person in 2016 than in 1900? A little bit at a time. Long-run economic growth is normally a gradual process in which real GDP per capita grows at most a few percent per year. From 1900 to 2016, real GDP per capita in the United States increased an average of 1.9% each year.

To have a sense of the relationship between the annual growth rate of real GDP per capita and the long-run change in real GDP per capita, it's helpful to keep in mind the **Rule of 70,** a mathematical formula that tells us how long it takes real GDP per capita, or any other variable that grows gradually over time, to double. The approximate answer is:

(15-1) $\text{Number of years for variable to double} = \dfrac{70}{\text{Annual growth rate of variable}}$

(Note that the Rule of 70 can only be applied to a positive growth rate.) So, if real GDP per capita grows at 1% per year, it will take 70 years to double. If it grows at 2% per year, it will take only 35 years to double. In fact, U.S. real GDP per capita rose, on average, 1.9% per year over the last century.

Applying the Rule of 70 to this information implies that it should have taken 37 years for real GDP per capita to double; it would have taken 111 years—three periods of 37 years each—for U.S. real GDP per capita to double three times. That is, the Rule of 70 implies that over the course of 111 years, U.S. real GDP per capita should have increased by a factor of $2 \times 2 \times 2 = 8$. And this does turn out to be a pretty good approximation of reality. Between 1900 and 2016—a period of 116 years—real GDP per capita rose just over eightfold.

Figure 15-3 shows the average annual rate of growth of real GDP per capita for selected countries from 1980 to 2017. Some countries were notable success stories: for example, China, although still quite poor, has made spectacular progress. India, although not matching China's performance, has also achieved impressive

FIGURE 15-3 Comparing Recent Growth Rates

The average annual rate of growth of real GDP per capita from 1980 to 2017 is shown here for selected countries. China and, to a lesser extent, India and Ireland achieved impressive growth. The United States and France had moderate growth. Once considered an economically advanced country, Argentina had more sluggish growth. Still others, such as Zimbabwe, slid backward.

Data from: World Development Indicators.

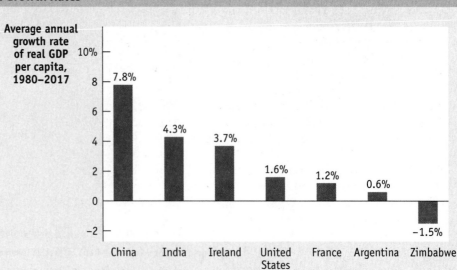

CHANGE IN LEVELS VERSUS RATE OF CHANGE

When studying economic growth, it's important to understand the difference between a *change in level* and a *rate of change*. When we say that real GDP "grew," we mean that the level of real GDP increased. For example, we might say that U.S. real GDP grew during 2017 by $392 billion.

If we knew the level of U.S. real GDP in 2016, we could also represent the amount of 2017 growth in terms of a rate of change. For example, if U.S. real GDP in 2016 had been $17,659 billion, then U.S. real GDP in 2017 would have been $17,659 billion + $392 billion = $18,051 billion.

We could calculate the rate of change, or the growth rate, of U.S. real GDP during 2017 as: (($18,051 billion − $17,659 billion)/$17,659 billion) ×100 = ($392 billion/$17,659 billion) × 100 = 2.2%. Remember that statements about economic growth over a period of years almost always refer to changes in the growth rate.

When talking about growth or growth rates, economists often use phrases that appear to mix the two concepts, which can be confusing. For example, when we say that "U.S. growth fell during the 1970s," we mean that the U.S. growth rate of real GDP was lower in the 1970s compared to the 1960s. When we say that "growth accelerated during the early 1990s," we mean that the growth rate increased year after year in the early 1990s—for example, going from 3% to 3.5% to 4%.

growth. The same is true for Bangladesh, as discussed in the following Economics in Action.

Some countries, though, have had very disappointing growth. Argentina was once considered a wealthy nation. In the early years of the twentieth century, it was in the same league as the United States and Canada. But since then it has lagged far behind more dynamic economies. And still others, like Zimbabwe, have slid backward.

What explains these differences in growth rates? To answer that question, we need to examine the sources of long-run economic growth, which we turn to next.

ECONOMICS >> *in Action*
An Economic Breakthrough in Bangladesh

Western news media rarely mention Bangladesh: it's not a political hot spot, it doesn't have oil, and it's overshadowed by its immense neighbor, India. Yet it is home to more than 160 million people—and although it is still very poor, it is nonetheless one of the greatest economic success stories of the past generation.

As recently as the 1980s, real GDP per capita in Bangladesh—which achieved independence from Pakistan in 1971, after a brutal war—was barely higher than it had been in 1950, when the country was so poor that it literally lived on the edge of starvation. In the early 1990s, however, the nation began a process of political and economic reform, making the transition from military rule to democracy, freeing up markets, and achieving monetary and fiscal

Although Bangladesh remains a very poor country, a high growth rate has improved living standards over the last 25 years.

stability. And growth took off, most notably with the rise of Bangladesh as a major exporter of clothing to Western markets. Real GDP per capita grew at over 3% per year, from the late 1980s through 2010, doubling over the 20-year period from 1990 to 2010.

By 2015 real GDP per capita was almost $2\frac{1}{2}$ times what it had been in 1990. Other measures also showed dramatic improvements in the quality of life: life expectancy rose by a dozen years, child mortality fell by 70%, school enrollment rose sharply, especially for girls.

Make no mistake, Bangladesh is still incredibly poor by American standards. Wages are very low, although rising, while working conditions are often terrible and dangerous—a point highlighted in 2013, when a factory complex collapsed, killing more than a thousand workers. But compared with its own past,

>> **Quick Review**

• Economic growth is measured using real GDP per capita.

• In the United States, real GDP per capita increased eightfold since 1900, resulting in a large increase in living standards.

• Many countries have real GDP per capita much lower than that of the United States. About 25% of the world's population has living standards worse than those existing in the United States in the early 1900s.

• The long-term rise in real GDP per capita is the result of gradual growth. The **Rule of 70** tells us how many years at a given annual rate of growth it takes to double real GDP per capita.

• Growth rates of real GDP per capita differ substantially among nations.

Bangladesh has achieved a lot of progress—and demonstrated that economic growth brings real human benefits, too.

>> **Check Your Understanding** 15-1

Solutions appear at back of book.

1. Why do economists use real GDP per capita to measure economic progress rather than some other measure, such as nominal GDP per capita or real GDP?

2. Apply the Rule of 70 to the data in Figure 15-3 to determine how many years it will take each of the countries listed there (except Zimbabwe) to double its real GDP per capita. Would India's real GDP per capita exceed that of the United States in the future if growth rates remain as shown in Figure 15-3? Why or why not?

3. Although China and India currently have growth rates much higher than the U.S. growth rate, the typical Chinese or Indian household is far poorer than the typical American household. Explain why.

The Sources of Long-Run Growth

Long-run economic growth depends almost entirely on one ingredient: rising *productivity*. However, a number of factors affect the growth of productivity. Let's look first at why productivity is the key ingredient and then examine what affects it.

The Crucial Importance of Productivity

Sustained economic growth occurs only when the amount of output produced by the average worker increases steadily. The term **labor productivity,** or **productivity** for short, is used to refer either to output per worker or, in some cases, to output per hour. (The number of hours worked by an average worker differs to some extent across countries, although this isn't an important factor in the difference between living standards in, say, India and the United States.) In this book we'll focus on output per worker. For the economy as a whole, productivity—output per worker—is simply real GDP divided by the number of people working.

You might wonder why we say that higher productivity is the only source of long-run growth. Can't an economy also increase its real GDP per capita by putting more of the population to work? The answer is, yes, but . . . .

For short periods of time, an economy can experience a burst of growth in output per capita by putting a higher percentage of the population to work. That happened in the United States during World War II, when millions of women who previously worked only in the home entered the paid workforce. The percentage of adult civilians employed outside the home rose from 50% in 1941 to 58% in 1944, and you can see the resulting bump in real GDP per capita during those years in Figure 15-1.

Over the longer run, however, the rate of employment growth is never very different from the rate of population growth. Over the course of the twentieth century, for example, the population of the United States rose at an average rate of 1.3% per year and employment rose 1.5% per year. Real GDP per capita rose 1.9% per year; of that, 1.7%—that is, almost 90% of the total—was the result of rising productivity. In general, overall real GDP can grow because of population growth, but any large increase in real GDP *per capita* must be the result of increased output *per worker*. That is, it must be due to higher productivity.

So increased productivity is the key to long-run economic growth. But what leads to higher productivity?

Labor productivity, often referred to simply as **productivity,** is output per worker.

Explaining Growth in Productivity

There are three main reasons why the average U.S. worker today produces far more than his or her counterpart a century ago. First, the modern worker has far more *physical capital,* such as machinery and office space, to work with. Second, the modern worker is much better educated and so possesses much more *human capital.* Finally, modern firms have the advantage of a century's *technological progress.* Let's look at each of these factors.

Increases in Physical Capital Economists define **physical capital** as manufactured resources such as buildings and machines. Physical capital makes workers more productive. For example, a worker operating a backhoe can dig a lot more feet of trench per day than one equipped only with a shovel.

The average U.S. private-sector worker today is backed up by more than $350,000 worth of physical capital—far more than a U.S. worker had 100 years ago and far more than the average worker in most other countries has today.

Increases in Human Capital It's not enough for workers to have good equipment—they must also know what to do with it. **Human capital** refers to the improvement in labor created by the education and knowledge embodied in the workforce.

The human capital of the United States has increased dramatically over the past century. A century ago, although most Americans were able to read and write, very few had an extensive education. In 1910, only 13.5% of Americans over 25 had graduated from high school and only 3% had four-year college degrees. By 2015, the percentages were 88% and 33%, respectively. It would be impossible to run today's economy with a population as poorly educated as the population of a century ago.

Analyses based on *growth accounting,* described later in this chapter, suggest that education—and its effect on productivity—is an even more important determinant of growth than increases in physical capital.

Technological Progress Probably the most important driver of productivity growth is **technological progress,** which is broadly defined as an advance in the technical means of the production of goods and services. We'll see shortly how economists measure the impact of technology on growth. Workers today are able to produce more than those in the past, even with the same amount of physical and human capital, because technology has advanced over time. It's important to realize that economically important technological progress need not be flashy or rely on cutting-edge science. Historians have noted that past economic growth has been driven not only by major inventions, such as the railroad or the semiconductor chip, but also by thousands of modest innovations, such as the flat-bottomed paper bag, patented in 1870, which made packing groceries and many other goods much easier, and the Post-it® note, introduced in 1980, which has had surprisingly large benefits for office productivity. Experts attribute much of the productivity surge that took place in the United States late in the twentieth century to new technology adopted by service-producing companies like Walmart rather than to high-technology companies.

Accounting for Growth: The Aggregate Production Function

Productivity is higher, other things equal, when workers are equipped with more physical capital, more human capital, better technology, or any combination of the three. But can we put numbers to these effects? To do this, economists make use of estimates of the **aggregate production function,** which shows how productivity depends on the quantities of physical capital per worker and human capital per worker as well as the state of technology.

Physical capital consists of human-made resources such as buildings and machines.

Human capital is the improvement in labor created by the education and knowledge embodied in the workforce.

Technological progress is an advance in the technical means of the production of goods and services.

The **aggregate production function** is a hypothetical function that shows how productivity (real GDP per worker) depends on the quantities of physical capital per worker and human capital per worker as well as the state of technology.

An aggregate production function exhibits **diminishing returns to physical capital** when, holding the amount of human capital per worker and the state of technology fixed, each successive increase in the amount of physical capital per worker leads to a smaller increase in productivity.

In general, all three factors tend to rise over time, as workers are equipped with more machinery, receive more education, and benefit from technological advances. What the aggregate production function does is allow economists to disentangle the effects of these three factors on overall productivity.

An example of an aggregate production function applied to real data comes from a comparative study of Chinese and Indian economic growth by the economists Barry Bosworth and Susan Collins of the Brookings Institution. They used the following aggregate production function:

GDP per worker = $T \times$ (Physical capital per worker)$^{0.4} \times$ (Human capital per worker)$^{0.6}$

where T represented an estimate of the level of technology and they assumed that each year of education raises workers' human capital by 7%. Using this function, they tried to explain why China grew faster than India between 1978 and 2004. About half the difference, they found, was due to China's higher levels of investment spending, which raised its level of physical capital per worker faster than India's. The other half was due to faster Chinese technological progress.

In analyzing historical economic growth, economists have discovered a crucial fact about the estimated aggregate production function: it exhibits **diminishing returns to physical capital.** That is, when the amount of human capital per worker and the state of technology are held fixed, each successive increase in the amount of physical capital per worker leads to a smaller increase in productivity.

Figure 15-4 and the table to its right give a hypothetical example of how the level of physical capital per worker might affect the level of real GDP per worker, holding human capital per worker and the state of technology fixed. In this example, we measure the quantity of physical capital in dollars.

FIGURE 15-4 Physical Capital and Productivity

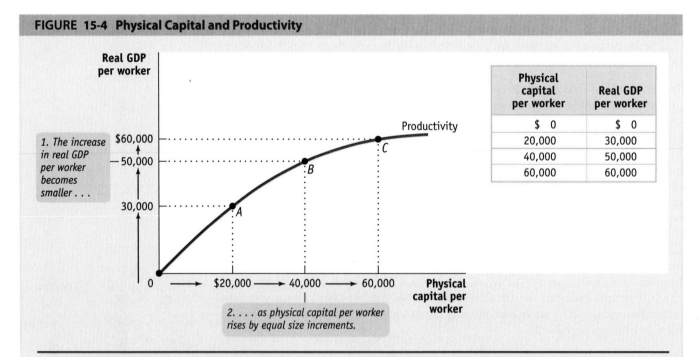

Physical capital per worker	Real GDP per worker
$ 0	$ 0
20,000	30,000
40,000	50,000
60,000	60,000

1. The increase in real GDP per worker becomes smaller . . .

2. . . . as physical capital per worker rises by equal size increments.

The aggregate production function shows how, in this case, holding human capital per worker and technology fixed, productivity increases as physical capital per worker rises. Other things equal, a greater quantity of physical capital per worker leads to higher real GDP per worker but is subject to diminishing returns: each successive addition to physical capital per worker produces a smaller increase in productivity. Starting at the origin, 0, a $20,000 increase in physical capital per worker leads to an increase in real GDP per worker of $30,000, indicated by point A. Starting from point A, another $20,000 increase in physical capital per worker leads to an increase in real GDP per worker but only of $20,000, indicated by point B. Finally, a third $20,000 increase in physical capital per worker leads to only a $10,000 increase in real GDP per worker, indicated by point C.

To see why the relationship between physical capital per worker and productivity exhibits diminishing returns, think about how having farm equipment affects the productivity of farmworkers. A little bit of equipment makes a big difference: a worker equipped with a tractor can do much more than a worker without one. And a worker using more expensive equipment will, other things equal, be more productive: a worker with a $40,000 tractor will normally be able to cultivate more farmland in a given amount of time than a worker with a $20,000 tractor because the more expensive machine will be more powerful, perform more tasks, or both.

But will a worker with a $40,000 tractor, holding human capital and technology constant, be twice as productive as a worker with a $20,000 tractor? Probably not: there's a huge difference between not having a tractor at all and having even an inexpensive tractor; there's much less difference between having an inexpensive tractor and having a better tractor. And we can be sure that a worker with a $200,000 tractor won't be 10 times as productive: a tractor can be improved only so much. Because the same is true of other kinds of equipment, the aggregate production function shows diminishing returns to physical capital.

Diminishing returns to physical capital imply a relationship between physical capital per worker and output per worker like the one shown in Figure 15-4. As the productivity curve for physical capital and the accompanying table illustrate, more physical capital per worker leads to more output per worker. But each $20,000 increment in physical capital per worker adds less to productivity.

As you can see from the table, there is a big payoff for the first $20,000 of physical capital: real GDP per worker rises by $30,000. The second $20,000 of physical capital also raises productivity, but not by as much: real GDP per worker goes up by only $20,000. The third $20,000 of physical capital raises real GDP per worker by only $10,000. By comparing points along the curve you can also see that as physical capital per worker rises, output per worker also rises—but at a diminishing rate.

Going from the origin at 0 to point *A*, a $20,000 increase in physical capital per worker, leads to an increase of $30,000 in real GDP per worker. Going from point *A* to point *B*, a second $20,000 increase in physical capital per worker, leads to an increase of only $20,000 in real GDP per worker. And from point *B* to point *C*, a $20,000 increase in physical capital per worker, increased real GDP per worker by only $10,000.

It's important to realize that diminishing returns to physical capital is an "other things equal" phenomenon: additional amounts of physical capital are less productive *when the amount of human capital per worker and the technology are held fixed*. Diminishing returns may disappear if we increase the amount of human capital per worker, or improve the technology, or both at the same time the amount of physical capital per worker is increased.

For example, a worker with a $40,000 tractor who has also been trained in the most advanced cultivation techniques may in fact be more than twice as productive as a worker with only a $20,000 tractor and no additional human capital.

But diminishing returns to any one input—regardless of whether it is physical capital, human capital, or number of workers—is a pervasive characteristic of production. Typical estimates suggest that in practice a 1% increase in the quantity of physical capital per worker increases output per worker by only one-third of 1%, or 0.33%.

In practice, all the factors contributing to higher productivity rise during the course of economic growth: both physical capital and human capital per worker increase, and technology advances as well. To disentangle the effects of these factors, economists use **growth accounting,** which estimates the contribution of each major factor in the aggregate production function to economic growth. For example, suppose the following are true:

- The amount of physical capital per worker grows 3% per year.
- According to estimates of the aggregate production function, each 1% rise in physical capital per worker, holding human capital and technology constant, raises output per worker by one-third of 1%, or 0.33%.

Growth accounting estimates the contribution of each major factor in the aggregate production function to economic growth.

IT MAY BE DIMINISHED . . . BUT IT'S STILL POSITIVE

It's important to understand what *diminishing returns to physical capital* means and what it doesn't mean. As we've already explained, it's an "other things equal" statement: holding the amount of human capital per worker and the technology fixed, each successive increase in the amount of physical capital per worker results in a smaller increase in real GDP per worker.

But this doesn't mean that real GDP per worker eventually falls as more and more physical capital is added. It's just that the increase in real GDP per worker gets smaller and smaller, albeit remaining at or above zero. So an increase in physical capital per worker will never reduce productivity.

But due to diminishing returns, at some point increasing the amount of physical capital per worker no longer produces an economic payoff: at this point the increase in output is so small that it is not worth the cost of the additional physical capital.

In that case, we would estimate that growing physical capital per worker is responsible for 3%×0.33=1 percentage point of productivity growth per year. A similar but more complex procedure is used to estimate the effects of growing human capital. The procedure is more complex because there aren't simple dollar measures of the quantity of human capital.

Growth accounting allows us to calculate the effects of greater physical and human capital on economic growth. But how can we estimate the effects of technological progress? We do this by estimating what is left over after the effects of physical and human capital have been taken into account. For example, let's imagine that there was no increase in human capital per worker so that we can focus on changes in physical capital and in technology.

In Figure 15-5, the lower curve shows the same hypothetical relationship between physical capital per worker and output per worker shown in Figure 15-4. Let's assume that this was the relationship given the technology available in 1945. The upper curve also shows a relationship between physical capital per worker and productivity, but this time given the technology available in 2015. (We've chosen a 70-year stretch to allow us to use the Rule of 70.) The 2015 curve is shifted up compared to the 1945 curve because technologies developed over the previous 70 years make it possible to produce more output for a given amount of physical capital per worker than was possible with the technology available in 1945. (Note that the two curves are measured in constant dollars.)

Let's assume that between 1945 and 2015 the amount of physical capital per worker rose from $20,000 to $60,000. If this increase in physical capital per worker had taken place without any technological progress, the economy would have moved from *A* to *C*: output per worker would have risen, but only from $30,000 to $60,000, or 1% per year (using the Rule of 70 tells us that a 1% growth rate over 70 years doubles output). In fact, however, the economy moved from *A* to *D:* output rose from $30,000 to $120,000, or 2% per year. There was an increase in both physical capital per worker and technological progress, which shifted the aggregate production function.

In this case, 50% of the annual 2% increase in productivity—that is, 1% in annual productivity growth—is due to higher **total factor productivity,** the amount of output that can be produced with a given amount of factor inputs. So when total factor productivity increases, the economy can produce more output with the same quantity of physical capital, human capital, and labor.

Most estimates find that increases in total factor productivity are central to a country's economic growth. And economists believe that technological progress drives increases in total factor productivity. By reducing the limitations on growth by a given amount of physical capital, technological progress is crucial to economic growth.

The Bureau of Labor Statistics estimates the growth rate of both labor productivity and total factor productivity for nonfarm businesses in the United States. According to the Bureau's estimates, over the period from 1948 to 2017 American labor productivity rose 2.2% per year. Less than half of that rise, approximately

Total factor productivity is the amount of output that can be achieved with a given amount of factor inputs.

FIGURE 15-5   Technological Progress and Productivity Growth

Technological progress raises productivity at any given level of physical capital per worker, and therefore shifts the aggregate production function upward. Here we hold human capital per worker fixed. We assume that the lower curve (the same curve as in Figure 15-4) reflects technology in 1945 and the upper curve reflects technology in 2015. Holding technology and human capital fixed, tripling physical capital per worker from $20,000 to $60,000 leads to a doubling of real GDP per worker, from $30,000 to $60,000. This is shown by the movement from point *A* to point *C*, reflecting an approximately 1% per year rise in real GDP per worker. In reality, technological progress raised productivity at any given level of physical capital—shown here by the upward shift of the curve—and the actual rise in real GDP per worker is shown by the movement from point *A* to point *D*. Real GDP per worker grew 2% per year, leading to a quadrupling during the period. The extra 1% in growth of real GDP per worker is due to higher total factor productivity.

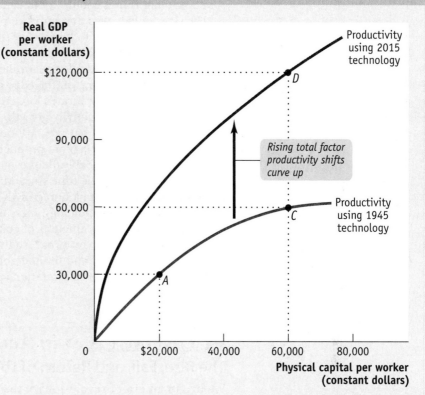

49%, is explained by increases in physical and human capital per worker; the rest is explained by rising total factor productivity—that is, by technological progress.

What About Natural Resources?

We have not yet mentioned natural resources, which certainly have an effect on productivity. Other things equal, countries that are abundant in valuable natural resources, such as highly fertile land or rich mineral deposits, have higher real GDP per capita than less fortunate countries.

The most obvious modern example is the Middle East, where enormous oil deposits have made a few sparsely populated countries very rich. For example, the United Arab Emirates (UAE) has about the same level of real GDP per capita as Germany, but the UAE's wealth is based on oil, not manufacturing, the source of Germany's high output per worker.

But other things are often not equal. In the modern world, natural resources are a much less important determinant of productivity than human or physical capital for the great majority of countries. For example, some nations with very high real GDP per capita, such as Japan, have very few natural resources. Some resource-rich nations, such as Nigeria (which has sizable oil deposits), are very poor.

Historically, natural resources played a much more prominent role in determining productivity. In the nineteenth century, the countries with the highest real GDP per capita were those abundant in rich farmland and mineral deposits: the United States, Canada, Argentina, and Australia. As a consequence, natural resources figured prominently in the development of economic thought.

In a famous book published in 1798, *An Essay on the Principle of Population,* the English economist Thomas Malthus made the fixed quantity of land in the world the basis of a pessimistic prediction about future productivity. As population grew, he pointed out, the amount of land per worker would decline. And this, other things equal, would cause productivity to fall.

His view, in fact, was that improvements in technology or increases in physical capital would lead only to temporary improvements in productivity because they would always be offset by the pressure of rising population and more workers on the supply of land. In the long run, he concluded, the great majority of people were condemned to living on the edge of starvation. Only then would death rates be high enough and birth rates low enough to prevent rapid population growth from outstripping productivity growth.

It hasn't turned out that way, although many historians believe that Malthus's prediction of falling or stagnant productivity was valid for much of human history. Population pressure probably did prevent large productivity increases until the eighteenth century. But in the time since Malthus wrote his book, any negative effects on productivity from population growth have been far outweighed by other, positive factors—advances in technology, increases in human and physical capital, and the opening up of enormous amounts of cultivable land in the New World.

It remains true, however, that we live on a finite planet, with limited supplies of resources such as oil and limited ability to absorb environmental damage. We address the concerns these limitations pose for economic growth in the final section of this chapter.

ECONOMICS >> *in Action*
The Rise, Fall, and Return of the Productivity Paradox

We live in an era of revolutionary technological change—or that's what everyone says. And to be fair, there are good reasons for the excitement. After all, your smartphone is thousands of times faster and can store millions of times more data than the computers available to the astronauts who landed on the moon. But is the dramatic increase in computing power translating into equally dramatic economic growth? Economists have been asking that question for decades—and the answer still isn't clear.

From today's perspective, the cutting-edge technologies introduced in the 1980s—desktop computers that could display text in any color you wanted as long as it was green, cell phones the size of small bricks, and so on—look pretty primitive. But they were a big improvement on what came before. Yet the economic payoff was surprisingly hard to see.

As Figure 15-6 shows, the big technological changes of the 1980s took place in the middle of a prolonged slump in the growth of total factor productivity. During the 21 years from 1974 to 1995, the average annual growth rate of total factor productivity was only 0.6%, a little over a quarter of what it had been during the previous 25 years. In 1987 Robert Solow, the Nobel-winning father of the modern theory of economic growth, famously noted that "you can see the computer age everywhere but in the productivity statistics." What was going on?

Some economists argued that the explanation of the so-called *productivity paradox* was that there's a big difference between having a new technology and knowing what to do with it. They predicted that computers would eventually pay off once business practices evolved to take advantage of personal computers, local area networks, and the internet.

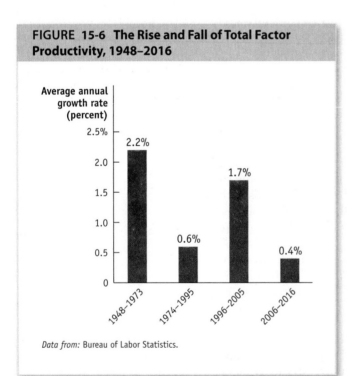

FIGURE 15-6 The Rise and Fall of Total Factor Productivity, 1948–2016

Data from: Bureau of Labor Statistics.

And this optimistic view was seemingly borne out by developments in the mid-1990s. Total factor productivity surged after around 1995, with much of the surge taking place in formerly staid sectors like retailing, where companies like Walmart took advantage of information technology to achieve big efficiency gains in seemingly prosaic areas like inventory management (using bar-code technology, as illustrated in this chapter's Business Case). The productivity paradox was over. Or was it?

After the spike from 1996 to 2005, growth in total factor productivity slowed to a crawl after 2005. Once again, new technology seemed to be everywhere: smartphones, tablets, and high-speed wireless internet were post-2005 developments. Despite these innovations, the productivity paradox was back with a vengeance.

The larger lesson here is that advances in technology can be exciting and ultimately very useful, but it may take many years of figuring out how to use them before there is a significant impact on living standards.

>> Check Your Understanding 15-2

Solutions appear at back of book.

1. Predict the effect of each of the following events on the growth rate of productivity.
   a. The amounts of physical and human capital per worker are unchanged, but there is significant technological progress.
   b. The amount of physical capital per worker grows at a steady pace, but the level of human capital per worker and technology are unchanged.

2. Output in the economy of Erewhon has grown 3% per year over the past 30 years. The labor force has grown at 1% per year, and the quantity of physical capital has grown at 4% per year. The average education level hasn't changed. Estimates by economists say that each 1% increase in physical capital per worker, other things equal, raises productivity by 0.3%. (*Hint:* % change in (X/Y)=% change in X – % change in Y.)
   a. How fast has productivity in Erewhon grown?
   b. How fast has physical capital per worker grown?
   c. How much has growing physical capital per worker contributed to productivity growth? What percentage of productivity growth is that?
   d. How much has technological progress contributed to productivity growth? What percentage of productivity growth is that?

3. Multinomics, Inc., is a large company with many offices around the country. It has just adopted a new computer system that will affect virtually every function performed within the company. Why might a period of time pass before employees' productivity is improved by the new computer system? Why might there be a temporary decrease in employees' productivity?

>> Quick Review

• Long-run increases in living standards arise almost entirely from growing **labor productivity,** often simply referred to as **productivity.**

• An increase in **physical capital** is one source of higher productivity, but it is subject to **diminishing returns to physical capital.**

• **Human capital** and **technological progress** are also sources of increases in productivity.

• The **aggregate production function** is used to estimate the sources of increases in productivity. **Growth accounting** has shown that rising **total factor productivity,** interpreted as the effect of technological progress, is central to long-run economic growth.

• Natural resources are less important today than physical and human capital as sources of productivity growth in most economies.

Why Growth Rates Differ

In 1800, according to estimates by the economic historian Angus Maddison, Mexico had somewhat higher real GDP per capita than Japan. Today, Japan has higher real GDP per capita than most European nations and Mexico is a relatively poor country, though by no means among the poorest. The difference? Over the long run—since 1800—real GDP per capita grew at 1.7% per year in Japan but at only 1.1% per year in Mexico.

As this example illustrates, even small differences in growth rates have large consequences over the long run. So why do growth rates differ across countries and across periods of time?

Explaining Differences in Growth Rates

Using the model of the aggregate production function, we were able to predict that economies with rapid growth tend to be economies that add physical capital, increase their human capital, or experience rapid technological progress. Striking economic success stories, like Japan in the 1950s and 1960s or China more recently, tend to be countries that do all of the three.

1. Rapidly add to their physical capital through high savings and investment spending.
2. Increase their human capital by improving educational institutions.
3. Use research and development to make fast technological progress.

Evidence also points to the importance of government policies, property rights, political stability, and good governance in fostering the sources of growth. (We'll look at the role of government.)

Savings and Investment Spending One reason for differences in growth rates between countries is that some countries are increasing their stock of physical capital much more rapidly than others, through high rates of investment spending. In the 1960s, Japan was the fastest-growing major economy; it also spent a much higher share of its GDP on investment goods than did other major economies. In recent years, China has been the fastest-growing major economy, and it similarly spends a very large share of its GDP on investment goods. In 2015, investment spending was 43% of China's GDP, compared with only 20% in the United States.

Where does the money for high investment spending come from? From savings. Investment spending must be paid for either out of savings from domestic households or by savings from foreign households—that is, an inflow of foreign capital.

Foreign capital has played an important role in the long-run economic growth of some countries, including the United States, that relied heavily on foreign funds during its early industrialization. For the most part, however, countries that invest a large share of their GDP are able to do so because they have high domestic savings. In fact, China in 2015 saved an even higher percentage of its GDP than it invested at home. The extra savings were invested abroad, largely in the United States.

One reason for differences in growth rates, then, is that countries add different amounts to their stocks of physical capital because they have different rates of savings and investment spending.

Education Just as countries differ substantially in the rate at which they add to their physical capital, there have been large differences in the rate at which countries add to their human capital through education.

A case in point is the comparison between Argentina and China. In both countries the adult literacy rate has risen steadily over time, but it has risen much faster in China.

Figure 15-7 shows the percentage of people over the age of 15 who can both read and write in China, which we have highlighted as an example of spectacular long-run growth, and in Argentina, a country whose growth has been disappointing. Thirty-five years ago, Argentina had a much more educated population, while many Chinese were still illiterate. Today, the average educational level and adult literacy rate in China is still slightly below that in Argentina—but that's mainly because there are still many elderly adults in China who never

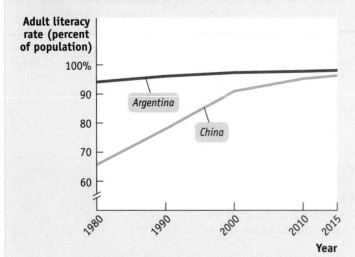

FIGURE 15-7 China's Students Are Catching Up, 1980–2015

Although China still lags behind Argentina in adult literacy, it is rapidly catching up. China's success at adding human capital is one key to the spectacular rise in its long-run growth rate in recent decades.

Data from: World Development Indicators, World Bank.

received basic education. In terms of secondary and tertiary education, China has outstripped once-rich Argentina.

Research and Development The advance of technology is a key force behind economic growth. What drives technological progress?

Scientific advances make new technologies possible. To take the most spectacular example in today's world, the semiconductor chip—which is the basis for all modern information technology—could not have been developed without the theory of quantum mechanics in physics.

But science alone is not enough: scientific knowledge must be translated into useful products and processes. And that often requires devoting a lot of resources to **research and development,** or **R&D,** spending to create new technologies and apply them to practical use.

Although some research and development is conducted by governments, much R&D is paid for by the private sector. The United States became the world's leading economy in large part because American businesses were among the first to make systematic research and development a part of their operations. Developing new technology is one thing; applying it is another. There have often been notable differences in the pace at which different countries take advantage of new technologies. For example, since 2000, Italy has suffered a significant decline in its total factor productivity, while the United States has moved ahead (see the Economics in Action on Italy at the end of this section). The sources of these national differences are the subject of a great deal of economic research.

The Role of Government in Promoting Economic Growth

Governments can play an important role in promoting—or blocking—all three sources of long-term economic growth: physical capital, human capital, and technological progress. They can affect growth directly through subsidies to the three factors that enhance growth that we just examined, or by creating an environment that either fosters or hinders growth. Government policies can increase the economy's growth rate through the following six main channels.

1. Government Subsidies to Infrastructure Governments play an important direct role in building **infrastructure:** roads, power lines, ports, information networks, and other large-scale physical capital projects that provide a foundation for economic activity. Although some infrastructure is provided by private companies, much of it is either provided by the government or requires a great deal of government regulation and support.

Poor infrastructure, such as a power grid that frequently fails and cuts off electricity, is a major obstacle to economic growth in many countries. To provide good infrastructure, an economy must not only be able to afford it, but it must also have the political discipline to maintain it.

Perhaps the most crucial infrastructure is something we, in an advanced country, rarely think about: basic public health measures in the form of a clean water supply and disease control. Poor health infrastructure is a major obstacle to economic growth in poor countries, especially those in Africa.

2. Government Subsidies to Education In contrast to physical capital, which is mainly created by private investment spending, much of an economy's human capital is the result of government spending on education. In the United States, various levels of government fund the bulk of primary and secondary education. Government funding subsidizes a significant share of higher education as well: over 70% of students attend public colleges and universities. In addition, the federal government significantly subsidizes research performed at private colleges and universities.

Research and development, or **R&D,** is spending to create and implement new technologies.

Roads, power lines, ports, information networks, and other underpinnings for economic activity are known as **infrastructure.**

Differences in the rate at which countries add to their human capital largely reflect government policy. As we saw in Figure 15-7, the adult literacy rate in China has been increasing more rapidly than in Argentina. This isn't because China is richer than Argentina; until recently, China was, on average, poorer than Argentina. Instead, it reflects the fact that the Chinese government has made education and raising the literacy rate high priorities.

3. Government Subsidies to R&D Technological progress is largely the result of private initiative. But in the more advanced countries, important R&D is done by government agencies as well. For example, the internet grew out of a system, the Advanced Research Projects Agency Network (ARPANET), created by the U.S. Department of Defense, then extended to educational institutions by the National Science Foundation.

4. Maintaining a Well-Functioning Financial System Governments play an important indirect role in making high rates of private investment spending possible. Both the amount of savings and the ability of an economy to direct savings into productive investment spending depend on the economy's institutions, especially its financial system. A well-regulated and well-functioning financial system is very important for economic growth because in most countries it is the principal way in which savings are channeled into investment spending.

If a country's citizens trust their banks, they will place their savings in bank deposits, which the banks will then lend to their business customers. But if people distrust their banks, they will hoard gold or foreign currency, keeping their savings in safe deposit boxes or under the mattress, where it cannot be turned into productive investment spending. A well-functioning financial system requires appropriate government regulation to assure depositors that their funds are protected from loss.

5. Protection of Property Rights *Property rights* are the rights of owners of valuable items to dispose of those items as they choose. A subset, *intellectual property rights*, are the rights of an innovator to accrue the rewards of her innovation. The state of property rights generally, and intellectual property rights in particular, are important factors in explaining differences in growth rates across economies. Why? Because no one would bother to spend the effort and resources required to innovate if someone else could appropriate that innovation and capture the rewards. So, for innovation to flourish, intellectual property rights must receive protection.

Sometimes this is accomplished by the nature of the innovation: it may be too difficult or expensive to copy. But, generally, the government has to protect intellectual property rights. A *patent* is a government-created temporary monopoly given to an innovator for the use or sale of his or her innovation. It's a temporary rather than permanent monopoly because while it's in society's interests to give an innovator an incentive to invent, it's also in society's interests to eventually encourage competition.

6. Political Stability and Good Governance There's not much point in investing in a business if rioting mobs are likely to destroy it, or in saving your money if someone with political connections can steal it. Political stability and good governance (including the protection of property rights) are essential ingredients in fostering economic growth in the long run.

Long-run economic growth in successful economies, like that of the United States, has been possible because there are good laws, institutions that enforce those laws, and a stable political system that maintains those institutions. The law must say that your property is really yours so that someone else can't take it away. The courts and the police must be honest so that they can't be bribed to ignore the law. And the political system must be stable so that laws don't change capriciously.

Americans take these preconditions for granted, but they are by no means guaranteed. Aside from the disruption caused by war or revolution, many countries find that their economic growth suffers due to corruption among the government officials who should be enforcing the law. For example, until 1991 the Indian government imposed many bureaucratic restrictions on businesses, which often had to bribe government officials to get approval for even routine activities—a tax on business, in effect. Economists have argued that a reduction in this burden of corruption is one reason Indian growth has been much faster in recent years.

Even when the government isn't corrupt, excessive government intervention can be a brake on economic growth. If large parts of the economy are supported by wasteful government subsidies, protected from imports, subject to unnecessary monopolization, or otherwise insulated from competition, productivity tends to suffer because of a lack of incentives. As we'll see in the next section, excessive government intervention is one often-cited explanation for slow growth in Latin America.

ECONOMICS >> *in Action*
What's the Matter with Italy?

Italy was once considered a remarkable economic success story. A century ago it was still a poor country—so poor that in the late nineteenth and early twentieth century millions of Italians emigrated to the United States and other destinations in search of a better life. After World War II, however, Italy experienced decades of rapid growth, with real GDP per capita quadrupling between 1950 and 1990. By the end of that growth spurt, as you can see from Figure 15-8, Italy was significantly richer than the United Kingdom, the nation that had led the Industrial Revolution.

But at that point Italian growth stalled. Real GDP per capita was stagnant after the late 1990s, and began falling after 2008, when Italy's economy suffered a severe downturn as a result of the European debt crisis. What went wrong?

Part of the answer involves slow growth of the factors of production. Italy's low birth rate has meant a rapidly aging population, with a declining percentage of working age adults. Italy has also lagged in education, with the lowest college-educated share of the population in the European Union. Italy also seems to be having trouble taking advantage of technological progress. In fact, measured total factor productivity in Italy has declined since 2000. Why?

Some economists suggest that the explanation may lie in its business culture. In particular, Italian management practices have been widely criticized because promotion and financial rewards all too often reflect seniority rather than performance, giving few incentives to adopt new technology and best business practices.

Underlying this low-performance culture may be a lack of effective competition in many markets, which means that even badly run companies can stay in business indefinitely. The absence of competition within the Italian economy points to a government policy failure, perhaps arising from the relationship between established firms and government being too cozy. In an economy dominated by established firms, there's little incentive to invest or innovate. Italy's troubles show that even countries with a history of economic success can stumble. Achieving economic growth, it turns out, isn't easy.

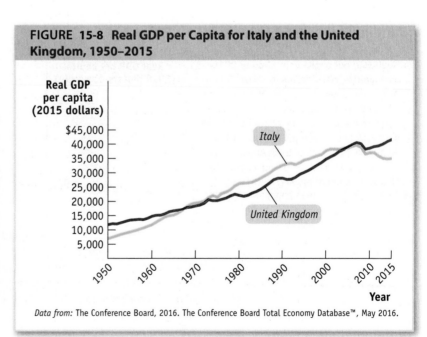

FIGURE 15-8 Real GDP per Capita for Italy and the United Kingdom, 1950–2015

Data from: The Conference Board, 2016. The Conference Board Total Economy Database™, May 2016.

>> ***Quick Review***

- Countries differ greatly in their growth rates of real GDP per capita due to differences in the rates at which they accumulate physical capital and human capital as well as differences in technological progress. A prime cause of differences in growth rates is differences in rates of domestic savings and investment spending as well as differences in education levels, and **research and development,** or **R&D,** levels. R&D largely drives technological progress.
- Government actions can promote or hinder the sources of long-term growth.
- Government policies that directly promote growth are subsidies to **infrastructure,** particularly public health infrastructure, subsidies to education, subsidies to R&D, and the maintenance of a well-functioning financial system.
- Governments improve the environment for growth by protecting property rights (particularly intellectual property rights through patents), by providing political stability, and through good governance. Poor governance includes corruption and excessive government intervention.

>> ***Check Your Understanding*** **15-3**

Solutions appear at back of book.

1. Explain the link between a country's growth rate, its investment spending as a percent of GDP, and its domestic savings.
2. U.S. centers of academic biotechnology research have closer connections with private biotechnology companies than do their European counterparts. What effect might this have on the pace of innovation and development of new drugs in the United States versus Europe?
3. During the 1990s in the former Soviet Union a lot of property was seized and controlled by those in power. How might this have affected the country's growth rate at that time? Explain.

Success, Disappointment, and Failure

As Figure 15-2 illustrates, rates of long-run economic growth differ quite a lot around the world. We'll now look at three regions of the world that have had quite different experiences with economic growth over the last several decades. Figure 15-9 shows trends since 1960 in real GDP per capita in 2010 dollars for three countries: Argentina, Nigeria, and South Korea. (As in Figure 15-1, the vertical axis is drawn in logarithmic scale.) We have chosen these countries because each is a particularly striking example of what has happened in its region. South Korea's amazing rise is part of a broad "economic miracle" in East Asia. Argentina's slow progress, interrupted by repeated setbacks, is more or less typical of the disappointing growth that has characterized Latin America. Like Argentina, Nigeria also had little growth in real GDP until 2000. Since then both countries have fared better.

East Asia's Miracle

In 1960 South Korea was a very poor country. In fact, in 1960 its real GDP per capita was lower than that of India today. But, as you can see from Figure 15-9, beginning in the early 1960s South Korea began an extremely rapid economic ascent: real GDP per capita grew about 7% per year for more than 30 years. Today South

FIGURE 15-9 Success and Disappointment

Real GDP per capita from 1960 to 2016, measured in 2010 dollars, is shown for Argentina, South Korea, and Nigeria, using a logarithmic scale. South Korea and some other East Asian countries have been highly successful at achieving economic growth. Argentina, like much of Latin America, has had several setbacks, slowing its growth. Nigeria's standard of living in 2016 was only barely higher than it had been in 1960, an experience shared by many African countries. Neither Argentina nor Nigeria exhibited much growth over the 56-year period, although both have had significantly higher growth in recent years.

Data from: World Development Indicators.

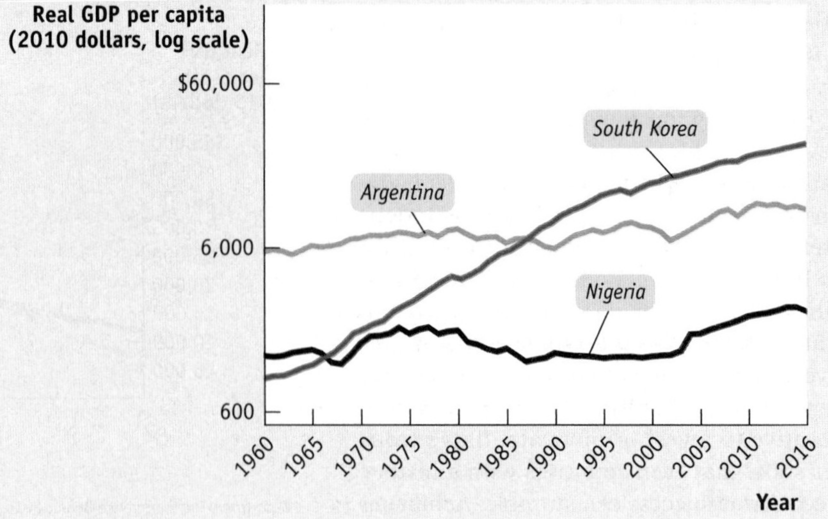

Korea, though still somewhat poorer than Europe or the United States, looks very much like an economically advanced country.

South Korea's economic growth is unprecedented in history: it took the country only 35 years to achieve growth that required centuries elsewhere. Yet South Korea is only part of a broader phenomenon, often referred to as the East Asian economic miracle. High growth rates first appeared in South Korea, Taiwan, Hong Kong, and Singapore but then spread across the region, most notably to China. Since 1975, the whole region has increased real GDP per capita by 6% per year, more than three times America's historical rate of growth.

How have the Asian countries achieved such high growth rates? The answer is that all of the sources of productivity growth have been firing on all cylinders. Very high savings rates, the percentage of GDP that is saved nationally in any given year, have allowed the countries to significantly increase the amount of physical capital per worker. Very good basic education has permitted a rapid improvement in human capital. And these countries have experienced substantial technological progress.

Why were such high rates of growth unheard of in the past? Most economic analysts think that East Asia's growth spurt was possible because of its *relative* backwardness. That is, by the time that East Asian economies began to move into the modern world, they could benefit from adopting the technological advances that had been generated in technologically advanced countries such as the United States.

In 1900, the United States could not have moved quickly to a modern level of productivity because much of the technology that powers the modern economy, from jet planes to computers, hadn't been invented yet. In 1970, South Korea probably still had lower labor productivity than the United States had in 1900, but it could rapidly upgrade its productivity by adopting technology that had been developed in the United States, Europe, and Japan over the previous century. This was aided by a huge investment in human capital through widespread schooling.

The East Asian experience demonstrates that economic growth can be especially fast in countries that are playing catch-up to other countries with higher GDP per capita. On this basis, many economists have suggested a general principle known as the **convergence hypothesis.** This principle says that differences in real GDP per capita among countries tend to narrow over time because countries that start with lower real GDP per capita tend to have higher growth rates. We'll look at the evidence on the convergence hypothesis in the upcoming Economics in Action.

Even before we get to that evidence, however, we can say right away that starting with a relatively low level of real GDP per capita is no guarantee of rapid growth, as the examples of Latin America and Africa both demonstrate.

Latin America's Disappointment

In 1900, Latin America was not considered an economically backward region. Natural resources, including both minerals and cultivable land, were abundant. Some countries, notably Argentina, attracted millions of immigrants from Europe in search of a better life. Measures of real GDP per capita in Argentina, Uruguay, and southern Brazil were comparable to those in economically advanced countries.

Since about 1920, however, growth in Latin America has been disappointing. As Figure 15-9 shows in the case of Argentina, growth has been disappointing for many decades, until 2000 when it finally began to increase. The fact that South Korea is now much richer than Argentina would have seemed inconceivable a few generations ago.

Why did Latin America stagnate? Comparisons with East Asian success stories suggest several factors. The rates of savings and investment spending in Latin America have been much lower than in East Asia, partly as a result of irresponsible

According to the **convergence hypothesis,** international differences in real GDP per capita tend to narrow over time.

government policy that has eroded savings through high inflation, bank failures, and other disruptions. Education—especially broad basic education—has been underemphasized: even Latin American nations rich in natural resources often failed to channel that wealth into their educational systems. And political instability, leading to irresponsible economic policies, has taken a toll.

In the 1980s, many economists came to believe that Latin America was suffering from excessive government intervention in markets. They recommended opening the economies to imports, selling off government-owned companies, and, in general, freeing up individual initiative. The hope was that this would produce an East Asian–type economic surge. So far, however, only one Latin American nation, Chile, has achieved sustained rapid growth.

Slow and uneven economic growth in sub-Saharan Africa has led to extreme and ongoing poverty for many of its people.

Africa's Troubles and Promise

Africa south of the Sahara is home to more than 1 billion people, more than three times the population of the United States. On average, they are very poor, nowhere close to U.S. living standards 100 or even 200 years ago. And economic progress has been both slow and uneven, as the example of Nigeria, the most populous nation in the region, suggests. In fact, real GDP per capita in sub-Saharan Africa actually fell 13% from 1980 to 1994, although it has recovered since then. The consequence of this poor growth performance has been intense and continuing poverty.

Several factors are probably crucial to explaining this disheartening story. Perhaps first and foremost is the problem of political instability. In the years after 1975, large parts of Africa experienced devastating civil wars (often with outside powers backing rival sides) that killed millions of people and made productive investment spending impossible. The threat of war and general anarchy also inhibited other important preconditions for growth, such as education and provision of basic infrastructure.

Property rights are also a major problem. The lack of legal safeguards means that property owners are often subject to extortion because of government corruption, making them averse to owning property or improving it. This is especially damaging in a country that is very poor.

While many economists see political instability and government corruption as the leading causes of underdevelopment in Africa, some—most notably Jeffrey Sachs of Columbia University and the United Nations—believe the opposite. They argue that Africa is politically unstable because it is poor. And Africa's poverty, they go on to claim, stems from its extremely unfavorable geographic conditions—much of the continent is landlocked, hot, infested with tropical diseases, and cursed with poor soil.

Sachs, along with economists from the World Health Organization, has highlighted the importance of health problems in Africa. In poor countries, worker productivity is often severely hampered by malnutrition and disease. In particular, tropical diseases such as malaria can only be controlled with an effective public health infrastructure, something that is lacking in much of Africa. Economists have been studying certain regions of Africa to determine whether modest amounts of aid given directly to residents for the purposes of increasing crop yields, reducing malaria, and increasing school attendance can produce self-sustaining gains in living standards.

Although the example of African countries represents a warning that long-run economic growth cannot be taken for granted, there are some signs of hope. As we saw in Figure 15-9, Nigeria's per capita GDP, after decades of stagnation, turned upward after 2000, and it achieved an average annual growth rate of 3% from 2008 through 2015.

Left Behind by Growth?

Historically, rising real GDP per capita has translated into rising real income for the great majority of a nation's residents. However, there's no guarantee that this will happen. In fact, if the share of the nation's income going to a particular group of citizens falls over time, that group may be left behind while others benefit from growth. That group may even suffer a decline in their real income while the overall income of the nation is rising.

This isn't just a theoretical possibility. In the United States, and to a lesser extent in other wealthy countries, the share of income going to families near the top of the income distribution, and especially to the 1% of families with the highest incomes, has grown substantially since 1980. Figure 15-10 shows one consequence of this rise in inequality. The figure compares the growth since 1953 of real per capita GDP in the United States and the real income of the *median family*—the family at the exact middle of the income scale, with half of all families richer and half poorer. Both numbers are shown as indexes, with 1953 = 100.

Until 1980 the two numbers grew at nearly the same rate because the distribution of income was quite stable. After 1980, however, a growing share of income went to a relatively small number of people at the top. As a result, the income of the median family—which arguably reflects the experience of the typical American—rose much more slowly than real GDP per capita. Many American families, in other words, were to some extent left behind by economic growth.

It is important, however, to acknowledge two qualifications to this trend in the United States. First, in the broad sweep of history it is still true that economic growth raises the standard of living of the great majority of the population. Second, it would be wrong to imagine that global economic growth, even in recent decades, has mainly benefited a well-off minority. On the contrary, from a worldwide perspective the most conspicuous aspect of recent growth has been the rise

FIGURE 15-10 The Growing Income Divide, 1953–2016

In the United States, from 1953 through 1980, both real per capita GDP and the real income of the median family grew at nearly identical rates because the distribution of income was quite stable. After 1980, however, the share of national income going to the richest Americans rose significantly. And while real GDP per capita continued to grow, real median income—the income earned by families in the middle of the income distribution—lagged behind. This means that since 1980 many of those families in the middle have been left behind by economic growth.

Data from: U.S. Census; FRED.

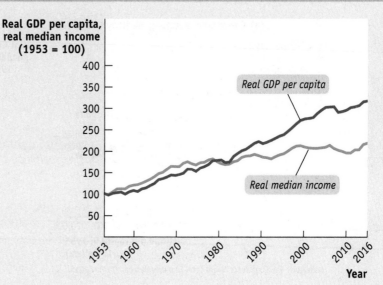

of a *global middle class*—rapidly rising incomes among hundreds of millions of previously poor people in China and other emerging economies.

ECONOMICS >> *in Action*
Are Economies Converging?

In the 1950s, much of Europe seemed quaint and backward to American visitors, and Japan seemed very poor. Today, a visitor to Paris or Tokyo sees a city that looks about as rich as New York. Although real GDP per capita is still somewhat higher in the United States, the differences in the standards of living among the United States, Europe, and Japan are relatively small.

Many economists have argued that this convergence in living standards is normal; the convergence hypothesis says that relatively poor countries should have higher rates of growth of real GDP per capita than relatively rich countries. And if we look at today's relatively well-off countries, the convergence hypothesis seems to be true.

Panel (a) of Figure 15-11 shows data for a number of today's wealthy economies measured in 2015 dollars. On the horizontal axis is real GDP per capita in 1955; on the vertical axis is the average annual growth rate of real GDP per capita from 1955 to 2015. There is a clear negative relationship as can be seen from the line fitted through the points. The United States was the richest country in this group in 1955 and had the slowest rate of growth. Japan, Ireland, and Spain were the poorest countries in 1955 and had the fastest rates of growth. These data suggest that the convergence hypothesis is true.

But economists who looked at similar data realized that these results depend on the countries selected. If you look at successful economies that have a high standard of living today, you find that real GDP per capita has converged. But looking across the world as a whole, including countries that remain poor, there is little evidence of convergence.

Panel (b) of Figure 15-11 illustrates this point, using data for regions rather than individual countries (other than the United States). In 1955, East Asia and Africa were both very poor regions. Over the next 60 years, the East Asian regional economy grew quickly, as the convergence hypothesis would have predicted, but

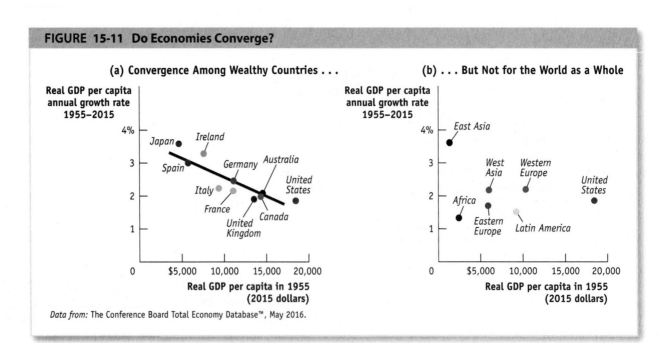

FIGURE 15-11 Do Economies Converge?

(a) Convergence Among Wealthy Countries . . .

(b) . . . But Not for the World as a Whole

Data from: The Conference Board Total Economy Database™, May 2016.

the African regional economy grew very slowly. In 1955, Western Europe had higher real GDP per capita than Latin America. But, contrary to the convergence hypothesis, the Western European regional economy grew much more quickly over the next 60 years, widening the gap between the regions rather than narrowing it, as the hypothesis would predict.

So the convergence hypothesis isn't all wrong. Economists still believe that countries with relatively low real GDP per capita tend to have higher rates of growth than countries with relatively high real GDP per capita, *other things equal.* But other things—education, infrastructure, rule of law, and so on—are often not equal. Statistical studies find that when you adjust for differences in these other factors, poorer countries do tend to have higher growth rates. This result is known as *conditional convergence.*

Because other factors differ, however, there is no clear tendency toward convergence in the world economy as a whole. Western Europe, North America, and parts of Asia are becoming more similar in real GDP per capita, but the gap between these regions and the rest of the world is growing.

>> Check Your Understanding 15-4

Solutions appear at back of book.

1. Some economists think the high rates of growth of productivity achieved by many Asian economies cannot be sustained. Why might they be right? What would have to happen for them to be wrong?

2. Consider Figure 15-11, panel (b). Based on the data there, which regions support the convergence hypothesis? Which do not? Explain.

3. Some economists think the best way to help African countries is for wealthier countries to provide more funds for basic infrastructure. Others think this policy will have no long-run effect unless African countries have the financial and political means to maintain this infrastructure. What policies would you suggest?

Is World Growth Sustainable?

Earlier in the chapter we described the views of Thomas Malthus, the early-nineteenth-century economist who warned that the pressure of population growth would tend to limit the standard of living. Malthus was right about the past: for around 58 centuries, from the origins of civilization until his own time, limited land supplies effectively prevented any large rise in real incomes per capita. Since then, however, technological progress and rapid accumulation of physical and human capital have allowed the world to defy Malthusian pessimism.

But will this always be the case? Some skeptics have expressed doubt about whether **sustainable long-run economic growth** is possible—that is, growth that can continue in the face of the limited supply of natural resources and with less negative impact on the environment.

Natural Resources and Growth, Revisited

In 1972 a group of scientists called The Club of Rome made a big splash with a book titled *The Limits to Growth*, which argued that long-run economic growth wasn't sustainable due to limited supplies of nonrenewable resources such as oil and natural gas. These "neo-Malthusian" concerns at first seemed to be validated by a sharp rise in resource prices in the 1970s. Since then, however, resource prices have gone up and down, with no clear trend.

Figure 15-12 shows the real price of oil—the price of oil adjusted for inflation in the rest of the economy. The rise, and fall, of concern about resource-based limits to growth have more or less followed the rise and fall of oil prices shown in the figure.

>> **Quick Review**

• East Asia's spectacular growth was generated by high savings and investment spending rates, emphasis on education, and adoption of technological advances from other countries.

• Poor education, political instability, and irresponsible government policies are major factors in the slow growth of Latin America.

• In sub-Saharan Africa, severe instability, war, and poor infrastructure—particularly affecting public health—resulted in a catastrophic failure of growth. But economic performance in recent years has been much better than in preceding years.

• The **convergence hypothesis** seems to hold only when other things that affect economic growth—such as education, infrastructure, property rights, and so on—are held equal.

Sustainable long-run economic growth is long-run growth that can continue in the face of the limited supply of natural resources and with less negative impact on the environment.

FIGURE 15-12 The Real Price of Oil, 1950–2017

The real prices of natural resources, like oil, rose dramatically in the 1970s and then fell just as dramatically in the 1980s. In 2005 the real prices of natural resources have soared, although by late 2014 real oil prices returned to the levels last seen in the 1990s.

Data from: Energy Information Administration; FRED.

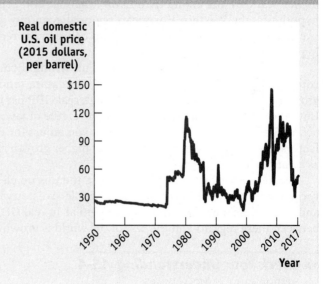

Differing views about the impact of limited natural resources on long-run economic growth turn on the answers to three questions:

1. How large are the supplies of key natural resources?
2. How effective will technology be at finding alternatives to natural resources?
3. Can long-run economic growth continue in the face of resource scarcity?

It's mainly up to geologists to answer the first question. Unfortunately, there's wide disagreement among the experts, especially about the prospects for future oil production. Some analysts believe there is enough untapped oil in the ground for world oil production to continue to rise for several decades. Others, including a number of oil company executives, believe that the growing difficulty of finding new oil fields will cause oil production to stop growing and eventually begin a gradual decline in the fairly near future. Some analysts believe that we have already reached that point.

The answer to the second question, whether there are alternatives to natural resources, will come from engineers. However, there are already many alternative natural resources being exploited. Since 2005 there have been dramatic developments in energy production, with large amounts of previously unreachable oil and gas extracted through fracking, and with a huge decline in the cost of electricity generated by wind and solar power.

The third question, whether economies can continue to grow in the face of resource scarcity, is mainly a question for economists. And most, though not all, economists are optimistic. They believe that modern economies can find ways to work around limits on the supply of natural resources. One reason for this optimism is the fact that resource scarcity leads to high resource prices. These high prices, in turn, provide strong incentives to conserve the scarce resource and find alternatives. For example, after the sharp oil price increases of the 1970s, American consumers turned to smaller, more fuel-efficient cars as U.S. industry greatly intensified its efforts to reduce energy bills.

Given such responses to prices, economists generally tend to see resource scarcity as a problem that modern economies handle fairly well, and not as a fundamental limit to long-run economic growth. Environmental issues, however, pose a more difficult problem for economies because dealing with them requires effective political action.

Economic Growth and the Environment

Economic growth, other things equal, tends to increase the adverse impact of human activity on the environment, including an increase in pollution, the loss of wildlife habitats, the extinction of species, and reduced biodiversity. As we saw in this chapter's opening story, China's spectacular economic growth has also brought a spectacular increase in air pollution in its cities.

In analyzing economic growth and its environmental impact, it is useful to distinguish between *local* environmental degradation, which affects a geographically limited area, and *global* environmental degradation, which is far-reaching, and with worldwide impact. As we'll see, it has proven to be far more difficult to address global environmental degradation and, in particular, the problem of *climate change.*

In fact, the improved air quality in the cities of today's advanced economies indicates that local environmental harm can be greatly reduced when there is sufficient political will and when resources are devoted to finding a solution. Decades ago, before regulations virtually eliminated the use of coal heat, air pollution in London was so bad that it killed 4,000 people over two weeks in 1952. And as recounted in the opening story, the smog that once afflicted Los Angeles has disappeared thanks to regulations mandating cleaner-burning gasoline. In both of these cases, government intervention and expending some resources made everyone better off.

However, tackling *climate change*—the change in the earth's climate due to human activities, such as pollution—has been a much harder problem to solve because policies must be implemented on a global scale, requiring the cooperation of many countries. There is broad scientific consensus that burning fossil fuels—coal, oil, and natural gas—leads to increasing levels of carbon dioxide in the atmosphere. Carbon dioxide is a type of *greenhouse gas.* Such gases trap the sun's energy, raising the planet's temperature, and lead to climate change, which, in turn, imposes high human, economic, and environmental costs. These costs include extreme weather, increased flooding, the disruption of agriculture, including crop failures, and more. A recent estimate put the cost of unmitigated climate change at 20% of world gross domestic product by 2100. Moreover, these costs tend to fall more heavily on poor countries.

The problem of climate change is linked to economic growth: the larger the economy, the more homes, factories, and vehicles, will have to be powered, typically by burning fossil fuels. At present, world energy consumption is overwhelmingly dependent upon fossil fuels, which account for 83% of total consumption, while clean, renewable sources account for only 12.5%. Why? Because historically, fossil fuels have been cheaper to use. Most of today's wealthy countries grew their economies through industrialization and the burning of fossil fuels over the last century. To reduce the global emission of greenhouse gases, developed countries and large rapidly developing countries, such as China and India, will have to undertake a transition from a heavy reliance on fossil fuels to greater use of clean, renewable energy sources such as wind and solar power. Until recently, effective action against climate change had been stymied by disagreement among countries on how to pay the cost of shifting from fossil fuel to clean energy sources. As Figure 15-13 shows, today's wealthy economies have historically been responsible for most of the carbon dioxide emissions—and carbon dioxide alone accounts for almost 76% of all global greenhouse gas emissions. But newly emerging economies like China and India are responsible for the recent growth. Inevitably, rich countries are reluctant to pay the price of reducing emissions only to have their efforts frustrated by rapidly growing emissions from new players. But relatively poor countries like China and India consider it unfair that they should be expected to bear the burden of protecting an environment threatened by the past actions of rich nations.

In 2015, in acknowledgment of the seriousness of the problem, 196 countries came together under the **Paris Agreement,** committing to reduce their emissions of greenhouse gases in an effort to limit the rise in the earth's temperature to no

Under the **Paris Agreement** of 2015, 196 countries agreed to reduce their greenhouse gas emissions in an effort to limit the rise in the earth's temperature to no more than 2 degrees centigrade.

FIGURE 15-13 Climate Change and Growth

Greenhouse gas emissions are positively related to growth. As shown here by the United States and Europe, wealthy countries have historically been responsible for the great bulk of carbon dioxide emissions—which make up more than three-quarters of all greenhouse gas emissions—because of their richer and faster-growing economies. As China and other emerging economies have grown, they began to emit much more carbon dioxide. China has since overtaken the United States and Europe in emissions.

Data from: Energy Information Administration.

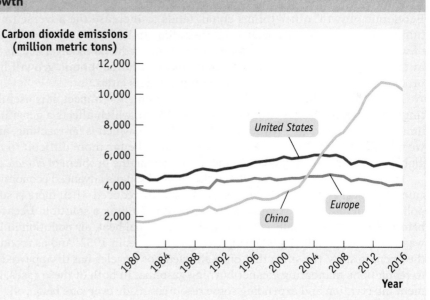

more than 2 degrees centigrade. The linchpin of the agreement was cooperation between China, India, and the United States. China and India agreed to limit their emissions, and the United States, along with other rich countries, committed to develop various forms of public and private financing to help poorer countries pay the cost. Despite the United States originally committing to the Paris Agreement, in 2017 the Trump administration announced plans for the United States to withdraw from it, effective November 4, 2020. Is it possible to maintain long-run growth while averting the effects of climate change? The answer, according to most economists who have studied the issue, is yes. While there will be economic costs, those costs have been falling as technological innovation in clean energy sources advances. The best available estimates show that even a large reduction in greenhouse gas emissions over the next few decades would cause only a modest reduction in the long-term rise in real GDP per capita.

To achieve long-run economic growth with environmental protection, governments will need to use regulations and environmental standards, and institute policies that create market incentives to encourage individuals and firms to make the transition to clean energy sources. Finally, governments—both rich and poor—will need to continue to cooperate with one another. Getting political consensus around the necessary policies will be key.

The answer is blowing in the wind.

ECONOMICS >> *in Action*
What Is the Cost of Limiting Carbon?

You may be surprised to learn that taking action against climate change in the United States doesn't necessarily require new legislation. Under U.S. law, the Environmental Protection Agency (EPA) is obliged to regulate pollutants that endanger public health, and in 2007 the Supreme Court ruled that carbon dioxide emissions meet that criterion.

So the EPA initiated a series of steps to limit carbon emissions. First, it set new fuel-efficiency standards to reduce emissions from motor vehicles. Then, it introduced rules limiting emissions from new power plants. Finally, in June 2014 it announced plans to limit emissions from existing power plants. This was a crucial step because coal-burning power plants account for a large part of carbon emissions, both in the United States and in other countries.

But how would these rules affect the U.S. economy? Critics argued that the EPA rules would cripple economic growth. For the most part, however, economists disagreed. The EPA's own analysis suggested that by 2030 its rules would cost the U.S. economy about $9 billion annually in today's dollars—equivalent to 0.05% of the $19 trillion of goods and services produced annually—a trivial sum.

Still, these EPA's rules would, at best, make a small dent in the problem of climate change. How much would a program that really deals with the problem cost? In 2014 the United Nations International Panel on Climate Change (IPCC) estimated that global measures limiting the rise in temperatures to 2 degrees centigrade would impose gradually rising costs, reaching about 5% of output by the year 2100. The impact on the world's rate of economic growth would, however, be small—a reduction of approximately 0.06 percentage points each year. The IPCC's numbers were more or less in line with other estimates. Most independent studies have found that environmental protection need not greatly reduce growth.

At a fundamental level, the key insight here is that given the right incentives modern economies can find many ways to reduce emissions, ranging from the use of renewable energy sources (which have grown much cheaper) to inducing consumers to choose goods with lower environmental impact. Economic growth and environmental damage don't have to go together.

>> Check Your Understanding 15-5
Solutions appear at back of book.

1. Are economists typically more concerned about the limits to growth imposed by environmental degradation or those imposed by resource scarcity? Explain, noting the role of negative externalities (costs imposed by individuals or firms on others without the requirement to pay compensation), in your answer.

2. What is the link between greenhouse gas emissions and growth? What is the expected effect on growth from emissions reduction? Why is international burden sharing of greenhouse gas emissions reduction a contentious problem?

>> Quick Review

• Economists generally believe that environmental degradation poses a major challenge to **sustainable long-run economic growth.** They also generally believe that modern economies can find ways to alleviate limits to growth from natural resource scarcity through the price response that promotes conservation and the creation of alternatives.

• Economic growth tends to harm the environment unless actions are taken to protect it. Local environmental degradation can be addressed through political will and resources. Global environmental degradation is harder to address because it requires cooperation across many countries.

• The accumulation of greenhouse gases, a by-product of burning fossil fuels, has led to climate change, the raising of the earth's temperature. In order to avert the impact of climate change, effective government intervention is required.

• Developed countries and rapidly growing large countries need to shift from a heavy reliance on fossil fuels to using clean, energy sources like solar and wind power. This will come at a modest cost to the rise in real GDP per capita, a cost that is falling as technological innovation in clean energy sources advances.

• In the **Paris Agreement** of 2015, 196 countries agreed to reduce their greenhouse gas emissions in an effort to limit the rise in the earth's temperature.

SOLVED PROBLEM   Tracking India's Economic Growth

In the early 1980s, India adopted a series of governmental reforms with two main goals: promoting industrial production and opening the economy to international trade. These policies led to a 300% increase in real GDP per capita in India, and over the last thirty-five years, India has ranked as one of the fastest growing economies in the world.

By comparing the economy in India from 1981 to 1985 and then from 2006 to 2010, show that changes in the economic environment from the early 1980s contributed to the overall economic growth experienced throughout India. What was India's long-run growth rate during each of these five-year periods? Use real GDP per capita to measure growth. At the current long-run growth rate, approximately how long should it take for GDP to double in India?

Year	Real GDP per capita
1981	$439
1982	444
1983	466
1984	473
1985	486
2011	$1,414
2012	1,472
2013	1,547
2014	1,642
2015	1,753

Year	Growth rate
1982	1.1%
1983	5.0
1984	1.5
1985	2.7
2012	4.1%
2013	5.1
2014	6.1
2015	6.8

STEP | 1 Compare the economy in India across time from 1981 to 1985 and then from 2011–2015. [*Hint:* The Federal Reserve Economic Database (FRED) site fred.stlouisfed.org provides statistics over time on real GDP per capita for various countries.] *Read pages 406–408.*

Go to the website fred.stlouisfed.org. Under the search box enter "GDP per capita India" and select the option for "Constant GDP per capita." Scroll over the graph and copy the numbers from 1981–1985 and 2011–2015.

Real GDP per capita in India from the World Bank site in constant U.S. dollars (reference year 2010) is shown in the table.

STEP | 2 Using the numbers in the accompanying table, find the growth rate in real GDP in India over the same periods, and discuss the difference in growth rates in the early 1980s with those of the early 2010s. *Read the Pitfalls on page 409.*

The rate of change, or growth rate, in real GDP per capita between year 1 and year 2 is calculated using the following formula:

$$\left(\frac{(\text{real GDP per capita in year 2} - \text{real GDP per capita in year 1})}{(\text{real GDP per capita in year 1})} \right) \times 100$$

Thus, the growth rate below between 1981 and 1982 is calculated as follows:

$$\left(\frac{(\$444 - \$439)}{\$439} \right) \times 100 = 1.1\%$$

As you can see from the numbers in the table, India experienced modest growth from 1981 through 1985 but significant growth from 2011 through 2015.

STEP | 3 What was the average long-run growth during each five-year period? How long will it take India's GDP to double if the economy continues to grow at the long-run average from 2011–2015? *Read pages 408–409 and look closely at Equation 15-1.*

Summing the above growth rates from 1981 to 1985 and dividing by 4, we find an average growth rate of 2.6%. The average growth from 2011 to 2015 is 5.5%. According to the rule of 70, if India continues to grow at an average of 5.5% it would take 70/5.5 = 12.7 years for real GDP per capita to double in India.

SUMMARY

1. Growth is measured as changes in real GDP per capita in order to eliminate the effects of changes in the price level and changes in population size. Levels of real GDP per capita vary greatly around the world: About a quarter of the world's population lives in countries that are still poorer than the United States was in 1900. GDP per capita in the United States is about eight times as high as it was in 1900.

2. Growth rates of real GDP per capita also vary widely. According to the **Rule of 70,** the number of years it takes for real GDP per capita to double is equal to 70 divided by the annual growth rate of real GDP per capita.

3. The key to long-run economic growth is rising **labor productivity,** or just **productivity,** which is output per worker. Increases in productivity arise from increases in **physical capital** per worker and **human capital** per worker as well as **technological progress.** The

aggregate production function shows how real GDP per worker depends on these three factors. Other things equal, there are **diminishing returns to physical capital:** holding human capital per worker and technology fixed, each successive addition to physical capital per worker yields a smaller increase in productivity than the one before. Equivalently, more physical capital per worker results in a lower, but still positive, increase in productivity. **Growth accounting,** which estimates the contribution of each factor to a country's economic growth, has shown that rising **total factor productivity,** the amount of output produced from a given amount of factor inputs, is key to long-run growth. It is usually interpreted as the effect of technological progress. In contrast to earlier times, natural resources are a less significant source of productivity growth in most countries today.

4. The large differences in countries' growth rates are largely due to differences in their rates of accumulation of physical and human capital as well as differences in technological progress. Although inflows of foreign savings from abroad help, a prime factor is differences in domestic savings and investment spending rates, since most countries that have high investment spending on physical capital finance it by high domestic savings. Technological progress is largely a result of **research and development,** or **R&D.**

5. Governments can help or hinder growth. Government policies that directly foster growth are subsidies to **infrastructure,** particularly public health infrastructure, subsidies to education and R&D, and maintenance of a well-functioning financial system that channels savings into investment spending, education, and R&D. Governments can enhance the environment for growth by protecting property rights (particularly intellectual property rights through patents), by being politically stable, and by providing good governance. Poor governance includes corruption and excessive government intervention.

6. The world economy contains examples of success and failure in the effort to achieve long-run economic growth. East Asian economies have done many things right and achieved very high growth rates. The low growth rates of Latin American and African economies over many years led economists to believe that the

convergence hypothesis, the claim that differences in real GDP per capita across countries narrow over time, fits the data only when factors that affect growth, such as education, infrastructure, and favorable government policies and institutions, are held equal across countries. In recent years, there has been an uptick in growth among some Latin American and sub-Saharan African countries, largely due to a boom in commodity exports.

7. Economists generally believe that environmental degradation poses a major challenge to **sustainable long-run economic growth.** Addressing environmental degradation requires effective governmental intervention, but the problem of natural resource scarcity is often well handled by the market price response.

8. Climate change is linked to growth and there is broad consensus that government action is needed to address it. To avert the impact of climate change, countries will need to shift from a heavy reliance on fossil fuel to using clean, renewable energy sources. This will come at a modest cost to the rise in real GDP per capita, a cost that is falling as technological innovation in clean energy sources advances. Countries also need to cooperate with each other to realize the terms of the 2015 **Paris Agreement,** in which 196 signatory countries agreed to reduce their greenhouse gas emissions in an effort to limit the rise in earth's temperature.

how government can help growth (handwritten)

KEY TERMS

Rule of 70, p. 408
Labor productivity, p. 410
Productivity, p. 410
Physical capital, p. 411
Human capital, p. 411
Technological progress, p. 411
Aggregate production function, p. 411

Diminishing returns to physical capital, p. 412
Growth accounting, p. 413
Total factor productivity, p. 414
Research and development (R&D), p. 419

Infrastructure, p. 419
Convergence hypothesis, p. 423
Sustainable long-run economic growth, p. 427
Paris Agreement, p. 429

DISCUSSION QUESTIONS

1. The accompanying table shows data from the World Bank, World Development Indicators, for real GDP per capita in 2010 U.S. dollars for Argentina, Ghana, South Korea, and the United States for 1960, 1980, 2000, and 2015.

   a. Complete the table by expressing each year's real GDP per capita as a percentage of its 1960 and 2015 levels.

   b. How does the growth in living standards from 1960 to 2015 compare across these four nations? What might account for these differences?

	Argentina			Ghana			South Korea			United States		
		Percentage of			Percentage of			Percentage of			Percentage of	
Year	Real GDP per capita (2010 dollars)	1960 real GDP per capita	2015 real GDP per capita	Real GDP per capita (2010 dollars)	1960 real GDP per capita	2015 real GDP per capita	Real GDP per capita (2010 dollars)	1960 real GDP per capita	2015 real GDP per capita	Real GDP per capita (2010 dollars)	1960 real GDP per capita	2015 real GDP per capita
1960	$5,853	?	?	$1,053	?	?	$1,103	?	?	$17,037	?	?
1980	8,408	?	?	901	?	?	3,911	?	?	28,734	?	?
2000	8,544	?	?	975	?	?	15,105	?	?	45,056	?	?
2015	12,128	?	?	1,696	?	?	25,023	?	?	51,486	?	?

2. The following table provides approximate statistics on per capita income levels and growth rates for regions defined by income levels. According to the Rule of 70, starting in 2015 the high-income countries are projected to double their per capita GDP in approximately 70 years, in 2085. Throughout this question, assume constant growth rates for each of the regions are equal to their average value between 2000 and 2015.

Region	Real GDP per capita (2015)	Average annual growth rate of real GDP per capita (2000–2015)
High-income countries	$41,038	1.0%
Middle-income countries	4,584	4.4
Low-income countries	588	2.3

Data from: World Bank.

a. Calculate the ratio of per capita GDP in 2015 of the following:

   i. Middle-income to high-income countries

   ii. Low-income to high-income countries

   iii. Low-income to middle-income countries

b. Calculate the number of years it will take the low-income and middle-income countries to double their per capita GDP.

c. Calculate the per capita GDP of each of the regions in 2085. (*Hint:* How many times does their per capita GDP double in 70 years, the number of years from 2015 to 2085?)

d. Repeat part a with the projected per capita GDP in 2085.

e. Compare your answers to parts a and d. Comment on the change in economic inequality between the regions.

3. The country of Androde is currently using Method 1 for its production function. By chance, scientists stumble onto a technological breakthrough that will enhance Androde's productivity. This technological breakthrough is reflected in another production function, Method 2. The accompanying table shows combinations of physical capital per worker and output per worker for both methods, assuming that human capital per worker is fixed.

Method 1		Method 2	
Physical capital per worker	Real GDP per worker	Physical capital per worker	Real GDP per worker
0	0.00	0	0.00
50	35.36	50	70.71
100	50.00	100	100.00
150	61.24	150	122.47
200	70.71	200	141.42
250	79.06	250	158.11
300	86.60	300	173.21
350	93.54	350	187.08
400	100.00	400	200.00
450	106.07	450	212.13
500	111.80	500	223.61

a. Using the data in the accompanying table, draw the two production functions in one diagram. Androde's current amount of physical capital per worker is 100. In your figure, label that point A.

b. Starting from point A, over a period of 70 years, the amount of physical capital per worker in Androde rises to 400. Assuming Androde still uses Method 1, in your diagram, label the resulting point of production B. Using the Rule of 70, calculate by how many percent per year output per worker has grown.

c. Now assume that, starting from point A, over the same period of 70 years, the amount of physical capital per worker in Androde rises to 400, but that during that time period, Androde switches to Method 2. In your diagram, label the resulting point of production C. Using the Rule of 70, calculate by how many percent per year output per worker has grown now.

d. As the economy of Androde moves from point A to point C, what share of the annual productivity growth is due to higher total factor productivity?

4. The Bureau of Labor Statistics regularly releases the "Productivity and Costs" report for the previous month. Go to www.bls.gov and find the latest report. (On the Bureau of Labor Statistics home page, from the tab "Subjects," select the link to "Productivity: Labor

Productivity & Costs"; then, from the heading "LPC News Releases," find the most recent "Productivity and Costs" report.) What were the percent changes in business and nonfarm business productivity for the previous quarter? How does the percent change in that quarter's productivity compare to the percent change from the same quarter a year ago?

5. Why would you expect real GDP per capita in California and Pennsylvania to exhibit convergence but not in California and Baja California, a state of Mexico that borders the United States? What changes would allow California and Baja California to converge?

6. According to the U.S. Energy Information Administration, the proven oil reserves existing in the world in 2015 consisted of 1,663 billion barrels. In that year, the U.S. Energy Information Administration reported that the world daily oil production was 80.58 million barrels a day.

   a. At this rate, for how many years will the proven oil reserves last? Discuss the Malthusian view in the context of the number you just calculated.

   b. In order to do the calculations in part a, what did you assume about the total quantity of oil reserves over time? About oil prices over time? Are these assumptions consistent with the Malthusian view on resource limits?

   c. Discuss how market forces may affect the amount of time the proven oil reserves will last, assuming that no new oil reserves are discovered and that the demand curve for oil remains unchanged.

7. The accompanying table shows the annual growth rate for the years 2000–2014 in per capita emissions of carbon dioxide (CO_2) and the annual growth rate in real GDP per capita for selected countries.

Country	2000–2014 Average annual growth rate	
	Real GDP per capita	CO_2 emissions per capita
Argentina	1.69%	1.17%
Bangladesh	4.33	4.47
Canada	0.96	0.01
China	9.24	7.48
Germany	1.20	−0.41
Ireland	1.30	−2.56
Japan	0.70	0.11
South Korea	3.51	2.32
Mexico	0.67	0.42
Nigeria	5.03	−1.30
Russia	4.16	1.35
South Africa	1.64	−0.02
United Kingdom	1.02	−2.20
United States	0.85	−1.27

Data from: Energy Information Administration; World Bank.

   a. Rank the countries in terms of their growth in CO_2 emissions, from highest to lowest. What five countries have the highest growth rate in emissions? What five countries have the lowest growth rate in emissions?

   b. Now rank the countries in terms of their growth in real GDP per capita, from highest to lowest. What five countries have the highest growth rate? What five countries have the lowest growth rate?

   c. Would you infer from your results that CO_2 emissions are linked to growth in output per capita?

   d. Do high growth rates necessarily lead to high CO_2 emissions?

PROBLEMS

interactive activity

1. The following table shows the average annual growth rate in real GDP per capita for Argentina, Ghana, and South Korea using data from the World Bank, World Development Indicators, for the past few decades.

Years	Average annual growth rate of real GDP per capita		
	Argentina	Ghana	South Korea
1965–1975	1.92%	−1.13%	8.29%
1975–1985	−1.42	−2.29	7.08
1985–1995	1.54	1.70	8.06
1995–2005	1.14	2.16	4.28
2005–2015	3.11	4.45	3.02

   a. For each 10-year period and for each country, use the Rule of 70 where possible to calculate how long it would take for that country's real GDP per capita to double.

   b. Suppose that the average annual growth rate that each country achieved over the period 2005–2015 continues indefinitely into the future. Starting from 2015, use the Rule of 70 to calculate, where possible, the year in which a country will have doubled its real GDP per capita.

2. What roles do physical capital, human capital, technology, and natural resources play in influencing long-run economic growth of aggregate output per capita?

3. How have U.S. policies and institutions influenced the country's long-run economic growth?

4. Over the next 100 years, real GDP per capita in Groland is expected to grow at an average annual rate of 2.0%. In Sloland, however, growth is expected to be somewhat slower, at an average annual growth rate of 1.5%. If both countries have a real GDP per capita today of $20,000, how will their real GDP per capita differ in 100 years? [*Hint:* A country that has a real GDP today of

$x and grows at $y\%$ per year will achieve a real GDP of $x \times (1+(y/100))^z$ in z years.]

5. The accompanying table shows data from the World Bank, World Development Indicators, for real GDP per capita (2010 U.S. dollars) in France, Japan, the United Kingdom, and the United States in 1960 and 2015. Complete the table. Have these countries converged economically?

	1960		2015	
	Real GDP per capita (2010 dollars)	**Percentage of U.S. real GDP per capita**	**Real GDP per capita (2010 dollars)**	**Percentage of U.S. real GDP per capita**
France	$12,992	?	$41,330	?
Japan	8,369	?	44,657	?
United Kingdom	13,869	?	40,933	?
United States	17,037	?	51,486	?

6. The accompanying table shows data from the World Bank, World Development Indicators for real GDP per capita (2010 U.S. dollars) for Argentina, Ghana, South Korea, and the United States in 1960 and 2015. Complete the table. Have these countries converged economically?

	1960		2015	
	Real GDP per capita (2010 dollars)	**Percentage of U.S. real GDP per capita**	**Real GDP per capita (2010 dollars)**	**Percentage of U.S. real GDP per capita**
Argentina	$5,853	?	$12,128	?
Ghana	1,053	?	1,696	?
South Korea	1,103	?	25,023	?
United States	17,037	?	51,486	?

7. Access the Discovering Data exercise for Chapter 15 online to answer the following questions.

a. What was the ratio of Japanese GDP per capita relative to the United States in 1950 and 1991?

b. Why has Japan's GDP converged to that of the United States?

c. Rank the countries in order of richest to poorest (with 1 being the richest) in 1960 and 2010.

d. What was the ratio of GDP per capita for Spain relative to the United States in 1960 and 2010?

e. Which two countries experienced the fastest rate of convergence from 1960 through 2010?

f. Why are lower-income countries, like South Korea in 1960, able to grow faster than rich countries?

g. If countries continue along a similar path, will Japan, South Korea, Chile, or Spain be the first country to reach the level of real GDP per capita in the United States?

WORK IT OUT Interactive step-by-step help with solving this problem can be found online.

8. You are hired as an economic consultant to the countries of Albernia and Brittania. Each country's current relationship between physical capital per worker and output per worker is given by the curve labeled "Productivity₁" in the accompanying diagram. Albernia is at point A and Brittania is at point B.

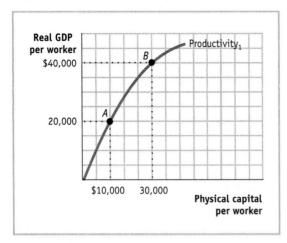

a. In the relationship depicted by the curve Productivity₁, what factors are held fixed? Do these countries experience diminishing returns to physical capital per worker?

b. Assuming that the amount of human capital per worker and the technology are held fixed in each country, can you recommend a policy to generate a doubling of real GDP per capita in Albernia?

c. How would your policy recommendation change if the amount of human capital per worker could be changed? Assume that an increase in human capital doubles the output per worker when physical capital per worker equals $10,000. Draw a curve on the diagram that represents this policy for Albernia.

DIFFERENT GENERATIONS, DIFFERENT POLICIES

UNEMPLOYMENT AND INFLATION are the two great evils of macroeconomics, and policy makers do their best to keep both under control. Sometimes, however, this task isn't straightforward, as we learned in Chapter 14: Policies to control inflation can worsen unemployment and policies aimed at reducing unemployment can cause inflation. So at times it's hard to know whether inflation or unemployment poses the bigger risk to the economy.

Policy makers at the Federal Reserve, also known as the Fed, found themselves facing such a quandary in 2011, when the unemployment rate, at around 9%, was very high by historical standards, but inflation had spiked to almost 4%, twice the widely accepted policy target of 2%. So should policy remain expansionary, to fight unemployment, or should it be contractionary, to reduce inflation?

In the end, the Fed decided to keep its foot on the gas and continue with a strongly expansionary monetary policy—it reduced interest rates with the goal of boosting the economy. Fed officials believed that the inflation surge was a blip caused by a temporary rise in oil prices, and that it would soon dissipate. Time proved them right: once the oil price rise ran its course, inflation quickly fell back below 2%. The Fed's counterpart in Europe, the European Central Bank, or ECB, faced a similar situation: a 10% unemployment rate and 3% inflation. Yet it made the opposite policy choice: contractionary monetary policy—raising interest rates with the goal of slowing the economy.

In response to increased inflation in 2011, Fed chair Bernanke made the right policy choice, while ECB president Trichet did not. The *AD–AS* model explains why.

Why did these two central banks, facing similar circumstances, move in opposite directions? Differences in the ages of the two bank leaders may provide a clue: Jean-Claude Trichet, President of the ECB, was 68, while Ben Bernanke, the chairman of the Fed, was 57. The eleven-year age difference may seem inconsequential, but it was in fact significant because it corresponded to differences in the kinds of economic problems that dominated when each man was coming of age.

In fact, Neil Irwin of the *New York Times* has found a strong correlation between the ages of policy makers and their policy stances. Those like Mr. Trichet, who spent their young adulthood during the high-inflation 1970s, were more likely to call for interest-rate hikes and tightening monetary policy to head off inflation than were younger policy makers, like Mr. Bernanke, who, in contrast, were more concerned about unemployment and growth.

Bernanke understood that an economic slump can arise from different types of shocks. This understanding requires a model of the economy that can distinguish between different types of short-run economic fluctuations.

So why was Bernanke right in this case? Because the recessions of the 1970s were very different from the severe slump that began in 2007 and was still afflicting the economy in 2011. The recessions of the 1970s were largely caused by *supply shocks,* while the Great Recession of 2007–2009 was the result of a *demand shock.* Unlike Trichet, Bernanke understood that an economic slump can arise from two different types of shocks.

In this chapter we will develop the *AD–AS model* to help you understand how these shocks affect the economy. We'll proceed in three steps. First, we'll develop the concept of *aggregate demand.* Then we'll turn to the parallel concept of *aggregate supply.* Finally, we'll put the two concepts together. •

WHAT YOU WILL LEARN

- How does the **aggregate demand curve** illustrate the relationship between the aggregate price level and the quantity of aggregate output demanded?

- How does the **aggregate supply curve** illustrate the relationship between the aggregate price level and the quantity of aggregate output supplied?

- Why is the aggregate supply curve different in the short run compared to the long run?

- How is the **AD–AS model** used to analyze economic fluctuations?

- How can monetary policy and fiscal policy stabilize the economy?

> The **aggregate demand curve** shows the relationship between the aggregate price level and the quantity of aggregate output demanded by households, businesses, the government, and the rest of the world.

Aggregate Demand

The Great Depression, the great majority of economists agree, was the result of a massive negative demand shock. What does that mean? In Chapter 3 we learned that when economists talk about a fall in the demand for a particular good or service, they're referring to a leftward shift of the demand curve. Similarly, when economists talk about a negative demand shock to the economy as a whole, they're referring to a leftward shift of the **aggregate demand curve,** a curve that shows the relationship between the aggregate price level and the quantity of aggregate output demanded by households, firms, the government, and the rest of the world.

Figure 16-1 shows what the aggregate demand curve may have looked like in 1933, at the end of the 1929–1933 recession. The horizontal axis shows the total quantity of domestic goods and services demanded, measured in 2009 dollars. We use real GDP to measure aggregate output and will often use the two terms interchangeably. The vertical axis shows the aggregate price level, measured by the GDP deflator.

With these variables on the axes, we can draw a curve, *AD*, showing how much aggregate output would have been demanded at any given aggregate price level. Since *AD* is meant to illustrate aggregate demand, the point labeled 1933 on the curve corresponds to actual data from that year, when the aggregate price level was 7.3 and the total quantity of domestic final goods and services purchased was $778 billion in 2009 dollars.

The aggregate demand curve in Figure 16-1 is downward sloping, indicating a negative relationship between the aggregate price level and the quantity of aggregate output demanded. A higher aggregate price level, other things equal, reduces the quantity of aggregate output demanded; a lower aggregate price level, other things equal, increases the quantity of aggregate output demanded. According to Figure 16-1, if the price level in 1933 had been 4.2 instead of 7.3, the total quantity of domestic final goods and services demanded would have been $1,000 billion in 2009 dollars instead of $778 billion.

The first key question about the aggregate demand curve is: why should the curve be downward sloping?

FIGURE 16-1 The Aggregate Demand Curve

The aggregate demand curve shows the relationship between the aggregate price level and the quantity of aggregate output demanded. The curve is downward sloping due to the wealth effect of a change in the aggregate price level and the interest rate effect of a change in the aggregate price level. Corresponding to the actual 1933 data, here the total quantity of goods and services demanded at an aggregate price level of 7.3 is $778 billion in 2009 dollars. According to our hypothetical curve, however, if the aggregate price level had been only 4.2, the quantity of aggregate output demanded would have risen to $1,000 billion.

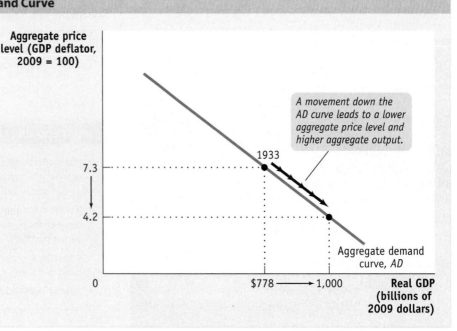

Why Is the Aggregate Demand Curve Downward Sloping?

In Figure 16-1, the curve *AD* is downward sloping. Why? Recall the basic equation of national income accounting:

(16-1) $GDP = C + I + G + X - IM$

where *C* is consumer spending, *I* is investment spending, *G* is government purchases of goods and services, *X* is exports to other countries, and *IM* is imports. If we measure these variables in constant dollars—that is, in prices of a base year—then $C + I + G + X - IM$ is the quantity of domestically produced final goods and services demanded during a given period. *G* is decided by the government, but the other variables are private-sector decisions. To understand why the aggregate demand curve slopes downward, we need to understand why a rise in the aggregate price level reduces *C* and *I*.

You might think that the downward slope of the aggregate demand curve is a natural consequence of the *law of demand* defined back in Chapter 3. That is, since the demand curve for any one good is downward sloping, isn't it natural that the demand curve for aggregate output is also downward sloping? This turns out, however, to be a misleading parallel. The demand curve for any individual good shows how the quantity demanded depends on the price of that good, *holding the prices of other goods and services constant*. The main reason the quantity of a good demanded falls when the price of that good rises—that is, the quantity of a good demanded falls as we move up the demand curve—is that people switch their consumption to other goods and services.

But when we consider movements up or down the aggregate demand curve, we're considering *a simultaneous change in the prices of all final goods and services*. Furthermore, changes in the composition of goods and services in consumer spending aren't relevant to the aggregate demand curve: if consumers decide to buy fewer clothes but more cars, this doesn't necessarily change the total quantity of final goods and services they demand.

Why, then, does a rise in the aggregate price level lead to a fall in the quantity of all domestically produced final goods and services demanded? There are two main reasons: the *wealth effect* and the *interest rate effect* of a change in the aggregate price level

The Wealth Effect An increase in the aggregate price level, other things equal, reduces the purchasing power of many assets. Consider, for example, someone who has $5,000 in a bank account. If the aggregate price level were to rise by 25%, what used to cost $5,000 would now cost $6,250, and would no longer be affordable. And what used to cost $4,000 would now cost $5,000, so that the $5,000 in the bank account would now buy only as much as $4,000 would have bought previously. With the loss in purchasing power, the owner of that bank account would probably scale back his or her consumption plans. Millions of other people would respond the same way, leading to a fall in spending on final goods and services, because a rise in the aggregate price level reduces the purchasing power of everyone's bank account.

Correspondingly, a fall in the aggregate price level increases the purchasing power of consumers' assets and leads to more consumer demand. The **wealth effect of a change in the aggregate price level** is the effect on consumer spending caused by the effect of a change in the aggregate price level on the purchasing power of consumers' assets. Because of the wealth effect, consumer spending, *C*, falls when the aggregate price level rises, leading to a downward-sloping aggregate demand curve.

The Interest Rate Effect Economists use the term *money* in its narrowest sense to refer to cash and bank accounts on which people can use a debit card and write checks. People and firms hold money because it reduces the cost and inconvenience

The **wealth effect of a change in the aggregate price level** is the effect on consumer spending caused by the effect of a change in the aggregate price level on the purchasing power of consumers' assets.

The **interest rate effect of a change in the aggregate price level** is the effect on consumer spending and investment spending caused by the effect of a change in the aggregate price level on the purchasing power of consumers' and firms' money holdings.

of making transactions. An increase in the aggregate price level, other things equal, reduces the purchasing power of a given amount of money holdings. To purchase the same basket of goods and services as before, people and firms now need to hold more money. So, in response to an increase in the aggregate price level, the public tries to increase its money holdings, either by drawing down its savings in bank accounts, by borrowing more, or by selling assets such as bonds. This reduces the funds available for lending to other borrowers and drives interest rates up.

A rise in the interest rate reduces investment spending because it raises the cost of borrowing. It also reduces consumer spending because, with higher interest rates paid on their savings accounts, households save more of their disposable income. So a rise in the aggregate price level depresses investment spending, *I*, and consumer spending, *C*, through its effect on the purchasing power of money holdings, an effect known as the **interest rate effect of a change in the aggregate price level.** This also leads to a downward-sloping aggregate demand curve.

We'll have a lot more to say about money and interest rates in Chapter 19 on monetary policy. For now, the important point is that the aggregate demand curve is downward sloping due to both the wealth effect and the interest rate effect of a change in the aggregate price level.

Shifts of the Aggregate Demand Curve

In Chapter 3, where we introduced the analysis of supply and demand in the market for an individual good or service, we stressed the importance of the distinction between *movements along* the demand curve and *shifts of* the demand curve. The same distinction applies to the aggregate demand curve. Figure 16-1 shows a *movement along* the aggregate demand curve, a change in the aggregate output demanded as the aggregate price level changes.

But there can also be *shifts of* the aggregate demand curve, changes in the quantity of goods and services demanded at any given price level, as shown in Figure 16-2. When we talk about an increase in aggregate demand, we mean a

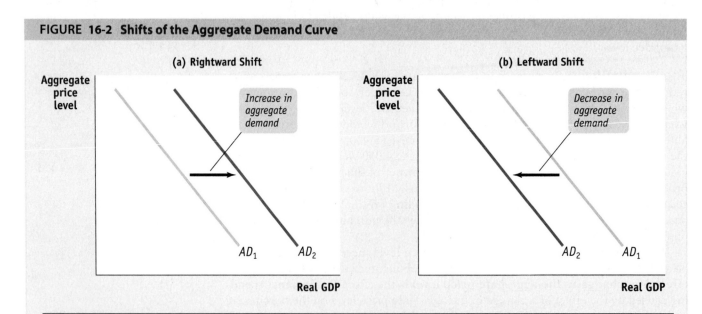

FIGURE 16-2 Shifts of the Aggregate Demand Curve

Panel (a) shows the effect of events that increase the quantity of aggregate output demanded at any given aggregate price level, such as improvements in business and consumer expectations or increased government spending. Such changes shift the aggregate demand curve to the right, from AD_1 to AD_2. Panel (b) shows the effect of events that decrease the quantity of aggregate output demanded at any given aggregate price level, such as a fall in wealth caused by a stock market decline. This shifts the aggregate demand curve leftward from AD_1 to AD_2.

shift of the aggregate demand curve to the right, as shown in panel (a) by the shift from AD_1 to AD_2. A rightward shift occurs when the quantity of aggregate output demanded increases at any given aggregate price level. A decrease in aggregate demand means that the AD curve shifts to the left, as in panel (b). A leftward shift implies that the quantity of aggregate output demanded falls at any given aggregate price level.

A number of factors can shift the aggregate demand curve. Among the most important factors are changes in expectations, changes in wealth, and the size of the existing stock of physical capital. In addition, both fiscal and monetary policy can shift the aggregate demand curve. We'll now examine each of the factors that shift the aggregate demand curve. For an overview of them, see Table 16-1.

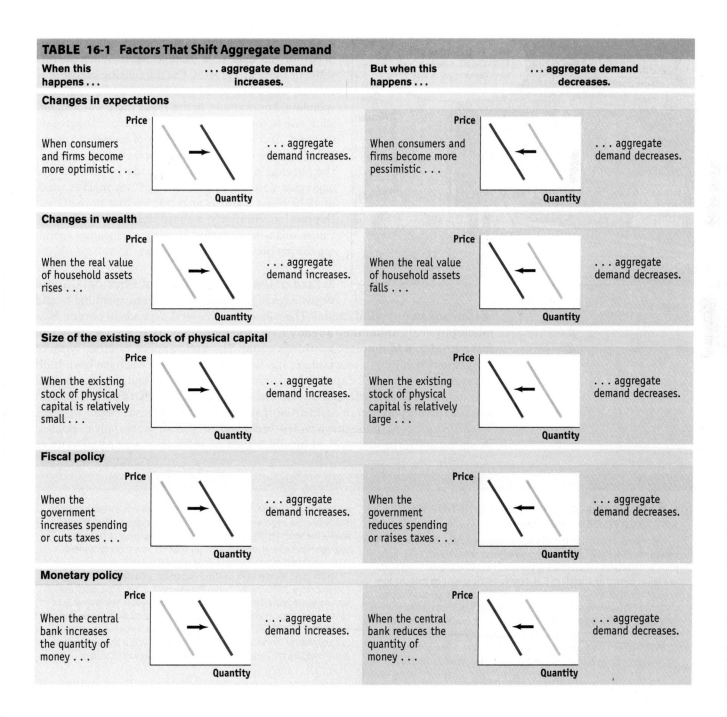

TABLE 16-1 Factors That Shift Aggregate Demand

When this happens . . .	. . . aggregate demand increases.	But when this happens . . .	. . . aggregate demand decreases.
Changes in expectations			
When consumers and firms become more optimistic . . .	. . . aggregate demand increases.	When consumers and firms become more pessimistic . . .	. . . aggregate demand decreases.
Changes in wealth			
When the real value of household assets rises . . .	. . . aggregate demand increases.	When the real value of household assets falls . . .	. . . aggregate demand decreases.
Size of the existing stock of physical capital			
When the existing stock of physical capital is relatively small . . .	. . . aggregate demand increases.	When the existing stock of physical capital is relatively large . . .	. . . aggregate demand decreases.
Fiscal policy			
When the government increases spending or cuts taxes . . .	. . . aggregate demand increases.	When the government reduces spending or raises taxes . . .	. . . aggregate demand decreases.
Monetary policy			
When the central bank increases the quantity of money . . .	. . . aggregate demand increases.	When the central bank reduces the quantity of money . . .	. . . aggregate demand decreases.

1. Changes in Expectations Both consumer spending and planned investment spending depend in part on people's expectations about the future. Consumers base their spending not only on the income they have now but also on the income they expect to have in the future. Firms base their planned investment spending not only on current conditions but also on the sales they expect to make in the future. As a result, changes in expectations can push consumer spending and planned investment spending up or down. If consumers and firms become more optimistic, aggregate spending rises; if they become more pessimistic, aggregate spending falls.

In fact, short-run economic forecasters pay careful attention to surveys of consumer and business sentiment. In particular, forecasters watch the Consumer Confidence Index, a monthly measure calculated by the Conference Board, and the Michigan Consumer Sentiment Index, a similar measure calculated by the University of Michigan.

2. Changes in Wealth Consumer spending depends in part on the value of household assets. When the real value of these assets rises, the purchasing power they embody also rises, leading to an increase in aggregate spending. For example, in the 1990s there was a significant rise in the stock market that increased aggregate demand. And when the real value of household assets falls (because of a stock market crash, for instance), the purchasing power they embody is reduced and aggregate demand also falls. The stock market crash of 1929 was a significant factor leading to the Great Depression. Similarly, a sharp decline in real estate values was a major factor depressing consumer spending during the 2007–2009 recession.

3. Size of the Existing Stock of Physical Capital Firms engage in planned investment spending to add to their stock of physical capital. Their incentive to spend depends in part on how much physical capital they already have: the more they have, the less they will feel a need to add more, other things equal. The same applies to other types of investment spending. For example, if a large number of houses have been built in recent years, this will depress the demand for new houses and, as a result, will also tend to reduce residential investment spending. In fact, that's part of the reason for the deep slump in residential investment spending that began in 2006. The housing boom of the previous few years had created an oversupply of houses: by spring 2009, the inventory of unsold houses on the market was equal to more

---

PITFALLS

A MOVEMENT ALONG VERSUS A SHIFT OF THE AGGREGATE DEMAND CURVE

As we've seen, one reason the *AD* curve is downward sloping is the wealth effect of a change in the aggregate price level: a higher aggregate price level reduces the purchasing power of households' assets and leads to a fall in consumer spending, *C*. But we've also just learned that changes in wealth lead to a shift of the *AD* curve. Aren't those two principles contradictory? Which one is right—does a change in wealth move the economy along the *AD* curve or does it shift the *AD* curve? The answer is: both are correct—*it depends on the source of the change in wealth.*

A movement along the *AD* curve occurs when a change in the aggregate price level changes the purchasing power of consumers'

existing wealth (the real value of their assets). This is the *wealth effect of a change in the aggregate price level*—a change in the aggregate price level is the source of the change in wealth. For example, a fall in the aggregate price level increases the purchasing power of consumers' assets and leads to a movement down the *AD* curve.

In contrast, a change in wealth *independent of a change in the aggregate price level* shifts the *AD* curve. For example, a rise in the stock market or a rise in real estate values leads to an increase in the real value of consumers' assets at any given aggregate price level. In this case, the source of the change in wealth is a change in the values of assets without any change in the aggregate price level—that is, a change in asset values holding the prices of all final goods and services constant.

than 14 months of sales, and prices of new homes had fallen more than 25% from their peak. This gave the construction industry little incentive to build even more homes.

4. Fiscal Policy One of the key insights of macroeconomics is that the government can have a powerful influence on aggregate demand and that, in some circumstances, this influence can be used to improve economic performance. The use of either government spending—government purchases of final goods and services and government transfers—or tax policy to stabilize the economy is known as *fiscal policy*. In practice, governments often respond to recessions by increasing spending, cutting taxes, or both. They often respond to inflation by reducing spending or increasing taxes.

The effect of government purchases of final goods and services, *G*, on the aggregate demand curve is *direct* because government purchases are themselves a component of aggregate demand. So an increase in government purchases shifts the aggregate demand curve to the right and a decrease shifts it to the left. History's most dramatic example of how increased government purchases affect aggregate demand was the effect of wartime government spending during World War II.

Because of the war, U.S. federal purchases surged 400%. This increase in purchases is usually credited with ending the Great Depression. In the 1990s Japan used large public works projects —such as government-financed construction of roads, bridges, and dams—in an effort to increase aggregate demand in the face of a slumping economy. Similarly, in 2009, in the wake of the Great Recession, the United States began spending more than $100 billion on infrastructure projects such as improving highways, bridges, public transportation, and more, to stimulate overall spending.

In contrast, changes in either tax rates or government transfers influence the economy *indirectly*, through their effect on disposable income. A lower tax rate means that consumers get to keep more of what they earn, increasing their disposable income. An increase in government transfers also increases consumers' disposable income. In either case, this increases consumer spending and shifts the aggregate demand curve to the right. A higher tax rate or a reduction in transfers reduces the amount of disposable income received by consumers. This reduces consumer spending and shifts the aggregate demand curve to the left.

5. Monetary Policy We opened this chapter by talking about the problems faced by the Federal Reserve in 2011. The Federal Reserve controls *monetary policy*—the use of changes in the quantity of money or the interest rate to stabilize the economy. We've just discussed how a rise in the aggregate price level, by reducing the purchasing power of money holdings, causes a rise in the interest rate. That, in turn, reduces both investment spending and consumer spending.

But what happens if the quantity of money in the hands of households and firms changes? In modern economies, the quantity of money in circulation is largely determined by the decisions of a *central bank* created by the government. As we'll learn in Chapter 18, the Federal Reserve, the U.S. central bank, is a special institution that is neither exactly part of the government nor exactly a private institution. When the central bank increases the quantity of money in circulation, households and firms have more money, which they are willing to lend out. The effect is to drive the interest rate down at any given aggregate price level, leading to higher investment spending and higher consumer spending.

That is, increasing the quantity of money shifts the aggregate demand curve to the right. Reducing the quantity of money has the opposite effect: households and firms have fewer money holdings than before, leading them to borrow more and lend less. This raises the interest rate, reduces investment spending and consumer spending, and shifts the aggregate demand curve to the left.

During the 1979 oil crisis, the interest rate effect from a rise in the aggregate price level pushed the economy up the *AD* curve, leading to a fall in aggregate output.

ECONOMICS >> *in Action*
Moving Along the Aggregate Demand Curve, 1979–1980

When looking at data, it's often hard to distinguish between changes in spending that represent *movements along* the aggregate demand curve and *shifts of* the aggregate demand curve. One telling exception, however, is what happened right after the oil crisis of 1979. Faced with a sharp increase in the aggregate price level—the rate of consumer price inflation reached 14.8% in March of 1980—the Federal Reserve stuck to a policy of increasing the quantity of money slowly. The aggregate price level was rising steeply, but the quantity of money circulating in the economy was growing slowly. The net result was that the purchasing power of the quantity of money in circulation fell.

This led to an increase in the demand for borrowing and a surge in interest rates. The *prime rate*, which is the interest rate banks charge their best customers, climbed above 20%. High interest rates, in turn, caused both consumer spending and investment spending to fall: in 1980 purchases of durable consumer goods like cars fell by 5.3% and real investment spending fell by 8.9%.

In other words, in 1979–1980 the economy responded just as we'd expect if it were moving upward along the aggregate demand curve from right to left: due to the wealth effect and the interest rate effect of a change in the aggregate price level, the quantity of aggregate output demanded fell as the aggregate price level rose. This does not explain, of course, why the aggregate price level rose. But as we'll see in the upcoming section on the *AD–AS* model, the answer to that question lies in the behavior of the *short-run aggregate supply curve*.

>> Check Your Understanding 16-1

Solutions appear at back of book.

1. Determine the effect on aggregate demand of each of the following events. Explain whether it represents a movement along the aggregate demand curve (up or down) or a shift of the curve (leftward or rightward).
   a. A rise in the interest rate caused by a change in monetary policy
   b. A fall in the real value of money in the economy due to a higher aggregate price level
   c. News of a worse-than-expected job market next year
   d. A fall in tax rates
   e. A rise in the real value of assets in the economy due to a lower aggregate price level
   f. A rise in the real value of assets in the economy due to a surge in real estate values

>> Quick Review

- The **aggregate demand curve** is downward sloping because of the **wealth effect of a change in the aggregate price level** and the **interest rate effect of a change in the aggregate price level.**

- The aggregate demand curve shifts in response to changes in consumer spending caused by changes in wealth and changes in expectations about future income. It also shifts in response to changes in investment spending caused by changes in expectations about future sales and by the size of the existing stock of physical capital.

- Fiscal policy affects aggregate demand directly through government purchases and indirectly through changes in taxes or government transfers. Monetary policy affects aggregate demand indirectly through changes in the interest rate.

‖ Aggregate Supply

Between 1929 and 1933, the worst years of the Great Depression, there was a sharp fall in aggregate demand—a reduction in the quantity aggregate output demanded at any given price level. One consequence of the economy-wide decline in demand was a fall in the prices of most goods and services. By 1933, the GDP deflator (one of the price indexes we defined in Chapter 13) was 26% below its 1929 level, and other indexes were down by similar amounts. A second consequence was a decline in the output of most goods and services: by 1933, real GDP was 27% below its 1929 level. A third consequence, closely tied to the fall in real GDP, was a surge in the unemployment rate from 3% to 25%.

The association between the plunge in real GDP and the plunge in prices wasn't an accident. Between 1929 and 1933, the U.S. economy was moving down its **aggregate supply curve,** which shows the relationship between the economy's aggregate price level (the overall price level of final goods and services in the economy) and the total quantity of final goods and services, or aggregate output, that producers are willing to supply. (As you will recall, we use real GDP to measure aggregate output. So we'll often use the two terms interchangeably.) More specifically, between 1929 and 1933 the U.S. economy moved down its *short-run aggregate supply curve.*

The Short-Run Aggregate Supply Curve

The period from 1929 to 1933 demonstrated that there is a positive relationship in the *short run* between the aggregate price level and the quantity of aggregate output supplied. That is, a rise in the aggregate price level is associated with a rise in the quantity of aggregate output supplied, other things equal; a fall in the aggregate price level is associated with a fall in the quantity of aggregate output supplied, other things equal. To understand why this positive relationship exists, consider the most basic question facing a producer: is producing a unit of output profitable or not? Let's define profit per unit:

(16-2) Profit per unit of output =
Price per unit of output – Production cost per unit of output

Thus, the answer to the question depends on whether the price the producer receives for a unit of output is greater than or less than the cost of producing that unit of output. At any given point in time, many of the costs that producers face are fixed per unit of output and can't be changed for an extended period of time. Typically, the largest source of inflexible production cost is the wages paid to workers. *Wages* here refer to all forms of worker compensation, such as employer-paid health care and retirement benefits in addition to earnings.

Wages are typically an inflexible production cost because the dollar amount of any given wage paid, called the **nominal wage,** is typically determined by contracts that were signed some time ago. And even when there are no formal contracts, there are often informal agreements between management and workers, making companies reluctant to change wages in response to economic conditions. For example, companies usually will not reduce wages during poor economic times—unless the downturn has been particularly long and severe—for fear of generating worker resentment. Correspondingly, they typically won't raise wages during better economic times—until they are at risk of losing workers to competitors—because they don't want to encourage workers to routinely demand higher wages.

As a result of both formal and informal agreements, then, the economy is characterized by **sticky wages:** nominal wages that are slow to fall even in the face of high unemployment and slow to rise even in the face of labor shortages. It's important to note, however, that nominal wages cannot be sticky forever: ultimately, formal contracts and informal agreements will be renegotiated to take into account changed economic circumstances.

To understand how the fact that many costs are fixed in nominal terms gives rise to an upward-sloping short-run aggregate supply curve, it's helpful to know that prices are set somewhat differently in different kinds of markets. In *perfectly competitive markets,* producers take prices as given; in *imperfectly competitive markets,* producers have some ability to choose the prices they charge. In both kinds of markets, there is a short-run positive relationship between prices and output, but for slightly different reasons.

Let's start with the behavior of producers in perfectly competitive markets; remember, they take the price as given. Imagine that, for some reason, the

The **aggregate supply curve** shows the relationship between the aggregate price level and the quantity of aggregate output supplied in the economy.

The **nominal wage** is the dollar amount of the wage paid.

Sticky wages are nominal wages that are slow to fall even in the face of high unemployment and slow to rise even in the face of labor shortages.

The short-run aggregate supply curve shows the relationship between the aggregate price level and the quantity of aggregate output supplied that exists in the short run, the time period when many production costs can be taken as fixed.

aggregate price level falls, which means that the price received by the typical producer of a final good or service falls. Because many production costs are fixed in the short run, production cost per unit of output doesn't fall by the same proportion as the fall in the price of output. So the profit per unit of output declines, leading perfectly competitive producers to reduce the quantity supplied in the short run.

On the other hand, suppose that for some reason the aggregate price level rises. As a result, the typical producer receives a higher price for its final good or service. Again, many production costs are fixed in the short run, so production cost per unit of output doesn't rise by the same proportion as the rise in the price of a unit. And since the typical perfectly competitive producer takes the price as given, profit per unit of output rises and output increases.

Now consider an imperfectly competitive producer that is able to set its own price. If there is a rise in the demand for this producer's product, it will be able to sell more at any given price. Given stronger demand for its products, it will probably choose to increase its prices as well as its output, as a way of increasing profit per unit of output. In fact, industry analysts often talk about variations in an industry's *pricing power*: when demand is strong, firms with pricing power are able to raise prices—and they do.

Conversely, if there is a fall in demand, firms will normally try to limit the fall in their sales by cutting prices.

Both the responses of firms in perfectly competitive industries and those of firms in imperfectly competitive industries lead to an upward-sloping relationship between aggregate output and the aggregate price level. The positive relationship between the aggregate price level and aggregate output in the short run is illustrated by an upward-sloping **short-run aggregate supply curve.** Along this curve, producers are willing to supply during the time period when many production costs, particularly nominal wages, can be taken as fixed.

Figure 16-3 shows a hypothetical short-run aggregate supply curve, *SRAS*, that matches actual U.S. data for 1929 and 1933. On the horizontal axis is aggregate output (or, equivalently, real GDP)—the total quantity of final goods and services supplied in the economy—measured in 2009 dollars. On the vertical axis is the aggregate price level as measured by the GDP deflator, with the value for the year

---

FIGURE 16-3 The Short-Run Aggregate Supply Curve

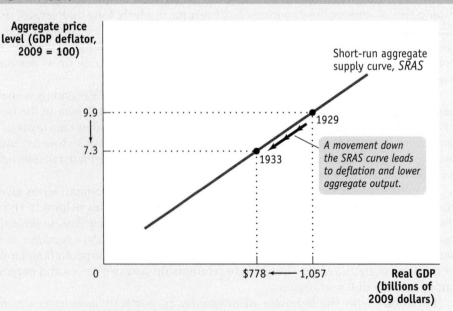

The short-run aggregate supply curve shows the relationship between the aggregate price level and the quantity of aggregate output supplied in the short run, the period in which many production costs such as nominal wages are fixed. It is upward sloping because a higher aggregate price level leads to higher profit per unit of output and higher aggregate output given fixed nominal wages. Here we show numbers corresponding to early in the Great Depression, from 1929 to 1933. When deflation occurred and the aggregate price level fell from 9.9 (in 1929) to 7.3 (in 1933), firms responded by reducing the quantity of aggregate output supplied from $1,057 billion to $778 billion measured in 2009 dollars.

2009 equal to 100. In 1929, the aggregate price level was 9.9 and real GDP was $1,057 billion. In 1933, the aggregate price level was 7.3 and real GDP was only $778 billion. The movement down the *SRAS* curve corresponds to the deflation and fall in aggregate output experienced over those years.

What's Truly Flexible and What's Truly Sticky? Most macroeconomists agree that the picture shown in Figure 16-3 is correct: there is, other things equal, a positive short-run relationship between the aggregate price level and aggregate output. But many would argue that the details are a bit more complicated.

So far we've stressed a difference in the behavior of the aggregate price level and the behavior of nominal wages. That is, we've said that the aggregate price level is flexible but nominal wages are sticky in the short run. Although this assumption is a good way to explain why the short-run aggregate supply curve is upward sloping, empirical data on wages and prices don't wholly support a sharp distinction between flexible prices of final goods and services and sticky nominal wages.

On one side, some nominal wages are in fact flexible even in the short run because some workers are not covered by a contract or informal agreement with their employers. Since some nominal wages are sticky but others are flexible, we observe that the *average nominal wage*—the nominal wage averaged over all workers in the economy—falls when there is a steep rise in unemployment. For example, nominal wages fell substantially in the early years of the Great Depression.

On the other side, some prices of final goods and services are sticky rather than flexible. For example, some firms, particularly the makers of luxury or name-brand goods, are reluctant to cut prices even when demand falls. Instead they prefer to cut output even if their profit per unit hasn't declined.

These complications, as we've said, don't change the basic picture. When the aggregate price level falls, some producers cut output because the nominal wages they pay are sticky. And some producers don't cut their prices in the face of a falling aggregate price level, preferring instead to reduce their output. In both cases, the positive relationship between the aggregate price level and aggregate output is maintained. So, in the end, the short-run aggregate supply curve is still upward sloping.

Shifts of the Short-Run Aggregate Supply Curve

Figure 16-3 shows a *movement along* the short-run aggregate supply curve, as the aggregate price level and aggregate output fell from 1929 to 1933. This was precipitated by a sharp fall in aggregate demand—a leftward shift of the aggregate demand curve. But there can also be *shifts of* the short-run aggregate supply curve. Panel (a) of Figure 16-4 shows a *decrease in short-run aggregate supply*—a leftward shift of the short-run aggregate supply curve. Aggregate supply decreases when producers reduce the quantity of aggregate output they are willing to supply at any given aggregate price level. Panel (b) shows an *increase in short-run aggregate supply*—a rightward shift of the short-run aggregate supply curve. Aggregate supply increases when producers increase the quantity of aggregate output they are willing to supply at any given aggregate price level.

To understand why the short-run aggregate supply curve can shift, it's important to recall that producers make output decisions based on their profit per unit of output. The short-run aggregate supply curve illustrates the relationship between the aggregate price level and aggregate output: because some production costs are fixed in the short run, a change in the aggregate price level leads to a change in producers' profit per unit of output and, in turn, leads to a change in aggregate output.

But three other factors besides the aggregate price level can affect profit per unit and, in turn, aggregate output: changes in commodity prices, in nominal

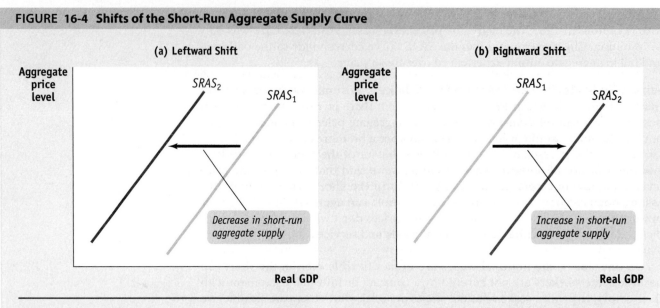

FIGURE 16-4 Shifts of the Short-Run Aggregate Supply Curve

Panel (a) shows a decrease in short-run aggregate supply: the short-run aggregate supply curve shifts leftward from $SRAS_1$ to $SRAS_2$, and the quantity of aggregate output supplied at any given aggregate price level falls. Panel (b) shows an increase in short-run aggregate supply: the short-run aggregate supply curve shifts rightward from $SRAS_1$ to $SRAS_2$, and the quantity of aggregate output supplied at any given aggregate price level rises.

wages, and in productivity. Changes in these factors will shift the short-run aggregate supply curve.

To develop some intuition, suppose that something happens that raises production costs—say, an increase in the price of oil. At any given price of output, a producer now earns a smaller profit per unit of output. As a result, producers reduce the quantity supplied at any given aggregate price level, and the short-run aggregate supply curve shifts to the left. If, in contrast, something happens that lowers production costs—say, a fall in the nominal wage—a producer now earns a higher profit per unit of output at any given price of output. This leads producers to increase the quantity of aggregate output supplied at any given aggregate price level, and the short-run aggregate supply curve shifts to the right.

1. Changes in Commodity Prices In the opening story, we saw how the views of Jean-Claude Trichet, the president of the ECB, were shaped by the high inflation of the 1970s. The origins of that inflationary period lay in a sharp and sustained increase in the price of a very important commodity—oil. The high price of oil sharply raised costs for producers around the world.

A *commodity* is a standardized input bought and sold in bulk quantities. An increase in the price of a commodity, such as oil, raises production costs across the economy and reduces the quantity of aggregate output supplied at any given aggregate price level. This shifts the aggregate supply curve to the left. Conversely, a decline in commodity prices reduces production costs, leading to an increase in the quantity supplied at any given aggregate price level and a rightward shift of the short-run aggregate supply curve.

Why isn't the influence of commodity prices already captured by the short-run aggregate supply curve? Because commodities—unlike, say, soft drinks—are not a final good. Hence their prices are not included in the calculation of the aggregate price level. Further, commodities represent a significant cost of production to most suppliers, just like nominal wages do. So changes in commodity prices have large impacts on production costs. And in contrast to noncommodities, the prices of commodities can sometimes change drastically due to industry-specific shocks to supply—such as wars in the Middle East or rising Chinese demand that leaves less oil for the United States.

2. Changes in Nominal Wages At any given point in time, the dollar wages of many workers are fixed because they are set by contracts or informal agreements made in the past. Nominal wages can change, however, once enough time has passed for contracts and informal agreements to be renegotiated.

Suppose, for example, that there is an economy-wide rise in the cost of health care insurance premiums paid by employers as part of employees' wages. From the employers' perspective, this is equivalent to a rise in nominal wages because it is an increase in employer-paid compensation. So this rise in nominal wages increases production costs and shifts the short-run aggregate supply curve to the left.

Conversely, suppose there is an economy-wide fall in the cost of such premiums. This is equivalent to a fall in nominal wages from the point of view of employers; it reduces production costs and shifts the short-run aggregate supply curve to the right.

An important historical fact is that during the 1970s the surge in the price of oil had the indirect effect of also raising nominal wages. This "knock-on" effect occurred because many wage contracts included *cost-of-living allowances* that automatically raised the nominal wage when consumer prices increased. Through this channel, the surge in the price of oil—which led to an increase in overall consumer prices—ultimately caused a rise in nominal wages.

So the economy, in the end, experienced two leftward shifts of the aggregate supply curve: the first generated by the initial surge in the price of oil, the second generated by the induced increase in nominal wages. The negative effect on the economy of rising oil prices was greatly magnified through the cost-of-living allowances in wage contracts. As a result of that experience, cost-of-living allowances in today's wage contracts are rare.

3. Changes in Productivity An increase in productivity means that a worker can produce more units of output with the same quantity of inputs. For example, the introduction of barcode scanners in retail stores greatly increased the ability of a single worker to stock, inventory, and resupply store shelves. As a result, the cost to a store of "producing" a dollar of sales fell, profit rose, and the quantity supplied increased. (Think of Walmart and the increase in the number of its stores as an increase in aggregate supply.) So, a rise in productivity, whatever the source, increases producers' profit per unit produced and shifts the short-run aggregate supply curve to the right.

Conversely, a fall in productivity—say, due to new regulations that require workers to spend more time filling out forms—reduces the number of units of output a worker can produce with the same quantity of inputs. Consequently, the cost per unit of output rises, leading to a fall in profit per unit produced, and quantity supplied falls. This shifts the short-run aggregate supply curve to the left.

For a summary of the factors that shift the short-run aggregate supply curve, see Table 16-2.

The Long-Run Aggregate Supply Curve

We've just seen that in the short run a fall in the aggregate price level leads to a decline in the quantity of aggregate output supplied because nominal wages are sticky in the short run. But, as mentioned earlier, contracts and informal agreements are renegotiated in the long run. So in the long run, nominal wages will fully adjust to changes in the aggregate price level (they are flexible, not sticky). This fact greatly alters the long-run relationship between the aggregate price level

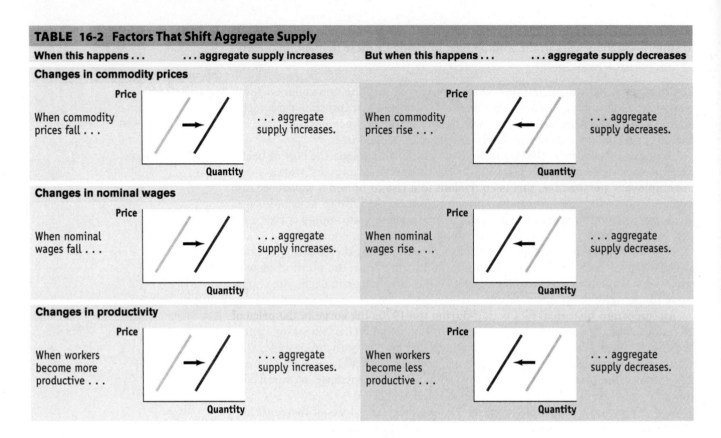

TABLE 16-2 Factors That Shift Aggregate Supply

When this happens . . .	. . . aggregate supply increases	But when this happens . . .	. . . aggregate supply decreases
Changes in commodity prices			
When commodity prices fall . . .	. . . aggregate supply increases.	When commodity prices rise . . .	. . . aggregate supply decreases.
Changes in nominal wages			
When nominal wages fall . . .	. . . aggregate supply increases.	When nominal wages rise . . .	. . . aggregate supply decreases.
Changes in productivity			
When workers become more productive . . .	. . . aggregate supply increases.	When workers become less productive . . .	. . . aggregate supply decreases.

and aggregate supply. In fact, in the long run, the aggregate price level has *no* effect on the quantity of aggregate output supplied.

To see why, let's conduct a thought experiment. Imagine that you could wave a magic wand—or maybe a magic barcode scanner—and cut *all prices* in the economy in half at the same time. By "all prices" we mean the prices of all inputs, including nominal wages, as well as the prices of final goods and services. What would happen to aggregate output, given that the aggregate price level has been halved and all input prices, including nominal wages, have been halved?

The answer is: nothing. Consider Equation 16-2 again: each producer would receive a lower price for its product, but costs would fall by the same proportion. As a result, every unit of output profitable to produce before the change in prices would still be profitable to produce after the change in prices. So a halving of *all* prices in the economy has no effect on the economy's aggregate output. In other words, changes in the aggregate price level now have no effect on the quantity of aggregate output supplied.

In reality, of course, no one can change all prices by the same proportion at the same time. But now, we'll consider the *long run, the period of time in which all prices, including production costs such as nominal wages, are fully flexible.* In the long run, inflation or deflation has the same effect as someone changing all prices by the same proportion. *As a result, changes in the aggregate price level do not change the quantity of aggregate output supplied in the long run.* That's because changes in the aggregate price level, which is composed of prices of final goods and services, will be accompanied by equal proportional changes in *all* input prices, including nominal wages.

The **long-run aggregate supply curve,** illustrated in Figure 16-5 by the curve *LRAS,* shows the relationship between the aggregate price level and the quantity of aggregate output supplied that holds when all prices, including nominal wages, are fully flexible. The long-run aggregate supply curve is vertical because changes in the aggregate price level have *no* effect on aggregate output in the long run.

The **long-run aggregate supply curve** shows the relationship between the aggregate price level and the quantity of aggregate output supplied that would exist if all prices, including nominal wages, were fully flexible.

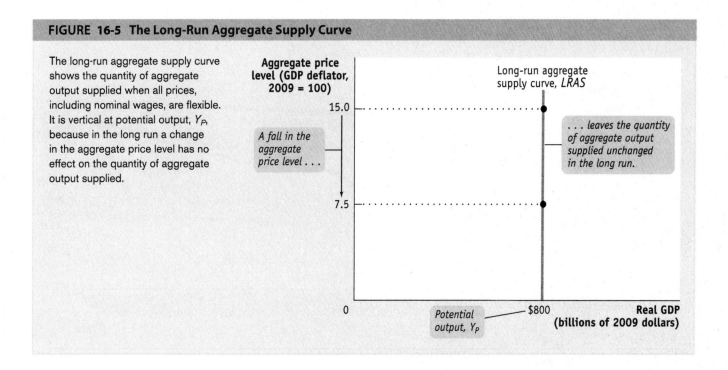

FIGURE 16-5 The Long-Run Aggregate Supply Curve

The long-run aggregate supply curve shows the quantity of aggregate output supplied when all prices, including nominal wages, are flexible. It is vertical at potential output, Y_P, because in the long run a change in the aggregate price level has no effect on the quantity of aggregate output supplied.

Aggregate price level (GDP deflator, 2009 = 100)

15.0

A fall in the aggregate price level . . .

7.5

0

Long-run aggregate supply curve, *LRAS*

. . . leaves the quantity of aggregate output supplied unchanged in the long run.

Potential output, Y_P

$800

Real GDP (billions of 2009 dollars)

At an aggregate price level of 15.0, the quantity of aggregate output supplied is $800 billion in 2009 dollars. If the aggregate price level falls by 50% to 7.5, the quantity of aggregate output supplied is unchanged in the long run at $800 billion in 2009 dollars.

It's important to understand not only that the *LRAS* curve is vertical but also that its position along the horizontal axis is significant. The horizontal intercept in Figure 16-5, $800 billion (in 2009 dollars), is the economy's **potential output,** Y_P: the level of real GDP the economy produces if all prices, including nominal wages, were fully flexible.

In reality, the actual level of real GDP is almost always either above or below potential output. We'll see why later in this chapter, when we discuss the *AD–AS* model. Still, an economy's potential output is an important measure because it defines the trend around which actual aggregate output fluctuates from year to year.

In the United States, the Congressional Budget Office, or CBO, estimates annual potential output for the purpose of federal budget analysis. In Figure 16-6, the CBO's estimates of U.S. potential output from 1990 to 2018 are represented by the orange line and the actual values of U.S. real GDP over the same period are represented by the blue line. Years shaded purple on the horizontal axis correspond to periods in which actual aggregate output fell short of potential output; years shaded green correspond to periods in which actual aggregate output exceeded potential output.

As you can see, U.S. potential output has risen steadily over time—implying a series of rightward shifts of the *LRAS* curve. What has caused these rightward shifts? The answer lies in the factors related to long-run growth that we discussed in Chapter 15, such as increases in physical capital and human capital as well as technological progress. Over the long run, as the size of the labor force and the productivity of labor both rise, the level of real GDP that the economy is capable of producing also rises. Indeed, one way to think about long-run economic growth is that it is the growth in the economy's potential output. We generally think of the long-run aggregate supply curve as shifting to the right over time as an economy experiences long-run growth.

Potential output is the level of real GDP the economy would produce if all prices, including nominal wages, were fully flexible.

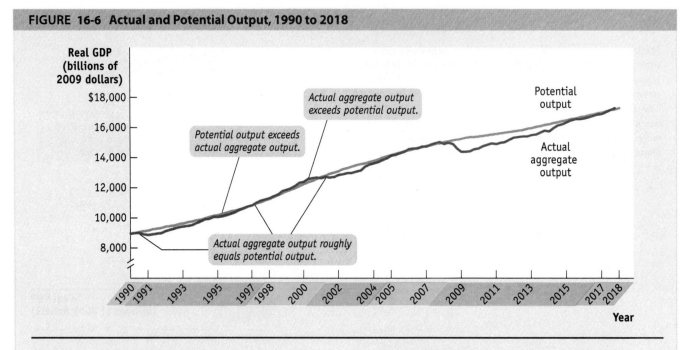

FIGURE 16-6 Actual and Potential Output, 1990 to 2018

This figure shows the performance of actual and potential output in the United States from 1990 to 2018. The orange line shows estimates of U.S. potential output, produced by the Congressional Budget Office, and the blue line shows actual aggregate output. The purple-shaded years are periods in which actual aggregate output fell below potential output, and the years shaded green are periods in which actual aggregate output exceeded potential output. As shown, significant shortfalls occurred in the recessions of the early 1990s and after 2000. Actual aggregate output was significantly above potential output in the boom of the late 1990s, and a huge shortfall occurred after the recession of 2007–2009.

Data from: Congressional Budget Office; Bureau of Economic Analysis; Federal Reserve Bank of St. Louis.

From the Short Run to the Long Run

As you can see in Figure 16-6, the economy normally produces more or less than potential output: actual aggregate output was below potential output in the early 1990s, above potential output in the late 1990s, below potential output for most of the 2000s, and significantly below potential output after the recession of 2007–2009. So the economy is normally on its short-run aggregate supply curve—but not on its long-run aggregate supply curve. So, why is the long-run curve relevant? Does the economy ever move from the short run to the long run? And if so, how?

The first step to answering these questions is to understand that the economy is always in one of only two states with respect to the short-run and long-run aggregate supply curves. It can be on both curves simultaneously by being at a point where the curves cross (as in the few years in Figure 16-6 in which actual aggregate output and potential output roughly coincided). Or it can be on the short-run aggregate supply curve but not the long-run aggregate supply curve (as in the years in which actual aggregate output and potential output *did not* coincide).

But that is not the end of the story. If the economy is on the short-run but not the long-run aggregate supply curve, the short-run aggregate supply curve will shift over time until the economy is at a point where both curves cross—a point where actual aggregate output is equal to potential output.

Figure 16-7 illustrates how this process works. In both panels *LRAS* is the long-run aggregate supply curve, $SRAS_1$ is the initial short-run aggregate supply curve, and the aggregate price level is at P_1. In panel (a) the economy starts at the initial production point, A_1, which corresponds to a quantity of aggregate output supplied, Y_1, that is higher than potential output, Y_P. Producing an aggregate output

FIGURE 16-7   From the Short Run to the Long Run

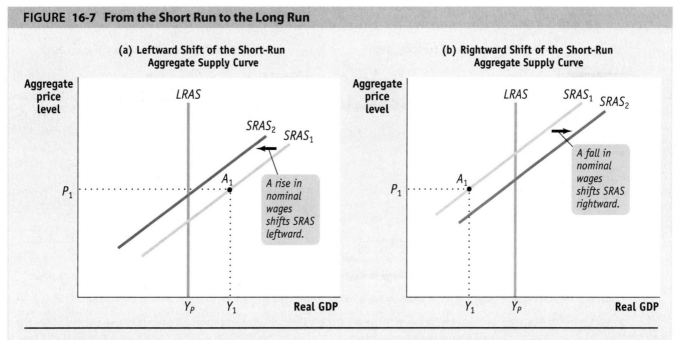

(a) Leftward Shift of the Short-Run Aggregate Supply Curve

Aggregate price level

LRAS

$SRAS_2$ $SRAS_1$

A_1

A rise in nominal wages shifts SRAS leftward.

P_1

Y_P Y_1 Real GDP

(b) Rightward Shift of the Short-Run Aggregate Supply Curve

Aggregate price level

LRAS $SRAS_1$ $SRAS_2$

A fall in nominal wages shifts SRAS rightward.

A_1

P_1

Y_1 Y_P Real GDP

In panel (a), the initial short-run aggregate supply curve is $SRAS_1$. At the aggregate price level, P_1, the quantity of aggregate output supplied, Y_1, exceeds potential output, Y_P. Eventually, low unemployment will cause nominal wages to rise, leading to a leftward shift of the short-run aggregate supply

curve from $SRAS_1$ to $SRAS_2$. In panel (b), the reverse happens: at the aggregate price level, P_1, the quantity of aggregate output supplied is less than potential output. High unemployment eventually leads to a fall in nominal wages over time and a rightward shift of the short-run aggregate supply curve.

level (such as Y_1) that is higher than potential output (Y_P) is possible only because nominal wages haven't yet fully adjusted upward.

Until this upward adjustment in nominal wages occurs, producers are earning high profits and producing a high level of output. But a level of aggregate output higher than potential output means a low level of unemployment. Because jobs are abundant and workers are scarce, nominal wages will rise over time, gradually shifting the short-run aggregate supply curve leftward. Eventually it will be in a new position, such as $SRAS_2$.

In panel (b), the initial production point, A_1, corresponds to an aggregate output level, Y_1, that is lower than potential output, Y_P. Producing an aggregate output level (such as Y_1) that is lower than potential output (Y_P) is possible only because nominal wages haven't yet fully adjusted downward. Until this downward adjustment occurs, producers are earning low (or negative) profits and producing a low level of output. An aggregate output level lower than potential output means high unemployment. Because workers are abundant and jobs are scarce, nominal wages will fall over time, shifting the short-run aggregate supply curve gradually to the right. Eventually it will be in a new position, such as $SRAS_2$.

We'll see shortly that these shifts of the short-run aggregate supply curve will return the economy to potential output in the long run.

ECONOMICS >> *in Action*
Sticky Wages in the Great Recession

We've asserted that the aggregate supply curve is upward sloping in the short run mainly because of *sticky wages*—in particular, because employers are reluctant to cut nominal wages (and workers are unwilling to accept wage cuts) even when labor is in excess supply. But what is the evidence for wage stickiness?

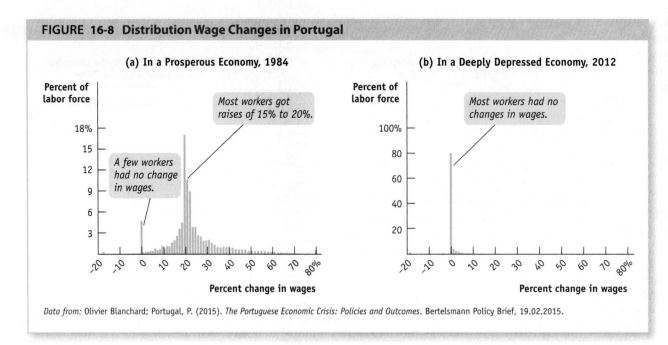

FIGURE 16-8 Distribution Wage Changes in Portugal

Data from: Olivier Blanchard; Portugal, P. (2015). *The Portuguese Economic Crisis: Policies and Outcomes.* Bertelsmann Policy Brief, 19.02.2015.

The answer is that we can look at what happens to wages at times when we might have expected to see many workers facing wage cuts because similar workers are unemployed and would be willing to work for less. If wages are sticky, what we would expect to find at such times is that many workers' wages don't change at all: there's no reason for employers to give them a raise, but because wages are sticky, they don't face cuts either.

And that is exactly what you find during and after the Great Recession of 2007–2009. Figure 16-8 shows an especially striking illustration: the case of Portugal, which suffered a severe, prolonged slump starting in 2008, with the unemployment rate peaking at more than 17% in early 2013.

Panel (a) shows the distribution of Portuguese wage changes—the percentage of all workers whose wage went up by a given amount—in prosperous times, namely 1984, when the economy was doing fairly well and there was also significant inflation. As you can see, most workers were getting raises of between 15% and 20%, but they were spread over a significant range. Panel (b), by contrast, shows the distribution of wage changes in 2012, when the Portuguese economy was deeply depressed and inflation was near zero. Under those circumstances you might have expected to see widespread wage cuts. But employers are reluctant to cut wages. So what we saw instead was that most workers' wages, nearly 80%, were completely flat, as shown by the spike you see at zero. That is, because wages were sticky, most wages were neither rising nor falling.

>> Check Your Understanding 16-2

Solutions appear at back of book.

1. Determine the effect on short-run aggregate supply for each of the following events. Explain whether it represents a movement along the *SRAS* curve or a shift of the *SRAS* curve.
   a. A rise in the consumer price index (CPI) leads producers to increase output.
   b. A fall in the price of oil leads producers to increase output.
   c. A rise in legally mandated retirement benefits paid to workers leads producers to reduce output.

2. Suppose the economy is initially at potential output and the quantity of aggregate output supplied increases. What information would you need to determine whether this was due to a movement along the *SRAS* curve or a shift of the *LRAS* curve?

The *AD–AS* Model

From 1929 to 1933, the U.S. economy moved down the short-run aggregate supply curve as the aggregate price level fell. In contrast, from 1979 to 1980 the U.S. economy moved up the aggregate demand curve as the aggregate price level rose. In each case, the cause of the movement along the curve was a shift of the other curve. In 1929–1933, it was a leftward shift of the aggregate demand curve—a major fall in consumer spending. In 1979–1980, it was a leftward shift of the short-run aggregate supply curve—a dramatic fall in short-run aggregate supply caused by the surging price of oil. Although the aggregate price level did not fall during the Great Recession, economists agree that it was caused by a leftward shift of the aggregate demand curve, similar to the 1929–1933 episode.

So to understand the behavior of the economy, we must put the aggregate supply curve and the aggregate demand curve together. The result is the ***AD–AS* model,** the basic model we use to understand economic fluctuations.

Short-Run Macroeconomic Equilibrium

We'll begin our analysis by focusing on the short run. Figure 16-9 shows the aggregate demand curve and the short-run aggregate supply curve on the same diagram. The point at which the *AD* and *SRAS* curves intersect, E_{SR}, is the **short-run macroeconomic equilibrium:** the point at which the quantity of aggregate output supplied is equal to the quantity demanded by domestic households, businesses, the government, and the rest of the world. The aggregate price level at E_{SR}, P_E, is the **short-run equilibrium aggregate price level.** The level of aggregate output at E_{SR}, Y_E, is the **short-run equilibrium aggregate output.**

We saw in the supply and demand model that a shortage of any individual good causes its market price to rise but a surplus of the good causes its market price to fall. These forces ensure that the market reaches equilibrium. The same logic applies to short-run macroeconomic equilibrium. If the aggregate price level is above its equilibrium level, the quantity of aggregate output supplied exceeds the quantity of aggregate output demanded. This leads to a fall in the aggregate price level and pushes it toward its equilibrium level.

If the aggregate price level is below its equilibrium level, the quantity of aggregate output supplied is less than the quantity of aggregate output demanded. This

In the ***AD–AS* model,** the aggregate supply curve and the aggregate demand curve are used together to analyze economic fluctuations.

The economy is in **short-run macroeconomic equilibrium** when the quantity of aggregate output supplied is equal to the quantity demanded.

The **short-run equilibrium aggregate price level** is the aggregate price level in the short-run macroeconomic equilibrium.

Short-run equilibrium aggregate output is the quantity of aggregate output produced in the short-run macroeconomic equilibrium.

FIGURE 16-9 The *AD–AS* Model

The *AD–AS* model combines the aggregate demand curve and the short-run aggregate supply curve. Their point of intersection, E_{SR}, is the point of short-run macroeconomic equilibrium where the quantity of aggregate output demanded is equal to the quantity of aggregate output supplied. P_E is the short-run equilibrium aggregate price level, and Y_E is the short-run equilibrium level of aggregate output.

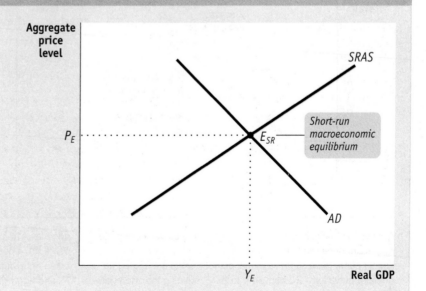

An event that shifts the aggregate demand curve is a **demand shock.**

leads to a rise in the aggregate price level, again pushing it toward its equilibrium level. In the discussion that follows, we'll assume that the economy is always in short-run macroeconomic equilibrium.

We'll also make another important simplification based on the observation that in reality there is a long-term upward trend in both aggregate output and the aggregate price level. We'll assume that a fall in either variable really means a fall compared to the long-run trend. For example, if the aggregate price level normally rises 4% per year, a year in which the aggregate price level rises only 3% would count, for our purposes, as a 1% decline. In fact, since the Great Depression there have been very few years in which the aggregate price level of any major nation actually declined—Japan's period of deflation since 1995 is one of the few exceptions. There have, however, been many cases in which the aggregate price level fell relative to the long-run trend.

Short-run equilibrium aggregate output and the short-run equilibrium aggregate price level can change either because of shifts of the *AD* curve or because of shifts of the *SRAS* curve. Let's look at each case in turn.

Shifts of Aggregate Demand: Short-Run Effects

An event that shifts the aggregate demand curve, such as a change in expectations or wealth, the effect of the size of the existing stock of physical capital, or the use of fiscal or monetary policy, is known as a **demand shock.** The Great Depression was caused by a negative demand shock, the collapse of wealth and of business and consumer confidence that followed the stock market crash of 1929 and the banking crisis of 1930–1931.

The Depression was ended by a positive demand shock—the huge increase in government purchases during World War II. In 2008 the U.S. economy experienced another significant negative demand shock as the housing market turned from boom to bust, leading consumers and firms to scale back their spending.

Figure 16-10 shows the short-run effects of negative and positive demand shocks. A negative demand shock shifts the aggregate demand curve, *AD*, to the

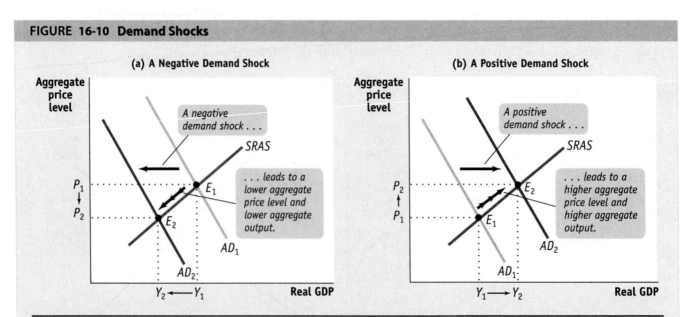

FIGURE 16-10 Demand Shocks

A demand shock shifts the aggregate demand curve, moving the aggregate price level and aggregate output in the same direction. In panel (a), a negative demand shock shifts the aggregate demand curve leftward from AD_1 to AD_2, reducing the aggregate price level from P_1 to P_2 and aggregate output from Y_1 to Y_2. In panel (b), a positive demand shock shifts the aggregate demand curve rightward, increasing the aggregate price level from P_1 to P_2 and aggregate output from Y_1 to Y_2.

left, from AD_1 to AD_2, as shown in panel (a). The economy moves down along the $SRAS$ curve from E_1 to E_2, leading to lower short-run equilibrium aggregate output and a lower short-run equilibrium aggregate price level. A positive demand shock shifts the aggregate demand curve, AD, to the right, as shown in panel (b). Here, the economy moves up along the $SRAS$ curve, from E_1 to E_2. This leads to higher short-run equilibrium aggregate output and a higher short-run equilibrium aggregate price level. Demand shocks cause aggregate output and the aggregate price level to move in the same direction.

> An event that shifts the short-run aggregate supply curve is a **supply shock.**

Shifts of the *SRAS* Curve

An event that shifts the short-run aggregate supply curve, such as a change in commodity prices, nominal wages, or productivity, is known as a **supply shock.** A *negative* supply shock raises production costs and reduces the quantity producers are willing to supply at any given aggregate price level, leading to a leftward shift of the short-run aggregate supply curve. The U.S. economy experienced severe negative supply shocks following disruptions to world oil supplies in 1973 and 1979.

In contrast, a *positive* supply shock reduces production costs and increases the quantity supplied at any given aggregate price level, leading to a rightward shift of the short-run aggregate supply curve. The United States experienced a positive supply shock between 1995 and 2000, when the increasing use of the internet and other information technologies caused productivity growth to surge.

The effects of a negative supply shock are shown in panel (a) of Figure 16-11. The initial equilibrium is at E_1, with aggregate price level P_1 and aggregate output Y_1. The disruption in the oil supply causes the short-run aggregate supply curve to shift to the left, from $SRAS_1$ to $SRAS_2$. As a consequence, aggregate output falls and the aggregate price level rises, an upward movement along the AD curve. At

FIGURE 16-11 Supply Shocks

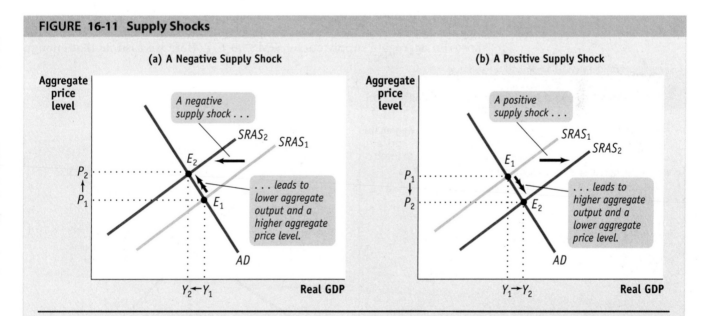

A supply shock shifts the short-run aggregate supply curve, moving the aggregate price level and aggregate output in opposite directions. Panel (a) shows a negative supply shock, which shifts the short-run aggregate supply curve leftward and causes *stagflation*—lower aggregate output and a higher aggregate price level. Here the short-run aggregate supply curve shifts from $SRAS_1$ to $SRAS_2$, and the economy moves from E_1 to E_2. The aggregate price level rises from P_1 to P_2, and aggregate output falls from Y_1 to Y_2. Panel (b) shows a positive supply shock, which shifts the short-run aggregate supply curve rightward, generating higher aggregate output and a lower aggregate price level. The short-run aggregate supply curve shifts from $SRAS_1$ to $SRAS_2$, and the economy moves from E_1 to E_2. The aggregate price level falls from P_1 to P_2, and aggregate output rises from Y_1 to Y_2.

Stagflation is the combination of inflation and falling aggregate output.

the new equilibrium, E_2, the short-run equilibrium aggregate price level, P_2, is higher, and the short-run equilibrium aggregate output level, Y_2, is lower than before.

The combination of inflation and falling aggregate output shown in panel (a) has a special name: **stagflation,** for "stagnation plus inflation." Stagflation is unpleasant: falling aggregate output leads to rising unemployment, while the purchasing power of consumers is squeezed by rising prices. Stagflation in the 1970s created a mood of economic pessimism, and deeply affected those who lived through it, like Jean-Claude Trichet. It also, as we'll see, poses a dilemma for policy makers.

A positive supply shock, shown in panel (b), has exactly the opposite effects. A rightward shift of the *SRAS* curve from $SRAS_1$ to $SRAS_2$ results in a rise in aggregate output and a fall in the aggregate price level, a downward movement along the *AD* curve. The favorable supply shocks of the late 1990s led to a combination of full employment and declining inflation. That is, the aggregate price level fell compared with the long-run trend. This combination produced, for a time, a great wave of national optimism.

The distinctive feature of supply shocks, both negative and positive, is that, unlike demand shocks, they cause the aggregate price level and aggregate output to move in *opposite* directions.

There's another important contrast between supply shocks and demand shocks. As we've seen, monetary policy and fiscal policy enable the government to shift the *AD* curve, meaning that governments are in a position to create the kinds of shocks shown in Figure 16-10. It's much harder for governments to shift the *AS* curve. Are there good policy reasons to shift the *AD* curve? We'll turn to that question soon. First, however, let's look at the difference between short-run macroeconomic equilibrium and *long-run macroeconomic equilibrium*.

Long-Run Macroeconomic Equilibrium

Figure 16-12 combines the aggregate demand curve with both the short-run and long-run aggregate supply curves. The aggregate demand curve, *AD*, crosses the short-run aggregate supply curve, *SRAS*, at E_{LR}. Here we assume that enough

---

FIGURE 16-12 Long-Run Macroeconomic Equilibrium

Here the point of short-run macroeconomic equilibrium also lies on the long-run aggregate supply curve, *LRAS*. As a result, short-run equilibrium aggregate output is equal to potential output, Y_P. The economy is in long-run macroeconomic equilibrium at E_{LR}.

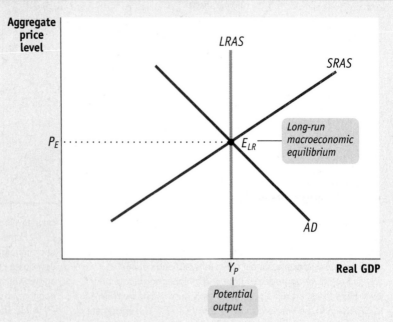

time has elapsed that the economy is also on the long-run aggregate supply curve, *LRAS*. As a result, E_{LR} is at the intersection of all three curves—*SRAS*, *LRAS*, and *AD*. So short-run equilibrium aggregate output is equal to potential output, Y_P. Such a situation, in which the point of short-run macroeconomic equilibrium is on the long-run aggregate supply curve, is known as **long-run macroeconomic equilibrium.**

To see the significance of long-run macroeconomic equilibrium, let's consider what happens if a demand shock moves the economy away from long-run macroeconomic equilibrium. In Figure 16-13, we assume that the initial aggregate demand curve is AD_1 and the initial short-run aggregate supply curve is $SRAS_1$. So the initial macroeconomic equilibrium is at E_1, which lies on the long-run aggregate supply curve, *LRAS*. The economy, then, starts from a point of short-run and long-run macroeconomic equilibrium, and short-run equilibrium aggregate output equals potential output at Y_1.

Now suppose that for some reason—such as a sudden worsening of business and consumer expectations—aggregate demand falls and the aggregate demand curve shifts leftward to AD_2. This results in a lower equilibrium aggregate price level at P_2 and a lower equilibrium aggregate output level at Y_2 as the economy settles in the short run at E_2. The short-run effect of such a fall in aggregate demand is what the U.S. economy experienced in 1929–1933: a falling aggregate price level and falling aggregate output.

Aggregate output in this new short-run equilibrium, E_2, is below potential output. When this happens, the economy faces a **recessionary gap.** A recessionary gap inflicts a great deal of pain because it corresponds to high unemployment. The large recessionary gap that had opened up in the United States by 1933 caused intense social and political turmoil. And the devastating recessionary gap that opened up in Germany at the same time played an important role in Hitler's rise to power.

The economy is in **long-run macroeconomic equilibrium** when the point of short-run macroeconomic equilibrium is on the long-run aggregate supply curve.

There is a **recessionary gap** when aggregate output is below potential output.

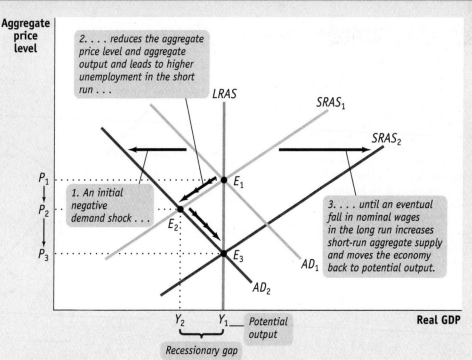

FIGURE 16-13 Short-Run Versus Long-Run Effects of a Negative Demand Shock

In the long run the economy is self-correcting: demand shocks have only a short-run effect on aggregate output. Starting at E_1, a negative demand shock shifts AD_1 leftward to AD_2. In the short run the economy moves to E_2 and a recessionary gap arises: the aggregate price level declines from P_1 to P_2, aggregate output declines from Y_1 to Y_2, and unemployment rises. But in the long run nominal wages fall in response to high unemployment at Y_2, and $SRAS_1$ shifts rightward to $SRAS_2$. Aggregate output rises from Y_2 to Y_1, and the aggregate price level declines again, from P_2 to P_3. Long-run macroeconomic equilibrium is eventually restored at E_3.

2. . . . reduces the aggregate price level and aggregate output and leads to higher unemployment in the short run . . .

1. An initial negative demand shock . . .

3. . . . until an eventual fall in nominal wages in the long run increases short-run aggregate supply and moves the economy back to potential output.

Recessionary gap

There is an **inflationary gap** when aggregate output is above potential output.

But this isn't the end of the story. In the face of high unemployment, nominal wages eventually fall, as do any other sticky prices, ultimately leading producers to increase output. As a result, a recessionary gap causes the short-run aggregate supply curve to gradually shift to the right over time. This process continues until $SRAS_1$ reaches its new position at $SRAS_2$, bringing the economy to equilibrium at E_3, where AD_2, $SRAS_2$, and $LRAS$ all intersect. At E_3, the economy is back in long-run macroeconomic equilibrium; it is back at potential output Y_1 but at a lower aggregate price level, P_3, reflecting a long-run fall in the aggregate price level. In the end, the economy is *self-correcting* in the long run.

What if, instead, there was an increase in aggregate demand? The results are shown in Figure 16-14, where we again assume that the initial aggregate demand curve is AD_1 and the initial short-run aggregate supply curve is $SRAS_1$, so that the initial macroeconomic equilibrium, at E_1, lies on the long-run aggregate supply curve, $LRAS$. Initially, then, the economy is in long-run macroeconomic equilibrium.

Now suppose that aggregate demand rises, and the AD curve shifts rightward to AD_2. This results in a higher aggregate price level, at P_2, and a higher aggregate output level, at Y_2, as the economy settles in the short run at E_2. Aggregate output in this new short-run equilibrium is above potential output, and unemployment is low in order to produce this higher level of aggregate output. When this happens, the economy experiences an **inflationary gap.**

As in the case of a recessionary gap, the story doesn't end here. In the face of low unemployment, nominal wages will rise, as will other sticky prices. An inflationary gap causes the short-run aggregate supply curve to shift gradually to the left as producers reduce output in the face of rising nominal wages. This process continues until $SRAS_1$ reaches its new position at $SRAS_2$, bringing the economy to equilibrium at E_3, where AD_2, $SRAS_2$, and $LRAS$ all intersect. At E_3, the economy is back in long-run macroeconomic equilibrium. It is back at potential output, but at a higher price level, P_3, reflecting a long-run rise in the aggregate price level. Again, the economy is self-correcting in the long run.

FIGURE 16-14 Short-Run Versus Long-Run Effects of a Positive Demand Shock

Starting at E_1, a positive demand shock shifts AD_1 rightward to AD_2, and the economy moves to E_2 in the short run. This results in an inflationary gap as aggregate output rises from Y_1 to Y_2, the aggregate price level rises from P_1 to P_2, and unemployment falls to a low level. In the long run, $SRAS_1$ shifts leftward to $SRAS_2$ as nominal wages rise in response to low unemployment at Y_2. Aggregate output falls back to Y_1, the aggregate price level rises again to P_3, and the economy self-corrects as it returns to long-run macroeconomic equilibrium at E_3.

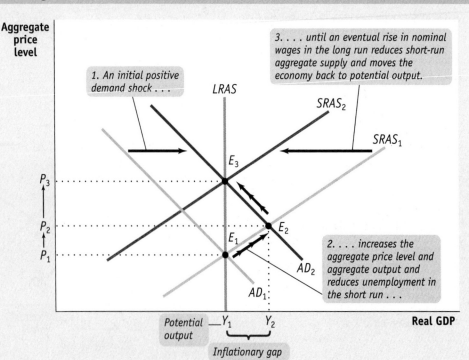

To summarize the analysis of how the economy responds to recessionary and inflationary gaps, we can focus on the **output gap,** the percentage difference between actual aggregate output and potential output. The output gap is calculated as follows:

(16-3) $\text{Output gap} = \dfrac{\text{Actual aggregate output } - \text{ Potential output}}{\text{Potential output}} \times 100$

Our analysis says that the output gap always tends toward zero.

If there is a recessionary gap, so that the output gap is negative, nominal wages eventually fall, moving the economy back to potential output and bringing the output gap back to zero. If there is an inflationary gap, so that the output gap is positive, nominal wages eventually rise, also moving the economy back to potential output and again bringing the output gap back to zero. So in the long run the economy is **self-correcting:** shocks to aggregate demand affect aggregate output in the short run but not in the long run.

> The **output gap** is the percentage difference between actual aggregate output and potential output.
>
> The economy is **self-correcting** when shocks to aggregate demand affect aggregate output in the short run, but not in the long run.

ECONOMICS >> *in Action* 🌐
Supply Shocks Versus Demand Shocks in Practice

How often do supply shocks and demand shocks, respectively, cause recessions? The verdict of most, though not all, macroeconomists is that recessions are mainly caused by demand shocks. But when a negative supply shock does happen, the resulting recession tends to be especially severe.

Let's get specific. Officially there have been twelve recessions in the United States since World War II. However, two of these, in 1979–1980 and 1981–1982, are often treated as a single *double-dip recession* (that is, a recession followed by a temporary recovery, which is then followed by another recession), bringing the total number down to eleven. Of these eleven recessions, only two—the recession of 1973–1975 and the double-dip recession of 1979–1982—showed the distinctive combination of falling aggregate output and a surge in the price level that we call stagflation. In each case, the cause of the supply shock was political turmoil in the Middle East—the Arab–Israeli war of 1973 and the Iranian revolution of 1979—that disrupted world oil supplies and sent oil prices skyrocketing. In fact, economists sometimes refer to the two slumps as "OPEC I" and "OPEC II," after the Organization of the Petroleum Exporting Countries, the world oil cartel. A third recession that began in 2007 and lasted until 2009 was at least partially exacerbated, if not at least partially caused, by a spike in oil prices.

So eight of eleven postwar recessions were purely the result of demand shocks, not supply shocks. The few supply-shock recessions, however, were the worst as measured by the unemployment rate. Figure 16-15 shows the U.S. unemployment rate since 1948, with the dates of the 1973 Arab–Israeli war and the 1979 Iranian revolution marked on the graph. Some of the highest unemployment rates since World War II came after these big negative supply shocks.

There's a reason the aftermath of a supply shock tends to be particularly severe for the economy: macroeconomic policy has a much harder time dealing with supply shocks than with demand shocks. We'll see in a moment why supply shocks present such a problem.

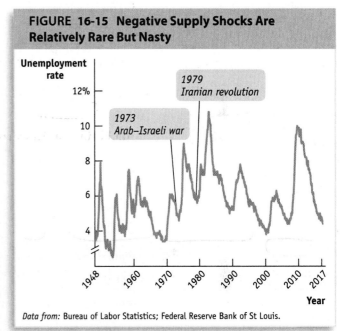

FIGURE 16-15 Negative Supply Shocks Are Relatively Rare But Nasty

Data from: Bureau of Labor Statistics; Federal Reserve Bank of St Louis.

- The **AD–AS model** is used to study economic fluctuations.

- **Short-run macroeconomic equilibrium** occurs at the intersection of the short-run aggregate supply and aggregate demand curves. This determines the **short-run equilibrium aggregate price level** and the level of **short-run equilibrium aggregate output.**

- A **demand shock,** a shift of the *AD* curve, causes the aggregate price level and aggregate output to move in the same direction. A **supply shock,** a shift of the *SRAS* curve, causes them to move in opposite directions. **Stagflation** is the consequence of a negative supply shock.

- A fall in nominal wages occurs in response to a **recessionary gap,** and a rise in nominal wages occurs in response to an **inflationary gap.** Both move the economy to **long-run macroeconomic equilibrium,** where the *AD, SRAS,* and *LRAS* curves intersect.

- The **output gap** always tends toward zero because the economy is **self-correcting** in the long run.

>> *Check Your Understanding* 16-3
Solutions appear at back of book.

1. Describe the short-run effects of each of the following shocks on the aggregate price level and on aggregate output.
   a. The government sharply increases the minimum wage, raising the wages of many workers.
   b. Solar energy firms launch a major program of investment spending.
   c. Congress raises taxes and cuts spending.
   d. Severe weather destroys crops around the world.

2. A rise in productivity increases potential output, but some worry that demand for the additional output will be insufficient even in the long run. How would you respond?

Macroeconomic Policy

We've just seen that the economy is self-correcting in the long run: it will eventually trend back to potential output. Most macroeconomists believe, however, that the process of self-correction can typically take a decade or more. In particular, if aggregate output is below potential output, the economy can suffer an extended period of depressed aggregate output and high unemployment before it returns to normal.

This belief is the background to one of the most famous quotations in economics: John Maynard Keynes's declaration, "In the long run we are all dead."

Economists usually interpret Keynes as having recommended that governments not wait for the economy to correct itself. Instead, it is argued by many economists, but not all, that the government should use monetary and fiscal policy to get the economy back to potential output in the aftermath of a shift of the aggregate demand curve. This is the rationale for an active **stabilization policy,** which is the use of government policy to reduce the severity of recessions and rein in excessively strong expansions.

Can stabilization policy improve the economy's performance? If we reexamine Figure 16-6, the answer certainly appears to be yes. Under active stabilization policy, the U.S. economy returned to potential output in 1996 after an approximately five-year recessionary gap. Likewise, in 2001 it also returned to potential output after an approximately four-year inflationary gap.

These periods are much shorter than the decade or more that economists believe it would take for the economy to self-correct in the absence of active stabilization policy. In fact, recovery from the Great Recession took longer—seven years—partly because of political constraints on fiscal policy. And recovery would have taken even longer if Ben Bernanke had not undertaken strongly expansionary monetary policy, as recounted in the opening story. However, as we'll see shortly, the ability to improve the economy's performance is not always guaranteed. It depends on the kinds of shocks the economy faces.

Policy in the Face of Demand Shocks

Imagine that the economy experiences a negative demand shock, like the one shown in Figure 16-13. As we've discussed in this chapter, monetary and fiscal policy shift the aggregate demand curve. If policy makers react quickly to the fall in aggregate demand, they can use monetary or fiscal policy to shift the aggregate demand curve back to the right. And if policy were able to perfectly anticipate shifts of the aggregate demand curve, it could short-circuit the whole process shown in Figure 16-13. Instead of going through a period of low aggregate output and falling prices, the government could manage the economy so that it would stay at E_1.

Stabilization policy is the use of government policy to reduce the severity of recessions and rein in excessively strong expansions.

Why might a policy that short-circuits the adjustment shown in Figure 16-13 and maintains the economy at its original equilibrium be desirable? For two reasons.

1. The temporary fall in aggregate output that would happen without policy intervention is a bad thing, particularly because such a decline is associated with high unemployment.

2. Price stability is generally regarded as a desirable goal. So preventing deflation—a fall in the aggregate price level—is a good thing.

Does this mean that policy makers should always act to offset declines in aggregate demand? Not necessarily. Some policy measures to increase aggregate demand, especially those that increase budget deficits, may have long-term costs in terms of lower long-run growth. Furthermore, in the real world, policy makers aren't perfectly informed, and the effects of their policies aren't perfectly predictable. This creates the danger that stabilization policy will do more harm than good. That is, attempts to stabilize the economy may end up creating more instability. Despite these qualifications, most economists believe that a good case can be made for using macroeconomic policy to offset major negative shocks to the *AD* curve.

Should policy makers also try to offset positive shocks to aggregate demand? It may not seem obvious that they should. After all, even though inflation may be a bad thing, isn't more output and lower unemployment a good thing? Not necessarily.

Most economists now believe that any short-run gains from an inflationary gap must be paid back later. So policy makers today usually try to offset positive as well as negative demand shocks. For reasons we'll explain in Chapter 19, attempts to eliminate recessionary gaps and inflationary gaps usually rely on monetary rather than fiscal policy. In 2007 and 2008 the Federal Reserve sharply cut interest rates in an attempt to head off a rising recessionary gap; earlier in the decade, when the U.S. economy seemed headed for an inflationary gap, it raised interest rates to generate the opposite effect.

But how should macroeconomic policy respond to supply shocks?

The British economist Sir John Maynard Keynes (1883–1946), probably more than any other single economist, created the modern field of macroeconomics.

Responding to Supply Shocks

Back in panel (a) of Figure 16-11 we showed the effects of a negative supply shock: in the short run such a shock leads to lower aggregate output but a higher aggregate price level. As we've noted, policy makers can respond to a negative *demand* shock by using monetary and fiscal policy to return aggregate demand to its original level. But what can or should they do about a negative *supply* shock?

In contrast to the aggregate demand curve, there are no easy policies that shift the short-run aggregate supply curve. That is, there is no government policy that can easily affect producers' profitability and so compensate for shifts of the short-run aggregate supply curve. So the policy response to a negative supply shock cannot aim to simply push the curve that shifted back to its original position.

And if you consider using monetary or fiscal policy to shift the aggregate demand curve in response to a supply shock, the right response isn't obvious. Two bad things are happening simultaneously: a fall in aggregate output, leading to a rise in unemployment, *and* a rise in the aggregate price level. Any policy that shifts the aggregate demand curve helps one problem only by making the other worse. If the government acts to increase aggregate demand and limit the rise in unemployment, it reduces the decline in output but causes even more inflation. If it acts to reduce aggregate demand, it curbs inflation but causes a further rise in unemployment.

It's a trade-off with no good answer. In the end, the United States and other economically advanced nations suffering from the supply shocks of the 1970s eventually chose to stabilize prices even at the cost of higher unemployment. This was the same policy that Jean-Claude Trichet adopted in 2011, when he chose to forgo expansionary monetary policy after he mistook a temporary blip in oil prices as a supply shock.

FIGURE 16-16 Has Stabilization Policy Been Stabilizing?

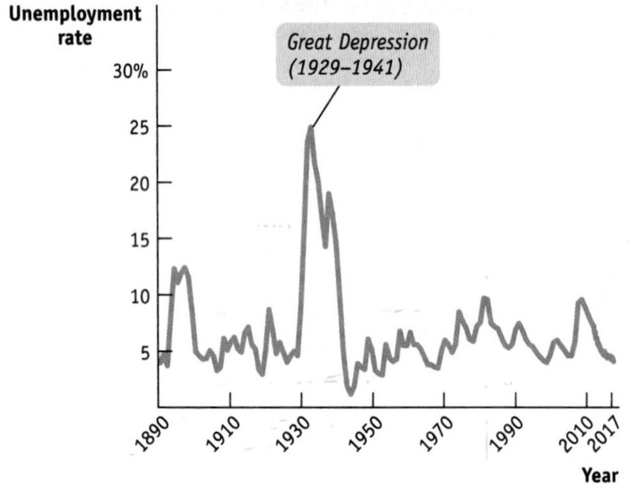

Data from: Christina Romer, "Spurious Volatility in Historical Unemployment Data." *Journal of Political Economy* 94, no. 1 (1986): 1–37 (years 1890–1928); Bureau of Labor Statistics (years 1929–2017).

ECONOMICS >> *in Action*
Is Stabilization Policy Stabilizing?

We've described the theoretical rationale for stabilization policy as a way of responding to demand shocks. But does stabilization policy actually stabilize the economy? We can try to answer this question by looking at the long-term historical record.

Before World War II, the U.S. government didn't really have a stabilization policy, largely because macroeconomics as we know it didn't exist, and there was no consensus about what to do. Since World War II, and especially since 1960, active stabilization policy has become standard practice.

So, has the economy actually become more stable since the government began trying to stabilize it? The answer is a qualified yes. It's qualified for two reasons. One is that data from the pre–World War II era are less reliable than modern data. The other is that the severe and protracted slump that began in 2007 has shaken confidence in the effectiveness of government policy. Still, there seems to have been a reduction in the size of fluctuations.

Figure 16-16 shows the number of unemployed as a percentage of the nonfarm labor force since 1890. (We focus on nonfarm workers because farmers, though they often suffer economic hardship, are rarely reported as unemployed.) Even ignoring the huge spike in unemployment during the Great Depression, unemployment seems to have varied a lot more before World War II than after. It's also worth noticing that the peaks in postwar unemployment, in 1975, 1982, and to some extent in 2010, corresponded to major supply shocks—the kind of shock for which stabilization policy has no good answer.

It's possible that the greater stability of the economy reflects good luck rather than policy. But on the face of it, the evidence suggests that stabilization policy is indeed stabilizing.

>> *Quick Review*

- **Stabilization policy** is the use of fiscal or monetary policy to off-set demand shocks. There can be drawbacks, however. Such policies may lead to a long-term rise in the budget deficit and lower long-run growth because of crowding out. And, due to incorrect predictions, a misguided policy can increase economic instability.

- Negative supply shocks pose a policy dilemma because fighting the slump in aggregate output worsens inflation, and fighting inflation worsens the slump.

>> *Check Your Understanding* 16-4
Solutions appear at back of book.

1. Suppose someone says, "Using monetary or fiscal policy to pump up the economy is counterproductive—you get a brief high, but then you have the pain of inflation."
   a. Explain what this means in terms of the *AD–AS* model.
   b. Is this a valid argument against stabilization policy? Why or why not?

2. In 2008, in the aftermath of the collapse of the housing bubble and a sharp rise in the price of commodities, particularly oil, there was much internal disagreement within the Fed about how to respond, with some advocating lowering interest rates and others contending that this would set off a rise in inflation. Explain the reasoning behind each one of these views in terms of the *AD–AS* model.

SOLVED PROBLEM   A Shocking Analysis

During the financial crisis in autumn 2008, the financial system delivered a sobering shock to the economy when the stock market lost about half of its value. Soon afterward, consumer spending came to a screeching halt. Within six months of the crash, GDP fell by 2.5% and the price level fell by 2.8%. Show how an analysis of aggregate demand and aggregate supply could have predicted this short-run effect on aggregate output and the aggregate price level. Assuming no government intervention, what would you have predicted in the long run?

STEP | 1 Begin by drawing and labeling the aggregate demand curve. Then draw and label the short-run aggregate supply curve. Next, find the initial equilibrium price and output levels and label them on your graph as well. *Read pages 455–456 and review Figure 16-9.*

The aggregate demand curve and the short-run aggregate supply curve are shown in the following diagram. The initial equilibrium point is labeled E_1, the initial price level is labeled P_1, and the initial output level is labeled Y_1.

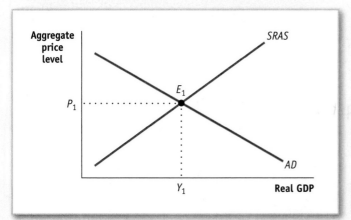

STEP | 2 Using your graph from Step 1, analyze the short-run effect of the stock market fall on aggregate demand and aggregate supply by drawing a new curve representing aggregate demand after the stock market fall. *Read pages 456–457 and review Figure 16-10, panel (a).*

A decrease in household wealth will reduce consumer spending. Beginning at the equilibrium point, E_1 in the diagram below, the aggregate demand curve will shift from AD_1 to AD_2. The economy will be in short-run macroeconomic equilibrium at point E_2. The aggregate price level will be lower than at P_1, and aggregate output will be lower than output at the original equilibrium point.

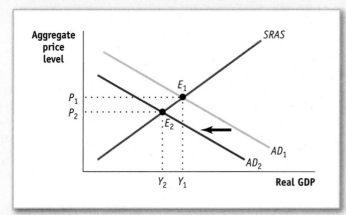

STEP | 3 Draw the long-run aggregate supply curve through the initial equilibrium point E_1, and label the recessionary gap. *Read pages 458–461 and review Figures 16-12 and 16-13.*

The long-run aggregate supply curve is drawn in the following diagram. The economy now faces a recessionary gap between Y_1 and Y_2.

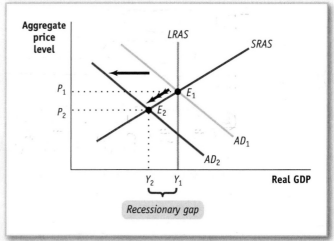

STEP | 4 What would you predict in the long run? *Read pages 458–461 and review Figure 16-13.*

As wage contracts are renegotiated, nominal wages will fall and the short-run aggregate supply curve will shift gradually to the right over time until it reaches $SRAS_2$ and intersects AD_2 at point E_3. At E_3, the economy is back at its potential output but at a much lower aggregate price level, as shown in the following diagram.

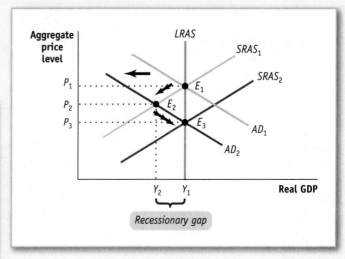

Quantity of
Price level vs. Output Demanded

SUMMARY

1. The **aggregate demand curve** shows the relationship between the aggregate price level and the quantity of aggregate output demanded.

Price/
wealth

2. The aggregate demand curve is downward sloping for two reasons. The first is the **wealth effect of a change in the aggregate price level**—a higher aggregate price level reduces the purchasing power of households' wealth and reduces consumer spending. The second is the **interest rate effect of a change in the aggregate price level**—a higher aggregate price level reduces the purchasing power of households' and firms' money holdings, leading to a rise in interest rates and a fall in investment spending and consumer spending.

3. The aggregate demand curve shifts because of changes in expectations, changes in wealth not due to changes in the aggregate price level, and the effect of the size of the existing stock of physical capital. Policy makers can use fiscal policy and monetary policy to shift the aggregate demand curve.

4. The **aggregate supply curve** shows the relationship between the aggregate price level and the quantity of aggregate output supplied.

Price level vs. Qoutput S

?

5. The **short-run aggregate supply curve** is upward sloping because **nominal wages** are **sticky** in the short run: a higher aggregate price level leads to higher profit per unit of output and increased aggregate output in the short run.

6. Changes in commodity prices, nominal wages, and productivity lead to changes in producers' profits and shift the short-run aggregate supply curve.

7. In the long run, all prices, including nominal wages, are flexible and the economy produces at its **potential output.** If actual aggregate output exceeds potential output, nominal wages will eventually rise in response to low unemployment and aggregate output will fall. If potential output exceeds actual aggregate output, nominal wages will eventually fall in response to high unemployment and aggregate output will rise. So the **long-run aggregate supply curve** is vertical at potential output.

8. In the ***AD–AS* model,** the intersection of the short-run aggregate supply curve and the aggregate demand curve is the point of **short-run macroeconomic equilibrium.** It determines the **short-run equilibrium aggregate price level** and the level of **short-run equilibrium aggregate output.**

9. Economic fluctuations occur because of a shift of the aggregate demand curve (a *demand shock*) or the short-run aggregate supply curve (a *supply shock*). A **demand shock** causes the aggregate price level and aggregate output to move in the same direction as the economy moves along the short-run aggregate supply curve. A **supply shock** causes them to move in opposite directions as the economy moves along the aggregate demand curve. A particularly nasty occurrence is **stagflation**—inflation and falling aggregate output—which is caused by a negative supply shock.

10. Demand shocks have only short-run effects on aggregate output because the economy is **self-correcting** in the long run. In a **recessionary gap,** an eventual fall in nominal wages moves the economy to **long-run macroeconomic equilibrium,** where aggregate output is equal to potential output. In an **inflationary gap,** an eventual rise in nominal wages moves the economy to long-run macroeconomic equilibrium. We can use the **output gap,** the percentage difference between actual aggregate output and potential output, to summarize how the economy responds to recessionary and inflationary gaps. Because the economy tends to be self-correcting in the long run, the output gap always tends toward zero.

11. The high cost—in terms of unemployment—of a recessionary gap and the future adverse consequences of an inflationary gap lead many economists to advocate active **stabilization policy:** using fiscal or monetary policy to offset demand shocks. There can be drawbacks, however, because such policies may contribute to a long-term rise in the budget deficit and crowding out of private investment, leading to lower long-run growth. Also, poorly timed policies can increase economic instability.

12. Negative supply shocks pose a policy dilemma: a policy that counteracts the fall in aggregate output by increasing aggregate demand will lead to higher inflation, but a policy that counteracts inflation by reducing aggregate demand will deepen the output slump.

KEY TERMS

Aggregate demand curve, p. 438
Wealth effect of a change in the aggregate price level, p. 439
Interest rate effect of a change in the aggregate price level, p. 440

Aggregate supply curve, p. 445
Nominal wage, p. 445
Sticky wages, p. 445
Short-run aggregate supply curve, p. 446

Long-run aggregate supply curve, p. 450
Potential output, p. 451
AD–AS model, p. 455
Short-run macroeconomic equilibrium, p. 455

DISCUSSION QUESTIONS

1. Your study partner is confused by the upward-sloping short-run aggregate supply curve and the vertical long-run aggregate supply curve. How would you explain this?

2. Suppose that in Wageland all workers sign annual wage contracts each year on January 1. No matter what happens to prices of final goods and services during the year, all workers earn the wage specified in their annual contract. This year, prices of final goods and services fall unexpectedly after the contracts are signed. Answer the following questions using a diagram and assume that the economy starts at potential output.

   a. In the short run, how will the quantity of aggregate output supplied respond to the fall in prices?

   b. What will happen when firms and workers renegotiate their wages?

3. Suppose that all households hold all their wealth in assets that automatically rise in value when the aggregate price level rises (an example of this is what is called an "inflation-indexed bond"—a bond whose interest rate, among other things, changes one-for-one with the inflation rate). What happens to the wealth effect of a change in the aggregate price level as a result of this allocation of assets? What happens to the slope of the aggregate demand curve? Will it still slope downward? Explain.

4. The Conference Board publishes the Consumer Confidence Index (CCI) every month based on a survey of 5,000 representative U.S. households. It is used by many economists to track the state of the economy. A press release by the Board on December 27, 2016, stated: "The Conference Board Consumer Confidence Index®, which had increased considerably in November, posted another gain in December. The Index now stands at 113.7 (1985 = 100), up from 109.4 in November."

   a. As an economist, is this news encouraging for economic growth?

   b. Explain your answer to part a with the help of the AD–AS model. Draw a typical diagram showing two equilibrium points (E_1) and (E_2). Label the vertical axis "Aggregate price level" and the horizontal axis "Real GDP." Assume that all other major macroeconomic factors remain unchanged.

   c. How should the government respond to this news if the economy is below potential output? If it is above potential output?

5. Using aggregate demand, short-run aggregate supply, and long-run aggregate supply curves, explain the process by which each of the following government policies will move the economy from one long-run macroeconomic equilibrium to another. Illustrate with diagrams. In each case, what are the short-run and long-run effects on the aggregate price level and aggregate output?

   a. There is an increase in taxes on households.

   b. There is an increase in the quantity of money.

   c. There is an increase in government spending.

6. In the accompanying diagram, the economy is in long-run macroeconomic equilibrium at point E_1 when an oil shock shifts the short-run aggregate supply curve to $SRAS_2$. Based on the diagram, answer the following questions.

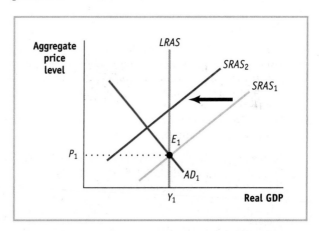

   a. How do the aggregate price level and aggregate output change in the short run as a result of the oil shock? What is this phenomenon known as?

   b. What fiscal or monetary policies can the government use to address the effects of the supply shock? Use a diagram that shows the effect of policies chosen to address the change in real GDP. Use another diagram to show the effect of policies chosen to address the change in the aggregate price level.

   c. Why do supply shocks present a dilemma for government policy makers?

PROBLEMS

interactive activity

1. A fall in the value of the dollar against other currencies makes U.S. final goods and services cheaper to foreigners even though the U.S. aggregate price level stays the same. As a result, foreigners demand more American aggregate output. Your study partner says that this represents a movement down the aggregate demand curve because foreigners are demanding more in response to a lower price. You, however, insist that this represents a rightward shift of the aggregate demand curve. Who is right? Explain.

2. The economy is at point A in the accompanying diagram. Suppose that the aggregate price level rises from P_1 to P_2. How will aggregate supply adjust in the short run and in the long run to the increase in the aggregate price level? Illustrate with a diagram.

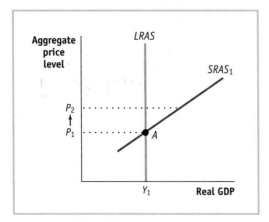

3. Suppose that the economy is currently at potential output. Also suppose that you are an economic policy maker and that a college economics student asks you to rank, if possible, your most preferred to least preferred type of shock: positive demand shock, negative demand shock, positive supply shock, negative supply shock. How would you rank them and why?

4. Explain whether the following government policies affect the aggregate demand curve or the short-run aggregate supply curve and how.

   a. The government reduces the minimum nominal wage.

   b. The government increases Temporary Assistance to Needy Families (TANF) payments, government transfers to families with dependent children.

   c. To reduce the budget deficit, the government announces that households will pay much higher taxes beginning next year.

   d. The government reduces military spending.

5. In Wageland, all workers sign annual wage contracts each year on January 1. In late January, a new computer operating system is introduced that increases labor productivity dramatically. Explain how Wageland will move from one short-run macroeconomic equilibrium to another. Illustrate with a diagram.

6. There were two major shocks to the U.S. economy in 2007, leading to the severe recession of 2007–2009. One shock was related to oil prices; the other was the slump in the housing market. This question analyzes the effect of these two shocks on GDP using the *AD–AS* framework.

   a. Draw typical aggregate demand and short-run aggregate supply curves. Label the horizontal axis "Real GDP" and the vertical axis "Aggregate price level." Label the equilibrium point E_1, the equilibrium quantity Y_1, and equilibrium price P_1.

   b. Data taken from the Department of Energy indicate that the average price of crude oil in the world increased from $54.63 per barrel on January 5, 2007, to $92.93 on December 28, 2007. Would an increase in oil prices cause a demand shock or a supply shock? Redraw the diagram from part a to illustrate the effect of this shock by shifting the appropriate curve.

   c. The Housing Price Index, published by the Office of Federal Housing Enterprise Oversight, calculates that U.S. home prices fell by an average of 3.0% in the 12 months between January 2007 and January 2008. Would the fall in home prices cause a supply shock or demand shock? Redraw the diagram from part b to illustrate the effect of this shock by shifting the appropriate curve. Label the new equilibrium point E_3, the equilibrium quantity Y_3, and equilibrium price P_3.

   d. Compare the equilibrium points E_1 and E_3 in your diagram for part c. What was the effect of the two shocks on real GDP and the aggregate price level (increase, decrease, or indeterminate)?

7. Using aggregate demand, short-run aggregate supply, and long-run aggregate supply curves, explain the process by which each of the following economic events will move the economy from one long-run macroeconomic equilibrium to another. Illustrate with diagrams. In each case, what are the short-run and long-run effects on the aggregate price level and aggregate output?

   a. There is a decrease in households' wealth due to a decline in the stock market.

   b. The government lowers taxes, leaving households with more disposable income, with no corresponding reduction in government purchases.

8. The economy is in short-run macroeconomic equilibrium at point E_1 in the accompanying diagram. Based on the diagram, answer the following questions.

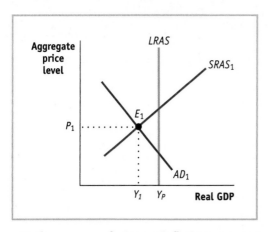

a. Is the economy facing an inflationary or a recessionary gap?

b. What policies can the government implement that might bring the economy back to long-run macroeconomic equilibrium? Illustrate with a diagram.

c. If the government did not intervene to close this gap, would the economy return to long-run macroeconomic equilibrium? Explain and illustrate with a diagram.

d. What are the advantages and disadvantages of the government implementing policies to close the gap?

9. The late 1990s in the United States were characterized by substantial economic growth with low inflation; that is, real GDP increased with little, if any, increase in the aggregate price level. Explain this experience using aggregate demand and aggregate supply curves. Illustrate with a diagram.

WORK IT OUT **Interactive step-by-step help with solving this problem can be found online.**

10. In each of the following cases, in the short run, determine whether the events cause a shift of a curve or a movement along a curve. Determine which curve is involved and the direction of the change.

a. As a result of an increase in the value of the dollar in relation to other currencies, American producers now pay less in dollar terms for foreign steel, a major commodity used in production.

b. An increase in the quantity of money by the Federal Reserve increases the quantity of money that people wish to lend, lowering interest rates.

c. Greater union activity leads to higher nominal wages.

d. A fall in the aggregate price level increases the purchasing power of households' and firms' money holdings. As a result, they borrow less and lend more.

When we think about innovation and technological progress, we tend to focus on the dramatic changes: cars replacing horses and buggies, electric light bulbs replacing gaslights, computers replacing adding machines and typewriters. However, much more progress is incremental and almost invisible to most people, yet has huge effects over time. Consider, for example, the simple barcode scanner.

Barcodes were first used commercially in 1974, when a 10-pack of Wrigley's chewing gum was rung up with a scanner produced by the National Cash Register Corporation (now NCR Corp). Since then barcodes and their two-dimensional descendants—visual patterns that are meaningless to human eyes but are instantly recognizable by scanners and smartphones—have become ubiquitous, used to identify and route everything from shipping containers to airline passengers.

The benefits from machine-readable labels are enormous, extending well beyond what consumers in the checkout line can see. For example, retailers use them to continuously track sales, telling them when to reorder merchandise and restock shelves, what to keep in their warehouses, how productive individual workers are, and more. Grocery retailing is a labor-intensive industry, and economists estimate that the adoption of barcode technology reduced labor costs by as much as 40%. Ultimately, barcode technology helped drive the computerization of the entire retail industry.

You might think, then, that NCR, which remains a major player in point-of-service technologies like scanners, ATMs, and so forth, made a fortune from its leading role in this technology revolution. But while the company has done well, scanner sales in the early years weren't enormous: the adoption of barcode scanners was relatively slow compared with the spread of smartphones a couple of decades later. Only about a third of supermarkets adopted them in the first decade after that historic pack of gum.

Why? To realize the full potential of barcode technology, both retailers and firms had to spend substantial money upfront to buy the scanners and the information-processing systems they served. Equally important, manufacturers had to install the equipment to put barcodes on their products. This created a chicken-and-egg problem, with retailers waiting to have more scanner-readable products available and manufacturers waiting for more scanner-ready stores.

Over time this problem was resolved as retailers and manufacturers made the necessary investments, setting the stage for widespread use of information technology. In fact, after around 1990, retailing became one of the leading sources of overall productivity growth in the U.S. economy.

Adoption was slower in Europe. In the United States, big stores were the first to install scanners, and the technology fostered greater concentration of retailing at the expense of small mom-and-pop stores that couldn't afford to implement scanner technology. In Europe, however, government policies—especially land-use policy—protected these stores.

Eventually, however, Europe began to follow the trend, too. Barcode technology has spread from the United States to become almost universal, at least in advanced economies.

QUESTIONS FOR THOUGHT

1. Barcode technology spurred a lot of investment in retailing. How did it alter the retailing production function? What would a similar amount of investment have accomplished without the new technology?

2. The spread of barcodes was delayed in the United States because everyone was waiting for someone else to move. What policy could have been adopted to address the delays? Would it have been a good idea?

3. Use the case to explain why international growth rates vary.

4. Despite initial barriers, barcodes have spread globally. What does this imply about differences in economic growth across countries?

If you or someone you know bought a new car recently, the odds are pretty good that it was manufactured by one of two Japanese companies, Toyota or Honda. Together, these companies account for almost a quarter of total passenger car sales. But this was not always the case. In 1973, the two companies accounted for a mere 2.6% of U.S. auto sales. Over the course of the 1970s and early 1980s, the Japanese share quadrupled. Why?

Toyota did a lot of things right: during the 1960s it had perfected the technique of so-called *just-in-time production* or *lean manufacturing,* a production system that yielded lower costs, higher productivity, and higher quality compared to American production techniques. (You

may recall our discussion of lean production in an earlier Business Case.)

But Toyota was lucky as well. During the 1970s, Americans began to switch from enormous sedans to smaller cars, a market that American car companies had neglected. The few choices they did offer were of poor quality, and included the AMC Gremlin and Ford Pinto, among others. In contrast, Toyota, having long produced small, reliable, fuel-efficient cars for Japan, its home market, was ready to fill the gap.

But why the shift to smaller, fuel-efficient cars? One answer is that the United States experienced a series of severe recessions, which could have induced consumers to seek cheaper alternatives to traditional big cars. As it turns out, however, other recessions have not led to major downsizing in car purchases. Figure 16-17 shows the average number of miles per gallon for new passenger cars since 1975, which has generally trended upward, but increased at a much faster rate in the mid- to late 1970s and early 1980s, before stabilizing in the early 1990s—this despite the fact that many consumers were buying more fuel-efficient cars at that time. And, as you can see, there was only a slight increase in average mileage after 2007, even though the Great Recession that began that year was deeper and more prolonged than any slump since the 1930s.

So what was different in the 1970s? At that time, two bad things were happening: unemployment was rising sharply, but so was the price of gasoline. After 2007, as unemployment soared, gas prices fluctuated but eventually came down to levels well below those before the recession. So people bought fewer cars, but not, by and large, smaller cars.

The point is that Toyota got its big break not just by producing good cars, but also by producing the particular kind of good car that suited consumers during the economic troubles of the 1970s.

QUESTIONS FOR THOUGHT

1. Why do you think gas prices rose in the recessions of the 1970s but fell after the Great Recession?

2. What does this say about the causes of the recessions in each case?

3. In the 1970s, Toyota was able to increase its American sales despite interest rates on auto loans surging as high as 17.5%. In contrast, after 2007, auto loan rates fell to their lowest levels in history; car sales also declined. Explain why. (*Hint:* Examine the connection between inflation and interest rates on loans.)

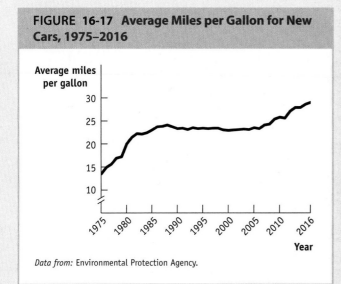

FIGURE 16-17 Average Miles per Gallon for New Cars, 1975–2016

Data from: Environmental Protection Agency.

17 Fiscal Policy

SPENDING OUR WAY OUT OF A RECESSION

THE U.S. ECONOMY entered the downturn that would eventually be dubbed the Great Recession at the end of 2007, but it didn't fall off a cliff until the fall of 2008, when it took a terrifying plunge, losing more than 6 million jobs over the 10 months between August 2008 and June 2009. Policy makers scrambled on multiple fronts to stabilize the situation, such as cutting interest rates and rushing emergency aid to troubled banks. However, advisers to then newly elected President Obama believed that these measures were insufficient to do any more than limit the bleeding. They believed that in order to restore the jobs being lost, the economy needed a boost—a *stimulus*—from the federal government's budget, in the form of increased spending and tax cuts.

The president took his advisers' advice, and the American Recovery and Reinvestment Act was signed into law on February 17, 2009. It increased federal spending, temporarily expanded federal assistance programs like food stamps and unemployment insurance, provided aid to financially strapped state and local governments, and cut some taxes. It came with a total price tag of about $830 billion, mostly falling in the first two years, when it peaked at about 10% of the federal budget. Policy makers argued that this stimulus package would provide crucial support to the severely depressed economy and accelerate the pace of recovery.

The Recovery Act was a classic example of *fiscal policy:* changes in taxes and government spending to stabilize the economy by shifting the aggregate demand curve. In this case the fiscal policy was *expansionary*, designed to shift the aggregate demand curve *out*; fiscal policies that shift the aggregate demand curve *in* are *contractionary*.

Fiscal policy is often controversial. In 2009, some believed it was a mistake to increase government spending at a time of widespread distress. One member of Congress spoke for many when he declared that the government should spend *less* in hard times: "American families are tightening their belts, but they don't see government tightening its belt." There were also concerns that the stimulus would widen the budget deficit. But most economists believe that expansionary fiscal policy is appropriate when the economy is depressed.

The qualification—"when the economy is depressed"—is important. In 2017, eight years after the Obama stimulus, the newly elected Trump administration passed new tax cuts. In some respects these measures looked similar to the Obama stimulus, but while some economists supported the Trump stimulus, most did not—including many who supported the Obama stimulus. Weren't they being inconsistent? In reality, no: in early 2009 the U.S. economy was deeply depressed and was heading further downward. By contrast, in early 2017 the economy was growing and was close to full employment. The economists who declined to support the Trump stimulus knew that stimulus, delivered at the wrong time, was likely to be counterproductive to the economy. They understood that, in making fiscal policy, timing is crucial.

In this chapter we'll see how fiscal policy fits into the model of economic fluctuations we studied in Chapter 16. We will also see why budget deficits and government debt can be problems, and why short-run and long-run considerations can pull fiscal policy in opposite directions. •

In making fiscal policy, timing is crucial. Expansionary fiscal policy was appropriate during the deeply depressed economy of 2009. But it is counterproductive if undertaken when the economy is strong, as it was in 2017.

WHAT YOU WILL LEARN

- What is fiscal policy and why is it an essential tool in managing economic fluctuations?

- Which policies constitute **expansionary fiscal policy** and which constitute **contractionary fiscal policy?**

- Why does fiscal policy have a multiplier effect, and how is this effect influenced by **automatic stabilizers?**

- Why do governments calculate the **cyclically adjusted budget balance?**

- Why can a large **public debt** and the government's **implicit liabilities** be a cause for concern?

FIGURE 17-1 Government Spending and Tax Revenue for Selected High-Income Countries in 2017

Government spending and tax revenue are represented as a percentage of GDP. France has a particularly large government sector, representing more than half of its GDP. The U.S. government sector, although sizable, is smaller than those of Canada and most European countries.

Data from: IMF World Economic Outlook.

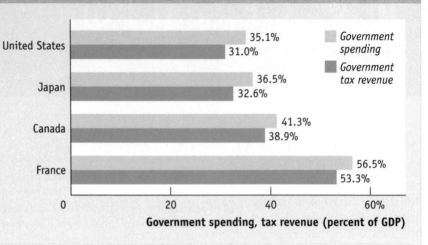

Government spending, tax revenue (percent of GDP)

United States — Government spending 35.1%, Government tax revenue 31.0%
Japan — Government spending 36.5%, Government tax revenue 32.6%
Canada — Government spending 41.3%, Government tax revenue 38.9%
France — Government spending 56.5%, Government tax revenue 53.3%

Fiscal Policy: The Basics

Modern governments in economically advanced countries spend a great deal of money and collect a lot in taxes. Figure 17-1 shows government spending and tax revenue as percentages of GDP for a selection of high-income countries in 2017. As you can see, the French government sector is relatively large, accounting for more than half of the French economy. The government of the United States plays a smaller role in the economy than those of Canada, Japan, and most European countries. But that role is still sizable, with the government playing a major role in the U.S. economy. As a result, changes in the federal budget—changes in government spending or in taxation—can have large effects on the American economy.

To analyze these effects, we begin by showing how taxes and government spending affect the economy's flow of income. Then we can see how changes in spending and tax policy affect aggregate demand.

FIGURE 17-2 Sources of Tax Revenue in the United States, 2018

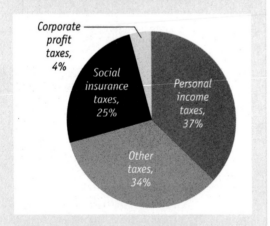

Corporate profit taxes, 4%
Social insurance taxes, 25%
Personal income taxes, 37%
Other taxes, 34%

Personal income taxes, taxes on corporate profits, and social insurance taxes account for most government tax revenue. The rest is a mix of property taxes, sales taxes, and other sources of revenue. (Percentages may not add to 100 due to rounding.)

Data from: Bureau of Economic Analysis.

Taxes, Purchases of Goods and Services, Government Transfers, and Borrowing

What kinds of taxes do Americans pay, and where does the money go? Figure 17-2 shows the composition of U.S. tax revenue in 2018. Taxes, of course, are required payments to the government. In the United States, taxes are collected at the national level by the federal government; at the state level by each state government; and at local levels by counties, cities, and towns. At the federal level, the taxes that generate the greatest revenue are income taxes on both personal income and corporate profits as well as *social insurance* taxes, which we'll explain shortly. At the state and local levels, the picture is more complex: these governments rely on a mix of sales taxes, property taxes, income taxes, and fees of various kinds.

Overall, taxes on personal income and corporate profits accounted for 41% of total government revenue in 2018; social insurance taxes accounted for 25%; and a variety of other taxes, collected mainly at the state and local levels, accounted for the rest.

Figure 17-3 shows the composition of total U.S. government spending in 2017, which takes two broad forms. One form is purchases of goods and services. This includes everything from ammunition for the military to the salaries of public school teachers (who are treated in the national accounts as providers of a service—education). The big items here are national defense and education. The category "Other goods and services" consists mainly of state and local spending on a variety of services, from police and firefighters to highway construction and maintenance.

The other form of government spending is government transfers, which are payments by the government to households for which no good or service is provided in return. In the United States, as well as in Canada and in Europe, government transfers represent a very large proportion of the budget. Most U.S. government spending on transfer payments is accounted for by the following four programs:

- Social Security, which provides guaranteed income to older Americans, disabled Americans, and the surviving spouses and dependent children of deceased or retired beneficiaries

- Medicare, which covers much of the cost of health care for Americans over age 65

- Medicaid, which covers much of the cost of health care for Americans with low incomes

- The Affordable Care Act (ACA), which seeks to make health insurance available and affordable to all Americans

The term **social insurance** is used to describe government programs that are intended to protect families against economic hardship. These include Social Security, Medicare, Medicaid, and the ACA, as well as smaller programs such as unemployment insurance and food stamps. The ACA works through a system of regulated private insurance markets, subsidies, and an expansion of Medicaid eligibility, and is much smaller than the other three large programs. Social insurance programs in the United States are largely paid for with special, dedicated taxes on wages—the social insurance taxes mentioned earlier. The ACA is an exception: it is funded mainly by taxes on private health insurance purchases.

How do tax policy and government spending affect the economy? The answer is that taxation and government spending have a strong effect on total aggregate spending in the economy.

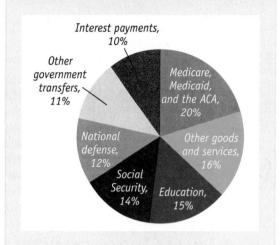

FIGURE 17-3 Government Spending in the United States, 2017

The two types of government spending are purchases of goods and services and government transfers. The biggest items in government purchases are national defense and education. The biggest items in government transfers are Social Security, Medicare, Medicaid, and the Affordable Care Act. (Percentages do not add to 100 due to rounding.)

Data from: Bureau of Economic Analysis.

Social insurance programs are government programs intended to protect families against economic hardship.

The Government Budget and Total Spending

Let's recall the basic equation of national income accounting:

(17-1) $GDP = C + I + G + X - IM$

The left-hand side of this equation is GDP, the value of all final goods and services produced in the economy. The right-hand side is aggregate spending, total spending on final goods and services produced in the economy. It is the sum of consumer spending (C), investment spending (I), government purchases of goods and services (G), and the value of exports (X) minus the value of imports (IM). It includes all the sources of aggregate demand.

The government directly controls one of the variables on the right-hand side of Equation 17-1: government purchases of goods and services (G). But that's not the only effect fiscal policy has on aggregate spending in the economy. Through changes in taxes and transfers, it also influences consumer spending (C) and, in some cases, investment spending (I).

To see why the budget affects consumer spending, recall that *disposable income,* the total income households have available to spend, is equal to the total income they receive from wages, dividends, interest, and rent, *minus* taxes, *plus* government transfers or

$$\text{Disposable income} = \text{Income} - \text{Taxes} + \text{Government},$$

where

$$\text{Income} = \text{Wages} + \text{Dividends} + \text{Interest} + \text{Rents received}$$

Expansionary fiscal policy is fiscal policy that increases aggregate demand.

So either an increase in taxes or a reduction in government transfers *reduces* disposable income. And a fall in disposable income, other things equal, leads to a fall in consumer spending. Conversely, either a decrease in taxes or an increase in government transfers *increases* disposable income. And a rise in disposable income, other things equal, leads to a rise in consumer spending.

The government's ability to affect investment spending is a more complex story, which we won't discuss in detail. The important point is that the government taxes profits, and changes in the rules that determine how much a business owes can increase or reduce the incentive to spend on investment goods.

Because the government itself is one source of spending in the economy, and because taxes and transfers can affect spending by consumers and firms, the government can use changes in taxes or government spending to *shift the aggregate demand curve*. And as we saw in Chapter 16, there are sometimes good reasons to shift the aggregate demand curve.

Expansionary and Contractionary Fiscal Policy

The government can shift the aggregate demand curve to close either a recessionary gap, created when aggregate output falls below potential output, or an inflationary gap, created when aggregate output exceeds potential output.

Figure 17-4 shows the case of an economy facing a recessionary gap. *SRAS* is the short-run aggregate supply curve, *LRAS* is the long-run aggregate supply curve, and AD_1 is the initial aggregate demand curve. At the initial short-run macroeconomic equilibrium, E_1, aggregate output is Y_1, below potential output, Y_P. What the government would like to do is increase aggregate demand, shifting the aggregate demand curve rightward to AD_2. This would increase aggregate output, making it equal to potential output. Fiscal policy that increases aggregate demand, called **expansionary fiscal policy**, normally takes one of three forms:

FIGURE 17-4 Expansionary Fiscal Policy Can Close a Recessionary Gap

The economy is in short-run macroeconomic equilibrium at E_1, where the aggregate demand curve, AD_1, intersects the *SRAS* curve. However, it is not in long-run macroeconomic equilibrium. At E_1, there is a recessionary gap of $Y_P - Y_1$. An expansionary fiscal policy—an increase in government purchases of goods and services, a reduction in taxes, or an increase in government transfers—shifts the aggregate demand curve rightward. It can close the recessionary gap by shifting AD_1 to AD_2, moving the economy to a new short-run macroeconomic equilibrium, E_2, which is also a long-run macroeconomic equilibrium.

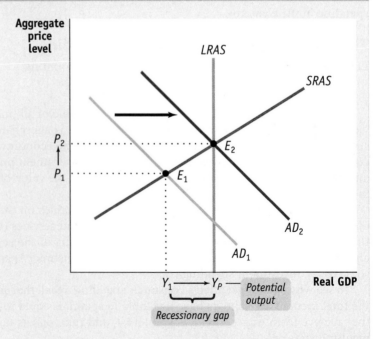

1. An increase in government purchases of goods and services

2. A cut in taxes

3. An increase in government transfers

Contractionary fiscal policy is fiscal policy that reduces aggregate demand.

The 2009 stimulus (or the Recovery Act) was a combination of all three: a direct increase in federal spending and aid to state governments to help them maintain spending, tax cuts for most families, and increased aid to the unemployed.

Figure 17-5 shows the opposite case—an economy facing an inflationary gap. Again, *SRAS* is the short-run aggregate supply curve, *LRAS* is the long-run aggregate supply curve, and AD_1 is the initial aggregate demand curve. At the initial equilibrium, E_1, aggregate output is Y_1, above potential output, Y_P.

Policy makers often try to head off inflation by eliminating inflationary gaps. To eliminate the inflationary gap shown in Figure 17-5, fiscal policy must reduce aggregate demand and shift the aggregate demand curve leftward to AD_2. This reduces aggregate output and makes it equal to potential output. Fiscal policy that reduces aggregate demand, called **contractionary fiscal policy,** is the opposite of expansionary fiscal policy. It is implemented in three possible ways:

1. A reduction in government purchases of goods and services

2. An increase in taxes

3. A reduction in government transfers

A classic example of contractionary fiscal policy occurred in 1968, when U.S. policy makers grew worried about rising inflation. President Lyndon Johnson imposed a temporary 10% surcharge on taxable income—everyone's income taxes were increased by 10%. He also tried to scale back government purchases of goods and services, which had risen dramatically because of the cost of the Vietnam War.

Can Expansionary Fiscal Policy Actually Work?

In practice, the use of fiscal policy—in particular, the use of expansionary fiscal policy in the face of a recessionary gap—is often controversial. Let's quickly

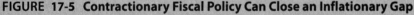

FIGURE 17-5 Contractionary Fiscal Policy Can Close an Inflationary Gap

The economy is in short-run macroeconomic equilibrium at E_1, where the aggregate demand curve, AD_1, intersects the *SRAS* curve. But it is not in long-run macroeconomic equilibrium. At E_1, there is an inflationary gap of $Y_1 - Y_P$. A contractionary fiscal policy—such as reduced government purchases of goods and services, an increase in taxes, or a reduction in government transfers—shifts the aggregate demand curve leftward. It closes the inflationary gap by shifting AD_1 to AD_2, moving the economy to a new short-run macroeconomic equilibrium, E_2, which is also a long-run macroeconomic equilibrium.

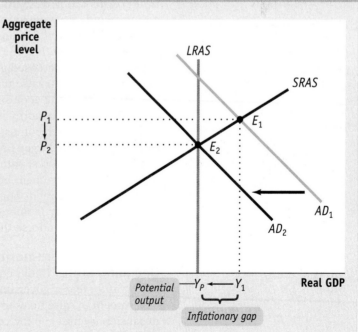

summarize the major points of the debate over expansionary fiscal policy, so we can understand when the critiques are justified and when they are not.

There are three main arguments against the use of expansionary fiscal policy.

- Government spending always crowds out private spending
- Government borrowing always crowds out private investment spending
- Government budget deficits lead to reduced private spending

The first of these claims is wrong in principle, but it has nonetheless played a prominent role in public debates. The second is valid under some, but not all, circumstances. The third argument, although it raises some important issues, isn't a good reason to believe that expansionary fiscal policy doesn't work.

Claim 1: "Government Spending Always Crowds Out Private Spending"

Some claim that expansionary fiscal policy can never raise aggregate spending and therefore can never raise aggregate income, with reasons that go something like this: "Every dollar that the government spends is a dollar taken away from the private sector. So any rise in government spending must be offset by an equal fall in private spending." In other words, every dollar spent by the government *crowds out*, or displaces, a dollar of private spending.

But the statement is wrong because it assumes that resources in the economy are always fully employed and, as a result, the aggregate income earned in the economy is always a fixed sum—which isn't true. In reality, whether or not government spending crowds out private spending depends upon the state of the economy. In particular, when the economy is suffering from a recessionary gap, there are unemployed resources in the economy, and output (and therefore income) is below its potential level. Expansionary fiscal policy during these periods puts unemployed resources to work and generates higher spending and higher income. Government spending crowds out private spending only when the economy is operating at full employment. So the argument that expansionary fiscal policy always crowds out private spending is wrong in principle.

Claim 2: "Government Borrowing Always Crowds Out Private Investment Spending"

How valid is the argument that government borrowing uses funds that would have otherwise been used for private investment spending—that is, it crowds out private investment spending. So how valid is the argument that government borrowing always reduces private investment spending?

Much like Claim 1, Claim 2 is wrong because whether crowding out occurs depends upon whether the economy is depressed or not. If the economy is not depressed, then increased government borrowing, by increasing the demand for loanable funds, can raise interest rates and crowd out private investment spending. However, if the economy is depressed, crowding out is much less likely to occur. When the economy is at far less than full employment, a fiscal expansion will lead to higher incomes, which in turn leads to increased savings at any given interest rate. This larger pool of savings allows the government to borrow without driving up interest rates. The stimulus of 2009 was a case in point: despite high levels of government borrowing, U.S. interest rates stayed near historic lows. In the end, government borrowing crowds out private investment spending only when the economy is operating at full employment (which is why most economists declined to endorse the Trump administration's tax cuts).

Claim 3: "Government Budget Deficits Lead to Reduced Private Spending"

Other things equal, expansionary fiscal policy leads to a larger budget deficit and greater government debt. And higher debt will eventually require the government to raise taxes to pay it off. So, according to the third argument against expansionary fiscal policy, consumers, anticipating that they must pay higher taxes in the future to pay off today's government debt, will cut their spending today in order to save money. This argument, first made by nineteenth-century economist David Ricardo, is known as *Ricardian equivalence*. It is an argument often taken to imply that expansionary fiscal policy will have no effect on the economy because far-sighted consumers will undo any attempts at expansion by the government. (And will also undo any contractionary fiscal policy, for that matter.)

In reality, however, it's doubtful that consumers behave with such foresight and budgeting discipline. Most people, when provided with extra cash (generated by the fiscal expansion), will spend at least some of it. So even fiscal policy that takes the form of temporary tax cuts or transfers of cash to consumers probably does have an expansionary effect.

Moreover, it's possible to show that even with Ricardian equivalence, a temporary rise in government spending that involves direct purchases of goods and services—such as a program of road construction—would still lead to a boost in total spending in the near term. That's because even if consumers cut back their current spending in anticipation of higher future taxes, their reduced spending will take place over an extended period as consumers save over time to pay the future tax bill. Meanwhile, the additional government spending will be concentrated in the near future, when the economy needs it.

So although the effects emphasized by Ricardian equivalence may reduce the impact of fiscal expansion, the claim that it makes fiscal expansion completely ineffective is neither consistent with how consumers actually behave nor a reason to believe that increases in government spending have no effect. So, in the end, it's not a valid argument against expansionary fiscal policy.

In Sum The extent to which we should expect expansionary fiscal policy to work depends upon the circumstances. Recall the conclusion in the chapter opening story: in making fiscal policy, timing is critical. When the economy has a recessionary gap—as it did when the 2009 stimulus was passed—economics tells us that this is just the kind of situation in which expansionary fiscal policy helps the economy. However, when the economy is already at full employment, as it was very close to in 2018 when the Trump tax cuts went into effect, expansionary fiscal policy is the wrong policy and will lead to crowding out, an overheated economy, and higher inflation.

A Cautionary Note: Lags in Fiscal Policy

Looking back at Figures 17-4 and 17-5, it may seem obvious that the government should actively use fiscal policy—always adopting an expansionary fiscal policy when the economy faces a recessionary gap and always adopting a contractionary fiscal policy when the economy faces an inflationary gap. But many economists caution against an extremely active stabilization policy, arguing that a government that tries too hard to stabilize the economy—through either fiscal policy or monetary policy—can end up making the economy less stable.

We'll leave discussion of the warnings associated with monetary policy to Chapter 19. In the case of fiscal policy, one key reason for caution is that there are important *time lags* between when the policy is decided upon and when it is implemented. To understand the nature of these lags, consider the three things that have to happen before the government increases spending to fight a recessionary gap.

1. The government has to realize that the recessionary gap exists: economic data take time to collect and analyze, and recessions are often recognized only months after they have begun.

    Although the Great Recession is generally considered to have begun in December 2007, as late as September 2008 some economists were still questioning whether the recession was real.

2. The government has to develop a spending plan, which can itself take months, particularly if politicians take time debating how the money should be spent and passing legislation.

3. It takes time to spend money. For example, a road construction project begins with activities such as surveying that don't involve spending large sums. It may be quite some time before the big spending begins. The Recovery Act was passed in the first quarter of 2009, but much of its effect on federal spending, especially purchases of goods and services, didn't come until 2011.

Because of these lags, an attempt to increase spending to fight a recessionary gap may take so long to get going that the economy has already recovered on its own. In fact, the recessionary gap may have turned into an inflationary gap by the time expansionary fiscal policy takes effect. In that case, expansionary fiscal policy will make things worse instead of better.

This doesn't mean that fiscal policy should never be actively used. In early 2009 there was good reason to believe that the slump facing the U.S. economy would be both deep and long and that a fiscal stimulus designed to arrive over the next year or two would almost surely push aggregate demand in the right direction. In fact, as we'll see later in this chapter, the 2009 stimulus arguably faded out too soon, leaving the economy still deeply depressed when it ended. But the problem of lags makes the actual use of both fiscal and monetary policy harder than you might think from a simple analysis like the one we have just given.

ECONOMICS >> *in Action*
A Tale of Two Stimuli

There were some broad similarities between the Obama stimulus of 2009 and proposals that were floated by the Trump administration soon after it took office in early 2017, including the passing of new tax cuts that started in 2018 and the proposal of new infrastructure spending. Yet many economists who supported the Obama stimulus were dubious about the Trump plan, because the state of the economy had changed.

Figure 17-6 shows two indicators that played an important role in policy discussions at both times. One is the unemployment rate. The other is the *quits rate*, the fraction of workers voluntarily leaving their jobs each month. This rate is widely viewed as an indication of how good the labor market is: workers are reluctant to quit if they believe new jobs are very hard to find. For this reason, the quits rate is a useful backup to the unemployment rate: if you're unsure whether the unemployment rate is giving an accurate read on the situation, you can check whether the quits rate is telling the same story.

What you can see from Figure 17-6 is that in early 2009 the United States showed all the signs of a deeply depressed economy, in the grip of an accelerating plunge, with

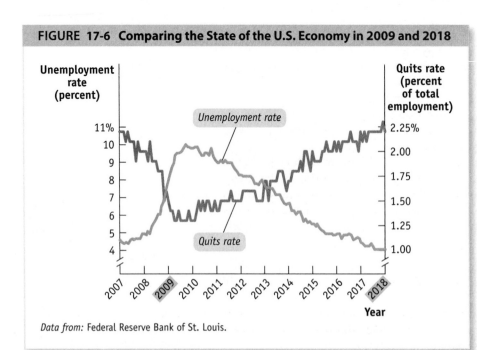

FIGURE 17-6 **Comparing the State of the U.S. Economy in 2009 and 2018**

Data from: Federal Reserve Bank of St. Louis.

unemployment high and rising and the quits rate low and falling. By early 2018, when the tax cuts took effect, however, the data were telling the opposite story: a low unemployment rate and a high quits rate indicated that jobs were relatively plentiful.

This difference meant that the case for expansionary fiscal policy was much weaker in 2018 than it had been in 2009: under 2018 conditions it was, in fact, likely that increased government spending would crowd out private spending, and that increased government borrowing would crowd out private investment. It was possible to favor the Trump administration's proposals for a variety of reasons. But the macroeconomics of fiscal policy made the potential downside much higher than it had been in 2009.

>> Check Your Understanding 17-1

Solutions appear at back of book.

1. In each of the following cases, determine whether the policy is an expansionary or contractionary fiscal policy.
   a. Several military bases around the country, which together employ tens of thousands of people, are closed.
   b. The number of weeks an unemployed person is eligible for unemployment benefits is increased.
   c. The federal tax on gasoline is increased.

2. Explain why federal disaster relief, which quickly disburses funds to victims of natural disasters such as hurricanes, floods, and large-scale crop failures, will stabilize the economy more effectively after a disaster than relief that must be legislated.

3. Is the following statement true or false? Explain. "When the government expands, the private sector shrinks; when the government shrinks, the private sector expands."

‖ Fiscal Policy and the Multiplier

An expansionary fiscal policy, like the 2009 stimulus, pushes the aggregate demand curve to the right. A contractionary fiscal policy pushes the aggregate demand curve to the left. For policy makers, however, knowing the direction of the shift isn't enough: they need estimates of *how much* a given policy will shift the aggregate demand curve. To get these estimates, they use the concept of the multiplier.

Multiplier Effects of an Increase in Government Purchases of Goods and Services

Suppose that a government decides to spend $50 billion building bridges and roads. The government's purchases of goods and services will directly increase total spending on final goods and services by $50 billion. But there will also be an indirect effect: the government's purchases will start a chain reaction throughout the economy.

The firms that produce the goods and services purchased by the government earn revenues that flow to households in the form of wages, profits, interest, and rent. This increase in disposable income leads to a rise in consumer spending. The rise in consumer spending, in turn, induces firms to increase output, leading to a further rise in disposable income, which leads to another round of consumer spending increases, and so on.

In this case, the *multiplier* is the ratio of the total change in real GDP caused by the change in the government's purchases of goods and services. More generally, real GDP can change with any *autonomous change in aggregate spending*, not just a change in consumer spending. An **autonomous change in aggregate spending** is the initial rise or fall in the desired level of spending by firms, households, or

>> Quick Review

• The main channels of fiscal policy are taxes and government spending. Government spending takes the form of purchases of goods and services as well as transfers.

• In the United States, most government transfers are accounted for by **social insurance** programs designed to alleviate economic hardship—principally Social Security, Medicare, Medicaid, and the Affordable Care Act (ACA).

• The government controls *G* directly and influences *C* and *I* through taxes and transfers.

• **Expansionary fiscal policy** is implemented by an increase in government spending, a cut in taxes, or an increase in government transfers. **Contractionary fiscal policy** is implemented by a reduction in government spending, an increase in taxes, or a reduction in government transfers.

• Arguments against the effectiveness of expansionary fiscal policy based upon crowding out are valid only when the economy is at or close to full employment. The argument that expansionary fiscal policy won't work because of Ricardian equivalence—that consumers will cut back spending today to offset expected future tax increases—appears to be untrue in practice. What is clearly true is that time lags can reduce the effectiveness of fiscal policy, and potentially render it counterproductive.

Expansionary or contractionary fiscal policy will start a chain reaction throughout the economy.

An **autonomous change in aggregate spending** is an initial change in the desired level of spending by firms, households, or government at a given level of real GDP.

The **multiplier** is the ratio of the total change in real GDP caused by an autonomous change in aggregate spending to the size of that autonomous change.

The **marginal propensity to consume,** or **MPC,** is the increase in consumer spending when disposable income rises by $1.

government at a given level of GDP. Formally, the **multiplier** is the ratio of the total change in real GDP caused by an autonomous change in aggregate spending to the size of that autonomous change.

If we sum the effect from all these rounds of consumer spending increases, how large is the total effect on aggregate output? To answer this question, we need to introduce the concept of the **marginal propensity to consume,** or **MPC:** the increase in consumer spending when disposable income rises by $1. When consumer spending changes because of a rise or fall in disposable income, MPC is that change in consumer spending divided by the change in disposable income:

$$(17\text{-}2) \quad MPC = \frac{\Delta \text{Consumer spending}}{\Delta \text{Disposable income}}$$

where the symbol Δ (delta) means "change in." For example, if consumer spending goes up by $5 billion when disposable income goes up by $10 billion, MPC is $5 billion/$10 billion = 0.5.

Now, consider a simple case in which there are no taxes or international trade, so that any change in GDP accrues entirely to households. We also assume that the aggregate price level is fixed, so that any increase in nominal GDP is also a rise in real GDP, and that the interest rate is fixed. In that case the multiplier is $1/(1 - MPC)$. So, if the marginal propensity to consume is 0.5, the multiplier is $1/(1 - 0.5) = 1/0.5 = 2$. Given a multiplier of 2, a $50 billion increase in government purchases of goods and services would increase real GDP by $100 billion. Of that $100 billion, $50 billion is the initial effect from the increase in G, and the remaining $50 billion is the subsequent effect arising from the increase in consumer spending.

What happens if government purchases of goods and services are instead reduced? The math is exactly the same, except that there's a minus sign in front: if government purchases of goods and services fall by $50 billion and the marginal propensity to consume is 0.5, real GDP falls by $100 billion.

Multiplier Effects of Changes in Government Transfers and Taxes

Expansionary or contractionary fiscal policy need not take the form of changes in government purchases of goods and services. Governments can also change transfer payments or taxes. In general, however, a change in government transfers or taxes shifts the aggregate demand curve by *less* than an equal-sized change in government purchases, resulting in a smaller effect on real GDP.

To see why, imagine that instead of spending $50 billion on building bridges, the government simply hands out $50 billion in the form of government transfers. In this case, there is no direct effect on aggregate demand, as there was with government purchases of goods and services. Real GDP goes up because households spend some of that $50 billion—but they won't spend it all.

Table 17-1 shows a hypothetical comparison of two expansionary fiscal policies assuming an *MPC* equal to 0.5 and a multiplier equal to 2: one in which the government directly purchases $50 billion in goods and services and one in which the government makes transfer payments instead, sending out $50 billion in checks to consumers. In each case there is a first-round effect on real GDP, either from purchases by the government or from purchases by the consumers who received the checks, followed by a series of additional rounds as rising real GDP raises disposable income.

However, the first-round effect of the transfer program is smaller. Because we have assumed that the *MPC* is 0.5, only $25 billion of the $50 billion is spent, with the other $25 billion saved. And as a result, all the further rounds are smaller, too. In the end, the transfer payment increases real GDP by only $50 billion, equal to $MPC \times 1/(1 - MPC)$. In comparison, a $50 billion increase in government purchases produces a $100 billion increase in real GDP, equal to $1/(1 - MPC)$.

Overall, when expansionary fiscal policy takes the form of a rise in transfer payments, real GDP may rise by either more or less than the initial government outlay—that is, the multiplier may be either more or less than 1, depending upon the size of the *MPC*. In Table 17-1, with an *MPC* equal to 0.5, the multiplier is exactly 1: a $50 billion rise in transfer payments increases real GDP by $50 billion. If the *MPC* is less than 0.5, so that a smaller share of the initial transfer is spent, the multiplier on that transfer is *less* than 1. If a larger share of the initial transfer is spent, the multiplier is *more* than 1.

TABLE 17-1 **Hypothetical Effects of a Fiscal Policy When *MPC* = 0.5**		
Effect on real GDP	**$50 billion rise in government purchases of goods and services**	**$50 billion rise in government transfer payments**
First round	$50 billion	$25 billion
Second round	$25 billion	$12.5 billion
Third round	$12.5 billion	$6.25 billion
. . .	. . .	. . .
Total effect	$100 billion	$50 billion
Total effect in terms of multiplier	$\Delta Y = \Delta G \times 1/(1 - MPC)$	$\Delta Y = \Delta TR \times MPC \times 1/(1 - MPC)$

A tax cut has an effect similar to the effect of a transfer. It increases disposable income, leading to a series of increases in consumer spending. But the overall effect is smaller than that of an equal-sized increase in government purchases of goods and services: the autonomous increase in aggregate spending is smaller because households save part of the amount of the tax cut.

We should also note that taxes introduce a further complication—they typically change the size of the multiplier. That's because in the real world governments rarely impose **lump-sum taxes,** in which the amount of tax a household owes is independent of its income. With lump-sum taxes there is no change in the multiplier. Instead, the great majority of tax revenue is raised via taxes that are not lump-sum, and so tax revenue depends upon the level of real GDP.

In practice, economists often argue that the size of the multiplier determines *who* among the population should get tax cuts or increases in government transfers. For example, compare the effects of an increase in unemployment benefits to a cut in taxes on profits distributed to shareholders as dividends. Consumer surveys suggest that the average unemployed worker will spend a higher share of any increase in his or her disposable income than would the average recipient of dividend income. That is, people who are unemployed tend to have a higher *MPC* than people who own a lot of stocks because the latter tend to be wealthier and tend to save more of any increase in disposable income. If that's true, a dollar spent on unemployment benefits increases aggregate demand more than a dollar's worth of dividend tax cuts.

How Taxes Affect the Multiplier

The increase in government tax revenue when real GDP rises isn't the result of a deliberate decision or action by the government. It's a consequence of the way the tax laws are written, which causes most sources of government revenue to increase *automatically* when real GDP goes up. For example, income tax receipts increase when real GDP rises because the amount each individual owes in taxes depends positively on his or her income, and households' taxable income rises when real GDP rises. Sales tax receipts increase when real GDP rises because people with more income spend more on goods and services. And corporate profit tax receipts increase when real GDP rises because profits increase when the economy expands.

The effect of these automatic increases in tax revenue is to reduce the size of the multiplier. Remember, the multiplier is the result of a chain reaction in which higher real GDP leads to higher disposable income, which leads to higher consumer spending, which leads to further increases in real GDP. The fact that the government siphons off some of any increase in real GDP means that at each stage

Lump-sum taxes are taxes that don't depend on the taxpayer's income.

Automatic stabilizers are government spending and taxation rules that cause fiscal policy to be automatically expansionary when the economy contracts and automatically contractionary when the economy expands.

Discretionary fiscal policy is fiscal policy that is the result of deliberate actions by policy makers rather than rules.

of this process, the increase in consumer spending is smaller than it would be if taxes weren't part of the picture. The result is to reduce the multiplier.

Many macroeconomists believe it's a good thing that taxes reduce the multiplier. In the previous chapter we argued that most, though not all, recessions are the result of negative demand shocks. The same mechanism that makes tax revenue increase when the economy expands makes tax revenue decrease when the economy contracts. Since tax receipts decrease when real GDP falls, the effects of these negative demand shocks are smaller than in a world in which there were no taxes. The decrease in tax revenue reduces the adverse effect of the initial fall in aggregate demand.

The automatic decrease in government tax revenue generated by a fall in real GDP—caused by a decrease in the amount of taxes households pay—acts like an automatic expansionary fiscal policy implemented in the face of a recession. Similarly, when the economy expands, the government finds itself automatically pursuing a contractionary fiscal policy—a tax increase. Government spending and taxation rules that cause fiscal policy to be automatically expansionary when the economy contracts and automatically contractionary when the economy expands, without requiring any deliberate action by policy makers, are called **automatic stabilizers.**

The rules that govern tax collection aren't the only automatic stabilizers, although they are the most important ones. Some types of government transfers also play a stabilizing role. For example, more people receive unemployment insurance when the economy is depressed than when it is booming. The same is true of Medicaid and food stamps. So transfer payments tend to rise when the economy is contracting and fall when the economy is expanding. Like changes in tax revenue, these automatic changes in transfers tend to reduce the size of the multiplier because the total change in disposable income that results from a given rise or fall in real GDP is smaller.

As in the case of government tax revenue, many macroeconomists believe that it's a good thing that government transfers reduce the multiplier. Expansionary and contractionary fiscal policies that are the result of automatic stabilizers are widely considered helpful to macroeconomic stabilization because they blunt the extremes of the business cycle.

But what about fiscal policy that *isn't* the result of automatic stabilizers? **Discretionary fiscal policy** is the direct result of deliberate actions by policy makers rather than automatic adjustment. For example, during a recession, the government may pass legislation that cuts taxes and increases government spending to stimulate the economy. In general, economists tend to support the use of discretionary fiscal policy only in the case of a severe recession or sustained economic weakness.

During the Great Depression, the Works Progress Administration (WPA), an example of discretionary fiscal policy, put millions of unemployed Americans to work constructing bridges, roads, buildings, dams, and parks.

ECONOMICS >> *in Action*
Austerity and the Multiplier

We've explained the logic of the fiscal multiplier, but what empirical evidence do economists have about multiplier effects in practice? Until a few years ago, the answer would have been that we didn't have nearly as much evidence as we'd like.

The problem was that large changes in fiscal policy are fairly rare, and usually happen at the same time other things are taking place, making it hard to separate the effects of spending and taxes from those of other factors. For example, the U.S. government drastically increased spending during World War II. But it also instituted rationing of many consumer goods and restricted construction of new homes in order to conserve resources for the war effort. So it is hard to distinguish the effects of the increase in government spending from the transformation of a peacetime economy to a war economy.

However, recent events offer considerable new evidence. In the wake of the Global Financial Crisis of 2009, several European governments found themselves facing debt crises. As loans they had taken out came due, these governments were either unable to raise new funds or were forced to pay extremely high interest rates. As a result, they had to turn to the rest of Europe for aid. In an attempt to reduce budget deficits, a condition of this aid was *austerity*—sharp cuts in spending plus tax increases. Austerity is a form of contractionary fiscal policy. So by comparing the economic performance of countries forced into austerity with the performance of countries that weren't, we get a relatively clear view of the effects of changes in spending and taxes.

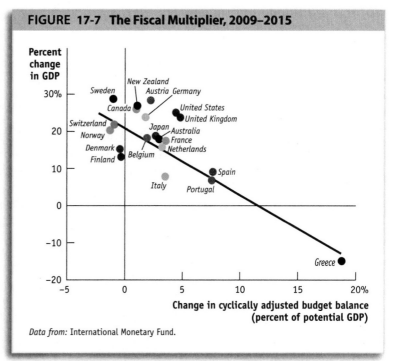

FIGURE 17-7 The Fiscal Multiplier, 2009–2015

Data from: International Monetary Fund.

Figure 17-7 compares the amount of austerity imposed in a number of countries between 2009 and 2015 to the growth in their GDP over the same period. Austerity is measured on the horizontal axis by the change in the *cyclically adjusted budget balance*, defined later in this chapter. As you can see, Greece stands out. It was forced to impose severe spending cuts and suffered a huge fall in output. But even without Greece there is a clear negative relationship. A line fitted through the scatterplot has a slope of –1.8. That is, the figure suggests that spending cuts and tax increases had an average multiplier of 1.8. Put another way, a contractionary fiscal policy that took $1 out of the economy resulted in a $1.80 fall in GDP.

Economists have offered a number of qualifications and caveats to this result, given that this wasn't truly a controlled experiment. Yet, recent experience strongly supports the proposition that fiscal policy does indeed move GDP in the predicted direction, with a multiplier of more than 1.

>> Check Your Understanding 17-2
Solutions appear at back of book.

1. Explain why a $500 million increase in government purchases of goods and services will generate a larger rise in real GDP than a $500 million increase in government transfers.

2. Explain why a $500 million reduction in government purchases of goods and services will generate a larger fall in real GDP than a $500 million reduction in government transfers.

3. The country of Boldovia has no unemployment insurance benefits and a tax system using only lump-sum taxes. The neighboring country of Moldovia has generous unemployment benefits and a tax system in which residents must pay a percentage of their income. Which country will experience greater variation in real GDP in response to demand shocks, positive and negative? Explain.

‖ The Budget Balance

Headlines about the government's budget tend to focus on just one point: whether the government is running a surplus or a deficit and, in either case, how big. People usually think of surpluses as good: when the federal government ran a record

>> **Quick Review**

• The **multiplier** is the ratio of the total change in real GDP caused by an **autonomous change in aggregate spending** to the size of that autonomous change. The multiplier is determined by the **marginal propensity to consume (MPC)**.

• Changes in taxes and government transfers also move real GDP, but by less than equal-sized changes in government purchases.

• Taxes reduce the size of the multiplier unless they are **lump-sum taxes.**

• Taxes and some government transfers act as **automatic stabilizers** as tax revenue responds positively to changes in real GDP and some government transfers respond negatively to changes in real GDP. Many economists believe that it is a good thing that they reduce the size of the multiplier. In contrast, economists tend to support the use of **discretionary fiscal policy** only during severe recessions or periods of sustained economic weakness.

surplus in 2000, many people regarded it as a cause for celebration. Conversely, people usually think of deficits as bad: when the U.S. federal government ran record deficits from 2009 to 2011, many people regarded it as a cause for concern.

How do surpluses and deficits fit into the analysis of fiscal policy? Are deficits ever a good thing and surpluses a bad thing? To answer those questions, let's look at the causes and consequences of surpluses and deficits.

The Budget Balance as a Measure of Fiscal Policy

What do we mean by surpluses and deficits? The budget balance is the difference between the government's revenue, in the form of tax revenue, and its spending, both on goods and services and on government transfers, in a given year. That is, the budget balance—savings by government—is defined by Equation 17-3:

(17-3) $S_{Government} = T - G - TR$

where T is the value of tax revenues, G is government purchases of goods and services, and TR is the value of government transfers. A budget surplus is a positive budget balance and a budget deficit is a negative budget balance.

Other things equal, expansionary fiscal policies—increased government purchases of goods and services, higher government transfers, or lower taxes—reduce the budget balance for that year. That is, expansionary fiscal policies make a budget surplus smaller or a budget deficit bigger. Conversely, contractionary fiscal policies—reduced government purchases of goods and services, lower government transfers, or higher taxes—increase the budget balance for that year, making a budget surplus bigger or a budget deficit smaller.

You might think this means that changes in the budget balance can be used to measure fiscal policy. In fact, economists often do just that: they use changes in the budget balance as a "quick-and-dirty" way to assess whether current fiscal policy is expansionary or contractionary. But they always keep in mind two reasons this quick-and-dirty approach is sometimes misleading:

1. Two different changes in fiscal policy that have equal-sized effects on the budget balance may have quite unequal effects on the economy. As we have already seen, changes in government purchases of goods and services have a larger effect on real GDP than equal-sized changes in taxes and government transfers.

2. Often, changes in the budget balance are themselves the result, not the cause, of fluctuations in the economy.

To understand the second point, we need to examine the effects of the business cycle on the budget.

The Business Cycle and the Cyclically Adjusted Budget Balance

Historically there has been a strong relationship between the federal government's budget balance and the business cycle. The budget tends to move into deficit when the economy experiences a recession, but deficits tend to get smaller or even turn into surpluses when the economy is expanding. Figure 17-8 shows the federal budget deficit as a percentage of GDP from 1964 to 2018. Shaded areas indicate recessions; unshaded areas indicate expansions. As you can see, the federal budget deficit increased around the time of each recession and usually declined during expansions. In fact, in the late stages of the long expansion from 1991 through early 2001, the deficit actually became negative—the budget deficit became a budget surplus.

The relationship between the business cycle and the budget balance is even clearer if we compare the budget deficit as a percentage of GDP with the unemployment rate, as we do in Figure 17-9. The budget deficit almost always rises when the unemployment rate rises and falls when the unemployment rate falls.

FIGURE 17-8 The U.S. Federal Budget Deficit and the Business Cycle, 1964–2018

The budget deficit as a percentage of GDP tends to rise during recessions (indicated by shaded areas) and fall during expansions.

Data from: Federal Reserve Bank of St. Louis.

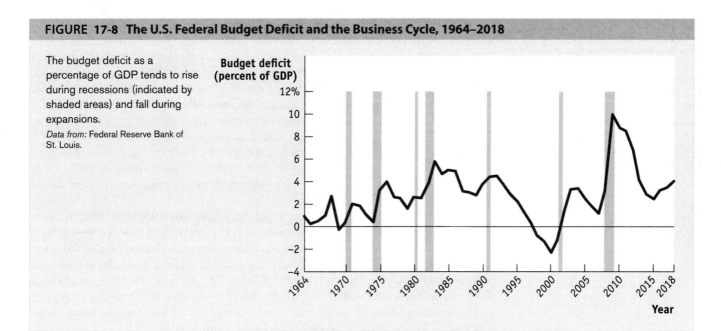

Is this relationship between the business cycle and the budget balance evidence that policy makers engage in discretionary fiscal policy, using expansionary fiscal policy during recessions and contractionary fiscal policy during expansions? Not necessarily. To a large extent the relationship in Figure 17-9 reflects automatic stabilizers at work. As we saw earlier in the discussion of automatic stabilizers, government tax revenue tends to rise and some government transfers, like unemployment benefit payments, tend to fall when the economy expands. Conversely, government tax revenue tends to fall and some government transfers tend to rise when the economy contracts. So the budget tends to move toward surplus during expansions and toward deficit during recessions even without any deliberate action on the part of policy makers.

In assessing budget policy, it's often useful to separate movements in the budget balance due to the business cycle from movements due to discretionary

FIGURE 17-9 The U.S. Federal Budget Deficit and the Unemployment Rate, 1964–2018

There is a close relationship between the budget balance and the business cycle: a recession moves the budget balance toward deficit, but an expansion moves it toward surplus. Here, the unemployment rate serves as an indicator of the business cycle, and we should expect to see a higher unemployment rate associated with a higher budget deficit. This is confirmed by the figure: the budget deficit as a percentage of GDP moves closely in tandem with the unemployment rate.

Data from: Federal Reserve Bank of St. Louis.

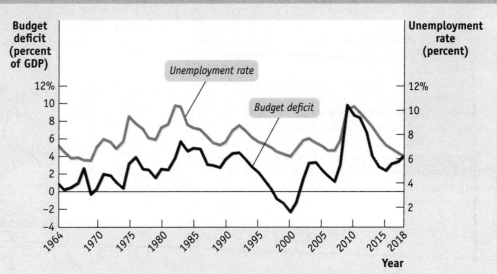

The **cyclically adjusted budget balance** is an estimate of what the budget balance would be if real GDP were exactly equal to potential output.

fiscal policy changes. The former are affected by automatic stabilizers and the latter by deliberate changes in government purchases, government transfers, or taxes. It's important to realize that business-cycle effects on the budget balance are temporary: both recessionary gaps (in which real GDP is below potential output) and inflationary gaps (in which real GDP is above potential output) tend to be eliminated in the long run. Removing their effects on the budget balance sheds light on whether the government's taxing and spending policies are sustainable in the long run.

In other words, do the government's tax policies yield enough revenue to fund its spending in the long run? As we'll learn shortly, this is a fundamentally more important question than whether the government runs a budget surplus or deficit in the current year.

To separate the effect of the business cycle from the effects of other factors, many governments produce an estimate of what the budget balance would be if there were neither a recessionary nor an inflationary gap. The **cyclically adjusted budget balance** is an estimate of what the budget balance would be if real GDP were exactly equal to potential output. It takes into account the extra tax revenue the government would collect and the transfers it would save if a recessionary gap were eliminated—or the revenue the government would lose and the extra transfers it would make if an inflationary gap were eliminated.

Figure 17-10 shows the actual budget deficit and the Congressional Budget Office estimate of the cyclically adjusted budget deficit, both as a percentage of potential GDP, from 1965 to 2018. As you can see, the cyclically adjusted budget deficit doesn't fluctuate as much as the actual budget deficit. In particular, large actual deficits, such as those of 1975, 1983, and 2009 (indicated by the purple bars), are mostly due to a depressed economy.

Should the Budget Be Balanced?

Persistent budget deficits can cause problems for both the government and the economy. Yet politicians are often tempted to run deficits because this allows them to cater to voters by cutting taxes without cutting spending or by increasing spending without increasing taxes. As a result, there are occasional attempts by policy makers to force fiscal discipline by introducing legislation—even a constitutional amendment—forbidding the government from running budget deficits. This is usually stated as a

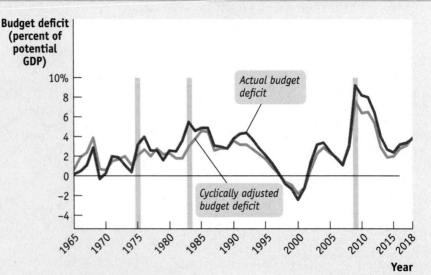

FIGURE 17-10 The Actual Budget Deficit Versus the Cyclically Adjusted Budget Deficit, 1965–2018

The cyclically adjusted budget deficit is an estimate of what the budget deficit would be if the economy was at potential output. It fluctuates less than the actual budget deficit because years of large budget deficits also tend to be years when the economy has a large recessionary gap. The large actual deficits in 1975, 1983, and 2009 (which are reported in the following year) are indicated by the vertical purple bars. These deficits were mostly due to a depressed economy.

Data from: Congressional Budget Office.

requirement that the budget be balanced—that revenues at least equal spending each fiscal year. Would it be a good idea to require a balanced budget annually?

Most economists don't think so. They believe that the government should only balance its budget on average—that it should be allowed to run deficits in bad years, offset by surpluses in good years. They don't believe the government should be forced to run a balanced budget *every year* because this would undermine the role of taxes and transfers as automatic stabilizers.

As we've learned, the tendency of tax revenue to fall and transfers to rise when the economy contracts helps to limit the size of recessions. But falling tax revenue and rising transfer payments generated by a downturn in the economy push the budget toward deficit. If constrained by a balanced-budget rule, the government would have to respond to this deficit with contractionary fiscal policies that would tend to deepen a recession.

Yet policy makers concerned about excessive deficits sometimes feel that rigid rules prohibiting—or at least setting an upper limit on—deficits are necessary. In fact, as the following Economics in Action explains, state and local governments do have such rules, which had a major impact on fiscal policy during the Great Recession and in its aftermath.

ECONOMICS >> *in Action*
Trying to Balance Budgets in a Recession

When the Great Recession struck, the U.S. federal government's budget deficit increased from just $160 billion to $1.4 trillion, partly because of stimulus measures but mainly because of automatic stabilizers: revenue fell sharply, while some expenditures, especially unemployment benefits, rose. Many observers worried about this deficit, but most economists thought that trying to balance the budget in the face of a recession would actually make that recession worse.

When it comes to government spending in America, however, the federal government isn't the only player. State and local governments account for about 40% of total government spending, and most government employment. (Most government employees are in positions that deliver essential services, such as schoolteachers, police officers, and firefighters.) And almost all of these state and local governments have rules requiring that they balance their budgets all the time.

There are a number of reasons for these rules, which make sense for each individual state or city. Taken together, however, the rules mean that for a large part of government in America, automatic stabilizers don't work. In fact, state and local governments cut back sharply in the face of a depressed economy, especially after 2010, when federal aid from the 2009 stimulus ended. Figure 17-11 shows the number of state and local employees from 2000 to 2018; as you can see, from 2009 until 2013 (the period shaded in purple), there were large cuts, mainly layoffs of teachers, in the face of falling revenues.

These actions at the state and local levels didn't fully offset the effects of automatic stabilizers at the federal level, but they still probably caused the recession to be deeper and the recovery slower than it would have been if we didn't have multiple levels of government, with the lower levels required to run balanced budgets.

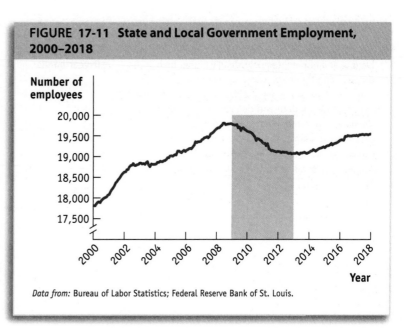

FIGURE 17-11 State and Local Government Employment, 2000–2018

Data from: Bureau of Labor Statistics; Federal Reserve Bank of St. Louis.

>> Check Your Understanding 17-3
Solutions appear at back of book.

1. Why is the cyclically adjusted budget balance a better measure of whether government policies are sustainable in the long run than the actual budget balance?

2. Explain why states required by their constitutions to balance their budgets are likely to experience more severe economic fluctuations than states not held to that requirement.

Long-Run Implications of Fiscal Policy

At the end of 2009, the government of Greece ran into a financial wall. Like most other governments in Europe (and the U.S. government, too), the Greek government was running a large budget deficit, which meant that it needed to keep borrowing more funds, both to cover its expenses and to pay off existing loans as they came due. But governments, like countries or individuals, can only borrow if lenders believe it's likely that they will eventually be willing or able to repay their debts. By 2009 many lenders had lost faith in Greece's financial future, and they were no longer willing to lend to the Greek government. Those few who were willing to lend demanded very high interest rates to compensate them for the risk of loss.

Figure 17-12 compares interest rates on 10-year bonds issued by the governments of Greece and Germany. At the beginning of 2007, Greece could borrow at almost the same rate as Germany, widely considered a very safe borrower. In 2009 its borrowing costs started to climb, and by the end of 2011 Greece had to pay an interest rate around 10 times the rate Germany paid.

What precipitated the crisis? In 2009 it became clear that the Greek government had used creative accounting to hide just how much debt it had already taken on. Government debt is, after all, a promise to make future payments to lenders. By 2010 it seemed likely that the Greek government had already promised more than it could possibly deliver.

Lenders became deeply worried that the level of Greek government debt was unsustainable—that is, it was unlikely to repay what was owed. As a result, Greece found itself largely shut out of private debt markets. In order to prevent a

---

FIGURE 17-12 Greek and German Long-Term Interest Rates

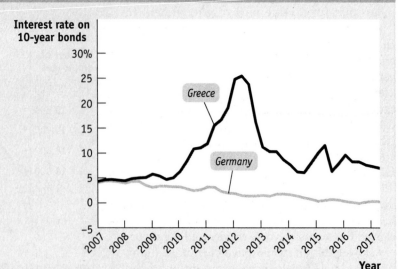

As late as 2008, the government of Greece could borrow at interest rates only slightly higher than those facing Germany, widely considered a very safe borrower. But in early 2009, as it became clear that both Greek debt and deficits were larger than previously reported, lenders lost confidence in the government's ability to repay its debts and sent Greek borrowing costs skyrocketing.

Data from: Federal Reserve Bank of St. Louis; OECD "Main Economic Indicators Complete Database."

government collapse, it received emergency loans from other European nations and the International Monetary Fund. But these loans came with the requirement that the Greek government undertake austerity, by making severe spending cuts and sharply raising taxes. Austerity in Greece wreaked havoc with the economy, imposed severe economic hardship on citizens, and led to massive social unrest.

The 2009 crisis in Greece shows why no discussion of fiscal policy is complete without taking into account the long-run implications of government budget surpluses and deficits, especially the implications for government debt. We now turn to those long-run implications.

Deficits, Surpluses, and Debt

When a family spends more than it earns over the course of a year, it has to raise the extra funds either by selling assets or by borrowing. And if a family borrows year after year, it will eventually end up with a lot of debt.

The same is true for governments. With a few exceptions, governments don't raise large sums by selling assets such as national parkland. Instead, when a government spends more than the tax revenue it receives—when it runs a budget deficit—it almost always borrows the extra funds. And governments that run persistent budget deficits end up with substantial debts.

To interpret the numbers that follow, you need to know a slightly peculiar feature of federal government accounting. For historical reasons, the U.S. government does not keep books by calendar years. Instead, budget totals are kept by **fiscal years,** which run from October 1 to September 30 and are labeled by the calendar year in which they end. For example, fiscal 2018 began on October 1, 2017, and ended on September 30, 2018.

At the end of fiscal 2018, the U.S. federal government had total debt equal to $21.5 trillion. However, part of that debt represented special accounting rules specifying that the federal government as a whole owes funds to certain government programs, especially Social Security. We'll explain those rules shortly. For now, however, let's focus on **public debt:** federal government debt held by individuals and institutions outside the government. At the end of fiscal 2018, the federal government's public debt was "only" $15.8 trillion, or 78% of GDP. Federal public debt at the end of 2018 was larger than at the end of 2017 because the government ran a deficit in 2018: a government that runs persistent budget deficits will experience a rising level of public debt. Why is this a problem?

Potential Dangers Posed by Rising Government Debt

There are two reasons to be concerned when a government runs persistent budget deficits that result in government debt that rises over time.

1. Crowding Out When the economy is at full employment and the government borrows funds in the financial markets, it is competing with firms that plan to borrow funds for investment spending. As a result, the government's borrowing may crowd out private investment spending, increasing interest rates, and reducing the economy's long-run rate of growth.

2. Financial Pressure and Default Today's deficits, by increasing the government's debt, place financial pressure on future budgets. The impact of current deficits on future budgets is straightforward. Like individuals, governments must pay their bills, including interest payments on their accumulated debt. When a government is deeply in debt, those interest payments can be substantial. In fiscal 2018, the U.S. federal government paid 1.6% of GDP, or $325 billion, in interest on its debt. The more heavily indebted government of Italy paid interest of 4% of its GDP in 2018, according to estimates.

A **fiscal year** runs from October 1 to September 30 and is labeled according to the calendar year in which it ends.

Public debt is government debt held by individuals and institutions outside the government.

Other things equal, a government paying large sums in interest must raise more revenue from taxes or spend less than it would otherwise be able to afford—or it must borrow even more to cover the gap. And a government that borrows to pay interest on its outstanding debt pushes itself even deeper into debt. This process can eventually push a government to the point where lenders question its ability to repay. Like a consumer who has maxed out his or her credit cards, it will find that lenders are unwilling to lend any more funds. The result can be that the government defaults on its debt—it stops paying what it owes. Default is often followed by deep financial and economic turmoil.

Americans aren't used to the idea of government default, but it does happen. In the 1990s Argentina, a relatively high-income developing country, was widely praised for its economic policies—and it was able to borrow large sums from foreign lenders. By 2001, however, Argentina's interest payments were spiraling out of control, and the country defaulted. It eventually reached a settlement with most of its lenders under which it paid less than a third of the amount originally due.

Default creates havoc in a country's financial markets and badly shakes public confidence in both the government and the economy. Argentina's debt default was accompanied by a crisis in the country's banking system and a very severe recession. And even if a highly indebted government avoids default, a heavy debt burden typically forces it to slash spending or raise taxes, politically unpopular measures that can also damage the economy. In some cases, austerity measures intended to reassure lenders that the government can indeed pay end up depressing the economy so much that lender confidence continues to fall.

If it has its own currency, a government that has trouble borrowing can print money to pay its bills. But doing so can lead to another problem: inflation. In fact, budget problems are the main cause of very severe inflation. Governments do not want to find themselves in a position where the choice is between defaulting on their debts and inflating those debts away by printing money.

⊕ GLOBAL COMPARISON   THE AMERICAN WAY OF DEBT

How does the public debt of the United States stack up internationally? In dollar terms, we're number one—but this isn't very informative, since the U.S. economy and so the government's tax base are much larger than those of all but a few other nations. A more informative comparison is the ratio of public debt to GDP.

The figure shows the *net public debt* of a number of rich countries as a percentage of GDP in 2018. Net public debt is government debt minus any assets governments may have—an adjustment that can make a big difference. What you see here is that the United States is more or less in the middle of the pack.

It may not surprise you that Greece heads the list, and most of the other high-net-debt countries are European nations that have been making headlines for their debt problems. Interestingly, however, Japan is also high on the list because it has used massive public spending to prop up its economy ever since the 1990s. Investors, however, still consider Japan a reliable government, so its borrowing costs remain low despite high net debt.

In contrast to the other countries, Norway has a large *negative* net public debt thanks to oil. Norway is one of the world's largest oil exporters. Instead of spending its oil revenues immediately, the government of Norway has used them to build up an investment fund for future needs following the lead of traditional oil producers like Saudi Arabia. As a result, Norway has a huge stock of government assets rather than a large government debt.

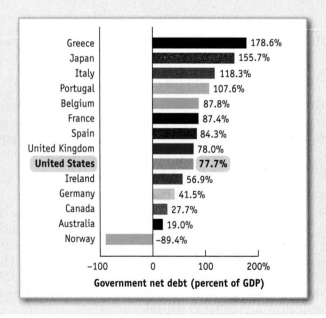

Government net debt (percent of GDP)

Country	Net debt
Greece	178.6%
Japan	155.7%
Italy	118.3%
Portugal	107.6%
Belgium	87.8%
France	87.4%
Spain	84.3%
United Kingdom	78.0%
United States	**77.7%**
Ireland	56.9%
Germany	41.5%
Canada	27.7%
Australia	19.0%
Norway	−89.4%

Data from: International Monetary Fund; World Economic Outlook, October 2018; Congressional Budget Office; Eurostat.

Concerns about the long-run effects of deficits need not rule out the use of expansionary fiscal policy to stimulate the economy when it is depressed. However, these concerns do mean that governments should try to offset budget deficits in bad years with budget surpluses in good years. In other words, governments should run a budget that is approximately balanced over time. Have they actually done so?

> The **debt–GDP ratio** is the government's debt as a percentage of GDP.

Deficits and Debt in Practice

Figure 17-13 shows the U.S. federal government's budget deficit and how its debt changed from 1940 to 2017. Panel (a) shows the federal deficit as a percentage of GDP. As you can see, the federal government ran huge deficits during World War II. It briefly ran surpluses after the war, but it has normally run deficits ever since, especially after 1980. This seems inconsistent with the advice that governments should offset deficits in bad times with surpluses in good times.

However, panel (b) of Figure 17-13 shows that for most of the period these persistent deficits didn't lead to runaway debt. To assess the ability of governments to pay their debt, we use the **debt–GDP ratio,** the government's debt as a percentage of GDP. We use this measure, rather than simply looking at the size of the debt, because GDP, which measures the size of the economy as a whole, is a good indicator of the potential taxes the government can collect. If the government's debt grows more slowly than GDP, the burden of paying that debt is actually falling compared with the government's potential tax revenue. Under these conditions the underlying economy is strong enough to generate future surpluses, allowing the government to pay off its debt, at a time of its own choosing, and avoid the potential dangers of financial pressure and default.

What we see from panel (b) is that although the federal debt grew in almost every year, the debt–GDP ratio fell for 30 years after the end of World War II. This shows that the debt–GDP ratio can fall, even when debt is rising, as long as GDP

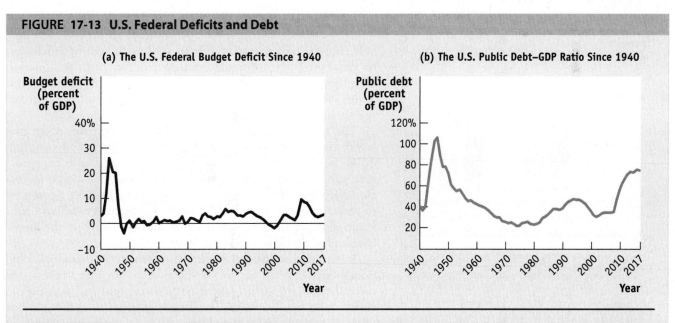

FIGURE 17-13 U.S. Federal Deficits and Debt

Panel (a) shows the U.S. federal budget deficit as a percentage of GDP from 1940 to 2017. The U.S. government ran huge deficits during World War II and has run smaller deficits ever since. Panel (b) shows the U.S. debt–GDP ratio. Comparing panels (a) and (b), you can see that in many years the debt–GDP ratio has declined in spite of government deficits. This seeming paradox reflects the fact that the debt–GDP ratio can fall, even when debt is rising, as long as GDP grows faster than debt.

Data from: Office of Management and Budget; Federal Reserve Bank of St. Louis.

Implicit liabilities are spending promises made by governments that are effectively a debt despite the fact that they are not included in the usual debt statistics.

grows faster than debt. Still, a government that runs persistent *large* deficits will have a rising debt–GDP ratio when debt grows faster than GDP. In the aftermath of the financial crisis of 2008, the U.S. government began running deficits much larger than anything seen since World War II, and the debt–GDP ratio began rising sharply. Similar surges in the debt–GDP ratio could be seen in a number of other countries after 2008. Economists and policy makers agreed that this was not a sustainable trend, that governments would need to get their spending and revenues back in line.

Implicit Liabilities

Looking at Figure 17-13, you might be tempted to conclude that until the 2008 crisis struck, the U.S. federal budget was in fairly decent shape: the return to budget deficits after 2001 caused the debt–GDP ratio to rise a bit, but that ratio was still low compared with both historical experience and some other wealthy countries. In fact, however, experts on long-run budget issues view the situation of the United States (and other countries such as Japan and Italy) with some alarm. The reason is the problem of *implicit liabilities*. **Implicit liabilities** are spending promises made by governments that are effectively a debt despite the fact that they are not included in the usual debt statistics.

The implicit liabilities of the U.S. government arise mainly from transfer programs that are aimed at providing security in retirement and protection from large health care bills:

- Social Security is the main source of retirement income for most older Americans.
- Medicare pays most of older Americans' medical costs.
- Medicaid provides health care to lower-income families.
- The Affordable Care Act subsidizes health insurance premiums for many low-to-moderate income families who are ineligible for Medicaid.

In each of these cases, the government has promised to provide transfer payments to future as well as current beneficiaries. So these programs represent a future debt that must be honored, even though the debt does not currently show up in the usual statistics. Together, these programs currently account for approximately half of federal spending.

The implicit liabilities created by these transfer programs worry fiscal experts. Figure 17-14 shows why. It shows actual 2018 spending on Social Security and major health care programs, measured as a percentage of GDP, together with Congressional Budget Office projections for spending in 2048. According to these projections, spending on Social Security will rise substantially over the next few decades and spending on the major health care programs will soar. Why?

In the case of Social Security, the answer is demography. Social Security is a pay-as-you-go system: current workers pay payroll taxes that fund the benefits of current retirees. So the ratio of the number of retirees drawing benefits to the number of workers paying into Social Security has a major impact on the system's finances.

There was a huge surge in the U.S. birth rate between 1946 and 1964, the years of what is commonly called the *baby boom*. Most baby boomers are currently of working age—which means they are paying taxes, not collecting benefits. But some are

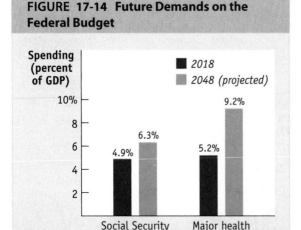

FIGURE 17-14 Future Demands on the Federal Budget

This figure shows actual spending on social insurance programs as a percentage of GDP in 2018 and Congressional Budget Office projections for these same programs in 2048. Partly as a result of an aging population, these programs will become much more expensive over time. But, it is the significant increases in health care spending that will pose the most serious problem for the federal budget in the future.

Data from: Congressional Budget Office.

starting to retire, and as more and more of them do so, they will stop earning taxable income and start collecting benefits.

As a result, the ratio of retirees receiving benefits to workers paying into the Social Security system will rise. In 2018 there were 36 retirees receiving benefits for every 100 workers paying into the system. But, by 2048, according to the Social Security Administration, that number will rise to 45. So as baby boomers move into retirement, benefit payments will continue to rise relative to the size of the economy.

The aging of the baby boomers, by itself, poses only a moderately sized long-run fiscal problem. The projected rise in health care spending is a much more serious concern. These projections also reflect the aging of the population, both because more people will be eligible for Medicare and because older people tend to have higher medical costs. But the main story behind projections of higher health care spending is the long-run tendency of such spending to rise faster than overall spending, for both government-funded and privately funded health care.

To some extent, the implicit liabilities of the U.S. government are already reflected in debt statistics. We mentioned earlier that the government had a total debt of $21.5 trillion at the end of fiscal 2018 but that only $15.8 trillion of that total was owed to the public. The main explanation for that discrepancy is that both Social Security and part of Medicare (the hospital insurance program) are supported by *dedicated taxes:* their expenses are paid out of special taxes on wages. At times, these dedicated taxes yield more revenue than is needed to pay current benefits.

In particular, since the mid-1980s the Social Security system has been taking in more revenue than it currently needs in order to prepare for the retirement of the baby boomers. This surplus in the Social Security system has been used to accumulate a *Social Security trust fund,* which was $2.9 trillion at the end of fiscal 2018.

The money in the trust fund is held in the form of U.S. government bonds, which are included in the $21.5 trillion in total debt. You could say that there's something funny about counting bonds in the Social Security trust fund as part of government debt. After all, these bonds are owed by one part of the government (the government outside the Social Security system) to another part of the government (the Social Security system itself). But the debt corresponds to a real, if implicit, liability: promises by the government to pay future retirement benefits. So many economists argue that the gross debt of $21.5 trillion, the sum of public debt and government debt held by Social Security and other trust funds, is a more accurate indication of the government's fiscal health than the smaller amount owed to the public alone.

>> Check Your Understanding 17-4
Solutions appear at back of book.

1. Explain how each of the following events would affect the public debt or implicit liabilities of the U.S. government, other things equal. Would the public debt or implicit liabilities be greater or smaller?
   a. A higher growth rate of real GDP
   b. Retirees living longer
   c. A decrease in tax revenue
   d. Government borrowing to pay interest on its current public debt
2. Suppose the economy is in a slump and the current public debt is quite large. Explain the trade-off of short-run versus long-run objectives that policy makers face when deciding whether or not to engage in deficit spending.
3. Explain how a contractionary fiscal policy like austerity can make it more likely that a government is unable to pay its debts.

>> Quick Review

• Large and persistent budget deficits lead to increases in **public debt.**

• Public debt that rises year after year can lead to financial pressure and government default. In less extreme cases, it can crowd out investment spending, reducing long-run growth. This suggests that budget deficits in bad **fiscal years** should be offset with budget surpluses in good fiscal years.

• However, if a country has rising GDP, economists believe it may safely run annual deficits as long as the **debt–GDP ratio** is stable or falling because GDP is growing faster than the debt.

• In addition to their official public debt, modern governments have implicit liabilities. The U.S. government has large **implicit liabilities** in the form of Social Security, Medicare, Medicaid, and the Affordable Care Act (ACA). With large implicit liabilities, a stable debt–GDP ratio may give a misleading sense of security.

SOLVED PROBLEM   Mind the Gap

The Congressional Budget Office is an independent federal agency that provides Congress with nonpartisan and timely economic data on budgetary matters. One of its tasks is to produce estimates of GDP and potential GDP and then make projections about recessionary or inflationary gaps. Congress then uses this information to make decisions about the need for expansionary or contractionary fiscal policies. The Congressional Budget Office estimated that actual U.S. GDP was $14.55 trillion and potential GDP was $15.33 trillion for 2008. Knowing this, what was the size of the recessionary gap in 2008? Assuming that the marginal propensity to consume is 0.5, what is the change in government purchases of goods and services necessary to increase GDP by this amount if there are no price changes?

As you have learned, in February 2009 Congress passed the American Recovery and Reinvestment Act that initially provided for a nominal stimulus of $787 billion. By March 2010, only $62 billion of the nominal stimulus had actually been spent. Based on our assumptions above, by how much would this amount of government spending be expected to increase nominal GDP?

STEP | 1 Find the size of the recessionary gap in 2008. *Read pages 486–488.*

As potential GDP is valued in 2008 dollars, the size of the recessionary gap in 2008 dollars was $15.33 trillion – $14.55 trillion = $0.78 trillion, or $780 billion.

STEP | 2 Find the multiplier. *Read pages 481–483.*

The multiplier is equal to $1/(1 - MPC)$, so in this case, the multiplier is $1/(1 - 0.5) = 2$.

STEP | 3 Find the change in government purchases of goods and services necessary to close the gap with a multiplier of 2. *Reread pages 481–483.*

With no price changes and a multiplier of 2, government purchases of goods and services need to increase by $390 billion in order to close a recessionary gap of $780 billion. Without a change in the aggregate price level, a shift of the aggregate demand curve results in an equivalent change in equilibrium GDP. This assumption has the same effect as assuming that the short-run aggregate supply curve is horizontal.

STEP | 4 By how much would $62 billion of government spending be expected to increase nominal GDP? *Use the multiplier from Step 2.*

With a multiplier of 2, $62 billion of government spending would be expected to increase nominal GDP by $124 billion. Through the first half of 2009, the recessionary gap continued to widen, reaching an estimated $1.13 trillion during the second quarter of 2009—larger than the estimated recessionary gap of $780 billion in 2008. During the last half of 2009 and the first quarter of 2010, the recessionary gap began to narrow, but slowly. The gap was still $956 billion at the end of 2011. Stimulus spending in 2009 and the first quarter of 2010 was not enough to quickly and significantly narrow a very wide recessionary gap.

SUMMARY

1. The government plays a large role in the economy, collecting a large share of GDP in taxes and spending a large share both to purchase goods and services and to make transfer payments, largely for **social insurance.** *Fiscal policy* is the use of taxes, government transfers, or government purchases of goods and services to shift the aggregate demand curve.

2. Government purchases of goods and services directly affect aggregate demand, and changes in taxes and government transfers affect aggregate demand indirectly by changing households' disposable income. **Expansionary fiscal policy** shifts the aggregate

demand curve rightward; **contractionary fiscal policy** shifts the aggregate demand curve leftward.

3. Only when the economy is at full employment is there potential for crowding out of private spending and private investment spending by expansionary fiscal policy. The argument that expansionary fiscal policy won't work because of Ricardian equivalence—that consumers will cut back spending today to offset expected future tax increases—appears to be untrue in practice. What is clearly true is that very active fiscal policy may make the economy less stable due to time lags in policy formulation and implementation.

4. Fiscal policy has a multiplier effect on the economy, the size of which depends on the fiscal policy and the **marginal propensity to consume (MPC).** The MPC determines the size of the **multiplier,** the ratio of the total change in real GDP caused by **an autonomous change in aggregate spending** to the size of that autonomous change. Except in the case of **lump-sum taxes,** taxes reduce the size of the multiplier. Expansionary fiscal policy leads to an increase in real GDP, and contractionary fiscal policy leads to a reduction in real GDP. Because part of any change in taxes or transfers is absorbed by savings in the first round of spending, changes in government purchases of goods and services have a more powerful effect on the economy than equal-sized changes in taxes or transfers.

5. Rules governing taxes—with the exception of lump-sum taxes—and some transfers act as **automatic stabilizers,** reducing the size of the multiplier and automatically reducing the size of fluctuations in the business cycle. In contrast, **discretionary fiscal policy** arises from deliberate actions by policy makers rather than from the business cycle.

6. Some of the fluctuations in the budget balance are due to the effects of the business cycle. In order to separate the effects of the business cycle from the effects of discretionary fiscal policy, governments estimate the **cyclically adjusted budget balance,** an estimate of the budget balance if the economy were at potential output.

7. U.S. government budget accounting is calculated on the basis of **fiscal years.** Persistently large budget deficits have long-run consequences because they lead to an increase in **public debt.** As a result, two potential dangers may arise: crowding out, which reduces long-run economic growth, and financial pressure leading to default, which brings economic and financial turmoil.

8. A widely used measure of fiscal health is the **debt–GDP ratio.** This number can remain stable or fall even in the face of persistent budget deficits if GDP rises over time. With large **implicit liabilities,** a stable debt–GDP ratio may give a misleading sense of security. The largest implicit liabilities of the U.S. government come from Social Security, Medicare, Medicaid, and the Affordable Care Act (ACA), the costs of which are increasing due to the aging of the population and rising medical costs.

KEY TERMS

Social insurance, p. 475
Expansionary fiscal policy, p. 476
Contractionary fiscal policy, p. 477
Autonomous change in aggregate spending, p. 482
Multiplier, p. 482

Marginal propensity to consume (MPC), p. 482
Lump-sum taxes, p. 483
Automatic stabilizers, p. 484
Discretionary fiscal policy, p. 484
Cyclically adjusted budget balance, p. 488

Fiscal year, p. 491
Public debt, p. 491
Debt–GDP ratio, p. 493
Implicit liabilities, p. 494

DISCUSSION QUESTIONS

1. Show why a $10 billion reduction in government purchases of goods and services will have a larger effect on real GDP than a $10 billion reduction in government transfers by completing the accompanying table for an economy with a marginal propensity to consume (MPC) of 0.6. The first and second rows of the table are filled in for you: on the left side of the table, in the first row, the $10 billion reduction in government purchases decreases real GDP and disposable income, YD, by $10 billion, leading to a reduction in consumer spending of $6 billion (MPC × change in disposable income) in row 2. However, on the right side of the table, the $10 billion reduction in transfers has no effect on real GDP in round 1 but does lower YD by $10 billion, resulting in a decrease in consumer spending of $6 billion in round 2.

a. When government purchases decrease by $10 billion, what is the sum of the changes in real GDP after the 10 rounds?

b. When the government reduces transfers by $10 billion, what is the sum of the changes in real GDP after the 10 rounds?

c. Using the formula for the multiplier for changes in government purchases and for changes in transfers, calculate the total change in real GDP due to the $10 billion decrease in government purchases and the $10 billion reduction in transfers. What explains the difference? [*Hint:* The multiplier for government purchases of goods and services is $1/(1 - MPC)$. But since each $1 change in government transfers only leads to an initial change in real GDP of $MPC \times \$1$, the multiplier for government transfers is $MPC/(1 - MPC)$.]

Rounds	Decrease in G = −$10 billion (billions of dollars)			Decrease in TR = −$10 billion (billions of dollars)		
	Change in G or C	Change in real GDP	Change in YD	Change in TR or C	Change in real GDP	Change in YD
1	ΔG = −$10.00	−$10.00	−$10.00	ΔTR = −$10.00	−$0.00	−$10.00
2	ΔC = −6.00	−6.00	−6.00	ΔC = −6.00	−6.00	−6.00
3	ΔC = ?	?	?	ΔC = ?	?	?
4	ΔC = ?	?	?	ΔC = ?	?	?
5	ΔC = ?	?	?	ΔC = ?	?	?
6	ΔC = ?	?	?	ΔC = ?	?	?
7	ΔC = ?	?	?	ΔC = ?	?	?
8	ΔC = ?	?	?	ΔC = ?	?	?
9	ΔC = ?	?	?	ΔC = ?	?	?
10	ΔC = ?	?	?	ΔC = ?	?	?

2. The government's budget surplus in Macroland has risen consistently over the past five years. Two government policy makers disagree as to why this has happened. One argues that a rising budget surplus indicates a growing economy; the other argues that it shows that the government is using contractionary fiscal policy. Can you determine which policy maker is correct? If not, why not?

3. Figure 17-10 shows the actual budget deficit and the cyclically adjusted budget deficit as a percentage of GDP in the United States from 1965 to 2018. Assuming that potential output was unchanged, use this figure to determine which of the years from 1990 to 2018 the government used expansionary fiscal policy and in which years it used contractionary fiscal policy.

4. In 2016, the policy makers of the economy of Eastlandia projected the debt–GDP ratio and the ratio of the budget deficit to GDP for the economy for the next 10 years under different scenarios for growth in the government's deficit. Real GDP is currently $1,000 billion per year and is expected to grow by 3% per year, the public debt is $300 billion at the beginning of the year, and the deficit was $30 billion in 2016.

Year	Real GDP (billions of dollars)	Debt (billions of dollars)	Budget deficit (billions of dollars)	Debt (percent of real GDP)	Budget deficit (percent of real GDP)
2016	$1,000	$300	$30	?	?
2017	1,030	?	?	?	?
2018	1,061	?	?	?	?
2019	1,093	?	?	?	?
2020	1,126	?	?	?	?
2021	1,159	?	?	?	?
2022	1,194	?	?	?	?
2023	1,230	?	?	?	?
2024	1,267	?	?	?	?
2025	1,305	?	?	?	?
2026	1,344	?	?	?	?

a. Complete the accompanying table to show the debt–GDP ratio and the ratio of the budget deficit to GDP for the economy if the government's budget deficit remains constant at $30 billion over the next 10 years. (Remember that the government's debt will grow by the previous year's deficit.)

b. Redo the table to show the debt–GDP ratio and the ratio of the budget deficit to GDP for the economy if the government's budget deficit grows by 3% per year over the next 10 years.

c. Redo the table again to show the debt–GDP ratio and the ratio of the budget deficit to GDP for the economy if the government's budget deficit grows by 20% per year over the next 10 years.

d. What happens to the debt–GDP ratio and the ratio of the budget deficit to GDP for the economy over time under the three different scenarios?

5. In which of the following cases does the size of the government's debt and the size of the budget deficit indicate potential problems for the economy?

a. The government's debt is relatively low, but the government is running a large budget deficit as it builds a high-speed rail system to connect the major cities of the nation.

b. The government's debt is relatively high due to a recently ended deficit-financed war, but the government is now running only a small budget deficit.

c. The government's debt is relatively low, but the government is running a budget deficit to finance the interest payments on the debt.

d. The government's debt is relatively high and the government is running a budget deficit to finance new infrastructure spending.

6. How did or would the following affect the current public debt and implicit liabilities of the U.S. government?

a. In 2003, Congress passed and President George W. Bush signed the Medicare Modernization Act, which provides seniors and individuals with disabilities with a prescription drug benefit. Some of the benefits under this law took effect immediately, but other benefits will not begin until sometime in the future.

b. The age at which retired persons can receive full Social Security benefits is raised to age 70 for future retirees.

c. Social Security benefits for future retirees are limited to those with low incomes.

d. Because the cost of health care is increasing faster than the overall inflation rate, annual increases in Social Security benefits are increased by the annual increase in health care costs rather than the overall inflation rate.

e. The Affordable Care Act (ACA), which went into effect in 2014, created incentives for hospitals to find ways to save the government money.

PROBLEMS
interactive activity

1. The accompanying diagram shows the current macroeconomic situation for the economy of Albernia. You have been hired as an economic consultant to help the economy move to potential output, Y_P.

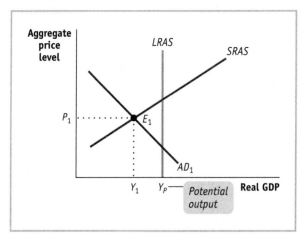

a. Is Albernia facing a recessionary or inflationary gap?

b. Which type of fiscal policy—expansionary or contractionary—would move the economy of Albernia to potential output, Y_P? What are some examples of such policies?

c. Illustrate the macroeconomic situation in Albernia with a diagram after the successful fiscal policy has been implemented.

2. The accompanying diagram shows the current macroeconomic situation for the economy of Brittania; real GDP is Y_1, and the aggregate price level is P_1. You have been hired as an economic consultant to help the economy move to potential output, Y_P.

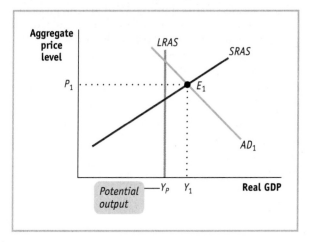

a. Is Brittania facing a recessionary or inflationary gap?

b. Which type of fiscal policy—expansionary or contractionary—would move the economy of Brittania to potential output, Y_P? What are some examples of such policies?

c. Illustrate the macroeconomic situation in Brittania with a diagram after the successful fiscal policy has been implemented.

3. An economy is in long-run macroeconomic equilibrium when each of the following aggregate demand shocks occurs. What kind of gap—inflationary or recessionary—will the economy face after the shock, and what type of fiscal policies would help move the economy back to potential output? How would your recommended fiscal policy shift the aggregate demand curve?

a. A stock market boom increases the value of stocks held by households.

b. Firms come to believe that a recession in the near future is likely.

c. Anticipating the possibility of war, the government increases its purchases of military equipment.

d. The quantity of money in the economy declines and interest rates increase.

4. During a 2008 interview, then German Finance Minister Peer Steinbrück said, "We have to watch out that in Europe and beyond, nothing like a combination of downward economic [growth] and high inflation rates emerges—something that experts call stagflation." Such a situation can be depicted by the movement of the short-run aggregate supply curve from its original position, $SRAS_1$, to its new position, $SRAS_2$, with the new equilibrium point E_2 in the accompanying figure. In this question, we try to understand why stagflation is particularly hard to fix using fiscal policy.

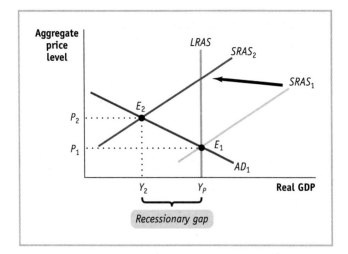

a. What would be the appropriate fiscal policy response to this situation if the primary concern of the government was to maintain economic growth? Illustrate the effect of the policy on the equilibrium point and the aggregate price level using the diagram.

b. What would be the appropriate fiscal policy response to this situation if the primary concern of the government was to maintain price stability? Illustrate the effect of the policy on the equilibrium point and the aggregate price level using the diagram.

c. Discuss the effectiveness of the policies in parts a and b in fighting stagflation.

5. In each of the following cases, either a recessionary or inflationary gap exists. Assume that the aggregate supply curve is horizontal, so that the change in real GDP arising from a shift of the aggregate demand curve equals the size of the shift of the curve. Calculate both the change in government purchases of goods and services and the change in government transfers necessary to close the gap.

a. Real GDP equals $100 billion, potential output equals $160 billion, and the marginal propensity to consume is 0.75.

b. Real GDP equals $250 billion, potential output equals $200 billion, and the marginal propensity to consume is 0.5.

c. Real GDP equals $180 billion, potential output equals $100 billion, and the marginal propensity to consume is 0.8.

6. Most macroeconomists believe it is a good thing that taxes act as automatic stabilizers and lower the size of the multiplier. However, a smaller multiplier means that the change in government purchases of goods and services, government transfers, or taxes needed to close an inflationary or recessionary gap is larger. How can you explain this apparent inconsistency?

7. You are an economic adviser to a candidate for national office. She asks you for a summary of the economic consequences of a balanced-budget rule for the federal government and for your recommendation on whether she should support such a rule. How do you respond?

8. Your study partner argues that the distinction between the government's budget deficit and debt is similar to the distinction between consumer savings and wealth. He also argues that if you have large budget deficits, you must have a large debt. In what ways is your study partner correct and in what ways is he incorrect?

9. Access the Discovering Data exercise for Chapter 17 online to answer these questions.

a. Which of these six countries—the United States, France, Italy, Greece, Germany, and the United Kingdom—had the largest amount of government debt as a percent of GDP as of 2015? Which had the smallest?

b. Calculate the percentage change in government debt from 2007 through 2015 for the same six countries. Which country experienced the largest percentage increase in government debt from 2007 through 2015? Which experienced the smallest?

c. Using the six countries as a reference point, what conclusions can you draw about the relationship between government debt and economic growth?

10. Unlike households, governments are often able to sustain large debts. For example, in 2016, the U.S. government's total debt reached $19.5 trillion, approximately equal to 106.1% of GDP. At the time, according to the U.S. Treasury, the average interest rate paid by the government on its debt was 1.3%. However, running budget deficits becomes hard when very large debts are outstanding.

a. Calculate the dollar cost of the annual interest on the government's total debt assuming the interest rate and debt figures cited above.

b. If the government operates on a balanced budget before interest payments are taken into account, at what rate must GDP grow in order for the debt–GDP ratio to remain unchanged?

c. Calculate the total increase in national debt if the government incurs a deficit of $600 billion in 2017.

d. At what rate would nominal GDP have to grow in order for the debt–GDP ratio to remain unchanged when the deficit in 2017 is $600 billion?

e. Why is the debt–GDP ratio the preferred measure of a country's debt rather than the dollar value of the debt? Why is it important for a government to keep this number under control?

WORK IT OUT Interactive step-by-step help with solving this problem can be found online.

11. The accompanying table shows how consumers' marginal propensities to consume in a particular economy are related to their level of income.

Income range	Marginal propensity to consume
$0–$20,000	0.9
$20,001–$40,000	0.8
$40,001–$60,000	0.7
$60,001–$80,000	0.6
Above $80,000	0.5

a. Suppose the government engages in increased purchases of goods and services. For each of the income groups in the table, what is the value of the multiplier—that is, what is the "bang for the buck" from each dollar the government spends on government purchases of goods and services in each income group?

b. If the government needed to close a recessionary or inflationary gap, at which group should it primarily aim its fiscal policy of changes in government purchases of goods and services?

18 | Money, Banking, and the Federal Reserve System

"THE PRODUCT IS CAREFULLY CREATED in rural facilities throughout the Peruvian countryside using cheap labor, then hoarded in stash houses controlled by violent gangs in Lima. Once there, the goods are packed into parcels, loaded onto planes or hidden inside luggage, pottery, hollowed-out Bibles, sneakers, children's toys or massive shipping containers bound for major U.S. ports of entry, such as Miami." So began a 2016 *Washington Post* report on Operation Sunset, a huge raid carried out by Peruvian authorities in cooperation with the U.S. Secret Service. But what was the target of this raid? It wasn't a drug bust; it was a fake money bust.

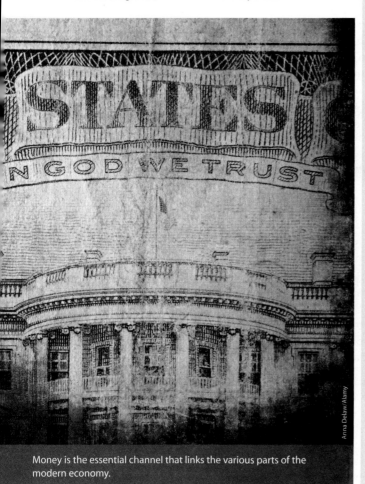

Anna Delaw/Alamy

Money is the essential channel that links the various parts of the modern economy.

In recent years, Peru has become a major source for the production of counterfeit U.S. currency; the so-called "Peruvian note" is considered to be the best counterfeit in the business. Workers employed by criminal syndicates meticulously add decorative details to printed bills by hand, creating high-quality fakes that are very hard to detect.

The funny thing is that elaborately decorated pieces of paper have little or no intrinsic value. Indeed, a $100 bill printed with blue or orange ink wouldn't be worth the paper it was printed on.

But if the ink on that piece of paper is just the right shade of green, people will think that it's *money* and will accept it as payment for very real goods and services. Why? Because they believe, correctly, that they can do the same thing: exchange that piece of green paper for real goods and services.

In fact, here's a riddle: If a fake $100 bill from Peru enters the United States and is successfully exchanged for a good or service with nobody ever realizing it's a fake, who gets hurt? Accepting a fake $100 bill isn't like buying a car that turns out to be a lemon or a meal that turns out to be inedible. As long as the bill's counterfeit nature remains undiscovered, it will pass from hand to hand just like a real $100 bill.

The answer to the riddle is that the actual victims of the counterfeiting are U.S. taxpayers, because counterfeit dollars reduce the revenues available to pay for the operations of the U.S. government. Accordingly, the Secret Service diligently monitors the integrity of U.S. currency, promptly investigating any reports of counterfeit dollars. The efforts of the Secret Service attest to the fact that money isn't like ordinary goods and services, and it certainly is not like a piece of colored paper.

In this chapter we'll look at what money is, the role that it plays, the workings of a modern monetary system, and the institutions that sustain and regulate it, including the *Federal Reserve*. ●

WHAT YOU WILL LEARN

- What are the various roles that **money** plays and what forms does it take?
- Why is the level of the **money supply** so important to the state of the economy?
- How do the actions of private banks and the Federal Reserve determine the money supply?
- How does the Federal Reserve use **open-market operations** to change the **monetary base**?

Money is any asset that can easily be used to purchase goods and services.

Currency in circulation is cash held by the public.

Checkable bank deposits are bank accounts that can be accessed using checks, debit cards, and digital payments.

The **money supply** is the total value of financial assets in the economy that are considered money.

Without a liquid asset like money, making purchases would be much harder.

The Meaning of Money

In everyday conversation, people often use the word *money* to mean wealth. If you ask, "How much money does Bill Gates, the founder of Microsoft, have?" the answer will be something like, "Oh, $80 billion or so, but who's counting?" That is, the number will include the value of the stocks, bonds, real estate, and other assets he owns.

But the economist's definition of money doesn't include all forms of wealth. The dollar bills in your wallet are money; other forms of wealth—such as stocks, bonds, and real estate—aren't money. What, according to economists, distinguishes money from other forms of wealth?

What Is Money?

Money is defined in terms of what it does: **money** is any asset that can easily be used to purchase goods and services. An asset is *liquid* if it can easily be converted into cash. Money consists of cash itself, which is liquid by definition, as well as other assets that are highly liquid.

You can see the distinction between money and other assets by asking yourself how you pay for your morning jolt of java. The person at the register will accept dollar bills in return for a double mocha latte—but he or she likely won't accept stock certificates or a collection of vintage baseball cards. If you want to convert stock certificates or vintage baseball cards into a latte, you have to sell them—trade them for money—and then use the money to buy your drink.

Of course, the vast majority of stores allow you to buy goods with a debit card linked to your bank account, and many of us pay larger bills (like tuition) with checks written on our accounts. Does that make your bank account money, even if you haven't converted it into cash? Yes. **Currency in circulation**—actual cash in the hands of the public—is considered money. So are **checkable bank deposits**—bank accounts that can be accessed using checks, debit cards, and digital payments.

Some definitions of money include assets other than currency and checkable bank deposits. There are two widely used definitions of the **money supply,** the total value of financial assets in the economy that are considered money.

1. The narrower definition of money considers only the most liquid assets to be money: currency in circulation, checkable bank deposits, and traveler's checks. (Once popular, traveler's checks are rarely used now, but they are still included in the Fed's definition of the money supply.)

2. The broader definition includes the three categories just noted plus other assets that are "almost" checkable, such as savings account deposits that can easily be transferred into a checking account with a phone call or a few taps on a smartphone. Both definitions of the money supply, however, make a distinction between those assets that can easily be used to purchase goods and services and those that can't.

Money plays a crucial role in generating *gains from trade* because it makes indirect exchange possible. Think of what happens when a cardiac surgeon buys a new refrigerator. The surgeon has valuable services to offer—namely, heart operations. The owner of the store has valuable goods to offer—refrigerators and other appliances. It would be extremely difficult for both parties if, instead of using money, they had to directly barter the goods and services they sell. In a barter system, a cardiac surgeon and an appliance store owner could trade only if the store owner happened to want a heart operation and the surgeon happened to want a new refrigerator.

This is known as the problem of finding a *double coincidence of wants:* in a barter system, two parties can trade only when each wants what the other has to offer.

Money solves this problem: individuals can trade what they have to offer for money and trade money for what they want.

Because the ability to make transactions with money rather than relying on bartering makes it easier to achieve gains from trade, the existence of money increases welfare, even though money does not directly produce anything.

Let's take a closer look at the roles money plays in the economy.

Roles of Money

Money plays three main roles in any modern economy: it is a *medium of exchange,* a *store of value,* and a *unit of account.*

1. Medium of Exchange Our cardiac surgeon/refrigerator example illustrates the role of money as a **medium of exchange**—an asset that individuals use to trade for goods and services rather than for consumption. People can't eat dollar bills; rather, they use dollar bills to trade for goods and services.

In normal times, the official money of a given country—the dollar in the United States, the peso in Mexico, and so on—is also the medium of exchange in virtually all transactions in that country. During troubled economic times, however, other goods or assets often play that role instead. For example, during economic turmoil people often turn to other countries' moneys as the medium of exchange: U.S. dollars have played this role in troubled Latin American countries, as have euros in troubled Eastern European countries. In a famous example, cigarettes functioned as the medium of exchange in World War II prisoner-of-war camps: even nonsmokers traded goods and services for cigarettes because the cigarettes could in turn be easily traded for other items. Inmates at federal penitentiaries, where smoking is now banned, reportedly use canned mackerel for many transactions. During the extreme German inflation of 1923, goods such as eggs and lumps of coal became, briefly, mediums of exchange.

2. Store of Value To act as a medium of exchange, money must also be a **store of value**—a means of holding purchasing power over time. To see why this is necessary, imagine trying to operate an economy in which ice-cream cones were the medium of exchange. Such an economy would quickly suffer from, well,

> A **medium of exchange** is an asset that individuals acquire for the purpose of trading goods and services rather than for their own consumption.
>
> A **store of value** is a means of holding purchasing power over time.

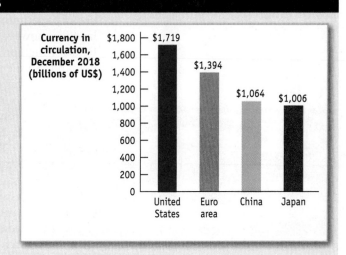

GLOBAL COMPARISON   THE BIG MONEYS

Americans tend to think of the dollar as the world's leading currency—and it does remain the currency most likely to be accepted in payment around the globe. But there are other important currencies, too. One simple measure of a currency's importance is the value of the quantity of that currency in circulation. This figure shows the value, in billions of dollars, of the quantity of four major currencies in circulation as of December 2018. The euro, used by a group of countries whose combined economies are roughly comparable in size to America's, is used almost as often as the dollar. China, with its rapidly growing economy, has a currency (the yuan) that isn't far behind the euro. And Japan's yen isn't far behind the big three, despite its much smaller economy, largely because the Japanese make much more use of cash, as opposed to checks, credit cards, or debit cards, than either Europeans or Americans.

Data from: Federal Reserve Bank of St. Louis; European Central Bank; Bank of Japan; The People's Bank of China.

A **unit of account** is a measure used to set prices and make economic calculations.

Commodity money is a good used as a medium of exchange that has intrinsic value in other uses.

Commodity-backed money is a medium of exchange with no intrinsic value but whose ultimate value is guaranteed by a promise that it can be converted into valuable goods.

monetary meltdown: your medium of exchange would often turn into a sticky puddle before you could use it to buy something else. Of course, money is by no means the only store of value. Any asset that holds its purchasing power over time is a store of value. So the store-of-value role is a necessary but not distinctive feature of money.

3. Unit of Account Finally, money normally serves as the **unit of account**—the commonly accepted measure individuals use to set prices and make economic calculations. To understand the importance of this role, consider a historical fact: during the Middle Ages, peasants typically were required to provide landowners with goods and labor rather than money. A peasant might, for example, be required to work on the lord's land one day a week and hand over one-fifth of his harvest.

Today, rents, like other prices, are almost always specified in money terms. That makes things much clearer: imagine how hard it would be to decide which apartment to rent if modern landlords followed medieval practice. Suppose, for example, that Mr. Smith says he'll let you have a place if you clean his house twice a week and bring him a pound of steak every day, whereas Ms. Jones wants you to clean her house just once a week but wants four pounds of chicken every day. Who's offering the better deal? It's hard to say. If, instead, Smith wants $600 a month and Jones wants $700, the comparison is easy. In other words, without a commonly accepted measure, the terms of a transaction are harder to determine, making it more difficult to make transactions and achieve gains from trade.

Goods with value, like gold and silver, were used as a medium of exchange for centuries.

Types of Money

In some form or another, money has been in use for thousands of years. For most of that period, people used **commodity money:** the medium of exchange was a good, normally gold or silver, that had intrinsic value in other uses. These alternative uses gave commodity money value independent of its role as a medium of exchange. For example, cigarettes, which served as money in World War II prisoner-of-war camps, were also valuable because many prisoners smoked. Gold was valuable because it was used for jewelry and ornamentation, aside from the fact that it was minted into coins.

By 1776, the year in which the United States declared independence and Adam Smith published *The Wealth of Nations,* there was widespread use of paper money in addition to gold or silver coins. Unlike modern dollar bills, however, this paper money consisted of notes issued by private banks, which promised to exchange their notes for gold or silver coins on demand. So the paper currency that initially replaced commodity money was **commodity-backed money,** a medium of exchange with no intrinsic value whose ultimate value was guaranteed by a promise that it could always be converted into valuable goods on demand.

The big advantage of commodity-backed money over simple commodity money, like gold and silver coins, was that it tied up fewer valuable resources. Although a note-issuing bank still had to keep some gold and silver on hand, it had to keep only enough to satisfy demands for redemption of its notes. And it could rely on the fact that on a normal day only a fraction of its paper notes would be redeemed. So the bank needed to keep only a portion of the total value of its notes in circulation in the form of gold and

By issuing paper notes to function as money instead of gold and silver coins, banks were able to free up valuable resources.

silver in its vaults. It could then lend out the remaining gold and silver to those who wished to use it. This allowed society to use the remaining gold and silver for other purposes, all with no loss in the ability to achieve gains from trade.

In a famous passage in *The Wealth of Nations*, Adam Smith described paper money as a "waggon-way through the air." Smith was making an analogy between money and an imaginary highway that did not absorb valuable land beneath it. An actual highway provides a useful service but at a cost: land that could be used to grow crops is instead paved over. If the highway could be built through the air, it wouldn't destroy useful land. As Smith understood, when banks replaced gold and silver money with paper notes, they accomplished a similar feat: they reduced the amount of real resources used by society to provide the functions of money.

At this point you may ask: why make any use at all of gold and silver in the monetary system, even to back paper money? In fact, today's monetary system goes even further than the system Smith admired, having eliminated any role for gold and silver. A U.S. dollar bill isn't commodity money, and it isn't even commodity-backed. Rather, its value arises entirely from the fact that it is generally accepted as a means of payment, a role that is ultimately decreed by the U.S. government. Money whose value derives entirely from its official status as a means of exchange is known as **fiat money** because it exists by government fiat, a historical term for a policy declared by a ruler.

Fiat money has two major advantages over commodity-backed money. First, it is even more of a "waggon-way through the air"—creating it doesn't use up any real resources beyond the paper it's printed on. Second, the supply of money can be adjusted based on the needs of the economy, instead of being determined by the amount of gold and silver that prospectors happen to discover.

Fiat money, though, poses some risks. In the opening story, we described one such risk—counterfeiting. Counterfeiters usurp a privilege of the U.S. government, which has the sole legal right to print dollar bills. And the benefit that counterfeiters get by exchanging fake bills for real goods and services comes at the expense of the U.S. federal government, which covers a small but nontrivial part of its own expenses by issuing new currency to meet a growing demand for money. Another larger risk is that governments that can create money whenever they feel like it will be tempted to abuse the privilege.

A Short History of the Dollar   U.S. dollar bills are pure fiat money: they have no intrinsic value, and they are not backed by anything that does. But American money wasn't always like that. In the early days of European settlement, the colonies that would become the United States used commodity money, partly consisting of gold and silver coins minted in Europe. But because such coins were scarce on this side of the Atlantic, the colonists relied on a variety of other forms of commodity money. For example, settlers in Virginia used tobacco as money and settlers in the Northeast used *wampum*, made from a clamshell.

Later in American history, commodity-backed paper money came into widespread use. But this wasn't paper money as we now know it, issued by the U.S. government and bearing the signature of the Secretary of the Treasury. Before the Civil War, the U.S. government didn't issue any paper money. Instead, dollar bills were issued by private banks, which promised that their bills could be redeemed for gold or silver coins on demand. These promises weren't always credible because banks sometimes failed, leaving holders of their bills with worthless pieces

> **Fiat money** is a medium of exchange whose value derives entirely from its official status as a means of payment.

Not until the Civil War did the U.S. government issue official paper money.

A **monetary aggregate** is an overall measure of the money supply.

Near-moneys are financial assets that can't be directly used as a medium of exchange but can be readily converted into cash or checkable bank deposits.

of paper. Understandably, people were reluctant to accept currency from any bank rumored to be in financial trouble. In this private money system, some dollars were less valuable than others.

A curious legacy of that time was notes issued by the Citizens' Bank of Louisiana, based in New Orleans, that became among the most widely used bank notes in the southern states. These notes were printed in English on one side and French on the other. (At the time, many people in New Orleans, originally a colony of France, spoke French.) Thus, the $10 bill read *Ten* on one side and *Dix*, the French word for *ten*, on the other. These $10 bills became known as *dixies*, probably the source of the nickname of the U.S. South.

The U.S. government began issuing official paper money, called *greenbacks*, in 1862 as a way to pay for the ongoing Civil War. At first greenbacks had no fixed value in terms of commodities. After 1873, the U.S. government guaranteed the value of a dollar in terms of gold, effectively turning dollars into commodity-backed money.

In 1933, when President Franklin D. Roosevelt broke the link between dollars and gold, his own federal budget director—who feared that the public would lose confidence in the dollar if it wasn't ultimately backed by gold—declared ominously, "This will be the end of Western civilization." It wasn't. The link between the dollar and gold was restored a few years later, then dropped again—seemingly for good—in August 1971. Despite the warnings of doom, the U.S. dollar went on to become the world's most widely used currency.

Measuring the Money Supply

The Federal Reserve calculates the size of two **monetary aggregates,** overall measures of the money supply, which differ in how strictly money is defined. The two aggregates are known, rather cryptically, as M1 and M2. (There used to be a third aggregate named—you guessed it—M3, but in 2006 the Federal Reserve stopped measuring it, determining that it was no longer useful.)

M1, the narrowest definition, contains only currency in circulation (also known as cash), checkable bank deposits, and traveler's checks. M2 adds several other kinds of assets, often referred to as **near-moneys**—financial assets that aren't directly usable as a medium of exchange but can be readily converted into cash or checkable bank deposits, such as savings accounts. Examples are time deposits such as small-denomination *certificates of deposit (CDs)*, which aren't checkable but can be withdrawn at any time before their maturity date by paying a penalty. Because currency and checkable deposits are directly usable as a medium of exchange, M1 is the most liquid measure of money.

Figure 18-1 shows the actual composition of M1 and M2 as of February 2018, in billions of dollars. M1 was valued at $3,614.1 billion, with about 43% accounted for by currency in circulation, almost all the rest accounted for by checkable bank deposits, and a tiny slice accounted for by traveler's checks. In turn, M1 made up 26% of M2, valued at $13,858.4 billion. M2 consists of M1 plus other types of assets: two types of bank deposits, known as savings deposits and time deposits,

---

PITFALLS

WHAT'S NOT IN THE MONEY SUPPLY

Financial assets like stocks and bonds are not part of the money supply under any definition because they're not liquid enough.

M1 consists, roughly speaking, of assets you can use to buy groceries or a cup of coffee: currency, checkable deposits, and traveler's checks. M2 is broader, because it includes things like savings accounts that can easily and quickly be converted into M1. For example, you can switch funds between your savings and checking accounts at an ATM or using your smartphone.

By contrast, converting a stock or a bond into cash requires selling the stock or bond—something that usually takes some time and involves paying a broker's fee. That makes these assets much less liquid than bank deposits. So stocks and bonds, unlike bank deposits, aren't considered money.

FIGURE 18-1   Monetary Aggregates, February 2018

The Federal Reserve uses two definitions of the money supply, M1 and M2. As panel (a) shows, more than half of M1 consists of checkable bank deposits with currency in circulation making up virtually all of the rest. M2, as panel (b) shows, has a much broader definition: it includes M1 plus a range of other deposits and deposit-like assets, making it almost four times as large. (Numbers may not add to 100% due to rounding.)

Data from: Federal Reserve Bank of St. Louis.

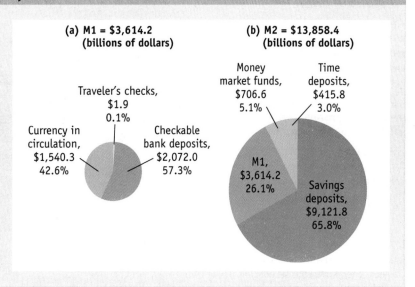

(a) M1 = $3,614.2
(billions of dollars)

Traveler's checks, $1.9 0.1%

Currency in circulation, $1,540.3 42.6%

Checkable bank deposits, $2,072.0 57.3%

(b) M2 = $13,858.4
(billions of dollars)

Money market funds, $706.6 5.1%

Time deposits, $415.8 3.0%

M1, $3,614.2 26.1%

Savings deposits, $9,121.8 65.8%

both of which are considered noncheckable, plus money market funds, which are mutual funds that invest only in liquid assets and bear a close resemblance to bank deposits. These near-moneys pay interest, although cash (currency in circulation) does not, and they typically pay higher interest rates than any offered on checkable bank deposits.

ECONOMICS >> *in Action*
From Bucks to Bitcoin

There is $1.7 trillion of currency in circulation in the United States, more than $5,000 for every man, woman, and child. Most individuals don't carry this amount in their wallets. So where is all the cash?

Much of it can be found in cash registers. Businesses as well as individuals need to hold cash. However, the largest proportion of these huge currency holdings—approximately 60%—is in the hands of foreign residents who so distrust their national currencies that the U.S. dollar has become a widely accepted medium of exchange and store of value.

Cash is also widely used to keep transactions hidden—by criminals such as drug dealers, or businesspeople looking to avoid paying taxes on their income.

The desire to shield transactions from the eyes of authorities helps to explain the growth of Bitcoin, a virtual currency created in 2009. It is basically a computing algorithm that creates electronic tokens that are accepted by some as currency.

But what leads people to place faith in a virtual currency—to accept it in place of "real" money? As with the dollar, faith in Bitcoin arose from the belief that someone else, at a later date, would accept it in exchange for something real. As long as there are people who want to hide transactions, that's not an unreasonable belief. Bitcoin has become increasingly popular as merchants have started to accept it to avoid credit card fees.

One drawback to Bitcoin is its susceptibility to hacking. Despite that, the attractions of Bitcoin, and another new virtual currency, Ethereum, are so great that their combined value in December 2018 was approximately $76 billion.

>> Quick Review

• **Money** is any asset that can easily be used to purchase goods and services. **Currency in circulation** and **checkable bank deposits** are both part of the **money supply.**

• Money plays three roles: a **medium of exchange,** a **store of value,** and a **unit of account.**

• Historically, money took the form first of **commodity money,** then of **commodity-backed money.** Today the dollar is pure **fiat money.**

• The money supply is measured by two **monetary aggregates:** M1 and M2. M1 consists of currency in circulation, checkable bank deposits, and traveler's checks. M2 consists of M1 plus various kinds of **near-moneys.**

>> Check Your Understanding 18-1
Solutions appear at back of book.

1. Suppose you hold a gift card, good for certain products at participating stores. Is this gift card money? Why or why not?

2. Although most bank accounts pay some interest, depositors can get a higher interest rate by buying a certificate of deposit, or CD. The difference between a CD and a checking account is that the depositor pays a penalty for withdrawing the money before the CD comes due—a period of months or even years. Small CDs are counted in M2 but not in M1. Explain why they are not part of M1.

3. Explain why a system of commodity-backed money uses resources more efficiently than a system of commodity money.

The Monetary Role of Banks

Roughly 43% of M1, the narrowest definition of the money supply, consists of currency in circulation—$1 bills, $5 bills, and so on. It's obvious where currency comes from: it's printed by the U.S. Treasury. But the rest of M1 consists of checkable bank deposits; savings deposits account for the great bulk of M2, the broader definition of the money supply. By either measure, then, bank deposits are a major component of the money supply. And this fact brings us to our next topic: the monetary role of banks.

What Banks Do

A bank is a *financial intermediary* that uses liquid assets, in the form of bank deposits, to finance the illiquid investments of borrowers. Banks can create liquidity because they don't need to keep all of the funds deposited with it in the form of highly liquid assets. Except in the case of a *bank run*—which we'll get to shortly—all of a bank's depositors won't want to withdraw their funds at the same time. So a bank can provide its depositors with liquid assets yet still invest much of the depositors' funds in illiquid assets, such as mortgages and business loans.

Banks can't, however, lend out all the funds placed in their hands by depositors because they have to satisfy any depositor who wants to withdraw his or her funds. In order to meet these demands, a bank must keep substantial quantities of liquid assets on hand. In the modern U.S. banking system, these assets take the form either of currency in the bank's vault or deposits held in the bank's own account at the Federal Reserve. As we'll see shortly, the latter can be converted into currency more or less instantly. Currency in bank vaults and bank deposits held at the Federal Reserve are called **bank reserves.** Because bank reserves are in bank vaults and at the Federal Reserve, not held by the public, they are not part of currency in circulation.

To understand the role of banks in determining the money supply, we start by introducing a simple tool for analyzing the financial position of a bank or business: a **T-account.** A T-account summarizes the financial position of a bank or business in a single table by showing assets on the left and liabilities on the right.

Figure 18-2 shows the T-account for a hypothetical business that *isn't* a bank—Samantha's Smoothies. According to Figure 18-2, Samantha's Smoothies owns a building worth $30,000 and has $15,000 worth of smoothie-making business equipment. These are assets, so they're on the left side of the table. To finance its opening, the business borrowed $20,000 from a local bank. That's a liability, so the loan is on the right side of the table. By looking at the T-account, you can immediately see what Samantha's Smoothies owns and what it owes. Oh, and it's called a T-account because the lines in the table make a T-shape.

Bank reserves are the currency banks hold in their vaults plus their deposits at the Federal Reserve.

A **T-account** is a tool for analyzing a business's financial position by showing, in a single table, the business's assets (on the left) and liabilities (on the right).

FIGURE 18-2 A T-Account for Samantha's Smoothies

A T-account summarizes a business's financial position. Its assets, in this case consisting of a building and some smoothie-making machinery, are on the left side. Its liabilities, consisting of the money it owes to a local bank, are on the right side.

Assets		Liabilities	
Building	$30,000	Loan from bank	$20,000
Smoothie-making machines	$15,000		

Samantha's Smoothies is an ordinary, nonbank business. Now let's look at the T-account for a hypothetical bank, First Street Bank, which is the repository of $1 million in bank deposits. Figure 18-3 shows First Street Bank's financial position. The loans First Street Bank has made are on the left side because they're assets: they represent funds that borrowers are expected to repay. The bank's only other assets, in this example, are its reserves, which can take the form of either cash in the bank's vault or deposits at the Federal Reserve. On the right side are the bank's liabilities, which in this example consist entirely of deposits made by customers at First Street Bank. These are liabilities of the bank because they represent funds that must ultimately be repaid to depositors.

Notice that in this example First Street Bank's assets are larger than its liabilities. And that's the way it is supposed to be. Banks are required by law to maintain assets that are larger, by a specific percentage, than their liabilities.

We will assume that First Street Bank holds reserves equal to 10% of its customers' bank deposits. The fraction of bank deposits that a bank holds as reserves is its **reserve ratio.** In the modern American system, the Federal Reserve—which, among other things, regulates banks operating in the United States—sets a minimum required reserve ratio that banks must maintain. To understand why banks are regulated in this way, let's consider a problem banks can face: bank runs.

The Problem of Bank Runs

A bank can lend out most of the funds deposited in its care because in normal times only a small fraction of its depositors want to withdraw their funds on any given day. But what would happen if, for some reason, all or at least a large fraction of its depositors tried to withdraw their funds during a short period of time, such as over a couple of days? If a significant share of its depositors demanded their money back at the same time, the bank wouldn't be able to raise enough cash to meet those demands. The reason for this cash shortfall is that banks convert most of their depositors' funds into loans made to borrowers. That's how banks earn revenue—by charging interest on loans. And bank loans are illiquid: they can't easily be converted into cash on short notice.

To see why, imagine that First Street Bank has lent $100,000 to Drive-a-Peach Used Cars, a local dealership. To raise cash to meet demands for withdrawals, First Street Bank can sell its loan to Drive-a-Peach to someone else—another bank

The **reserve ratio** is the fraction of bank deposits that a bank holds as reserves.

FIGURE 18-3 Assets and Liabilities of First Street Bank

First Street Bank's assets consist of $1,200,000 in loans and $100,000 in reserves. Its liabilities consist of $1,000,000 in deposits—money owed to people who have placed funds in First Street's hands.

Assets		Liabilities	
Loans	$1,200,000	Deposits	$1,000,000
Reserves	$100,000		

A **bank run** is a phenomenon in which many of a bank's depositors try to withdraw their funds due to fears of a bank failure.

Deposit insurance guarantees that a bank's depositors will be paid even if the bank can't come up with the funds, up to a maximum amount per account.

or an individual investor. But if First Street Bank tries to sell the loan quickly, potential buyers will be wary: they will suspect that First Street Bank wants to sell the loan because there is something wrong and the loan might not be repaid. As a result, First Street Bank can sell the loan quickly only by offering it for sale at a deep discount—say, a discount of 40%, for a sale price of $60,000.

The upshot is that if a significant number of First Street Bank's depositors suddenly decided to withdraw their funds, the bank's efforts to raise the necessary cash quickly would force it to sell off its assets very cheaply. Inevitably, this leads to a *bank failure:* the bank would be unable to pay off its depositors in full because its liabilities exceed its assets.

What might start this whole process? That is, what could lead First Street Bank's depositors to rush to pull their money out? A plausible answer is a spreading rumor that the bank is in financial trouble. Even if depositors aren't sure the rumor is true, they are likely to play it safe and get their money out while they still can. And it gets worse: a depositor who simply thinks that *other* depositors are going to panic and try to get their money out will realize that this could "break the bank." So he or she joins the rush. In other words, fear about a bank's financial condition can be a self-fulfilling prophecy: depositors who believe that other depositors will rush to the exit will rush to the exit themselves.

A **bank run,** then, is a phenomenon in which many of a bank's depositors try to withdraw their funds due to fears of a bank failure. Moreover, bank runs aren't bad only for the bank in question and its depositors. Historically, they have often proved contagious, with a run on one bank leading to a loss of faith in other banks, causing additional bank runs.

The upcoming Economics in Action describes an actual case of just such a contagion, the wave of bank runs that swept across the United States in the early 1930s. In response to that experience and similar experiences in other countries, the United States and most other modern governments established a system of bank regulations that protect depositors and prevent most bank runs.

Bank Regulation

Should you worry about losing money in the United States due to a bank run? As long as it's a conventional bank, the answer is no. After the banking crises of the 1930s, the United States and most other countries put into place a system designed to protect depositors and the economy as a whole against bank runs. This system has four main features: *deposit insurance, capital requirements,* and *reserve requirements.* In addition, banks have access to the *discount window,* a source of cash when it's needed.

1. Deposit Insurance Almost all banks in the United States advertise themselves as a "member of the FDIC"—the Federal Deposit Insurance Corporation. The FDIC provides **deposit insurance,** a guarantee that depositors will be paid from FDIC funds, even if the bank is unable to satisfy withdrawals, up to a maximum amount per account. The FDIC currently guarantees the first $250,000 per depositor, per insured bank.

It is worth noting that deposit insurance doesn't just protect depositors if a bank fails. It also greatly reduces the potential for bank failures from bank runs by eliminating the main reason for bank runs: since depositors know their funds are safe if a bank should fail, they have no incentive to rush to withdraw their accounts because of a rumor that the bank is in trouble.

2. Capital Requirements Although deposit insurance protects the banking system against bank runs, it creates a well-known incentive problem. Because depositors are protected from loss, they have no incentive to monitor their bank's financial health, allowing risky behavior by the bank to go undetected. At the same time, the owners of banks have an incentive to engage in overly risky investment behavior, such as making questionable loans at high interest rates. That's because if all goes well, the owners profit; if things go badly, the government covers the losses through federal deposit insurance.

To reduce the incentive for excessive risk taking, regulators require that bank owners hold substantially more assets than the value of bank deposits. That way, the bank still has assets larger than its deposits even if some of its loans go bad, and losses will accrue against the bank's assets, not the government. The excess of a bank's assets over its bank deposits and other liabilities is called the *bank's capital*. Bank capital is sometimes referred to as the bank's *net worth* or *owner's equity*. For example, First Street Bank has capital of $300,000, equal to ($1,200,000 + $100,0000) − $1,000,000. This is equivalent to $300,000/($1,200,000 + $100,000) = 23% of the total value of its assets. In practice, banks' capital is required to equal at least 7% of the value of their assets.

3. Reserve Requirements Another regulation used to reduce the risk of bank runs is **reserve requirements,** rules set by the Federal Reserve that specify the minimum reserve ratio for banks. For example, in the United States, the minimum reserve ratio for checkable bank deposits is 10%.

4. The Discount Window One final protection against bank runs is the fact that the Federal Reserve, which we discuss more thoroughly later in this chapter, stands ready to lend money to banks in trouble, an arrangement known as the **discount window.** The ability to borrow money means a bank can avoid being forced to sell its assets at fire-sale prices in order to satisfy the demands of a sudden rush of depositors demanding cash. Instead, it can turn to the Fed and borrow the funds it needs to pay off depositors.

Limits to Regulation's Reach: Shadow Banking The modern U.S. banking system is well-protected against old-fashioned bank runs. Unfortunately, as many investors learned to their horror in 2008, although old-fashioned bank runs may be a thing of the past, new-fashioned bank runs—which look very different but have many of the same effects—can still happen.

The reason is the rise of shadow banking, a variety of financial arrangements that aren't exactly banking in the traditional sense, but serve more or less the same purposes as conventional banking. These arrangements are undertaken by nondepository financial firms, including investment banks, insurance companies, hedge fund companies, and money market fund companies. Because they don't accept deposits, firms in the shadow banking sector aren't fully covered by the protections or regulations that have made conventional, depository banking so safe. We'll say more about shadow banking later in the chapter.

ECONOMICS >> *in Action*
It's a Wonderful Banking System

For many in the generation that lived through the Great Depression, memories of bank runs, with fearful depositors rushing to reclaim their funds, were vivid and long lasting. There was a wave of bank runs in late 1930, a second wave in the spring of 1931, and a third wave in early 1933. By the end, more than a third of the nation's banks had failed. To bring the panic to an end, on March 6, 1933, the newly inaugurated president, Franklin Delano Roosevelt, declared a national *bank holiday,* closing all banks for a week to give bank regulators time to close unhealthy banks and certify healthy ones.

Since then, regulation has protected the United States and other wealthy countries against most bank runs. But recent decades have seen several waves of bank runs in developing countries. For example, bank runs played a role in

Reserve requirements are rules set by the Federal Reserve that determine the minimum reserve ratio for banks.

The **discount window** is an arrangement in which the Federal Reserve stands ready to lend money to banks in trouble.

Panicky IndyMac depositors lined up to pull their money out of the troubled California bank in July 2008.

an economic crisis that swept Southeast Asia in 1997–1998 and in the severe economic crisis in Argentina that began in late 2001. And a panic with strong resemblance to a wave of bank runs swept world financial markets in 2008.

Notice that we said *most bank runs*. There are some limits on deposit insurance; in particular, as we've learned, in the United States currently only the first $250,000 of an individual depositor's funds in an insured bank is covered. As a result, there can still be a run on a bank perceived as troubled. In fact, that's exactly what happened in July 2008 to IndyMac Bank, a Pasadena-based lender that had made a large number of questionable home loans. As questions about IndyMac's financial soundness were raised, depositors began pulling out funds, forcing federal regulators to step in and close the bank. In Britain the limits on deposit insurance are much lower, which exposed the bank Northern Rock to a classic bank run in September 2007. Unlike the bank runs of the 1930s, however, most depositors at both IndyMac and Northern Rock got all their funds back—and the panics at these banks didn't spread to other institutions.

>> *Quick Review*

- A **T-account** is used to analyze a bank's financial position. A bank holds **bank reserves**—currency in its vaults plus deposits held in its account at the Federal Reserve. The **reserve ratio, *rr,*** is the ratio of bank reserves to customers' bank deposits.

- Because bank loans are illiquid, but a bank is obligated to return depositors' funds on demand, **bank runs** are a potential problem. Although they took place on a massive scale during the 1930s, they have been largely eliminated in the United States through bank regulation in the form of **deposit insurance,** capital requirements, and **reserve requirements,** as well as through the availability of the **discount window.** The emergence of shadow banking, however, has shown the limits of regulation to prevent bank runs in the conventional banking sector.

>> *Check Your Understanding* 18-2

Solutions appear at back of book.

1. Suppose you are a depositor at First Street Bank. You hear a rumor that the bank has suffered serious losses on its loans. Every depositor knows that the rumor isn't true, but each thinks that most other depositors believe the rumor. Why, in the absence of deposit insurance, could this lead to a bank run? How does deposit insurance change the situation?

2. A con artist has a great idea: he'll open a bank without investing any capital and lend all the deposits at high interest rates to real estate developers. If the real estate market booms, the loans will be repaid and he'll make high profits. If the real estate market goes bust, the loans won't be repaid and the bank will fail—but he will not lose any of his own wealth. How would modern bank regulation frustrate his scheme?

‖ Determining the Money Supply

Without banks, there would be no checkable deposits, so the quantity of currency in circulation would equal the money supply. In that case, the money supply would be solely determined by whoever controls government minting and printing presses. But banks do exist, and through their creation of checkable bank deposits they affect the money supply in two ways.

1. Banks reduce the money supply by removing some currency from circulation: dollar bills that are sitting in bank vaults, as opposed to sitting in people's wallets, aren't part of the money supply.

2. Much more importantly, banks increase the money supply by making loans, the total value of which is much larger than their reserves. As a result, they make the money supply larger than just the value of currency in circulation.

Our next topic is how banks create money and what determines the amount of money they create.

How Banks Create Money

To see how banks create money, let's examine what happens when someone decides to deposit currency in a bank. Consider the example of Silas, a miser, who keeps a shoebox full of cash under his bed. Suppose Silas realizes that it would be safer, as well as more convenient, to deposit that cash in the bank and to use his debit card when shopping. Assume that he deposits $1,000 into a checkable account at First Street Bank. What effect will Silas's actions have on the money supply?

Panel (a) of Figure 18-4 shows the initial effect of his deposit. First Street Bank credits Silas with $1,000 in his account, so the economy's checkable bank deposits rise by $1,000. Meanwhile, Silas's cash goes into the vault, raising First Street's reserves by $1,000 as well.

This initial transaction has no effect on the money supply. Currency in circulation, part of the money supply, falls by $1,000. Checkable bank deposits, also part of the money supply, rise by the same amount.

But this is not the end of the story, because First Street Bank can now lend out part of Silas's deposit. Assume that it holds 10% of Silas's deposit—$100—in reserves and lends the rest out in cash to Silas's neighbor, Maya. The effect of this second stage is shown in panel (b). First Street's deposits remain unchanged, and so does the value of its assets. But the composition of its assets changes: by making the loan, it reduces its reserves by $900, so that they are only $100 larger than they were before Silas made his deposit. In the place of the $900 reduction in reserves, the bank has acquired an IOU, its $900 cash loan to Maya.

So by putting $900 of Silas's cash back into circulation by lending it to Maya, First Street Bank has, in fact, increased the money supply. That is, the sum of currency in circulation and checkable bank deposits has risen by $900 compared to what it had been when Silas's cash was still under his bed. Although Silas is still the owner of $1,000, now in the form of a checkable deposit, Maya has the use of $900 in cash from her borrowings.

And this may not be the end of the story. Suppose that Maya uses her cash to buy a television from Acme Merchandise. What does Anne Acme, the store's owner, do with the cash? If she holds on to it, the money supply doesn't increase any further. But suppose she deposits the $900 into a checkable bank deposit— say, at Second Street Bank. Second Street Bank, in turn, will keep only part of that deposit in reserves, lending out the rest, creating still more money.

FIGURE 18-4   Effect on the Money Supply of Turning Cash into a Checkable Deposit at First Street Bank

(a) Initial Effect Before Bank Makes a New Loan

Assets		Liabilities	
Loans	No change	Checkable deposits	+$1,000
Reserves	+$1,000		

(b) Effect When Bank Makes a New Loan

Assets		Liabilities	
Loans	+$900	No change	
Reserves	−$900		

When Silas deposits $1,000 (which had been stashed in a shoebox under his bed) into a checkable bank account, there is initially no effect on the money supply: currency in circulation falls by $1,000, but checkable bank deposits rise by $1,000. The corresponding entries on the bank's T-account, depicted in panel (a), show deposits initially rising by $1,000 and the bank's reserves initially rising by $1,000. In the second stage, depicted in panel (b), the bank holds 10% of Silas's deposit ($100) as reserves and lends out the rest ($900) to Maya. As a result, its reserves fall by $900 and its loans increase by $900. Its liabilities, including Silas's $1,000 deposit, are unchanged. The money supply, the sum of checkable bank deposits and currency in circulation, has now increased by $900–the $900 now held by Maya.

TABLE 18-1 How Banks Create Money

	Currency in circulation	Checkable bank deposits	Money supply
First stage Silas keeps his cash under his bed.	$1,000	$0	$1,000
Second stage Silas deposits cash in First Street Bank, which lends out $900 to Maya, who then pays it to Anne Acme.	900	1,000	1,900
Third stage Anne Acme deposits $900 in Second Street Bank, which lends out $810 to another borrower.	810	1,900	2,710

Assume that Second Street Bank, like First Street Bank, keeps 10% of any bank deposit in reserves and lends out the rest. Then it will keep $90 in reserves and lend out $810 of Anne's deposit to another borrower, further increasing the money supply.

Table 18-1 shows the process of money creation we have described so far. To simplify the table we will assume that, at first, the money supply consists only of Silas's $1,000. After he deposits the cash into a checkable bank deposit and the bank makes a loan, the money supply rises to $1,900. After the second deposit and the second loan, the money supply rises to $2,710. And the process will, of course, continue from there. (Although we have considered the case in which Silas places his cash in a checkable bank deposit, the results would be the same if he put it into any type of near-money.)

This process of money creation may sound familiar. In Chapter 17 we described the *multiplier process:* an initial increase in real GDP leads to a rise in consumer spending, which leads to a further rise in real GDP, which leads to a further rise in consumer spending, and so on. What we have here is another kind of multiplier—the *money multiplier*. We'll now see what determines the size of this multiplier.

Reserves, Bank Deposits, and the Money Multiplier

In tracing out the effect of Silas's deposit in Table 18-1, we assumed that the funds a bank lends out always end up being deposited either in the same bank or in another bank—so funds disbursed as loans come back to the banking system, even if not to the lending bank itself.

In reality, some of these loaned funds may be held by borrowers in their wallets and not deposited in a bank, meaning that some of the loaned amount "leaks" out of the banking system. Such leaks reduce the size of the money multiplier, just as leaks of real income into savings reduce the size of the real GDP multiplier. (Bear in mind, however, that the leak here comes from the fact that borrowers keep some of their funds in currency, rather than the fact that consumers save some of their income.)

Excess reserves are a bank's reserves over and above its required reserves.

But let's set that complication aside for a moment and consider how the money supply is determined in a checkable-deposits-only monetary system, where funds are always deposited in bank accounts and none are held in wallets as currency. That is, in our checkable-deposits-only monetary system, any and all funds borrowed from a bank are immediately deposited into a checkable bank account. We'll assume that banks are required to satisfy a minimum reserve ratio of 10% and that every bank lends out all of its **excess reserves,** reserves over and above the amount needed to satisfy the minimum reserve ratio.

Now suppose that for some reason a bank suddenly finds itself with $1,000 in excess reserves. What happens? The answer is that the bank will lend out that $1,000, which will end up as a checkable bank deposit somewhere in the banking system, launching a money multiplier process very similar to the process shown in Table 18-1.

"There's money in there that could be used for other purposes."

In the first stage, the bank lends out its excess reserves of $1,000, which becomes a checkable bank deposit somewhere. The bank that receives the $1,000 deposit keeps 10%, or $100, as reserves and lends out the remaining 90%, or $900, which again becomes a checkable bank deposit somewhere. The bank receiving this $900 deposit again keeps 10%, which is $90, as reserves and lends out the remaining $810. The bank receiving this $810 keeps $81 in reserves and lends out the remaining $729, and so on. As a result of this process, the total increase in checkable bank deposits is equal to a sum that looks like:

> The **monetary base** is the sum of currency in circulation and bank reserves.

$$\$1,000 + \$900 + \$810 + \$729 + \ldots$$

We'll use the symbol rr for the reserve ratio. More generally, the total increase in checkable bank deposits that is generated when a bank lends out $1,000 in excess reserves is:

(18-1) Increase in checkable bank deposits from $1,000 in excess reserves =
$$\$1,000 + (\$1,000 \times (1 - rr)) + (\$1,000 \times (1 - rr)^2) + (\$1,000 \times (1 - rr)^3) + \ldots$$

An infinite series of this form can be simplified to:

(18-2) Increase in checkable bank deposits from $1,000 in excess reserves =
$$\$1,000/rr$$

Given a reserve ratio of 10%, or 0.1, a $1,000 increase in excess reserves will increase the total value of checkable bank deposits by $1,000/0.1 = $10,000. In fact, the total value of checkable bank deposits will be equal to the value of bank reserves divided by the reserve ratio. *Or to put it a different way, in a checkable-deposits-only monetary system, if the reserve ratio is 10%, each $1 of reserves held by a bank supports $1/rr = $1/0.1 = $10 of checkable bank deposits.*

The Money Multiplier in Reality

In reality, the determination of the money supply is more complicated than our simple model suggests because it depends not only on the ratio of reserves to bank deposits but also on the fraction of the money supply that individuals choose to hold in the form of currency. In fact, we already saw this in our example of Silas depositing the cash under his bed: when he chose to hold a checkable bank deposit instead of currency, he set in motion an increase in the money supply.

To define the money multiplier in practice, it's important to recognize that the Federal Reserve controls the *sum* of bank reserves and currency in circulation, called the *monetary base*, but it does not control the allocation of that sum between bank reserves and currency in circulation. Consider Silas and his deposit one more time: by taking the cash from under his bed and depositing it in a bank, he reduced the quantity of currency in circulation but increased bank reserves by an equal amount—leaving the *monetary base*, on net, unchanged. The **monetary base,** which is the quantity the monetary authorities control, is the sum of currency in circulation and reserves held by banks.

The monetary base is different from the money supply in two ways.

1. Bank reserves, which are part of the monetary base, aren't considered part of the money supply. A $1 bill in someone's wallet is considered money because it's available for an individual to spend, but a $1 bill held as bank reserves in a bank vault or deposited at the Federal Reserve isn't considered part of the money supply because it's not available for spending.

2. Checkable bank deposits, which are part of the money supply because they are available for spending, aren't part of the monetary base.

FIGURE 18-5 The Monetary Base and the Money Supply

The monetary base is equal to bank reserves plus currency in circulation. It is different from the money supply, consisting mainly of checkable or near-checkable bank deposits plus currency in circulation. Each dollar of bank reserves backs several dollars of bank deposits. As a result, in normal economic times, the money supply is larger than the monetary base, making the circle at right larger than the circle on the left. However, in extraordinary economic times, as in the aftermath of the 2008 financial crisis, the monetary base grew, overtaking the money supply, making the circle at right smaller than the circle on the left.

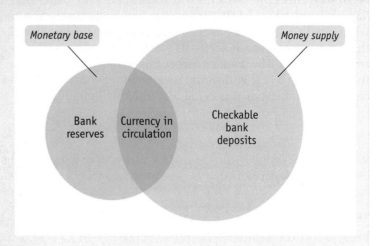

The **money multiplier** is the ratio of the money supply to the monetary base.

Figure 18-5 illustrates the two concepts. The circle on the left represents the monetary base, consisting of bank reserves plus currency in circulation. The circle on the right represents the money supply, consisting mainly of currency in circulation plus checkable or near-checkable bank deposits. As the figure indicates, currency in circulation is part of both the monetary base and the money supply. But bank reserves aren't part of the money supply, and checkable or near-checkable bank deposits aren't part of the monetary base. In practice, most of the monetary base actually consists of currency in circulation, which also makes up about half of the money supply.

Now we can formally define the **money multiplier:** it's the ratio of the money supply to the monetary base. Before the financial crisis of 2008, it was about 1.6, as calculated from official Federal Reserve statistics. After the crisis, it fell to about 0.7. Even before the crisis it was a lot smaller than $1/0.1 = 10$, which would be the money multiplier in a checkable-deposits-only system with a reserve ratio of 10% (the minimum required ratio for most checkable deposits in the United States).

The reason the actual money multiplier has been smaller than 10 is that people hold significant amounts of cash, and a dollar of currency in circulation, unlike a dollar in reserves, doesn't support multiple dollars of the money supply. In fact, before the crisis, currency in circulation accounted for more than 90% of the monetary base.

At the beginning of 2009, currency in circulation had dropped to only 40% of the monetary base. Nearly a decade later, in 2017, the percentage remained the same. What happened, basically, is that the Federal Reserve dramatically expanded the monetary base in response to the financial crisis. The Fed undertook this action in an effort to stabilize the economy after Lehman Brothers, a key financial institution, failed in September 2008. However, banks saw few opportunities for safe, profitable lending at the time. So rather than lending out the increase in the monetary base, they parked it at the Federal Reserve in the form of deposits that counted as part of the monetary base. As a result, currency in circulation no longer dominated the monetary base, as the surge in deposits at the Fed made the monetary base larger than M1. As a result, the actual money multiplier fell to less than 1 as banks held much more than the required 10% in reserves at the Fed. In May 2017, the money multiplier stood at 0.9.

The collapse of Lehman Brothers in 2008 and the ensuing financial crisis prompted the Federal Reserve to dramatically increase the monetary base in order to stabilize the economy.

ECONOMICS >> *in Action*
Multiplying Money Down

In our hypothetical example illustrating how banks create money, we described Silas the miser taking the currency from under his bed and turning it into a checkable bank deposit. This led to an increase in the money supply as banks engaged in successive waves of lending backed by Silas's funds. It follows that if something happened to make Silas revert to old habits, taking his money out of the bank and putting it back under his bed, the result would be less lending and, ultimately, a decline in the money supply. That's exactly what happened as a result of the bank runs of the 1930s.

Table 18-2 shows what happened between 1929 and 1933, as bank failures shook the public's confidence in the banking system:

TABLE 18-2 The Effects of Bank Runs, 1929–1933

	Currency in circulation	Checkable bank deposits	M1
	(billions of dollars)		
1929	$3.90	$22.74	$26.64
1933	5.09	14.82	19.91
Percent change	+31%	–35%	–25%

Data from: U.S. Census Bureau (1975), *Historical Statistics of the United States.*

- The second column shows the public's holdings of currency. This increased sharply, as many Americans decided that money under the bed was safer than money in the bank after all.

- The third column shows the value of checkable bank deposits. This fell sharply, through the multiplier process, when individuals pulled their cash out of banks. Loans also fell because banks that survived the waves of bank runs increased their excess reserves, just in case another wave began.

- The fourth column shows the value of M1, the first of the monetary aggregates we described earlier. It fell sharply because the total reduction in checkable or near-checkable bank deposits was much larger than the increase in currency in circulation.

>> Check Your Understanding 18-3
Solutions appear at back of book.

1. Assume that total reserves are equal to $200 and total checkable bank deposits are equal to $1,000. Also assume that the public does not hold any currency. Now suppose that the required reserve ratio falls from 20% to 10%. Trace out how this leads to an expansion in bank deposits.

2. Take the example of Silas depositing his $1,000 in cash into First Street Bank and assume that the required reserve ratio is 10%. But now assume that each time someone receives a bank loan, he or she keeps half the loan in cash. Explain the resulting expansion in the money supply.

>> Quick Review

- Banks create money when they lend out **excess reserves,** generating a multiplier effect on the money supply.

- In a checkable-deposits-only system, $1 of bank reserves supports $1/*rr* checkable deposits. So the money supply would be equal to bank reserves divided by the reserve ratio. In reality, however, the public holds some funds as cash rather than in checkable deposits.

- The Fed controls the **monetary base,** equal to bank reserves plus currency in circulation. The **money multiplier** is equal to the money supply divided by the monetary base. It is smaller than $1/*rr* because people hold some funds as cash.

The Federal Reserve System

Who's in charge of ensuring that banks maintain enough reserves? Who decides how large the monetary base will be? The answer, in the United States, is an institution known as the Federal Reserve (or, informally, as the *Fed*). The Federal Reserve is a **central bank**—an institution that oversees and regulates the banking system and controls the monetary base.

Other central banks include the Bank of England, the People's Bank of China, the Bank of Japan, and the European Central Bank, or ECB. The ECB acts as a common central bank for 19 European countries: Austria, Belgium, Cyprus, Estonia, Finland, France, Germany, Greece, Ireland, Italy, Latvia, Lithuania, Luxembourg, Malta, the Netherlands, Portugal, Slovakia, Slovenia, and Spain. The world's oldest central bank is Sweden's Sveriges Riksbank, which awards the Nobel Prize in economics.

A **central bank** is an institution that oversees and regulates the banking system and controls the monetary base.

The Structure of the Fed

The legal status of the Fed, which was created in 1913, is unusual: it is not exactly part of the U.S. government, but it is not really a private institution either. Strictly speaking, the Federal Reserve system consists of two parts: the Board of Governors and the 12 regional Federal Reserve Banks.

The Board of Governors, which oversees the entire system from its offices in Washington, D.C., is constituted like a government agency: its seven members are appointed by the president and must be approved by the Senate. However, they are appointed for 14-year terms, to insulate them from political pressure in their conduct of monetary policy.

Although the chairperson of the Fed is appointed more frequently—every four years—it's traditional for chairs to be reappointed and serve much longer terms. For example, William McChesney Martin was chair of the Fed from 1951 until 1970. Alan Greenspan, appointed in 1987, served as the Fed's chair until 2006. Ben Bernanke, Greenspan's successor, served until 2014. Janet Yellen, who followed Ben Bernanke, became the first chair to not be reappointed to a second term. Jerome Powell was her successor at the Fed.

The 12 Federal Reserve Banks each serve a region of the country, providing various banking and supervisory services. One of their jobs, for example, is to audit the books of private-sector banks to ensure their financial health. Each regional bank is run by a board of directors chosen from the local banking and business community. The Federal Reserve Bank of New York plays a special role: it carries out *open-market operations*, usually the main tool of monetary policy. Figure 18-6 shows the 12 Federal Reserve districts and the city in which each regional Federal Reserve Bank is located.

Decisions about monetary policy are made by the Federal Open Market Committee, which consists of the Board of Governors plus five of the regional bank presidents. The president of the Federal Reserve Bank of New York is always on the committee, and the other four seats rotate among the 11 other regional bank presidents. The chairman of the Board of Governors normally also serves as the chairman of the Open Market Committee.

The effect of this complex structure is to create an institution that is ultimately accountable to the voting public because the Board of Governors is chosen by the

FIGURE 18-6 The Federal Reserve System

The Federal Reserve System consists of the Board of Governors in Washington, D.C., plus 12 regional Federal Reserve Banks. This map shows each of the 12 Federal Reserve districts.

Data from: Board of Governors of the Federal Reserve System.

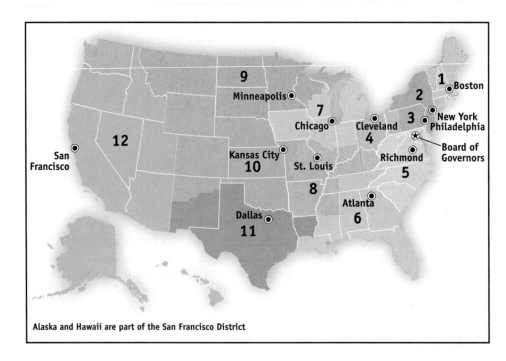

Alaska and Hawaii are part of the San Francisco District

president and confirmed by the Senate, all of whom are themselves elected officials. But the long terms served by board members, as well as the indirectness of their appointment process, largely insulate them from short-term political pressures.

What the Fed Does: Reserve Requirements and the Discount Rate

The Fed has three main policy tools at its disposal: *reserve requirements,* the *discount rate,* and, most importantly, *open-market operations.*

In our discussion of bank runs, we noted that the Fed sets a minimum reserve ratio requirement, currently equal to 10% for checkable bank deposits. Banks that fail to maintain at least the required reserve ratio on average over a two-week period face penalties.

What does a bank do if it looks as if it has insufficient reserves to meet the Fed's reserve requirement? Normally, it borrows additional reserves from other banks via the **federal funds market,** a financial market that allows banks that fall short of the reserve requirement to borrow reserves (usually just overnight) from banks that are holding excess reserves. The interest rate in this market is determined by supply and demand—but the supply and demand for bank reserves are both strongly affected by Federal Reserve actions. As we'll see in the next chapter, the **federal funds rate,** the interest rate at which funds are borrowed and lent in the federal funds market, plays a key role in modern monetary policy.

Alternatively, banks in need of reserves can borrow from the Fed itself via the *discount window.* The **discount rate** is the rate of interest the Fed charges on those loans. Normally, the discount rate is set 1 percentage point above the federal funds rate in order to discourage banks from turning to the Fed when they are in need of reserves. Beginning in the fall of 2007, however, the Fed reduced the spread between the federal funds rate and the discount rate as part of its response to an ongoing financial crisis. As a result, by the spring of 2008 the discount rate was only 0.25 percentage points above the federal funds rate. And in mid-2017, the discount rate was still only 0.60 percentage points above the federal funds rate.

In order to alter the money supply, the Fed can change reserve requirements, the discount rate, or both. If the Fed reduces reserve requirements, banks will normally lend a larger percentage of their deposits, leading to more loans and an increase in the money supply via the money multiplier. Alternatively, if the Fed increases reserve requirements, banks are forced to reduce their lending, leading to a fall in the money supply via the money multiplier.

If the Fed reduces the spread between the discount rate and the federal funds rate, the cost to banks of being short of reserves falls. Banks respond by increasing their lending, and the money supply increases via the money multiplier. If the Fed increases the spread between the discount rate and the federal funds rate, bank lending falls—and so will the money supply via the money multiplier.

Under current practice, however, the Fed doesn't use changes in reserve requirements to actively manage the money supply. The last significant change in reserve requirements was in 1992. The Fed normally doesn't use the discount rate either, although, as we mentioned earlier, there was a temporary surge in lending through the discount window beginning in 2007 in response to a financial crisis. Ordinarily, monetary policy is conducted almost exclusively using the Fed's third policy tool: open-market operations.

Open-Market Operations

Like the banks it oversees, the Federal Reserve has assets and liabilities. The Fed's assets normally consist of holdings of debt issued by the U.S. government, mainly short-term U.S. government bonds with a maturity of less than one year, known as U.S. Treasury bills. Remember, the Fed isn't exactly part of the U.S. government,

The **federal funds market** allows banks that fall short of the reserve requirement to borrow funds from banks with excess reserves.

The **federal funds rate** is the interest rate at which funds are borrowed and lent in the federal funds market.

The **discount rate** is the rate of interest the Fed charges on loans to banks.

FIGURE 18-7 The Federal Reserve's Assets and Liabilities

The Federal Reserve holds its assets mostly in short-term government bonds called U.S. Treasury bills. Its liabilities are the monetary base—currency in circulation plus bank reserves.

Assets	Liabilities
Government debt (Treasury bills)	Monetary base (currency in circulation + bank reserves)

An **open-market operation** is a purchase or sale of government debt by the Fed.

so U.S. Treasury bills held by the Fed are a liability of the government but an asset of the Fed. The Fed's liabilities consist of currency in circulation and bank reserves. Figure 18-7 summarizes the normal assets and liabilities of the Fed in the form of a T-account.

In an **open-market operation** the Federal Reserve buys or sells U.S. Treasury bills, normally through a transaction with *commercial banks* (banks that accept deposits and make loans), and *investment banks* (that create and trade assets but don't accept deposits). The Fed never buys U.S. Treasury bills directly from the federal government. There's a good reason for this: when a central bank buys government debt directly from the government, it is lending directly to the government—in effect, the central bank is printing money to finance the government's budget deficit. This has historically been a formula for disastrously high levels of inflation.

The two panels of Figure 18-8 show the changes in the financial position of both the Fed and commercial banks that result from open-market operations. When the Fed buys U.S. Treasury bills from a commercial bank, it pays by crediting the bank's reserve account by an amount equal to the value of the Treasury bills. This is illustrated in panel (a): the Fed buys $100 million of U.S. Treasury

FIGURE 18-8 Open-Market Operations by the Federal Reserve

(a) An Open-Market Purchase of $100 Million

	Assets		Liabilities	
Federal Reserve	Treasury bills	+$100 million	Monetary base	+$100 million

	Assets		Liabilities
Commercial banks	Treasury bills	−$100 million	No change
	Reserves	+$100 million	

(b) An Open-Market Sale of $100 Million

	Assets		Liabilities	
Federal Reserve	Treasury bills	−$100 million	Monetary base	−$100 million

	Assets		Liabilities
Commercial banks	Treasury bills	+$100 million	No change
	Reserves	−$100 million	

In panel (a), the Federal Reserve increases the monetary base by purchasing U.S. Treasury bills from private commercial banks in an open-market operation. Here, a $100 million purchase of U.S. Treasury bills by the Federal Reserve is paid for by a $100 million addition to private bank reserves, generating a $100 million increase in the monetary base. This will ultimately lead to an increase in the money supply via the money multiplier as banks lend out some of these new reserves. In

panel (b), the Federal Reserve reduces the monetary base by selling U.S. Treasury bills to private commercial banks in an open-market operation. Here, a $100 million sale of U.S. Treasury bills leads to a $100 million reduction in private bank reserves, resulting in a $100 million decrease in the monetary base. This will ultimately lead to a fall in the money supply via the money multiplier as banks reduce their loans in response to a fall in their reserves.

bills from commercial banks, which increases the monetary base by $100 million because it increases bank reserves by $100 million. When the Fed sells U.S. Treasury bills to commercial banks, it debits the banks' accounts, reducing their reserves. This is shown in panel (b), where the Fed sells $100 million of U.S. Treasury bills. Here, bank reserves and the monetary base decrease.

You might wonder where the Fed gets the funds to purchase U.S. Treasury bills from banks. The answer is that it simply creates them with a mouse click—or the stroke of a pen—that credits the banks' accounts with extra reserves. (The Fed prints money to pay for Treasury bills only when banks want the additional reserves in the form of currency.) Remember, the modern dollar is fiat money, which isn't backed by anything. So the Fed can create additional monetary base at its own discretion.

The change in bank reserves caused by an open-market operation doesn't directly affect the money supply. Instead, it starts the money multiplier in motion. After the $100 million increase in reserves shown in panel (a) of Figure 18-8, commercial banks will (under normal circumstances) lend out all of their additional reserves, immediately increasing the money supply by $100 million. Some of those loans would be deposited back into the banking system, increasing reserves again and permitting a further round of loans, and so on, leading to a rise in the money supply. An open-market sale has the reverse effect: bank reserves fall, requiring banks to reduce their loans, leading to a fall in the money supply.

Although economists often say, loosely, that the Fed controls the money supply—checkable deposits plus currency in circulation, that statement is not completely accurate. *The Fed literally only controls the monetary base—bank reserves plus currency in circulation. But by increasing or reducing the monetary base, the Fed can exert a powerful influence on both the money supply and interest rates*. This influence is the basis of monetary policy, the subject of the next chapter.

The European Central Bank

We've seen that the Fed is only one of a number of central banks around the world. In general, other central banks operate in much the same way as the Fed. That's especially true of the only other central bank that rivals the Fed in terms of importance to the world economy: the European Central Bank.

The European Central Bank (ECB) was created in January 1999 when 11 European nations abandoned their national currencies, adopted the euro as their common currency, and placed their joint monetary policy in the ECB's hands. More countries have joined since then, with Lithuania becoming the nineteenth European nation to adopt the euro in 2015. The ECB instantly became an extremely important institution: although no single European nation has an economy anywhere near as large as that of the United States, the combined economies of the eurozone, the group of countries that have adopted the euro as their currency, are roughly as big as the U.S. economy. As a result, the ECB and the Fed are the two giants of the monetary world.

Like the Fed, the ECB has a special status: it's not a private institution, but it's not exactly a government agency either. In fact, it can't be a government agency because there is no pan-European government!

First of all, the ECB, which is located in Frankfurt, Germany, isn't really the counterpart of the whole Federal Reserve system: it's the equivalent of the Board of Governors in Washington. The European counterparts of the regional Federal Reserve Banks are Europe's national central banks: the Bank of France, the Bank of Italy, and so on. Until 1999, each of these national banks was its country's equivalent to the Fed. For example, the Bank of France controlled the French monetary base.

Today these national banks, like regional Feds, provide various financial services to local banks and businesses and conduct open-market operations, but the making of monetary policy has moved upstream to the ECB. Still, the various European national central banks aren't small institutions: in total, they employ more than 50,000 people.

In the eurozone, each country chooses who runs its own national central bank. The ECB's Executive Board is the counterpart of the Fed's Board of Governors; its members are chosen by unanimous consent of the eurozone national governments. The counterpart of the Federal Open Market Committee is the ECB's Governing Council. Just as the Fed's Open Market Committee consists of the Board of Governors plus a rotating group of regional Fed presidents, the ECB's Governing Council consists of the Executive Board plus the heads of the national central banks.

Like the Fed, the ECB is also ultimately answerable to voters, and it tries to maintain its independence from short-term political pressures.

ECONOMICS >> *in Action*
The Fed's Balance Sheet, Normal and Abnormal

Figure 18-7 showed a simplified version of the Fed's balance sheet. Here, liabilities consisted entirely of the monetary base and assets consisted entirely of Treasury bills. This is an oversimplification because the Fed's operations are more complicated in reality and its balance sheet contains a number of additional things. But, in normal times, Figure 18-7 is a reasonable approximation: the monetary base typically accounts for 90% of the Fed's liabilities, and 90% of its assets are in the form of claims on the U.S. Treasury (as in Treasury bills).

But in late 2007 it became painfully clear that we were no longer in normal times. The source of the turmoil was the bursting of a huge housing bubble, which led to massive losses for financial institutions that had made mortgage loans or held mortgage-related assets. This led to a widespread loss of confidence in the financial system.

Not only were conventional deposit-taking commercial banks in trouble, but so were nondepository financial institutions like investment banks and insurance companies, which make up the shadow banking sector. Because they carried a lot of debt, faced huge losses from the collapse of the housing bubble, and held illiquid assets, panic hit the shadow banking sector. Within hours the financial system was frozen as financial institutions experienced what were, essentially, bank runs.

For example, in 2008, many investors became worried about the health of Bear Stearns, a Wall Street investment bank that engaged in complex financial deals, buying and selling financial assets with borrowed funds. When confidence in Bear Stearns dried up, the firm was unable to raise the funds needed to deliver on its end of these deals and it quickly spiraled into collapse. This was followed by the collapse of another investment bank, Lehman Brothers, and set off widespread panic in financial markets.

The Fed sprang into action to contain what was becoming a meltdown across the entire financial sector. It greatly expanded its discount window—making huge loans to deposit-taking banks as well as nondepository financial institutions. This gave financial institutions the liquidity that the financial market had denied them. And as these firms took advantage of the ability to borrow cheaply from the Fed, they pledged their assets on hand as collateral—a motley collection of real estate loans, business loans, and so on.

Examining Figure 18-9, we see that starting in mid-2008, the Fed sharply reduced its holdings of traditional securities like Treasury bills, as its "lending to financial institutions" skyrocketed—referring to discount window lending, but also to loans the

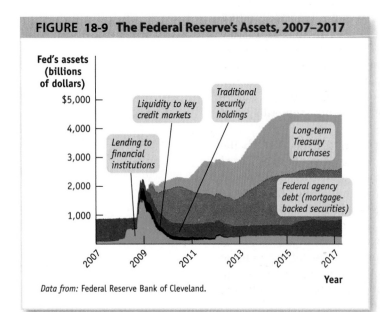

FIGURE 18-9 The Federal Reserve's Assets, 2007–2017

Data from: Federal Reserve Bank of Cleveland.

Fed made directly to firms like Bear Stearns. "Liquidity to key credit markets" covers purchases by the Fed of assets like corporate bonds, which was necessary to keep interest rates on loans to firms from soaring. Finally, "Federal agency debt" is the debt of Fannie Mae and Freddie Mac, the government-sponsored home mortgage agencies, which the Fed was also compelled to buy in order to prevent collapse in the mortgage market.

As the crisis subsided in late 2009, the Fed didn't return to its traditional asset holdings. Instead, it shifted into long-term Treasury bills and increased its purchases of Federal agency debt. The whole episode was very unusual—a major departure from the way the Fed normally conducts business, but one that it deemed necessary to stave off financial and economic collapse. It was also a graphic illustration of the fact that the Fed does much more than just determine the size of the monetary base.

>> Check Your Understanding 18-4

Solution appears at back of book.

1. Assume that any money lent by a bank is always deposited back in the banking system as a checkable deposit, that the reserve ratio is 10%, and that banks don't hold excess reserves. Explain the effects of a $100 million open-market purchase of U.S. Treasury bills by the Fed on the value of checkable bank deposits. What is the size of the money multiplier?

The Evolution of the American Banking System

Up to this point, we have been describing the U.S. banking system and how it works. To fully understand that system, however, it is helpful to understand how and why it was created—a story that is closely intertwined with the story of how and when things went wrong. The key elements of twenty-first century U.S. banking weren't created out of thin air: efforts to change both the regulations that govern banking and the Federal Reserve system that resulted from the 2008 crisis have propelled financial reform to the forefront.

The Crisis in American Banking in the Early Twentieth Century

The creation of the Federal Reserve system in 1913 marked the beginning of the modern era of American banking. From 1864 until 1913, American banking was dominated by a federally regulated system of national banks. They alone were allowed to issue currency, and the currency notes they issued were printed by the federal government with uniform size and design. How much currency a national bank could issue depended on its capital. Although this system was an improvement on the earlier period in which banks issued their own notes with no uniformity and virtually no regulation, the national banking regime still suffered numerous bank failures and major financial crises—at least one and often two per decade.

The main problem afflicting the system was that the money supply was not sufficiently responsive: it was difficult to shift currency around the country to respond quickly to local economic changes. (In particular, there was often a tug-of-war between New York City banks and rural banks for adequate amounts of currency.) Rumors that a bank had insufficient currency to satisfy demands for withdrawals would quickly lead to a bank run. A bank run would then spark a contagion, setting off runs at other nearby banks, sowing widespread panic and devastation in the local economy. In response, bankers in some locations pooled their resources to create local clearinghouses that would jointly guarantee a member's liabilities in the event of a panic, and some state governments began offering deposit insurance on their banks' deposits.

In both the Panic of 1907 and the financial crisis of 2008, large losses from risky speculation destabilized the banking system.

Despite these recurrent crises, calls for monetary reform went unheeded until the Panic of 1907, which led to a four-year national recession, drove home just how vulnerable the system had become.

This crisis originated in institutions in New York known as *trusts*, bank-like institutions that accepted deposits but that were originally intended to manage only inheritances and estates for wealthy clients. Because these trusts were supposed to engage only in low-risk activities, they were less regulated, had lower reserve requirements, and had lower cash reserves than national banks, allowing them to pay their depositors higher returns. As a result, trusts grew rapidly: by 1907, the total assets of trusts in New York City were as large as those of national banks. Meanwhile, the trusts declined to join the New York Clearinghouse, a consortium of New York City national banks that guaranteed one anothers' soundness.

The Panic of 1907 began with the failure of the Knickerbocker Trust, a large New York City trust that failed when it suffered massive losses in unsuccessful stock market speculation. Quickly, other New York trusts came under pressure, and frightened depositors began queuing in long lines to withdraw their funds. The New York Clearinghouse declined to step in and lend to the trusts, and even healthy trusts came under serious assault. Within two days, a dozen major trusts had gone under. Credit markets froze, and the stock market fell dramatically as stock traders were unable to get credit to finance their trades; business confidence evaporated.

Fortunately, New York City's wealthiest man, the banker J. P. Morgan, quickly stepped in to stop the panic. Understanding that the crisis was spreading and would soon engulf healthy institutions, trusts and banks alike, he worked with other bankers, wealthy men such as John D. Rockefeller, and the U.S. Secretary of the Treasury to shore up the reserves of banks and trusts so they could withstand the onslaught of withdrawals. Once people were assured that they could withdraw their money, the panic ceased. Although the panic itself lasted little more than a week, it and the stock market collapse decimated the economy. A four-year recession ensued, with production falling 11% and unemployment rising from 3% to 8%.

Responding to Banking Crises: The Creation of the Federal Reserve

Concerns over the frequency of banking crises and the unprecedented role of J. P. Morgan in saving the financial system prompted the federal government to initiate banking reform. In 1913 the national banking system was eliminated and the Federal Reserve system was created as a way to compel all deposit-taking institutions to hold adequate reserves and to open their accounts to inspection by regulators. The Panic of 1907 convinced many that the time for centralized control of bank reserves had come. In addition, the Federal Reserve was given the sole right to issue currency to make the money supply sufficiently responsive to satisfy economic conditions around the country.

Although the new regime standardized and centralized the holding of bank reserves, it did not eliminate the potential for bank runs because banks' reserves were still less than the total value of their deposits. The potential for more bank runs became a reality during the Great Depression. Plunging commodity prices hit American farmers particularly hard, precipitating a series of bank runs in 1930, 1931, and 1933, each of which started at midwestern banks and then spread throughout the country.

After the failure of a particularly large bank in 1930, federal officials realized that the economy-wide effects compelled them to take a less hands-off approach and to intervene more vigorously. In 1932, the Reconstruction Finance Corporation (RFC) was established and given the authority to make loans to banks in order to stabilize the banking sector. Also, the Glass-Steagall Act of 1933, which created federal deposit insurance and increased the ability of banks to borrow from the Federal Reserve system, was passed. However, the beast had not yet been tamed. Banks became fearful of borrowing from the RFC because doing so signaled weakness to the public.

As noted earlier, the new president, Franklin Delano Roosevelt, was inaugurated during the catastrophic bank run of 1933. He immediately declared a "bank holiday," closing all banks until regulators could get a handle on the problem.

In March 1933, emergency measures were adopted that gave the RFC extraordinary powers to stabilize and restructure the banking industry by providing capital to banks through either loans or outright purchases of bank shares. With the new rules, regulators closed nonviable banks and recapitalized viable ones by allowing the RFC to buy preferred shares in banks (shares that gave the U.S. government more rights than regular shareholders) and by greatly expanding banks' ability to borrow from the Federal Reserve. By 1933, the RFC had invested over $18 billion (2017 dollars) in bank capital—one-third of the total capital of all banks in the United States at that time—and purchased shares in almost one-half of all banks. The RFC loaned more than $36 billion (2017 dollars) to banks during this period.

Economic historians uniformly agree that the banking crises of the early 1930s greatly exacerbated the severity of the Great Depression, rendering monetary policy ineffective as the banking sector broke down, and currency withdrawn from banks and stashed under beds reduced the money supply.

Although the powerful actions of the RFC stabilized the banking industry, new legislation was needed to prevent future banking crises. The Glass-Steagall Act of 1933 separated banks into two categories, **commercial banks,** depository banks that are covered by deposit insurance, and nondepository **investment banks,** which engaged in creating and trading financial assets such as stocks and corporate bonds and that were not covered by deposit insurance.

Regulation Q prevented commercial banks from paying interest on checking accounts in the belief that this would promote unhealthy competition between banks. In addition, investment banks were much more lightly regulated than commercial banks. The most important measure for the prevention of bank runs, however, was the adoption of federal deposit insurance (with an original limit of $2,500 per deposit).

These measures were clearly successful, and the United States enjoyed a long period of financial and banking stability. As memories of the bad old days dimmed, Depression-era bank regulations were lifted. In 1980, Regulation Q was eliminated; by 1999, the Glass-Steagall Act had been so weakened that offering services like trading financial assets was no longer off-limits to commercial banks.

The Savings and Loan Crisis of the 1980s

Along with banks, the banking industry also included **savings and loans** (also called S&Ls or **thrifts**), institutions designed to accept savings and turn them into long-term mortgages for home-buyers. S&Ls were covered by federal deposit insurance and were tightly regulated for safety. However, trouble hit in the 1970s, as high inflation led savers to withdraw their funds from low-interest-paying S&L accounts and put them into higher-interest-paying money market accounts. In addition, the high inflation rate severely eroded the value of the S&Ls' assets, the long-term mortgages they held on their books.

A **commercial bank** accepts deposits and is covered by deposit insurance.

An **investment bank** trades in financial assets and does not accept deposits, so it is not covered by deposit insurance.

A **savings and loan (thrift)** is another type of deposit-taking bank, usually specializing in issuing home loans.

Bank-like activities undertaken by nondepository financial firms such as investment banks and hedge funds, but without regulatory oversight or protection, are known as **shadow banking**.

To improve the S&Ls' competitive position vis-à-vis banks, Congress eased regulations to allow S&Ls to undertake much more risky investments in addition to long-term home mortgages. However, the new freedom did not bring with it increased oversight, leaving S&Ls with less oversight than banks. Not surprisingly, during the real estate boom of the 1970s and 1980s, S&Ls engaged in overly risky real estate lending. Also, corruption occurred when some S&L executives used their institutions as private piggy banks.

During the late 1970s and early 1980s, political interference from Congress kept insolvent S&Ls open when a bank in a comparable situation would have been quickly shut down by regulators. By the early 1980s, numerous S&Ls had failed. Because accounts were covered by federal deposit insurance, the liabilities of a failed S&L became liabilities of the federal government, and depositors had to be paid from taxpayer funds. From 1986 through 1995, the federal government closed over 1,000 failed S&Ls, costing U.S. taxpayers over $124 billion.

In a classic case of shutting the barn door after the horse has escaped, in 1989 Congress put in place comprehensive oversight of S&L activities. It also empowered Fannie Mae and Freddie Mac to take over much of the home mortgage lending previously done by S&Ls. *Fannie Mae* and *Freddie Mac* are quasi-governmental agencies created during the Great Depression to make homeownership more affordable for low- and moderate-income households. The S&L crisis led to a steep slowdown in the finance and real estate industries, leading to the recession of the early 1990s.

Back to the Future: The Financial Crisis of 2008 and Its Aftermath

The bank regulations introduced in the 1930s led to a long era of relative financial stability. But by the early twenty-first century, a new problem had emerged: these regulations didn't cover **shadow banking**—activities, as we explained earlier, that don't look like traditional banking but serve similar purposes while posing significant risks. In 2008 shadow banking was at the center of a crisis that in important ways resembled the crisis of the 1930s.

Shadow Banking and Its Vulnerabilities
The details of shadow banking can be complex. However, much of the shadow banking system involves financial intermediaries—nondepository financial firms like investment banks, insurance companies, hedge funds, and money market funds. These firms borrow short-term—often taking out loans that must be repaid the next day—and use the borrowed funds to buy relatively illiquid assets to put up as collateral. This looks like banking to those lending funds to intermediaries, because their loans are a lot like bank deposits. For example, a corporation with extra cash on hand might lend that extra cash on an overnight basis to a Wall Street investment bank. That way it can get a higher interest rate than if it parked the funds in ordinary bank deposits, and under normal circumstances it can still count on having access to the money with only one day's notice.

Meanwhile, the financial intermediary doesn't have to keep enough cash on hand to repay all of its debts every day. Many of the lenders will simply roll over their loans each day, relending the funds. And when a lender does demand repayment, the borrower will simply raise the cash from another lender. So the shadow banking firm's relationship to its lenders is a lot like a conventional bank's relationship with its depositors, except for two significant differences: there is no deposit insurance and there is much less regulation of the intermediary's actions.

It is a system that can work seamlessly in normal times, but it can also go terribly wrong as it did when the housing bubble it helped to create burst in 2007, leading to the Great Recession.

Subprime Lending and the Housing Bubble
The story of the 2008 crisis begins with low interest rates: by 2003, U.S. interest rates were at historically low levels, partly because of Federal Reserve policy and partly because of large inflows

of capital from other countries, especially China. These low interest rates helped cause a boom in housing, which in turn pulled the U.S. economy out of recession. As housing boomed, however, financial institutions took on greater risks that were not well understood.

Traditionally, people were only able to borrow money to buy homes if they could show that they had sufficient income to meet the mortgage payments. Home loans to people who don't meet the usual criteria for borrowing, called **subprime lending,** were only a minor part of overall lending. But in the booming housing market of 2003 to 2006, subprime lending started to seem like a safe bet. According to conventional thinking, since housing prices kept rising, borrowers who were unable to make their mortgage payments could always pay off their mortgages by selling their homes. As a result, subprime lending exploded.

For the most part, these subprime loans were not made by traditional banks that lend out depositors' money. Instead, most of the loans were made by *loan originators*, companies specializing in making subprime loans and quickly selling them off to other investors in the shadow banking market. Large-scale sales of subprime mortgages were made possible by **securitization:** the assembly of pools of loans and sale of shares of the income from these pools. Again, according to conventional thinking at the time, these shares were considered relatively safe investments, based on the belief that large numbers of home-buyers were unlikely to default on their payments simultaneously.

But that's exactly what happened. The housing boom turned out to be a bubble, and when home prices started falling in late 2006, significant numbers of subprime borrowers were unable either to meet their mortgage payments or sell their houses for enough to pay off their mortgages. As a result, they defaulted and investors in securities backed by subprime mortgages suffered heavy losses.

These securities were largely held by shadow banking institutions, but also by some traditional, depository banks. Like the trusts that played a key role in the Panic of 1907, these largely unregulated shadow banks offered higher returns to investors but left them extremely vulnerable in a crisis. Without the safety net of deposit insurance, mortgage-related losses led to a collapse of trust in the financial system.

Figure 18-10 shows one measure of the severity of the loss of trust: the quantity of *asset-backed commercial paper,* an important asset class in shadow banking.

Subprime lending is lending to home-buyers who don't meet the usual criteria for qualifying for a loan.

In **securitization,** a pool of loans is assembled and shares of that pool are sold to investors.

"Honey we're homeless."

FIGURE 18-10 Measuring Lost Trust

In the mid-2000s the use of asset-backed commercial paper—short-term loans created by securitization of mortgages and other debts, and an important component of shadow banking—grew rapidly in volume. But it went into rapid decline after the housing boom went bust, a sign of extreme financial stress as liquidity in the financial system dried up.

Data from: Federal Reserve Bank of St. Louis.

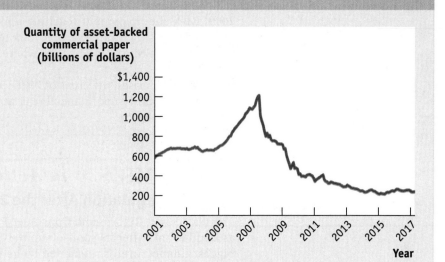

In the mid-2000s this paper—backed by short-term loans taken out using assets often created by securitization of mortgages and other debts—grew rapidly in volume. After the housing bust, it went into rapid decline, a sign of extreme financial stress. Although this was not a 1930s-style crash in the money supply in an official sense, it functioned in much the same way because commercial paper was an essential source of liquidity in the financial system.

Crisis and Response Starting in 2007, the bursting of the housing bubble, followed by large losses on the part of financial firms and the collapse in trust in the financial system, led to major disruptions for the economy as a whole. All firms—financial and nonfinancial—found it difficult to borrow, even for short-term operations. Individuals found home loans unavailable and credit card limits reduced. Prices of many assets tumbled, severely reducing household wealth.

Overall, the negative economic effect of the financial crisis bore a strong and extremely troubling resemblance to the banking crisis of the early 1930s, which sparked the Great Depression. Policy makers, noticing the resemblance, tried to prevent a repeat performance. Beginning in August 2007, the Federal Reserve provided liquidity to stop a cascade of defaults, by lending funds to a wide range of institutions and buying commercial paper. The Fed and the Treasury Department also stepped in to rescue individual firms that were deemed too crucial to be allowed to fail, such as the investment bank Bear Stearns and the insurance company AIG.

In September 2008, however, under political pressure to punish "irresponsible bankers," policy makers allowed one major investment bank, Lehman Brothers, to fail. They quickly regretted the decision. Within days of Lehman's failure, widespread panic gripped the financial markets. In response, the U.S. government intervened further to support the financial system. The U.S. Treasury injected capital directly into banks—supplying them with cash in return for shares. The effect was to partly *nationalize* the financial system (take public ownership). The Federal Reserve engaged in novel forms of open-market operations, such as providing massive liquidity through discount window lending and buying a large quantity of other assets—mainly long-term government debt and the debt of Fannie Mae and Freddie Mac (as shown in Figure 18-9 by the huge surge in Fed assets after September 2008).

The Aftermath of the Crisis After many terrifying months, in the fall of 2010 the financial system stabilized, and major institutions had repaid much of the money the federal government had injected during the crisis. However, the recovery of the banks was not matched by a successful turnaround for the overall economy. Although the recession that began in December 2007 officially ended in June 2009, with unemployment reaching a high of 10% in October 2009, unemployment fell very slowly afterward. It took nearly nine years, until May 2016, for the unemployment rate to fall back to where it had been before the start of the Great Recession.

Like earlier crises, the crisis of 2008 led to changes in banking regulation, most notably the Dodd-Frank financial regulatory reform act discussed in the following Economics in Action.

ECONOMICS >> *in Action*
Financial Regulation After the 2008 Crisis

The Wall Street Reform and Consumer Protection Act of 2010—generally known as Dodd-Frank, after its sponsors in the Senate and House, respectively—was the biggest financial reform enacted since the 1930s. How did it change financial regulation?

For traditional depository banks, the main change was the creation of a new agency, the Consumer Financial Protection Bureau. Its mission was to protect borrowers from being exploited through seemingly attractive financial deals they didn't understand.

The main thrust of Dodd-Frank, however, was the regulation of shadow banking institutions. Under the law, a financial institution could be designated as "systematically important"—that is, like Lehman Brothers, it was important enough to the financial system that it could trigger a banking crisis, even though it wasn't a depository bank.

Under Dodd-Frank, these systemically important institutions were subjected to depository bank–style regulation, such as relatively high capital requirements and limits on risk taking. In addition, the federal government asserted *resolution authority*, the right to seize troubled nondepository financial institutions in much the same way that it seized troubled banks.

The Dodd-Frank Act extended old-fashioned bank regulation to today's more complex financial system. More recently, the Trump Administration has rolled back some of its provisions.

Dodd-Frank also mandated that most *derivatives*, complex financial instruments that also played a significant role in the 2008 crisis, could be bought and sold on public exchanges in order to make them more transparent and reduce risk.

Overall, the purpose of Dodd-Frank was to extend the spirit of old-fashioned bank regulation to the more complex financial system of the twenty-first century. How well is it working? Relatively well, according to the evidence so far:

- The new rules on systemically important institutions seem to have reduced the incentive to create shadow banks that bypass regulations on conventional banks. An example is the case of GE Capital, an unregulated bank once owned by General Electric. Although it was the main source of profits for its parent company, General Electric sold it off in the wake of Dodd-Frank.

- Resolution authority seems to have led to a reduction in the so-called *too big to fail subsidy:* the lower cost of borrowing enjoyed by big financial institutions compared to smaller ones because it was assumed that only the big ones would be bailed out in a crisis.

- The Consumer Financial Protection Bureau is widely considered to have been quite effective at punishing and deterring financial fraud.

That said, we won't know how effective Dodd-Frank has been until the next period of financial turbulence.

>> Check Your Understanding 14-5

Solutions appear at back of book.

1. What are the similarities between the Panic of 1907, the S&L crisis, and the crisis of 2008?

2. Why did the creation of the Federal Reserve fail to prevent the bank runs of the Great Depression? What measures stopped the bank runs?

3. Why were extraordinary measures needed to deal with the financial crisis of 2008?

>> Quick Review

- The Federal Reserve system was created in response to the Panic of 1907.

- Widespread bank runs in the early 1930s resulted in greater bank regulation and the creation of federal deposit insurance. Banks were separated into two categories: **commercial** (covered by deposit insurance) and **investment** (not covered).

- In the **savings and loan (thrift)** crisis of the 1970s and 1980s, insufficiently regulated S&Ls incurred huge losses from risky speculation in housing.

- Unregulated **shadow banking** activities created a vulnerability in the financial system. In the mid-2000s, **securitization** spread loans from **subprime lending** throughout the shadow banking sector, and among some traditional banks, leading to a financial crisis when the housing bubble burst. The Federal Reserve and U.S. Treasury undertook extraordinary steps to stabilize financial markets.

- In 2010, Congress passed the Dodd-Frank Act. The law extended both financial regulations—to avoid another financial crisis—and protections against consumer financial fraud.

SOLVED PROBLEM   Multiplying Money

The economic stimulus of 2009, which we learned about in the previous chapter, was initially a $787 billion package of spending, aid, and tax cuts intended to help the struggling U.S. economy and reverse a severe recession. It is the most recent example we have of fiscal stimulus in action. As part of this Act, the U.S. government issued tax rebate checks to eligible households. On average, rebate checks totaled $950.00.

Economists have estimated that each household initially spent about $450.00 of the rebate. Since the public holds about 50% of M1 in the form of currency, the average household deposited about $250.00 of the remaining $500.00 and held the other $250.00 in cash. In light of this data, approximately how much will the money supply increase in response to the average household's deposit? (*Hint:* Create a table that shows the change in the money supply for ten rounds.) Assume that banks lend out the full amount of any excess reserves.

STEP | 1 **Find the required reserve ratio in the United States.** *Review pages 510–511 to find and understand the U.S. reserve ratio.*

The required reserve ratio in the United States is 10%.

STEP | 2 **Make a table that shows on line 1 the initial deposit, the required reserves, the excess reserves, the loans that a bank makes, and the amount held in currency from the initial loans made by the bank.** *Review pages 515–517 to help determine the required reserves, excess reserves, and the loans made.*

The amount held in currency from the initial loans made by the bank is the amount in the loan that "leaks" out of the banking system, which is also discussed in the section, "Reserves, Bank Deposits, and the Money Multiplier." The first line of this table is shown here.

Round	Deposits	Required reserves	Excess reserves	Loans	Held as currency
1	$250.00	$25.00	$225.00	$225.00	$112.50

The deposit amount is $250.00. As determined in Step 1, the required reserves are 10% of this deposit amount: $10\% \times \$250.00 = \$25.00$. The excess reserves are therefore $250.00 − $25.00 = $225.00. We have assumed that banks loan out all of their excess reserves, so they loan out $225.00. Of this amount, the public will hold 50% in currency: $50\% \times \$225.00 = \$112.50$.

STEP | 3 **Extend this table for 10 rounds.** *Review pages 515–517.*

If, after the first round, the public has held $112.50 of $225.00 in loans as currency, then the second round will begin with a deposit of $112.50 = $225.00 − $112.50. Each round begins with the difference between the loan amount and the amount held in currency from the previous round. The extended table is shown here.

Round	Deposits	Required reserves	Excess reserves	Loans	Held as currency
1	$250.00	$25.00	$225.00	$225.00	$112.50
2	112.50	11.25	101.25	101.25	50.63
3	50.63	5.06	45.56	45.56	22.78
4	22.78	2.28	20.50	20.50	10.25
5	10.25	1.03	9.23	9.23	4.61
6	4.61	0.46	4.15	4.15	2.08
7	2.08	0.21	1.87	1.87	0.93
8	0.93	0.09	0.84	0.84	0.42
9	0.42	0.04	0.38	0.38	0.19
10	0.19	0.02	0.17	0.17	0.09
Total after 10 rounds	$454.39	$45.44	$408.95	$408.95	$204.48

Round 2 is constructed in the same manner as Round 1. The round begins with a deposit of $112.50. The bank holds $11.25 of this as reserves, and so the excess reserves and the amount loaned out is $112.50 – $11.25 = $101.25. Of this, the ~~household~~ keeps $50.63 in currency.

STEP | **4** **Determine the increase in the money supply that results from the aver~~age~~ household deposit.** *Review pages 516–517.*

The approximate increase in the money supply from the average household de~~posit is~~ $408.95.

[handwritten note: Chapter 18 money, Banking + Federal Reserve]

SUMMARY

1. **Money** is any asset that can easily be used to purchase goods and services. **Currency in circulation** and **checkable bank deposits** are both considered part of the **money supply.** Money plays three roles: it is a **medium of exchange** used for transactions, a **store of value** that holds purchasing power over time, and a **unit of account** in which prices are stated.

2. Over time, **commodity money,** which consists of goods possessing value aside from their role as money, such as gold and silver coins, was replaced by **commodity-backed money,** such as paper currency backed by gold. Today the dollar is pure **fiat money,** whose value derives solely from its official role.

3. The Federal Reserve calculates two measures of the money supply. *[handwritten: most fluid]* **M1** is the narrowest **monetary aggregate,** containing only currency in circulation, *[handwritten: least fluid]* traveler's checks, and checkable bank deposits. **M2** includes a wider range of assets called **near-moneys,** mainly other forms of bank deposits that can easily be converted into checkable bank deposits.

4. Banks allow depositors immediate access to their funds, but they also lend out most of the funds deposited in their care. To meet demands for cash, they maintain **bank reserves** composed of both currency held in vaults and deposits at the Federal Reserve. The **reserve ratio** is the ratio of bank reserves to bank deposits. A **T-account** summarizes a bank's financial position, with loans and reserves counted as assets and deposits counted as liabilities.

5. Banks have sometimes been subject to **bank runs,** most notably in the early 1930s. To avert this danger, depositors are now protected by **deposit insurance;** bank owners face capital requirements that reduce the incentive to make overly risky loans with depositors' funds; and banks must satisfy **reserve requirements.**

6. When currency is deposited in a bank, it starts a multiplier process in which banks lend out **excess reserves,** leading to an increase in the money supply—so banks create money. If the entire money supply consisted of

checkable b~~ank deposits~~ equal to the~~se~~ ratio. In rea~~lity~~ currency in~~circulation~~ the ratio of the money supply to the monetary base.

7. The monetary base is controlled by the Federal Reserve, the **central bank** of the United States. The Fed regulates banks and sets reserve requirements. To meet those requirements, banks borrow and lend reserves in the **federal funds market** at the **federal funds rate.** Through the *discount window* facility, banks can borrow from the Fed at the **discount rate.**

8. **Open-market operations** by the Fed are the principal tool of monetary policy: the Fed can increase or reduce the monetary base by buying U.S. Treasury bills from banks or selling U.S. Treasury bills to banks.

9. In response to the Panic of 1907, the Fed was created to centralize the holding of reserves, inspect banks' books, and make the money supply sufficiently responsive to varying economic conditions.

10. The Great Depression sparked widespread bank runs in the early 1930s, which greatly worsened and lengthened it. Federal deposit insurance was created, and the government recapitalized banks by lending to them and by buying shares of banks. By 1933, banks had been separated into two categories: **commercial banks** (which accept deposits and are covered by deposit insurance) and **investment banks** (which don't accept deposits and are not covered). Public acceptance of deposit insurance finally stopped the bank runs of the Great Depression.

11. The **savings and loan (thrift)** crisis of the 1980s arose because insufficiently regulated S&Ls engaged in overly risky speculation and incurred huge losses. Depositors in failed S&Ls were compensated with taxpayer funds because they were covered by deposit insurance. The crisis caused steep losses in the financial and real estate sectors, resulting in a recession in the early 1990s.

12. The emergence of **shadow banking,** bank-like activities undertaken by nondepository financial firms not subject to regulatory oversight or protection, once again made the financial system vulnerable to bank-run type panics. In the mid-2000s, **securitization** of mortgage loans from **subprime lending** spread through the shadow banking sector and among some traditional depository banks. When the housing bubble burst in 2007, losses by financial institutions led to panic and a widespread collapse of the financial system in 2008. To prevent another Great Depression, the Federal Reserve and U.S. Treasury undertook extraordinary actions to provide support to the financial system, such as injecting capital into banks through the purchase of bank shares, providing massive liquidity through discount window lending, and buying large amounts of long-term government debt and government-sponsored agency debt. By 2010, the financial system had stabilized but the economy did not fully recover until 2016.

13. In 2010, Congress passed a financial regulation reform act, known as Dodd-Frank, in order to prevent another crisis. Its main purpose was to extend old-fashioned bank regulation to today's more complex financial system. It also extended protection for consumers against financial fraud.

KEY TERMS

Money, p. 504
Currency in circulation, p. 504
Checkable bank deposits, p. 504
Money supply, p. 504
Medium of exchange, p. 505
Store of value, p. 505
Unit of account, p. 506
Commodity money, p. 506
Commodity-backed money, p. 506
Fiat money, p. 507
Monetary aggregate, p. 508

Near-moneys, p. 508
Bank reserves, p. 510
T-account, p. 510
Reserve ratio, p. 511
Bank run, p. 512
Deposit insurance, p. 512
Reserve requirements, p. 513
Discount window, p. 513
Excess reserves, p. 516
Monetary base, p. 517
Money multiplier, p. 518

Central bank, p. 519
Federal funds market, p. 521
Federal funds rate, p. 521
Discount rate, p. 521
Open-market operation, p. 522
Commercial bank, p. 527
Investment bank, p. 527
Savings and loan (thrift), p. 527
Shadow banking, p. 528
Subprime lending, p. 529
Securitization, p. 529

DISCUSSION QUESTIONS

1. The following table shows the components of M1 and M2 in billions of dollars for the month of December in the years 2006 to 2016, reported by the Federal Reserve Bank of St. Louis. Complete the table by calculating M1, M2, currency in circulation as a percentage of M1, and currency in circulation as a percentage of M2. What trends or patterns about M1, M2, currency in circulation as a percentage of M1, and currency in circulation as a percentage of M2 do you see? What might account for these trends?

Year	Currency in circulation	Traveler's checks	Checkable deposits	Savings deposits	Time deposits	Money market funds	M1	M2	Currency in circulation as a percentage of M1	Currency in circulation as a percentage of M2
2006	$750.2	$6.7	$611.3	$3,694.9	$1,206.1	$772.2	?	?	?	?
2007	760.6	6.3	609.5	3,898.4	1,276.1	923.3	?	?	?	?
2008	816.3	5.5	785.1	4,089.4	1,457.9	1,012.5	?	?	?	?
2009	863.7	5.1	829.7	4,813.1	1,188.3	771.1	?	?	?	?
2010	918.8	4.7	919.0	5,331.3	933.2	668.1	?	?	?	?
2011	1,001.5	4.3	1,164.1	6,032.0	775.8	658.6	?	?	?	?
2012	1,090.5	3.8	1,367.0	6,685.0	643.7	638.6	?	?	?	?
2013	1,160.2	3.5	1,496.5	7,131.5	567.3	635.7	?	?	?	?
2014	1,252.2	2.9	1,675.0	7,580.9	519.0	616.9	?	?	?	?
2015	1,337.9	2.5	1,739.3	8,185.1	408.4	640.3	?	?	?	?
2016	1,418.4	2.2	1,902.0	8,842.3	371.6	712.6	?	?	?	?

Data from: Federal Reserve Bank of St. Louis.

2. Ryan Cozzens withdraws $400 from his checking account at the local bank and keeps it in his wallet.

   a. How will the withdrawal change the T-account of the local bank and the money supply?

   b. If the bank maintains a reserve ratio of 10%, how will it respond to the withdrawal? Assume that the bank responds to insufficient reserves by reducing the amount of deposits it holds until its level of reserves satisfies its required reserve ratio. The bank reduces its deposits by calling in some of its loans, forcing borrowers to pay back these loans by taking cash from their checking deposits (at the same bank) to make repayment.

   c. If every time the bank decreases its loans, checkable bank deposits fall by the amount of the loan, by how much will the money supply in the economy contract in response to Ryan's withdrawal of $400?

   d. If every time the bank decreases its loans, checkable bank deposits fall by the amount of the loan and the bank maintains a reserve ratio of 20%, by how much will the money supply contract in response to a withdrawal of $400?

3. In Westlandia, the public holds 50% of M1 in the form of currency, and the required reserve ratio is 20%. Estimate how much the money supply will increase in response to a new cash deposit of $500 by completing the accompanying table. (*Hint:* The first row shows that the bank must hold $100 in minimum reserves—20% of the $500 deposit—against this deposit, leaving $400 in excess reserves that can be loaned out. However, since the public wants to hold 50% of the loan in currency, only $400 × 0.5 = $200 of the loan will be deposited in

round 2 from the loan granted in round 1.) How does your answer compare to an economy in which the total amount of the loan is deposited in the banking system and the public doesn't hold any of the loan in currency? What does this imply about the relationship between the public's desire for holding currency and the money multiplier?

4. Show the changes to the T-accounts for the Federal Reserve and for commercial banks when the Federal Reserve sells $30 million in U.S. Treasury bills. If the public holds a fixed amount of currency (so that all new loans create an equal amount of checkable bank deposits in the banking system) and the minimum reserve ratio is 5%, by how much will checkable bank deposits in the commercial banks change? By how much will the money supply change? Show the final changes to the T-account for the commercial banks when the money supply changes by this amount.

5. As shown in Figure 18-9, the portion of the Federal Reserve's assets made up of U.S. Treasury bills has declined since 2007. Go to www.federalreserve.gov. On the top of the page, under "Data" and "Money Stock and Reserve Balances," select the link "Factors Affecting Reserve Balances – H.4.1." Click on the link for the current release.

   a. Under "Condition Statement of Federal Reserve Banks," find the row "Reserve Bank Credit." What is the total amount of reserve bank credit under "Average of Daily Figures" for the most current week ended? What is the amount displayed for "U.S. Treasury securities"? What percentage of the Federal Reserve's total reserve bank credit is currently made up of U.S. Treasury bills?

   b. Do the Federal Reserve's assets consist primarily of U.S. Treasury securities, as they did in January 2007, the beginning of the graph in Figure 18-9, or does the Fed still own a large number of other assets, as it did in early 2017, the end of the graph in Figure 18-9?

Round	Deposits	Required reserves	Excess reserves	Loans	Held as currency
1	$500.00	$100.00	$400.00	$400.00	$200.00
2	200.00	?	?	?	?
3	?	?	?	?	?
4	?	?	?	?	?
5	?	?	?	?	?
6	?	?	?	?	?
7	?	?	?	?	?
8	?	?	?	?	?
9	?	?	?	?	?
Total after 10 rounds	?	?	?	?	?

PROBLEMS

interactive activity

1. For each of the following transactions, what is the initial effect (increase or decrease) on M1? On M2?

   a. You sell a few shares of stock and put the proceeds into your savings account.

   b. You sell a few shares of stock and put the proceeds into your checking account.

   c. You transfer money from your savings account to your checking account.

   d. You discover $0.25 under the floor mat in your car and deposit it in your checking account.

   e. You discover $0.25 under the floor mat in your car and deposit it in your savings account.

2. There are three types of money: commodity money, commodity-backed money, and fiat money. Which type of money is used in each of the following situations?

   a. Bottles of rum were used to pay for goods in colonial Australia.

   b. Salt was used in many European countries as a medium of exchange.

   c. For a brief time, Germany used paper money (the "Rye Mark") that could be redeemed for a certain amount of rye, a type of grain.

   d. The town of Ithaca, New York, prints its own currency, the Ithaca HOURS, which can be used to purchase local goods and services.

3. Indicate whether each of the following is part of M1, M2, or neither:

   a. $95 on your campus meal card

   b. $0.55 in the change cup of your car

   c. $1,663 in your savings account

   d. $459 in your checking account

   e. 100 shares of stock worth $4,000

   f. A $1,000 line of credit on your Target credit card

4. Tracy Williams deposits $500 that was in her sock drawer into a checking account at the local bank. The reserve ratio is 10%.

   a. How does the deposit initially change the T-account of the local bank? How does it change the money supply?

   b. If the bank maintains a reserve ratio of 10%, how will it respond to the new deposit?

   c. If every time the bank makes a loan, the loan results in a new checkable bank deposit in a different bank equal to the amount of the loan, by how much could the total money supply in the economy expand in response to Tracy's initial cash deposit of $500?

   d. If every time the bank makes a loan, the loan results in a new checkable bank deposit in a different bank equal to the amount of the loan and the bank maintains a reserve ratio of 5%, by how much could the money supply expand in response to Tracy's initial cash deposit of $500?

5. The government of Eastlandia uses measures of monetary aggregates similar to those used by the United States, and the central bank of Eastlandia imposes a required reserve ratio of 10%. Given the following information, answer the questions below.

   > Bank deposits at the central bank = $200 million
   > Currency held by public = $150 million
   > Currency in bank vaults = $100 million
   > Checkable bank deposits = $500 million
   > Traveler's checks = $10 million

   a. What is M1?

   b. What is the monetary base?

   c. Are the commercial banks holding excess reserves?

   d. Can the commercial banks increase checkable bank deposits? If yes, by how much can checkable bank deposits increase?

6. What will happen to the money supply under the following circumstances in a checkable-deposits-only system?

   a. The required reserve ratio is 25%, and a depositor withdraws $700 from his checkable bank deposit and holds it as cash.

   b. The required reserve ratio is 5%, and a depositor withdraws $700 from his checkable bank deposit and holds it as cash.

   c. The required reserve ratio is 20%, and a customer deposits $750 to her checkable bank deposit and holds it as cash.

   d. The required reserve ratio is 10%, and a customer deposits $600 to her checkable bank deposit and holds it as cash.

7. Although the U.S. Federal Reserve doesn't use changes in reserve requirements to manage the money supply, the central bank of Albernia does. The commercial banks of Albernia have $100 million in reserves and $1,000 million in checkable deposits; the initial required reserve ratio is 10%. The commercial banks follow a policy of holding no excess reserves. The public holds no currency, only checkable deposits in the banking system.

a. How will the money supply change if the required reserve ratio falls to 5%?

b. How will the money supply change if the required reserve ratio rises to 25%?

8. Using Figure 18-6, find the Federal Reserve district in which you live. Go to www.federalreserve.gov/fomc/ and determine if the president of the regional Federal Reserve bank in your district is currently a voting member of the Federal Open Market Committee (FOMC).

9. The Congressional Research Service estimates that at least $45 million of counterfeit U.S. $100 notes produced by the North Korean government are in circulation.

a. Why do U.S. taxpayers lose because of North Korea's counterfeiting?

b. As of December 2016, the interest rate earned on one-year U.S. Treasury bills was 0.87%. At a 0.87% rate of interest, what is the amount of money U.S. taxpayers are losing per year because of these $45 million in counterfeit notes?

10. The accompanying figure shows new U.S. housing starts, in thousands of units per month, between January 1980 and December 2016. The graph shows a large drop in new housing starts from 1984–1991 and 2006–2009. New housing starts are related to the availability of mortgages.

a. What caused the drop in new housing starts from 1984–1991?

b. What caused the drop in new housing starts from 2006–2009?

c. How could better regulation of financial institutions have prevented these two instances?

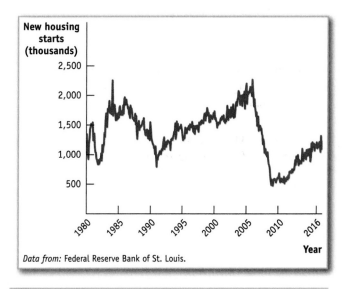

Data from: Federal Reserve Bank of St. Louis.

WORK IT OUT **Interactive step-by-step help with solving this problem can be found online.**

11. Show the changes to the T-accounts for the Federal Reserve and for commercial banks when the Federal Reserve buys $50 million in U.S. Treasury bills. If the public holds a fixed amount of currency (so that all loans create an equal amount of deposits in the banking system), the minimum reserve ratio is 10%, and banks hold no excess reserves, by how much will deposits in the commercial banks change? By how much will the money supply change? Show the final changes to the T-account for commercial banks when the money supply changes by this amount.

Chapter 18

Money, Banking

...JN IN GOVERNMENT

WHEN Nicholas Lemann, a writer for *The New Yorker* magazine, sought to write an article on arguably the most powerful person in the U.S. government, he didn't visit the White House. Instead, he visited the Federal Reserve in Washington, D.C., the home of the Fed's Board of Governors and its chairperson (at the time, Janet Yellen and currently Jerome Powell). As he later wrote, "There is an old saw that the Fed chair(person) is the most powerful person in the government. In the wake of the financial crisis, that may actually be an understatement."

Yet, at the Federal Reserve, unlike at the nearby White House, there is no pomp and circumstance: no aides dashing around, no splendidly dressed military guards, no ornate paintings on the walls, and no Secret Service. Instead, workers at the Fed are casually

dressed—and often look like graduate students. For example, each day at the New York Federal Reserve Bank, where the Fed's financial operations are performed, billions of dollars worth of long-term U.S. government bonds are bought and sold in a small room with just five employees. Struck by the ordinariness of it all, Lemann wrote, "Can a spectacle so lacking in the indicia of importance—no pageantry, no emotions, not even speaking—really be the beating heart of capitalism?"

The answer is yes. The source of the power of the Fed chair and the Board of Governors comes from their ability to set *monetary policy*. It's hard to overstate the importance of the Fed's monetary policy to the U.S. economy—for price stability, for job creation, and for the smooth functioning of the financial system. Roughly half the recessions that have occurred since World War II can be attributed, at least partly, to policies undertaken by the Federal Reserve to fight inflation. And during many other periods, Fed policy played a critical role in fighting slumps and promoting recovery. More recently, during the financial crisis of 2008 and the ensuing Great Recession, the Fed was at the very center of the fight to keep the economy from plunging into an abyss.

How does the Fed accomplish all this? Through changes in the money supply and interest rates, which are implemented by its unassuming-looking employees trading billions of dollars daily in U.S. government bonds. (And, as we learned in Chapter 18, to a lesser extent, the Fed can influence the money supply by changing the reserve requirements for banks.)

In this chapter we'll learn how monetary policy works—how actions by the Federal Reserve can have a powerful effect on the economy. We'll start by looking at the *demand for money* from households and firms. Then we'll see how the Fed's ability to change the *supply of money* allows it to move interest rates in the short run and thereby affect real GDP. We'll look at U.S. monetary policy in practice and compare it to the monetary policy of other central banks. We'll conclude by examining monetary policy's long-run effects. •

WHAT YOU WILL LEARN

- What is the **money demand curve?**
- Why does the **liquidity preference model** determine the interest rate in the short run?
- How does the Federal Reserve implement monetary policy?
- Why is monetary policy the main tool for stabilizing the economy?
- Why do economists believe in **monetary neutrality?**

A **certificate of deposit (CD)** is a bank-issued asset in which customers deposit funds for a specified amount of time and earn a specified interest rate.

The Demand for Money

In the previous chapter we learned about the various types of monetary aggregates: M1, the most commonly used definition of the money supply, consists of currency in circulation (cash), plus checkable bank deposits, plus traveler's checks; and M2, a broader definition of the money supply, consists of M1 plus deposits that can easily be transferred into checkable deposits. We also learned why people hold money—to make it easier to purchase goods and services. Now we'll go deeper, examining what determines how much money individuals and firms want to hold at any given time.

The Opportunity Cost of Holding Money

Most economic decisions involve trade-offs at the margin. That is, individuals decide how much of a good to consume by determining whether the benefit they'd gain from consuming a bit more of any given good is worth the cost. The same decision process is used when deciding how much money to hold.

Individuals and firms find it useful to hold some of their assets in the form of money because of the convenience that cash provides: money can be used to make purchases directly, but other assets can't. But there is a price to be paid for that convenience: money normally yields no rate of return, or a lower rate of return, than nonmonetary assets.

As an example of how convenience makes it worth incurring some opportunity costs, consider the substantial sums that Americans hold in cash and in zero-interest bank accounts linked to debit cards or money transmitters like PayPal and Venmo. By doing so they forgo the interest that could have been earned by putting those funds into an interest-bearing asset like a certificate of deposit. A **certificate of deposit,** or **CD,** is a bank-issued asset that allows customers to deposit their funds for a specified amount of time, and, in return, the bank pays a specified interest rate. For example, as of March 2019 the bank Capital One was offering a five-year CD paying 3.10% annually and a one-year CD paying 2.70%. But CDs also carry a penalty if funds are withdrawn before the specified amount of time—whether five years or one year—has elapsed.

There is a price to be paid for the convenience of holding money.

So, making sense of the demand for money is about understanding how individuals and firms trade off the benefit of holding monetary assets that provide convenience but little or no interest (like cash and zero-interest bank accounts), versus the benefit of holding nonmonetary assets that provide more interest but less convenience (like CDs). And that trade-off is affected by the interest rate. (As before, when we say *the interest rate* it is with the understanding that we mean a nominal interest rate—that is, it's unadjusted for inflation.)

Next, we'll examine how that trade-off changed dramatically from June 2007 to June 2009, when there was a big fall in interest rates.

Table 19-1 illustrates the opportunity cost of holding money in a specific month, June 2007. The first row shows the interest rate on one-month certificates of deposit—that is, the interest rate individuals could get if they were willing to tie their funds up for one month.

In June 2007, one-month CDs yielded 5.30%. The second row shows the interest rate on interest-bearing demand deposits. Funds in these accounts were more accessible than those in CDs, but the price of that convenience was a much lower interest rate, only 2.30%. Finally, the last row shows the interest rate on currency—cash in your wallet—which was, of course, zero.

TABLE 19-1 Selected Interest Rates, June 2007

One-month certificates of deposit (CDs)	5.30%
Interest-bearing demand deposits	2.30%
Currency	0

Data from: Federal Reserve Bank of St. Louis.

Table 19-1 shows the opportunity cost of holding money at one point in time, but the opportunity cost of holding money changes when the overall level of interest rates changes. Specifically, when the overall level of interest rates falls, the opportunity cost of holding money falls, too.

Table 19-2 illustrates this point by showing how selected interest rates changed between June 2007 and June 2009, a period when the Federal Reserve was slashing rates in an (unsuccessful) effort to fight off a rapidly worsening recession. A comparison between interest rates in those two months illustrates what happens when the opportunity cost of holding money falls sharply. Over the course of two years the federal funds rate, which is the rate the Fed controls most directly, fell by 5.05 percentage points. The interest rate on one-month CDs fell almost as much, 5.02 percentage points. These interest rates are **short-term interest rates**—rates on financial assets that come due, or mature, within less than a year.

TABLE 19-2 Interest Rates and the Opportunity Cost of Holding Money

	June 2007	June 2009
Federal funds rate	5.25%	0.20%
One-month certificates of deposit (CDs)	5.30%	0.28%
Interest-bearing demand deposits	2.30%	0.14%
Currency	0	0
CDs minus interest-bearing demand deposits (percentage points)	**3.00**	**0.14**
CDs minus currency (percentage points)	**5.30**	**0.28**

Data from: Federal Reserve Bank of St. Louis.

As short-term interest rates fell, the interest rate on money didn't fall by the same amount. The interest rate on currency, of course, remained at zero. The interest rate paid on demand deposits did fall, but by much less than short-term interest rates. As a comparison of the two columns of Table 19-2 shows, the opportunity cost of holding money fell. The last two rows of Table 19-2 summarize this comparison: they give the differences between the interest rates on CDs and demand deposits and between the interest rates on CDs and currency.

These differences—the opportunity cost of holding money rather than interest-bearing assets—declined sharply between June 2007 and June 2009. This reflects a general result: *the higher the short-term interest rate, the higher the opportunity cost of holding money; the lower the short-term interest rate, the lower the opportunity cost of holding money.*

The fact that the federal funds rate in Table 19-2 and the interest rate on one-month CDs fell by almost the same percentage is not an accident: all short-term interest rates tend to move together, with rare exceptions. The reason short-term interest rates tend to move together is that CDs and other short-term assets (like one-month and three-month U.S. Treasury bills) are in effect competing for the same business. Any short-term asset that offers a lower-than-average interest rate will be sold by investors, who will move their wealth into a higher-yielding short-term asset. The selling of the asset, in turn, forces its interest rate up, because investors must be rewarded with a higher rate to induce them to buy it.

Conversely, investors will move their wealth into any short-term financial asset that offers an above-average interest rate. The purchase of the asset drives its interest rate down when sellers find they can lower the rate of return on the asset and still find willing buyers. So, interest rates on short-term financial assets tend to be roughly the same because no asset will consistently offer a higher-than-average or a lower-than-average interest rate.

Table 19-2 contains only short-term interest rates. At any given moment, **long-term interest rates**—rates of interest on financial assets that mature, or come due, a number of years into the future—may be different from short-term interest rates. The difference between short-term and long-term interest rates is sometimes important as a practical matter.

It's short-term rates rather than long-term rates that affect money demand, because the decision to hold money involves trading off the convenience of holding cash versus the payoff from holding assets that mature in the short term—a year or less. For the moment, however, let's ignore the distinction between short-term and long-term rates and assume that there is only one interest rate.

Short-term interest rates are the interest rates on financial assets that mature within less than a year.

Long-term interest rates are interest rates on financial assets that mature a number of years in the future.

The **money demand curve** shows the relationship between the interest rate and the quantity of money demanded.

The Money Demand Curve

Because the overall level of interest rates affects the opportunity cost of holding money, the quantity of money individuals and firms want to hold is, other things equal, negatively related to the interest rate. In Figure 19-1, the horizontal axis shows the quantity of money demanded and the vertical axis shows the interest rate, r, which you can think of as a representative short-term interest rate such as the rate on one-month CDs.

The relationship between the interest rate and the quantity of money demanded by the public is illustrated by the **money demand curve**, MD, in Figure 19-1. The money demand curve slopes downward because, other things equal, a higher interest rate increases the opportunity cost of holding money, leading the public to reduce the quantity of money it demands. For example, if the interest rate is very low—say, 1%—the interest forgone by holding money is relatively small. As a result, individuals and firms will tend to hold relatively large amounts of money to avoid the cost and nuisance of converting other assets into money when making purchases.

By contrast, if the interest rate is relatively high—say, 15%, a level it reached in the United States in the early 1980s—the opportunity cost of holding money is high. People will respond by keeping only small amounts in cash and deposits, converting assets into money only when needed.

You might ask why we draw the money demand curve with the interest rate—as opposed to rates of return on other assets, such as stocks or real estate—on the vertical axis. The answer is that for most people the relevant question in deciding how much money to hold is whether to put the funds in the form of other assets that can be turned fairly quickly and easily into money. Stocks don't fit that definition because there are significant transaction fees when you sell stock (which is why stock market investors are advised not to buy and sell too often). Real estate doesn't fit the definition either because selling real estate involves even larger fees and can take a long time as well. So the relevant comparison is with assets that are "close to" money—assets like CDs that are less liquid than money but more liquid than stocks or real estate. And as we've already seen, the interest rates on all these assets normally move closely together.

FIGURE 19-1 The Money Demand Curve

The money demand curve illustrates the relationship between the interest rate and the quantity of money demanded. It slopes downward: a higher interest rate leads to a higher opportunity cost of holding money and reduces the quantity of money demanded. Correspondingly, a lower interest rate reduces the opportunity cost of holding money and increases the quantity of money demanded.

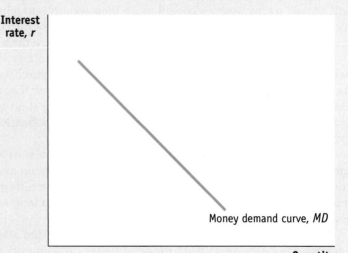

Shifts of the Money Demand Curve

A number of factors other than the interest rate affect the demand for money. When one of these factors changes, the money demand curve shifts. Figure 19-2 shows shifts of the money demand curve: an increase in the demand for money corresponds to a rightward shift of the *MD* curve, raising the quantity of money demanded at any given interest rate; a decrease in the demand for money corresponds to a leftward shift of the *MD* curve, reducing the quantity of money demanded at any given interest rate.

The most important factors causing the money demand curve to shift are changes in the aggregate price level, changes in real GDP, changes in credit markets and banking technology, and changes in institutions.

Changes in the Aggregate Price Level Americans keep a lot more cash on hand and funds in their checking accounts today than they did in the 1950s. One reason is that they have to if they want to be able to buy anything: almost everything costs more now than it did when you could get a burger, fries, and a drink at McDonald's for 45 cents and a gallon of gasoline for 29 cents. So, other things equal, higher prices increase the demand for money (a rightward shift of the *MD* curve), and lower prices decrease the demand for money (a leftward shift of the *MD* curve).

We can actually be more specific than this: other things equal, the demand for money is *proportional* to the price level. That is, if the aggregate price level rises by 20%, the quantity of money demanded at any given interest rate, such as r_1 in Figure 19-2, also rises by 20%—the movement from M_1 to M_2. Why? Because if the price of everything rises by 20%, it takes 20% more money to buy the same basket of goods and services. And if the aggregate price level falls by 20%, at any given interest rate the quantity of money demanded falls by 20%—shown by the movement from M_1 to M_3 at the interest rate r_1. As we'll see later, the fact that money demand is proportional to the price level has important implications for the long-run effects of monetary policy.

FIGURE 19-2 Increases and Decreases in the Demand for Money

The demand curve for money shifts when non-interest-rate factors that affect the demand for money change. An increase in money demand shifts the money demand curve to the right, from MD_1 to MD_2, and the quantity of money demanded rises at any given interest rate. A decrease in money demand shifts the money demand curve to the left, from MD_1 to MD_3, and the quantity of money demanded falls at any given interest rate.

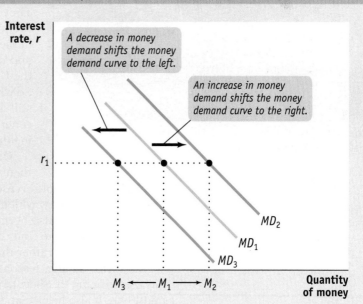

Changes in Real GDP Households and firms hold money as a way to facilitate purchases of goods and services. The larger the quantity of goods and services they buy, the larger the quantity of money they will want to hold at any given interest rate. So, an increase in real GDP—the total quantity of goods and services produced and sold in the economy—shifts the money demand curve rightward. A fall in real GDP shifts the money demand curve leftward.

Changes in Credit Markets and Banking Technology As late as the 1960s, almost all small purchases—lunch, groceries, and more—were made using cash because alternatives were few. Since then, however, the need for cash has been greatly reduced by a series of innovations, from widely available credit cards to debit cards to apps like PayPal that let you pay with your smartphone. ATMs and then online banking also made it much easier to transfer funds between accounts, so it became less necessary to hold a surplus of funds in checking accounts in order to make payments. All of these developments make it easier for people to make purchases and reduce the demand for money, shifting the demand curve for money to the left.

Changes in Institutions Changes in institutions can increase or decrease the demand for money. For example, until Regulation Q was eliminated in 1980, U.S. banks weren't allowed to offer interest on checking accounts. So the interest you would forgo by holding funds in a checking account instead of an interest-bearing asset made the opportunity cost of holding funds in checking accounts very high. When banking regulations changed, allowing banks to pay interest on checking account funds, the demand for money rose and shifted the money demand curve to the right.

No matter what they are shopping for, Japanese consumers tend to pay with cash rather than plastic.

ECONOMICS >> *in Action*
A Yen for Cash

Japan, say financial experts, is still a "cash society." Visitors from the United States or Europe are surprised at how little use the Japanese make of credit cards or debit cards. They do make many purchases with smartphones, yet they still carry remarkably large amounts of cash around in their wallets. Yet Japan is one of the most economically and technologically advanced countries, and superior to the United States in some areas, such as transportation. So why do the citizens of this economic powerhouse often still do business the way Americans and Europeans did a generation ago? The answer highlights the factors affecting the demand for money.

One reason the Japanese use cash so much is that their institutions never made the switch to heavy reliance on plastic. For complex reasons, Japan's retail sector is still dominated by small mom-and-pop stores, which are reluctant to invest in information technology. Japan's banks have also been slow about pushing transaction technology; visitors are often surprised to find that ATMs outside of major metropolitan areas close early in the evening rather than staying open all night.

But there's another reason the Japanese hold so much cash: there's little opportunity cost to doing so. Short-term interest rates in Japan have been below 1% since the mid-1990s. It also helps that the Japanese crime rate is quite low, so you are unlikely to have your wallet stolen. So why not hold cash?

1. Explain how each of the following would affect the quantity of money demanded. Does the change cause a movement along the money demand curve or a shift of the money demand curve?
   a. Short-term interest rates rise from 5% to 30%.
   b. All prices fall by 10%.
   c. New wireless technology automatically charges supermarket purchases to credit cards, eliminating the need to stop at the cash register.
   d. To avoid paying a sharp increase in taxes, residents of Laguria shift their assets into overseas bank accounts. These accounts are harder for tax authorities to trace but also harder for their owners to tap and convert funds into cash.
2. Which of the following will increase the opportunity cost of holding cash? Which will reduce it? Explain.
   a. In order to attract new customers, the new internet payment firm, PayBuddy, announces it will pay 0.5% interest on cash balances in a PayBuddy account.
   b. To attract more deposits, banks raise the interest paid on six-month CDs.
   c. In an effort to increase holiday sales, stores offer one-year zero-interest deals on purchases made with store credit cards.

Money and Interest Rates

Consistent with its statutory mandate, the Committee seeks to foster maximum employment and price stability. The economic outlook has strengthened in recent months. The Committee expects that, with further gradual adjustments in the stance of monetary policy, economic activity will expand at a moderate pace in the medium term and labor market conditions will remain strong. Inflation on a 12-month basis is expected to move up in coming months and to stabilize around the Committee's 2 percent objective over the medium term. Near-term risks to the economic outlook appear roughly balanced, but the Committee is monitoring inflation developments closely.

In view of realized and expected labor market conditions and inflation, the Committee decided to raise the target range for the federal funds rate to 1-1/2 to 1-3/4 percent. The stance of monetary policy remains accommodative, thereby supporting strong labor market conditions and a sustained return to 2 percent inflation.

So read part of a press release from the Federal Reserve issued on March 21, 2018. We learned about the federal funds rate in the previous chapter: it's the rate at which banks lend reserves to each other to meet the required reserve ratio. As the statement implies, at each of its eight-times-a-year meetings, a group called the Federal Open Market Committee sets a target value for the federal funds rate. It's then up to Fed officials to achieve that target. This is done by the Open Market Desk at the Federal Reserve Bank of New York, which buys and sells short-term U.S. government debt, known as Treasury bills, to achieve that target.

As we've already seen, other short-term interest rates, such as the rates on CDs, move with the federal funds rate. So when the Fed raised its target for the federal funds rate in March 2018, many other short-term interest rates also rose by about the same amount.

How does the Fed go about achieving a *target federal funds rate?* And more to the point, how is the Fed able to affect interest rates at all?

According to the **liquidity preference model of the interest rate,** the interest rate is determined by the supply and demand for money.

The **money supply curve** shows how the quantity of money supplied varies with the interest rate.

The Equilibrium Interest Rate

Recall that, for simplicity, we're assuming there is only one interest rate paid on nonmonetary financial assets, both in the short run and in the long run. To understand how the interest rate is determined, consider Figure 19-3, which illustrates the **liquidity preference model of the interest rate;** this model says that the interest rate is determined by the supply and demand for money in the market for money. Figure 19-3 combines the money demand curve, *MD*, with the **money supply curve,** *MS*, which shows how the quantity of money supplied by the Federal Reserve varies with the interest rate.

The Federal Reserve can increase or decrease the money supply: it usually does this through *open-market operations,* buying or selling Treasury bills, but it can also lend via the *discount window* or change *reserve requirements.* Let's assume for simplicity that the Fed, using one or more of these methods, simply chooses the level of the money supply that it believes will achieve its interest rate target. Then the money supply curve is a vertical line, *MS* in Figure 19-3, with a horizontal intercept corresponding to the money supply chosen by the Fed, $\overline{M}$. The money market equilibrium is at *E*, where *MS* and *MD* cross. At this point the quantity of money demanded equals the money supply, $\overline{M}$, leading to an equilibrium interest rate of r_E.

To understand why r_E is the equilibrium interest rate, consider what happens if the money market is at a point like *L*, where the interest rate, r_L, is below r_E. At r_L the public wants to hold the quantity of money M_L, an amount larger than the actual money supply, $\overline{M}$. This means that at point *L*, the public wants to shift some of its wealth out of interest-bearing assets such as CDs into money.

This result has two implications.

1. The quantity of money demanded is *more* than the quantity of money supplied.

2. The quantity of interest-bearing nonmoney assets demanded is *less* than the quantity supplied.

So those trying to sell nonmoney assets will find that they have to offer a higher interest rate to attract buyers. As a result, the interest rate will be driven up from r_L until the public wants to hold the quantity of money that is actually available, $\overline{M}$. That is, the interest rate will rise until it is equal to r_E.

FIGURE 19-3 Equilibrium in the Money Market

The money supply curve, *MS*, is vertical at the money supply chosen by the Federal Reserve, $\overline{M}$. The money market is in equilibrium at the interest rate r_E: the quantity of money demanded by the public is equal to $\overline{M}$, the quantity of money supplied.

At a point such as *L*, the interest rate, r_L, is below r_E and the corresponding quantity of money demanded, M_L, exceeds the money supply, $\overline{M}$. In an attempt to shift their wealth out of nonmoney interest-bearing financial assets and raise their money holdings, investors drive the interest rate up to r_E. At a point such as *H*, the interest rate r_H exceeds r_E and the corresponding quantity of money demanded, M_H, is less than the money supply, $\overline{M}$. In an attempt to shift out of money holdings into nonmoney interest-bearing financial assets, investors drive the interest rate down to r_E.

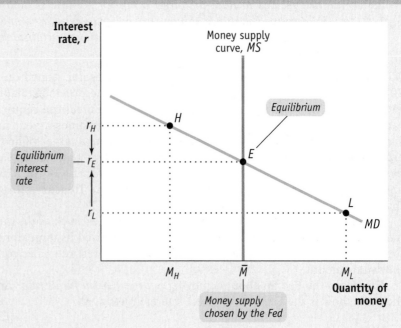

Now consider what happens if the money market is at a point such as H in Figure 19-3, where the interest rate r_H is above r_E. In that case, the quantity of money demanded, M_H, is less than the quantity of money supplied, $\overline{M}$. Correspondingly, the quantity of interest-bearing nonmoney assets demanded is greater than the quantity supplied. Those trying to sell interest-bearing nonmoney assets will find that they can offer a lower interest rate and still find willing buyers. This leads to a fall in the interest rate from r_H. It falls until the public wants to hold the quantity of money that is actually available, $\overline{M}$. Again, the interest rate will end up at r_E.

The **target federal funds rate** is the Federal Reserve's desired federal funds rate.

Monetary Policy and the Interest Rate

Let's examine how the Federal Reserve can use changes in the money supply to change the interest rate. Figure 19-4 shows what happens when the Fed increases the money supply from $\overline{M}_1$ to $\overline{M}_2$. The economy is originally in equilibrium at E_1, with an equilibrium interest rate of r_1 and money supply, $\overline{M}_1$. An increase in the money supply by the Fed to $\overline{M}_2$ shifts the money supply curve to the right, from MS_1 to MS_2, and leads to a fall in the equilibrium interest rate to r_2. Why? Because r_2 is the only interest rate at which the public is willing to hold the quantity of money actually supplied, $\overline{M}_2$.

So an increase in the money supply drives the interest rate down. Conversely, a reduction in the money supply drives the interest rate up. By adjusting the money supply up or down, the Fed can set the interest rate.

In practice, at each meeting the Federal Open Market Committee decides on the interest rate to prevail for the next six weeks, until its next meeting. The Fed sets a **target federal funds rate,** a desired level for the federal funds rate. This target is then enforced by the Open Market Desk of the Federal Reserve Bank of New York which adjusts the money supply through the purchase and sale of Treasury bills until the actual federal funds rate equals the target rate. The other tools of monetary policy, lending through the discount window and changes in reserve requirements, aren't used on a regular basis (although the Fed used discount window lending in its efforts to address the 2008 financial crisis).

FIGURE 19-4 The Effect of an Increase in the Money Supply on the Interest Rate

The Federal Reserve can lower the interest rate by increasing the money supply. Here, the equilibrium interest rate falls from r_1 to r_2 in response to an increase in the money supply from $\overline{M}_1$ to $\overline{M}_2$. In order to induce people to hold the larger quantity of money, the interest rate must fall from r_1 to r_2.

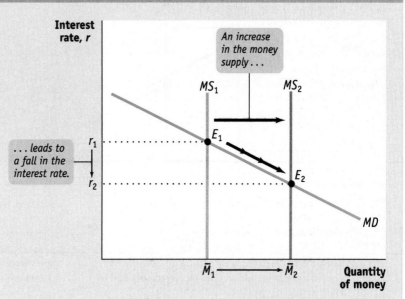

Figure 19-5 shows how this works. In both panels, r_T is the target federal funds rate. In panel (a), the initial money supply curve is MS_1 with money supply $\overline{M}_1$, and the equilibrium interest rate, r_1, is above the target rate. To lower the interest rate to r_T, the Fed makes an open-market purchase of Treasury bills that leads to an increase in the money supply via the money multiplier. This is illustrated in panel (a) by the rightward shift of the money supply curve from MS_1 to MS_2 and an increase in the money supply to $\overline{M}_2$. This drives the equilibrium interest rate down to the target rate, r_T.

Panel (b) shows the opposite case. Again, the initial money supply curve is MS_1 with money supply $\overline{M}_1$. But this time the equilibrium interest rate, r_1, is below the target federal funds rate, r_T. In this case, the Fed will make an open-market sale of Treasury bills, leading to a fall in the money supply to $\overline{M}_2$ via the money multiplier. The money supply curve shifts leftward from MS_1 to MS_2, driving the equilibrium interest rate up to the target federal funds rate, r_T.

Long-Term Interest Rates

Earlier we mentioned that long-term interest rates—rates on bonds or loans that mature in several years—don't necessarily move with short-term interest rates. How is that possible, and what does it say about monetary policy?

For example, in March of 2018 after the Fed raised the federal funds rates, the short-term interest rate in the United States was 1.70%. But long-term interest rates—rates on bonds or loans that mature in several years—were different and higher. The interest rate on 10-year government bonds was 2.84%.

Why were these long-term rates so different? Because long-term rates reflect expected future monetary policy, which in turn largely depends on the future economic outlook.

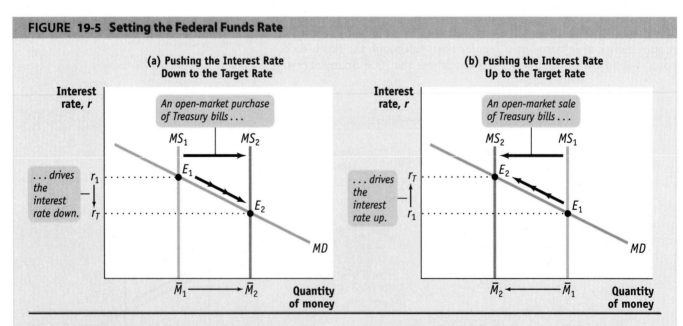

FIGURE 19-5 Setting the Federal Funds Rate

The Federal Reserve sets a target for the federal funds rate and uses open-market operations to achieve that target. In both panels the target rate is r_T. In panel (a) the initial equilibrium interest rate, r_1, is above the target rate. The Fed increases the money supply by making an open-market purchase of Treasury bills, pushing the money supply curve rightward, from MS_1 to MS_2, and driving the interest rate down to r_T. In panel (b) the initial equilibrium interest rate, r_1, is below the target rate. The Fed reduces the money supply by making an open-market sale of Treasury bills, pushing the money supply curve leftward, from MS_1 to MS_2, and driving the interest rate up to r_T.

Consider the case of Min, who has already decided to place $10,000 in U.S. government bonds for the next two years. However, she hasn't decided whether to put the money in one-year bonds, at a 4% rate of interest, or two-year bonds, at a 5% rate of interest. If she buys the one-year bond, then in one year, Min will receive the $10,000 she paid for the bond (the *principal*) plus interest earned. If instead she buys the two-year bond, Min will have to wait until the end of the second year to receive her principal and her interest.

You might think that the two-year bonds are a clearly better deal—but they may not be. Suppose that Min expects the rate of interest on one-year bonds to rise sharply next year. If she puts her funds in one-year bonds this year, she will be able to reinvest the money at a much higher rate next year. And this could give her a two-year rate of return that is higher than if she put her funds into the two-year bonds today.

For example, if the rate of interest on one-year bonds rises from 4% this year to 8% next year, putting her funds in a one-year bond today and in another one-year bond a year from now will give her an annual rate of return over the next two years of about 6%, better than the 5% rate on two-year bonds.

The same considerations apply to all investors deciding between short-term and long-term bonds. If they expect short-term interest rates to rise, investors may buy short-term bonds even if long-term bonds bought today offer a higher interest rate today. If they expect short-term interest rates to fall, investors may buy long-term bonds even if short-term bonds bought today offer a higher interest rate today.

As the example suggests, long-term interest rates largely reflect the average expectation in the market about what's going to happen to short-term rates in the future. What happened in 2018 is that investors expected the U.S. economy to continue growing in the near future, which led to the expectation that the Fed would raise short-term rates.

Expected monetary policy is not, however, the whole story: risk is also a factor. Let's return to Min's decision: whether to buy one-year or two-year bonds. Suppose that there is some chance she will need to cash in her investment after just one year—say, to meet an emergency medical bill. If she buys two-year bonds, she would have to sell those bonds to meet the unexpected expense. But what price will she get for those bonds? It depends on what has happened to interest rates in the rest of the economy. As we've learned, bond prices and interest rates move in opposite directions: if interest rates rise, bond prices fall, and vice versa.

This means that Min will face extra risk if she buys two-year rather than one-year bonds, because, if a year from now bond prices fall and she must sell her bonds in order to raise cash, she will lose money on the bonds. Owing to this risk factor, long-term interest rates are, on average, higher than short-term rates in order to compensate long-term bond purchasers for the higher risk they face (although this relationship is reversed when short-term rates are unusually high).

As we will soon see, the fact that long-term rates don't necessarily move with short-term rates is sometimes an important consideration for monetary policy.

Advertising during the two world wars increased the demand for government long-term bonds from savers who might have been otherwise reluctant to tie up their funds for several years.

ECONOMICS >> *in Action*
Up the Down Staircase

We began this section with the Fed's March 2018 announcement that it was raising its target interest rate. By historical standards, however, the target rate was still quite low. As Figure 19-6 shows, in early 2007, before the financial crisis, the target rate was 5.25%. But when the financial crisis hit in 2008, the Fed drastically cut rates in an effort to fight the Great Recession, and kept them close to zero for seven years.

FIGURE 19-6 The Fed's Target, 2007–2019

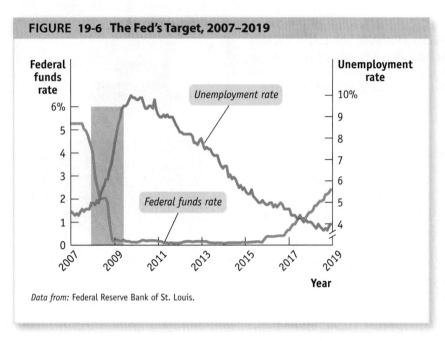

Data from: Federal Reserve Bank of St. Louis.

Why did the Fed keep rates so low? Because a severe recession followed by a slow recovery kept unemployment—also shown in the figure—very high, while inflation stayed low, for a very long time. In effect, the Fed believed that it needed to keep the pedal to the metal.

By late 2015, however, the economy had clearly improved, with unemployment, in particular, down roughly to its pre-crisis level. And in December 2015 the Federal Open Market Committee began inching back toward a more historically normal monetary policy, a process still underway in March 2018. But "inching" is the word: in the aftermath of that March 2018 rate hike, the federal funds rate was still well below what it had been a decade earlier.

Why was the Fed moving so slowly? For one thing, while the economy had clearly recovered from the worst of the Great Recession, it was hardly experiencing an inflationary boom. In fact, the Fed's preferred measure of inflation was still a bit below its target.

Also, a significant number of economists worried that changes in the economic environment, in particular an aging population and slowing productivity growth, meant that maintaining full employment would require keeping interest rates more or less permanently low by historical standards. Investors seemed to agree: long-term interest rates in early 2018 were only about 2.75%, which implied that, for the foreseeable future, investors didn't expect the Fed to return to the kind of interest rates it used to target.

But was this expectation right? Should the Fed have moved more quickly—or not moved at all? Time will tell. But, the changes in the Fed's target over the period from 2007 to 2018 offer a clear illustration of the forces that drive monetary policy.

>> **Quick Review**

• According to the **liquidity preference model of the interest rate,** the equilibrium interest rate is determined by the money demand curve and the **money supply curve.**

• The Federal Reserve can move the interest rate through open-market operations that shift the money supply curve. In practice, the Fed sets a **target federal funds rate** and uses open-market operations to achieve that target.

• Long-term interest rates reflect expectations about what's going to happen to short-term rates in the future. Because of risk, long-term interest rates tend to be higher than short-term rates.

>> Check Your Understanding 19-2

Solutions appear at back of book.

1. Assume that there is an increase in the demand for money at every interest rate. Draw a diagram showing the effect of this on the equilibrium interest rate for a given money supply.

2. Now assume that the Fed is following a policy of targeting the federal funds rate. What will the Fed do in the situation described in Question 1 to keep the federal funds rate unchanged? Illustrate with a diagram.

3. Malia must decide whether to buy a one-year bond today and another one a year from now, or to buy a two-year bond today. In which of the following scenarios is she better off taking the first action? The second action?
   a. This year, the interest on a one-year bond is 4%; next year, it will be 10%. The interest rate on a two-year bond is 5%.
   b. This year, the interest rate on a one-year bond is 4%; next year, it will be 1%. The interest rate on a two-year bond is 3%.

Monetary Policy and Aggregate Demand

We saw how fiscal policy can be used to stabilize the economy in Chapter 17. Now we will see how monetary policy, which we've defined as changes in the money supply, and the interest rate, can play the same role.

Expansionary and Contractionary Monetary Policy

In Chapter 16 we learned that monetary policy shifts the aggregate demand curve. We can now explain how that works: through the effect of monetary policy on the interest rate.

Figure 19-7 illustrates the process. Suppose, first, that the Federal Reserve wants to reduce interest rates, so it expands the money supply. As you can see in the top portion of the figure, a lower interest rate, in turn, will lead, other things equal, to more investment spending. This will in turn lead to higher consumer spending, through the multiplier process, and to an increase in aggregate output demanded. In the end, the total quantity of goods and services demanded at any given aggregate price level rises when the quantity of money increases, and the *AD* curve shifts to the right. Monetary policy that increases the demand for goods and services is known as **expansionary monetary policy.**

Suppose, alternatively, that the Federal Reserve wants to increase interest rates, so it contracts the money supply. You can see this process illustrated in the bottom portion of the diagram. Contraction of the money supply leads to a higher interest rate. The higher interest rate leads to lower investment spending, then to lower consumer spending, and then to a decrease in aggregate output demanded. So, the total quantity of goods and services demanded falls when the money supply is reduced, and the *AD* curve shifts to the left. Monetary policy that decreases the demand for goods and services is called **contractionary monetary policy.** (It is also commonly called *tight monetary policy.*)

Expansionary monetary policy is monetary policy that increases aggregate demand.

Contractionary monetary policy is monetary policy that decreases aggregate demand.

"I told you the Fed should have tightened."

FIGURE 19-7   Expansionary and Contractionary Monetary Policy

EXPANSIONARY

Increase money supply → Lower interest rate → Higher investment spending raises income → Higher consumer spending (via multiplier) → Increase in aggregate demand and *AD* curve shifts to the right

Aggregate price level — *Real GDP*; AD_1, AD_2

CONTRACTIONARY

Decrease money supply → Higher interest rate → Lower investment spending reduces income → Lower consumer spending (via multiplier) → Decrease in aggregate demand and *AD* curve shifts to the left

Aggregate price level — *Real GDP*; AD_2, AD_1

The top portion of the diagram shows what happens when the Fed adopts an expansionary monetary policy and increases the money supply. Interest rates fall, leading to higher investment spending, which raises income, which, in turn, raises consumer spending and shifts the *AD* curve to the right. The bottom portion shows what happens when the Fed adopts a contractionary monetary policy and reduces the money supply. Interest rates rise, leading to lower investment spending and a reduction in income. This lowers consumer spending and shifts the *AD* curve to the left.

Monetary Policy in Practice

How does the Fed decide whether to use expansionary or contractionary monetary policy? And how does it decide how much is enough? As we've learned, policy makers try to both fight recessions and ensure *price stability:* low (though usually not zero) inflation. Actual monetary policy reflects a combination of these goals.

In general, the Fed and other central banks tend to engage in expansionary monetary policy when actual real GDP is below potential output. Panel (a) of Figure 19-8 shows the U.S. output gap, defined in Chapter 16 as the percentage difference between actual real GDP and potential output, versus the federal funds rate since 1985. (Recall that the output gap is positive when actual real GDP exceeds potential output.) As you can see, the Fed tends to raise interest rates when the output gap is rising (when the economy is developing an inflationary gap) and cut rates when the output gap is falling. (The exception is the period from 2009 to 2016 when the federal funds rate was stuck near zero, a phenomenon called the *zero lower bound on interest rates*.)

The big exception was the late 1990s, when the Fed left rates steady for several years even as the economy developed a positive output gap (which went along with a low unemployment rate). One reason the Fed was willing to keep interest rates low in the late 1990s was that inflation was low.

Panel (b) of Figure 19-8 compares the inflation rate, measured as the rate of change in consumer prices excluding food and energy, with the federal funds rate. You can see how low inflation during the mid-1990s, the early 2000s, and the late 2000s helped encourage loose monetary policy in the late 1990s, in 2002–2003, and again beginning in 2008.

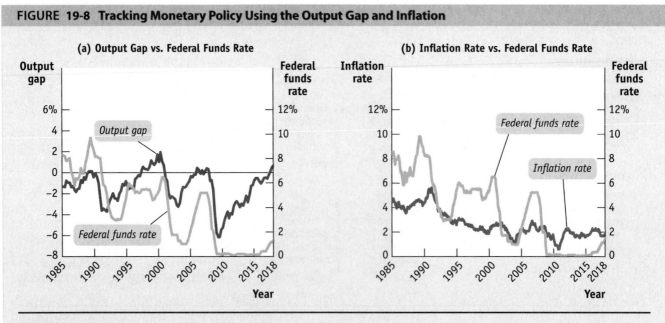

FIGURE 19-8 Tracking Monetary Policy Using the Output Gap and Inflation

Panel (a) shows that the federal funds rate usually rises when the output gap is rising, and falls when the output gap is falling. Panel (b) illustrates that the federal funds rate tends to be high when inflation is high and low when inflation is low.

Data from: Federal Reserve Bank of St. Louis.

The Taylor Rule Method of Setting Monetary Policy

In 1993 Stanford economist John Taylor suggested that monetary policy should follow a simple rule that takes into account concerns about both the business cycle and inflation. He also suggested that actual monetary policy often looks as if the Federal Reserve was, in fact, more or less following the proposed rule. A **Taylor rule for monetary policy** is a rule for setting interest rates that takes into account the inflation rate and the output gap or, in some cases, the unemployment rate.

A widely cited example of a Taylor rule is a relationship among Fed policy, inflation, and unemployment estimated by economists at the Federal Reserve Bank of San Francisco. These economists found that between 1988 and 2008 the Fed's behavior was well summarized by the following Taylor rule:

Federal funds rate = 2.07 + 1.28 × inflation rate − 1.95 × unemployment gap

where the inflation rate was measured by the change over the previous year in consumer prices excluding food and energy, and the unemployment gap was the difference between the actual unemployment rate and Congressional Budget Office estimates of the natural rate of unemployment.

Figure 19-9 compares the federal funds rate predicted by this rule with the actual federal funds rate from 1985 to early 2018. As you can see, the Fed's decisions were quite close to those predicted by this particular Taylor rule from 1985 through the end of 2008. We'll talk about what happened after 2008 shortly.

Inflation Targeting

Until January 2012, the Fed did not explicitly commit itself to achieving a particular inflation rate. However, in January 2012, the Fed announced that it would set its policy to maintain an approximately 2% inflation rate per year. With that statement, the Fed joined a number of other central banks that have explicit inflation targets. So, rather than using a Taylor rule to set monetary policy, they instead announce the inflation rate that they want to achieve—the *inflation target*—and set policy in an attempt to hit that target. This method of setting monetary policy, called **inflation targeting,** involves having the central bank announce the

A **Taylor rule for monetary policy** is a rule that sets the federal funds rate according to the level of the inflation rate and either the output gap or the unemployment rate.

Inflation targeting occurs when the central bank sets an explicit target for the inflation rate and sets monetary policy in order to hit that target.

FIGURE 19-9 The Taylor Rule and the Federal Funds Rate

The purple line shows the federal funds rate predicted by the San Francisco Fed's version of the Taylor rule, which relates the interest rate to the inflation rate and the unemployment rate. The green line shows the actual federal funds rate. The actual rate tracked the predicted rate quite closely through the end of 2008. After that, however, the Taylor rule called for negative interest rates, which is a difficult and problematic goal to achieve.

Data from: Bureau of Labor Statistics; Congressional Budget Office; Federal Reserve Bank of St. Louis; Glenn D. Rudebusch, "The Fed's Monetary Policy Response to the Current Crisis," *FRBSF Economic Letter* #2009–17 (May 22, 2009).

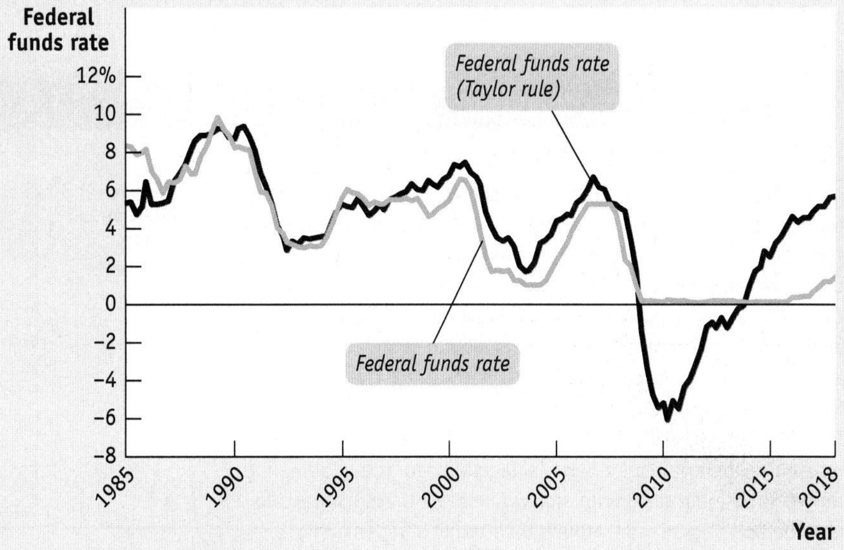

inflation rate it is trying to achieve and set policy in an attempt to hit that target. The central bank of New Zealand, which was the first country to adopt inflation targeting, specified a range for that target of 1% to 3%.

Other central banks commit themselves to achieving a specific number. For example, the Bank of England has committed to keeping inflation at 2%. In practice, there doesn't seem to be much difference between these versions: central banks with a target range for inflation seem to aim for the middle of that range, and central banks with a fixed target tend to give themselves considerable wiggle room.

One major difference between inflation targeting and the Taylor rule method is that inflation targeting is forward-looking rather than backward-looking. That is, the Taylor rule method adjusts monetary policy in response to *past* inflation, but inflation targeting is based on a forecast of future inflation.

Advocates of inflation targeting argue that it has two key advantages over a Taylor rule: *transparency* and *accountability*. First, economic uncertainty is reduced because the central bank's plan is transparent: the public knows the objective of an inflation-targeting central bank. Second, the central bank's success can be judged by seeing how closely actual inflation rates have matched the inflation target, making central bankers accountable.

Critics of inflation targeting argue that it's too restrictive because there are times when other concerns—like the stability of the financial system—should take priority over achieving any particular inflation rate. Indeed, starting in late 2013 the Taylor rule rate and the federal funds rate diverged significantly, as the Fed kept the interest rate close to zero while the Taylor rule rate climbed. The Fed's actions were motivated by the fear that an interest rate rise could push the persistently weak economy back into turmoil and recession.

Many American macroeconomists have had positive things to say about inflation targeting—including Ben Bernanke (the Fed chair from 2006 through early 2014). And in January 2012 the Fed declared that what it means by the "price stability" it seeks is 2% inflation, although there was no explicit commitment about when this inflation rate would be achieved.

The Zero Lower Bound Problem

As Figure 19-9 shows, a Taylor rule based on inflation and the unemployment rate does a good job of predicting Federal Reserve policy from 1985 through 2008. After that, however, things go awry, and for a simple reason: with very high

---

🌐 GLOBAL COMPARISON   INFLATION TARGETS

This figure shows the target inflation rates of six central banks that have adopted inflation targeting. The central bank of New Zealand introduced inflation targeting in 1990. Today it has an inflation target range of 1% to 3%. The central banks of Canada and Sweden have the same target range but also specify 2% as the precise target. The central bank of Norway has a target of 2.5%, with an allowable range from 1.5% to 3.5%, while the central bank of Britain specifies an inflation target of 2%. Since 2012, the U.S. Federal Reserve also targets inflation at 2%.

In practice, these differences in detail don't seem to lead to significantly different results. New Zealand aims for the middle of its range, at 2% inflation; Britain, Norway, and the United States allow considerable wiggle room around their target inflation rates.

Data from: IMF.

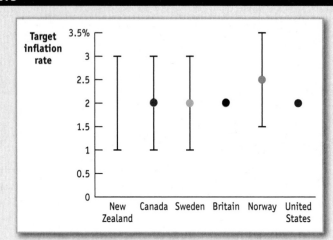

unemployment and low inflation, the same Taylor rule called for an interest rate significantly less than zero, which is a difficult and problematic goal to achieve.

Negative interest rates are a problem because people always have the alternative of holding cash, which offers a zero interest rate. Why, then, would they ever buy a bond yielding an interest rate less than zero?

Until 2014 most economists believed that it was basically impossible for interest rates to go below zero. That year, however, the central bank of Switzerland did the previously unthinkable, setting rates slightly below zero. It turns out that even at a slightly negative interest rate, there are limits to how much cash the public is willing to hold, because storing cash is expensive: you need vaults that are secure against loss. By 2015, the Swiss equivalent of the federal funds rate was –0.75%, and both the European Central Bank and the Bank of Japan also had slightly negative rates.

So, the zero lower bound isn't an absolute limit. Still, no central bank has tried to push rates significantly below zero, say down to –3% or –6%, which is what the Taylor rule suggested for the United States in 2009 and 2010. This is explained partly because rates that low would lead to the hoarding of cash. Also, negative interest rates are widely believed to cause big problems for the banking system, with adverse effects on the economy as a whole. This set of circumstances leads to what is called the **zero lower bound for interest rates:** interest rates cannot fall much below zero without causing significant problems.

The Fed has never been willing to push rates below zero. This in turn means that when inflation is low and the economy is operating far below potential, normal monetary policy—open-market purchases of short-term government debt to expand the money supply—runs out of room to operate because short-term interest rates are already at or near zero. Economists refer to this situation as *running up against the zero lower bound.*

In November 2010 the Fed began an attempt to circumvent the problem caused by its inability to reduce interest rates further despite economic weakness; this attempt went by the somewhat obscure name *quantitative easing.* Instead of purchasing only short-term government debt, it began buying longer-term government debt—five-year or six-year bonds, rather than three-month Treasury bills. And, as we know, long-term interest rates don't exactly follow short-term rates. At the time the Fed began this program, short-term rates were near zero, but rates on longer-term bonds were between 2% and 3%. The Fed hoped that direct purchases of these longer-term bonds would drive down interest rates on long-term debt, exerting an expansionary effect on the economy.

Later the Fed expanded the program, also purchasing mortgage-backed securities, which normally offer somewhat higher rates than U.S. government debt. Here, too, the hope was that these rates could be driven down, with an expansionary effect on the economy. As with ordinary open-market operations, quantitative easing was undertaken by the Federal Reserve Bank of New York.

Was this policy effective? The Federal Reserve believes that it helped the economy. However, the pace of recovery remained disappointingly slow. Starting in 2016, the Fed began to slowly raise rates by an amount less than a Taylor rule would have predicted, reflecting the sluggish pace of the recovery.

The **zero lower bound for interest rates** means that interest rates cannot fall much below zero without causing significant problems.

ECONOMICS >> *in Action*
What the Fed Wants, the Fed Gets

What's the evidence that the Fed can actually cause an economic contraction or expansion? You might think that finding such evidence is just a matter of looking at what happens to the economy when interest rates go up or down. But it turns out that there's a big problem with that approach: the Fed usually changes interest rates in an attempt to tame the business cycle, raising rates if the economy

FIGURE 19-10 When the Fed Wants a Recession

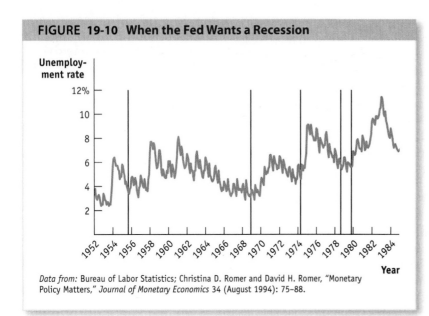

Data from: Bureau of Labor Statistics; Christina D. Romer and David H. Romer, "Monetary Policy Matters," *Journal of Monetary Economics* 34 (August 1994): 75–88.

is expanding and reducing rates if the economy is slumping. So in the actual data, it often looks as if low interest rates go along with a weak economy and high rates go along with a strong economy.

In a famous paper titled "Does Monetary Policy Matter?", macroeconomists Christina Romer and David Romer solved this problem by focusing on episodes in which monetary policy wasn't a reaction to the business cycle. Specifically, they used minutes from the Federal Open Market Committee and other sources to identify episodes "in which the Federal Reserve in effect decided to attempt to create a recession to reduce inflation." Rather than just using monetary policy as a tool of macroeconomic stabilization, sometimes it is used to eliminate *embedded inflation*—inflation that people believe will persist into the future. In such a case, the Fed needs to create a recessionary gap—not just eliminate an inflationary gap—to wring embedded inflation out of the economy.

Figure 19-10 shows the unemployment rate between 1952 and 1984 and also identifies five dates on which, according to Romer and Romer, the Fed decided that it wanted a recession (the vertical lines). In four out of the five cases, the decision to contract the economy was followed, after a modest lag, by a rise in the unemployment rate. On average, Romer and Romer found the unemployment rate rises by 2 percentage points after the Fed decides that unemployment needs to go up.

So yes, the Fed gets what it wants.

>> Quick Review

• The Federal Reserve can use **expansionary monetary policy** to increase aggregate demand and **contractionary monetary policy** to reduce aggregate demand. The Federal Reserve and other central banks generally try to tame the business cycle while keeping the inflation rate low but positive.

• Under a **Taylor rule for monetary policy,** the target federal funds rate rises when there is high inflation and either a positive output gap or very low unemployment; it falls when there is low or negative inflation and either a negative output gap or high unemployment.

• In contrast, some central banks set monetary policy by **inflation targeting,** a forward-looking policy rule, rather than by using the Taylor rule, a backward-looking policy rule. Although inflation targeting has the benefits of transparency and accountability, some think it is too restrictive. Until 2008, the Fed followed a loosely defined Taylor rule. Starting in early 2012, it began inflation targeting with a target of 2% per year.

• There is a **zero lower bound for interest rates**—they cannot fall much below zero without causing significant problems—that limits the effectiveness of monetary policy.

• Because it is subject to fewer lags than fiscal policy, monetary policy is the main tool for macroeconomic stabilization.

>> Check Your Understanding 19-3

Solutions appear at back of book.

1. Suppose the economy is currently suffering from an output gap and the Federal Reserve uses an expansionary monetary policy to close that gap. Describe the short-run effect of this policy on the following.
   a. The money supply curve
   b. The equilibrium interest rate
   c. Investment spending
   d. Consumer spending
   e. Aggregate output

2. In setting monetary policy, which central bank—one that operates according to a Taylor rule or one that operates by inflation targeting—is likely to respond more directly to a financial crisis? Explain.

Money, Output, and Prices in the Long Run

Through its expansionary and contractionary effects, monetary policy is generally the policy tool of choice to help stabilize the economy. However, not all actions by central banks are productive. In particular, central banks sometimes print money, not to fight a recessionary gap but to help the government pay its bills, an action that typically destabilizes the economy.

What happens when a change in the money supply pushes the economy away from, rather than toward, long-run equilibrium? As we've learned, the economy is self-correcting in the long run: a demand shock has only a temporary effect on aggregate output. If the demand shock is the result of a change in the money supply, we can make a stronger statement: in the long run, changes in the quantity of money affect the aggregate price level, but they do not change real aggregate output or the interest rate. To see why, let's look at what happens if the central bank permanently increases the money supply.

Short-Run and Long-Run Effects of an Increase in the Money Supply

To analyze the long-run effects of monetary policy, it's helpful to think of the central bank as choosing a target for the money supply rather than the interest rate. In assessing the effects of an increase in the money supply, we return to the analysis of the long-run effects of an increase in aggregate demand.

Figure 19-11 shows the short-run and long-run effects of an increase in the money supply when the economy begins at potential output, Y_1. The initial short-run aggregate supply curve is $SRAS_1$, the long-run aggregate supply curve is $LRAS$, and the initial aggregate demand curve is AD_1. The economy's initial equilibrium is at E_1, a point of both short-run and long-run macroeconomic equilibrium because it is on both the short-run and the long-run aggregate supply curves. Real GDP is at potential output, Y_1.

Now suppose there is an increase in the money supply. Other things equal, an increase in the money supply reduces the interest rate, which increases investment spending, which leads to a further rise in consumer spending, and so on. So an increase in the money supply increases the quantity of goods and services

---

FIGURE 19-11   The Short-Run and Long-Run Effects of an Increase in the Money Supply

When the economy is already at potential output, an increase in the money supply generates a positive short-run effect, but no long-run effect, on real GDP.

Here, the economy begins at E_1, a point of short-run and long-run macroeconomic equilibrium. An increase in the money supply shifts the AD curve rightward, and the economy moves to a new short-run macroeconomic equilibrium at E_2 and a new real GDP of Y_2. But E_2 is not a long-run equilibrium: Y_2 exceeds potential output, Y_1, leading over time to an increase in nominal wages. In the long run, the increase in nominal wages shifts the short-run aggregate supply curve leftward, to a new position at $SRAS_2$.

The economy reaches a new short-run and long-run macroeconomic equilibrium at E_3 on the $LRAS$ curve, and output falls back to potential output, Y_1. When the economy is already at potential output, the only long-run effect of an increase in the money supply is an increase in the aggregate price level from P_1 to P_3.

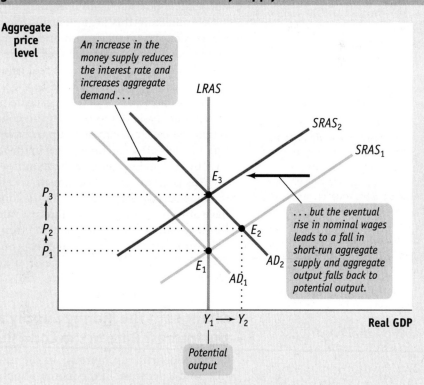

An increase in the money supply reduces the interest rate and increases aggregate demand . . .

. . . but the eventual rise in nominal wages leads to a fall in short-run aggregate supply and aggregate output falls back to potential output.

According to the concept of **monetary neutrality,** changes in the money supply have no real effects on the economy.

demanded, shifting the AD curve rightward, to AD_2. In the short run, the economy moves to a new short-run macroeconomic equilibrium at E_2. The price level rises from P_1 to P_2, and real GDP rises from Y_1 to Y_2. That is, both the aggregate price level and aggregate output increase in the short run.

But the aggregate output level, Y_2, is above potential output. As a result, nominal wages will rise over time, causing the short-run aggregate supply curve to shift leftward. This process stops only when the $SRAS$ curve ends up at $SRAS_2$ and the economy ends up at point E_3, a point of both short-run and long-run macroeconomic equilibrium. The long-run effect of an increase in the money supply, then, is that the aggregate price level has increased from P_1 to P_3, but aggregate output is back at potential output, Y_1. In the long run, a monetary expansion raises the aggregate price level but has no effect on real GDP.

We won't describe the effects of a monetary contraction in detail, but the same logic applies. In the short run, a fall in the money supply leads to a fall in aggregate output as the economy moves down the short-run aggregate supply curve. In the long run, however, the monetary contraction reduces only the aggregate price level, and real GDP returns to potential output.

Monetary Neutrality

How much does a change in the money supply change the aggregate price level in the long run? The answer is that a change in the money supply leads to an equal proportional change in the aggregate price level in the long run. For example, if the money supply falls 25%, the aggregate price level falls 25% in the long run; if the money supply rises 50%, the aggregate price level rises 50% in the long run.

How do we know this? Consider the following thought experiment: suppose all prices in the economy—prices of final goods and services and also factor prices, such as nominal wage rates—double. And suppose the money supply doubles at the same time. What difference does this make to the economy in real terms? The answer is none. All real variables in the economy—such as real GDP and the real value of the money supply (the amount of goods and services it can buy)—are unchanged. So there is no reason for anyone to behave any differently.

We can state this argument in reverse: if the economy starts out in long-run macroeconomic equilibrium and the money supply changes, restoring long-run macroeconomic equilibrium requires restoring all real values to their original values. This includes restoring the real value of the money supply to its original level. So if the money supply falls 25%, the aggregate price level must fall 25%; if the money supply rises 50%, the aggregate price level must rise 50%; and so on.

This analysis demonstrates the concept known as **monetary neutrality,** in which changes in the money supply have no real effects on the economy. In the long run, the only effect of an increase in the money supply is to raise the aggregate price level by an equal percentage. Economists argue that *money is neutral in the long run.*

This is, however, a good time to recall the dictum of John Maynard Keynes: "In the long run we are all dead." In the long run, changes in the money supply don't have any effect on real GDP, interest rates, or anything else except the price level. But it would be foolish to conclude from this that the Fed is irrelevant. Monetary policy does have powerful real effects on the economy in the short run, often making the difference between recession and expansion. And that matters a lot for society's welfare.

Changes in the Money Supply and the Interest Rate in the Long Run

In the short run, an increase in the money supply leads to a fall in the interest rate, and a decrease in the money supply leads to a rise in the interest rate. In the long run, however, changes in the money supply don't affect the interest rate.

FIGURE 19-12 The Long-Run Determination of the Interest Rate

The economy is initially at E_1, a long-run macroeconomic equilibrium. In the short run, an increase in the money supply, from $\overline{M}_1$ to $\overline{M}_2$ pushes the interest rate down from r_1 to r_2. The economy moves to E_2, a short-run equilibrium. In the long run, however, the aggregate price level rises in proportion to the increase in the money supply, leading to an increase in money demand at any given interest rate in proportion to the increase in the aggregate price level, as shown by the shift from MD_1 to MD_2. The result is that the quantity of money demanded at any given interest rate rises by the same amount as the quantity of money supplied. The economy moves to long-run equilibrium at E_3 and the interest rate returns to to r_1.

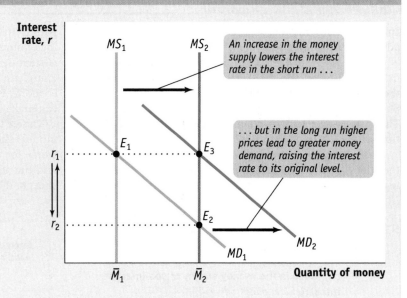

An increase in the money supply lowers the interest rate in the short run . . .

. . . but in the long run higher prices lead to greater money demand, raising the interest rate to its original level.

Figure 19-12 shows why. It shows the money supply curve and the money demand curve before and after the Fed increases the money supply. We assume that the economy is initially at E_1, in long-run macroeconomic equilibrium at potential output, and with money supply $\overline{M}_1$. The initial equilibrium interest rate, determined by the intersection of the money demand curve MD_1 and the money supply curve MS_1, is r_1.

Now suppose the money supply increases from $\overline{M}_1$ to $\overline{M}_2$. In the short run, the economy moves from E_1 to E_2 and the interest rate falls from r_1 to r_2. Over time, however, the aggregate price level rises, and this raises money demand, shifting the money demand curve rightward from MD_1 to MD_2. The economy moves to a new long-run equilibrium at E_3, and the interest rate rises to its original level at r_1.

And it turns out that the long-run equilibrium interest rate is the original interest rate, r_1. We know this for two reasons. First, due to monetary neutrality, in the long run the aggregate price level rises by the same proportion as the money supply; so if the money supply rises by, say, 50%, the aggregate price level will also rise by 50%. Second, the demand for money is, other things equal, proportional to the aggregate price level.

So, a 50% increase in the money supply raises the aggregate price level by 50%, which increases the quantity of money demanded at any given interest rate by 50%. As a result, the quantity of money demanded at the initial interest rate, r_1, rises exactly as much as the money supply—so that r_1 is still the equilibrium interest rate. In the long run, then, changes in the money supply do not affect the interest rate.

>> Check Your Understanding 19-4

Solutions appear at back of book.

1. Assume the central bank increases the quantity of money by 25%, even though the economy is initially in both short-run and long-run macroeconomic equilibrium. Describe the effects, in the short run and in the long run (giving numbers where possible), on the following.
   a. Aggregate output
   b. Aggregate price level
   c. Interest rate
2. Why does monetary policy affect the economy in the short run but not in the long run?

>> Quick Review

- According to the concept of **monetary neutrality,** changes in the money supply do not affect real GDP, they only affect the aggregate price level. Economists believe that money is neutral in the long run.

- In the long run, the equilibrium interest rate in the economy is unaffected by changes in the money supply.

SOLVED PROBLEM   The Great Mistake of 1937

In 1937, policy makers at the Fed and in the Roosevelt administration decided that the Great Depression that began in 1929 was over. They believed that the economy no longer needed special support and began phasing out the policies they instituted in the early years of the decade. Spending was cut back, and monetary policy was tightened. The result was a serious relapse in 1938, referred to at the time as the "second Great Depression."

Many economists think that this setback was caused by the policy makers who pulled back too soon, tightening both fiscal and monetary policy, before the economy was on the path to full recovery. Everything else being equal, a tightening of monetary policy causes a drop in GDP. If the economy is starting to heat up and a boom is on its way, this tightening can be important to preventing inflation. But, if the economy is in a fragile state, a tightening of monetary policy can make things worse by decreasing GDP even further.

Using the liquidity preference model and the AD–AS model, show how in 1937 monetary policy made things worse for the economy by decreasing GDP in the short run and putting further downward pressure on prices in the short and long run.

STEP | 1 Draw the money demand curve, *MD*, and the money supply curve, *MS*, in order to show how the liquidity preference model predicts that a decrease in the money supply raises interest rates. *Review pages 546–547.*

A decrease in the money supply shifts the *MS* curve to the left, from $\overline{M}_1$ to $\overline{M}_2$, as in the accompanying diagram. The interest rate increases from r_1 to r_2 because of the downward-sloping money demand curve.

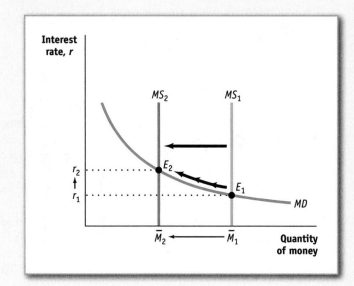

STEP | 2 Draw the short-run and long-run effects of a decrease in the money supply on GDP and prices by drawing the *LRAS* curve, the *AD* curves, and the *SRAS* curves before and after a decrease in the money supply. *Review pages 557–558 and Figure 19-11.*

Other things being equal, a decrease in the money supply increases the interest rate, which reduces investment spending and leads to a further fall in consumer spending. So, as shown in the accompanying diagram, a decrease in the money supply decreases the quantity of goods and services demanded, shifting the *AD* curve leftward to AD_2. The price level falls from P_1 to P_2, and real GDP falls from Y_1 to Y_2.

However, the aggregate output level Y_2 is below potential output. As a result, nominal wages will fall over time, causing the *SRAS* curve to shift rightward. Prices fall further, to P_3, but GDP returns to potential output at Y_1. The economy ends up at point E_3, a point of both short-run and long-run equilibrium.

So, in 1937, monetary policy simply made things worse for the economy by decreasing GDP in the short run, and putting further downward pressure on prices in the short and long run.

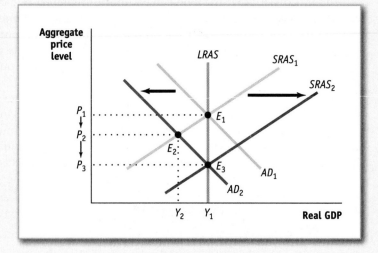

OC oo holding money

SUMMARY

1. The **money demand curve** arises from a trade-off between the opportunity cost of holding money and the liquidity that money provides. Americans hold substantial sums in cash and in zero-interest bank accounts linked to debit cards or money transmitters like PayPal and Venmo. By doing so they forgo the interest that could have been earned by putting those funds into an interest-bearing asset like a **certificate of deposit (CD).** The opportunity cost of holding money depends on **short-term interest rates,** not **long-term interest rates.** Changes in the aggregate price level, real GDP, technology, and institutions shift the money demand curve.

2. According to the **liquidity preference model of the interest rate,** the interest rate is determined in the money market by the money demand curve and the **money supply curve.** The Federal Reserve can change the interest rate in the short run by shifting the money supply curve. In practice, the Fed uses open-market operations to achieve a **target federal funds rate,** which other short-term interest rates generally track. Although long-term interest rates don't necessarily move with short-term interest rates, they reflect expectations about what's going to happen to short-term rates in the future.

3. **Expansionary monetary policy** reduces the interest rate by increasing the money supply. This increases investment spending and consumer spending, which in turn increases aggregate demand and real GDP in the short run. **Contractionary monetary policy** raises the interest rate by reducing the money supply. This reduces investment spending and consumer spending, which in turn reduces aggregate demand and real GDP in the short run.

4. The Federal Reserve and other central banks try to stabilize the economy, limiting fluctuations of actual output around potential output, while also keeping inflation low but positive. Under a **Taylor rule for monetary policy,** the target federal funds rate rises when there is high inflation and either a positive output gap or very low unemployment; it falls when there is low or negative inflation and either a negative output gap or high unemployment. Some central banks, including the Fed, engage in **inflation targeting,** which is a forward-looking policy rule, whereas the Taylor rule method is a backward-looking policy rule. Because monetary policy is subject to fewer implementation lags than fiscal policy, it is the preferred policy tool for stabilizing the economy. However, because interest rates cannot fall much below zero without causing significant problems, there is a **zero lower bound for interest rates.** As a result, the effectiveness of monetary policy is limited.

5. In the long run, changes in the money supply affect the aggregate price level but not real GDP or the interest rate. Data show that the concept of **monetary neutrality** holds: changes in the money supply have no real effect on the economy in the long run.

KEY TERMS

Certificate of deposit (CD), p. 540
Short-term interest rates, p. 541
Long-term interest rates, p. 541
Money demand curve, p. 542
Liquidity preference model of the interest rate, p. 546

Money supply curve, p. 546
Target federal funds rate, p. 547
Expansionary monetary policy, p. 551
Contractionary monetary policy, p. 551
Taylor rule for monetary policy, p. 553

Inflation targeting, p. 553
Zero lower bound for interest rates, p. 555
Monetary neutrality, p. 558

DISCUSSION QUESTIONS

1. **a.** Go to www.treasurydirect.gov. Under "Individuals," go to "Treasury Securities & Programs." Click on "Treasury bills." Under "at a glance," click on "rates in recent auctions." What is the investment rate for the most recently issued 52-week T-bills?

   b. Go to the website of your favorite bank. What is the interest rate for one-year CDs?

   c. Why are the rates for one-year CDs higher than for 52-week Treasury bills?

2. Go to www.treasurydirect.gov. Under "Individuals," go to "Treasury Securities & Programs." Click on "Treasury notes." Under "at a glance," click on "rates in recent auctions." Use the list of Note, Bond, and TIPS Auction Results to answer the following questions.

   a. What are the interest rates on 2-year and 10-year notes?

   b. How do the interest rates on the 2-year and 10-year notes relate to each other? Why is the interest rate on the 10-year note higher (or lower) than the interest rate on the 2-year note?

3. According to the European Central Bank website, the treaty establishing the European Community "makes clear that ensuring price stability is the most important contribution that monetary policy can make to achieve a favorable economic environment and a high level of employment." If price stability is the only goal of monetary policy, explain how monetary policy would be conducted during recessions. Analyze both the case of a recession that is the result of a demand shock and the case of a recession that is the result of a supply shock.

PROBLEMS

interactive activity

1. Access the Discovering Data exercise for Chapter 19 Problem 1 online to answer the following questions.

   a. What is the target federal funds rate?

   b. Is the target federal funds rate different from the target federal funds rate in the previous FOMC statement? If yes, by how much does it differ?

   c. Does the statement comment on current macroeconomic conditions in the United States? How does it describe the U.S. economy?

2. How will the following events affect the demand for money? In each case, specify whether there is a shift of the demand curve or a movement along the demand curve and its direction.

   a. There is a fall in the interest rate from 12% to 10%.

   b. Thanksgiving arrives and, with it, the beginning of the holiday shopping season.

   c. Increasingly, merchants are adopting electronic payment systems that allow more consumers to use PayPal and Apple Pay to make purchases.

   d. The Fed engages in an open-market purchase of U.S. Treasury bills.

3. An economy is facing the recessionary gap shown in the accompanying diagram. To eliminate the gap, should the central bank use expansionary or contractionary monetary policy? How will the interest rate, investment spending, consumer spending, real GDP, and the aggregate price level change as monetary policy closes the recessionary gap?

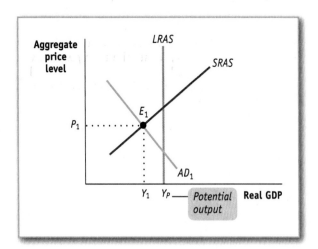

4. An economy is facing the inflationary gap shown in the accompanying diagram. To eliminate the gap, should the central bank use expansionary or contractionary monetary policy? How will the interest rate, investment spending, consumer spending, real GDP, and the aggregate price level change as monetary policy closes the inflationary gap?

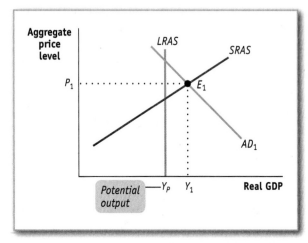

5. In the economy of Eastlandia, the money market is initially in equilibrium when the economy begins to slide into a recession.

   a. Using the accompanying diagram, explain what will happen to the interest rate if the central bank of Eastlandia keeps the money supply constant at $\overline{M}_1$.

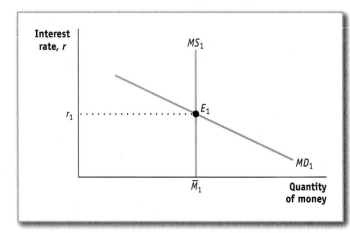

   b. If the central bank is instead committed to maintaining an interest rate target of r_1, then as the economy slides into recession, how should the central bank react? Using your diagram from part a, demonstrate the central bank's reaction.

6. Suppose that the money market in Westlandia is initially in equilibrium and the central bank decides to decrease the money supply.

    a. Using a diagram like the one in Problem 5, explain what will happen to the interest rate in the short run.

    b. What will happen to the interest rate in the long run?

7. An economy is in long-run macroeconomic equilibrium with an unemployment rate of 5% when the government passes a law requiring the central bank to use monetary policy to lower the unemployment rate to 3% and keep it there. How could the central bank achieve this goal in the short run? What would happen in the long run? Illustrate with a diagram.

8. The effectiveness of monetary policy depends on how easy it is for changes in the money supply to change interest rates. By changing interest rates, monetary policy affects investment spending and the aggregate demand curve. The economies of Albernia and Brittania have very different money demand curves, as shown in the accompanying diagram. In which economy will changes in the money supply be a more effective policy tool? Why?

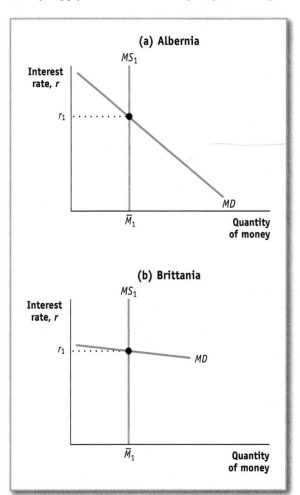

(a) Albernia

(b) Brittania

9. During the Great Depression, businesspeople in the United States were very pessimistic about the future of economic growth and reluctant to increase investment spending even when interest rates fell. How did this limit the potential for monetary policy to help alleviate the Depression?

10. Access the Discovering Data exercise for Chapter 19 Problem 10 online to answer the following questions.

    a. How does the relationship between the effective federal funds rate and the Taylor rule change throughout the Great Recession?

    b. Compare the long-term and short-term interest rate before and after the Great Recession.

WORK IT OUT Interactive step-by-step help with solving this problem can be found online.

---

11. Because of the economic slowdown associated with the 2007–2009 recession, the Federal Open Market Committee of the Federal Reserve, between September 18, 2007, and December 16, 2008, lowered the federal funds rate in a series of steps from a high of 5.25% to a rate between 0% and 0.25%. The idea was to provide a boost to the economy by increasing aggregate demand.

    a. Use the liquidity preference model to explain how the Federal Open Market Committee lowers the interest rate in the short run. Draw a typical graph that illustrates the mechanism. Label the vertical axis "Interest rate" and the horizontal axis "Quantity of money." Your graph should show two interest rates, r_1 and r_2.

    b. Explain why the reduction in the interest rate causes aggregate demand to increase in the short run.

    c. Suppose that in 2022 the economy is at potential output but that this is somehow overlooked by the Fed, which continues its monetary expansion. Demonstrate the effect of the policy measure on the *AD* curve. Use the *LRAS* curve to show that the effect of this policy measure on the *AD* curve, other things equal, causes the aggregate price level to rise in the long run. Label the vertical axis "Aggregate price level" and the horizontal axis "Real GDP."

The Solana power plant covers three square miles of the Arizona desert in Gila Bend, about 70 miles from Phoenix. Whereas most solar installations rely on photovoltaic panels that convert light directly into electricity, Solana uses a system of mirrors to concentrate the sun's heat on black pipes, which convey that heat to tanks of molten salt. The heat in the salt is, in turn, used to generate electricity. The advantage of

this arrangement is that the plant can keep generating power long after the sun has gone down, greatly enhancing its efficiency.

Solana is one of only a small number of concentrated thermal solar plants operating or under construction, and as Figure 19-13 shows, solar power has been rapidly rising in importance, with the amount of solar-generated electricity increasing over 800% between 2006 and 2016. There are a number of reasons for this sudden rise, but the 2009 stimulus—which put substantial sums into the promotion of green energy—was a major factor. Solana, in particular, was built by the Spanish company Abengoa with the aid of a $1.45 billion federal loan guarantee. Abengoa also received $1.2 billion for a similar plant in the Mojave Desert.

While Solana is a good example of stimulus spending at work, it is also a good example of why such spending tends to be politically difficult. There were many protests over federal loans to a non-American firm, although Abengoa had the necessary technology, and the construction jobs created by the project were, of course, in the United States. Also, the long-term financial viability of solar power projects depends in part on whether government subsidies and other policies favoring renewable energy will continue, which isn't certain.

In terms of the goals of the stimulus, however, Solana seems to have done what it was supposed to: it generated jobs at a time when borrowing was cheap and many construction workers were unemployed.

FIGURE 19-13 The Solar Sunrise, 2006–2016

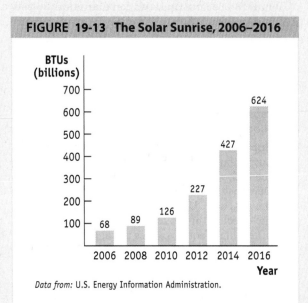

Data from: U.S. Energy Information Administration.

QUESTIONS FOR THOUGHT

1. How did the political reaction to government funding for the Solana project differ from the reaction to more conventional government spending projects such as roads and schools? What does the case tell us about how to assess the value of a fiscal stimulus project?

2. In Chapter 17 we talked about the problem of lags in discretionary fiscal policy. What does the Solana case tell us about this issue?

3. Is the depth of a recession a good or a bad time to undertake an energy project? Why or why not?

It's always nice when someone shows his or her appreciation by giving you a gift. Over the past few years, more people have been showing their appreciation by giving gift cards, prepaid plastic cards issued by a retailer that can be redeemed for merchandise. The best-selling single item for more than 80% of the top 100 American retailers, says GiftCardUSA.com, is their gift cards.

What could be more simple and useful than allowing the recipient to choose what he or she wants? And isn't a gift card more personal than cash or a check?

Yet a number of firms are now making a profit from the fact that gift card recipients are often willing to sell their cards at a discount—sometimes at a fairly sizable discount—to turn them into cold, impersonal dollars and cents. Meanwhile, other people are willing to buy those cards, and turn them into goods *they* want.

Cardcash.com is one such site. At the time of writing, it offers to pay cash to a seller of a Walmart gift card equivalent to 89% of the card's face value. For example, the seller of a Walmart card with a value of $100 would receive $89. Cardcash.com profits by reselling the card at a premium over what it paid. So it would sell a Walmart gift card for more than 89% of its face value. The amount of cash offered to sellers of cards will vary by retailer. Cardcash offers cash equal to only 70% of a Gap card's face value, for example.

Many consumers will sell at a sizable discount to turn gift cards into cash. But retailers promote the use of gift cards over cash because much of the value of gift cards issued never gets used, a phenomenon known as *breakage*.

How does breakage occur? People lose cards. Or they spend only $47 of a $50 gift card, and never return to the store to spend that last $3. Also, retailers have imposed fees on the use of cards or made them subject to expiration dates, which customers forget about. And if a retailer goes out of business, the value of outstanding gift cards disappears with it.

In addition to breakage, retailers benefit when customers intent on using up the value of their gift card find that it is too difficult to spend exactly the amount of the card. Instead, they end up spending even more than the card's face value, sometimes even more than they would have without the gift card.

Gift cards are so beneficial to retailers that instead of rewarding customer loyalty with rebate checks (once a common practice), they have switched to dispensing gift cards. As one commentator noted in explaining why retailers prefer gift cards to rebate checks, "Nobody neglects to spend cash."

QUESTIONS FOR THOUGHT

1. Why are gift card owners willing to sell their cards for a cash amount less than their face value?

2. Why do gift cards for Walmart sell for a smaller discount than those for the Gap?

3. Use your answer from Question 2 to explain why cash never "sells" at a discount.

4. Explain why retailers prefer to reward loyal customers with gift cards instead of rebate checks.

5. There are now laws restricting retailers' ability to impose fees and expiration dates on their gift cards and mandate greater disclosure of their terms. Why do you think Congress enacted this legislation?

Officially, PayPal, the electronic funds–transfer firm—which is also the owner of Venmo, a mobile-phone payment service that has become extremely popular—isn't considered a bank. Instead, regulators consider it a *money transmitter*, an entity that sends your money someplace rather than holding it and keeping it safe.

However, as users accumulate substantial sums in their PayPal accounts, that distinction has started to look questionable. Venmo users, in particular, often seem willing to let incoming payments sit in their accounts until the funds are spent. As a result, PayPal's accounts were estimated to total more than $13 billion in 2016. If those billions were considered bank deposits, PayPal would be considered among the 50 largest banks in the United States.

At first glance, leaving significant sums in PayPal accounts seems counterintuitive for two reasons. First, these accounts aren't protected by federal deposit insurance. Second, they pay no interest. But upon closer examination, this behavior makes good economic sense. People will typically hold only a tiny fraction of their wealth in their PayPal account, thereby making the lack of federal deposit insurance an acceptable risk. And interest rates on bank accounts are so low at the time of this writing (around 0.06% in Spring 2019) that losing that interest is a reasonable price to pay to avoid the hassle of moving funds back and forth between a bank account and a PayPal or Venmo account.

The result is that many people are behaving like one user quoted by the *Wall Street Journal*, who now waits a while before transferring funds out of her Venmo account to her regular bank account: "I'm starting to intentionally keep my money in there a little bit longer."

But will PayPal/Venmo or something like it begin to make major inroads into traditional banking? Some analysts think so. Others suggest, however, that conventional banks will find ways to make mobile payments easier, and that rising interest rates will lure customers back to conventional bank deposits. Time will tell.

QUESTIONS FOR THOUGHT

1. PayPal accounts aren't counted as part of the money supply. Should they be? Why or why not?

2. In 2010, only around 25% of mobile phones in the United States were smartphones. In 2017, that number increased to more than 80%. How does this situation play into the PayPal story, and how does it fit into the broader pattern of monetary history?

3. How might future actions by the Federal Open Market Committee affect the future of PayPal and similar services?

20

International Trade, Capital Flows, and Exchange Rates

THE EVERYWHERE PHONE

WHAT DO AMERICANS DO with their time? The answer is that they largely spend it staring at small screens. A 2018 study found that college students spend up to ten hours a day looking at a smartphone (especially an iPhone) or a tablet, slightly more time than is spent watching TV.

The production and consumption of smartphones are examples of today's hyperglobal world with its soaring levels of international trade.

Where do these small screens come from? Specifically, where does an iPhone come from?

Apple, which sells the iPhone, is an American company. But if you said that iPhones come from America, you're mostly wrong: Apple develops products, but contracts almost all of the manufacturing of those products to other companies, which are mainly overseas. But it's not really right to answer "China," either, even though that's where iPhones are assembled. You see, assembly—the last phase of iPhone production, in which the pieces are put together in the familiar metal-and-glass case—only accounts for a small fraction of the phone's value.

In fact, a study of the iPhone estimated that of the average factory price of $229 per phone, only around $10 stayed in the Chinese economy. A substantially larger amount went to South Korean manufacturers, who supplied the display and memory chips. There were also substantial outlays for raw materials, sourced all over the world. And the biggest share of the price—more than half—consisted of Apple's profit margin, which was largely a reward for research, development, and design.

So where do iPhones come from? Lots of places. And the case of the iPhone isn't unusual: the car you drive, the clothing you wear, even the food you eat are generally the end products of complex *supply chains* that span the globe.

Has this always been true? Yes and no. Large-scale international trade isn't new. By the early twentieth century, middle-class residents of London already ate bread made from Canadian wheat and beef from the Argentine Pampas, while wearing clothing woven from Australian wool and Egyptian cotton. In recent decades, however, new technologies for transportation and communication have interacted with pro-trade policies to produce an era of *hyperglobalization* in which international trade has soared, thanks to complex chains of production like the one that puts an iPhone in front of your nose. As a result, now, more than ever before, we must have a full picture of international trade to understand how national economies work.

This chapter examines the interaction of national economies. We begin with a discussion of the economics of international trade. With that foundation established, we move on to discuss how trade and capital flows are part of the balance of payments accounts. Finally, we look at the various factors that influence exchange rates. •

WHAT YOU WILL LEARN

- What is comparative advantage and why does it lead to international trade?
- What are the sources of comparative advantage?
- Who gains and who loses from international trade?
- Why do trade protections like **tariffs** and **import quotas** create inefficiency?
- What are the **balance of payments accounts?**
- What determines international capital flows?
- What roles do the **foreign exchange market** and the **exchange rate** play?

Goods and services purchased from other countries are **imports;** goods and services sold to other countries are **exports.**

Globalization is the phenomenon of growing economic linkages among countries.

Comparative Advantage and International Trade

The United States buys smartphones—and many other goods and services—from other countries. At the same time, it sells many goods and services to other countries. Goods and services purchased from abroad are **imports;** goods and services sold abroad are **exports.**

As illustrated by the opening story, international trade plays an increasingly important role in the world economy. Panel (a) of Figure 20-1 shows the ratio of goods crossing national borders to *world GDP*—the total value of goods and services produced in the world as a whole—since 1870. As you can see, the long-term trend has been upward, although there have been some periods of declining trade—for example, the sharp but brief dip in trade during the global financial crisis of 2008 and its aftermath.

Panel (b) shows imports and exports as a percentage of GDP for a number of countries. It shows that foreign trade is significantly more important for many other countries than it is for the United States.

Foreign trade isn't the only way countries interact economically. In the modern world, investors from one country often invest funds in another nation; many companies are multinational, with subsidiaries operating in several countries; and a growing number of people work in a country different from the one in which they were born. The growth of all these forms of economic linkages among countries is often called **globalization.**

Globalization isn't a new phenomenon. As you can see from panel (a) of Figure 20-1, there was rapid growth in trade between 1870 and the beginning of World War I, as railroads and steamships effectively made the shipping of goods

FIGURE 20-1 The Growing Importance of International Trade

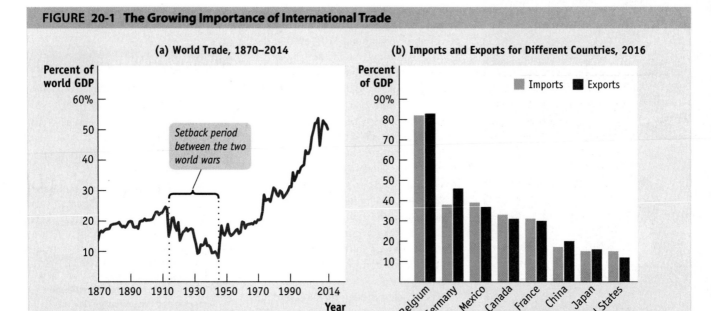

Panel (a) shows the long-term history of the ratio of world trade to world production. The trend has been generally upward, thanks to technological progress in transportation and communication, although there was a long setback during the period between the two world wars. Panel (b) demonstrates that international trade is significantly more important to many other countries than it is to the United States.

Data from: [panel (a)] Klasing, M. J., and P. Milionis, "Quantifying the Evolution of World Trade, 1870–1949," *Journal of International Economics* (2013); and Feenstra, Robert C., Robert Inklaar, and Marcel P. Timmer, "The Next Generation of the Penn World Table," *American Economic Review* 105, no. 10 (2015): 3150–3182, available for download at www.ggdc.net/pwt; [panel (b)] World Development Indicators.

long distances both faster and cheaper, effectively shrinking the world. This growth of trade was accompanied by large-scale international investment and migration. However, globalization went into reverse for almost 40 years after World War I, as governments imposed limits on trade of the kind analyzed later in this chapter. And by several measures, globalization didn't return to 1913 levels until the 1980s.

Since then, however, there has been a further dramatic increase in international linkages, sometimes referred to as **hyperglobalization,** exemplified by the way the manufacturing of iPhones and other high-tech goods involves supply chains of production that span the globe, and in which each stage of a good's production takes place in a different country—all made possible by advances in communication and transportation technology. (For a real-life example, see the business case that follows this chapter.)

> **Hyperglobalization** is the phenomenon of extremely high levels of international trade.

One big question in international economics is whether hyperglobalization will continue in the decades ahead. As you can see from looking closely at Figure 20-1, the big rise in the ratio of exports to world GDP leveled off around 2005. Since then, there have been many reports about companies deciding that the money they saved by buying goods from suppliers thousands of miles away is more than offset by the disadvantages of long shipping times and other inconveniences. (Even now, it takes around two weeks for a container ship from China to arrive in California, and a month to reach the East Coast.) As a result, there has been some move toward *reshoring*, bringing production closer to markets. If this turns out to be a major trend, world trade could level off or even decline as a share of world GDP, although it would remain very important.

To understand why international trade occurs and why economists believe it is beneficial to the economy, we will first review the concept of comparative advantage.

Production Possibilities and Comparative Advantage, Revisited

To produce phones, any country must use resources—land, labor, and capital—that could have been used to produce other things. The potential production of other goods a country must forgo to produce a phone is the opportunity cost of that phone.

In some cases, it's easy to see why the opportunity cost of producing a good is especially low in a given country. Consider, for example, shrimp—much of which now comes from seafood farms in Vietnam and Thailand. It's a lot easier to produce shrimp in Vietnam, where the climate is nearly ideal and there's plenty of coastal land suitable for shellfish farming, than it is in the United States.

Conversely, other goods are not produced as easily in Vietnam as in the United States. For example, Vietnam doesn't have the base of skilled workers and technological know-how that makes the United States so good at producing high-technology goods. So the opportunity cost of a ton of shrimp, in terms of other goods such as aircraft, is much less in Vietnam than it is in the United States.

The opportunity cost of smartphone assembly in China is lower, giving it a comparative advantage.

In other cases, matters are a little less obvious. It's as easy to assemble smartphones in the United States as it is in China, and Chinese electronics workers are, if anything, less productive than their U.S. counterparts. But Chinese workers are a lot less productive than U.S. workers in other areas, such as automobile and chemical production. This means that diverting a Chinese worker into assembling phones reduces output of other goods less than diverting a U.S. worker into assembling phones. That is, the opportunity cost of smartphone assembly in China is less than it is in the United States.

Notice that we said the opportunity cost of phone *assembly*. As we've seen, most of the value of a "Chinese-made" phone actually comes from other countries.

FIGURE 20-2 Comparative Advantage and the Production Possibility Frontier

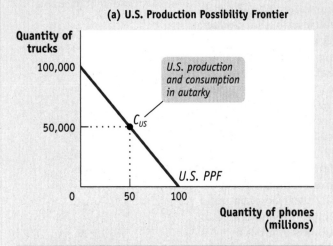

(a) U.S. Production Possibility Frontier

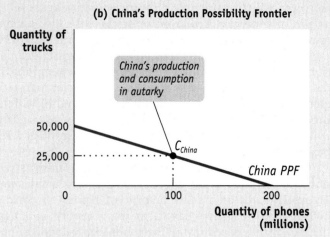

(b) China's Production Possibility Frontier

The U.S. opportunity cost of 1 million phones in terms of trucks is 1,000: for every 1 million phones, 1,000 trucks must be forgone. The Chinese opportunity cost of 1 million phones in terms of trucks is 250: for every additional 1 million phones, only 250 trucks must be forgone. As a result, the United States has a comparative advantage in truck production, and China has a comparative advantage in phone production. In autarky, each country is forced to consume only what it produces: 50,000 trucks and 50 million phones for the United States; 25,000 trucks and 100 million phones for China.

For the sake of exposition, however, let's ignore that complication and consider a hypothetical case in which China makes phones from scratch.

So we say that China has a comparative advantage in producing smartphones. Let's repeat the definition of comparative advantage from Chapter 2: *A country has a comparative advantage in producing a good or service if the opportunity cost of producing the good or service is lower for that country than for other countries.*

Figure 20-2 provides a hypothetical numerical example of comparative advantage in international trade. We assume that only two goods are produced and consumed, phones and Caterpillar heavy trucks. (The United States doesn't export many ordinary trucks, but Caterpillar, which makes earth-moving equipment, is a major exporter.) And we assume that there are only two countries in the world, the United States and China. The figure shows hypothetical production possibility frontiers for the United States and China.

As in Chapter 2, we simplify the model by assuming that the production possibility frontiers are straight lines, as shown in Figure 2-1, rather than the more realistic bowed-out shape in Figure 2-2. The straight-line shape implies that the opportunity cost of a phone in terms of trucks in each country is constant—it does not depend on how many units of each good the country produces. The analysis of international trade under the assumption that opportunity costs are constant, which makes production possibility frontiers straight lines, is known as the **Ricardian model of international trade,** named after the English economist David Ricardo, who introduced this analysis in the early nineteenth century.

In Figure 20-2 we show a situation in which the United States can produce 100,000 trucks if it produces no phones, or 100 million phones if it produces no trucks. Thus, the slope of the U.S. production possibility frontier, or *PPF*, is $-100,000/100 = -1,000$. That is, to produce an additional million phones, the United States must forgo the production of 1,000 trucks. Likewise, to produce one more truck, the United States must forgo 1,000 phones (equal to 1 million phones divided by 1,000 trucks).

The **Ricardian model of international trade** analyzes international trade under the assumption that opportunity costs are constant.

Similarly, China can produce 50,000 trucks if it produces no phones or 200 million phones if it produces no trucks. Thus, the slope of China's *PPF* is −50,000/200 = −250. That is, to produce an additional million phones, China must forgo the production of 250 trucks. Likewise, to produce one more truck, China must forgo 4,000 phones (1 million phones divided by 250 trucks).

Economists use the term **autarky** to refer to a situation in which a country does not trade with other countries. We assume that in autarky the United States chooses to produce and consume 50 million phones and 50,000 trucks. We also assume that in autarky China produces and consumes 100 million phones and 25,000 trucks.

The trade-offs facing the two countries when they don't trade are summarized in Table 20-1. As you can see, the United States has a comparative advantage in the production of trucks because it has a lower opportunity cost in terms of phones than China has: producing a truck costs the United States only 1,000 phones, while it costs China 4,000 phones. Correspondingly, China has a comparative advantage in phone production: 1 million phones costs only 250 trucks, while it costs the United States 1,000 trucks.

> **Autarky** is a situation in which a country does not trade with other countries.

TABLE 20-1 U.S. and Chinese Opportunity Costs of Phones and Trucks

	U.S. Opportunity Cost		Chinese Opportunity Cost
1 million phones	1,000 trucks	>	250 trucks
1 truck	1,000 phones	<	4,000 phones

As we learned in Chapter 2, each country can do better by engaging in trade than it could by not trading. A country can accomplish this by specializing in the production of the good in which it has a comparative advantage and exporting that good, while importing the good in which it has a comparative disadvantage.

Let's see how this works.

The Gains from International Trade

Figure 20-3 illustrates how both countries can gain from specialization and trade, by showing a hypothetical rearrangement of production and consumption that allows *each* country to consume more of *both* goods. Again, panel (a) represents the United States and panel (b) represents China. In each panel we indicate again the autarky production and consumption assumed in Figure 20-2.

FIGURE 20-3 The Gains from International Trade

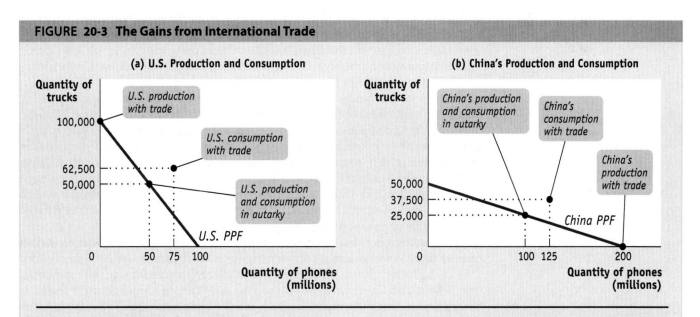

Trade increases world production of both goods, allowing both countries to consume more. Here, each country specializes its production as a result of trade: the United States concentrates on producing trucks, and China concentrates on producing phones. Total world production of both goods rises, which means that it is possible for both countries to consume more of both goods.

TABLE 20-2 How the United States and China Gain from Trade

		In Autarky		With Trade		
		Production	Consumption	Production	Consumption	Gains from trade
United States	Million phones	50	50	0	75	+25
	Trucks	50,000	50,000	100,000	62,500	+12,500
China	Million phones	100	100	200	125	+25
	Trucks	25,000	25,000	0	37,500	+12,500

Once trade becomes possible, however, everything changes. With trade, each country can move to producing only the good in which it has a comparative advantage—trucks for the United States and phones for China. Because the world production of both goods is now higher than in autarky, trade makes it possible for each country to consume more of both goods.

Table 20-2 sums up the changes as a result of trade and shows why both countries can gain. The left part of the table shows the autarky situation, before trade, in which each country must produce the goods it consumes. The right part of the table shows what happens as a result of trade. After trade, the United States specializes in the production of trucks, producing 100,000 trucks and no phones; China specializes in the production of phones, producing 200 million phones and no trucks.

The result is a rise in total world production of both goods. As you can see in the table, gains from trade enable

- The United States to consume both more trucks (12,500 more) and phones (25 million more) than before, even though it no longer produces phones, because it can import phones from China.

- China can also consume more of both goods (12,500 more trucks and 25 million more phones), even though it no longer produces trucks, because it can import trucks from the United States.

The key to this mutual gain is the fact that trade liberates both countries from self-sufficiency—from the need to produce the same mixes of goods they consume. Because each country can concentrate on producing the good in which it has a comparative advantage, total world production rises, making a higher standard of living possible in both nations.

In this example we have simply assumed the post-trade consumption bundles of the two countries. In fact, the consumption choices of a country reflect both the preferences of its residents and the *relative prices*—the prices of one good in terms of another in international markets. Although we have not explicitly given the price of trucks in terms of phones, that price is implicit in our example: China sells the United States the 75 million phones the United States consumes in return for the 37,500 trucks China consumes, so 1 million phones are traded for 500 trucks. This tells us that the price of a truck on world markets must be equal to the price of 2,000 phones.

One requirement that the relative price must satisfy is that no country pays a relative price greater than its opportunity cost of obtaining the good in autarky. That is, the United States won't pay more than 1,000 trucks for one million phones from China, and China won't pay more than 4,000 phones for each truck from the United States. Once this requirement is satisfied, the actual relative price in international trade is determined by supply and demand—and we'll turn to supply and demand in international trade in the next section. However, first let's look more deeply into the nature of the gains from trade.

Comparative Advantage Versus Absolute Advantage

It's easy to accept the idea that Vietnam and Thailand have a comparative advantage in shrimp production: they have a tropical climate that's better suited to shrimp farming than that of the United States (even along the Gulf Coast), and they have a lot of usable coastal area. So the United States imports shrimp from Vietnam and Thailand. In other cases, however, it may be harder to understand why we import certain goods from abroad.

U.S. imports of phones from China are a case in point. There's nothing about China's climate or resources that makes it especially good at assembling electronic devices. In fact, it almost surely would take fewer hours of labor to assemble a smartphone or a tablet in the United States than in China.

Why, then, do we buy phones assembled in China? Because the gains from trade depend on *comparative advantage*, not absolute advantage. Yes, it would take less labor to assemble a phone in the United States than in China. That is, the productivity of Chinese electronics workers is less than that of their U.S. counterparts. But what determines comparative advantage is not the amount of resources used to produce a good but the opportunity cost of that good—in this case, the quantity of other goods forgone in order to produce a phone. And the opportunity cost of phones is lower in China than in the United States.

The tropical climates of Vietnam and Thailand give them a comparative advantage in shrimp production.

Here's how it works: Chinese workers have low productivity compared with U.S. workers in the electronics industry. But Chinese workers have even lower productivity compared with U.S. workers in other industries. Because Chinese labor productivity in industries other than electronics is relatively very low, producing a phone in China, even though it takes a lot of labor, does not require forgoing the production of large quantities of other goods.

In the United States, the opposite is true: very high productivity in other industries (such as automobiles) means that assembling electronic products in the United States, even though it doesn't require much labor, requires sacrificing lots of other goods. So the opportunity cost of producing electronics is less in China than in the United States. Despite its lower labor productivity, China has a comparative advantage in the production of many consumer electronics, although the United States has an absolute advantage.

The source of China's comparative advantage in consumer electronics is reflected in global markets by the wages Chinese workers are paid. That's because a country's wage rates, in general, reflect its labor productivity. In countries where labor is highly productive in many industries, employers are willing to pay high wages to attract workers, so competition among employers leads to an overall high wage rate. In countries where labor is less productive, competition for workers is less intense and wage rates are correspondingly lower.

As the Global Comparison shows, there is indeed a strong relationship between overall levels of productivity and wage rates around the world. Because China has generally low productivity, it has a relatively low wage rate. Low wages, in turn, give China a cost advantage in producing goods when its productivity is only moderately low, like consumer electronics. As a result, it's cheaper to produce these goods in China than in the United States.

The kind of trade that takes place between low-wage, low-productivity economies like China and high-wage, high-productivity economies like the United States gives rise to two common misperceptions.

- The *pauper labor fallacy* is the belief that when a country with high wages imports goods produced by workers who are paid low wages, this must hurt the standard of living of workers in the importing country.

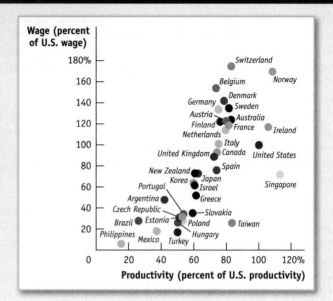

GLOBAL COMPARISON   PRODUCTIVITY AND WAGES AROUND THE WORLD

It's true that both the pauper labor argument and the sweatshop labor argument are fallacies. The real explanation for low wages in poor countries is low overall productivity.

The graph shows estimates of labor productivity, measured by the value of output (GDP) per worker, and wages, measured by the hourly compensation of the average worker, for several countries in 2014. Both productivity and wages are expressed as percentages of U.S. productivity and wages; for example, productivity and wages in Japan were 62% and 73%, respectively, of their U.S. levels. You can see the strong positive relationship between productivity and wages. The relationship isn't perfect. For example, Norway has higher wages than its productivity might lead you to expect. But simple comparisons of wages give a misleading sense of labor costs in poor countries: their low wage advantage is mostly offset by low productivity.

Data from: The Conference Board.

• The *sweatshop labor fallacy* is the belief that trade must be bad for workers in poor exporting countries because those workers are paid very low wages by our standards.

Both fallacies miss the nature of gains from trade: it's to the advantage of both countries if the poorer, lower-wage country exports goods in which it has a comparative advantage, even if its cost advantage in these goods depends on low wages. That is, both countries are able to achieve a higher standard of living through trade.

It's particularly important to understand that buying a good made by someone who is paid much lower wages than most U.S. workers doesn't necessarily imply that you're taking advantage of that person. It depends on the alternatives. Because workers in poor countries have low productivity across the board, they are offered low wages whether they produce goods exported to America or goods sold in local markets. A job that looks terrible by rich-country standards can be a step up for someone in a poor country.

International trade that depends on low-wage exports can nonetheless raise the exporting country's standard of living. This is especially true of very-low-wage nations. For example, Bangladesh and similar countries would be much poorer than they are—their citizens might even be starving—if they weren't able to export goods such as clothing based on their low wage rates.

Sources of Comparative Advantage

International trade is driven by comparative advantage, but where does comparative advantage come from? Economists who study international trade have found three main sources of comparative advantage: international differences in *climate*, international differences in *factor endowments*, and international differences in *technology*.

Differences in Climate One key reason the opportunity cost of producing shrimp in Vietnam and Thailand is less than in the United States is that shrimp need warm water—Vietnam has plenty of that, but America doesn't. In general, differences in climate play a significant role in international trade. Tropical countries export tropical products like coffee, sugar, bananas, and shrimp. Countries in the temperate zones export crops like wheat and corn. Some trade is even driven by the difference in seasons between the northern and southern hemispheres: winter deliveries of Chilean grapes and New Zealand apples have become commonplace in U.S. and European supermarkets.

Differences in Factor Endowments The United States does more trade with Canada than with any other country (China comes in second). Among other things, Canada sells us a lot of forest products—lumber and products derived from lumber, like pulp and paper. These exports don't reflect the special skill of Canadian lumberjacks. Canada has a comparative advantage in forest products because its forested area is much greater compared to the size of its labor force than the ratio of forestland to the labor force in the United States.

Forestland, like labor and capital, is a *factor of production:* an input used to produce goods and services. (Recall from Chapter 2 that the factors of production are land, labor, physical capital, and human capital.) Due to history and geography, the mix of available factors of production differs among countries, providing an important source of comparative advantage. The relationship between comparative advantage and factor availability is found in an influential model of international trade, the *Heckscher–Ohlin model,* developed by two Swedish economists in the first half of the twentieth century.

Two key concepts in the model are *factor abundance* and *factor intensity.* Factor abundance refers to how large a country's supply of a factor is relative to its supply of other factors. **Factor intensity** refers to the ranking of goods according to which factor is used in relatively greater quantities in production compared to other factors. So oil refining is a capital-intensive good because it tends to use a high ratio of capital to labor, but phone production is a labor-intensive good because it tends to use a high ratio of labor to capital.

According to the **Heckscher–Ohlin model,** *a country that has an abundant supply of a factor of production will have a comparative advantage in goods whose production is intensive in that factor.* So a country that has a relative abundance of capital will have a comparative advantage in capital-intensive industries such as oil refining, but a country that has a relative abundance of labor will have a comparative advantage in labor-intensive industries such as phone production.

The basic intuition behind this result is simple and based on opportunity cost.

- The opportunity cost of a given factor—the value that the factor would generate in alternative uses—is low for a country when it is relatively abundant in that factor.
- Relative to the United States, China has an abundance of low-skilled labor.
- As a result, the opportunity cost of the production of low-skilled, labor-intensive goods is lower in China than in the United States.

World trade in clothing is the most dramatic example of the validity of the Heckscher–Ohlin model in practice. Clothing production is a labor-intensive activity: it doesn't take much physical capital, nor does it require a lot of human capital in the form of highly educated workers. So you would expect labor-abundant countries such as China and Bangladesh to have a comparative advantage in clothing production. And they do.

The fact that international trade is the result of differences in factor endowments helps explain another fact: international specialization of production is often *incomplete.* That is, a country often maintains some domestic production of a good that it imports. A good example of this is the United States and oil. Saudi Arabia exports oil to the United States because Saudi Arabia has an abundant supply of oil relative to its other factors of production; the United States exports medical devices to Saudi Arabia because it has an abundant supply of expertise in medical technology relative to its other factors of production. But the United States also produces oil domestically because the size of its domestic oil reserves

The **factor intensity** of a good is a measure of which factor is used in relatively greater quantities than other factors in production.

According to the **Heckscher–Ohlin model,** a country has a comparative advantage in a good whose production is intensive in the factors that are abundantly available in that country.

A greater endowment of forestland gives Canada a comparative advantage in forest products.

in Texas and Alaska (and now, increasingly, its oil shale reserves elsewhere) makes it economical to do so.

In our supply and demand analysis in the next section, we'll consider incomplete specialization by a country to be the norm. We should emphasize, however, that the fact that countries often incompletely specialize does not in any way change the conclusion that there are gains from trade.

Differences in Technology In the 1970s and 1980s, Japan became by far the world's largest exporter of automobiles, selling large numbers to the United States and the rest of the world. Japan's comparative advantage in automobiles wasn't the result of climate. Nor can it easily be attributed to differences in factor endowments: aside from a scarcity of land, Japan's mix of available factors is quite similar to that in other advanced countries. Instead, Japan's comparative advantage in automobiles was based on the superior production techniques developed by its manufacturers, which allowed them to produce more cars with a given amount of labor and capital than their American or European counterparts.

Japan's comparative advantage in automobiles was a case of comparative advantage caused by differences in technology—the techniques used in production.

The causes of differences in technology are somewhat mysterious. Sometimes they seem to be based on knowledge accumulated through experience—for example, Switzerland's comparative advantage in watches reflects a long tradition of watchmaking. Sometimes, however, they are the result of a set of innovations that for some reason occur in one country but not in others.

Technological advantage, however, is often transitory. By adopting *lean production* (techniques designed to improve manufacturing productivity through increased efficiency), American auto manufacturers have closed much of the gap in productivity with their Japanese competitors. In addition, Europe's aircraft industry has closed a similar gap with the U.S. aircraft industry. At any given point in time, however, differences in technology are a major source of comparative advantage.

ECONOMICS >> *in Action*
How Hong Kong Lost Its Shirts

The rise of Hong Kong was one of the most improbable-sounding economic success stories of the twentieth century. When a communist regime took over China in 1949, Hong Kong—which was still at that point a British colony—became in effect a city without a hinterland, largely cut off from economic relations with the territory just over the border. Since Hong Kong had until that point made a living largely by serving as a point of entry into China, you might have expected the city to languish. Instead, however, Hong Kong prospered, to such an extent that today the city—now returned to China, but governed as a special autonomous region—has a GDP per capita comparable to that of the United States.

During much of its ascent, Hong Kong's rise rested, above all, on its clothing industry. In 1980 Hong Kong's garment and textile sectors employed almost 450,000 workers, close to 20% of total employment. These workers overwhelmingly made apparel—shirts, trousers, dresses, and more—for export, especially to the United States.

Since then, however, the Hong Kong clothing industry has fallen sharply in size—in fact, it has almost disappeared. So, too, have Hong Kong's apparel exports. Figure 20-4 shows Hong Kong's share of U.S. apparel

FIGURE 20-4 Education, Skill Intensity, and Trade

Share of U.S. apparel imports (percent)

Data from: U.S. International Trade Administration.

imports since 1990, along with the share of a relative newcomer to the industry, Bangladesh. As you can see, Hong Kong has more or less dropped off the chart, while Bangladesh's share has risen significantly in recent years.

Why did Hong Kong lose its comparative advantage in making shirts, pants, and so on? It wasn't because the city's garment workers became less productive. Instead, it was because the city got better at other things. Apparel production is a labor-intensive, relatively low-tech industry; comparative advantage in that industry has historically always rested with poor, labor-abundant economies. Hong Kong no longer fits that description; Bangladesh does. Hong Kong's garment industry was a victim of the city's success.

>> Check Your Understanding 20-1
Solutions appear at back of book.

1. In the United States, the opportunity cost of 1 ton of corn is 50 bicycles. In China, the opportunity cost of 1 bicycle is 0.01 ton of corn.
   a. Determine the pattern of comparative advantage.
   b. In autarky, the United States can produce 200,000 bicycles if no corn is produced, and China can produce 3,000 tons of corn if no bicycles are produced. Draw each country's production possibility frontier assuming constant opportunity cost, with tons of corn on the vertical axis and bicycles on the horizontal axis.
   c. With trade, each country specializes its production. The United States consumes 1,000 tons of corn and 200,000 bicycles; China consumes 3,000 tons of corn and 100,000 bicycles. Indicate the production and consumption points on your diagrams, and use them to explain the gains from trade.
2. Explain the following patterns of trade using the Heckscher–Ohlin model.
   a. France exports wine to the United States, and the United States exports movies to France.
   b. Brazil exports shoes to the United States, and the United States exports shoe-making machinery to Brazil.

Supply, Demand, and International Trade

Simple models of comparative advantage are helpful for understanding the fundamental causes of international trade. However, to analyze the effects of international trade at a more detailed level and to understand trade policy, it helps to return to the supply and demand model. We'll start by looking at the effects of imports on domestic producers and consumers, then turn to the effects of exports.

The Effects of Imports

Figure 20-5 shows the U.S. market for phones, ignoring international trade for a moment. It introduces a few new concepts: the *domestic demand curve,* the *domestic supply curve,* and the *domestic or autarky price.*

The **domestic demand curve** shows how the quantity of a good demanded by residents of a country depends on the price of that good. Why "domestic"? Because people living in other countries may demand the good, too. Once we introduce international trade, we need to distinguish between purchases of a good by domestic consumers and purchases by foreign consumers. So the domestic demand curve reflects only the demand of residents of our own country.

Similarly, the **domestic supply curve** shows how the quantity of a good supplied by producers inside our own country depends on the price of that good. Once we introduce international trade, we need to distinguish between the supply of domestic producers and foreign supply—supply brought in from abroad.

The **domestic demand curve** shows how the quantity of a good demanded by domestic consumers depends on the price of that good.

The **domestic supply curve** shows how the quantity of a good supplied by domestic producers depends on the price of that good.

FIGURE 20-5 Consumer and Producer Surplus in Autarky

In the absence of trade, the domestic price is P_A, the autarky price at which the domestic supply curve and the domestic demand curve intersect. The quantity produced and consumed domestically is Q_A. Consumer surplus is represented by the blue-shaded area, and producer surplus is represented by the red-shaded area.

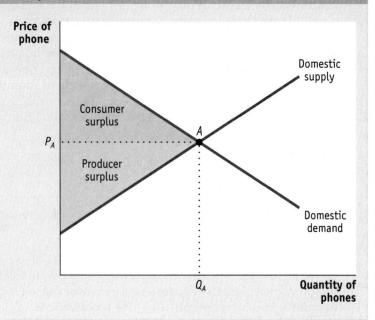

In autarky, with no international trade in phones, the equilibrium in this market would be determined by the intersection of the domestic demand and domestic supply curves, point A. The equilibrium price of phones would be P_A, and the equilibrium quantity of phones produced and consumed would be Q_A. As always, both consumers and producers gain from the existence of the domestic market. In autarky, consumer surplus would be equal to the area of the blue-shaded triangle in Figure 20-5. Producer surplus would be equal to the area of the red-shaded triangle. And total surplus would be equal to the sum of these two shaded triangles.

Now let's imagine opening up this market to imports. To do this, we must make an assumption about the supply of imports. The simplest assumption, which we will adopt here, is that unlimited quantities of phones can be purchased from abroad at a fixed price, known as the world price of phones. Figure 20-6 shows a situation in which the **world price** of a phone, P_W, is lower than the price of a phone that would prevail in the domestic market in autarky, P_A.

Given that the world price is below the domestic price of a phone, it is profitable for importers to buy phones abroad and resell them domestically. The imported phones increase the supply of phones in the domestic market, driving down the domestic market price. Phones will continue to be imported until the domestic price falls to a level equal to the world price.

The result is shown in Figure 20-6. Because of imports, the domestic price of a phone falls from P_A to P_W. The quantity of phones demanded by domestic consumers rises from Q_A to Q_D, and the quantity supplied by domestic producers falls from Q_A to Q_S. The difference between the domestic quantity demanded and the domestic quantity supplied, $Q_D - Q_S$, is filled by imports.

Now let's turn to the effects of imports on consumer surplus and producer surplus. Because imports of phones lead to a fall in their domestic price, consumer surplus rises and producer surplus falls. Figure 20-7 shows how this works. We label four areas: W, X, Y, and Z. The autarky consumer surplus we identified in Figure 20-5 corresponds to W, and the autarky producer surplus corresponds to the sum of X and Y. The fall in the domestic price to the world price leads to an increase in consumer surplus; it increases by X and Z, so consumer surplus now equals the sum of W, X, and Z. At the same time, producers lose X in surplus, so producer surplus now equals only Y.

The **world price** of a good is the price at which that good can be bought or sold abroad.

FIGURE 20-6 The Domestic Market with Imports

Here the world price of phones, P_W, is below the autarky price, P_A. When the economy is opened to international trade, imports enter the domestic market, and the domestic price falls from the autarky price, P_A, to the world price, P_W. As the price falls, the domestic quantity demanded rises from Q_A to Q_D and the domestic quantity supplied falls from Q_A to Q_S. The difference between domestic quantity demanded and domestic quantity supplied at P_W, the quantity $Q_D - Q_S$, is filled by imports.

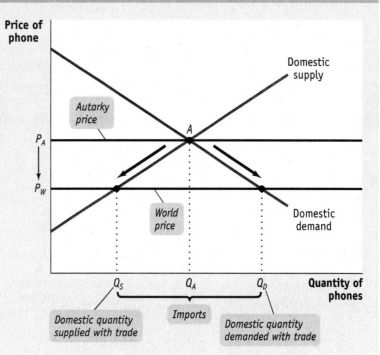

The table in Figure 20-7 summarizes the changes in consumer and producer surplus when the phone market is opened to imports. Consumers gain surplus equal to the areas $X + Z$. Producers lose surplus equal to X. So the sum of producer and consumer surplus—the total surplus generated in the phone market—increases by Z. As a result of trade, consumers gain and producers lose, but the gain to consumers exceeds the loss to producers.

This is an important result. We have just shown that opening up a market to imports leads to a net gain in total surplus, which is what we should have expected given the proposition that there are gains from international trade.

However, we have also learned that although the country as a whole gains, some groups—in this case, domestic producers of phones—lose as a result of international trade. As we'll see shortly, the fact that international trade typically creates losers as well as winners is crucial for understanding the politics of trade policy.

We turn next to the case in which a country exports a good.

The Effects of Exports

Figure 20-8 shows the effects on a country when it exports a good, in this case trucks. For this example, we assume that unlimited quantities of trucks can be sold abroad at a given world price, P_W, which is higher than the price that would prevail in the domestic market in autarky, P_A.

The higher world price makes it profitable for exporters to buy trucks domestically and sell them overseas. The purchases of domestic trucks drive the domestic price up until it is equal to the world price. As a result, the quantity demanded by domestic consumers falls from Q_A to Q_D and the quantity supplied by domestic producers rises from Q_A to Q_S. This difference between domestic production and domestic consumption, $Q_S - Q_D$, is exported.

FIGURE 20-7 The Effects of Imports on Surplus

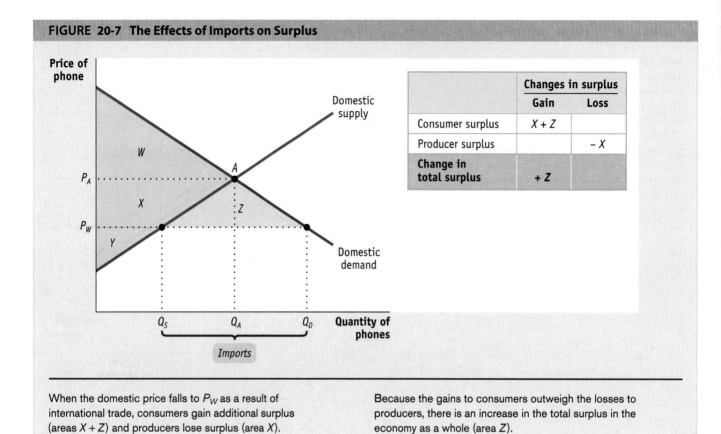

	Changes in surplus	
	Gain	**Loss**
Consumer surplus	$X + Z$	
Producer surplus		$-X$
Change in total surplus	**$+ Z$**	

When the domestic price falls to P_W as a result of international trade, consumers gain additional surplus (areas $X + Z$) and producers lose surplus (area X).

Because the gains to consumers outweigh the losses to producers, there is an increase in the total surplus in the economy as a whole (area Z).

Like imports, exports lead to an overall gain in total surplus for the exporting country but they also create losers as well as winners. Figure 20-9 shows the effects of truck exports on producer and consumer surplus. In the absence of trade, the price of each truck would be P_A. Consumer surplus in the absence of

FIGURE 20-8 The Domestic Market with Exports

Here the world price, P_W, is greater than the autarky price, P_A. When the economy is opened to international trade, some of the domestic supply is now exported. The domestic price rises from the autarky price, P_A, to the world price, P_W. As the price rises, the domestic quantity demanded falls from Q_A to Q_D and the domestic quantity supplied rises from Q_A to Q_S. The portion of domestic production that is not consumed domestically, $Q_S - Q_D$, is exported.

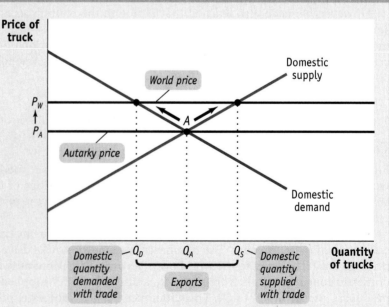

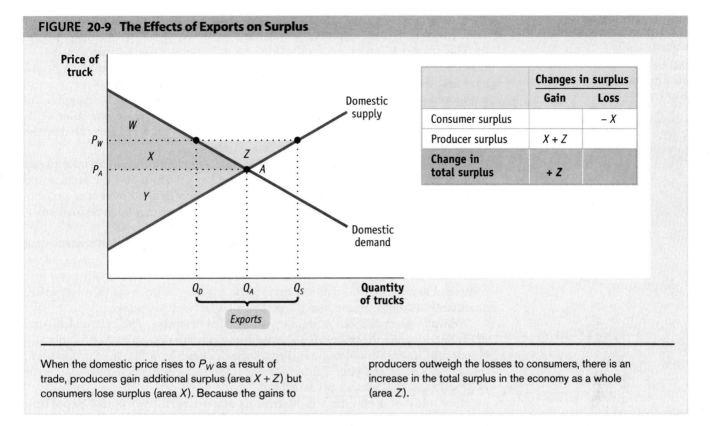

FIGURE 20-9 The Effects of Exports on Surplus

	Changes in surplus	
	Gain	**Loss**
Consumer surplus		– X
Producer surplus	X + Z	
Change in total surplus	**+ Z**	

When the domestic price rises to P_W as a result of trade, producers gain additional surplus (area $X + Z$) but consumers lose surplus (area X). Because the gains to producers outweigh the losses to consumers, there is an increase in the total surplus in the economy as a whole (area Z).

trade is the sum of areas W and X, and producer surplus is area Y. As a result of trade, price rises from P_A to P_W, consumer surplus falls to W, and producer surplus rises to $Y + X + Z$. So producers gain $X + Z$, consumers lose X, and, as shown in the table accompanying the figure, the economy as a whole gains total surplus in the amount of Z.

We have learned, then, that imports of a particular good hurt domestic producers of that good but help domestic consumers, whereas exports of a particular good hurt domestic consumers of that good but help domestic producers. In each case, the gains are larger than the losses.

International Trade and Wages

So far we have focused on the effects of international trade on producers and consumers in a particular industry. For many purposes this is a very helpful approach. However, producers and consumers are not the only parts of society affected by trade—so are the owners of factors of production. In particular, the owners of labor, land, and capital employed in producing goods that are exported, or goods that compete with imported goods, can be deeply affected by trade.

Moreover, the effects of trade aren't limited to just those industries that export or compete with imports because *factors of production can often move between industries*. So now we turn our attention to the long-run effects of international trade on income distribution—how a country's total income is allocated among its various factors of production.

To begin our analysis, consider the position of Maria, who is initially employed as an accountant in an industry that is shrinking as a result of growing international trade. Suppose, for example, that she works in the U.S. apparel (clothing) industry, which formerly employed millions of people but has largely been displaced by imports from low-wage countries. Maria is likely to find a new job

Exporting industries produce goods and services that are sold abroad.

Import-competing industries produce goods and services that are also imported.

in another industry, such as health care, which has been expanding rapidly over time. How will the move affect her earnings?

The answer is, there probably won't be much effect. According to the U.S. Bureau of Labor Statistics, accountants earn roughly the same amount in health care that they do in what's left of the apparel industry—about $80,000 a year. So we shouldn't think of Maria as a producer of apparel who is hurt by competition from imports. Instead, we should think of her as a worker with particular skills who is affected by imports mainly by the extent to which those imports change the wages of accountants in the economy as a whole.

The wage rate of accountants is a *factor price*—the price employers have to pay for the services of a factor of production. One key question about international trade is how it affects factor prices—not just narrowly defined factors of production like accountants, but broadly defined factors such as capital, unskilled labor, and college-educated labor.

Earlier in this chapter we described the Heckscher–Ohlin model of trade, which states that comparative advantage is determined by a country's factor endowment. This model also suggests how international trade affects factor prices in a country: compared to autarky, international trade tends to raise the prices of factors that are abundantly available and reduce the prices of factors that are scarce.

We won't work this out in detail, but the idea is simple. The prices of factors of production, like the prices of goods and services, are determined by supply and demand. If international trade increases the demand for a factor of production, that factor's price will rise; if international trade reduces the demand for a factor of production, that factor's price will fall.

Now think of a country's industries as consisting of two kinds: **exporting industries,** which produce goods and services that are sold abroad, and **import-competing industries,** which produce goods and services that are also imported from abroad. Compared with autarky, international trade leads to higher production in exporting industries and lower production in import-competing industries. This indirectly increases the demand for factors used by exporting industries and decreases the demand for factors used by import-competing industries.

In addition, the Heckscher–Ohlin model says that a country tends to export goods that are intensive in its abundant factors and to import goods that are intensive in its scarce factors. *So international trade tends to increase the demand for factors that are abundant in our country compared with other countries, and to decrease the demand for factors that are scarce in our country compared with other countries. As a result, the prices of abundant factors tend to rise, and the prices of scarce factors tend to fall as international trade grows.*

In other words, international trade tends to redistribute income toward a country's abundant factors and away from its less abundant factors.

U.S. exports tend to be human-capital-intensive (such as high-tech design and Hollywood movies) while U.S. imports tend to be unskilled-labor-intensive (such as phone assembly and clothing production). This suggests that the effect of international trade on the U.S. factor markets is to raise the wage rate of highly educated American workers and reduce the wage rate of unskilled American workers.

This effect has been a source of much concern in recent years. Wage inequality—the gap between the wages of high-paid and low-paid workers—has increased substantially over the last 30 years. Some economists believe that growing international trade is an important factor in that trend. If international trade has the effects predicted by the Heckscher–Ohlin model, its growth raises the wages of highly educated American workers, who already have relatively high wages, and lowers the wages of less educated American workers, who already have relatively low wages.

But keep in mind another phenomenon: trade reduces the income inequality between countries as poor countries improve their standard of living by exporting to rich countries.

How important are these effects? In some historical episodes, the impacts of international trade on factor prices have been very large. As we explain in the following Economics in Action, the opening of transatlantic trade in the late nineteenth century had a large negative impact on land rents in Europe, hurting landowners but helping workers and owners of capital.

The effects of trade on wages in the United States have generated considerable controversy in recent years. Most economists who have studied the issue agree that growing imports of labor-intensive products from newly industrializing economies, and the export of high-technology goods in return, have helped cause a widening wage gap between highly educated and less educated workers in this country. However, most economists believe that it is only one of several forces explaining the growth in American wage inequality.

ECONOMICS >> *in Action* 🌐
Trade, Wages, and Land Prices in the Nineteenth Century

International trade redistributes income toward a country's abundant factors and away from its less abundant factors.

Beginning around 1870, there was an explosive growth of world trade in agricultural products, based largely on the steam engine. Steam-powered ships could cross the ocean much more quickly and reliably than sailing ships. Until about 1860, steamships had higher costs than sailing ships, but after that costs dropped sharply. At the same time, steam-powered rail transport made it possible to bring grain and other bulk goods cheaply from the interior to ports. The result was that land-abundant countries—the United States, Canada, Argentina, and Australia—began shipping large quantities of agricultural goods to the densely populated, land-scarce countries of Europe.

This opening up of international trade led to higher prices of agricultural products, such as wheat, in exporting countries and a decline in their prices in importing countries. Notably, the difference between wheat prices in the midwestern United States and England plunged.

The change in agricultural prices created winners and losers on both sides of the Atlantic as factor prices adjusted. In England, land prices fell by half compared with average wages; landowners found their purchasing power sharply reduced, but workers benefited from cheaper food. In the United States, the reverse happened: land prices doubled compared with wages. Landowners did very well, but workers found the purchasing power of their wages dented by rising food prices.

>> Check Your Understanding 20-2
Solutions appear at back of book.

1. Due to a strike by truckers, trade in food between the United States and Mexico is halted. In autarky, the price of Mexican grapes is lower than that of U.S. grapes. Using a diagram of the U.S. domestic demand curve and the U.S. domestic supply curve for grapes, explain the effect of the strike on the following.
   a. U.S. grape consumers' surplus
   b. U.S. grape producers' surplus
   c. U.S. total surplus
2. What effect do you think the strike will have on Mexican grape producers? Mexican grape pickers? Mexican grape consumers? U.S. grape pickers?

>> Quick Review

• The intersection of the **domestic demand curve** and the **domestic supply curve** determines the domestic price of a good. When a market is opened to international trade, the domestic price is driven to equal the **world price.**

• If the world price is lower than the autarky price, trade leads to imports and the domestic price falls to the world price. There are overall gains from international trade because the gain in consumer surplus exceeds the loss in producer surplus.

• If the world price is higher than the autarky price, trade leads to exports and the domestic price rises to the world price. There are overall gains from international trade because the gain in producer surplus exceeds the loss in consumer surplus.

• Trade leads to an expansion of **exporting industries,** which increases demand for a country's abundant factors, and a contraction of **import-competing industries,** which decreases demand for its scarce factors.

An economy has **free trade** when the government does not attempt either to reduce or to increase the levels of exports and imports that occur naturally as a result of supply and demand.

Policies that limit imports are known as **trade protection** or simply as **protection.**

A **tariff** is a tax levied on imports.

‖ The Effects of Trade Protection

Ever since David Ricardo laid out the principle of comparative advantage in the early nineteenth century, most economists have advocated **free trade.** That is, they have argued that government policy should not attempt either to reduce or to increase the levels of exports and imports that occur naturally as a result of supply and demand.

Despite the free-trade arguments of economists, however, many governments use taxes and other restrictions to limit imports. Less frequently, governments offer subsidies to encourage exports. Policies that limit imports, usually with the goal of protecting domestic producers in import-competing industries from foreign competition, are known as **trade protection** or simply as **protection.**

Let's look at the two most common protectionist policies, *tariffs* and *import quotas,* then turn to the reasons governments follow these policies.

The Effects of a Tariff

A **tariff** is a form of excise tax, one that is levied only on sales of imported goods. For example, the U.S. government could declare that anyone bringing in phones must pay a tariff of $100 per unit. In the distant past, tariffs were an important source of government revenue because they were relatively easy to collect. But in the modern world, tariffs are usually intended to discourage imports and protect import-competing domestic producers rather than as a source of government revenue.

The tariff raises both the price received by domestic producers and the price paid by domestic consumers. Suppose, for example, that our country imports phones, and a phone costs $200 on the world market. As we saw earlier, under free trade the domestic price would also be $200. But if a tariff of $100 per unit is imposed, the domestic price will rise to $300, because it won't be profitable to import phones unless the price in the domestic market is high enough to compensate importers for the cost of paying the tariff.

Figure 20-10 illustrates the effects of a tariff on imports of phones. As before, we assume that P_W is the world price of a phone. Before the tariff is imposed,

FIGURE 20-10 The Effect of a Tariff

A tariff raises the domestic price of the good from P_W to P_T. The domestic quantity demanded shrinks from Q_D to Q_{DT}, and the domestic quantity supplied increases from Q_S to Q_{ST}. As a result, imports—which had been $Q_D - Q_S$ before the tariff was imposed—shrink to $Q_{DT} - Q_{ST}$ after the tariff is imposed.

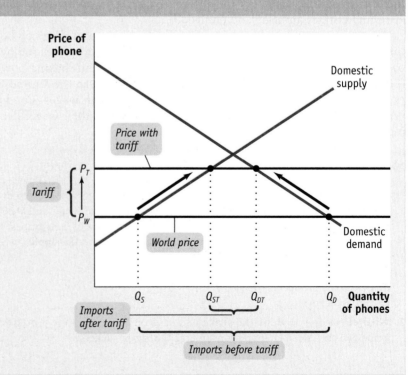

imports have driven the domestic price down to P_W, so that pre-tariff domestic production is Q_S, pre-tariff domestic consumption is Q_D, and pre-tariff imports are $Q_D - Q_S$.

Now suppose that the government imposes a tariff on each phone imported. As a consequence, it is no longer profitable to import phones unless the domestic price received by the importer is greater than or equal to the world price plus the tariff. So the domestic price rises to P_T, which is equal to the world price, P_W, plus the tariff. Domestic production rises to Q_{ST}, domestic consumption falls to Q_{DT}, and imports fall to $Q_{DT} - Q_{ST}$.

A tariff, then, raises domestic prices, leading to increased domestic production and reduced domestic consumption compared to the situation under free trade. Figure 20-11 shows the effects on surplus. There are three effects:

1. The higher domestic price increases producer surplus, a gain equal to area A.

2. The higher domestic price reduces consumer surplus, a reduction equal to the sum of areas A, B, C, and D.

3. The tariff yields revenue to the government. How much revenue? The government collects the tariff—which, remember, is equal to the difference between P_T and P_W on each of the $Q_{DT} - Q_{ST}$ units imported. So total revenue is $(P_T - P_W) \times (Q_{DT} - Q_{ST})$. This is equal to area C.

The welfare effects of a tariff are summarized in the table in Figure 20-11. Producers gain, consumers lose, and the government gains. But consumer losses are greater than the sum of producer and government gains, leading to a net reduction in total surplus equal to areas $B + D$.

An excise tax creates inefficiency, or deadweight loss, because it prevents mutually beneficial trades from occurring. The same is true of a tariff, where the

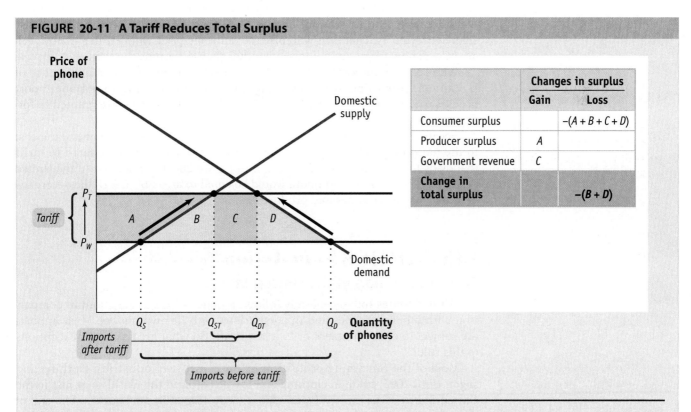

FIGURE 20-11 A Tariff Reduces Total Surplus

	Changes in surplus	
	Gain	Loss
Consumer surplus		$-(A + B + C + D)$
Producer surplus	A	
Government revenue	C	
Change in total surplus		$-(B + D)$

When the domestic price rises as a result of a tariff, producers gain additional surplus (area A), the government gains revenue (area C), and consumers lose surplus (areas $A + B + C + D$).

Because the losses to consumers outweigh the gains to producers and the government, the economy as a whole loses surplus (areas B and D).

An **import quota** is a legal limit on the quantity of a good that can be imported.

deadweight loss imposed on society is equal to the loss in total surplus represented by areas $B + D$.

Tariffs generate deadweight losses because they create inefficiencies in two ways:

1. Some mutually beneficial trades go unexploited: some consumers who are willing to pay more than the world price, P_W, do not purchase the good, even though P_W is the true cost of a unit of the good to the economy. The cost of this inefficiency is represented in Figure 20-11 by area D.

2. The economy's resources are wasted on inefficient production: some producers whose cost exceeds P_W produce the good, even though an additional unit of the good can be purchased abroad for P_W. The cost of this inefficiency is represented in Figure 20-11 by area B.

The Effects of an Import Quota

An **import quota,** another form of trade protection, is a legal limit on the quantity of a good that can be imported. For example, a U.S. import quota on Chinese phones might limit the quantity imported each year to 50 million units. Import quotas are usually administered through licenses: a number of licenses are issued, each giving the license-holder the right to import a limited quantity of the good each year.

A quota on sales has the same effect as an excise tax, with one difference: the money that would otherwise have accrued to the government as tax revenue under an excise tax becomes license-holders' revenue under a quota—also known as quota rents. Similarly, an import quota has the same effect as a tariff, with one difference: the money that would otherwise have been government revenue becomes quota rents to license-holders.

Look again at Figure 20-11. An import quota that limits imports to $Q_{DT} - Q_{ST}$ will raise the domestic price of phones by the same amount as the tariff we considered previously. That is, it will raise the domestic price from P_W to P_T. However, area C will now represent quota rents rather than government revenue.

Who receives import licenses and so collects the quota rents? In the case of U.S. import protection, the answer may surprise you: the most important import licenses—mainly for clothing, and to a lesser extent for sugar—are granted to foreign governments.

Because the quota rents for most U.S. import quotas go to foreigners, the cost to the nation of such quotas is larger than that of a comparable tariff (a tariff that leads to the same level of imports). In Figure 20-11 the net loss to the United States from such an import quota would be equal to areas $B + C + D$, the difference between consumer losses and producer gains.

ECONOMICS >> *in Action*
Trade Protection in the United States

The United States today generally follows a policy of free trade, both in comparison with other countries and in comparison with its own history. Most imports are subject to either no tariff or to a low tariff. So what are the major exceptions to this rule?

Most of the remaining protection involves just two industries: clothing and sugar. Until 2005, trade in clothing and textiles around the world—not just in the United States—was limited by an elaborate system of import quotas. The end of that system led to a sharp drop in welfare losses (as shown in Figure 20-12), but the United States maintains relatively high tariffs on clothing imports.

The U.S. government also maintains a system of import quotas on sugar, which raise sugar's price above world levels and cost consumers several hundred million dollars a year.

The most important thing to know about current U.S. trade protection is how limited it really is, and how little cost it imposes on the economy. Every two years the U.S. International Trade Commission, a government agency, produces estimates of the impact of "significant trade restrictions" on U.S. welfare. As Figure 20-12 shows, over the past two decades both average tariff levels and the welfare loss from trade restrictions as a share of national income, which weren't all that big to begin with, have fallen sharply.

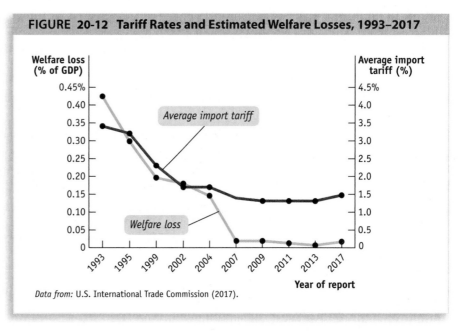

FIGURE 20-12 Tariff Rates and Estimated Welfare Losses, 1993–2017

Data from: U.S. International Trade Commission (2017).

>> Check Your Understanding 20-3

Solutions appear at back of book.

1. Suppose the world price of butter is $0.50 per pound and the domestic price in autarky is $1.00 per pound. Use a diagram similar to Figure 20-10 to show the following.

   a. If there is free trade, domestic butter producers want the government to impose a tariff of no less than $0.50 per pound. Compare the outcome with a tariff of $0.25 per pound.

   b. What happens if a tariff greater than $0.50 per pound is imposed?

2. Suppose the government imposes an import quota rather than a tariff on butter. What quota limit would generate the same quantity of imports as a tariff of $0.50 per pound?

‖ Capital Flows and the Balance of Payments

In 2018 people living in the United States sold trillions of dollars' worth of stuff to people living in other countries and bought trillions' of dollars worth of stuff in return. What kind of stuff? All kinds. Residents of the United States (including firms operating in the United States) sold airplanes, bonds, software licenses, wheat, and many other items to residents of other countries. U.S. residents bought cars, stocks, oil, and many other items from residents of other countries.

How can we keep track of these transactions? In Chapter 13 we learned that economists keep track of the domestic economy using the national income and product accounts. Economists keep track of international transactions using a different but related set of numbers, the *balance of payments accounts.*

Balance of Payments Accounts

A country's **balance of payments accounts** are a summary of the country's transactions with other countries for a given year.

To understand the basic idea behind the balance of payments accounts, let's consider a small-scale example: not a country, but a family farm. Let's say that we

>> Quick Review

• Most economists advocate **free trade,** although many governments engage in **trade protection** of import-competing industries. The two most common protectionist policies are tariffs and import quotas. In rare instances, governments subsidize exporting industries.

• A **tariff** is a tax on imports. It raises the domestic price above the world price, leading to a fall in trade and domestic consumption and a rise in domestic production. Domestic producers and the government gain, but domestic consumer losses more than offset this gain, leading to deadweight loss.

• An **import quota** is a legal quantity limit on imports. Its effect is like that of a tariff, except that revenues—the quota rents—accrue to the license holder, not to the domestic government.

A country's **balance of payments accounts** are a summary of the country's transactions with other countries for a given year.

know the following about how last year went financially for the Costas, who own a small artichoke farm in California:

- They made $100,000 by selling artichokes.
- They spent $70,000 on running the farm, including purchases of new farm machinery, and another $40,000 buying food, paying utility bills, replacing their worn-out car, and so on.
- They received $500 in interest on their bank account but paid $10,000 in interest on their mortgage.
- They took out a new $25,000 loan to help pay for farm improvements but didn't use all the money immediately. So they put the remaining $5,500 in the bank.

TABLE 20-3 The Costas' Financial Year

	Sources of cash	Uses of cash	Net
Sales and purchases of goods and services	Artichoke sales: $100,000	Farm operation and living expenses: $110,000	–$10,000
Interest payments	Interest received on bank account: $500	Interest paid on mortgage: $10,000	–$9,500
Loans and deposits	Funds received from new loan: $25,000	Funds deposited in bank: $5,500	+$19,500
Total	$125,500	$125,500	$0

How could we summarize the Costas' transactions for the year? One way would be with a table like Table 20-3, which shows sources of cash coming in and uses of cash going out, characterized under a few broad headings. The first row of Table 20-3 shows sales and purchases of goods and services: sales of artichokes; purchases of groceries, heating oil, that new car, and so on. The second row shows interest payments: the interest the Costas received from their bank account and the interest they paid on their mortgage. The third row shows loans and deposits: cash coming in from a loan and cash deposited in the bank.

In each row we show the net inflow of cash from that type of transaction. So the net in the first row is –$10,000, because the Costas spent $10,000 more than they earned. The net in the second row is –$9,500, the difference between the interest the Costas received on their bank account and the interest they paid on the mortgage. The net in the third row is $19,500: the Costas brought in $25,000 with their new loan but put only $5,500 of that sum in the bank.

The last row shows the sum of cash coming in from all sources and the sum of all cash used. These sums are equal, by definition: every dollar has a source, and every dollar received gets used somewhere. (What if the Costas hid money under the mattress? Then that would be counted as another "use" of cash.)

A country's balance of payments accounts is a table that summarizes the country's transactions with the rest of the world for a given year in a manner very similar to the way we just summarized the Costas' financial year.

Table 20-4 shows a simplified version of the U.S. balance of payments accounts for 2017. Where the Costas family's accounts show sources and uses of cash, a country's balance of payments accounts show payments from foreigners—sources of cash for the United States as a whole—and payments to foreigners—uses of cash for the United States as a whole.

Row 1 of Table 20-4 shows payments that arise from U.S. sales to foreigners and U.S. purchases from foreigners of goods and services in 2017. For example, the number in the second column of row 1, $2,331 billion, incorporates items such as the value of U.S. wheat exports and the fees foreigners paid to U.S. consulting companies in 2017. The number in the third column of row 1, $2,900 billion, incorporates items such as the value of U.S. oil imports and the fees U.S. companies paid to Indian call centers—the people who often answer your 1-800 calls—in 2017.

Row 2 shows U.S. *factor income* in 2017—the income that foreigners paid to American residents for the use of American-owned factors of production, as well as income paid by Americans to foreigners for the use of foreign-owned factors of production. Factor income mostly consists of investment income, such as interest paid by Americans on loans from overseas, profits of American-owned corporations that operate overseas, and the like. For example, the profits earned by Disneyland Paris, which is owned by the U.S.-based Walt Disney Company, are included in the $926 billion figure in the second column of row 2. The profits earned by the U.S. operations of Japanese auto companies are included in the $710 billion figure shown in the third column of row 2. Factor income also includes some labor income. For example, the wages of an American engineer who worked temporarily on a construction site in Dubai are counted in the $926 billion figure in the second column.

Row 3 shows *transfers* for the United States in 2017—funds sent by American residents to residents of other countries and vice versa. The figure in the second column of row 3, $150 billion, includes payments sent home by skilled American workers who work abroad. The third column accounts for the major portion of international transfers. That figure, $265 billion, is composed mainly of remittances that immigrants who reside in the United States, such as the millions of Mexican-born workers employed in the United States, send to their families in their country of origin.

Row 4 of the table shows net payments accruing from sales and purchases of assets between American residents and foreigners in 2017. Such payments involve a wide variety of transactions, from Chinese companies purchasing U.S. firms to U.S. purchases of European stocks and bonds. The details of these transactions are complex, and if you add up all purchases the value is very large, which is why we focus only on the net value. Overall, according to official figures, and as you can see in the table, U.S. residents sold $376 billion more in assets than they purchased.

In laying out Table 20-4, we have separated rows 1, 2, and 3 into one group, to distinguish them from row 4, reflecting a fundamental difference in how these two groups of transactions affect the future. When a U.S. resident sells a good such as wheat to a foreigner, that's the end of the transaction. But a financial asset, such as a bond, is different: it is a promise to pay interest and principal in the future. So when a U.S. resident sells a bond to a foreigner, that sale creates a liability: the U.S. resident will have to pay interest and repay principal in the future. The balance of payments accounts distinguish between transactions that don't create liabilities and those that do.

Transactions that don't create liabilities are considered part of the **balance of payments on current account,** often referred to simply as the **current account:** the balance of payments on goods and services plus net international transfer payments and factor income. This corresponds to rows 1, 2, and 3 in Table 20-4. In practice, row 1 of the table, amounting to –$569 billion, corresponds to the most important part of the current account: the **balance of payments on goods and services,** the difference between the value of exports and the value of imports during a given period.

In economic news reports, you may see references to another measure, the **merchandise trade balance,** sometimes referred to as the **trade balance** for short. It is the difference between a country's exports and imports of goods alone—not including services. Economists sometimes focus on the merchandise trade balance, even though it's an incomplete measure, because data on international trade in services aren't as accurate as data on trade in physical goods, and they are also slower to arrive.

TABLE 20-4 The U.S. Balance of Payments in 2017 (billions of dollars)

		Payments from foreigners	Payments to foreigners	Net
1	Sales and purchases of goods and services	$2,331	$2,900	–$569
2	Factor income	926	710	216
3	Transfers	150	265	–115
	Current account (1 + 2 + 3)			**–468**
4	Asset sales and purchases (financial account)	1,588	1,212	376
	Financial account (4)			**376**
	Statistical discrepancy			**–92**

Data from: Bureau of Economic Analysis.

A country's **balance of payments on current account,** or **current account,** is its balance of payments on goods and services plus net international transfer payments and factor income.

A country's **balance of payments on goods and services** is the difference between its exports and its imports during a given period.

The **merchandise trade balance,** or **trade balance,** is the difference between a country's exports and imports of goods.

A country's **balance of payments on financial account,** or simply its **financial account,** is the difference between its sales of assets to foreigners and its purchases of assets from foreigners for a given period.

Transactions that involve the sale or purchase of assets, and therefore do create future liabilities, are considered part of the **balance of payments on financial account,** or the **financial account** for short, for a given period. This corresponds to row 4 in Table 20-4, which was $376 billion in 2017. (Until a few years ago, economists often referred to the financial account as the *capital account.* We'll use the modern term, but you may run across the older term.)

So how does it all add up? The rows shaded purple in Table 20-4 show the bottom lines: the overall U.S. current account and financial account for 2017. As you can see:

- The United States ran a *current account deficit:* the amount it paid to foreigners for goods, services, factors, and transfers was more than the amount it received.

- Simultaneously, it ran a *financial account surplus:* the value of the assets it sold to foreigners was more than the value of the assets it bought from foreigners.

- In the official data, the U.S. current account deficit and financial account surplus didn't offset each other: the financial account surplus in 2017 was $92 billion smaller than the current account deficit (shown in the final row of the table). But that was just a statistical error, reflecting the imperfection of official data. (The discrepancy may have reflected foreign purchases of U.S. assets that official data somehow missed.)

In fact, it's a basic rule of balance of payments accounting that the current account and the financial account must sum to zero:

(20-1) Current account (CA) + Financial account $(FA) = 0$

or

$$CA = -FA$$

Why must Equation 20-1 be true? We already saw the fundamental explanation in Table 20-3, which showed the accounts of the Costas family: in total, the sources of cash must equal the uses of cash. The same applies to balance of payments accounts. Figure 20-13, a variant on the circular-flow diagram we encountered first in Chapter 2, may help you visualize how this adding up works. Instead of showing the flow of money *within* an economy, Figure 20-13 shows the flow of money *between* national economies.

FIGURE 20-13 The Balance of Payments

The blue arrows represent payments that are counted in the current account. The green arrows represent payments that are counted in the financial account. Because the total flow into the United States must equal the total flow out of the United States, the sum of the current account plus the financial account is zero.

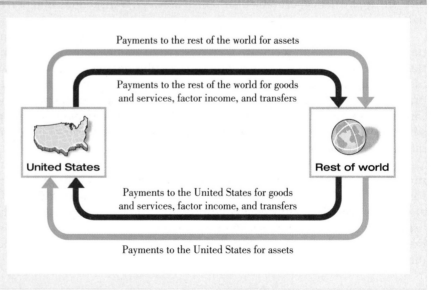

Payments to the rest of the world for assets

Payments to the rest of the world for goods and services, factor income, and transfers

United States

Rest of world

Payments to the United States for goods and services, factor income, and transfers

Payments to the United States for assets

Money flows into the United States from the rest of the world as payment for U.S. exports of goods and services, as payment for the use of U.S.-owned factors of production, and as transfer payments. These flows, indicated by the lower blue arrow, are the positive components of the U.S. current account. Money also flows into the United States from foreigners who purchase U.S. assets. They make up the positive component of the U.S. financial account and are shown by the lower green arrow.

At the same time, money flows from the United States to the rest of the world as payment for U.S. imports of goods and services, as payment for the use of foreign-owned factors of production, and as transfer payments. These flows, indicated by the upper blue arrow, are the negative components of the U.S. current account. Money also flows from the United States to purchase foreign assets. They make up the negative component of the U.S. financial account and are shown by the upper green arrow.

As in all circular-flow diagrams, the flow into a box and the flow out of a box are equal. This means that the sum of the blue and green arrows going into the United States (at the bottom of the diagram) is equal to the sum of the blue and green arrows going out of the United States (at the top of the diagram). That is,

(20-2)
Positive current account entries + Positive financial account entries =
    (lower blue arrow)   (lower green arrow)
Negative current account entries + Negative financial account entries
    (upper blue arrow)   (upper green arrow)

Equation 20-2 can be rearranged as follows:

(20-3)
Positive current account entries – Negative current account entries +
Positive financial account entries – Negative financial account entries = 0

Equation 20-3 is equivalent to Equation 20-1: once we have summed up the positive and negative entries within each account, the current account plus the financial account is equal to zero.

But what determines the current account and the financial account?

🌐 GLOBAL COMPARISON   BIG SURPLUSES

As we've seen, the United States generally runs a large deficit in its current account. In fact, America leads the world in its current account deficit; other countries run bigger deficits as a share of GDP, but they have much smaller economies, so the U.S. deficit is much bigger in absolute terms.

For the world as a whole, however, deficits on the part of some countries must be matched with surpluses on the part of other countries. So who are the surplus nations offsetting U.S. deficits, and what if anything do they have in common?

The accompanying figure shows the average current account surplus of the six countries that ran the largest surpluses over the period from 2007 to 2016. You may not be surprised to see China topping the list. For a time China had a deliberate policy of keeping its currency weak relative to other currencies. And Saudi Arabia, with its vast oil reserves, generates a current account surplus by exporting a lot of oil.

Germany, Japan, the Netherlands, and Switzerland run current account surpluses for more or less the same reasons: they are rich nations with high savings rates, giving them a lot of money to invest. They also have slow long-run growth, which reduces the opportunities for domestic investment. So, much of their savings goes abroad, which means that they run deficits on the financial account and surpluses on the current account.

The current account surpluses of Germany and the Netherlands have also grown thanks to the declining value of the euro. A lower euro has reduced the cost of their manufacturing goods on world markets, allowing them to export more.

Overall, the surplus countries are a diverse group. If your picture of the world is simply one of American deficits versus Chinese surpluses, you're missing a large part of the story.

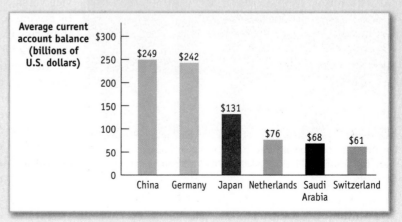

Data from: IMF World Economic Outlook, 2017.

Underlying Determinants of International Capital Flows

International differences in investment opportunities generate international differences in the demand for capital. A country with a rapidly growing economy, other things equal, will offer more investment opportunities and a higher return to investors than a country with a slowly growing economy. So, a country with a rapidly growing economy will typically have a higher demand for capital than the country with a slowly growing economy. As a result, capital tends to flow from slowly growing to rapidly growing economies.

International differences in the supply of funds reflect differences in savings across countries. These may be the result of differences in private savings rates, which vary among countries. They may also reflect differences in savings by governments. In particular, government budget deficits, which reduce overall national savings, can lead to capital inflows.

Now we can put together the demand for capital generated by investment opportunities within a country, with the supply for capital generated by savings within a country, to explain differences in interest rates across countries. Other things equal, countries with a high demand for capital and/or a low supply of capital will have higher interest rates. As a result, they will be the recipients of capital inflows.

Conversely, other things equal, countries with a low demand for funds and/or a high supply of funds will have lower interest rates. As a result, they will be the sources of capital outflows. The classic example of international capital flows—the flow of capital from Britain to the United States and other New World economies from 1870 to 1914—is described in the upcoming Economics in Action. During that era, the United States was rapidly industrializing and had a high demand for capital. But Britain, which had already industrialized, had a slowly growing economy with a large amount of accumulated savings.

Two-Way Capital Flows

International investment opportunities and differences in savings rates are important determinants of the direction of *net* capital flows—the excess of inflows into a country over outflows, or vice versa. The direction of *net* flows, other things equal, is also determined by differences in interest rates between countries. However, *gross* flows take place in both directions: for example, the United States both sells assets to foreigners and buys assets from foreigners. Why does capital move in both directions?

Oi qi jx/AP Images

Many American companies have opened plants in China to access the growing Chinese market and take advantage of low labor costs.

The answer to this question is that in the real world, as opposed to the simple model just described, there are other motives for international capital flows besides seeking a higher rate of interest.

Individual investors often seek to diversify against risk by buying stocks in several countries. Stocks in Europe may do well when stocks in the United States do badly, or vice versa, so investors in Europe try to reduce their risk by buying some U.S. stocks, as U.S. investors try to reduce their risk by buying some European stocks. The result is capital flows in both directions.

Meanwhile, corporations often engage in international investment as part of their business strategy—for example, auto companies may find that they can compete better in an overseas market if they assemble some of their cars in that location. Such business investments can also lead to two-way capital flows, as, say, European car makers build plants in the United States even as U.S. computer companies open facilities in Europe.

Finally, some countries, including the United States, are international banking centers: people from all over the world put money in U.S. financial institutions, which then invest many of those funds overseas.

The result of these two-way flows is that modern economies are typically both debtors (countries that owe money to the rest of the world) and creditors (countries to which the rest of the world owes money). Due to years of both capital inflows and outflows, at the end of 2017, the United States had accumulated foreign assets worth $27.6 trillion, and foreigners had accumulated assets in the United States worth $35.5 trillion.

ECONOMICS >> *in Action*
The Golden Age of Capital Flows

Technology, it's often said, shrinks the world. Jet planes have put most of the world's cities within a few hours of one another, while fiber-optic cables and satellites transmit information instantly around the globe. So you might think that international capital flows must now be larger than ever.

But if international capital flows are measured as a share of world savings and investment, that belief turns out not to be true. The golden age of capital flows actually preceded World War I—from 1870 to 1914.

These capital flows went mainly from European countries, especially Britain, to what were then known as *zones of recent settlement*, countries that were attracting large numbers of European immigrants. Among the big recipients of capital inflows were Australia, Argentina, Canada, and the United States.

The large capital flows reflected differences in investment opportunities. Britain, a mature industrial economy with limited natural resources and a slowly growing population, offered relatively limited opportunities for new investment. The zones of recent settlement, with rapidly growing populations and abundant natural resources, offered investors a higher return and attracted capital inflows. Estimates suggest that over this period Britain sent about 40% of its savings abroad, largely to finance railroads and other large projects. No country has matched that record in modern times.

Why can't we match the capital flows of our great-great-grandfathers? Economists aren't completely sure, but they have pointed to two causes: migration restrictions and political risks.

During the golden age of capital flows, capital movements were complementary to population movements: the big recipients of capital from Europe were also places to which large numbers of Europeans were moving. These large-scale population movements were possible before World War I because there were few legal restrictions on immigration. In today's world, by contrast, migration is limited by extensive legal barriers. Although there are still important migration flows, such as the wave of refugees into Europe in recent years, overall they play a much smaller economic role than the flows of the late nineteenth and early twentieth century.

The other explanation for our inability to match the golden age of capital flows is political risk. Modern governments often limit foreign investment because they fear it will diminish their national autonomy. And due to political or security concerns, governments sometimes seize foreign property, a risk that deters investors from sending more than a relatively modest share of their wealth abroad. In the nineteenth century such actions were rare, partly because some major destinations of investment were still European colonies, partly because in those days governments had a habit of sending troops and gunboats to enforce the claims of their investors.

>> Check Your Understanding 20-4

Solutions appear at back of book.

1. Which of the balance of payments accounts do the following events affect?
   a. Boeing, a U.S.-based company, sells a newly built airplane to China.
   b. Chinese investors buy stock in Boeing from American residents.
   c. A Chinese company buys a used airplane from American Airlines and ships it to China.
   d. A Chinese investor who owns property in the United States buys a corporate jet, which he will keep in the United States so he can travel around America.

2. What effect do you think the collapse of the U.S. housing bubble in 2008, and the ensuing Great Recession, had on international capital flows into the United States?

The Role of the Exchange Rate

We've just seen how differences in the supply of loanable funds from savings and the demand for loanable funds for investment spending lead to international capital flows. We've also learned that a country's balance of payments on current account plus its balance of payments on financial account add to zero: a country that receives net capital inflows must run a matching current account deficit, and a country that generates net capital outflows must run a matching current account surplus.

The behavior of the financial account—reflecting inflows or outflows of capital—is best described by equilibrium in the global loanable funds market. At the same time, the balance of payments on goods and services, the main component of the current account, is determined by decisions in the international markets for goods and services.

So, given that the financial account reflects the movement of capital and the current account reflects the movement of goods and services, what ensures that the balance of payments really does balance? That is, what ensures that the two accounts actually offset each other?

Not surprisingly, a price is what makes these two accounts balance. Specifically, that price is the *exchange rate*, which is determined in the *foreign exchange market*.

Understanding Exchange Rates

Currencies are traded in the **foreign exchange market.**

The prices at which currencies trade are known as **exchange rates.**

In general, goods, services, and assets produced in a country must be paid for in that country's currency. American products must be paid for in dollars; European products must be paid for in euros; Japanese products must be paid for in yen. Occasionally, sellers will accept payment in foreign currency, but they will then exchange that currency for domestic money.

International transactions, then, require a market—the **foreign exchange market**—in which currencies can be exchanged for each other. This market determines **exchange rates,** the prices at which currencies trade. (The foreign exchange market is, in fact, not located in any one geographic spot. Rather, it is a global electronic market that traders around the world use to buy and sell currencies.)

Table 20-5 shows exchange rates among the world's three most important currencies as of 3 P.M., EDT, on April 27, 2017. Each entry shows the price of the "row" currency in terms of the "column" currency. For example, at that time US$1 exchanged for €0.9198, so it took €0.9198 to buy US$1. Similarly, it took US$1.0872 to buy €1. These two numbers reflect the same rate of exchange between the euro and the U.S. dollar: 1/1.0872 = 0.9198.

TABLE 20-5 Exchange Rates, April 27, 2017, 3 P.M.

	U.S. dollars	Yen	Euros
One U.S. dollar exchanged for	1	111.26	0.9198
One yen exchanged for	0.0089	1	0.0082
One euro exchanged for	1.0872	120.99	1

There are two ways to write any given exchange rate. In this case, there were €0.9198 to US$1 and US$1.0872 to €1. Which is the correct way to write it? The answer is that there is no fixed rule. In most countries, people tend to express the exchange rate as the price of a dollar in domestic currency. However, this rule isn't universal, and the U.S. dollar–euro rate is commonly quoted both ways. The important thing is to be sure you know which one you are using, as explained in the accompanying Pitfalls.

When discussing movements in exchange rates, economists use specialized terms to avoid confusion. When a currency becomes more valuable in terms of other currencies, economists say that the currency **appreciates.** When a currency becomes less valuable in terms of other currencies, it **depreciates.** Suppose, for example, that the value of €1 went from $1 to $1.25, which means that the value of US$1 went from €1 to €0.80 (because $1/1.25 = 0.80$). In this case, we would say that the euro appreciated and the U.S. dollar depreciated.

By the way, although *appreciate* and *depreciate* are the technical, more or less official terms for a rise or fall of a currency against other currencies, you will also often hear it said that an appreciating currency is getting "stronger," or a depreciating currency is getting "weaker." It's important to realize that these terms, while widely used, shouldn't be taken as value judgments: a strong dollar isn't necessarily a good thing and a weak dollar isn't necessarily a bad thing.

Movements in exchange rates, other things equal, affect the relative prices of goods, services, and assets in different countries. Suppose, for example, that the price of an American hotel room is US$100 and the price of a French hotel room is €100. If the exchange rate is €1 = US$1, these hotel rooms have the same price. If the exchange rate is €1.25 = US$1, the French hotel room is 20% cheaper than the American hotel room. If the exchange rate is €0.80 = US$1, the French hotel room is 25% more expensive than the American hotel room.

But what determines exchange rates? Supply and demand in the foreign exchange market.

PITFALLS

WHICH WAY IS UP?

What does it mean when someone says that "The U.S. exchange rate is up"?

It could mean either that the dollar appreciated or that it depreciated. It depends on how the exchange rate is measured. Sometimes the exchange rate is measured as the price of a dollar in terms of foreign currency. But sometimes it is measured as the price of foreign currency in terms of dollars. So, be particularly careful when using published statistics. Most countries other than the United States state their exchange rates in terms of the price of a dollar in their domestic currency—for example, Mexican officials will say that the exchange rate is 10, meaning 10 pesos per dollar. But Britain, for historical reasons, usually states its exchange rate the other way. On April 27, 2017, US$1 was worth £0.7749, and £1 was worth US$1.2905. More often than not, this number is reported as an exchange rate of 1.2905. In fact, on occasion, professional economists and consultants embarrass themselves by getting the direction in which the pound is moving wrong!

By the way, Americans generally follow other countries' lead: we usually say that the exchange rate against Mexico is 10 pesos per dollar but that the exchange rate against Britain is 1.29 dollars per pound. But this rule isn't reliable; exchange rates against the euro can be stated both ways.

So, always check before using exchange rate data by asking yourself: which way is the exchange rate being measured?

The Equilibrium Exchange Rate

Imagine, for the sake of simplicity, that there are only two currencies in the world: U.S. dollars and euros. Europeans wanting to purchase American goods, services, and assets come to the foreign exchange market, wanting to exchange euros for U.S. dollars. That is, Europeans demand U.S. dollars from the foreign exchange market and, correspondingly, supply euros to that market. Americans wanting to buy European goods, services, and assets come to the foreign exchange market to exchange U.S. dollars for euros. That is, Americans supply U.S. dollars to the foreign exchange market and, correspondingly, demand euros from that market. (International transfers and payments of factor income also enter into the foreign exchange market, but to make things simple we'll ignore these.)

Figure 20-14 shows how the foreign exchange market works. The quantity of dollars demanded and supplied at any given euro–U.S. dollar exchange rate is shown on the horizontal axis, and the euro–U.S. dollar exchange rate is shown on the vertical axis. The exchange rate plays the same role as the price of a good or service in an ordinary supply and demand diagram.

The figure shows two curves, the demand curve for U.S. dollars and the supply curve for U.S. dollars. The key to understanding the slopes of these curves is that the level of the exchange rate affects exports and imports. When a country's currency appreciates (becomes more valuable), exports fall and imports rise.

When a currency becomes more valuable in terms of other currencies, it **appreciates.**

When a currency becomes less valuable in terms of other currencies, it **depreciates.**

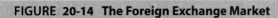

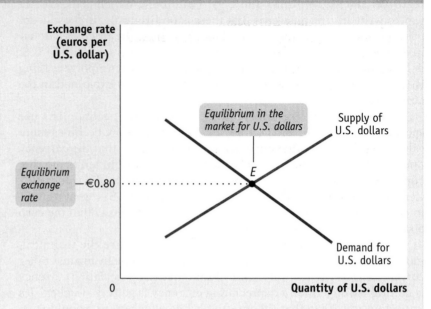

FIGURE 20-14 The Foreign Exchange Market

The foreign exchange market matches up the demand for a currency from foreigners who want to buy domestic goods, services, and assets with the supply of a currency from domestic residents who want to buy foreign goods, services, and assets. Here the equilibrium in the market for dollars is at point *E*, corresponding to an equilibrium exchange rate of €0.80 per US$1.

When a country's currency depreciates (becomes less valuable), exports rise and imports fall.

To understand why the demand curve for U.S. dollars slopes downward, recall that the exchange rate, other things equal, determines the prices of American goods, services, and assets relative to those of European goods, services, and assets.

If the U.S. dollar rises against the euro (the dollar appreciates), American products will become more expensive to Europeans relative to European products. So Europeans will buy less from the United States and will acquire fewer dollars in the foreign exchange market: the quantity of U.S. dollars demanded falls as the number of euros needed to buy a U.S. dollar rises.

If the U.S. dollar falls against the euro (the dollar depreciates), American products will become relatively cheaper for Europeans. Europeans will respond by buying more from the United States and acquiring more dollars in the foreign exchange market: the quantity of U.S. dollars demanded rises as the number of euros needed to buy a U.S. dollar falls.

A similar argument explains why the supply curve of U.S. dollars in Figure 20-14 slopes upward: the more euros required to buy a U.S. dollar, the more dollars Americans will supply. Again, the reason is the effect of the exchange rate on relative prices. If the U.S. dollar rises against the euro, European products look cheaper to Americans—who will demand more of them. This will require Americans to convert more dollars into euros.

The **equilibrium exchange rate** is the exchange rate at which the quantity of U.S. dollars demanded in the foreign exchange market is equal to the quantity of U.S. dollars supplied. In Figure 20-14, the equilibrium is at point *E*, and the equilibrium exchange rate is 0.80. That is, at an exchange rate of €0.80 per US$1, the quantity of U.S. dollars supplied to the foreign exchange market is equal to the quantity of U.S. dollars demanded.

To understand the significance of the equilibrium exchange rate, it's helpful to consider a numerical example of what equilibrium in the foreign exchange market looks like. A hypothetical example is shown in Table 20-6. The first row shows European purchases of U.S. dollars, either to buy U.S. goods and services or to buy U.S. assets. The second row shows U.S. sales of U.S. dollars, either to buy

The **equilibrium exchange rate** is the exchange rate at which the quantity of a currency demanded in the foreign exchange market is equal to the quantity supplied.

European goods and services or to buy European assets. At the equilibrium exchange rate, the total quantity of U.S. dollars Europeans want to buy is equal to the total quantity of U.S. dollars Americans want to sell.

Remember that the balance of payments accounts divide international transactions into two types. Purchases and sales of goods and services are counted in the current account. (Again, we're leaving out transfers and factor income to keep things simple.) Purchases and sales of assets are counted in the financial account. At the equilibrium exchange rate, then, we have the situation shown in Table 20-6: the sum of the balance of payments on current account plus the balance of payments on financial account is zero.

Now let's briefly consider how a shift in the demand for U.S. dollars affects equilibrium in the foreign exchange market. Suppose that for some reason capital flows from Europe to the United States increase due to a change in the preferences of European investors. The effects are shown in Figure 20-15. The demand for U.S. dollars in the foreign exchange market increases as European investors convert euros into dollars to fund their new investments in the United States. This is shown by the shift of the demand curve from D_1 to D_2. As a result, the U.S. dollar appreciates against the euro: the number of euros per U.S. dollar at the equilibrium exchange rate rises from XR_1 to XR_2.

What are the consequences of this increased capital inflow for the balance of payments? The total quantity of U.S. dollars supplied to the foreign exchange market still must equal the total quantity of U.S. dollars demanded. So the increased capital inflow to the United States—an increase in the balance of payments on financial account—must be matched by a decline in the balance of payments on current account. What causes the balance of payments on current account to decline? The appreciation of the U.S. dollar. A rise in the number of euros per U.S. dollar leads Americans to buy more European goods and services and Europeans to buy fewer American goods and services.

TABLE 20-6 A Hypothetical Equilibrium in the Foreign Exchange Market

	Current account	Financial account	Totals
European purchases of U.S. dollars (trillions of dollars)	To buy U.S. goods and services: 1.0	To buy U.S. assets: 1.0	**2.0**
U.S. sales of U.S. dollars (trillions of dollars)	To buy European goods and services: 1.5	To buy European assets: 0.5	**2.0**
U.S. balance of payments	–0.5	+0.5	

FIGURE 20-15 An Increase in the Demand for U.S. Dollars

An increase in the demand for U.S. dollars might result from a change in the preferences of European investors. The demand curve for U.S. dollars shifts from D_1 to D_2. So, the equilibrium number of euros per U.S. dollar rises—the dollar appreciates against the euro. As a result, the balance of payments on current account falls as the balance of payments on financial account rises.

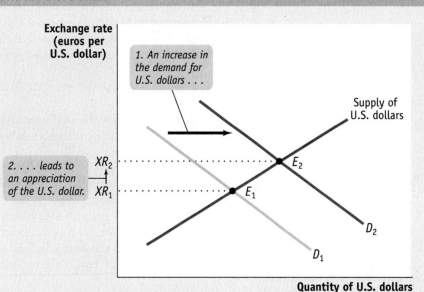

TABLE 20-7 A Hypothetical Example of Effects of Increased Capital Inflows

	Current account	Financial account	Totals
European purchases of U.S. dollars (trillions of dollars)	To buy U.S. goods and services: 0.75 (down 0.25)	To buy U.S. assets: 1.5 (up 0.5)	2.25
U.S. sales of U.S. dollars (trillions of dollars)	To buy European goods and services: 1.75 (up 0.25)	To buy European assets: 0.5 (no change)	2.25
U.S. balance of payments	–1.0 (down 0.5)	+1.0 (up 0.5)	

Table 20-7 shows a hypothetical example of how this might work. Europeans are buying more U.S. assets, increasing the balance of payments on the financial account from 0.5 to 1.0. This is offset by a reduction in European purchases of U.S. goods and services and a rise in U.S. purchases of European goods and services, both the result of the dollar's appreciation.

So any change in the U.S. balance of payments on financial account generates an equal and opposite reaction in the balance of payments on current account. Movements in the exchange rate ensure that changes in the financial account and in the current account offset each other.

Let's briefly run this process in reverse. Suppose there is a reduction in capital flows from Europe to the United States—again due to a change in the preferences of European investors. The demand for U.S. dollars in the foreign exchange market falls, and the dollar depreciates: the number of euros per U.S. dollar at the equilibrium exchange rate falls. This leads Americans to buy fewer European products and Europeans to buy more American products. Ultimately, this generates an increase in the U.S. balance of payments on current account. So a fall in capital flows into the United States leads to a weaker dollar, which in turn generates an increase in U.S. net exports.

Inflation and Real Exchange Rates

In 1993 one U.S. dollar exchanged, on average, for 3.1 Mexican pesos. By 2019, the peso had fallen against the dollar by more than 80%, with an average exchange rate of more than 19 pesos per dollar. Did Mexican products also become drastically cheaper relative to U.S. products over that 24-year period? Did the price of Mexican products expressed in terms of U.S. dollars also fall by more than 80%? The answer to both questions is no, because Mexico had much higher inflation than the United States over that period. In fact, the relative price of U.S. and Mexican products fluctuated both up and down between 1993 and 2017, with no clear trend.

To take account of the effects of differences in inflation rates, economists calculate **real exchange rates,** exchange rates adjusted for international differences in aggregate price levels. Suppose that the exchange rate we are looking at is the number of Mexican pesos per U.S. dollar. Let P_{US} and P_{Mex} be indexes of the aggregate price levels in the United States and Mexico, respectively. Then the real exchange rate between the Mexican peso and the U.S. dollar is defined as:

(20-4) $\text{Real exchange rate} = \text{Mexican pesos per U.S. dollar} \times \dfrac{P_{US}}{P_{Mex}}$

To distinguish it from the real exchange rate, the exchange rate unadjusted for aggregate price levels is sometimes called the *nominal* exchange rate.

To understand the significance of the difference between the real and nominal exchange rates, let's consider the following example. Suppose that the Mexican peso depreciates against the U.S. dollar, with the exchange rate going from 10 pesos per U.S. dollar to 15 pesos per U.S. dollar, a 50% change. But suppose that at the same time the price of everything in Mexico, measured in pesos, increases by 50%, so that the Mexican price index rises from 100 to 150. At the same time, suppose that there is no change in U.S. prices, so that the U.S. price index remains at 100. Then the initial real exchange rate is:

$\text{Pesos per dollar before depreciation} \times \dfrac{P_{US}}{P_{Mex}} = 10 \times \dfrac{100}{100} = 10$

Real exchange rates are exchange rates adjusted for international differences in aggregate price levels.

After the peso depreciates and the Mexican price level increases, the real exchange rate is:

$$\text{Pesos per dollar after depreciation} \times \frac{P_{US}}{P_{Mex}} = 15 \times \frac{100}{150} = 10$$

In this example, the peso has depreciated substantially in terms of the U.S. dollar, but the *real* exchange rate between the peso and the U.S. dollar hasn't changed at all. And because the real peso–U.S. dollar exchange rate hasn't changed, the nominal depreciation of the peso against the U.S. dollar will have no effect either on the quantity of goods and services exported by Mexico to the United States or on the quantity of goods and services imported by Mexico from the United States.

To see why, consider again the example of a hotel room. Suppose that this room initially costs 1,000 pesos per night, which is $100 at an exchange rate of 10 pesos per dollar. After both Mexican prices and the number of pesos per dollar rise by 50%, the hotel room costs 1,500 pesos per night—but 1,500 pesos divided by 15 pesos per dollar is $100, so the Mexican hotel room still costs $100. As a result, a U.S. tourist considering a trip to Mexico will have no reason to change plans.

The same is true for all goods and services that enter into trade: *the current account responds only to changes in the real exchange rate, not the nominal exchange rate.* A country's products become cheaper to foreigners only when that country's currency depreciates in real terms, and those products become more expensive to foreigners only when the currency appreciates in real terms. As a consequence, economists who analyze movements in exports and imports of goods and services focus on the real exchange rate, not the nominal exchange rate.

It's the real exchange rate, not the nominal exchange rate, that counts in decisions about buying and selling abroad.

Figure 20-16 illustrates just how important it can be to distinguish between nominal and real exchange rates. The line labeled "Nominal exchange rate" shows the number of pesos it took to buy a U.S. dollar from 1993 to 2017. As you can see, the peso depreciated massively over that period. But the line labeled "Real exchange rate" shows the real exchange rate: it was calculated using Equation 20-4, with price indexes for both Mexico and the United States set so that 1993 = 100. In real terms,

---

FIGURE 20-16   Real Versus Nominal Exchange Rates, 1993–2017

Between November 1993 and February 2017, the price of a dollar in Mexican pesos increased dramatically. But because Mexico had higher inflation than the United States, the real exchange rate, which measures the relative price of Mexican goods and services, ended up roughly where it started.

Data from: Federal Reserve Bank of St. Louis.

the peso depreciated between 1994 and 1995, but not by nearly as much as the nominal depreciation. By 2013, the real peso–U.S. dollar exchange rate was just about back where it started, although it rose again over the next two years.

Purchasing Power Parity

A useful tool for analyzing exchange rates, closely connected to the concept of the real exchange rate, is known as *purchasing power parity*. The **purchasing power parity** between two countries' currencies is the nominal exchange rate at which a given basket of goods and services would cost the same amount in each country. Suppose, for example, that a basket of goods and services that costs $100 in the United States costs 1,000 pesos in Mexico. Then the purchasing power parity is 10 pesos per U.S. dollar: at that exchange rate, 1,000 pesos = $100, so the market basket costs the same amount in both countries.

Let's consider an example. *The Economist* magazine publishes an annual comparison of the cost in different countries of one particular consumption item that is found around the world—a McDonald's Big Mac. The magazine finds the price of a Big Mac in local currency, then computes two numbers: the price of a Big Mac in U.S. dollars using the prevailing exchange rate and the exchange rate at which the price of a Big Mac would equal the U.S. price.

If purchasing power parity held for Big Macs, the dollar price of a Big Mac would be the same everywhere. If purchasing power parity is a good theory for the long run, the exchange rate at which a Big Mac's price matches the U.S. price should offer some guidance about where the exchange rate will eventually end up.

Table 20-8 shows *The Economist* estimates for selected countries as of January 2017, ranked in increasing order of the dollar price of a Big Mac. The countries with the cheapest Big Macs, and therefore by this measure with the most undervalued currencies, are Mexico, India, and China, all developing countries.

Calculations of purchasing power parities are usually made by estimating the cost of buying broad market baskets containing many goods and services—everything from cars and groceries to housing and internet service. But as Table 20-8 illustrates, nominal exchange rates almost always differ from purchasing power parities. Some of these differences are systematic: in general, aggregate price levels are lower in poor countries than in rich countries because services tend to be cheaper in poor countries. But even among countries at roughly the same level of economic development, nominal exchange rates vary quite a lot from purchasing power parity.

Figure 20-17 shows the nominal exchange rate between the Canadian dollar and the U.S. dollar, measured as the number of Canadian dollars per U.S. dollar, from 1990 to 2018, together with an estimate of the purchasing power parity exchange rate between the United States and Canada over the same period. The purchasing power parity didn't change much over the whole period because the United States and Canada had about the same rate of inflation. For most of the 1990s through 2005, the nominal exchange rate was above the purchasing power parity, so a market basket was much cheaper in Canada than in the United States. But from 2005 to 2018, the Canadian dollar appreciated, making a market basket more expensive in Canada.

Over the long run, however, purchasing power parities are pretty good at predicting actual changes in nominal exchange rates. In particular, nominal exchange rates between

The **purchasing power parity** between two countries' currencies is the nominal exchange rate at which a given basket of goods and services would cost the same amount in each country.

TABLE 20-8 Purchasing Power Parity and the Price of a Big Mac

Country	Big Mac price		Local currency per dollar	
	In local currency	In U.S. dollars	Implied PPP	Actual exchange rate
Mexico	Peso 49	$2.23	9.68	21.95
India	Rupee 170	2.49	33.60	68.33
China	Yuan 19.6	2.83	3.87	6.93
Japan	¥ 380	3.26	75.10	116.67
Britain	£ 3.09	3.73	0.61	0.83
Euro area	€ 3.88	4.06	0.77	0.96
United States	$5.06	5.06	1.00	1.00
Brazil	Real 16.5	5.12	3.26	3.22
Switzerland	SFr 6.50	6.35	1.28	1.02

Data from: The Economist.

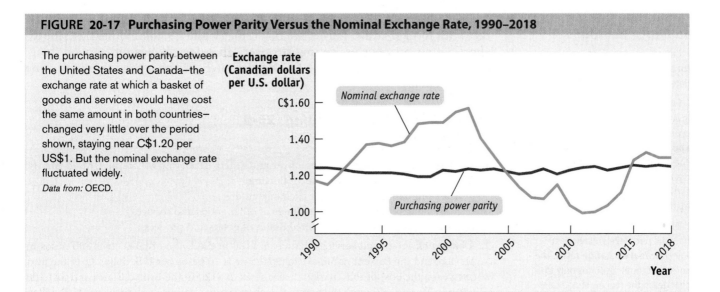

FIGURE 20-17 Purchasing Power Parity Versus the Nominal Exchange Rate, 1990–2018

The purchasing power parity between the United States and Canada–the exchange rate at which a basket of goods and services would have cost the same amount in both countries–changed very little over the period shown, staying near C$1.20 per US$1. But the nominal exchange rate fluctuated widely.

Data from: OECD.

countries at similar levels of economic development tend to fluctuate around levels that lead to similar costs for a given market basket.

ECONOMICS >> *in Action*
Strong Dollar Woes

Does the exchange rate really matter for business? To answer this question, let's consider what happened to U.S. corporations from 2014 to 2015.

Over the course of these two years, the dollar strengthened sharply against many currencies, especially the euro and the Japanese yen. The dollar's rise largely reflected the weakness of other economies: troubles in Europe and Japan kept interest rates and investment demand low, and capital flowed to the United States, which was experiencing steady job growth and overall was doing a much better job recovering from the Great Recession.

While the strong dollar reflected (relatively) good news for the U.S. economy as a whole, it was bad news for U.S. companies that sell a lot to overseas markets—companies like Proctor and Gamble, which sells toothpaste and other toiletries around the world, or Johnson and Johnson, whose Huggies diapers protect many foreign babies' bottoms. Such companies reported large hits to their profits, and began either losing ground to foreign competitors or shifting some of their own production abroad.

Figure 20-18 illustrates the overall picture. It compares the U.S. *effective exchange rate,* a measure of the average value of the dollar against other currencies, with *real net exports,* exports minus imports, measured in 2009 dollars. From early 2014 to early 2016 the dollar rose about 15% on average, then stayed at that higher level into 2017, while real net exports moved considerably deeper into deficit.

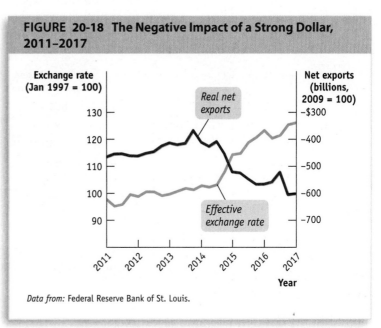

FIGURE 20-18 The Negative Impact of a Strong Dollar, 2011–2017

Data from: Federal Reserve Bank of St. Louis.

In other words, the exchange rate does matter a lot for businesses that compete with foreign rivals. Earlier we noted that while it's common to describe an appreciating currency as "getting stronger," that doesn't mean it's a good thing. And the stronger dollar of 2014 to 2015 definitely wasn't a good thing for some U.S. companies.

>> *Check Your Understanding* 20-5

Solutions appear at back of book.

1. Mexico discovers huge reserves of oil and starts exporting oil to the United States. Describe how this would affect the following.
   a. The nominal peso–U.S. dollar exchange rate
   b. Mexican exports to the United States of other goods and services
   c. Mexican imports from the United States of goods and services

2. A basket of goods and services that costs $100 in the United States costs 800 pesos in Mexico, and the current nominal exchange rate is 10 pesos per U.S. dollar. Over the next five years, the cost of that market basket rises to $120 in the United States and to 1,200 pesos in Mexico, although the nominal exchange rate remains at 10 pesos per U.S. dollar. Calculate the following.
   a. The real exchange rate now and five years from now, if today's price index in both countries is 100
   b. Purchasing power parity today and five years from now

SOLVED PROBLEM | Trade Is Sweet

The United States has a long-standing policy of trade protection in the sugar industry. As part of the sugar program, the United States Department of Agriculture limits imports to less than 15% of domestic consumption. The policy is controversial, with producers of sodas, candy bars, and other sweetened snacks pitted against sugar growers as well as some public health advocates.

Using the following hypothetical U.S. domestic demand and supply schedule for sugar, determine how many tons of sugar the United States produces in autarky and the equilibrium price per ton.

Price of sugar ($ per metric ton)	Quantity of sugar demanded (millions of tons)	Quantity of sugar supplied (millions of tons)
$650	4	12
600	6	10
550	8	8
500	10	6
450	12	4
400	14	2
350	16	0

If the world price of sugar is $500 per ton, will the United States import or export sugar? How much will they import if there were no import restrictions?

STEP | 1 In autarky, how many tons of sugar does the United States produce, and at what price are they bought and sold? *Review page 577.*

In autarky, the United States produces 8 million tons of sugar, and sugar is sold at $550 per metric ton. This is the quantity and price at which "Quantity of sugar demanded" equals "Quantity of sugar supplied" in the table. At this price and production level, the market is in equilibrium.

STEP | 2 If the world price of sugar is $500 per ton, will the United States import or export sugar? *Review pages 577–579.*

As shown in Figure 20-6, if the world price is less than the autarky price, then a country will import. In this case, the world price is $500 per metric ton, and as determined in Step 1, the autarky price is $550 per metric ton, so the United States will import sugar.

STEP | 3 Determine how much will be imported or exported. *Review pages 577–579.*

Domestic demand at a world price of $500 per ton is 10 million tons, and domestic supply at a world price of $500 per ton is 6 million tons. Since there is a shortage of 4 million tons, the United States will import 4 million tons of sugar if there are no import restrictions.

But in reality, because of the sugar program the United States could not import the required amount of sugar, resulting in higher prices.

SUMMARY

1. International trade is of growing importance to the United States and of even greater importance to most other countries. International trade, like trade among individuals, arises from comparative advantage: the opportunity cost of producing an additional unit of a good is lower in some countries than in others. Goods and services purchased from abroad are **imports;** those sold abroad are **exports.** Foreign trade, like other economic linkages between countries, has been growing rapidly, a phenomenon called **globalization. Hyperglobalization,** the phenomenon of extremely high levels of international trade, has occurred as advances in communication and transportation technology have allowed supply chains of production to span the globe.

2. The **Ricardian model of international trade** assumes that opportunity costs are constant. It shows that there are gains from trade: two countries are better off with trade than in **autarky.**

3. In practice, comparative advantage reflects differences between countries in climate, factor endowments, and technology. The **Heckscher–Ohlin model** shows how differences in factor endowments determine comparative advantage: goods differ in **factor intensity,** and countries tend to export goods that are intensive in the factors they have in abundance.

4. The **domestic demand curve** and the **domestic supply curve** determine the price of a good in autarky. When international trade occurs, the domestic price is driven to equality with the **world price,** the price at which the good is bought and sold abroad.

5. If the world price is below the autarky price, a good is imported. This leads to an increase in consumer surplus, a fall in producer surplus, and a gain in total surplus. If the world price is above the autarky price, a good is exported. This leads to an increase in producer surplus, a fall in consumer surplus, and a gain in total surplus.

6. International trade leads to expansion in **exporting industries** and contraction in **import-competing industries.** This raises the domestic demand for abundant factors of production, reduces the demand for scarce factors, and so affects factor prices, such as wages.

7. Most economists advocate **free trade,** but in practice many governments engage in **trade protection.** The two most common forms of **protection** are tariffs and quotas. On rare occasions, export industries are subsidized.

8. A **tariff** is a tax levied on imports. It raises the domestic price above the world price, hurting consumers, benefiting domestic producers, and generating government revenue. As a result, total surplus falls. An **import quota** is a legal limit on the quantity of a good that can be imported. It has the same effects as a tariff, except that the revenue goes not to the government but to those who receive import licenses.

9. A country's **balance of payments accounts** summarize its transactions with the rest of the world. The **balance of payments on current account,** or **current account,** includes the **balance of payments on goods and services** together with balances on factor income and transfers. The **merchandise trade balance,** or **trade balance,** is a frequently cited component of the balance of payments on goods and services. The **balance of payments on financial account,** or **financial account,** measures capital flows. By definition, the balance of payments on current account plus the balance of payments on financial account is zero.

10. Capital flows respond to international differences in interest rates and other rates of return; they can be usefully analyzed using an international version of the loanable funds model, which shows how a country in which the interest rate would be low in the absence of capital flows sends funds to a country in which the interest rate would be high in the absence of capital flows. The underlying determinants of capital flows are international differences in savings and opportunities for investment spending.

11. Currencies are traded in the **foreign exchange market;** the prices at which they are traded are **exchange rates.** When a currency rises against another currency, it **appreciates;** when it falls, it **depreciates.** The **equilibrium exchange rate** matches the quantity of that currency supplied to the foreign exchange market to the quantity demanded.

12. To correct for international differences in inflation rates, economists calculate **real exchange rates,** which multiply the exchange rate between two countries' currencies by the ratio of the countries' price levels. The current account responds only to changes in the real exchange rate, not the nominal exchange rate. **Purchasing power parity** is the exchange rate that makes the cost of a basket of goods and services equal in two countries. While purchasing power parity and the nominal exchange rate almost always differ, purchasing power parity is a good predictor of actual changes in the nominal exchange rate.

KEY TERMS

Imports, p. 568
Exports, p. 568
Globalization, p. 568
Hyperglobalization, p. 569
Ricardian model of international trade, p. 570
Autarky, p. 571
Factor intensity, p. 575
Heckscher–Ohlin model, p. 575
Domestic demand curve, p. 577
Domestic supply curve, p. 577
World price, p. 578

Exporting industries, p. 582
Import-competing industries, p. 582
Free trade, p. 584
Trade protection, p. 584
Protection, p. 584
Tariff, p. 584
Import quota, p. 586
Balance of payments accounts, p. 587
Balance of payments on current account (current account), p. 589
Balance of payments on goods and services, p. 589

Merchandise trade balance (trade balance), p. 589
Balance of payments on financial account (financial account), p. 590
Foreign exchange market, p. 594
Exchange rates, p. 594
Appreciates, p. 595
Depreciates, p. 595
Equilibrium exchange rate, p. 596
Real exchange rate, p. 598
Purchasing power parity, p. 600

DISCUSSION QUESTIONS

1. Both Canada and the United States produce lumber and footballs with constant opportunity costs. The United States can produce either 10 tons of lumber and no footballs, or 1,000 footballs and no lumber, or any combination in between. Canada can produce either 8 tons of lumber and no footballs, or 400 footballs and no lumber, or any combination in between.

   a. Draw the U.S. and Canadian production possibility frontiers in two separate diagrams, with footballs on the horizontal axis and lumber on the vertical axis.

   b. In autarky, if the United States wants to consume 500 footballs, how much lumber can it consume at most? Label this point *A* in your diagram. Similarly, if Canada wants to consume 1 ton of lumber, how many footballs can it consume in autarky? Label this point *C* in your diagram.

   c. Which country has the absolute advantage in lumber production?

   d. Which country has the comparative advantage in lumber production?

   Suppose each country specializes in the good in which it has the comparative advantage, and there is trade.

   e. How many footballs does the United States produce? How much lumber does Canada produce?

   f. Is it possible for the United States to consume 500 footballs and 7 tons of lumber? Label this point *B* in your diagram. Is it possible for Canada at the same time to consume 500 footballs and 1 ton of lumber? Label this point *D* in your diagram.

2. According to data from the U.S. Census Bureau, since 2000, the value of U.S. imports of men's and boy's

apparel from China has more than tripled from a rel- atively small $244 million in 2000 to $926 million in 2014. What prediction does the Heckscher–Ohlin model make about the wages received by labor in China?

3. The accompanying table indicates the U.S. domestic demand schedule and domestic supply schedule for commercial jet airplanes. Suppose that the world price of a commercial jet airplane is $100 million.

Price of jet (millions)	Quantity of jets demanded	Quantity of jets supplied
$120	100	1,000
110	150	900
100	200	800
90	250	700
80	300	600
70	350	500
60	400	400
50	450	300
40	500	200

a. In autarky, how many commercial jet airplanes does the United States produce, and at what price are they bought and sold?

b. With trade, what will the price for commercial jet airplanes be? Will the United States import or export airplanes? How many?

4. In the economy of Scottopia in 2016, exports equaled $400 billion of goods and $300 billion of services and imports equaled $500 billion of goods and $350 billion of services; the rest of the world purchased $250 bil- lion of Scottopia's assets. What was the merchandise trade balance for Scottopia? What was the balance of payments on current account? What was the balance of payments on financial account? What was the value of Scottopia's purchases of assets from the rest of the world?

5. Based on the exchange rates for the trading days of 2016 and 2017 shown in the accompanying table, did the U.S. dollar appreciate or depreciate over the year? Did the movement in the value of the U.S. dollar make American goods and services more or less attractive to foreigners?

April 1, 2016	April 1, 2017
US$1.42 to buy 1 British pound sterling	US$1.25 to buy 1 British pound sterling
32.26 Taiwan dollars to buy US$1	30.40 Taiwan dollars to buy US$1
US$0.77 to buy 1 Canadian dollar	US$0.75 to buy 1 Canadian dollar
112.09 Japanese yen to buy US$1	111.39 Japanese yen to buy US$1
US$1.14 to buy 1 euro	US$1.07 to buy 1 euro
0.96 Swiss franc to buy US$1	1.00 Swiss franc to buy US$1

6. In each of the following scenarios, suppose that the two nations are the only trading nations in the world. Given inflation and the change in the nominal exchange rate, which nation's goods become more attractive?

a. Inflation is 10% in the United States and 5% in Japan; the U.S. dollar–Japanese yen exchange rate remains the same.

b. Inflation is 3% in the United States and 8% in Mex- ico; the price of the U.S. dollar falls from 12.50 to 10.25 Mexican pesos.

c. Inflation is 5% in the United States and 3% in the euro area; the price of the euro falls from $1.30 to $1.20.

d. Inflation is 8% in the United States and 4% in Can- ada; the price of the Canadian dollar rises from US$0.60 to US$0.75.

PROBLEMS

interactive activity

1. For each of the following trade relationships, explain the likely source of the comparative advantage of each of the exporting countries.

a. The United States exports software to Venezuela, and Venezuela exports oil to the United States.

b. The United States exports airplanes to China, and China exports clothing to the United States.

c. The United States exports wheat to Colombia, and Colombia exports coffee to the United States.

2. Shoes are labor-intensive and satellites are capital- intensive to produce. The United States has abundant capital. China has abundant labor. According to the Heckscher–Ohlin model, which good will China export? Which good will the United States export? In the United States, what will happen to the price of labor (the wage) and to the price of capital?

3. Before the North American Free Trade Agreement (NAFTA) gradually eliminated import tariffs on goods, the autarky price of tomatoes in Mexico was below the world price and in the United States was above the world price. Similarly, the autarky price of poultry in Mexico was above the world price and in the United States was below the world price. Draw diagrams with domestic supply and demand curves for each country and each of the two goods. (You will need to draw four diagrams.) As a result of NAFTA, the United States now imports tomatoes from Mexico and the United States now exports poultry to Mexico. How would you expect the following groups to be affected?

a. Mexican and U.S. consumers of tomatoes. Illustrate the effect on consumer surplus in your diagram.

b. Mexican and U.S. producers of tomatoes. Illustrate the effect on producer surplus in your diagram.

c. Mexican and U.S. tomato workers.

d. Mexican and U.S. consumers of poultry. Illustrate the effect on consumer surplus in your diagram.

e. Mexican and U.S. producers of poultry. Illustrate the effect on producer surplus in your diagram.

f. Mexican and U.S. poultry workers.

4. The accompanying table shows the U.S. domestic demand schedule and domestic supply schedule for oranges. Suppose that the world price of oranges is $0.30 per orange.

Price of orange	Quantity of oranges demanded (thousands)	Quantity of oranges supplied (thousands)
$1.00	2	11
0.90	4	10
0.80	6	9
0.70	8	8
0.60	10	7
0.50	12	6
0.40	14	5
0.30	16	4
0.20	18	3

a. Draw the U.S. domestic supply curve and domestic demand curve.

b. With free trade, how many oranges will the United States import or export?

Suppose that the U.S. government imposes a tariff on oranges of $0.20 per orange.

c. How many oranges will the United States import or export after introduction of the tariff?

d. In your diagram, shade the gain or loss to the economy as a whole from the introduction of this tariff.

5. How would the following transactions be categorized in the U.S. balance of payments accounts? Would they be entered in the current account (as a payment to or from a foreigner) or the financial account (as a sale of assets to or purchase of assets from a foreigner)? How will the balance of payments on the current and financial accounts change?

a. A French importer buys a case of California wine for $500.

b. An American who works for a French company deposits her paycheck, drawn on a Paris bank, into her San Francisco bank.

c. An American buys a bond from a Japanese company for $10,000.

d. An American charity sends $100,000 to Africa to help local residents buy food after a harvest shortfall.

6. The accompanying diagram shows foreign-owned assets in the United States and U.S.-owned assets abroad, both as a percentage of foreign GDP. As you can see from the diagram, both increased around five-fold from 1980 to 2016.

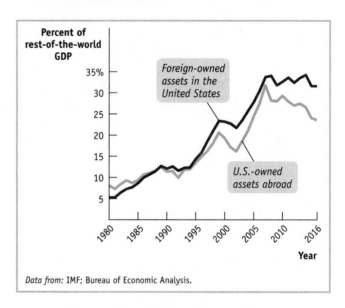

Data from: IMF; Bureau of Economic Analysis.

a. As U.S.-owned assets abroad increased as a percentage of foreign GDP, does this mean that the United States, over the period, experienced net capital outflows?

b. Does this diagram indicate that world economies were more tightly linked in 2016 than they were in 1980?

7. In the economy of Popania in 2016, total Popanian purchases of assets in the rest of the world equaled $300 billion and purchases of Popanian assets by the rest of the world equaled $400 billion; Popania exported goods and services equal to $350 billion. What was Popania's balance of payments on financial account in 2016? What was its balance of payments on current account? What was the value of its imports?

8. Go to http://fx.sauder.ubc.ca. Using the table labeled "The Most Recent Cross-Rates of Major Currencies," determine whether the British pound (GBP), the Canadian dollar (CAD), the Japanese yen (JPY), the euro (EUR), and the Swiss franc (CHF) have appreciated or depreciated against the U.S. dollar (USD) since April 1, 2017. The exchange rates on April 1, 2017 are listed in the table in Discussion Question 5.

WORK IT OUT Interactive step-by-step help with solving these problems can be found online.

---

9. Assume Saudi Arabia and the United States face the production possibilities for oil and cars shown in the accompanying table.

Saudi Arabia		United States	
Quantity of oil (millions of barrels)	**Quantity of cars (millions)**	**Quantity of oil (millions of barrels)**	**Quantity of cars (millions)**
0	4	0	10.0
200	3	100	7.5
400	2	200	5.0
600	1	300	2.5
800	0	400	0

a. What is the opportunity cost of producing a car in Saudi Arabia? In the United States? What is the opportunity cost of producing a barrel of oil in Saudi Arabia? In the United States?

b. Which country has the comparative advantage in producing oil? In producing cars?

c. Suppose that in autarky, Saudi Arabia produces 200 million barrels of oil and 3 million cars; and suppose that the United States produces 300 million barrels of oil and 2.5 million cars. Without trade, can Saudi Arabia produce more oil *and* more cars? Without trade, can the United States produce more oil *and* more cars?

Suppose now that each country specializes in the good in which it has the comparative advantage, and the two countries trade. Also assume that for each country the value of imports must equal the value of exports.

d. What is the total quantity of oil produced? What is the total quantity of cars produced?

e. Is it possible for Saudi Arabia to consume 400 million barrels of oil and 5 million cars and for the United States to consume 400 million barrels of oil and 5 million cars?

f. Suppose that, in fact, Saudi Arabia consumes 300 million barrels of oil and 4 million cars and the United States consumes 500 million barrels of oil and 6 million cars. How many barrels of oil does the United States import? How many cars does the United States export? Suppose a car costs $10,000 on the world market. How much, then, does a barrel of oil cost on the world market?

10. Suppose the United States and Japan are the only two trading countries in the world. What will happen to the value of the U.S. dollar if the following occur, other things equal?

a. Japan relaxes some of its import restrictions.

b. The United States imposes some import tariffs on Japanese goods.

c. Interest rates in the United States rise dramatically.

d. A report indicates that Japanese cars last much longer than previously thought, especially compared with American cars.

It's a very good bet that as you read this, you're wearing something manufactured in Asia. And if you are, it's also a good bet that the Hong Kong company Li & Fung was involved in getting your garment designed, produced, and shipped to your local store. From Levi's to Walmart, Li & Fung is a critical conduit from factories around the world to the shopping mall nearest you.

The company was founded in 1906 in Guangzhou, China. According to Victor Fung, the company's chairman, his grandfather's "value added" was that he spoke English, allowing him to serve as an interpreter in business deals between Chinese and foreigners. When Mao's Communist Party seized control in mainland China, the company moved to Hong Kong. There, as Hong Kong's market economy took off during the 1960s and 1970s, Li & Fung grew as an export broker, bringing together Hong Kong manufacturers and foreign buyers.

The real transformation of the company came, however, as Asian economies grew and changed. Hong Kong's rapid growth led to rising wages, making Li & Fung increasingly uncompetitive in garments, its main business. So the company reinvented itself: rather than being a simple broker, it became a "supply chain manager." Not only would it allocate production of a good to a manufacturer, it would also break production down, allocate production of the inputs, and then allocate final assembly of the good among its 12,000+ suppliers around the globe. Sometimes production would be done in sophisticated economies like those of Hong Kong or even Japan, where wages are high but so is quality and productivity; sometimes it would be done in less advanced locations like mainland China or Thailand, where labor is less productive but cheaper.

For example, suppose you own a U.S. retail chain and want to sell garment-washed blue jeans. Rather than simply arrange for production of the jeans, Li & Fung will work with you on their design, providing you with the latest production and style information, like what materials and colors are trendy. After the design has been finalized, Li & Fung will arrange for the creation of a prototype, find the most cost-effective way to manufacture it, and then place an order on your behalf. Through Li & Fung, the yarn might be made in South Korea and dyed in Taiwan, and the jeans sewn in Thailand or mainland China. And because production is taking place in so many locations, Li & Fung provides transport logistics as well as quality control.

Li & Fung has been enormously successful. In 2018, the company had a market value of $10.8 billion, with offices and distribution centers in more than 50 countries.

QUESTIONS FOR THOUGHT

1. Why do you think it was profitable for Li & Fung to go beyond brokering exports to becoming a supply chain manager, breaking down the production process and sourcing the inputs from various suppliers across many countries?

2. What principle do you think underlies Li & Fung's decisions on how to allocate production of a good's inputs and its final assembly among various countries?

3. Why do you think a retailer prefers to have Li & Fung arrange international production of its jeans rather than purchase them directly from a jeans manufacturer in mainland China?

4. What is the source of Li & Fung's success? Is it based on human capital, on ownership of a natural resource, or on ownership of capital?

Solutions to *Check Your Understanding* Questions

This section offers suggested answers to the *Check Your Understanding* questions found within chapters.

CHAPTER ONE

1-1 Check Your Understanding

1. **a.** This statement is a feature of a market economy. The invisible hand refers to the way in which the individual pursuit of self-interest can lead to good results for society as a whole.

   b. This statement is not a feature of a market economy. In a market economy, production and consumption decisions are the result of decentralized decisions by many firms and individuals. In a command economy, a central authority makes decisions about production and consumption.

   c. This statement is a feature of a market economy. Sometimes the pursuit of one's own interests does not promote the interests of society as a whole. This can lead to market failure.

   d. This statement is not a feature of a market economy. Although the economy grows over time, fluctuations are regular features of market economies.

1-2 Check Your Understanding

1. **a.** This illustrates the concept of opportunity cost. Given that a person can only eat so much at one sitting, having a slice of chocolate cake requires that you forgo eating something else, such as a slice of coconut cream pie.

   b. This illustrates the concept that resources are scarce. Even if there were more resources in the world, the total amount of those resources would be limited. As a result, scarcity would still arise. For there to be no scarcity, there would have to be unlimited amounts of everything (including unlimited time in a human life), which is clearly impossible.

   c. This illustrates the concept that people usually exploit opportunities to make themselves better off. Students will seek to make themselves better off by signing up for the tutorials of teaching assistants with good reputations and avoiding those teaching assistants with poor reputations. It also illustrates the concept that resources are scarce. If there were unlimited spaces in tutorials with good teaching assistants, they would not fill up.

   d. This illustrates the concept of marginal analysis. Your decision about allocating your time is a "how much" decision: how much time spent exercising versus how much time spent studying. You make your decision by comparing the benefit of an additional hour of exercising to its cost, the effect on your grades of one fewer hour spent studying.

2. **a.** Yes. The increased time spent commuting is a cost you will incur if you accept the new job. That additional time spent commuting—or equivalently, the benefit you would get from spending that time doing something else—is an opportunity cost of the new job.

   b. Yes. One of the benefits of the new job is that you will be making $50,000. But if you take the new job, you will have to give up your current job; that is, you have to give up your current salary of $45,000. So $45,000 is one of the opportunity costs of taking the new job.

   c. No. A more spacious office is an additional benefit of your new job and does not involve forgoing something else. So it is not an opportunity cost.

1-3 Check Your Understanding

1. **a.** This illustrates the concept that markets usually lead to efficiency. Any seller who wants to sell a book for at least $30 does indeed sell to someone who is willing to buy a book for $30. As a result, there is no way to change how used textbooks are distributed among buyers and sellers in a way that would make one person better off without making someone else worse off.

   b. This illustrates the concept that there are gains from trade. Students trade tutoring services based on their different abilities in academic subjects.

   c. This illustrates the concept that when markets don't achieve efficiency, government intervention can improve society's welfare. In this case the market, left alone, will permit bars and nightclubs to impose costs on their neighbors in the form of loud music, costs that the bars and nightclubs have no incentive to take into account. This is an inefficient outcome because society as a whole can be made better off if bars and nightclubs are induced to reduce their noise.

   d. This illustrates the concept that resources should be used as efficiently as possible to achieve society's goals. By closing neighborhood clinics and shifting funds to the main hospital, better health care can be provided at a lower cost.

   e. This illustrates the concept that markets move toward equilibrium. Here, because books with the same amount of wear and tear sell for about the same price, no buyer or seller can be made better off by engaging in a different trade than he or she undertook. This means that the market for used textbooks has moved to an equilibrium.

2. **a.** This does not describe an equilibrium situation. Many students should want to change their behavior and switch to eating at the restaurants. Therefore, the situation described is not an equilibrium. An equilibrium will be established when students are equally as well off eating at the restaurants as eating at the dining hall—which would happen if, say, prices at the dining hall were higher than at the restaurants.

   b. This does describe an equilibrium situation. By changing your behavior and riding the bus, you would not be made better off. Therefore, you have no incentive to change your behavior.

1-4 Check Your Understanding

1. **a.** This illustrates the principle that government policies can change spending. The tax cut would increase people's after-tax incomes, leading to higher consumer spending.

   b. This illustrates the principle that one person's spending is another person's income. As oil companies decrease their spending on labor by laying off workers and pay remaining workers lower wages, those workers' incomes fall. In turn, those workers decrease their consumer spending, causing restaurants and other consumer businesses to lose income.

   c. This illustrates the principle that overall spending sometimes gets out of line with the economy's productive capacity. In this case, spending on housing was too high relative to the economy's capacity to create new housing. This first led to a rise in house prices, and then—as a result—to a rise in overall prices, or *inflation*.

‖ CHAPTER TWO

2-1 Check Your Understanding

1. **a.** False. An increase in the resources available to Boeing for use in producing Dreamliners and small jets changes the production possibility frontier by shifting it outward. This is because Boeing can now produce more small jets and Dreamliners than before. In the accompanying figure, the line labeled "Boeing's original *PPF*" represents Boeing's original production possibility frontier, and the line labeled "Boeing's new *PPF*" represents the new production possibility frontier that results from an increase in resources available to Boeing.

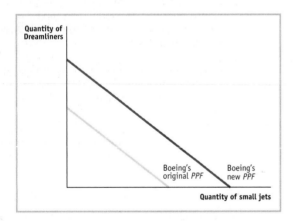

   b. True. A technological change that allows Boeing to build more small jets for any amount of Dreamliners built results in a change in its production possibility frontier. This is illustrated in the accompanying figure: the new production possibility frontier is represented by the line labeled "Boeing's new *PPF*," and the original production frontier is represented by the line labeled "Boeing's original *PPF*." Since the maximum quantity of Dreamliners that Boeing can build is the same as before, the new production possibility frontier intersects the vertical axis at the same point as the original frontier. But since the maximum possible quantity of small jets is now greater than before, the new frontier intersects the horizontal axis to the right of the original frontier.

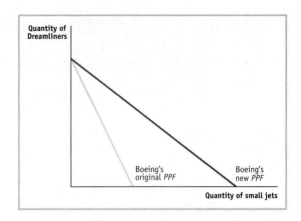

   c. False. The production possibility frontier illustrates how much of one good an economy must give up to get more of another good only when resources are used efficiently in production. If an economy is producing inefficiently—that is, inside the frontier—then it does not have to give up a unit of one good to get another unit of the other good. Instead, by becoming more efficient in production, this economy can have more of both goods.

2. **a.** The United States has an absolute advantage in automobile production because it takes fewer Americans (6) to produce a car in one day than it takes Italians (8). The United States also has an absolute advantage in washing machine production because it takes fewer Americans (2) to produce a washing machine in one day than it takes Italians (3).

   b. In Italy the opportunity cost of a washing machine in terms of an automobile is $3/8$: $3/8$ of a car can be produced with the same number of workers and in the same time it takes to produce 1 washing machine. In the United States the opportunity cost of a washing machine in terms of an automobile is $2/6 = 1/3$: $1/3$ of a car can be produced with the same number of workers and in the same time it takes to produce 1 washing machine. Since $1/3 < 3/8$, the United States has a comparative advantage in the production of washing machines: to produce a washing machine, only $1/3$ of a car must be given up in the United States but $3/8$ of a car must be given up in Italy. This means that Italy has a comparative advantage in automobiles. This can be checked as follows. The opportunity cost of an automobile in terms of a washing machine in Italy is $8/3$, equal to $2\frac{2}{3}$: $2\frac{2}{3}$ washing machines can be produced with the same number of workers and in the time it takes to produce 1 car in Italy. And the opportunity cost of an automobile in terms of a washing machine in the United States is $6/2$, equal to 3 : 3 washing machines can be produced with the same number of workers and in the time it takes to produce 1 car in the United States. Since $2\frac{2}{3} < 3$, Italy has a comparative advantage in producing automobiles.

   c. The greatest gains are realized when each country specializes in producing the good for which it has a comparative advantage. Therefore, the United States should specialize in washing machines and Italy should specialize in automobiles.

3. At a trade of 10 U.S. large jets for 15 Brazilian small jets, Brazil gives up less for a large jet than it would if it were building large jets itself. Without trade, Brazil gives up 3 small jets for each large jet it produces. With trade, Brazil gives up only 1.5 small jets for each large jet from

the United States. Likewise, the United States gives up less for a small jet than it would if it were producing small jets itself. Without trade, the United States gives up ¾ of a large jet for each small jet. With trade, the United States gives up only ⅔ of a large jet for each small jet from Brazil.

4. An increase in the amount of money spent by households results in an increase in the flow of goods to households. This, in turn, generates an increase in demand for factors of production by firms. So, there is an increase in the number of jobs in the economy.

2-2 Check Your Understanding

1. **a.** This is a normative statement because it stipulates what should be done. In addition, it may have no "right" answer. That is, should people be prevented from all dangerous personal behavior if they enjoy that behavior—like skydiving? Your answer will depend on your point of view.

   b. This is a positive statement because it is a description of fact.

2. **a.** True. Economists often have different value judgments about the desirability of a particular social goal. But despite those differences in value judgments, they will tend to agree that society, once it has decided to pursue a given social goal, should adopt the most efficient policy to achieve that goal. Therefore economists are likely to agree on adopting policy choice B.

   b. False. Disagreements between economists are more likely to arise because they base their conclusions on different models or because they have different value judgments about the desirability of the policy.

‖ CHAPTER THREE

3-1 Check Your Understanding

1. **a.** The quantity of umbrellas demanded is higher at any given price on a rainy day than on a dry day. This is a rightward *shift of* the demand curve, since at any given price the quantity demanded rises. This implies that any specific quantity can now be sold at a higher price.

   b. The quantity of summer Caribbean cruises demanded rises in response to a price reduction. This is a *movement along* the demand curve for summer Caribbean cruises.

   c. The demand for roses increases the week of Valentine's Day. This is a rightward *shift of* the demand curve.

   d. The quantity of gasoline demanded falls in response to a rise in price. This is a *movement along* the demand curve.

3-2 Check Your Understanding

1. **a.** The quantity of houses supplied rises as a result of an increase in prices. This is a *movement along* the supply curve.

   b. The quantity of strawberries supplied is higher at any given price. This is a rightward *shift of* the supply curve.

   c. The quantity of labor supplied is lower at any given wage. This is a leftward *shift of* the supply curve compared to the supply curve during school vacation. So, in order to attract workers, fast-food chains have to offer higher wages.

   d. The quantity of labor supplied rises in response to a rise in wages. This is a *movement along* the supply curve.

   e. The quantity of cabins supplied is higher at any given price. This is a rightward *shift of* the supply curve.

3-3 Check Your Understanding

1. **a.** The supply curve shifts rightward. At the original equilibrium price of the year before, the quantity of grapes supplied exceeds the quantity demanded. This is a case of surplus. The price of grapes will fall.

   b. The demand curve shifts leftward. At the original equilibrium price, the quantity of hotel rooms supplied exceeds the quantity demanded. This is a case of surplus. The rates for hotel rooms will fall.

   c. The demand curve for second-hand snowblowers shifts rightward. At the original equilibrium price, the quantity of second-hand snowblowers demanded exceeds the quantity supplied. This is a case of shortage. The equilibrium price of second-hand snowblowers will rise.

3-4 Check Your Understanding

1. **a.** The market for large cars: this is a rightward shift in demand caused by a decrease in the price of a complement, gasoline. As a result of the shift, the equilibrium price of large cars will rise and the equilibrium quantity of large cars bought and sold will also rise.

   b. The market for fresh paper made from recycled stock: this is a rightward shift in supply due to a technological innovation. As a result of this shift, the equilibrium price of fresh paper made from recycled stock will fall and the equilibrium quantity bought and sold will rise.

   c. The market for movies at a local movie theater: this is a leftward shift in demand caused by a fall in the price of a substitute, on-demand films. As a result of this shift, the equilibrium price of movie tickets will fall and the equilibrium number of people who go to the movies will also fall.

2. Upon the announcement of the new chip, the demand curve for computers using the earlier chip shifts leftward, as demand decreases, and the supply curve for these computers shifts rightward, as supply increases.

   a. If demand decreases relatively more than supply increases, then the equilibrium quantity falls, as shown here:

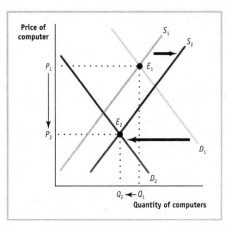

If supply increases relatively more than demand decreases, then the equilibrium quantity rises, as shown here:

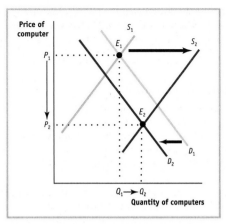

b. In both cases, the equilibrium price falls.

‖ CHAPTER FOUR

4-1 Check Your Understanding

1. a. A consumer buys each pepper if the price is less than (or just equal to) the consumer's willingness to pay for that pepper. The demand schedule is constructed by asking how many peppers will be demanded at any given price. A producer will continue to supply peppers as long as the price is greater than, or just equal to, the producer's cost. The supply schedule is constructed by asking how many peppers will be supplied at any price. The following table illustrates the demand and supply schedules.

$0.20 on his first and $0.00 on his second pepper. Total producer surplus is $1.10. Total surplus in this market is therefore $1.00 + $1.10 = $2.10.

2. a. If Josey consumes one fewer pepper, she loses $0.60 (her willingness to pay for her second pepper); if Casey consumes one more pepper, he gains $0.30 (his willingness to pay for his fourth pepper). This results in an overall loss of consumer surplus of $0.60 − $0.30 = $0.30.

   b. Cara's cost of the last pepper she supplied (the third pepper) is $0.40, and Jamie's cost of producing one more (his third pepper) is $0.70. Total producer surplus therefore falls by $0.70 − $0.40 = $0.30.

   c. Josey's willingness to pay for her second pepper is $0.60; this is what she would lose if she were to consume one fewer pepper. Cara's cost of producing her third pepper is $0.40; this is what she would save if she were to produce one fewer pepper. If we therefore reduced quantity by one pepper, we would lose $0.60 − $0.40 = $0.20 of total surplus.

4-2 Check Your Understanding

1. a. Fewer homeowners are willing to rent out their driveways because the price ceiling has reduced the payment they receive. This is an example of a fall in price from a price ceiling, leading to a fall in the quantity supplied. It is shown in the accompanying diagram by the movement from point E to point A along the supply curve, a reduction in quantity of 400 parking spaces.

Price of pepper	Quantity of peppers demanded	Quantity of peppers demanded by Casey	Quantity of peppers demanded by Josey	Quantity of peppers supplied	Quantity of peppers supplied by Cara	Quantity of peppers supplied by Jamie
$0.90	1	1	0	8	4	4
0.80	2	1	1	7	4	3
0.70	3	2	1	7	4	3
0.60	4	2	2	6	4	2
0.50	5	3	2	5	3	2
0.40	6	3	3	4	3	1
0.30	8	4	4	3	2	1
0.20	8	4	4	2	2	0
0.10	8	4	4	2	2	0
0.00	8	4	4	0	0	0

b. The quantity demanded equals the quantity supplied at a price of $0.50, the equilibrium price. At that price, a total quantity of five peppers will be bought and sold.

c. Casey will buy three peppers and receive a consumer surplus of $0.40 on his first, $0.20 on his second, and $0.00 on his third pepper. Josey will buy two peppers and receive a consumer surplus of $0.30 on her first and $0.10 on her second pepper. Total consumer surplus is therefore $1.00. Cara will supply three peppers and receive a producer surplus of $0.40 on her first, $0.40 on her second, and $0.10 on her third pepper. Jamie will supply two peppers and receive a producer surplus of

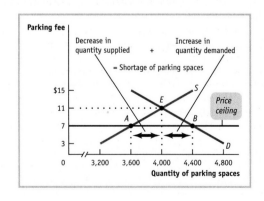

b. The quantity demanded increases by 400 spaces as the price decreases. At a lower price, more fans are willing to drive and rent a parking space. It is shown in the diagram by the movement from point E to point B along the demand curve.

c. Under a price ceiling, the quantity demanded exceeds the quantity supplied; as a result, shortages arise. In this case, there will be a shortage of 800 parking spaces. It is shown by the horizontal distance between points A and B.

d. Price ceilings result in wasted resources. The additional time fans spend to guarantee a parking space is wasted time.

e. Price ceilings lead to inefficient allocation of a good—here, the parking spaces—to consumers.

f. Price ceilings lead to black markets.

2. a. False. By lowering the price that producers receive, a price ceiling leads to a decrease in the quantity supplied.

b. True. A price ceiling leads to a lower quantity supplied than in an efficient, unregulated market. As a result, some people who would have been willing to pay the market price, and so would have gotten the good in an unregulated market, are unable to obtain it when a price ceiling is imposed.

c. True. Those producers who still sell the product now receive less for it and are therefore worse off. Other producers will no longer find it worthwhile to sell the product at all and so will also be made worse off.

3. a. Since the apartment is rented quickly at the same price, there is no change (either gain or loss) in producer surplus. So any change in total surplus comes from changes in consumer surplus. When you are evicted, the amount of consumer surplus you lose is equal to the difference between your willingness to pay for the apartment and the rent-controlled price. When the apartment is rented to someone else at the same price, the amount of consumer surplus the new renter gains is equal to the difference between his or her willingness to pay and the rent-controlled price. So this will be a pure transfer of surplus from one person to another only if both your willingness to pay and the new renter's willingness to pay are the same. Since under rent control apartments are not always allocated to those who have the highest willingness to pay, the new renter's willingness to pay may be either equal to, lower than, or higher than your willingness to pay. If the new renter's willingness to pay is lower than yours, this will create additional deadweight loss: there is some additional consumer surplus that is lost. However, if the new renter's willingness to pay is higher than yours, this will create an increase in total surplus, as the new renter gains more consumer surplus than you lost.

b. This creates deadweight loss: if you were able to give the ticket away, someone else would be able to obtain consumer surplus, equal to his or her willingness to pay for the ticket. You neither gain nor lose any surplus, since you cannot go to the concert whether or not you give the ticket away. If you were able to sell the ticket, the buyer would obtain consumer surplus equal to the difference between his or her willingness to pay for the ticket and the price at which you sell the ticket. In addition, you would obtain producer surplus equal to the difference between the price at which you sell the ticket and your cost of selling the ticket (which, since you won the ticket, is presumably zero). Since the restriction to neither sell nor give away the ticket means that this surplus cannot be obtained by

anybody, it creates deadweight loss. If you could give the ticket away, as described above, there would be consumer surplus that accrues to the recipient of the ticket; and if you give the ticket to the person with the highest willingness to pay, there would be no deadweight loss.

c. This creates deadweight loss. If students buy ice cream on campus, they obtain consumer surplus: their willingness to pay must be higher than the price of the ice cream. Your college obtains producer surplus: the price is higher than your college's cost of selling the ice cream. Prohibiting the sale of ice cream on campus means that these two sources of total surplus are lost: there is deadweight loss.

d. Given that your dog values ice cream equally as much as you do, this is a pure transfer of surplus. As you lose consumer surplus, your dog gains equally as much consumer surplus.

4-3 Check Your Understanding

1. a. Some gas station owners will benefit from getting a higher price. Q_F indicates the sales made by these owners. But some will lose; there are those who make sales at the market equilibrium price of P_E but do not make sales at the regulated price of P_F. These missed sales are indicated on the graph by the fall in the quantity demanded along the demand curve, from point E to point A.

b. Those who buy gas at the higher price of P_F will probably receive better service; this is an example of *inefficiently high quality* caused by a price floor since gas station owners compete on quality rather than price. But opponents are correct to claim that consumers are generally worse off—those who buy at P_F would have been happy to buy at P_E, and many who were willing to buy at a price between P_E and P_F are now unwilling to buy. This is indicated on the graph by the fall in the quantity demanded along the demand curve, from point E to point A.

c. Proponents are wrong because consumers and some gas station owners are hurt by the price floor, which creates "missed opportunities"—desirable transactions between consumers and station owners that never take place. The deadweight loss, the amount of total surplus lost because of missed opportunities, is indicated by the shaded area in the accompanying figure. Moreover, the inefficiency of wasted resources arises as consumers spend time and money driving to other states. The price floor also tempts people to engage in black market activity. With the price floor, only Q_F units are sold. But at prices between P_E and P_F, there are drivers who cumulatively want to buy more than Q_F and owners who are willing to sell to them, a situation likely to lead to illegal activity.

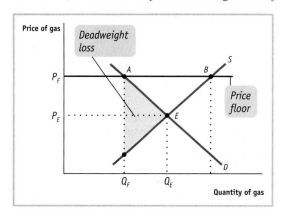

4-4 Check Your Understanding

1. **a.** The price of a ride is $7 since the quantity demanded at this price is 6 million: $7 is the *demand price* of 6 million rides. This is represented by point *A* in the accompanying figure.

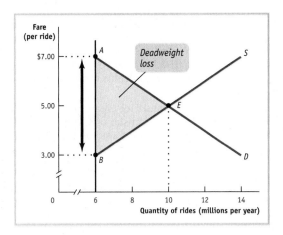

b. At 6 million rides, the supply price is $3 per ride, represented by point *B* in the figure. The wedge between the demand price of $7 per ride and the supply price of $3 per ride is the quota rent per ride, $4. This is represented in the figure above by the vertical distance between points *A* and *B*.

c. The quota discourages 4 million mutually beneficial transactions. The shaded triangle in the figure represents the deadweight loss.

d. At 9 million rides, the demand price is $5.50 per ride, indicated by point *C* in the accompanying figure, and the supply price is $4.50 per ride, indicated by point *D*. The quota rent is the difference between the demand price and the supply price: $1. The deadweight loss is represented by the shaded triangle in the figure. As you can see, the deadweight loss is smaller when the quota is set at 9 million rides than when it is set at 6 million rides.

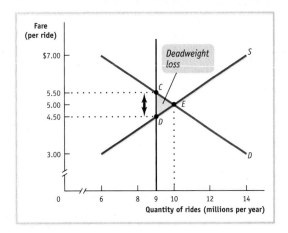

2. The accompanying figure shows a decrease in demand by 4 million rides, represented by a leftward shift of the demand curve from D_1 to D_2: at any given price, the quantity demanded falls by 4 million rides. (For example, at a price of $5, the quantity demanded falls from 10 million to 6 million rides per year.) This eliminates the effect of a quota limit of 8 million rides. At point E_2, the new market

equilibrium, the equilibrium quantity is equal to the quota limit; as a result, the quota has no effect on the market.

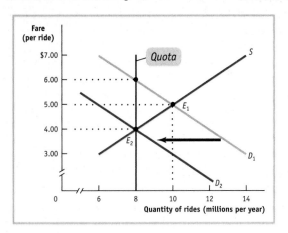

‖ CHAPTER FIVE

5-1 Check Your Understanding

1. By the midpoint method, the percent change in the price of strawberries is

$$\frac{\$1.00 - \$1.50}{(\$1.50 + \$1.00)/2} \times 100 = \frac{-\$0.50}{\$1.25} \times 100 = -40\%$$

Similarly, the percent change in the quantity of strawberries demanded is

$$\frac{200,000 - 100,000}{(100,000 + 200,000)/2} \times 100 = \frac{100,000}{150,000} \times 100 = 67\%$$

Dropping the minus sign, the price elasticity of demand using the midpoint method is 67%/40% = 1.7.

2. By the midpoint method, the percent change in the quantity of movie tickets demanded in going from 4,000 tickets to 5,000 tickets is

$$\frac{5,000 - 4,000}{(4,000 + 5,000)/2} \times 100 = \frac{1,000}{4,500} \times 100 = 22\%$$

Since the price elasticity of demand is 1 at the current consumption level, it will take a 22% reduction in the price of movie tickets to generate a 22% increase in quantity demanded.

3. Since price rises, we know that quantity demanded must fall. Given the current price of $0.50, a $0.05 increase in price represents a 10% change, using the method in Equation 5-2. So the price elasticity of demand is

$$\frac{\text{Change in quantity demanded}}{10\%} = 1.2$$

so that the change in quantity demanded (10% × 1.2) equals 12%. A 12% decrease in quantity demanded represents 100,000 × 0.12, or 12,000 ice-cream sandwiches.

5-2 Check Your Understanding

1. **a.** Elastic demand. Consumers are highly responsive to changes in price. For a rise in price, the quantity effect (which tends to reduce total revenue) outweighs the

price effect (which tends to increase total revenue). Overall, this leads to a fall in total revenue.

b. Unit-elastic demand. Here the revenue lost to the fall in price is exactly equal to the revenue gained from higher sales. The quantity effect exactly offsets the price effect.

c. Inelastic demand. Consumers are relatively unresponsive to changes in price. For consumers to purchase a given percent increase in output, the price must fall by an even greater percent. The price effect of a fall in price (which tends to reduce total revenue) outweighs the quantity effect (which tends to increase total revenue). As a result, total revenue decreases.

d. Inelastic demand. Consumers are relatively unresponsive to price, so the percent fall in output is smaller than the percent rise in price. The price effect of a rise in price (which tends to increase total revenue) outweighs the quantity effect (which tends to reduce total revenue). As a result, total revenue increases.

2. a. The demand of an accident victim for a blood transfusion is very likely to be perfectly inelastic because there is no substitute and it is necessary for survival. The demand curve will be vertical, at a quantity equal to the needed transfusion quantity.

b. Students' demand for green erasers is likely to be perfectly elastic because there are easily available substitutes: nongreen erasers. The demand curve will be horizontal, at a price equal to that of nongreen erasers.

5-3 Check Your Understanding

1. By the midpoint method, the percent increase in Chelsea's income is

$$\frac{\$18,000 - \$12,000}{(\$12,000 + \$18,000)/2} \times 100 = \frac{\$6,000}{\$15,000} \times 100 = 40\%$$

Similarly, the percent increase in her consumption of albums is

$$\frac{40 - 10}{(10 + 40)/2} \times 100 = \frac{30}{25} \times 100 = 120\%$$

So Chelsea's income elasticity of demand for albums is 120%/40% = 3.

2. Sanjay's consumption of expensive restaurant meals will fall more than 10% because a given percent change in income (a fall of 10% here) induces a larger percent change in consumption of an income-elastic good.

3. The cross-price elasticity of demand is 5%/20% = 0.25. Since the cross-price elasticity of demand is positive, the two goods are substitutes.

5-4 Check Your Understanding

1. By the midpoint method, the percent change in the number of hours of web-design services contracted is

$$\frac{500,000 - 300,000}{(300,000 + 500,000)/2} \times 100 = \frac{200,000}{400,000} \times 100 = 50\%$$

Similarly, the percent change in the price of web-design services is

$$\frac{\$150 - \$100}{(\$100 + \$150)/2} \times 100 = \frac{\$50}{\$125} \times 100 = 40\%$$

The price elasticity of supply is 50%/40% = 1.25. So supply is elastic.

2. a. True. An increase in demand raises price. If the price elasticity of supply of milk is low, then relatively little additional quantity supplied will be forthcoming as the price rises. As a result, the price of milk will rise substantially to satisfy the increased demand for milk. If the price elasticity of supply is high, then there will be a relatively large increase in quantity supplied when the price rises. As a result, the price of milk will rise only by a little to satisfy the higher demand for milk.

b. False. It is true that long-run price elasticities of supply are generally larger than short-run elasticities of supply. But this means that short-run supply curves are generally steeper, not flatter, than long-run supply curves.

c. True. When supply is perfectly elastic, the supply curve is a horizontal line. So a change in demand has no effect on price; it affects only the quantity bought and sold.

5-5 Check Your Understanding

1. a. Without the excise tax, Zhang, Yves, Xavier, and Walter sell, and Ana, Bernice, Chizuko, and Dagmar buy one can of soda each, at $0.40 per can. So the quantity bought and sold is 4.

b. At a price to consumers of $0.60, only Ana and Bernice are willing to buy a can of soda. At a price paid to producers of only $0.20, only Zhang and Yves are willing to sell. So the quantity bought and sold is 2.

c. Without the excise tax, Ana's individual consumer surplus is $0.70 − $0.40 = $0.30; Bernice's is $0.60 − $0.40 = $0.20; Chizuko's is $0.50 − $0.40 = $0.10; and Dagmar's is $0.40 − $0.40 = $0.00. Total consumer surplus is $0.30 + $0.20 + $0.10 + $0.00 = $0.60. With the tax, Ana's individual consumer surplus is $0.70 − $0.60 = $0.10 and Bernice's is $0.60 − $0.60 = $0.00. Total consumer surplus post-tax is $0.10 + $0.00 = $0.10. So the total consumer surplus lost because of the tax is $0.60 − $0.10 = $0.50.

d. Without the excise tax, Zhang's individual producer surplus is $0.40 − $0.10 = $0.30; Yves's is $0.40 − $0.20 = $0.20; Xavier's is $0.40 − $0.30 = $0.10; and Walter's is $0.40 − $0.40 = $0.00. Total producer surplus is $0.30 + $0.20 + $0.10 + $0.00 = $0.60. With the tax, Zhang's individual producer surplus is $0.20 − $0.10 = $0.10 and Yves's is $0.20 − $0.20 = $0.00. Total producer surplus post-tax is $0.10 + $0.00 = $0.10. So the total producer surplus lost because of the tax is $0.60 − $0.10 = $0.50.

e. With the tax, two cans of soda are sold, so the government tax revenue from this excise tax is 2 × $0.40 = $0.80.

f. Total surplus without the tax is $0.60 + $0.60 = $1.20. With the tax, total surplus is $0.10 + $0.10 = $0.20, and government tax revenue is $0.80. So deadweight loss from this excise tax is $1.20 − ($0.20 + $0.80) = $0.20.

2. a. The demand for gasoline is inelastic because there is no close substitute for gasoline itself and it is difficult for drivers to arrange substitutes for driving, such as taking public transportation. As a result, the deadweight loss from a tax on gasoline would be relatively small, as shown in the accompanying diagram.

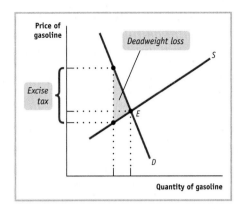

b. The demand for milk chocolate bars is elastic because there are close substitutes: dark chocolate bars, milk chocolate kisses, and so on. As a result, the deadweight loss from a tax on milk chocolate bars would be relatively large, as shown in the accompanying diagram.

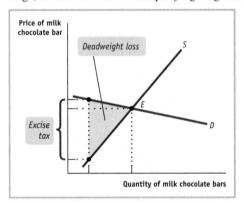

‖ CHAPTER SIX

6-1 Check Your Understanding

1. a. The fixed input is the 10-ton machine, and the variable input is electricity.

b. As you can see from the declining numbers in the third column of the accompanying table, electricity does indeed exhibit diminishing returns: the marginal product of each additional kilowatt of electricity is less than that of the previous kilowatt.

Quantity of electricity (kilowatts)	Quantity of ice (pounds)	Marginal product of electricity (pounds per kilowatt)
0	0	
		1,000
1	1,000	
		800
2	1,800	
		600
3	2,400	
		400
4	2,800	

c. A 50% increase in the size of the fixed input means that Bernie now has a 15-ton machine. So the fixed input

is now the 15-ton machine. Since it generates a 100% increase in output for any given amount of electricity, the quantity of output and marginal product are now as shown in the accompanying table.

Quantity of electricity (kilowatts)	Quantity of ice (pounds)	Marginal product of electricity (pounds per kilowatt)
0	0	
		2,000
1	2,000	
		1,600
2	3,600	
		1,200
3	4,800	
		800
4	5,600	

6-2 Check Your Understanding

1. a. As shown in the accompanying table, the marginal cost for each pie is found by multiplying the marginal cost of the previous pie by 1.5. Variable cost for each output level is found by summing the marginal cost for all the pies produced to reach that output level. So, for example, the variable cost of three pies is $1.00 + $1.50 + $2.25 = $4.75. Average fixed cost for Q pies is calculated as $9.00/$Q$ since fixed cost is $9.00. Average variable cost for Q pies is equal to variable cost for the Q pies divided by Q; for example, the average variable cost of five pies is $13.19/5, or approximately $2.64. Finally, average total cost can be calculated in two equivalent ways: as TC/Q or as $AVC + AFC$.

Quantity of pies	Marginal cost of pie	Variable cost of pie	Average fixed cost of pie	Average variable cost of pie	Average total cost of pie
0		$0.00	–	–	–
	$1.00				
1		1.00	$9.00	$1.00	$10.00
	1.50				
2		2.50	4.50	1.25	5.75
	2.25				
3		4.75	3.00	1.58	4.58
	3.38				
4		8.13	2.25	2.03	4.28
	5.06				
5		13.19	1.80	2.64	4.44
	7.59				
6		20.78	1.50	3.46	4.96

b. The spreading effect dominates the diminishing returns effect when average total cost is falling: the fall in AFC dominates the rise in AVC for pies 1 to 4. The diminishing returns effect dominates when average total cost is rising: the rise in AVC dominates the fall in AFC for pies 5 and 6.

c. Alicia's minimum-cost output is 4 pies; this generates the lowest average total cost, $4.28. When output is less than 4, the marginal cost of a pie is less than the average total cost of the pies already produced. So making an additional pie lowers average total cost. For example, the marginal cost of pie 3 is $2.25, whereas the average total cost of pies 1 and 2 is $5.75. So making pie 3 lowers average total cost to $4.58, equal to (2×$5.75+$2.25)/3. When output is more than 4, the marginal cost of a pie is greater than the average total cost of the pies already produced. Consequently, making an additional pie raises average total cost. So, although the marginal cost of pie 6 is $7.59, the average total cost of pies 1 through 5 is $4.44. Making pie 6 raises average total cost to $4.96, equal to (5×$4.44+$7.59)/6.

6-3 Check Your Understanding

1. a. The accompanying table shows the average total cost of producing 12,000, 22,000, and 30,000 units for each of the three choices of fixed cost. For example, if the firm makes choice 1, the total cost of producing 12,000 units of output is $8,000+(12,000×$1.00) = $20,000. The average total cost of producing 12,000 units of output is therefore $20,000/12,000 = $1.67. The other average total costs are calculated similarly.

	12,000 units	22,000 units	30,000 units
Average total cost from choice 1	$1.67	$1.36	$1.27
Average total cost from choice 2	1.75	1.30	1.15
Average total cost from choice 3	2.25	1.34	1.05

So if the firm wanted to produce 12,000 units, it would make choice 1 because this gives it the lowest average total cost. If it wanted to produce 22,000 units, it would make choice 2. If it wanted to produce 30,000 units, it would make choice 3.

b. Having historically produced 12,000 units, the firm would have adopted choice 1. When producing 12,000 units, the firm would have had an average total cost of $1.67. When output jumps to 22,000 units, the firm cannot alter its choice of fixed cost in the short run, so its average total cost in the short run will be $1.36. In the long run, however, it will adopt choice 2, making its average total cost fall to $1.30.

c. If the firm believes that the increase in demand is temporary, it should not alter its fixed cost from choice 1 because choice 2 generates higher average total cost as soon as output falls back to its original quantity of 12,000 units: $1.75 versus $1.67.

2. a. This firm is likely to experience constant returns to scale. To increase output, the firm must hire more workers, purchase more computers, and pay additional telephone charges. Because these inputs are easily available, their long-run average total cost is unlikely to change as output increases.

b. This firm is likely to experience decreasing returns to scale. As the firm takes on more projects, the costs of communication and coordination required to implement the expertise of the firm's owner are likely to increase.

As a result, the firm's long-run average total cost will increase as output increases.

c. This firm is likely to experience increasing returns to scale. Because diamond mining requires a large initial set-up cost for excavation equipment, long-run average total cost will fall as output increases.

3. The accompanying diagram shows the long-run average total cost curve (*LRATC*) and the short-run average total cost curve corresponding to a long-run output choice of 5 cases of salsa (*ATC₅*). The curve *ATC₅* shows the short-run average total cost for which the level of fixed cost minimizes average total cost at an output of 5 cases of salsa. This is confirmed by the fact that at 5 cases per day, *ATC₅* touches *LRATC*, the long-run average total cost curve.

If Selena expects to produce only 4 cases of salsa for a long time, she should change her fixed cost. If she does *not* change her fixed cost and produces 4 cases of salsa, her average total cost in the short run is indicated by point *B* on *ATC₅*; it is no longer on the *LRATC*. If she changes her fixed cost, though, her average total cost could be lower, at point *A*.

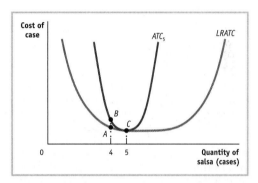

|| CHAPTER SEVEN

7-1 Check Your Understanding

1. a. With only two producers in the world, each producer will represent a sizable share of the market. So the industry will not be perfectly competitive.

b. Because each producer of natural gas from the North Sea has only a small market share of total world supply of natural gas, and since natural gas is a standardized product, the natural gas industry will be perfectly competitive.

c. Because each designer has a distinctive style, high-fashion clothes are not a standardized product. So the industry will not be perfectly competitive.

d. The market described here is the market in each city for tickets to baseball games. Since there are only one or two teams in each major city, each team will represent a sizable share of the market. So the industry will not be perfectly competitive.

7-2 Check Your Understanding

1. a. The firm should shut down immediately when price is less than minimum average variable cost, the shut-down price. In the accompanying diagram, this is optimal for prices in the range 0 to P_1.

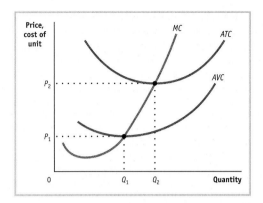

b. When price is greater than minimum average variable cost (the shut-down price) but less than minimum average total cost (the break-even price), the firm should continue to operate in the short run even though it is making a loss. This is optimal for prices in the range P_1 to P_2 and for quantities Q_1 to Q_2.

c. When price exceeds minimum average total cost (the break-even price), the firm makes a profit. This happens for prices in excess of P_2 and results in quantities greater than Q_2.

2. This is an example of a temporary shut-down by a firm when the market price lies below the shut-down price, the minimum average variable cost. In this case, the market price is the price of a lobster meal and variable cost is the variable cost of serving such a meal, such as the cost of the lobster, employee wages, and so on. In this example, however, it is the average variable cost curve rather than the market price that shifts over time, due to seasonal changes in the cost of lobsters. Maine lobster shacks have relatively low average variable cost during the summer, when cheap Maine lobsters are available. During the rest of the year, their average variable cost is relatively high due to the high cost of imported lobsters. So the lobster shacks are open for business during the summer, when their minimum average variable cost lies below price. But they close during the rest of the year, when price lies below their minimum average variable cost.

7-3 Check Your Understanding

1. a. A fall in the fixed cost of production generates a fall in the average total cost of production and, in the short run, an increase in each firm's profit at the current output level. So in the long run new firms will enter the industry.

The increase in supply drives down price and profits. Once profits are driven back to zero, entry will cease.

b. An increase in wages generates an increase in the average variable and the average total cost of production at every output level. In the short run, firms incur losses at the current output level, and so in the long run some firms will exit the industry. (If the average variable cost rises sufficiently, some firms may even shut down in the short run.) As firms exit, supply decreases, price rises, and losses are reduced. Exit will cease once losses return to zero.

c. Price will rise as a result of the increased demand, leading to a short-run increase in profits at the current output level. In the long run, firms will enter the industry, generating an increase in supply, a fall in price, and a fall in profits. Once profits are driven back to zero, entry will cease.

d. The shortage of a key input causes that input's price to increase, resulting in an increase in average variable and average total costs for producers. Firms incur losses in the short run, and some firms will exit the industry in the long run. The fall in supply generates an increase in price and decreased losses. Exit will cease when losses have returned to zero.

2. In the accompanying diagram, point X_{MKT} in panel (b), the intersection of S_1 and D_1, represents the long-run industry equilibrium before the change in consumer tastes. When tastes change, demand falls and the industry moves in the short run to point Y_{MKT} in panel (b), at the intersection of the new demand curve D_2 and S_1, the short-run supply curve representing the same number of egg producers as in the original equilibrium at point X_{MKT}. As the market price falls, an individual firm reacts by producing less—as shown in panel (a)—as long as the market price remains above the minimum average variable cost. If market price falls below minimum average variable cost, the firm would shut down immediately. At point Y_{MKT} the price of eggs is below minimum average total cost, creating losses for producers. This leads some firms to exit, which shifts the short-run industry supply curve leftward to S_2. A new long-run equilibrium is established at point Z_{MKT}. As this occurs, the market price rises again, and, as shown in panel (c), each remaining producer reacts by increasing output (here, from point Y to point Z). All remaining producers again make zero profits. The decrease in the quantity of eggs supplied in the industry comes entirely from the exit of some producers from the industry. The long-run industry supply curve is the curve labeled LRS in panel (b).

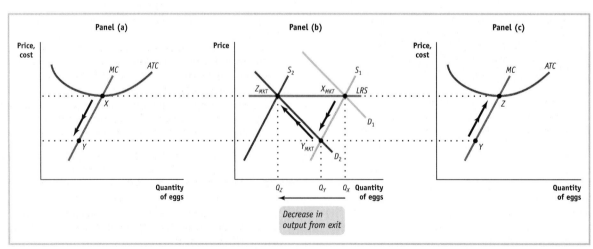

‖ CHAPTER EIGHT

8-1 Check Your Understanding

1. a. This does not support the conclusion. Texas Tea has a limited amount of oil, and the price has risen in order to equalize supply and demand.

b. This supports the conclusion because the market for home heating oil has become monopolized, and a monopolist will reduce the quantity supplied and raise the price to generate profit.

c. This does not support the conclusion. Texas Tea has raised its price to consumers because the price of its input, home heating oil, has increased.

d. This supports the conclusion. The fact that other firms have begun to supply heating oil at a lower price implies that Texas Tea must have earned sufficient profits to attract the other firms to Frigid.

e. This supports the conclusion. It indicates that Texas Tea enjoys a barrier to entry because it controls access to the only Alaskan heating oil pipeline.

2. a. Extending the length of a patent increases the length of time during which the inventor can reduce the quantity supplied and increase the market price. Since this increases the period of time during which the inventor can earn economic profits from the invention, it increases the incentive to invent new products.

b. Extending the length of a patent also increases the period of time during which consumers have to pay higher prices. So, determining the appropriate length of a patent involves making a trade-off between the desirable incentive for invention and the undesirable high price to consumers.

3. a. When a large number of other people use Passport credit cards, then any one merchant is more likely to accept the card. The larger the customer base, then, the more likely a Passport card will be accepted for payment.

b. When a large number of people own a car with a new type of engine, it will be easier to find a knowledgeable mechanic who can repair it.

c. When a large number of people use such a website, the more likely it is that you will be able to find a buyer for something you want to sell or a seller for something you want to buy.

8-2 Check Your Understanding

1. a. The price at each output level is found by dividing the total revenue by the number of emeralds produced; for example, the price when 3 emeralds are produced is $252/3 = $84. The price at the various output levels is then used to construct the demand schedule in the accompanying table.

Quantity of emeralds demanded	Price of emerald	Marginal revenue	Quantity effect component	Price effect component
1	$100			
		$86	$93	–$7
2	93			
		66	84	–18
3	84			
		28	70	–42
4	70			
		–30	50	–80
5	50			

b. The marginal revenue schedule is found by calculating the change in total revenue as output increases by one unit. For example, the marginal revenue generated by increasing output from 2 to 3 emeralds is ($252 – $186) = $66.

c. The quantity effect component of marginal revenue is the additional revenue generated by selling one more unit of the good at the market price. For example, as shown in the accompanying table, at 3 emeralds, the market price is $84; so when going from 2 to 3 emeralds, the quantity effect is equal to $84.

d. The price effect component of marginal revenue is the decline in total revenue caused by the fall in price when one more unit is sold. For example, as shown in the table, when only 2 emeralds are sold, each emerald sells at a price of $93. However, when Emerald, Inc. sells an additional emerald, the price must fall by $9 to $84. So the price effect component in going from 2 to 3 emeralds is (–$9) × 2 = –$18. That's because 2 emeralds can only be sold at a price of $84 when 3 emeralds in total are sold, although they could have been sold at a price of $93 when only 2 in total were sold.

e. In order to determine Emerald, Inc.'s profit-maximizing output level, you must know its marginal cost at each output level. Its profit-maximizing output level is the one at which marginal revenue is equal to marginal cost.

2. As the accompanying diagram shows, the marginal cost curve shifts upward to $400. The profit-maximizing price rises and quantity falls. Monopolist profit falls from $3,200 to $300 × 6 = $1,800. Perfectly competitive industry profits, though, are unchanged at zero.

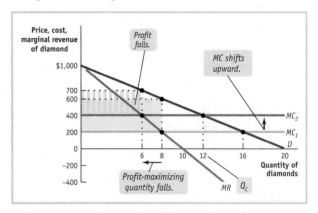

8-3 Check Your Understanding

1. a. Cable internet service is a natural monopoly. So the government should intervene only if it believes that price exceeds average total cost, where average total cost is based on the cost of laying the cable. In this case it should impose a price ceiling equal to average total cost. Otherwise, it should do nothing.

b. The government should approve the merger only if it fosters competition by transferring some of the company's landing slots to another, competing airline.

2. a. False. As can be seen from Figure 8-8, panel (b), the inefficiency arises from the fact that some of the consumer surplus is transformed into deadweight loss (the yellow area), not that it is transformed into profit (the green area).

b. True. If a monopolist sold to all customers who have a valuation greater than or equal to marginal cost, all mutually beneficial transactions would occur and there would be no deadweight loss.

3. As shown in the accompanying diagram, a profit-maximizing monopolist produces Q_M, the output level at which $MR = MC$. A monopolist who mistakenly believes that $P = MR$ produces the output level at which $P = MC$ (when, in fact, $P > MR$, and at the true profit-maximizing level of output, $P > MR = MC$). This misguided monopolist will produce the output level Q_C, where the demand curve crosses the marginal cost curve—the same output level produced if the industry were perfectly competitive. It will charge the price P_C, which is equal to marginal cost, and make zero profit. The entire shaded area is equal to the consumer surplus, which is also equal to total surplus in this case (since the monopolist receives zero producer surplus). There is no deadweight loss since every consumer who is willing to pay as much as or more than marginal cost gets the good. A smart monopolist, however, will produce the output level Q_M and charge the price P_M. Profit equals the green area, consumer surplus corresponds to the blue area, and total surplus is equal to the sum of the green and blue areas. The yellow area is the deadweight loss generated by the monopolist.

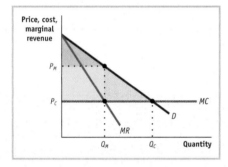

8-4 Check Your Understanding

1. **a.** False. A price-discriminating monopolist will sell to some customers that a single-price monopolist will refuse to—namely, customers with a high price elasticity of demand who are willing to pay only a relatively low price for the good.

   b. False. Although a price-discriminating monopolist does indeed capture more of the consumer surplus, inefficiency is lower: more mutually beneficial transactions occur because the monopolist makes more sales to customers with a low willingness to pay for the good.

   c. True. Under price discrimination consumers are charged prices that depend on their price elasticity of demand. A consumer with highly elastic demand, is more sensitive to a price change, and will pay a lower price than a consumer with inelastic demand, who is less sensitive to a price change.

2. **a.** This is not a case of price discrimination because all consumers, regardless of their price elasticities of demand, value the damaged merchandise less than undamaged merchandise. So the price must be lowered to sell the merchandise.

   b. This is a case of price discrimination. Senior citizens have a higher price elasticity of demand for restaurant meals (their demand for restaurant meals is more responsive to price changes) than other patrons. Restaurants lower the price to high-elasticity consumers (senior citizens). Consumers with low price elasticity of demand will pay the full price.

   c. This is a case of price discrimination. Consumers with a high price elasticity of demand will pay a lower price by

collecting and using discount coupons. Consumers with a low price elasticity of demand will not use coupons.

   d. This is not a case of price discrimination; it is simply a case of supply and demand.

‖ CHAPTER NINE

9-1 Check Your Understanding

1. **a.** The world oil industry is an oligopoly because a few countries control a necessary resource for production, oil reserves.

   b. The microprocessor industry is an oligopoly because two firms possess superior technology and so dominate industry production.

   c. The wide-body passenger jet industry is an oligopoly because there are increasing returns to scale in production.

2. **a.** The firm is likely to act noncooperatively and raise output, which will generate a negative price effect. But because the firm's current market share is small, the negative price effect will fall much more heavily on its rivals' revenues than on its own. At the same time, the firm will benefit from a positive quantity effect.

   b. The firm is likely to act noncooperatively and raise output, which will generate a fall in price. Because its rivals have higher costs, they will lose money at the lower price while the firm continues to make profits. So, the firm may be able to drive its rivals out of business by increasing its output.

3. **a.** This is not likely to be interpreted as evidence of tacit collusion. Considerable variation in market shares indicates that firms have been competing to capture one another's business.

   b. This is not likely to be interpreted as evidence of tacit collusion. Because these features make it more unlikely that consumers will switch products in response to lower prices, this is a way for firms to avoid any temptation to gain market share by lowering prices. This is a form of product differentiation used to avoid direct competition.

   c. This is likely to be interpreted as evidence of tacit collusion. In the guise of discussing sales targets, firms can create a cartel by designating quantities to be produced by each firm.

   d. This is likely to be interpreted as evidence of tacit collusion. By raising prices together, each firm in the industry is refusing to undercut its rivals by leaving its price unchanged or lowering it. Because it could gain market share by doing so, refusing to do it is evidence of tacit collusion.

9-2 Check Your Understanding

1. When Margaret builds a missile, Nikita's payoff from also building a missile is –10; it is –20 if he does not. The same set of payoffs holds for Margaret when Nikita builds a missile: her payoff is –10 if she also builds one, –20 if she does not. So it is a Nash (or noncooperative) equilibrium for both Margaret and Nikita to build missiles, and their total payoff is $(-10)+(-10) = -20$. But their total payoff is greatest when neither builds a missile: their total payoff is $0+0 = 0$. But this outcome—the cooperative outcome—is unlikely. If Margaret builds a missile but Nikita does not, Margaret gets a payoff of +8, rather than the 0 she gets if she doesn't build a missile. So Margaret is better off if she

builds a missile but Nikita doesn't. Similarly, Nikita is better off if he builds a missile but Margaret doesn't: he gets a payoff of +8, rather than the 0 he gets if he doesn't build a missile. So both players have an incentive to build a missile. Both will build a missile, and each gets a payoff of –10. So unless Nikita and Margaret are able to communicate in some way to enforce cooperation, they will act in their own individual interests and each will build a missile.

2. **a.** Future entry by several new firms will increase competition and drive down industry profits. As a result, there is less future profit to protect by behaving cooperatively today. So, each oligopolist is more likely to behave noncooperatively today.

   b. When it is very difficult for a firm to detect if another firm has raised output, then it is very difficult to enforce cooperation by playing tit for tat. So it is more likely that a firm will behave noncooperatively.

   c. When firms have coexisted while maintaining high prices for a long time, each expects cooperation to continue. So the value of behaving cooperatively today is high, and it is likely that firms will engage in tacit collusion.

9-3 Check Your Understanding

1. **a.** Ladders are not differentiated as a result of monopolistic competition. A ladder producer makes different ladders (tall ladders versus short ladders) to satisfy different consumer needs, not to avoid competition with rivals. So, two tall ladders made by two different producers will be indistinguishable by consumers.

   b. Soft drinks are an example of product differentiation as a result of monopolistic competition. For example, several producers make colas; each is differentiated in terms of taste, which fast-food chains sell it, and so on.

   c. Department stores are an example of product differentiation as a result of monopolistic competition. They serve different clienteles who have different price sensitivities and different tastes. They also offer different levels of customer service and are situated in different locations.

   d. Steel is not differentiated as a result of monopolistic competition. Different types of steel (beams versus sheets) are made for different purposes, not to distinguish one steel manufacturer's products from another's.

2. **a.** Perfectly competitive industries and monopolistically competitive industries both have many sellers, so it may be hard to distinguish between them solely in terms of number of firms. And in both market structures, there is free entry into and exit from the industry in the long run. But, in a perfectly competitive industry, one standardized product is sold; in a monopolistically competitive industry, products are differentiated. So, you should ask whether products are differentiated in the industry.

   b. In a monopoly there is only one firm, but a monopolistically competitive industry contains many firms. So, you should ask whether or not there is a single firm in the industry.

‖ CHAPTER TEN

10-1 Check Your Understanding

1. **a.** The negative externality is the pollution caused by the wastewater runoff, an uncompensated cost imposed by the poultry farms on their neighbors.

   b. Since poultry farmers do not account for the negative externality of their actions into account when making decisions about how much wastewater to generate, they will create more runoff than is socially optimal in the absence of government intervention or a private deal. They will produce runoff up to the point at which the marginal social benefit of an additional unit of runoff is zero; however, their neighbors experience a high, positive level of marginal social cost of runoff from this output level. So, the quantity of wastewater runoff is inefficient: reducing runoff by one unit would reduce total social benefit by less than it would reduce total social cost.

   c. At the socially optimal quantity of wastewater runoff, the marginal social benefit is equal to the marginal social cost. This quantity is lower than the quantity of wastewater runoff that would be created in the absence of government intervention or a private deal.

2. Yasmin's reasoning is not correct: allowing some late returns of books is likely to be socially optimal. Although you impose a marginal social cost on others every day that you are late in returning a book, there is some positive marginal social benefit to you of returning a book late—for example, you get a longer period to use it in working on a term paper.

   The socially optimal number of days that a book is returned late is the number at which the marginal social benefit equals the marginal social cost. A fine so stiff that it prevents any late returns is likely to result in a situation in which people return books although the marginal social benefit of keeping them another day is greater than the marginal social cost—an inefficient outcome. In that case, allowing a patron with an overdue book another day before it has to be returned would increase total social benefit more than it would increase total social cost. So, charging a moderate fine that reduces the number of days that books are returned late to the socially optimal number of days is appropriate.

10-2 Check Your Understanding

1. This is a misguided argument. Allowing polluters to sell emissions permits makes polluters face the cost of polluting in the form of the opportunity cost of the permit. If a polluter chooses not to reduce its emissions, it cannot sell its emissions permits. As a result, it forgoes the opportunity of making money from the sale of the permits. So, despite the fact that the polluter receives a monetary benefit from selling the permits, the scheme has the desired effect: to make polluters internalize the externality of their actions.

2. **a.** If the emissions tax is smaller than the marginal social cost at Q_{OPT}, a polluter will face a marginal cost of polluting (equal to the amount of the tax) that is less than the marginal social cost at the socially optimal quantity of pollution. Since a polluter will produce emissions up to the point at which the marginal social benefit is equal to its marginal cost, the resulting amount of pollution will be larger than the socially optimal quantity. As a result, there is inefficiency: if the amount of pollution is larger than the socially optimal quantity, the marginal social cost exceeds the marginal social benefit. A reduction in emissions levels will increase social surplus.

   If the emissions tax is greater than the marginal social cost at Q_{OPT}, a polluter will face a marginal cost of polluting (equal to the amount of the tax) that is greater than the marginal social cost at the socially optimal quantity of pollution. This will lead the polluter to reduce emissions below the socially optimal quantity.

This also is inefficient: whenever the marginal social benefit is greater than the marginal social cost, an increase in emissions levels will raise social surplus.

b. If the total amount of allowable pollution is set too high, the supply of emissions permits will be high and so the equilibrium price at which permits are traded will be low. That is, polluters will face a marginal cost of polluting (the price of a permit) that is "too low"—lower than the marginal social cost at the socially optimal quantity of pollution. As a result, pollution will be greater than the socially optimal quantity. This is inefficient and lowers total surplus.

If the total level of allowable pollution is set too low, the supply of emissions permits will be low and so the equilibrium price at which permits are traded will be high. That is, polluters will face a marginal cost of polluting (the price of a permit) that is "too high"—higher than the marginal social cost at the socially optimal quantity of pollution. As a result, pollution will be lower than the socially optimal quantity. This also is inefficient and lowers total surplus.

c. A carbon tax will increase the cost of using fossil fuels, including the prices of gasoline and coal. As the cost of fossil fuels increases, consumers will reduce their use of fossil fuels as energy sources. They will be increasingly likely to purchase more fuel-efficient cars and invest in solar technology for their homes.

10-3 Check Your Understanding

1. College education provides a positive externality through the creation of knowledge. And student aid acts like a Pigouvian subsidy on higher education. If the marginal social benefit of higher education is indeed $29 billion, then student aid is an optimal policy.

2. a. Planting trees generates a positive externality since many people (not just those who plant the trees) benefit from the increased air quality and lower summer temperatures. Without a subsidy, people will plant too few trees, setting the marginal social cost of planting a tree—what they forgo by planting a tree—too low. (Although too low, it may still be more than zero since a homeowner gains some personal benefit from planting a tree.) A Pigouvian subsidy will induce people to plant more trees, bringing the marginal social benefit of planting a tree in line with the marginal social cost.

b. Water-saving toilets generate a positive externality because they discourage wasting water, thereby reducing the need to pump water from rivers and aquifers. Without a subsidy, homeowners will use water until the marginal social cost of water usage is equal to zero since water is costless to them. A Pigouvian subsidy on water-saving toilets will induce homeowners to reduce their water usage so that the marginal social benefit of water is in line with the marginal social cost.

c. Discarded plastic drink bottles create a negative externality by degrading the environment. Without a tax, people will discard plastic bottles freely—until the marginal social cost of discarding a bottle (what they must forgo in discarding a bottle) is zero. A Pigouvian tax or subsidy on drink bottles will bring the marginal social benefit of a drink bottle in line with its marginal social cost. This can be done two ways: a tax or a subsidy. A tax will induce drink manufacturers to shift away from plastic bottles that pollute to less-polluting containers, like

paper cartons. A subsidy for disposing of the containers in an environmentally sound way, such as recycling, will induce drink consumers to dispose of the bottles in a way that reduces the negative externality.

10-4 Check Your Understanding

1. a. Use of a public park is nonexcludable, but it may or may not be rival in consumption, depending on the circumstances. For example, if both you and I use the park for jogging, then your use will not prevent my use—use of the park is nonrival in consumption. In this case the public park is a public good. But use of the park is rival in consumption if there are many people trying to use the jogging path at the same time or when my use of the public tennis court prevents your use of the same court. In this case the public park is a common resource.

b. A cheese burrito is both excludable and rival in consumption. Hence it is a private good.

c. Information from a password-protected website is excludable but nonrival in consumption. So, it is an artificially scarce good.

d. Publicly announced information on the path of an incoming hurricane is nonexcludable and nonrival in consumption. So, it is a public good.

2. a. With 10 Homebodies and 6 Revelers, the marginal social benefit schedule of money spent on the party is as shown in the accompanying table.

Money spent on party	Marginal social benefit
$0	
	$(10 \times \$0.05) + (6 \times \$0.13) = \$1.28$
1	
	$(10 \times \$0.04) + (6 \times \$0.11) = \$1.06$
2	
	$(10 \times \$0.03) + (6 \times \$0.09) = \$0.84$
3	
	$(10 \times \$0.02) + (6 \times \$0.07) = \$0.62$
4	

The efficient spending level is $2, the highest level for which the marginal social benefit is greater than the marginal cost ($1).

b. With 6 Homebodies and 10 Revelers, the marginal social benefit schedule of money spent on the party is as shown in the accompanying table.

Money spent on party	Marginal social benefit
$0	
	$(6 \times \$0.05) + (10 \times \$0.13) = \$1.60$
1	
	$(6 \times \$0.04) + (10 \times \$0.11) = \$1.34$
2	
	$(6 \times \$0.03) + (10 \times \$0.09) = \$1.08$
3	
	$(6 \times \$0.02) + (10 \times \$0.07) = \$0.82$
4	

The efficient spending level is now $3, the highest level for which the marginal social benefit is greater than the marginal cost ($1). The efficient level of spending has increased from that in part a because with relatively more Revelers than Homebodies, an additional dollar spent on the party generates a higher level of social benefit compared to when there are relatively more Homebodies than Revelers.

c. When the numbers of Homebodies and Revelers are unknown but residents are asked their preferences, Homebodies will pretend to be Revelers to induce a higher level of spending on the public party. That's because a Homebody still receives a positive individual marginal benefit from an additional $1 spent, despite the fact that his or her individual marginal benefit is lower than that of a Reveler for every additional $1. In this case the "reported" marginal social benefit schedule of money spent on the party will be as shown in the accompanying table.

Money spent on party	Marginal social benefit
$0	
	$16 \times \$0.13 = \$2.08$
1	
	$16 \times \$0.11 = \$1.76$
2	
	$16 \times \$0.09 = \$1.44$
3	
	$16 \times \$0.07 = \$1.12$
4	

As a result, $4 will be spent on the party, the highest level for which the "reported" marginal social benefit is greater than the marginal cost ($1). Regardless of whether there are 10 Homebodies and 6 Revelers (part a) or 6 Homebodies and 10 Revelers (part b), spending $4 in total on the party is clearly inefficient because marginal cost exceeds marginal social benefit at this spending level.

As a further exercise, consider how much Homebodies gain by this misrepresentation. In part a, the efficient level of spending is $2. So, by misrepresenting their preferences, the 10 Homebodies gain, in total, $10 \times (\$0.03 + \$0.02) = \$0.50$—that is, they gain the marginal individual benefit in going from a spending level of $2 to $4. The 6 Revelers also gain from the misrepresentations of the Homebodies; they gain $6 \times (\$0.09 + \$0.07) = \$0.96$ in total. This outcome is clearly inefficient—when $4 in total is spent, the marginal cost is $1 but the marginal social benefit is only $0.62, indicating that too much money is being spent on the party.

In part b, the efficient level of spending is actually $3. The misrepresentation by the 6 Homebodies gains them, in total, $6 \times \$0.02 = \$0.12$, but the 10 Revelers gain $10 \times \$0.07 = \$0.70$ in total. This outcome is also clearly inefficient—when $4 is spent, marginal social benefit is only $\$0.12 + \$0.70 = \$0.82$ but marginal cost is $1.

CHAPTER ELEVEN

11-1 Check Your Understanding

1. a. A pension guarantee program is a social insurance program. The possibility of an employer declaring bankruptcy and defaulting on its obligation to pay employee pensions creates insecurity. By providing pension income to those employees, such a program alleviates this source of economic insecurity.

b. The SCHIP program is a poverty program. By providing health care to children in low-income households, it targets its spending specifically to the poor.

c. The Section 8 housing program is a poverty program. By targeting its support to low-income households, it specifically helps the poor.

d. The federal flood program is a social insurance program. For many people, the majority of their wealth is tied up in the home they own. The potential for a loss of that wealth creates economic insecurity. By providing assistance to those hit by a major flood, the program alleviates this source of insecurity.

2. The poverty threshold is an absolute measure of poverty. It defines individuals as poor if their incomes fall below a level that is considered adequate to purchase the necessities of life, irrespective of how well other people are doing. And that measure is fixed: in 2018, for instance, it took $12,140 for an individual living alone to purchase the necessities of life, regardless of how well-off other Americans were. In particular, the poverty threshold is not adjusted for an increase in living standards: even if other Americans are becoming increasingly well-off over time, in real terms (that is, how many goods an individual at the poverty threshold can buy) the poverty threshold remains the same.

3. a. To determine mean (or average) income, we take the total income of all individuals in this economy and divide it by the number of individuals. Mean income is $(\$39,000 + \$17,500 + \$900,000 + \$15,000 + \$28,000)/5 = \$999,500/5 = \$199,900$. To determine median income, look at the accompanying table, which ranks the five individuals in order of their income.

	Income
Vijay	$15,000
Kelly	17,500
Oskar	28,000
Sephora	39,000
Raul	900,000

The median income is the income of the individual in the exact middle of the income distribution: Oskar, with an income of $28,000. So the median income is $28,000.

Median income is more representative of the income of individuals in this economy: almost everyone earns income between $15,000 and $39,000, close to the median income of $28,000. Only Raul is the exception: it is his income that raises the mean income to $199,900, which is not representative of most incomes in this economy.

b. The first quintile is made up of the 20% (or one-fifth) of individuals with the lowest incomes in the economy. Vijay makes up the 20% of individuals with the lowest incomes. His income is $15,000, so that is the average income of the first quintile. Oskar makes up the 20% of individuals with the third-lowest incomes. His income is $28,000, so that is the average income of the third quintile.

4. As the Economics in Action pointed out, much of the rise in inequality reflects growing differences among highly educated workers. That is, workers with similar levels of education earn very dissimilar incomes. As a result, the principal source of rising inequality in the United States today is reflected by statement b: the rise in the bank CEO's salary relative to that of the branch manager.

11-2 Check Your Understanding

1. The Earned Income Tax Credit (EITC), a negative income tax, applies only to those workers who earn income; over a certain range of incomes, the more a worker earns, the higher the amount of EITC received. A person who earns no income receives no income tax credit. By contrast, poverty programs that pay individuals based solely on low income still make those payments even if the individual does not work at all; once the individual earns a certain amount of income, these programs discontinue payments. As a result, such programs contain an incentive not to work and earn income, since earning more than a certain amount makes individuals ineligible for their benefits. The negative income tax, however, provides an incentive to work and earn income because its payments increase the more an individual works.

2. The second column of Table 11-3 gives the percentage reduction in the overall poverty rate by government programs. So the reduction in the overall poverty rate by the U.S. welfare state is given by adding up the numbers in that second column, which gives a 16.7% reduction in the overall poverty rate. For those aged 65 or over, the welfare state cuts the poverty rate by 43.5%, the amount given by adding up the numbers in the last column of Table 11-3.

11-3 Check Your Understanding

1. a. The program benefits you and your parents because the pool of all college students contains a representative mix of healthy and less healthy people, rather than a selected group of people who want insurance because they expect to pay high medical bills. In that respect, this insurance is like *employment-based health insurance*. Because no student can opt out, the school can offer health insurance based on the health care costs of its average student. If each student had to buy his or her own health insurance, some students would not be able to obtain any insurance and many would pay more than they do to the school's insurance program.

   b. Since all students are required to enroll in its health insurance program, even the healthiest students cannot leave the program in an effort to obtain cheaper insurance tailored specifically to healthy people. If this were to happen, the school's insurance program would be left with an adverse selection of less healthy students and so would have to raise premiums, beginning the adverse selection death spiral. But since no student can leave the insurance program, the school's program can continue to base its premiums on the average student's probability of requiring health care, avoiding the adverse selection death spiral.

11-4 Check Your Understanding

1. a. Recall one of the principles from Chapter 1: one person's spending is another person's income. A high sales tax on consumer items is the same as a high marginal tax rate on income. As a result, the incentive to earn income by working or by investing in risky projects is reduced, since the payoff, after taxes, is lower.

   b. If you lose a housing subsidy as soon as your income rises above $25,000, your incentive to earn more than $25,000 is reduced. If you earn exactly $25,000, you obtain the housing subsidy; however, as soon as you earn $25,001, you lose the entire subsidy, making you worse off than if you had not earned the additional dollar.

2. Over the past 40 years, polarization in Congress has increased. Forty years ago, some Republicans were to the left of some Democrats. Today, the rightmost Democrats appear to be to the left of the leftmost Republicans.

CHAPTER TWELVE

12-1 Check Your Understanding

1. a. This is a microeconomic question because it addresses decisions made by consumers about a particular product.

   b. This is a macroeconomic question because it addresses consumer spending in the overall economy.

   c. This is a macroeconomic question because it addresses changes in the overall economy.

   d. This is a microeconomic question because it addresses changes in a particular market, in this case the market for economists.

   e. This is a microeconomic question because it addresses choices made by consumers and producers about which mode of transportation to use.

   f. This is a microeconomic question because it addresses changes in a particular market.

   g. This is a macroeconomic question because it addresses changes in a measure of the economy's overall price level.

2. a. When people can't get credit to finance their purchases, they will be unable to spend money. This will weaken the economy, and, as others see the economy weaken, they will also cut back on their spending in order to save for future bad times. As a result, the credit shortfall will spark a compounding effect through the economy as people cut back their spending, making the economy worse, leading to more cutbacks in spending, and so on.

   b. If you believe the economy is self-regulating, then you would advocate doing nothing in response to the slump.

   c. If you believe in Keynesian economics, you would advocate that policy makers undertake monetary and fiscal policies to stimulate spending in the economy.

12-2 Check Your Understanding

1. We talk about business cycles for the economy as a whole because recessions and expansions are not confined to a few industries—they reflect downturns and upturns for the economy as a whole. In downturns, almost every sector of the economy reduces output and the number of people employed. Moreover, business cycles are an international phenomenon, sometimes moving in rough synchrony across countries.

2. A recession can hurt people throughout society. They cause large numbers of workers to lose their jobs and make it

hard to find new jobs. Recessions hurt the standard of living of many families and are usually associated with a rise in the number of people living below the poverty line, an increase in the number of people who lose their houses because they can't afford their mortgage payments, and a fall in the percentage of Americans with health insurance. Recessions also hurt the profits of firms.

12-3 Check Your Understanding

1. Countries with high rates of population growth will have to maintain higher long-run growth rates of overall output than countries with low rates of population growth in order for them to achieve an increased standard of living per person, since aggregate output will have to be divided among a larger number of people.

12-4 Check Your Understanding

1. **a.** As some prices have risen but other prices have fallen, there may be overall inflation or deflation. The answer is ambiguous.

   b. As all prices have risen significantly, this sounds like inflation.

   c. As most prices have fallen and others have not changed, this sounds like deflation.

12-5 Check Your Understanding

1. **a.** This situation reflects comparative advantage. Canada's comparative advantage results from the development of oil—Canada now has an abundance of oil.

   b. This situation reflects comparative advantage. China's comparative advantage results from an abundance of labor; China is good at labor-intensive activities such as assembly.

   c. This situation reflects macroeconomic forces. Germany has been running a huge trade surplus because of underlying decisions regarding savings and investment spending, with its savings in excess of its investment spending.

   d. This situation reflects macroeconomic forces. The United States was able to begin running a large trade deficit because the technology boom made the United States an attractive place to invest, with investment spending outstripping U.S. savings.

‖ CHAPTER THIRTEEN

13-1 Check Your Understanding

1. Let's start by considering the relationship between the total value added of all domestically produced final goods and services and aggregate spending on domestically produced final goods and services. These two quantities are equal because every final good and service produced in the economy is either purchased by someone or added to inventories. And additions to inventories are counted as spending by firms. Next, consider the relationship between aggregate spending on domestically produced final goods and services and total factor income. These two quantities are equal because all spending that is channeled to firms to pay for purchases of domestically produced final goods and services is revenue for firms. Those revenues must be paid out by firms to their factors of production in the

form of wages, profit, interest, and rent. Taken together, this means that all three methods of calculating GDP are equivalent.

2. You would be counting the value of the steel twice—once as it was sold by American Steel to American Motors and once as part of the car sold by American Motors.

13-2 Check Your Understanding

1. **a.** In 2015 nominal GDP was $(1,000,000 \times \$0.40) + (800,000 \times \$0.60) = \$400,000 + \$480,000 = \$880,000$. A 25% rise in the price of french fries from 2015 to 2016 means that the 2016 price of french fries was $1.25 \times \$0.40 = \$0.50$. A 10% fall in servings means that $1,000,000 \times 0.9 = 900,000$ servings were sold in 2016. As a result, the total value of sales of french fries in 2016 was $900,000 \times \$0.50 = \$450,000$. A 15% fall in the price of onion rings from 2015 to 2016 means that the 2016 price of onion rings was $0.85 \times \$0.60 = \$0.51$. A 5% rise in servings sold means that $800,000 \times 1.05 = 840,000$ servings were sold in 2016. As a result, the total value of sales of onion rings in 2016 was $840,000 \times \$0.51 = \$428,400$. Nominal GDP in 2016 was $\$450,000 + \$428,400 = \$878,400$. To find real GDP in 2016, we must calculate the value of sales in 2016 using 2015 prices: $(900,000$ french fries $\times \$0.40) + (840,000$ onion rings $\times \$0.60) = \$360,000 + \$504,000 = \$864,000$.

   b. The change in nominal GDP from 2015 to 2016 was $((\$878,400 - \$880,000)/\$880,000) \times 100 = -0.18\%$, a decline. But a comparison using real GDP shows a decline of $((\$864,000 - \$880,000)/\$880,000) \times 100 = -1.8\%$. That is, a calculation based on real GDP shows a drop 10 times larger (1.8%) than a calculation based on nominal GDP (0.18%). In this case, the calculation based on nominal GDP underestimates the true magnitude of the change.

2. A price index based on 2010 prices will contain a relatively high price of electronics and a relatively low price of housing compared to a price index based on 2015 prices. This means that a 2010 price index used to calculate real GDP in 2013 will magnify the value of electronics production in the economy, but a 2015 price index will magnify the value of housing production in the economy.

13-3 Check Your Understanding

1. This market basket costs, pre-frost, $(100 \times \$0.20) + (50 \times \$0.60) + (200 \times \$0.25) = \$20 + \$30 + \$50 = \$100$. The same market basket, post-frost, costs $(100 \times \$0.40) + (50 \times \$1.00) + (200 \times \$0.45) = \$40 + \$50 + \$90 = \$180$. So the price index is $(\$100/\$100) \times 100 = 100$ before the frost and $(\$180/\$100) \times 100 = 180$ after the frost, implying a rise in the price index of 80%. This increase in the price index is less than the 84.2% increase calculated in the text. The reason for this difference is that the new market basket of 100 oranges, 50 grapefruit, and 200 lemons contains proportionately more of the items that have experienced relatively lower price increases (the lemons, whose price has increased by 80%) and proportionately fewer of the items that have experienced relatively large price increases (the oranges, whose price has increased by 100%). This shows that the price index can be very sensitive to the composition of the market basket. If the market basket contains a large proportion of goods whose prices have risen faster than the prices of other goods, it will lead to a higher estimate of the increase in the price level. If it contains a large proportion of goods whose prices have risen more slowly than the prices of

other goods, it will lead to a lower estimate of the increase in the price level.

2. **a.** A market basket determined 10 years ago will contain fewer cars than at present. Given that the average price of a car has grown faster than the average prices of other goods, this basket will underestimate the true increase in the cost of living because it contains relatively too few cars.

   b. A market basket determined 20 years ago will not contain broadband internet access. So it cannot track the fall in prices of internet access over the past few years. As a result, it will overestimate the true increase in the cost of living.

3. Using Equation 13-3, the inflation rate from 2015 to 2016 is $((242.821 - 237.846)/237.846) \times 100 = 2.09\%$.

CHAPTER FOURTEEN

14-1 Check Your Understanding

1. Software improvements developed by employment websites that enable job-seekers to find jobs more quickly will reduce the unemployment rate over time. However, websites that induce discouraged workers to begin actively looking for work again will lead to an increase in the unemployment rate over time.

2. **a.** Rosa is not counted as unemployed because she is not actively looking for work, but she is counted in broader measures of labor underutilization as a discouraged worker.

   b. Anthony is not counted as unemployed; he is considered employed because he has a job.

   c. Kanako is unemployed; she is not working and is actively looking for work.

   d. Sergio is not unemployed, but underemployed; he is working part time for economic reasons. He is counted in broader measures of labor underutilization.

   e. Natasha is not unemployed, but she is a marginally attached worker. She is counted in broader measures of labor underutilization.

3. Both parts a and b are consistent with the relationship, illustrated in Figure 14-5, between above-average or below-average growth in real GDP and changes in the unemployment rate: during years of above-average growth, the unemployment rate falls, and during years of below-average growth, the unemployment rate rises. However, part c is not consistent: it implies that a recession is associated with a fall in the unemployment rate, which is incorrect.

14-2 Check Your Understanding

1. **a.** When the pace of technological advance quickens, there will be higher rates of job creation and destruction as old industries disappear and new ones emerge. As a result, frictional unemployment will be higher as workers leave jobs in declining industries in search of jobs in expanding industries.

   b. When the pace of technological advance quickens, there will be greater mismatch between the skills employees have and the skills employers are looking for, leading to higher structural unemployment.

   c. When the unemployment rate is low, frictional unemployment will account for a larger share of total unemployment because other sources of unemployment will be diminished. So the share of total unemployment composed of the frictionally unemployed will rise.

2. A binding minimum wage represents a price floor below which wages cannot fall. As a result, actual wages cannot move toward equilibrium. So, a minimum wage causes the quantity of labor supplied to exceed the quantity of labor demanded. Because this surplus of labor reflects unemployed workers, it affects the unemployment rate. Collective bargaining has a similar effect—unions are able to raise the wage above the equilibrium level to a level like W_U in the accompanying diagram. This will act like a minimum wage by causing the number of job-seekers to be larger than the number of workers firms are willing to hire. Collective bargaining causes the unemployment rate to be higher than it otherwise would be, as shown in the accompanying diagram.

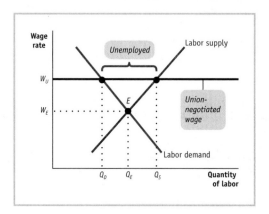

3. An increase in unemployment benefits at the peak of the business cycle reduces the cost to individuals of being unemployed, causing them to spend more time searching for new jobs. So the natural rate of unemployment would increase.

14-3 Check Your Understanding

1. Shoe-leather costs as a result of inflation will be lower because it is now less costly for individuals to manage their assets in order to economize on their money holdings. This reduction in the costs associated with converting other assets into money translates into lower shoe-leather costs.

2. If inflation came to an unexpected and complete stop over the next 15 or 20 years, the inflation rate would be zero, which of course is less than the expected inflation rate of 2% to 3%. Because the real interest rate is the nominal interest rate minus the inflation rate, the real interest rate on a loan would be higher than expected, and lenders would gain at the expense of borrowers. Borrowers would have to repay their loans with funds that have a higher real value than had been expected.

CHAPTER FIFTEEN

15-1 Check Your Understanding

1. Economic progress raises the living standards of the average resident of a country. An increase in overall real GDP does not accurately reflect an increase in an average

resident's living standard because it does not account for growth in the number of residents. If, for example, real GDP rises by 10% but population grows by 20%, the living standard of the average resident falls: after the change, the average resident has only $(110/120) \times 100 = 91.7\%$ as much real income as before the change. Similarly, an increase in nominal GDP per capita does not accurately reflect an increase in living standards because it does not account for any change in prices. For example, a 5% increase in nominal GDP per capita generated by a 5% increase in prices implies that there has been no change in living standards. Real GDP per capita is the only measure that accounts for both changes in the population and changes in prices.

2. Using the Rule of 70, the number of years it will take for China to double its real GDP per capita is $(70/7.8) = 8.97$, or approximately 9 years; India: $(70/4.3) = 16.28$, or approximately 16 years; Ireland: $(70/3.7) = 18.9$, or approximately 19 years; the United States: $(70/1.6) = 43.75$, or approximately 44 years; France: $(70/1.2) = 58.33$, or approximately 58 years; and Argentina: $(70/0.6) = 116.67$, or approximately 117 years. Since the Rule of 70 can only be applied to a positive growth rate, we cannot apply it to the case of Zimbabwe, which experienced negative growth. If India continues to have a higher growth rate of real GDP per capita than the United States, then India's real GDP per capita will eventually surpass that of the United States.

3. The United States began growing rapidly over a century ago, but China and India have begun growing rapidly only recently. As a result, the living standard of the typical Chinese or Indian household has not yet caught up with that of the typical American household.

15-2 Check Your Understanding

1. **a.** Significant technological progress will result in a positive growth rate of productivity even though physical capital per worker and human capital per worker are unchanged.

   b. The growth rate of productivity will fall but remain positive due to diminishing returns to physical capital.

2. **a.** If output has grown 3% per year and the labor force has grown 1% per year, then productivity—output per person—has grown at approximately $3\% - 1\% = 2\%$ per year.

   b. If physical capital has grown 4% per year and the labor force has grown 1% per year, then physical capital per worker has grown at approximately $4\% - 1\% = 3\%$ per year.

   c. According to estimates, each 1% rise in physical capital, other things equal, increases productivity by 0.3%. So, as physical capital per worker has increased by 3%, productivity growth that can be attributed to an increase in physical capital per worker is $0.3 \times 3\% = 0.9\%$. As a percentage of total productivity growth, this is $0.9\%/2\% \times 100\% = 45\%$.

   d. If the rest of productivity growth is due to technological progress, then technological progress has contributed $2\% - 0.9\% = 1.1\%$ to productivity growth. As a percentage of total productivity growth, this is $1.1\%/2\% \times 100\% = 55\%$.

3. It will take a period of time for workers to learn how to use the new computer system and to adjust their routines. And because there are often setbacks in learning a new system, such as accidentally erasing your computer files, productivity at Multinomics may decrease for a period of time.

15-3 Check Your Understanding

1. A country that has high domestic savings is able to achieve a high rate of investment spending as a percent of GDP. This, in turn, allows the country to achieve a high growth rate.

2. It is likely that the United States will experience a greater pace of innovation and development of new drugs because closer links between private companies and academic research centers will lead to research and development more directly focused on producing new drugs rather than on pure research.

3. It is likely that these events resulted in a fall in the country's growth rate because the lack of property rights would have dissuaded people from making investments in a productive capacity.

15-4 Check Your Understanding

1. The conditional version of the convergence hypothesis says that countries grow faster, other things equal, when they start from relatively low GDP per capita. From this we can infer that they grow more slowly, other things equal, when their real GDP per capita is relatively higher. This points to lower future Asian growth. However, other things might not be equal: if Asian economies continue investing in human capital, if savings rates continue to be high, if governments invest in infrastructure, and so on, growth might continue at an accelerated pace.

2. The regions of East Asia, Western Europe, and the United States support the convergence hypothesis because a comparison among them shows that the growth rate of real GDP per capita falls as real GDP per capita rises. Eastern Europe, West Asia, Latin America, and Africa do not support the hypothesis because they all have much lower real GDP per capita than the United States but have either approximately the same growth rate (West Asia and Eastern Europe) or a lower growth rate (Africa and Latin America).

3. The evidence suggests that both sets of factors matter: better infrastructure is important for growth, but so is political and financial stability. Policies should try to address both areas.

15-5 Check Your Understanding

1. Economists are typically more concerned about environmental degradation than resource scarcity. The reason is that in modern economies the price response tends to alleviate the limits imposed by resource scarcity through conservation and the development of alternatives. However, because environmental degradation involves a cost imposed by individuals or firms on others without the requirement to pay compensation (known as a *negative externality*), effective government intervention is required to address it. As a result, economists are more concerned about the limits to growth imposed by environmental degradation because a market response would be inadequate.

2. Growth increases a country's greenhouse gas emissions. The current best estimates, however, are that a large reduction in emissions will result in only a modest reduction in growth. The international burden sharing of greenhouse gas emissions reduction is contentious because rich countries are reluctant to pay the costs of reducing their emissions only to see newly emerging countries like China rapidly increase their emissions. Yet most of the current accumulation of gases is due to the past actions of rich countries. Poorer countries like China are equally reluctant to sacrifice their growth to pay for the past actions of rich countries.

CHAPTER SIXTEEN

16-1 Check Your Understanding

1. **a.** This is a shift of the aggregate demand curve. A decrease in the quantity of money raises the interest rate, since people now want to borrow less and lend more. A higher interest rate reduces investment and consumer spending at any given aggregate price level. So the aggregate demand curve shifts to the left.

    b. This is a movement up along the aggregate demand curve. As the aggregate price level rises, the real value of money holdings falls. This is the interest rate effect of a change in the aggregate price level: as the value of money falls, people want to hold more money. They do so by borrowing more and lending less. This leads to a rise in the interest rate and a reduction in consumer and investment spending. So it is a movement along the aggregate demand curve.

    c. This is a shift of the aggregate demand curve. Expectations of a poor job market, and so lower average disposable incomes, will reduce people's consumer spending today at any given aggregate price level. So the aggregate demand curve shifts to the left.

    d. This is a shift of the aggregate demand curve. A fall in tax rates raises people's disposable income. At any given aggregate price level, consumer spending is now higher. So the aggregate demand curve shifts to the right.

    e. This is a movement down along the aggregate demand curve. As the aggregate price level falls, the real value of assets rises. This is the wealth effect of a change in the aggregate price level: as the value of assets rises, people will increase their consumption plans. This leads to higher consumer spending. So it is a movement along the aggregate demand curve.

    f. This is a shift of the aggregate demand curve. A rise in the real value of assets in the economy due to a surge in real estate values raises consumer spending at any given aggregate price level. So the aggregate demand curve shifts to the right.

16-2 Check Your Understanding

1. **a.** This represents a movement along the SRAS curve because the CPI—like the GDP deflator—is a measure of the aggregate price level, the overall price level of final goods and services in the economy.

    b. This represents a shift of the SRAS curve because oil is a commodity. The SRAS curve will shift to the right because production costs are now lower, leading to a

higher quantity of aggregate output supplied at any given aggregate price level.

    c. This represents a shift of the SRAS curve because it involves a change in nominal wages. An increase in legally mandated benefits to workers is equivalent to an increase in nominal wages. As a result, the SRAS curve will shift leftward because production costs are now higher, leading to a lower quantity of aggregate output supplied at any given aggregate price level.

2. You would need to know what happened to the aggregate price level. If the increase in the quantity of aggregate output supplied was due to a movement along the SRAS curve, the aggregate price level would have increased at the same time as the quantity of aggregate output supplied increased. If the increase in the quantity of aggregate output supplied was due to a rightward shift of the LRAS curve, the aggregate price level might not rise. Alternatively, you could make the determination by observing what happened to aggregate output in the long run. If it fell back to its initial level in the long run, then the temporary increase in aggregate output was due to a movement along the SRAS curve. If it stayed at the higher level in the long run, the increase in aggregate output was due to a rightward shift of the LRAS curve.

16-3 Check Your Understanding

1. **a.** An increase in the minimum wage raises the nominal wage and, as a result, shifts the short-run aggregate supply curve to the left. As a result of this negative supply shock, the aggregate price level rises and aggregate output falls.

    b. Increased investment spending shifts the aggregate demand curve to the right. As a result of this positive demand shock, both the aggregate price level and aggregate output rise.

    c. An increase in taxes and a reduction in government spending both result in negative demand shocks, shifting the aggregate demand curve to the left. As a result, both the aggregate price level and aggregate output fall.

    d. This is a negative supply shock, shifting the short-run aggregate supply curve to the left. As a result, the aggregate price level rises and aggregate output falls.

2. As the rise in productivity increases potential output, the long-run aggregate supply curve shifts to the right. If, in the short run, there is now a recessionary gap (aggregate output is less than potential output), nominal wages will fall, shifting the short-run aggregate supply curve to the right. This results in a fall in the aggregate price level and a rise in aggregate output. As prices fall, we move along the aggregate demand curve due to the wealth and interest rate effects of a change in the aggregate price level. Eventually, as long-run macroeconomic equilibrium is reestablished, aggregate output will rise to be equal to potential output.

16-4 Check Your Understanding

1. **a.** An economy is overstimulated when an inflationary gap is present. This will arise if an expansionary monetary or fiscal policy is implemented when the economy is currently in long-run macroeconomic equilibrium. This shifts the aggregate demand curve to the right, in the short run raising the aggregate price level and aggregate

output and creating an inflationary gap. Eventually nominal wages will rise and shift the short-run aggregate supply curve to the left, and aggregate output will fall back to potential output. This is the scenario envisaged by the speaker.

b. No, this is not a valid argument. When the economy is not currently in long-run macroeconomic equilibrium, an expansionary monetary or fiscal policy does not lead to the outcome described above. Suppose a negative demand shock has shifted the aggregate demand curve to the left, resulting in a recessionary gap. An expansionary monetary or fiscal policy can shift the aggregate demand curve back to its original position in long-run macroeconomic equilibrium. In this way, the short-run fall in aggregate output and deflation caused by the original negative demand shock can be avoided. So, if used in response to demand shocks, fiscal or monetary policy is an effective policy tool.

2. Those within the Fed who advocated lowering interest rates were focused on boosting aggregate demand in order to counteract the negative demand shock caused by the collapse of the housing bubble. Lowering interest rates will result in a rightward shift of the aggregate demand curve, increasing aggregate output but raising the aggregate price level. Those within the Fed who advocated holding interest rates steady were focused on the fact that fighting the slump in aggregate demand in the face of a negative supply shock could result in a rise in inflation. Holding interest rates steady relies on the ability of the economy to self-correct in the long run, with the aggregate price level and aggregate output only gradually returning to their levels before the negative supply shock.

‖ CHAPTER SEVENTEEN

17-1 Check Your Understanding

1. a. This is a contractionary fiscal policy because it is a reduction in government purchases of goods and services.

b. This is an expansionary fiscal policy because it is an increase in government transfers that will increase disposable income.

c. This is a contractionary fiscal policy because it is an increase in taxes that will reduce disposable income.

2. Federal disaster relief that is quickly disbursed is more effective than legislated aid because there is very little time lag between the time of the disaster and the time it is received by victims. So, it will stabilize the economy after a disaster. In contrast, legislated aid is likely to entail a time lag in its disbursement, potentially destabilizing the economy.

3. This statement implies that expansionary fiscal policy will result in crowding out of the private sector, and that the opposite, contractionary fiscal policy, will lead the private sector to grow. Whether this statement is true or not depends upon whether the economy is at full employment; it is only then that we should expect expansionary fiscal policy to lead to crowding out. If, instead, the economy has a recessionary gap, then we should expect that the private sector grows along with the fiscal expansion, and contracts along with a fiscal contraction.

17-2 Check Your Understanding

1. A $500 million increase in government purchases of goods and services directly increases aggregate spending by $500 million, which then starts the multiplier in motion. It will increase real GDP by $500 million $\times 1/(1-MPC)$. A $500 million increase in government transfers increases aggregate spending only to the extent that it leads to an increase in consumer spending. Consumer spending rises by $MPC \times \$1$ for every $1 increase in disposable income, where MPC is less than 1. So a $500 million increase in government transfers will cause a rise in real GDP only MPC times as much as a $500 million increase in government purchases of goods and services. It will increase real GDP by $500 million $\times MPC/(1-MPC)$.

2. This is the same issue as in Problem 1, but in reverse. If government purchases of goods and services fall by $500 million, the initial fall in aggregate spending is $500 million. If there is a $500 million reduction in government transfers, the initial fall in aggregate spending is $MPC \times \$500$ million, which is less than $500 million.

3. Boldovia will experience greater variation in its real GDP than Moldovia because Moldovia has automatic stabilizers while Boldovia does not. In Moldovia the effects of slumps will be lessened by unemployment insurance benefits that will support residents' incomes, while the effects of booms will be diminished because tax revenues will go up. In contrast, incomes will not be supported in Boldovia during slumps because there is no unemployment insurance. In addition, because Boldovia has lump-sum taxes, its booms will not be diminished by increases in tax revenue.

17-3 Check Your Understanding

1. The actual budget balance takes into account the effects of the business cycle on the budget deficit. During recessionary gaps, it incorporates the effect of lower tax revenues and higher transfers on the budget balance; during inflationary gaps, it incorporates the effect of higher tax revenues and reduced transfers. In contrast, the cyclically adjusted budget balance factors out the effects of the business cycle and assumes that real GDP is at potential output. Since, in the long run, real GDP tends to potential output, the cyclically adjusted budget balance is a better measure of the long-run sustainability of government policies.

2. In recessions, real GDP falls. This implies that consumers' incomes, consumer spending, and producers' profits also fall. So in recessions, states' tax revenue (which depends in large part on consumers' incomes, consumer spending, and producers' profits) falls. In order to balance the state budget, states have to cut spending or raise taxes. But that deepens the recession. Without a balanced-budget requirement, states could use expansionary fiscal policy during a recession to lessen the fall in real GDP.

17-4 Check Your Understanding

1. a. A higher growth rate of real GDP implies that tax revenue will increase. If government spending remains constant and the government runs a budget surplus, the size of the public debt will be less than it would otherwise have been.

b. If retirees live longer, the average age of the population increases. As a result, the implicit liabilities of the government increase because spending on programs for older Americans, such as Social Security and Medicare, will rise.

c. A decrease in tax revenue without offsetting reductions in government spending will cause the public debt to increase.

d. Public debt will increase as a result of government borrowing to pay interest on its current public debt.

2. In order to stimulate the economy in the short run, the government can use fiscal policy to increase real GDP. This entails borrowing, which increases the size of the public debt further and leads to undesirable consequences: in extreme cases, governments can be forced to default on their debts. Even in less extreme cases, a large public debt is undesirable because government borrowing crowds out borrowing for private investment spending. This reduces the amount of investment spending, reducing the long-run growth of the economy.

3. A contractionary fiscal policy like austerity reduces government spending, which in turn reduces income and reduces tax revenue. With less tax revenue, the government is less able to pay its debts. Also, a failing economy causes lenders to have less confidence that a government is able to pay its debts and leads them to raise interest rates on the debt. Higher interest rates on the debt make it even less likely the government can repay.

‖ CHAPTER EIGHTEEN

18-1 Check Your Understanding

1. The defining characteristic of money is its liquidity: how easily it can be used to purchase goods and services. Although a gift card can easily be used to purchase a very defined set of goods or services (the goods or services available at the store issuing the gift card), it cannot be used to purchase any other goods or services. A gift card is therefore not money, since it cannot easily be used to purchase all goods and services.

2. Again, the important characteristic of money is its liquidity: how easily it can be used to purchase goods and services. M1, the narrowest definition of the money supply, contains only currency in circulation, checkable bank deposits, and traveler's checks. CDs aren't checkable—and they can't be made checkable without incurring a cost because there's a penalty for early withdrawal. This makes them less liquid than the assets counted in M1.

3. Commodity-backed money uses resources more efficiently than simple commodity money, like gold and silver coins, because commodity-backed money ties up fewer valuable resources. Although a bank must keep some of the commodity—generally gold and silver—on hand, it only has to keep enough to satisfy demand for redemptions. It can then lend out the remaining gold and silver, which allows society to use these resources for other purposes, with no loss in the ability to achieve gains from trade.

18-2 Check Your Understanding

1. Even though you know that the rumor about the bank is not true, you are concerned about other depositors pulling their money out of the bank. And you know that if enough other depositors pull their money out, the bank will fail. In that case, it is rational for you to pull your money out before the bank fails. All depositors will think like this, so even if they all know that the rumor is false, they may still rationally pull their money out, leading to a bank run. Deposit insurance leads depositors to worry less about the possibility of a bank run. Even if a bank fails, the FDIC will currently pay each depositor up to $250,000 per account. This will make you much less likely to pull your money out in response to a rumor. Since other depositors will think the same, there will be no bank run.

2. The aspects of modern bank regulation that would frustrate this scheme are *capital requirements* and *reserve requirements*. Capital requirements mean that a bank has to have a certain amount of capital—the difference between its assets (loans plus reserves) and its liabilities (deposits). The con artist could not open a bank without putting any of his own wealth in because the bank needs a certain amount of capital—that is, it needs to hold more assets (loans plus reserves) than deposits. So, the con artist would be at risk of losing his own wealth if his loans turn out badly.

18-3 Check Your Understanding

1. Since they only have to hold $100 in reserves, instead of $200, banks now lend out $100 of their reserves. Whoever borrows the $100 will deposit it in a bank, which will lend out $100 \times (1 - rr) = \$100 \times 0.9 = \$90$. Whoever borrows the $90 will put it into a bank, which will lend out $90 \times 0.9 = \$81$, and so on. Overall, deposits will increase by $\$100/0.1 = \$1,000$.

2. Silas puts $1,000 in the bank of which the bank lends out $\$1,000 \times (1 - rr) = \$1,000 \times 0.9 = \$900$. Whoever borrows the $900 will keep $450 in cash and deposit $450 in a bank. The bank will lend out $\$450 \times 0.9 = \$405$. Whoever borrows the $405 will keep $202.50 in cash and deposit $202.50 in a bank. The bank will lend out $\$202.50 \times 0.9 = \$182.25$, and so on. Overall, this leads to an increase in deposits of $\$1,000 + \$450 + \$202.50 + \ldots$ But it decreases the amount of currency in circulation: the amount of cash is reduced by the $1,000 Silas puts into the bank. This is offset, but not fully, by the amount of cash held by each borrower. The amount of currency in circulation therefore changes by $-\$1,000 + \$450 + \$202.50 + \ldots$ The money supply therefore increases by the sum of the increase in deposits and the change in currency in circulation, which is $\$1,000 - \$1,000 + \$450 + \$450 + \$202.50 + \$202.50 + \ldots$ and so on.

18-4 Check Your Understanding

1. An open-market purchase of $100 million by the Fed increases banks' reserves by $100 million as the Fed credits their accounts with additional reserves. In other words, this open-market purchase increases the monetary base (currency in circulation plus bank reserves) by $100 million. Banks lend out the additional $100 million. Whoever borrows the money puts it back into the banking system in the form of deposits. Of these deposits, banks lend out $100 million $\times (1 - rr) = \$100$ million $\times 0.9 = \$90$ million. Whoever borrows the money deposits it back into the banking system. And banks lend out $90 million $\times 0.9 = \$81$ million, and so on. As a result, bank deposits increase by $100 million $+ \$90$ million $+ \$81$ million $+ \ldots = \$100$ million/ $rr = \$100$ million/0.1 = \$1,000$ million $= \$1$ billion. Since in this simplified example all money lent out is deposited back into the banking system, there is no increase of currency in circulation, so the increase in bank deposits is equal to the increase in the money supply.

In other words, the money supply increases by $1 billion. This is greater than the increase in the monetary base by a factor of 10: in this simplified model in which deposits are the only component of the money supply and in which banks hold no excess reserves, the money multiplier is $1/rr = 10$.

18-5 Check Your Understanding

1. The Panic of 1907, the S&L crisis, and the crisis of 2008 all involved losses by shadow bank–like financial institutions that were less regulated than traditional depository banks. In the crises of 1907 and 2008, there was a widespread loss of confidence in the financial sector and a collapse of credit markets. Like the crisis of 1907 and the S&L crisis, the crisis of 2008 exerted a powerful negative effect on the economy.

2. The creation of the Federal Reserve failed to prevent bank runs because it did not eradicate the fears of depositors that a bank collapse would cause them to lose their money. The bank runs eventually stopped after federal deposit insurance was instituted and the public came to understand that their deposits were now protected.

3. Extraordinary measures were needed to address the financial crisis of 2008 because the failure of unregulated shadow banks, like Lehman Brothers, led to increased panic in markets as asset prices tumbled and credit markets froze for households and businesses. The failure of shadow banks also put the entire financial system at risk of failure, both the financially sound traditional depository banks and nondepository financial institutions that were eventually deemed too critical to the economy to fail.

‖ CHAPTER NINETEEN

19-1 Check Your Understanding

1. **a.** By increasing the opportunity cost of holding money, a high interest rate reduces the quantity of money demanded. This is a movement up and to the left along the money demand curve.

   b. A 10% fall in prices reduces the quantity of money demanded at any given interest rate, shifting the money demand curve leftward.

   c. This technological change reduces the quantity of money demanded at any given interest rate. So it shifts the money demand curve leftward.

   d. This will increase the demand for money at any given interest rate. With more of the economy's assets in overseas bank accounts that are difficult to access, people will want to hold more cash to finance purchases. The money demand curve shifts to the right.

2. **a.** The 0.5% interest paid on cash balances will reduce the opportunity cost of holding cash for PayBuddy customers because they now forgo less by holding cash.

   b. An increase in the interest paid on six-month CDs raises the opportunity cost of holding cash because holding cash requires forgoing the higher interest paid.

   c. One year of zero-interest financing on holiday purchases increases the opportunity cost of holding cash. A holiday shopper need not convert interest-paying assets into cash in order to avoid paying interest on credit card purchases. So what a shopper forgoes by paying for holiday

purchases with cash instead of charging it on a credit card has increased.

19-2 Check Your Understanding

1. In the accompanying diagram, the increase in the demand for money is shown as a rightward shift of the money demand curve, from MD_1 to MD_2. This raises the equilibrium interest rate from r_1 to r_2.

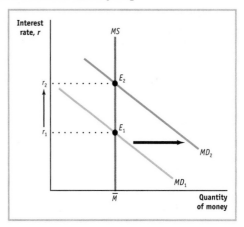

2. In order to prevent the interest rate from rising, the Federal Reserve must make an open-market purchase of Treasury bills, shifting the money supply curve rightward. This is shown in the accompanying diagram as the move from MS_1 to MS_2.

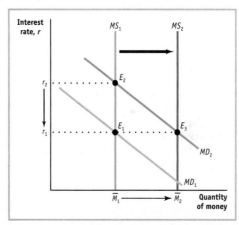

3. **a.** Malia is better off buying a one-year bond today and a one-year bond next year because this allows her to get the higher interest rate one year from now.

   b. Malia is better off buying a two-year bond today because it gives her a higher interest rate in the second year than if she bought two one-year bonds.

19-3 Check Your Understanding

1. **a.** The money supply curve shifts to the right.

   b. The equilibrium interest rate falls.

   c. Investment spending rises, due to the fall in the interest rate.

   d. Consumer spending rises, due to the multiplier process.

   e. Aggregate output rises because of the rightward shift of the aggregate demand curve.

2. The central bank that uses a Taylor rule is likely to respond more directly to a financial crisis than one that uses inflation targeting because with a Taylor rule the central bank does not have to set policy to meet a pre-specified inflation target. Additionally, under the Taylor rule, central banks will respond directly to a change in the unemployment rate because in a financial crisis unemployment is more likely to increase than inflation is to decrease.

19-4 Check Your Understanding

1. a. Aggregate output rises in the short run, then falls back to potential output in the long run.

b. The aggregate price level rises in the short run, but by less than 25%. It rises further in the long run, for a total increase of 25%.

c. The interest rate falls in the short run, then rises back to its original level in the long run.

2. In the short run, a change in the interest rate alters the economy because it affects investment spending, which in turn affects aggregate demand and real GDP through the multiplier process. However, in the long run, changes in consumer spending and investment spending will eventually result in changes in nominal wages and the nominal prices of other factors of production. For example, an expansionary monetary policy will eventually cause a rise in factor prices; a contractionary monetary policy will eventually cause a fall in factor prices. In response, the short-run aggregate supply curve will shift to move the economy back to long-run equilibrium. So in the long run, monetary policy has no effect on the economy.

‖ CHAPTER TWENTY

20-1 Check Your Understanding

1. a. To determine comparative advantage, we must compare the two countries' opportunity costs for a given good. Take the opportunity cost of 1 ton of corn in terms of bicycles. In China, the opportunity cost of 1 bicycle is 0.01 ton of corn; so the opportunity cost of 1 ton of corn is 1/0.01 bicycles = 100 bicycles. The United States has the comparative advantage in corn since its opportunity cost in terms of bicycles is 50, a smaller number. Similarly, the opportunity cost in the United States of 1 bicycle in terms of corn is 1/50 ton of corn = 0.02 ton of corn. This is greater than 0.01, the Chinese opportunity cost of 1 bicycle in terms of corn, implying that China has a comparative advantage in bicycles.

b. Given that the United States can produce 200,000 bicycles if no corn is produced, it can produce 200,000 bicycles × 0.02 ton of corn/bicycle = 4,000 tons of corn when no bicycles are produced. Likewise, if China can produce 3,000 tons of corn if no bicycles are produced, it can produce 3,000 tons of corn × 100 bicycles/ton of corn = 300,000 bicycles if no corn is produced. These points determine the vertical and horizontal intercepts of the U.S. and Chinese production possibility frontiers, as shown in the accompanying diagram.

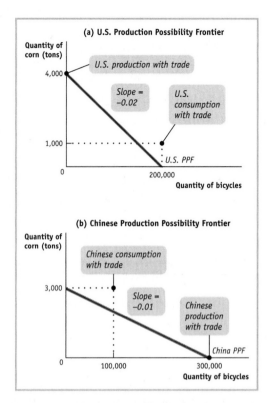

(a) U.S. Production Possibility Frontier

(b) Chinese Production Possibility Frontier

c. The diagram shows the production and consumption points of the two countries. Each country is clearly better off with international trade because each now consumes a bundle of the two goods that lies outside its own production possibility frontier, indicating that these bundles were unattainable in autarky.

2. a. According to the Heckscher–Ohlin model, this pattern of trade occurs because the United States has a relatively larger endowment of factors of production, such as human capital and physical capital, that are suited to the production of movies, but France has a relatively larger endowment of factors of production suited to wine-making, such as vineyards and the human capital of vintners.

b. According to the Heckscher–Ohlin model, this pattern of trade occurs because the United States has a relatively larger endowment of factors of production, such as human and physical capital, that are suited to making machinery, but Brazil has a relatively larger endowment of factors of production suited to shoe-making, such as unskilled labor and leather.

20-2 Check Your Understanding

1. In the accompanying diagram, P_A is the U.S. price of grapes in autarky and P_W is the world price of grapes under international trade. With trade, U.S. consumers pay a price of P_W for grapes and consume quantity Q_D, U.S. grape producers produce quantity Q_S, and the difference, $Q_D - Q_S$, represents imports of Mexican grapes. As a consequence of the strike by truckers, imports are halted, the price paid by American consumers rises to the autarky price, P_A, and U.S. consumption falls to the autarky quantity, Q_A.

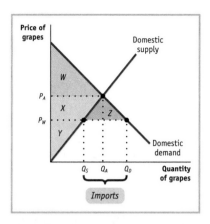

a. Before the strike, U.S. consumers enjoyed consumer surplus equal to areas $W + X + Z$. After the strike, their consumer surplus shrinks to W. So consumers are worse off, losing consumer surplus represented by $X + Z$.

b. Before the strike, U.S. producers had producer surplus equal to the area Y. After the strike, their producer surplus increases to $Y + X$. So U.S. producers are better off, gaining producer surplus represented by X.

c. U.S. total surplus falls as a result of the strike by an amount represented by area Z, the loss in consumer surplus that does not accrue to producers.

2. Mexican grape producers are worse off because they lose sales of exported grapes to the United States, and Mexican grape pickers are worse off because they lose the wages that were associated with the lost sales. The lower demand for Mexican grapes caused by the strike implies that the price Mexican consumers pay for grapes falls, making them better off. U.S. grape pickers are better off because their wages increase as a result of the increase of $Q_A - Q_S$ in U.S. sales.

20-3 Check Your Understanding

1. a. If the tariff is $0.50, the price paid by domestic consumers for a pound of imported butter is $0.50 + $0.50 = $1.00, the same price as a pound of domestic butter. Imported butter will no longer have a price advantage over domestic butter, imports will cease, and domestic producers will capture all the feasible sales to domestic consumers, selling amount Q_A in the accompanying figure. If the tariff is $0.25, the price paid by domestic consumers for a pound of imported butter is $0.50 + $0.25 = $0.75, $0.25 cheaper than a pound of domestic butter. American butter producers will gain sales in the amount of $Q_2 - Q_1$ as a result of the $0.25 tariff. But this is smaller than the amount they would have gained under the $0.50 tariff, the amount $Q_A - Q_1$.

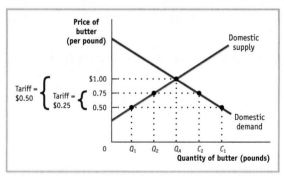

b. As long as the tariff is at least $0.50, increasing it more has no effect. At a tariff of $0.50, all imports are effectively blocked.

2. All imports are effectively blocked at a tariff of $0.50. So such a tariff corresponds to an import quota of 0.

20-4 Check Your Understanding

1. a. The sale of the new airplane to China represents an export of a good to China and so enters the current account.

   b. The sale of Boeing stock to Chinese investors is a sale of a U.S. asset and so enters the financial account.

   c. Even though the plane already exists, when it is shipped to China it is an export of a good from the United States. So the sale of the plane enters the current account.

   d. Because the plane stays in the United States, the Chinese investor is buying a U.S. asset. So this is identical to the answer to part b: the sale of the jet enters the financial account.

2. The collapse of the U.S. housing bubble and the ensuing recession led to a dramatic fall in interest rates in the United States because of the deeply depressed economy. Consequently, capital inflows into the United States dried up.

20-5 Check Your Understanding

1. a. The increased purchase of Mexican oil will cause U.S. individuals (and firms) to increase their demand for the peso. To purchase pesos, individuals will increase their supply of U.S. dollars to the foreign exchange market, causing a rightward shift in the supply curve of U.S. dollars. This will cause the peso price of the dollar to fall (the amount of pesos per dollar will fall). The peso has appreciated and the U.S. dollar has depreciated as a result.

   b. This appreciation of the peso means it will take more U.S. dollars to obtain the same quantity of Mexican pesos. If we assume that the price level (measured in Mexican pesos) of other Mexican goods and services does not change, other Mexican goods and services become more expensive to U.S. households and firms. The dollar cost of other Mexican goods and services will rise as the peso appreciates. So Mexican exports to the United States of goods and services other than oil will fall.

   c. Assuming that the U.S. price level (measured in U.S. dollars) does not change, the appreciation of the peso will make U.S. goods and services cheaper in terms of pesos. So Mexican imports from the United States of goods and services will rise.

2. a. The real exchange rate equals

$$\text{Pesos per U.S. dollar} \times \frac{\text{Aggregate price level in the United States}}{\text{Aggregate price level in Mexico}}$$

   Today, the aggregate price levels in both countries are both equal to 100. The real exchange rate today is $10 \times (100/100) = 10$. The aggregate price level in five years, in the United States, will be $100 \times (120/100) = 120$, and in Mexico it will be $100 \times (1,200/800) = 150$. The real exchange rate in five years, assuming the nominal exchange rate does not change, will be $10 \times (120/150) = 8$.

   b. Today, a basket of goods and services that costs $100 costs 800 pesos, so the purchasing power parity is 8 pesos per U.S. dollar. In five years, a basket that costs $120 will cost 1,200 pesos, so the purchasing power parity will be 10 pesos per U.S. dollar.

Glossary

A

absolute advantage the advantage an individual or country has in an activity if that individual or country can do it better than others.

absolute value the value of a number without regard to a plus or minus sign.

accounting profit a business's revenue minus the explicit cost and depreciation; usually larger than economic profit.

AD–AS model the basic model used to understand fluctuations in aggregate output and the aggregate price level. It uses the aggregate supply curve and the aggregate demand curve together to analyze the behavior of the economy in response to shocks or government policy.

administrative costs (of a tax) the resources used for its collection, for the method of payment, and for any attempts to evade the tax.

aggregate demand curve a graphical representation that shows the relationship between the aggregate price level and the quantity of aggregate output demanded by households, firms, the government, and the rest of the world. The aggregate demand curve has a negative slope due to the wealth effect of a change in the aggregate price level and the interest rate effect of a change in the aggregate price level.

aggregate output the economy's total quantity of output of final goods and services.

aggregate price level a measure of the overall level of prices in the economy.

aggregate production function a hypothetical function that shows how productivity (real GDP per worker) depends on the quantities of physical capital per worker and human capital per worker as well as the state of technology.

aggregate supply curve a graphical representation that shows the relationship between the aggregate price level and the total quantity of aggregate output supplied in the economy.

antitrust policy efforts undertaken by the government to prevent oligopolistic industries from becoming or behaving like monopolies.

appreciation a rise in the value of one currency in terms of other currencies.

autarky a situation in which a country does not trade with other countries.

automatic stabilizers government spending and taxation rules that cause fiscal policy to be automatically expansionary when the economy contracts and automatically contractionary when the economy expands without requiring any deliberate actions by policy makers. Taxes that depend on disposable income are the most important example of automatic stabilizers.

autonomous change in aggregate spending an initial rise or fall in aggregate spending at a given level of real GDP.

average cost an alternative term for average total cost; the total cost divided by the quantity of output produced.

average fixed cost the fixed cost per unit of output.

average total cost total cost divided by quantity of output produced. Also referred to as average cost.

average variable cost the variable cost per unit of output.

B

balance of payments accounts a summary of a country's transactions with other countries, including two main elements: the balance of payments on current account and the balance of payments on financial account.

balance of payments on current account (current account) transactions that don't create liabilities; a country's balance of payments on goods and services plus net international transfer payments and factor income.

balance of payments on financial account (financial account) international transactions that involve the sale or purchase of assets, and therefore create future liabilities.

balance of payments on goods and services the difference between the value of exports and the value of imports during a given period.

bank reserves currency held by banks in their vaults plus their deposits at the Federal Reserve.

bank run a phenomenon in which many of a bank's depositors try to withdraw their funds because of fears of a bank failure.

bar graph a graph that uses bars of varying height or length to show the comparative sizes of different observations of a variable.

barrier to entry something that prevents other firms from entering an industry. Crucial in protecting the profits of a monopolist.

barter a transaction in which people directly exchange goods or services that they have for goods or services that they want.

black market a market in which goods or services are bought and sold illegally, either because it is illegal to sell them at all or because the prices charged are legally prohibited by a price ceiling.

break-even price the market price at which a firm earns zero profits.

business cycle the short-run alternation between economic recessions and expansions.

business-cycle peak the point in time at which the economy shifts from expansion to recession.

business-cycle trough the point in time at which the economy shifts from recession to expansion.

C

cartel an agreement among several producers to obey output restrictions in order to increase their joint profits.

causal relationship the relationship between two variables in which the value taken by one variable directly influences or determines the value taken by the other variable.

central bank an institution that oversees and regulates the banking system and controls the monetary base.

certificate of deposit (CD) a bank-issued asset in which customers deposit funds for a specified amount of time and earn a specified interest rate.

chained dollars method of calculating real GDP that splits the difference between growth rates calculated using early base years and the growth rates calculated using late base years.

checkable bank deposits bank accounts on which people can write checks.

circular-flow diagram a diagram that represents the transactions in an economy by flows around a circle.

clean energy sources energy sources that do not emit greenhouse gases. Renewable energy sources are also clean energy sources.

climate change the man-made change in Earth's climate from the accumulation of greenhouse gases caused by the use of fossil fuels.

Coase theorem the proposition that even in the presence of externalities an economy can always reach an efficient solution as long as transaction costs are sufficiently low.

collusion cooperation among producers to limit production and raise prices so as to raise one another's profits.

commercial bank a bank that accepts deposits and is covered by deposit insurance.

commodity output of different producers regarded by consumers as the same good; also referred to as a standardized product.

commodity-backed money a medium of exchange that has no intrinsic value whose ultimate value is guaranteed by a promise that it can be converted into valuable goods on demand.

commodity money a medium of exchange that is a good, normally gold or silver, that has intrinsic value in other uses.

comparative advantage the advantage an individual or country has in producing a good or service if the opportunity cost of producing the good or service is lower for that individual or country than for others.

competitive market a market in which there are many buyers and sellers of the same good or service, none of whom can influence the price at which the good or service is sold.

complements pairs of goods for which a rise in the price of one good leads to a decrease in the demand for the other good.

constant returns to scale long-run average total cost is constant as output increases.

consumer price index (CPI) a measure of the cost of the market basket of a typical urban American family.

consumer surplus a term often used to refer both to individual consumer surplus and to total consumer surplus.

contractionary fiscal policy fiscal policy that reduces aggregate demand by decreasing government purchases, increasing taxes, or decreasing transfers.

contractionary monetary policy monetary policy that, through the raising of the interest rate, reduces aggregate demand and therefore output.

convergence hypothesis a principle of economic growth that holds that

international differences in real GDP per capita tend to narrow over time because countries that start with lower real GDP per capita tend to have higher growth rates.

copyright gives the creator of a literary or artistic work sole rights to profit from that work.

cost the lowest price at which a seller is willing to sell a good.

cost-benefit analysis the estimation and comparison of the social costs and social benefits of providing a public good.

cross-price elasticity of demand a measure of the effect of the change in the price of one good on the quantity demanded of the other; it is equal to the percent change in the quantity demanded of one good divided by the percent change in the price of another good.

currency in circulation actual cash held by the public.

curve a line on a graph, which may be curved or straight, that depicts a relationship between two variables.

cyclical unemployment the difference between the actual rate of unemployment and the natural rate of unemployment due to downturns in the business cycle.

cyclically adjusted budget balance an estimate of what the budget balance would be if real GDP were exactly equal to potential output.

D

deadweight loss the loss in total surplus that occurs whenever an action or a policy reduces the quantity transacted below the efficient market equilibrium quantity.

debt–GDP ratio government debt as a percentage of GDP; frequently used as a measure of a government's ability to pay its debts.

decreasing returns to scale long-run average total cost increases as output increases.

deflation a fall in the overall level of prices.

demand curve a graphical representation of the demand schedule, showing the relationship between quantity demanded and price.

demand price the price of a given quantity at which consumers will demand that quantity.

demand schedule shows how much of a good or service consumers will want to buy at different prices.

demand shock an event that shifts the aggregate demand curve. A positive demand shock is associated with higher demand for aggregate output at any price level and shifts the curve to the right. A negative demand shock is associated with lower demand for aggregate output at any price level and shifts the curve to the left.

dependent variable the determined variable in a causal relationship.

deposit insurance a guarantee that a bank's depositors will be paid even if the bank can't come up with the funds, up to a maximum amount per account.

depreciation a fall in the value of one currency in terms of other currencies.

diminishing returns to an input the effect observed when an increase in the quantity of an input, while holding the levels of all other inputs fixed, leads to a decline in the marginal product of that input.

diminishing returns to physical capital the effect on an aggregate production function when the amount of human capital per worker and the state of technology are held fixed: each successive increase in the amount of physical capital per worker leads to a smaller increase in productivity.

discount rate the rate of interest the Federal Reserve charges on loans to banks that fall short of reserve requirements.

discount window a protection against bank runs in which the Federal Reserve stands ready to lend money to banks in trouble.

discouraged workers nonworking people who are capable of working but have given up looking for a job given the state of the job market.

discretionary fiscal policy fiscal policy that is the direct result of deliberate actions by policy makers rather than rules.

disinflation the process of bringing the inflation rate down.

domestic demand curve a demand curve that shows how the quantity of a good demanded by domestic consumers depends on the price of that good.

domestic supply curve a supply curve that shows how the quantity of a good supplied by domestic producers depends on the price of that good.

dominant strategy a player's best action regardless of the action taken by the other player.

duopolist one of the two firms in a duopoly.

duopoly an oligopoly consisting of only two firms.

E

economic growth the growing ability of the economy to produce goods and services.

economic profit a business's revenue minus the opportunity cost of resources; usually less than the accounting profit.

economics the social science that studies the production, distribution, and consumption of goods and services.

economy a system for coordinating society's productive activities.

efficiency wages wages that employers set above the equilibrium wage rate as an incentive for workers to deliver better performance.

efficient describes a market or economy that takes all opportunities to make some people better off without making other people worse off.

elastic demand when the price elasticity of demand is greater than 1.

emissions tax a tax that depends on the amount of pollution a firm produces.

employment the number of people currently employed in the economy, either full time or part time.

environmental standards rules established by a government to protect the environment by specifying actions by producers and consumers.

equilibrium an economic situation in which no individual would be better off doing something different.

equilibrium exchange rate the exchange rate at which the quantity of a currency demanded in the foreign exchange market is equal to the quantity supplied.

equilibrium price the price at which the market is in equilibrium, that is, the quantity of a good or service demanded equals the quantity of that good or service supplied; also referred to as the market-clearing price.

equilibrium quantity the quantity of a good or service bought and sold at the equilibrium (or market-clearing) price.

equity fairness; everyone gets his or her fair share. Since people can disagree about what's "fair," equity isn't as well defined a concept as efficiency.

excess reserves a bank's reserves over and above the reserves required by law or regulation.

exchange rate the price at which currencies trade, determined by the foreign exchange market.

excise tax a tax on sales of a good or service.

excludable referring to a good, describes the case in which the supplier can prevent those who do not pay from consuming the good.

expansion period of economic upturn in which output and employment are rising; most economic numbers are following their normal upward trend; also referred to as a recovery.

expansionary fiscal policy fiscal policy that increases aggregate demand by increasing government purchases, decreasing taxes, or increasing transfers.

expansionary monetary policy monetary policy that, through the lowering of the interest rate, increases aggregate demand and therefore output.

explicit cost a cost that involves actually laying out money.

exporting industries industries that produce goods or services that are sold abroad.

exports goods and services sold to other countries.

external benefit a benefit that an individual or firm confers on others without receiving compensation.

external cost an uncompensated cost that an individual or firm imposes on others; also known as negative externalities.

externalities external benefits and external costs.

F

factor intensity the difference in the ratio of factors used to produce a good in various industries. For example, oil refining is capital-intensive compared to clothing manufacture because oil refiners use a higher ratio of capital to labor than do clothing producers.

factor markets markets in which firms buy the resources they need to produce goods and services.

factors of production the resources used to produce goods and services.

federal funds market the financial market that allows banks that fall short of reserve requirements to borrow funds from banks with excess reserves.

federal funds rate the interest rate at which funds are borrowed and lent in the federal funds market.

fiat money a medium of exchange whose value derives entirely from its official status as a means of payment.

final goods and services goods and services sold to the final, or end, user.

firm an organization that produces goods and services for sale.

fiscal policy changes in government spending and taxes designed to affect overall spending.

fiscal year the time period used for much of government accounting, running from October 1 to September 30. Fiscal years are labeled by the calendar year in which they end.

fixed cost a cost that does not depend on the quantity of output produced; the cost of a fixed input.

fixed input an input whose quantity is fixed for a period of time and cannot be varied.

forecast a simple prediction of the future.

foreign exchange market the market in which currencies can be exchanged for each other.

fossil fuels fuel derived from fossil sources such as coal and oil.

free entry and exit describes an industry that potential producers can easily enter or current producers can easily leave.

free trade trade that is unregulated by government tariffs or other artificial barriers; the levels of exports and imports occur naturally, as a result of supply and demand.

free-rider problem the problem that results when individuals have no incentive to pay for their own consumption of a good, they will take a "free ride" on anyone who does pay; a problem with goods that are nonexcludable.

frictional unemployment unemployment due to time workers spend in job search.

G

gains from trade an economic principle that states that by dividing tasks and trading, people can get more of what they want through trade than they could if they tried to be self-sufficient.

game theory the study of behavior in situations of interdependence.

GDP deflator a price measure for a given year that is equal to 100 times the ratio of nominal GDP to real GDP in that year.

GDP per capita GDP divided by the size of the population; equivalent to the average GDP per person.

Gini coefficient a number that summarizes a country's level of income inequality based on how unequally income is distributed across quintiles.

globalization the phenomenon of growing economic linkages among countries.

government transfer a government payment to an individual or a family.

greenhouse gases gas emissions that trap heat in Earth's atmosphere.

gross domestic product (GDP) the total value of all final goods and services produced in the economy during a given period, usually a year.

growth accounting an estimation of the contribution of each of the major factors (physical and human capital, labor, and technology) in the aggregate production function.

H

Heckscher–Ohlin model a model of international trade in which a country has a comparative advantage in a good whose production is intensive in the factors that are abundantly available in that country.

horizontal axis the number line along which values of the x-variable are measured; also referred to as the x-axis.

horizontal intercept the point at which a curve hits the horizontal axis; it indicates the value of the x-variable when the value of the y-variable is zero.

household a person or a group of people who share income.

human capital the improvement in labor created by the education and knowledge embodied in the workforce.

Hyperglobalization the phenomenon of extremely high levels of international trade.

I

imperfect competition a market structure in which no firm is a monopolist, but producers nonetheless have market power they can use to affect market prices.

implicit cost a cost that does not require the outlay of money; it is measured by the value, in dollar terms, of forgone benefits.

implicit liabilities spending promises made by governments that are effectively a debt despite the fact that they are not included in the usual debt statistics. In the United States, the largest implicit liabilities arise from Social Security and Medicare, which promise transfer payments to current and future retirees (Social Security) and to the elderly (Medicare).

import-competing industries industries that produce goods or services that are also imported.

import quota a legal limit on the quantity of a good that can be imported.

imports goods and services purchased from other countries.

incentive anything that offers rewards to people who change their behavior.

income distribution the way in which total income is divided among the owners of the various factors of production.

income-elastic demand when the income elasticity of demand for a good is greater than 1.

income elasticity of demand the percent change in the quantity of a good demanded when a consumer's income changes divided by the percent change in the consumer's income.

income-inelastic demand when the income elasticity of demand for a good is positive but less than 1.

increasing returns to scale long-run average total cost declines as output increases.

independent variable the determining variable in a causal relationship.

individual choice the decision by an individual of what to do, which necessarily involves a decision of what not to do.

individual consumer surplus the net gain to an individual buyer from the purchase of a good; equal to the difference between the buyer's willingness to pay and the price paid.

individual demand curve a graphical representation of the relationship between quantity demanded and price for an individual consumer.

individual producer surplus the net gain to an individual seller from selling a good; equal to the difference between the price received and the seller's cost.

individual supply curve illustrates the relationship between quantity supplied and price for an individual consumer.

industry supply curve a graphical representation that shows the relationship between the price of a good and the total output of the industry for that good.

inefficient allocation to consumers a form of inefficiency in which people who want a good badly and are willing to pay a high price don't get it, and those who care relatively little about the good and are only willing to pay a low price do get it; often a result of a price ceiling.

inefficient allocation of sales among sellers a form of inefficiency in which sellers who are willing to sell at the lowest price are unable to make sales while sales go to sellers who are only willing to sell at a higher price.

inefficiently high quality a form of inefficiency in which sellers offer high-quality goods at a high price even though buyers would prefer a lower quality at a lower price; often the result of a price floor.

inefficiently low quality a form of inefficiency in which sellers offer low-quality goods at a low price even though buyers would prefer a higher quality at a higher price; often a result of a price ceiling.

inelastic demand when the price elasticity of demand is less than 1.

inferior good a good for which a rise in income decreases the demand for the good.

inflation a rise in the overall level of prices.

inflation rate the percent change per year in a price index—typically the consumer price index.

inflation targeting an approach to monetary policy that requires that the central bank try to keep the inflation rate near a predetermined target rate.

inflationary gap exists when aggregate output is above potential output.

infrastructure physical capital, such as roads, power lines, ports, information networks, and other parts of an economy, that provides the underpinnings, or foundation, for economic activity.

in-kind benefit a benefit given in the form of goods or services.

input a good or service used to produce another good or service.

interaction (of choices) my choices affect your choices, and vice versa; a feature of most economic situations. The results of this interaction are often quite different from what the individuals intend.

interdependence when a firm's decision significantly affects the profits of other firms in the industry.

interest rate (of a loan) the price, calculated as a percentage of the amount borrowed, that a lender charges a borrower for the use of the borrower's savings for one year.

interest rate effect of a change in the aggregate price level the effect on consumer spending and investment spending caused by a change in the purchasing power of consumers' money holdings when the aggregate price level changes. A rise (fall) in the aggregate price level decreases (increases) the purchasing power of consumers' money holdings. In response, consumers try to increase (decrease) their money holdings, which drives up (down) interest rates, thereby decreasing (increasing) consumption and investment.

intermediate goods and services goods and services, bought from one firm by another firm, that are inputs for production of final goods and services.

internalize the externality when individuals take into account external costs and external benefits.

investment bank a bank that trades in financial assets and is not covered by deposit insurance.

invisible hand refers to the way in which the individual pursuit of self-interest can lead to good results for society as a whole.

J

job search the time spent by workers looking for employment.

jobless recovery a period in which the real GDP growth rate is positive but the unemployment rate is still rising.

K

Keynesian economics a theory that states that economic slumps are caused by inadequate spending and they can be mitigated by government intervention.

L

labor force the sum of employment and unemployment.

labor force participation rate the percentage of the population age 16 or older that is in the labor force.

labor productivity output per worker; also referred to as simply productivity.

law of demand the principle that a higher price for a good or service, other things equal, leads people to demand a smaller quantity of that good or service.

license the right, conferred by the government or an owner, to supply a good.

linear relationship the relationship between two variables in which the slope is constant and therefore is depicted on a graph by a curve that is a straight line.

liquidity preference model of the interest rate a model of the market for money in which the interest rate is determined by the supply and demand for money.

long run the time period in which all inputs can be varied.

long-run aggregate supply curve a graphical representation that shows the relationship between the aggregate price level and the quantity of aggregate output supplied that would exist if all prices, including nominal wages,

were fully flexible. The long-run aggregate supply curve is vertical because the aggregate price level has no effect on aggregate output in the long run; in the long run, aggregate output is determined by the economy's potential output.

long-run average total cost curve a graphical representation showing the relationship between output and average total cost when fixed cost has been chosen to minimize average total cost for each level of output.

long-run economic growth the sustained upward trend in the economy's output over time.

long-run industry supply curve a graphical representation that shows how quantity supplied responds to price once producers have had time to enter or exit the industry.

long-run macroeconomic equilibrium the point at which the short-run macroeconomic equilibrium is on the long-run aggregate supply curve; so short-run equilibrium aggregate output is equal to potential output.

long-run market equilibrium an economic balance in which, given sufficient time for producers to enter or exit an industry, the quantity supplied equals the quantity demanded.

long-term interest rate the interest rate on financial assets that mature a number of years into the future.

lump-sum taxes taxes that don't depend on the taxpayer's income.

M

macroeconomics the branch of economics that is concerned with the overall ups and downs in the economy.

marginal analysis the study of marginal decisions.

marginal benefit the additional benefit derived from producing one more unit of a good or service.

marginal cost the additional cost incurred by producing one more unit of a good or service.

marginal decision a decision made at the "margin" of an activity to do a bit more or a bit less of that activity.

marginal product the additional quantity of output produced by using one more unit of a given input.

marginal propensity to consume (*MPC*) the increase in consumer spending when disposable income rises by $1. Because consumers normally spend part but not all of an additional dollar of disposable income, *MPC* is between 0 and 1.

marginal revenue the change in total revenue generated by an additional unit of output.

marginal revenue curve a graphical representation showing how marginal revenue varies as output varies.

marginal social benefit of pollution the additional gain to society as a whole from an additional unit of pollution.

marginal social cost of pollution the additional cost imposed on society as a whole by an additional unit of pollution.

marginally attached workers nonworking individuals who say they would like a job and have looked for work in the recent past but are not currently looking for work.

market basket a hypothetical set of consumer purchases of goods and services.

market-clearing price the price at which the market is in equilibrium, that is, the quantity of a good or service demanded equals the quantity of that good or service supplied; also referred to as the equilibrium price.

market economy an economy in which decisions about production and consumption are made by individual producers and consumers.

market failure refers to the way in which the individual pursuit of self-interest can lead to bad results for society as a whole.

market power the ability of a firm to raise prices.

market share the fraction of the total industry output accounted for by a given producer's output.

markets for goods and services markets in which firms sell goods and services that they produce to households.

maximum the highest point on a nonlinear curve, where the slope changes from positive to negative.

mean household income the average income across all households.

means-tested a program available only to individuals or families whose incomes fall below a certain level.

median household income the income of the household lying at the exact middle of the income distribution.

medium of exchange an asset that individuals acquire for the purpose of trading for goods and services rather than for their own consumption.

menu cost the real cost of changing a listed price.

merchandise trade balance (trade balance) the difference between a country's exports and imports of goods alone—not including services.

microeconomics the branch of economics that studies how people make decisions and how those decisions interact.

midpoint method a technique for calculating the percent change in which changes in a variable are compared with the average, or midpoint, of the starting and final values.

minimum the lowest point on a nonlinear curve, where the slope changes from negative to positive.

minimum-cost output the quantity of output at which the average total cost is lowest—the bottom of the U-shaped average total cost curve.

minimum wage a legal floor on the wage rate. The wage rate is the market price of labor.

model a simplified representation of a real situation that is used to better understand real-life situations.

monetary aggregate an overall measure of the money supply. The most common monetary aggregates in the United States are M1, which includes currency in circulation, traveler's checks, and checkable bank deposits, and M2, which includes M1 as well as near-moneys.

monetary base the sum of currency in circulation and bank reserves.

monetary neutrality the concept that changes in the money supply have no real effects on the economy in the long run and only result in a proportional change in the price level.

monetary policy changes in the quantity of money in circulation designed to alter interest rates and affect the level of overall spending.

money any asset that can easily be used to purchase goods and services.

money demand curve a graphical representation of the relationship between the interest rate and the quantity of money demanded. The money demand curve slopes downward because, other things equal, a higher interest rate increases the opportunity cost of holding money.

money multiplier the ratio of the money supply to the monetary base.

money supply the total value of financial assets in the economy that are considered money.

money supply curve a graphical representation of the relationship between the quantity of money supplied by the Federal Reserve and the interest rate.

monopolist a firm that is the only producer of a good that has no close substitutes.

monopolistic competition a market structure in which there are many competing producers in an industry, each producer sells a differentiated product, and there is free entry and exit into and from the industry in the long run.

monopoly an industry controlled by a monopolist.

monopsony when there is only one buyer of a good.

monopsonist a firm that is the sole buyer in a market.

movement along the demand curve a change in the quantity demanded of a good that results from a change in that good's price.

movement along the supply curve a change in the quantity supplied of a good that results from a change in the price of that good.

multiplier the ratio of total change in real GDP caused by an autonomous change in aggregate spending to the size of that autonomous change.

N

Nash equilibrium (also known as a noncooperative equilibrium) when each player in a game chooses the action that maximizes his or her payoff given the actions of other players, ignoring the effects of his or her action on the payoffs received by those other players.

national income and product accounts method of calculating and keeping track of consumer spending, sales of producers, business investment spending, government purchases, and a variety of other flows of money between different sectors of the economy; also referred to as national accounts.

natural monopoly exists when increasing returns to scale provide a large cost advantage to having all output produced by a single firm.

natural rate of unemployment the normal unemployment rate around which the actual unemployment rate fluctuates; the unemployment rate that arises from the effects of frictional and structural unemployment.

near-money a financial asset that can't be directly used as a medium of exchange but can be readily converted into cash or checkable bank deposits.

negative externalities external costs.

negative income tax a program that supplements the income of low-income working families.

negative relationship a relationship between two variables in which an increase in the value of one variable is associated with a decrease in the value of the other variable. It is illustrated by a curve that slopes downward from left to right.

network externality the increase in the value of a good to an individual is greater when a large number of others own or use the same good.

nominal GDP the value of all final goods and services produced in the economy during a given year, calculated using the prices current in the year in which the output is produced.

nominal interest rate the interest rate in dollar terms.

nominal wage the dollar amount of any given wage paid.

noncooperative behavior actions by firms that ignore the effects of those actions on the profits of other firms.

noncooperative equilibrium (also known as a Nash equilibrium) when each player in a game chooses the action that maximizes his or her payoff given the actions of other players, ignoring the effects of his or her action on the payoffs received by those other players.

nonexcludable referring to a good, describes the case in which the supplier cannot prevent those who do not pay from consuming the good.

nonlinear curve a curve in which the slope is not the same between every pair of points.

nonlinear relationship the relationship between two variables in which the slope is not constant and therefore is depicted on a graph by a curve that is not a straight line.

nonrival in consumption referring to a good, describes the case in which the same unit can be consumed by more than one person at the same time.

normal good a good for which a rise in income increases the demand for that good—the "normal" case.

normative economics the branch of economic analysis that makes prescriptions about the way the economy should work.

O

oligopolist a firm in an industry with only a small number of producers.

oligopoly an industry with only a small number of producers.

omitted variable an unobserved variable that, through its influence on other variables, creates the erroneous appearance of a direct causal relationship among those variables.

open economy an economy that trades goods and services with other countries.

open-market operation a purchase or sale of U.S. Treasury bills by the Federal Reserve, normally through a transaction with a commercial bank.

opportunity cost the real cost of an item: what you must give up in order to get it.

optimal output rule profit is maximized by producing the quantity of output at which the marginal revenue of the last unit produced is equal to its marginal cost.

origin the point where two axes meet.

other things equal assumption the assumption that all other relevant factors remain unchanged.

output gap the percentage difference between actual aggregate output and potential output.

P

Paris Agreement a commitment by 196 countries, signed in 2015, to reduce their greenhouse gas emissions in an effort to limit the rise in the earth's temperature to no more than 2 degrees centigrade.

patent gives an inventor a temporary monopoly in the use or sale of an invention.

payoff the reward received by a player in a game, such as the profit earned by an oligopolist.

payoff matrix shows how the payoff to each of the participants in a two-player game depends on the actions of both. Such a matrix helps us analyze situations of interdependence.

perfect price discrimination when a monopolist charges each consumer his or her willingness to pay—the maximum that the consumer is willing to pay.

perfectly competitive industry an industry in which all producers are price-takers.

perfectly competitive market a market in which all participants are price-takers.

perfectly elastic demand the case in which any price increase will cause the quantity demanded to drop to zero; the demand curve is a horizontal line.

perfectly elastic supply the case in which even a tiny increase or reduction in the price will lead to very large changes in the quantity supplied, so that the price elasticity of supply is infinite; the perfectly elastic supply curve is a horizontal line.

perfectly inelastic demand the case in which the quantity demanded does not respond at all to changes in the price; the demand curve is a vertical line.

perfectly inelastic supply the case in which the price elasticity of supply is zero, so that changes in the price of the good have no effect on the quantity supplied; the perfectly inelastic supply curve is a vertical line.

physical capital manufactured resources, such as buildings and machines.

pie chart a circular graph that shows how some total is divided among its components, usually expressed in percentages.

Pigouvian subsidy a payment designed to encourage activities that yield external benefits.

Pigouvian taxes taxes designed to reduce external costs.

positive economics the branch of economic analysis that describes the way the economy actually works.

positive externalities external benefits.

positive relationship a relationship between two variables in which an increase in the value of one variable is associated with an increase in the value of the other variable. It is illustrated by a curve that slopes upward from left to right.

potential output the level of real GDP the economy would produce if all prices, including nominal wages, were fully flexible.

poverty program a government program designed to aid the poor.

poverty rate the percentage of the population living below the poverty threshold.

poverty threshold the annual income below which a family is officially considered poor.

price ceiling the maximum price sellers are allowed to charge for a good or service; a form of price control.

price controls legal restrictions on how high or low a market price may go.

price discrimination when a seller charges different prices to different consumers for the same good.

price elasticity of demand the ratio of the percent change in the quantity demanded to the percent change in the price as we move along the demand curve (dropping the minus sign).

price elasticity of supply a measure of the responsiveness of the quantity of a good supplied to the price of that good; the ratio of the percent change in the quantity supplied to the percent change in the price as we move along the supply curve.

price floor the minimum price buyers are required to pay for a good or service; a form of price control.

price index a measure of the cost of purchasing a given market basket in a given year, where that cost is normalized so that it is equal to 100 in the selected base year; a measure of overall price level.

price regulation a limitation on the price a monopolist is allowed to charge.

price stability a situation in which the overall level of prices is changing slowly or not at all.

price-taking consumer a consumer whose actions have no effect on the market price of the good or service he or she buys.

price-taking firm's optimal output rule the profit of a price-taking firm is maximized by producing the quantity of output at which the market price is equal to the marginal cost of the last unit produced.

price-taking producer a producer whose actions have no effect on the market price of the good or service it sells.

price war a collapse of prices when tacit collusion breaks down.

principle of marginal analysis the proposition that the optimal quantity is the quantity at which marginal benefit is equal to marginal cost.

Prisoners' dilemma a game based on two premises: (1) Each player has an incentive to choose an action that benefits itself at the other player's expense, and (2) When both players act in this way, both are worse off than if they had acted cooperatively.

private good a good that is both excludable and rival in consumption.

private health insurance when each member of a large pool of individuals pays a fixed amount annually to a private company that agrees to pay most of the medical expenses of the pool's members.

producer price index (PPI) a measure of changes in the prices of goods purchased by producers.

producer surplus refers to either individual producer surplus or total producer surplus.

product differentiation the attempt by a firm to convince buyers that its product is different from the products of other firms in the industry.

production function the relationship between the quantity of inputs a firm uses and the quantity of output it produces.

production possibility frontier illustrates the trade-offs facing an economy that produces only two goods. It shows the maximum quantity of one good that can be produced for any given quantity produced of the other.

productivity output per worker; a shortened form of the term labor productivity.

public debt government debt held by individuals and institutions outside the government.

public good a good that is both nonexcludable and nonrival in consumption.

public ownership when goods are supplied by the government or by a firm owned by the government to protect the interests of the consumer in response to natural monopoly.

purchasing power parity (between two countries' currencies) the nominal exchange rate at which a given basket of goods and services would cost the same amount in each country.

Q

quantity control an upper limit on the quantity of some good that can be bought or sold; also referred to as a quota.

quantity demanded the actual amount of a good or service consumers are willing to buy at some specific price.

quantity supplied the actual amount of a good or service producers are willing to sell at some specific price.

quota an upper limit on the quantity of some good that can be bought or sold; also referred to as a quantity control.

quota limit the total amount of a good under a quota or quantity control that can be legally transacted.

quota rent the difference between the demand price and the supply price at the quota limit; this difference, the earnings that accrue to the license-holder, is equal to the market price of the license when the license is traded.

R

real exchange rate the exchange rate adjusted for international differences in aggregate price levels.

real GDP the total value of all final goods and services produced in the economy during a given year, calculated using the prices of a selected base year.

real income income divided by the price level.

real interest rate the nominal interest rate minus the inflation rate.

real wage the wage rate divided by the price level.

recession a period of economic downturn when output and unemployment are falling; also referred to as a contraction.

recessionary gap exists when aggregate output is below potential output.

renewable energy sources inexhaustible sources of energy (unlike fossil fuel sources, which are exhaustible).

research and development (R&D) spending to create new technologies and prepare them for practical use.

reserve ratio the fraction of bank deposits that a bank holds as reserves. In the United States, the minimum required reserve ratio is set by the Federal Reserve.

reserve requirements rules set by the Federal Reserve that set the minimum reserve ratio for banks. For checkable bank deposits in the United States, the minimum reserve ratio is set at 10%.

resource anything, such as land, labor, and capital, that can be used to produce something else.

reverse causality the error committed when the true direction of causality between two variables is reversed.

Ricardian model of international trade a model that analyzes international trade under the assumption that opportunity costs are constant.

rival in consumption referring to a good, describes the case in which one unit cannot be consumed by more than one person at the same time.

Rule of 70 a mathematical formula that states that the time it takes real GDP per capita, or any other variable that grows gradually over time, to double is approximately 70 divided by that variable's annual growth rate.

S

savings and loans (thrifts) deposit-taking banks, usually specialized in issuing home loans.

scarce in short supply; a resource is scarce when there is not enough of the resource available to satisfy all the various ways a society wants to use it.

scatter diagram a graph that shows points that correspond to actual observations of the x- and y-variables; a curve is usually fitted to the scatter of points to indicate the trend in the data.

securitization the pooling of loans and mortgages made by a financial institution and the sale of shares in such a pool to other investors.

self-correcting describes an economy in which shocks to aggregate demand affect aggregate output in the short run but not in the long run.

self-regulating economy an economy in which problems such as unemployment are resolved without government intervention, through the working of the invisible hand.

shadow banking bank-like activities undertaken by nondepository financial firms such as investment banks and hedge funds, but without regulatory oversight and protection.

shift of the demand curve a change in the quantity demanded at any given price, represented by the change of the original demand curve to a new position, denoted by a new demand curve.

shift of the supply curve a change in the quantity supplied of a good or service at any given price, represented graphically by the change of the original supply curve to a new position, denoted by a new supply curve.

shoe-leather costs the increased costs of transactions caused by inflation.

short run the time period in which at least one input is fixed.

shortage the insufficiency of a good or service that occurs when the quantity demanded exceeds the quantity supplied; shortages occur when the price is below the equilibrium price.

short-run aggregate supply curve a graphical representation that shows the positive relationship between the aggregate price level and the quantity of aggregate output supplied that exists in the short run, the time period when many production costs, particularly nominal wages, can be taken as fixed. The short-run aggregate supply curve has a positive slope because a rise in the aggregate price level leads to a rise in profits, and therefore output, when production costs are fixed.

short-run equilibrium aggregate output the quantity of aggregate output produced in short-run macroeconomic equilibrium.

short-run equilibrium aggregate price level the aggregate price level in short-run macroeconomic equilibrium.

short-run individual supply curve a graphical representation that shows how an individual producer's profit-maximizing output quantity depends on the market price, taking fixed cost as given.

short-run industry supply curve a graphical representation that shows how the quantity supplied by an industry depends on the market price, given a fixed number of producers.

short-run macroeconomic equilibrium the point at which the quantity of aggregate output supplied is equal to the quantity demanded.

short-run market equilibrium an economic balance that results when the quantity supplied equals the quantity demanded, taking the number of producers as given.

short-term interest rate the interest rate on financial assets that mature within less than a year.

shut-down price the price at which a firm ceases production in the short run because the market price has fallen below the minimum average variable cost.

single-payer system a health care system in which the government is the principal payer of medical bills funded through taxes.

single-price monopolist offers its product to all consumers at the same price.

slope a measure of the steepness of a line. The slope of a line is measured by "rise over run"—the change in the y-variable between two points on the line divided by the change in the x-variable between those same two points.

social insurance government programs—like Social Security, Medicare, unemployment insurance, and food stamps—designed to provide protection against unpredictable financial distress.

socially optimal quantity of pollution the quantity of pollution that society would choose if all the costs and benefits of pollution were fully accounted for.

specialization a situation in which different people each engage in the different task that he or she is good at performing.

stabilization policy the use of government policy to reduce the severity of recessions and to rein in excessively strong expansions. There are two main tools of stabilization policy: monetary policy and fiscal policy.

stagflation the combination of inflation and falling aggregate output.

standardized product output of different producers regarded by consumers as the same good; also referred to as a commodity.

sticky wages nominal wages that are slow to fall even in the face of high unemployment and slow to rise even in the face of labor shortages.

store of value an asset that is a means of holding purchasing power over time.

strategic behavior when a firm attempts to influence the future behavior of other firms.

structural unemployment unemployment that results when there are more people seeking jobs in a labor market than there are jobs available at the current wage rate, even when the economy is at the peak of the business cycle.

subprime lending lending to homebuyers who don't meet the usual criteria for borrowing.

substitutes pairs of goods for which a rise in the price of one of the goods leads to an increase in the demand for the other good.

sunk cost a cost that has already been incurred and is not recoverable.

supply and demand model a model of how a competitive market works.

supply curve a graphical representation showing the relationship between quantity supplied and price.

supply price the price of a given quantity at which producers will supply that quantity.

supply schedule a list or table showing how much of a good or service producers will supply at different prices.

supply shock an event that shifts the short-run aggregate supply curve. A negative supply shock raises production costs and reduces the quantity supplied at any aggregate price level, shifting the curve leftward. A positive supply shock decreases production costs and increases the quantity supplied at any aggregate price level, shifting the curve rightward.

surplus the excess of a good or service that occurs when the quantity supplied exceeds the quantity demanded; surpluses occur when the price is above the equilibrium price.

sustainable long-run economic growth long-run growth that can continue in the face of the limited supply of natural resources and the impact of growth on the environment.

T

T-account a simple tool that summarizes a business's financial position by showing, in a single table, the business's assets and liabilities, with assets on the left and liabilities on the right.

tacit collusion cooperation among producers, without a formal agreement, to limit production and raise prices so as to raise one anothers' profits.

tangent line a straight line that just touches a nonlinear curve at a particular point; the slope of the tangent line is equal to the slope of the nonlinear curve at that point.

target federal funds rate the Federal Reserve's desired level for the federal funds rate. The Federal Reserve adjusts the money supply through the purchase and sale of Treasury bills until the actual rate equals the desired rate.

tariff a tax levied on imports.

tax rate the amount of tax people are required to pay per unit of whatever is being taxed.

Taylor rule for monetary policy a rule for setting the federal funds rate that takes into account both the inflation rate and the output gap.

technological progress an advance in the technical means of the production of goods and services.

technology the technical means for the production of goods and services.

technology spillover an external benefit that results when knowledge spreads among individuals and firms.

time-series graph a two-variable graph that has dates on the horizontal axis and values of a variable that occurred on those dates on the vertical axis.

tit for tat involves playing cooperatively at first, then doing whatever the other player did in the previous period.

total consumer surplus the sum of the individual consumer surpluses of all the buyers of a good in a market.

total cost the sum of the fixed cost and the variable cost of producing a given quantity of output.

total cost curve a graphical representation of the total cost, showing how total cost depends on the quantity of output.

total factor productivity the amount of output that can be produced with a given amount of factor inputs.

total producer surplus the sum of the individual producer surpluses of all the sellers of a good in a market.

total product curve a graphical representation that shows how the quantity of output depends on the quantity of the variable input, for a given quantity of the fixed input.

total revenue the total value of sales of a good or service. It is equal to the price multiplied by the quantity sold.

total surplus the total net gain to consumers and producers from trading in a market; the sum of the consumer surplus and the producer surplus.

tradable emissions permits licenses to emit limited quantities of pollutants that can be bought and sold by polluters.

trade when individuals provide goods and services to others and receive goods and services in return.

trade deficit when the value of the goods and services bought from foreigners is more than the value of the goods and services sold to consumers abroad.

trade protection (protection) policies that limit imports.

trade surplus when the value of goods and services bought from foreigners is less than the value of the goods and services sold to them.

trade-off a comparison of the costs and benefits of doing something.

transaction costs the expenses of negotiating and executing a deal.

truncated cut; in a truncated axis, some of the range of values are omitted, usually to save space.

U

underemployment the number of people who work part time because they cannot find full-time jobs.

unemployment the total number of people who are actively looking for work but aren't currently employed.

unemployment rate the percentage of the total number of people in the labor force who are unemployed.

unit of account a measure used to set prices and make economic calculations.

unit-of-account costs costs arising from the way inflation makes money a less reliable unit of measurement.

unit-elastic demand the case in which the price elasticity of demand is exactly 1.

U-shaped average total cost curve a distinctive graphical representation of the relationship between output and average total cost; the average total cost curve falls at low levels of output, then rises at higher levels.

V

value added (of a producer) the value of its sales minus the value of its purchases of intermediate goods and services.

variable a quantity that can take on more than one value.

variable cost a cost that depends on the quantity of output produced; the cost of a variable input.

variable input an input whose quantity the firm can vary at any time.

vertical axis the number line along which values of the y-variable are measured; also referred to as the y-axis.

vertical intercept the point at which a curve hits the vertical axis; it shows the value of the y-variable when the value of the x-variable is zero.

W

wasted resources a form of inefficiency in which people expend money, effort, and time to cope with the shortages caused by a price ceiling.

wealth effect of a change in the aggregate price level the effect on consumer spending caused by the change in the purchasing power of consumers' assets when the aggregate price level changes. A rise in the aggregate price level decreases the purchasing power of consumers' assets, so consumers decrease their consumption; a fall in the aggregate price level increases the purchasing power of consumers' assets, so consumers increase their consumption.

wedge the difference between the demand price of the quantity transacted and the supply price of the quantity transacted for a good when the supply of the good is legally restricted. Often created by a quantity control, or quota.

welfare state the collection of government programs designed to alleviate economic hardship.

willingness to pay the maximum price a consumer is prepared to pay for a good.

world price the price at which a good can be bought or sold abroad.

X

x-axis the line along which values of the x-variable are measured; also referred to as the horizontal axis.

Y

y-axis the line along which values of the y-variable are measured; also referred to as the vertical axis.

Z

zero lower bound for interest rates statement of the fact that interest rates cannot fall below zero.